Leading Issues in African-American Studies

Leading Issues in African-American Studies

**Edited by
Nikongo BaNikongo**

CAROLINA ACADEMIC PRESS
Durham, North Carolina

Library of Congress Cataloging-in-Publication Data

Ba-Nikongo, Nikongo.
    Leading issues in African-American studies / Nikongo BaNikongo.
        p.   cm.
    Includes bibliographical references (p.   ).
    ISBN 0-89089-669-0
    1. Afro-Americans—Study and teaching.   2. Afro-Americans.
I. Title.
E184.7.B33   1997
305.896'073—dc21   97-5379
                                                                CIP

Carolina Academic Press
700 Kent Street
Durham, North Carolina 27701
Telephone (919) 489-7486
Fax (919) 493-5668
www.cap-press.com

Printed in the United States of America

Contents

Leading Issues in African-American Studies

Section I

A Range of Controversial Issues

1

The Scope of Contending Issues

Nikongo BaNikongo

Many scholars still have significant difficulty defining Afro-American Studies. Whether or not it is a separate and distinct discipline remains, among many, a matter of some controversy. The writer Jeffrey Woodyard argues that it is in fact a discipline although it did not actually approach that stage until the 1980s. Everything prior to that he refers to as pre-paradigmatic.

To the extent that it has achieved institutional acceptance with its separate programs, departments and granting of advance degrees, it warrants now going beyond the semantic and treating Afro-American Studies as a field in and of itself. But what is it? History asks, what happened in the past? Political Science asks, what are the dimensions of power? Economics ask, what are the modes of production, distribution and consumption? Sociology asks, what are the structures and organization and functioning of individuals, groups and society? What does Afro-American Studies ask?

The definition which the student gets of Afro-American Studies is almost totally dependent on where the definition is given, from whom and the objective the giver has in mind. Most lecturers in the discipline consider that it is basically a social science which investigates the historical, political, economic and sociological dimensions of life in the Afro-community. Still others include significant emphasis on the humanities and even fine arts. At some level, then, Afro-American Studies becomes a study of everything and anything that is relevant to the Afro-community.

The pan-academic approach to Afro-American Studies is not very popular. It is more likely to find greater emphasis on one end of the spectrum than the other. If the academic fields of inclusion present some controversy, so too does its geographic scope. Here again much depends on and differs from place to place. Many schools confine their interest to the life experiences of African peoples in the United States; these schools are more likely to call their departments Afro-American Studies. Many others broaden the geographic scope to include the investigation of African peoples wherever they are found; these schools are more likely to refer to their departments as Africana Studies or Africana & Afro-American Studies.

Utilization of the broader geographic scope approach does present some academic problems of its own. This is most clearly seen in discussions of the evolution of the discipline. Clearly the study of Africa and Afro-America in American institutions followed distinct paths but they evolved closely enough to treat as a single time period if one assumes that the genesis was, as most writers would have it, in the 1960s. The problem is that scholars of Afro-American Studies are in much disagreement as to dating the earliest beginnings of the more narrow approach of Afro-American Studies and in so doing the date falls anywhere along a continuum from the 1830s to the 1960s.

What there is less controversy around is dating the arrival of Africans here in what is now the United States. Until Van Sertima, it was generally regarded that the experience began ca. 1619. However, with the publication of his most popular, "They Came Before Columbus," Ivan Van Sertima has forced a discussion of an African presence in the Americas long before 1500. Moreover, the historical periodization of the experience of Africans in the United States finds little congruence though much overlap.

In looking at the major periods in the Afro-American experience, many writers make reference to a Rural and Urban period, the first running from ca. 1619 to ca. 1945, the second from ca. 1945 to the Present. Equally popular is the bifurcation of the experience between the "Enslavement Period," ca. 1619 to ca. 1864, and the "Free Period," ca. 1865 to the Present. While both approaches have value, they are analytically restrictive. The approach I have devised at Howard University is to present five sub-periods: the first, ca. 1619 to ca. 1864, the Period of Enslavement; the second, ca. 1865 to ca. 1945, the Period of Neo-Enslavement; the third, ca. 1945 to ca. 1968, the Classic Civil Rights Period; the fourth, ca. 1969 to ca. 1979, the Age of Affirmative Action; and the fifth, ca. 1980 to the Present, the Post Civil Rights Period.

It is hardly surprising that controversy abounds among much every aspect of Afro-American Studies. What is constant is that everyone is trying to be "Afrocentric." But what is "Afrocentricity" anyway? The best known and perhaps the most prolific writer on the subject matter probably provides the best answer when he says, "the Afrocentrist will not question the idea of the centrality of African ideals and values but will argue over what constitutes those ideals and values."

Part of the intrigue of Afro-American studies lies in the fact that there is perhaps as much disagreement as there is agreement on the various and sundry topics of concern. At the very least, the range of opinions may be subdivided between points of view associated with those whom Wilson refers to as "the Liberals" and those points of view associated with individuals more like himself whom he dubs "the Conservatives." Wilson, however, contends that the "Liberal Viewpoint" has lost its popularity or at least its credibility and that the "Conservative Viewpoint" is now, and has been for some time, dominant.

It's safe to say that the camp referred to as "the Liberals" is regarded as the one for whom the political, economic, cultural and social malaise of the Afro-community can be traced directly and blamed on racism, past and present. For the Afro-conservative camp, understanding the problem of the community requires much less emphasis on the sins of the dominant society and much greater understanding of the "values, attitudes, and lifestyles" of the Afro-community itself. This conservative perspective has amply been explained by writers like Wilson, Loury, Sowell, Steele, and Robinson. Racism, they argue must be distinguished between its "historic" versus its "contemporary" effects, the former being much more formidable and really affecting the life opportunities of the community in ways that the latter simply doesn't. We live, after all, as they would argue in a period of a "declining significance of race."

Whether or not "race matters," to steal and twist Cornel West's phrase, as a determinant of the life chances and opportunities of the Afro-community may be less important than its implications for the cohesiveness of the community itself. If what is being observed is the evolution of two Afro-Americas, one affluent and becoming increasingly so, the other poor and falling into greater poverty, it becomes increasingly difficult to make appeals on a matter of race in an atmosphere where race no longer matters. Sociologically, a disjuncture between the affluent and the "truly disadvantaged" undermines any ability of the majority of the Afro-minority to act with group strength and to sustain its demands for affirmative action policies and programs. But then again from the perspective of many, Afro-cohesiveness neither is nor should be necessary as individuals become part and parcel of a larger "melting pot." Such a perspective has not in any way served to minimize the problematique but rather to add to its complexity. Indeed it is but one facet of the contending issues in Afro-American Studies today.

A major area of contention has to do with the issue of identity. While it is clear that cultural boundaries persist between the dominant society and the Afro-community, a healthy debate rages on as to whether an attempt ought to be made at continually narrowing that divide. The debate centers on the question of name identification. African slaves and their descendants in the United States have undergone a myriad of name changes over their stay here. The writer Alkalimat traces these nomenclatures from African through Colored, Negro, Non-White, Minority and Black. Later we get added to the difficulty, Afro-American and African-American. For Alkalimat, it demonstrates the continuing alienation and estrangement of a people but also perhaps an unending search for identity. It shows as well, that while a significant percentage of the community is in a constant struggle to re-connect with something, anything African, significant others wish to emphasize their uniqueness of being part and parcel of the American experience while still others see no value in clinging to any semblance of Africanity and abandon it altogether.

The varying perspectives account for the designation by many of themselves as "Africans," others as decidedly "Afro/African-Americans," and many as simply Americans. It is not necessarily correct to assume that those who emphasize their "Americanism" have some how lost consciousness or are divorced from reality nor is it that those who insist on "Afro/African-Americanism" are less conscious than others. One finds that persons who fall into these two categories, particularly the latter, wish to emphasize and are proud of the role of their foreparents in contributing if not being primarily responsible for the making of an American society which boast an economic outlook that is unparalleled.

A similar arena of diverse views exists on the role of Afro-Americans in the affairs of the larger African world, i.e., African and the Afro-Caribbean. The two perspectives are very clear. On the one hand, some writers argue that African-Americans have a long history of caring and being involved in the situation of Africans outside the United States. This concern has been demonstrated from the earliest arrival through the centuries and continues to the modern period, the argument holds. The role of the Congressional Black Caucus and the activities of W.E.B. Du Bois are given as working examples of that demonstrated concern.

Other writers disagree with the above perspective. They argue instead that that which masquerades as "Pan-Africanism" was at each juncture little more than expediency for some other purpose. The crux of the argument here is that African-

Americans cared little and knew less about the bulk of their ethnic population abroad. It is not an attempt to question the concern of African-Americans for Africans elsewhere, as much as it is to demonstrate realistically a paucity of knowledge of larger group interests.

Defining the group has itself presented significant difficulties. In the United States, the extent of miscegenation have prompted many not only to ask "what color is Black?" but also to raise tenuous issues of bi-racialism and identity. For most of the American experience, any mixture of Caucasian and African assured that the offspring of such a union would be classified as "Black." Most likely the individual would be socialized in the culture of the community and view himself/herself as "Black only." It was rare that a person of such background would think of himself/herself as "bi-racial." Bi-racialism was simply seen as a farce in a society premised so much on race as a determinator of privilege and which left no room for ambiguity of ethnicity. Mulattos therefore viewed themselves as "Black," associated and identified themselves with the Afro-community if not by choice, surely by circumstance. This may not have held true in every instance and may have had nuances from one geographic location to the other, but held true for the most part.

Today, an increasing number of mulattos are looking to celebrate their "dual-heritage." No longer are they content with being lumped in with a group to which they believe they only partially belong. In Affirmative Action fact sheets, in various censuses and statistical compilations, they have demanded a separate category distinct from that of others. For many in the African-American community, the actions of these mulattos border on naivete if not on ignorance. For more and more mulattos, however, it represents a coming of age and organizations are being formed to lend support to their efforts.

In a significant number of instances, mulattos tend to be the offsprings of African and Jewish inter-personal relationships. The relationship between the African-American and Jewish communities has been under strain for some time. A century old history of working together has been unraveling owing in part to what has always been an uneasy alliance and a marriage of convenience. On many key political and economic issues Jews and Africans have found themselves at odds. Differences in their attitudes toward affirmative action education policy and Israeli-Arab relations are but two areas of soreness. Added to these is Jewish displeasure with much of African-American political leadership particularly with regard to individuals such as Jesse Jackson and Louis Farrakhan.

While some effort is afoot at repairing the strained relationship which exist, many writers insist that the Jewish community was never and is not now a "friend" to the Afro-community. They argue that the role of Jews in founding and funding African-American civil rights organizations was an act of self-preservation in a time when American society was as openly hostile to Jews as it was to African-Americans. Moreover, while both the Jewish and African-American communities for a long period in American history suffered from political denial and social outcastness, unlike African-Americans, Jews never suffered from economic deprivation.

The line of argument advanced above is rejected by those who praise the role of Jews in assisting the African-American community not only financially but with their physical presence in the Civil Rights Movement and with their lives as well. Proponents of this line of thinking look to the "commonality" of the experience and the "similarity" of the struggle of the two communities. Moreover, they conclude, despite present tensions, there is more which binds the communities together than that which sets them apart; the conclusion, "Jews are not our enemies."

As to where the enemy actually resides is the basis of widespread debate and difference among scholars of the African-American experience. The dominant theme seems to retain the notion that the main enemy of the African-American community is present and continuing racism. This school of thought holds that the social and economic malaise of the Afro-community can be traced directly to the effects of racism then and now. They believe that racism may well have changed in its form, but its content remains the same and that while it may be less overt, it has not declined in significance. Affirmative action policies and programs have not only failed but were never intended to work. Anderson points out that it was under the control of African-Americans and that Caucasian-Americans would not devise a policy to undermine they own position in the society.

Ben Wattenberg once wrote an article entitled, "The Good News Is That the Bad News Is Wrong." He suggested that cries of racism were unfounded and that they were devised to maintain African-American political and community leadership in power. He is not a member of the African-American community, but no less well-known scholarly members have echoed similar arguments. The enemy they argue is not racism, not an enemy outside but rather an enemy within the community itself. Loury speaks of "The Moral Quandary of the Black Community" as being mostly responsible for their present situation. Robinson suggests that "Black Men Are Their Own Worst Enemies" by refusing to educate themselves and making the system work for them. Steele goes further by arguing that racism becomes a crutch upon which African-Americans hang their frailties, failings and shortcomings, an excuse they use for seeking rights rather that wishing to be judged by "The Content Of Our Character."

How can we blame intra-community violence, high rates of high-school dropouts, teenage pregnancy, non-supportive fathers, and other "social ills" on racism? This is the question posed by those who reject racism as our major foe. It is, in their minds, our thoughts about ourselves and our attitudes toward work as well as our "destructive" cultural values that comprise our worst problem. The enemy for these scholars, then, is not racism, "the enemy is us."

Depending on how one assesses the nature of the enemy determines what is viewed as acceptable solutions. One perspective holds that Affirmative Action policies and programs are good, necessary and deserved. This perspective believes that centuries of denial politically, socially and economically have combined and conspired to place African-Americans at a distinct and decisive disadvantage. Let alone, the community would have developed the resources and knowhow to advance, develop and experience upward social mobility consonant with other groups; but this was not the case. Their experience not only retarded their historical progress but handicapped their contemporary efforts at self-sufficiency. Affirmative action from this vantage point should be thought more of in terms of "Remedial Action" or actions designed to remedy or repair past injustices; such programs and policies are not only necessary, but they are good and deserved.

For how long? This is the question posed by those who reject the above argument. These rejectionists believe that Affirmative Action programs and policies have lasted long enough, if not too long. They argue that such policies tend to produce lasting dependency, cycles of poverty and laziness. We live in an America, they say, where individual effort and hard work are sufficient to guarantee success and where laws protect every person equally against discrimination and offer recourse wherever it exists. Besides, some writers point out, other groups have been "equally" discriminated in American society and have risen above it to lead successful lives through perseverance and dedication to hard work. Furthermore, not only is the political atmosphere not conducive to continuing notions of Affirmative Action, but one is hard-pressed to sustain an argument that today's "whites" are somehow responsible for the sins of their fathers. From this point of view, then, Affirmative Action policies and programs are not only undeserved, but they are bad and unnecessary. The issue remains a major part of the intra-community debate.

The Afro-centric debate, issues of identity, the causes of underclassness, these are but a few of the issues making for lively debate in the discipline of Afro-American Studies today. Several other topics no less important are included. Questions of "Correct Adoption" practices, political affiliation, alliances and strategies, religion, and male-female relationships to name a few, add to the myriad of controversial concerns. Here, in this collection, we attempt to present the complexities of the debate.

As a final note, since the articles in this volume have their origins in many different sources and reflect many different backgrounds and viewpoints, we have maintained, as much as possible, the writing style, citation style, and language of each individual author.

Section II

The Afrocentric Debate

2

Afrocentricity: Implications for Higher Education

Jerome H. Schiele

The concept of cultural diversity in higher education in the United States has been significantly restricted. Discussions and debates have primarily focused on enhancing the presence of students and faculty of color, with a special emphasis on recruitment and retention (Carter & Wilson, 1994; Pettigrew, 1991; Epps, 1989; Blackwell, 1988, 1987; Oliver & Brown, 1988). In other words, cultural diversity has been primarily conceptualized as the diversification of racial characteristics of students and faculty. A more important dimension of cultural diversity, which has received scant attention, is the diversification of the philosophical foundation of higher education.

Although there appears to be considerable diversity in the knowledge base of higher education in the United States, the philosophical underpinnings of higher education are primarily shaped by one dominant world view. That is, to the extent that a society's institutions of higher education reflect the predominant values found in that society, it is reasonable to assume that the predominant values undergirding the philosophical foundation of higher education in the United States are Eurocentric in nature. Eurocentric means that these values exclusively emanate from a European-American view of the world. Thus, by being Eurocentric, the philosophical base of higher education in the United States has become ethnocentric and uninclusive. This has resulted in the omission of world views of other ethnic groups found in the United States, and, more specifically, in institutions of higher education.

In order to diversify the philosophical foundation of higher education, alternative world view or philosophical models[1] need to be considered and integrated. One alternative philosophical model is the Afrocentric model (also referred to in this paper as Afrocentricity). With this in mind, the thrust of this article is to discuss some *beginning* ideas on how Afrocentricity can be promoted and integrated

---

An earlier version of this essay appeared in *Journal of Black Studies* 25, 2 (December 1994): 150–69 and is adapted/reprinted with the permission of the copyright holder/author.

1. For the purpose of this paper, a philosophical model is defined as a system of ideas and beliefs about the nature and structure of elements (i.e., people, animals, & things) found in the world and universe. In essence, it is a world view. There are three traditional philosophical models of this world: Afrocentricity, Eurocentricity, and Asiancentricity. For an excellent discussion of these models from a social science perspective, see Cook & Kono (1977).

in institutions of higher education in the United States. The promotion and integration of Afrocentricity, as an alternative philosophical model, would not only help diversify the philosophical base of higher education, but it would also serve to broaden the world views and conceptual frameworks of students, professors, and administrators.

What Is Afrocentricity?

The concept Afrocentricity has been used to convey a variety of meanings. This has lead to considerable misunderstanding about Afrocentricity and, consequently, has prompted some to question its validity (Nicholson, 1991; Shannker, 1991; Mercer, 1991; Ravitch, 1991; Schlesinger, 1991).

Afrocentricity, or Afrocentrism, has received the most attention in primary and secondary education (Schiele, 1991a). There, Afrocentricity has been largely associated with the exposure of African-American children, and others, to the historical accomplishments of people of African descent. Viewed as a major component of what is referred to as the curriculum of inclusion or multicultural education, the integration of Afrocentric content in primary and secondary schools is predicated on the assumption that African-American children will perform better, academically, if they have knowledge of the past accomplishments of their ancestors. A second dominant view in the popular literature is that Afrocentricity is a new black nationalist movement that advocates racial separation and exposes white racism and culpability. For example, Nicholson (1991) maintains that the return to nationalistic sentiments via Afrocentrism is a result of the belief among African Americans that the civil rights movement failed to improve the overall status of African Americans.

Although Afrocentricity is, in part, associated with African history and can be said to reflect black nationalist thought (Schiele, 1991a), it has been more appropriately described as a philosophical model based on traditional African philosophical assumptions (Abarry, 1990; Schiele, 1990; Bell et al., 1990; Asante, 1990, 1988; Baldwin & Hopkins, 1990; Nobles, 1988, 1980; Carruthers, 1989, 1981; Akbar, 1984, 1979; Dixon, 1976; Boykin & Toms, 1985; Boykin, 1983; Baldwin, 1980; Khatib et al., 1979). Much of the thrust of this research, which has primarily emanated from African-American social scientists, is based on the assumption that "...any meaningful and authentic study of peoples of African descent must begin and proceed with Africa as the center, not periphery..." (Abarry, 1990, p.123). This observation is further predicated on the assumptions that there are distinct cultural differences between African and European peoples (Kambon, 1992; Herskovits, 1941; Diop, 1978; Baldwin, 1980; Nobles, 1980; Dixon, 1976) and that western social science has negated the worldview or cultural reality of African people (Kambon, 1992; Schiele, 1990; Carruthers, 1989; Asante, 1987; Baldwin & Bell, 1985; Akbar, 1984).

As a philosophical model, Afrocentricity is viewed as being distinct from and oppositional to Eurocentricity (Baldwin, 1985; Kambon, 1992; Diop, 1978; Asante, 1988; Khatib et al., 1979), which is the philosophical foundation of the United States. Hence, Afrocentricity has a distinct set of cosmological, ontological, epistemological and axiological attributes. Cosmologically, the Afrocentric model views the structure of reality from a perspective of interdependency. That is, all elements of the universe, such as people, animals, inanimate objects, etc., are viewed as interconnected (Baldwin & Hopkins, 1990; Bell et al., 1990; Nobles, 1980; Mbiti, 1970). There is no separation between the spiritual and the material (Asante, 1980); reality is viewed as being "both spiritual and material at once" (Meyers, 1985, p.34). The emphasis on an interdependent cosmological perspective is captured succinctly in the African notion that to destroy one component of the web of cosmic elements is to destroy the entire universe, even the creator (Mbiti, 1970; Nobles, 1980).

Ontologically, Afrocentricity assumes that all elements of the universe—including people—are spiritual, that is, are created from a similar universal substance (Akbar, 1984; Nobles, 1980; Mbiti, 1970). Spirituality is taken here to imply the nonmaterial or invisible substance that connects all elements of the universe. The focus on spirituality within the Afrocentric perspective supports and encourages the cosmological view of interdependency. Indeed, for elements to be considered interdependent, there must be a universal link, and, in African philosophy, that link is the nonmaterial spirit of the Creator (Akbar, 1984; Mbiti, 1970; Nobles, 1980; Zahan, 1979).

Epistemologically, the Afrocentric perspective places considerable emphasis on an affective way of obtaining knowledge (Schiele, 1991a, 1991b, 1990; Asante, 1988; Akbar, 1984; Nichols, 1987; Dixon, 1976). That is, knowing (i.e., understanding events and reality) through emotion or feeling is considered valid and critical from an Afrocentric standpoint. Indeed, a major premise of Afrocentricity is that "the most direct experience of self is through emotion or affect" (Akbar, 1984, p. 410). The focus on affect in Afrocentricity does not prevent recognition and use of rationality. Rather, affect, as a means of knowing, is viewed as offsetting the use of rationality (Akbar, 1984).

Axiologically, Afrocentricity significantly underscores the value of interpersonal relationships (Schiele, 1991a, 1990; Nichols, 1987; Hale-Benson, 1982; Dixon, 1976). The maintenance and enhancement of harmonious interpersonal relationships is considered the most important cultural value in Afrocentricity (Schiele, 1990a, 1990). This focus fosters a human-centered perspective towards life rather than an object or material perspective, wherein the value in maintaining and strengthening interpersonal bonds overrides the concern over acquiring material objects (Schiele, 1991a) and accumulating wealth. In order to further understand Afrocentricity, it is instructive to identify how it fundamentally differs from Eurocentricity in its conception of human beings. This not only serves to better elucidate Afrocentricity, but also to better understand Eurocentricity, which is the philosophical foundation of higher education in the United States.

Basic Distinctions between Afrocentric and Eurocentric Views of Human Beings

A fundamental difference in the conception of human beings between the Afrocentric and Eurocentric philosophical models is that whereas there is considerable emphasis on harmony and collectivity within the Afrocentric perspective, considerable emphasis is placed on domination, conflict, and fragmentation within the Eurocentric perspective (Welsing, 1991; Schiele, 1994, 1991a; Bell et al., 1990; Baldwin & Hopkins, 1990; Baldwin, 1985, 1980; Burgest, 1982, 1981; Wright, 1984; Dixon, 1976; Carruthers, 1972). Because of the focus on fragmentation and domination, the Eurocentric model tends to engender an individualistic and materialistic orientation towards life. That is, people are conceived primarily as individuals separate from other people and nature (Akbar, 1984; Dixon, 1984), who aggressively and competitively seek control over nature, material items (i.e., objects, property), and other people (Pinderhughes, 1985; Bell et al., 1990; Baldwin, 1985; Welsing, 1991; Wright, 1984; Dixon, 1976; Carruthers, 1972). To this extent, the Eurocentric philosophical system is considered unhumanistic in that the material needs (i.e., power, objects, physical gratification) of the individual are valued over the collective well-being of people. The unhumanistic character of Eurocentricity also emanates from the heavy emphasis it places on material and physical attributes of people as opposed to nonmaterial or intangible qualities (Bell et al., 1990; Akbar, 1984; Asante, 1981).

Unlike the fragmented and restricted view of human beings found in the Eurocentric perspective, Afrocentricity offers a more holistic conception of human beings. This is because Afrocentricity views people from a collective and spiritual perspective. Although Afrocentricity recognizes individual uniqueness (Akbar, 1984; Boykin & Toms, 1985; Boykin, 1983), it conceives individual identity as collective identity. That is, the individual can not be understood separate from other people (Akbar, 1984), because there is no perceptual separation of the individual from other people (Dixon, 1976). Thus, from an Afrocentric viewpoint, discerning similarities or commonalities of people takes precedence over discerning individual differences (Schiele, 1990).

The spiritual character of Afrocentricity stems from the assumption that spirituality is essential to the human makeup (Schiele, 1991a, 1990; Richards, 1989; Akbar, 1984; Khatib et al., 1979; Mbiti, 1970) and that nonmaterial attributes of people are just as important as other human qualities in defining and understanding human behavior (Akbar, 1984; Weems, 1974). Afrocentricity's focus on spirituality is also related to the high value given to the belief in a supreme being and on the high value placed on morality (Baldwin, 1985, 1981; Akbar, 1984, 1979; Boykin, 1983; Nobles, 1980). As Akbar (1984) has observed, spirituality and morality are inseparable within an Afrocentric framework.

The divergent views on human beings between the Afrocentric and Eurocentric worldviews has significant implications for higher education. One such implication is the manner in which the teacher/student relationship is conceived.

Conception of Teacher/Student Relationship

In order to begin a discussion on diversifying the philosophical foundation of higher education, vital changes in the conception of teacher/student relationships must come about. This observation is predicated on the assumption that the philosophical foundation of higher education is shaped significantly by the nature of the teacher/student relationship, that is, by the expectations academia ascribes to the student and the teacher. The student/teacher relationship is the most important social relationship in academia because the classroom is the locus of service delivery in higher education.

If applied to teacher/student relationships, the Afrocentric model would emphasize a relationship based on cooperation and harmony. The relationship would not be based on uncooperation, antagonism, or aloofness. This would require both the teacher and the student to assume a more humble and affable posture when relating to one another. The teacher would assume a nonelitist posture and would view students as people who are eager to learn. Every effort would be made by the teacher to foster a comfortable and inspirational learning milieu so that students can feel free to manifest their full potential as learners and as critical thinkers. Students, on the other hand, would view teachers not as persons who are "out to get them" but rather as persons who are attempting to elicit the "best" in them. Indeed, eliciting the best in students so that they can better know themselves and so that they can better tap into the universal wisdom and spirit of the creator (God) is an ancient concept of education that goes back to Nile Valley civilizations (see, Hilliard, 1989). In this regard, an Afrocentric viewpoint on higher education does not separate learning from becoming "God like" (Hilliard, 1989). The conception of teacher/student relations is illuminated further below as some roles (i.e., expectations) of the teacher and student are identified from an Afrocentric perspective.

Role of Teacher

As stated earlier, the affective approach to knowledge is considered valid and important within an Afrocentric framework. With this in mind, a major role or expectation of the teacher would be to emphasize and foster a subjective, as well as cognitive, experience of knowledge among students. Shakir (1989) calls this subjective experience of knowledge "feeling" intellect. According to Shakir, feeling intellect requires that the student have an emotional, learning experience, wherein he or she formulates and expresses an opinion about the content presented. In this regard, a primary objective of the educator, indeed of education, would be not only to transform the head of the student but also to transform the heart (Shakir, 1989).

Although fostering "feeling" intellect among students would be important, fostering "feeling" intellect among teachers is just as important. Teachers should view themselves as change agents, conduits through which students are transformed. However, in order for a teacher to effectively affect change in students, a transformation must first occur within the teacher. Therefore, the teacher must have a subjective experience of knowledge before he or she can encourage feeling intellect among students.

Additional roles of the teacher, within an Afrocentric framework, would be that of information provider and information receiver. Because of the heavy emphasis on fragmentation found in Eurocentricity, the role of information provider has been primarily assigned to the teacher, whereas the role of information receiver has been primarily assigned to the student. Within an Afrocentric framework, however, learning is viewed as interdependent and bidirectional rather than independent and unidirectional. Thus, the teacher would take on both roles, providing information to students as well as receiving information (feedback) from students. Although there would be considerable information exchange between students and teachers, a major distinction is that the teacher would serve as the guide or facilitator of the information exchange process, wherein she or he directs and manages the flow of information. An emphasis on the mutual exchange of information between the teacher and student has the potential to strengthen the teacher/student relationship, making education a more interconnected process. For this process to be complete, it is imperative that the student assume a different set of expectations.

Role of Student

Although roles of students vary across the various degree levels of higher education, the emphasis on fragmentation found in Eurocentricity has fostered a view of the "lone" or detached learner. The didactic style of the teacher lecturing to students and the focus on competitive learning have both contributed to this detached view of learning. Thus, Eurocentric educational systems tend to alienate students from teachers as well as from other students. This can have deleterious effects on learning.

One of the most adverse effects of the detached view of learning is that students often do not see themselves as a collective and interdependent social group. In this regard, Afrocentricity would view a classroom of students from a collective and interconnected perspective rather than from a detached and competitive one. Students would see themselves more as a group, than as individuals, who share a common experience (i.e., the course) with a common objective: survival and satisfactory completion of the course. The role of the student, therefore, would be that of a "cooperative" learner who is concerned with the collective survival of the class. To facilitate collective survival, efforts would be aimed at strengthening weaker students while providing continued support to students who are not as weak. From an Afrocentric perspective, a chief responsibility of the stronger student would be to provide ongoing tutelage and encouragement to students who are not as strong.

Another role of the student would be to cultivate "feeling" intellect just as much as cognitive intellect. It was stated earlier that "feeling" intellect requires the student to subjectively experience knowledge. This is currently de-emphasized in the Eurocentric system because learning and intelligence have been primarily associated with reasoning. Thus, the adage "I think; therefore, I know" is the chief value that shapes the learning process in Eurocentric educational institutions. From an Afrocentric perspective, the adage "I think and I feel; therefore, I know" provides the foundation on which learning is based. Feeling the knowledge then becomes just as important as experiencing it cognitively, that is, from a perspective of reasoning.

Some questions that would help a student to cultivate "feeling" intellect or a subjective experience of knowledge are as follows: How do I feel about the knowledge? That is, does the knowledge make me angry, sad, happy, etc.? Does the knowledge make me feel good about myself and the society to which I belong? How practical is the knowledge? What are the moral implications of the knowledge? Or, how can the knowledge be used to improve humanity? Questions such as these would allow the student to tap an additional source of intellectual inquiry, thereby providing him or her with a more complete experience of knowledge.

Before this additional source of intellect can be cultivated, there needs to be a serious effort made within academia to promote and integrate Afrocentric thought. Although this effort should be initiated by anyone who is interested in

Afrocentricity, African-American educators should take primary responsibility for disseminating Afrocentric content and ideas.

Afrocentricity and African-American Educators

Since Afrocentricity is based on traditional African philosophical assumptions, African-American educators have a special relationship with Afrocentricity's philosophical attributes. This observation is supported by those who maintain that slavery and Jim Crowism did not obliterate all that was reminiscent of Africa for African Americans (Nobles, 1988, 1980; Sudarkasa, 1988; Herskovits, 1941; Hale-Benson, 1982; Dixon, 1976; Asante, 1988). It is assumed that the behavior and lifestyle of contemporary African Americans continue to be shaped by traditional African philosophical assumptions, on which Afrocentricity is based. Indeed, empirical (i.e., statistical) evidence has recently been found to support this assumption (see Bell et al., 1990; Baldwin & Hopkins, 1990).

Afrocentricity is also said to have a self-affirming and psychologically liberating effect on African Americans (Asante, 1988; Akbar, 1984; Baldwin, 1985, 1984; Carruthers, 1989; Clark, 1991). This is because of the racist nature of the Eurocentric system (Clark, 1991; Baldwin, 1985; Akbar, 1984; Jochannon, 1976), wherein the value of European or "white" supremacy is implicitly, and in many instances, explicitly communicated. The result of this racist element is that it portrays anyone who is nonwhite or European as pathological, unintelligent, or immoral. As Baldwin (1985) observes, Eurocentricity "is anti-African because it projects European supremacy and African inferiority as the natural order" (p. 217). Hence, it is believed that for African Americans to accept Eurocentric values is to participate in their (our) own oppression and psychological degradation. Afrocentricity, therefore, provides a mode through which African Americans in general, and African-American educators in specific, can be liberated from the distorted and pervasive view of African inferiority found in Eurocentricity.

Because of Eurocentric cultural oppression, too many African-American educators suffer from what Kambon (1992) calls psychological/cultural misorientation. This misorientation occurs when African Americans accept the definitions of reality avouched by European Americans without any regard for or consideration of an Afrocentric view of reality (Kambon, 1992). Psychological/cultural misorientation has restricted too many African-American educators' view of scholarship, higher education, and theory development, and, therefore, causes many to remain incarcerated within Eurocentric standards of scholarship, higher education, and theory development. Many of these African-American educators view Afrocentricity as mere folklore or "feel good" curriculum that should and can not be integrated into higher education. What these educators fail to acknowledge is that the current Eurocentric educational enterprise is nothing more than a formal application of European American folklore (i.e., traditional values and practices) and the exaltation of European American civilization (i.e., a "feel good" curriculum). Thus, African-American educators who are amenable and adhere to Afrocentric concepts of higher education and theory development unfortunately have to bear the brunt of responsibility for disseminating Afrocentricity because of the severe psychological/cultural misorientation of many of our brothers and sisters.

To the extent that Afrocentricity has a special meaning for all African Americans, African-American students and administrators also bear some of the responsibility for promoting Afrocentric thought in higher education. African-American educators, however, should assume primary responsibility because their academic (i.e., occupational) role specifically prescribes that they disseminate (via teaching) and produce (via scholarly writing) knowledge. Hence the dissemination and creation of knowledge is a major task of the educator in higher education. Albeit administrators and students disseminate and produce knowledge, these are not their primary occupational tasks.

There are several ways through which African-American educators can promote and integrate Afrocentricity in higher education. Three modes are as follows: 1) promoting Afrocentricity among students, colleagues, and administrators; 2) integrating Afrocentric content in the class; and 3) applying and integrating Afrocentricity in scholarly and professional activities.

Afrocentricity Among Students, Colleagues, & Administrators

In the various academic roles wherein African-American educators interact with students, colleagues, and administrators, Afrocentric ideas can and should be disseminated. In the role of academic advisor, for example, African-American educators can use some of the time spent on advising students to discuss and explain the Afrocentric perspective. This discussion does not have to be limited to African-American students but to all students. Indeed, based on this writer's experience as a professor in a predominantly white university, a noticeable amount—although not an overwhelming majority—of white students have found Afrocentricity to be interesting and valid. African-American students have been more interested primarily because Afrocentricity affirms an African world view.

Afrocentric ideas may be disseminated more rapidly among students if the educator identifies and works with a few vocal and prominent students who are actively involved in campus politics. This would create a "snowball" effect, in which those few students would serve as messengers to other students and faculty on campus. If enough students become interested in Afrocentricity, it could have a similar effect as when African-American college students of the late 1960s and early 1970s became increasingly aware of the need for Black Studies programs and departments.

Other academic roles that can be used by African-American educators to promote Afrocentricity are those of colleague and committee member. Often, informal discussions with colleagues are characterized by the sharing of information and new ideas. This is an excellent time to share information about Afrocentricity, especially with colleagues who are comfortable and flexible enough to contemplate a world view that significantly challenges Eurocentric ideas and values. Informal discussions with colleagues can sometimes lead to scholarly collaborations as well as significant changes in curriculum policy.

The discussions that are generated in the various standing and non-standing committees also provide an opportunity to share information on Afrocentricity. These discussions are often philosophical, especially discussions in committees that deal specifically with student and curricula concerns. When these discussions arise, this would be an opportune time to plug a few words in for Afrocentricity, that is, to interject an Afrocentric perspective into the discussion. Since Afrocentricity may be an especially threatening and politically inflammatory perspective for many European-American—and even some African-American—faculty, it is preferable that African-American senior faculty with tenure—or who may have significant clout in the department—take the lead in interjecting an Afrocentric viewpoint. This does not imply that junior and untenured faculty should not participate in a discussion of Afrocentric ideas; rather, this suggestion recognizes that junior and untenured faculty are more politically vulnerable to a critique of their ideas.

Some African-American faculty, especially department chairpersons, have considerable interaction with administrators. Hence, the role of administrative liaison could be exploited by African-American educators to advance Afrocentric concepts among administrators. The exposure of Afrocentricity to administrators is critical because they possess the political power needed to initiate substantive change, thus, increasing the likelihood of Afrocentricity being integrated throughout the university or college. To this extent, educators should target administrators who they believe are amenable to Afrocentricity. Although Afrocentricity has special significance for African Americans (Schiele, 1991a), it should not be presumed that African-American administrators are inherently more receptive than other administrators. The role of administrator is very political, and, because Afrocentricity is often viewed as controversial, administrators of any ethnicity may be extremely circumspect in associating themselves with Afrocentric faculty and thought.

Afrocentricity in the Class

It was stated earlier that in order to truly integrate Afrocentricity in higher education, there would have to be a change in the conception of teacher/student relationships. However, Afrocentric content can be integrated in the classes taught by African-American educators without altering the current character of teacher/student relationships. This may be especially relevant for African-American educators who teach social science and humanities related content. These courses, more so than the biological and physical sciences, deal more with cultural issues and concerns of a society. Because of the cosmological attributes of Afrocentricity, however, biological and physical scientists may also be able to integrate an Afrocentric perspective, especially as it relates to examining the order and structure of natural phenomena.

An excellent curriculum content area to integrate Afrocentric thought is social research. Presently this writer teaches social research within a School of Social Work. Although research is often viewed as a technical curriculum content area, its major objective is to provide society with a means through which reality can be determined. Thus, research fundamentally addresses the philosophical area of inquiry known as epistemology. Research, and social science in general, also reflect and defend the cultural values of the society in which they exist (Akbar, 1984). In this regard, research in Eurocentric societies—in addition to other societies where Eurocentric values have been superimposed—is heavily shaped by Eurocentric conceptions of epistemology, human inquiry, logic, and behavioral normality. It is with this in mind that this writer introduces Afrocentric content in research classes, with a special focus on how Afrocentricity, as contrasted with Eurocentricity, views epistemology, human inquiry, logic, and normality. Asante's (1990) discussion of Afrocentricity and knowledge, Akbar's (1984) discussion of Afrocentric social science and Kershaw's (1992) examination of Afrocentric method are excellent references to assist one in interpreting an Afrocentric perspective on research. There are probably as many ways to integrate Afrocentric content in the class as there are academic courses. A primary requirement is that the educator become as familiar and comfortable as possible with Afrocentric content so that she or he does not misinform and misguide the student.

Afrocentricity in Scholarly & Professional Activities

A significant expectation of the educator in higher education is to produce and disseminate knowledge. The production and dissemination of knowledge is usually achieved through two modes: 1) conference/community presentations, and 2) scholarly publications. In both modes, Afrocentric ideas can and should be applied.

Applying Afrocentricity in scholarly activities is essential for primarily two reasons. First, although the promotion of Afrocentricity among an educator's students and colleagues and the integration of it in an educator's class are important, the inclusion of Afrocentric ideas in published works and in conference/community presentations ensures the exposure of Afrocentricity to a wider audience. Second, the permanency of written communications allows an educator to promote Afrocentricity even when he or she is involved in some other activity. It also allows an educator to promote Afrocentricity when he or she is deceased, which guarantees the survival of Afrocentric thought for future generations.

For applied academic disciplines, Afrocentricity may also be promoted through professional practice. Medicine, social work, education, clinical and counseling psychology, nursing, law, business, and public health are examples of applied disciplines that have firm foundations in higher education. Educators in these fields who are also practitioners should be creative and think of ways in which Afrocentricity can be integrated to serve their respective clientele. Practitioners who serve African-American clients should especially consider applying Afrocentricity in their service delivery. Indeed, in social work and psychology this has been done (see, for example, Brisbane & Womble, 1991; Meyers, 1988; Phillips, 1990; Schiele, 1996, 1994, 1993).

The connection between applying Afrocentricity in professional practice and integrating Afrocentricity in the curriculum should not be de-emphasized. Frequently, in applied fields, the integration of knowledge in the curriculum is brought on by advancements and innovations in the field. Thus, the extent to which an educator of an applied discipline incorporates Afrocentricity in his or her professional practice is the extent to which he or she can use Afrocentricity to generate new knowledge to be included in the curriculum. In addition, the application of Afrocentric ideas in professional practice prevents Afrocentricity from solely becoming an intellectual, classroom discourse.

Summary and Conclusion

This chapter has presented some beginning ideas on how the Afrocentric world view can be promoted and integrated in higher education. Although some work towards this goal can emanate from ideas presented in this chapter, additional work needs to be pursued. The significance of this work is associated with the significance of educational institutions. Educational institutions are primary socialization agents of a society, and they have a vital influence on how we view the world, various groups, and ourselves. At present, the Eurocentric world view predominates higher education in the United States, which means that all who matriculate are given a heavy—if not exclusive—dose of Eurocentrism. Moreover, the predominance of the Eurocentric world view in higher education has created an illusion that the Eurocentric view of the world is the *only* view of the world.

Afrocentricity provides an alternative to the Eurocentric view of higher education and the world. It offers students, professors, and administrators of African descent an opportunity to reaffirm their world view, which has been repudiated and defamed within the Eurocentric framework. In addition, Afrocentricity has the potential to assist European-American students, professors, and administrators in overcoming the misconception—whether consciously or unconsciously manifested—that Europe and the western world hold exclusive rights to knowledge. Along these lines, a major outcome of integrating Afrocentric thought in higher education is that it will help *equalize* how African Americans and European-Americans view themselves and each other in relation to the contributions that have emanated from their respective philosophical models.

References

Abarry, A.S. (1990). "Afrocentricity: Introduction." *Journal of Black Studies*, 21(2), 123–125.

Akbar, N. (1984). "Africentric social sciences for human liberation." *Journal of Black Studies*, 14(4), 395–414.

Akbar, N. (1979). "African roots of Black personality," in W.D. Smith, H. Kathleen, M.H. Burlew, & W.M. Whitney (eds.), *Reflections on Black psychology*, (pp. 79–87). Washington, D.C.: University Press of America.

Asante, M.K. (1990). *Kemet, Afrocentricity, and knowledge*. Trenton, NJ: Africa World Press, Inc.

Asante, M.K. (1988). *Afrocentricity*. Trenton, NJ: Africa World Press, Inc.

Asante, M.K. (1987). *The Afrocentric idea*. Philadelphia, PA: Temple University Press.

Asante, M.K. (1981). "Black male-female relationships: An Afrocentric context," in L. Gary (ed.), *Black men*. Beverly Hills, CA: Sage.

Asante, M.K. (1980). "International/intercultural relations," in M.K. Asante and A.S.Vandi (eds.) *Contemporary Black thought: Alternative analyses in social and behavioral science*, (pp. 43–58). Beverly Hills, CA: Sage Publications.

Baldwin, J. (1985). "Psychological aspects of European cosmology in American society." *The Western Journal of Black Studies*, 9(4), 216–223.

Baldwin, J. (1984). "African self-consciousness and the mental health of African-Americans." *Journal of Black Studies*, 15(2), 177–194.

Baldwin, J. (1980). "The psychology of oppression," in M.K. Asante & A. Vandi (eds.), *Contemporary Black thought: Alternative analyses in social and behavioral science*, (pp. 95–110). Beverly Hills, CA: Sage.

Baldwin, J. (1981). "Notes on an Africentric theory of Black personality." *The Western Journal of Black Studies* 5, 172–179.

Baldwin, J. and Hopkins, R. (1990). "African-American and European-American cultural differences as assessed by the worldviews paradigm: An empirical analysis." *The Western Journal of Black Studies*, 14(1), 38–52.

Baldwin, J. and Bell, Y. (1985). "The African self-consciousness scale: An Africentric personality questionnaire." *The Western Journal of Black Studies*, 9(2), 62–68.

Bell, Y.R., Bouie, C.L. and Baldwin, J.A. (1990). "Afrocentric cultural consciousness and African-American male-female relationships." *Journal of Black Studies*, 21(2), 162–189.

Blackwell, J.E. (1988). "Faculty issues: The impact on minorities." *The Review of Higher Education*, 11(4), 417–434.

Blackwell, J.E. (1987). *Mainstreaming outsiders: The production of Black professionals.* 2nd ed. Dix Hills, NY: General Hall Pub. Co.

Boykin, W. (1983). "The academic performance of Afro-American children," in J. Spence (ed.), *Achievement and achievement motives*, (pp. 324–371). San Francisco, CA: W. Freeman.

Boykin, W. and Toms, F. (1985). "Black child socialization: A conceptual framework," in H.P. McAdoo (ed.) *Black children.* Beverly Hills, CA: Sage.

Brisbane, F.L. and Womble, M. (1991). *Working with African Americans: The professional's handbook.* Chicago: HRDI International Press.

Burgest, D.R. (1982). "Worldviews: Implications for social theory and third world people," in D.R. Burgest (ed.), *Social work practice with minorities*, (pp. 45–56). Metuchen, NJ: The Scarecrow Press.

Burgest, D.R. (1981). "Theory on White supremacy and Black oppression." *Black Books Bulletin*, 7(2), 26–30.

Carruthers, J.H. (1989). "Towards the Development of a Black Social Theory." Paper presented at the Howard University, Graduate Student Council's Distinguished Lecture Series, Washington, D.C., February 9.

Carruthers, J.H. (1981). "Reflections on the history of the Afrocentric worldview." *Black Books Bulletin*, 7(1), 4–7.

Carruthers, J.H. (1972). *Science and oppression.* Chicago: The Center for Inner City Studies.

Carter, D. & Wilson, R. (1994). *Minorities in higher education.* Washington, DC: American Council on Education.

Clark, J.H. (1991). *Notes for an African world revolution: Africans at the crossroads.* Trenton, NJ: Africa World Press, Inc.

Cook, N. & Kono, S. (1977). "Black psychology: The third great tradition." *Journal of Black Psychology*, 3(2), 18–30.

Diop, C.A. (1978). *The cultural unity of Black Africa.* Chicago: Third World Press.

Dixon, V. (1976). "World views and research methodology," in L. King, V. Dixon, and W. Nobles (eds.), *African philosophy: Assumptions and paradigms for research on Black persons*, (pp. 51–93). Los Angeles: Fanon Center Publications.

Epps, E.G. (1989). "Academic culture and the minority professor." *Academe*, 75(5), 23–26.

Hale-Benson, J. (1982). *Black children: Their roots, culture, and learning styles.* Provo, UT: Brigham Young University Press.

Herskovits, M.J. (1941). *The myth of the negro past.* New York: Harper & Row.

Hilliard, A.G. (1989). "Kemetic concepts in education," in I.V. Sertima (ed., 3rd printing), *Nile valley civilizations.* Atlanta: Morehouse College.

Jochannon, Y. Ben (1976). *Black clergy without a Black theology.* New York: Alkebulan Books.

Kambon, K. (aka Joe Baldwin), (1992). *The African personality in america: An Africancentered framework.* Tallahassee, FL: Nubian Nation Publication.

Kershaw, T. (1992). "Afrocentrism and the Afrocentric method." *The Western Journal of Black Studies*, 16(3), 160–168.

Khatib, S., Akbar, N., McGee, D. and Nobles, W. (1979). "Voodoo or IQ: An introduction to African psychology," in W.D. Smith, K.H. Burlew, M.H. Mosley and W.M. Whitney (eds.) *Reflections on Black psychology*. Washington, DC: University Press of America.

Mbiti, J. (1970). *African religions and philosophy*. Garden City, NY: Anchor Books.

Mercer, J. (1991). "Nile valley scholars bring new light and controversy to African studies." *Black Issues in Higher Education*, 7(26), 1, 12–17.

Meyers, L.J. (1988). *An Afrocentric world view: Introduction to an optimal psychology*. Dubuque, IA: Kendall-Hunt.

Meyers, L.J. (1985). "Transpersonal psychology: The role of the Afrocentric paradigm." *The Journal of Black Psychology*, 12(1), 31–42.

Nichols, E. (1987). "Counseling perspectives for a multi-ethnic and pluralistic work force." Paper presented at the National Association of Social Workers Annual Conference, New Orleans, LA, September.

Nicholson, D. (1991). "Afrocentrism and the tribalization of America." *New York Teacher*, 32(11), 15.

Nobles, W.W. (1988). "African-American family life: An instrument of culture," in H.P. McAdoo (2nd Ed.), *Black families* (pp. 44–53). Beverly Hills, CA: Sage.

Nobles, W.W. (1980). "African philosophy: Foundations for Black psychology," in R. Jones (3rd Ed.), *Black psychology*, (pp. 23–35). New York: Harper and Row.

Oliver, J. and Brown, L. (1988). "The development and implementation of a minority recruitment plan: Process, strategy and results." *Journal of Social Work Education*, 24(2), 175–185.

Pettigrew, L.E. (1991). "Recruiting students of color: Some do's and don'ts." *Black Issues in Higher Education*, 8(3), 64.

Phillips, F.B. (1990). "NTU psychotherapy: An Afrocentric approach." *The Journal of Black Psychology*, 17(1), 55–74.

Pinderhughes, E. (1985). "Race, ethnicity, class: As practitioner and client variables," in M.W. Day (ed.), *The socio-cultural dimensions of mental health*, (pp. 22–36). New York: Vintage Press.

Ravitch, D. (1991). "Multiculturalism: E pluribus plures." *The American Scholar*, Summer, 337–354.

Richards, D.M. (1989). *Let the circle be unbroken: The implications of African spirituality in the Diaspora*. New York: Dept. of Black & Puerto Rican Studies, Hunter College.

Schiele, J.H. (1996). "Afrocentricity: An emerging paradigm in social work practice." *Social Work*, 41(3), 284–294.

Schiele, J.H. (1994). "Afrocentricity as an alternative world view for equality." *Journal of Progressive Human Services*, 5(1), in press.

Schiele, J.H. (1993). "Cultural oppression, African Americans, and social work practice." *Black Caucus: Journal of the National Association of Black Social Workers*, Fall (2), 20–34.

Schiele, J.H. (1991a). "Afrocentricity for all." *Black Issues in Higher Education*, 8(15), 27.

Schiele, J.H. (1991b). "An epistemological perspective on intelligence assessment among African-American children." *Journal of Black Psychology*, 17(2), 23–36.

Schiele, J.H. (1990). "Organizational theory from an Afrocentric perspective." *Journal of Black Studies*, 21(2), 145–161.

Schlesinger, A. (1991). "The disuniting of America: What we all stand to lose if multicultural education takes the wrong approach." *American Educator*, 15(3), 14, 21–27, 28–31, 32–33.

Shakir, A.A. (1989). "Tougaloo renaissance: Reflecting, renewing, and rededicating." President's Inaugural Address given at Tougaloo College, Tougaloo, Mississippi, May 13.

Shannker, A. (1991). "Afrocentric education." *New York Teacher*, 32(15), 12.

Sudarkasa, N. (1988). "Interpreting the African heritage in Afro-American family organization," in H.P. McAdoo (2nd Ed.), *Black families*, (pp. 27–43). Beverly Hills, CA: Sage.

Weems, L. (1974). "Black community research needs: Methods, model, and modalities," in L.E. Gary (ed.), *Social Research and the Black Community: Selected Issues and Priorities*. Washington, DC: Institute for Urban Affairs.

Welsing, F.C. (1991). *The Isis papers: The keys to the colors*. Chicago: Third World Press.

Wright, B.E. (1984). *The psychopathic racial personality and other essays*. Chicago: Third World Press.

Zahan, D. (1979). *The religion, spirituality, and thought of traditional africa*. Chicago: University of Chicago Press.

3

Organizational Theory from an Afrocentric Perspective

Jerome H. Schiele

Although possessing widely differing assumptions about organizational and human nature, organizational theories all have one thing in common: they reflect the conceptual frameworks of western social science, which are derivatives of western ideology and thought. By exclusively reflecting the values and notions of western society, these theories are circumscribable and biased and omit different conceptualizations of human beings and society found in other cultures. To this extent, and because western social science has negated the world view of African people (Carruthers, 1989; Asante, 1987; Akbar, 1984; Karenga, 1982), it has been argued that there be developed an alternative social science model reflective of the cultural background and cultural reality of African people (Asante 1988, 1980a; Baldwin, 1986; Baldwin and Bell, 1985; Akbar, 1985, 1984; Williams, 1981; Semmes, 1981; Nobles, 1980, 1978; Dixon, 1976). This alternative model is known as the Afrocentric model. To date, most work along these lines has applied the Afrocentric model to individual and group behavior, but its application to organizational theory has been neglected.

The purpose of this article is to reconceptualize organizational theory by employing the Afrocentric paradigm. Drawing from some of the tenets of the Afrocentric paradigm, this article identifies and discusses some of the characteristics of an Afrocentric organization and the extent to which these characteristics are congruent or incongruent with western theories of organizations. Hence this chapter offers an alternative conceptual paradigm for the study of formal organizations in general, and human service organizations in specific.[1]

The addition of a new conceptual paradigm for the study of human service organizations will contribute to the diversification—and strengthening—of the total body of human service organization theory and knowledge. In addition, the application of the Afrocentric model to organizational theory will help to

An earlier version of this essay appeared in *Journal of Black Studies* 21, 2 (December 1990): 145–161 and is adapted/reprinted with the permission of the copyright holder/author.

1. Within the study of formal organizations, there is the study of human service organizations. Human service organizations are organizations that process, sustain or change individuals. Within these organizations, human beings are considered the "raw material". Some examples are welfare organizations, hospitals, schools, mental health agencies, and churches. For a detailed discussion, see Y. Hasenfeld. *Human Service Organizations*. Englewood Cliffs, N.J.: Prentice-Hall, 1983, and Y. Hasenfeld and R. English. *Human Service Organizations*. Ann Arbor, Mich.: University of Michigan Press, 1974.

broaden its conceptual knowledge base as a social science model. To this end, this article seeks to contribute to the study of Afrocentric concepts and issues (i.e., Afrology)[2] and to highlight the worldview of African people in the context of organizational theory.

Tenets of Afrocentric Paradigm

The Afrocentric paradigm is predicated on traditional African philosophical assumptions that emphasize the interconnectedness and interdependency of natural phenomena. From this perspective, all modalities and realities are viewed as one, and there is no demarcation between the spiritual and material, substance and form (Asante, 1980b). Indeed, in African philosophy, "the anthropocentric ontology was a complete unity which nothing could destroy" (Nobles, 1980: 26). Accordingly, all natural phenomena are functionally connected and to destroy one part is to destroy the whole existence of the universe, even the creator (Nobles, 1980). As Asante (1980b: 50) observes, "the continuity from material to spiritual is the universal basis of the Afrocentric viewpoint". In addition, the Afrocentric paradigm views affect, rhythm, rituals, and symbols as valid determiners of human activity and reality (Akbar, 1984; Nichols, 1976; Dixon, 1976).

The tenets of the Afrocentric model reflect its collective, rhythmic, nonmaterial or spiritual, and affective character. The following is a nonexhaustive enumeration of the tenets of the Afrocentric paradigm, which reflect the model's assumptions about human beings and human behavior. The tenets are derived from the works of several scholars (see Asante, 1988, 1980a, 1980b; Baldwin, 1986, 1981; Akbar, 1985, 1984, 1976; Boykin and Toms, 1985; Boykin, 1983; Hale-Benson, 1982; Williams, 1981; Nobles, 1980, 1978; Khatib et al., 1979; Nichols, 1976; Dixon, 1976; Mbiti, 1970). The underlying theme of most of these scholars' works is that because traditional African philosophical assumptions continue to be a major part of the African-American's ethos, there is a need for a social science model or conceptual paradigms that reflect the cultural background and reality of African people. The tenets are as follows:

1) Human beings are conceived collectively.
2) Human beings are spiritual.
3) Human beings are good.
4) The affective approach to knowledge is epistemologically valid.
5) Much of human behavior is nonrational.
6) The axiology or highest value lies in interpersonal relations.

Before specifically addressing the applicability of these tenets to organizational theory, the next section will examine some basic distinctions between the Afrocentric model and mainstream theories of organizations.

---

2. For a detailed discussion on Afrology, see M. K. Asante. *Afrocentricity*. Trenton, N.J.: Africa World Press, Inc., 1988.

Distinctions between Afrocentric and Mainstream Organizational Theories

There are some fundamental distinctions in the conceptions of organizations between the Afrocentric model and mainstream (i.e., western) organizational theories. Albeit there are similarities between the Afrocentric model and some mainstream organizational theories, a major difference between the Afrocentric model and mainstream organizational theories lies in, what this writer will refer to as, "organizational normality" (i.e., that which is considered the standard or acceptability of reality for organizations). Many mainstream or western organizational theories—with the exception of the Neo-Marxist perspective—concentrate on the factors affecting organizational productivity (i.e., how fast, how much and how well something is produced or, in the case of human service organizations, how well and how efficient people are processed, sustained or changed). This focus is in the theory of bureaucracy's principle of rationality (Weber, 1946), in the scientific management's notion of maximum productivity (Hasenfeld, 1983), in the human relation's assumption that increased worker satisfaction will induce increased productivity (Kaplan and Tausky, 1977), in the decision-making theory's concepts of "satisficing" and "performance gap" (Hasenfeld, 1983), in the energy expended by Lawrence and Lorsch to identify the attributes of a "highly effective organization" (Lawrence and Lorsch, 1967), in the natural system model's emphasis on goal displacement and how this displacement causes the unattainment of formal, official goals (Scott, 1967), and in the political economy's focus on how the distribution of power and the availability of resources both within and without organizations shape the choice of service technologies used for production. As Perrow (1978) astutely observes, even when such theories as the natural systems and human relations theories reject mechanical and rationalistic notions of organizations and accept informal, humanistic and natural characteristics, these characteristics are viewed as constraints on the organization in becoming more efficient (rational) in achieving its announced goals—in other words, constraining its rate of production.

Another fundamental characteristic of mainstream or western theories of organizations is the emphasis placed on the individual organization member. Even the human relations model, with its focus on small group processes, uses this group process to affect the individual's job satisfaction and productivity. Part of this individual focus is a function of the manner in which "individual" is conceived in the western tradition, especially in western social science. Akbar (1984) comments on this observation in his discussion of what he calls the Eurocentric social science model. Akbar maintains that one of the salient attributes of the Eurocentric model is its individualistic character. Individualism is emphasized in the Eurocentric model, according to Akbar, because human identity is conceived insularly: it is assumed that the individual can be understood separate from others. By focusing on this conception of human identity, Akbar contends that the individual's corporate identity (e.g., significant others such as family members, community members, and friends) is of secondary importance in conceiving the individual.

The limited conception of human identity found in the Eurocentric model is reflected in the way the "client" is conceived in human service organization theory. Throughout the human service organization literature, "client" is usually conceived as one individual, as if she or he lives in a vacuum and is not a part of a social group.

Unlike the Eurocentric model's conception of identity, individual identity is conceived as a collective identity within the Afrocentric model (Akbar, 1984; Baldwin, 1981; Nobles, 1980). Although this model emphasizes collectivity, it does not reject the notion of uniqueness (Boykin and Toms, 1985; Akbar, 1984; Boykin, 1983). Rather, it rejects the idea that the individual can be understood separate from others (Akbar, 1984). For example, Mbiti (1970: 141) uses the African adage "I am because we are and because we are, therefore I am" to capture the essence of this collective identity. Similarly, Cook and Kono (1977: 26) state that in Black or African psychology "individuality in the sense of self in opposition to the group disappears and is replaced by a common understanding and a common goal". Moreover, Asante's (1988) concept of the "collective cognitive imperative" (i.e., the full spiritual and intellectual commitment to a vision by a group), Nobles' (1980) concept of "experimental communality" or the sharing of a particular experience by a particular group of people, and Baldwin's (1981) concept of "African self consciousness"[3] are important in understanding a fundamental characteristic of Africentrism, which is its emphasis on discerning similarities or commonalities of a people and their condition, instead of discerning and emphasizing individual differences. Because of this, Africentrism gives preeminence to the group; the welfare of the group takes precedence over the welfare of the individual. This group orientation has also been discussed by Hunt (1974), who asserts that the black perspective on public management is a collective orientation, wherein the public demands and interests of blacks as a group supplant the needs of blacks as individuals.

An important issue that needs to be addressed if further work is to be done with the Afrocentric approach to organizations is the question of the validity of the collective orientation assumption of black or African-Americans. In recent years, especially after the passage of civil rights and affirmative action legislation, a significant number of African-Americans with advanced training and education have enjoyed economic progress, while, concomitantly, the economic condition of a broad number of African-Americans has worsened (Wilson, 1987, 1980). This apparent economic class schism within the African-American community may have attenuated the collective bond and identity of African-Americans. Further conceptual work, therefore, is needed to grapple with innovative ways of responding to the effects of social class distinctions.

Assuming that the collective orientation assumption is valid—and being mindful that the Afrocentric model is predicated on "traditional" African philosophical assumptions—the interests of the organization as a whole or collective would be the primary concern within an Afrocentric framework, albeit individual interests and concerns would be recognized. Thus, from an Afrocentric perspective, organizational and group survival replaces productivity as the overriding concern. Organizational normality, therefore, would not be defined by the quantity or efficiency of production (as is the case in the western theories of organizations) but

---

3. Joseph Baldwin defines "African self consciousness" as the conscious level process of communal phenomenology. He also views it as a basic core of black personality. For a detailed discussion, see J. Baldwin. "Notes on an afrocentric theory of Black personality." *Western J. of Black Studies* 5, 3: 172–179, 1981.

rather the way in which an organization preserves itself (i.e., whether the behaviors employed by organizational members maintain the survival of the organization). Although this view of survival is similar to the concept of survival found in the Natural Systems model—in that organizational survival is given high importance—a fundamental difference is that survival in the Natural Systems model places considerable emphasis on goal attainment, as if goal attainment and survival were synonymous. Survival in the Afrocentric perspective conceives survival in itself as paramount. Though goal attainment would be important within an Afrocentric organization, survival in an organization based on Afrocentric principles would include more than just goal attainment. It would, for example, include the maintenance of common objectives, concerns, and sentiments among organizational members.

In addition to the maintenance of common objectives, concerns and sentiments among organizational members, the Afrocentric model's concept of survival also transcends the boundaries of the organization and extends into the community. This focus highlights organization-community relations more strongly than any existing human service organization theory. Just as it is unthinkable to understand the individual separate from others in the Afrocentric model so would it be to understand the organization separate from the community to which it is a part and to which it serves. Therefore, to a considerable extent, the organization and the community are viewed as one, in that the organization's purpose is a reflection of the community's purpose. To the extent that this bond exists between the organization and the community, it is assumed that the survival of the organization is significantly related to the survival of the community and vice versa. Hence, the collective survival notion found in the Afrocentric model involves the coalescence of individual, organizational, and community identity.

Fundamentally, the Afrocentric model differs from existing organizational theories in its view of organizational normality, its concept of human identity, and its notion of organizational survival. Further differences are highlighted below as tenets of the Afrocentric model are applied to describe how an Afrocentric organization might look like and what it might emphasize.

Afrocentric Tenets and Organizational Theory

As this section elucidates the tenets and their application to organizational theory, it also discusses the extent to which these tenets are congruent or incongruent with tenets of mainstream, western-oriented organizational theories. This is achieved by presenting each tenet and discussing its applicability to the study of human service organizations. The first tenet is presented below.

Human Beings Are Conceived Collectively

As was previously mentioned, the Afrocentric model places considerable emphasis on a collective conceptualization of human beings and collective survival. Hence, organizational unity would be a primary goal of an Afrocentric organization. To encourage an orientation toward organizational unity, low internal differentiation of work tasks would probably suit an organization based on Afrocentric principles. This would help constrain the emergence of well-defined organizational subunits or subdivisions, which cause organizational members to become more committed to the goals and interests of their particular subunits than to the goals and interests of the organization as a whole (Selznick, 1946). Because of the Afrocentric model's emphasis on group similarities or group "oneness", the value of superordinate and subordinate relationships would be downplayed in favor of consensus group processes. There would be a more equitable distribution of power, unlike the Weberian model.

The human relations model probably comes the closest to an approximation of the latter in that it argues against a strict hierarchical power structure and extensive division of labor and encourages the participation of subordinates in the decision-making process (Kaplan and Tausky, 1977). However, the human relations model still views these persons as "subordinates", implying that they are less competent than their superiors in making decisions. The Afrocentric paradigm would carry the argument against a rigid hierarchical power structure even further.

Human Beings Are Spiritual

In the Afrocentric model, there is recognition of the spiritual or nonmaterial aspect of human beings. Akbar (1984: 408) observes "when men and women are reduced to their lowest terms they are invisible and of an universal substance" and that without the inclusion of the spiritual or metaphysical element of humans, the human makeup is incomplete. Hence the inclusion and recognition of the spiritual element of humans in the Afrocentric model is indicative of its holistic perspective: mind, body, and soul are believed to be interdependent and interrelated phenomena (Asante, 1987; Akbar, 1984; Nobles, 1980; Weems, 1974; Mbiti, 1970); thus, for example, "to have a good body means that one has a good mind, and vice versa; one cannot exist without the other" (Weems, 1974: 32).

As it relates to organizational theory, much emphasis would be placed on enhancing the spirituality of organizational members in the Afrocentric paradigm. Spirituality, as defined by Boykin and Toms (1985: 41), is "conducting one's life as though its essence were vitalistic rather than mechanistic and as though transcending forces significantly govern the lives of people". Spirituality, according to Akbar (1984: 409), also implies morality, in that "morality and spirituality are inseparable".

To the degree that spirituality implies morality, there is recognition of "organizational morality" in the Afrocentric model. Organizational morality refers to an organizational state in which members of an organization have the highest regard for human life and dignity and consistently display behaviors that reflect this value. This respect is not assumed to be held exclusively for organizational members but also for clients and others served by the human service organization. To this end, humanistic values, such as client and worker self-worth, worker empathy and concern for the welfare of clients and co-workers, are moved from a status of obscurity to the forefront of organizational priorities. This is especially relevant to human service organizations whose purpose is to promote the general well-being of individuals in society (Hasenfeld, 1983). Further conceptual work, however, is needed to build on this notion of organizational spirituality/morality.

Nonetheless, the development and maintenance of organizational members' spirituality would be viewed as a critical factor in shaping the mental and physical performance of members. It would be assumed that without a well nourished and developed spirit, the mental and physical performance of organizational members will be at a minimum.

Human Beings Are Good

Consistent with the notions of spirituality and morality, the Afrocentric paradigm recognizes the fundamental goodness of human beings. This model rejects a pessimistic perspective of human nature and posits that humans have a proclivity towards enhancing life in a constructive manner (Asante, 1988, 1980a; Akbar, 1984).

This notion of inherent goodness is congruent with the human relation model's assumption "that man is basically good" (Kaplan and Tausky, 1977: 171) and is incongruent with the scientific model or McGregor's (1960) theory X which posits that human beings must be controlled, coerced, and threatened with punishment to work, as if adults were recalcitrant children. Contrarily, the Afrocentric model views human beings as having the capacity for self mastery, self direction, and self regulation (Akbar, 1984). Hence, from an Afrocentric organizational perspective, there would be no need to practice rigid supervision and control. Further conceptual work in this area is needed, especially as it relates to how an Afrocentric perspective would, for example, deal with accountability, the hiring and firing of workers, and the reprehension of workers.

The Affective Approach To Knowledge Is Epistemologically Valid

In the Afrocentric model, emphasis is placed on an affective epistemology. For example, Akbar (1984: 410) maintains that a major premise of Afrocentric social science is that "the most direct experience of self is through emotion or affect". Consistent with this focus on affect, Nichols (1976), in his typology of the philosophical aspects of cultural differences, shows that the epistemology or valid way of knowing for African-Americans is affective, where one knows through symbolic imagery and rhythm. Dixon (1976) defines symbolic imagery as the use of phenomena, such as words, gestures and objects, to convey multiple meanings, and, like Nichols, asserts that Africans throughout the diaspora generally know reality through the synthesis of symbolic imagery and affect. Other scholars have also discussed the importance of affect in the lives of African-Americans (Asante, 1988, 1980a; Boykin, 1983; Hale-Benson, 1982; Baldwin, 1981; Brown, 1978; Boykin, 1977; Senghor, 1962). Indeed, feeling has been said to be a major criterion when examining the aesthetics of African-Americans (Asante, 1988). The focus on affect in the Afrocentric model, however, does not preclude recognition and use of rationality. Instead, affect, as a means of knowing, is viewed as offsetting the use of rationality (Akbar, 1984).

As it relates to organizations, this affective, epistemological character of the Afrocentric model has a significant implication for evaluating worker performance. Instead of the considerable emphasis placed on quantifying worker performance, which is characteristic of bureaucracies (Lipsky, 1980), a more balanced approach would be used in Afrocentric organizations that would include both quantitative and subjective (qualitative) means of determining worker performance. One example of a qualitative means of performance evaluation is the use of field or naturalistic observations. By observing the worker while executing his or her daily work tasks, the observer can discern the intricate attributes of the worker and the worker's immediate work milieu. These intricacies are difficult to tap and observe when exclusively relying on quantitative measures. As Lipsky (1980: 168) states, "actual performance is virtually impossible to measure...aspects of performance can be measured...but the most important dimensions of service performance defy calibration". To fortify the validity of performance evaluations, qualitative measures would be considered appropriate and necessary for an organization based on Afrocentric principles.

Much of Human Behavior Is Nonrational

Consistent with the epistemology of affect, the Afrocentric paradigm views much of human behavior as deriving from feeling in lieu of reasoning (Akbar, 1984). This is not to imply that humans are without rationality, but that humans are influenced by a multitude of positive and negative life experiences resulting from social interaction. The emotions elicited by these experiences can have an unpredictable effect on the decisions, actions, and mood of people that sometimes obviate the exercise and use of rationality.

Moreover, this nonrationalistic perspective of human behavior refutes the assumption that human beings are invariably rational, mechanistic, and objective. Such a rationalistic perspective prevents understanding of much of the human experience by omitting the influence of affect (Akbar, 1984) and values that shape human biases.

Because of the pervasive influence of the Weberian school of organizational theory, there is an implicit and, to a great extent, explicit assumption that organizations should strive for rationality or efficiency (i.e., that the organization employs the most efficient unit of activity to attain its goals). Implied in such an objective is that in order to employ the most efficient unit of activity, there certainly must be rational people to develop and implement these activities. In contrast, the Afrocentric paradigm would not place so much emphasis on efficiency or rationality because (1) it would recognize the important role of affect in the lives of people; (2) it would realize that people are not infallible, impervious superbeings; and (3) because of its de-emphasis on the rate of production, time and speed would be downplayed in organizational processes.

The Axiology or Highest Value Lies in Interpersonal Relations

Nichols (1976) shows that the axiology or highest value for African-Americans lies in the interpersonal relationships between and among people. The maintenance and enhancement of the interpersonal relationship is considered the most preeminent value in the Afrocentric paradigm. Such an emphasis fosters a human centered orientation to life in lieu of an object or material orientation. Accordingly, the acquisition of an object or material item would not take precedence over maintaining and strengthening interpersonal ties.

The focus on interpersonal relationships in existing organizational models is best represented in the human relations model, with its emphasis on increasing interpersonal competence (Kaplan and Tausky, 1977), warm personal ties (Litwak, 1978), and collegial relationships (Litwak, 1978; Kaplan and Tausky, 1977). The strengthening of interpersonal competence and relationships in the human relations model, however, is used as a strategy to increase workers' satisfaction, through increased participation, in order to affect worker performance and increase work efforts. Thus, increased interpersonal ties is viewed as a means to achieve an end. This weakens and undermines the human relation model's interpersonal character and assertion.

Conversely, in the Afrocentric model, the strengthening of interpersonal relationships between and among organizational members would be perceived as an end in itself. As was mentioned, the major focus in Africentrism is not on how much or how fast something is produced but rather the way in which the organization preserves itself. Accordingly, how can an organization preserve or sustain itself, and remain unified, without valuable, interpersonal bonds among and between its members? Meaningful and indelible interpersonal bonds among organizational members would facilitate a human service organization to uniformly serve and represent its community, providing the community with a model for unity through the practice of an interpersonal, human centered axiology.

Implications for Research and Practice

Although this chapter has described several characteristics of an Afrocentric organizational paradigm, additional conceptual work needs to be explored to fully develop an Afrocentric organizational model. For example, since organizational survival is a primary concern of the Afrocentric perspective, several research questions emerge for an Afrocentric oriented organization to function in an Eurocentric or western oriented society: (1) How can collectively oriented people in an Afrocentric organization maintain a collective orientation in a society that is, to a considerable extent, antithetical to a collective, communal focus; (2) How would an Afrocentric oriented organization, with its de-emphasis on efficiency, survive in a society that places substantial value on efficiency; (3) How would other external factors, such as legal and legislative mandates, affect the de-emphasis on efficiency in an Afrocentric organization; (4) How would this type of organization establish a communal bond with members of a community who are influenced by the dominant, western value of individualism; and (5) What role would social class and race play in shaping organization-community relations? These are just a few research questions that speak to organization-environment relations.

Other examples of areas needing exploration are as follows: (1) What techniques or methods would be appropriate for an Afrocentric human service organization; (2) How would goals be formulated in an organization based on Afrocentric principles; and (3) What should be the appropriate size of an Afrocentric organization? These, and other, research efforts should contribute significantly to the application of the Afrocentric model to the study of formal organizations in general and human service organizations in specific.

In addition to the latter research implications, the Afrocentric model can also be useful for African-American managers, and others, working in human service organizations. For example, the interpersonal, human centered axiology found in the Afrocentric model can assist managers in strengthening the primary function of human service organizations which is to protect, sustain and promote the personal well-being of individuals in society (Hasenfeld, 1983). This humanistic focus can also be employed to improve interpersonal relations between and among organizational members, and it would offset the concern over efficiency.

The Afrocentric model's focus on organizational collectivity and low internal differentiation can be used by human service personnel to preclude the heavy emphasis placed upon subunit or subdivision interests created by high internal differentiation. As a result, this focus will help alleviate internal, organizational conflict and will facilitate greater interest among workers in the goals of the entire organization. This focus is especially needed for human service organizations that serve the African-American community. The African-American community, especially low-income African-American communities, face many social problems and are in critical need of assistance. Human service organizations that serve these communities and that experience considerable, internal organizational conflict can impede the attainment of the overall goals of the organization and the community, thus hindering the community from receiving adequate services and resources for social change.

The Afrocentric model's emphasis on community relations can be used by members of human service organizations to better understand the dynamics and importance of organization-community relations. Often, the needs of a community, as perceived by indigenous persons, are omitted in the planning and delivery of human services. The Afrocentric framework will help sensitize members of a human service organization to the needs, objectives and idiosyncrasies of the community being served. This sensitization will not only help foster better organization-community relations; it will also aid in the planning and administering of appropriate human services—services that are congruent with the needs and objectives of the community rather than the needs and objectives of a nonindigenous, organizational elite.

Summary and Conclusion

This chaper has offered an alternative conceptual framework for the study of formal organizations in general but human service organizations in specific—the Afrocentric paradigm. Drawing from several underlying tenets of the Afrocentric model, it was argued that an Afrocentric organization would be characterized by an unified, collective membership maintaining survival; a close identification between the community and the organization; a de-emphasis on the rate of production and efficiency; low internal differentiation; an emphasis on consensus decision-making; a positive, not negative, outlook on worker tendencies; a strong emphasis on enhancing members' spirituality; a balanced (i.e., qualitative and quantitative) means of evaluating worker performance; and an interpersonal, human centered axiology.

Because of its affective, collective, metaphysical/spiritual, and humanistic character, the Afrocentric paradigm offers a more complete representation of human qualities and needs. Rational (efficient), objective, and material/object oriented models fail to take into consideration the humanism of people and the circumstances that preclude the use of rationality. This lack of consideration, found in western organizational theories, has fostered a brand of human service organizations that concern themselves not with the human needs and concerns of their members and clients, but with becoming more efficient (rational) in the fruition of their announced, and often times unattainable, goals. It is time that human service organizations accept a model that is more consistent with and reflective of the human experience. The Afrocentric model best represents that experience.

References

Akbar, N. (1985). "Our destiny: Authors of a scientific revolution," in H.P. McAdoo (ed.) *Black Children*. Beverly Hills: Sage Publications.

———. (1984). "Afrocentric social sciences for human liberation." *Journal of Black Studies*, 14, 4: 395–414.

———. (1976) "Rhythmic patterns in African personality," in L. King, V. Dixon and W. Nobles (eds.), *African philosophy: Assumptions and paradigms for research on Black people*. Los Angeles: Fanon Center Publicantions.

Asante, M.K. (1988). *Afrocentricity*. Trenton, NJ: Africa World Press, Inc.

———. (1987). *The Afrocentric Idea*. Philadelphia, PA: Temple University Press.

———. (1980a). *Afrocentricity: The Theory of Social Change*. Buffalo: Amulefi Publishers.

———. (1980b). "International/intercultural relations," in M.K. Asante and A.S.Vandi (eds.), *Contemporary Black Thought: Alternative Analyses in Social and Behavioral Science*. Beverly Hills: Sage Publications.

Baldwin, J. (1986). "African (Black) Psychology: Issues and synthesis." *Journal of Black Studies*, 16, 3: 235–249.

———. (1981). "Notes on an Afrocentric theory of Black personality." *The Western Journal of Black Studies*, 5: 172–179.

Baldwin, J. and Bell, Y. (1985). "The African self-consciousness scale: An Afrocentric personality questionnaire." *The Western Journal of Black Studies*, 9, 2: 62–68.

Boykin, W. (1983). "The academic performance of Afro-American children," in J. Spence (ed.), *Achievement and Achievement Motives*. San Francisco: W. Freeman.

———. (1977). "Experimental psychology from a Black perspective: Issues and examples." *The Journal of Black Psychology*, 3, 1: 29–50.

Boykin, W. and Toms, F. (1985). "Black child socialization: A conceptual framework," in H.P. McAdoo (ed.), *Black Children*. Beverly Hills: Sage Publications.

Brown, I. (1978). *Psychology of the Black Experience: A Cultural Integrity Viewpoint*. Unpublished manuscript.

Carruthers, J. (1989). *Towards the Development of a Black Social Theory*. Paper presented at the Howard University, Graduate Student Council's Distinguished Lecture Series, Washington, D.C., February 9.

Cook, N. and Kono, S. (1977). "Black psychology: The third great tradition." *The Journal of Black Psychology*, 3, 2: 18–20.

Dixon, V. (1976). "World views and research methodology," in L. King, V. Dixon, and W. Nobles (eds.), *African Philosophy: Assumptions and Paradigms for Research on Black Persons*. Los Angeles: Fanon Center Publications.

Hale-Benson, J. (1982). *Black Children: Their Roots, Culture, and Learning Styles*. Provo, UT: Brigham Young University Press.

Hasenfeld, Y. (1983). *Human Service Organizations*. Englewood Cliffs, N.J.: Prentice-Hall.

Hunt, D. (1974). "The black perspective on public management." *Public Administration Review*, 34, 6: 520–525.

Kaplan, H. and Tausky, C. (1977). "Humanism in organizations: A critical appraisal." *Public Administration Review*, 37, 5: 171–180.

Karenga, M. (1982). *Introduction to Black Studies*. Englewood, CA: Kawaida Publications

Khatib, S., Akbar, N., McGee, D. and Nobles, W. (1979). "Voodoo or IQ: An introduction to African psychology," in W.D. Smith, K.H. Burlew, M.H. Mosley and W.M. Whitney (eds.), *Reflections on Black Psychology*. Washington, DC: University Press of America.

Lawrence, P.R. and Lorsch, J.W. (1967). *Organization and Environment: Managing Differentiation and Integration*. Cambridge, MA: Harvard Graduate School of Business Administration.

Lipsky, M. (1980). *Street-level Bureaucracy*. New York: Russell Sage Foundation.

Litwak, E. (1978). "Organizational constructs and mega bureaucracy," in R.S. Sarri and Y. Hansenfeld (eds.), *The Management of Human Services*. New York: Columbia University Press.

Mbiti, J. (1970). *African Religions and Philosophy*. Garden City, NY: Anchor Books.

McGregor, D. (1960). *The Human Side of Enterprise*. New York: McGraw-Hill.

Nichols, E. (1976). *The Philosophical Aspects of Cultural Differences*. Unpublished manuscript.

Nobles, W. (1980). "African philosophy: Foundations for Black psychology," in R. Jones (3rd Ed.), *Black Psychology*. New York: Harper and Row.

———. (1978). *African Consciousness and Liberation Struggles: Implications for the Development and Construction of Scientific Paradigms*. Unpublished manuscript.

Perrow, C. (1978). "Demystifying organizations," in R.S. Sarri and Y. Hasenfeld (eds.), *The Management of Human Services*. New York: Columbia University Press.

Scott, R. (1967). "The factory as a social service organization: Goal displacement in workshops for the blind." *Social Problems*, 15: 160–175.

Selznick, P. (1946). "Foundation for the theory of organization." *American Sociological Review*, 13: 25–35.

Semmes, C.E. (1981). "Foundations of an afrocentric social science: Implication for curriculum-building, theory, and research in Black Studies." *Journal of Black Studies*, 12, 1: 3–17.

Senghor, L. (1962). "What is negritude?" *Negro Digest*, 6: 3–6.

Weber, M. (1946). *From Max Weber: Essays in Sociology*. New York: Oxford University Press.

Weems, L. (1974). "Black community research needs: Methods, model, and modalities," in L.E. Gary (ed.), *Social Research and the Black Community: Selected Issues and Priorities*. Washington, DC: Institute for Urban Affairs.

Williams, R.L. (1981). *The Collective Black Mind: An Afro-Centric Theory of Black Personality*. St. Louis: Williams & Associates.

Wilson, W.J. (1987). *The Truly Disadvantaged: The Inner City, The Underclass, and Public Policy*. Chicago: University of Chicago Press.

———. (1980). *The Declining Significance of Race: Blacks and Changing American Institutions*. Chicago: University of Chicago Press.

4

Ethnicity and Color in Ancient Egypt

Prince Brown, Jr.

Egypt's primacy on the world's stage historically and culturally is an undisputed fact. In general it can be argued, with some confidence, that it is anterior to all other human cultures of which there is any record. Accordingly, it is much written about and is the subject of extended debates and controversies. One emerging controversy focuses on the question of the ethnicity and color of the Ancient Egyptians. Afrocentrists are now being taken to task for their interpretation that ancient Egypt was essentially an indigenous black African civilization (Diop, 1974; ben-Jochannan, 1989; Jackson, 1972; Hilliard; 1992; Williams, 1987). They are being accused of "distorting the archaeological and historical record" and in the process drawing "academically unsound" conclusions (Young, 1992, p. 2). Afrocentrists would contend that they are righting those records, allowing them to represent positions free of nationalistic and ethnic biases. Afrocentrists agree with their critic, Robert S. Bianchi (Egyptian advisor to the Journal Archaeology), that "only by a rigorous inspection of the data combined with academic integrity can such politicizing of history be stopped..." (Young, 1992, p. 2).

Background to the Controversy

Africans and African Americans have long argued that the writing of history has been manipulated to provide a role model for Europeans and their descendants. A key tool in the manipulation of history has been racism. The discussion about the ethnicity and color of the ancient Egyptians and the contention that Grecian civilization was inspired, in large measure, by the cultural traditions of Egypt (Coleman, 1992; Bernal, 1992) have taken on new urgency with the publication of Martin Bernal's two volume work, *Black Athena*.

Bernal has earned the enmity of many white scholars for the unmistakable message in his title, *Black Athena*, that Grecian civilization is simply a continuation of a "black" African tradition. And, in fact, African (Diop, 1974; ben-Jochannan, [1970] 1989), African American (Parker, 1917; Woodson, 1918; Jackson, 1972; Williams, 1987; Drake, 1987, 1990), and African Caribbean (James, 1954) scholars had made the claim earlier. All of these writers drew on work that had firmly established Bernal's point. Indeed, in 1872, 115 years before Bernal, W. Winwood Reade wrote that:

Egypt from the earliest times had been the university of Greece. It has been visited, according to tradition, by Orpheus and Homer: there Solon had studied law-making, there the rules and principles of the Pythagorean order had been obtained, there Thales had taken lessons in geometry, there Democritus had laughed and Xenophanes had sneered. And now every intellectual Greek made the voyage to that country; it was regarded as a part of education, as a pilgrimage to the cradle-land of their mythology...In that country Herodotus resided several years...To Egypt came the divine Plato, and drank long and deeply of its ancient lore (Reade, [1872] 1943, pp. 60–61).

C.F. Volney, a French naturalist, was no less emphatic. Writing in 1791 (196 years before Bernal) he commented as follows upon viewing the ruins of the ancient Egyptian city of Thebes:

There a people, now forgotten, discovered, while others were yet barbarians, the elements of the arts and sciences. A race of men now rejected from society for their sable skin and frizzled hair, founded on the study of the laws of nature, those civil and religious systems which still govern the universe (Volney, [1791] 1991, pp. 16–17).

The following selection from Volney's extensive notes at the bottom of these same pages leaves no doubt about the point he wishes to make:

It would be easy to multiply citations upon this subject; from all which it follows, that we have the strongest reasons to believe that the country neighboring to the tropic was the cradle of the sciences, and of consequence that the first learned nation was a nation of Blacks; for it is incontrovertible, that, by the term Ethiopians, the ancients meant to represent a people of black complexion, thick lips, and woolly hair (Volney, [1791] 1991, p. 17n).

It is a testimony to the prevalence of institutional racism in scholarly writings that the works of Africans, and Africans in the diaspora, have traditionally been ignored by mainstream white intellectuals (with some few exceptions). It was only after Bernal, a white professor of Classics at Cornell University, discoursed on the subject that whites responded to the African and African American challenge to their scholarship. Some writers like the African Caribbean scholar, J.A. Rogers, is still largely ignored. This is despite the fact that his work is the result of extensive travels (Europe, Africa, America), drawing on numerous original sources, while giving meticulous attention to the slightest detail.

Two important points need to be kept in mind here: first, the claims and positions being taken by Afrocentrists are not, as some have suggested, fanciful flights of imagination intended to provide role models for African American youths (Young, 1992, p. 2; Schlesinger, 1991); rather, they are mainly based on data and scholarship of early white European researchers writing before about the mid-1800s. That is, before Euro-American scholarship became dominated by the "colonial mentality," accompanied by the need to invent "race." The second point is that some of the earliest challenges to the spread of ideological, political, self-interested scholarship being offered as scientific, cultural history came from a small group of white writers (Haddon & Huxley, 1936; Montagu, 1972; Gould, 1981; Harris, 1968) rather than Afrocentrists.

Indeed, in a work published in 1851, Thomas Smyth called attention to the deliberate destruction of the Egyptian archaeological record by European researchers (362–364n). Smyth's review of the literature relative to the origin and ethnicity of the ancient Egyptians is fully consistent with that being put forth by present-day Afrocentric writers.[1] Afrocentrists are now being labelled racists for making the same points. It is also to be noted that such criticisms come from the American historian, Arthur M. Schlesinger, who readily admits that he is not an expert on African history[2] (1991, p. 41).

Color, Race and Ethnicity

The scholarship of human relations is made cumbersome by the use of ill-defined concepts like "race" (Outlaw, 1990; King, 1971; Marger, 1991; Shanklin, 1994), its confused and often interchangeable use with "ethnicity" and an overemphasis on the significance of "color" (Shils, 1967). It is not the intent to debate these concepts here. "Race" is a social construct (Omi & Winant, 1986; Levin, 1991) and is, therefore, not a concern of this paper. Color is an incident of evolutionary factors and social practices; it has no innate bearing on ethnicity and ethnicity does not determine color. It is, nevertheless, true that evolutionary patterns have resulted in specific ethnic groups sharing certain physical characteristics that are in no way related to moral, psychological, intellectual and cultural disposition. These connections have been alleged by intellectuals intent on exploiting unproven and meaningless associations to the advantage of the ethnic groups with which they affiliate. For example, intellectuals of the former slave state of South Carolina were foremost in defense of "color" slavery. James H. Hammond, Governor, US Senator, and slaveholder spoke as follows to his colleagues in the Senate in 1858:

> In all social systems there must be a class to do the menial duties, to perform the drudgery of life. That is a class requiring but a low order of intellect and but little skill. Its requisites are vigor, docility, fidelity. Such a class you must have...It constitutes the very mud-sill of society...Fortunately for the South we have found a race adapted to that purpose to her hand...We do not think whites should be slaves either by law or necessity. Our slaves are black, of another, inferior race. The status in which we have placed them is an elevation. They are elevated from the condition in which God first created them; by being made our slaves (McKitrick, 1963, pp. 122–123).

Twenty years earlier Chancellor William Harper of the South Carolina College had offered his "Memoir on Slavery":

> If there are sordid, servile, and laborious offices to be performed, is it not better that there should be sordid, servile, and laborious beings to perform them? If

---

1. See Appendix No.1., Chapters I and II, pp. 353–375.
2. Schlesinger criticizes African American educators and psychologists who advocate Afrocentrism for what he alleges is their lack of knowledge about African history. But, in fact, these theorists have access to numerous historical references from scholars whose works provide documentation for an Afrocentric view. The writings, for example, of St. Clair Drake, Chancellor Williams, G.F.M. James, and Yosef A. ben-Jochannan are listed in the bibliography to this paper. Readers interested in African history may consult UNESCO International Scientific Committee's, *General History of Africa*, Volumes 1–8, 1889. Another valuable work is Basil Davidson's, *Africa in History*, 1991.

there were infallible marks by which individuals of inferior intellect, could be selected at their birth—would not the interests of society be served...And if this race be generally marked by such inferiority is it not fit they should fill them (Fredrickson, 1988, p. 22)?

The social construction of "race" (Delacampagne, 1990) has led to the institution of the practice of "racism." It is to be noted that John E. Coleman, in attempting to refute the thesis that Grecian civilization derived from Egyptian influence does not deny the existence of racism in scholarship (1992, p. 52). What does not follow so readily is his insistence that racism impacts only minimally the conclusions researchers reach. Marvin Harris, in his exhaustive study: *The Rise of Anthropological Theory*, draws a different conclusion. He points out the "overarching 'racial' determinism of every major mid-nineteenth-century figure," with the exception of John S. Mill and Henry T. Buckle, "who is customarily assigned a formative role in the development of anthropology as a distinctive discipline" (1968, p. 78). Following Harris, Christian Delacampagne's research has led to the conclusion that we are forced to recognize "racist" attitudes at work "in the majority of the philosophers of the Enlightenment" (1990, p. 86).

Given their value orientation to realize harmonious multiethnic societies, some intellectuals respond to the quest to ascertain the ethnicity and color of the ancient Egyptians with the question: What does it matter what they looked like? They harbor the fear that historical "truth" might mitigate against the kind of society they deem desirable. Their "morally correct" value position framed in the context of abstract humanism (often preached but little practiced) is clearly not widely shared as evidenced by the practice of slavery and "racism" in the Western tradition. What they desire does not in anyway change historical facts. The position is anti-intellectual and anti-science if the ultimate objective of these traditions is to know history and reality as completely and accurately as is possible. Indeed, accurate history, and its potential to function as a liberating force was not lost on Frederick Douglas. He wrote as follows in a letter to his son in 1887 while visiting Cairo:

> It has been the fashion of American writers, to deny that the Egyptians were Negroes and claim that they are of the same race of themselves. This has, I have no doubt, been largely due to a wish to deprive the Negro of the moral support of Ancient Greatness and to appropriate the same to the white race (McFeely, 1991, pp. 331–332).

Moreover, the question is also relevant with regards to its significant future social implications. The earlier assertion that "race" is a fallacious concept biologically makes clear that there is no intent here to make any special claims about any group of people or any set of human traits. Given the social history of human beings the question matters because those who have labelled themselves "white" and proclaimed their alleged superiority have made it matter. It matters because millions of African ethnics over hundreds of years have lost their lives because of the association of dark skin with slavery and lack of moral and intellectual development (Jordan, 1974) in Western scholarship. To confront colorphobia is to begin the process of enabling meaningful consideration of the equality of all humanity.

Scholarship is not value neutral, nor is it without consequences. This is what Arthur Schlesinger (1991) understands in his polemical diatribe directed at the aspirations of African Americans. This is what African Americans understand when they demand that their interpretations of history be added to—and integrated with—that of European and Euro-Americans in the academic enterprise. The African American historian, Roger Wilkins, understands the myriad value orientations and consequences of the ability to define self and others when he writes, "The greatest power" is what it has "always been: the power to define reality where blacks are concerned and to manage perceptions and therefore arrange politics and culture to reinforce those definitions" (1992, p. 46). The problem is especially troublesome when it can be shown that the work of scholars like Franz Boas, who enjoys a staunch reputation as an egalitarian, "can be described as equivocal at best and racist at worst" (Williams, 1993, p. 7). Reginald Horsman describes the effect of Euro-American writers exercising their power to define subordinate-status groups:

> In the first half of the nineteenth century many in the United States were anxious to justify the enslavement of the blacks and the expulsion and possible extermination of the Indians…In this era popular periodicals, the press, and many American politicians eagerly sought scientific proof for racial distinctions and for the prevailing American and world order; the intellectual community provided the evidence they needed (Horsman, 1981).

The likelihood of the evolution of the ideal multiethnic society is enhanced if Europeans come to understand that their ancestors alone did not create civilization; and for continental Africans and those in the diaspora to understand that their ancestors made significant and determinative contributions. The opinions of Hammond, Harper and Horsman make clear that we do not live in a color-blind society. While white Americans know this, many refuse to acknowledge it publicly. This, for African Americans, however, is a reality that must be lived with everyday. They understand the promise of the multiethnic society but reject the suggestion of white writers like Schlesinger (1991) that African American protest and challenges to Eurocentric scholarship delays, rather than hastens, its arrival.

Afrocentrists are arguing that scholarship can be historically accurate and still have positive consequences. They are accusing many European and Euro-Americans of writing history in ways which deny valid African contributions and denigrate and misinterpret African cultural integrity and traditions. As the primary beneficiaries of the social, economic, and political traditions that have shaped the world—descendants of Europeans are content with the view of history as their intellectuals have written it. Afrocentrists, on the other hand, realize that society's collective well-being is intrinsically tied to a view of history and the evolution of culture that is inclusive of humanity rather than exclusive of the majority of Non-European ethnics. Finally, Africans and African Americans know that they too have a history—and, therefore, a culture—the viability of which is signaled by their very survival. They, too, can examine the historical and archaeological record, interpret them, and define themselves.

This is precisely what the late African American historian and Africanist, William Leo Hansberry, began doing at Howard University in the 1920s. His work is the result of extensive investigations of research sources in the U.S. and Europe.

Hansberry describes Africa and Africans as seen by classical writers and is able to draw relationships which show their influence on Grecian culture during its formative period; that is, before there was a unified Greece (Harris, 1977). Further, his work is notable for its use of original sources, as well as the demonstration of the usefulness of the (Greek) mythic tradition in assisting archaeological research. Indeed, these sources were invaluable to Heinrich Schliemann (the discoverer of ancient Troy) and Sir Arthur Evans whose research on the island of Crete led him to hypothesize a significant African presence (Harris, 1977, pp. 29–32). The power of the African cultural influence in both Greece and Rome is evidenced by the fact that every major fiction and non-fiction writer [Homer, Hesiod, Pindar, Ovid, Virgil, Aeschylus, Sophocles, Euripides, Herodotus, Diodorus Siculus, Josephus, Dion Cassius, Aristotle, Pliny the Elder, Claudius Ptolemy, Strabo] (Harris, 1977, pp. 26, 28) who was an eye-witness to ancient history deemed it necessary to write about Africans—their customs, physiognomy, traditions, and civilizations.

In addition to Afrocentrists, scholars from other ex-colonial societies are beginning to challenge the Eurocentric view of human history (Gidiri, 1974), and together are winning over some Euro-American thinkers with their logic and factual presentations (McIntosh, McIntosh, and Togola, 1989). A few other mainstream white writers are calling attention to the racist tradition in European and Euro-American anthropology. Bettina Arnold has shown "How Hitler's archaeologists distorted European prehistory to justify racist and territorial goals" (1992). In the United States, Marvin Harris (1968) and Ashley Montagu (1972) have helped to establish the antiracist tradition in scholarship. Thus the question of the ethnicity and color of the ancient Egyptians has relevance not only for continental and diasporan Africans, but for the entire world community. Self perception and ultimately the sense of destiny scholars and researchers bring to their work as a result of the ethnic group with which they are socially identified play no small part in what they offer as rigorous logic and objectively derived facts.

Witness the musings of archaeologist, J.E. Manchip White, offering explanations as to why the Nubian Pharaoh, Piankhi, withdrew after capturing the seat of government in Egypt. Claiming caucasoid status for the Egyptians, White suggests that the "Negroes, felt ill-at-ease among the fair-skinned Egyptians" (1970, p. 190). For him, "white" is such an overwhelming presence that the simple blacks, as Nubians are described on the preceding page, sense their inferiority and defer accordingly. He does not explain the incompatibility of this logic with the fact that the Nubians had just subdued their alleged "betters" and could have done with them as they wished.

Assigning the status "white" to the ancient Egyptians was/is an activity initiated by European and Euro-American researchers as an essential part of the on-going effort to claim pre-eminence [for those labelled "white"] among human groups. It has politicized the failed effort to biologically construct "race" (Levin, 1991; Shanklin, 1994), and has further confused useless schemes which attempt "racial" classification (Montagu, 1972; King, 1971; Marger, 1991; Lewontin et al., 1984).

J.E. Manchip White (1970) is caught up in the dilemma that has plagued Eurocentric Egyptologists since they first became fully aware of Northeast African civilization: how to reconcile the outstanding accomplishments of Egyptian-Nubian-Ethiopian culture with the phenotype and morphology of the peoples occupying these regions. Unable to locate a "pure" white race to which it could be attributed, they tried to locate the center of this complex as close to Europe as possible. Thus, one reads in White that "the civilization of Lower Egypt [the delta] was almost certainly more advanced...than the civilization of Upper Egypt" (1970, p.

142). When this approach proved unconvincing, one is told that "it is indisputable that Asian ideas were reaching Upper Egypt" (1970, p. 142). Throughout the text this subtlety of language is offered in place of physical evidence and logical thought: "It seems likely (p. 141), "there seems little doubt" (p. 128), and "It seems almost certain." Another strategy was to attribute Northeast African civilization to Southwest Asians. It does not contradict the logic and sensibilities of Euro-American scholars that the major focus of the "Oriental" Institute of the University of Chicago is Ancient Egypt and Nubia in Africa. The final solution is to declare the inhabitants of Egypt "white" even though this requires tortuous massaging of their own "racial" indicators. This scheme leads to brown, red and even black Egyptians—who we are told are really Caucasians. It is worth noting that only in North Africa would these same people be considered "white"; and even there Europeans do not treat them as their equals. In the United States they would suffer all of the indignities traditionally directed at African Americans.

The purpose of the effort to classify the Egyptians "white" becomes clear when the chapter headings of classical archaeologist, James Breasted's influential work: *The Conquest of Civilization* (1926), is perused. Breasted declares Egypt to be part of the Oriental Cultural sphere despite the fact that it is the anterior culture—with a civilization that evolved thousands of years before Islam became a cultural force in the world—and is physically on the African continent. Even more informative, however, is a subheading of Chapter IV on Western Asia: Babylonia—which reads: "The Scene of the Evolution of Civilization and the Great White Race." In the tradition of Arnold Toynbee (1961), Breasted helped to popularize the view that civilization was primarily a white accomplishment. While the Egyptians had a dark-complexion, other more dependable "racial" indicators signal their white status (Davis, 1991, p. 19).

Ever-changing circumstances and events impact the evolutionary process to account for the physical characteristics of a particular group of people, in a given location, at a point in time. Group traits are only fixed in the person of a specific individual and change due to genetic and social factors bearing upon offsprings within the group and between members of different groups. That this observation is fact undermines the utility of "race" and leads logically to a discussion of ethnicity as the fundamental concept distinguishing human groups. Physical isolation has functioned as an enforcer of traits only so long as groups remained truly isolated. Even limited contact begins to modify the phenotype of individual group members. When we move beyond the predilection of certain European and Euro-Americans to write human social history to their advantage—evolutionary theory and the historical and archaeological research record point to the ancient Egyptians as a black-complexioned, indigenous African population. Consider, as just one example, the words of Count Constantin de Volney [1757–1820] who personally studied the Megaliths of Egypt, and whose works are typically ignored by European and American writers.

> But returning to Egypt, the lesson she teaches history contains many reflections for philosophy. What a subject for mediation, to see the present barbarism and ignorance of the Copts, descendants of the alliance between the profound genius of the Egyptians and the brilliant mind of the Greeks! Just think that this race of black men, today our slave and the object of our scorn, is the very race to which we owe our arts, sciences, and even the use of Speech! Just imagine, finally, that it is in the midst of peoples who call themselves the greatest friends

of liberty and humanity that one has approved the most barbarous slavery and questioned whether black men have the same kind of intelligence as Whites! (quoted in Diop, 1974, pp. 27–28).

The list is long of noted white scholars who searched in vain for a white presence in ancient Africa. They include Sir Gaston Maspero, who was a director of the Cairo Museum, and Jean Eapart, a Belgian Egyptologist (Diop, 1974, p. 83). This is what Bernal (1987) and Davidson (1991, p. 45) have called the European "Aryan Model" of the birth of Egyptian civilization. Indeed, the overriding concern of 19th century European and American scholars with assigning whites a formative role in establishing Egyptian culture is the best evidence that the claim cannot be substantiated by data available to them. As recently as 1959, Harvard anthropologist, William Howells, claimed that early "white" skulls were found in prehistoric East Central Africa (pp. 322–325), even though physical anthropology has not been able to assign a "racial" label to early hominid remains.

Once the assertion that Northeast Africans were really dark-complexioned whites became dogma, Professor Breasted, founder of the Oriental Institute, could then write:

> On the South of the Northwest Quadrant lay the teeming black world of Africa, separated from the Great White Race by an impassable desert barrier, the Sahara, which forms so large a part of the Southern Flatlands. Isolated thus and at the same time unfitted by ages of tropical life for any effective intrusion among the White Race, the negro and negroid peoples remained without any influence on the development of early civilization. We may then exclude both of these external races—the straight-haired, round-headed, yellow-skinned Mongoloids on the east, and the wooly-haired, long-headed, dark skinned Negroids on the south—from any share in the origins...subsequent development of civilization (1926, p. 113).

Several years before Breasted, Professor Charles Seignobos of the University of Paris (History of Ancient Civilization) opined on the origins of civilization as follows:

> Almost all civilized peoples belong to the white race. The people of other races have remained savage or barbarian, like the men of prehistoric times. It is within the limits of Asia and Africa that the first civilized peoples had their development—the Egyptians in the Nile Valley, the Chaldeans in plains of the Euphrates. They were people of sedentary and peaceful pursuits. Their skin was dark, the hair short and thick, the lips strong. Nobody knows their origin with exactness and scholars are not agreed on the name to give them (some terming them Cushites, others Hamites). Later, between the 20th and 25th centuries B.C., came bands of martial shepherds who had spread over all Europe and the west of Asia—the Aryans and the Semites (quoted in Jackson, 1972, p. 193). Such internally contradictory scholarship cannot possibly with-stand rigorous review. It invites critique.

Writing about ancient kingdoms and empires of the Western Sudan on the Atlantic coast of Africa, Lady Lugard informs us that the Fulani (long a dominant ethnic group in that region) are "a partly white race." Suggesting that they are immigrants to Africa, one reads:

Whether Phoenician, Egyptian, Indian, or simply Arab, they are evidently a race distinct from the Negroid and other black types by which they have been surrounded and notwithstanding the marked effects produced on some portions of their people by intermarriage with Negro women, they have kept the distinctive qualifications of their race through a known period of two thousand years. The Fulah of today is as distinct from the pure Negro as was the first Fulah of whom we have record. How long they may have existed in Africa before any record of them was made it is with our present knowledge impossible to say. The Hausa and the Songhay are other races which, though black, are absolutely distinct from the pure Negro type (Lugard 1964 [1906], p. 22).

Likewise, we are told by another writer that the Ethiopians on the east coast of Africa are not an indigenous people (Osgood, 1928, p. 121). None of these writers explain why there are so many "Blacks" in Africa who are really "Whites," but no "Whites" in Europe who are really "Blacks." Moret & Davy contend that animal and vegetable species and minerals were introduced into Egypt from without (1970 [1926], p. 164). And, finally, McIntosh, McIntosh & Togola (1989, p. 77) points to the claim by some writers that the central Southeast African Zimbabwe culture and its megaliths are of foreign origin. It would appear that, if these authors are to be believed, nothing in Africa is African. African structures and cultures of the greatest antiquity are the work of black-complexioned Mediterranean "whites" and Southwest Asian caucasoids (White, 1970). To be sure, there are "Negroes" in Africa, but their presence anywhere is an enigma (Wendt, 1962, p. 169; Howells, 1959, p. 339) and, further, according to M.D. Jeffreys, nowhere are they associated with the development of culture (cited in Jackson, 1972, p. 203).

In recent times some European scholars have partitioned Africa geographically using "racial" language. The Southern Mediterranean and the Sahara region is popularly referred to as "white" Africa, the sub-Sahara is "black" Africa (Maquet, 1972). The effect of this bit of scholarship is to complete the "caucasianization" of North Africa. Its modern-day populations which defy any kind of "racial" label (*General History of Africa*, Vol.1, pp. 100–103) are declared white—thereby giving credence to Arnold Toynbee's statement that: "The Black Race has not helped to create any civilization, while the Polynesian White Race has helped to create one civilization, the Brown Race two, the Yellow Race three, the Red Race and Nordic White Race four apiece, the Alpine White Race, nine, and the Mediterranean White Race, ten" (1961, p. 238). Eurocentrics offer these and other such related contentions to the world as objective scholarship. Africans and African Americans called it—racism.

The naive idea that though "black" in appearance—people could in some more fundamental and significant way be "white" remains a dominant theme in the modern literature (Davis, 1991). Euro-American writers have made much of this dogma. Writing in the prestigious National Geographic Magazine, W.H. Osgood offered the following:

> Although surrounded by Negro tribes and having some admixture of Negro blood brought in through centuries of slaving-holding, the Ethiopian is by no means a Negro. He is dark-skinned, with hair usually kinky and lips frequently thick, but he has a good high-bridged nose, well-set eyes, and a firm chin. To this he adds a proud and dignified bearing and a warlike, patriotic spirit, which mark him in an outstanding manner (1928, p. 122).

The implication is clear. It is his "proud...dignified bearing and warlike patriotic spirit" which make him white, since the physical description would make him a classic example of the category anthropologist label: Negro/Black/African. It is the intellectual duty of all scholars, not just African and African Americans, to challenge work which ascribes abstract qualities to morphological features and use them to facilitate human oppression.

William Howells of Harvard University attempted to give the assertion anthropological, and therefore, scientific, sanction by claiming that ancient white skulls had been identified in prehistoric East Central Africa (1959, p. 323), and that the Watussi, and by an indirect inference, the Masai can be traced to an ancient "white" strain (1959, p. 322). All of this is offered without the slightest bit of evidence as Physical Anthropology is not able to assign a "racial" label to prehistoric hominid skeletal remains. The physiognomy of the modern Watussi and Masai is self-evident. Howells' intent is not to be lost—modern anthropological research now firmly locates the origin of humanity in East Central Africa.

Whenever possible the tendency has been to convolute, dilute or deny outright the role of ethnic Africans in the development of civilization. When it is not possible to disregard the evidence of an indigenous African presence, the situation is treated with contempt and derision. Consider the case of the 25th Egyptian dynasty dominated by Ethiopian Kings. Sir Arthur Weigall, an Englishman who served the Egyptian government as Inspector-General of Antiquities, has labelled it "that astonishing epoch of nigger dominion" (1969 [1928], p. 186). W. Winford Reade would write in 1872, with the typical European air of superiority, about "nigger minstrels from Central Africa..." (1943 [1872], p. 1). The 1959 edition of William Howells', *Mankind in the Making*, still considered it helpful to the reader's understanding to describe the Watussi as "horse-faced" (1959, p. 322). For the philosopher, G.W.F. Hegel, Africans were totally without virtue (1956, pp. 91–93). Mavis Campbell cites Gilbert Murray in an effort to explain the motivation for such unflattering descriptors of certain human groups:

> ...when one reads such a list of charges against any tribe or nation, either ancient or in modern times, one can hardly help concluding that somebody wanted to annex their land (Campbell, 1974, p. 296).

In 1884–85 the colonial powers, meeting in Berlin, reached agreement on the manner in which Africa would be divided and administered for the political and economic benefit of Europeans (Pakenham, 1991, p. 251–255). The looting of Africa's human and natural resources was a political as well as a military exercise.

The African Ethnicity of the Ancient Egyptians

The African and African American challenge to racist scholarship is rooted in several classes of evidence and research which point rather definitively to the origin and ethnicity of the ancient Egyptians. They range from findings in Physical Anthropology to Art History to Archaeological and Historical research. Specifically, with regard to anthropology, the generalization known as Gloger's rule applies: "Within the same species the tendency is for more heavily pigmented populations to be closer to the equator and lighter populations to be farther from it" (Stein & Rowe, 1989, p. 166). This idea is not unrelated to the principle of natural selection: the tendency of certain organisms to select those genes which best assure their adaptation to and survival in a given environment (Ubelaker et al., 1990). While people are described as being "yellow, brown, red, black, and white," only one body chemical, Melanin, gives rise to human skin color. Melanin functions in equatorial regions to produce darker skin color (Stein & Rowe, 1989, p. 167). It is, therefore, unlikely, that light-complexioned peoples would evolve in areas subject to prolonged and intense exposure to sunlight (Nelson & Jurmain, 1988, pp. 154–157). Studies clearly demonstrate that, in general, the distribution of human skin color conforms to the biological principles cited above (Stein & Rowe, 1989, p. 167). This is one of the central messages in a National Geographic, made for television documentary aired in 1988 entitled: "Mysteries of Mankind." John Jackson (1972, pp. 184–205) cites several pioneering researchers, Eugen Georg (1931), Professor Ernest Albert Hooton (1931), and Sir Harry Johnson (1899) whose efforts to explain human phenotype led to conclusions consistent with Gloger's rule.

The earliest known Greek literature—the Homeric epics—refer to Africans as "Ethiopians" and described them as black-skinned with woolly hair. This description remains the same in all subsequent references to the phenotype of Northeast Africans by early Greek and Roman writers (Snowden, 1983, pp. 37–59; Rogers, 1952, pp. 29–36). Individuals in human populations deemed homogenous are not mirror images of each other. This assumption, nevertheless, drives efforts to differentiate between Egyptians and Ethiopians by writers whose socialization and training predispose them to search for "racial" distinctions (Toynbee, 1961; White, 1970; Snowden, 1971, 1983; Davis, 1991). Europeans of the 18th century were well aware of phenotype variation among so-called "Negroes" or "Ethiopians."

> These negroes are sometimes of so deep a brown that the skin appears to be quite black: sometimes their skin is as light as a mulatto's. The average tint is a rich deep bronze. Their eyes are dark, though blue eyes are occasionally seen; their hair is black, though sometimes of a rusty red, and is always of a woolly texture. To this rule there are no exceptions—it is the one constant character, the one infallible sign by which the race may be detected (Reade 1943 [1872], p. 217).

It should also be kept in mind that the descriptions of Africans were written hundreds of years after thousands of "whites," Assyrians, Persians, Greeks, Romans...Vizigoths, Byzantines, Arabs, Portuguese, and Spaniards (Oliver, 1991, p. 159) had entered Egypt as traders, students, soldiers and conquerors (Reade, 1943). It is not surprising, then, to find human variation most pronounced on the Southern shore of the Mediterranean and less so as one moves southward. Herodotus' description of the Egyptians and Ethiopians is one of the earliest written accounts. Contemplating the origins of the dark-complexioned Colchians living on the Black Sea in Asia, he writes:

> ...it is undoubtedly a fact that the Colchians are of Egyptian descent...My own idea on the subject was based first on the fact that they have black skins and woolly hair (not that that amounts to much, as other nations have the

same), and secondly, and more especially, on the fact that the Colchians, the
Egyptians, and the Ethiopians are the only races which from ancient times have
practised circumcision.

...And now I think of it, there is a further point of resemblance between the
Colchians and Egyptians: they share a method of weaving linen different from
that of any other people; and there is also a similarity between them in language and way of living (1988, pp. 167–168).

It is to be noted that Diodorus' description of Ethiopians, "black-skinned, flat-
nosed and woolly-haired (Snowden, 1971, p. 6) is consistent with Herodotus'.

The research of C.A. Diop led to citations of other Greek writers who were
equally as clear with their description of Egyptians. One of his sources is the
Greek writer, Lucien, who relates an encounter between two conversationalists:

Lycinus (describing a young Egyptian): This boy is not merely black, he has
thick lips and his legs are too thin. His hair worn in a plait behind shows that
he is not a freeman.
Timoaus: But that is a sign of really distinguished birth in Egypt, Lycinus. All
freeborn children plait their hair until they reach manhood. It is the exact opposite of the custom of our ancestors who thought it seemly for old men to secure their hair with a gold broach to keep it in place (Diop, 1991, p. 17).

Not only is the description explicit about the complexion of the Egyptians, it
also draws attention to certain operative rules in human evolutionary theory:
Bergmann's rule states that "within the same species, populations living near the
equator have less body bulk" than those dwelling farther away. Allen's rule states
that "populations of the same species living near the equator tend to have more
protruding body parts and longer limbs than do those living farther away..."
(Stein & Rowe, 1989, p. 166).

A final eyewitness description of Egyptians and Ethiopians is that of Aristotle
[384–322 B.C.], the icon of the Western intellectual tradition. In a piece entitled,
Physiognomonics, he writes:

Too black a hue marks the coward, as witness Egyptians and Ethiopians, and
so does also too white a complexion, as you may see from women...and very
woolly hair also signifies cowardice, as may be seen in Ethiopians (1991, pp.
1247–1248).

It should be kept in mind that Aristotle would have been very familiar with
Arab Asians as well as other North Africans.

The most significant turning point in the cultural history of Africa was the
Arab conquest of the whole of Northern Africa. It was this development that
brought foreign influence to the continent in a manner that is still decisive today.
"With this event the biography of ancient Africa is closed, and the history of Asi-
atic Africa begins" (Reade, 1943, p. 129). Reade's intent is clear: up until this
point the culture of Africa, including Egypt, was indigenous. Islamic influence did
not come to Africa until (641 A.D.), hundreds of years after the decline of Egypt
and after it had suffered military defeat by the Assyrians, Persians, Greeks, and
Romans. Arabs and Europeans had long been attracted to the Nile Valley region
where even those who came as conquerors had been, largely, culturally absorbed.

Further, while Arabic/Muslim culture came to dominate Northern and Western Africa, the majority physical type remains African in character. The population consisted primarily of converts to Islam rather than immigrants from the Arabian peninsula.

Some of the earliest archaeological interpretations of Egyptian artifacts also shed light on this question. We can cite verbatim the opinion of Champollion the Younger (he deciphered the Rosetta Stone), who wrote that: "We find there [in the royal tombs] Egyptians and Africans represented in the same way, which could not be otherwise; but the Namou (the Asians) and the Tamhou (Europeans) present significant and curious variants" (quoted in Diop, 1974, p. 47). Consistent with the verbal description offered by Herodotus, Diodorus, and Aristotle, Champollion's review of artifactual evidence did not distinguish between Egyptians and Ethiopians; but clearly differentiate between them and Asians and Europeans. Egypt was indeed a meeting place for the various ethnic groups living on the Mediterranean. They included "The Ethiopic, deb or black, with curly hair, long legs, thick lips, and very swarthy colour; the second a brown race, the Misraim; and the third a fairer tribe of Caucasians, the last comers, and a privileged body of conquerors, but not the authors of the civilization or the religion of the land" (Smyth 1851, pp. 364–365).

It is possible to cite other equally convincing evidence and sources on the origin of the indigenous Egyptians. They were not, as writers like White (1970) and Breasted (1926) projected, Southwest Asian caucasoids. Prior to the invasion of Egypt by the Hyksos [1700–1600 B.C.] (Moret & Davy, 1970, pp. 243–255), there is no evidence of any kind to indicate large scale immigration of non-Africans into Africa. Egyptian civilization, was at this point, a *fait accompli*. There is no evidence of an earlier civilization capable of reproducing itself on a grander scale in Egypt.

> Moreover, apart from some stations of uncertain age in Palestine, no trace of man earlier than 4000 B.C. exists in Syria or Mesopotamia. By that date the Egyptians had their feet on the threshold of their history proper. It is, then, reasonable to attribute the precocious development of Egypt's first inhabitants to their own genius and to the exceptional conditions presented by the Nile Valley. Nothing proves that it was due to the incursion of more civilized strangers. The very existence of such, or at least of their civilization, remains to be proved (Moret & Davy, 1970, p. 122).

Likewise, the German scholar, Herbert Wendt, is unequivocal in his assessment of the origin of the ancient Egyptians and their civilization. He declares that the Neolithic Egyptians were related to the modern Galla, Somali, and Masai of East Africa. "Egyptian skeletons, statues and countless pictures of Egyptians in their temples and monuments show the same 'racial' characteristics as the Nubians and the Nilotic tribes, the brown-skinned hunters of the steppes and the savannah husbandmen of the Sudan" (1962, p. 58).

> Therefore Egypt was a great Kingdom created by Africans, the most important African Kingdom in the history of the world. Of African origin were such great personalities in world history as Ramses the great, the Sun-king Akhnaton, the many Pharaohs...Of African inspiration are the Pyramids, the golden burial-chambers, and statues, plastic arts, temple friezes and other great Egyptian works of art. The Sphinx is an African monument, the hieroglyphs are an African script, and Ammon, Isis and Osiris are African gods. So great was the

achievement of the Africans in the Nile Valley that all the great men of ancient Europe journeyed there—the philosophers Thales and Anaximander, the mathematician Pythagoras, the statesman Solon and an endless stream of historians and geographers....(1962, p. 58).

Sir E.A. Wallace Budge established himself years ago as the foremost European Egyptologist. He is the translator of *The Book of the Dead* from the Hieroglyphics into English, and was Keeper of the Egyptian and Assyrian Antiquities in the British Museum. He wrote in his 1902 volume: *Egypt,* that "the historic native of Egypt, both in the old and new stone ages, was African" (quoted in ben-Jochannan, 1989, p. 43). Forced by the data to acknowledge that "Egypt from the earliest times had been the university of Greece" (1943, p. 60), and the reality of the dark complexion of the Egyptians, Winwood Reade hastens to fashion a scenario that makes these facts palatable to the European mind. The Egyptians, we read, are very likely Asian caucasoids from Babylonia who enslaved and intermarried with the negroes already living there (1943, pp. 376–377). This explains, according to Reade, the "dash of the 'tar-brush' plainly to be read by the practised eye in the portraits, though not in the conventional faces, of the monuments" (1943, p. 377). Contrast Reade's interpretation with that of Count Volney upon seeing the Sphinx:

> On seeing that head, typically Negro in all its features...In other words, the ancient Egyptians were true negroes of the same type as all native-born Africans. That being so, we can see how their blood, mixed for several centuries with that of the Romans and the Greeks, must have lost the intensity of its original color. We can even state as a general principle that the face is a kind of monument able, in many cases, to attest or shed light on historical evidence on the origins of peoples (quoted in Diop, 1974, p. 27).

It is finally being acknowledged that Ethiopia/Nubia was an early black civilization. A recent report of work being done by Dr. Bruce B. Williams of the University of Chicago lends credible support to the antiquity of Egyptian-Nubian contact, with Nubia being the founding culture (Wilford, 1992). This is consistent with Alfred Haddon's findings in his research on the antiquity of Ethiopia and Egypt. According to him the Egyptians locate their origin in central Northeast Africa (1925, p. 4). Again, this view is substantiated by Diodorus who reports that the Egyptians were "colonists" of the Ethiopians; and further, many Egyptian funerary customs, priestly functions, laws and writing forms were derived from Ethiopian sources (cited in Snowden, 1983, p. 51). The late Cheikh A. Diop cites shared traditions in antiquity as well as modern customs as the basis for his position that Egyptian culture was/is an extension of that of Ethiopia (1974, pp. 146–147).

As recently as 1986 a version of the "whites founded all civilizations" thesis was still being offered in a major textbook (*The Heritage of World Civilization*) on the subject. Conceding the fact that the Nubian/Ethiopians were dark-complexioned, ethnic Africans, one reads that:

> The royal line that emerged to rule at the new Kushite capital of Napata was Egyptian in culture and probably largely Caucasoid in race in their early centuries of power (Craig et al., 1986, p. 357).

In this version Caucasoids led a Negroid people "up" the path to civilization. The tendency to claim biologically endowed superiority appears to be a universal failing of dominant group intellectuals from ancient times to the present. When, in fact, the outstanding characteristic that they do share has been their monopoly, or near-monopoly, of the most efficient instruments of war which they rarely hesitate to use. Over time this monopoly of force is buttressed by the use of history and other academic disciplines as propaganda tools. Thus, whenever in the writing of human social history, Europeans encounter the faintest echoes of civilization—black-complexioned peoples become "white," their outstanding accomplishments are attributed to peoples other than themselves, and they are said to display profound intellectual and moral flaws. Consequently, African ethnics and their descendants are intent on joining in the writing of history. They are signalling their refusal to continue to be victimized by a mindset forged in the crucible of colonialism.

Conclusion

This article has offered an overview of the substantial evidentiary base supporting the Afrocentric challenge to traditional scholarship on Africa and diasporan Africans. Critics of Afrocentrism have overstated its position in their efforts to maintain intellectual hegemony and to define reality in the interest of the groups with which they identify. The Afrocentric position makes no claim of innate superiority, and is part of an emerging multicultural perspective which calls for inclusion of peoples of African descent rather than exclusion of Europeans in writing history. Further, sufficient materials exist to write such a work with minimum distortion and misinterpretation of the historical, archaeological, anthropological, and literary and artistic record. It is this record which drives the Afrocentric challenge; a record available for investigation by any person having an interest in these issues.

Afrocentrism emphasizes the role of culture and ethnicity in shaping the development of human societies rather than continuing to give attention to the specious, ideological concept of "race." It does not hesitate to point out the connection between intellectual activity and structural arrangements in society in its quest to alleviate human oppression.

References

Arnold, Bettina (1992). "The Past as Propaganda." *Archaeology*, July/August, p. 30.

Aristotle (1991). "Physiognomonics." in *The Complete Works of Aristotle*, Jonathan Barnes, ed., Vol. I. Princeton, NJ: Princeton University Press.

ben-Jochannan, Yosef A.A. (1989). *Black Man of the Nile And His Family*. Baltimore, MD: Black Classic Press.

Bernal, Martin (1987). *Black Athena: The Afro-Asiatic Roots of Classical Civilization. Vol. I: The Fabrication of Ancient Greece, 1785–1985*. New Brunswick, NJ: Rutgers University Press.

———. (1991). *Vol. II: The Archaeological and Documentary Evidence*. New Brunswick, NJ: Rutgers University Press.

————. (1992). "The Case for Massive Egyptian Influence in The Aegean." *Archaeology*, September/October, p. 53.

Breasted, James H. (1926). *The Conquest of Civilization*. New York: Harper & Brothers

Campbell, Mavis (1974). "Aristotle and Black Slavery: A Study in Race Prejudice." in *Race: The Journal of The Institute of Race Relations*, Vol. 15, No. 3, London.

Coleman, John E. (1992). "Did Egypt Shape the Glory That Was Greece?" *Archaeology*, September/October, p. 48.

Craig, Albert M., et al. *The Heritage of World Civilizations: Volume 1 to 1600*. New York: Macmillan Publishing Company, 1986.

Davidson, Basil (1991). "The Ancient World and Africa: Whose Roots?" in *Egypt Revisited*, Ivan Van Sertima, ed. New Brunswick, NJ: Transaction Publishers.

Davis, James F. (1991). *Who is Black*. University Park, PA: The Pennsylvania State University Press.

Delacampagne, Christian (1990). "Racism and the West: From Praxis to Logos," in *Anatomy of Racism*, David T. Goldberg, ed. Minneapolis: University of Minnesota Press.

Diop, Cheikh A. (1974). *The African Origin of Civilization*. New York: Lawrence Hill & Company.

————. (1991). "Origin of the Ancient Egyptians," in *Egypt Revisited*, Ivan Van Sertima, ed. New Brunswick: Transaction Publishers.

Drake, St. Clair (1987). "Black Folk Here and There," in *History and Anthropology*, Vol. 1. Los Angeles: Center for Afro-American Studies, University California Press.

————. (1990). "Black Folk Here and There." an Essay in *History and Anthropology*, (Vol. 2). Los Angeles: Center for Afro-American Studies, University California Press.

Fredrickson, George M. (1988). *The Arrogance of Race*. Middletown, CT: Wesleyan University Press.

Gidiri, A. (1974). "Imperialism and Archaeology." *Race*, Vol. 15, No. 4, p. 431.

Gould, Stephen J. (1981). *The Mismeasure of Man*. New York: W.W. Norton & Co.

Haddon, Alfred (1925). *The Races of Man and Their Distribution*. New York: Macmillan Press.

Haddon, Alfred and Huxley, Julian (1936). *We Europeans*. New York: Harper.

Harris, Joseph E., ed. (1977). *African and Africans as Seen by Classical Writers*. Washington, DC: Howard University Press.

Harris, Marvin (1968). *The Rise of Anthropological Theory*. New York: Thomas Y. Crowell Company.

Herodotus (1988). *The Histories*. Trans. by Aubrey de Selincourt. New York: Viking Penguin Inc.

Hilliard, III, Asa G. (1992). "The Meaning to KMT (Ancient Egyptian) History for Contemporary African American Experience," *Phylon*, Vol. 49, Nos. 1, 2, pp. 10–22.

Horsman, Reginald (1981). *Race and Manifest Destiny*. Cambridge, MA: Harvard University Press.

Howells, William (1959). *Mankind in the Making*. New York: Doubleday & Company.

Jackson, John G. (1972). *Man, God, and Civilization*. Secaucus, NJ: Citadel Press.

James, George F.M. (1954). *Stolen Legacy*. New York: Philosophical Library.

Jordan, Winthrop D. (1974). *The White Man's Burden: Historical Origins of Racism in the United States*. New York: Oxford University Press.

King, James C. (1971). *The Biology of Race*. New York: Harcourt Brace Jovanovich.

Lewontin, R.C., Rose, Steven and Kamin, Leon J. (1984). *Not In Our Genes: Biology, Ideology, and Human Nature*. New York: Pantheon Books.

Levin, Michael D. (1991). "Population Differentiation and Racial Classification." *Encyclopedia of Human Biology*, Vol. 6. Academic Press Inc.

Lugard, Lady (1964). *A Tropical Dependency*. London: Frank Cass & Co. Ltd.

Maquet, Jacques (1972). *Civilizations of Black Africa*. New York: Oxford University Press.

Marger, Martin N. (1991). *Race and Ethnic Relations*. Belmont, CA: Wadsworth Publishing Company.

McFeely, William S. (1991). *Frederick Douglas*. New York: W.W. Norton & Company.

McIntosh, Roderick J., McIntosh, Susan K., and Togola, Tereba (1989). "People Without History." *Archaeology*, Vol. 42, No. 1, January/ February.

McKitrick, Eric L. (1963). *Slavery Defended: The Views of the Old South*. New Jersey: Prentice Hall, Incorporated.

Montagu, Ashley (1972). *Statement on Race*. New York: Oxford University Press.

Moret, A. and Davy, G. (1970). *From Tribe to Empire [1926]*. New York: Cooper Square Publishers, Inc.

Nelson, Harry and Jurmain, Robert (1988). *Introduction to Physical Anthropology*. New York: West Publishing Company.

Oliver, Roland (1992). *The African Experience*. New York: HarperCollins Publishers.

Omi, Michael and Winant, Howard (1986). *Racial Formation in the US: From the 1960s to the 1980s*. London: Routledge & Kegan Paul.

Outlaw, Lucius (1990). "Toward a Critical Theory of 'Race,' " in *Anatomy of Racism*, David T. Goldberg, ed. Minneapolis: University of Minnesota Press.

Osgood, Wilfred H. (1928). "Nature and Man in Ethiopia." *The National Geographic Magazine*, Vol. LIV, No. 2, August.

Pakenham, Thomas (1991). *The Scramble for Africa*. New York: Avon Books.

Parker, George W. (1917). "The African Origin of the Grecian Civilization." *The Journal of Negro History*. Vol. 2, No. 2, April.

Reade, Winwood (1943). *The Martyrdom Of Man*. London: Watts & Co.

Rogers, Joel A. (1952). *Nature Knows No Color-line*.

Schlesinger, Jr., Arthur M. (1991). *The Disuniting of America*. Knoxville, TN: Whittle Direct Books.

Shanklin, Eugenia (1994). *Anthropology & Race*. Belmont, CA: Wadsworth Publishing Company.

Shils, Edward (1967). "Color, the Universal Intellectual Community, and the Afro-Asian Intellectual." *Daedalus*, Spring.

Smyth, Thomas. (1851). *The Unity of the Human Races*. Edinburgh: Johnstone and Hunter.

Snowden, Jr., Frank M. (1971). *Blacks in Antiquity*. Cambridge, MA: Harvard University Press.

———. (1983). *Before Color Prejudice*. Cambridge, MA: Harvard University Press.

Stein, Philip L., and Rowe, Bruce M. (1989). *Physical Anthropology*. New York: McGraw-Hill Publishing Company.

Toynbee, Arnold J. (1961). *A Study of History*. New York: Oxford University Press.

Ubelaker, Douglas H., Bass, W., Jantz, R., and Smith, F. (1990). *A Review of Human Origins*. 6th Ed. Knoxville, TN: University of Tennessee.

UNESCO (1989). *General History of Africa*. Berkeley, CA: University of California Press.

Volney, C.F. (1991). *The Ruins of Empire*. Baltimore, MD: Black Classic Press.

Weigall, Arthur (1969). *Personalities of Antiquity* [1928]. Freeport, NY: Books For Libraries Press.

Wendt, Herbert (1962). *It Began in Babel: The Story of the Birth and Development of Races and Peoples*. Boston: Houghton Mifflin Co.

White, J.E. Manchip (1970). *Ancient Egypt: Its Culture and History*. New York: Dover Publications, Inc.

Wilford, John N. (1992). "Nubian Treasures Reflect Black Influence on Egypt." *The New York Times*, Feb. 11, pp. B5, B8.

Wilkins, Roger (1992). "White Out." *Mother Jones*, November/ December (1992). p. 44.

Williams, Chancellor (1987). *The Destruction of Black Civilization*. Chicago: Third World Press.

Williams, Jr., Vernon J. (1993). "Franz U. Boas and the Conflict Between Science and Values, 1894–1915." *The American Philosophical Association Newsletter (APA)*. Vol. 92, No. 1, pp. 7–16.

Woodson, Carter G. (1918). "The Beginnings of The Miscegenation of The Whites and Blacks." *The Journal of Negro History*, Vol. 3, No. 4, October.

Young, Peter A. (1992). "Was Nefertiti Black?" *Archaeology*, September/October, p. 2.

5

Afrocentricity: Problems of Method and Nomenclature

Erskine Peters

Evident in contemporary American culture are numerous types of "Afrocentricities." These "Afrocentricities" have been appropriated into almost every domain along the cultural continuum from the sacred to the secular. Some rap groups distinguish themselves from other rap groups by designating themselves "Afrocentric;"[1] some feminist/womanist, eco-feminist,[2] gay[3] and lesbian groups do the same. Some christian ministers[4] and churches label themselves "Afrocentric" and some erotic and pornographic videos[5] do so too. Many of these varying notions of Afrocentricity are what James Stewart alludes to in stating that " 'popular afrocentricism'[6] is being confused increasingly with systematic intellectual

---

1. See, for example, H.E.A.L [Human Education Against Lies], KRS 1, "Family Got to Get Busy," *Civilization Against Technology*, Elektra/Asylum Records, 1991. See also Robin Roberts, " 'Ladies First': Queen Latifah's Afrocentric Feminist Music Video." *African American Review*, Vol. 28, No. 2: 245–257. See especially page 246 where Queen Latifah is quoted as saying, "To Me Afrocentricity is a way of living. . . . It's about being into yourself and being proud of your origins."

2. See, for example, Shamara Shantu Riley, "Ecology Is a Sistah's Issue Too: The Politics of Emergent Afrocentric Ecowomanism," in Carol J. Adams, ed., *Ecofeminism and the Sacred*. Continuum Publishing Company, 1993, pp. 191–204.

3. There is, for example, the magazine *SBC*, published in Los Angeles, CA, whose subtitle reads "For the Afrocentric Homosexual Man."

4. For a discussion of my thoughts about some of the major problems with the African-American christian ministry, see Erskine Peters, *African Americans in the New Millennium*, pp. 16–25.

5. See, for example, an erotic series called "In Loving Color," a Sean Michaels and Video Team Production, labelled "An Afrocentric Production."

6. The best intellectual valorization of popular Afrocentrism is set forth by Ronald Walters when he writes that "there are some indications that the concept of Afrocentricity has taken hold at the grass-roots level within African-American communities in the 1990s. This has happened largely as an antithesis to and as a result of the three-decade movement for racial integration within the schools and other institutions dominated by whites that control the socialization of Black youth. The current dysfunctional condition of urban Black educational institutions and the connection between this condition and the rise of serious youthful crime, drug involvement and other antisocial behavior have called for a response by Black people themselves. And Blacks have embarked upon an indigenous reinvention of aspects of their life encompassing such cultural artifacts as Rap music, break dancing, inventive language, and now the movement for the 'infusion' of African and African-American studies in the schools" (Ronald W. Walters, *Pan Africanism in the African Diaspora: An Analysis of Modern Afrocentric Political Movements*. Wayne State University Press, 1993, p. 372).

approaches to the field."[7] The crucial issue is whether the reference to Africa in the word "Afrocentric" is a tribute designation indicating that traditional African worldviews have something supremely and expressly foundational to offer or whether the reference is a mere label of behavioral and racial differentiation, a mere way of expressing resentment for the European, instead of a profound way of relocating one's world view.

The use and coinage of so many different terms in this essay is employed only to highlight the great disparities existing under the rubric of so-called "Afrocentricity." The various terms are used to show that there is little or no consistent logic at work in much of popular as well as intellectual designations of the Afrocentric and to show that when there is consistency it is not necessarily grounded in indigenous and traditional African values.

Before moving to the focal discussion of this essay, as a point of information, a few words should be said about the key players in the post-mid-twentieth century Afrocentric movement. Four of the major theoretical figures to be considered when undertaking a formal study of Afrocentricity are John Henrik Clarke, Jacob H. Carruthers, Molefi Asante, and James B. Stewart.[8]

(1) *John Henrik Clarke*: The key founding figure of the post-mid-twentieth century Afrocentric movement is perhaps John Henrik Clarke. Based on the work of political historian Ronald Walters in *Pan Africanism in the African Diaspora*, Clarke advocated, via the Pan-Africanist oriented Black Caucus of the African Studies Association, the establishment, in 1968, of the African Heritage Association, as a reconstructive challenge to the Eurocentric scholarship and governance of the African Studies Association that had been established in 1956.[9] Speaking on behalf of the "adoption of the Pan Africanist (or Afrocentric) perspective" (Walters 1993, p. 368) at the Twelfth Annual meeting of the two-thousand member African Studies Association, Clarke explained that "this perspective defines that all black people are African people and rejects the division of African peoples by geographical locations based on colonialist spheres of influence" (Walters, p. 368). According to Walters, the "concept of 'Afro-centrism' emerged from this political struggle as a product of expressing the need of this collection of Black scholars to articulate the ideology of Pan Africanism as applied to the study of the land of their parents" (Walters, p. 369). Walters emphasizes that "the first point made in the collectively drafted objectives of the newly formed AHSA would indicate that in the field of education, AHSA's purpose was the 'reconstruction of African history and cultural studies along *Afrocentric* lines while effecting an intellectual union among black scholars the world over" (Walters, p. 369). Articulating his Pan-Africanist/Afrocentrist challenge before the Black Caucus of the ASA, Clarke summed up the thrust of their collective thought by declaring that "[w]hen pseudo political independence was given to Africa, the one thing the Eu-

---

7. See James B. Stewart, "Reaching For Higher Ground: Toward An Understanding of Black/Africana Studies." *The Afrocentric Scholar* Vol. 1 No. 1, (May 1992): 2. Careful study of Stewart's article is critical for anyone attempting or interested in becoming a serious Afrocentric scholar.

8. Numerous other proponents of Afrocentricity like Maulana Karenga, Yosef A. A. ben-Jochannan, etc., are discussed in Stewart (1992), Semmes (1992), and Azibo (1992).

9. Ronald W. Walters, *Pan Africanism in the African Diaspora: An Analysis of Modern Afrocentric Political Movements*. Wayne State University Press, 1993, pp. 366–67.

ropean did not give up was his domination over the direction of African history" (Qtd. in Fraser 1969, p. 21). Stating that "how a man thinks about himself determines how he acts, Clarke added that "the one thing the Europeans did not want us to do is to think that we can rule nations and institutions. And, more dangerous, that we could question his institutions. We have come to this point in our history where we must not only question old institutions, but we must make new institutions distinctly our own..." (Fraser, p. 21).[10] A direct result of the AHSA challenge, Walters's own Walters's Afrocentric emphasis, as he defines it, is in determining "what forces drive African-origin peoples to continue identifying with the source of their cultural origin and in determining how...these forces affect the quality of relationship both among Africans in the Diaspora and between Africans on the continent" (Walters, p. 14).

(2) *Jacob H. Carruthers*: Foundational Afrocentric proponent Jacob H. Carruthers, of the Kemetic Institute in Chicago and co-founder of the Association for the Study of Classical African Civilization, and author of *Essays in Ancient Egyptian Studies* (1984), sounded the Afrocentric mandate not only through argumentation but very importantly through demonstration. Having taking seriously the call for Pan-Africanist/Afrocentric studies made in the 1960s, Carruthers immersed himself so deeply in the study of ancient and traditional African cultures that by 1978 he was able to deliver a body of penetrating and sophisticated lectures stating and demonstrating, through an emphasis on Kemetic/ Tawitic/Ancient Egyptian culture, the Afrocentric rationale. Carruthers's intellectual and academic justification for using Tawi (his preferred term for Ancient Egypt, meaning "The United Two Lands") as a starting point is reflected in Mongameli Mabona's statement that "to arrive at the proper estimation of the cultural values of any society, it is necessary to grasp first the philosophy or rather the metaphysical attitude which underlies these values. History and archaeology show that there has been in Africa a civilization which extended from Egypt to Angola from Timbuctu to Zimbabwe. This civilization consisted of a complex of cultures which in their structure showed a marvelous formal and thematic uniformity[11] to be observed in their literature and mythologies" (Qtd. in Carruthers, p. 13).

Stated in Carruthers's own terms, the Afrocentric mandate is to formulate "an African worldview" as an "essential beginning point for all research which is based upon the *interests* of African people. There can be no African history, no African social science without an African worldview." Carruthers adds that "[by] African, I do not mean merely a history or social science of Africa but a world history and a universal method of analysis designed by and for Africans" (Carruthers, p. 17).

(3) *Molefi Asante*: Molefi Asante holds the singular historical position of having spearheaded the founding of the first African-American Studies Ph.D. granting

---

10. C. Gerald Fraser, "Black Caucus Deliberations at Montreal: Who Should Control African Studies and For What Ends?" *Africa Report* (December 1969): 20–21.

11. One very important aspect of the work of early Egyptologist Wallace Budge is that in translating and interpreting *The Book of the Dead* (which some have made us aware ought to be translated as "The Book of Coming Forth By Day," and which I propose ought probably be translated as "A Book *For* the Dead," the "dead" being all of us the so-called living!), Budge consistently worked to relate the Kemetic/Ancient Egyptian spiritual system and its symbols to the spiritual systems and symbols of the other regions of Africa, thus working always to illustrate African cultural continuity.

program in the United States and the world, for that matter. Particularly because of his tireless efforts at promoting the Afrocentric perspective and because of his long record of publishing on the topic, Asante's presence as founding Chairperson of the Temple University's African-American Studies doctorate program identifies it historically with his Afrocentric theoretical efforts. Asante's prominence and popularity as the most easily identifiable proponent of Afrocentricity merits him therefore special attention in several parts of this essay.

Asante has published perhaps the most single-authored texts with "Afrocentricity" in the title. Included in these are *The Afrocentric Idea* (1987), *Afrocentricity* (1988), and *Kemet, Afrocentricity and Knowledge* (1990). What Asante attempts in *Afrocentricity* (1988), and most of his works, is to present the Afrocentric mandate. However, so busy is he in writing and re-writing the mandate that he rarely convincingly, or demonstrably, writes African culture. Consequently, it is difficult to find Afrocentricity demonstrated sufficiently in his thought even when bringing together several of his books.

No matter what spiritual and intellectual admiration one might hold for Kemet/Ancient Egypt, Asante's premise, evolving out of that of the Association for the Study of Classical African Civilization, that "the centerpiece of Afrocentric theory [is] a reconnection in our minds, of Egypt to Africa" (Asante 1988, p. ix) is troubling and problematic. This premise assumes that African Americans already relate easily to the rest of the African continent, a matter which even today is highly disputable. A major part of the problem of the premise is that it stems from the Association's adoption of the highly valorized, Euro-elitist word "classical," a word which resonates easily as meaning classical like Greece, like Rome, like all the so-called prestigious artifacts of the Europeans. In general, the book *Afrocentricity* serves its purpose as a mandate, but the problem with the rhetoric of any mandate is in its preoccupation with argumentation. The student must be careful therefore not to mistake the mandate for the cultural model, that is, for Africa itself. The reader of *Afrocentricity* is left with Afrocentric argumentation but not with enough African-based conceptual models of social, political, philosophical, and economic being. As a result, in critiquing the black Christian ministry (a truly important subject), for example, a hollowness rings through Asante's statement that "[t]hose ministers who formulate clear political and social philosophies based on the African center will completely alter the church's emphasis" (Asante 1988, p. 76). Asante's statement rings with hollowness because no specific textual references or models of African-based spiritual thought and behavior are presented. In another instance, for example, too, Asante's formulations set forth in the section title "Nijia: The Way," while composing a nice general meditation for reflection, lack the specificity of African-based categories concerning the nature of life and existence. Thus, one necessarily raises the question of how one is to make a truly Afrocentric argument with so few (and even then vague) references to models of thinking and being in Africa.

Even in the later *Kemet, Afrocentricity, and Knowledge* (1991), Asante still spends more time in argument with the European, racist historical legacy than he does on presenting Kemet itself. More disturbing, however, is the fact that Asante too often is not aware of the imperialist nature of his logic. To see this, one need only reflect, for example, on the empire logic implicit in Asante's statement that "[a] fundamental position of my argument is that all African societies find Kemet a common source for intellectual and philosophical ideas" (Asante 1991, p. 92).

This sounds dangerously much like the erroneous historical paradigm which argues that European culture brought civilization to the rest of the globe. For might it not have been that in order to build the Kemetic empire that the Kemites collected and synthesized all the wisdom it could find in the regions of Africa with which it had contact? For Asante to set forth such a position as "fundamental" is like espousing wholeheartedly that the big life, the imperial life is the good life and that a thatched-roof village, for example, has little to offer that is good, original, or philosophically sufficient.

The problem with Asante's work is that there is never enough elaboration upon traditional Africa, its values, social, political, and economic systems. Asante emphasizes the use of traditional African communication and language functions as a theoretical building block for creating what he calls "Africology." Yet, even his limiting himself to this very restricted theoretical model is never fully nor adequately elaborated to demonstrate how the use of his theoretical model would be operative for analyzing the complex social, philosophical, aesthetic, political, and economic layers of the cultures of African peoples. The result is that Asante promulgates a disposition more than he promulgates an adequately comprehensive theory. What is discussed in Asante's several books never engages its subject on a comprehensive enough level to cover, for example, what Shaha Mfundishi Maasi and Mfundishi J. H. Hassan K. Salim articulate in their book *Kupigani Ngumi* when they identify forty-two significant aspects of the indigenous African value systems, ranging from the African conception of time to the conception of marriage and the definition of love.[12] Maasi and Salim provide a comprehensive world view[13] into which one can place one's evolving Afrocentric self whether one agrees with all the points set forth in their book or not. However, one comes away from Asante simply not having learned very much about African culture and values. Unfortunately, as a key proponent of Afrocentricity, and perhaps now the most well-known one, Asante himself leaves the door open for all types of "Afrocentric" claims by attempting to be theoretical before he is sufficiently foundational.[14] In consequence, one might wish to ponder Paul Gilroy's critique of Asante's brand of Afrocentricism reflected in Gilroy's contention that Asante's formulation "is stubbornly focused around the reconstitution of individual consciousness rather than around the reconstruction of the black nation in exile or elsewhere" (Gilroy 1992, p. 305).[15] While this particular criticism may strike one as extreme, its implications certainly merit attention. West African-born scholar Manthia Diawara even goes so far as to accuse "Afrocentric academics" of fixing "blackness by reducing it to Egypt and *kente* cloths," adding that "Afrocentricism has become a religion, a camp movement, where one can find refuge from

---

12. See Shaha Mfundishi Maasi and Mfundishi J. H. Hassan K. Salim, *Kupigana Ngumi: Root Symbols of The Ntchru and Ancient Kmt, Volume 1.* The Pan-Afrakan Kupigana Ngumi Press and Black Gold Press, 1992, pp. 189–95.

13. A similar effort is made from a philosophical and proverbial perspective in Erskine Peters, *African Openings to the Tree of Life.* Regent Press, 1983.

14. The reader should study Stewart's discussion of Asante's theoretical limitations (Stewart 1992, pp. 44–46). Stewart also discusses how Asante's formulations coincide with the limitations of Henry Louis Gates, Jr., whose theoretical posture I address later in this discussion.

15. Paul Gilroy, "It's a Family Affair," in *Black Popular Culture*. A project of Michelle Wallace edited by Gina Dent. Bay Press, 1992, pp. 303–316.

the material realities of being black in Washington, D.C., London, or Nairobi" (Diawara 1992, p. 289).[16] While the criticisms of Gilroy and Diawara are indeed harsh, their arguments are not wholly untenable.

(4) *James B. Stewart*: Those interested in understanding how to establish a rigorous and cogent Afrocentric methodological perspective, especially on a scholarly level, should study and refer continuously to James B. Stewart's careful analysis titled "Reaching For Higher Ground: Toward an Understanding of Black/Africana Studies" published in the inaugural issue of *The Afrocentric Scholar* (May 1992). Stewart's discussion demonstrates a mastery of the history of the evolution of all the major endeavors in the United States to articulate an Afrocentric theoretical methodology. Moreover, in the last ten pages of his article Stewart synthesizes the best elements from all of the important proponents of Afrocentric theory, thus providing serious scholars with what is perhaps the best, most comprehensive methodological formulation available. Stewart's methodological formulations are the logical complement to the type of thoroughly itemized value system set forth by Maasi and Salim. Neither can substitute for the other but for both delineation of and emphasis on the indigenous African value system is essential. In effect, Stewart suggests that "for the sake of argument let Afrocentricity refer to the degree of overlap between an idealized model of thought and behavior generated from an interpretation of traditional African thought and practice and an individual's actual thought and behavior" (Stewart 1992, p. 38). To clarify his point further, Stewart argues that "the process of becoming Afrocentric, then, can be disaggregated into three components: (a) increasing the causal connection between an individual's expressed ideology and observed behavior, (b) increasing the degree of overlap between an individual's ideology and behavior and the modal thought and behavior of African Americans (or Africans) depending on the selected reference group, and (c) increasing the degree of overlap between an individual's current expressed ideology and behavior and the ideology and behavior patterns advocated by 'strong claim' Afrocentrists" (Stewart, p. 38).

In conjunction with Stewart (since Stewart's article is very terse), one might want to read, as a preface to the intellectual history of Afrocentric thought, Clovis Semmes's (a.k.a. Jabulani K. Makalani) wonderfully lucid, though scholarly, sections on "African-Centered Thought" and "Afrocentric Forms." In the span of twenty pages in *Cultural Hegemony and African-American Development*,[17] Semmes, beginning with nineteenth-century United States African-American history, provides an excellent summary for understanding the historical evolution of what has come to be popularized as Afrocentricity.

What emerges when there are major discrepancies in the evolution of the Afrocentric self as a result of placing inadequate emphasis on indigenous and traditional Africa is the main subject of the present essay. Hence in considering the notion of Afrocentricity, several fundamental issues need to be raised in order to arrive at a common understanding of the factors and concepts upon which a functional and effective idea of Afrocentricity can be predicated. As we can already

---

16. See Manthia Diawara, "Afro-Kitsch," in *Black Popular Culture*, a project of Michelle Wallace edited by Gina Dent. Bay Press, 1992, pp. 285–91.

17. Clovis Semmes, *Cultural Hegemony and African American Development*. Praeger Publishers, 1992.

see, under the rubric of Afrocentricity, there are several factors at work. Which of these factors does or even should have preeminence is arguable; nevertheless, some of these factors are composed of and determined by very problematic dimensions.

Overall, there appear to be four discernible aspects of Afrocentricity at work in written and oral discourse of Afrocentric proponents, both professors and students. First, there is a form of Afrocentricity which is derived from an understanding of African cultural world view or cosmology. Second, there is a form of Afrocentricity which, in its emphasis on the African person as the neglected being, might be called Afrosubjectivity. Here the African descendant in America is assured primacy as the subject irrespective of intellectual inconsistencies, etc.

Third, there is also at work what might be called "Afrosynthicity." In the discourse of Afrosynthicity, the interest is generalized toward the exploration of Afro-America as a cultural and political entity emphasizing Afro-America's need to assert its sheer autonomous existence. The impulse here is basically nationalistic. In Afrosynthetic discourse, Africa is utilized for whatever purpose is convenient for the subject at hand. What is often revealed in this Afrosynthetic discourse is an identity crisis that is related to matters that go beyond the initial separation from Africa and profoundly into the imbibing of the European personality (e.g. African American machismo modeled along the lines of John Wayne and his frontier antecedents). Fourth, there is, of course, what might be called Afrosyncretism. This is probably the earliest form of scholarly discourse which has emphasized the threads of African culture to have survived in the Americas. In this category, one would find, for example, the important work of Lorenzo Dow Turner, Melville Herskovits, Roger Bastide, Robert Farris Thompson, et al.

When relating to anything labeled Afrocentric, one ought at least be discriminating enough to know which mode is at work, and discriminating enough to know especially that a fundamental Afrocentricity, based on African values, is not always at work. Indeed, one author may at various times work quite appropriately in various modes. But, again, it seems crucial that one recognize what mode is operative because under the rubric of Afrocentricity, African essences can be and have been so easily misrepresented.

In the interest of respect for Africa and esteem for the African ancestors, one might advocate that the concept of Afrocentricity have at least a generalized African cosmology as its fundamental determinant. That is to say, African values and African worldview would determine, shape, and order the various facets of the thought examined or espoused and would therefore be a determinant of the discourse. But certainly, in order to adhere to this prescription for the Afrocentric, one needs first to do the requisite homework that would allow her or him to give a reasonable articulation of African philosophic, gnostic, social, political, and economic being. In its highest sense, this form of Afrocentricity is reflected in Joseph Baldwin's statement that "the Africentric paradigm...as it has evolved over the past 20 years...consists of four basic characteristics: (a) It generates the construction of African social reality from the framework of the history, culture and philosophy of African civilization; (b) It recognizes and articulates the basic continuity of the African worldview throughout the diverse populations...(c) It recognizes and articulates the basic distinctness and independence of the African worldview...(d) It projects the African survival thrust as the center of social reality" (Azibo 1992, p. 67).[18]

Asante argues in *The Afrocentric Idea* that "Afrocentricity proposes a cultural reconstruction that incorporates the African perspective as a part of an entire human transformation...."[19] In his words, an understanding of "the African foundations of human societies" would provide one with another way of seeing.[20] Thus, Asante is primarily urging that Afrocentricity be grounded foremost in cultural comprehension of Africa.

More explicitly, Asante, as a proponent of Afrocentricity, defines it as "placing African ideals at the center of an analysis that involves African culture and behavior."[21] Asante footnotes his definition by adding, "I maintain that African Americans can never achieve their full psychological potential until they find congruence between who they are and what their environment says they ought to be. To be Afrocentric is to place Africans and the interest of Africa at the center of our approach to problem solving."[22]

In Asante's total definition, however, there is, a conflation of an ideology of Afrocentrism with an ideology of ethnocentrism. The convergence of these ideologies is not very philosophically compatible. Asante's phrase "the interest of Africa" can suggest so many things. Indeed the phrase can suggest as much or more about the Europeanized worldview of African-Americans than about what is truly African or in the actual interests of continental Africans. If the former is the case, then the African-American, as a Europeanized being, may fall more under the influence of ethnocentrism than Afrocentricism.

It might further be argued that the origin of the tension within Asante's total definition of the Afrocentric, that is, that "to be Afrocentric is to place Africans and the interest of Africa at the center of our approach to problem solving,"[23] is in the fact that the ethnocentric is so often merely the *egocentric writ large*. Because the egocentric is so typically narrow-visioned, inclinations toward it are problematic. Of course, egocentrism in the case of oppressed peoples is often almost politically mandated for sheer survival. Nevertheless, the egocentric is narrow-visioned and is definitely a liability when it works in collusion with the ethnocentric.

Afrocentric ideals, at large, that is ideals based upon fundamental African values and cosmology, seem to push beyond the boundaries of ethnocentrism. This transcendent attribute is mainly due to the fact that indigenous African thought has not developed extremely rigid categorizations of humanity and nature, as has European thought. The Afrocentric, therefore, would remain more cosmic in its world view. Whereas, since the Eurocentric has developed more rigid categorizations of humanity and nature, it has by its own logic become tremendously ethno-

---

18. Quoted in Daudi Ajani ya Azibo, "Articulating the Distinction Between Black Studies and the Study of Blacks: The Fundamental Role of Culture and the African-Centered Worldview." *The Afrocentric Scholar: The Journal of the National Council For Black Studies* Vol. 1, No. 1 (May 1992): 64–97.

19. Molefi K. Asante, *The Afrocentric Idea*. Philadelphia: Temple University Press, 1987, p. 5.

20. *Ibid.*, pp. 4–5.

21. *Ibid.*, p. 6.

22. See *The Afrocentric Idea* , note #3, pp. 197–198.

23. *Ibid.*

centric, terrestrially oriented and limited as opposed to having a more cosmic orientation toward the inter-connectedness of existence as would the Afrocentric.

There may be something of a paradox in the conceptualization of African culture as being more cosmically oriented, when one remembers that so much of traditional African society is quite characteristically unit-oriented or "tribal." On the surface Africa's social and political demography is so often based on small organizational units, leading one to think with regard to localization and particularity. Nevertheless, this orientation toward the smaller units was an aspect of African social genius and seems not to have rigidified boundaries of being. For above all, African cultural orientation is indeed a cosmic orientation. This cosmic orientation is rooted in the belief lying at the heart of virtually all African cultural units that the universe is a potent conglomerate of active energies, natural and human, seen and not seen and that all units of being are reflections of these energies. Herein lies the foundation for universal interconnectedness. Everything comes from and reflects the same source.

To think about the incongruence of the Afrocentric and the ethnocentric in more specific terms, it may be useful to note the pre-occupation of many Afro-Americans with the need to pin down the ethnic-racial identity of the ancient Egyptians. The need to clarify that the ancient Egyptians were not white, by which is really meant, not Anglo-Saxon, is a significant intellectual, philosophical, and political point in light of the fraudulent history that the modern Anglo-Saxons have created about themselves by appropriating unto themselves the creation of civilization as well as all claims to culture and civilization.

As a reaction to this fraudulence, the question is often raised from the African-American audience in public lectures on Africa about the racial identity of the Egyptians. The same point is sometimes hammered upon by Afrocentric lecturers and scholars to the extent that all parties, by the logic outlined above, make a precarious slip from the Afrocentric cosmic orientation of thinking into the racio-ethnocentric, terrestrial-orientation of thinking. In slipping unwittingly into the racio-ethnocentric, terrestrial orientation, the lecturers, scholars and audience miss a true comprehension of the glory of the Egypt they wish to claim and of the Egypt with which they, because of various needs, wish to identify. That is, they often end up identifying with very specific points about Ancient Egypt to the extent that they overlook the cosmic points that really should be made via true identification with Egypt. Again that is, if one focuses too much on racial specificity, then one may disregard the spiritual lessons the Egyptian priesthood sought for millennia to pass down and to teach.

In conjunction with the foregoing point, even after careful study and great appreciation of some of the historically indispensable theoretical and methodological essays in the inaugural issue of *The Afrocentric Scholar: The Journal of the National Council For Black Studies*, one may very well still stand at issue with the use of Kmet/Ancient Egypt as the almost exclusive model for representing and valorizing African civilization. The almost singular use of Kmetic/Egyptian model may veritably and inadvertently reinforce pathologies of African Americans (derived from European hegemony) with respect, for instance, to equating physical beauty with not being "too black" and having relatively long hair; with respect to equating power and self-worth with empire. African Americans must beware of their special psychological challenge which demands a real rather than abstract association with and appreciation for the Africa of the thatched roof village as well as with imperial Africa. Otherwise one may find that one is still operating out of a European paradigm of what is valuable and what is beautiful. Thus, why not cite, for example, as often as one cites Egypt the civilizations of the Dogon via the cosmology articulated Ogotommeli,[24] or the cosmogony of the Zulu as is relayed through authors like Mazisi Kunene in *Anthem of the Decades*[24] and Vusamazulu Credo Mutwa in *Indaba My Children*[25] and the recent, very extraordinarily informative presentations of the Dagara worldview by Malidoma and Sobonfu Some in *Of Water and the Spirit* and *We Have No Word for Sex*.[26] This admonition about metal models is crucial most of all because the multi-layeredness of African self-hatred can create peculiar zones of self-deception, even among the most outstanding intellectuals. This admonition is also important because when speaking of *the* African worldview, the truly Africentric person ought to be able to demonstrate how the African worldview manifests itself throughout various regions of Africa.

Interest in the issue of the identity of the Ancient Egyptians is complicated by the motive of the question and by the point-of-view that determines the answer. Therefore, if the conscious or subconscious motive of the interest is in affirming one's human superiority as a race, it is doubtful whether one will arrive at a creditable answer about the fundamental essence of Ancient Egypt. To put the matter in the form of a question, can an egocentric frame of reference provide an adequate interpretation of anything that is truly African? It seems logical to say that had the Ancient Egyptians, those African folk who crystallized Ancient Egypt's being and essence, been caught in racio-ethnocentric thinking Egypt never would have occupied the grand historical space of several millennia that it did. To the contrary, it was the cosmic-centric orientation that became crystallized along the Nile by ancient Africans that allowed them to surrender their ethnocentrism to a broader world view, a world view that gave primacy to cosmic law, not social law, about humanity. It was cosmic law, not parochial, social or racial law by which talent was defined and which determined even the eligibility to hold the office of Pharaoh. It was this African cultural orientation which placed emphasis on cosmic force and cosmic law that deterred atrophy in ancient Egyptian civilization and allowed it to endure for several millennia.

It is useful to consider infantile American civilization by contrast, a civilization which has operated and still does operate from the Eurocentric, racio-ethnocentric orientation. In merely two centuries as a nation, America suffers from a critical crisis of atrophy. This condition of atrophy is possibly largely due to American reluctance to embrace the law of cosmic humanity, giving preference to the terrestrial, racio-ethnocentric orientation, thereby stifling through neglect, marginalization, and alienation, the genius of its total lot of human resources.

---

24. See Marcel Griaule, *Conversations With Ogotemmeli: Introduction to Dogon Religious Ideas*. New York: Oxford University Press, 1965.

25. See Mazisi Kunene, *Anthem of the Decades*. Portsmouth: Heineman Educational Books, Inc., 1981.

25. See Vusamazulu Credo Mutwa, *Indaba, My Children: African Tribal History, Legends, Customs, and Religious Beliefs*. London: Kahn and Averill, 1966.

26. See Malidoma Patrice Some, *Of Water and the Spirit: Ritual, Magic and Initiation in the Life of An African Shaman*. G. P. Putnam's Sons, 1994; and Malidoma and Sobonfu Some, *We Have No Word For Sex: An Indigenous View of Intimacy* (an audiotape). Oral Tradition Archives, Box 51155, Pacific Grove, CA 93950.

The pertinence of an allusion to the Egyptians will be more apparent if it is kept in mind that in his conceptualization of Afrocentricity, Asante asserts that "The Afrocentric analysis reestablishes the centrality of the ancient Kemetic (Egyptian) civilization and the Nile Valley cultural complex as points of reference in much the same way as Greece and Rome serve as reference points for the European world" (Asante 1987, p. 9). In addition to the problem just discussed, another problem is inherent in this proposition of Asante, and it is certainly a problem against which the Afrocentric student must be on guard.

The problem presently referred to is the problem of structural analogue inherent in Asante's proposition. That is, the proposition is determined to a great extent by Eurocentric thinking rather than by purported Afrocentric thinking. Thus one might raise the question again: what are the ramifications of thinking in terms of Asante's proposition, viz., that Egypt serves the Afrocentric world view "the same way Greece and Rome serve as reference points for the European world"? There are indeed many intellectual liabilities in Asante's formulation of his proposition. Are Asante's follower's picking up on his intended meaning? Hence the need to be intellectually and philosophically clear on why Egypt might be central to Afrocentric thinking. Is it because Egypt was a great empire and African Americans want to identify with the idea of empire, a successful African civilization along European lines? Or is it because African Americans truly value Egypt's philosophical and gnostic essence?

To put it more simply, for what reason is it that African Americans really desire to claim the pyramids? As monuments to empire or as symbols of an adept process of being and system of knowing? While I do think it is Asante's intention to claim the latter, many African-American students, in their Eurocentric and philistine thought processes, while quoting Asante, are unwittingly claiming the former. In effect, then, one can begin to understand why Paul Gilroy, a diasporic African not from the United States, feels the need to reject the term "Afrocentric," recognizing it really as what he calls "Americentricism," that is, a form of African-oriented thought biased toward a psychology of African descendants with a United States psychology (Gilroy 1992, p. 307). Gilroy's key point is that too often the Afrocentric thought emanating from the United States "attempts to construct a sense of black particularity *outside* of a notion of national identity. Its founding problem lies in the effort to figure sameness across national boundaries and between nation-states" (Gilroy 1992, p. 306).

Gilroy's interest in the way United States African Americans define the Afrocentric is reflected in the complication of Afrocentric representation in Patricia Hill Collins's *Black Feminist Thought*,[27] when from a black feminist perspective reputed African and universal women values conflate. Although she refers to African-based emphasis on the use of dialogue as a humanizing factor for all members of the African indigenous community (Collins 1991, p. 212), still problematic in Collins's use of the Afrocentric is the inclination to view the concept more in light of United States African-American oppression instead of in light of traditional African value systems. Thus for Collins to say that "an Afrocentric feminist epistemology is rooted in the everyday experiences of African-American

---

27. Patricia Hill Collins, *Black Feminist Thought: Knowledge, Consciousness, and the Politics of Empowerment*. Routledge, Chatman, and Hall, Inc., 1991.

women" (Collins 1991, p. 207) is inadequate as Afrocentric, that is, inadequate in establishing within African-American thought systems a foundational relationship with the potency of indigenous African ways of thinking. The crucial points of emphasis in African indigenous cultures, such as emphasis on gaining fundamental understanding and mastery of the female and male cosmic/personal energies, are never discussed or mentioned. The indigenous African ways to "knowledge, consciousness, and...empowerment" (words from the subtitle of Collins's book) are never investigated as gateways to empowerment and liberation.[28]

Thus one returns to Asante's definition of Afrocentricity and asks the critical question, how shall one define those crucial words in his phrase "the interest of Africa"? A necessary word of caution would be that African Americans would do well to guard their individual and collective intellect from slipping from the Afrocentric into the more ego-determined, American ethnocentric frame of reference. There is a thin line here which can make a critical difference in the value of the intellectual model one purports to be interested in constructing and reconstructing. A present fear is that too many younger proponents of Afrocentricity, particularly college students, are not aware that their mental structures are still working in the celebration of imperialism.

The most germane Afrocentric theory must be able to predicate itself upon the most rudimentary and most unitary form of African village culture. If this is not so, then it seems difficult to assert that Afrocentricity is really working toward the affirmation or validation of Africa. That is, must one have the great empires of Mali, Benin, and Kmet in order to determine the essential value and greatness of Africa?

Some of what is called Afrocentric is better identified as Afrosubjectivity and/ or Afrosubjectivism or maybe even Afro-narcissism. It is worth keeping in mind that, as stated by Lawrence Cahoone, "Subjectivity is consciousness. That is to say, subjectivity is that feature of or activity of human individuals by which humans have awareness of appearances or phenomena, by which things show themselves or are manifest or present to us; it is the awareness of anything whatsoever, the field or totality of experiences. Subjectivity is conceived in various and sometimes ambiguous ways: as an activity, as a metaphysical substance, as the things which appear, and that which allows them to appear" (Cahoone 1988, p. 19). To be even more specific, Cahoone's definition of subjectivism states, "Subjectivism is the conviction that the *distinction between subjectivity and non-subjectivity is the most fundamental distinction in an inquiry*" (Cahoone, p. 20). Consequently, one must learn to be aware of the disposition of the self. Although subjectivism can take on metaphysical, ethical, or other meanings, it is to its problematic methodological and/or systemic dualism that one must be alert. Too often Afrocentrists are not aware of the intellectual necessity and importance of making this recogni-

---

28. The student wishing to have an African-based understanding of consciousness, knowledge, and empowerment may wish to begin by studying the following: (1) Ra Un Nefer Amen, *Metu Neter*, Volumes 1 & 2 (Khamit Corporation 1990, 1994; (2) Maya Deren, *Divine Horsemen: The Voodoo Gods of Haiti* (Dell 1970); Henry and Margaret Drewal, *Gelede: Art and Female Power Among the Yoruba* (Indiana University Press 1983); Erskine Peters, *African Openings to the Tree of Life* (Regent Press 1983); and the works of Malidoma and Sobonfu Some, including *Of Water and the Spirit* (G.P. Putnam's Sons 1994) and *We Have No Word For Sex* (audio tape from Oral Tradition Archives, Pacific Grove California 1994).

tion. That is to say, Afrocentrists are often too unaware of their involvement with subjectivism, a very European phenomenon, historically speaking.

All of this is to say that subjectivism privileges the perceiving consciousness. But frequently, the Afrocentrist's perceiving consciousness is the European or Western aspect of her or his personality, which personality is sometimes a denied identity. African thinking is not necessarily the thinking which is privileged in some of what is labelled Afrocentric thought. From a more definite Afrocentric point of view, one should be inclined to raise the question, do human consciousness and human intellectuality mandate the privileging of the subject under any circumstance? Might not there be some possibility and some value in thinking with double-consciousness, not so much in the Du Boisean sense, but in the Ancient Egyptian sense of thinking "mdu-ntrically"[29] (hieroglyphically), thinking, that is, with regard to synthesis, thinking simultaneously in reference to or from the perspective of both subject and object? When Molefi Asante speaks about "the possibilities of a world where Africa . . . is subject and not object [and where, as a result] such a posture is necessary and rewarding for Africans and Europeans" (Asante 1987, p. 3), he is speaking, of course, from a perspective that there is value in African cosmology. One should be careful, therefore, not to confuse the idea of Africa as subject with specific problems of Western subjectivity which are reflected in the self-absorption of the individual and individualized self. To restate the problem articulated above: subjectivity in terms of self-absorption does occur, unfortunately, and too often, in some of our thinking, that is labelled Afrocentric.

Giving additional attention to the matter of the "subject," one may pursue the vitally related issue whether Afrocentricity lends itself to the unqualified appropriation of various aspects of U.S. African-American culture simply because those cultural phenomena are identified with the U.S. African-American subject? There is little benefit in arguing defensively, as some do, that there is nothing wrong with U.S. African-American culture. It would seem that one value of the Afrocentric would be to serve as criteria for critiquing the U.S. African-American phenomenon of culture as well as the general western phenomenon of culture. Afrocentricity ought be able to illuminate from a long-term perspective just what things are dysfunctional within U.S. African-American culture. The generally astute Adolph Reed, for example, even takes a defensive posture regarding the possible short-comings of Afro-American culture.[30]

A serious and influential component of Afro-American culture, Afro-American Christianity, for one, definitely needs a surgical critique. Consider, for example, the messianic aspect of Christianity which has become so integral as a determinant in the U.S. African-American cultural worldview. An Afrocentric critique of the Judeo-Christian messianic view with the generally non-messianic African cultural view might be fruitful, for example, to U.S. African-American intellectual and political as well as ontological development or reconstruction.

Can an Afrocentric concept be established simply on the basis of conceptual opposition of a Eurocentric tradition and an Afro-American phenomenon? Ought not the intellectual criteria always be rooted somewhere in Africa or, at least, validated by fundamental African values? Is the U.S. African-American subject, in all

29. "Mdu ntr" means divine words in Kmetic language and is a more appropriate term than the word "hieroglyphics."

30. Adolf Reed Jr., "Steel Trap," *The Nation*, March 4, 1991, pp. 274ff.

his/her European complications to be so unequivocally and mistakenly identified or equated with Afrocentricity? If so, perhaps there is a real need to argue for and make plentiful use of distinct terms which will designate that which is peculiarly related to U.S. African American life as "Afrocentric" and that which is truly related to African cultural, historical and philosophic foundations and the African diasporic continuum as "Africentric."

It would be useful to analyze some specific instances in which what is labelled Afrocentricity falls victim to what is really some form of Afrosubjectivity. In "Black Heroes and the Afrocentric Values in Theatre,"[31] for instance, Barbara Molette's argument for an Afrocentric concept of the hero is significantly undermined by the logistics of the oppositional paradigm she employs. Her oppositional mode of argument is a form of refutation which simply allows her to set herself in subjective opposition rather than intellectual opposition to the dominant and privileged European culture. Her oppositional strategy is set in motion by her very essential subjectivity, a subjectivity stimulated by the need to engage in debunking rather than by the need to engage in analysis.

The subjective emphasis, as exhibited in Barbara Molette's work, causes the presumed analyst to overlook crucial dimensions of the opposed worldview as she attempts to promote her own worldview. Thus, having been taken in by her own African-American subjectivity Molette characterizes the Eurocentric heroic tradition as requiring "the trait of aggressiveness in order to achieve the status of hero" (Molette 1985, p. 449). By contrast, asserts Molette, African culture does not require the aggressive trait as part of its criteria for hero status. "Instead," Molette contends, [the African concept of the hero] "might involve the use of nonaggressive athletic skill to resolve a crisis accompanied by the exhibition of bravery, courage, and wit" (Molette, p. 449). One has to raise the question here of who it is Molette assumes to be her audience and what it is that she presumes about that audience. Indeed a concept of the European hero might also "involve the use of nonaggressive athletic skill to resolve a crisis accompanied by the exhibition of bravery, courage, and wit." Even a non-reading television watcher would have difficulty complying with such an over-generalization in Molette's definition of the Eurocentric hero. Certainly, then, one need not expect the acquiescence of an audience of readers who are even lightly versed in European history, literature, or theatre. Even more improbable is Molette's assertion that "a nonracist, nonsexist concept of magnitude is necessary in order to identify and understand Black characters who are heroic" (Molette, p. 449). If such a definition of the heroic which includes the nonsexist dimension is to hold ground, what then is any reasonably enlightened person to do with a hero like Bigger Thomas in *Native Son*, not to mention the real life ones. There are other complications in Molette's logic as well, which need not be belabored here, including, most ironically, her indiscriminate use of the comic hero and most surprisingly, her use of a virtually untranslatable French word (*panache*) to express what she feels epitomizes the Afrocentric comic hero.

Thus Molette may very well be stimulated by important Afrocentric values with regard to her interest in defining and distinguishing between the African and European conceptualizations of the hero, the comic hero in particular; however,

---

31. See Barbara Molette, "Black Heroes and the Afrocentric Values in Theatre," *Journal of Black Studies*, Vol. 15, No. 4 (June 1985): 447–462.

the foundation for her definition, based a great deal in aspects of her subjectivity, i.e., her obviously primary need to debunk the European, is unreliable. Suffice it to say therefore that the oppositional paradigm, a naively subjective paradigm, generated by the less than academic need to debunk rather than to enlighten, when not handled with intellectual fullness, can become very problematic and ineffective in its attempts to establish an Afrocentric value system and Afrocentric intellectual model or strategy. By contrast, the work of Cheryl Townsend Gilkes establishes itself in many respects as intellectually Afrocentric. This is demonstrated in her article " 'Mother to the Motherless, Father to the Fatherless': Power, Gender, and Community in an Afrocentric Biblical Tradition."[32] Gilkes's work exemplifies Afrocentricity by making the African cultural linkage with Afro-America demonstrable by highlighting and examining certain assumptions taken for granted in the Afro-American folk tradition, by virtue of their being rooted in the traditional African worldview. Thus, Gilkes shows how a worldview constituted of both feminine and masculine deities was carried over into the New World experience of Africans as they encountered and metamorphosed Christianity.

Gilkes demonstrates how in their embracing of the Judaeo-Christian patriarchal deity, the Africans in America have nevertheless in their syncretic spiritual culture recast the Judaeo-Christian God and attributed to it maternal as well as paternal qualities. Hence, the Judaeo-Christian deity in African-American tradition is readily referred to in prayers, sermons, and gospel songs, though not in "scripture reading," as "the mother to the motherless and father to the fatherless" (Gilkes 1989, p. 57). Because their conceptualization of deity, as both masculine and feminine complements forms and essences, was rooted in their traditional African spiritual reality and heritage, "it never occurred to black people [in America] that this combined feminine and masculine image of God could possibly be an issue" as it would have been in Europeanized Christianity, Wilkes argues (Gilkes, p. 57), adding that "the images of God in songs, sermons, prayers, and testimonies are important Afrocentric expressions in the United States" (Gilkes, p. 58).

To further clarify her point of view, Gilkes states that "Black people imaged a God of power as both male and female although they were initially presented with a patriarchal God in an androcentric text" (Gilkes, p. 58). To support her argument, Gilkes's exploration of the biblical scriptures reveals that the reference to God as "father to the fatherless" appears in Psalm 68 and only in those specific terms. The Africans broadened the gender reference in order to embrace a more African conceptualization of divinity as partaking of the masculine and the feminine.

But in the case of some of Gilkes's other Afrocentric references where does one draw the line? For when Gilkes moves into the discussion of the crucial issue of black liberation and the creation of a liberationist Christian theology, is she correct in designating this issue of black American liberation as Afrocentric since she does not demonstrate how the issue of liberation has origins in traditional African cultural determinants? The critical legitimacy of the issue of liberation is not at all to be underplayed for its ramifications for the lives of African descendants in America. Nevertheless, if the term Afrocentric is to be used to designate that

---

32. See Cheryl Townsend Gilkes, " 'Mother to the Motherless, Father to the Fatherless': Power, Gender, and Community in an Afrocentric Biblical Tradition," *Semeia: An Experimental Journal for Biblical Criticism*, Vol. 47 (1989): 57–85.

which is African derived, then the question must be asked whether the situation that mandates liberation is of African origin.

More specifically is the political situation of African Americans fundamentally tied to any particular African cultural derivatives? Should one critique the political situation from an African cultural perspective, one could very easily validate what is being done as Afrocentric. But is the issue of our political situation necessarily Afrocentric simply because one is focusing on matters related to African descendants? To probe further in to the matter demarcation, could an African-American who is sold, for example, on Marxism but whose focus is exclusively the situation of black people be appropriately called Afrocentric? One notices often that in the Afrocentricity of intellectual and popular culture, it is African American issues rather than African values that are foregrounded. This is not to say, though, that the issues themselves do not have value implications.

The area most fraught with problems is the realm of more abstract thinking where one is required to do more extrapolation and transferring of the African-based value systems and worldview. Nevertheless the transmissibility of an African-based worldview is what Linda James-Myers achieves in the articulation of her potent theory of *optimal psychology* set forth in her various articles and her book *Understanding An Afrocentric World View: Introduction To An Optimal Psychology* (1988).[33] Very exemplary, too, of African-based interpretation is Paul Carter Harrison's *The Drama of Nommo* (1972)[34] and the work of Kariamu Welsh Asante related to African-American dance and her development of the Umfundalai dance technique.[35]

A sub-category of Afrosubjectivism might be marked off as Afro-significationism. The root term, "signifying," is thought of here as the dominant form of sarcasm in Afro-American verbal culture. In this context, signifying is defined as a verbal or gestural strategy employing rhetorical indirectness or directness and is used for the purpose of ridicule. The tone of the sarcasm may run the gamut from mild to caustic.

In effect, Afro-significationism is defined in this discussion as a mode of intellectualism in which intellectual engagement is overridden by signifying itself; that is, intellectual analysis is overridden, laced with, or determined by the motive of counterhegemonic discursive retaliation. This is the mode of discursive engagement with European critical theory, which, at least in one respect, characterizes some of the recent and prolific work of Houston A. Baker, Jr., and virtually all of the work of Henry Louis Gates, Jr.[36] The extent of Baker's and Gates's awareness,

---

33. See the following by Linda James-Myers: (1) *Understanding An Afrocentric Worldview: Introduction to an Optimal Psychology*. Dubuque, IA: Kendall/Hunt Publishers, 1988; (2) "Traditional African Medicine and Optimal Theory." *The Journal of Black Psychology*, Vol. 19, No. 1: 25–47.

34. See Paul Carter Harrison, *The Drama of Nommo*. New York: Grove Press, Inc., 1972

35. See, for example, Kariamu Welsh-Asante, *African Dance: An Artistic, Historical, and Philosophical Inquiry*. Trenton: Africa World Press, 1994; (2) "Images of Women in African Dance: Sexuality and Sensuality as Dual Unity." *Sage*, Vol. 8, No. 2 (Fall 1994): 16 ff.; (3) "African-American Dance in Curricula-Modes of Inclusion." *Journal of Physical Education, Recreation and Dance*, Vol. 64, No. 2 (February 1993): 48–51; and (4) "Philosophy and Dance in Africa: The Views of Cabral and Fanon." *The Journal of Black Studies*, Vol. 21, No. 2 (December 1990): 224–32.

36. As illustrations of works by Houston A. Baker, Jr., and Henry Louis Gates, Jr., I cite Houston A. Baker, Jr., "To Move Without Moving: An Analysis of Creativity and Commerce

their intellectualism, partly determined by this psychology, is unclear but suffice it to say that a crucial aspect of their discursive representation is structured implicitly, and perhaps even very unconsciously, around their signifying in the extreme about intellectual merit and achievement and intellectual discourse in the Western philosophic tradition, especially as this tradition began increasingly, within the past two decades to be courted and imitated by literary critics.

Perhaps owing to this type of involvement, graduate students in particular will frequently undertake to cite the work of Baker and Gates as examples of Afrocentric literary criticism. When placed in historical and critical perspective, the work of Baker and Gates over the past decade has more value as an implicitly signifying mode, a mode of mimetic productivity, than as lucid and compelling Afrocentric literary and cultural interpretation. Much of the writing of Baker and Gates, in consequence of their emphases on demonstrating and reflecting the adaptability and suitability of African-American culture for European critical theory, signifies indeed about the nature of current critical discursive productivity in the academy. Unfortunately, though, too often their excessive enthusiasm to be like the postmodernist, neo-hegemonic authorities gives to their literary and cultural enterprise a detractive and negative value. Hence the language of European theory so dominates the discourse of Baker in his discussion of the blues that the blues itself has to struggle with the discourse to retain any kind of prominence as subject. And with Gates's almost exploitative use of Elegba figure and others aspects of West African mythology in *The Signifying Monkey*, in the conscious or unconscious service of European theory, the result is even more devastating. The outcome of the work of both critics is the further compromising of African culture to validate itself.

Some of Baker and Gates's productions might be likened to the troubled and dubious achievements of celebrated cinematographer Spike Lee. One need only remember that Lee's mode of presentation and emphasis is heavily determined by sense that to market to African Americans successfully the subject must be one of-African-American controversy. The suitability of the comparison of Baker and Gates with Lee would become even clearer if one were to be reminded that in Spike Lee's posture as a satirist, the troublesome aspects of Lee's problematic achievements stem very much from his deficiencies in the areas of both dramaturgical irony and verbal irony. That is, as with Baker and Gates who often appear so mesmerized by the magical power of the language of European discourse, Lee too seems more captivated by the mandate to produce the black controversial subject than he is conscious of the need to exert over his production the ultimate in African-based verbal and dramaturgical control. Nevertheless, Spike Lee, too, is often labeled Afrocentric.

This point of view regarding Gates is corroborated by Boyi[37] who agrees that Gates arrives at his "Afrocentric" point, after his romance with validation of

---

in Ralph Ellison's Trueblood Episode," *PMLA: Publications of the Modern Language Association of America*, Vol. 98, No. 5 (October, 1983): 828–845 and Baker's *Blues, Ideology, and Afro-American Literature: A Vernacular Theory*. University of Chicago Press, 1984. Regarding Gates, I cite especially *The Signifying Monkey: A Theory of Afro-American Literary Criticism*. Oxford University Press, 1988.

37. Boyi is quoted in Stewart (1992): 30–31.

African culture through European theory, and that his efforts to set interpretative examples do not reach far enough into rich realm of indigenous African cultural paradigms (Qtd. in Stewart, pp. 30–31). The fixations of Baker and Gates also lead, of course, to consideration of questions about audience constituency and to fundamental questions of who (not with regard to race, but intellectual integrity) is perceived as the most valued audience constituent. This problem of audience value brings us back to the essential issue, the trap of subjectivity, the matter of self-consciousness and the determinants of self-consciousness.

In attempting to define the maturing African-American literary imagination as Afrocentric, Carol Blackshire-Belay[38] sets forth several good points in proposing that this "maturing imagination" can be defined by seeing "first and foremost [that] the writer uses language that reflects the culture. Second, [that] the writer understands the universality of African peoples' experience, that is, the emotions and attitudes are universal to the African audience. Third, [that] the writer transcends the local or fixed boundary of imagination in style, imagery, and form. [And] lastly, the writer shows a quest for justice, harmony, and peace" (Blackshire-Belay 1992, p. 6). Not overlooked by Blackshire-Belay in her proposal, however, are the myriad complications for arriving at a mature Afrocentric disposition. In dealing with the literary arts, for example, she allows therefore for factoring in and accounting for such crucial and problematic matters as the writer's voice and audience even with respect to the most favored African-American writers. Blackshire-Belay questions, for instance, "whether the voices of Hurston and Ellison and Wright were meant for a [black] or for white audience," whether blacks were only "a sideshow in their discourse," whether the object "was to explain [blacks] to whites," and whether [blacks] were for these writers and others "the aesthetic material for a larger social point than the narrative discourse?" (Blackshire-Belay 1992, p. 7).

The truly complicating factors of these issues notwithstanding, true immersion into indigenous African philosophical systems ought to offer one more spiritual intellectual potency for resolving and managing these and a range of other issues that complicate diasporic African existence. Unfortunately, though, diasporic Africans are so westernized in their thinking processes that like their colonizers and enslavers, they, too, are easily prone to dismiss the value of anything seen as very old or ancient or African.

This Afrosubjectivism is not unlike the Cartesian rationalist dictum, *Cogito ergo sum*—"I think therefore I am" from which Afrosubjectivism definitively stems. And as with the classical European tradition of thinking, too often in so-called Afrocentric thinking, too, existence itself becomes vulnerable to being defined as the privilege of the human in the West. Specifically, existence remains the singular privilege of rational perception.

In an effort to ascertain his own existence, Rene Descartes, in the *Meditations*, arrived at the position that such a verification of existence could be made only via the possession of consciousness. The Cartesian postulate, in its most popular facet, that *to think* was *to be*, was conceived in and eventually embraced by a world which postulated an hierarchical ordering of racial humanity.[39] The Euro-

---

38. Carol Aisha Blackshire-Belay, ed., *Language and Literature in the African American Imagination*. Greenwood Press, 1992.

39. It is important to remember, though, that the popular facet of Cartesian metaphysics, as represented in Descartes's *Meditations*, "underscore[s] the contingency of thinking by the

pean eventually identified the Cartesian "I" primarily with himself and therefore attributed the primacy of thinking and reasoning unto himself, the European human, subsequently attempting to appropriate all of the great thinking ever done unto himself, and even further, subsequently becoming massively engaged in the material production and distribution of thought (the European self) and things (things, too, are manifestations of thought) through the printed word and book selling. This engagement with the reproduction of his own thinking self was to serve for the European as tangible justification for claiming for himself the primary status in the order of being.

A true Africanist philosopher might formulate her/his conceptualization of existence in other terms. Hence K. K. B. FU-KIAU maintains in his discussion of the African concept of being, "African society in general, and Bantu in particular, perceive a human being as a power, a phenomenon of perpetual veneration from conception to death—a perpetual reality that cannot be denied..." (FU-KIAU 1991, p. 8). Thus, the Africanist philosopher might say, for example, "I be; therefore I am." This conceptualization would therefore not appropriate existence as the singular engagement of the human. It would not encourage a bifurcation of the human and the natural in the way that bifurcation happened in the evolution of the European worldview under the Cartesian incentive coupled with the rationalist emphasis, a line of emphasis which had its historical descent through the groundwork of Aristotle and the cultivation of medieval Christian scholastic philosophy, coming later to be combined with the rationalist emphasis found in the evolution of Protestant theology and its privileging of the individual self.

The question that remains for the true Afrocentrist is, does he or she really wish to become entwined in the snares of subjectivism? And, will African Americans expend their energy attempting to become latter-day modernists, self-absorbed, appropriationist individualists? Such may be precisely what they may indeed become if they are not critical of the intellectual categories by which they operate.

If Afrocentrists are about the business of improving upon the past and present Columbian New World, it would be well for advocates and practitioners to keep in mind that the Afrocentrist is very much a product of the West and is therefore very susceptible to the Western pitfalls, particularly the pitfall of subjectivism and narcissism. Admonitions for the European and European American are, therefore, also applicable to the African American. Fred Dallmayr, author of *The Twilight of Subjectivity*, reminds us that, as Ortega y Gasset reflected on the "Cartesian legacy of the 'thinking substance' or the 'thinking subject,' he raised the following very pertinent proposition: "Suppose," said Ortega y Gasset, that this idea of subjectivity which is the root of modernity should be superseded, suppose it should be invalidated in whole or in part by another idea, deeper and firmer. This would mean that a new climate, a new era, was beginning."[40] What role is the Afrocentric worldview playing in this invalidation of the Cartesian legacy of subjectivity—a legacy which aided in the reification and institutionalization of chattel

---

argument that the ego, as a dependent and imperfect thing, has no power to sustain its existence, and therefore depends every moment on the power of God," according to Hiram Caton in *The Origin of Subjectivity*. New Haven: Yale University Press, 1973, p. 150.

40. Fred Dallmayr, *The Twilight of Subjectivity: Contributions to a Post-Individualistic Theory of Politics*. Amherst: University of Massachusetts Press, 1981, p. 1.

slavery and subsequent racist oppression? Is Afrocentricity in its current modes playing a role of simple replacement, thereby perpetuating the negative phenomenological structures of that legacy, or is it playing a more radically phenomenological role of structural displacement? Hopefully, postmodern humankind (society, culture) will be able to triumph over the phenomenological dilemma to which Martin Heidegger contends it is fated in declaring that "Whatever and however we may try to think, we think within the sphere of tradition."[41]

In conclusion and to re-state the problem: Is Afrocentricity the focus on the condition of the African-American racial self and its manifold predicaments (economic, psychological, sociological, etc.) as a result of American slavery and Euro-American racism, or is Afrocentricity the affirmation of ancient and traditional African values? Both are essential areas of intellectual inquiry and are not mutually exclusive intellectual dimensions.

Perhaps for our pronouncements and inquiries more than one term is necessary: "Afrocentric," "Afracentric," and "Africentric." The first term, "Afrocentric" might be used to designate matters peculiar to the enslaved Africans and their descendants in the Americas, issues peculiar to the African-American racial self and its manifold predicaments. The second term, "Afracentric," could refer to matters relating to women, in particular. This second term might need its own subcategories, however, since there are some issues more peculiar to women of African descent in America which are not necessarily of significance to continental African women. This effort at distinction and discrimination in the nomenclature is crucial because there are dimensions of the African-American worldview which certainly ought not always carry the presumption of being essentially African. That is, African-American issues and characteristics are not universally African. Many aspects of African-American ontology are American determined, not African determined, such aspects of being which derive, for example, from basic bourgeois, the individualistic worldview of Americans rather than of Africans. The third term, "Africentric," could be the more foundational designation, bearing definite and precise grounding in indigenous African thought and customs. "Africentric" would refer specifically to African cultural attributes, ontologies, epistemologies, and axiologies with respect to their purposeful, illuminative, and regenerative agency for Africa and the African diaspora.

But again, perhaps only one term is really necessary and that is the most fundamentally reflective and comprehensive one which advocated here to be "Africentricity," resonating with Azibo's definition of "Africentricity" that states: "A matured apprehension of the concept of Africentricity reveals its meaning to be no more or less than construing, interpreting, negotiating, and otherwise acting on the world using the system of conceptual thought generated from the African deep structure, also known as the African worldview. The cultural factors and cultural aspects as developed by the African...thus paramatrize Africentricity. When an African actually employs this conceptual universe, she or he is *located* Africentrically....Distortion in the meaning of Africentricity often arises" when one is Africentrically oriented but not Africentrically located (Azibo, p. 84), that is, when the theory is not reflected in the behavior.

---

41. Quoted in Dalia Judovitz, *Subjectivity and Representation in Descartes*. New York: Cambridge University Press, 1988, p. vi.

References

Asante, Molefi Kete. *The Afrocentric Idea*. Philadelphia: Temple University Press, 1987.
———. *Afrocentricity*. Trenton: Africa World Press, Inc., 1988.
———. *Kemet, Afrocentricity and Knowledge*. Trenton: Africa World Press, Inc., 1990.
Azibo, Daudi Ajani ya. "Articulating the Distinction between Black Studies and the Study of Blacks: The Fundamental Role of Culture and the African-Centered Worldview." *The Afrocentric Scholar*. Volume 1, Number 1 (May 1992): 64–97.
Blackshire-Belay, Carol Aisha, ed. *Language and Literature in the African American Imagination*. Greenwood Press, 1992.
Cahoone, Lawrence E. *The Dilemma of Modernity: Philosophy, Culture, and Anti-Culture*. Albany: State University of New York Press, 1988.
Carruthers, Jacob. H. *Essays in Ancient Egyptian Studies*. Los Angeles: University of Sankore Press, 1984.
Caton, Hiram. *The Origin of Subjectivity*. New Haven: Yale University Press, 1973.
Collins, Patricia Hill. *Black Feminist Thought: Knowledge, Consciousness, and the Politics of Empowerment*. New York: Routledge, Chapman and Hall, Inc., 1991.
Dallmayr, Fred. *The Twilight of Subjectivity: Contributions to a Post-Individualistic Theory of Politics*. Amherst: University of Massachusetts Press, 1981.
Diawara, Manthia. "Afro-Kitsch," in *Black Popular Culture*. Seattle: Bay Press, 1992: 285–91.
Fraser, C. Gerald. "Black Caucus Deliberations at Montreal: Who Should Control African Studies and For What Ends?" *Africa Report* (December 1969): 20–21.
FU-KIAU, Kimbwandende Kia Bunseki. *Self-Healing, Power and Therapy: Old teachings From Africa*. New York: Vantage Press, Inc., 1991.
Gilkes, Cheryl Townsend. " 'Mother to the Motherless, Father to the Fatherless': Power, Gender, and Community in an Afrocentric Biblical Tradition." *SEMEIA: An Experimental Journal For Biblical Criticism*. Volume 47 (1989): 57–85.
Gilroy, Paul. "It's a Family Affair," in *Black Popular Culture*. Ed. Gina Dent. Seattle: Bay Press, 1992: 303–16.
Judovitz, Dalia. *Subjectivity and Representation in Descartes*. New York: Cambridge University Press, 1988.
Maasi, Shaha Mfundishi, et al. *Kupigana Ngumi: Root Symbols of the Ntchru and Ancient Kmt, Volume 1*. Plainfield, N.J.: The Pan-Afrakan Kupigana Press and Black Gold Press, 1992.
Molette, Barbara. "Black Heroes and the Afrocentric Values in Theatre." *Journal of Black Studies*, Volume 15, Number 4 (June 1985): 447–462.
Peters, Erskine. *African Americans in the New Millennium*. Oakland: Regent Press, 1991.
———. *African Openings to the Tree of Life*. Oakland: Regent Press, 1983.
Reed, Adolph Jr. "Steel Trap." *The Nation* (March 4, 1991): 274–79.
Riley, Shamara Shantu. "Ecology Is a Sistah's Issue Too: The Politics of Emergent Afrocentric Ecowomanism," in *Ecofeminism and the Sacred*. Ed. Carol J. Adams. New York: Continuum Publishing Company, 1993: 191–204.
Roberts, Robin. " 'Ladies First': Queen Latifah's Afrocentric Feminist Music Video." *African American Review*, Volume 28, Number 2 (1994): 245–257.
Semmes, Clovis E. (aka Jabulani K. Makalani). *Cultural Hegemony in African American Development*. Westport: Praeger Publishers, 1992.
Stewart, James B. "Reaching For Higher Ground: Toward an Understanding of Black/Africana Studies." *The Afrocentric Scholar* Volume 1, Number 1 (May 1992): 1–63.
Walters, Ronald W. *Pan-Africanism in the African Diaspora: An Analysis of Modern Afrocentric Political Movements*. Detroit: Wayne State University Press, 1993.

Section III

In Search of Identity

6

Racial Identity Development of African American Adolescents

Deborah L. Plummer

Racial Identity Development of African American Adolescents: The Exploratory Stage

Establishing a racial identity, an ethnographic dimension of the self-concept, is one of several developmental tasks of adolescence. For African American adolescents, establishing a racial identity is a critical part of identity formation and therefore a crucial topic for study and research in Black psychology and African American studies. Although models of racial identity development (Cross, 1971; Jackson, 1975; Taylor, 1976; Thomas, 1971) have made a significant contribution to the understanding of African American personality they have primarily focused on adult patterns of development. Historically, the study of racial identity development has been neglected or minimized in the study of adolescence, but has recently burgeoned as an area of study (Phinney, 1989; Phinney & Tarver, 1988; Plummer, 1995). Thus, the purpose of this essay is to explore the developmental tasks inherent in establishing racial identity for African American adolescents. It discusses this period as an exploratory stage to capture the transitory nature of the racial identity resolution.

Adolescent Racial Identity Development

Racial identity can be defined as the developmental process by which a person incorporates race. It is the psychological connection one has with race rather than the mere identification of skin color. For example, the use of the term "oreo" to refer to

An earlier version of this essay appeared in *Journal of Black Psychology* 21, 2 (May 1995): 168–180. and is adapted /reprinted with the permission of the copyright holder/author.

an assimilated Black who is "White on the inside and Black on the outside", speaks to the concept of racial identity attitudes. Until recently relatively nothing has been written in adolescent development textbooks on racial identity. This was largely due to the fact that most empirical studies on adolescent identity have used White Europeans as subjects. As a result, there was virtually nothing written on adolescent racial identity development as compared to physical, cognitive, social and personality development. The dearth of research studies on racial identity development is even more notably missing when discussing African American adolescents.

Likewise, African American theorists of racial identity have taken an adult perspective. Most have assumed that adolescents do not have a psychological connection with racial identity and have accepted their parents' or society's label of racial identity (Parham, 1993; Spencer, 1982). Racial identity attitudes of African American children, late adolescents (college-aged students) and adults have been the focus of research efforts in racial identity development (Aboud, 1987; Baldwin, 1985; Carter, 1991; Cross, 1971, 1978, 1991; Cross, Parham & Helms, 1991; Helms, 1990; Hopson & Hopson, 1990; Jackson, 1975; Kambon, 1992; Looney, 1988; Parham, 1993; Spencer, 1982). There are few theoretical and empirical studies of racial identity attitudes in adolescence, in general, and fewer yet of African American adolescents' racial identity development (Phinney, 1989). Because adolescence is a time of change in every aspect of a young person's life, their racial identity attitudes are often considered unstable or not representative of their own attitudes. Nevertheless, adolescents' intellectual, moral, social and personality development have been researched for particular developmental characteristics; thus it seems logical that racial identity attitudes of adolescents should be worth exploring.

Of the racial identity development models, Cross's (1971, 1991) model of nigrescence (the process of becoming Black), represents a comprehensive statement of Black racial identity development and offers a framework for understanding adolescent racial identity development. Cross describes four themes of self-concept issues concerning race and parallel attitudes that the individual holds about Blacks and Whites as a reference group. A brief description of each of the themes is as follows:

> *Pre-encounter*—The African American with these attitudes conceptualizes life from a White European frame of reference. This person may deny or devalue his or her Blackness. People with pre-encounter attitudes are considered to be in pre-discovery of ownership of their racial identity. They may have little understanding of the sociopolitical implications of race in America and prefer to think in terms of a "colorless or colorblind" society.
>
> *Encounter*—Encounter attitudes describe the awakening process experienced by the African American. This awakening is often the result of a critical incident in one's life that leads the individual to reconceptualize issues of race in society and to reorganize racial feelings in one's personal life. For example, experiencing a White European individual with racist attitudes and practices or experiencing an African American outside of the context of a stereotype may act as a catalyst to racial identity attitude change.
>
> *Immersion*—Encounter attitudes move the African American into ownership of his or her racial identity. The person makes a conscious decision to "become Black," embrace African values and moves into the Immersion stage. Immersion attitudes are illustrated by an investment in African American culture evidenced by wearing ethnic clothing and hairstyles, choosing African entertainment forms, and associating primarily with other African Americans. Immersion attitudes are pro-Black.

Internalization—Internalization attitudes are those that illustrate a heightened awareness of the meaning of being African American. The person has a high degree of comfort with oneself as a racial being and insists on being acknowledged as African American while recognizing and appreciating other ethnic/racial heritages.

Cross (1987) further defines reference group orientation as a construct that includes ethnographic dimensions of the self-concept (racial identity, group identity, race awareness, racial ideology, race evaluation, race esteem, race image, and racial self-identification). Personal identity describes dynamics and structures of the self (self-esteem, self-worth, self-confidence, self-evaluation, interpersonal confidence, ego-ideal, personality traits, introversion-extroversion, and levels of anxiety). Reference group orientation together with personal identity equals self-concept (Cross, 1987). Thus healthy racial identity attitudes are only one aspect of ego development, and racial identity achievement is only one aspect of global identity achievement.

Among the researchers who have sought to employ and expand Cross' model, Parham (1989a, 1989b) has proposed a framework for understanding racial identity attitudes within the life span development theory. Parham suggests that a person's frame of reference for race is potentially influenced by his or her life stage and the tasks associated with that developmental period of life. An assumption of Parham's extension of Cross's model is that manifestations of African American identity in childhood and adolescence reflect parental and/or societal views of race. Therefore, ownership of one's racial identity does not happen until late adolescence or early adulthood. Similarly, Phinney (1989) states that adolescents simply may not be interested in ethnicity or may have absorbed ethnic attitudes from parents and other adults. Thus their attitudes are representation of Marcia's (1966, 1980) foreclosed status—making a commitment without exploration, usually on the basis of parental values.

Because nearly all of the work on adolescent identity development is based on the work of James Marcia, it is important to understand his concepts as groundwork for understanding adolescent racial identity development. Marcia's four identity status are described more fully in the next paragraph.

Marcia (1966, 1980) expanded on the work of Erikson's central adolescent dilemma of identity versus role confusion. He proposes that the process of adolescent identity formation has two parts, a crisis and a commitment. Crisis describes the period of decision-making when old values and choices are reexamined. An outcome of this reevaluation process is a commitment to a specific role or a specific ideology. Thus, four different statuses are possible—identity achievement, moratorium, foreclosure, and identity diffusion. In identity achievement the person has been through a crisis and reached a commitment. Moratorium describes a crisis in progress with no commitment being made. Foreclosure describes a commitment that has been made without the crisis of reevaluation process. Identity diffusion describes the adolescent who is not in a crisis and has not made a commitment.

Like Marcia's model which defines four statuses of identity formation based on the variables of crisis and commitment, Cross' nigrescence model includes the notion that achieved racial identity is the result of a racial identity crisis which involves searching and exploration and ends in resolution and commitment to African American identity.

Phinney (1990) extended Marcia's concepts to define three rough stages of ethnic identity for adolescents. The first stage is that of "unexamined ethnic identity" characterized by acceptance of images and stereotypes proposed by society or endorsement of parental racial identity attitudes. This stage is equivalent to Marcia's foreclosed status and Cross' Pre-encounter theme. The second stage is the "ethnic identity search" characterized by a crisis and then further exploration of racial identity. This second stage is equivalent to Marcia's crisis in ego identity and Cross' encounter stage. The final stage proposed by Phinney for adolescent ethnic identity development is "resolution of conflicts and contradictions." The adolescent may choose to adopt society's attitudes or wholeheartedly accept his/her ethnic group's patterns and values. This stage is analogous to Marcia's status of identity achievement and the stage has similarities to Cross' Internalization theme. In Phinney's third stage, like Cross' Internalization theme, the adolescent achieves resolution and experiences a degree of comfort as a ethnic/racial person. The adolescent in Phinney's third stage may choose distance from his/her racial group, embracing a bicultural identity or wholehearted adoption of his/her racial group's values and customs as resolution to his/her racial identity struggle. However, Cross's Internalization stage differs from Phinney's third stage in that it does not embrace adoption of negative stereotypes or rejection of one's racial group as a resolution to the nigrescence struggle. Cross's Internalization stage describes self-actualized, healthy racial identification attitudes that result in inner peace (Cross, 1991).

What should be noted in the comparison of Phinney's and Cross's stages is Phinney's use of the term ethnic instead of racial identity. In her studies she discusses African American teens as moving toward a clear ethnic identity, thus, it can be assumed that she uses the terms race and ethnicity interchangeably. Helms (1990) among others stresses the importance of the term racial when referring to racial identity attitudes. Race (as opposed to ethnicity) is clearly a emotionally-loaded term, holds special significance in American culture and is therefore critical to more fully understanding the African American personality and racial identity development.

Adolescent Racial Identity Resolution Patterns

Adolescents most likely continue their racial identity struggle beyond the racial socialization of childhood and come to some resolution of this struggle, however temporary, in the adolescent period. For African American adolescents, establishing a racial identity is an added aspect of creating a personal identity (Phinney & Tarver, 1988). This identity search differs from other aspects of ego identity in the sense of which Erikson and Marcia describe it because there is no choice about establishing a racial identity (Bee, 1994). The African American adolescent can only struggle with the process and define his or her form of racial identity resolution. Outside social forces—peer groups, school, work settings—demand that African American adolescents establish a position on their connection with their race.

Plummer (1995) examined the patterns of racial identity expression for 285 African American adolescents between the ages of 14 and 18. In this study using the Black Racial Identity Attitude Scale (RIAS-B, Helms & Parham, 1985), the adolescents widely endorsed Cross's Internalization attitudes. This is not surprising when one thinks that many African American adolescents have enjoyed many of the psychological privileges of being African American since their birth. They have generally been able to celebrate African American culture openly, view African American television programs and films, and have witnessed African American professionals in positions of influence. They may have grown up with a sense of pride in their race, unlike perhaps their grandparents who struggled with negative feelings of being "colored" or "Negro" (Plummer, 1996). Thus, as Phinney (1989) and Plummer (1996) have suggested, for African American adolescents who come from nurturing environments the struggle with racial identity may not be part of the global search for identity that Erikson describes as central to adolescent development. Their internalization attitudes may have been stabilized as part of their self-concept during childhood. Because parents of African American children typically prepare their children for the status of being Black in America, this process of racial socialization provides the child with skills to operate in predominately White environments (Peters, 1985). Therefore, by the time a child reaches adolescence, his or her racial identity attitudes may be clearly defined although not fully mature.

On the other hand, it is difficult to determine whether these same racial identity internalization attitudes expressed in adolescence could be a form of Pre-encounter themes. In Cross' current organization of the nigrescence model, he defines another form of the Pre-encounter stage that assigns low salience to race. Adolescents who state that "I'm not African American; I'm just American" might fit into this stage. The same psychological privileges noted above that could lead to internalization attitudes could also lead to a type of racial comfort that assigns little significance to racial differences. Conceivably, adolescents who express pre-encounter (low salience) attitudes do not necessarily differ in their value structure from those with Internalization attitudes but differ in their value *orientation* (Cross, 1995). They may view themselves as "Black" but see no difference in their opportunities and worldviews than their White counterparts.

Adolescent Internalization attitudes may also be just a part of adolescent egocentrism which persists in many adolescent behaviors and in adolescent thinking. Because their worldviews are narrow and their lived experience limited, it is conceivable that their Internalization attitudes are premature and more characteristic of idealized thought than an integrated analysis of racial identity struggle.

Another explanation for adolescent Internalization attitudes could be modeling of parental racial identity attitudes. Spencer (1982) and Parham (1993) have suggested that adolescent manifestations of racial identity are really reflections of parental attitudes. Plummer (1996) in a cross-sectional study of racial identity across the life span, found that African American adolescents mirrored almost exactly middle-aged African American adults in their expression of racial identity attitudes. African American young adults were found to have a dissimilar pattern of racial identity expression from both the African American adolescents and middle-aged adults. Middle-aged adults and adolescents, as in other aspects of development, may have a reciprocal interaction of racial identity attitudes. In other words, the influence may be bidirectional with parents or teachers influencing adolescents and adolescents influencing their adult models.

Parents, teachers, and other significant adult role models do have a direct influence on the pattern of development for adolescents. Thus, Internalization attitudes may result from the fact that these adolescents have grown up in homes that have supported and nurtured positive African American personalities. Parham (1989b) and Baldwin (1985) support the notion that it is possible that if one's

African personality is nurtured developmentally in a supportive environment (i.e. strong identification with African cultural values, connectedness to the Creator, love, self-pride and promotion of one's people) that the individual may develop a positive African self-consciousness or have Internalization attitudes beginning at birth and continuing through his or her adult years. This does not assume that African American adolescents, as with adolescents in general, do not struggle with creating a overall personal identity, for racial identity is only one aspect of reference group orientation (Cross, 1987).

Issues in Adolescent Racial Identity Development

Exploring racial identity attitudes of adolescents clearly has its methodological limitations. Besides for the individual differences in the developmental process for adolescents, overall cognitive and gender differences exist. In addition, the issue of meaningful and accurate assessment measures presents a challenge in researching adolescent racial identity development.

Cognitive development, particularly the ability to abstract, is most likely directly related to achieved racial identity. Abstract thinking is required to move beyond a label of race to its psychological significance. Most likely there is a greater difference in expression of racial identity attitudes between early adolescents (ages 12, 13) and late adolescents (ages 17, 18). In late adolescents the ability to abstract as a cognitive process is realized. Thus, late adolescents would be able to achieve racial identity resolution in a more permanent basis than early adolescents.

One of the recurrent questions in studies of general identity formation has been whether males and females achieve identity in the same way. The evidence is mixed depending on the area of identity achievement. Gender differences do exist in adolescent physical, intellectual, social, personality and moral development (Craig, 1992). Similarly, racial identity development differs in its resolution for African American adolescent males and females. Plummer (1995) found that African American females endorsed significantly less Pre-encounter attitudes than their male counterparts. Gender differences in racial identity expression warrant continued study.

In addition, meaningful assessment measures for racial identity attitudes of adolescents are sorely needed. The process of racial socialization process of children has been well mapped (Phinney & Rotherham, 1987) but adolescent attitudes that are the product of this socialization need to be continually defined. Measures with items that capture the experience of adolescents' racial identity struggle and reflect their psychological connection with race are needed.

Conclusion

Racial identity attitudes, like other adolescent attitudes, are in the exploratory stage. Often African American adolescent racial identity development is manifested in behaviors such as interracial dating, choosing schools and careers that are more mainstream culture and making other life decisions without the awareness of racial and political implications. It is important to continue to explore with African American adolescents their racial identity attitudes and provide them with culture-specific and multicultural experiences which will continually challenge their alleged racial identity achievement.

In addition, specific delineation of adolescent racial identity development tasks are needed. Measurements that assess these tasks need to be developed and other measures that correlate with the variables of racial identity development need to be identified and administered in conjunction with racial identity scales.

The formation of a personal identity has traditionally been viewed as a positive outcome of adolescence. For African American adolescents defining themselves as African American would clearly be a part of their developmental task for this stage. This essay has examined African American adolescent racial identity development and its patterns of expression. By doing so it is hoped that exploring racial identity attitudes of African American adolescent remain a vital part of adolescent personality development theory.

References

Aboud, F. (1987). "The development of ethnic self-identification and attitudes." In J. Phinney & M. Rotherham (eds.), *Children's ethnic socialization: Pluralism and development* (pp. 32–55). Newbury Park, CA: Sage.

Baldwin, J. (1985). "African self-consciousness and mental health of African-Americans." *Journal of Black Studies*, 15, 177–194.

Bee, H. (1994). *Lifespan Development*. New York: Harper Collins.

Carter, R.T. (1991). "Racial identity attitudes and psychological functioning." *Journal of Multicultural Counseling and Development*, 19, 105–114.

Craig, G. (1992). *Human Development* (6th ed.). Englewood Cliffs, NJ: Prentice Hall.

Cross, W.E. (1971). The Negro-to-Black conversion experience: Toward a psychology of Black liberation. *Black World*, 20, 13–27.

Cross, W.E. (1978). "The Cross and Thomas models of psychological nigrescence." *Journal of Black Psychology*, 5, 13–19.

Cross, W.E. (1987). "A two-factor theory of Black identity: Implications for the study of identity development in minority children." In J. Phinney & M. Rotherham (eds.), *Children's ethnic socialization: Pluralism and Development* (pp. 117–133). Newbury Park, CA: Sage.

Cross, W.E. (1991). *Shades of Black: Diversity in African American Identity*. Philadelphia, PA: Temple University Press.

Cross, W.E. (1995). "The psychology of nigrescence: Revising the Cross model." In J.G. Ponterotto, J. Casas, L.A. Suzuki, & C.M. Alexander, (eds.), *Handbook of Multicultural Counseling* (pp. 93–122). Thousand Oaks: CA: Sage Publications.

Cross, W.B., Parham, T.A. & Helms, J.E. (1991). "The stages of Black identityy development: Nigrescence Models." In R.E. Jones (ed.), *Black Psychology* (3rd ed., pp. 319–339). New York: Harper & Row.

Helms, J.E. (1990). *Black and White racial identity: Theory, Research and Practice*. New York: Greenwood.

Helms, J.E. & Parham T.A. (1985). "Black racial identity attitude scale (form RIAS-B)." In J.E. Helms (ed.), *Black and White Racial Identity: Theory, Research and Practice* (pp. 245–247). New York: Greenwood.

Hopson, D.P. & Hopson, D.S. (1990). *Different and Wonderful: Raising Black Children in a Race-conscious Society*. New York: Simon & Schuster.

Jackson, B. (1975). "Black identity development." *Journal of Educational Diversity*, 2, 19–25.

Kambon, K.K.K. (1992). *The African Personality in America.* Tallahassee, FL: Nubian Nation Productions.

Looney, J. (1988). "Ego development and Black identity." *Journal of Black Psychology*, 15, 41–56.

Marcia, J. (1966). development and validation of ego-identity status. *Journal of Personality and Social Psychology*, 3, 551–558.

Marcia, J. (1980). "Identity in adolescence." In J. Adelson (ed.), *Handbook of Adolescent Psychology* (pp. 159–187). New York: Wiley.

Parham, T.A. (1989a). "Nigrescence: The transformation of Black consciousness across the life cycle." In R.E. Jones (ed.), *Black Adult Development and Aging* (pp. 151–166). Berkeley, CA: Cobb & Henry.

Parham, T.A. (1989b). "Cycles of psychological nigrescence." *The Counseling Psychologist*, 17, 187–226.

Parham, T.A. (1993). *Psychological storms; The African American Struggle for Identity.* Chicago: African American Images.

Peters, M.F. (1985). "Racial socialization of young Black children." In H. McAdoo & J. McAdoo (eds.), *Black Children: Social, Educational and Parental Environments.* Newbury Park, CA: Sage.

Phinney, J.S. (1989). "Stages of ethnic identity development in minority group adolescents." *Journal of Early Adolescence*, 9, 34–49.

Phinney, J.S. (1990). Ethnic identity in adolescents and adults: Review of research. *Psychological Bulletin*, 108, 499–514.

Phinney, J.S. & Rotheram, M. (Eds.). (1987). *Children's Ethnic Socialization: Pluralism and development.* Newbury Park, CA: Sage.

Phinney, J.S., & Tarver, S. (1988). "Ethnic identity search and commitment in Black and White eighth-graders." *Journal of Early Adolescence*, 13, 171–183.

Plummer, D.L. (1995). "Patterns of racial identity development of African American adolescent males and females." *Journal of Black Psychology*, 21, 168–180.

Plummer, D.L. (1996). "Black racial identity attitudes and stages of the life span: An exploratory investigation." *Journal of Black Psychology*, 22, 169–181.

Spencer, M.B. (1982). "Personal and group identity of Black children: An alternative synthesis." *Genetic Psychology Monographs*, 106, 59–84.

Taylor, J. (1976). "The Pittsburgh Project-Part I: Toward community growth and survival." In W.E. (ed.), *The Third Conference on Empirical Research in Black Psychology* (pp. 34–46). Washington, DC: National Institute of Education.

Thomas, C. (1971). *Boys no more.* Beverly Hills, CA: Glencoe.

7

Between Two Worlds: Psychosocial Issues of Black/White Interracial Young Adults in the U.S.A.

Ursula M. Brown

For most of U.S. history, children of mixed black and white racial heredity have been categorized as black, even if they are fair-skinned blond and blue-eyed. Adams (*1973*) and Drake and Cayton (*1945*) believed that despite initial resistance, interracial children eventually adapt to this societally imposed identity restriction, and that by the time they reach adulthood they "almost always" view themselves as black. The consistent labeling as black, together with socialization in the black community, were seen by these scholars as gradually conditioning the interracial child toward a black identity.

Arnold (*1984*), Funderburg (*1994*), Jacobs (*1977*), Piskacek and Golub (*1973*), Porter *(1971)*, Poussaint (*1984*) and Spickard (*1989*) noted that society's insistence that interracial children are simply black, when in reality they incorporate a dual racial heritage, undermines the formation of a healthy racial identity, creates conflicts and/or jeopardizes positive self-esteem. With whiteness idealized and blackness frequently associated with negative stereotypes, discrimination and oppression, the negation of the white part of their identity becomes even more difficult for them. An article in *The New York Times (Atkins, 1991)* suggested that adaptation to the societally prescribed black identity may be less common and more difficult than has been generally assumed. Atkins noted a mushrooming of support groups for interracial or multiracial students in major universities throughout the U.S., including New York University, Harvard, Yale, Kansas State, University of Michigan, Stanford and University of California.

Due to the extreme sparsity of empirical research in the area of psychosocial development in interracial children, understanding of the presence or absence, as well as the nature of relationships between racial identity, conflict and self-esteem is at a rudimentary level at best. Also, the impact of demographic and physical factors, as well as experiences in the sociocultural environment, are only poorly

An earlier version of part of this essay appeared in *American Journal of Orthopsychiatry* 65, 1 (January 1995): 125–130 and is adapted/reprinted with the permission of the copyright holder/author.

understood. This dearth of information has deprived interracial families, social scientists, as well as mental health professionals, of knowledge necessary to provide meaningful support to interracial children and their psychosocial challenges.

The Civil Rights Movement of the 1960s and the 1967 Supreme Court decision, *Loving vs. Virginia*, opened the doors to interracial marriages. The U.S. Bureau of the Census counted 51,000 black/white interracial marriages in 1960 and 296,000 in 1994. This represents an increase of 580% in 34 years. Expansion of our knowledge of one of the most important developmental tasks faced by interracial children, the formation of a stable and clear racial identity, has become increasingly important.

The findings presented here are excerpts from a larger research project (*Brown, 1991 and 1995*). The data presented here will examine aspects of racial identity, conflict, self-esteem, demographic, physical and experiential factors in interracial young adults. In addition, the relationship among these variables will be explored. In view of the general lack of knowledge about interracial people, a retrospective and cross-sectional research design was chosen. The data presented here was obtained from three measurements.

Method

Sample

The two major criteria for participants in this study were: 1) being an offspring of one socially defined black (African-American) and one socially defined white (European-American) parent; and 2) being between 18 and 35 years of age. This age group had been chosen for the following reasons:

Eighteen marks the end of adolescence and the beginning of adulthood. In general, at this developmental juncture ego identity has been tentatively defined and one begins, according to Erikson (*1959*) to experience an inner sense of sameness and continuity. Whether or not Erikson's observation holds true for the interracial person has not been well established. Consequently, the age range for the purpose of this study had been originally 18 through 25. The initial difficulties in finding potential study candidates brought an expansion of the age category to 35.

The participants of this study consisted of 119 American-born interracial young adults. The mean age of respondents was 21.4 years. While a few high school seniors participated in this study, more than half (61.3%) attended college. The remaining sample came from all walks of life, including professionals, housewives, sales clerks, secretaries, maintenance workers and welfare mothers. At the time of the interview, all of the participants resided in northeastern states such as New York, New Jersey, Pennsylvania, Connecticut, Massachusetts, Washington, D.C. and Maryland.

The study sample was obtained mainly by word of mouth. This was done after attempts to find a sample by various traditional methods (newspaper ads, fliers, talks to student organizations) had failed. The "snowball method," in which one referral produced one or more subsequent referrals, proved to be more successful. Interviews were usually held at places convenient to the respondents, including homes, dormitories, empty classrooms, study lounges, cafes and restaurants.

Measures

The *Brown Interracial Young Adult Interview* (*1991*), a semi-structured interview, consists of 67 questions and 256 variables. The interview measures: a) demographics; b) degree to which respondents identify as a black, white, or interracial person; c) degree of conflict experienced with regard to racial identity; d) resolution of the racial identity question; and e) experiences within the social milieu that influenced the identity outcome. Among the experiences examined were racial labeling, contact and acceptance by blacks, whites, or interracial people, quality of relationship with family members, exposure to culture, and influence of racial status laws. Questions with fixed alternative responses were posed by the researcher. Open-ended questions were used to gain understanding of the more complex and frequently more sensitive issues surrounding racial identity.

To assure the reliability of the data, items were measured repeatedly. Racial identity measures included race identification as part of demographic data questions, racial self-definition on forms asking for racial group membership information, how participants would view themselves racially in the absence of societal pressures, and racial self-perceptions during various phases of life. Finally, participants were asked whether they had ever considered trying, or actually tried, to "pass" as white.

To measure conflict, questions about how participants saw themselves racially had an "undecided" or "unsure" option. Participants were also asked directly if they had experienced doubts or uncertainties about their racial identity while growing up, which time periods were particularly problematic in regard to racial identity, and the degree to which they felt they had resolved the racial identity question in adulthood.

Self-esteem was measured by using the *Coopersmith Self-Esteem Inventory, Adult Form* (*1987*). This instrument is a 25-item self-report questionnaire and is intended to measure the way a person evaluates and maintains an evaluation about him or herself. Participants respond to each item by indicating that the item is either "like me" or unlike me." Computed test-retest reliability estimates from college students who were administered the short form ranged from .80 for males to .82 for females. Studies of construct validity (*Adair, 1984; Sewell, 1985*) have shown the measure to correlate with reading achievement, perceived popularity, test anxiety, family adjustment and the like. The reliability estimates (Cronbach Alpha) range from .78 to .81 for different sub-samples of college students.

Finally, *Spivey's Physical Description* (*1984*), consisting of two parts, was used to measure the racial appearance or phenotype of participants. The first part of this measure provides a 7-item check list measuring skin color, hair texture, eye color, various facial features, and body type. Each item was rated on a scale varying from 3 to 7 points. The second part, a 5-item measure, gave a "first impression" of the participant's racial background on the basis of his or her total appearance. In some cases, this "First Impression" list yielded a more accurate measure of the respondent's appearance than the itemized "Skin Color and Characteristics Scale." For instance, some of the participants had the coloring of a white person, but the facial features, hair texture, body build, etc. of a black person, or vice versa.

Each participant was evaluated for categorical inclusion by the researcher immediately after the interview; therefore, these ratings were subjective and did not profit from inter-rater reliability checks.

Table 1. Public versus Private Racial Identities (N=119)

Category Choice	Public (%)	Private (%)
Black	64.7	19.3
White	0.8	5.0
Hispanic	0.8	—
Asian	—	—
Native American	—	—
Other	33.6	5.9
Interracial	—	66.4
Undecided	—	3.4

Items concerning racial identity, conflict, self-esteem, experiential and physical characteristics were grouped together to form scales. The reliability of these scales as estimated by Cronbach's Alpha was high for the racial identity scales (.84 to .76) and adequate for conflict (.50). The Cronbach alpha for experiential factors ranged from .75 to .42. The self-esteem and physical characteristic scales were .80 and .80, respectively. The data were coded and entered into the computer. The analysis included descriptive statistics and both a bivariate and multivariate data analysis.

Results

Racial Identity

The popular belief that racial identity formation in interracial children is mostly a linear journey toward blackness was not confirmed. Rather, it was found that racial identity varied among participants and was a multidimensional process influenced by a physiological and psychological dual racial makeup, experiences in the social environment, racial appearance and/or personal idiosyncracies. Some participants had black identities and a few had white ones. The majority, however, indicated that they would define themselves as interracial if given the choice. There was also a difference in how participants defined themselves publicly and how they saw themselves privately.

As can be seen in Table 1, the majority of participants (64.7%) reported choosing the black racial category on forms requesting racial group membership information. However, in the absence of external pressures, more (66.4%) indicated that they would identify themselves as interracial, while a few (5%) said they would define themselves as white if they had a choice. Participants who chose the "other" category on forms frequently added that they were interracial, bi-racial, mulatto, or a human being.

The compartmentalization into public and private identities seemed to help participants preserve their interracial self-perception while conforming to societal pressures to disregard their white roots. For some participants, this important coping mechanism apparently developed in response to a gradual conditioning process within the family as well as the requirements of the larger social milieu.

Table 2. Primary and Secondary Racial Identities (N=119)

Degree of Identification	Black	White	Interracial
Not at all	3.4	20.1	2.5
Somewhat	48.7	63.9	26.1
Very much	47.9	16.0	71.4

For others, it was the result of a conscious and frequently sudden decision after their interracial or white self-perceptions came under fire. This frequently occurred when participants entered the working world or college. A 23-year-old college senior explained:

> I thought of myself as mixed. It was not a problem for me until someone said, "Well how can you consider yourself interracial? You are black!" That was in my "Race Awareness" class. (The professor....was trying to get us to say whether we consider ourselves black or white.) [The professor explained] "You can't be both. If there was a war, blacks on one side and whites on the other, which side would you go on?" I said: "Probably neither, because I would have to choose between my father and mother, and I don't have a favorite." But since I could not answer, he was yelling at me, "People see you as black." "That is just describing my color [the participant responded] "but if I go by what I know, I can't consider myself black." I remember I was very upset, and I wanted to drop out of class after that....But ever since then I have been filling out forms...by what people see me as rather than what I should put down. I know a lot of my friends are the same way. Well, my black friends, anyway. I don't want to have every single day an argument.

As Table 2 demonstrates, many participants identified to different degrees with all three identity options, to the parts as well as the sum of their racial heritages. They emerged as primary and secondary identities. This is not surprising since the racial make-up of participants was different than that of their racially homogeneous black and white parents, a difference that frequently seemed to make complete racial identification with either parent difficult. Consequently, the black identity and particularly the white identity (an illegal identity for interracial people, even if they look white) often, though not always, emerged as secondary. In contrast, the interracial identity, reflecting the actual dual racial makeup of participants, frequently emerged as primary.

Racial identity seemed to fluctuate during the various developmental phases. For grade school, 25.2% of the respondents recalled black, 21.8% white, and 33.6% interracial identities. The remainder were unsure how they had viewed themselves racially at that time, or remembered seeing themselves as "human" or as "a person." For high-school, 29.4% of respondents remembered black identities (a slight increase), 54.6% interracial (a considerable increase), and 10.9% white (a 50% reduction). The proportion of respondents remembering black identities after high school remained stable at 29.4%, while interracial identities grew to 57.1%, and white identities dropped to 4.2%. These findings suggest that some participants "blackened out" as they approached adulthood. However, the majority of participants increasingly saw themselves as interracial. Only a few respondents reported white racial identities in the post-adolescent years.

Table 3. Conflict and Resolution of Racial Identity (N=119)

Measure	Conflict (%)	Resolution (%)
None	23.5	16.8
Somewhat	42.9	21.0
Large Extent	31.9	62.2
Not Sure	1.7	—

Conflict

The potential for conflict was present in all three racial identities. The interracial identity is not an officially legitimate one in the United States, and black or white identity only reflects half of the respondents' heredity. In addition, the white identity is fraudulent in legal terms for interracial people. It was, therefore, not surprising that the majority of participants (74.8%) had experienced conflict and/or uncertainty about their racial identity while growing up. More than one-third (37.8%) continued to struggle with the question of racial group membership (see Table 3) as adults.

For some respondents, the compartmentalization of public and private identities did not relieve their emotional turmoil sufficiently. They continued to feel misidentified by society, rendered invisible, and pressured to deny their white parent and their own whiteness. Some participants indicated that they would be unable to resolve their racial identity conflicts unless they were recognized as interracial. The 62.2% who reported satisfactory resolution of the racial identity question had come to terms with the realization that their bi-racial background would not be recognized, found that their public and private black identities coincided, or were quite public about their interracial self-perceptions.

The data failed to verify the common assumption that the most successful racial identity for people of interracial heredity is the black one, but it confirmed the high emotional cost associated with white identity. As Table 4 shows, the black identity tended to correlate with some conflict reduction, while the white identity was associated with significant degrees of conflict.

Only the interracial identity was associated with significantly diminished conflict. In the multiple regression analysis, interracial identity emerged as the only identity to predict low conflict. These results suggest that the interracial identity is the most conducive to the emotional well-being of interracial children.

Self-Esteem

The concern that racial identity conflicts of interracial children would jeopardize their self-esteem was verified by the findings of this study. Conflict about

Table 4. Correlations between Conflict and Racial Identity (N=119)

Racial Identity	Degree of Conflict
Black	−0.15*
White	0.29**
Interracial	−0.24**

*$p \leq .10$ (two-tailed); ** $p \leq .01$ (two tailed).

racial identity emerged as the most salient predictor of low self-esteem in the multiple regression analysis. It is important to note, however, while many of the respondents reported emotional upset about their racial identities, only those with high degrees of conflict seemed adversely affected in regard to self-esteem.

Quite unexpectedly, respondents were found to have significantly higher self-esteem than the norm group (t=2.50, df=343, p≤.05). The mean for this sample was 76.7 and standard deviations 16.9. The norm established by Coopersmith for adults (age 20–34) was 71.1 and the standard deviation 18.8. Caution is warranted in interpreting these results. It is quite feasible that the significant differences in self-esteem levels may be due to sample bias. Many of the participants came from middle class backgrounds and/or were found in highly selective and reputable universities (Harvard, Yale, Princeton, Columbia, Wesleyan, Tufts, Hunter, CUNY, Rutgers, Bucknell Lock Haven University and Mary Mount Manhattan College).

One cannot rule out, however, the possibility that various coping mechanisms successfully protected the self-esteem of respondents. The compartmentalization of a public black and private interracial or, in some instances, white identities, were perhaps the most common defensive maneuvers. Other coping mechanisms were denial ("I am black" or "I am white," rather than "I am interracial"), rationalizations ("I can't view myself as interracial, since it is not a legitimate racial category") or sublimation through high educational and professional achievements. Avoidance was used by a few participants with white identities who had been victimized by racism and subsequently abandoned their white social circle and their identifications with the white world. Instead, they adopted black identities and immersed themselves into a more accepting black world. Similarly, some participants with white identities avoided contact with blacks for fear that their "forbidden" identities would make them targets of hostility or ridicule. Also, black associations jeopardized their intentions to cross-racial boundaries.

Another reason for the elevated self-esteem scores may have been family support. Ongoing and open dialogue about racial issues seemed to characterize the family interaction of many, but not all, participants. The importance of familiarizing and instilling pride in both racial heritages was seen by many participants as a crucial prerequisite to self-acceptance.

Demographic Factors

Most of the demographic factors (age, gender, parental income, educational and occupational status) were unrelated to racial identity. However, self-esteem and conflict about racial group membership was found to be significantly correlated to some of the demographic variables.

Gender: Female participants were found to have significantly low self-esteem (r=−.20, p≤.05) and tended to have conflicts about racial identity (r=.16, p≤.10). The underlying reasons for these results are not readily apparent. There are, however, a variety of possibilities. Gender identification between parent and child usually occurs between two people whose racial characteristics are similar and where laws do not prohibit the identification with the whiteness of the parent. The majority of the interracial females of this study identified with a mother whose racial status as well as racial characteristics often (but not always) differed from their own (of the 70 female participants, 51 had white and only 19 had black mothers). Consequently, identification may have been more difficult and problematic. With many of the participants living in white or racially-mixed communities where the beauty ideal continues, for the most part, to be white, the identification with a white mother and the wish to be white may have been constantly reinforced. The frustration of being close, but ultimately unable to become white, or not being permitted to be interracial (which would have allowed a partial identification with a white mother), may have been a constant source of irritation. Self-esteem was adversely affected as a result.

Given the fact that many of the participants indicated that they had "good" or "excellent" relationships with their mothers, it is reasonable to assume that many of the mothers may have been aware of their daughters' difficulties. Various supportive measures, such as validation of their child's feelings and assurances about their attractiveness, may have ameliorated their daughters' conflicts. However, some of the white mothers had internalized racism from the white world. Therefore, they seemed to be unable to provide the needed support. A young woman with light brown skin, curly, sandy-colored hair and an expressive face poignantly elaborated:

> *I think my mother really 'freaked out' when I was born and there was this little black child instead of a little 'Heidi' looking child. She did everything she could to make me look like she looks . . . so she could identify with me. . . . I always felt self-conscious about being close to her or when she was with her family. I felt I was a stigma to her. I would always ask people what do I look like? . . . what do I look like? If they told me I looked black, I was very depressed. If they told me I looked white, I would be very happy. I could never get a handle on my self-image. I wanted to look like my 'mommy,' but was always getting feedback that my mother and I were fundamentally different. . . .*

Education: The degree of conflict and/or uncertainty participants experienced about their racial identities was significantly and positively associated with the level of education they had reached (r=.18, p≤.05). The qualitative data showed that conflicts seemed to be especially prevalent when participants entered college. Pressures to assume a black, in favor of an interracial or white, identity frequently mounted at this juncture of life. These pressures often started when filling out college applications that lacked an interracial category. Defining themselves as black on these forms often initiated efforts by the black college community to reach out to the respondents and integrate them into their formal and informal social networks. However, to be accepted in the black college community, participants frequently had to show evidence that they had disassociated themselves from their white roots. Respondents with strong black identities, or participants who felt traumatized and rejected while growing up in a mostly white community, seemed to have little difficulties in complying with these pressures. However, participants with strong interracial or occasional white identities frequently felt upset and angry about these demands. Failure to adopt black identities, however, made them seem like traitors to the black cause and invited various expressions of hostility, ridicule, and even ostracism. While many of the participants coped with these pressures by going underground with their interracial identities, others did not. They fought openly for recognition as interracial people and formed student organizations that addressed their unique needs. Others withdrew from the black community or, in some instances, from the college in question altogether.

Pressures in the white college community seemed to be more subtle. To fit into such a community, participants frequently felt pushed into "acting white" and disregarding their black cultural heritage. This seemed to arouse loyalty conflicts towards their black parent, relatives and friends, and/or anxiety about losing the black part of themselves. Consequently, the entry into college frequently elicited a belated identity crisis. For some of the respondents, the reexamination and reevaluation of the racial identity question during this period led to a transformation of their racial identities. For others, it brought about a consolidation or a strengthening of an existing racial identity.

Sometimes the departure from college or other important junctures in life, such as the entry into the work force, marriage, etc., invited a reworking of racial identities that had been formed as a result of external or internal pressures.

Some of the respondents felt burdened by their interracial heritage. They thought that their life would have been easier if they were just black or just white. Others felt that they were enriched by it.

Physical Characteristics

Pettigrew (*1964*) attributed the vehement opposition to interracial marriage in the United States to the erroneous belief that racial mixing would result in an inundation of the white population by blacks. Pettigrew argued that race mixing would achieve just the opposite. The findings of this study support Pettigrew's argument. The majority of the participants (49.6%) were categorized by the researcher as having the appearance of a light-skinned black person, 26.9% as a dark-skinned white person, and 11.8% as a fair-skinned white person. Less than twelve percent (11.8%) of the participants were seen as having the appearance of a medium-dark-skinned black person.

The racial appearance of the respondents had an important impact on how they viewed themselves racially. A positive and significant correlation was found between black racial characteristics and the black identity (r=.18, p≤.05). Since all participants were assigned black racial group membership even if they looked white, it is reasonable to assume that tremendous perceptual adjustments were required by some participants to reconcile discrepant physical and social realities. Some of these participants compensated for their lack of physical blackness by immersing themselves into black culture and black social circles. Others dated or married darker skinned partners so they would be more readily recognized as an authentic black person. Finally, a few tried to cross over into the white world. Of course, the emotional cost of such a step was extremely high. It frequently required abandoning families and friends and living in constant fear that their misrepresentation would be discovered.

Experiential Factors

Contact/Acceptance in the Community: Interracial families traditionally lived in black communities, where they often found protection from a rejecting white world (*Adams, 1973*). Changes brought about the Black Power Movement of the 1960s, which granted blacks the right to live in the community of their choice, seemed to have brought a major shift in this pattern. As Table 5 demonstrates, the majority of the participants grew up in racially-integrated or white communities.

**Table 5. Number of Participants Living in Various Communities
of Different Racial Composition (N = 119)**

Community	Mostly Black	Mostly White	Racially Mixed	Other People of Color	N/A
# 1	19.3%	37. %	41.9%	.9%	1.7%
# 2	16.0	42.9	29.4	3.4	8.4
# 3	12.6	30.3	31.1	—	26.4
# 4	5.9	16.8	21.8	.8	54.6
# 5	2.5	9.2	9.2	.8	78.2
# 6	—	8.4	3.4	—	88.2
# 7	—	5.0	2.5	—	92.4
# 8	1.7	.8	—	—	97.5
# 9	—	.8	.8	—	98.3
#10	.8	—	—	—	99.2

* Rows add up to 100% (except where due to rounding error).

Some caution must be exercised in interpreting these results, for many of the participants came from middle class backgrounds. Therefore, sample bias may have contributed to these findings.

The emotional well-being of participants was frequently influenced by the racial makeup of the community they lived in. Within the white community, incorporating a black racial heritage seemed to invite racial discrimination and negative stereotyping. This was especially true for participants who looked black, or if it became known that they had a black parent. The longer participants lived in a white neighborhood, the more significant their identifications with whites ($r=.22$, $p \leq .05$), and the greater their conflicts ($r=.27$, $p \leq .01$). Having been deprived of contact and bonds with black people, their knowledge of the black experience and culture often was at a rudimentary level, at best. Instead, the message that blacks are "bad" or "inferior" had been internalized. Their own blackness, as a result, was experienced as alien, a source of shame and self-hatred. The interracial identity which linked them to blackness was, therefore, significantly negated ($r=-.23, p \leq .05$). Considering that the interracial identity most closely reflected their racial constitution and was associated with the least conflict, this loss seemed to be especially unfortunate.

The adolescent period and dating in the white community was identified as particularly painful. Due to the strong taboo against cross-racial dating, many of the respondents had never been asked out for a date. Or, being fearful of rejection, because of their mixed racial heritage, they refrained from pursuing potential dating partners. As a result, they were often left intensely lonely and sad, and with a deep sense that there was something wrong with them. The entry into college and/or a multi-racial environment presented often a welcomed rescue from a world which could not accept what they represented.

Black community living, for a variety of reasons, did not always offer a better alternative. The means for white (2.96) and for the black community acceptance (3.02) were not significantly different from each other ($t=.46$, $df=118$, $p \leq .64$). Showing physical and/or cultural evidence of white roots frequently stimulated questions about their racial group loyalties and their authenticity as a black person. This exerted constant pressures on respondents to prove their blackness, rid themselves of their whiteness and/or hide their white relatives. Some of them, to dispel doubts about their racial group loyalties, avoided white friends and deeply immersed themselves into black political causes, culture and/or dress. A 31-year-old woman who had the appearance of a light-skinned black person recalled:

> *The emphasis in my home was on African-American culture. However, I used to be ostracized [by other blacks] as though I had a disability because I had a white parent. Since I wear dread locks, things have changed for the better because it is a sign that I take pride in my African heritage.*

The longer participants lived in the black community, the lower their self-esteem (r=−.20, p≤.05). Of course, it is quite feasible that these low self-esteem scores, in part, may have been related to the devastating effects of poverty, racial discrimination, neglect and abuse that continue to characterize many black communities. However, the constant feeling of not being "black enough" seemed to gnaw on the self-esteem of many of the participants. The emergence of the black acceptance variable as a significant positive predictor of the black identity, and salient negative predictors of the interracial and white identities, suggests that black acceptance had a powerful impact on the racial identity outcome of respondents.

There was an overwhelming consensus among participants (83.2%) that they would live in a racially-mixed community if they had a choice. A 23-year-old fair-skinned woman who grew up in a predominantly white community said:

> *I definitely like a mixed neighborhood. There is a lack of stress on race. You don't have to choose sides and be constantly tested. With blacks, you always have to prove that you are black enough. With whites, you have to worry that they know you are black.*

The means for racially-integrated (3.70) and black community acceptance (3.02) differed significantly from each other (t=−6.41, df=118, p≤.01). Similarly, the means for the white (2.96) and racially-integrated community acceptance showed significant differences (t=−7.56, df=118, p≤.01).

Exposure to Culture: With America being a white-dominated culture and many participants having been raised in white or racially-mixed communities, the imbalance between black and white cultural exposure that many participants reported was not surprising. The means for black (8.91) and white (14.27) cultural exposure within the family were significantly different from each other (t=−9.67, df=118, p≤.01). Similarly, the means for black (2.02) and white (3.51) cultural exposure within the school system showed significant differences (t=−16.45, df=118, p≤.01).

While some families seemed to make conscious efforts to compensate for the overall sparsity of black cultural representation, such attempts were much less apparent from the school system. Most participants did not enjoy regular exposure to black culture until college. It is unclear from the results whether the greater immersion into black studies at that time were the result of greater availability of such courses, more interest, or an increase of pressures to embrace their blackness.

Within both the family (r=−.30, p≤.00) and the school (r=−.21, p≤.05), immersion into black culture significantly diminished conflict and/or uncertainty about racial identity. Contact with black role models, familiarity with black history and culture were identified by various participants as a powerful antidote against negative stereotypes associated with blackness. Ultimately, it facilitated the integration of the black and white identity parts into a unified whole.

The exposure to black culture not only helped participants to own their blackness as part of an interracial identity configuration, but also assume to significant degrees the black identity prescribed by racial status laws (r=.36, p≤.01).

Racial Status: Within the United States, the dual racial heritage of interracial people is not recognized. Anyone with any black ancestry is considered black, even they look white. Almost three-quarters (71%) of the participants reported being influenced to various degrees by these legal stipulations. The more they shaped their racial identities according to these laws, the more significant their conflicts about racial identity (r=.19, p≤.05), the stronger their black (r=.28, p≤.01) and the weaker their interracial identities (r=−.27, p≤.01). The emotional cost of the racial misidentification was further emphasized by the negative and significant correlation between conflict and self-esteem (r=−.32, p≤.01).

As discussed earlier, many of the participants coped with these laws by privately holding on to their interracial self-perceptions, while publicly embracing the socially prescribed black identity. Their dual genetic and psychological makeup seemed to outweigh societal forces in how they regarded themselves racially. Slightly over two-thirds (66.4%) of the participants indicated that they would identify as interracial if they had a choice. This response came after years of societal conditioning toward a black identity. The resentment that many of them harbored for not having a racial category that accurately defined their dual racial background was poignantly captured by a 26-year-old student. She said:

> I don't want to be categorized either as black or white because I am neither, but every time I have to fill out a form I am confronted with the fact that there is no category for me. It's like I don't exist.

Racial Labeling:The racial background of family members influenced whether they stressed the institutionally endorsed or the bi-racial background of the participants. More specifically, black family members tended to emphasize the respondents' blackness (r=.15, p≤.10), while white family members to significant degrees provided an interracial label (r=.25, p≤.01). Only a small number of the respondents reported the provision of white racial labels.

Why some family members stressed a particular racial identity is not clear. However, one may assume that some family members felt more pressured by external forces than others. Parents who provided an interracial or, in some instances, white label, seemed to be more readily guided by their own beliefs, the physical characteristics of their children and/or clues from their children's racial self-perceptions.

Participants who were consistently prepared by their families that society would regard them as black had strong black identities (r=.56, p≤.01) and enjoyed significant conflict reduction (r=−.19, p≤.05). Such conditioning seemed to overshadow eventually internal messages and ultimately make societal and self-perceptions more congruent. Conflict reduction was enjoyed as a result.

A 21-year-old college student with a strong black identity and the physical appearance of a light-skinned black person elaborated how the racial labeling approach of his parents was effective in diminishing the uncertainties he had about racial group membership. He commented:

We always talked about it [race]. She [white mother] never wanted me to limit myself to one definition. He [black father] was a lot more strict about it. My father gave me background and pride in being black. My parents always made it clear to me who I am and how I would be perceived. It was never a mystery to me. Both of their approaches were positive.

Excessive pressures towards a black identity seemed to invite anger and resentment, especially if the participant's identity did not coincide with parental and societal views. A 20-year-old light-skinned black man, who grew up with a black mother and a black stepfather, explained:

I never could communicate with my family...really talk to them...I had to make my own rules...Everyone saw me as black, no buts! I am still confused...I am not sure whether I relate to the black or the white side...I want to be in the middle...and sometimes you wonder whether you wonder all your life 'what are you?' or whether you are going to make your own path.

The lack of communication that often resulted from the parental intolerance of their child's ambivalent feelings and identity fluctuations seemed to deprive participants of the opportunity to successfully negotiate the emotional stumbling blocks on the road towards a racial identity. Often, there was premature closure to their racial identity struggle. Intense pressure from parents to assume a black identity frequently originated from fears that their child would get hurt unless they managed to change their racial self-perceptions to the socially prescribed one.

Some family members tried to foster a white identity. Such efforts significantly encouraged the illegal white identity (r=.49, p≤.01) and, not surprisingly, significant degrees of conflict (r=.23, p≤.05). The emotional turmoil seemed to be increased if physical characteristics, identification with a black parent and/or fears of being caught in the deception did not permit compliance with the parent's wish. The encouragement to "pass" as white seemed to be especially toxic when it originated from a white parent. Participants frequently interpreted such communications that their blackness was undesirable and/or that it represented a stigma to their white parent. The anger and shame they experienced in light of the perceived parental devaluation was frequently coupled with guilt that their blackness may invite social rejection of their white parent. Fears of losing the parent's love as a result intensified their emotional turmoil. The wish to spare them from the racial discrimination and hardships that blacks within this white-dominated society must frequently contend with seemed to be much more readily heard when it came from a black parent.

Participants seemed to be admiring and appreciative of parents who emphasized both sides of their racial heritage. A 25-year-old woman saw her parents' recognition of her interracial heritage as well as their conscious efforts to expose her to an interracial lifestyle as a key ingredient in the formation of a successful interracial identity. She remembered:

My parents encouraged us [she had several younger siblings] to be proud of our racial heritages. They were intelligent about this. They knew I was half of each. They did not deny that or suggest to identify with one.

As this account suggests, many parents seemed to either directly or indirectly acknowledge the interracial heritage of respondents rather than providing deliberate and consistent interracial labels. The significant relationship between interracial labeling and interracial identity was, therefore, unexpected. Caution must be exercised when interpreting the strong correlations between racial labeling and racial identity, for some respondents seemed unsure how their families viewed their racial group membership. They indicated that race was not an important issue in their families. Rather, character and other personal attributes were stressed. After some probing, however, most participants could remember instances where racial group membership was either explicitly (providing a direct label) or implicitly (being included with a special racial group) mentioned. It is, therefore, possible that the answers of the participants in part may have been projections of how they viewed themselves racially.

Discussion

The present study failed to provide evidence that most interracial people view themselves as black when they reach adulthood. Rather, the majority of participants increasingly saw themselves as interracial. However, there were some respondents who embraced black identities and a few whose identities were white. The significant reduction of emotional turmoil associated with interracial identity may be attributed to the fact that a synthesis of black and white identities had been achieved and a new, integrated and unified identity configuration had been formed; consequently, these respondents did not need to invest their emotional energies in denying an important part of themselves, a task seen by some participants as impossible. A 21-year-old student explained:

> When you mix salt and pepper, it's impossible to separate the grains. You have a new spice, not just salt and not just pepper. The same is true when you are interracial.

The societal misidentification of participants seemed to arouse conflicts in many, complicating their quest for a clear racial identity. The inability to openly embrace and express both parts of their racial heritage was a constant underlying emotional irritant for many of these young adults. Even when they had adopted the socially prescribed black identity, being half-white frequently rendered their authenticity as a black person questionable, especially among blacks. This put constant pressure on them to prove their blackness and to disregard their whiteness (including their white relatives).

The task that confronted the families of participants in supporting them towards a clear racial identity was bewildering. If they validated the reality of their interracial constitution and reinforced the development of an interracial identity, they clashed with U.S. racial status laws and societal racial labelling. If, on the other hand, they conformed to societal expectation and tried to convince the respondents that he or she is just black, their actual racial make-up was misrepresented. This potentially undermined the participant's emotional well-being as well as the parent-child relationship. Also, the negation of the white identity part may have been equated by some parents as an annihilation of themselves or their spouses and, therefore, represented a source of resentment and conflict.

Thus, the lack of a social and institutional sanction for their dual racial heritage imposed a heavy emotional burden on participants as well as their families. Ultimately, it complicated immensely their quest of a clear racial identity.

Limitations of Study

The present study constitutes groundwork for more definitive studies, offering insights into certain phenomena and associations among various factors rather than establishing causal relationships between dependent and independent variables. Generalization of the findings about any particular developmental phase or beyond the age group of 18–35 is limited by lack of detailed information. In addition, the findings are restricted to young adults born in the United States with one black parent of African-American descent and one white parent of European-American heritage. Since the study was not based on a probability sample, it was biased in the direction of over-sampling in the more highly educated middle class.

The retrospective research design that asked participants to report recalled experiences is another limitation of the study; since memory is prone to distortion, some of the findings may be biased. In addition, characteristics of the interviewer may have had a bearing on responses. Participants were informed of the researcher's personal interest in the project, based on her having raised two children of her own interracial marriage; still, her white racial and European cultural heritage may have skewed some of the responses.

Despite these limitations, however, the data provide important insight into an area that has been largely neglected.

Conclusion

Trying to fit into a socially prescribed racial mold that accommodates only half of the respondents' racial makeup seemed to be an enormous struggle. It discouraged a simple and natural unfolding of racial identity and put pressure on these young adults to deny an important part of their physiological and psychological existence. To pretend that interracial children are just black is irrational and racist, and to define them as "other" is dehumanizing and degrading. Social and legal sanction for their dual racial background (now under consideration by such governmental agencies as the Bureau of the Census) would go far toward reducing the emotional stumbling blocks faced by interracial people. Unfortunately, in a society that has traditionally used racial classifications to legitimize social inequalities and oppression, the psychological benefits associated with such a category may be seriously compromised. The splintering of black and interracial groups into two separate entities would decrease the size of each. This could jeopardize their already precarious political and socioeconomic position and undermine their ability to obtain social and economic justice. How to reconcile these conflicting psychological and sociological needs of interracial people is a new and complex challenge to social scientists. In an increasingly multiracial society where communities of color are often divided against one another, it is a challenge that deserves careful consideration.

References

Adams, P. (1973). "Counseling with interracial couples and their children in the South." In J. Stuart and L.E. Abt (eds.), *Interracial marriage: Expectations and reality* (pp. 54–61). New York: Grossman.

Arnold, M. (1984). *The effect of racial identification on self-concept in interracial children.* Doctoral dissertation, St. Louis University (University Microfilms International No. 8418608).

Atkins, E. (1991, June 5). "When life isn't simply black or white." *New York Times,* p. C1.

Brown, U. (1995). "Black/white interracial young adults: Quest for a racial identity." *American Journal of Orthopsychiatry,* 65 (1): 125–130.

Brown, U. (1991). *A study of racial identity, conflict, self-esteem and experiential factors in young adults with one black and one white parent.* Doctoral dissertation, New York University (University Microfilms International No. 9222937).

Coopersmith, S. (1987). *Coopersmith self-esteem inventories.* Manual. Palo Alto: Consulting Psychologist Press.

Drake, S., & Cayton, H. (1945). *Black metropolis.* New York: Harcourt Brace.

Erikson, E. (1959). *Identity and life cycle, psychological issues.* Monograph. New York: International Universities Press.

Erikson, E. (1968). *Identity: youth and crisis.* New York and London: Norton and Company.

Funderburg, L. (1994). *Black, white, other: Bi-racial Americans talk about racial identity.* New York: Morrow and Company.

Jacobs, J. (1977). *Black/white interracial families: Marital process, identity development in young children.* Doctoral dissertation. Wright Institute, Berkeley, CA. (University Microfilms International No. 78-3173).

Loving v. Virginia, 388 U.S. 1 (1967).

Pettigrew, T. (1964). *A profile of the American Negro.* Princeton, Toronto, New York, London: VanNostrand Co.

Piskacek, V. and Golub, M. (1973). *Children of interracial marriage: expectations and realities.* Eds. Irving Stuart and L.E. Abt. New York: Grossman Publishers.

Porter, J. (1971). *Black child, white child.* Cambridge, MA: Harvard University Press.

Poussaint, A. (1984). "Study of interracial children presents positive picture." *Bulletin, Interracial Books for Children,* 15 (6): 9–10.

Spickard, P. (1989). *Mixed blood: Intermarriage and ethnic identity in twentieth century America.* Madison: University of Wisconsin Press.

Spivey, P. (1984). *Interracial adolescents: Self-image, racial self-concept and family process.* Doctoral dissertation, City University of New York.

United States Bureau of the Census (1994). *Current population reports,* pp. 20–483, Household and Family Characteristics.

8

The End of Africanity?
The Bi-Racial Assault
on Blackness

Rhett S. Jones

Black people have coped with, when they have not overcome, slavery, racism, economic exploitation, political oppression, and a host of other afflictions in the United States and the thirteen colonies of British North America that preceded its formation. At present African Americans confront the grave problems of black-on-black crime, drugs, unemployment, underemployment, and perhaps most serious of all, the disorganization of black families.

Blacks not only survived these and many other problems, but managed at the same time to create one of the most remarkable cultures in human history. The slaves, without property, wealth, political power, full control over their own families, or even full control over their own bodies, created a culture in which African Americans delivered respect to one another. Respect in the slave community was not based on money or power, as the slaves had neither, but rather on reputation, which in turn was based on treatment of children, respect for the elderly, belief in God, and meeting one's responsibilities to the community.

This culture, the racial unity on which it rests, and the idea of blackness or Africanity itself is now under attack. This paper places the assault of Africanity in historic and hemispheric context and examines the reasons why it is being launched at this time.

African Americans who consider themselves to be bi-racial or multi-racial are in the forefront of efforts to deconstruct blackness. Like most black Americans these persons are of mixed racial ancestry, but unlike most black Americans, they are attempting to carve out for themselves a separate racial identity, distinct from the mass of blacks. They want their non-African ancestry recognized. When asked to identify themselves racially they do not want to call themselves black, instead they wish to be called bi-racial or multi-racial, and some even wish to list the different races from which they are descended. Some have said they do not mind calling themselves black, providing they can also point out that they are at the same time not entirely black. Others have lobbied state legislatures and the fed-

An earlier version of this essay appeared in *Western Journal of Black Studies* 18, 4 (Winter 1994): 201–210 and is adapted/reprinted with the permission of the copyright holder/author.

eral government to establish a category of bi-racial or multi-racial so that on printed forms they will not have to check black or "other."

The bi-racial movement is, of course, larger than those who are of mixed black and non-black ancestry, but it is in the African American community that it has produced most discussion. For persons of mixed white-Latino, white-Asian American, or white-Native American ancestry bi-racialism is not an important issue because it has a long history of being recognized and acknowledged. The rules of race in the United States permit these persons to acknowledge their mixed race ancestry, and indeed to claim to be both white and non-white. For example, in the West, persons who are regarded as white may run for office and make mention of a Native American grandmother in an attempt to attract the Indian vote. And in Florida the same person may at times present herself as white, and at other times as a Latina. With the exception of blacks, all people of color have been permitted to follow the path laid down by Europeans who migrated to the United States in that they are regarded as assimilating minorities (Davis, 1991). Their racial ancestry is of interest, and they may point out that one of their parents is not white, but this is only an issue of passing curiosity. It is understood that they are in the process of becoming white Americans.

According to a number of studies (Quan, 1982; Loewen, 1988; Wong, 1993) over the course of the twentieth century Chinese and Chinese Americans in Mississippi were able to move from being regarded as black in the state's bi-racial system to being regarded as white. In the opening statement of his book, Loewen, 1988: iii) quotes a conversation with a white Baptist minister in Mississippi:

> 'You're either a white man or a nigger, here, Now, that's the whole story. When I first came to the delta, the Chinese were classed as nigras.' ['And now they are called whites?'] 'That's right!'

Blacks could not follow the Chinese into whiteness. And because of the one-drop rule it is impossible for a politician, otherwise thought of as white, to run for office and make mention of his black grandmother as a ploy to attract the African American vote. The one-drop rule holds that any person of known African ancestry, regardless of his/her physical appearance, is black. It applies only to blacks, and is not applied to Asian Americans, Latinos, and Native Americans. The one-drop rule made it illegal in many states for whites, and in some states Native Americans, to intermarry with blacks. But even before anti-miscegenation laws were struck down in 1967 by the Supreme Court they were for the most part focused on African Americans. According to Fuchs (1990: 139–140):

> Japanese, Chinese, and Filipinos even escaped the anti-miscegenation statutes of several mainland states, probably because they were difficult to enforce, but also because they were not made to apply to them by the courts in every state. In Louisiana, for example, the state supreme court in 1938 decided that African ancestry was the only definition of color. In a subsequent decision, the court made it plain that to be a Filipino was not to be colored but white. It made no difference that some Filipinos had much darker skin color than some African-Americans. That was, of course, the whole point of caste, to confine [black] people by blood lines (not by color alone) in a subjugated status.

Not only does the one-drop rule apply only to Afro-Americans, but it exists only in the United States. All of the nations of the western hemisphere are multi-racial, including within their borders varying numbers of people from Europe, Asia, and Africa, as well as the descendants of the original inhabitants. As is the case in the United States, race relations in these nations, and the colonies that preceded them have been characterized by miscegenation, but unlike the United States, most of these nations acknowledge racial intermixture. So, for example, in Haiti the term "mulatre" is applied to persons of mixed European and African ancestry, while the term "mulatto" is applied to the same persons in Mexico. Only in the United States is the reality of sexual relations between whites and non-whites denied, and then only when the non-white partner is black. There are no mulattos in the United States, only blacks.

Ironically, many of the bi-racials who are at the forefront of efforts to deconstruct blackness claim they are not primarily concerned with it, but with whiteness. As Reddy (1994) sees it, claims of white superiority in the United States rest on the idea that whites are a pure race and not only created civilization, technology, rational thought, but played the central role in all the achievements of mankind. Blacks, on the other hand, never created any great civilizations, this argument runs, and are fortunate to have been transported to America where they benefit from contact with whites. By insisting that the white race is not a pure one, Reddy argues, and celebrating their mixed race ancestry, bi-racials undermine the idea of race purity and the racist thought it makes possible. Liem (1994) agrees, noting that bi-racialism disturbs conventional ideas about race and therefore challenges racism.

Zack (1993: 164) sees the person who insists on having her bi-racial ancestry acknowledged as claiming an identity "that looks to the future rather than to the past, an identity founded on freedom and resistance to oppression rather than immanence and acceptance of tradition." She (Zack, 1993: 164) continues:

> An American who identifies herself as mixed black and white race is a new person racially, because old racial categories do not allow her to identify herself in this way. It is such a person's very newness racially that gives her the option of racelessness. To be raceless in contemporary racial and racist society is, in effect, to be anti-race. If 'authenticity' is a definition of the self in the face of oppression, then the authenticity of a person of mixed race may rest on her resistance to biracial racial categories—the racial authenticity of mixed race could therefore be the racial position of anti-race.

The bi-racials take the position that those who continue to fight as blacks against racist oppression are essentially the prisoners of past conceptual categories. By refusing to abandon their Africanity and failing to insist that they are partially white, these backward looking African Americans enable European Americans to continue the ideas of race purity that make possible racism.

Eluding Africanity: Racial Constructs Outside the United States

But ideas of race purity and the ideology of racism are not as closely linked as this argument suggests. The history of race in American nations outside the United States makes this clear. While these countries acknowledge racial intermixture in their racial terminology, they remain racist. *In Slave and Citizen: The Negro in the Americas*, the book that pioneered the comparative study of racism and slavery in the Americas, Tannenbaum (1946) argued that slaves were treated better in Latin America than in the United States for two reasons. First, the Roman Catholic Church insisted on the spiritual equality of the races, and while this did not mean that the church advocated either the end of slavery or racial equality, it did mean that blacks were entitled to full membership in the Church, and that they therefore had the right to be baptized, to be married and to benefit from all the other sacraments. In many North American Protestant denominations there was no agreement that blacks were human beings nor were they regarded as the spiritual equals of whites. The second part of what has come to be known as the Tannenbaum Thesis suggests that while slavery was natural, normative, and common in Spain and Portugal, the institution had died out in Britain. When the Spaniards and Portuguese settled their American colonies they routinely imported to the New World a form of labor common in the Old. But the English settlers had to create and justify what for them was a new institution. Their rationalizations eventually evolved into racism.

In the half-century since it first appeared, the Tannenbaum Thesis has been subjected to a variety of criticism from persons trained in a number of different disciplines. While conceding that patterns of race relations varied in different parts of the Americas, historian Greene (1942), anthropologist Harris (1964), historian McManus (1973), and folklorist Piersen (1988) concluded the explanation for this variance was demographic rather than the cultural reasons advanced by Tannenbaum. They argued that in those areas where blacks were numerous and therefore viewed as threatening they were likely to be treated more harshly than in those areas where they were small in number. Prior to publication of Tannenbaum's book Williams (1944) had argued that economic forces shaped and determined different patterns of race relations in the Americas, an argument further developed by Aptheker (1956) and Genovese (1971, 1976).

Despite their disagreements over the causes of racial discrimination, scholars agreed that racism was a force throughout the Americas, although it manifested itself in different racial structures. The sociologist Hoetink (1967) contrasted the two-tiered system of race relations in the United States, which recognized only blacks and whites, with the three-tiered system of race in Latin America which recognized whites, mulattos, and blacks. A number of scholars (Morner, 1967; Mellafe, 1975; Rout, 1976) provided descriptions of the elaborate racial terminologies constructed by Spanish and Portuguese settlers demonstrating thereby the many intermediate racial categories between whites and blacks.

In discussions of the Tannenbaum Thesis, slavery and race relations in Brazil emerged as central (Jones, 1990). Writing in an era when Jim Crow laws made racial segregation legal in the South, and de facto racial segregation was characteristic of the West and North, Tannenbaum viewed Brazil as the ideal to which the United States should aspire. Tannenbaum's argument was buttressed by the translation of Gilberto Freyre's massive study, *The Masters and the Slaves: A Study in the Development of Brazilian Slavery* (1946), of slavery in his country in which he argued that the Portuguese colonizers of Brazil drew no hard and fast line between the races, and that blacks were free to rise in the system. Many North American students of the Brazilian race relations observed that blacks occupied high positions in church, military, education, and politics in Brazil. Elkins

(1959), Klein (1967), and Morner (1967) were among the scholars influenced by these arguments, although they modified them in many significant respects. Three informative anthologies on the comparative study of race in the Americas (Foner and Genovese, 1969; Cohen and Greene, 1972; Winks, 1972) devoted considerable attention to Brazil.

Hoetink (1967, 1973) concluded that while Tannenbaum and Freyre may have been right in suggesting that some persons of African descent found the system more open to them in Brazil, than did their brethren in the United States, this did not mean that the Portuguese were any less bigoted than the English. Hoetink suggested that because the Portuguese had a conception of whiteness that was darker than that held by the English, Brazil provided greater opportunities for persons of mixed racial ancestry than did the United States. These persons could approximate the "somatic norm image" of the Portuguese and hence were regarded as white. Similarly, Degler (1971) suggested that a "mulatto escape hatch" existed in Brazil which enabled those persons of African ancestry who were light-skinned and possessed European facial features to rise in Brazil society, while those who were phenotypically African could not.

In the United States where the one-drop rule determined ideas about race most blacks neither understood nor appreciated the Brazilian distinction between mixed-race and black. The collection of essays collected by Hellwig (1992) demonstrates that many blacks in the United States believed that Brazil was a racial paradise. Such otherwise shrewd observers of race relations as Oliver Cromwell Cox, E. Franklin Frazier, and Robert S. Abbott believed that Brazil provided a model of race relations the United States would do well to emulate. More recently, however, African Americans, influenced by the writings of such black Brazilians as Do Nascimento (1989), the work of Ghanaian born Anani Dzidzienyo (1983, 1985a, 1993) and the research of Brazilian social scientists themselves, have accepted the idea that while Brazilians view race in different ways than Americans, Brazil is as racist the United States. In both nations blacks are discriminated against, must cope with powerful negative stereotypes, and are able to rise in the system only when their behavior demonstrates they have consciously and deliberately rejected behavioral patterns the white controlled society considers African.

In suggesting that their attacks on the purity of whiteness will undercut and discredit racism, bi-racials seem curiously ignorant of, or unwilling to systematically explore, the history of race relations outside the United States. Skidmore (1974) shows that Brazilians have long held a conception of whiteness that is not based on race purity, and instead have advocated a "whitening" process in which, over time, blacks would gradually be absorbed into the white population. In a reversal of the one-drop rule, the Brazilian assumption has been that as whites are the dominant, superior, and more powerful race they will absorb blacks into the white race with little difficulty. The resultant race while white, would include persons of African ancestry, and therefore would not be pure in the sense that the bi-racials in the United States use the term. The Brazilian example suggests that even where racists do not view whites as constituting a pure race, they remain racists. Zack (1993: 75) is one of the bi-racials who understands this:

> It has been estimated that between 70 and 80 percent of all designated black Americans have some degree of white ancestry. If Americans, like Brazilians,

were racist but more benevolent toward individuals, then 70 to 80 percent of all designated black Americans could be redesignated not-black. This is not to suggest that such redesignation would alleviate the problems of black Americans—the traditions of racial discrimination are too powerful in American life for any mere linguistic change to erase the kinds of racism that are an integral part of American life.

Why then suggest that millions of black Americans who have sought the end of slavery, Jim Crow, and racism for centuries as black people that they should become not-black? Leaving aside what this would mean for the 20 to 30 percent of "all designated black Americans" who having no white ancestry would be separated from other blacks by the new racial category, why do bi-racials such as Zack urge those Afro-Americans who have white ancestors to abandon Africanity?

The answer is simple. Because race in the United States is bi-polar, in order to deconstruct whiteness bi-racials must attack blackness. Whites and blacks have very different reasons for opposing the bi-racial movement, but bi-racials do not always distinguish between these reasons, nor the different histories that have shaped them. Blacks and whites are not equal and by asserting they want to be something other than black, the bi-racials are not making a politically neutral statement in which they equally condemn whites and blacks for their shared simplistic ideas about race, but making an anti-black statement. To be sure, they are attacking whiteness, the glue that binds European Americans together and makes possible racism, but at the same time they are attacking blackness, the glue that binds African Americans together at a time when black America needs the unity Africanity provides perhaps more than any other time in their history.

Escaping Africanity: Racial Constructs in the United States

The issue is complicated by the fact that bi-racials seem to be more hostile toward blacks than toward whites. While at first glance this seems strange, the social scientific literature demonstrates that intermediate racial groups—and those like the bi-racials who would like to create an intermediate status for themselves—often vent their hostilities on the group beneath them, rather than the group above them. It is, after all, less risky to attack the powerless than to attack the powerful, and such attacks help the intermediate group to distance itself from the lower group. This is no where more clear than in the evolution of racial attitudes among Native Americans.

The growth of racism in the United States and the end of Indian military power placed Native Americans on the east coast in a vulnerable position. The Indians, writes McLoughlin (1984: 254) worked to give themselves "a status superior to that of the black man, a necessity forced upon the Indian by the slave status of black people in America and the efforts of white Europeans to place the Indian in the same caste." So long as the Native peoples were sufficiently powerful to hold their own against the encroaching whites, they were free to hold whatever attitudes they wished toward blacks. Some of them freely accepted runaway slaves into their tribes, others simply ignored them, and still others returned the fugitives to their owners, Some Indians made a practice of stealing slaves or encouraging them to runaway, and then selling them to other whites. So long as they were powerful militarily the Indians decided how they would treat blacks, just as they decided how they would treat whites, and how they would treat one another. But as it became clear that Euro-Americans were winning the military struggle, Indian peoples prudently and practically took into consideration white attitudes toward blacks.

Among the most watchful and adaptive of these tribes were the Cherokee. Many of the Cherokee adopted the emergent Euro-American culture to avoid the near-destruction of such coastal tribes as the Catawba and Uchee. According to McLoughlin (1986: 336):

> However, as the Cherokee gradually accepted the white man's style of plantation agriculture and realized how whites felt about 'people of color,' their attitude toward Africans changed.... At first reluctantly and later without compunction, the Cherokee concluded that their survival as a nation depended upon their clearly distinguishing themselves from Africans. To treat blacks as equals would not raise the blacks in white eyes but would simply lower the red man. 'Civilization' for the Cherokee became the adoption of the southern white attitude toward black labor. To own slaves became both a source of wealth and a source of respect.

Conscious of their increasingly vulnerable position, the Cherokee quickly mastered and accepted the racial terminology of European Americans. In a 1793 letter sent by Little Turkey, one of the Cherokee leaders, to the governor of Tennessee, the Spaniards were described as "a lying, deceitful, treacherous people, and...not real white people, and what few I have seen of them looked like mulattos, and I would never have anything to say to them" (Perdue, 1979: 48). Whether Little Turkey actually believed the Spaniards were mulattos is beside the point. He clearly understood the nuances of race and sought to use his knowledge to the advantage of his people.

Like all other peoples, the Cherokee had what anthropologists term creation myths, accounts of the beginning of the world. Under contact with whites and blacks, these myths, which originally made no mention of race, evolved to explain racial differences and to distance the Cherokee, and other Indians, from blacks. A Cherokee chief told a white man in the 1820s that the Great Spirit, having first created three men, one white, one black, and one red, then spoke to them (McLoughlin, 1984: 257):

> "White man, you are pale and weak, but I made you first, and will give your first choice; go to the boxes, open them and look in, and choose which you will take for your portion.' The white man [took the box that] was filled with pens, and ink, and paper, and compasses, and such things as your people now use. The Great Spirit spoke again and said, 'Black man, I made you next, but I do not like you. You may stand aside. The Red man is my favourite, he shall come forward and take the next choice.' [The red man chose] a box filled with tomahawks, knives, war clubs, traps, and such things as are useful in war and hunting. The Great Spirit laughed when he saw how well his red son knew how to choose. Then he said to the negro, 'You may have what is left, the third box is for you.' That was filled with axes, and hoes, with buckets to carry water in, and long whips for driving oxen, which meant that the negro must work for both the red and white man, and it has been so ever since.

In the reconstruction of their past and their treatment of blacks, whether slave or free, the Cherokee and other eastern tribes sought to make certain that whites understood that Indians were different from blacks and that they should not together be regarded as people of color. To achieve this goal Native peoples had to deny and disassociate themselves from persons of mixed black and Indian ancestry, whom whites were now defining as black. Prior to accepting this Euro-American conception of blackness, Native Americans had sometimes intermarried with, adopted, and accepted blacks into their tribes, but they were now found themselves forced to reject their own kin in order to carve out a middle place for themselves between whites and black.

The notable exception to this tendency in North America, at least up through the early nineteenth century, were the Seminole who, far from accepting the negative white view of blackness, refused to abandon those Africans and descendants of Africans who had intermarried with and become part of the tribe. Bateman (1990: 18) concludes that, "Because the Seminole were themselves an amalgam of peoples of diverse cultural and linguistic background, the blacks who settled and allied with them became an integral part of the Seminole people." As the Seminole were, for much of the period of the late eighteenth and early nineteenth century, able to remain isolated from direct military and social pressure from the United States, it may be that they maintained ideas about the nature of race different from those held by Euro-Americans. Whatever may be the explanation, slavery among the Seminole "began to assume characteristics greatly different from slavery in the neighboring tribes" (Littlefield, 1977: 5). According to Katz (1986: 52), "By the nineteenth century Black Seminoles had become key advisors and valuable interpreters for the nation. They were familiar with English, Spanish, and the Muskogee or Hitchiti Seminole languages."

Unlike the Seminole, and like the Cherokee, the Chinese of Mississippi separated themselves from blacks. The majority of Chinese who settled in the Mississippi Delta arrived between 1910 and 1930 (Wong, 1993: 20). They were to work as sharecroppers and thereby provide the plantation owners with an alternative source of labor to that of blacks. Whites feared that blacks would leave Mississippi for the North in such large numbers that they would lack workers, but while many Afro-Americans did leave the state, enough remained to continue to serve as the backbone of the state's labor force. In the meantime the Chinese arrivals realized that sharecropping would not enable them to get ahead in American society. But they soon discovered a niche for themselves. In the early to mid-twentieth century close to 80 percent of the Mississippi Chinese were grocers. They were able, in this capacity, to serve both races and to provide arenas in which the two races could informally meet. They rapidly prospered in ways in which those grocers who were limited to serving only black or white clientele could not.

According to Wong (1993: 21):

> The relationship between the Chinese grocers and the black members of the community grew over the years. Not only did the Chinese run businesses in the black community, but they also lived there. Therefore, they were subject to the same discrimination and prejudice that blacks received from whites. Consequently, the Chinese grocers were more friendly than white grocers toward black customers. Most Chinese grocers, for instance, 'did not require the deferential courtesy forms customarily demanded by whites.' The Chinese grocers

were thus able to monopolize a portion of the market in the black community. For Chinese grocers, being in a position in between white and black was very rewarding, financially as well as socially.

This passage somewhat understates the relationship between the Chinese and blacks for not only did the Chinese live in the black community, but they often intermarried and/or cohabited with blacks.

As the Chinese community grew and prospered, its successful members sought to take their children out of Mississippi's inferior Afro-American schools and move them to Euro-American ones. Cohn (1967: 235) argues that whites had no objection to admitting Chinese children to white schools, but feared if the doors were open to them, children of mixed Chinese/African American ancestry would attend. To permit children of part-African ancestry to attend Euro-American schools would, of course, violate the one-drop rule. To win acceptance for their children in the school system and to provide them with better opportunities, the Chinese cut ties with the black community. "By pressuring Chinese men to end their relationships with black women and to abandon their bi-racial children, or by forcing Chinese-black families to leave the community, the Chinese hoped" to eliminate Chinese-black American relationships (Wong, 1993: 22).

Those Chinese who were willing to abandon black wives and children and cut social ties with blacks, prospered and were accepted by whites. Their children were enrolled in white schools, they joined white churches, and they became members of many white social organizations. But (Loewen, 1988: 136–137):

> A vastly different fate befell those Chinese who refused to give up their Negro wives, usually because they had children by them. Even though some of them in past years were eminent in the Chinese community, their position is now extremely marginal. They do not participate to any substantial extent in the social life of any of the racial groups around them. Typically, these families have no social life whatever, beyond the nuclear family itself. One [of the 'white' Chinese] put it this way: 'We didn't associate at all with those Chinese. Well, we did associate with them but just as little as we could.'

This man and those like him have escaped blackness, are accepted by whites, and smugly comfortable in their escape, give little thought to those Chinese who chose to remain linked with African Americans.

Attacking Africanity: Bi-Racial Strategies

The bi-racials approach to race has more in common with that of the Cherokee and the Mississippi Chinese than that of the Seminole, as they attempt to distance themselves from blacks in the hope of persuading white America that they are not black. Like the Cherokee and the Mississippi Chinese, the bi-racials focus on blackness, not whiteness. While they claim to be attacking whiteness they have little to say about white people, being centrally concerned and fearful that whites will think of them as black.

This is no where more clear than in a collection of essays by undergraduates who consider themselves bi-racial (Anderson, 1994). Anderson's study makes it clear that while these young people are primarily interested in constructing a bi-racial identity, they are also interested in distancing themselves from blacks. One student wrote, "Obviously there was no escaping the amount of pigment in my body, but I did not want to be prejudged *as black* [emphasis mine]...The most comfortable identity for me was that of a multiracial Caribbean American" (Anderson, 1994: 7). Another student observed, "Because my identity contained the elements of both sides I could relate to Asians much better than the blacks" (Anderson, 1994: 4). This student does not explain why he had better relations with Asians than with blacks, but does point out that while in high school he joined the Afro-Latino Society because he was expected to do so, not because he wanted to. Clearly, both students felt they were regarded as black, that they were pressured to be black, and that they did not want to be black.

Attempts to escape from blackness are not limited to undergraduates. Zack (1993: xi) begins her book, *Race and Mixed Race*:

> I was born in Brooklyn in 1944. My mother was a single parent and I was an only child. She was an artist...If racial identification had been required, I would have identified as myself as my mother had brought me up to do: I was 'Jewish.'...My mother had a close friend while I was growing up who was married to someone else. He regularly drank too much and was rarely sober when he visited my mother. He seemed to be indifferent to children although— or because—he and his wife had ten. He rarely spoke to me. He faded out of our lives when I was twelve. When I was sixteen I found out that he had been my father.

The words, carefully chosen by a philosopher, while at one level merely descriptive, are revealing. Zack's white mother is an "artist." The black man who "had been my father" drank too much. As it is not mentioned, presumably he had no occupation, or at least not one Zack's mother shared with her, or which she recalls, or cares to recall.

Zack (1993: xi) does recall that, "During my student years, race was not an issue for me: I did not have to identify myself racially on any forms, and I do not remember any official person in the New York City public school system, in college, or in graduate school asking me what race I was." Unlike most other Americans of African descent who came to adulthood over the course of the 1950s and 1960s race played no role in Zack's life. "Race did not seem to be preeminent in my life—until 1990 when I returned to academia. Between 1970 and 1990, academia had become racialized. *Now* [emphasis mine] race is a big issue" (Zack, 1993: xii).

Zack is fortunate for historically race has always been a "big issue" for most African Americans, and it continues to be even for those who do not want to be regarded as black. Reddy (1994) observes that bi-racial students see themselves as passing for black, by which she means that it will be assumed they are black unless they make it clear that they are bi-racial. In a 1992 forum held by such students at Brown University they argued that if they do not make it clear that they have a white parent, they will have to listen to attacks being made on whites, and therefore on their parents, by blacks who assume that as they appear to be black they will have no objection to anti-white statements. For this reason bi-racial students try to make it clear as soon as possible after meeting Afro-Americans that they are not black, but bi-racial. But as all bi-racials fall within the phenotypical range of those who are regarded as black in the United States, their pronouncements are usually received by African Americans with surprise and hostility. Most blacks, aware of the mixed ancestry of African Americans in the United States, see the bi-racials as attempting to claim a privileged status for themselves.

In this they are not alone. Blackness is such a despicable status in the Americas that persons of African descent have made, and continue to make, repeated efforts to escape it. Dzidzienyo (1985b), long-time student of race relations in Brazil, explained that nation's proliferation of intermediate racial categories between white and black, with the simple explanation that in Brazil "No one wants to be black." Zack (1993: 75) understands why whites would not want Afro-Americans with white ancestors to be regarded as white, "But it is not clear on the face of it why a black person...would want to impose a black designation on a racially mixed person." If a person can escape from this despised position into a non-black category, then as Zack sees it, he/she should be allowed to do so.

But in the United States only those persons who want to escape blackness seem interested in changing America's racial categories by creating a new category of bi-racials. Sundiata (1994: G-22) asks, "What will be the effect of change on Asians, Hispanics and Native Americans? There is no evidence that these groups wish to have interracial offspring put within a new 'multiracial' designation." Neither the Cherokee nor the Chinese in Mississippi sought to be considered as bi-racial, they were content to have escaped being thought of as black or somehow linked to Africanity. Nor is there any evidence that European Americans, many of whom might by virtue of Native American, Asian, or African ancestry claim to be bi-racial, have any wish to be regarded as other than white. To be sure there are a number of Euro-Americans, dubbed by unsympathetic Native Americans as "Indian wanabees," who do not want to be white. But these persons do not want to be termed bi-racial either, instead they wish to parlay such Native American heritage as they may possess into full tribal membership. The bi-racial movement is largely composed of persons of African ancestry who do not want to be black.

A number of factors explain why the bi-racial assault on blackness has emerged at this particular time. First, the end of segregation made it possible for persons of obvious African ancestry to freely move about public places. This freedom is unparalleled in the twentieth century for less than a generation ago guide books were published for traveling blacks indicating where they could eat, use the restroom, or rent a hotel room. There was a "gentleman's agreement" in many communities which prevented apartments being rented or homes being sold to blacks, and often the agreement was backed up by force of law. In many states, not all of them Southern, it was legal to sell property with the restriction that it might not be re-sold to an Afro-American. In this era, all persons of African ancestry were on the same side of a color line that was firmly and clearly drawn. But now that segregation no longer exists some bi-racials are emboldened to separate themselves from blacks. Free to move about where they wish, they no longer need the black support system created by their ancestors. For them blackness is not only out of date, but seems likely to permanently link them to an inferior race.

At the same time the African American culture so painfully constructed by the slaves is itself in disarray. The same racial segregation which so oppressed black Americans was a source of strength. Denied entry into the larger white society, one which rested on wealth, property, education, and political power the slaves created a separate culture of their own (Jones, 1993: 11). Within this culture they delivered respect to one another based on how members of the slave community treated one another. As racism continued after emancipation so too did this culture, only where it had previously operated underground and hidden from whites it now surfaced. Free, blacks were able to establish institutions—churches, fraternal organizations, insurance groups, newspapers, women's clubs, colleges, burial societies, and schools—in which they publicly recognized, celebrated, rewarded, praised, and supported one another. By Euro-American standards these institutions had neither wealth nor political power, but they provided African Americans with a sense of achievement. The distinguished black sociologist, E. Franklin Frazier misunderstood the purpose of these institutions when he derided the Black Bourgeoisie in his book by the same title (1957). Frazier ridiculed middle-class blacks for their social pretensions, noting that most of them lacked the resources that would have made for middle-class standing in the white community. But that was just the point. They were not in the white community, but the organizations they created enabled these black Americans to give one another a sense of status, recognition, and prestige.

Integration made it possible for a tiny handful of blacks to become vice-presidents in Fortune 500 companies, generals in the United States Army, bishops in the Roman Catholic Church, and professors in Ivy League Universities, while hundreds of others achieved similar middle-rung status in other white institutions. For the first time in the nation's history, so many African Americans entered the middle class that one sociologist (Wilson, 1978) boldly entitled his book *The Declining Significance of Race*. Social scientists differ over how many blacks have achieved middle-class status, but clearly many black Americans believed that neither the culture that had carried their ancestors through slavery and its aftermath, nor the institutions this culture created were any longer necessary. These organizations were not allowed to silently wither away as many publicly questioned the need for black professional organizations, sororities, colleges, publications, and other black institutions. As the bi-racial movement demonstrates, it is but a short step from questioning the need for black institutions to questioning the need for blackness.

Two other factors made this step easy to take. The end of legal segregation in housing—while covertly evaded in many areas—and the growth of the black middle-class meant that some blacks were able to move out of black neighborhoods. Up through the 1970s most blacks regardless of occupation, education, and income lived in black neighborhoods, a fact that reinforced African American solidarity. But now many blacks who had been successful no longer lived in black neighborhoods and were therefore able enter into informal relationships with whites that would have been both unthinkable and impossible a decade earlier. Second, and paradoxically, this same period produced the "white backlash," in which millions of whites in their votes and in the policies they supported indicated they thought blacks had come too far too fast. Three times, beginning in 1980, Euro-American voters elected to the presidency men whose policies sought to turn back the racial clock. Under the guise of a color-blind policy these men sought, and with considerable success, achieved the goal of restoring the whites first policy that had long been characteristic of the United States. It is against the backdrop of these events that the bi-racial attack on blackness is taking place.

Of course, there is no such thing as a bi-racial community in the United States, but with African American culture in disarray, middle-class blacks fleeing the black community, and a white backlash gaining force, bi-racials doubtless saw it to their advantage to escape blackness. They face a real problem though. Most African Americans don't care to join them.

Perhaps three-quarters of the black American population has ancestors who are not African and therefore have as much right to claim a bi-racial identity as do the bi-racials. For while the idea of whiteness is based on race purity, the idea of blackness is not. The Afro-American population includes persons who are the descendants of virtually every racial and ethnic group on the face of the earth. Moreover, many blacks know the racial identity of their non-black ancestors, and some—especially those with Native American or white ancestors—know a considerable amount of their non-African family background. If they wish, they could clearly lay claim to a bi-racial or multi-racial status. It is instructive, however, that in their attempts to be recognized as non-black, the bi-racials have not appealed to this mass of blacks to join them and also be classified as bi-racial. Instead they have concentrated their energies in getting whites to recognize bi-racials as something other than black.

In order to win black Americans to their cause bi-racials would need to answer a number of difficult questions. First, there is the question of the application of the term bi-racial. Given that those who are children of white-Latino, white-Asian American, and white-Native American parents seem little interested in being bi-racial is the term to apply only to those who are the children of a black and non-black parent? And how far back does bi-raciality go? Is it only for this generation of mixed children? Or may all black Americans claim to be bi-racial? And since, under the laws of the United States most of the ancestors of present day African Americans, however racially mixed they may have been, will simply be listed in the public records as black—or its historical equivalent—how is it to be determined that present day blacks are in fact racially mixed? Could they simply present themselves for physical inspection, relying on skin color, hair texture, lip shape, or eye color as proof of their non-black ancestry? Or would a mere declaration of mixed ancestry suffice? And what of those who, although of "pure" African ancestry shall attempt to pass for bi-racial? Shall they be legally punished or will a simple public declaration that they are black, not bi-racial, be sufficient punishment and humiliation?

Bi-racials have not spent much time in answering these questions because their primary appeals have been made not to blacks, but to whites. Although most African Americans qualify for bi-racial status, few would accept it even if it became an option. Unlike Brazil and the other nations of this hemisphere, there is no tradition of escaping blackness in the United States. There is no intermediate racial tier by means which persons can acknowledge white relatives and black, so that historically the only way in which one could escape Africanity was to pass, to cut all ties with black kin and become white. Some Afro-Americans have been willing to take this step, just as were some Mississippi Chinese and some Cherokee in order to obtain better opportunities for their children and themselves in a racist social order.

Conclusion

The bi-racial assault on Africanity is born out of a great deal of pain. The people who are its leaders say they resent having to choose between their parents, resent having to deny a part of themselves, and resent being forced to consider themselves black, when they do not feel black. They focus much of this resentment on African Americans. Ironically the very people from whom they seek to escape and the very idea they seek to deconstruct might offer them comfort and guidance.

The black community in the United States has never had the luxury of excluding persons because of their racial ancestry, nor to do them justice, have its members been much interested in doing so. The reason for this is while European American and African American culture have much in common they differ in their ideas as to the cause of behavior. Because most Afro-Americans know they are of mixed racial ancestry, race does figure significantly as a causal factor in African American culture. Most, but not all white Americans, really believe that race determines behavior and that blacks behave in ways that are different from and inferior to those of whites because as a degraded, despicable and inferior people, they simply cannot help themselves. If most whites did not believe this the nation would not remain racist. Most, but not all black Americans, really believe that moral choice determines behavior and that (some) whites behave in racist ways because they choose to be racists.

Blacks do not believe in biological determinism which is why black hatemongering groups have so small a following—despite considerable media attention—in the black community. This is not to say there are no black bigots, nor is it to say that the black community is perfect. Jones (1977) demonstrated that at least through the mid-1970s most blacks who wrote on African American history accepted white stereotypes of Native peoples in an attempt to demonstrate the superiority of Africans over Indians. It is to say that when Martin Luther King, Jr., looked forward to a time in the United States when people would be judged by the content of their character and not the color of their skin he merely urged white people to do what black people had long done, judge people by their actions not by their race.

Armed with this belief, African Americans have achieved so much in the battle against race hate as black people that most are little minded to put aside blackness on the grounds that if whites recognize some blacks as bi-racial this will undercut racism. Most blacks have no intention of claiming a special bi-racial status for themselves while leaving behind those blacks who can make no such claim. Bi-racials who mislike this reality may, of course, and should continue their appeals to whites for special recognition. Those who understand it should rejoin the African American community and continue the struggle for racial justice. There will be time enough to talk about being bi-racial and multi-racial when that struggle is won and whites are no longer regarded as superior to blacks.

References

Anderson, Wanni W. (1994). "Structuring Biracial and Multiracial Identities Across Cultures." Paper presented at Annual Meeting of the Association for Asian American Studies, Ann Arbor, MI, April 7.
Aptheker, Herbert (1956). *Toward Negro Freedom*. New York: New Century Publishers.

Bateman, Rebecca B. (1990). "Africans and Indians: A Comparative Study of the Black Carib and Black Seminole." *Ethnohistory,* 37 (Winter): 1–24.

Cohen, David W. and Jack P. Greene, eds. (1972). *Neither Slave Nor Free: The Freedmen of African Descent in the Slave Societies of the New World.* Baltimore: Johns Hopkins University Press.

Cohn, David L. (1967). *Where I Was Born and Raised.* Notre Dame: University of Notre Dame Press.

Davis, F. James (1991). *Who is Black? One Nation's Definition.* University Park: University of Pennsylvania Press.

Degler, Carl (1971). *Neither Black nor White: Slavery and Race Relations in Brazil and the United States.* New York: Macmillan.

Do Nascimento, Abdias (1989). *Brazil: Mixture or Massacre?—Essays in the Genocide of a Black People.* Dover, MA: The Majority Press.

Dzidzienyo, Anani (1983). "Blackness and Politics in Brazil" in Rhett S. Jones, ed. *Politics and the African Legacy.* Providence: Rhode Island Black Studies Consortium.

——— (1985a). "The African Connection and the Afro-Brazilian Condition" in Pierre-Michel Fontaine, ed. *Race Class and Power in Brazil.* Los Angeles: Center for Afro-America Studies, University of California.

——— (1985b). Personal communication.

——— (1993). "Brazilian Race Relations Studies: Old Problems, New Ideas?" *Humboldt Journal of Social Relations,* 19 (2): 109–129.

Elkins, Stanley M. (1959). *Slavery: A Problem in American Institutional and Intellectual Life.* Chicago: University of Chicago Press.

Foner, Laura and Eugene D. Genovese, eds. (1969). *Slavery in the New World: A Reader in Comparative History.* Englewood Cliffs, NJ: Prentice-Hall.

Frazier, E. Franklin (1957). *Black Bourgeoisie: The Rise of a New Middle Class in the United States.* Glencoe, IL: The Free Press.

Freyre, Gilberto (1946). *The Masters and the Slaves: A Study in the Development of Brazilian Civilization.* Translated by Samuel Putnam. New York: Knopf.

Fuchs, Lawrence H. (1990). *The American Kaleidoscope: Race, Ethnicity, and the Civic Culture.* Hanover, NH: University Press of New England.

Genovese, Eugene D. (1971). *The World the Slaveholders Made: Two Essays in Interpretation.* New York: Vintage Books.

——— (1976). *Roll, Jordan, Roll: The World the Slaves Made.* New York: Vintage Books.

Greene, Lorenzo Johnston (1942). *The Negro in Colonial New England.* New York: Columbia University Press.

Harris, Marvin (1964). *Patterns of Race in the Americas.* New York: Walker.

Hellwig, David J., ed. (1992). *African-American Reflections on Brazil's Racial Paradise.* Philadelphia: Temple University Press.

Hoetink, Harmannus (1967). *The Two Variants in Caribbean Race Relations: A Contribution to the Sociology of Segmented Societies.* Translated by Eva M. Hooykaas. New York: Oxford.

——— (1973). *Slavery and Race Relations in the Americas. An Inquiry Into Their Nature and Nexus.* New York: Harper and Row.

Jones, Rhett S. (1977). "Black over Red: The Image of Native Americans in Black History." *Umoja I,* (Summer): 13–29.

——— (1990). "Brazilian Race Relations in Hemispheric Perspective: Review Essay." *Trotter Institute Review,* 4 (Summer): 15–18.

——— (1993). "Double Burdens, Double Responsibilities: Eighteenth Century Black Males and the African American Struggle." *Journal of African American Male Studies I,* (Winter): 1–14.

Katz, William Loren (1986). *Black Indians: A Hidden Heritage.* New York: Atheneum.

Klein, Herbert S. (1967). *Slavery in the Americas: A Comparative Study of Virginia and Cuba*. Chicago: University of Chicago Press.

Liem, Ramsay (1994). Discussant's comments on "Crossing Boundaries? Interracial Marriages and Multiracial Children." Meeting of the Southern New England Consortium on Race and Ethnicity, Providence, RI, February 5.

Littlefield, Daniel F., Jr. (1977). *Africans and Seminoles: From Removal to Emancipation*. Westport, CT: Greenwood Press.

Loewen, James W. (1988). *The Mississippi Chinese: Between Black and White*. Prospect Heights, IL: Waveland Press.

McLoughlin, William G. with William H. Conser, Jr. and Virginia Duffy McLoughlin (1984). *The Cherokee Ghost Dance: Essays on the Southeastern Indians, 1789–1861*. Macon, GA: Mercer University Press.

McLoughlin, William G. (1986). *Cherokee Renascence in the New Republic*. Princeton, NJ: Princeton University Press.

McManus, Edgar J. (1973). *Black Bondage in the North*. Syracuse, NY: Syracuse University Press.

Mellafe, Rolando (1975). *Negro Slavery in Latin America*. Translated by J.W.S. Judge. Berkeley: University of California Press.

Morner, Magnus (1967). *Race Mixture in the History of Latin America*. Boston: Little, Brown.

Perdue, Theda (1979). *Slavery and the Evolution of Cherokee Society, 1540–1866*. Knoxville: University of Tennessee Press.

Piersen, William D. (1988). *Black Yankees: The Development of an Afro-American Subculture in Eighteenth Century New England*. Amherst: University of Massachusetts Press.

Quan, Robert Seto (1982). *Lotus among the Magnolias: The Mississippi Chinese*. Jackson: University of Mississippi Press.

Reddy, Maureen (1994). "Crossing the Color Line: Race, Mothering, and Culture." Paper presented at the Meeting of the Southern New England Consortium on Race and Ethnicity, Providence, RI, February 5.

Rout, Leslie B., Jr. (1976). *The African Experience in Spanish America*. New York: Cambridge University Press.

Skidmore, Thomas (1974). *Black Into White: Race and Nationality in Brazilian Thought*. New York: Oxford.

Sundiata, Ibrahim K. (1994). "How Black is Black?" *Boston Globe* June 5: G-22.

Tannenbaum, Frank (1946). *Slave and Citizen: The Negro in the Americas*. New York: Knopf.

Williams, Eric (1944). *Capitalism and Slavery*. Chapel Hill: University of North Carolina Press.

Wilson, William J. (1978). *The Declining Significance of Race: Blacks and Changing American Institutions*. Chicago: University of Chicago Press.

Winks, Robin, ed. (1972). *Slavery: A Comparative Perspective*. New York: New York University Press.

Wong, Vivian Wu (1993). "The Chinese in Mississippi: A Race in Between." *Trotter Review*, 7 (Fall): 20–22.

Zack, Naomi (1993). *Race and Mixed Race*. Philadelphia: Temple University Press.

9

Mixed Black and White Race and Public Policy

Naomi Zack

There is so much myth involved in the classification of Americans into black and white racial categories that the facts about race are part of the subject of Racial Theory. Racial Theory is the intellectual structure within which it is possible to develop an understanding of how *race* is socially constructed. In that theoretical context, the ordinary concept of race in the United States, which purports to be about something hereditary and physical, has no scientific foundation; neither does this concept have an ethical rationale which ensures just treatment for individuals or a maximization of benefits for all concerned groups. In this paper, I mean to sketch the historical, empirical and emancipatory context for permitting American individuals of mixed black and white race to identify themselves racially. Such permission would be a matter of future public policy in many different political, intellectual, scientific and educational contexts—it would reflect a massive paradigm shift in emancipatory black and white racial thought and action, just as the historical denial of permission has reflected white racism and racial oppression. Because the case of black and white racial mixture has always been the site of the most stringent impositions of racial purity in American culture, argument for self-identification in that case is an important beginning for unraveling racial mythology, in general.

The One-Drop Rule

The racial categories of black and white race form a rigid, asymmetrical classification system in the United States. On a folk level, it is assumed that an individual is either black or white, but not both.[1] However, there have been individuals acknowledged as having both black and white ancestors since seventeenth century colonial days so something besides the facts of heredity, as they are understood in

An earlier version of this essay appeared in *Hypatia* 10, 1 (Winter 1995): 120–132 and is adapted/reprinted with the permission of the copyright holder/author.

1. For more comprehensive discussions of the inadequacy of the American folk concepts of black and white race, see Naomi Zack, *Race and Mixed Race*, Philadelphia: Temple University Press, 1993, Ch. 2; also, Naomi Zack, "Race, Nominalism and Reference," forthcoming in the American Philosophical Association *Newsletter on Philosophy and the Black Experience*.

other cases of ancestral diversity, must be at work here.[2] At work is the one-drop rule, which has been reflected in the United States census since 1920. According to the one-drop rule, an individual is racially black if he or she has one black ancestor anywhere in her genealogical line of descent, and this holds regardless of whether, or how many, white, Asian or Native American ancestors were also present. By contrast, a person is white only if she has no non-white ancestors. That is the logic behind American racial designations and its only basis is the public policy which was associated with black chattel slavery. Nevertheless, Americans assume that there are biological foundations for racial classifications. That there are no such foundations is worth a few minutes to review.

The Biology of Race

First of all, the drop in the one-drop rule refers to a drop of blood. It used to be believed that ancestors literally passed their blood on to their descendants and that this blood mixed with the blood of other ancestors whenever a child was conceived. We now know that that this is nonsense: maternal and foetal blood circulate separately; blood is not passed on but its type is copied genetically; there are no general racial blood types—human blood types are distinguished for transfusion purposes and full siblings may have incompatible blood types.[3]

According to biological anthropologists, the racial unit is not an individual but a population that has more of some physical traits than other populations. There probably never have been pure races because racial populations have rarely been isolated from members of other racial populations. Social taboos may substitute for geographical isolation in breeding populations, but no such taboo has ever been completely effective; and even if such a taboo were effective, the physical traits which would be designated as racial traits would be a matter of cultural choice, and not biology.[4] Biologically, there is no *general* genetic marker for race. There are genes associated with particular physical traits which have been socially designated as racial traits, but there is no gene for white race, black race, Asian race or any other race, which has been scientifically identified during the centuries in which the modern idea of race has been in circulation.[5] It is important, in this regard, to note the contrast with sex. While all individuals do not neatly divide into XX or XY on a chromosomal level, due to borderline and more complex combinations of X and Y, nevertheless, X and Y are identifiable as general sexual

---

2. For a book-length treatment of the history of mixed black and white race in the United States, conducted within the traditional racial paradigm, see Joel Williamson, *New People*, New York: Free Press, 1980.

3. For the facts on blood and race, see Zack, *Race and Mixed Race*, Ch. 2, and references therein.

4. For a discussion of race and breeding, see Zack, *Race and Mixed Race*, Ch. 4.

5. For an argument about the *modernity* of contemporary concepts of race, see Martin Bernal, *Black Athena*, New Brunswick: Rutgers University Press, 1987, pp. 439–45, 454–5. See also, Naomi Zack, "Slavery without Race," in *Bachelors of Science: Seventeenth Century Identity, Then and Now*, Ch. 14, Philadelphia: Temple University Press, forthcoming, 1995–6.

markers which determine more specific sexual characteristics.[6] Even after all of the social constructions of sex and gender are filtered out, the overwhelming majority of individuals are XX or XY. This general XX-ness or XY-ness causes or explains less general physical characteristics, which themselves have underlying genes. For example, the presence of XX predicts the presence of the gene for ovaries. If it were the case that all of the specific physical sexual characteristics varied along continua and that XX and XY did not exist, then there would be no general genetic basis for sex. That is the situation with race. The specific physical characteristics that different cultures have designated as racial in different ways, vary, without any underlying general genetic marker that causes them or can be used to explain their presence. Once one realizes this, it becomes clear that *race* is what cultures take it to be. As a *general* biological characteristic, which is how racist cultures construct race, race does not exist. But given racist constructions, race has a powerful social reality and it is therefore an extraordinarily complex subject to both refer to and dissolve at the same time.

Due to the one-drop rule, an American classified as black may have more genes which cause physical characteristics considered to be white, than an American classified as white. The presence of a black ancestor does not ensure the presence of any of the genes of that ancestor beyond the second generation. This is because individuals get one-half of their genes from each parent and there is no guarantee that they have genes from all four grandparents—the "racial" genes, i.e., the genes underlying perceptible traits that that the culture has designated as "racial" traits, might be just as likely to drop out as the non-racial ones. Lest it seem contradictory to speak—even in quotes—of racial genes, in the same breath with a claim that there are no genes for race, it should be remembered that a racial gene is a gene for a trait that has been *culturally* determined to be a racial trait. There is nothing specifically *racial* in a biological sense about a "racial" gene. "Racial" genes are genes that underly skin color, hair texture and other physical characteristics of human beings. They otherwise have nothing extra, physically or genetically, to distinguish them from other "non-racial" genetic differences, except that these "racial" genes have been designated, picked out, identified, as "racial." Finally, it should also be noted that so-called racial genes do not get inherited in clumps. Most genes are subject to dispersal and recombination at conception and the genes behind the physical traits which society has picked out as racial are no more likely to get passed on together than are genes for traits to which society attaches no racial significance.[7] This is why individuals who are otherwise presumed to be of the same race, do not all have the same racial traits.

Groups of individuals from the same geographical area, such as a part of precolonial Africa, may share some biological traits among their members, such as dark brown skin and curly hair. But the designation of these traits as racial is a purely cultural construction. Ever since the colonial period racial designation has accompanied the oppression and exploitation, or domination, of the groups so

---

6. For a discussion of the development of X and Y as chromosomal markers of sex, see Daniel J. Kevles, *In the Name of Eugenics*, Berkeley: University of California Press, 1985, pp. 238–250.

7. For discussions of variations in racial genes, see N.P. Dubinin, "Race and Contemporary Genetics," and L.C. Dunn, "Race and Biology," both in Leo Kuper, ed. *Race, Science and Society*, New York: Columbia University Press, 1965, pp. 68–83 and 61–67.

designated. During the seventeenth, eighteenth and nineteenth centuries, the domination of what are now called third world populations was practiced by Europeans on a global scale. The physical differences from Europeans of these third world peoples and the assumed difference in geographical origins of their ancestors became the basis of modern European concepts of race. Until the 1920s, social scientists also assumed that cultural differences among racially designated groups were physically inherited. [8]

The American History of the One-Drop Rule

In colonial America, prisoners from Africa were worked as slaves, along with Europeans and Native Americans. By the end of the eighteenth century, these African slaves were known as "n"egroes—the 'n' was always lower case until the Harlem Renaissance—and only "n"egroes could be enslaved in the United States.[9] By that time, those individuals who were then called "negroes" and who historians after the 1930s refer to as "Negroes", but who should probably be referred to as American slaves, had been conceptualized as a distinct race from whites, lower in biological hierarchy and intellectually and morally inferior to whites.[10] So, first African prisoners were made slaves and then they were defined as a "race" of "negroes." Every member of this "race" of "negroes" was posited as having the characteristics of a population which was essentially different from the "white" population. (Unfortunately, the limitations of this paper preclude investigation of the development of cultural constructions of racial whiteness, not to mention the racialization of the indigenous American population.) Why was that difference necessary to posit, as a matter of public policy? Because the white population, as a matter of public policy, based on Enlightenment political theory, was constructed as having a human birthright of freedom.[11] The next conceptual step in the American racializing program, insofar as it was connected with the institution of slavery, entailed an identification of enslavement itself as a determinant of race.

The common assumption among contemporary historians is that in English North America, "Negroes" were enslaved because they were "n"egroes.[12] In fact, the situation was worse than that: African prisoners and their descendants were enslaved and kept in slavery for the simple reason that they or their ancestors were first enslaved. This was accomplished through the mediating concept of race, specifically the concept of "negro race."

The final North American public policy regarding the children of female slaves was beneficial to the economic interests of the owners of female slaves. As owners of living things, these owners wanted to have secure ownership of the offspring of

---

8. For accounts and discussions of the history of the concept of race in the social sciences, see Michael Leiris, "Race and Culture, in Kuper, *Race, Science and Society*, pp. 135–72; R. Fred Wacker, *Ethnicity, Pluralism and Race*, Westport: Greenwood, 1983.

9. For descriptions of nineteenth century racial hierarchies and source references, see Zack, *Race and Mixed Race*, pp. 58–61, 78–9.

10. Ibid., pp. 116–122.

11. See John Immerwahr and Michael Burke, "Race and the Modern Philosophy Course," *Teaching Philosophy* 16, 1 (March 1993): 26–27.

12. For example, Immerwahr and Burke write, "Only blacks were slaves and slaves were slaves *because* they were black." Ibid., p. 27.

what they already owned. Since only "n"egroes could be owned as slaves, the only way that they could own the children of their slaves were if those children were "n"egroes. As everyone has always known, many of children women slaves gave birth to had fathers who were not slaves and not "n"egroes. Therefore, to protect the economic interests of slave owners in English North America, the institution of slavery gave birth to the one-drop rule, as a matter of public policy.

By contrast, in Louisiana under French rule and throughout Latin America, manumission of children with slave mothers and free white fathers was common, all through the period of slavery. Those children were recognized as mixed black and white race.[13]

It became illegal to import slaves into the United States, in the 1830s. Then the cotton gin increased the speed with which cotton could be processed and the need for slave labor to grow cotton increased. The large scale miscegenation of the slave population due to generations of sexual exploitation of female slaves by free whites, as well as intra-racial miscegenation within the "n"egro population, resulted in an otherwise embarrassing number of "whiter" slave offspring, who, if they were not automatically designated "n"egroes, because only negroes could be enslaved, would have presented a disastrous loss of capital for the slave economy. After Louisiana came under the rule of Anglo-Americans, and throughout slavery in the United States, after the 1850s, all of the children of slave mothers, regardless of their paternity, were assumed to have the racial status of their mothers. (This was of course contrary to English custom and law that supported patriarchal descent in all other matters of lineage and property.)[14]

Even though, originally, the economics of slavery determined the public policy of the one-drop rule, the abolition of slavery did not mitigate the application of this rule. Between the Civil War and 1915 the one drop rule became the law in most states, where it was expressed in so-called anti-miscegenation laws that proscribed inter-racial marriage.[15] Ironically, this policy was locked in place among African-Americans during the Harlem Renaissance, when many prominent mixed-race black spokespersons explicitly took up Negro identities to the conceptual obliteration of their white ancestors. At the time, there was no choice in the matter because the United States census no longer recognized a category of mixed race and anyone who was "black" according to the one-drop rule was not accepted as white in American society.[16] Even though the anti-miscegenation laws were struck down by the United States Supreme Court in 1967, the one-drop rule has never been successfully challenged as a basis for racial classification. Officially, and according to custom, an American is black given one black ancestor, no matter how many white ancestors she has and regardless of her social experiences.

---

13. The classic work on the comparison between North and South America on this issue has become Carl N. Degler, *Neither Black nor White: Slavery and Race Relations in Brazil and the United States,* New York: Macmillan, 1971.

14. See Zack, *Race and Mixed Race,* pp. 57–61.

15. Ibid., pp. 79–82. For further details on the history of anti-miscegenation laws, see Robert J. Sickels, *Race, Marriage and the Law,* Albuquerque: University of New Mexico Press, 1972.

16. Zack, *Race and Mixed Race,* pp. 95–112.

Mixed Black and White Race and Present Public Policy, in Theory

The American history of racial categorization was unjust. This might occasion a yawn against the widespread understanding that the United States has a long history of racial injustice. However, we are still trapped in the rigidity of notions of biological racial difference that presuppose pseudo-scientific ideas of race. And the one-drop rule is still public policy.

Whites assume that this is how blacks want it and blacks continue to reproduce it for a variety of reasons that include hard-won affirmative action benefits, which reinforce "pure" racial identities; family and community loyalty; and continuing devaluation and oppression against individuals with African ancestry by individuals without African ancestry.

However, many individuals of mixed black and white race, especially of first generation "mixture," experience the one-drop rule not only as racist in itself, against them, but as fundamentally supportive of the false categories of race. The whole idea of race requires an assumption of a population stable in certain physical characteristics, which will "breed true." That is, the idea of race rests on fantasies of racial purity.

However, the question is not whether it is better for an individual with black and white ancestors to be designated white or partly black and partly white, than all black, because addressing the question in those terms accepts a foundation of the unjust treatment of blacks by whites. Rather, these are the pertinent questions: Since there is no such thing as race and our present legacy of racial categories is shot through with pseudo-science, and racist habits and beliefs, how should "race" be determined? Who should decide what race I am to myself? How should anyone determine the "race" of another person? Notice that there are two levels to these questions. If race is a fiction, then the person of pure race is in the same position regarding these questions as the person of mixed race. But, if race is held down as a social constant, then, in the context of the nonsense of the one-drop rule, the person of mixed black and white race presents a special problem to herself and others.

I would like to stay on the level that all notions of race are fictions, but I don't think that is yet feasible at this time in American culture. Therefore, I am provisionally going to go along with the fiction that there are such things as black and white race, as a basis on which to consider the ongoing one-drop rule from the standpoint of an individual of mixed black and white race. How should mixed black and white individuals identify themselves and be racially identified by others, at this time?

I think that the only emancipatory answer to that question has to be provided by the individuals themselves. It has been estimated that between 75% and 90% of all African-Americans have some white ancestry. Within this group, the group likely to self-identify as mixed race is probably no more than 10% or 15%.[17] However, if there is no scientific foundation to the concept of race, that is, if races do not exist, then neither do mixed races exist. The facts of racial mixture, namely the existence of individuals of mixed race, undermine the very notion of race, which presupposes racial "purity." Since there never have been pure races, it

---

17. Williamson, *New People*, pp. 9–16; 125.

is impossible to calculate degrees of racial mixture. Still, despite these puzzles, on a folk level, Americans take race very seriously and it is only fair that those individuals who do not fit into any one of the recognized racial categories have an opportunity to identify themselves, that is, to choose their own racial identities.

As it stands now, most people "choose" a racial identity after they have learned how others identity them. This is a passive process of choice, closer to socially approved assent than free choice. Children with a black parent and a white parent, and even greater degrees of racial diversity, are now obligated to "choose" which box to check as they move through the various institutional processes of racial identification in the culture. They choose the box which "best" applies to them, but nothing in official or social reality permits them a choice of *all* that applies them in racial terms.

Broadly speaking, even given the racial fictions in place, every person defines for herself what it means to be what she is racially by learning about her family history. Using present energy and making commitments for the future, she invents her racial identity at the same time that she tells herself she is discovering it. This is an existential point. The person of mixed race is as entitled to this existential process, with its self-defining illusion of invention masquerading as discovery, as is the person of presumptively pure race. In the present case, she has a right to be mixed race rather than black race or white race. At present, she can only be white if she lies about the presence of a black ancestor. And she can only eschew all racial identity, should she chooses to invent herself on the ground of her discovery that race is a fiction, if she refuses to participate in many cultural contexts that might otherwise benefit her. This right for a mixed race person to be mixed race seems to be a fundamental requirement for psychological and social health but it is as difficult to create a general justification for it as it is to justify the right of human beings to selfhood. In fact, the generality of the justification can only be anchored by something beyond American law and culture, as I will try to do in a moment.

In the present order of race, United States federal racial classification systems only allow for four racial categories—black, white, hispanic, Asian and Native American, with an added ethnic rider of Hispanic or non-Hispanic. Where categories of "other" have been added to state forms, according to "Directive 15" the components of "other" in individual cases are reassessed and if an individual has a black ancestor, the individual is reclassified as black.[18]

In June 1993, the United States House of Representatives Subcommittee on Census, Statistics and Postal Personnel heard public testimony concerning the inclusion of a multi-racial category in the United States census. As of this writing, the outcome of those hearings is inconclusive. It is not merely that even liberal public record keeping is constrained by outmoded concepts of race in the population at large. The inconclusiveness is further diffused by the expressed concern of African American interest groups that if part of their presently designated constitutency of African Americans redesignates itself as multi-racial, the remaining constituency will lose affirmative action gains.[19] Nonetheless, many black and

---

18. See Carlos A. Fernandez, "Testimony of the Association of MultiEthnic Americans," and Susan Graham, "The Grass Roots Advocacy," both reprinted in Naomi Zack, ed., *Microdiversity: Writings in Mixed Race Culture and Identity*," forthcoming.

19. See Lawrence Wright, "One Drop of Blood," *The New Yorker*, July 25, 1994, pp. 46–55.

white mixed-race Americans continue to wonder whether one-drop black racial identification, based on biological fiction, should be supported at the expense of more accurate description and record keeping. It is difficult to see how anyone except the mixed race individuals themselves, would have a right to decide that matter. According to international moral-political rights theories, as stated in the United Nations Charter, the right of Americans of mixed race to identify themselves and be identified, i.e., recognized, as a distinct racial category would seem to be related to other social and political rights of self-determination. The analogue to national self-determination in this political sense, for mixed black and white Americans, is racial self-identification. As with emerging nations, united within themselves by geography, self-identification precedes identification and recognition by others.

Mixed race people do not constitute geographically continuous, potentially sovereign entities as groups, so there is no issue of political independence at stake. But neither do racially pure groups present a basis for national sovereignty—except within separatist movements, which in the United States, at least, have been motivated by extremist and supremacist ideologies. There has, of course, been some geographically-based political districting of black racial interests, in the United States in recent years, for the presumed benefit of blacks. If some of the people in those districts revise their identification as racially mixed and not-black, there is concern that the remaining blacks would not benefit as much as when the group was larger.[20] But, the resulting groups could form coalitions and, the racism against blacks that presupposes general differences among populations that do not exist, will have been undermined to the extent that everyone publically acknowledges that some American blacks have white ancestors and are therefore not, strictly speaking, "black." If all blacks are not black because some of them are also white, then the rigid differences that people mistakenly assume have a biological foundation would begin to soften in the American mind. This would in turn undermine racism as a psychological attitude based on an assumption of strong physical difference.

Furthermore, the United Nations Charter expresses an international moral-political consensus that all individuals are entitled to the same rights, regardless of race and color (Article 2): If blacks and whites have a right to identify themselves as such, then so do mixed black and white individuals. The United Nations Charter also stipulates that no one may be compelled to belong to an association (Article 20, 2): If the one-drop rule does not have the biological foundation it has been assumed to have in American history, then no one should be compelled to be black. And, if race itself is a fiction, then no one should be compelled to identify herself or be identified by others in any way at all racially, if she so chooses. Failure to identify in some specific way racially, or in any way racially, ought not to put anyone at a disadvantage to those who do so identify.

In that United Nations' context of freedom of association, racial identification has not yet been addressed because it has up to now been assumed that racial identification has a neutral, factual foundation. Indeed, the international theoretical work on race has primarily focused on the promulgation of social and biological science findings in the first half of the twentieth century, which concluded that

---

20. Ibid.

cultural differences among racial groups are matters of historical contingency rather than physical heredity.[21] But, since there is no empirical, factual foundation for the American one-drop rule of black racial classification, in many cases of mixed race, there are no neutral, factual determinants for racial identification. Given this absence of an assumed biological foundation for racial identification, if it is, for whatever reason, necessary that mixed race individuals be identified by race, those individuals have a right to chose their racial identifications, based on the United Nations Charter right to freedom of association.

In situations where an individual's chosen racial designation is at odds with how others classify her, care should be taken by those others to precisely refine the empirical basis on which they make their identifications. And in many cases, the reliance on socially coerced self-identification, e.g., the one-drop rule, is so strong that experts will have to dispense with rational categories altogether. There is an interesting example of this in recent American Medical Association policy recommendations for the detection of sickle cell anemia in infants. It used to be believed that infants of non-white racial groups were at higher risk for this disease. However, medical practitioners have come to realize that they have no reliable criteria for identifying all infants racially so the recommended procedure for detection is to test all infants for sickle cell anemia, regardless of the racial group to which they seem to belong or are said to belong.[22]

Mixed race individuals would also have a right to reject all racial identification, just as a full right to freedom in religious affiliation would include the choice of no religious affiliation, or the choice of atheism. I have so far been suggesting that black and white mixed race Americans would chose to identify as mixed race or non-racial. But even that is too stringent a projection once the false categories begin to crumble. Some mixed black and white raced people will choose to be black. Others will choose to be white. And still others will choose to identify based on Asian or Native American ancestry.

Mixed Black and White Race and Present Public Policy, in Fact

Parallel to the foregoing theoretical justification for self-identification for individuals of mixed race, there is a demographic and grass roots basis for such self-identification which public policy theorists and planners need to allow into their awareness as specific contexts make relevant. Statistically, mixed-race births in the United States have increased 26 times as much as pure race births over recent decades.[23] And now, for the first time in American history, due to the success of the Civil Rights Movement, albeit it incomplete and begrudged, there is a generation of mixed black and white individuals who are not ashamed of their racial ori-

---

21. For the United Nations' positions on race, culture and heredity, see "Four Statements on the Race Question" (drafted at Unesco House, Paris), in Kuper, *Race, Science and Society*, Appendix, pp. 344–364.

22. J. Jarrett Clinton, "From the Agency for Health Care Policy and Research," *Journal of the American Medical Association*, 270, 18 (Nov. 10, 1991): 2158.

23. For the statistics on the increase of mixed-race marriages and births, see "Special Reports," *I-Pride Newsletter*, 15, 1 (January 1993): 20–21.

gins, and whose parents do not experience a need to apologize for having brought them into the world.

Project RACE (Reclassify All Children Equally), an organization originating from efforts to change racial designations of school children in Georgia, has been lobbying legislatures in recent years to include multi-racial categories on the U. S. Census, and in local record keeping. The membership of the Association of Multi-Ethnic Americans, consisting of mixed-race families and their children, actively support one another through social and cultural events and newsletters in which they share their experiences in the larger society which does not recognize their existence, as mixed-race.[24]

When people from different racial categories have children, as they always have done despite the existence of social or legal strictures, and whether they do so as a result of exploitation, accident, ignorance, or love, fairness in a racial society requires that those children receive the same degree of racial respect as presumptively racially-pure children, especially since it is widely assumed that racial identities are constructed in childhood in ways closely connected with self-esteem on a deep motivational level. It is not known to what extent the importance of a child's positive feelings about race is a result of racism at large in the culture. Neither is it known whether it would be consistent with other aspects of mental health and social adjustment for individuals to eschew all racial identity—even in a racist society. However, before the studies can be conducted that will provide empirical answers to these questions, the conceptual framework or theoretical assumptions that would otherwise underly such studies has to be reexamined. There is no reason to believe that social scientists are not as burdened by racial mythology as other people.

At this time, for the first time in American academic letters, a small, rapidly increasing number of scholars from varied disciplines are beginning to express these issues of microdiversity, and the subject of mixed race is becoming a recognized addition to curricula that address diversity and multiculturalism. Paul Spickard, F. James Davis, Maria P.P. Root, and I have recently published book-length works on the topic of mixed race in the United States and further work is in press as of this writing. (The popular print media and commercial publishing houses are not far behind, or ahead, as the case may be.[25]) The general scholarly topic is *Racial Theory*, the specialization at issue is *Mixed Race* (or *Multirace*), but in practical policy making contexts, the facts which need to be addressed are the facts of *microdiversity*. This term 'microdiversity' points to the reality that many individuals are racially diverse within themselves and not merely diverse as members of groups that are believed, in often erroneous ways, to be racially different from other groups.

The map of the emancipatory scholarship of microdiversity is now on the drawing board: it may be filled in by tracing out the complex varieties of microdiversity which exist in reality; or it may blaze a route to a neo-universalist rejection of the concept of race in both scholarly and popular culture. In historical ana-

---

24. See *Project Race Newsletter*, April 1993 (Roswell, GA).

25. Paul Spickard, *Mixed Blood: Inter-marriage and Ethnic Identity in Twentieth-Century America*, Madison: University of Wisconsin Press, 1989; F. James Davis, *Who is Black?*, University Park: Penn State Press, 1991; Maria P.P. Root, *Racially Mixed People in America*, Newbury Park: Sage, 1992; Naomi Zack, *Race and Mixed Race* (loc. cit.).

lyzes, microdiversity intersects with critiques of patriarchy because the one-drop rule is a legacy of white male slave owners; and in feminist analyzes of contemporary culture, microdiversity intersects with gender because mixed-race women are still stereotyped as exotic, erotic and morally defective.

In terms of present practice and policy, microdiversity has indeterminate connections with affirmative action. Since the aim of both affirmative action and the scholarship of microdiversity is to improve the institutional situations of individuals who would otherwise be overlooked or abused, both become redundant if they succeed. In the meantime, if affirmative action is just and effective, the facts of microdiversity strengthen its mandate because people of mixed race have never before been positively acknowledged to exist. So long as Americans believe in races, they will believe in racial whiteness and whites will probably continue to be generally better off than non-whites. And if affirmative action programs continue to be the chosen strategy for achieving equality, then mixed-race individuals, insofar as they do not belong to the white, privileged, dominant group, would continue to qualify as affirmative action clients (or "patients").

I want to close with a word of caution. Tigers have to be dismounted with great care. It's one thing to understand within a safe forum that race is a biological fiction. In American culture at large, the fiction of race continues to operate as fact and in situations of backlash against emancipatory progress, the victims of racial oppression, non-whites, are insulted and injured further for their progress against oppression. If those who practice such second-order oppression begin to employ the truth that race is a fiction, gains already secured against first order oppression (or in redress of it) could be jeopardized. This is a risk many will find daunting but the answer is not to back off from the truth but to realize that it will take a while to replace the fictitious cultural realities. If the truth, about mixed black and white race and race in general were to be (affirmatively) taught throughout the American educational system it would take about two generations to have a real effect on the culture—the first generation would learn it in school and teach it to their children.

References

Bernal, Martin (1987). *Black Athen.* New Brunswick: Rutgers University Press.
Clinton, J. Jarrett (1991). "From the Agency for Health Care Policy and Research," *Journal of the American Medical Association*, 270, 18M (Nov. 10): 2158.
Davis, F. James (1991). *Who is Black?* University Park: Penn State Press.
Degler, Carl N. (1971). *Neither Black nor White: Slavery and race relations in Brazil and the United States.* New York: Macmillan.
Dubinin, N.P. (1965). "Race and Contemporary Genetics," in Leo Kuper, ed. *Race, Science and Society.* New York: Columbia University Press, pp. 31–67.
Dunn, L.C. (1965). "Race and Biology," in Leo Kuper, ed. *Race, Science and Society*, New York: Columbia University Press, pp. 68–94.
Fernandez, Carlos A. (1995). "Testimony of the Association of MultiEthnic Americans," in Naomi Zack, *American Mixed Race: Exploring Microdiversity.* Lanham: Rowman and Littlefield.
Graham, Susan (1995). "The Grass Roots Advocacy," in Naomi Zack, *American Mixed Race: Exploring Microdiversity.* Lanham: Rowman and Littlefield.

Immerwahr, John and Michael Burke (1993). "Race and the Modern Philosophy Course," *Teaching Philosophy*, 16, 1 (March): 26–27.

Kevles, Daniel J. (1985). *In the Name of Eugenics*. Berkeley: University of California Press.

Leiris, Michael (1965). "Race and Culture," in Leo Kuper, ed. *Race, Science and Society*, New York: Columbia University Press, pp. 135–72.

Root, Maria P.P. (1992). *Racially Mixed People in America*. Newbury Park: Sage.

Sickels, Robert J. (1972). *Race Marriage and the Law*. Albuquerque: University of New Mexico Press.

Spickard, Paul (1989). *Mixed Blood: Inter-marriage and Ethnic Identity in Twentieth-Century America*. Madison: University of Wisconsin Press.

Wacker, R. Fred (1983). *Ethnicity, Pluralism and Race*. Westport: Greenwood.

Williamson, Joel (1980). *New People*. New York: Free Press.

Wright, Lawrence (1994). "One Drop of Blood," *The New Yorker*, (July 25): 46–55.

Zack, Naomi (1993). *Race and Mixed Race*. Philadelphia: Temple University Press.

——— (1994). "Race and Philosophic Meaning," American Philosophical Association *Newsletter on Philosophy and the Black Experience*, 93, 2 (Fall).

——— ed. (1995). *American Mixed Race: Exploring Microdiversity*. Lanham: Rowman and Littlefield.

——— (1996). *Bachelors of Science: Seventeenth Century Identity Then and Now*. Philadelphia: Temple University Press.

Section IV

Class and Culture

10

Black Underclass and Culture

Anthony J. Lemelle, Jr.

The way we approach looking at culture will influence our positions on social policy. At the same time our culture will to a great extent, though perhaps not entirely, determine how we go about our day-to-day activities. One of the major issues confronting the American culture today is the debate about the definition of culture. In historical actuality, the definition of culture is an enduring problem for Eurocentric scholarship. Edward B. Tylor and Alfred L. Kroeber were two anthropologists considered to be noted authorities on the definitions of culture in the Eurocentric tradition. Tylor argued that "culture is that complex whole which includes knowledge, belief, art, morals, law, custom, and any other capabilities and habits acquired by man as a member of society."[1] Kroeber felt that culture should be understood as that part of human existence that consciously evolves primarily in response to physical and environmental needs.[2]

What the definitions of culture in the Eurocentric tradition share are the assumptions that cultures may be ranked, Western civilization is the parent of the finest culture in history, and that the functions of the mind rather than body, feeling, emotion, and spirit are the basic substance of cultures. This definition of culture contrasts with an Afrocentric definition of culture. African philosophical traditions hold that it is impossible to divide mind, body, and spirit.[3] Also when there are hierarchical divisions in African societies, there is a general understanding that life has dealt certain cards to individuals which are not necessarily the content of the individual's character but merely represents varying situations.[4]

The Afrocentric perspective begins with questioning the assumption that cultures may be ranked. And, it is doubtful that individuals may be ranked as in the sense of the Eurocentric tradition.

The Eurocentric perspective has employed a policy of divide and conquer which functions to keep issues unclear and allows its agents to use smoke and mirror tactics to reproduce their political and economic dominance. The policy of divide and conquer is applied in processes with individuals, groups and cultural

---

1. Edward B. Tylor, *Primitive Culture*, Vol. I (London: John Murray, 1891), p. 1.
2. Alfred Louis Kroeber, *The Nature of Culture* (Chicago: University of Chicago Press, 1952), pp. 23–25.
3. Nathan Huggins, "The Seamless Web," in *Black Odyssey: The African-American Ordeal in Slavery* (New York: Vintage Books, 1990).
4. John S. Mbiti, *African Religions and Philosophy* (Garden City, N.Y.: Anchor Books, 1970).

productions. For example, in the Eurocentric tradition, universities divided and compartmentalized knowledge, they strictly police the turf of differing disciplines. If we were to study American political culture under the domination of Eurocentric values, it would mean to count voting behavior, explain the political processes as they are communicated by white men of power and politicians, and to discuss the virtually all white male political history.

In contrast to the Eurocentric method of producing knowledge, Afrocentric scholars make use of interdisciplinary methods in their scholarship. Therefore, the political functions of culture are an integral part of Afrocentric scholarship. Increasingly under the banner of postmodernity, white scholars are writing a deconstruction of Eurocentric scholastic assumptions. But these resistance approaches were first developed by African and African diaspora scholars. Very often the Eurocentric scholars will embrace a black scholar to emulate or parrot their values. Following a technology for the reproduction of their dominance, the Eurocentric scholars attempt to erase the black collaborationist process. This paper will elaborate the process of the reproduction of Eurocentric dominance in terms of political culture. It will discuss the historical impact of that dominance and what its reproduction means in the day-to-day life of the Afro-community in the United States. I contend that the so-called black underclass culture is in actuality the greater part of African-American culture. We miss this fact when we buy into the Eurocentric narrative of black history which constructs Africans in America as deviants and criminals. Finally, I will discuss rhythm-and-blues music as an example of black underclass culture.

Black People's Burden

Any young person attending public, and most private, primary and secondary schools in the United States will be taught that the so-called Founding Fathers were men of the highest moral and ethical standing in the history of nations. Students learn that these founders were intellectually superior to national citizens not just in the United States but all over the world. Instructors stress Thomas Jefferson's and Benjamin Franklin's visits to Europe. At the same time the instructors diligently erase the violent orientation towards Africans Americans shared by these men of questionable moral make-up. For example, both Jefferson and Franklin were virulent white supremacists who wrote policies which still impact on both the life chances and quality of life for African Americans.

Benjamin Franklin wrote a famous essay entitled *Observations Concerning the Increase of Mankind* where he noticed that the number of "purely white People" in the world was proportionately very small. He reflected on the fact that all of Africa was black or tawny, Asia chiefly tawny and America was almost all so with the exception of the white newcomers. According to Franklin, the English were the "principle Body of white People": "And while we are...Scouring our Planet, by clearing America of Woods, and so making the Side of our globe reflect a brighter Light to the Eyes of Inhabitants in Mars and Venus, why should we in the Sight of Superior Beings, darken its People? why increase the Sons of Africa, by Planting them in America, where we have so fair an opportunity, by excluding all

Blacks and Tawneys, of increasing the lovely white...?"[5] When Franklin mentions increasing/decreasing populations, he is producing a policy of gene pool control which is commonly understood as genocide.

Jefferson also had a disdain for Africans and promoted both population transfer and genocide policies directed toward Africans in the United States. He referred to Africans as the "blot" which had to be completely removed from "American" soil. One of Jefferson's biggest concerns was the "amalgamation with the other colour...which produces a degradation to which no lover of his country, no lover of excellence in the human character can innocently consent."[6]

Jefferson spent a great deal of time reflecting on his problem. His problem may be simply stated: on the one hand, he passionately hated black people; but in order for him to be a self-sufficient, rugged individual he relied on unpaid black labor. He concluded: To send them off all at once was not practical. He calculated that the population transfer would take twenty-five years. What was Jefferson's greatest concern regarding his genocide policy recommendations? After all, he was a slaver. He knew the amount of loss of life associated with the trans-Atlantic slave trade. Yet Jefferson was more concerned with the cost in dollars to the slavers rather than the life chances of the slaves. According to Jefferson's numbers:

> The value of the slaves would amount to $600 million, and the cost of transportation and provisions would add up to $300 million. "It cannot be done in this way," he decided. The only "practicable" plan, he thought, was to deport the future generation of blacks: Black infants would be taken from their mothers.... Since a newborn infant was worth only $25.50, Jefferson calculated, the estimated loss of slave property would be reduced from $600 million to only $37.5 million.[7]

Many scholars have decided to erase the significance of Jefferson's passionate hate for Africans, but is this a major intellectual error? Such scholars will equivocate, generally suggesting that Jefferson had some major ideas about justice and equality. They will add that no human is perfect. Yet, are not Jefferson's ideas on justice and equality found in sources which endure with greater fidelity and integrity? Some will note that promoting Franklin and Jefferson, who appear to be major anti-African bigots, is to join in on spiritual, intellectual and physical hate of Africans and the African diaspora. For example, is sending black children to schools which carry names commemorative of anti-African figures conscionable?

It is exactly for these kinds of historical reasons that many African, African-American, and other African-diaspora scholars have rejected the Eurocentric cultural dominance where white men of power control the scholarship and police the canons. Some black scholars find Eurocentricism more appealing than Afrocentricism, in spite of the practical and political problems that the love of Europe presents for Africans. Ultimately, these scholars are rejected by the majority of African Americans while white men of power reward them with special positions

5. Benjamin Franklin, "Observations Concerning the Increase of Mankind (1751)," in Leonard W. Labaree, ed., *The Papers of Benjamin Franklin* (New Haven, Conn.: Yale University Press, 1959), vol. 4, p. 234.

6. Edwin M. Betts, ed., *Thomas Jefferson's Farm Book* (Princeton, N.J.: Princeton University Press, 1953), p. 38.

7. Ronald Takaki, *Iron Cages: Race and Culture in 19th-Century America* (New York: Oxford University Press, 1990), p. 45.

at prestigious and not-so-prestigious institutions. Many of the best of the Euro-centric black scholars are given high visibility; they have invited speaking engagements which are out of proportion with normal expectations; they are unrealistically provided space in the major white publications; they are sought to speak on areas completely out of their expertise, as long as the topic has to do with black people. The Eurocentric black scholars hate African derived culture and initiatives to better the life chances and quality of life of black people. First, what is culture and what is its social function? What is Afrocentricity and why is it so important for black culture?

Culture and Its Function

Much of African-American culture developed in response to white cultural imperialism. White cultural imperialism is a force relationship of dominance which is institutionalized through lying, cheating, stealing, and murdering. As the black political historian Manning Marable demonstrates in his study of black America, U.S. social and political institutions are structured in fraud.[8] The consequence of white cultural imperialism is cultural hegemony. Antonio Gramsci, an Italian intellectual, defined cultural hegemony as "an order in which a certain way of life and thought is dominant, in which one concept of reality is diffused throughout society in all its institutional and private manifestations, informing with its spirit all taste, morality, customs, religious and political principles, and all social relations, particularly in their intellectual and moral connotation."[9]

Hegemony means that there are particular periods of history in social life which constitutes a historical bloc of forces. The historical bloc of U.S. dominance reassures the reproduction of a stable, self-reproducing, hierarchical order of capital relations. Through hegemony the powerful are able to win the voluntary consent of the ruled because the ruled accept their subordinate position for the sake of being able to have certain desires, fantasies, and socially constructed identities.[10] Under liberal democracy in late capitalism, the powerful allow normal men to dominate women, behave as sportsmen and managers. The limited freedoms under hegemony allows room for some variation of life-styles but place and location are very important for the operation of the social system. The most important aspect of the system is to hide the way institutions systematically administer different rewards to specific interest groups. After all, it is thought by the "sane" in the social system that we are all alike, free, equal, and capable of achieving on the basis of our own merit.

Raymond Williams, a radical scholar of culture, modified Gramsci's concept of hegemony. He demonstrated that the plurality of cultures or life-styles in any

---

8. Manning Marable, "Inequality and the Burden of Capitalist Democracy: A Point of View on Black History," in *How Capitalism Underdeveloped Black America* (Boston: South End Press, 1983), pp. 1–19.

9. Gwynn Williams, "The Concept of 'Egemonia' in the Thought of Antonio Gramsci: Some Notes on Interpretation," *Journal of the History of Ideas*, vol. 21, 1960: 587.

10. Antonio Gramsci, *Selections From Prison Notebooks*, Quintin Hoare and Geoffrey Norwell, eds. and trans. (New York: International Publishers, 1971), pp. 206–276.

given social formation is merely an illusion. While some will find pleasure for a short time by indulging in the illusion, in the long run the political hegemony of a particular group is the view of the world that prevails. More over, the irony of the dominance of the particular hegemonic group is that the illusion itself allows for it to prevail. For Williams, culture is nothing more but the complex network of social practices which indicate or determine positions of domination, equality, or subordination. The melting pot view of culture which is normative in the United States is incapable of allowing this definition of culture because the melting pot view hides the conflicts of interests in the society. It attempts to talk about and represent differences within an articulation of unity but when the out-groups come into real conflict within institutions, the struggles become the evidence that there is no totalizing and permanent hegemony.[11]

Stuart Hall, a black scholar noted for his cultural studies, interprets Gramsci's concept of hegemony not "as a moment of simple unity, but a process of unification (never totally achieved), founded on strategic alliances between different sectors, not on their pre-given identity."[12] Many scholars have written about class groups, or political party groups, as if there is an automatic correspondence between belonging to a particular group and social practices. Hall shows that there is a problem with such thinking. If we think in the terms of automatically associating class, political, or ideological practices with particular groups, we preclude explaining "how ethnic and racial difference can be constructed as a set of economic, political, and ideological antagonisms, *within* a class which is subject to roughly similar forms of exploitation with respect to ownership of and expropriation from the 'means of production'."[13]

Stuart Hall, Raymond Williams, and Antonio Gramsci share in recognizing that there are patterned ways to reproduce social order which may be referred to as culture. They all recognize that there is a political function for culture. And they recognize that resistance is a dimension of social order when exploitation, inequality, and oppression are elements of a society. This understanding of culture is precisely the dimension of culture that Amilcar Cabral, agronomist and Secretary-General of the African Party for the Independence of Guinea and the Cape Verde Islands, suggested in his theory of culture during the national liberation movements.

In one study, Cabral contrasts the differences between French and Portuguese forms of colonialism, as well as historical and political differences between the resistance movements of Algeria and Guinea-Bissau.[14] Cabral argues that it is 'popular culture' which forms the basis of the anti-colonial political struggle. Frantz Fanon, the Algerian theorist of the anti-colonial movement, argues that it is 'the people' who form the basis for the struggle against colonial oppression. For Fanon, national culture cannot exist within the history and domination of colonialism; for Cabral, the operations of national culture are in a dialectical relationship with history. Cabral concludes:

---

11. Raymond Williams, *Marxism and Literature* (New York: Oxford University Press, 1977).

12. Stuart Hall, "Gramsci's Relevance for the Study of Race and Ethnicity," *Journal of Communication Inquiry*, 10 (Summer 1986): 5–27.

13. Ibid.

14. Amilcar Cabral, *Return to the Source: Selected Speeches of Amilcar Cabral* (New York: Monthly Review Press, 1973).

> Whatever may be the conditions of a people's political and social factors... it is generally within the culture that we find the seed of opposition, which leads to the structuring and development of the liberation movement.[15]

Culture for Fanon is constituted by 'tradition' or 'custom' rather than by the culture proper. Fanon's view of culture is shared by many postmodern writers. For example, Edward W. Said, a noted cultural critic of the West, in his book *Culture and Imperialism* describes culture as the best of the tradition and custom of a people.[16] With these kinds of binary distinctions, such theorists construct categories like elite, high, and real culture which is in opposition to lowly popular culture. And, of course, in so doing, they anoint themselves the elite experts and representatives of the best and highest cultural traditions. In addition, they fancy themselves capable of discerning for the masses what is best in the society.

For Cabral culture is never totalizing and colonialism, or oppression, equally is never totalizing. Colonialism's cultural hegemony does not extend to the subaltern groups beyond the metropole. Cabral argues, the "multiplicity of social and ethnic groups... complicates the effort to determine the role of culture in the liberation movement." Cabral continues:

> In our time it is common to affirm that all peoples have a culture. The time is past when in an effort to perpetuate the domination of people, culture was considered an attribute of privileged peoples or nations, and when, out of either ignorance or malice, culture was confused with technical power, if not with skin colour or the shape of one's eyes.... The liberation movement must furthermore embody the mass character, the popular character of the culture—which is not and never could be the privilege sectors of the society.[17]

Finally, for our concern with the process of cultural hegemony when one national group colonizes another, Cabral emphasizes the role of the Eurocentric black scholars whom he calls the black petite bourgeoisie. Cabral points out that:

> The colonizer not only creates a system to repress the cultural life of the colonized people; he also provokes and develops the cultural alienation of a part of the population, either by so-called assimilation of indigenous elites and popular masses... notably the urban and peasant *petite bourgeoisie*, assimilates the colonizer's mentality, considers itself culturally superior to its own people and ignores or looks down upon their cultural values.[18]

Afrocentricity and Black Culture

Afrocentricity is not a new intellectual movement. It has a long and distinguished history. Like any other scholarly undertaking and discipline, Afrocentric learning contains debates, disagreements, resolutions, and argumentations. Afro-

---

15. Ibid., p. 43.
16. Edward W. Said, *Culture and Imperialism* (New York: Vintage, 1994), pp. 3–19.
17. Cabral, op. cit., pp. 39–46.
18. Ibid.

centricity is a cultural development and, as we have said up to this point about culture generally, there are no pure cultures. Likewise, there is no pure Afrocentric moment. One leader of the modern Afrocentric position is Molefi Kete Asante. Asante relies on many Afrocentric scholars to construct cogent and systematic arguments advancing Afrocentricity. Some of the scholars who influence his works are Cheikh Anta Diop, John Henrik Clarke, Theophile Obenga, and Chukwunyere Kamalu. My point is that Afrocentricity is a traditional and established perspective consisting of both internal and external debates.

Asante defines Afrocentricity in the following way:

> Afrocentricity is primarily an orientation to data. There are certainly data and facts which may be used by Afrocentrists in making analyses, but the principal component of the theoretical piece has to do with an orientation, a location, a position. Thus, I have explained in several books and articles that Afrocentricity is a *perspective which allows Africans to be subjects of historical experiences rather than objects* on the fringes of Europe.[19]

While Afrocentricity does not represent the only intellectual perspective available in black culture, it is clearly a major perspective. There are other perspectives such as the Eurocentric perspectives of a black scholar like Henry Louis Gates, Jr., a professor who is associated with Duke, Cornell, Yale, Harvard, and Oxford universities; or other black professors of his ilk like Cornel West, Thomas Sowell, Glenn Loury, Shelby Steele, and K. Anthony Appiah. Any black intellectual should be clear about the differences these scholars represent and the political implications of their representations. It seems clear that the masses of African Americans, particularly among the youth, are agents for a lived Afrocentricity.

Black Eurocentric scholars often claim that the young are misguided and are superficially only dealing in symbolic representations like Malcolm X caps and tee shirts. Have these scholars elevated themselves above the community? Are we to presume that they know something, perhaps learned at white elite universities, that others in the African-American community have, due to a lack of privilege, not acquired? Or rather, is there a historical place for this kind of thinking and agency in the African-American experience?

African-American Colonization and the Underclass

The framework of a colonial interpretation is the worldwide imperialism of specific European nations and the United States which used capitalism as its main instrument to oppress Africans all over the world. It is commonly agreed that capitalist expansion began in the fifteenth century and resulted in the majority of the nonwhite world becoming victims of the European colonial powers. Usually so-

---

19. Molefi Kete Asante, *Malcolm X as Cultural Hero and Other Afrocentric Essays* (Trenton, N.J.: Africa World Press, 1993).

cial theorists refer to three forms of colonialism: external colonialism, neocolonialism, and internal colonialism. External colonialism involves management of a country's culture, politics, and economy by an outside colonial power. There are many forms of this; in fact, every colonial project has its specificity. Neocolonialism is a contemporary form of colonialism in which, through revolution, colonized countries overthrow the colonizers, but the colonizers continue to direct the economies of the colonized through international capitalists and corporations. Finally, when there is a large in-migration of whites into a colonized country or a large in-migration of people of color into a colonial power's country that results in the control and exploitation of non-European groups, the country is internally colonized.

In the United State's internal colonialism, non-European groups are usually residentially segregated, "superexploited" in employment and wealth, and culturally stigmatized, and have some of their leaders co-opted by whites. Eurocentric hegemony is the order of the day.

A key element of Eurocentric hegemony is the attempt to control the definition of the social order, as I discussed earlier, to leave the impression that there is a system of equality where social rewards are distributed on the basis of merit. However, an empirical examination of this claim does not substantiate its merit. What the Eurocentric explanations miss is that African-American culture became inextricably linked to resistance and protest, which the Eurocentrist redefined over time as deviance and criminality. Today's so-called black family structure, and the black community's relationship to education, employment, crime, and civic life are a composite of resistance. From the perspective of most blacks, the Eurocentric scholars and policy-makers are unable to veil the illegitimacy of the goal of assimilation.

Given the internal colonial experience of African Americans, the concept of the underclass has not been fully developed in the sociological and social welfare literature to meet the needs of a precise analysis. Ken Auletta described the underclass as persons who feel "excluded from society," who reject "commonly accepted values," and who suffer "from behavioral as well as income deficiencies." Auletta goes on to describe the bottom stratum of the stratification hierarchy.[20] His definition is clearly a value judgement and, more properly, an economic definition of the underclass. A sociological definition of the underclass should consider relative poverty and relative deprivation, which will assist in explaining an aspect of the black community resistance behavior in the working, middle and upper-middle strata. The point is that if we look at any of those stratification categories, African Americans will form an aggregate fraction at the bottom of each of the strata. In general then, all African Americans are in the underclass: they are the underclass of the upper-middle class, the underclass of the middle-class, and the underclass of the working-class. I am suggesting that relative deprivation assists in explaining the perpetuation of the resistance aspect of black culture across class strata. Economics alone will not explain black culture; economics, which I am using in the broadest sense including the economics of colonialism, imperialism, relative deprivation, and the rest, is one aspect of culture.

---

20. Ken Auletta, *The Underclass* (New York: Random House, 1982), pp. xiii–xviii. Also see, William J. Wilson, "The Urban Underclass," in Leslie W. Dunbar, ed., *Minority Report* (New York: Pantheon Books, 1984), pp. 75–117.

Culture of Resistance

We may only imagine what might have become of the slaves had they not used their cultural know-how to survive. I thought about the fact that the slave Frederick Douglass would have "perished" had he not been a thief:

> I suffered much from hunger, but much more from cold. In hottest summer and coldest winter, I was kept almost naked—no shoes, no stockings, no jacket, no trousers, nothing on but a course tow linen shirt, reaching only to my knees. I had no bed. I must have perished with cold, but that, the coldest nights, I used to steal a bag, and there sleep on the cold, damp, clay floor...[21]

Many will wonder what other adjustments Douglass made given his social situation. How did he have sex given the fact that he had no bed? The inhumanity revealed through this passage in his *Narrative* has haunted me for years. It is remarkable that from these kinds of situations and similar ones, slaves contributed the first authentic U.S. literary genre in the form of the slave narrative. Several works have recovered the relationship between African cultural "survivals" and African-American cultural productions. I propose glossing rhythm-and-blues music from my Afrocentric position to highlight the value of popular black culture in the survival of African Americans. Naturally, my position is that there is a traceable linkage between what preceded each generation and their cultural reproduction of black social life. By suggesting this, I question whether there has been a "decline" in cultural values as the Eurocentrists would have us to believe.

Rhythm and Blues as Black Underclass Cultural Resistance

A distinctive African-American contribution to United States culture was the blues music genre. Three types of blues music emerged in successive historical periods: primitive blues, classical blues, and rhythm and blues. Primitive blues blossomed from work songs in which the African tradition of call-and-response was used; workers used such songs to coordinate their movements. Very often, prisoners made up work songs or sang known ones as they worked in chain gangs. Classical blues, a fusion of the early English ballad and the African shout and call-and-response ritual, evolved as the most prominent style of the blues genre. Its three-line structure, a feature of the shout, was in turn incorporated in later musical styles. A song's first two lines were repeated; in jazz, this repetition became known as the "riff," which also became a central feature of rhythm and blues.

The highest development of the blues genre came in the form of rhythm and blues. This development occurred in roughly the 1930's, at a time when large dance and show bands formed into jazz bands. The jazz bands appealed to middle-class audiences, especially on the East Coast; but the black neighborhoods located in northern urban areas appreciated the subculture of rhythm and blues. Rhythm-and-blues music was often lyrically explicit in proclaiming its resistance stance.

---

21. Frederick Douglass, *The Narrative of the Life of Frederick Douglass, An American Slave: Written by Himself* (New York: New American Library, 1968), p. 43.

Rhythm-and-blues artists developed regional sounds; the largest of such traditions to emerge were the Northeastern and Southwestern sounds. When the Great Depression destroyed the race record labels where blacks were compelled to produce music before the 1930s, the new rhythm-and-blues recordings came from artists who had moved north to Kansas City and St. Louis. A few of the black artists were able to integrate into the white music world in a marginal way; most had to remain in the black music market. The lyrics from the black productions drew upon the immense inventory of expressions and phrases of black culture, which often carried hidden messages and double meanings.

The Northeastern artists relied heavily on the classical blues tradition. They were closer to white orchestral styles, and whites often came to clubs located on the "chitlin' circuit" (clubs where black artists traveled to perform in cities such as Chicago, Washington, D.C., Philadelphia, and New York) to see performers such as Duke Ellington and Fletcher Henderson. The southwestern bands were committed to "swinging" the sound and to a rugged presentation; these artists included such shouting blues singers as Jimmy Witherspoon and Joe Turner.

Rhythm-and-blues music transmitted norms to African Americans, both urban and rural, that black society thought to be vital to its existence. Very often such values had to be hidden in the double meanings of rhythm-and-blues lyrics. Companies including Savoy Records in New York, Chess Records in Chicago, and Atlantic Records in New York channeled blues to the most remote rural areas. These companies often sent representatives to the South to discover new blues lyrics, music, and artists.

Rhythm-and-blues music introduced fury, outrage, and passion to the blues worldview. Even more, rhythm and blues was not uninterested in indecent and erotic subjects. Rhythm-and-blues artists aired subjects as diverse as a homosexual taking a woman's man, penis size, desire for sex, and the sacrifices necessary to obtain money. A rich tradition of depth and breadth was created in an antagonistic society that was so oppressive that African Americans would often have to voice political concerns through music, since their political participation was precluded by white custom.

Rhythm and blues also promoted a communal usufruct. Lyrics of one rhythm-and-blues song often appear in other songs; the tradition is to borrow lines and communicate them within the rhythm-and-blues community. This tradition meant that each song called for an answer. In the rhythm-and-blues tradition, the speaker and the chorus become a single voice in the performance. The subject of the performance is the community's subject, and so the community participates in each public performance. When the rhythm-and-blues performer is on stage, members of the audience stand in witness to the testimony of the artist and often respond by shouting during the performance. The rhythm-and-blues artist does not reflect personal experience but rather the experiences of the community; the artist is merely a spokesperson.

Rhythm-and-blues lyrics follow the African narrative style with little exception. The narrative style has been traced to the African fable. In the fable, there is usually an evil spirit (perhaps an animal) with whom all the community is familiar; there is also a young man who makes reparation for injustice. "The Boll Weevil Blues" is an example. The weevil is the dreaded enemy of the cotton planter; the cotton planter is the enemy of the cotton picker. In the blues story, the struggle is between the weevil and the captain, who represents the planter-class, while the

picker patronizes the weevil. The weevil then becomes the living symbol of liberation. The blues text stresses mockery, sarcasm, tragedy, and accusation, which is
masked by melancholy.

Failure of Eurocentric Reason

Many holding Eurocentric values despise rhythm-and-blues music and the
forms of music which grew out of the blues tradition, such as, funk and rap.
Many have argued that the music has lost its social consciousness and its
uniqueness as a black art form. Some suggest that the music has become influenced more by commercialism than by human artistic creativity. What these
perspectives overlook is the ingenuity of the artist to use the vectors of communication to reproduce a popular African American culture which is a culture
and politic of resistance. Rap music is a recent contribution to African-American music tradition.

Rap music resulted from combining a set of developments in rhythm and blues,
including the essential African narrative, the call-and-response ritual, and communal usufruct, then pushing these themes to limits to which the African-American art form had not been taken before. For one thing, rap music relied on "sampling," which is the process of taking rhythm-and-blues music and writing rap
lines over the music. This act is probably the most subversive in terms of using
such a practice in a political economy that has private property as its strongest
commitment. With rap music, Eurocentric culture was faced with the eruption to
the perennial double standard: white artists had been allowed to present risque
productions at their pleasure, but black artists felt that they were unfairly sanctioned by white power. The first time this situation confronted rappers occurred
when two members of the group 2 Live Crew were arrested in Fort Lauderdale,
Florida, after a concert for singing lyrics that a state judge ruled obscene. The second was when the rap group from Houston, the Geto Boys, had their album withdrawn on the eve of its release by Geffen Records because the lyrics were considered to be explicitly violent and sexual. And the third incident was the charge of
anti-Semitism against the group Public Enemy when one of the group's members,
Richard Griffin, accurately pointed to a relationship between the state of Israel
and the fascist Republic of South Africa.

The black middle-class generally agreed with the white media that there were
problems with these black cultural productions. While the black middle-class engaged in the liberal-integrationist politics of their historical agenda (led for the
most part by Jesse Jackson), President Bill Clinton saw the opportunity to appropriate the black political agenda represented in the rap music through two strategic moves. First, he worked for the elevation of Jackson protege Ron Brown to
Democratic National Committee chairman and subverted Jackson's authority by
pitting Brown's conservative posture against Jackson's "left" tendencies. Second,
in June 1992, at the National meeting of the Rainbow Coalition in Washington,
D.C., Clinton accused the rap artist Sister Souljah of being a black racist and suggested Jackson's complicity in her "reverse racism." These events represented
both historical and typical white male behavior, and black Eurocentrist integrationist behavior toward African-American culture.

A Eurocentrist approach to the analysis of African-American culture precludes an objective and historically consistent view of the ways that blacks have resisted oppression and sustained themselves in the face of a brutal, cold, and the violent social system that is organized according to white male reason. It alienates the theorist from her/his community and produces in the theorist a feeling of being better than the community. At the same time, the Eurocentric approach produces a priestly practice with respect to the assessment of productive politics for African Americans.

Asante summed it up best when he wrote:

> I believe the essential historical qualities of the African American can be seen to have the following characteristics:
>
> 1. Recognizing an irreducible commitment to the project of liberation and freedom: This means that the African American recognizes a different history than the European...
>
> 2. Having roots in the great mythic, oral, and literary works of people of African descent.
>
> 3. Resonating with the rhythms, textures, and arts of the African world, that is, the arts produced by the people of the African world.
>
> 4. Serving the historical moment on the basis of classical transformations... which we may have forgotten but which exist in the context of our current situations.[22]

---

22. Asante, op. cit., p. 18.

11

The Black Middle Class as a Racial Class

Rutledge M. Dennis

About forty years ago, E. Franklin Frazier (1957) ignited an emotional and intellectual debate among black Americans, the reverberations of which have not yet abated, when he wrote a trenchant account of the psychology and sociology of the black middle class. A decade later, Martin Luther King (1967) continued Frazier's critique of this middle class by asserting that "It's time for the Negro middle class to rise up from its stool of indifference, to retreat from its flight into unreality and bring its full resources—its heart, its mind, and its checkbook to the aid of the less fortunate brother." Three years later, Nathan Hare (1970), one of Frazier's former students, entered the fray with an even more vitriolic attack on the black middle class. The issues raised, and the accusations hurled, by these scholars continue to shape the discourse surrounding the contemporary black middle class (Blackwell, 1985; Cruse, 1987; Landry, 1988; Hooks and West, 1991; Lehmann, 1991; Billingsley, 1992; Cose, 1993). Given the ideology of race in American social thought, Frazier's poignant arguments are best viewed within the context of an anomaly: the strange phenomenon of the emergence of a "middle" class in a society where race relations were predicated on white supremacy which meant, historically, centuries of preferential treatment for white Americans. Indeed, as Du Bois (1901) earlier declared, the very idea of a black middle class within a racially divided country amounts to a "double paradox" or a "paradox within a paradox."

Given the race and class parameters of the United States, any analysis of the black middle class must address, simultaneously, class as well as racial issues. The term *racial class* will be used to describe this unique situation. Viewing the class as a racial class suggests several features: that any comparisons made between it and any version of the white middle class must be carefully delimited (Early, 1994; Martin and Martin, 1978; Willie, 1979, 1991). Second, that discussions relative to race cannot be rigidly demarcated from discussions involving class.

This paper examines two dimensions of the black middle class as a racial class: its historical formation and development as a class, and its class consciousness. A delineation of these features illustrates how this class is not only different in origins from the white middle class; it also demonstrates how, and against great odds, blacks have sought to carve out niches, as much as doing so is possible, in a society which has historically devalued and undermined them.

An earlier version of this essay appeared in *Research in Race and Ethnic Relations* and is adapted/reprinted with the permission of the copyright holder/author.

Racial Class Formation

In his brief social history of the Black North (New York, Philadelphia, and Boston), Du Bois (circa 1901, 1969) charts the emergence of the black middle class, the bulk of whom, he notes, are descendants of free black parentage. Frazier (1932), likewise, traces the lineage of one branch of the early black middle class from the "time that they were first introduced into the Virginia colony in 1619." Indeed, using the research findings of the noted historian G. Carter Woodson, Frazier (1932:24) even goes as far to say that the free families in 1830 were " ... enjoying in the South at least their greatest prosperity."

Thomas Sowell (1981) also analyzes the important role of the "free person of color." According to Sowell, many among this group had been able to acquire their freedom "by one means or another," while others gained their freedom by virtue of the fact that they were the sons and daughters of slave masters. The unique position of the "free persons of color" is crucial to understanding how and why this group became the leadership and decision-making elite in the nineteenth century; likewise, it explains this group's key role in the growth of the middle class. Sowell (1981:195–196) explains it as follows:

> The lives of most "free persons of color" were narrowly circumscribed, economically, politically, and legally. They were usually poor, unskilled workers, lacked basic civil rights in most of the South and much of the North, and had little or no legal protection against fraud or even violence by whites. Nevertheless, they were years—or even generations—ahead of the slaves in their acculturation to American society. Most "free persons of color" could read and write in 1850, although only 1 or 2 percent of the slaves could do so ... In short, "free persons of color" had a large head start over the rest of the black population in their adjustment to American society. There were enduring consequences to this head start. The descendants of "free persons of color" remained prominent among Negro leadership in many fields, into the twentieth century ...

The historian John Hope Franklin (1967) also discusses the role of the "free persons of color," but he highlights, as does Sowell, a group seldom mentioned when analyzing the Ante-bellum and Post-bellum periods: the large number of skilled slaves who were generally town and city dwellers. Because they were highly skilled, they, too, after 1865, would constitute a part of that small, but important, middle class.

Yet another part of the middle class after 1865 would be comprised of those who were house servants or domestic slaves, in contrast to those who were field hands or field slaves. The Post-bellum status of those domestic servants was derived from their greater exposure to white American culture and values. According to Thorpe (1961), of the enslaved, house slaves and their children, due to their exposure to the slave master's culture (speech, dress, religion, etc.) were, after 1865, able to play a leadership and class role, out of proportion to their number in the larger black population. Many writers have sought to construct an antagonistic relationship between the two groups, however, Blassingame's (1972) careful and detailed study of the slave community does not support this view. Though agreeing that domestic servants did have a few advantages, he also examines their many disadvantages. More importantly, he notes (p. 210) that rather than the oft-repeated antagonistic relationship, "[D]omestic servants were the field slave's most important windows on the outside world and aids in trying to fathom the planter's psyche."

The relative political freedom experienced in the North during the post-1865 years, along with greater opportunities for educational and occupational advancement, made it possible for Northern blacks to experience a degree of upward mobility impossible in the South. In Du Bois' 1901 study (p. 2), he cites this as a factor in the growing class division within black communities in the North: "there is a sharper division of the Negroes into classes and a greater difference in attainment and training than one finds in the South." Similar patterns of racial class formation have been described for Chicago (Drake and Cayton, 1945; Spear, 1967) and New York (Osofsky, 1968). Landry (1988) draws the distinction between the old and new middle class, linking the growth of the new middle class to the need for services in the fast-growing communities in the large urban centers. These four books, like Du Bois' Philadelphia study, document the occupations which represented middle classness in various stages of the evolution of the black middle class. They also examine the very tenuous and fragile links which occupationally defined middle classness for blacks in contrast to whites.

In his Philadelphia study Du Bois traces the formation of the black middle class from those who comprise the following occupations: the professions, composing the smallest percentage and the highest income (teachers, lawyers, physicians, and clergymen); merchants; clerks; and skilled tradesmen. In his 1901 observations of black life in New York City and Boston, Du Bois included the following occupations as middle class in New York: teachers, physicians, merchants, clerks, mail carriers, and clergymen. In Boston this class included those in the following occupations: lawyers, teachers, clergymen, mercantile trade, real estate, merchants, undertakers, clerks, and salesmen. Drake and Cayton (1945) document similar occupations for the black middle class in Chicago.

Du Bois' (circa 1901, 1969:29) observation that this class comprises a very small proportion of the communities in New York, Boston, and Philadelphia is not startling news. Rather, it is to be expected. His important observation, however, is that, unlike the white middle class, the black middle class has great difficulties in passing its knowledge and financial resources to its children. This fact is intricately linked to the classes' inability to receive adequate wages and promotions in competitive situations with whites. This racial division of labor served to slow rather than terminate the growth of the black middle class. It did mean, however, that blacks in semi-skilled or non-skilled labor would be pushed further down the occupational and wage ladder.

Since the white professional class had no desire to service a pariah or outcast group, the door was opened for black professionals to fill the void. Many of these professionals, especially doctors, dentists, lawyers, and teachers were largely confined to black clients, patients and students since whites generally refused to patronize their businesses. Here we may note three features which operated hand in glove in the formation of the black middle class: structured inequality, group exclusion, and the ideology of race. Each re-inforced the other.

Lacking a legacy of middle classness, the members of this small black middle class were transfixed between their collective past and their future aspirations, both personal and collective. Their plight was all the more ambiguous because they were navigating in uncharted waters: there was no aggregate of middle class role models, hence, there were no guidelines for the road on which they had embarked. They were confronted with a dilemma: whites did not want to associate with them and did exclude them, yet tried to undermine them and did not want them to succeed. On the other hand, this class had a collective experience and a common fate with the less fortunate, but it was pulled by a desire to move beyond its racial status. It identified with the problems of the less fortunate members of the group but did not want to live as they lived. It wanted to assert its class role but was prevented from doing so. Thus, its class role had to be fulfilled within the context of its racial role within the community.

Osofsky (1968:16) describes the special ordeal of this emerging class and quotes Du Bois (1903) on the perilous passage in the making of this class: "The rise of a nation, the pressing forward of a social class means a bitter struggle, a hard and soul-sickening battle with the world such as few of the more favored classes know or appreciate."

When Du Bois examines Southern life the formation of the black middle class has different contours. In his Farmville, Virginia study (Du Bois, 1898) farmers, teachers, grocers, and artisans comprise the black middle class. In another essay (Du Bois, 1969) he includes farmers, landlords, and mechanics. Beyond the category of teachers, there is an absence of a professional class to the extent that such a class existed in his study of the North. Given the differences in regional economics (industrialism in the North and agrarianism in the South), this would be expected. In this sense, the formation of the black middle class in the South parallels the formation of the white middle class in that region, just as the black middle class in the North follows, to some extent, the white Northern middle class pattern.

The formation of middle classness in the South is consistent with the three determinants which assisted in the formation of the black middle class in the North: structured inequality, group exclusion, and the ideology of race. But the three determinants would operate more rigidly and more violently in the South. The structured inequality would be deeper, group exclusion more intense, and racial ideology more formal and legal. E. Franklin Frazier (1957a) paints a picture of a very rigid class structure among Southern blacks, between house servants and field slaves and between slaves and "free coloreds." According to him, there was virtual class warfare between the groups.

The position of blacks in general, and more specifically the middle class, was very tenuous, fragile, and subject to the racial winds which constantly traversed the South. The difference between the two regions with respect to blacks amounts to one of degree. The three determinants worked similarly in the North and the South because both regions wanted separate black and white worlds. By constructing two separate worlds and enforcing this separation through laws, traditions, and customs in the South, and by tradition, custom, and habit in the North, both regions assisted in the formation of a permanent black racial class.

The formation of a black middle class occurs in the United States for the same reasons middle classes appear in all industrial nations: urbanization, industrialization and consumerism. This black middle class emerges, but unlike the larger white middle class, it is a marginal class in as much as its racial status is an obstacle to its class opportunities. It is an economic and social class based on education, income, and occupation, but it is defined more by its race, hence it is primarily a racial class. Chapter Nine of Du Bois' *The Philadelphia Negro* (pp. 97–146) examines the many occupations made possible by the rapid social change in the city. This rapid social change provided new opportunities for enterprising individuals from the lower and working classes, as well as those individuals who were reared in families which had already begun the emotional and psychological movement into the middle class, though they may have lacked many of the financial and cultural attributes of this class.

The studies cited in this section demonstrate that the black middle class emerges, North and South, due to consistent and persistent themes in American life: racial politics, structured inequality, and group exclusion. The evolution of this class as a racial class is indeed a paradox, for its middle classness is intricately linked to its racial status, thus, it emerges as a special class, a racial class. In this sense, it could not simply become a class for itself in as much as, unlike the white middle class, it could not, even if it wanted to, totally disengage itself from the non-middle class within its midst. Though its status as a racial class made it distinct, Willie (1976:58) notes that this class is very much like the white middle class in that "its members are success-oriented, upwardly mobile, [and] materialistic...They immerse themselves in work and leave little time for leisure. Education, occupation, hard work and thrift are accepted as the means for the achievement of success."

In one sense, slavery, racism, and jim crowism created the foundation upon which this class developed. But despite these features, or it might be, because of these features, it can be said that this class created itself, against great odds. Taking advantage of the limited opportunities available, black Americans pushed and shoved against, as Du Bois said, "the veil." As they did, they operated within the only society they knew; they sought to create, shape, and influence the cultural forces within their communities and beyond. This enabled them to pursue their dreams of the "good life" as they had defined it.

Race and Class Consciousness

Du Bois' analysis of Philadelphia, and Allan H. Spear (1967) and Drake and Cayton's (1945) study of Chicago reiterate a central theme: that the emerging black middle class was torn between its racial ideal—integration, and the urban Northern reality—segregation. How to deal with this lack of correspondence between the ideal and the reality became a major issue. According to both Du Bois (1969:41) and Spear (1967:53–62) the intraracial battle lines were drawn between Northern-born blacks who generally wanted to use the politics of protest to support the abolition of the color line. Many among this group were reluctant to create or build institutions, fearing that doing so might harden the color line. On the other side were many migrants from the South who, in the South, lived under, practiced, and supported the concept of racial solidarity, self-help, and a collectivist group economics. The Southern-born sought to shame the Northern-born, accusing them of running away from their race. This push was assisted by white hostility and resistance to greater racial cooperation.

Spear (1967:91) indicates that the black middle class and black middle class leadership emerge in conjunction with the rise of institution-building in Chicago:

> The rise of the new middle-class leadership was closely interrelated with the development of Chicago's black ghetto. White hostility and population growth

combined to create the physical ghetto on the South Side. The response of Negro leadership, on the other hand, created the institutional ghetto. Between 1900 and 1915, Chicago's Negro leaders built a complex of community organizations, institutions, and enterprises that made the South Side not simply an area of Negro concentration but a city within a city.

Du Bois' Philadelphia study attests to similar institution-building there as well. In both cases, however, there was great reluctance of many within the middle class to create strong internal infrastructures within the black community. They feared that the very institutions and organizations being created to serve the immediate needs might, over time, in fact contribute to the very segregation being fought. Despite the apprehensions, however, many believed that blacks had no choice in the matter: A people herded together, because of race, within tightly controlled urban boundaries, sharing a common racial memory of discrimination and exclusion, and confronted with the reality of having to create their own world, had to first define then carve out for itself a collective strategy for group survival. Thus, many reasoned, the dangers of long-term segregation would be offset by the need to construct community life to enable communities to tend to their communal needs.

Over time, it was natural that the institutional and organizational building would create and sustain a degree of racial consciousness. Such a consciousness was partially ignited by an already existing white racial consciousness which unabashedly proclaimed white supremacy as the political, economic, and cultural ideology. Thus, as blacks became more immersed in institutions such as churches, lodges, social clubs, unions, schools, and the professional groups which were primarily black, there was the sense that these groups would be used to break down the wall of shame and discrimination even as they were being used to fulfill everyday needs. Black racial consciousness was fueled by the racial conflicts, hostility, and the exclusionary policies of whites. As Spear notes, these racial policies by whites forced even those blacks who saw no benefits in racial consciousness to move in that direction.

The institutions and organizations, having been created, shaped and molded a sense of racial identity, racial consciousness, and racial solidarity (see Dennis, 1991). In many ways this consciousness was singular in spite of Du Bois' analysis of "double consciousness" as a major theme in black life (Dennis, 1980, 1995). That Du Bois himself understood the singularity of racial consciousness, in contrast to a doubleness, can be shown by his description of the rise of racial awareness, identity, and consciousness among blacks in New York (Du Bois, 1969, circa 1901:16):

> ...let us follow the life of the average New York negro. He is first born to a colored father and mother...The child's neighbors as he grows up, are colored, for he lives in a colored district...The young man's friends and associates are therefore all negroes. When he goes to work he works alongside colored men in most cases; his social circle, his clubs and organizations throughout the city are all confined to his own race, and his contact with the whites is practically confined to economic relationships, the streets, and street cars, with occasionally some intercourse at public amusements.

If the passage above describes the growing racial identity and consciousness of the "average citizen," what might be said of the middle class citizen? And how did this middle class define its racial class role vis-à-vis the average citizen? Given its income, education, life style, and professional status, can it be assumed that this middle class had a heightened or diminished sense of racial identity and consciousness? Even if the middle class were opposed to community building, the fact is that it did do so, becoming the institutional and organizational leaders.

Du Bois views the black middle class at times in a most ambiguous light: on one hand, it is torn between its class aspirations in an upwardly mobile class society; on the other hand, it is divided, perplexed, and angry because of a racial status that cannot be transcended in a racist society. Yet as divided as the class may have been, the process of institution-building had to proceed with a relatively high level of group consciousness and solidarity, points emphasized by Du Bois, Spear, Drake and Cayton, and later Frazier. A point also, by the way, recognized by the non-middle class in black communities. Whites may have viewed all blacks as a collective with little distinctions between individuals and groups; blacks, however, knew better, and responded to these differences.

One of the major issues in any discussion of the black middle class involves the oft made claim that this class does indeed have a consciousness, but that it is the consciousness of a white middle class. A close reading of the sociology, politics, and economics of this class casts doubt on this thesis. That the black middle class became conscious of itself as a racial class can be seen in a variety of institutions and organizations. They made their middle classness felt in the middle class churches they found and attended; the middle class fraternities and sororities; the middle class private social clubs; insurance societies; loan associations, labor unions; hospitals; and an assortment of middle class professional and occupational groups.

That the middle class played a pivotal role cannot be questioned. But it often was a struggle as Du Bois (circa 1899:177–178) succinctly describes it:

> It is the germ of a great middle class, but in general its members are curiously hampered by the fact that, being shut off from the world about them, they are the aristocracy of their own people, with all the responsibility of an aristocracy, and yet they, on the other hand, are not prepared for this role, and their own masses are not used to looking to them for leadership. As a class they feel strongly the centrifugal forces of class repulsion among their own people, and, indeed, are compelled to feel it in sheer self-defense. They do not relish being mistaken for servants; they shrink from the free and easy worship of most of the Negro churches, and they shrink from all such display and publicity as will expose them to the veiled insult and depreciation which the masses suffer. Consequently this class, which ought to lead, refuses to head any race movement on the plea that thus they draw the very color line against which they protest. On the other hand their ability to stand apart, refusing on one hand all responsibility for the masses of the Negroes and on the other hand seeking no recognition from the outside world...

This statement by Du Bois can be viewed as a classic case of the contradictions which abound in discussions of the black middle class. Whereas Du Bois paints an accurate picture of the formation of this class, when he moves towards a description of its role in the black community he lapses into inconsistencies. For example, on page 392 of the Philadelphia study he castigates the middle class and upper classes because they "should recognize their duty toward the masses." Yet on the very next page (393) he contradicts that assertion by acknowledging that the middle and upper classes are engaged in activities to assist in the betterment of the lower classes "...the Negro must learn the lesson that other nations learned so laboriously and imperfectly, that his better classes have their chief excuse for being in the work they may do toward lifting the rabble... *that they do something already to grapple with these social problems of their race is true, but they do not yet do nearly as much as they must, nor do they clearly recognize their responsibility* [my emphasis]. Du Bois does not clearly spell out in specific terms what particular activities he wants performed by the middle class. Later speaking of middle class leaders, Du Bois (circa 1931, 1970:56) lauds this group for having "worked unselfishly for the uplift of the masses of Negro folk...There is no other group of leaders on earth who have so largely made common cause with the lowest of their race as educated American Negroes, and it is their foresight and sacrifice and theirs alone that have saved the American freedman from annihilation and degradation."

In a review of the interracial activities at the turn of the century we have seen how structured inequality, racial exclusion, and the ideology of race created two communities in Philadelphia, Farmville and New York (Du Bois), Chicago (Drake and Cayton; Spear), and Harlem (Osofsky). We have also seen the factors which contributed to the rise and development of the black middle class and the occupations associated with this class; how and why this class became involved in community development; how and why racial pride, racial identity, and racial consciousness emerged as important weapons in the racial struggle between blacks and whites; and how the black middle class role was viewed and accepted.

Ironically, it is E. Franklin Frazier who offers one of the most lucid explanations for the presence of racial pride and racial consciousness among middle class blacks. This is ironic because Frazier (1957) was one of the principal architects of the view which excoriates the black middle class from the 1950s onward. Writing on youth from middle class families, Frazier (circa 1940, 1967:55) proffered the view of this class: "they show more sophistication toward their racial status, that they show more consciousness of their social status, and that they are likely to exhibit a greater degree of race consciousness...the nascent race consciousness of this class is accompanied by a critical attitude toward the deficiencies of the Negro and a deeper resentment of the discrimination practiced by whites." In this passage Frazier captures both the class and race ambivalences of the black middle class, but the quote is light years away from his 1957 statement which attributes a high level of self-hatred for this class and the great disdain, according to Frazier, it expresses towards members of the lower class.

The contemporary black middle class can be defined, as some researchers have, as a "new" class (Landry, 1987). Landry contrasts the old and the new middle classes, and he concludes that the thread permeating both classes remains the same: the world of uncertainty at work and in social settings. The article by Richard Lacayo (March 13, 1989) characterizes the uncertainty as a Du Boisian "double consciousness" in which members of the black middle class "...speak again and again of 'living in two worlds.' In one they are judged by their credentials and capabilities. In the other, race still comes first." But in a departure from the double theme, Lacayo notes that the black side of the double conscious may be the stronger of the two, asserting that "Like other ethnic and racial groups, upwardly mobile African Americans often fear that assimilation will mean a loss of identity." In other words, blacks are experiencing the centrifugal as well as the centripetal forces operating in the American society: they fear being too marginalized simultaneously with being too assimilated. Out of this dilemma has emerged, according to Lacayo, a movement towards "conserving black traditions."

Ellis Cose's (1993) recent book analyzes the hurt and rage of the black middle class. Amid the hurt and pain, the book examines the degree to which race consciousness still permeates that class—though this consciousness is often fueled by the many slights, mistreatments, and insults experienced by this class. If Lacayo is correct and members of the black middle class do live "between two worlds," we should not, however, conclude necessarily that their identity has been placed in limbo between these worlds. Despite the theory of living "between two worlds," and there may be gaps between emotional and physical worlds, there is a degree to which Lacayo is not describing anything more about the black middle class that Du Bois had not much earlier analyzed. In fact, much of the discontent expressed in the Cose book and the Lacayo article relate to the frustrations on the job and job-related conflicts. Occupational and wage competition with white Americans are issues for middle class blacks in the marketplace; on these issues, whites continue to be the reference groups against which blacks compare their economic gains, as it should be. However, in many other areas of life, other blacks continue to be the reference group for middle class blacks. For example Karen DeWitt (1975:14) speaks to this point when she argues that, contrary to popular beliefs, members of the black middle class do identify with each other: "while middle and upper-income blacks may share behavioral similarities with their [white] counterparts, there is no sense of peoplehood, and ultimately peoplehood is more significant." As one of DeWitt's interviewer remarks (Ibid): "We define our lives in terms of each other and the children. If I'm going to be compared to anybody, I'd rather be compared with another black professional. We have made it under similar circumstances."

Awareness of these circumstances has fostered middle class racial consciousness, though this consciousness has a different form from that of the working and lower classes. For example, one is not likely to find many members of the middle class among The Nation of Islam, just as they were not found in large numbers among Garvey's UNIA movement (Cruse, 1987). A modified racial consciousness tends to be more acceptable to this class, one which does not require a radical break with certain mainstream values and assumptions. Alphonso Pinkney (1975:156) addresses this point in his comparison of middle and upper class blacks and whites:

> Middle and upper-class blacks are hardly distinguishable from white Americans of comparable social class level in many cultural patterns. There is even some evidence that they frequently overconform to middle-class standards of behavior in religious observations, in dress, in sexual behavior, and in child-rearing practices. But this does not mean that black culture is a myth...

The pre-1960s represented a racial and class consciousness in the direction of integration. For many blacks that meant an abandonment of black institutions and organizations (Cruse, 1987; hooks and West, 1991; Early, 1994) Groups such as the NAACP, the Urban League, the pre-mid 1960s CORE, SCLC, and the early SNCC epitomized the politics and philosophy of this thrust. The Black Power and Pan-African movements of the mid-1960s and the 1970s pointed black America in yet a new direction and ushered in new levels of racial as well as class consciousness. Here, the integration-Black Power dichotomy is presented as an "ideal type" in as much as there existed a multiplicity of criss-crosses and movements back and forth between the two bipolar types. Indeed, as black life became more diversified, as had the larger society, it would be possible for many members of the middle class to have their feet in several camps (see Allen, 1969; Blackwell, 1985; Amiri Baraka and Neal, 1968; Toure and Hamilton, 1994).

Recent interest in genealogy, travels to Africa and the Caribbean, as well as interest in black contemporary and folk art, artifacts, and music, among many members of the black middle class, indicate that we may be in the midst of a cultural renaissance. If this assertion is correct, the middle class, because it has the necessary cash reserves and the surplus funds, and because it retains organizational and leadership positions within communities, will be the pacesetter.

What is being examined here are merely the visible and manifest cultural tendencies reflecting patterns of middle class life. There may be as many members of the middle class who do not manifest these cultural tendencies, but this does not negate, nor does it lessen the impact of new cultural forces in the general population. A number of new cultural innovations have surfaced, many of these primarily within and by the middle classes: the origins and growing popularity of Kwanzaa; the creation of "rite of passage" ceremonies for black teenagers; the growing number of middle class newlyweds who integrate African practices into their traditional Western weddings. Another visible example of the contemporary cultural resurgence has been the overwhelming popularity of black colleges and universities; this, after a decade or so wondering whether these colleges and universities would survive the last two decades of the twentieth century.

A glance at the magazine rack in any medium or large city will illustrate the growing middle class's purchasing power, for there is a variety of magazines directed towards the black middle class. Such would not exist if the black middle class were simply a shadow of the white middle class, rather than a racial class unto itself with a sense of its own racial class consciousness. There are those who wish this racial class to have racial consciousness but not class consciousness, just as there are those who would nullify its racial consciousness but keep its class consciousness. Both groups lack a fundamental understanding of the unique role and position of this racial class in the American society.

The examples of black middle class consciousness presented above do not presage any vision cutting ties to the larger society; rather, it suggests a new assertiveness and confidence that it is possible to fully participate in the larger society while at the same time adhere to those particular attributes of one's historic heritage and culture. For contrary to one side of Du Bois' theme on double consciousness, it is possible to be both black and an American.

Conclusion

The black middle class has had a unique evolution as a racial class. It is a class whose major defining attribute has been its ethnicity. Out of its varied history has emerged the nuts and bolts used in the construction of black community life. Du Bois painted the black middle class as ambiguous, uncertain, aloof, and angry that race prevented it from playing its "proper" class role. Later, Frazier provided the middle class with few redeeming values and virtues. Yet it is to this class that we look when we trace the history of black communities. Mind you, it is not only this class, for this class relied upon and needed the support of the vast working and lower classes which comprised the bulk of the population. But this class played an inordinate role in whatever foundations were laid for strictly communal developments.

Albert Murray (1970) castigates those who seek to divide black communities along rigid class lines. Viewing such attempts as mere political posturing, he accuses advocates of inciting class warfare among blacks. Given the fact that the legacy of middle classness among blacks is extremely small, and given the fact that the vast numbers of those who join the contemporary "new" middle class class have working class parents and grandparents (see McAdoo, 1975; Landry, 1988; Billingsley, 1992) it is doubtful that any warfare will occur. It does not, however, discount tensions between the middle and working classes, but the greatest tension will probably occur between the black and white middle classes as many middle class gains over the past twenty-five years may be stalled due to middle class white fears of the preferential treatment of minorities. The current debate over affirmative action is a harbinger of things to come. But if the past history of the black middle tells us anything, it is that this class will fight the "new" racism just as it fought the old version. It will fight, not by giving up its class role to immerse itself in its racial role; rather, it will use both roles as it has done historically, thus affirming its unique status as a racial class.

Bibliography

Allen, Robert (1969). *Black Awakening in Capitalist America*. Garden City: Doubleday and Company.

Baraka, Amiri and Larry Neal (1968). *Black Fire*. New York: William Morrow and Company.

Blackwell, James (1985). *The Black Community: Diversity and Unity*. New York: Harper and Row.

Billingsley, Andrew (1968). *Black Families in White America*. Englewood Cliffs: Prentice-Hall.

Billingsley, Andrew (1992). *Climbing Jacob's Ladder*. New York: Simon and Schuster.

Blassingame, John (1972). *The Slave Community*. New York: Oxford University Press.

Cose, Ellis (1993). *The Rage of a Privileged Class*. New York: Harper Collins.

Cox, Oliver (1974). *Race Relations*. New York: Harper and Row.

Cruse, Harold (1967). *Rebellion or Revolution*. New York: William Morrow.

Cruse, Harold (1987). *Plural But Equal*. New York: William Morrow.

Davis, George and C. Watson (1982). *Black Life in Corporate America*. Garden City: Doubleday.

Dennis, Rutledge M. and C. Henderson (1980). "Intellectuals and Double Consciousness" in C. Hedgepeth (Ed.), *Afro-American Perspectives in the Humanities*. San Diego: Collegiate.

Dennis, Rutledge M. (1991). "Dual Marginality and Discontent Among Black Middletown Youth" in Rutledge Dennis (Ed.), *Research in Race and Ethnic Relations*. Greenwich, Ct.: JAI Press.

Dennis, Rutledge M. (1995). "The Racial Socialization of White Youth" in Benjamin Bowser and R. Hunt (Eds.), *Impacts of Racism on White Americans*. [Second Edition]. Newbury Park: Sage.

Dennis, Rutledge M. (1995). "Du Bois' Concept of Double Consciousness: Myth and Reality" in John Stone and Rutledge Dennis (Eds.), *Race and Ethnicity: Comparative Perspectives*. Boston: Blackwell.

DeWitt, Karen (1975). "The Black Middle Class" in *Potomac* (January 26): 12–14, 25.

Drake, St. Clair and H. Cayton (1945). *Black Metropolis: A Study of Negro Life in a North-ern City*. New York: Harper and Row.

Du Bois, W.E.B. (1898). "The Negroes of Farmville: A Social Study," *Bulletin of the United States Department of Labor*, Vol. 3 (January): 1–38.

Du Bois, W.E.B. (1899). *The Philadelphia Negro: A Social Study.* Philadelphia: University of Pennsylvania.

Du Bois, W.E.B. (1903). *The Souls of Black Folks*. Chicago: A.C. McClurg.

Du Bois, W.E.B. (1970). "The Negro Bourgeoisie" in M.Weinberg (Ed.) *W.E.B. Du Bois: A Reader* (1970). New York: Harper and Row.

Du Bois, W.E.B. (1969). [1901] *The Black North in 1901*. New York: Arno Press.

Duneier, Mitchell (1992). *Slim's Table*. Chicago: University of Chicago Press.

Early, Gerald (1994). *Daughters: On Family and Fatherhood*. New York: Addison-Wesley Publishers.

Franklin, John Hope (1967). *From Slavery to Freedom*. New York: Alfred A. Knopf.

Frazier, E. Franklin (1932). *The Free Negro Family*. Chicago: University of Chicago Press.

Frazier, E. Franklin (1940). *Negro Youth at the Crossways*. Washington, DC: American Council on Education.

Frazier, E. Franklin (1957). *Black Bourgeoisie*. New York: Free Press.

Frazier, E. Franklin (1957). *The Negro in the United States*. New York: Macmillan.

Hacker, Andrew (1980). *The End of the American Era*. New York: Atheneum.

Hare, Nathan (1970). *Black Anglo-Saxons*. New York: Collier Books.

hooks, bell and Cornel West (1991). *Breaking Bread*. Boston: South End Press.

King, Jr., Martin Luther (1968). *Where Do We Go From Here?* Boston: Beacon Press.

Lacayo, Richard (1989). "Between Two Worlds," *Time* (March 13): 58–68.

Landry, Bart (1987). *The New Black Middle Class*. Berkeley: University of California.

Lehmann, Nicholas (1991). *The Promised Land*. New York: Alfred A. Knopf.

Martin, Elmer and J. Martin (1978). *The Black Extended Family*. Chicago: University of Chicago Press.

McAdoo, Harriette (1975). "The Impact of the Extended Family Structure on the Upward Mobility of Blacks," *Journal of African-American Issues*, Vol. 3, No. 4: 279–295.

Osofsky, Gilbert (1968). *Harlem: The Making of a Ghetto*. New York: Harper and Row.

Pinkney, Alphonso (1975). *Black Americans*. Englewood Cliffs: Prentice-Hall.

Sowell, Thomas (1981). *Ethnic America*. New York: Basic Books.

Spear, Allan (1967). *Black Chicago*. Chicago: University of Chicago Press.

Thorpe, Earl (1961). *The Mind of The Negro*. Baton Rouge: Ortlieb Press.

Toure, Kwame (1967). *Black Power: The Politics of Liberation in America*. New York: Vintage Books.

Willie, Charles (1979). *The Caste and Class Controversy*. Bayside, NY: General Hall.

Willie, Charles (1991). "Caste, Class, and Ramily Life Chances" pp. 65–84 in *Research in Race and Ethnic Relations*, Vol. 6, Rutledge Dennis (Ed.). Greenwich, CT: JAI Press.

Section V

Race and Aesthetics

12

Rising Tide or Ebb Tide? Recent Changes in the Black Middle Class in the U.S., 1980–1990

Frank Harold Wilson

Background

At the beginning of the post-World War II period, the black middle class in the United States was much smaller than present. According to Gunnar Myrdal, this middle class was a small group of professionals and business people whose existence in the racial caste order derived from monopolizing specialized services to the black masses (Myrdal, 1944; 689–704). Myrdal's description captured an economic situation where the status of blacks was constrained by institutional structures of racial discrimination, de jure segregation, poverty, and marginalization that largely excluded them from upwardly mobile, high-paying, and prestigious employment in the industrial economy and occupational structure. Historic and continuing post-World War II discrimination were reflected in most blacks working as servants, domestics, unskilled laborers, and farmers. This description did not capture nor anticipate the dynamic changes in class accompanying the wartime and post-World War II black migration to the cities.

E. Franklin Frazier examined the early post-World War II structural changes in the economy through the 1950s and offered a different assessment. In *The Black Bourgeoisie* (1957), he saw in the growth and differentiation of the American occupational structure the bases for the increased mobility of blacks into professional, managerial, clerical/sales, and crafts occupations and the formation of a new middle class. Because the wartime and post-war geographic mobility from the South was a condition of this occupational mobility, Frazier noted that the entry of blacks into the cities of the North was directly correlated with blacks' greater relative incomes (Frazier, 1957). Only two years after the publication of

An earlier version of this essay appeared in *Research in Race and Ethnic Relations* 1995, 8, 21–56 and is adapted/reprinted with the permission of the copyright holder/author.

The Black Bourgeoisie, the Census Bureau began publishing poverty status data which showed 9.9 million blacks or 55 percent of the black population below the poverty line (U.S. Bureau of Census, 1978; 28). While Frazier's observations captured large-scale and dramatic economic structural changes among blacks that primarily involved the expansion of working-class and lower-middle class occupations (See: Farley and Allen, 1989; table 9.1), these trends occurred alongside a persistence of racial caste.

Frazier's analysis preceded the height of the civil rights movement, the War on Poverty of the 1960s, and the most rapid growth period of the black middle class. The growth of black incomes during the 1960s resulted in the U.S. percentage of blacks below the poverty line decreasing from 55 percent in 1960 to 33 percent in 1970. Blacks in professional, clerical, craftsmen, and operatives occupations grew importantly, while nonfarm and agricultural labor shrank. The rising tides of the black middle class, working class, and poor during the 1960s and 1970s would be organizationally mobilized via the civil rights movements and black power movements and be institutionally codified via federal policies of equal opportunity and affirmative action. These rising tides of Black Americans would soon meet storms of resistance, reaction, counterrevolution, and conservatism.

William Julius Wilson in *The Declining Significance of Race: Blacks and Changing American Institutions* (1978) would address the economic and political changes bearing on black class changes through the 1970s. Wilson argued that with the growth of corporate and government sectors during the 1950s and 1960s, college educated and talented blacks experienced dramatic movement into white collar employment and occupational upgrading (Wilson, 1978; 126–129). Although the rates of black occupational upgrading slowed during the early 1970s, he notes that blacks continued to experience more rapid occupational upgrading than whites (Wilson, 1978; 130). This "declining significance of race" experienced by young, highly educated, and talented blacks was accompanied by the increasing growth, isolation, and falling behind of the black underclass. By 1987, in *The Truly Disadvantaged: The Inner City, The Underclass, and Public Policy*, Wilson continued to argue the dislocation and marginalization of the black ghetto poor or underclass and the mobility of the black middle class from the ghetto.

Controversies remain concerning the continuity of the trends described by Frazier and Wilson and how these anticipate and capture the economic developments affecting the black community by social class through the 1980s. Landry, for example, argues that during the 1973–75 and 1980–82 recessions, middle class blacks fared worse and lost ground relative to middle class whites (Landry, 1987; 194–195). He notes that these negative structural effects of the recession were felt earlier and continued longer among blacks, were reflected in a slowed growth of the black middle class. Between 1973 and 1982, the percentage of blacks in the middle class nationally increased only one percent—from 5.8 to 6.8 (Landry, 1987; 196). Furthermore, blacks continued to be overrepresented in the lower black middle class of sales and clerical workers vis-à-vis the upper middle class of professionals and administrators (Landry, 1987; 198). Careful contextualization of occupational and income changes by race since the 1970s also raises questions of whether the black community is becoming increasingly differentiated largely due to social class or race. Recent studies such as Wilson, Tienda, and Wu indicate that the persistently high gap in black and white unemployment is explained not only by residence, differential access to employment opportunities, and different occupational distributions, but also by segmented labor markets by race and labor market discrimination. At levels of higher education, the racial difference in unemployment remained rather than decreased (Wilson, Tienda, Wu, 1993).

This chapter will shed light on the black middle class controversy by reviewing the theories and examining census data on economic and occupational changes from 1980 to 1990 as evidence. While the black middle class continued to grow nationally, these recent trends show a black middle class that is increasingly precarious, characterized by a widening of the racial gap in earnings, and growing unevenly. This chapter will show that the changes accompanying the growing black middle class are complex and characterized by racial, class, and gender differentials. The chapter is organized as follows. First, theoretical perspectives of the American economy and black middle class will be reviewed. Second, census data will be used to examine changes in black income, occupational distributions, and occupational segregation. Third, the implications of these findings for theorizing and research on racial stratification and public policy will be discussed.

Theories of the American Economy, Occupational Structure, and Changing Black Middle Class

During the post-World War II years through the 1980s, macroeconomic changes have been reflected and reproduced in important class changes among Black Americans. Although nearly all observers agree that the structure of blacks in the economy and black social classes have changed, there are different interpretations and assessments of what this development means. Questions concerning the black middle class, working class, and lower class, and their relationships are subject to controversy. There are two competing models of social stratification and social mobility by race that are usually found in the social science literature that can be extended to account for the status of blacks in general and the black middle class in particular: 1) black middle class formation and growth as integration into the post-industrial economy; 2) black middle class formation and growth as dual labor market integration and segregation into the post-industrial economy and occupational structure.

These models differ with respect to the assumptions of the underlying logic of the American economy and occupational structure, the causes of black class growth and decline, the salient variables and relationships, and the future of both the black middle class and lower classes in American society.

Integration Models of Black Middle Class Changes

Integration perspectives view the different outcomes of blacks' education, occupations, and earnings as largely a function of their human capital and the degree of match/mismatch between changing black social and economic characteristics relevant to generating income and the changing communities and labor markets where—blacks are situated. These perspectives view the economy as a capitalist market one in which competition, profit, rationality, innovation, and growth drive it. In this post-industrial economy, there is expected to be stronger relationships among schooling, occupational status, and earnings for both blacks and whites. Unlike an earlier economy and occupational structure where highly educated blacks experienced discrimination (Blau and Duncan, 1965), this contemporary economy and occupational structure are characterized by a decreasing significance of race for highly educated and talented blacks (Wilson, 1978; Featherman and Hauser, 1978). The black lower class and underclass are increasingly isolated and left behind due to historic discrimination and lower human capital (Wilson, 1987). Integration perspectives argue that the black middle class is bifurcated and fundamentally different from blacks in other social classes.

The integrative perspectives have "progress" themes which emphasize blacks' increasing status attainment as an important phenomenon in quantitative and qualitative terms (Jaynes and Williams, 1989; Kilson, 1983; Wilson, 1978; Freeman, 1976; Wattenberg and Scammon, 1973). Research which has validated this hypothesis has shown gains in college attendance and graduation since the 1970s, the greatest convergence in racial incomes among younger blacks with college completion, the rapid entry and growth of blacks in new middle class occupations, and the steady breaking down of employment barriers in the private and public sectors. Where black middle class persons have lower earnings than similar white persons, this is assumed to be a product of the lower human capital characteristics and historic discrimination. For working class and lower class blacks, factors such as lower human capital characteristics, productivity, access to job information networks, and residence in central cities where post-industrial employment has moved from the traditionally high-wage manufacturing activities (and blacks do not have the high-tech training and skills) largely explain what has happened (Kasarda, 1988; Kasarda, 1985). Higher black unemployment grows out of deprivations in blacks' human capital and the growing mismatch.

Macrosociological factors are also relevant to understanding integrative perspectives of blacks changing economic status. First, government interventions in the economy such as affirmative action, compliance, and set-aside programs are argued to have improved equality of opportunity undercutting discrimination in employment and business. Public policies such as Kennedy's Executive Order 11246 (1961) establishing an obligation on the part of federal contractors to undertake "affirmative action" to ensure equal employment, Congressional enactment of Title VI of the Civil Rights Act of 1964 ending unfair employment treatment of against minorities and women, Nixon's Executive Order 11478 (1969) requiring federal departments and agencies to set plans for equal employment opportunity, and the Civil Rights Act of 1991 are exemplary. Second, because discrimination is perceived as an exogenous "taste" or aberration that contradicts competition, young blacks and blacks in general are expected, with all other factors equal, to have an edge with similarly educated and trained whites. The preferential treatment given blacks in the post-industrial economy predicts that blacks should be entering new occupations more rapidly than whites and moving up the ladder at least as fast. To the extent blacks experience higher unemployment across classes these may be viewed as statistical artifacts. Third, the growth of the post-industrial economy is characterized by a convergence of high-paying and low-paying occupational opportunities across regions. Unlike earlier, earnings for middle class blacks across metropolitan areas in the South and North are now more similar. The poverty, which was traditionally higher among blacks in the South, is now characterized by higher levels in the Midwest and Northeast. The integration perspectives minimize and make invisible the effects of outright institutional and class-based discrimination among blacks in the marketplace while acknowledging historic discrimination. Fourth, to the extent that blacks in middle class occupations earn less than similar whites, these should be viewed in the context of the mismatch between education, training, skills, and changing regional and metropolitan labor markets. It is argued that because the black middle class primarily resides in older metropolitan centers characterized by declining economies rather than migrating to newer metropolitan centers characterized by growth, the chances of translating education, training, and skills into higher status occupations and earnings are constrained.

Segmentation Models of Black Middle Class Changes

Segmentation perspectives argue that while the economic integration of blacks is nominally driven by competition, growth, equality, and diversity, counterveiling historic and contemporary structures of racial stratification, institutional discrimination, and occupational segregation result in significantly different patterns for contemporary Black Americans in general and the black middle class specifically. Accompanying the changes in the post-industrial economy, these perspectives underscore the dynamic yet persistent structures and processes that dichotomize business and labor markets into primary and secondary sectors which differ in working conditions, wages, and stability. Primary labor markets consist of the more rapidly growing advanced segments of the economy which have relatively more sustained growth, high wages, strong benefits, secure working environments, and favorable probabilities of upward career occupational mobility. Primary businesses consist of those leading international, national, and regional companies. Secondary labor markets consist of slow growing and declining segments of the economy which experience instability, lower wages, marginal benefits, insecure working environments, and greater probabilities of horizontal and downward mobility. Secondary businesses consist of those local-oriented and small businesses most subject to marginal profits, turnover, and failures.

Segmentation perspectives view the post-World War II economic growth as a transformation characterized by uneven processes of growth and decline driven by global competition, deindustrialization, corporate centralization, automation, and the management of social control. Concomitantly, the growth of the state is driven by organizational relationships and norms of corporate liberalism, governmental reform, and intergovernmental transfer programs which increase its adaptability while insulating it from power contests and conflicts (Piven and Cloward, 1972). The growth of the black middle class is primarily explained by macrosociological processes of state growth, political centralization, bureaucratization, home rule, empowerment, and other interventions which have variably and unevenly integrated blacks into the economy (Darrity, 1990; Collins, 1989;

Hill, 1987; Jones, 1986; Collins, 1983). Simultaneously, the growth of the black poor and underclass result out of a logic of capitalist surplus labor where complex forces of agricultural modernization, industrialization, and automation increasingly render blacks into lower paying, part-time, and unemployed ranks of cities. Racial segregation further isolates and distances blacks from the rapid growth industries of the economy. For blacks of all classes, these perspectives view the changing economy as crystallized around a racial division of labor that has race and class consequences for participation and mobility.

These macrosociological factors are most salient to explaining segmentation perspectives. First, the changing economic status of blacks in the post-industrial economy is importantly characterized by externalities linked to the expansion of corporate and public administration (Collins, 1983). While recognizing that the black middle class has grown recently, these perspectives emphasize that these trends are cyclical rather than linear events. The corporate liberalism, governmental reforms, and intergovernmental transfer programs relevant to the formation and growth of the post-World War II middle class in general and the black middle class specifically are predicted to have a logic of development characterized by structural and intraclass conflicts which may undermine the bases of this class in the long run. Second, the role of deindustrialization, automation, redlining, and disinvestment have disproportionately and adversely affected the development of inner city communities, the wealth of black middle classes, and business formation. The marginalization of urban black communities and black labor is reflected in a precarious black middle class vulnerable to horizontal and downward movement. Third, despite governmental policies such as Affirmative Action, segmentation perspectives emphasize that both majority group management and organized labor competition with blacks result in a persistence of institutional discrimination in employment, promotion, lower wages, and less career mobility for the black middle class. Fourth, the contemporary earnings returns for black college graduates have less convergence than described during the 1970s. The greatest convergence in income is now predicted to be found among persons with post-secondary school experience/training short of college completion. The segmentation/segregation perspectives emphasize a persistence of discrimination that cuts across occupations. To the extent that blacks in middle class occupations are growing, they are expected to be strongly represented and concentrated in occupations and industries that are declining economic activities or low-paying employment.

The Changing Economic and Occupational Status of the Black Middle Class

How may the black middle class during the 1980s be characterized? Do economic and occupational statistics suggest increasing integration or segmentation? In an attempt to shed light on these questions, the next portion of this paper is an empirical assessment. The empirical assessment of selected structural economic changes among Black Americans is focused on the following: 1) black income changes; 2) black changes in middle class occupations; 3) black middle class changes in occupational segregation. These statistics provide a context for describing and analyzing the continuity and discontinuity between the 1980s and earlier.

Black Income Changes, 1980–1990

Changes in black income provide a context for interpreting the intergroup and intragroup dynamics of Black Americans in the larger class structure and the status of the black middle class. Black income changes may be examined in terms of at least two dimensions—concentration changes and distributional changes. Gini ratios are used for income distributions to describe the extent of concentration. Sometimes called the coefficient of population concentration (Shryock and Siegal, 1975; 178–180), ginis, when examined over time, provide an important dimension of changing racial differentials in income concentration that permit an assessment of the convergence-divergence issue.

Since the 1970s, national income data shows the gini ratio increasing steadily. Between 1970 and 1990, the overall gini score increased 44 points—from .394 to .438. This increase reflects a pattern of increasing shares of aggregate income earned by families in the two highest quintiles and decreasing shares earned by families in the lowest quintiles. The overall income distribution increased less rapidly during the 1970s when the gini gained 9 points going from .394 (1970) to .403 (1980). Since 1980, the gini concentration coefficient gained 25 points—from .403 to .428.

Racial differentials show that black income distributions are relatively more asymmetrical than other racial groups in the U.S. Between 1970 and 1990, the gini increased 42 points going from .422 to .464. Only 17 points of this increase occurred in the 1970s; a 25-point increase occurred in the 1980s. The concentration of white income distribution increased less rapidly going from .387 (1970) to .419 (1990)—a 32-point increase. It is instructive that during the 1970s, the white gini increased only 7 points. Between 1980 and 1990, the white income concentration increased 25 points—from .394 to .419 (1980 and 1990 figures respectively). Although the point increase among white income during the 1980s was the same as blacks, the beginning of period levels were much lower. In fact, the unevenness of black income concentration during the 1960s was considerably higher than those for other racial groups during the 1990s.

In *The Declining Significance of Race* (1978), William Julius Wilson argued that the black class structure in the contemporary United States was becoming more differentiated and polarized. This schism in the black community was exemplified by what he perceived as a more rapid growth of income inequality among black families than white families. Based on his examination of shares of aggregate income during the 1970s, Wilson noted that while the upper two-fifths of black families made greater gains, the lower two-fifths experienced substantial losses (Wilson, 1978; Wilson, 1979; 13–15). These latter sociological facts partly validated the bases of his hypothesis of the increasing significance of class among Black Americans. Independent observation of income shifts between 1970 and 1980 confirms these observations (see table 1). While the upper two quintiles of black families increased their share of aggregate income from 68 to 70 percent, the share of the lower two-fifths decreased from 15.2 to 13.8 percent. At the same

Table 1. Mean Income of Families by Quintiles and Percent of Aggregate Income Received by Each Fifth and Top Five Percent, 1970–1990.

	1970	1980	1990	1970–1980	1980–1990
Black					
Top 5 Percent	15.2	15.6	17.3	+4.7	+1.7
Highest Fifth	43.1	44.8	47.3	+1.7	+2.5
Fourth Fifth	24.9	25.4	25.3	+ .5	− .1
Third Fifth	16.8	16.0	15.6	+ .8	− .4
Second Fifth	10.6	9.6	8.6	−1.0	−1.0
Lowest Fifth	4.6	4.2	3.3	− .4	− .9
White					
Top 5 Percent	15.4	15.1	17.1	− .3	+2.0
Highest Fifth	40.5	40.9	43.6	+ .4	+2.7
Fourth Fifth	23.6	24.0	23.6	+ .4	− .4
Third Fifth	17.7	17.6	16.6	− .1	−1.0
Second Fifth	12.5	11.9	11.1	− .6	− .8
Lowest Fifth	5.8	5.6	5.1	− .2	− .5
Mean Income of Families in Dollars					
Black					
Top 5 Percent	74,580	81,510	99,563	6,930	18,053
Highest Fifth	52,867	58,564	67,860	5,697	9,296
Fourth Fifth	30,604	33,193	36,295	2,589	3,102
Third Fifth	20,641	20,966	22,394	325	1,428
Second Fifth	12,990	12,546	12,325	−444	−221
Lowest Fifth	5,619	5,519	4,721	−100	−798
Mean	24,542	26,158	28,714	1,616	2,556
White					
Top 5 Percent	117,172	124,763	159,082	7,591	34,319
Highest Fifth	76,724	84,459	101,161	7,735	16,702
Fourth Fifth	44,712	49,593	54,723	4,881	5,130
Third Fifth	33,476	36,234	38,568	2,758	2,334
Second Fifth	23,721	24,615	25,778	894	1,163
Lowest Fifth	10,909	11,455	11,834	546	379
Mean	37,908	41,272	46,406	3,364	5,134
Black/White Ratios					
Top 5 Percent	63.6	65.3	62.6	+1.7	−2.7
Highest Fifth	68.9	69.3	67.1	− .4	−2.2
Fourth Fifth	68.4	66.9	66.3	−1.5	− .6
Third Fifth	61.7	57.9	58.1	−3.8	+ .2
Second Fifth	54.8	48.2	47.8	−6.6	− .4
Lowest Fifth	51.5	48.1	39.8	−3.4	−8.2
Mean	61.0	63.3	61.8	+2.3	−1.5

Source: U.S. Bureau of the Census, Current Population Reports, Series P-60, Money Income of Households, Families, and Persons in the United States: 1991. Washington, D.C.: U.S. Government Printing Office, 1992.

time, the upper two quintiles of white income increased 1 percent—from 64 to 65 percent and the lower two fifths decreased .8 percent—from 18.3 to 17.5. It is instructive that while Wilson focuses on racial intragroup comparisons with respect to aggregate income distributions, he did not examine racial intergroup differences of income received and understated the race-based changes during the 1970s.

The 1980s are characterized by a continuity of income gains among the highest quintile of black families and losses among the lowest two quintiles of black families. Unlike the 1970s, income improvements among the fourth and third fifths of black families reversed to losses. Among whites, the highest income families grew in absolute and relative shares of income more rapidly than similar black families. Losses in aggregate income remained substantially greater among the two lowest quintiles of black families. In none of these quintiles did black incomes experience improvements.

Close observation of these quintiles with respect to mean income of families is revealing of the divergence or "falling behind" patterns that began during the 1970s. These show that mean family incomes of blacks at each level generally remained below two-thirds of the white family income. With the exception of the top five percent which experienced a 1.7 increase during the 1970s and the third fifth which remained virtually unchanged during the 1980s, these data show that blacks have been experiencing income losses at all levels. During the 1970s, these losses in income were greatest among the working class, the poor, and lower middle class. During the 1980s, the poorest of the poor have fallen behind much faster. Still, the fourth fifth and third fifth of black incomes, which captures much of the lower middle and working class, have slowed in momentum.

Finally, the 1990 actual mean incomes of blacks are depressed roughly one strata downward compared to whites. The mean income for the top five percent of black families ($99,563) was comparable but slightly lower than that received for the highest fifth of white families ($101,161). The mean income for the highest fifth of black families ($67,860) was $13,000 higher than the fourth fifth of whites. The fourth fifth of black families ($36,295) earned less than the third fifth of white families ($38,568). The lowest fifth of black families has continued to experience the most rapid dislocation and marginalization. Not only has this strata experienced large relative losses but actual losses in incomes as well. These income trends underscore the slowed growth and inertia in the black middle class.

Black Changes in Middle Class Occupations, 1980–1990

In this analysis of middle class changes, the occupations of principal interest are listed under five divisions based on the 1980 Standard Occupational Classification Manual and International Labor Office Classification (U.S. Department of Commerce, 1980; International Labor Office, 1988): 1) executive, administrative, and managerial; 2) professional specialty; 3) technicians and technologists; 4) marketing and sales; 5) administrative support (including clerical). Although these do not cover all middle-income occupations, these cover the principal upper- and lower-middle class occupations.

Executive, administrative, and managerial occupations include the upper- and middle-management activities which are focused on achieving the broader objectives of industrial, commercial, governmental, and other economies while directly

Table 2. Black Population in Middle Class Occupations, 1980–1990

	1980	1990	Change
Executive, Administrative, Managerial			
Officials & administrators, pub. adm.	30,109	61,481	31,372
Finanacial Managers	12,524	30,275	17,751
Managers, marketing, advertising, &			
public relations	12,823	23,858	11,035
Administrators, education & related	38,584	67,310	28,726
Managers, medicine and health	8,673	25,530	16,857
Other Specified Managers	33,028	145,249	112,221
Managers and administrators, n.e.c.			
Salaried	209,931	202,112	–7,819
Self-employed	16,522	12,026	–4,496
Management related occupations			
Accountants and auditors	51,990	106,046	54,056
Personnel, training, & labor relations specialists	44,259	19,690	–24,569
Buyers and purchasing agents	13,612	25,734	12,122
Inspectors and Compliance Officers	16,244	25,851	9,607
Other management related	28,578	135,448	106,870
Professional Specialty Occupations			
Engineers, architects, and surveyors			
Architects	2,887	4,327	1,440
Engineers			
Civil Engineers	4,924	7,984	3,060
Electrical & electronic engineers	9,383	19,338	9,955
Industrial engineers	5,395	6,475	1,080
Mechanical engineers	4,567	4,568	1
Other engineers	10,655	20,415	9,760
Surveyors and mapping scientists	671	235	–436
Computer systems analysts & scientists	9,421	24,917	15,496
Operations and systems researchers and analysts	4,781	20,111	15,324
Mathematical scientists	2,825	3,523	698
Natural scientists			
Chemists, except biochemists	4,965	8,617	3,652
Other natural scientists	6,541	8,504	1,963
Health diagnosing occupations	17,898	28,070	10,172
Health assessment & treating			
Registered nurses	94,845	165,520	70,675
Other health assessment & treating	36,836	50,908	14,072
Teachers, except post-secondary	354,176	435,558	81,382
Social scientists & urban planners	5,418	21,841	16,423
Social & recreational workers	88,021	167,382	79,361
Lawyers and judges	14,839	27,320	12,481
Writers, artists, entertainers, and athletes	55,642	105,042	49,410
Other professional specialty	94,952	304,148	209,196
Total	1,346,525	2,099,481	752,956

Sources: U.S. Bureau of Census, 1980 Census of Population, U.S. Summary (Occupations by Industry), table 1; 1990 Census of Population (Supplementary Reports) CP-S-1-1, table 1.

Table 2. (continued) Percent Black in Middle Class Occupations, 1980–1990

	1980	1990	Change
Executive, Administrative, Managerial			
Officials & administrators, pub. adm.	8.3	12.1	3.8
Financial Managers	3.1	4.8	1.7
Managers, marketing, advertising, &			
public relations	1.9	3.9	2.0
Administrators, education & related	10.1	10.8	0.7
Managers, medicine and health	8.0	10.9	2.9
Other Specified Managers	6.0	7.6	1.6
Managers and administrators, n.e.c.			
Salaried	4.6	4.1	−0.5
Self-employed	2.9	2.9	0.0
Management related occupations			
Accountants and auditors	5.2	6.6	1.4
Personnel, training, & labor relations specialists	10.8	4.2	−6.6
Buyers and purchasing agents	3.7	5.2	1.5
Inspectors and Compliance Officers	8.1	11.5	3.4
Other management related	4.9	9.2	4.3
Professional Specialty Occupations			
Engineers, architects, and surveyors			
Architects	2.8	2.8	0.0
Engineers			
Civil Engineers	2.5	3.2	0.7
Electrical and electronic engineers	2.9	4.1	1.2
Industrial engineers	2.8	3.7	0.9
Mechanical engineers	2.3	2.5	0.2
Other engineers	2.2	3.2	1.0
Surveyors and mapping scientists	2.3	2.1	−0.2
Computer systems analysts & scientists	4.7	5.3	.6
Operations and systems researchers and analysts	6.0	8.0	2.0
Mathematical scientists	6.1	6.2	0.1
Natural scientists			
Chemists, except biochemists	4.9	6.1	1.2
Other natural scientists	3.2	3.2	0.0
Health diagnosing occupations	2.8	3.2	0.4
Health assessment & treating occupations			
Registered nurses	7.5	8.8	1.3
Other health assessment & treating	8.6	8.1	−0.5
Teachers, except post-secondary	9.7	9.6	−0.1
Social scientists & urban planners	2.5	5.7	3.2
Social & recreational workers	18.5	14.8	−3.7
Lawyers and judges	2.8	3.5	0.7
Writers, artists, entertainers, and athletes	4.3	5.0	0.7
Other professional specialty occupations	7.0	8.1	1.1

Sources: U.S. Bureau of Census, 1980 Census of Population, U.S. Summary (Occupations by Industry), table 1; 1990 Census of Population (Supplementary Reports) CP-S-1-1, table 1.

Table 2. (continued) Black Population in Middle Class Occupations, 1980–1990

	1980	1990	Change
Technicians & Related Support Occupations			
Health technologists and technicians			
Licensed practical nurses	76,300	79,136	2,836
Other health technologists/technicians	56,690	108,525	51,835
Engineering & science technicians			
Electrical & electronic technicians	15,810	29,083	13,273
Industrial & mechanical engineering	1,211	2,297	1,086
Drafting & surveying technicians	16,159	18,377	2,218
Other engineering & science	28,263	18,127	−10,136
Technicians, except health, engineering, and science			
Airplane pilots and navigators	647	1,886	1,239
Air traffic controllers and broadcast			
equipment operators	7,367	8,327	960
Computer programmers	17,545	39,284	21,739
Other technicians, except h.e. & s.	27,842	63,012	35,170
Sales Occupations			
Supervisors and proprietors, sales			
Salaried	39,653	149,738	110,085
Self-employed	12,937	10,644	−2,293
Sales representatives, finance and			
business services	59,186	114,631	55,445
Sales representatives, commodities except retail	30,600	46,311	15,711
Sales workers, retail & personal services			
Cashiers	159,241	409,423	250,182
Other sales occupations	165,816	274,958	109,142
Sales related occupations	931	778	−153
Administrative Support Occupations			
Supervisors, administrative support	97,689	111,542	13,853
Computer equipment operators	47,474	91,065	43,591
Secretaries, stenographers, typists			
Secretaries	218,522	295,199	76,677
Stenographers and typists	115,561	122,069	6,508
Receptionists	40,763	73,590	32,827
Other information clerks	38,776	87,207	48,431
File clerks	46,584	49,701	3,117
Other records processing except financial	77,089	83,871	6,782
Bookkeepers, accounting, & auditing	78,289	107,828	29,539
Payroll & timekeeping clerks	12,930	16,977	4,047
Other financial records processing	23,311	30,346	7,035
Telephone operators	41,798	44,525	2,727
Mail and message distributing	140,191	215,012	74,821
Production coordinators & expediters	31,657	44,987	13,330
Traffic shipping & receiving clerks	62,836	88,349	25,513
Stock & inventory clerks	68,744	99,197	30,453
Other material recording, scheduling	27,345	43,664	16,319
Adjusters and investigators	55,586	137,216	81,630
Data-entry keyers	61,578	113,968	52,390
Other administrative support	349,158	401,991	52,833
Total	2,352,079	3,632,841	1,280,762

Table 2. (continued) Percent Black in Middle Class Occupations, 1980–1990

	1980	1990	Change
Technicians & Related Support Occupations			
Health technologists and technicians			
Licensed practical nurses	17.9	18.3	0.4
Other health technologists/technicians	10.5	7.8	−2.7
Engineering & science technicians			
Electrical & electronic technicians	6.0	7.2	1.2
Industrial & mechanical engineering	4.8	5.1	0.3
Drafting & surveying technicians	4.4	4.4	0.0
Other engineering & science	6.3	7.6	1.3
Technicians, except health, engineering, and science			
Airplane pilots and navigators	0.9	1.7	0.8
Air traffic controllers and broadcast			
equipment operators	6.7	10.1	3.4
Computer programmers	5.6	5.9	0.3
Other technicians, except h.e. & s.	6.7	8.0	1.3
Sales Occupations			
Supervisors and proprietors, sales			
Salaried	3.6	5.0	1.4
Self-employed	2.9	2.4	−0.5
Sales representatives, finance and			
business services	3.3	4.6	1.3
Sales representatives, commodities except retail	2.4	2.9	0.5
Sales workers, retail & personal services			
Cashiers	9.3	14.3	5.0
Other sales occupations	4.9	6.9	2.0
Sales related occupations	3.6	4.0	0.4
Administrative Support Occupations			
Supervisors, administrative support	9.2	12.1	2.9
Computer equipment operators	11.6	13.6	2.0
Secretaries, stenographers, typists			
Secretaries	5.6	7.3	1.7
Stenographers and typists	14.7	16.4	1.7
Receptionists	7.9	9.0	1.1
Other information clerks	10.3	11.5	1.2
File clerks	16.8	18.5	1.7
Other records processing except financial	11.1	13.6	2.5
Bookkeepers, accounting, & auditing	4.3	5.6	1.3
Payroll & timekeeping clerks	8.1	9.5	1.4
Other financial records processing	8.7	10.1	2.4
Telephone operators	14.3	19.1	4.8
Mail and message distributing	18.1	20.8	2.7
Production coordinators & expediters	8.8	9.2	0.4
Traffic shipping & receiving clerks	13.0	13.6	.6
Stock & inventory clerks	12.0	13.9	1.9
Other material recording, scheduling	11.0	11.8	0.8
Adjusters and investigators	10.8	12.0	1.2
Data-entry keyers	16.3	17.8	1.5
Other administrative support	11.7	6.4	−5.3

supporting management (U.S. Department of Commerce, 1980; 33). Professional occupations include activities which increase knowledge, apply scientific or artistic concepts and theories, teach about the aforementioned, or engage in any combination of these three activities (International Labor Office, 1988; 47).

Technologists and technicians provide technical assistance in engineering and scientific research, development, testing and related activities, as well as independently operating and programming technical equipment and systems (U.S. Department of Commerce, 1980; 97). Marketing and sales occupations are concerned with selling goods and services, purchasing commodities and properties for resale, and with conducting wholesale or retail businesses on own or owner's behalf or in partnership (U.S. Department of Commerce, 1980; 106). Administrative support occupations include activities concerned with the preparation, transcription, transfer, systematizing, and preservation of written communications and records, gathering and distribution of information, operation of office machines and electronic data-processing equipment, communications distribution including telephone operators, mail distribution, and related activities (U.S. Department of Commerce, 1980; 121).

In 1980, the 3,698,604 blacks in these broad occupational listings made up roughly two-fifths (or 39.6%) of all blacks in the labor force. A decomposition of these strata by individual categories show the following contributions to the black occupational structure: administrative support (11.5%), professional specialty (8.9%), executive, administrative, and managerial (5.5%), sales (5%), technical specialty (2.7%). Viewed indigenously, blacks in these middle class occupations had 1,635,881 persons in administrative support (52%), 829,648 in professional specialty (20.5%), 516,877 in executive, administrative, managerial (11.2%), 468,364 in sales (10.7%), and 247,834 in technical specialty (5.6%).

Intergroup comparisons showed blacks as generally most underrepresented in the more prestigious and high-paying occupations. Of the total U.S. labor force, blacks made up 9.7 percent of administrative support occupations, 8.5 percent of the technicians and technologists, 6.9 percent of professional specialty occupations, 5.1 percent of executive, administrative, and managerial, and 4.8 percent of the marketing and sales occupations. The variability of black representation within individual occupations was substantial. The largest absolute numbers of blacks in professional occupations included teachers (354,176), health assessment and treatment occupations (131,681), other professional specialty occupations (94,952), social and recreational workers (88,021), and cultural activities such as writers, artists, entertainers, and athletes (55,642). The next largest strata of professions for blacks were to be found among engineers (34,924), health diagnosing occupations (17,898), lawyers and judges (14,839), natural scientists (11,506), and computer systems analysts and scientists (9,421). Among the executive/administrative ranks, the largest numbers of blacks were found among unclassified managers and administrators (226,453). The next strata were found within accountants and auditors (51,990), managers in medicine and health fields (38,584), public administration (30,109), managers, marketing, advertising, and public relations (12,823), financial managers (12,524), and other specified managers (8,673).

In relative terms, the largest percentages of blacks in executive and professional occupations were to be found among social and recreational workers (18.5%), personnel training and labor relations specialists (10.8%), educational administrators (10.1%), teachers (9.7%), other health assessment and treating occupations (8.6%), officials and administrators, public administration (8.3%), and inspectors and compliance officers (8.1%). Blacks made up 5 to 8 percent of the work force in these occupations: managers, medicine and health (8.0%), registered nurses (7.5%), mathematical scientists (6.1%), other specified managers (6.0%), operations and systems researchers and analysts (6.0%), and accountants and auditors (5.2%). The smallest, selective, and most isolated conditions of blacks were found in self-employed managers (2.9%), lawyers and judges (2.8%), architects (2.8%), social scientists and urban planners (2.5%), surveyors and mapping scientists (2.3%), and managers in marketing, advertising, and public relations (1.9%).

Within the technical, sales, and administrative support occupations the largest numbers of blacks were found in other administrative support occupations (349,158), secretaries (218,522), sales related occupations (165,816), cashiers (159,241), and mail and message distribution occupations (140,191). Blacks were principally represented in administrative support activities involving special tasks, stenographic, typing, and computing equipment and secondarily represented in administrative support activities involving supervision, accounting, auditing, and informational distribution. Within technological and technical occupations, blacks were particularly visible in the health fields and less visible in engineering and other fields. Among sales occupations, black participation was disproportionately concentrated in cashiers and sales work and limited in sales representatives, supervisory, and proprietor occupations.

Relatively speaking, the largest percentages of blacks were found among mail and message distribution occupations (18.1%), licensed practical nurses (17.9%), file clerks (16.8%), data entry keyers (16.3%), stenographers and typists (14.7%), telephone operators (14.3%), traffic shipping and receiving clerks (13.0%), stock inventory clerks (12.0%), other administrative support (11.7%), and computer equipment operators (11.6%). Blacks were least represented among airplane pilots and navigators (0.9%), sales representatives in commodities (2.4%), self-employed supervisors and proprietors, sales (2.9%), sales representatives, finance and business (3.3%), salaried supervisors and proprietors, sales related (3.6%), bookkeepers, accounting and auditing clerks (4.3%), drafting and surveying technicians (4.4%), industrial and mechanical engineering technicians (4.8%), computer programmers (5.6%), and secretaries (5.6%).

During the 1980s, blacks employed in these middle class occupations increased 2,273,312—from 3,501,553 (1980) to 5,774,865 (1990). The rate of growth in these occupations (64.9 percent) exceeded the overall black rate of growth in the economy (37.5 percent). In 1990, blacks in these occupations made up 44.9 percent of the black work force—up from 39.6 in 1980.

Decomposing the contribution of each of these occupational categories to the make-up of blacks employed in middle-class work in 1980 had 17.6 percent in administrative support, 9.5 percent in professional specialty, 7.9 percent in sales, 6.9 percent in executive, managerial, and administrative, and 3 percent in technical/technicians. Although absolute increases occurred in each occupational category, it is instructive that most of the movement was accounted for by two broad occupational listings—sales, executive, managerial, and administrative. The dynamics of the post-industrial economy were now indigenously reflected in 39.1 percent of black middle class employees in administrative support, 21.1 percent in professional specialty, 17.5 percent in sales, 15.6 percent in executive, administrative, and managerial, and 6.7 percent in technical occupations. In the total U.S.

labor force, black representation increased in percentage terms most in sales—from 5 to 7 (a 2 percent increase) and administrative support—from 9.7 to 11.4 (a 1.7 percent increase). Slow but steady growth resulted in blacks making up 8.8 percent of the technicians (+ 0.3), 7.3 percent of the professional specialty occupations (+ 0.4), and 6.2 percent of the executives, administrators, and managers (+ 0.6).

Between 1980 and 1990, black employment in the executive, administrative, managerial, and professional occupations experienced the greatest increases in management-related occupations (158,086), other specified managers (112,221), teaching (81,382), social and recreational workers (79,361), and registered nurses (70,675). The next leading growth occupations for blacks were found among writers, artists, entertainers, and athletes (49,410), officials and administrators, public administration (31,372), and engineers (23,856).

Rates of growth were usually most rapid in lines of work having smaller base black occupational representation. The most rapid rates of growth for blacks were found among managers and administrators, n.e.c. (340%), social scientists and urban planners (303%), computer systems analysts and scientists (164%), financial managers (142%), electrical engineering (106%), and administrators in public administration (105%). Robust growth did occur among social and recreational workers (90%), buyers and purchasing agents (89%), writers, artists, entertainers, and athletes (89%), educational administrators (86%), lawyers and judges (84%), registered nurses (75%), chemists (74%), civil engineers (62%), inspectors and compliance officers (59%), health diagnosing occupations (57%), and architects (50%). Growth was slower among teachers (38%), mathematical scientists (25%), and industrial engineers (20%). There were four occupations among this strata experiencing decreases of blacks—surveyors and mapping scientists (–65%), personnel, training and labor relations specialists (–66%), self-employed managers and administrators, n.e.c. (–27%), and salaried managers and administrators (–4%). Although the decreases among surveyors and mapping scientists and self-employed managers have continuities in the larger population, the losses among personnel, training, and labor relations specialists and salaried managers, n.e.c. are discontinuous with overall and white trends.

Among the technical, sales, and administrative support occupations, the largest scale increases occurred in cashiers (250,182), supervisors and proprietors, sales occupations (110,085), other sales occupations, retail and personal services (109,142), adjusters and investigators (81,630), secretaries (76,677), and mail and message distributing occupations (74,821). It is important to note that these occupations accounted for nearly four-fifths (or 78.9%) of all black increases in technical, sales, and administrative support occupations. Within the total U.S. population, increases in these same categories accounted for 87.4 percent of all increases suggesting that black growth was in fact slower. The next leading growth occupations for blacks include sales representatives for finance and business services (55,445), administrative support occupations (52,833), data-entry keyers (52,390), other health technologists and technicians (51,835), other information clerks (48,431), other technicians (35,170), receptionists (32,827), stock and inventory clerks (30,453), and bookkeepers, accounting, and auditing clerks (29,539).

Decade rates of growth were very rapid in these occupations: other health technologists and technicians (442%), salaried supervisors and proprietors, sales occupations (278%), other administrative support occupations (235%), airline pilots and navigators (191%), adjusters and investigators (147%), other technicians (126%), other information clerks (125%), and computer programmers (124%). It is significant that within each of the aforementioned occupational categories, black participation at least doubled. Recent movement and expansion was particularly robust among sales representatives, commodities (94%), computer equipment operators (92%), industrial and mechanical engineering technicians (90%), data-entry keyers (85%), electrical and electronic technicians (83%), receptionists (80%), and other sales occupations (66%). Conversely, the slowest occupational growth for blacks occurred among licensed practical nurses (4%) file clerks (6.7%), telephone operators (6.5%), stenographers and typists (5.6%), and other records processing occupations. Decreases occurred among other engineering and science technicians (–35.8%), self-employed supervisors and proprietors (–17.7%), and sales related occupations (–16.4%). Within the overall and white population these latter occupations registered decade decreases.

Gender Differentials in Black Middle Class Occupational Changes

To what extent are decade occupational changes among blacks continuous or discontinuous with overall trends when disaggregated by gender? Are the macroeconomic changes in the economy during the 1980s that are preliminarily reflected in black entry, growth, and mobility across these occupations suggestive of increased integration or has the recent black movement been more illustrative of segregation by race and gender? For purposes of this discussion, black changes in these same middle class occupations are examined separately for men and women (see table 3).

Decade changes show black men experiencing relatively more stability than mobility in status. When percentage increases in the national work force are examined, blacks did experience important increases among other specified managers (4.7%), social scientists and urban planners (2.7%), public administrators (2.3%), operations and systems researchers and analysts (2.0%), and as inspectors and compliance officers (2.0%). Black men increased at least 1 percent of the labor force during the 1980s in these occupations: financial managers, other specified managers, accountants and auditors, buyers and purchasing agents, and chemists. At the same time, a majority of these executive, administrative, managerial, and professional occupations were characterized by slow to stationary growth. Contractions in the larger work force were reflected in net losses for black men employed as personnel, training, and labor relations specialists, surveying and mapping specialists, other natural scientists, registered nurses, and social and recreational workers. The latter occupational category, one of the traditional professional specialties among blacks, experienced the strongest absolute losses for black men.

Black men employed in technical, sales, and administrative support occupations experienced similar patterns. The greatest percentage growth was found in nontraditional areas such as secretarial, filing clerks, and payroll and timekeeping clerks, where black men make up a small numeric part of the work force. In marketing and sales occupations, only cashiers and sales occupations relating to retail

Table 3. Percent Black Men in Middle Class Occupations, 1980–1990

	1980	1990	Change
Executive, Administrative, Managerial			
Officials & administrators, pub. adm.	6.9	9.2	2.3
Financial Managers	2.4	3.6	1.2
Managers, marketing, advertising, & public relations	1.6	2.5	0.9
Administrators, education & related	8.3	9.1	0.8
Managers, medicine and health	6.0	10.7	4.7
Other Specified Managers	5.7	7.0	1.3
Managers and administrators, n.e.c.			
Salaried	3.2	3.3	0.1
Self-employed	2.9	3.1	0.2
Management related occupations			
Accountants and auditors	3.6	5.0	1.4
Personnel, training, & labor relations specialists	8.8	3.7	−5.1
Buyers and purchasing agents	2.9	4.2	1.3
Inspectors and Compliance Officers	6.6	8.6	2.0
Other management related	3.5	8.1	4.6
Professional Specialty Occupations			
Engineers, architects, and surveyors			
Architects	2.7	2.8	0.1
Engineers			
Civil Engineers	2.4	2.9	0.5
Electrical and electronic engineers	2.6	3.6	1.0
Industrial engineers	2.5	3.2	0.7
Mechanical engineers	2.2	2.6	0.4
Other engineers	2.1	2.9	0.8
Surveyors and mapping scientists	2.2	1.7	−0.5
Computer systems analysts & scientists	3.8	4.2	0.4
Operations and systems researchers and analysts	4.2	6.2	2.0
Mathematical scientists	3.7	3.8	0.1
Natural scientists			
Chemists, except biochemists	4.4	5.5	1.1
Other natural scientists	2.5	2.5	0.0
Health diagnosing occupations	2.4	2.6	0.2
Health assessment & treating			
Registered nurses	10.3	9.7	−0.6
Other health assessment & treating	6.3	7.0	0.7
Teachers, except postsecondary	6.9	7.8	0.9
Social scientists & urban planners	2.6	5.3	2.7
Social & recreational workers	16.5	11.5	−5.0
Lawyers and judges	2.3	2.6	0.3
Writers, artists, entertainers, and athletes	4.6	5.5	0.9
Other professional specialty	5.6	6.4	0.8

Sources: U.S. Bureau of Census, 1980 Census of Population, U.S. Summary (Occupations by Industry), table 1; 1990 Census of Population (Supplementary Reports) CP-S-1-1, table 1.

Table 3. (cont.) Percent Black Men in Middle Class Occupations, 1980–1990

	1980	1990	Change
Technicians & Related Support Occupations			
Health technologists and technicians			
Licensed practical nurses	19.6	20.5	0.9
Other health technologists/technicians	11.7	6.3	−5.4
Engineering & science technicians			
Electrical & electronic technicians	5.3	6.4	1.1
Industrial & mechanical engineering	4.4	4.4	0.0
Drafting & surveying technicians	4.3	4.2	−0.1
Other engineering & science	5.2	6.1	0.9
Technicians, except health, engineering, and science			
Airplane pilots and navigators	0.8	1.5	0.7
Air traffic controllers and broadcast			
equipment operators	5.6	8.8	3.2
Computer programmers	4.5	4.6	0.1
Other technicians, except h.e. & s.	5.6	7.1	1.5
Sales Occupations			
Supervisors and proprietors, sales			
Salaried	3.3	4.1	0.8
Self-employed	2.9	2.4	−0.5
Sales representatives, finance and business services	3.0	3.9	0.9
Sales representatives, commodities except retail	2.1	2.5	0.4
Sales workers, retail & personal services			
Cashiers	9.6	11.6	2.0
Other sales occupations	4.5	6.1	1.6
Sales related occupations	3.4	3.0	−0.4
Administrative Support Occupations			
Supervisors, administrative support	8.3	11.4	3.1
Computer equipment operators	11.4	12.9	1.5
Secretaries, stenographers, typists			
Secretaries	8.4	12.5	4.1
Stenographers and typists	14.9	16.5	1.6
Receptionists	13.6	13.9	0.3
Other information clerks	10.1	11.3	1.2
File clerks	15.4	19.9	4.5
Other records processing except financial	10.7	13.2	2.5
Bookkeepers, accounting, & auditing	6.5	9.2	2.7
Payroll & timekeeping clerks	8.5	11.6	3.1
Other financial records processing	7.9	9.2	1.3
Telephone operators	14.4	17.0	2.6
Mail and message distributing	16.3	19.2	2.9
Production coordinators & expediters	7.4	8.2	0.8
Traffic shipping & receiving clerks	13.8	14.6	0.8
Stock & inventory clerks	12.3	14.5	2.2
Other material recording, scheduling	10.0	10.8	0.8
Adjusters and investigators	6.9	9.5	2.6
Data-entry keyers	15.6	16.3	0.7
Other administrative support	11.9	4.9	−7.0

Table 3. (cont.) Percent Black Women in Middle Class Occupations, 1980–1990

	1980	1990	Change
Executive, Administrative, Managerial			
Officials & administrators, pub. adm.	11.5	15.6	4.1
Finanacial Managers	4.6	6.1	1.5
Managers, marketing, advertising, & public relations	3.4	7.0	3.6
Administrators, education & related	13.0	12.4	−0.6
Managers, medicine and health	10.0	11.0	1.0
Other Specified Managers	6.7	8.3	1.7
Managers and administrators, n.e.c.			
Salaried	8.5	5.7	−2.8
Self–employed	3.0	2.6	−0.4
Management related occupations			
Accountants and auditors	7.9	8.2	0.3
Personnel, training, & labor relations specialists	13.0	9.3	−3.7
Buyers and purchasing agents	5.1	6.3	1.2
Inspectors and Compliance Officers	17.1	20.8	3.7
Other management related	6.8	9.6	2.8
Professional Specialty Occupations			
Engineers, architects, and surveyors			
Architects	3.2	2.6	−0.6
Engineers			
Civil Engineers	5.8	5.9	0.1
Electrical and electronic engineers	9.0	9.2	0.2
Industrial engineers	5.5	6.7	1.2
Mechanical engineers	7.5	5.5	−2.0
Other engineers	6.3	6.3	0.0
Surveyors and mapping scientists	4.0	6.2	2.2
Computer systems analysts & scientists	7.6	7.8	0.2
Operations and systems researchers and analysts	10.7	10.4	−0.3
Mathematical scientists	10.0	9.6	−0.4
Natural scientists			
Chemists, except biochemists	7.1	7.6	0.5
Other natural scientists	5.8	5.0	−0.8
Health diagnosing occupations	5.3	5.5	0.2
Health assessment & treating occupations			
Registered nurses	7.4	8.7	1.3
Other health assessment & treating	10.4	8.6	−1.8
Teachers, except postsecondary	10.8	10.2	−0.6
Social scientists & urban planners	2.5	6.1	3.6
Social & recreational workers	19.5	17.8	−1.7
Lawyers and judges	6.4	6.2	−0.2
Writers, artists, entertainers, and athletes	3.7	4.5	0.8
Other professional specialty	9.2	8.6	−0.6

Sources: U.S. Bureau of Census, 1980 Census of Population, U.S. Summary (Occupations by Industry), table 1; 1990 Census of Population (Supplementary Reports) CP-S-1-1, table 1.

Table 3. (cont.) Percent Black Women in Middle Class Occupations, 1980–1990

	1980	1990	Change
Technicians & Related Support Occupations			
Health technologists and technicians			
Licensed practical nurses	17.9	18.3	0.4
Other health technologists/technicians	10.0	9.8	−0.2
Engineering & science technicians			
Electrical & electronic technicians	12.1	12.6	0.5
Industrial & mechanical engineering	7.1	9.4	2.3
Drafting & surveying technicians	5.1	5.5	0.4
Other engineering & science	9.3	10.9	1.6
Technicians, except health, engineering, and science			
Airplane pilots and navigators	2.6	7.5	4.9
Air traffic controllers and broadcast			
equipment operators	8.9	14.5	5.6
Computer programmers	8.0	8.6	0.6
Other technicians, except h.e. & s.	8.7	9.1	0.4
Sales Occupations			
Supervisors and proprietors, sales			
Salaried	4.4	6.6	2.2
Self-employed	2.9	2.5	−0.4
Sales representatives, finance and business services	3.8	5.6	1.8
Sales representatives, commodities except retail	4.3	4.4	0.1
Sales workers, retail & personal services			
Cashiers	9.2	15.1	5.9
Other sales occupations	5.2	7.5	2.3
Sales related occupations	3.8	4.9	1.1
Administrative Support Occupations			
Supervisors, administrative support	10.3	12.6	2.3
Computer equipment operators	11.8	14.1	2.3
Secretaries, stenographers, typists			
Secretaries	5.6	7.3	1.7
Stenographers and typists	14.7	16.4	1.7
Receptionists	7.6	8.7	1.1
Other information clerks	10.3	11.6	1.3
File clerks	17.1	18.2	1.1
Other records processing except financial	11.3	13.7	2.4
Bookkeepers, accounting, & auditing	4.0	5.2	1.2
Payroll & timekeeping clerks	8.0	9.2	1.2
Other financial records processing	8.9	10.3	1.4
Telephone operators	14.3	19.4	5.1
Mail and message distributing	22.3	23.5	1.2
Production coordinators & expediters	10.3	9.9	−0.4
Traffic shipping & receiving clerks	10.7	11.1	0.4
Stock & inventory clerks	11.6	13.0	1.4
Other material recording, scheduling	12.7	13.1	0.4
Adjusters and investigators	13.1	13.0	0.1
Data-entry keyers	16.3	18.1	1.8
Other administrative support	11.6	8.7	−2.9

and personal services experienced increases greater than 1 percent; all others were less than 1 percent. Within the technologists and technicians ranks, only in the fields of air traffic controllers and broadcast operators (3.2 % increase), other technicians except h.e. & s. (1.5% increase) and electrical and electronic technicians (1.1 % increase) did employment improve at least 1 percent.

Black women experienced the greatest percentage increases nationally in the female work force as official and administrators, public administration (4.1%), inspectors and compliance officers (3.7%), managers, marketing and advertising (3.6%), social scientists and urban planners (3.6%), other management related (2.8%), surveyors and mapping scientists (2.2%), other specified managers (1.7%), industrial engineering (1.2%), buyers and purchasing agents (1.2%), and managers in medicine and health (1.0%). Still, the 1980s were particularly characterized by uneven growth and decline for black women. Growth occupations for black women in the upper middle class strata were primarily in administrative areas of public administration, marketing and advertising, public relations, inspectors and compliance officers, and secondarily in specific professions such as mechanical engineering and as social scientists and urban planners. It is instructive that while experiencing absolute increases in most professional specialty occupations, black women still experience the highest occupational segregation.

At the same time, black women in the lower middle class strata experienced increases in administrative support occupations such as cashiers (5.9%), air traffic controllers/broadcast equipment operators (5.6%), telephone operators (5.1%), and airline pilots and navigators (4.9%). Decreases were found among other health technicians (–0.2%), self-employed supervisors (–0.4%), production coordinators and expeditors (–0.4%), and other administrative support (–2.9%).

Trends in Occupational Segregation

In an attempt to summarize the recent changes in middle class occupational distributions, indexes of occupational dissimilarity have been calculated. These indexes are frequently used as measures of the degree of occupational segregation between groups and are interpreted as the percentage of workers of either group that would have to change occupations to equalize the distributions. For purposes of analysis, occupational dissimilarity measures in this discussion focus on: 1) racial differences of same gender (black men and white men, black women and white women); 2) racial and gender differences (black men and white women, white men and black women); 3) gender differences of same race (black men and women, white men and women).

Farley and Allen examined overall trends in the indexes by race and sex between 1940 and 1980 using broad occupational categories (Farley and Allen, 1987; 264–265). These showed that occupational distributions converged most rapidly between black and white women. During this 40-year time span, racial differences between women decreased 45 points—from 63 to 18 and racial differences between men decreased 19 points—from 43 to 24. Other researchers such as Albelda note that while the period levels of occupational segregation have been highest between white men and black women, these decreases have also been greatest. He concludes that while improvements in occupational segregation by

Table 4. Indexes of Dissimilarity for Selected Middle Class Occupations by Race and Gender, 1980–1990

	1980	1990	Change
Executive, Managerial, Administrative, and Professional			
Black Men and White Men	23.8	22.6	−1.2
Black Women and White Women	16.3	13.9	−2.4
Black Men and White Women	36.6	37.2	+0.6
White Men and Black Women	60.1	53.2	−6.9
Black Men and Black Women	44.4	42.1	−2.3
White Men and White Women	48.2	47.1	−1.1
Technical, Sales, and Administrative Support (including Clerical)			
Black Men and White Men	29.9	21.3	−8.6
Black Women and White Women	22.4	17.0	−5.4
Black Men and White Women	46.4	31.8	−14.6
White Men and Black Women	59.4	46.1	−13.3
Black Men and Black Women	47.9	35.9	−12.0
White Men and White Women	54.9	38.9	−16.0

Sources of Raw Data: U.S. Bureau of Census, 1980 Census of Population, U.S. Summary (Occupations by Industry), table 1; 1990 Census of Population (Supplementary Reports) CP-S-1-1, table 1.

race have been substantial, changes in occupational segregation by gender have been small. The Farley and Allen and Albelda studies examined occupational segregation through 1980 and 1981 respectively.

These data confirm earlier findings showing the greatest movement and largest decreases of occupational segregation in the strata of technical, sales, and administrative support occupations (see table 4). In 1980, occupational segregation was greatest between white men and black women (59.4) followed by white men and women (54.9), black men and women (47.9), black men and white women (46.4), black and white men (29.9), and black and white women (22.4). Unlike earlier decades, decreases in gender segregation during the 1980s between white men and women (−16) exceeded segregation decreases between black men and white women (−14.6), white men and black women (−13.3), and black men and women (−12). Similar to earlier, decreases in occupational segregation between black and white men (−8.6) and black and white women (−5.4) changed more slowly. The findings suggest the salience of race and gender interaction in very dynamic economic activities.

Changes in segregation were slower, smaller, and stable in the upper middle-class executive, managerial, administrative, and professional specialty occupations. In 1980, occupational segregation was greatest between white men and black women (60.1) followed by white men and women (48.2), black men and women (44.4), black men and white women (36.6), black and white men (23.8), and black and white women (16.3). Between 1980 and 1990, the greatest movement occurred in work situations between white men and black women (−6.9). Small decreases between black and white women (−2.4) and black men and women (−2.3) were comparable as were decreases between black and white men (−1.2) and white men and women (−1.1). However, occupational segregation between black men and white women (+0.6) showed the most stability. This latter pattern of persistent occupational segregation runs counter to the other comparisons. Despite black women's changes, they continue to be most segregated from white men and black men in these occupations.

Implications and Summary

How can the decade changes and differentials in black employment growth in middle class occupations be explained? What are the salient relationships between the changing status of blacks in the middle class and larger changes in the U.S. economy and division of labor? From a macrosociological perspective, these recent changes are interconnected with the restructuring of the American economy from industrial to service activities, the modernization of work involving increased use of high-tech, automation, and information, and a "new federalism" role of the state in civil rights and affirmative action interventions. It is important to underscore that the growth of blacks in these selected middle class occupations occurred in an economic context where the relative distribution of income by race for upper-, middle-, and other income blacks fell behind. The growth of the black middle class during the 1980s, with decreasing shares of income, is relatedly suggestive of a precarious status characterized by this class's lower investments and savings and higher underemployment and unemployment. During the 1980s, the growth of blacks in middle class occupations occurred in an economic context of decreased income, savings, and capital investment and increased underemployment and unemployment.

Dynamics of black middle class growth were not uniform and should be viewed in both intragroup and intergroup contexts. Blacks employed in these occupations increased from 39.6 (1980) to 44.9 (1990) and their rate of growth (64.9%) exceeded the overall rate of growth for all blacks employed in the economy (37.5%). In absolute terms, black persons experienced largest employment increases in occupations such as cashiers, management-related occupations, other specified managers, sales supervisors and proprietors, retail and personal services, adjusters and investigators, teaching, social and recreation workers, secretaries, mail and message distribution workers, and registered nurses. In relative terms, rates of growth were particularly rapid among salaried supervisors and proprietors, airline pilots and navigators, computer systems analysts and scientists, adjusters and investigators, financial managers, other technicians, other information clerks, computer programmers, electrical engineers, administrators in public administration, sales representatives in commodities, computer equipment operators, social and recreational workers, industrial and mechanical engineering technicians, buyers and purchasing agents, writers, artists, and entertainers, educational administrators, and data keyers. Slow growth occurred among licensed practical nurses, stenographers and typists, telephone operators, other records processing occupations, and mechanical engineers. Although blacks experienced increases in most of the middle class occupations examined, decreasing employment opportunities were found in occupations such as surveyors and mapping specialists, unclassified self-employed managers and administrators, engineering and science technicians, self-employed supervisors and proprietors, and sales related occupations.

Gender patterns show that black men grew slowly in a majority of the upper-middle executive, administrative, managerial, and professional occupations and the lower-middle class technical, sales, and administrative support occupations.

Rapidly growing employment for black men occurred among operations and systems researchers and analysts, unclassified managers, managers in health and medicine, social scientists and urban planners, computer systems analysts and scientists, airplane pilots and navigators, supervisors and proprietors, cashiers, data entry keyers, and nontraditional clerical and administrative support occupations. Black women experienced greatest movement in administrative areas of public administration, marketing and advertising, public relations, inspectors and compliance officers, and professions such as social scientists and urban planners and mechanical engineers. Within the technical, sales, and administrative support occupations, black women grew most as cashiers, secretaries, supervisors of administrative support occupations, salaried sales supervisors, and as adjusters and investigators. Overall, these distributional changes are reflected in improvements in occupational segregation which show the greatest mobility and desegregation in the strata of administrative support, sales, and technical occupations with slower and smaller decreases of occupational segregation in the upper-middle class executive, managerial, administrative, and professional occupations. While black women experienced greater gains than black men across both strata of the middle class, their continued segregation from the higher paying occupations through 1990 remains greater than black men, white men, and white women. Black men's occupational movement continued in the lower middle class strata but appears to be slowing in the upper middle class.

This paper provides findings which inform the hypotheses and claims of both the integrationist and segmentation perspectives of the changing black middle class. The complex patterns and trends identified underscore the importance of examining the role of each perspective, their complementarity, and value added insights in understanding this phenomenon. At the same time, there are other points where the integrationist and segmentation perspectives offer contradictory insights of the dynamics bearing on the contemporary structure of the American economy and the future of the black middle class.

Continued growth of blacks in the middle class and the increased desegregation of blacks across these broad occupational strata are partly suggestive of progress themes in integration perspectives. Distributional changes across most of the individual occupational listings indicate that black middle class entry and movement have been steady. Continuous with earlier post-World War II decades, the quantitative growth of economic activities has been also characterized by qualitative changes of increased diversity and dispersion of the black middle class. Within the strata of upper middle class occupations, increases of blacks in "middle-level" management-related and administrative activities surpassed traditional professions such as teaching, social and recreational work, and nursing. Among sales occupations, the emergence of a large cohort of black salaried supervisors and proprietors is symbolic of the promises of capital development. Rapid growth areas of the post-industrial economy such as services, high tech, medicine/health, marketing/sales, real estate, and information are reflected and reproduced in dynamics of the black middle class. More so than earlier, these occupations are structurally connected to the private sector.

Contextualization and careful analysis of the changing relationships among the economy, occupations, and income suggest that the growth of the black middle class was generally reproduced in slow and uneven movements broadly characterized by persistent racial segmentation. This more sober assessment recognizes that while the occupations supportive of the black middle class continued to grow nationally, the economic activities accounting for this phenomenon were primarily within lower-middle class administrative support occupations such as adjusters and investigators, secretaries, mail and message distribution, and computer equipment operators and sales occupations such as cashiers, salaried supervisors/proprietors, and sales representatives. Within the upper-middle class executive, administrative, and managerial occupations it is significant that black growth was largest in activities involving public employment and quasi-public services—accountants, auditors, public administration, educational administration, inspectors and compliance officers, and health managers. These same governmental relationships bear on the high growth professional occupations of teaching, social and recreational work, and registered nurses. Outside of activities with these state relationships, improvements for blacks in these upper-middle class occupations, with a few exceptions, appear slow and incremental.

Other contemporary developments suggest further caution. First, accompanying the recent recessions since 1990, there are signs that blacks in many of the sales and administrative support occupations are being disproportionately affected by central city retailing closings and administrative reductions in force (Sharpe, 1993). Second, racially segmented occupations such as practical nursing, mail and message distributing, telephone operators, typists/stenographers, social and recreational work, and others where blacks have gained niches are potentially vulnerable at a time of increased deregulation, privatization, automation, and deracialization. Third, while the role of affirmative action and minority set-aside programs have continued for blacks, the momentum has slowed and reversed. In a zero-sum economy, the distributional benefits of these policies are increasingly competitive and are being shared by other important minority groups such as Hispanic- and Asian-Americans and white women. Fourth, to the extent that changing income inequality indicators continue to show the relative size of the larger middle class in the U.S. as decreasing (Duncan, Smeeding, and Rodgers, 1992; Thurow, 1987), the implications for a growing black middle class are problematic. In particular, the challenges of continued recruitment, employment, and promotion facing highly educated, talented, and trained black men in higher-paying administrative, professional, and technical activities and the persistent occupational segregation and lower pay of black women in the aforementioned activities are suggested. Although the movement of blacks into middle class occupations continued during the 1980s, this was not the rising tide depicted in "progress" assessments.

References

Albelda, Randy. (1986). "Occupational Segregation by Race and Gender, 1970–81." *Industrial and Labor Relations Review*, Vol. 39, No. 3: 404–411.

Benjamin, Lois (1991). *The Black Elite: Facing the Color Line in the Twilight of the Twentieth Century*. Chicago: Nelson Hall.

Blackwell, James (1987). *Mainstreaming Outsiders: The Production of Black Professionals*. Dix Hills, NY: General Hall.

Blau, Peter M. and Otis Dudley Duncan (1967). *The American Occupational Structure*. New York: John Wiley.

Braddock, Jomills H., II and James McPartland (1987). "How Minorities Continue to Be Excluded from Equal Employment Opportunities: Research on Labor Market and Institutional Barriers." *Journal of Social Issues*, Vol. 43: 5–39.

Collins, Sharon (1983). "The Making of the Black Middle Class." *Social Problems*, Vol. 30: 369–382.

———. (1989). "The Marginalization of Black Executives." *Social Problems*, Vol. 36: 317–331.

Darity, William, Jr. (1990). "Race and Inequality in the Managerial Age," pp. 29–82 in Wornie L. Reed (ed.). *Assessment of the Status of African-Americans: Social, Political, and Economic Issues in Black America*, Vol. IV. Boston: The William Monroe Trotter Institute, University of Massachusetts, Boston.

Duncan, Gregory, Timothy M. Smeeding, and Willard Rodgers (1992). "The Incredible Shrinking Middle Class." *American Demographics*, May, pp. 34–38.

Farley, Reynolds and Walter Allen (1987). *The Color Line and The Quality of Life in America*. New York: Russell Sage Foundation.

Feagin, Joe R. (1976). "The Continuing Significance of race: Antiblack Discrimination in Public Places." *American Sociological Review*, Vol. 56, No. 1, February, pp. 101–116.

Featherman, David and Robert Hauser (1976). "Changes in the Socio-Economic Stratification of the Races, 1962–1973." *American Journal of Sociology*, Vol. 82, November, pp. 621–649.

———. (1978). *Opportunity and Change*. New York: Academic Pres.

Frazier, E. Franklin (1957). *The Black Bourgeoisie: The Rise of A New Middle Class in the United States*. New York: The Free Press.

Freeman, Richard (1976). *Black Elite: The New Market for Highly Educated Black Americans*. New York: McGraw Hill.

Hill, Robert (1987). "The Black Middle Class: Past, Present and Future," pp. 43–64 in *The State of Black America*. Washington, DC: National Urban League.

International Labor Office. (1988). International Standard Classification of Occupations, ISCO-88. Geneva, Switzerland: International Labor Office.

Jaynes, Gerald and Robin Williams, Jr. (1989). *A Common Destiny: Blacks and American Society*. Washington, DC: National Academy Press.

Jones, Edward (1986). "Black Managers: The Dream Deferred." *Harvard Business Review*, May/June, pp. 84–93.

Kasarda, John D. (1985). "Urban Change and Minority Opportunities," in Paul Peterson (ed.). *The New Urban Reality*. Washington, DC: Brookings Institute.

———. (1988). "Jobs, Migration, and Emerging Urban Mismatches," in Michael G.H. McGeary and Laurence E. Lynn (eds.). *Urban Change and Poverty*. Washington, DC: National Academy Press.

Kilson, Martin (1983). "The Black Bourgeoisie Revisited: From E. Franklin Frazier to the Present." *Dissent*, Winter, pp. 85–96.

Landry, Bart (1987). *The New Black Middle Class*. Berkeley: University of California Press.

Myrdal, Gunnar (1944). *An American Dilemma: The Negro Problem and American Democracy*. New York: Random House.

Pinkney, Alphonso (1984). *The Myth of Black Progress*. New York: Cambridge University Press.

Piven, Frances Fox and Richard Cloward. *Regulating the Poor: The Functions of Public Welfare*. New York: Vintage Books, 1972.

Sharpe, Rochelle (1993). "In the latest recession only blacks suffered net employment loss." *Wall Street Journal*, September 14, pp. A1 and A12.

Shryock, Henry and Jacob Siegel (1975). *The Methods and Materials of Demography*. Washington, DC: U.S. Government Printing Office.

Thurow, Lester (1987). "A Surge in Inequality." *Scientific American*, May, Vol. 256, No. 5: 30–37.

U.S. Bureau of Census (1978). *The Social and Economic Status of the Black Population in the United States: An Historical View, 1790–1978.* Current Population Reports, Series P-23, No. 8. Washington, DC: U.S. Government Printing Office.

———. (1980). *Census of Population. U.S. Summary. Occupations by Industry.* Washington, DC: U.S. Government Printing Office.

———. (1992). *Census of Population* (Supplementary Reports). Detailed Occupation and Other Characteristics From the EEO File for the United States. 1990 CP-S-1-1. Washington, DC: U.S. Government Printing Office.

———. (1992). *Current Population Reports, Series P-60, Money Income of Households, Families, and Persons in the United States: 1991.* Washington, DC: Washington, DC U.S. Government Printing Office.

———. (1993). *Current Population Reports, Series P60–185, Poverty in the United States: 1992.* Washington, DC: U.S. Government Printing Office.

U.S. Department of Commerce, Office of Federal Statistical Policy and Standards (1980). *Standard Occupational Classification Manual.* Washington, DC: U.S. Government Printing Ofice.

Wattenberg, Ben and Michael Scammon (1973). "Black Progress and Liberal Rhetoric." *Commentary,* Vol. 55: 35–44.

Willie, Charles V. (1991). "The Inclining Significance of Race," pp. 10–21 in Charles V. Willie (ed.). *Caste and Class Controversy on Race and Poverty.* Dix Hills, NY: General Hall.

Wilson, Franklin, Tienda, Marta, and Lawrence Wu (1993). "Racial Equality in the Labor Market: Still An Elusive Goal?" Paper presented at the Annual Meeting of the American Sociological Association.

Wilson, William Julius (1978). *The Declining Significance of Race: Blacks and Changing American Institutions.* Chicago: University of Chicago Press.

———. (1979). "The Declining Significance of Race: Myth or Reality?" in Joseph Washington (ed.). *The Declining Significance of Race: A Dialogue Among White and Black Social Scientists.* Philadelphia: Center for Afro-American Studies, University of Pennsylvania.

———. (1987). *The Truly Disadvantaged: The Inner City, the Underclass, and Public Policy.* Chicago: University of Chicago Press.

13

Music Making History: Africa Meets Europe in the United States of the Blues

William L. Benzon

> After emancipation...all those people who had been slaves, they needed the music more than ever now; it was like they were trying to find out in this music what they were supposed to do with this freedom: playing the music and listening to it—waiting for it to express what they needed to learn, once they had learned it wasn't just white people the music had to reach to, nor even to their own people, but straight out to life and to what a man does with his life when it finally is his.
> —Sidney Bechet, *Treat It Gentle*

> I went to the depot and set my suitcase down
> The blues overtake me and tears come rolling down
> —Blind Lemon Jefferson, *Easy Rider Blues*

> When I am elected President of the United States, my first executive order will be to change the name of the White House! To the Blues House.
> —Dizzy Gillespie, 1964 presidential campaign

Introduction: Music in Society and Culture

The cultural character of the United States of America has been dominated by two interacting cultural systems.[1] One of these derives from Europe and the other

---

1. This essay is a revision of "The United States of the Blues: On the Crossing of African and European Cultures in the 20th Century," *Journal of Social and Evolutionary Systems* 16 (4): 401–438, 1993, and is adapted/reprinted with the permission of the copyright holder.

One of the difficulties of writing this piece is that I have had to refer to African and European Americans as though there were clearly distinct and more or less internally homogeneous groups. In fact, of course, the boundaries are not clear and there are significant regional, class and ethnic differences within these two broad groups. Still, so much about American society and culture has depended on the destructive fiction that black is black and white is white that I have reasonable confidence that the my argument can serve as a useful

189

from Africa. The European system dominates in matters of intellectual and scientific culture and, despite the birth of modern democracy in the American Revolution, I think we need to concede the point in political matters as well. The United States may well be the first modern democratic state, but that democracy, and the state apparatus, has deep roots in Europe.

When we turn to expressive culture, matters are quite different. In some expressive domains, literature, architecture, and perhaps even painting, the European influences have dominated through most of American history. But in other domains the cultures of sub-Saharan Africa have had a profound, even a determining, influence. Sport is one such arena (Ashe, 1988; cf. Early, 1989, pp. 115–195, 208–214). Religion is another. With its dramatic conversions, speaking in tongues, vigorous song, and theatrical preaching, the fundamentalist strain of American religion took the impress of African America almost two centuries ago (cf. Bloom, 1992, pp. 48, 238; Philips, 1990, p. 231; Small, 1987, pp. 88 ff.; Williamson, 1984, p. 38). Throughout the nineteenth century, minstrel shows were a major form of popular entertainment and carried the African influence in comedy, song, and dance (Chase, 1966, pp. 259–300; Crouch, 1976; Handy, 1941; Southern, 1983, 228 ff.; Watkins, 1994). This influence came to full force in American popular music of the twentieth century, where the African-American element drives the train. Whether or not that influence has been so profound that we should remove the United States from the honor roll of Western nations is not clear to me, though I think it a reasonable possibility.

This New World dialog between Africa and Europe has not, of course, been an equal opportunity affirmative action interaction. Throughout American history white racism and domination have undermined the egalitarian and democratic ideals which have otherwise been so important in the nation's history. Thus the determinative effect which African America has exercised in expressive culture has been against the grain of political and economic power. That raises a question: How and why is it that a racist European America has allowed African America such cultural power? This is as deep and important as any question one can pose about society and culture in the United States of America (cf. Morrison, 1992).

To begin our exploration we need to make a clarification prompted by the current movement for multicultural education, a major purpose of which is to combat racism by fostering respect for diverse cultures. That purpose rests on a weak premise, for the most vicious racism is not primarily about culture. Such racism is, in Elisabeth Young-Bruehl's (1996) terminology, an ideology of desire; it is an active psychosocial formation whereby the racist attempts to alleviate his or her own psychological conflicts by hating and dominating members of another social group. The fact that members of the hated group may eat different foods, wear different clothes, sing different songs, dance different dances, and worship different gods is, at best, a secondary aspect of prejudice; such things give the racist something to hide behind when justifying his or her actions and attitudes, but they aren't what motivates the racism. We need to be clear on this matter for we are going to be investigating both cultural interaction and racism. What interests

reference point for studies which incorporate a realistic demographic diversity. I should also note that I do not assume that all white folks are racist, or that black folks automatically acquire some mysterious moral virtue because they have been racially oppressed.

me is how a certain social and psychosocial phenomenon, racism, has resulted in a certain multicultural process: European Americans learning to make music and to dance like African Americans.

I also wish to make a point about the fundamental importance of rhythm and music in human life. Recent work on expressive culture by David Hays (1992, pp. 189–190, 196–197) and on dance and military drill by William McNeill (1995) suggests that muscular bonding, to use McNeill's term, is essential to human society. By muscular bonding McNeill means a sense of community and solidarity created by moving together in groups, groups which dance together or engage in military drill together. If Hays and McNeill are on the right track, and I am assuming they are, then music and dance are not secondary matters, subordinate to speaking, writing and calculation in cultural importance. On the contrary, they are the necessary foundation of social cohesion and health; they have causal force in society and can foster social change. Thus the African American achievement in those arenas is as important as any cultural achievement by any group, anywhere, at any time. The fact that so many European Americans have adopted and adapted African-American dance and music for their own is a social and cultural phenomenon of the highest importance.

Nor is this phenomenon limited to North America, for African-American music has by now influenced culture all over the world. As Eldridge Cleaver observed almost three decades ago in *Soul on Ice* (1968, p. 203):

> And although modern science and technology are the same whether in New York, Paris, London, Accra, Cairo, Berlin, Moscow, Tokyo, Peking, or Sao Paulo, jazz is the only true international medium of communication current in the world today, capable of speaking creatively, with equal intensity and relevance, to the people in all those places.

Since then soul and rock and hip-hop have made the world tour as well. People the world over have adopted and adapted African-American expressive practice to suit their own needs.

Improvisation and Composition in Cultural Style

In her seminal study *Patterns of Culture*, Ruth Benedict (1934) argued that each culture exhibits a pattern by which its various customs, beliefs, and attitudes are integrated. Cultures are not miscellaneous grab-bags of traits, they are patterned wholes. European and African America do have cultural differences. My purpose in this section is to explore those differences through examining music. However, in the time-honored manner of those who infer the existence of fire from observations of smoke I assume those music differences reflect differences in the structures and processes in the societies which produce the music (see Small, 1987).

My thinking on this topic begins in my experience as a musician who has performed both in European styles, symphony orchestra, concert band, brass band, and African-derived styles, jazz, rhythm and blues, world beat. It is obvious to me that these are two very different musical worlds. At times I am astounded as I attempt simultaneously to contemplate them both. It is a rich world indeed that is home to such musics. At the same time I wonder: if these musics are so differ-ent, what does that difference imply about the cultures from which these musics originate?

In one view, human nature is everywhere the same. Different cultures are just different "languages" for articulating and expressing that same nature. That is not my view. To be sure, the human biological heritage is much the same from group to group. But that biological heritage includes a nervous system which takes over two decades to develop (Benzon and Hays, 1988, pp. 314 ff.) and which is, especially during the early phases of that development, open to environ-mental influence. Nurture thus has plenty of opportunity to influence human na-ture. Because of that we must consider cultural differences to be intrinsic, not ex-trinsic. One does not "wear" a culture as easily and superficially as one wears a suit of clothes, nor can one move from one culture to another as easily as one moves from business to casual attire.

Expressive culture is essential to organizing the biological seeds of desire and feeling into a way of life (Geertz, 1973, pp. 80 ff.; Hays, 1992; Benzon, 1993a). Expressive differences reflect different ways of shaping actions to meet desire, of interpreting the feelings which accompany those actions and desires. Thus the dif-ferences between European and more-or-less European-derived music and African-influenced music betoken different cultural styles. To get a sense of those styles, let us begin by comparing the two musics.

Note that, while my argument is about the interaction of African-American and European-American music in general, I want to confine my discussion in this sec-tion to a comparison of jazz and classical music. I have two reasons for this: 1) There are many genres of both black and white music in the United States. Dis-cussing them all would be complex, but that complexity would not appreciably alter my central points of contrast.[2] 2) Jazz is the only form of African-American music which has developed to the same level of sophistication as classical music (see Benzon, 1993b). Classical music thus represents Western culture at its most so-phisticated while jazz represents an equally sophisticated African-derived culture.

Let us begin with feeling: Do the two musics provide cultural stylization for the same range of emotions? The most relevant work on emotion in music has been done by Manfred Clynes (1977) as part of a general investigation of emotional expression. Clynes has found basic temporal patterns, pulsations or rhythms, through which we express our feelings. He calls these patterns essentic forms. His investigations have involved people from both Western and non-Western societies and he has found the same patterns in all his subjects. This suggests that the es-sentic forms are biologically given and not cultural conventions. While the set of essentic forms seems to be open-ended, there are seven basic ones: love, grief, awe (or reverence), joy, anger, hate, and sex.

Although these essentic forms are biologically given, whether or not they are incorporated into music depends on the codes of a culture's stylization—to use the term favored by Albert Murray. A given culture isn't obligated to codify the full biological legacy of humankind; or, to give the matter a different spin, no cul-ture can work out all the possible ramifications of human biological possibility.

---

2. For an enumeration of the various genres of African-American music, see Berendt (1975, p. 5), Keil (1966, pp. 217–224), and Maultsby (1990, p. 186). For more recent gen-res, you can consult George (1988, 1992).

African America has included sexuality directly in the codes of its music while Europe (and European America) has done so only indirectly, unless, of course, following the example and tutelage of African America. To say that jazz is comfortable with sexuality is not, of course, to imply that it is obsessed with it. Jazz embraces a full range of emotional expression, with sexuality taking its place in that range. And, correlatively, to say that classical music cannot deal with sexuality is not to say that the essentic form for sexuality never appears in classical music, only that its appearance is not routine.

Now, in saying this, we must confront a problem, for sexuality is at the center of racist stereotyping. In talking of the sexual nature of jazz are we thus falling into a racist trap? No, and for two reasons. In the first place, the racist places a negative value on sexuality while I am implying either a neutral or a positive value (take your pick). More deeply, the racist thinks he is talking about biological nature; he is asserting that folks with dark brown skin, flat noses, and tightly curled black hair are hypersexual and out of control because it is in their blood. I am not making any assertions about "blood" (that is to say, about genetics); I am talking about culture. Certain folks have chosen to give public shared expression to sexuality by allowing sexually expressive rhythms in their music and dance. Getting these rhythms into that music and dance requires the kind of discipline and control which comes from patient and dedicated practice and has nothing to do with the wanton license running riot in the racist imagination. It is one of the paradoxes of expressive culture that the highest expression of such discipline comes in performance which is effortless and free. On this matter, however, jazz and classical music come out the same. Regardless of the differences between their emotional patterns, both require discipline and both come alive only in freedom and ease.

Thus we need not feel the anxiety of political correctness in asserting that the sexuality which is so very obvious in jazz—to both its devotees and its detractors—is not at all obvious in classical music. In saying this I should note that, while Clynes has investigated music, he has not, to my knowledge, done a comparative study of the appearance of the various essentic forms in various musics. Nor have I done so. Thus in talking about the presence of sexuality in jazz and its absence in classical music I am only giving my subjective estimate of what is going on in these musics. It is not, however, a wildly idiosyncratic estimate.

In discussing these matters with friends, some have lobbied strongly on behalf of the sensuousness of "Là ci darem" from Mozart's *Don Giovanni*, which is lovely music; but how common is this in classical music? I've recently become fond of a passage about a third of the way into the "Arietta" of Beethoven's C minor Sonata (No. 32, Op. 111) where, after anticipatory probing, the music breaks into marvelous waterfalls of jazzy descending right-hand figures ending in rocking chords which are met by rolling ascending left-hand figures.[3] When I played this passage for a friend, without telling him what he was listening to, he

---

3. It is worth noting that Beethoven notated these rhythms using time signatures he did not use in any other of his some thirty-odd piano sonatas, a fact which underlines how exceptional these rhythms are in classical music. The Arietta consists of a theme, five variations, and a coda. The theme and first variation are written in 9/16 time; the second variation is in 6/16, the third in 12/32, and the remaining variations and coda are in 9/16. The second and especially the third variations are the jazziest.

said it sounded like someone trying to bridge the gap between Mozart and Fats Waller. While classical critics are able to note the jazz affinity here, they are clearly uneasy. Thus Wilfrid Mellers in his study, *Beethoven and the Voice of God* (1983) notes that "the metre becomes a boogie rhythm, rendered seraphic. This is not a joke" (p. 259). Of course it is not a joke, but the fact that a distinguished critic feels impelled to talk like that is a sign of how atypical, and threatening, sexuality is in this music. Sexuality is there, but as an exception, not a common occurrence. Then we have the famous Liebestod from Wagner's *Tristan and Isolde*, which is very passionate, but it isn't overtly sexy; the sex is thoroughly sublimated, with no release, only exhaustion. No doubt there is much sublimated sex in the romantic composers, but there is a difference between getting it straight and getting it tricked out in disguise, no matter how fine the cloth, how even the stitching, how elegant the fit. With the twentieth century the finery is peeled away; Ravel's *Bolero* is notorious, as is Stravinsky's *Rite of Spring*. Here the sexuality is overt, but both are late in the evolution of classical music, at the end of its major development, and their eroticism did not become a standard practice. A bit closer to the bone, those Europeans who didn't have the time or opportunity to learn the sophisticated stylings of the classical masters didn't have even sublimated sex in their music. They had no sexual stylization at all. That is, there was no publicly affirmed sexuality. When the opportunity came, those who wanted it learned it from African Americans.

I don't think we are dealing with a simple matter of rejecting sexuality. It is a more pervasive rejection of the body. Consider:

> Even the greatest Western music, on the order of Bach and Mozart and Beethoven, was spiritual rather than physical. The mind-body split that defined Western culture was in its music as well. When you felt transported by Mozart or Brahms, it wasn't your body that was transported. The sensation often described is a body yearning to follow where its spirit has gone... The classical dance that grew from this music had a stiff, straight back and moved in almost geometrical lines. The folk dances of the West were also physically contained, with linear gestures. The feet might move with wonderful flurries and intricate precision, but the hips and spine were kept rigid. (Ventura, 1987b, p. 86)

> The liveliest dances of Beethoven's last quartets no longer incite the feet to dance. Instead, the "heart inside dances." Beethoven found a new way of uncoupling the motoric output from the expression of essentic form by allowing inner forms to dance without corresponding motor outputs.... In his music the meaning of essentic form appears no longer as a communication directed at motoric outward expression. (Clynes, 1977, p. 85)

Ventura, writing an account of the migration of musical techniques from West African ritual to contemporary rock and roll, makes a more sweeping statement than Clynes, but they move in a similar direction. Classical music is somehow decoupled from the body, while African-American music is not.

We can see a minor consequence of this attitudinal difference in the rhetoric of critical censure. In criticizing the performances of particularly expressive musicians, such as the late Leonard Bernstein or the contemporary violinist, Nadja Salerno-Sonnenberg, classical critics sometimes question the propriety of the body movements and facial expressions of the performer, implying that such movement is mere self-indulgent exhibitionism.[4] Whatever role a musician's body movement has in enabling in his or her expressiveness, it is not clear why comment on that physical style should enter into a critical assessment of the performance. Would the same music have been acceptable if it had been delivered of a musician stiff of spine and serene of face? It is one thing for opponents of a musical style to criticize the body language of its performers, as opponents of rock and roll castigated Elvis Presley for his peripatetic pelvis, but the critics of classical gestural gyration are friendly to the music. On the other hand, I have never read a jazz critic make similar remarks. Thus, for example, while many critics didn't like what the late Miles Davis played in his last two decades, none of them ever complained that he moved in an unseemly way (for an example see Crouch, 1990a). The physically expressive classical musician seems to violate that uncoupling of body from music which Clynes talks about. But, since jazz is comfortable with the body, comment on the performer's movements has never been part of the jazz critic's arsenal of opprobrium.

This rejection of the body, in turn, translates into a musical technique which relegates rhythmic complexity to a secondary, if not tertiary, role. Relative rhythmic simplicity may well have been a precondition of the harmonic development which has been so important in classical music, for that development requires a precise vertical alignment of different instrumental lines which would be difficult to achieve if each part were rhythmically complex (Rockwell, 1983, p. 51). This was a precondition consistent with the overall rejection of bodily experience which has marked Western culture. However, when jazz musicians confronted classical music, that harmonic language was fully developed and they had no difficulty adapting it to the rhythmic intricacies of bop. African America thus discovered the miracle of linking the harmony of the spheres to the rhythms of the body.

Important though the basic pulse and rhythm are, jazz and classical music differ in many other ways. This is not the place to attempt a full comparison.[5] But one other difference demands attention, that between improvising and compos-

---

4. Harold Schonberg (1967, p. 357) notes that Bernstein's podium choreography was a source of contention. In an interview with Tim Page (1992, pp. 124–125), Ms. Salerno-Sonnenberg expressed irritation at "the implication that I sat around with my publicity agent and decided to play the way I do to attract attention. Do they think this is a joke? . . . And I've tried to play the violin without any facial expressions. I did a whole concert last year . . . and I spent the whole time concentrating on keeping my face straight. And I heard a tape of the concert afterwards, and it sounded as if I'd gone to sleep."
Expressive body movement is intrinsic to African musical performance (Blacking, 1974, pp. 109–111, Wilson, 1990, p. 29) and certainly remains in African-American performance. Given that Bernstein liked both jazz and rock, and that Salerno-Sonnenberg went to a Philadelphia school where she was one of only two white girls (Epstein, 1987, p. 85), is it possible that these classical performers have assimilated a measure of African style?
5. The literature on jazz has many comparisons between jazz and classical music—and other musics as well. But I don't know that a full comparison has been assembled in one place. Schuller (1968, pp. 6–66) and Dankworth (1968, 3–45) provide useful summaries of jazz practice with respect to rhythm, melody, harmony, timbre, form, and improvisation; those are the things which need to be compared with classical practice. Andre Hodier's (1956, pp. 139–157) discussion of "Melody in Jazz" is the best place to start making the comparison explicit; other chapters in the same book are useful as well (chapters 3, 10, 12, and 14). Paul Berliner's (1994) *Thinking in Jazz* is the best account of jazz improvisation by far. Erich Neumann's (1986) study of improvisation in Mozart is a useful point of entry to the study of classical improvisational practice. My essay on "Stages in the Evolution of

ing. Though there were limited opportunities for improvisation in classical music, especially in the Baroque and early Classical eras (cf. Neumann, 1986), it had become a thoroughly notated music by the early nineteenth century. Improvisation has always been important to jazz, even in the carefully crafted arrangements of the big band era. With the evolution of bop-style jazz, improvisation reached new sophistication and complexity (Benzon, 1993b; Schuller, 1989, p. 845).

If you think of improvisation as composition on the fly, then it is difficult to see how it could compare favorably with the carefully worked and reworked compositions of classical composers. However, the notion of jazz improvisation as spontaneous creation out of nothing is a romantic myth, a kissing cousin to natural rhythm. What happens on the bandstand reflects hours and months and years of study, thought, and practice, with musicians working out several approaches to improvising on each and every tune they play (Berliner, 1994). Yet, in one important respect, classical music is arguably the more sophisticated music. Jazz has not been able to create the large-scale architectures that classical composers have—Collier (1987, pp. 145 ff.) and Schuller (1989, pp. 148–153) have discussed this question in relation to the extended works of Duke Ellington. However, composition and improvisation are but means to an expressive end; their particular devices are subordinate to that purpose. It is a mistake to judge one set of technical devices as though they were functioning in the manner of another and rather different set of devices. What is relevant is how effective these devices are in achieving their expressive end.

In this context, the end is what David Hays (1992) has called a reorganizational epiphany. When Leonard Bernstein (1993, p. 284) says "By the time I come to the end of Beethoven's Fifth, I'm a new man," he is talking about reorganization. Over time such experience helps lessen psychological conflict, bringing about greater and greater psychological coherence. Given that both bop jazz and classical music achieve this end, their different techniques for achieving it must reveal much about their respective cultural patternings.[6]

Music" (1993) sketches a general comparative framework for understanding levels of musical sophistication and situates both jazz and classical music in it.

6. I'm in no position to offer an explicit account of how bop jazz and classical music achieve epiphanies. But I am willing to offer some speculation which gets part of the way there. My speculation begins with the common observation that music is much like mathematics; you take a small number of well-chosen rules and procedures and use them to create elaborate and sophisticated structures. These rules and procedures belong to what David Hays has called gnomonic structure (1992, p. 199; cf. Benzon and Hays, 1988, pp. 308–312; Benzon, 1981, pp. 252–256). The gnomonic rules are not linked to time and space. When enacted, however, those rules can generate complex structures of episodes, and the episodes do unfold in time. The note by note sequence of a performance is enacted by episodic structures.

To understand a performance in its totality you need mentally to recreate the particular gnomonic rules and procedures which generated that performance (cf. Hays, 1992; Benzon, 1993b). To understand what is going on note by note, moment by moment, you need to empathetically enact the episodic process which generates the notes. If the performance was improvised, then you need to recreate the improviser's procedures. If the performance was based on a composed text, then you need to recreate the composer's procedures.

It is my impression—I have no explicit quantitative evidence—that, minute by minute, bop improvisation (and later) tends to be denser in texture, less redundant, than most classical music. The rhythm is very active and has a more deeply branching phrase structure, to borrow a concept from linguistics, than a classical line of similar duration. The melodic lines tend to be angular and irregular, and the interaction between the soloist and the accompaniment is very rich. Classical compositions may often have a greater number of distinctly dif-

Unfortunately, I am not prepared to offer an explanation of how jazz and classical music achieve epiphanies, but I am willing to do a bit of beating around this particular bush. Trust is fundamental to the process, and psychoanalysis provides the clearest example of the role which trust plays in affective reorganization. The patient trusts in the good intentions and competence of the analyst and is thus willing to expose and express deep psychic hurts. This allows the analyst to guide the patient in working through inner conflicts to achieve more effective ways of dealing with the world. Trust is the womb in which reorganization grows. Similarly, I speculated in a paper on narrative (Benzon, 1993a) that the reader trusts a novel's narrator, which is the novelist's device for guiding reorganization. That trust allows the reader to experience imaginary events which might otherwise provoke too much anxiety. When those events are resolved at the end of the novel the reader has been changed a little, and in the direction of being more capable of dealing with the conflicts embodied in the novel.

I offer two illustrations of what musical trust is about and from which it can be argued that jazz and classical achieve that trust differently. I've logged many hours playing rhythm and blues in bars and nightclubs and have been puzzled about people's reluctance to dance to an unfamiliar tune, even if it has exactly the same beat as a familiar tune which had them happily dancing only minutes before. It is as though the unfamiliar melody makes it difficult for people to trust that the basic beat won't suddenly, in the middle of the tune, shift into some crazy Balkan eleven/eight meter, making chaos out of smooth, well-rehearsed four/four dance moves and transforming the dance from a romantic opportunity into a survival test. At a more sophisticated level, consider this anecdote told to me by a semi-professional jazz musician (Joe Wheeler, personal communication). He was playing piano in a lounge on New Year's Eve; the piano's action was thick and he struggled for half an hour until someone requested Thelonius Monk's "Round Midnight." For some reason, unexplained, his technical struggle disappeared and he began playing with imagination and liveliness well above his normal level. He continued that way for the entire evening, playing so well that he attracted the at-

---

ferent voices playing at a time, but, in the small scale, the individual lines and their interaction tend to be more regular and predictable than jazz improvisations. The upshot of this— and here the speculation quotient is even higher—is that a seven-minute bop performance may well make information processing demands comparable to those of a somewhat longer classical composition. We have experimental evidence that our sense of temporal duration depends, not on what happens during a given interval, but on how much storage space we devote to the memory of what happened in that interval (Ornstein, 1969). In particular our sense of duration for an interval can decrease if, after that interval, we learn a more efficient way to encode that experience in memory.

Let's return to the listener trying to understand a musical performance. The listener is listening to the unfolding structure of musical episodes and trying to infer the gnomonic rules on which the music is based. That inference cannot be complete until the last note. At that time the listener can "erase" all that he or she remembers of the elaborate episodic structure and replace it with the considerably more compact gnomonic structure. A considerable temporal duration has must been collapsed into a small one; in effect, the experience has been outside time. Improvisation and composition are two ways of achieving this.

Even granting provisional validity to this speculation, this temporal collapse does not quite add up to reorganizational epiphany. Even more speculation is required—though experimentally verified fact would be better. The overall point of this argument is simply to suggest a way we can begin to understand that composition and improvisation are different means to the similar expressive ends.

tention and admiration of the musicians playing for the dance in the adjacent ballroom. The fact that he was able to play so well for an entire evening indicates that he had the musical knowledge in his head and fingers. What he didn't have was sure access to the attitude, the behavioral mode (Benzon and Hays, 1990b, Hays, 1992), which allowed him fluently to implement that knowledge in performance. Getting into the mode is a matter of trust, of having faith in one's ability, and in the music itself.

But classical music and jazz have different ways of engineering that trust. In classical music creative responsibility has been divided between composers and performers. Composers create the overall structure and provide the fine texture while performers bring the music to life, providing the breathing nuance—recall Clynes' essentic forms—which binds texture and structure into living experience. When a classical performance begins, both performer and audience "know" that, in some sense, the work is already finished, existing in some ideal realm of composed Platonic essences. Trust is invested in that transcendent realm and all are moved. In contrast, the jazz musician, and audience, invest their trust in the immanent process through which the music grows and evolves. There are few composed essences in the jazz world; the improviser starts with a framework and from that constructs the music. As a practical matter, both classical and jazz musicians can experience states of ecstasy, of standing outside oneself as the music flows, but I'm willing to bet that, if we could trace the paths of neural energy implementing that ecstasy, we would find interesting differences between the two.[7]

The classical style of compositional essence parallels Western philosophical preoccupation with absolute truth, a preoccupation which has been severely stressed by the evolution of science beyond the certainties of the nineteenth century and by deconstructivist and postmodern thinking. The gap between the imagined musical essence—represented by notes on pages of paper—and the physical process of performing the music mirrors the Cartesian split between mind and body which has dogged Western metaphysics since the seventeenth century. Jazz immanence doesn't propose such a gap between the music itself and the process of performing the music. There is no gap between the ideal and the real, between musical space and performance time. In jazz, the music and the perfor-

---

7. Leonard Bernstein talked of completely forgetting "who you are or where you are and you write the piece right there. You just make it up as though you never heard it before...I always know when such a thing has happened because it takes so long to come back. It takes four or five minutes to know what city I'm in, who the orchestra is, who are the people making all that noise behind me, who am I? It's a very great experience and it doesn't happen often enough" (Epstein, 1987, p. 52). Karen Chester (personal communication), who currently produces Nadja Salerno-Sonnenberg's recordings tells me that Salerno-Sonnenberg sometimes gets similarly lost in her playing. The jazz musician Ira Sullivan said "I feel that I'm at my best when I can free myself completely from the effort of trying to put something out and feel more like I am the instrument being played—like opening the channel to God, or whatever it is. I suddenly get the feeling that I'm standing next to myself, but I'm not thinking that this is me playing" (Spitzer, 1972, p. 14). Jenny Boyd (1972, pp. 157–186) has collected a number of anecdotes, mostly from rock musicians, and Mickey Hart (1990) tells anecdotes about drumming and ecstasy. My own experience indicates that these various anecdotes, however interesting, lack descriptive nuance. These experiences are difficult to talk about, but we can do better. A systematic set of interviews with a variety of musicians—different styles and levels of accomplishment—and with attention to detail would be very illuminating.

mance are indistinguishable. Jazz can live and thrive on constructions which exist only in the act of creating them.

And, with this contrast, we return to our major theme—composition and improvisation as the organizing patterns of Western and African-American culture, respectively. It is not difficult, for example, to see a thematic similarity between classical music and football, on the one hand, and jazz and basketball, on the other hand (on games and cultural style, see Roberts, Sutton-Smith & Kendon, 1963). Football involves highly specialized players organized into elaborately structured units, enacting preplanned plays, and directed by a quarterback representing the coach/composer. Basketball uses a smaller number of players, whose roles are less rigorously specialized, and involves a free flowing style of play which is quite different from football. A football game is composed while a basketball game is improvised. African Americans dominate basketball but, while they are prominent in football, they have been kept from the key role of quarterback, the director of the coach's composition.

Similarly, it is not difficult to see a likeness between classical music, football, and the hierarchical structure of large corporations, the ones that are now "downsizing" and "delayering" to cut costs and gain flexibility. When we consider jazz and basketball in this context, what comes most quickly to my mind is the advice of current management gurus about the need for a very fluid corporate structure, one which changes quickly and has multifunctional workers organized into relatively flat structures. Thus Tom Peters (1992) uses the carnival as one of his key metaphors. Carnivals run lean, quickly adapt to changing markets, and have employees who play multiple roles. Carnivals, and the corporation of the twenty-first century, are improvisatory. Likewise, when Michael Maccoby (1990, pp. 474–475) talks of the need for "corporate men and women who can work interdependently within a corporate structure that stimulates and rewards individual initiative and continual improvement," he describes a pattern of vigorous individuality in service of a group creation which is a fundamental requirement of jazz. Duke Ellington's sidemen were all individualists who played their best music in Ellington's band; leaders such as Dizzy Gillespie, Art Blakey, and Miles Davis were known for so successfully fostering the growth of their musicians that many of them went on to become leaders themselves. Jazz culture stresses the importance of finding your own voice, your own style, even the basic sound a player gets from his or her instrument. In contrast, classical culture stresses adherence to an ideal sound and is doubtful about individuality, even from virtuoso soloists. Thus it is no surprise that the business world is beginning to see books with titles like *Leadership Jazz* (DePree, 1992) and *Jamming: The Art and Discipline of Business Creativity* (Kao, 1996).

These improvisatory corporations thus exhibit a pattern which reverses that which Henry Louis Gates, Jr. (1988, p. 122) finds in various important African-American novels (e.g., Zora Neale Hurston's *Their Eyes Were Watching God*, Ralph Ellison's *Invisible Man*). These novels use a Western literary form to express African-American content. The high-tech corporations have an African-American style with a white technological content. Unfortunately, few of these corporations are African-American enterprises. Between the informal mores and prejudices of the corporate world and the unfortunate relationship between much of African America and the educational system, the corporate world remains largely European American. However, to the extent that these more fluid corporations are run by relatively young men and women, they are run by people who have, for example, grown up listening and dancing to rock and roll and have thus been significantly influenced by African-American expressive style—a topic we'll return to later in this essay.[8] What I'm suggesting is that this new corporate style has not been created out of thin air. Rather, this new corporate style reflects a new personal style, and that personal style owes a debt to expressive devices developed in African America. If black folks hadn't invented jazz early in the century, then white folks would have been too stiff to have begun remaking their corporations in a more flexible manner as the century comes to a close.

One final contrast suggests itself. Classical music is the expression of a fully formed culture. Europe was under no pressure to conform to any standards other than its own. Jazz, however, is the creation of people under constant pressure to conform to conditions imposed on them. As Martin Williams (1983, p. 256) asserted, "Jazz is the music of a people who have been told by their circumstances that they are unworthy. And in jazz, these people discover their own worthiness." There is a sense, then, that jazz is the most advanced creation of a culture which has not been able to fully reveal and realize itself. Whether or not the next century will see that realization is a question as open as it is exciting.[9]

Society, Psyche, and Culture in North America

Cultures have interacted with and influenced one another at many times and places throughout human history. Much of this is no doubt aimless and opportunistic drifting and mixing in which songs, stories, tools, technologies, and social customs, etc., move from one group to another. Much of the interaction between Africans and Europeans in North America has, no doubt, been of this kind. However, over time the United States has evolved a social structure which puts a strong selective bias on the process. There is order and purpose to the cultural interaction between black and white society. In a way which defies existing categories of socio-cultural analysis, groups of people are influencing and reacting to each other on the group level.[10]

---

8. I have some direct experience on the relationship between high-tech improvisatory management style and rock and roll. In the early '90s I spent two years writing technical documentation for MapInfo, Corp., which makes software for analytic mapping. Sean O'Sullivan, one of the young founders and formerly chairman of the board, would end many of his electronic mail communications with an exhortation to "rock and roll." Half a year after I left, he resigned to pursue a career in rock and roll. To accommodate its rapid growth, MapInfo revised its management structure at least two times in the two years I was employed there. Change was explicitly recognized as being essential to survival.

9. When I originally wrote this section I had imagined, for example, that there was an "improvisational" philosophy still to be created, one which might well avoid the problems faced by current philosophy. Since then I have been reading Cornel West's (1989) history of pragmatism and suspect that pragmatism might well be that philosophy, or at least it may be the beginnings of that philosophy. If so, that suggests an interesting visual metaphor for the symbolic stratum of American culture. Imagine a double-helix—the structural form of DNA—in which one strand is jazz and the other pragmatism. Just what are the links connecting the two strands?

10. Such a social mechanism hasn't existed in all societies where whites have dominated blacks. European culture has mixed with African culture elsewhere, particularly the

Let us start with an analogy, courtesy of the old television program *Star Trek*. One episode centered on a being called an empath. If a person was ill or injured, the empath could touch that person, and through the touch, absorb the trauma into herself and thereby cure the person. The empath, however, was limited in her ability to absorb injury. That limitation provided the episodes's tension, for the Enterprise crew had more injuries than she could safely absorb. European America has used African America as such an empath, a circumstance which is at the heart of the standard canon of American literature. One of the books we find there contains a story about a poor white boy who flees his alcoholic and abusive father in the company of a slave. As Toni Morrison points out, in Mark Twain's *Huckleberry Finn,* "Jim permits his persecutors to torment him, humiliate him, and responds to the torment and humiliation with boundless love" (Morrison, 1992, p. 57). Huck and Tom inflicted their grievances on Jim and he absorbed them. The overall question is whether or not European America can be cured before African America is destroyed.

The Cultural Psychodynamics of Racism

I take it as given that Western culture is one of emotional restraint and repression. This repression, so my argument goes, is at the core of the psychodynamics of racism. We can begin with a curious and disappointing passage in Chapter 9, "Revolution," of W. E. B. Du Bois' *Dusk of Dawn* (1940, pp. 770–771). Du Bois says: "My own study of psychology under William James had predated the Freudian era, but it had prepared me for it. I now began to realize that in the fight against racial prejudice, we were not facing simply the rational, conscious determination of white folk to oppress us; we were facing age-long complexes sunk now largely to unconscious habit and irrational urge…" And that was it. He acknowledged the relevance of psychoanalytic thought, but did not use it in developing an analysis of racism. Subsequent intellectuals haven't done a great deal to write the discourse Du Bois only implied (for more implication, see Ellison, 1972,

---

Caribbean and Latin America, but not so fruitfully; this difference requires an explanation. The music of the Caribbean and South America has been strongly influenced by African rhythm; in fact, African rhythms survive there in purer form than they have in North America, presumably because the drum wasn't banished there as it was in North America. But Latin America has not produced a musical culture as fecund and sophisticated as jazz (Murray, 1976, p. 63; Crouch, 1990b, p. 79). Significantly, Latin America has not been as intensely racist as the United States (Fredrickson, 1988, pp. 189–205). Without intense racism, the socio-cultural mechanism I describe wouldn't function.

Fredrickson has attributed this difference between British North America and South America to the fact that, unlike Britain, Spain and Portugal were essentially feudal societies. In terms of the theory of cultural ranks (Benzon and Hays, 1990b), Britain was an emerging Rank 3 culture while Spain and Portugal were still Rank 2. In his view, the feudal mentality could easily accommodate a wide range of social statuses, with slaves merely being at the bottom. The British, however, were moving toward a capitalist system in which there was a wide gulf between the industrious and "worthy" middle class and a "worthless" lower class. Belief in a radical difference between black slaves and whites gave lower-class whites a scapegoat for the feelings of inferiority produced by this work ethic while, at the same time, the egalitarian milieu of North America forced the Southern aristocracy and white middle and lower class to seek solidarity in their mutual difference from black slaves (cf. remarks by Kenneth Clark in Terkel, 1992, pp. 334–338).

pp. 100, 311).[11] Economics has become a routine intellectual instrument in the examination of racism, but psychoanalysis has not.

Still, enough has been done to serve our purposes. Freud argued that, in general, much behavior is driven by unconscious desires. Moving beyond the individual psyche, he argued, perhaps most explicitly in *Civilization and Its Discontents* (1962), that Western civilization is built on a foundation of emotional repression. Racism is a society-wide manifestation of that repression. The basic point is simple: many of the characteristics racists have attributed to blacks are simply the repressed contents of their own hearts and minds which they have projected onto African Americans (Baldwin, 1963, p. 95 ff.; Gay, 1993, pp. 69 ff.; Morrison, 1992, pp. 37 ff., 51–52; Young-Bruehl, 1996). In particular, the heightened sexual desire and potency, and the greater emotionality, which whites have insisted on seeing in blacks has more to do with unconscious white desire than it does with black behavior.[12]

In an essay originally published in 1947, Talcott Parsons (1964, pp. 298–322) explored the dynamics of aggression, arguing that Western society is so structured that aggressive impulses are often generated in situations where they cannot be directly expressed, creating a need for ethnic and national "others" who can be scapegoated. Calvin Hernton explored the sexual dynamics of racism in a study originally published in 1965 (and reprinted in 1988). Erik Erikson made a general theoretical statement in the final chapter of his *Identity: Youth and Crisis* (1968, pp. 295–320). He argued that no culture has been able to adapt the full biological range of human desire and feeling to its patterns. Each culture cultivates some

---

11. I am certainly in no position to explain why Du Bois did not elaborate on the connections he saw between psychoanalytic theory and racism; however, since I fear that many other intellectuals have similar misgivings, I want to think about the matter. A recent remark by Charles Keil may provide a clue. The remark is a brief note which Keil originally wrote to Steven Feld in response to a long letter in which Feld discussed issues of sexuality, personal tragedy, and racism which occurred to him while thinking about the music of Aretha Franklin. Keil says to Feld, "I really appreciate the candor, the courage to jump into the song and sexuality issues that I've been afraid to write about too! . . . Maybe we should get together a group and try to think-talk our way through issues that are too weird and threatening to handle in scholarly or meditative isolation" (published in Keil and Feld, 1994, p. 223). Keil simply found these issues too anxiety-provoking to write about; perhaps Du Bois felt the same way. One cannot do effective intellectual work in a state of continuous and strong emotional arousal or anxiety. Where the subject matter provokes a strong emotional reaction, you must develop conceptual strategies which allow you to keep in touch with the subject matter while providing the detachment necessary for thought. It is a difficult balancing act.

However much the link between sexuality and racism has been neglected by intellectuals, it has been intensely studied by writers in such works as Richard Wright's *Native Son*, William Faulkner's *A Light in August*, Ralph Ellison's *Invisible Man*, Ishmael Reed's *Flight to Canada*, E.M. Forster's *A Passage to India*, and Jean Genet's play *The Screens*.

12. It would be a mistake, however, simply to view racism as individual psychopathology. As Elisabeth Young-Bruehl has observed (1996, p. 32), "many people have prejudices instead of the conventional forms of various pathologies, somewhat as people have perversions instead of neuroses if they act on their forbidden desires rather than repressing them." Psychopathology generally makes it more difficult for people to interact with others in ways which meet their needs. This is not generally the case with racists. On the contrary, their racist actions make it easier for them to interact with individuals in their own group, other racists, by displacing or projecting conflicts onto the objects of their racism. Racism is a social mechanism which allows individuals to deal with psychological conflicts in ways which do not threaten the group.

characteristics at the expense of others. The neglected characteristics may then co-alesce into a negative identity which members of a given society will often project or displace onto members of some other society or culture. Joel Kovel (1984) has undertaken an investigation of American racism in which he argues for different psychological processes in the North and the South. Most recently, Elisabeth Young-Bruehl (1996) has undertaken a psycho-social analysis of prejudice—including antisemitism, sexism, and homophobia in addition to racism—in which she identifies various kinds of prejudice and attempts to identify the historical conditions which give rise to them.

Such psycho-social mechanisms have shaped Europe's encounter with the peoples of Africa. Winthrop D. Jordan (1974) has shown that Europeans were disposed to see blacks in the image of the emotionality and sensuality they were rejecting in themselves. In the late Renaissance, blacks were likened to beasts; in Bacon's *New Atlantis* (1624) the "Spirit of Fornication" was depicted as "a little foul ugly Æthiop" (p. 19). Jordan notes that Englishmen "were especially inclined to discover attributes in savages which they found first, but could not speak of, in themselves" (pp. 22–23; see also Gilman, 1985). Thus before the European settlers of North America had any substantial contact with Africans, they had a lascivious place prepared in their minds through which to understand and interact with them. Shakespeare's Caliban was to be a lens through which the people of a whole continent would be viewed and interpreted.

Joel Williamson has taken this psychological line in examining the lynchings which once plagued this country, especially in the two decades straddling the turn of the century (Williamson, 1984, 117 ff.; see also Brundage, 1993; Du Bois, 1940, pp. 730, 747, 772; Fredrickson, 1988, pp. 172–182; Harrington, 1992, pp. 157–162). Many of the victims were black men often accused of some sexual offense against a white woman; in some cases the offense was real, in many it was not. Further, many of these lynchings were extravagant public exhibitions with widespread participation. That is, it wasn't a matter of a few drunken thugs breaking into the jail at night to get the offender—perhaps with the tacit approval of the sheriff—and then hanging him from a tree for all to see in the morning. Sometimes lynching preparations would go on for days, with newspaper articles about the alleged crime and the impending punishment, and with railroads offering special excursion fares to take people to the scene. The actual lynching would then take place in broad daylight, with thousands of people in attendance, vendors attending to the needs of these thousands, with photographers and reporters recording it all for posterity. People might take fingers of the victim as souvenirs. It was not unusual for tens or hundreds of men each to fire a bullet into the hanging body or bodies. Such public exhibitions seem much like the public tortures and executions of medieval Europe and obviously had the full approval of the local and regional community, with at least the tacit approval of national authorities. Williamson concludes that African-American males were being used as scapegoats for European-American discontent and that, while some of that discontent was certainly generated by current social displacement, some also stemmed from sexual and emotional repression.[13]

---

13. Lynchings were sporadic eruptions. While there were 156 lynchings in the peak year of 1892 (Williamson, p. 117), these were dispersed over a wide geographic area; lynchings would be relatively infrequent in each local community. Thus they were fine for an occasional

The thrust of these various studies is the same: racists are punishing others for their own sins. Western civilization has not created adequate means for directly incorporating a satisfying range of human emotion and behavior into its cultural practices. Consequently, it has been forced into racism as a one means of dealing with the resulting repression and self-hatred.

However, if the lynching is the prototypical scene of racist violence, there is a contrasting prototypical scene of racism, one which is not dominated by physical violence. Consider those night "black and tan" clubs, such as the Cotton Club, where the performers were black but the clientele was exclusively white. Why did all those white people seek black entertainment? No doubt most of them came for the erotic floor show, but some of them were interested in the music. Why? The question is not a new one, and the answer is obvious—in the same way that the applicability of Freud to racism is so obvious that it has been little discussed. European Americans have liked African-American music because it has expressive powers which are lacking in European and European-American music (Crouch, 1990b, p. 83; Keil, 1966, p. 49; Small, 1987, p. 154; Williams, 1983, p. 254). In particular, as we've seen above, African-American music is comfortable with sexuality, while European music is not.[14] People may have come to the Cotton Club to see black bodies enact jungle pseudo-rituals on stage; but they left with the expressive sound of African-American music boring into their brains.

In an important variant of the Cotton Club scenario, a white child—no doubt a descendant of Huck Finn—sneaks into the club to hear the black musicians play jazz. This variant was featured in Michael Curtiz's movie *Young Man With a Horn* (1950) where young Rick Martin idolized Art Hazzard. This movie was, in turn, based on Dorothy Baker's novel of the same name, based loosely on the life of Bix Beiderbecke, the first major white jazz musician. More recently, Hollywood producer George Lucas (responsible for the *Star Wars* and *Indiana Jones* movies) created a two-hour episode of his television show, *The Indiana Jones Chronicles*, in which young Indiana gets jazz lessons from Sidney Bechet (cf. Murray, 1970, pp. 101–102). I take this scene as a metaphor for the role of jazz (and African-influenced music in general) in the white world. While the jazz club is ostensibly a place of entertainment, it also functions on a deeper level as a school, one in which the teachers are black and the students are white. They are learning a cul-

---

quick and intense communal release; but lynchings would not alone be able to vent the pressure of continuous emotional repression. The institution of patrol, which began in the seventeenth century and continued into the nineteenth, is a different matter. It involved continual policing of blacks by white men (Williamson, pp. 18–19). By the nineteenth century, many able-bodied Southern white men were obligated to spend some of their time, week by week, patrolling the streets and roads at night to see that blacks were in their proper place. Patrols had the power to judge and punish infractions. Such continued vigilance would provide a continuously available way of working off repressed impulses.

14. In her biography of Josephine Baker, Phyllis Rose contrasts European exoticism with American racism (1989, p. 44): "Exoticism is frivolous, hangs out at nightclubs, will pay anything to have the black singer or pianist sit at its table. Racism is like a poor kid who grew up needing someone to hurt.... The racist is hedged around by dangers, the exoticism by used-up toys." What she means by exoticism is thus similar to what I mean in talking about the Cotton Club as a scene of racism. Whatever qualms I have about her term—I think talking about "exoticism" makes it a little too easy to lose sight of the fact that it is a form of racism, depending on the underlying psychodynamics of racism—her general discussion is an excellent one.

tural stylization of emotion which is more adequate to their needs than the one they learned at home, in school, or in church. Where the lyncher and his descendants are desperately trying to preserve the restrictiveness of his culture, the white jazz fan and his descendants are trying to break free from that restrictiveness by learning elements of a different culture.[15] In the night club scenario, Africa is the teacher and Europe the student (cf. Asante, 1987, p. 59).

Unfortunately the psychodynamics of racism doesn't end here. The need for projective psychological relief is an equal opportunity affirmative action agent of social destruction. Black Americans have demonized whites even as they have been demonized. The Black Muslims provide the most obvious example, with Elijah Muhammad's story of the evil Mr. Yacub who created a race of "blond, pale-skinned, cold-blue-eyed devils—savages, nude and shameless; hairy, like animals, they walked on all fours and they lived in trees." These white devils then turned a black "heaven on earth into a hell torn by quarreling and fighting" (Haley, 1965, p. 167; for different examples, see e.g. Crouch, 1990c, pp. 200–202, 231–244; Early, 1989, pp. 199–207; Young-Bruehl, 1996, pp. 481 ff.). Considering that African Americans have legitimate grievances against European Americans, the problem of sorting out the justified anger from the projective demonization seems hopeless. From that hopeless confusion Dr. Martin Luther King and El-Hajj Malik El-Shabazz—aka Malcolm X, Detroit Red, Malcolm Little—struggled to discriminate right from wrong and thereby exercised moral and political leadership which gave hope to millions.

Tertium Quid: The Artist and Negative European Identity

Europe was not, of course, limited to projecting its negative identity onto Africans. People of other races also bore this imprint, which is the central circumstance, for example, of E.M. Forster's *A Passage to India* (cf. Jan Mohammed, 1985). But we need not look solely to prejudices directed from one ethnic group to another. The romantic stereotype of the artist, as developed by and for the middle class during the nineteenth century, also embodied Europe's rejected affect. Thus, behind the much-discussed topic of black self-hatred we find the topic of white self-hatred.

We can see this romantic conception emerging in the Western imagination with Goethe's publication of *The Sufferings of Young Werther* in 1774. To be sure, Werther wasn't an artist in the sense of being vocationally dedicated to art, though he liked to paint and sketch. He was a love-addict who committed suicide because he would never be able to have the woman he loved; she was married to another. He serves as an archetype for the artist because he was a man of intense

---

15. I offer the "black and tan" nightclub and the lynching mostly as metaphors, each indicating a particular pattern of racist socio-cultural action. I find them to be useful conceptual tools, ways of summarizing two different complexes of attitudes and mechanisms, each conditioned by racism. But what is the underlying difference between these two scenarios, what is it that causes them to be different? One possibility is that the nightclub and the lynching are structured by two different kinds of racism. As the lynchings were mostly in the South while the "black and tan" nightclubs were in the urban North, perhaps Joel Kovel's (1984) distinction between (Southern) dominative and (Northern) aversive racism applies. We might also want to think about Elisabeth Young-Bruehl's (1996) distinction between ethnocentric prejudice (the nightclub?) and an ideology of desire (the lynching?).

feeling who was alienated from his society. As such, he proclaimed that "I have been drunk more than once, my passions have never been far from madness, and I regret neither; for, at my own level, I have come to appreciate why all extraordinary people who have achieved something great, something apparently impossible, have been inevitably decried by society as drunkards or madmen" (Goethe, translated by Steinhauer, 1970, p. 33).

The attitudes embodied in this book coalesced around the figure of the artist as a bohemian creature who dressed differently, thought differently, was given to vehement proclamations, perhaps a bit of debauchery, and who was, in general, somewhere between eccentric and crazy—the van Gogh and his ear syndrome. Thus, in his very influential *Silence* (1961, p. 127), the avant-garde composer John Cage approvingly quotes Rilke's remark that he had no interest in being psychoanalyzed because "I'm sure they would remove my devils, but I fear they would offend my angels." That is, madness is not just something which afflicts artists, among others, but rather it is the source of their creativity.

The trope of the rebellious artist, consumed with feeling, is a vehicle through which Western culture reminds itself of the affective life it has forsworn. The Western artist feels what the ordinary citizen cannot. Through identifying with the artist, the citizen gets access to those emotions which are otherwise held in check. The solid citizen dresses severely, works hard, and feels little or nothing; at leisure this good citizen reads a novel, attends a play, or an opera (perhaps *La Boheme*) and there encounters the artist who feels all that the citizen must deny. In that encounter the citizen gets safe and vicarious access to a richer emotional range. When the artist self-destructs, the citizen is reminded that emotion is dangerous. Thus the citizen is safely returned to the daily routine of emotional repression and drab dress.

The self-destructiveness of Western artists, so convention tells us, is simply the price they pay for their intense feeling. As long as we believe that they must pay that price, we accept our less intense, but safer, lives. We accept our repression because we believe it to be the only way to a secure life. We cannot tolerate the possibility that a life of strong feeling is not self-destructive but, on the contrary, could be deeply creative, nurturing, and sustaining. It is thus no accident that the artists in Western movies, novels and plays generally die. That is the only way we can tolerate them. The idea of a mentally balanced artist, whether painter, dancer, jazz musician, etc., doesn't make sense. Most Westerners would not be prepared to recognize such a person as a real artist. Western culture's emotional repression is thus no more hospitable to its own artists than it is to blacks. It must scapegoat both.[16]

The artist, the creator of expressive culture, thus serves as a *tertium quid* between European-American and African-American culture; it is a cultural position within European-derived culture through which white folks could permit themselves to learn from social outsiders of African-derived culture. The formal and informal institutional arrangements of white society place black society in the role of expressive outsider, a point brilliantly allegorized in Robert Zemeckis's film *Who Framed Roger Rabbit*? In the film's Los Angeles there are two worlds, that of human beings, and that of Toons, classic cartoon characters from Betty Boop to

---

16. Krin Gabbard (1995) has an essay on Spike Lee's *Mo' Better Blues* which is worth reading in this context. He points out that, in general, trumpet players in jazz movies generally have their musical wings clipped, as it were, before they end the movie easing into domestic bliss.

Elmer Fudd. The Toons and their world are consciously modeled on white stereotypes of blacks (Harmetz, 1988). The Toons are born entertainers; they sing, they dance, they tell jokes, they act in movies. And they are obviously outsiders, a whole society used by the humans to provide for human expressive needs.

Because European-American society came to assimilate African-American culture to the general role of the romantic artist, it has been possible for African Americans to pursue their own expressive imperatives while at the same time providing entertainment which European Americans not only like, but are willing to imitate. The system is deeply flawed; but it has been remarkably creative. Thus, over time, an economic arrangement, chattel slavery, has spawned a side effect which has transformed, not only American culture, but world culture, for African-American music is heard and emulated on all continents (Rothstein, 1991, p. 32; Wiora, 1965, pp. 158–160). The enslavement of Africans was justified by an ideology which mistook relative cultural simplicity for inherent inferiority and allowed Europeans to use Africans as a projective screen on which they viewed the same aspects of themselves which they had projected into their own artists. Over time that projection has evolved into a socio-cultural vehicle through which whites have adopted some of the expressive traits of those original Africans and their descendants. Thus, in a cultural sense, those Africans have become ancestors of us all.

Africa in America

Let us proceed with another text from W. E. B. Du Bois. This one is from *The Souls of Black Folk* (1903, p. 3), chapter one, paragraph three:

> After the Egyptian and Indian, the Greek and Roman, the Teuton and Mongolian, the Negro is a sort of seventh son, born with a veil, and gifted with second-sight in this American world, a world which yields him no true self-consciousness, but only lets him see himself through the revelation of the other world. It is a peculiar sensation, this double-consciousness, this sense of always looking at one's self through the eyes of others, of measuring one's soul by the tape of a world that looks on in amused contempt and pity.

One consequence of this double vision is a concern for "uplifting the race" which looks toward European-American standards (cf. Harrington, 1992, pp. 209–211). Thus Du Bois himself disapproved of jazz (1940, p. 702)—what would you expect from a middle-class man educated to the culture of Harvard and the University of Berlin?

However, African America has not been completely dominated by the European gaze. Africa survived, albeit highly transformed, and it is around this African core that black Americans forged a cultural identity of their own. The scholarly recognition of this African core begins in 1941, when Melville Herskovits published *The Myth of the Negro Past*. At the time, his thesis was a novel one—that American blacks had retained substantial traits and practices from African cultures. Herskovits, and others following in his wake, documented so many retentions that it is difficult for serious thinkers to continue denying the African influence.[17]

---

17. The publication of Herskovitz's book did not, however, end the idea that whatever culture African Americans had was, on the one hand, a response to poverty and oppression,

Music is one of the most obvious cases; but it is by no means a simple one. Slaves were often forbidden to perform their native music. In particular, the drums were widely banned in North America and, as a consequence, West African rhythms did not survive there (Gillespie, 1979, p. 318; Oliver, 1970, p. 56; Southern, 1983, p. 182), though they are prevalent in the Caribbean and in Latin America, where the drums were not banned. What did survive was a strong rhythmic pulse and a tendency to superimpose groups of three notes over a ground beat based on binary patterns (Schuller, 1968; Collier, 1978). Similarly, the blues scale, with its microtonal "blue" notes, seems to reflect both African and European tonal practice, though it doesn't exist on either continent (Schuller, 1968, pp. 44 ff.).

Most importantly for our purposes, the eroticism of African-American music is taken over from African music. This is an eroticism linked to religious ritual (cf. Jones, 1963, p. 92). Michael Ventura (1987a and 1987b) has given a succinct historical account of the route from African religious ceremony through New World voodoo to jazz and on to rock and roll, the point being that there is a comparatively recent historical linkage between African religious practice and African-American musical practice. Voodoo is a syncretic body or religious belief and practice in which West African deities are disguised as Christian saints; its ritual draws fairly directly on typical West African rituals (Mulira, 1990).

New Orleans is central to this development.[18] It was an exception to the general ban on drumming; slaves were permitted to practice their rituals, drumming and all, in Congo Square. Thus African ritual practice stayed alive well into the 1880s (Hobsbawm, 1993, p. 5). Since many whites watched the ceremony, Congo Square was, in effect, a precursor to those later clubs with black entertainment and white clientele (but see Starr, 1995, pp. 39–40). At the same time many Creoles were learning European music; for example, there was a Negro Philharmonic Society in the 1830s (Collier, 1978, p. 59; 1993, pp. 189 ff.). New Orleans was thus the scene of a most intimate mixing of African and European musical practice.

The resulting musical hybrid is one in which the sacred and the sexual are closely connected. This connection is not, of course, unknown in European culture. But it is one which was emphatically rejected in prevailing doctrine, with celibacy ordained for Catholic clergy while Protestant sects generally took a dim

---

and, on the other, taken over from white America. When Nathan Glazer and Patrick Moynihan published their classic *Beyond the Melting Pot: The Negroes, Puerto Ricans, Jews, Italians, and Irish of New York City* (1963), they credited the Jews with Broadway (p. 174) and the Puerto Ricans with Pablo Casals and "a passion for music and dancing" (pp. 129–130). That New York City was also the jazz capital of the world was never mentioned. When Charles Silberman published his 1964 *Crisis in Black and White* he was able to state definitively that "the Negro has been completely stripped of his past and severed from any culture save that of the United States" (p. 109, cf. pp. 167, 185). For recent review of some of the debate about African origins, see Holloway (1990, pp. ix–xiii) and Philips (1990, pp. 225–228).

18. While New Orleans is certainly the geographical focal point for the cultural mixing which produced jazz (Blassingame, 1979, pp. 36 ff.; Buerkle and Barker, 1973; Chase, 1966, pp. 301–314; Collier, 1978; Hobsbawm, 1993; Ventura, 1987a, pp. 36–42), it is certainly not the only city where blacks created a distinctively African-American music. Ross Russell (1971) makes a strong case for the independent creativity of Kansas City while Scott Brown's (1986) biography of James P. Johnson chronicles the role of New York City as an incubator of black piano virtuosity.

view of the body and its evil pleasures. African-American music embodies a different view, with a rich interplay between African-American sacred music and various secular forms—blues, rhythm and blues, soul, jazz.[19] Consider, for example, the remark by the great bluesman, B.B. King, that "Gospel singers sing about heavenly bodies and we blues singers sing about earthly ones" (Smith, 1988, p. 149). He clearly differentiates between blues and gospel, but implies that there is an abiding link as well. The outrageous androgynous Richard Penniman (Little Richard) has moved back and forth between preaching the gospel and singing rock and roll, and he's hardly the only African-American musician/ preacher, though he's the best known (Keil, 1966, pp. 147 ff.; Lincoln and Mamiya, 1990, p. 362). Similarly, soul music, with Ray Charles its prophet, Aretha Franklin the queen and James Brown the king, is based in gospel music (cf. for example, Peter Guralnick, 1986; Harrington, 1992, pp. 194–202)—a connection made in Robert Townsend's film, *The Five Heartbeats*, in which one of the musicians is a preacher's son and another overcomes his self-destructiveness by being born again. Between black popular music (and dance as well), with roots in black religion, and white derivatives from it, much of contemporary America's stylization of sexuality and secular love is derived from West African religious ceremony.

It is around this core of religious and musical practice that African America has forged a sense of cultural integrity and link to the African past. Black pride and cultural awareness was not invented in the nineteen sixties; it has a long history (Stuckey, 1987; Murray, 1970, pp. 171–188). One telling index of this awareness is the question of the name to be used in designating African Americans, an issue which has been discussed and debated among African Americans since the early nineteenth century (Stuckey, pp. 193–244). Playing the blues is a facet of African-American expressive culture. Knowing that the blues has a history, and that that history is yours, is an aspect of cultural nationalism. Such cultural nationalism often comes into defensive play when European Americans adopt versions of the blues for themselves.

Music in the Making of History: Blues Train to the Future

Now we are ready to enter into the heart of my argument, which is that the psycho-cultural blues train outlined in the previous section has been a driving force in twentieth-century American culture. When I say "driving force" I mean explicitly to assert that it has brought about change in the world, change not only in music, but in the persons and societies conditioned by the music.

The job of examining this blues train and understanding how how its systems interact in American culture began with *Blues People*, by Amiri Baraka, then writing as LeRoi Jones (1963), and has been followed by Charles Keil (1966, pp. 43 ff.)

---

19. Of course, this secularization of church music and its use for social dancing is not universally accepted. As Albert Murray (1976, p. 139) has observed, many "condemn all the good-time slow dragging, belly rubbing, hip grinding, flirtatious strutting, shouting, and stomping expressly because they regard such movements as not only sinful acts, but sinful ceremony to boot, which they seem to be clearly convinced is even worse."

and Nelson George (1988). They have uncovered a pattern of interaction between African-American and European-American musical culture which goes like this:

1. African Americans create a musical style.
2. European Americans adopt the style for their own use.
3. The most adventurous African Americans abandon the style and propose a new one.

This has happened successively with minstrelsy, ragtime, traditional and swing jazz, rock and roll, and perhaps most recently with hip-hop.

The first step is no more mysterious than any other manifestation of human creativity, though, as we have no recordings before this century, most of the initial cultural crossing is invisible to us. By now there should be no mystery about the second step. Whites adopt the style because it has stylistic resources they admire, allowing them to express aspects of their experience which are not easily accommodated by musical forms deriving from Europe. Or, since we want to avoid thinking in terms of music as expressing a pre-existing human essence, the African-American style shapes a cultural style more adequate to their biological nature than does the prevailing repertoire of European forms.

However, the white adaptation often seems anemic and lifeless—"white-bread" is the colloquial term—and, because it is generally more commercially successful, this is a source of resentment. And so, the theory goes, blacks propose another style in an effort to reclaim the music, to construct and affirm a unique ethnic identity. This part of the analysis is inadequate. The resentment is real, and it certainly is part of the motivation for stylistic innovation. African America has a strong need to protect the integrity of the expressive language it uses to construct public affirmation of its values. But too much emphasis on resentment and cultural possessiveness tends to deny black music a life of its own, to see it as primarily reacting against white borrowing.[20] Thus, when Baraka talks about the

---

20. While I understand how black people can feel that white people have stolen their music, this issue requires a bit of analysis. Cultural practices are not like bars of gold that can have only one owner. If you steal my golden eggs, then I no longer have them; I have lost something. If you play my music, you haven't taken anything from me; I can still play my music. When whites play black music they are not thereby depriving blacks of that music. In this context, the only sensible attitude is that the achievements of any culture constitute the common heritage of the human race. One need not be an Englishman to benefit from Newton's physics, a Moslem to benefit from al-Khowarizm's mathematics, nor black to benefit from Louis Armstrong's music.

However, when whites claim to have invented jazz (cf. Collier, 1978, pp. 124 ff.; Peretti, 1992, pp. 71, 187 ff.)—that *is* a kind of theft. It isn't clear to me, however, that the phenomenon of second-string white musicians achieving greater prominence than first-string blacks always represents cultural theft. The white musicians get the prominence because the more numerous white audience prefers them. One can question white taste, but that taste isn't an agent of cultural theft. However, as Paul Levinson has pointed out to me, in the 1950s a number of radio stations refused to play black "race" music, prompting record companies to issue white "covers" of the black records. That appears to be a kind of theft.

This leads to a broader economic issue, one which, it seems to me, is deeper than the income disparity between prominent second-string white performers and less prominent first-string blacks. Consider whatever expressive arena you will—jazz, all of African-American music, all of African-American entertainment, art, and sports. Add up all the money consumers spend on tickets, cover charges, recordings, magazines, biographies, videotapes, etc. Divide this into two piles, money spent by blacks and money spent by whites. Now consider

bop style of jazz as being a reaction to white swing music (Jones, pp. 181 ff.; Baraka, 1990, pp. 66–67) he misses the fact that jazz has a developmental imperative rooted in its own dynamics (Benzon, 1993b; cf. Keil, 1966, p. 45). The fact is, as Stanley Crouch (1990b, pp. 71–72) has noted, Baraka's resentment of whites leads him to devalue the music he ostensibly defends, reducing it to a defensive reflex and thereby denying the fecundity of its ultimately African roots and demeaning the freedom and dignity it achieves.

When one style of music becomes thoroughly known, the best musicians seek the challenge of creating a new style and a significant portion of the audience will be happy to follow them, for boredom afflicts us all. This is one kind of process when the new style is more sophisticated than the old, as was the case when jazz moved from traditional to swing, and then from swing to bop (Benzon, 1993b). Just why living systems of all kinds evolve toward more sophistication and complexity is not well understood, but that it happens is obvious (cf. Benzon and Hays, 1990a; cf. Csikszentmihalyi, 1993). However, we also see evolution from one state to another with no increase in complexity. Much of the stylistic change in music is of this kind. Independently of the imperatives of ethnic identity, such stylistic change would occur through a combination of boredom and the free flow of cultural ideas made possible population movement and by the various twentieth-century media.

As for the weakening of the music at the hands of white adaptors, there is nothing surprising in this. However much white audiences and musicians may admire black music, they have a different cultural background. When creating their own music they will borrow as much as they can and suit it to what their background will permit them. As John Rockwell has noted (1983, p. 167) this is a free choice, not something imposed on the white public by nefarious music moguls (cf. Ressner, 1990). And, in the last analysis, we have to acknowledge that some white adaptors—Benny Goodman, Frank Sinatra, and the Beatles come to mind—have made music that need apologize to no one.

The Blues: "Trouble In Mind"

European Americans readily acknowledged the expressive gifts of their African slaves (Chase, 1966, pp. 76 ff.) In the eighteenth century the Rev. John Davies of Virginia wrote a letter to John Wesley in which he observed that "the Negroes, above all of the human species I ever knew, have the nicest ear for music. They

---

the money made by all involved in producing the music, or sports, whatever—fees and salaries for performers and managers, salaries for those in the media, and so forth. This sum should equal that which consumers put in to the business. Divide this amount into two piles, that made by whites and that made by blacks.

Now compare the money consumers put into the business with the money the producers take out. If black producers take out less than black consumers put in, then the result is a net transfer of wealth from the black community to the white. As I don't know whether anyone has actually made such a calculation, I can't say whether or not white society has been able to use black music, entertainment, and sports to impoverish the black community. But, if the calculation worked out in that way, that would surely be a most serious kind of cultural theft. I have unhappy suspicions about how this calculation would work out; though perhaps a decade-by-decade breakdown would show that, as blacks have gotten more control over their business affairs, the amount of theft has been going down. That's progress.

have a kind of ecstatic delight in psalmody" (Chase, p. 80). African Americans provided a rich variety of music for themselves and at the behest of their white masters. For our purposes it is enough to acknowledge that this music, black and white—spirituals, work songs, dance tunes, "coon" songs, etc. (for historical sketches see Collier, 1978, pp. 3–55; Chase, 1966, pp. 232–323; Southern, 1983)—existed and that whites enjoyed and used it. But one genre requires special attention, that is the blues.

The blues did not come directly from Africa, but it certainly has African elements (Oliver, 1970). Just when it crystallized as a specific form is not certain, though the late nineteenth century is a good guess (Collier, 1978, p, 37; Palmer, 1981; Southern, 1983, pp. 330 ff.). More important than when and where is the matter of why: Why was the blues born? In *Blues People* Baraka suggested that the blues evolved when African Americans took their new-found freedom and confronted a society which had no place for them as free men and women (Jones, 1963, p. 55):

> With the old paternalistic society of the South went the simple role of the Negro in the Western world. Now the Negro was asked to throw himself into what was certainly still an alien environment and to deal with that environment in the same manner as his newly found white "brother" had been doing for centuries.... The post-slave society had no place for the black American, and if there were to be any area of the society where the Negro might have an integral function, that area would have to be one that he created for himself.

While the older musical forms, the dances, hymns and spirituals, the work songs, and so forth continued, a new musical form was needed to meet and fulfill the expressive demands presented by the new social and moral situation confronted by most African Americans. That form became known as the blues, and the blues came to be the foundation of much of African-American secular music up to rap and hip-hop. The blues is to African-American music what the sonnet is to English poetry, a basic form, to be mastered by all with aspirations to excellence, which has been put to the most various expressive uses.[21]

Thus, while often sorrowful, sadness is not the defining essence of the blues (Murray, 1976, pp. 57 ff.). The blues is more abstract and general than a particular emotional tone. Blues music is often joyful, ironic, confrontational, witty, and worldly wise. It is also a highly individual form of expression, both in lyrical content and in performance presentation; a solo performer sings about his or her own experience (Jones, 1963, pp. 65–76; Levine, 1977, pp. 222–223). In the more technical terms of musical device and structure, the blues is a set of expressive conventions and strategies—12-bar AAB form, I IV I V I harmony, call-and-response, the blues scale—within which African Americans have articulated a full view of life as generations of musicians improvise extensions, emendations, expostulations, emancipations, and ecstatically lubricious transubstantiations.

---

21. Charles Keil has recently speculated that the blues might not be as black as we think (Keil and Feld, pp. 198–200). The earliest blues recordings, made back in the teens, were made by whites; thus to the extent that those early recordings played a role in spreading the blues about, it was a white version that spread. It wasn't until about 1920 that we had extensive black blues recordings and it wasn't until the late 1920s that a black blues recording was a hit with blacks. If this speculation turns out to have merit, it might force some revision of Baraka's speculations about the origins of the blues.

As Dizzy Gillespie so often observed, before there was the universe, there was the blues.

While most early blues performers appear to have been male, in the second and third decades of the twentieth century a blues known as the classic blues emerged as a distinct genre, mostly performed by female vocalists, of which Bessie Smith became the best known. W. C. Handy, known as the Father of the Blues, collected and arranged many of these songs, with the "Memphis Blues," "St. Louis Blues" and "Beale Street Blues" among his best-known. The blues has developed many forms throughout the twentieth century, varying between regions, adopting electric instruments after World War II (Keil, 1966), and functioning as a cultural well from which other musical forms could draw inspiration and ideas. One of these forms became know as jazz, which began consolidating in the teens.

Jazz: "It Don't Mean a Thing If It Ain't Got That Swing"

If the blues is one tributary feeding into the jazz delta, then ragtime is the other. Straddling the turn of the century, ragtime was primarily a piano player's music and was strongly influenced by dance forms and the military march (Collier, 1978, p. 51). Scott Joplin was the best known exponent of the music, and his aspirations went far beyond what he was able to realize in his lifetime—his opera, *Treemonisha,* wouldn't receive a full performance until 1972, fifty-five years after his death in 1917 (Collier, 1978, pp. 51–53; Schonberg, 1981, pp. 160–163). Just when jazz finally emerged as a distinct style is uncertain. But it was going strong by the mid-teens.

New Orleans, or traditional jazz, is relatively simple in its devices, but, catalyzed by Louis Armstrong, it quickly evolved into the more sophisticated styling of swing. Jazz became the popular music of the second quarter of the century, naming first the Jazz Age of the twenties, and then the Swing Era of the thirties. Americans of all ages and ethnicity danced to the beat of the African diaspora. Jazz also traveled to Europe, where it was treated with an aesthetic and intellectual seriousness it did not enjoy at home. In time, jazz conquered the rest of the world (cf. Wiora, 1965, pp. 158–159).

Jazz attracted the attention of classical musicians (Ansermet, 1919) who began to incorporate some of its devices into their music as they had drawn on various European folk traditions (Bernstein, 1993, pp. 49–64; Hodier, 1956, pp. 245–263; Schuller, 1990). By this time, the classical tradition had taken its central techniques to their limits and many composers were casting about for new inspiration, new scales, different compositional devices, and more rhythm (Benzon, 1993b; Kramer, 1988; Wiora, 1965, pp. 194–195). At the same time, European artists such as Pablo Picasso were responding to African sculpture (Arnason, n.d., pp. 120–122; Clifford, 1988, pp. 196–200; Ogren, 1989, p. 146; Soyinka, 1987, p. 769) and Sigmund Freud was diagnosing the emotional ills of Western culture. Europeans were ready for a change and jazz gave it to them.

Popular though jazz was, it did not receive universal approval (Ulanov, 1952, pp. 107–108; Ogren, 1989, pp. 103–104, 156 ff.; Stowe, 1994, pp. 30 ff.). In particular, it was denounced for its sexuality. For example, a group of New York citizens formed a commission that complained about "slow jazz, which tempo in itself is the cause of most of the sensual and freakish dancing" (Collier, 1983, p. 121). In 1926 the city of New York passed the first in a series of regulations intended to restrict opportunities for live jazz performance, though the regulations were never stated in those terms (Chivigny, 1991). At one point, Duke Ellington was moved publicly to deny that jazz was responsible for a rash of sex crimes.[22] This disapproval, of course, did not keep whites from listening to the music nor from playing it; white teens and young adults followed the black and white swing bands (Stowe, 1994, pp. 43) and white players swelled the ranks beginning in the early twenties (Collier, 1978, pp. 123 ff.; Peretti, 1992).[23]

The net effect was an influx of African-American musical ideas into Tin Pan Alley and Broadway—for awhile black musicians and dancers thrived on Broadway (Douglas, 1995; Rose, 1989, pp. 46–80; Stearns and Stearns, 1994; Watkins, 1994). White swing bands, from Benny Goodman to Sammy Kaye conquered popular music, with the great black bands of Duke Ellington, Count Basie, Jimmie Lunceford and others playing to a more restricted house (Stowe, 1994). Inevitably, the white bands played sweeter and less expressively than the black. European America admired and desired the particular expressive vitality of jazz, but there were limits to how deeply it could accommodate itself to that expressiveness. Meanwhile the most adventurous jazz musicians—including Charlie Parker, Dizzy Gillespie, Thelonius Monk—invented bop during the early forties. Jazz is a music which slipped the yoke of racist oppression and, in bop, created a style which elevated improvisation to the same level of sophistication European classical music had achieved (Benzon, 1993b). Bop was Art with a capital "A." As A. B. Spellman (1970, p. 193) observed, "The bebop era was the first time that the black ego was expressed in America with self-assurance."

Bop artists went beyond their immediate tradition and explicitly searched other musics for techniques and inspiration. In the late forties Dizzy Gillespie (1979, pp. 317 ff.) hired a Cuban drummer, Chano Pozo. Since the drums had not been banned in Cuba, African rhythm survived there intact; when Gillespie brought Pozo to his band, he thus reestablished contact with African rhythm. Art Blakey traveled to Africa in 1948 and 1949 and brought African techniques and, later on, drummers back to America (Brown, 1988; Weinstein, 1992, pp. 50–51). In 1956 Dizzy Gillespie became the first jazz musician to go on a world tour sponsored by the U. S. State Department (Gillespie, 1979, pp. 411–427). His band was organized by the same Quincy Delight Jones, Jr. who would later become a vice president of Mercury Records and win fame and fortune as the producer of Michael Jackson's most successful albums (Ostransky, 1988). In the sixties Elvin Jones continued investigating African polyrhythms and studied Indian rhythms as

---

22. I don't know exactly when Ellington gave this particular testimony, but I am sure that he gave it. The September 1989 issue of *down beat* was an anniversary issue, with sections devoted to the 30s, 40s, etc. Each section contained pieces *down beat* printed in that year. The section for the thirties (p. 22) contained the story of Ellington's denial, but gave no publication information.

23. There have been, and are, very fine white jazz musicians—Jack Teagarden, Benny Goodman, Stan Getz, and Phil Woods come to mind. However, the primary innovators, the musicians who have made the deepest contributions to the language of jazz, have been overwhelmingly black. It is not clear why so few whites have made it to the top ranks, but two possibilities come to mind: 1) That no white musician can know the culture deeply enough to make a seminal contribution; 2) That white musicians have the option of going into classical music, an option effectively closed for blacks (cf. Harrington, 1992, pp. 228–234), and that is where the very best of them go.

well (cf. Feather, 1966, p. 169); he moved the drummer from an accompanying role to one of full collaboration with the horn-playing soloists. John Coltrane investigated Indian music to expand the possibilities of melodic improvisation in jazz. Jazz musicians have have continued to search the globe for musical ideas.

However, this increased sophistication had a cost, for it demanded greater sophistication from the listener than swing and traditional jazz. With sophistication in short supply, the jazz audience shrank and jazz ceased to be a strong and direct force in popular music. The blues continued to evolve independently of jazz and, in the late thirties and early forties, small "jump" bands developed as an offshoot of the big bands (Keil, 1966, pp. 61 ff.; Collier, 1978, pp. 449; Ventura, 1987b, pp. 88–89). This music would become that grab-bag called rhythm and blues and it would emerge on the far side of World War II and the Korean War as the seed bed and inspiration of rock and roll.

From the beginning, jazz had a white audience (Collier, 1983, pp. 88 ff.; 1993, pp. 219 ff.), an audience it would keep throughout its history to the present day. I am unaware of any figures from jazz's early days, but the following figures concerning interest in jazz, based on a 1982 study by the U. S. Bureau of the Census, are worth examining (Horowitz, 1990, p. 5):

Race	Number of Adults	Attend Live Events	Watch on TV	Listen to Radio	Listen to Recordings
Black	17,470,000	15%	28%	36%	36%
White	143,355,000	9%	17%	16%	18%
Other	3,750,000	9%	21%	23%	20%

While the percentage of black people is larger than the percentage of white people in all categories, the number of whites is so much larger that, in absolute terms, the white jazz audience is larger than the black; the percentages for "other" are between black and white in three of four categories while the absolute numbers are smaller than either. If we consider just those who attend lived events, the category implying the most substantial commitment, we have 2,620,500 blacks and 12,901,950 whites, almost five times the number of blacks. Just when the absolute number of white jazz fans became larger than the absolute number of blacks is not known; but these 1982 figures do not reflect a dramatically new situation. Similar percentages must have existed for decades. The inspiration and major innovators are black, but the audience has been largely white for most of jazz's history.

Rock: "Roll Over Beethoven"

The mid-fifties simultaneously gave us the civil rights movement and the birth of rock and roll. Both shocked mainstream America. The civil rights movement produced protest music which, in the sixties, would merge with rock to become a generalized music of political and cultural protest. It also provided a paradigm for political action which inspired the anti-war protests of the sixties.

As for rock and roll, its roots are in the rhythm and blues of musicians like Big Boy Crudup, Little Richard, Chuck Berry, Fats Domino, and Bo Diddley with musicians like Elvis Presley, Jerry Lee Lewis, and Bill Haley taking it into the white world (Ennis, 1992; Guralnick, 1994; Palmer, 1990; Puterbaugh, 1990; Ventura, 1987b, pp. 89 ff.). There it was soundly denounced by older whites for its lawless sensuality (Martin and Segrave, 1993; Schipper, 1990), and considerable political effort, including Congressional hearings, was marshaled in an effort to rid America of this nasty music. Once again the morals of America's youth were being undermined by sexy music. Writing in 1987 (pp. 68–81), the conservative scholar Allan Bloom gives a reasoned, if not reasonable, account of this rejection of rock and roll.

Unlike the swing era, however, this time music became a generational issue (Ennis, 1992, pp. 283–312; Hobsbawm, 1994, pp. 324–327; Palmer, 1990, p. 46). In the twenties, thirties, and forties, young and old alike, black or white, danced to much the same music. But rock and roll split the European-American world into youths and elders. Those who reached adulthood by the beginning of the fifties did not, by and large, dance to rock and roll, which thus became a music for adolescents (see Early, 1989, pp. 99 ff.). As those adolescents grew older, and their younger siblings moved into puberty, rock and roll became the expressive catalyst for a generation of cultural and political protest. By the mid-sixties, many of the best and brightest sons and daughters of the European-American middle class were joining the civil rights movement, protesting the war in Vietnam, chanting and meditating, taking hallucinogenic drugs, proclaiming and acting on sexual freedom, growing concerned about the environment, revising gender roles, and, in general, trying to create what became journalistically known as the counter-culture. All of this activity was reflected in the lyrics of rock and roll and energized by its beat. White middle-class youth had adopted black rhythm as the expressive catalyst for their assault on the culture they had inherited. They danced to a different drummer and dreamed of forming a new society grounded in those rhythms.

Rock and roll developed and became polymorphous, with many of the most important performers coming from England (Ennis, 1992; Gilmore, 1990). In various ways—the Beatles harmonically and melodically, Bob Dylan lyrically, and Jimi Hendrix with his outrageous jivometric guitar virtuosity—rock achieved a level of musical and lyrical sophistication comparable to the best of Broadway and Tin Pan Alley and of swing-era jazz. In the mid-fifties Bo Diddley had introduced what came to be known as the Bo Diddley beat into rock and roll; that beat was a standard West African rhythm which made its way here via the Caribbean. Other musicians mated rock with every conceivable musical style (Pond, 1990). One strain, heavy metal, substituted anger for the sexuality which rock had inherited from African America.

Meanwhile, the civil rights movement developed a more militant side and black cultural nationalism proliferated and became more visible to white America. As African-American cultural nationalism became national news, the musicians continued to produce new music. Marvin Gaye, Otis Redding, Aretha Franklin, James Brown, Stevie Wonder and Co. gave us soul; George Clinton, funk; and Ray Charles did everything. The electric urban blues of musicians such as B.B. King flourished and was recognized and adopted by European Americans. Jazz musicians confronted the same limitations of harmonic structures which classical composers encountered early in the century and developed an avant-garde that espoused jazz free of all rules and structures (see Benzon, 1993b; Collier, 1978, pp. 454–478; Litweiler, 1984). In some of this music, anger came to replace sexuality at the music's expressive core. At the same time, the foundations were laid for "classicizing" jazz. In the late sixties Rahsaan Roland Kirk began performing the whole history of jazz, from traditional New Orleans, through bop, to free jazz (Barkan, 1974), while the avant-garde Art Ensemble of Chicago made reference to that entire history, though not actually performing in those various styles (Rockwell, 1983, pp. 164–175). This effort would bear fruit in the eighties when a whole new generation of jazz musicians, led by the New Orleans trumpeter, Wynton Marsalis, would embrace older, more conservative, jazz styles as their primary expressive vehicle, consciously proclaiming that jazz has a history which performers must keep current through the playing of all its styles, not just the most recent ones.

On the whole, my sense is that this crossing of African- and European-American music was more extensive in its effects than that of the swing era. That it helped drive a wedge between the so-called baby boomers and their elders is the surest sign of this; and the broader cultural exploration catalyzed by rock and roll was more extensive than that of swing. Neither oriental religion nor drug use were new; nineteenth-century European musicians, poets, and intellectuals experimented with opium and hashish and knew Hindu literature, philosophy, and mystical practice. But the sixties and seventies saw members of various Eastern religious sects soliciting contributions in every airport, and hallucinogenic drug use became common recreation. None of this is directly African American, but African America provided the music which became the dominant and most widely shared expressive vehicle for all this activity. Blacks showed how to slip the yoke of repression and young whites proceeded to sew wild oats in every field they could find.

Finally, hidden in the background, the computer came of age. Computer courses began appearing in colleges during the middle sixties. I can remember my freshman year at the all-male Johns Hopkins when one of my classmates generated considerable interest with a female nude printed by a computer in a pattern of Xs and Os; that was 1965. Over the years, some students would become captivated by computers and become hackers, living for computing the way their Dionysian counterparts lived for sex, drugs, and rock and roll. Hacking developed into a counter-culture of its own (cf. Levy, 1984; Turkle, 1984). Yet, it shared a theme with the more publicized world of the flower-bedecked hippies: mind expansion. The hippies sought mind expansion in drugs and meditation; the hackers sought it in doing vastly clever things with computers, even attempting to make the machines think personal computers and video games were invented in the late seventies. Some of the hackers went into big business and some had counter-cultural dreams of changing the world through computers. During the middle eighties, computers would meet reggae and rock and roll in the world of science fiction, yielding cyberpunk.[24] And yet, as we'll see in the next section, African rhythm remained just around the corner.

---

24. One way to trace the links between the counter-culture of the sixties and the computer culture would be to follow the work of Stewart Brand, whose *The Last Whole Earth Catalog* published in 1971 quickly became something of a counter-culture bible. Brand published subsequent updates and established a quarterly magazine, *The Coevolution Quarterly*, which became *The Whole Earth Review*. In 1984 Brand published the *Whole Earth Software Catalog*, a guide to personal computing, and in 1987 wrote a book about MIT's Media Lab. More recently, Paul Levinson has reminded me, Brand had a role in founding *Wired*, a computer culture magazine with a graphic and verbal style deeply indebted to the sixties rock culture. Cyberpunk was defined by William Gibson's 1984 novel, *Neuromancer* (1984), in which video games meet reggae. *The Mississippi Review* devoted a special double issue to cyberpunk guest-edited by Larry McCaffery, Volume 16, numbers 2 and 3. For a brief chronology see Ravo and

Rap: "U Can't Touch This"

As the United States rolled into the late seventies, African America proposed a new music: rap, or hip-hop (George, 1988, 1992; Costello and Wallace, 1990; Gilroy, 1993, pp. 33–34, 103–110; Rose, 1994; Samuels, 1991). In the late seventies, black performers such as Michael Jackson and Lionel Richie became so successful in modifying their music to more effectively cross over to white audiences that a vacuum began to develop in popular music, which no longer satisfied the expressive needs of the black audience. Rap emerged to fill that vacuum. While rap, like all genres, has its antecedents—e.g., the tight rhythms of James Brown, the verbal games and poems of the street corner—it has features which make it a new point of musical departure:

1. It employs a technique of musical collage which depends on an extant library of recordings.
2. It is the most insistently rhythmic of the black genres, reducing melody and harmony to a minimal, and mostly background, role.
3. It has the most elaborate lyrics.
4. It often substitutes anger for the sensuality which had been basic to earlier forms.

The joint effect of these factors is that rap does not follow directly from the blues and gospel base which had been the cradle of African-American basic musical expression throughout this century—a point we will return to later. Rather, rap looks to verbal combat, oral narrative, and rhythm as its points of departure.

On the first point, rappers use fragments of extant recordings to create a background for the foreground rapping. This began in a multiple turntable technique in which one performer created a background of fragments from various sources while creating a strong rhythmic pulse through scratching a record with a turntable needle. With the advent of digital recording technology this evolved into an elaborate and sophisticated technique of digital collage. That makes it the first musical genre the existence of which depends on modern recording technology. It is one thing to make full use of recording technology to facilitate creating music which, in principle, could have been made otherwise; that has been going on in popular music at least since the Beatles recorded *Sgt. Pepper's Lonely Hearts Club Band* in the mid-sixties. Synthesizers and multitracking are enormously convenient; but, for the most part, music made with this technology could have been made more conventionally by different means. But the rappers take fragments from various different recordings and electronically combine them into a background which thus becomes a kind of archeological record of, mostly pop, mostly—though not exclusively—black, music. Technology has become intrinsic to rap's creation, not just a means of preserving and distributing the music.

Ironically, this most technological of musics is also relentlessly rhythmic. The rapper weaves his, or in some cases her, words over the hi-tech background which is not only highly rhythmic but, at times, is even anti-melodic and anti-harmonic

---

Cash (1993). David Porush has commented on cyberpunk's cultural and neural imperatives (1987, 1991). For a look at a journalistic fellow-traveller, pick up an issue of *Wired,* or better yet, of *Mondo 2000,* which features garish art direction, guidance on "smart" drugs (i.e., drugs which are supposed to enhance mental performance) and digital media, and interviews.

because the combined fragments are not in the same key. The resulting tonal clash works against even the fragmented melodies and harmonies to emphasize the rhythm. No other form of black American music is so insistently rhythmic as rap. Jazz rhythm may be more complex and sophisticated, but jazz also has considerable melodic and harmonic play. Rap has little beyond the rhythm—and the words. If, in the contemporary symbolic universe, the computer stands for disembodied mind, then rap rhythm violently links that mind to back the rhythmic body.

Such a move has deep roots in African-American culture. For example, after the Titanic sank, blacks began reciting a poem about that sinking in which a black boilerman, Shine, escapes despite attempts to keep him on board by offering him money and the sexual favors of a white woman, the captain's daughter (Jackson, 1974). In the popular mind, the Titanic was a symbol of technology triumphant; it was supposed to be unsinkable. Shine triumphed over that hubris and, in rejecting sex, countered white notions of black sexuality (cf. Jackson, p. 36). Charles Keil (1966, pp. 175–176) discusses this "nonmachine tradition" in his analysis of the concept of soul, a tradition which led many jazz musicians to form an ideological resistance to the electrical instrumentation of rock and roll. It is almost as though the rhythmic insistence was necessary to reclaim rap from the dangers of its intrinsic technological commitment.

Then, we have the words; among other things, they boast, and they finger the whiteman as a source of evil. Rap has more words than any other form of American music, except, perhaps, for the talking blues. Those words are manipulated as much for rhythmic effect as for what they say. Those words have, more than anything else, brought African-American verbal virtuosity (see Abrahams, 1970; Jackson, 1974) to mass public awareness—note that the Titanic poem mentioned above is in this tradition and is thus a precursor to rap. Between the words and the rhythm, rap is the most relentlessly and consciously Black, as in Not-White, form African America has produced. It is also the angriest. We have noted that avant-garde jazz musicians and heavy metal rockers created music steeped in anger. Avant-garde jazz has never had a large audience, while the heavy-metal audience is almost exclusively white, as are its musicians. Rap is the first mass-audience black form based on anger, giving it an ambivalent relationship to heavy-metal rock, one of its sources of musical samples (Costello and Wallace, 1990, pp. 67–68; George, 1992, p. 130). It is not clear what to make of this fact.

The mainstream media has, of course, focused on this anger as expressed in the genre of "gangsta" rap, objecting that it is sexist, racist, and excessively violent. Once again, as in the case of jazz and rock in prior generations, the nation's moral health is said to be imperiled, in this case by the misogyny, anti-white attitudes, and all-around violence of the gangstas. Whatever merits this line of criticism has, we should note that the misogyny was not invented by the gangstas. It is widespread in American society, certainly in those conservative circles most offended by rap (hooks, 1994, p. 116). Further, such criticism is focused too exclusively on only one segment of the hip-hop market and is oblivious to the fact there are oppositional forces within the hip-hop world. Thus, for example, female rappers will put out music explicitly criticizing and challenging sexist lyrics (Rose, 1994, pp. 146–182). The anti-white attitudes are no more defensible than is white racism, but one has a sense that much of the criticism and dismay has as much to do with an ethnocentric inability to understand how black people could possibly resent white society as with any consistent moral reasoning. Beyond this we can note that the general anger has been with us all along. Expressing it is, no doubt, a positive step. But, to the extent that that anger is motivated by a desire for an expressive culture which is Black beyond any possibility of White co-optation, that anger runs up against the relentless social psychodynamics of racism.

For, as relentlessly black as rap has been, since the mid-eighties its largest audience has been white, and male (Samuels, 1991; cf. Harrington, 1992, pp. 376–382). One is reminded of Gerald Early's (1989, p. 138) remark about a passage from Norman Mailer's account of the Ali-Foreman bout in Zaire where Mailer "expresses a very simple and very old idea here, namely, that the black male is metaphorically the white male's unconsciousness personified." The hidden psycho-social logic of racism has operated so that the anger black rappers express on their own behalf, and against whites, matches the anger white males feel—perhaps about themselves, or their elders, or both—but are not so willing to express. The anger which drove the rapper to create something which is, among other things, ethnically his, allows whites to feel their own anger though the rappers' performance while getting the vicarious thrill of an imaginary trip to the archetypal exotic Black Jungle Ghetto much as, half a century ago, their grandparents went to the Cotton Club to view erotic stage shows danced to hot jazz.

Yet, rap has not so far spawned a significant group of white rappers. Whites do perform it, but the majority of the performers, for both the white and black audience, remain black. Thus rap is not following the pattern set, first in the swing era, then in the rock and roll period, when the large white audience was served by white performers who imitated black models.

This suggests that the psycho-cultural dynamic of musical expression is undergoing a fundamental change. If, following Baraka, we think of the blues as an "expressive contract" between free blacks and white American society, then hiphop may represent a new aesthetic contract. The old contract was in force up until the Reagan presidential administration in the 1980s. This contract was based on a fundamental hope for the future and a belief in the possibility of social justice. All of the secular music of African-America was produced under the terms of this contract, as were the white imitations and reconstructions of black music. One aspect of this contract was that there would be little criticism or even mention of white racism in song lyrics. But, as hope began to falter in the 1980s, a new expressive contract became necessary. Hip-hop has emerged as the vehicle of that contract and pointed commentary on white racism is now an explicit part of America's expressive culture at the broadest level.

Meanwhile, the European-American division of the culture produced an art music which both had a large following and was not oriented toward nineteenth-century classical music. Called minimal, presumably because it had little or no harmonic movement, the music of musicians such as Philip Glass, Terry Riley, and Steve Reich was strongly influenced by various non-Western musics, including, jazz, Indian, West African, and Balinese gamelan (Rockwell, 1983, pp. 109–122; Glass, 1987; Page, 1992, pp. 66–83, 118–121). With its roots in the sixties, this music emerged to full public view in the eighties. While other music in the European tradition had taken elements from African-American and other non-Western musics, and put them to classical use, this assimilation had never been very deep. At its core, such music remained European in outlook. The minimalists absorbed non-Western lessons so deeply into their music that it must be considered a new departure from its founding expressive tradition just as hip-hop is a departure from its founding tradition. Where classical music had a narrative intent Philip Glass talks of the fundamentally meditative nature of his music. It achieves this aim through cyclic repetition of melodic fragments (cf. Sprenkle, 1986). Through this repetition the minimalists are restoring rhythmic complexity to the European tradition, thereby moving that tradition beyond the bounds of Western culture.

Thus, at the beginning of the nineties the North American crossing of Africa and Europe leaves us, on the one hand, with rap, which is a rhythmically intense point of departure from/within its African-American tradition of basic expression, and, on the other hand, with minimalism, a rhythmically intense point of departure from/within its European-American tradition of art music. There are hints that the classical world is loosening up; Nadja Salerno-Sonnenberg has recently observed that "The rules are less strict now, so we can appreciate the music more" (Roca, 1992, p. 6). Meanwhile, serious young men in Armani suits have been leading a strong jazz classicist movement based on styles from swing through bop to sixties modal jazz, and the jazz avant-garde has been raiding popular dance forms for rhythmic foundations on which to improvise spiky towers of sound. Aging rockers from the sixties continue to record and to tour while rock critics have been writing obituaries for a decade. Clearly, it is time for another spin of the evolutionary dice and Africa and Europe prepare to cross into the next millennium.

The Pattern So Far: "Freedom Over Me"

The critical question is, of course: is this process moving in some direction or is it just drifting in cultural space? One aspect of this question concerns the evolution of musical culture; the other aspect is whether or not there has been any change in the underlying psycho-social dynamic. Is the psychological pressure of racism easing up? And, if so, can we reasonably attribute some of that change to the social dynamics of expressive culture?

In the first phase of this musical evolution—jazz and swing—white America simply picked up on the music black America created and proceeded to develop its own version. At its best the white version has had lasting value; but, on the whole, it is in the black music that we find the most compelling players and performances. In the second phase—rock and roll—white America again picked up on black music, this time rhythm and blues. Rock and roll precipitated a generational split and, developing more richly than white swing had done, became the central expressive medium for a generation of social, political, and cultural protest and experimentation. Black music provided a catalytic vehicle for a generation of white Americans, moving them away from the Europe-dominated mainstream. It provided for occasions of muscular bonding, to recall William McNeill's (1995) phrase, which could solidify social networks among those seeking alternatives to middle-class American business-as-usual.

Beyond the music, the black protest of the civil rights movement provided an immediate precedent, example, and training ground for white anti-war protest; it was a source of social legitimacy and tactical example. I want to go out on still another speculative limb and argue that the civil rights movement owes a debt to jazz. I suggest that the political protests of the fifties and sixties are, in part, an indirect effect of the first phase, the jazz phase, of this overall expressive evolution; the musical expression of the 20s, 30s, and 40s had effects in society which helped enable the political expression of the 50s and 60s. Bop is important here, for with the creation of bop, African America created a rich and powerful art music, yet one which operated on very different principles from European classical music. That cultural achievement catalyzed a self-assurance without which the civil rights movement would have been difficult, if not impossible.

Organized political protest cannot be fueled by anger and outrage alone; it requires communal cohesion guided by a sense of dignity and of real possibility. The achievements of bop musicians contributed to that sense and that possibility (cf. Kofsky, 1970; Hobsbawm, 1993, pp. 229–247). To be sure, the civil rights movement got much of its leadership from the church, which is so central to African-American society (Lincoln and Mamiya, 1990)—a centrality which is being viciously highlighted by the racist burnings of black churches which have been occurring as I prepare this essay in the summer of 1996. But, as we saw above, the link between secular black music and the church is a close and intimate one, albeit often strained. Whatever the direct contribution of bop, and later, jazz musicians to the civil rights movement, the indirect effect—working through those who heard the music, and even those who only talked to those who heard the music— was surely significant. As Frank Kofsky (Kofsky, 1970, pp. 56 ff.) pointed out, when Charlie Parker played "Now's the Time" he was talking politics. How many of those who sang "We Shall Overcome" got to that point by listening to Parker tell them the time was ripe?

Then we need to consider the white counter-culture of the sixties. Its music, rock and roll, was directly influenced by rhythm and blues, which in turn evolved from earlier swing and blues. But the possibility of going beyond mere adolescent friskiness required the political climate of the civil rights movement, itself indebted to the spirit of jazz self-assertion. Thus black expressive energy influenced the counter-culture both directly through rhythm and blues and indirectly through the civil rights movement.

With the emergence of hip-hop the cultural dance takes a new turn. The black music which rock and roll took as its starting point followed naturally from the music which proceeded it. But rap represents a new point of African-American departure. Its anger is of its own time, but its expressive confidence, its willingness to break with the past, is a legacy of bop's assuredness and power. Similarly, bop is behind the minimalist wing of classical composition, providing paradigm and inspiration as an art music based on principles radically different from European art music. Rap anger and minimalist meditation inform the furthest extensions of the stylistic interaction between Africa and Europe. Only time will tell whether these are the catalytic engines of cultural forms steaming across a new savanna of human possibility.

Beyond the music, what has been so far achieved? Is there any evidence that European America is being cured of its psycho-social ills? Racism is still strong, and the projective psychodynamic which drives it still functions. However, that dynamic may be weakening; at least some whites have learned their lessons well and racist attitudes seem to be on the wane (Sniderman and Piazza, 1993). There is reason to believe that the sexual revolution has not been mere hype (Efron, 1985, pp. 7 ff.). For example, unmarried couples can now cohabitate openly and freely, something unthinkable in the *Father Knows Best* era and before. Attitudes have changed as well. In an interview with Peter Whitmer (1987, p. 127), the avant-garde novelist William S. Burroughs remarked:

[Skeptics about the 60s] don't seem to realize that forty years ago, four-letter words did not appear on printed pages; that when I was in my twenties and thirties [he was born in 1914], the idea that a Mexican or a black or a queer was anything but a second-class citizen was simply absurd. These were tremendous changes. Then, of course, the end of censorship.

Certainly there is much more writing and talk about sexuality. Much of it is superficial, such as that on television talk shows. But the talk exists, and that in itself is progress. In particular, there is a great deal of talk about the ugly consequences of misguided sexuality—e.g., child abuse. Such talk, which deeply questions the integrity of family dynamics, would have been impossible fifty or a hundred years ago. Before we can change our behavior and our hearts, we must be able to talk, from the heart, about that behavior. These changes in behavior and attitude have such strenuous opposition that we cannot confidently predict the future. Yet, if the talk continues, behavior may continue changing as well and the inheritors of the Western cultural legacy may create a more emotionally satisfying culture, one which no longer needs to use racism as a way of dealing with emotional conflict.

We need also to consider the revised appearance of African Americans on television and in the movies (Gates, 1989; Harrington, 1992, pp. 353–376). The 1977 miniseries *Roots,* based on Alex Haley's book, became the most highly rated program in network history. Blacks are no longer confined to subservient, marginal and low-life roles—maids, butlers, hookers, and hustlers—a circumstance indicating greater white willingness to see blacks as people, not merely as projective screens. Denzel Washington's portrayal of Don Pedro in Kenneth Branagh's 1993 film of Shakespeare's *Much Ado About Nothing* is a particularly striking example of color-blind casting. Bill Cosby took a black brush to the American Dream and created the most popular television show of the eighties.[25] Spike Lee catalyzed a sepia revolu-

---

25. This development certainly merits more attention than I am competent to give it. But I would like to offer some praise for Bill Cosby. Cosby's Huxtable family embodied widely shared values and aspirations which we might as well call The American Dream—interesting and remunerative careers for mother and father, attractive children, familial harmony, an elegant home and nice clothes all around. Previous African-American families on prime-time television were quite different. Fred Sanford (& Son) was a junkman living in the ghetto. George Jefferson (& family) was very successful, but also very insecure in the status attendant upon his material success. His insecurity may well be closer to reality than the Huxtables' easy self-assurance, but prime-time TV is mythology, not sociology. The myth is that everyone has a right to what the Huxtables have. That, by the way, these particular people are black, simply puts African-Americans at the center of this myth.

As a statement of the situation of black America *The Cosby Show* was certainly inadequate, and was criticized on that account (cf. Zoglin, 1987, p. 60; Gates, 1989, p. 40). But it is quite clear that Cosby never intended a full sociological treatment of contemporary African America. He was interested in mythologizing and, as mythologist, he was brilliant. As an example, consider the scene where, in honor of the forty-ninth wedding anniversary of Cliff's (played by Cosby) parents, the whole family performs to a record of Ray Charles' "Night Time is the Right Time." Cliff and his son Theo mime along with Ray's voice. Nice enough, and, from Cosby, some brilliant comic understatement. But the real focus is on the women and girls who take the roles of the Raelets. All of them, from mother Claire to young Rudy, swing their hips and sing. The song's statement is very simple and basic: "The night time, is the right time, to be with the one you love." And the way those ladies move makes it quite clear just why the night time is so right.

The attitude, the ethos, thus being expressed is absolutely scandalous in the context of conventional middle-class values. That children and grandchildren should honor their elders, yes

tion in cinema, creating mythically compelling depictions of black street life and rage (*Do the Right Thing*), the incendiary subject of inter-racial sex (*Jungle Fever*) and the polymorphic life of Malcolm X. Fears that *Do the Right Thing* would provoke riots (George, 1992, p. 35; Lee, 1991, p. 15) proved to be white projective paranoia, and, while some films did provoke largely black-on-black violence (George, 1992, pp. 152–156), that was different in kind and considerably less lethal than the rise in lynchings following the 1915 release of the thoroughly racist *Birth of a Nation* (Du Bois, 1940, pp. 729–730). African-American expressive genius is thus moving into a visual arena where one cannot pretend the blackness away—as one might pretend it away while listing to a record or the radio (for a chronology of expressive progress since 1971, see George, 1992, pp. 9–40).

To be sure, this cultural progress tragically parallels social conditions which, for many African Americans, are worse than they were twenty or thirty years ago (Hacker, 1992; Kondracke, 1989; Vann Woodward, 1989). But we should not allow the one face of this disparity to blind us to the other. The cultural progress is real, and so is the social regress. History works in mysterious ways and, if we are to influence its path into the future, we must take full note of its complexity, contradiction, and paradox.[26]

---

that is fine. But such a performance is hardly an honorable one. We should remember that, thirty years ago, when Elvis took his swinging pelvis to the Ed Sullivan show, his motions were censored. Now the same movements appear on a wholesome family TV show as a gift from granddaughters to admiring and loving grandparents. Such a thing would have been shocking on those stalwarts of fifties television, *Father Knows Best* or *Ozzie and Harriet*.

Such stylish and easy sensuality was central to *The Cosby Show*. It was most consistently present in the way Cosby moved and talked, but the other members of the family showed it in varying degrees. It was also present, of course, in the music, which included Stevie Wonder, Frank Foster and the Count Basie Orchestra, Dizzy Gillespie, Duke Ellington and John Coltrane (Cliff and Claire end one episode slow-slow-dancing to a recording of Ellington's "In a Sentimental Mood"), Joe Williams (jazz singer who played Claire's father), and Art Blakey. This style is, in the cultural psychodynamics we've been tracing, both a racist stereotype and a viable and vibrant cultural style. As stereotype it appeared in the various low-life characters— pimps, hookers, pushers, hustlers, thieves, and so forth—to which African-Americans have generally been relegated in movies and TV. Cosby's genius is to move this style into the middle-class, away from stereotypical low-life characters. Not only is he saying "African-Americans can be middle-class" he is also saying that "The middle-class can be sexy."

26. While I think about musical sophistication as distinct levels of cultural rank, a theoretical approach I have developed with David Hays (Benzon and Hays, 1990b; Hays, 1992; Benzon, 1993b), in the interests of readers unfamiliar with that theory, I have avoided it in the body of the essay. For those familiar with that work, or interested in becoming familiar with it, here is my sense of how the various musical genres mentioned in this essay fit into that framework:

Rank 1, Basic Expression: traditional jazz, most blues, rhythm and blues, most rock, rap.

Rank 2, Entertainment: swing-era jazz; fusion; some blues; the polystylistic Ray Charles; some rock, including the Beatles starting with *Sgt. Pepper's Lonely Hearts Club Band*, Bob Dylan, the Jimi Hendrix of *Electric Ladyland*, Frank Zappa, the Grateful Dead, the Talking Heads; the Broadway musical; singers such as Frank Sinatra, Tony Bennett, Judy Garland, Barbara Streisand.

Rank 3, Art: European classical; bop, and modal jazz.

Rank 4, Beyond art, candidates: such jazz as the Art Ensemble of Chicago and the World Saxophone Quartet; minimalist classical.

This classification should be treated cautiously and it is certainly subject to criticism and revision, both in the basic theory and in the application of that theory to music. Note partic-

Conclusion: Stepping Out on a New Savanna

Let's work our way to the end of this essay by considering a passage from Charles Keil's classic study, *Urban Blues* (1966, p. 197):

> Freedom cannot be given, dignity cannot be granted; but a deeper understanding of another way of life—perhaps even a profound respect for cultural differences—is possible. In the world of today and tomorrow it is necessary for survival. No nation on earth has yet achieved a lasting and productive cultural pluralism... The problem of the Negro in America is inextricably meshed with the problem of America in the world; and, as many confused prophets before me have noted, anything can happen, ranging from catastrophe to a golden age.

That is the issue before us. The United States is a single, highly diverse society, but it is culturally plural. At the heart of that society is a psycho-cultural engine which has crossed expressive practices of European and African ancestry. That same engine has killed many many people through direct and indirect racist violence. The question is whether or not the positive effects of the emerging expressive culture will be able to keep ahead and even gain on the effects of destructive violence. I know of no way to reason toward a strong conclusion on this issue. We simply do not have intellectual tools suitable to this task.

The full assimilation of African Americans to European-American culture is not a viable option. As long as emotional repression remains the norm in European-American culture, some means are needed to relieve that emotional strain. For too many whites, racist scapegoating remains an important source of strain relief. These people can't permit assimilation as it would threaten their emotional stability. On the other hand, African-American culture has positive features absent in European-American culture. Those who value this culture can't assimilate without destroying that expressive virtuosity and the social practices and values which nurture and support it.

The grimmest possibility is that this social engine will simply collapse and the United States will destroy itself in an orgy of "ethnic cleansing." Less grim, but by no means acceptable, is that the system will achieve some steady state in which expressive genres come and go, but the underlying psycho-cultural engine remains intact—I am reminded here of the centuries during which the Chinese dissipated psychological energy through binding the feet of their girls and women, a practice which may have killed ten percent of its victims (Fairbank, 1992). The only acceptable possibility is that a new social order will evolve in which expressive practices allow people to mature without such a heavy burden of emotional repression. In such a society assimilation would not be an issue.

The point of this essay is that fragments of such a society have already been evolving through the interaction between African and European America. That

---

ularly that the common stylistic designators—jazz, blues, pop, etc.—do not line up precisely with cultural rank.

This scheme reveals that the most active crossing from African America to European America took place at Ranks 1 and 2. It took a long time for Rank 3 European music to absorb African-American influence. When it finally did so, the result appears to be a music (minimalism) which has a foot in the next rank of cultural evolution.

evolution certainly has further to go and success is not certain. The possibility of success will surely increase if we become more aware of the psychological and social mechanisms driving this evolution. European America can afford that awareness only by acknowledging that Western culture is not eternal. The Western way has never been the only route to truth, love, beauty, and justice. And surely the political, scientific, and aesthetic ideals of the Western legacy will flourish more fully in a society freed of emotional repression and its correlative racism. Similarly, African America needs assurance that history is not a grand white conspiracy against peoples of color. Only with freedom and dignity thus assured can it grow beyond the mentality of victimization to assume the leadership responsibilities which the twenty-first century offers.

The West, as a particular set of cultural practices, ideas, and attitudes, is temporally bounded; it had a beginning and it must have an end as well (cf. West, 1993a, pp. 124–136; 1993b, pp. 116 ff.; 1993c, pp. 5 ff.). While it is common to place ancient Greece, Rome, and Israel within the bounds of Western culture, that intellectual reflex is anachronistic. That the West owes much to those cultures is certain, just as it is certain the West owes much to the mathematicians and natural philosophers of the Near and Far East. But were any Westerner to journey back to any of those cultures, she would surely find it exotic and alien. For example, the Greece we identify with elegant white temples is a dead Greece. In the days when those temples hosted the ceremonies and celebrants of a living religion they were painted in strong contrasting colors (Gombrich, 1951, p. 63). The contrast between pure white, on the one hand, and on the other, vivid blues and reds and yellows, is surely both a metaphor and a metonymy for the difference between ancient Greece considered as a Western nation and Greece as it actually was lived. Western culture originated in the cross-cultural flux of people, ideas, and attitudes in and between Europe and the Near East from the twelfth century through the European Renaissance. But the emergence of Western culture was not *a priori* inevitable and we should not pretend that it was by so casually assuming that Greece, Rome, and Israel were Western nations. Some of their culture traits survived in the West, but many did not.[27]

The Renaissance fixes the boundary at the beginning of Western culture, with its emotional repression and its correspondingly ambivalent interaction with Africa. What begins in time must also end in time. Western culture began to disperse at the turn of this century while simultaneously African America began driving the 20th Century Blues Unlimited into the forefront of cultural evolution.

While we continue to refer to modern physics, astronomy, chemistry, and biology as sciences, those disciplines have a theoretical and experimental style which differs as much from seventeenth, eighteenth, and nineteenth-century practice as that classical style differed from the natural philosophy which preceded it (Ben-

---

27. Despite much vigorous criticism of Eurocentric accounts of history and of non-European peoples, the notion that there is such as thing as Western culture has not been given much critical examination. "The West" is one essence which seems to have escaped current critiques of essentialism. Some preliminary steps toward such a critique can be found in James Clifford (1988, p. 272), Eric Wolf (1982, pp. 5–7), Marshall Hodgson (1993, pp. 6 ff., 255 ff.), and in Cornel West's (1993c, pp. 120–121, 125) remarks on the concept of Europe. I have been much concerned about the biological metaphor implicit in talking about entities such as French culture, Samoan culture, or Western culture as though they were analogues to biological species and have concluded that this way of thinking is nonsense (Benzon, in press).

zon and Hays, 1990b). Science continues, but the most advanced theorizing and experimentation is more sophisticated in kind and deserves a different name—one, I might add, more felicitous than a prefixed mongrel like "post-science." Similarly, the expressive regime of Western capital "A" Art—classical music, realistic painting and sculpture, the novel, and so forth—began to collapse at the turn of the century (Hays, 1992; Benzon, 1993a; Benzon, 1993b) with the most adventuresome workers seeking new forms. Political and economic institutions continue, but they are under great stress.

Even as the West is dissipating, post-Western culture is emerging and we are living, some even thriving, in it. Post-scientific thought, in physics, astronomy, chemistry, and biology, not to mention computing and other fields, is, by definition, post-Western. To think of it any other way is to misunderstand the course and nature of cultural evolution. With musicians—and athletes, dancers and preachers as well—as its unacknowledged legislators, the African-American blues train and its various crosses with European America, Europe itself, Asia and Latin America, and Africa itself is part of an era following Western domination of world history. These emerging cultures have strong African roots, but they are no more African than Western culture has been Greek, Roman, or Hebrew. They also have strong European roots. They are hybrids. Neither African nor European, they are emerging to sing and dance the united states of the blues on the new savanna of the 21st century.

Acknowledgements

This essay was written out of the conviction that the twentieth century owes as much to Daniel Louis Armstrong—a.k.a. Satchmo, Pops—as it does to Albert Einstein. I would like to dedicate it to Pops, to Rahsaan Roland Kirk and John Birks Gillespie, ambassadors from the United States of the Blues, and to Dave Dysert, who taught me jazz fundamentals. I am grateful to Ade Knowles and Druis Beasley Knowles for over a decade of fine music-making, friendship, and conversation on these issues. Art Efron has been an example of a thinker who has been driven to make emotionally tough arguments out of a sense of decency and truth. Bruce Jackson taught me the importance of African-American narrative tradition and was the first to encourage me to put my trumpeter's mouth in my writer's fingers and say what I know about black music and American culture. David Porush back-stopped my judgment of Beethoven and made insightful comments about rap and technology. David Hays, Paul Levinson, Martha Mills, and Fabrice Ziolkowski gave the manuscript a critical reading. I remain chief repository of factual error, interpretive misjudgment, and signifying monkey-shines.

References

Abrahams, R. D. (1970) *Deep Down in the Jungle*. Chicago: Aldine.

Ansermet, E-A. "Bechet and Jazz Visit Europe, 1919." Originally published in Revue Romande and reprinted in Ralph do Tolando, ed. *Frontiers of Jazz*. New York: Frederick Ungar Publishing, 1962, pp. 115–122.

Arnason, H. H. (n.d.) *History of Modern Art*. New York: Harry Abrams, Inc.

Asante, M. K. (1987) *The Afrocentric Idea*. Philadelphia: Temple University Press.

Ashe, A. (1988) *A Hard Road to Glory*. New York: Warner Books.

Baldwin, J. (1963) *The Fire Next Time*. New York: The Dial Press.

Baraka, A. (1990) "Jazz Criticism and Its Effect on the Art Form." In David Baker, ed. *New Perspectives on Jazz*. Washington and London: Smithsonian Institution Press, pp. 55–70.

Barkan, T. (1974) "Rahsaan Speaks His Peace." *down beat*, 41, No. 14, Aug. 15, pp. 13–14, 42.

Benedict, R. (1934) *Patterns of Culture*. Boston: Houghton-Mifflin.

Benzon, W. L. (1981) "Lust in Action: An Abstraction." *Language and Style*, 14, 251–270.

Benzon, W. L. (1993a) "The Evolution of Narrative and the Self." *Journal of Social and Evolutionary Systems*, 16 (2), 129–155.

Benzon, W. L. (1993b) "Stages in the Evolution of Music." *Journal of Social and Evolutionary Systems*, 16 (3), 273–296.

Benzon, W. L. (in press) "Culture as an Evolutionary Arena." *Journal of Social and Evolutionary Systems*.

Benzon, W. L., and D. G. Hays. (1988) "Principles and Development of Natural Intelligence." *Journal of Social and Biological Structures*, 11, pp. 293–322.

Benzon, W. L. and D. G. Hays (1990a) "Why Natural Selection Leads to Complexity." *Journal of Social and Biological Structures*, 13, pp. 33–40.

Benzon, W. L., and D. G. Hays. (1990b) "The Evolution of Cognition." *Journal of Social and Biological Structures*, 13, pp. 297–320.

Berendt, J. (1975) *The Jazz Book*. New York: Lawrence Hill.

Berliner, P. (1994) *Thinking in Jazz: The Infinite Art of Improvisation*. Chicago: University of Chicago Press.

Bernstein, L. (1993) *The Infinite Variety of Music*. New York: Anchor Books/Doubleday.

Blassingame, J. W. (1979) *The Slave Community*. New York, Oxford: Oxford University Press.

Blacking, J. (1974) *How Musical Is Man?* Seattle and London: University of Washington Press.

Bloom, A. (1987) *The Closing of the American Mind*. New York: Simon and Schuster.

Bloom, H. (1992) *The American Religion: The Emergence of the Post-Christian Nation*. New York: Simon and Schuster.

Brand. S. (1987) *The Media Lab*. New York: Viking.

Brown, S. E. (1986) *James P. Johnson: A Case of Mistaken Identity*. Metuchen and London: The Scarecrow Press and the Institute of Jazz Studies, Rutgers University.

Boyd, J. with H. George-Warren (1992) *Musicians In Tune*. New York: Fireside/Simon and Schuster.

Brown, T. D. (1988) "Drum Set, § II 6: Bop Drumming." In B. Kernfeld, ed. *The New Grove Dictionary of Jazz*, Vol. I: A-K. London: Macmillan Press, Ltd. p. 314.

Brundage, W. F. (1993) *Lynching in the New South: Georgia and Virginia, 1880–1930*. Urbana: University of Illinois Press.

Buerkle, J. V. and D. Barker (1973) *Bourbon Street Black*. New York: Oxford University Press

Cage, J. (1961) *Silence*. Middletown, Connecticut: Wesleyan University Press.

Chase, G. (1966) *America's Music*. New York: McGraw-Hill Book Company.

Chevigny, P. (1991) *Gigs*. New York: Routledge.

Cleaver, E. (1968) *Soul on Ice*. New York: Dell Publishing Co.

Clifford, J. (1988) *The Predicament of Culture*. Cambridge: Harvard University Press.

Clynes, M. (1977) *Sentics: The Touch of Emotions*. Garden City, New York: Anchor Press/Doubleday.

Collier, J. L. (1978) *The Making of Jazz*. Boston: Houghton Mifflin.

Collier, J. L. (1983) *Louis Armstrong: An American Genius*. New York: Oxford University Press.

Collier, J. L. (1987) *Duke Ellington*. New York, Oxford: Oxford University Press.

Collier, J. L. (1993) *Jazz: The American Theme Song*. New York: Oxford University Press.

Costello, M. & D. F. Wallace (1990) *Signifying Rappers*. New York: The Ecco Press.

Crouch, S. (1976) "The Minstrel Continuum." *Players*, 2, No. 3, January, pp. 38–42, 58–60.

Crouch, S. (1990a) "Play the Right Thing." *The New Republic*, 202, No. 7, February 12, pp. 30–37).

Crouch, S. (1990b) "Jazz Criticism and Its Effect on the Art Form." In David Baker, ed. *New Perspectives on Jazz*. Washington and London: Smithsonian Institution Press, pp. 71–87.

Crouch, S. (1990c) *Notes of a Hanging Judge*. New York: Oxford University Press.

Csikszentmihalyi, M. (1993) *The Evolving Self*. New York: HarperCollins.

Dankworth, A. (1968) *Jazz: An Introduction to its Musical Basis*. London: Oxford University Press.

DePree, M. (1992) *Leadership Jazz*. New York: Dell Publishing.

Douglas, A. (1995) *Terrible Honesty: Mongrel Manhattan in the 1920s*. New York: Farrar, Straus and Giroux.

Du Bois, W. E. B. (1903) *The Souls of Black Folk*. Chicago: A.C. McClurg.

Du Bois, W. E. B. (1940) *Dusk of Dawn*. Reprinted in *W.E.B. Du Bois: Writings,* ed. by Nathan Huggins. New York: Library of America, 1986.

Early, G. (1989) *Tuxedo Junction*. New York: The Ecco Press.

Ennis, P. (1992) *The Seventh Stream: The Emergence of Rocknroll in American Popular Music*. Hanover and London: Wesleyan University Press/University Press of New England.

Efron, A. (1985) "The Sexual Body: An Interdisciplinary Perspective." A special issue of *The Journal of Mind and Behavior*, 6, Nos. 1 & 2.

Ellison, R. (1972) *Shadow and Act*. New York: Vintage Books.

Epstein, H. (1987) *Music Talks: Conversations with Musicians*. New York: McGraw Hill.

Erikson, E. H. (1968) *Identity: Youth and Crisis*. New York: W.W. Norton.

Fairbank, J. K. (1992) *China: A New History*. Cambridge, MA: The Belknap Press of Harvard University Press.

Feather, L. (1966) *The Encyclopedia of Jazz in the Sixties*.

Freud, S. (1962) *Civilization and Its Discontents*. Translated by James Strachey. New York: W.W. Norton. Originally published as *Das Unbehagen in der Kultur*. Vienna: Internationaler Psychoanalytischer Verlag, 1930.

Fredrickson, G. M. (1988) *The Arrogance of Race*. Middletown, CT: Wesleyan University Press.

Gabbard, K. (1995) "Signifyin(g) the Phallus: Mo' Better Blues and Representations of Jazz Trumpet." In Krin Gabbard, ed. *Representing Jazz*. Durham, North Carolina: Duke University Press.

Gates, H. L. Jr. (1988) *The Signifying Monkey*. New York, Oxford: Oxford University Press.

Gates, H. L. Jr. (1989) *"TV's Black World Turns—But Stays Unreal."* The New York Times, Section 2, November 12, pp. 1, 40.

Gay, P. (1993) *The Cultivation of Hatred*. New York: W. W. Norton & Co.

Geertz, C. (1973) *The Interpretation of Culture*. New York: Basic Books.

George, N. (1988) *The Death of Rhythm and Blues*. Pantheon Books: New York.

George, N. (1992) *Buppies, B-Boys, Baps & Bohos*. New York: HarperCollins.

Gillespie, D., with Al Fraser. (1979) *To Be or Not to Bop*. New York: Doubleday.

Gilman, S. L. (1985) "Black Bodies, White Bodies: Toward an Iconography of Female Sexuality in Late Nineteenth-Century Art, Medicine, and Literature." *Critical Inquiry*, 12, pp. 204–242.

Gilmore, M. (1990) *"The Sixties."* Rolling Stone, Aug. 23, pp. 61–65, 142–144.

Gilroy, P. (1993) *The Black Atlantic: Modernity and Double Consciousness*. Cambridge, MA: Harvard University Press.

Glass, P. (1987) *Music by Philip Glass*. New York: Harper and Row.

Glazer, N. and P. Moynihan (1963) *Beyond the Melting Pot*. Cambridge, MA: The M.I.T. Press and Harvard University Press.

Goethe, Johann Wolfgang von. (1774) *The Sufferings of Young Werther*. Translated by Harry Steinhauer. New York: W. W. Norton, 1970.

Gombrich, E. (1951) *The Story of Art*. New York: Phaidon Publishers, Inc.

Guralnick, P. (1986) *Sweet Soul Music*. New York: Harper & Row.

Guralnick, P. (1994) *Last Train to Memphis: The Rise of Elvis Presley*. Boston: Little, Brown and Co.

Hacker, A. (1992) *Two Nations: Black and White, Separate, Hostile*, Unequal. New York: Ballantine Books.

Haley, A. (1965) *The Autobiography of Malcolm X*. New York: Grove Press.

Handy, W. C. (1941) *Father of the Blues*. Edited by Arna Bontemps. New York: Macmillan.

Harmetz, A. (1988) "How a 'Rabbit' was Framed." *The New York Times*, Section 2, June 19, pp. 1, 12.

Harrington, W. (1992) *Crossings: A White Man's Journey into Black America*. New York: HarperCollins.

Hart, M. with J. Stevens (1990) *Drumming at the Edge of Magic*. New York: HarperCollins.

Hays, D. G. (1992) "The Evolution of Expressive Culture." *Journal of Social and Evolutionary Systems*, 15, 187–216.

Hernton, C. C. (1988) *Sex and Racism in America*. New York: Grove Weidenfeld.

Herskovitz, M. J. (1988) *The Myth of the Negro Past*. Boston: Beacon Press. (Originally published 1941).

Hobsbawm, E. (1993) *The Jazz Scene*. New York: Pantheon.

Hobsbawm, E. (1994) *The Age of Extremes: A History of the World, 1914–1991*. New York: Pantheon.

Hodgson, M. (1993) *Rethinking World History*. Cambridge: Cambridge University Press.

Hodier, A. (1956) *Jazz: Its Evolution and Essence*. New York: Grove Press, Inc.

Holloway, J. E. ed. (1990) *Africanisms in American Culture*. Bloomington: Indiana University Press.

hooks, b. (1994) *Outlaw Culture: Resisting Representations*. New York: Routledge.

Horowitz, H. (1990) "The American Jazz Audience." In David Baker, ed. *New Perspectives on Jazz*. Washington and London: Smithsonian Institution Press, pp. 1–8.

Jackson, B. (1974) *Get Your Ass in the Water and Swim Like Me*. Cambridge, MA: Harvard University Press.

Jan Mohammed, A. R. (1985) "The Economy of Manichean Allegory: The Function of Racial Difference in Colonialist Literature." *Critical Inquiry*, 12, pp. 59–87.

Jones, L. (1963) *Blues People: Negro Music in White America*. New York: William Morrow and Company.

Jordan, W. (1974) *The White Man's Burden*. New York: Oxford University Press.

Kao, J. (1996) *Jamming: The Art and Discipline of Business Creativity*. New York: Harper Business.

Keil, C. (1966) *Urban Blues*. Chicago and London: University of Chicago Press.

Keil, C. and S. Feld (1994) *Music Grooves*. Chicago: University of Chicago Press.

Kofsky, F. (1970) *Black Nationalism and the Revolution in Music*. New York: Pathfinder Press.

Kondracke, M. (1989) "The Two Black Americas." *The New Republic*, 200, No. 6, Feb. 6, pp. 17–20.

Kovel, J. (1984) *White Racism: A Psychohistory*. New York: Columbia University Press.

Kramer, J. D. (1988) *The Time of Music*. New York: Schirmer Books.

Lee, S. (1991) *Five for Five*. New York: Stewart, Tabori & Chang.

Levine, L. W. (1977) *Black Culture and Black Consciousness*. New York: Oxford University Press.

Levy, S. (1984) *Hackers*. Garden City, NY: Anchor Press/Doubleday.

Lincoln, C. E. and L. H. Mamiya. (1990) *The Black Church in the African American Experience*. Durham and London: Duke University Press.

Litweiler, J. (1984) *The Freedom Principle: Jazz After 1958*. New York: Da Capo Press.

Maccoby, M. (1990) "American Character and the Organizational Man." *The World and I*, May, pp. 465–475.

Martin, L. and K. Segrave (1992) *Anti-Rock: The Opposition to Rock'n'Roll.* New York: Da Capo.

Maultsby, P.K. (1990) "Africanisms in African-American Music." In Joseph E. Holloway, ed. *Africanisms in American Culture.* Bloomington: Indiana University Press, pp. 185–210.

McNeill, W. H. (1995) *Keeping Together in Time: Dance and Drill in Human History.* Cambridge, MA: Harvard University Press.

Mellers, W. (1983) *Beethoven and the Voice of God.* London: Faber and Faber.

Morrison, T. (1992) *Playing in the Dark.* Cambridge, MA: Harvard University Press.

Mulira, J. G. (1990) "The Case of Voodoo in New Orleans." In Joseph E. Holloway, ed. *Africanisms in American Culture.* Bloomington: Indiana University Press, pp. 34–68.

Murray, A. (1970) *The Omni Americans.* New York: Da Capo Press.

Murray, A. (1976) *Stomping the Blues.* New York: Da Capo Press.

Murray, A. (1996) *The Blue Devils of Nada.* New York: Pantheon Books.

Neumann, F. (1986) *Ornamentation and Improvisation in Mozart.* Princeton, NJ: Princeton University Press.

Ogren, K. (1989) *The Jazz Revolution: Twenties America and the Meaning of Jazz.* New York, Oxford: Oxford University Press.

Oliver, P. (1970) *Savannah Syncopators: African Retentions in the Blues.* New York: Stein and Day.

Ornstein, R. (1969) *On the Experience of Time.* Harmondsworth, Middlesex: Penguin Books Ltd.

Ostransky, L. (1988) "Jones, Quincy (Delight, Jr.)." In B. Kernfeld, ed. *The New Grove Dictionary of Jazz,* Vol. I: A–K. London: Macmillan Press, Ltd.

Page, T. (1992) *Music from the Road.* New York, Oxford: Oxford University Press.

Palmer, R. (1981) *Deep Blues.* New York: Viking Penguin Inc.

Palmer, R. (1990) "The Fifties." *Rolling Stone,* April 19, pp. 44–48.

Parsons, T. (1964) *Essays in Sociological Theory.* New York: The Free Press.

Peretti, Burton W. (1992) *The Creation of Jazz.* Urbana and Chicago: University of Illinois Press.

Peters, T. (1992) *Liberation Management.* New York: Knopf.

Philips, J. E. (1990) "The African Heritage of White America." In Joseph E. Holloway, ed. *Africanisms in American Culture.* Bloomington: Indiana University Press, pp. 225–239.

Pond, S. (1990) "The Seventies." *Rolling Stone,* Sept. 20, pp. 51–54, 110.

Porter, L. (1988) "Blakey, Art." In B. Kernfeld, ed. *The New Grove Dictionary of Jazz,* Vol. I: A–K. London: Macmillan Press, Ltd., pp. 115–116.

Porush, D. (1987) "Cybernauts in Cyberspace: William Gibson's *Neuromancer.*" In George Slusser and Eric Rabkin, eds. *Aliens: The Anthropology of Science Fiction.* Carbondale: University of Southern Illinois Press, pp. 157–168.

Porush, D. (1991) "Frothing at the Synaptic Bath." In Larry McCaffery, ed. *Storming the Reality Studio: Essays on Cyberpunk and Virtual Reality.* Durham: Duke University Press, pp. 331–334.

Puterbaugh, P. (1990) "Little Richard." (interview) *Rolling Stone,* April 19, pp. 50–54, 126.

Ravo, N. and E. Hash (1993) "The Evolution of Cyberpunk." *The New York Times,* Section 2, August 8, p. 9.

Ressner, R. (1990) "Pat Boone." (interview) *Rolling Stone,* April 19, pp. 89–91, 124.

Roberts, J. M., B. Sutton-Smith, & A. Kendon (1963) "Strategy in Games and Folk Tales." Reprinted in Pierre Maranda, ed. *Mythology.* Harmondsworth, Middlesex: Penguin Books, Ltd., pp. 194–211.

Roca, O. (1992) "Notes on the Music." Published to go with Nadja Salerno-Sonnenberg, *It Ain't Necessarily So.* EMI Classics, CDC 7 54576 2.

Rockwell, J. (1983) *All American Music.* New York: Vintage Books.

Rose, P. (1989) *Jazz Cleopatra.* New York: Random House.

Rose, T. (1994) *Black Noise: Rap Music and Black Culture in Contemporary America.* Hanover and London: Wesleyan University Press/University Press of New England.

Rothstein, E. (1991) "Roll Over Beethoven." *The New Republic*, 204, No. 5, Feb. 4, pp. 29–34.

Russell, R. (1971) *Jazz Style in Kansas City and the Southwest*. Berkeley: University of California Press.

Samuels, D. (1991) "The Rap on Rap." *The New Republic*, 205, No. 20, November 11, pp. 24–29.

Schipper, H. (1990) "Dick Clark." (interview) *Rolling Stone*, April 19, pp. 67–70, 126.

Schonberg, H. C. (1967) *The Great Conductors*. New York: Simon and Schuster.

Schonberg, H. C. (1981) *Facing the Music*. New York: Summit Books.

Schuller, G. (1968) *Early Jazz*. New York and London: Oxford University Press.

Schuller, G. (1989) *Swing*. New York: W.W. Norton and Company.

Schuller, G. (1990) "The Influence of Jazz on the History and Development of Concert Music." In David Baker, ed. *New Perspectives on Jazz*. Washington and London: Smithsonian Institution Press, pp. 9–23.

Silberman, C. E. (1964) *Crisis in Black and White*. New York: Vintage Books.

Small, C. (1987) *Music of the Common Tongue: Survival and Celebration in Afro-American Music*. New York: Riverrun Press.

Smith, J. (1988) *Off the Record: An Oral History of Popular Music*. Unison Productions, Warner Books.

Sniderman, P. M. and T. Piazza (1993) *The Scar of Race*. Cambridge, MA: Harvard University Press.

Southern, E. (1983) *The Music of Black Americans*. 2nd ed. New York: W. W. Norton & Co.

Soyinka, W. (1987) "Nobel Lecture 1986: This Past Must Address Its Present." *PMLA*, 105, pp. 762–771.

Spellman, A. B. (1970) *Black Music: Four Lives in the Bebop Business*.

Sprenkle, R. (1986) "A Very American Music." *Johns Hopkins Magazine*, 38, No. 5, Oct., pp. 23–27.

Spitzer, D. D. (1972) "Ira Sullivan: Living Legend." *down beat*, 39, No. 3, Feb. 17, p. 14.

Starr, S. F. (1995) *Bamboula! The Life and Times of Louis Moreau Gottschalk*. New York: Oxford University Press.

Stearns, M. and J. Stearns (1994 [1968]) *Jazz Dance*. New York: Da Capo Press.

Stowe, D. W. (1994) *Swing Changes*. Cambridge, MA: Harvard University Press.

Stuckey, S. (1987) *Slave Culture: Nationalist Theory and the Foundations of Black America*. New York: Oxford University Press.

Terkel, S. (1992) *Race*. New York: The New Press.

Turkle, S. (1984) *The Second Self*. New York: Simon and Schuster.

Ulanov, B. (1952) *A History of Jazz in America*. New York: Viking Press.

Vann Woodward, C. (1989) "The Crisis of Caste." *The New Republic*, 201, No. 19, Nov. 6, pp. 38–44.

Ventura, M. (1987a) "Hear that Long Snake Moan, Part 1." *Whole Earth Review*, No. 54, pp. 28–43.

Ventura, M. (1987b) "Hear that Long Snake Moan, Part 2." *Whole Earth Review*, No. 55, pp. 82–93.

Watkins, M. (1994) *On the Real Side: Laughing, Lying, and Signifying— The Underground Tradition of African-American Humor*. New York: Simon and Schuster.

Weinstein, N. C. (1992) *A Night in Tunisia: Imagining of Africa in Jazz*. Metuchen, New Jersey: Scarecrow Press, Inc.

West, C. (1989) *The American Evasion of Philosophy*. Madison: The University of Wisconsin Press.

West, C. (1993a) *Beyond Eurocentrism and Multiculturalism. Volume One: Prophetic Thought in Postmodern Times*. Monroe, Maine: Common Courage Press.

West, C. (1993b) *Beyond Eurocentrism and Multiculturalism. Volume Two: Prophetic Reflections: Notes on Race and Power in America*. Monroe, Maine: Common Courage Press.

West, C. (1993c) *Keeping Faith: Philosophy and Race in America*. New York: Routledge.

Whitmer, P. O. (1987) *Aquarius Revisited*, Macmillan Publishing Company.

Williams, M. (1983) *The Jazz Tradition*. New York: Oxford University Press.

Williamson, J. (1984) *The Crucible of Race*. New York, Oxford: Oxford University Press.

Wilson, O. (1990) "The Influence of Jazz on the History and Development of Concert Music." In David Baker, ed. *New Perspectives on Jazz*. Washington and London: Smithsonian Institution Press, pp. 25–31.

Wiora, W. (1965) *The Four Ages of Music*. New York: W.W. Norton.

Wolfe, Eric (1982) *Europe and the People Without History*. Berkeley: University of California Press.

Young-Bruehl, E. (1996) *The Anatomy of Prejudices*. Cambridge, MA: Harvard University Press.

Zoglin, R. (1987) "Cosby, Inc." *Time*, Sept. 28, pp. 56–60.

14

Afrocentric Television Programming

Alice A. Tait
Robert L. Perry

You've taken my blues and gone—
You sing 'em on Broadway
And you sing 'em in Hollywood Bowl,
And you mixed 'em up with symphonies
And you fixed 'em
So they don't sound like me.
Yep, you done taken my blues and gone.

You also took my spirituals and gone.
You put me in *Macbeth* and *Carmen Jones*
And all kinds of *Swing Mikados*
And in everything but what's about me—
But someday somebody'll
Stand up and talk about me,
And write about me,
And put on plays about me!
I reckon it'll be
Me myself!

Yes, it'll be me.

—"Note on Commercial Theater," from
Selected Poems of Langston Hughes

Presence and Absence: An Introduction

We propose that historically and contemporarily African-Americans were and are severely under represented in the Eurocentric press, are portrayed stereotypically, depicted in low-status occupational roles, and denied news or public affairs

An earlier version of this essay appeared in *Western Journal of Black Studies;* 1994, 18, 4, Winter, 195–200 and is adapted/reprinted with the permission of the copyright holder/author.

programs to adequately serve their informational needs (Poindexter & Stroman, 1981; Gardner, 1983; Addessa, 1991; Entman, 1992). Specifically, we propose the social forces identified by the Kerner Commission Report directly and continuously affect the level of participation of African-Americans in television news media (Tait & Perry, 1987). Furthermore, where African-Americans were placed in programming policy-making positions, subsequent news content and coverage displayed an Afrocentric perspective.

The following theories discuss the potential impact of mass media on society and individuals, and serve to underscore the media's traditional impact on them both. The *agenda-setting* function of the media is the close relationship between the relative emphasis the media gives to different issues and the relative importance the public places on them (Cohen, 1963; Shaw & McCombs, 1977). Lazarsfeld and Merton (1960) described "*status conferral*" as coverage by the press that enhances the status or perceived importance of the person or event covered. *Meaning theory* describes the mass media as an important part of the process of communication in modern society. The media play a significant role in shaping and stabilizing the meanings experienced for the symbols of language. These meanings, in turn, shape behaviors towards those aspects of the social and physical order that are labeled by words. According to this theory, a medium like television can influence the public on how to interpret such labels as "women," "African-Americans," and "sexual attractiveness" (DeFleur & Ball-Rokeach, 1975).

Television presents African-Americans to the viewing public as deviant, threatening, and unintelligent subhumans. Based on the agenda-setting, status conferral, and meaning theories, television news makes an indelible impression because of its visual impact and its tendency, by means of inertia, to shape and stabilize the meanings experienced from the symbols of language. The way to correct these negative stereotypical images would be to develop programming which examines from a "Black perspective" the African-American experience. In the media world this would require station owners, writers, producers, and individuals who have the perspective to present the African-American experience. A paradigm for creating such foci of analyses that some African-American media scholars historically embraced, without the benefit of the label, is Afrocentrism. Afrocentricity involves a systematic exploration of relationships, social codes, cultural and commercial customs, mythoforms, oral traditions, and proverbs of the peoples of Africa and the African Diaspora. Afrocentricity is the belief in the centrality of Africans in Postmodern history.

"Njia: The Way" is the Afrocentricity doctrine, that is, the collective expression of the Afrocentric worldview. Njia represents the inspired Afrocentric spirit found in the traditions of African-Americans. There are six parts to a Njia meeting. They are: (1) Libation to Ancestors (honors ancestors), (2) Poetry and Music Creativity (free expression of creativity), (3) Nommo: Generative Word Power (includes Afrocentric discussions of all the problems of the world), (4) Affirmation (reinforces victorious beliefs), (5) Teaching from Njia (Afrocentric ideology), and (6) Libation to Posterity.

Nommo is especially relevant to an analysis of Afrocentric television programming. Nommo is an opportunity for the discussion of problems and the place where facts are disseminated. Historical, cultural, and political information can also be discussed during Nommo. An Afrocentric television program attempts to reflect all of these concepts in various forms. Afrocentric television programming is also a form of Nommo (Asante, 1988). *The Cosby Show,* although not explicating every avenue of African-American life, represents the prototypical Afrocentric television program as the images produced in the show were consistently reflective of African-American culture. The direction of the programming was African-American influenced. Conversely, the *Amos and Andy* show was the antithesis of Afrocentrism. In this work, Afrocentric theory is utilized to interpret how African-Americans are portrayed and should be portrayed in the influential mass media. The effects of the portrayal are inextricably intertwined to viewing habits, to the extent that viewing habits reify negative portrayals.

Research has indicated that television is significant in the lives of all African-Americans—with notable social class differences in the amount of significant effect—because they rely heavily on television as an important source of information about other African-Americans and the larger African-American community (Poindexter & Stroman, 1981). African-American children are also more likely to be influenced by television commercials and to adopt behavior patterns from televised models than non-African-American children. Since African-American children are the heaviest prime-time television viewers, the problems associated with *agenda-setting, status-conferral,* and *meaning* theories are thus magnified (Dates, 1980; Donohue & Donohue, 1977; Greenberg & Harneman, 1970; Neely, Heckel, & Leichtman, 1973; Heckel, McCarter & Nicholas, 1971; Thelen & Soltz, 1969).

Because the media sets an agenda, confers status, and interprets meaning, one effect of all this television viewing is that it legitimizes deviant, threatening, and unintelligent behavior. A self-fulfilling prophecy thus emerges: television creates the problem, and because of its power and appeal, perpetuates the problem by socializing African-American youth into believing that deviant behavior is acceptable and rewarding. Furthermore, non-African-American youth are provided with only the resultant negative stereotypes of African-American youth that continue to mar inter-ethnic relations. Research supports "cultivation analysis"; the belief that frequent exposure to television cultivates viewers' perceptions consistent with images projected by television. In this case, frequent exposure to television portrayals of African-Americans cultivates viewer beliefs and images consistent with the dominant cultural perspective on television (Gerbner et al., 1977, 1980, 1982; Dorr, 1982: Matabane, 1988; Gandy and Matabane, 1989; Meritt and Stroman, 1993).

From 1952–1969 a series of studies concluded that African-Americans changed from low to high media usage for political news (McCombs, 1968), used television as a primary source of general and especially political information (Becker & Stroman, 1978), were devoted to news and minimally researched public affairs programs, viewed local newscasts, and listened to radio news regularly. Older and more educated African-Americans, as opposed to younger and less educated African-Americans, were more likely to be regular viewers of public affairs programs. These observations suggest African-Americans viewed television as a credible source of information concerning other African-Americans, again, the agenda-setting function of mass media. One explanation for this attitude lies in the increased visibility of African-Americans, which resulted in *status conferral,* as other media-oriented African-Americans began to recognize their importance.

Given these trends as reported in the Eurocentric media, in order to further explicate this information in Afrocentric terms, it is necessary that the media directed at African-Americans embody both information and role-modeling. While the ideal is seldom achieved, historically, several other programs have attempted to report, record, and portray the African-American community from the perspective of its people. The most notable of these, *Profiles in Black* (Detroit, MI), a series about well-known African-Americans, *Black Journal* (Detroit, MI), *Tony Brown's Journal* (New York, NY), and *For My People* (Detroit, MI), are all representative programs dealing with a variety of contemporary and historical African-American issues.

Eurocentric Window Dressing

In the early days of television, African-Americans were rarely seen on the screen. A 1962 study, for example, found that three African-American faces appeared once every five hours (Lowenstein, Plotkin & Pugh, 1964). The drama of the civil rights movement, however, captured media attention. African-Americans became more visible and instilled a new awareness in the American public that they had been denied equality under the law and that they were determined to achieve it.

Television's role in publicizing the civil rights movement raised an important issue: to what extent and in what ways had television played a role in perpetuating the inequality that non-African-Americans were just beginning to perceive had been suffered by African-Americans? The first major study of this issue, popularly known as The Kerner Commission Report, investigated a series of racial disorders in order to discover what happened, why it happened, and what could be done to prevent it from happening again (Werner, 1968). The Commission Report concluded, among other things, the news media failed to communicate to the American people "on race relations, and problems of the underclass." Further, the commission found the media's routine portrayal of African-Americans as part of the society was low and "presented African-Americans as whites saw them, not as they saw themselves." The Kerner Commission was concerned about the effect—on whites as well as on African-Americans—of a television world that is "almost totally white in both appearance and attitude." Inherent in this statement, made by a culturally diverse commission, lies the importance of the Afrocentric idea being represented and needed in television programming.

This indictment of the media was directed toward its portrayal of African-Americans, and the ways in which African-Americans and whites perceived African-Americans, and how media portrayal and presentation of African-Americans contributed to the hypothesized psycho-socio effect of African-American negative self-esteem. The key to addressing the still unfulfilled Kerner Commission documented concern lies in the willingness and the media's ability to project an Afrocentric perspective.

In support of the Commission, Roberts (1975) concluded "the most notable quality of the newscasts...is the relatively few appearances made by African-Americans and their low visibility in those appearances." Visibility alone does not address the concern of the Commission, which was interested not only in appearance but with attitudes and values expressed by African-Americans. Contemporary programming, *Black Entertainment* and *The Cosby Show*, tend to take on more Afrocentric perspectives, as outlined by our definitions, but this is not true of television news in general. Thus, the struggle for African-American identity and value perspective television programming remains elusive.

The Kerner Commission's conclusion that a Eurocentric mass media will ultimately fail in its attempts to communicate with an audience that includes African-Americans and other Americans is no less valid as we approach the 21st century than when it was published 25 years ago. The continuance of this phenomena served in part to encourage the Federal Communications Commission (FCC), the agency which regulates the broadcast industry, to adopt policies and procedures designed to assure equal employment opportunities in all television and radio stations.

In 1968, however, the Kerner Commission suggested that the news media should perform another function—to condition viewer's expectations regarding what is "ordinary and normal" in society. The Commission found that African-Americans were not presented in the news as a matter of routine, nor were they presented within the context of the society. Primarily, they appeared in the context of disorder. This observation is still accurate in 1996.

From 1973–1992 researchers found that race relations as an issue was covered in a balanced manner during a typical week of news programming by the networks (Pride & Clark, 1973), but during particular incidents in which tensions were high, coverage of the race issue tended to exacerbate racial polarization (Warren, 1972). In stories covered during 1974, 1975, and 1977 by ABC, CBS, and NBC, African-Americans, Latinos, Asians, and Native Americans (ALANA) rarely appeared in or reported the news (Window Dressing on the Set, 1977); there was little news specifically devoted to the problems or achievements of these ethnic groups and women. Ziegler and White (1990) found in a sample of three composite weeks over two years (1987–89) that only seven percent of network correspondents were ALANA; they covered seven percent of the stories. Stroman, et al. (1995) reported that ABC, CBS, NBC and Fox tended to present African-American fictional characters with undeveloped backgrounds, unknown occupations and family connections and continuing restrictions in depictions especially for females. Finally, Foote (1994) stated that from 1988 through 1992, 29 ALANA correspondents appeared on the evening news broadcasts of ABC, CBS, and NBC. Seventeen were African-Americans, Asians (5), and Latinos (5).

Harold Lasswell (1948), a European mass media theorist, postulated in a serendipitous fashion some of the elements of Afrocentricity in his presentation of the unity of mass media functions; that is, that environment, social heritage and entertainment are inextricably intertwined as mass media functions. In presenting this hypothesis, Lasswell embraced the essence of the African aesthetic. However, results from research presented above and elsewhere in the present document indicated television news was potentially dysfunctional for African-Americans. In terms of the theorized mass media functions, therefore, the medium probably did not fulfill Lasswell's serendipitous thesis or the Afrocentric idea. Local newscasts also negatively stereotyped African-Americans (Gardner, 1983), sparsely covered African-American issues (Addessa, 1991), and promoted modern racism (Entman, 1992).

In order to more fully understand the extent of change since the Kerner Commission Report and the quality of that change, an analysis of African-American television management and ownership needs to be accomplished. Alter (1986) stated that ALANA believe news coverage of their communities could be better served if there were ALANA representation in management, a belief which coincided with the Kerner Commission's call for better coverage of racial issues. Most of the few African-American news directors in television were either heading low-budget operations or at ethnic stations (Stone, 1987). Alter (1986) stated "the desire to manage is partly healthy ambition and partly a reflection of unhappiness over how white-dominated news organizations cover the news."

In this section we explore several Nommo examples of African-American produced and directed programs. These programs were and are unique because they all sought to offer a diverse balanced perspective of African-Americans and embodied Afrocentric programming. According to Asante (1988), "When the oppressor seeks to use language and images (added) for the manipulation of our reality; Nommo, for ourselves and of ourselves, must continue the correct path of critical analysis. Such a path is not dictated necessarily by the oppressor's rhetoric but [by] Njia for the Afro-American intellectual. Objectivism, born of the history, culture, and materials of our existence must be at the base of our talk and our essaying." The goal of these programs was to document, explore and articulate African-American political, economic, and cultural issues. The programs themselves served as training programs by providing internships to African-Americans so they might enter the broadcasting market. *For My People*, *Profiles in Black* and WPGR-TV represent three examples.

An analysis of the conception, creative format, audience feedback, and content analysis of *Profiles in Black* demonstrated that *Profiles in Black* portrayed African- Americans realistically in its broadcasts, reversing the trend of portraying African-Americans as deviants (Tait, 1989). Gilbert Maddox, *Profiles in Black* host and producer, made the following observations, published by *The Detroit News*:

> We black people are moving in the direction of establishing identities, of gaining political, economic and social control of the black community. We are not opposed to the white community, but we want to make our own community as viable as possible.... The series will show the full range of people comprising the black population—the professionals who have succeeded, ADC mothers with their problems and hopes, young students, conservative and militant clergymen... (Judge, 1969)

Maddox demonstrates in this published statement essential ideas of Afrocentric theory by showing the interrelatedness of all African-Americans transcending social status and class. Maddox thus enlarges the American universal discourse because he embodies the whole spectrum of black culture and allows African-American voices to speak for themselves without imposing definitions.

A half-hour weekly television community service series, WWJ-TV (Detroit) filmed and broadcast *Profiles in Black* initially during prime time (Saturday, 8:30 p.m.) from November 1969 through December 1979. Developed because of WWJ-TV's desire to operate more effectively in the public interest and additionally, to employ increased numbers of African-Americans, *Profiles in Black* became WWJ's response to the Kerner Commission Report.

Maddox portrayed the African-American community's hopes and frustrations as well as highlighted their accomplishments and achievements. One technique he employed was to interview guests in their homes with their families to display their degree of community involvement. Maddox presented African-American professionals, politically active persons such as retired Congressman George

Crockett (a former judge) and Mayor Coleman Young; significant events such as the NAACP Freedom Fund dinner, that organization's annual fund raiser, usually featuring some nationally renowned speaker; the historical contributions of Paul Robeson and Malcolm X; contributions of the working class; Detroit's African-American and African-American controlled institutions such as Homes for Black Children: and the community's dissident voices, including those of the Minister of the Nation of Islam. These stories appealed to youths, adults, Anglo-Saxons, African-Americans, female and male audiences, and also showed alternative role models available in the African-American community (Maddox, 1978).

Throughout its ten-year history, *Profiles in Black* continued its presentation of public affairs programming for the Metropolitan Detroit viewer. According to Frank Angelo (1974): "Maddox...has done about as much as anyone in America to destroy stereotypes that whites have of Blacks—and too often Blacks have of themselves." Prior to producing, hosting and directing *Profiles in Black*, Maddox was responsible for a number of other programs with similar objectives to those of *Profiles in Black* , most notably: *Black and Unknown Bards, Negro History Series, Office of Economic Opportunity, Mayor's Development Team Report*, and *C.P.T. (Colored People's Time) Television Program*. Maddox's work as chronicled in this discussion revealed that he was deeply grounded in the applied aspects of Afrocentricity, before *Profiles in Black*, subsequent to, and concomitant to such scholars as M. Karenga (1982) and M. Asante (1988). *Profiles in Black* reflected Afrocentric programming.

One response to the inequities in the media was initiated by Project BAIT with the show *For My People*. Television was viewed as a way to serve "The Struggle," i.e. the Black Power struggle. The resulting television show, *For My People* was planned as a continuation of the Black Power Movement. David Rambeau is the executive producer/director and interviewer of *For My People*, the longest-running program dedicated to the news and public affairs information needs of African-Americans in Detroit. *For My People* airs weekly on Detroit FOX network affiliate WKBD Channel 50 (Rambeau Project BAIT files, 1987, p. 1, personal communication). The overall programming focus is community-based public affairs information and aired for the first time in December 1970. In 1971, *For My People* also began a 10-year run on WDET, Detroit's public radio station (Rambeau Project BAIT files, 1987, personal communication). *For My People* airs on WKBD Channel 50 on Saturday mornings between 6 am and 7 am, and at present is a one hour show but began as a half hour show. Channel 50 maintains records regarding issues discussed on *For My People* and guests which appear on the show.

For My People also airs seven-days-a-week on Detroit-based independent cable station Barden Cable on a rotating schedule. *For My People* airs on Barden Cable channel 67 to a possible audience of 119,000 subscribers in the city of Detroit only. Barden Cable does not maintain ratings information, nor has public access personnel indicated receiving any viewer responses as a result of the show (Winkfield, 1994).

Topics for discussion should focus primarily on economics/finance, politics, education, and social struggle (Project BAIT Manual, 1983, p. 1, personal communication). *For My People* interviews consist of an African-American Project BAIT interviewer and an African-American guest. Guests are ordinarily from a African-American organization, and discuss a topic from the African-American perspective that is of basic interest to the survival of prosperity of the African-American community (Project BAIT Manual, 1983, personal communication). Essentially Afrocentrism is a conscious effort to use African-Americans as sources and references on any subjects, and seek only the expertise of African-Americans. Whenever guests are solicited from any organization for the show, African-Americans are explicitly requested, the purpose of which is to hold local African-American political and economic leaders accountable to the issues discussed (Rambeau Interview, personal communication 1992).

Rambeau hopes that the interview format transmits Afrocentrism by directing the audience to view the discussion within the context of Afrocentrism (Rambeau Interview, 1992, personal communication). The production staff of *For My People* consists of Project BAIT workshop members who view Project BAIT as a "school" of art and communication. It offers hands-on training and experience in video production among other activities that encourage faculty and students to become actively involved in their community (Rambeau Project BAIT files, 1987, personal communication). To demonstrate the Afrocentric focus, the host of the interview wears a traditional African dashiki. As expressed by the producer/host/founder, David Rambeau, the Project BAIT Afrocentric ideals with regard to all projects, including *For My People,* are:

- That African-Americans are the focal point of any and all concerns.
- That any issue is validated with respect to its impact on the African-American community.
- That the discussion format of *For My People* is not accountable to represent, nor interested in the Eurocentric viewpoint.

Black Nationalist and Pan-Africanist ideology (referred to here as Afrocentrism) as outlined in the Project BAIT membership training manual of 1982 is as follows:

> BAIT is a Black Nationalist or/and Pan-Africanist organization. Study of either or both of these political positions can and must be done. We don't push this ideology on members but is should be clear to everyone that this is our position. Most folk enter without any kind of conscious position. Within the group we ask people to do certain tasks that if they possessed a nationalist philosophy they would do automatically. This is perhaps best since people generally don't (want) ideology, they want skills, jobs, etc. The leadership merely gives them assignments or tasks that fulfill a nationalist's ideology and ordinarily folk will be along simply because it is in their own best interest anyway. However, there must be some consciousness-raising in the group about our relationship to each other, to our community (that's why among other reasons we request that members bank at the Black bank) and to the other communities that we come in contact with. When there are differences of position on a particular question we don't make our decision on an arbitrary basis. We attempt to make our decisions in congruence with our philosophy of life, and that is Black nationalism." (BAIT Notes On Practice, 1982, p. 7, personal communication).

According to Rambeau, *For My People* is still on the air because it serves Channel 50 as a foil against complaints concerning equal representation because, within the African-American community, *For My People* covers news and public affairs programming by, for, and about African-American people.

The relationship between Afrocentricity and ownership can best be understood by reviewing the work of Fife (1979). She found that: African-American ownership does impact images in the news, such images are influenced by philosophies of ownership and philosophies of ownership are in turn influenced by community characteristics.

WGPR-TV debuted in September 1974, and holds the distinction of being the first black-owned and operated TV station in the United States. It was owned and operated by the International F.M. and A.M. Modern Masons and Eastern Star, a fraternal organization founded by Dr. William V. Banks, the first President and General Manager of WGPR, Inc., who also owns Detroit radio station WPGR-FM. CBS purchased WGPR-TV in September, 1993.

WPGR's philosophy was that African-American Detroiters deserved a television station attuned to their community in the same way that the "mainstream" media are attuned to the Anglo-Saxon community. WGPR's stated purpose was to provide African-American Detroiters the opportunity to have experiences with the broadcast industry, so they stressed training and community access. They emphasized an African-American perspective to the largest degree possible.

WGPR aired several hours daily of locally-produced programming including "Big City News," discontinued in 1992, a 30-minute, Monday through Friday newscast. Both the management and ownership saw "Big City News" (BCN) as focusing on the African-American community, while complementing mainstream media with alternative aspects on current events. BCN used the same newscast format as larger operations. Crews were sent out on assignments of general news events as well as specific events in the African-American community not covered by mainstream media. Management stresses that a BCN viewer could not watch other stations and still feel adequately informed on Detroit news, with the unique asset of getting that news from an African-American perspective. By "African-American perspective," management means that 1) the implications of issues for minorities are discussed, and 2) the participation of African-American leaders in area events is fairly and fully covered. BCN saw itself as "commitment coverage" to represent the African-American community.

To that end, WGPR monitored their syndicated news sources for stories about African-American issues to supplement local coverage. They sometimes contacted syndication services to complain about the dearth of African-American issues to supplement their local coverage. They included as many visible minorities in stories as possible, including neighborhood leaders as much as city-wide or national leaders. They especially tried to showcase "success stories" of African-Americans. Results from a content analysis of WPGR-TV programming showed that the programming reflects the station's philosophy.

Thus the essence of WGPR's television programming philosophy was Afrocentric because it placed African ideals at the center of its programming philosophy. The ownership did not separate itself from the community; it was a part of the community. It was also unique reporting in that it exemplified the "caring or nurturing mythoform" that is part of the Afrocentric idea (Asante, 1988).

For My People, Profiles in Black and WGPR-TV were directly successful in their attempts to address the issues raised by the 1968 Kerner Commission Report. Furthermore, it has been demonstrated that African-American producers and directors designed programs to present African-American family life and social issues as ordinary and normal subject matter. Such achievements were accomplished when African-Americans were in policy-making positions. However, even this sparse programming accomplishment could hardly have occurred without the Kerner Commission Report's findings and its subsequent effect on FCC policy.

Research discussed in this paper and conducted over a period of years documented the neglect of African-Americans in the news. Research designs of this study focused on African-Americans in the news and in the production of news programming. *For My People, Profiles in Black* and WGPR addressed issues raised by the Kerner Commission Report; to wit, that African-Americans were not being represented and were not, moreover, being presented in an Afrocentric context. The programs surveyed presented family and social issues from a patently African-American perspective.

One implication to be drawn from this initial study is that the strongest impact on the portrayal of African-Americans in the news appears to be achieved when African-Americans influence the conception and the news selection process. The studies indicated change is occurring, although from all accounts, such change appears to be painfully slow. We found that, although Afrocentricity had not been fully or faithfully articulated, these programs clearly operated within the spirit and context embraced by the philosophy.

References

Addessa, R. (1991). *Women, minorities and aids: The impact of broadcast deregulation on public discourse*, p. 3. Rita Addessa, Executive Director, Philadelphia Lesbian and Gay Task Force, 1501 Cherry Street, Philadelphia, PA 19103.

Alter, J. (1986, December). No room at the top. *Newsweek*, 108(22), 79–80.

Angelo, F. (1974, February 8). Gilbert Maddox TV host 'Profiles' breaks Black stereotypes. *Detroit Free Press*, 7–8.

Asante, M. K. (1988). *Afrocentricity*. New Jersey: Africa World Press, Inc.

Becker, B. & Stroman, C.A. (1978). Racial differences in gratifications. *Journalism Quarterly*, 55, 767–71.

Cohen, B. (1963). *The press and foreign policy*. Princeton: Princeton University Press.

Dates, J. (1980). Race, racial attitudes and adolescent perceptions of black television characters. *Journal of Broadcasting*, 24, 549–60.

DeFleur, M.& Ball-Rokeach, S. (1975). *Theories of mass communication* (3rd ed.). New York: David McKay Company, Inc., pp. 133–135.

Donohue, W. A. & Donohue, T. R. (1977). Black, white, white gifted, and emotionally disturbed children's perceptions of the reality in television programming. *Human Relations*, 30, 609–612.

Dorr, A. (1982). Television and its socializing effect on minority children. In G.L. Berry and C. Mitchell-Kernan (Eds.), *Television and the socialization of the minority child*. New York: Academic Press.

Entman, R. M. (1992). Blacks in the news: Television modern racism and cultural change. *Journalism Quarterly* (Summer), 341–61.

Fife, M. D. (1979, September). The Impact of minority ownership on broadcast program content: A case study of WGPR-TV's local news content, *Report to the National Association of Broadcasting*, Office of Research and Planning.

Foote, J. S. (1994, August). *Minority correspondents and the network evening news*. Paper presented at the Minorities and Communication Division, Association for Education in Journalism and Mass Communication, Atlanta, Georgia.

Gandy, O. H. & Matabane, P. W. (1989). Television and social perceptions among African Americans and Hispanics. In M.K. Asante and W. Gudykunst (Eds.), *Handbook of intercultural and international communication.* Beverly Hills: Sage.

Gardner, T. (1983). Cooperative communication strategies: Observations in a Black community. *Journal of Black Studies, 14,* 233.

Gerbner, G., Gross, L., Eleey, M. F., Jackson-Beeck, M., Jeffries-Fox, S., Signorielli, N. (1977). TV violence profile no. 8: The highlights. *Journal of Communication, 27*(2), 171–180.

Gerbner, G., Gross, L., Signorielli, N., Morgan, M. (1980). The "mainstreaming" of America: Violence profile no. 11. *Journal of Communication, 30*(3), 10–29.

Gerbner, G., Gross, L., Morgan, M., Signorielli, N. (1982). Charting the mainstream: Television's contributions to political orientations. *Journal of Communication, 32*(2), 100–127.

Greenberg, B. S. & Harneman, T. R. (1970). Racial attitudes and the impact of tv on Blacks. *Educational Broadcasting Review,* 4(2), 27–34.

Heckel, R. V., McCarter, R. E. & Nicholas, K. B. (1971). The effects of race and sex on the imitation of television models. *Journal of Social Psychology, 85,* 315–316.

Judge, F. (1969, November 27). Channel 4 to launch *Black Profiles. The Detroit News.*

Karenga, M. (1982). *Introduction to Black Studies.* Los Angeles: University of Sankore Press.

Lasswell, H. D. (1948). The structure and function of communication in society. In L. Bryson (Ed.), *The communication of ideas,* (pp. 37–51). New York: Harper & Bros.

Lazarsfeld, P. & Merton, R. (1960). Mass communication, popular taste and organized social action. In W. Schramm (Ed.), *Mass Media.* Urbana: University of Illinois Press.

Lowenstein, R., Plotkin, L. & Pugh, D. (1964). The Frequency of Appearances of Negroes on Television. *The Committee on Integration, New York Society for Ethnic Culture, 4.*

Maddox, G. A. (1978, August). An Overview of Profiles: Past and Future. *Report to WWJ-TV.*

Matabane, P. (1988). Television and the black audience: Cultivating moderate perspectives on racial integration. *Journal of Communication, 38*(4), 21–31.

McCombs, M. E. (1968). Negro use of television and newspapers for political information, 1952–1964. *Journal of Broadcasting, 12,* 261–66.

Merritt, B. & Stroman, C. A. (1993). Black family imagery and interactions on television: Is the image changing? *Journal of Black Studies, Summer.*

Neeley, J. T., Heckel, R. V., & Leichtman, H. M. (1973). The effect of race of model and response consequences to the model on imitation in children. *Journal of Social Psychology, 89,* 225–31.

Poindexter, P. M. & Stroman, C. A. (1981). Blacks and television: A review of the research literature. *Journal of Broadcasting, 25,* 103–21.

Pride, R. A. & Clark, D. H. (1973). Race relations in television news: A content analysis of the networks. *Journalism Quarterly, 50,* 319.

Roberts, C. (1975). The presentation of blacks in television network newscasts. *Journalism Quarterly, 52*(1), 50–55.

Shaw, D. L. & McCombs, M. (1977). *The emergence of american political issues: The agenda-setting function of the press.* St. Paul: West Publications.

Stone, V. A. (1987b) Minority employment in broadcast news 1976–1986. Paper presented at the annual meeting of the Association for Education in Journalism and Mass Communication, San Antonio, Texas.

Stroman, C. A., Merritt, B.& Matabane, P. (1995) African Americans on television: twenty-five years after Kerner. Paper presented at the Minorities and Communication Division, Association for Education in Journalism and Mass Communication, Washington, DC.

Tait, A. A. (1989). Profiles portrayal of African-Americans 1969–1979: Detroit's direct response to negative stereotypes. *Michigan Academician,* 21(4).

Tait, A. A. & Perry, R. L. (1987). The sociological implications of the civil rights movement for Black character development and generic programming within the television medium, 1955–1985. *The Negro Educational Review, 38,* 224–37.

Thelen, M. H. & Soltz, W. W. (1969). The effect of vicarious reinforcement on imitation in two social racial groups. *Child Development,* 40, 879–87.

Warren, D. (1972). Mass media and racial crisis: A study of the New Bethel Church incident in Detroit. *Journal of Social Issues,* 28(1), 111–132.

Werner, O. (1968). *Reports of the National Advisory Commission on Civil Disorders.* New York: Bantam Books.

Window dressing on the set: Women and minorities on television. (1977). United States Commission on Civil Rights, 4.

Winkfield, J. (1994). Unpublished Master's Thesis. Michigan State University.

Ziegler, D. & White, A. (1990). Women and minorities on network television news: An examination of correspondents and newsmakers. *Journal of Broadcasting & Electronic Media, Spring,* 215–223.

Section VI

Race Relations

15

Race and College Sport: A Long Way to Go

Richard E. Lapchick

As America confronts yet another racial crisis in the 1990s, the expectation remains that sport, 50 years after Jackie Robinson broke baseball's color barrier, can lead the way. College sport, in particular, has been portrayed as a beacon for democracy and equal opportunity.

This perception is taking place at a time when 75 percent of high school students indicated to public opinion analyst Lou Harris that they had seen or heard a racial act with violent overtones either very often or somewhat often in the previous 12 months.[1] Fifty-four percent of black high school students reported that they had been a victim of a racial incident.[2]

One in three students said that they would openly join in a confrontation against another racial or religious group if they agreed with the instigators. Another 17 percent, while they would not join, said they would feel that the victims deserved what they got.[3]

According to Harris, the nation's leading opinion analyst, too many of our children have learned how to hate. He concluded:

> America faces a critical situation. Our findings show that racial and religious harassment and violence are now commonplace among our young people rather than the exception. Far from being concentrated in any one area, confrontations occur in every region of the country and in all types of communities.[4]

One of the most hallowed assumptions about race and sport is that athletic contact between blacks and whites will favorably change racial perceptions. However, for this change to take place, coaches must be committed to helping guide players' social relations. The *Racism and Violence in American High Schools* survey conducted by Lou Harris for Northeastern University in 1993 showed that 70 percent of high school students reported that they had become friends with some-

An earlier version of this essay appeared in *Race and Class;* 1995, 36, 4, April–June, 87–94 and is adapted/reprinted with the permission of the copyright holder/author.

1. LH Associates, Inc. (for the Center for the Study of Sport in Society), *Racism and Violence in American High Schools: Project TEAMWORK Responds*, November, 1993, at 2.
2. *Id.*
3. Louis Harris and Associates, Inc. (for the Center for the Study of Sport in Society), *Youth Attitudes on Racism*, October, 1990, at 2.
4. *Id.*

one from a different racial or ethnic group through playing sports. Among blacks, a 77 percent majority reported this result; the comparable majority was 68 percent among whites and 79 percent among Hispanics. That, indeed, was encouraging news.[5]

Black Student-Athletes on Predominantly White Campuses

However, on predominantly white campuses, as in corporate boardrooms, the atmosphere naturally reflects the dominant white culture. Most campuses are not equal meeting grounds for white and black students, whether from urban or rural America.

American public opinion of college sport reached its nadir in the mid-1980s. In an attempt to create meaningful reform, many measures were passed. Among them were Proposition 48, 42 and 16. The wide-ranging debate and protest against Proposition 42 placed the issue of race among the central ethical issues in college sport in the 1990s. Proposition 42 would have prevented athletes who did not achieve certain academic standards from receiving a scholarship. The new debate over Proposition 16 in 1994–95 has again raised the racial specter in college sport to a new level.

The American Institutes for Research (AIR) produced a study for the NCAA in 1989 which suggested that there are low academic expectations for black athletes. Only 31 percent of the black athletes surveyed for the AIR study indicated that their coaches encouraged good grades. The study also suggested that black student-athletes are not receiving the education promised by colleges since they graduate at a significantly lower rate than whites. They have few black coaches or faculty members to model themselves after on campus.[6] All of this is drawing attention and public pressure. The Reverend Jesse Jackson founded the Rainbow Commission for Fairness in Athletics to change such imbalances.

While less than six percent of all students at Division 1-A institutions are black, 60 percent of the men's basketball players, 37 percent of the women's basketball players and 42 percent of the football players at those schools are black.[7]

All colleges and universities have some form of "special admittance" program in which a designated percentage of students who do not meet the normal admission standards of the school are allowed to enroll. According to the NCAA, about three percent of all students enter as "special admits." Yet more than 20 percent of football and basketball players enter under such programs. Thus, many enter with the academic odds already stacked against them.

---

5. *See* LH Associates, Inc. (for the Center for the Study of Sport in Society), *Survey of High School Athletes*, November, 1993.

6. *See* American Institutes for Research (AIR), *Studies of Intercollegiate Athletics, Report No.3: The Experiences of Black-Intercollegiate Athletes at NCAA Division I Institutions*, March, 1989.

7. *See* The National Collegiate Athletic Association, *1994 NCAA Division I Graduation-Rates Report*, June, 1994.

The 1989 NCAA AIR study presented a wealth of data. Those familiar with college athletics were not surprised by the study's findings which indicated that black athletes feel racially isolated on college campuses, are over represented in football and basketball, have high expectations of pro careers, and are uninvolved in other extracurricular activities. However, the results of the NCAA study stood in stark contrast to the findings published by the Women's Sports Foundation.[8] It was the first major study of minorities playing high school sports. It clearly established that in comparison to black non-athletes, black high school student-athletes feel better about themselves, are more involved in extracurricular activities other than sport, are more involved in the broader community, aspire to be community leaders and have better grade point averages and standardized test scores. Almost all those results contradict the view that most of white society has about the black athlete.

According to Lou Harris, it is apparent that most varsity athletes believe that their participation in high school team sports has helped them to become better students, better citizens and to avoid drugs:

> It is especially significant to note that the value of playing sports in all these areas was significantly higher for African-American student-athletes in particular and for football and basketball players in general. It merits considerable attention by colleges and universities where the experience of African-American student-athletes as well as their football and basketball players is significantly different and appears much more negative.[9]

The primary question which now must be asked is what happens to black athletes, and black students in general, between high school and college that seems to totally change how they perceive themselves. Among other things, many black students leave a high school that is either overwhelmingly black or at least partially integrated. If he is from an urban area, he leaves behind a core of black teachers and coaches. If he lives on campus or goes to school away from home, he leaves behind whatever positive support network existed in the community in which he was raised and leaves behind possible black role models who are not exclusively athletes.

The student athlete arrives in college to discover that the proportion of black students at Division-IA schools is approximately six percent. Furthermore, less than two percent of the faculty positions at colleges and universities are held by blacks. Finally, the athletic departments hire just slightly more blacks than the faculty and actually hire fewer blacks than the professional sports teams.

A great deal of emphasis has been placed on racial discrimination in professional sport, especially the hiring practices of professional franchises. In fact, a great deal of the research done at the Center for the Study of Sport in Society is devoted to the publication of the annual *Racial Report Card*. However, a look at the numbers of available employment positions in our colleges and universities indicates that it is less likely for blacks to be hired by higher education than in professional sport. While the militancy and struggle of the 1960s and 1970s have re-

---

8. *See* The Women's Sports Foundation, *Minorities In Sports: The Effect of Varsity Sports Participation on the Social, Educational, and Career Mobility of Minority Students*, August, 1989.

9. *See* LH Associates, 1993.

duced the negative self-perceptions of most young blacks, the stereotypes still exist for many whites. Those stereotypes come with all the taboos that go with them.

White and black athletes can meet on campus carrying a great deal of racial baggage. Their prejudices won't automatically evaporate with the sweat as they play together on a team. The key to racial harmony on a team is the attitude and leadership of the coach.

The coach must be committed to equality and clearly demonstrate this to the team. The history of young athletes, and students in general, makes it an up-hill task. Chances are that competition at the high school level bred some animosity; usually white teams play against black teams, reflecting urban residential housing patterns. There is virtually no playground competition between blacks and whites as few dare to leave their neighborhood.

On a college team, blacks and whites are competing for playing time, while in the society at large, black and white workers compete for jobs, public housing, even welfare. A primary difference is that whites may be apt to accept blacks on the team since it is perceived by some that they will help the team win more games and perhaps get them more exposure.

It is easy for white athletes, no matter what their racial attitudes might be, to accept blacks on their teams for two other reasons. First, they need not have any social contact with black teammates. Sports that blacks dominate are not sports like golf, tennis, and swimming where socializing is almost a requirement for competition. Players need not mingle after basketball, baseball, or football. More importantly, black male players need not mingle with white women after those games. Housing on campus, and social discrimination through fraternities and sororities, further isolates the black athletes. Whether in high school or college, the black student-athlete faces special problems as an athlete, as a student, and as a member of the campus community.

Most of white society believed we were on the road to progress until Al Campanis and Jimmy "The Greek" Snyder made us challenge our perceptions. Their statements on national television that blacks and whites are physically and mentally different were repugnant to much of the country and led to widespread self-examination. Like many whites who accept black dominance in sport, Campanis believed that blacks had less intellectual capacity. It makes things seem simple to people like Campanis: blacks sure can play, but they can't organize or manage affairs or lead whites. Marge Schott, speaking in private, reopened the wounds in 1992 when her remarks about blacks and Jews again stunned the world of sport.

Many people wouldn't see much to contradict this view if they looked to society at large. In 1995, white men and women were twice as likely to hold executive, administrative and managerial positions as black men. At the same time, blacks were twice as likely to hold positions of manual labor as whites. Decades of viewing this pattern could easily reinforce the Campanis viewpoint: whites are intelligent and blacks are physically powerful.

After fifty years of trying to determine the genetic superiority of blacks as athletes, science has proved little. Culture, class and environment still tell us the most. Instead of developing theories about why black Americans excel in sports, perhaps more time will now be spent on the achievement of black Americans in human rights, medicine, law, science, the arts and education who overcame the attitudes and institutions of whites to excel in fields where brains dictate the champions.

Coaches: A Study in Black and White

The coach becomes the black student-athlete's main contact, and the court frequently becomes the home where he is most comfortable. Nonetheless, there are some black athletes who feel that their white coaches discriminate against them and that their academic advisers give them different counseling. This may reflect a general distrust of whites or a strong perception that racism is the cause of certain events. Even well-intentioned acts can be interpreted by blacks as being racially motivated.

Over the years, there have been black student-athletes who have made a series of similar complaints irrespective of where their campus was located: subtle racism evidenced in different treatment during recruitment, poor academic advice, harsh discipline, positional segregation on the playing field and social segregation off it, blame for situations for which they are not responsible. There are also complaints of overt racism: racial abuse, blacks being benched in games more quickly than whites, marginal whites being kept on the bench while only blacks who play are retained, summer jobs for whites and good jobs for their wives.

To say that most or even many white coaches are racist is a great exaggeration. But most white coaches were raised with white values in a white culture. The norm for them is what is important for a white society.

Stereotypes of the Black Athlete

If white coaches accept stereotypical images of what black society is and what kind of men it produces, they may believe that blacks are less motivated, less disciplined, less intelligent (53 percent of all whites believe blacks are less intelligent) and more physically gifted. They may think that all blacks are raised in a culture bombarded by drugs, violence and sexuality and that they are more comfortable with other blacks.

They might believe those characteristics are a product of society or simply that they are the way God chose to make them. They might recognize themselves as racist, disliking blacks because of perceived negative traits. More than likely, however, he views himself as a coach trying to help. In either case, if he acts on these images, then his black players are victimized.

In one of the most important scandals of the 1980s, Memphis State, a 1985 NCAA Final Four participant, fell into disgrace. There were many allegations about the improprieties of the school and its coach, Dana Kirk.

One that could not be disputed was the fact that twelve years had gone by without Memphis State graduating a single black basketball player. Like several other urban institutions, Memphis State built a winning program with the talents of fine black athletes. The fact that none had graduated brought back memories of Texas Western's NCAA championship team which failed to graduate a single starter, all of whom were black. But this went on at Memphis State for more than a decade. The NAACP sued the school. Publicity finally led to the dismissal of Kirk. Indications are that Larry Finch, who replaced Kirk, who is white, has run a clean program. Perhaps the fact that Finch is black has resulted in a different approach to black players. In 1995, Memphis State has one of the nation's most open-minded and progressive presidents in Lane Rawlings.

I do not mean to single out Memphis State. In the 10 years since Dana Kirk was fired, I have been on more than 75 campuses. The pattern is frequently similar: the academic profile of black football and basketball players and their treatment as students is different from whites, and their graduation rate is lower at many schools.

Positional Segregation in College

The issue of positional segregation in college is becoming less of a factor. For years, whites played the "thinking positions." The controlling position in baseball is the pitcher; in football, it is the quarterback. Everyone loves the smooth, ball-handling guard in basketball. These are the glamour positions that fans and the press focus on. These have largely been white positions. College baseball still poses the greatest problem at all positions, as fewer and fewer blacks play college baseball. Less than three percent of Division 1-A college baseball players are black.[10]

However, in a major shift in college football, large numbers of black quarterbacks have been leading their teams since the late 1980s. Between 1960 and 1986, only seven black quarterbacks were among the top ten candidates for the Heisman Trophy and none finished higher than fourth. In 1987, 1988 and 1989, black quarterbacks Don McPherson (Syracuse), Rodney Peete (USC), Darien Hagan (Colorado), Reggie Slack (Auburn), Tony Rice (Notre Dame), Stevie Thompson (Oklahoma) and Major Harris (West Virginia) all finished among the top ten vote getters. In 1989, Andre Ware (Houston) became the first black quarterback to win the award. Florida State's Charlie Ward won it in 1993. In 1994, Nebraska won the national championship with a dramatic Orange Bowl victory behind the leadership of quarterback Tommie Frazier. Coach Osborne inserted Frazier into the starting line up after missing nearly the entire season with a blood clot.

Top point guards coming out of college are becoming more and more predominantly black. Recent stars such as Kenny Anderson, Tim Hardaway, Anfernee Hardaway and Jason Kidd are just a few of the more prominent black point guards. Hopefully, this bodes well for an end to positional segregation in college sport in the near future.

Can Black Athletes Speak Out?

The coach is the authority. Historically, athletes have rarely spoken out. This creates problems for all coaches who come up against an outspoken player. When the player is black and not a superstar, he will often be let go. Only the superstars like Bill Russell, Kareem Abdul-Jabbar, and Muhammad Ali can securely remain

---

10. Personal interview with Stanley Johnson of the NCAA on January 31, 1993.

because no one can afford to let them go. But even the greatest ones paid heavy prices for many years after their outspokenness.

Muhammad Ali, who had refused to go into the army, knew you had to be at the top to speak out if you were black. Ultimately, Ali had the money and influence to go all the way to the Supreme Court. Most blacks have neither the money nor the influence to make the system work.

In 1992, Craig Hodges spoke out about the Rodney King case in Los Angeles. Hodges was a great shooter but was a peripheral player on NBA the championship Chicago Bulls. He had won the Three point contest at the all-star game. After his remarks, he was cut by the Bulls and not one team picked him up.

Tommy Harper's case is also instructive. His contract was not renewed by the Boston Red Sox in December of 1985. The Red Sox said he was let go because he was not doing a good job as special assistant to the general manager. Harper, however, charged that he was fired because he spoke out against racist practices by the Red Sox.

Earlier in 1985 he said that the Sox allowed white players to receive passes to the whites-only Elks Club in Winter Haven, Florida, where they held spring training. (The Sox later stopped the tradition.) Harper sued and the Equal Employment Opportunity Commission ruled that the firing was a retaliatory action against Harper because he spoke out against discrimination. It took him a while to get back into baseball. As of this writing, he is a coach for the Montreal Expos.

There are positive examples as well. It did not go unnoticed that a group of black athletes at Auburn asked the president of the university to get a Confederate flag removed from a dormitory; it was removed. In 1987, the Pittsburgh basketball team wore ribbons as a protest against their school's investments in South Africa. In 1990, black athletes at the University of Texas at Austin led a protest against racism on campus. They had even been encouraged by members of the athletic department. Whether or not this will become a trend is hard to see, but the positive and widespread media coverage of their actions stood in dramatic contrast to early reactions to Russell, Ali and Abdul-Jabbar.

In 1969, fourteen black players on the University of Wyoming football team informed their athletic department of their intention to wear black arm bands during their upcoming game against Brigham Young University. The players' intent was to bring attention to the Morman church's doctrinal position which prevented blacks from holding the priesthood. After hearing of the players' plan, Wyoming's head football coach cited a long standing team policy which prevented players from engaging in protests of any kind. When the players showed up at his office wearing the arm bands just one day before the game, the coach interpreted their action as a defiance of the rule and a direct threat to his authority. He summarily dismissed all 14 players from the football team.

Although this incident remained a sore spot in the history of Wyoming athletics for nearly 24 years, the university held ceremonies to honor the players on September 24, 1993. The event was the result of the African American Studies Department working in conjunction with the school's administration to recognize the former players, signaling a new era in communications between student-athletes and the administration.

Interracial Dating and Sexual Stereotypes

The image of the black male involved with sex and violence took a profound turn in 1994 after O.J. Simpson was charged with a brutal double murder. Looking beyond the horror of the murders, the case once again brought out that fact that interracial dating is still a volatile issue in the 1990s. There is no question that it is far more common in the mid-1990s than it was in 1970 or even 1980 when Howie Evans, then a black assistant coach at Fordham and a columnist for the *Amsterdam News*, told me of the time when he used to work at a black community center in New York. Recruiters from predominantly white southern schools were coming there to recruit black women for their schools. Those coaches seemed to think that they understood the powerful sexual drives of black men, so they went out to get them some "safe" women friends from the North.

When I talk to black athletes after a lecture, I try to ask them about this. It doesn't matter where I am—Los Angeles, Denver, New York, Nashville or Norfolk—almost everyone says there is pressure, now usually very subtle, not to date white women. It doesn't matter how big the star is.

The black athletes also tell me that the assumption on campus is that they want white women more than black women. Not that blacks say they do, but that whites believe they do. If a white student wants to sleep with a coed, that's part of college life in our times. If a black student wants to do the same, that's the primal animal working out his natural instincts.

The Options for Black Athletes
Choosing a College

The effects of the actions of white coaches who act on stereotypical images of black athletes are not dissimilar. Study after study has shown the devastating consequences to the psyche of the person. As long as the act is perceived as being racially motivated—even if it is a well-intentioned act—the end result is the same.

Black student-athletes with pro aspirations would seem to have three choices, none of which are equal: he could choose to attend an historically black college, choose a predominantly white school with a black head coach, or choose a predominantly white school with a white head coach.

So what should the black athlete do? Should he attend a historically black college? After all, black colleges have turned out great pro athletes for years. But black college athletic programs started to decline when the white schools began to integrate. They don't have million-dollar booster clubs to compete with predominantly white schools to get star black athletes. Division I-A schools also offer the lure of bowl games, television coverage and a "good education."

NBA Players Association Director Charles Grantham told me that the black athlete who wants to turn pro has little realistic choice. "Exposure on TV means the scouts will see you and, if they like you, a higher position in the draft. That means more money, much more money."

The Southwestern Athletic Conference, which included Grambling, Jackson State and Southern, used to provide 35 to 40 players a year to the NFL in the early 1970s. By the 1990s, the numbers were between 6 to 10 in a big year.

Grambling's Eddie Robinson is the winningest coach in college history and has sent more players to the NFL than any coach. Could Eddie Robinson coach at Michigan or in the NFL? He has never had the opportunity to turn down a Division I-A job. Eddie Robinson is black; he became a coach before white institutions were ready for him.

Playing for a black coach at a predominantly white institution is another option for the black student-athlete. Many of today's black players would like to attend schools which have black coaches. For Division-I basketball players, that amounts to 45 schools, excluding the 16 historically black institutions.[11] The NCAA has 302 Division-I schools with approximately thirteen players per basketball team. Therefore, of the 3,926 slots for men's basketball players, approximately 793 fall under black basketball coaches.[12] The slots are far fewer in college football where there were only five black head coaches at the Division-I level at the close of the 1994 season. Finally, in Division I college baseball there is not a single black manager.[13]

Percentage of Black Employees in NCAA Member Institutions	
Athletic Administration	6.2%
Athletic Directors	3.6%
Associate Athletic Directors	4.5%
Assistant Athletic Directors	4.9%
Head Coaches	3.9%
Revenue-sport Head Coaches	12.9%
Assistant Head Coaches	9.8%

Source: The NCAA Minority Opportunities and Interests Committee's Four-Year Study of Race Demographics of Member Institutions, 1994.

The NCAA's 1994 Men's Final Four featured four teams that were comprised of 54 players, 29 of whom were black (54%), 24 of whom were white (44%), and one of which was Hispanic. On the other hand, alongside the court there were 39 coaches; 85 percent were white. There was not a single person of color on any of the four teams' medical staffs. The 15 athletic directors and associate athletic directors were all white. Of the 54 basketball administrators, there were only five who were black (9%). Of the 186 basketball support staff positions, whites occupied 174 (94%). Even the media covering the game were overwhelmingly white. Twelve of the 13 local radio and television broadcasters were white as well as 145 of the 150 local newspaper reporters.[14]

The 1995 National Championship football game which was played in the Orange Bowl was no different. The combined racial breakdown of the University of

---

11. Personal interview with Deb Kruger of the Black Coaches Association, January 25, 1995.

12. This number is an estimate arrived at by multiplying the number of Division I schools by the number of roster spots on a basketball team, then dividing the sum by the number of schools with black coaches.

13. This information was obtained by interview with the Black Coaches Association, February, 1995.

14. *See* Rainbow Commission for Fairness in Athletics, April, 1994.

Nebraska and University of Miami football programs demonstrates this. While nearly 63 percent of the players were black, 100 percent of the presidents, athletic directors, head coaches, associate athletic directors, sports information directors and medical staff were white.

There are many potential jobs available for blacks in coaching and in athletic departments. There are 906 NCAA members in all divisions, with an average of 15.8 teams per school.[15] That amounts to 14,315 teams. The National Association of Intercollegiate Athletics (NAIA) has 391 members with an average of 9.5 teams per school. That's another 3,715 teams. With an average of 2.5 coaches per team, college sport has approximately 45,075 coaching jobs. That excludes junior and community colleges.

When so very few positions are held by black Americans, there should be little wonder that black student-athletes feel isolated on campus. Pressure needs to be placed here to change these percentages. The coaches are available. According to the Black Coaches Association, it had 3,000 members. If there is to be a more promising future for the black student-athlete, then more black coaches and assistants will have to be hired.

How do present-day black coaches fare? In 1985, Nolan Richardson was hired by Arkansas and became the Southwest Conference's first black head basketball coach. When his first two teams lost thirty games, Arkansas newspapers wrote him off. When he led the team to the Final Four in 1990, Richardson was elevated to sainthood in the Arkansas media. When Arkansas won the 1994 National Championship, Richardson was clearly a star in the state. People were saying that his presence, and especially his success, was leading to improved race relations in northern Arkansas.

Georgetown's John Thompson made many people angry when he became the first black coach to win the national championship in 1984. This was especially true of some media figures who said he was arrogant and abrasive, and kept his team insulated from the public. They said his team was overly aggressive. The intensity of the attack varied but was prolonged over a decade. His personal leadership as the outspoken elder statesman of America's black coaches has enhanced his status in the black community and alienated many in the white community.

Thompson was breaking all the molds shaped by a stereotyping public. First, he was a big winner with a lot of black recruits coming to an increasingly multi-cultural campus. Second, these black players were not a freewheeling, footloose team but rather one of the more disciplined teams in the country. Even more importantly, at a time of great negative publicity concerning the academic abuse of college athletes, Thompson's players had one of the highest graduation rates in America. Was there some jealousy involved in the attacks? Didn't these same writers call aggressive white teams "hustling teams?" White coaches like John Wooden were called fatherly figures when they kept the press at arm's length from their teams.

Even if you accept the fact that Thompson's style was a tough one for the public to grapple with, this still doesn't explain the degree of the attacks against him. The racial issue seemed, once again, to be a factor. While there are several national writers who write balanced pieces on John Thompson and Georgetown, too many others clearly show us how far we have to go.

---

15. Personal interview with NCAA spokesperson, Phyllis Ton, on January 25, 1995.

For now, most black athletes will have to play for white coaches and many may have the problems mentioned. Academically, the black athlete may enter college at a disadvantage, one artificially maintained because he might be steered into easier courses. He may be less likely to get a degree. With prevailing stereotypes, some coaches will make assumptions about him they would never make about whites. Socially, he will be in an alien world, segregated in student housing, off-campus housing and on road trips. Increasingly, he will be forced to withdraw into the "safer" athletic subculture, becoming insulated from both black and white non-athletes.

The odds are surely not in favor of the black student-athlete. If, after enduring all these problems, he doesn't get a degree, then why does he subject himself to all of this in the first place? The answer is simple. He assumes that sports is his way out of poverty. How prevalent is this belief? The NCAA AIR study on the black college athlete showed that in 1989, approximately 45 percent of black basketball and football players at predominantly white schools think they will make the pros.[16] Less than one percent will. The Northeastern University study conducted by Lou Harris in 1993 showed that 51 percent of black high school student-athletes think they can make the pros as well.[17]

Sport has been promoted as the hope of black people. But too often those are empty hopes.

Black athletes become involved in a cycle that trades away their education for the promise of stardom that is very unlikely to ever be real. A black high school student has a better chance of becoming a doctor or attorney than he has of becoming a professional athlete. But those civic role models are not as visible as black athletes. Thus, for them, the professional athlete seems like the best model.

Unfortunately, some schools "pass" certain students-athletes to the next level without regard for academic achievement. They are conditioned to believe that academic work is not as necessary as working on their body. The promise of the pros is the shared dream, no matter how unrealistic.

The media is now reporting more on the problems. The NCAA has paid far greater attention to the racial issue in college sport. In the last ten years, things have gotten markedly better for black student-athletes. Their graduation rates have improved by more than 10 percent. The number of black coaches has increased. Public pressure for change, especially that coming from the Rainbow Commission for Fairness in Athletics founded by the Reverend Jesse Jackson, has finally been sustained over time.

Nonetheless, college sport has a long way to go before it fulfills its promise as a beacon of democracy and equal opportunity.

---

16. *See* AIR Study, 1989.
17. Harris, *supra* note 5.

16

Gender and Social Inequality: The Prevailing Significance of Race

Doris Y. Wilkinson

In every society there are at least two groups of people, besides the Negroes, who are characterized by high social visibility expressed in physical appearance, dress, and patterns of behavior, and who have been "suppressed." We refer to women and children. Their present status, as well as their history and their problems in society, reveal striking similarities to those of the Negroes.... It will, therefore, give perspective to the Negro problem and prevent faulty interpretations to sketch some of the important similarities between the Negro problem and the women's problem. [1]

A Parallel to the Negro Problem

In the perceptive appendix to *An American Dilemma*, Gunnar Myrdal clarified the meaning of "A Parallel to the Negro Problem." Concentrating on historical placement, status differentiation, and accompanying socially constructed attributes and behaviors, he interpreted what "marked" Americans of African ancestry in the United States. He observed that their position in the country's racially framed stratification system was analogous to that of free white women since both were under the control of a white male patriarchy. Taking into account the historically racialized social location and treatment of African slaves, without making gender distinctions among them, Myrdal noted that the ironic paternalistic conception of the slave as a family member "placed him beside women and children. The parallel goes, however, considerably deeper than being only a structural part in the defense ideology built up around slaves. Women [during the era of slavery] lacked a number of rights otherwise belonging to all free white citizens of full age." [2] Emphasizing the social position of white women, Myrdal recognized at the outset that:

An earlier version of this essay appeared in *Daedalus*; 1995, 124, 1, Winter, 167–178 and is adapted/reprinted with the permission of the copyright holder/author.

1. Gunnar Myrdal (1944). *An American Dilemma: The Negro Problem and Modern Democracy.* New York: Harper & Brothers, 1073.
2. Ibid.

A tremendous difference existed both in actual status of these different groups and in the tone of sentiment in the respective relations. In the decades before the Civil War, in the conservative and increasingly antiquarian ideology of the American South, woman was elevated as an ornament and looked upon with pride, while the Negro slave became increasingly a chattel and a ward. . . . [Yet,] from the very beginning, the fight in America for the liberation of the Negro slaves was, therefore, closely coordinated with the fight for women's emancipation.[3]

This essay will address aspects of this situation as applicable to the present racialized political arena in which "black-white" relations remain significant and polarized. Despite the growing concern with diversity—with all that is implied by the contemporary multiculturalism movement—race remains a principal determinant of social organization, affecting every aspect of employment, educational opportunity, health, and justice.

The Paradoxes of Race in a Gendered Society

In these last decades of the twentieth century, both intellectual discourse and academic scholarship are being greatly altered, indeed transformed, through the introduction of feminist perspectives, with a gender-fixed view providing new interpretations of the structure of postindustrial society.[4] New and reconstructed theoretical paradigms, deriving from poststructuralism, hermeneutics, and postmodernism, are modifying the ways in which contemporary political, economic, and social realities are interpreted. Where the humanities, the social sciences, and the natural sciences dwell increasingly on gender identities and emphasize the diverse conditions of oppression experienced by women, inequality in opportunity based on race tends to receive considerably less attention.

In academic discussions of inequality based on gender, considerable attention is given to women's traditional roles, the numerous workplace barriers that preclude upward mobility, and the disproportionately high male representation in many professional hierarchies, not least within the corporate world. Women are clearly underrepresented in the sciences; the "glass ceiling" restricts their movement into managerial positions in that domain and elsewhere. While there have been large changes in the labor force, in what women are now employed to do, there is increasing attention to problems created by sexual harassment in the workplace, conventional sexual stereotypes, and family violence, all adversely affecting the daily lives of women.[5]

In the contemporary, postmodern culture, gender is given considerable salience. Social class and race are not thought to be equally important as determinants of inequality. Where individuality, perceptions of self-worth, and patterns of interaction are weighed so heavily, social stratification—based on racial dis-

---

3. Ibid.

4. Doris Wilkinson, Maxine Baca Zinn, and Esther Chow, eds., "Race, Class and Gender," *Gender and Society* 6, September 1992, pp. 341–345.

5. Paula S. Rothenberg, ed., (1992). *Race, Class and Gender in the United States: An Integrated Study*, 2d ed. New York: St. Martin's Press.

tinctions and race-based animosities—figures less prominently. Women, because of today's characteristic role stereotyping and the resulting gender imbalance in the work force, are reduced to subordinate places.[6] Within academic and corporate settings, this inequality is constantly alluded to, and it is significant that such analysis is more commonly made by white female scholars and behavioral scientists than by those of African American descent or by their white male colleagues. In status ascription, identity, and group consciousness, gender description figures prominently. As long as race is not seen as the central element in defining the nation's opportunity structure, there can be no understanding of why the American race-based democracy continues to be confronted by the "dilemma" that Gunnar Myrdal so insightfully portrayed.

The salience of gendered differentiation in daily interaction and in the structure of society has contributed a meaningful dimension to intellectual dialogue and to scholarly accounts and interpretations of status arrangements.[7] Examining the importance of gender has enabled a more functional explication of the beliefs and customs that frame our complex political culture. At the same time, translating the ingrained, systemic, and pervasive influence of race and racism in the country's institutions and ideologies permits greater understanding of the construction and perpetuation of all forms of inequality. Delineating race as the central element in opportunity and in status arrangements provides an explanation for the permanence of an "American dilemma" within a race-based political economy.[8]

Events of the early 1940s, in the years just before Myrdal's classic work, provide a context for examining the premises of this discussion. The examples which follow focus on the prominence of race and the relatively inconsequential impact of gender in the persistence of structural inequality. Neither gender nor class has been significantly deterministic in the historical patterns of racial exclusion, segregation, and discrimination experienced by African Americans.

The Structure of Race Relations in the 1940s

When Gunnar Myrdal, a Swedish economist and social activist, wrote *An American Dilemma*, the United States was confronting a rapid transformation of its political culture and system of stratification. The Depression had ended and World War II was nearing its final phases. What was observed then about a democratic nation facing a moral paradox over its treatment of former African slaves remains salient today. It is, therefore, instructive to reexamine Myrdal's work.

---

6. Ibid.

7. Marietta Morrissey (1989). *Slave Women in the New World: Gender Stratification in the Caribbean*. Lawrence, Kans.: University Press of Kansas.

8. Frances Beale (1970). "Double Jeopardy: To Be Black and Female," in Toni Cade, ed., *The Black Woman: An Anthology*. New York: New American Library, 190. Jacquelyne Jackson, "A Critique of Lerner's Work on Black Women and Further Thoughts," *Journal of Social and Behavioral Sciences*, 21, Winter 1975, 63–89. Deborah K. King, "Multiple Jeopardies, Multiple Consciousness: The Context of a Black Feminist Ideology," *Signs: Journal of Women in Culture and Society*, 14, 1988, 42–72.

In 1944, Myrdal, Richard Sterner, and Arnold Rose wrote that "segregation is now becoming so complete that the white Southerner practically never sees a Negro except as his servant and in other standardized and formalized caste situations." Both ecological separation and racial distance were entrenched in the fabric of the nation's beliefs, values, and social class hierarchy. All housing, private and public, was segregated by custom and by law. In fact, the Federal Housing Administration assumed "the policy of segregation used by private institutions, like banks, mortgage companies, building and loan associations, and real estate companies." Myrdal commented on this dilemma: "It is one thing when private tenants, property owners, and financial institutions maintain and extend patterns of racial segregation in housing. It is quite another matter when a federal agency chooses to side with the segregationists."[9] Thus, interracial separation, spatial isolation, and all forms of ecological discrimination were among the myriad of racial restrictions confronting "the American Negro" and the country as a whole. Yet, the ideological dissonance Myrdal perceived as a phenomenon of white America was not a part of the oppressive circumstances or the cognitive understanding of the descendants of African slaves. Similarly, gender segregation was obliterated as an issue with equivalent meaning to the spatial and economic segregation and political disenfranchisement of Americans of African descent.

As the decade of the 1940s unfolded, an estimated 13 million Americans of African heritage were residing in the United States, representing 9.8 percent of the population. Most of the foreign-born Americans of African descent were from the West Indies. Although the descendants of former slaves and free persons were living in an evolving industrial country founded on democratic principles, their historical conditions, daily interactions, and life chances were vastly different from those of Euro-American men and women. As Myrdal observed, blacks and whites never encountered each other except in subordinated-superiorized role relationships.

Furthermore, there were no parallels in the social position of white women, slaves, or free blacks in the class system, nor were there parallels in their health status, and the conditions of oppression endured. Demographic data for 1940 show that a wider gap existed in life expectancy with regard to race than to gender. For example, life expectancy for white females was approximately 66.6 years, 62.1 years for white males, 54.9 years for African American females, and 51.5 years for African American or nonwhite males.[10] These comparative statistics, at that time as today, were empirical indicators of a major consequence of structural inequality based principally on a single ascriptive variable. Within racial categories today, significant variations persist in life expectancy. Life expectancy remains unequal for African American women and men, and throughout the 1940s infant and maternal mortality rates were predictably higher for nonwhites, most of whom were African American, than for whites. Racial inequality, not gender, is the foundation of these dissimilarities in life chances.

In spite of the organization of racial segregation in the country a half century ago, race and gender were systemic in the distribution of employment, privileges, and forms of opportunity throughout the North and the South. Data on the rep-

---

9. Myrdal (1944). *An American Dilemma*, 349–350. Also see: James E. Blackwell (1985). *The Black Community: Diversity and Unity*. New York: Harper & Row.

10. Peter M. Bergman and Mort N. Bergman (1969). *The Chronological History of the Negro in America*. New York: Harper & Row, 486–93.

resentation of African American workers among various types of occupations in the United States by region in 1940 vividly reveal the differential occupations and unequal economic situation of black men and women vis-a-vis white men and women. A disproportionate number of African American women worked in the service sector. Over one-half of employed black males were in non-farm labor with the majority in unskilled jobs, service work, or in machine operative positions. In addition, the weight of race and gender in unemployment figures was relatively constant; throughout the decade, the unemployment rate for white males remained less than that for African American males. A wide racial gap also existed for women—unemployment rates for white women were much lower than those for black women. This racially determined gender inequity characterized employment in Northern industrial cities, in the Midwest, and in the South, where vast disparities in employment rates and occupational statuses prevailed.[11]

In addition, housing discrimination was also normative and schools were separate and unequal. Race, not gender, was the principal determinant of this legislated inequality. Patterns of exclusion and isolation in the lives of African American women were the complete opposite of those encountered by Euro-American women. Black and white families lived in racially divided communities in all parts of the country; they were segregated by physical and socially constructed barriers. This racial distance occurred even when historical dwelling units and housing patterns dictated that they live on the same street. Myrdal felt that this ecological reality crystallized the "American Dilemma."

Following the Civil War and throughout the mid-twentieth century, racial customs and laws were interconnected in denying voting privileges, housing, and educational opportunities to African American families. Economic class was not the main component in the definitions of status, benefits, or advantages at any time between 1940 and 1970. Virtually not since slavery have economic class and gender affected where Americans of African ancestry would live, work, attend school, or worship. As previously noted, the Federal Housing Administration assented to the deliberate exclusion of "the Negro" from federal housing and even mandated the adoption of restrictive covenants for new housing based solely on race.[12] In addition, the Federal Housing Administration did not require that builders sell to African Americans.

Residential separation remains today. It is reinforced by lending institutions as well as real estate companies, and it is based on traditional customs and racial preferences. Gender is not a factor in housing discrimination based on race. While the masses of ethnic families in the United States live in ecologically distinct neighborhoods and communities, only African Americans remain spatially isolated and practically restricted to low income or predominantly black areas. Because of the variability in the amenities that accrue to those in particular residential communities, the salience of race linked to class transcends gender in interpretations of this form of inequality.

The economic conditions and health outcomes for African Americans just prior to and immediately following World War II and the Korean War negated the no-

---

11. Doris Wilkinson (1991). "The Segmented Labor Market and African American Women from 1890–1960: A Social History Interpretation," *Race and Ethnic Relations*, 6, 85–104.

12. Blackwell, *The Black Community*, 151–52.

tion of a quandary in the consciousness of Euro-Americans. Merging with institu-tionalized, federally supported, and racially-based preferential treatment, the system of justice also stood squarely against the descendants of African slaves. For them, gender was not a basis for the inequities encountered in the administration of justice. Specifically, the death penalty was applied with greater frequency to blacks than to whites convicted of capital crimes. In the 1990s, this tacitly approved practice of the differential allocation of fairness under the law has been relatively unchanged.[13] Any regional variations in police behavior and in judicial outcomes merely show the pervasiveness of a race-based political culture.

The Primacy of Race in a Gendered Social Order

The primary sociodemographic forces underlying inequality in the United States and in many other parts of the world, especially South Africa and England, are race and class. In order to understand the interrelations among status arrangements, the nature of social inequality, and the dynamics of the culture, these two stratifying factors require explication. A racially framed economy creates nearly permanent disenfranchised and disempowered strata almost independently of the interactive effects of gender and class. Therefore, any discussion of gender and structural differentiation exclusive of race leaves a much greater void in our knowledge base and hence in our comprehension of racialized realities.

Today gender is recognized as a crucial variable in the mapping of life experiences. Nonetheless, it is understandable why sex and gender discrimination were not examined extensively at the time *An American Dilemma* was written. The changing status of women and the gendering of society had not progressed as critical aspects of the transformation of American social organization and culture. At the same time, sexism has prevailed as an ideological force that has affected our values, beliefs, politics, the economy, the health sector, and other institutions. Given our country's multifaceted heritage, race has always been a far more fundamental basis of placement and intergroup exchange than has gender. Since Myrdal's analysis, economic class has emerged as a highly complex multidimensional variable and is somewhat more difficult to extricate from its interdependency with race.[14]

A half century after *An American Dilemma* and the Brown v. Board of Education of Topeka, Kansas, Decision, racial division continues to produce unequal eco-

---

13. Thomas J. Keil and Gennaro F. Vito, "Race and the Death Penalty in Kentucky Murder Trials: 1976–1991: A Study of Racial Bias as a Factor in Capital Sentencing," paper presented at the "Variations in Capital Punishment" panel, Academy of Criminal Justice Science, Chicago, Ill., 11 March 1994. Raymond Paternoster, "Prosecutorial Discretion in Requesting the Death Penalty: A Case of Victim-Based Racial Discrimination," *Law and Society Review*, 18, 1984, 437–78. M. Dwayne Smith, "Patterns of Discrimination in Assessments of the Death Penalty: The Case of Louisiana," *Journal of Criminal Justice*, 15, 1987, 279–86.

14. William J. Wilson (1978). *The Declining Significance of Race*. Chicago, Ill.: University of Chicago Press.

nomic, occupational, residential, and health outcomes between whites and blacks, as documented in labor force participation rates and health statistics for African American and Euro-American women between 1890 and 1960. This period spanned unparalleled changes in the country's political economy from one of slave-driven agricultural production and eventually complete racial exclusion, or "Jim Crowism," to an industrial order permeated by slowly evolving quasi-integration.

With rapid industrial growth and the diversification of the society, structural inequality evolved along gender and racial lines. Non-gender specific placement characterized the employment of Americans of African descent. Their restricted occupational outlets gave rise to a "secondary labor market." The original source for this employment discrimination was slavery. Racism provided the ideological justification for restricting opportunities and stratifying labor on the basis of race.

The institution of slavery in the United States set apart the work and employment privileges of African American males and females from those of European heritage.... In the process of equalizing the positions of African American men and women, enslavement embedded in the organization of work a virtually permanent caste-like component up to the mid-twentieth century. By establishing and legally validating rigid separation between the races, the institution generated vastly disparate ranking in the class system. Thus, it was inevitable that the descendants of slaves would inherit this structural pattern.[15]

Racial Oppression in the 1990s and Beyond

While political and economic inequities mirror sex differences and gender roles, and while these link with class placement in the framing of U.S. culture, racial ascription is far more pervasive in its impact, extent, intensity, historical meaning, and durability. Reflecting on Myrdal's thinking, the issue of class position does raise perplexing questions. However, the United States is guided in its customs, status hierarchies, beliefs, and normative domain by class domination intertwined with the injurious ideologies of racism and sexism. Whenever race is a part of the mosaic, it outweighs all other potential influences.

The Brown decision of 1954 recast the structural paradoxes surrounding education in the United States. Following that historic decision, the latent puzzles and concealed passions of race began to surface. Gender identity and sexual orientation were not at the forefront of the African American quest. Their central preoccupations were with the elimination of housing discrimination and restrictive covenants, access to quality health care, walking the streets without fear of police or other group harassment, the right to serve on juries and to receive justice in the courts, being treated with respect and dignity, being able to work, having voting privileges, and acquiring the chance to secure an education, including having quality schools for their children.

---

15. Wilkinson (1928). "The Segmented Labor Market and African American Women from 1890–1960," 88. See also Elizabeth Ross Haynes, "Negroes in Domestic Service in the United States," *Journal of Negro History*, 8, October 1928, 389–421.

Regardless of socioeconomic status and gender identity, segregation, discrimination, and restricted access have delimited the life experiences of all African Americans since the founding of the country and throughout most of the twentieth century. As shifts in the social class structure began to occur in the 1960s, African Americans who were successful or educated were seen as the enemies of the lower classes and of all "politically correct thinking" blacks. The notion was also propagated that Jews were the enemies of blacks, even though they had helped to build schools, had supported the NAACP, had participated in other Civil Rights organizations, and had marched alongside them in their struggle for freedom and equal protection under the Constitution.

In this century, race is the foundation of inequality for African Americans in all phases of life. White men and women in any social stratum, regardless of education, skills, ideological convictions, ethnic affiliations, gender, or sexual orientation, are aware that American society favors them over all African Americans. An example involving a Southern university in the 1990s will clarify this point. In one non-academic unit of the university, all of the supervisors, secretaries, and mid-level managers are white. Not one has a college degree. The "runners"— those who run back and forth across the campus to pick up the mail—are often black men with college degrees. In this unit, when a college educated African American female data entry clerk wanted to take some college classes, rules were passed stipulating that one could no longer take extensive breaks or enroll in more than one course. This attempt to prohibit a black female from continuing her education is an example of institutionalized racism. And yet, this practice is sanctioned at all levels of the division's administrative hierarchy.

Summary

Awareness of privilege associated with socially constructed status is a major dimension of group affiliation and shared behaviors. Independent of educational achievements and economic class, poor white men and women know that the entire social system treats them preferentially over blacks. Middle-class white males and females are aware that judges, lawyers, health professionals, Congress, legislators at local and state levels, and college and university administrators of predominantly white colleges and universities, among others, support and uphold their rights above all Americans of African descent. Being white in America, regardless of gender or qualifications, means being supported and privileged over Black Americans in all actions by "the system." This "system," anchored in the nation's cultural matrix, is an interlocking directorate and hierarchy dominated and controlled by men of one race. Myrdal and his associates recognized this phenomenon.

Gender contributes significantly to social inequalities. However, the United States is racially organized and hence its class structure is racially designed. White racism, along with class oppression and sexism, pervades the boundaries of the entire culture. Throughout this country's history and ensuing political economy, the extensiveness and permanence of the ideology of racism has been sustained. Recently, African American heterosexual women have been targeted as being the carriers, perpetrators, and/or victims of the acquired immune deficiency syndrome (AIDS)! This politically contrived racist defamation will inevitably affect the life chances, family functioning, employment options, and the entire future of African Americans. The direct link between race, not gender, and social inferiorization is evident in this calculated politicization of a world-wide health crisis. The shift in categorization of a disease that was disproportionately concentrated among homosexual men to heterosexual black females negates all logic. This attempt to reconstruct the origins and victims of the current pandemic clearly demonstrates the profound impact of race over gender and class in the United States.

We live in a social system where race endures as a politically charged attribute and where racism is a paramount belief configuration that reinforces a particular form of status domination and economic oppression. The ideology of racism determines, legitimizes, and reinforces the interlocking character of the race-class-gender triad. Myrdal was too early in his interpretations and descriptions to grasp this fundamental reality.

17

Ralph Bunche and the Howard School of Thought

Charles P. Henry

In late August of 1993, 33 young black intellectuals gathered at the Hudson River estate of NAACP president Joel Spingarn to discuss the problems of race in the midst of a depression. The meeting was planned by W.E.B. Du Bois, who like other officers of the NAACP, was feeling increased pressure to adjust the organization's traditional legal and political approach to the economic reality of the thirties. In fact, longtime race leaders like Du Bois and James Weldon Johnson would receive the brunt of the criticism coming from the young intellectuals.

Leading the attack were Abram Harris, E. Franklin Frazier and Ralph Bunche. Charging the older men with racial provincialism, the young radicals advocated black and white solidarity to force through the necessary reform legislation. The older "race men" and the NAACP, they stated, were caught up in the middle-class needs of the black business elite ignoring the economic needs of the black masses.[1]

Even though Harris, Bunche and Frazier were appointed to a special investigative committee to follow-up the Amenia Conference with specific recommendations for the NAACP, their report was debated but ultimately rejected. The young radicals went on to distinguished careers in academe and public service and their views began to diverge over the years. However, during the thirties they and other colleagues at Howard University produced a body of work that broke sharply with the preceding generation of black scholars and contributed to a paradigm that remained dominant until the sixties.

Race Relation Paradigms

There is a "mandatory requirement" that any discussion of paradigms begin with the work of Thomas Kuhn.[2] This requirement is followed by social scientists even though Kuhn was writing about scientific revolutions. Perhaps this is because if Kuhn is right that normal science can only interpret a dominant para-

---

An earlier version of this essay appeared in *National Political Science Review*; 1995, 5, 36–56 and is adapted/reprinted with the permission of the copyright holder/author.

1. Young, 1973, pp. 3–5; Wolters, 1970, pp. 219–223.
2. Kuhn, 1970.

digm, not correct it,[3] how much more true is this of social science, dependent as it is on the dominant culture to give it legitimacy. In short, the social science community is less insulated from society than the scientific community and therefore its paradigms may be less likely to challenge mainstream social norms.

Of course, in the area of race relations scientific, pseudo-scientific and social scientific theories have often merged to provide rationalizations for the racial status quo. According to Kuhn, any successful paradigm must attract an enduring group of adherents away from competing theories yet be sufficiently open-ended to leave problems to be resolved by those adherents. The theory is learned through its application to problem solving even though practitioners may work on entirely different applications.[4] Social Darwinists, for example, accepted Darwin's paradigm but applied it to an entirely different set of problems.

Kuhn states that it is "particularly in periods of acknowledged crises that scientists have turned to philosophical analysis as a device for unlocking the riddles of their field."[5] Almost all innovators, says Kuhn, are young with little commitment to prior traditions. In the social sciences, we might suspect that academics from marginalized groups would have less commitment to established views. However, the crucial question for both communities is who chooses the rules of debate when paradigms are in dispute or transition? As Kuhn states more than logic and the impact of nature are at work in winning the paradigm wars.[6]

Mack Jones has recently argued that the establishment of academic disciplines and the determination of their substantive content is a normative exercise that is necessarily parochial because a people's need to know is a function of their anticipation and control needs.[7] This means, says Jones, that a dominant paradigm "leads the practitioner to study the adversary community only to the extent that the adversary constitutes a problem."[8] For Jones this explains why American social science generally sees blacks as a problem but one which does not challenge the dominant paradigm of pluralist democracy. Such a paradigm conveys only a caricature of the oppressed or dominated people and hence has little prescriptive utility for their struggle to end their domination.

Jones views help explain the paradox of the centrality of black politics yet its marginalization in the discipline of political science. Michael Dawsen and Ernest Wilson III have documented this marginality as compared to the sister disciplines of history and sociology. Contending that the logical structure of a particular paradigm leads an analyst to structure the problem of racial or black politics in a particular way they examine the dominant theoretical paradigm, pluralist theory, and its main challengers—social stratification (Weberian theory), Marxism, modernization theory, social choice theory, and black nationalist theory. Among scholars interested in black politics they found that the most frequently used paradigms included pluralist, nationalist, and Weberian/modernization approaches. They also found that many of these scholars transcended paradigmatic differences and united their inquiries into black politics. Moreover, they found "that despite the

---

3. Ibid., p. 122.
4. Ibid., pp. 10, 47.
5. Ibid., p. 88.
6. Ibid., p. 94.
7. Barker, 1992, p. 30.
8. Ibid., p. 94.

paradigm or model in which black scholars worked, there were among many such scholars commonalties that transcended paradigmatic differences and united their inquiries into black politics."[9] These commonalties include a concern with tactics or strategy, a concern with the internal dynamics of the black community, frequent reference to historical antecedents, a concern about the gap between the promise and the performance of the America political system, and a tendency to blame white racism for unequal societal outcomes.[10]

Paradigms do indeed determine the approach which we take in defining and solving racial problems. Yet to fully understand contemporary paradigms we must examine their historical antecedents. None of the widely-used modern paradigms on race relations in general or black politics in particular is new. Where they differ now and in the past is in the varying interpretations and applications given to them by black and white proponents.

The Religious Paradigm on Race 1619 to 1860

From the arrival of the first slaves at Jamestown, Virginia, in 1619 until the Civil War the dominant perspective on race was shaped by a religious worldview. The central text for this view was the Christian Bible. Both pro-slavery and anti-slavery advocates debated the issue within the parameters set by the Bible. A key event in the hegemony of this view occurred in Virginia during the mid-1660s when, after considerable debate, the colonial assembly decided that it was possible to convert Africans to Christianity and still keep them in bondage. This enabled white Christians to continue their conversion of blacks without opposition and indeed with some support from slaveowners. The opposite decision by the Lutheran Church in South Africa severely restricted the spread of Christianity among the African population.[11]

White proponents of slavery promoted a Christianity that rationalized the institution of black slavery. The most common justification for the subordinate status of blacks was the "curse of Ham." The favorite biblical texts for these proponents came from the New Testament, especially the letters of Paul calling on servants to obey their masters and give unto Ceasar what is Ceasar's. Biblical promises of rewards in heaven, one assumes a segregated heaven, were used to pacify slaves concerned about injustice in this life.[12]

Developing simultaneously with "white Christianity" was a more radical "black Christianity." The slave's interpretation of the Bible often focused on Old Testament visions of "an eye and a tooth for a tooth." Heroes like Moses, Joshua, Daniel, Jonah, Gabriel, and David were preferred over Paul and the meek and mild Jesus. Obviously, the favorite book was Exodus and the spirituals were sometimes used to send secret messages. The best-known slave revolts of the 19th century were led by biblically inspired blacks—Denmark Vessey, Gabriel Prosser and Nat Turner. Of course, "black Christianity" had to be practiced in secret and

---

9. Dawson and Wilson, 1990, p. 223.
10. Ibid., pp. 223–4.
11. Raboteau, 1978; Levine, 1977; Fredrickson, 1981.
12. Ibid.

often co-existed with voduu. In fact, black Catholics in Louisiana integrated their Christianity with "vodoo" or "conjure" to produce a syncretic religion much like those found in Haiti and Cuba.[13]

Almost all black political writing from David Walker's Appeal through Reverend Henry Highland Garnet's call for slave resistance uses the Bible as the moral justification for action.[14] From the earliest slave narratives through the most popular novel of the 19th century—*Uncle Tom's Cabin*—literature by and about blacks revolves around religious themes.[15] Thus, while black and white applications of the Christian paradigm differ, the paradigm itself is not challenged.

The Biological/Genetic Paradigm—1860 to 1930

With the publication of Charles Darwin's *On the Origin of Species by Natural Selection* in 1859, a new paradigm rose to challenge and eventually replace the religious worldview on race. Darwin's work had been preceded by a wave of racist literature claiming to be scientific in the 1850s in Western Europe. Thus, although Darwin's work was not specifically concerned with the origins of races it was quickly applied to race.[16]

Social Darwinists, led by Herbert Spencer and William Graham Sumner, soon equated the survival of the fittest with the right of superior races to rule. Social Darwinism and organicism also reinforced the economic liberalism of the day. Lassiez-faire was reinterpreted as a mandate not to interfere with any form of human inequality and suffering. The poor were poor because they were biologically inferior and Negroes were slaves as a result of natural selection. Any attempt to interfere with "nature" through philanthropy or abolition would only hurt the superior race and lead to the multiplication of the inferior race.

Natural scientists developed sophisticated craneological and phrenological tests to support sociologists and anthropologists in the establishment of a hierarchy of races and promotion of a eugenics movement. The black response was to deny the superiority or inferiority of any race but to acknowledge biological differences. Black leaders stressed the complementarity of the races. The warm, sensitive, emotional, artistic temperament of the Negro balanced the cold, scientific, industrious nature of Caucasians.

Perhaps the leading black intellectual of the 19th century, Edward W. Blyden personified the black interpretation of the race paradigm. On the one hand, Blyden developed the concept of the "African personality." He stressed African religiosity, oneness with nature and communalism as unique racial traits. On the other hand, he was a great admirer of European culture and supported colonization as a means for grafting "European progress wholesale on African conservation and stagnation." Blyden did not approve of racial mixing because it diluted racial traits.[17]

---

13. Ibid.
14. Stuckey, 1972.
15. Gates, 1988.
16. Van den Berghe, 1967, p. 17.
17. Mudime, 1988; Lynch, 1970.

In the United States, Alexander Crummell, a major early influence of W.E.B. Du Bois, searched from the 1840s through the 1890s for the "innate" characteristics of races. Like his ideological opponent, Booker T. Washington, he tended to see blacks as an aesthetically gifted people, strongly enthusiastic, but lacking in discipline. Crummell acquired the reputation of championing blacks against mulattos. His emphasis on race pride and race destiny led him to organize the black cultural and intellectual elite into the American Negro Academy in 1897.[18]

It was at the first meeting of the Academy that its vice-president and social historian, Du Bois, read his paper on "The Conservation of Races." In this paper Du Bois sets forth a mystical notion of race interchanging it with "nation." He believed that racially growth was historically characterized by "the differentiation of spiritual and mental differences between great races of mankind and the integration of physical differences."[19] The German nation stood for science and philosophy; the English nation stood for "constitutional liberty and commercial freedom"; but the racial ideal of the Negro race had yet to be fulfilled.[20]

Only two years later in his *The Philadelphia Negro*, Du Bois introduces social science into his defense of the race. And in a critical review of Frederick L. Hoffman's *Race Traits and Tendencies of the American Negro* which asserts that Negroes were doomed to decline as a race because of weak genetic material, Du Bois cites relevant comparative data from European cities with which blacks compared favorably in terms of health and crime statistics.[21] While his intellectual peers Kelly Miller and Carter Woodson continued to focus on the primacy of race (prior to World War I only 14 black Americans had Ph.D.s from recognized universities) Du Bois began to give class increasing consideration. Thus while Miller and Woodson quarreled with the younger generation of black intellectuals, Du Bois supported them and invited dialogue. As such, Du Bois represents a transitional figure in the break from the biological paradigm.[22]

The push of the Great Depression and the pull of new anthropological evidence mark the end of the dominance of the biological explanations for black subordination.[23] While Du Bois now recognizes the importance of economics and encourages the NAACP to change its focus, he disappoints the "young radicals" by suggesting self-segregation in economic cooperatives as a viable economic strategy. While Du Bois is "convinced" of the essential truth of the Marxian philosophy, he asks is there any automatic power in socialism to override and suppress race prejudice?

> There are those who insist that the American Negro must stand or fall by his alliance with white Americans; that separation in any degree, physical or social, is impossible and that either, therefore, the Negro must take his stand with exploiting capitalists or with craft unions or with the communists. [24]

Du Bois says the question is already settled because Negroes form today a separate nation within a nation. What remains is to be organized along economic lines

---

18. Moses, 1978, p. 75.
19. Ibid., p. 135.
20. Ibid.
21. Toll, op. cit., p. 105.
22. Young, op. cit., pp. 9–16.
23. Remnants of the biological/genetic paradigm remain today in the debate over IQ testing. See Mensh, 1991.
24. Aptheker (ed.), 1985, p. 144.

that benefit the great majority of blacks. At the same time, blacks would continue the fight for political and civil equality.

The overthrow of the biological paradigm removed the major obstacle to racial assimilation. Robert Park, a transitional figure who worked for Booker T. Washington early in his career and trained E. Franklin Frazier and Charles S. Johnson late in his career, provided a theory of assimilation based on urban racial contact. While the young black intellectuals who opposed Du Bois assumed a Marxist posture throughout the thirties, by the early forties they had helped shape a new dominant paradigm based on the social psychology of Gunnar Myrdal. This new paradigm was assimilationist at its core and therefore never acceptable to Du Bois.

The Howard School

During the 1930's, Howard University was home for the most distinguished group of black scholars ever assembled on one campus. Of course, this concentration of intellectual talent was not coincidental. Segregation meant that the only positions available for black faculty, no matter how talented, were at black universities. In 1932, Bunche reported that of the 271 Howard faculty (including whites) 211 were Howard graduates.[25] As late as 1936, more than 80 percent of all black Ph.D.s were employed by Howard, Atlanta, and Fisk. By the 1940's government service and elite white universities had lured away many of Howard's most noted faculty members.

Among the distinguished faculty Howard in the 1930s were Ernest Everett Just, an internationally known biologist; philosopher Alain L. Locke, the first African American Rhodes Scholar and a leader of the Harlem Renaissance; Sterling A. Brown, English professor, author, poet, and critic; Law School Dean William H. Hastie, the first black governor of the Virgin Islands and the first black federal judge; Charles H. Houston, vice dean of the law school and architect of the NAACP legal strategy; Surgeon Charles R. Drew, the pioneer developer of blood plasma; Merze Tate, historian and specialist on disarmament; historian Rayford Logan; Charles Thompson, founder of the *Journal of Negro Education*; theologian and president Mordecai Johnson; linguist and sociologist Lorenzo Turner; historian Charles Wesley, founder of the *Journal of Negro History*; theologian Howard Thurman; chemist Percy Julian; William Leo Hansberry, a pioneer in African history; Kelly Miller, dean and professor of mathematics and sociology; W. Mercer Cook, professor of Romance Languages and later ambassador to Senegal and Gambia; economist Abram Harris; sociologist E. Franklin Frazier; and political scientist Ralph Bunche.[26] These latter three—Harris, Frazier, and Bunche—were social scientists with advanced degrees from elite white universities. They were active in campus politics, and as seen in the Amenia Conference, nationally known even though their careers were just developing.

Harris was the first of the three to arrive at Howard in 1927. A native of Richmond, Virginia, Harris graduated from Virginia Union and then attended the New York City School of Social Work. While in New York, Harris worked as a

---

25. Ralph Bunche Papers, UCLA, Box 135 "Conversation," March 7, 1932.
26. Logan, 1968.

research assistant for the National Urban League, came into contact with the city's left-wing intellectual community and developed an interest in black workers in the labor movement. By 1924, he had completed an M.A in economics from Pittsburgh with a thesis entitled "The Negro Laborer in Pittsburgh." Around this time, Harris developed a warm friendship with Du Bois that lasted until their separate splits with the NAACP in 1935. After teaching for a year at West Virginia Collegiate Institute (now West Virginia State) and a year as executive secretary of the Minneapolis Urban League, Harris began his doctoral studies in economics at Columbia. At the same time, he began teaching at Howard commuting regularly between the District of Columbia and New York. Harris's best-known work *The Black Worker* (1931), was written collaboratively with Sterling Spero and originally served as their joint doctoral dissertation.

Du Bois had written an enthusiastic review of the *The Black Worker* for *The Nation:* "...one of the first attempts in the economic field to make a synthesis of the labor movement and the Negro problem so as to interpret each in the light of the other and show them to be one question of American economics."[27] In his own journal, *The Crisis*, Du Bois "strongly recommended this book for reading, particularly by those American Negroes who do not yet realize that the Negro problem is primarily the problem of the Negro working man."[28]

In chapters of *The Black Worker* written by Harris, he takes Booker T. Washington to task emphasizing the old notion of the self-made man to exclusion of the "problems peculiar to wage earner in modern industry." Middle-class Negro leadership in general, Harris noted, always sided with capital and against organized labor. However, Harris urged blacks to try to avoid setting up separate unions, even if expedient, because it would hinder the development of class consciousness. Harris preferred the radical ideology of industrial unionism over more conservative trade unionism because they must be more concerned about neglecting any large section of workers.[29]

As early as 1927, Harris made clear that class not race was the dominant force in black oppression. Writing in *Social Forces* he states that "slavery was an economic system which involved white freemen as masters and black men as slaves. The Negro was not enslaved because his complexion, and nose and lip formation differed from the white man's." He goes on to add that "both the lower white and black classes were weak.... For a short period white and black bondsmen were on the same indefinite legal footing." This brief equality in status among the poor changed because "Negro labor being cheaper (more plentiful) than cheap white labor was more desired."[30]

Harris's sharpest attacks in the racial paradigm come in response to Du Bois. In 1935, Du Bois' published what some considered his finest scholarly work *Black Reconstruction in America*. Despite Du Bois' earlier praise of *The Black Worker* and Harris's stated admiration of Du Bois as the Negro intellectual to whom his generation owes the most, he proceeds to launch a fierce attack on the work. Du Bois, says Harris, is too bound by the racial paradigm of his generation to absorb Marxism:

---

27. Darity, 1989, p. 204.
28. Ibid.
29. Ibid., pp. 41–2.
30. Ibid., pp. 169–70.

> Dr. Du Bois concedes the inevitability of socialism and even the desirability of it, but is at the same time distrustful of white workers. He cannot believe that a movement founded upon working-class solidarity and cutting across racial lines can afford any immediate relief to the Negro's economic plight or have any practical realization in the near future. By temperament and habituation to the Negro equal rights struggle he is wholly unfitted to join, to say nothing of initiating, such a movement. He is a racialist whose discovery of Marxism as a critical instrument has been too recent and sudden for it to discipline his mental process or basically to change his social philosophy.[31]

Du Bois' ideological confusion, according to Harris leads him to convert the wholesale flight of Negroes from the plantations into a general strike against the slave regime while in fact the slaves had no real class consciousness nor any idea of what impact their "escape to freedom" would have on the outcome of the war. Moreover, had they pursued a truly radical agenda during Reconstruction, says Harris, their plans would never have been supported by Stevens and Summer, who were members of the capitalist class.[32]

Harris would extend his criticism of Du Bois' racial chauvinism in his other major economic study of the decade, *The Negro as Capitalist* (1936). This work came up just after Du Bois had set his new program for a Negro economic nation within the nation. Harris argued that Du Bois had not explained how a separate economy could function in the face of persistent industrial integration, business combination, and the centralization of capital control. In fact, Harris links Du Bois' proposal to those of the pre-Civil War proponents of a separate black economy, Martin Delany, whom he calls a "black Benjamin Franklin." The black businessman emerges as the villain who encourages black enterprise at the expense of white and black labor solidarity. Even groups like the New Negro Alliance who promoted "Don't Buy Where You Can't Work" campaigns were categorized with Du Bois as middle-class black chauvinists.[33] Throughout the thirties, then, Harris consistently rejected interracial conciliation as the strategy of Booker T. Washington and civil libertarianism and militant race-consciousness as the program of middle-class blacks. The first actively supported capitalism while the latter left untouched the material basis for racial inequality. While maintaining that white trade unions must change their racial practices he promoted class consciousness and class unity. In fact, blacks should pursue no actions that would inflame racial antagonism. Harris, unlike contemporary radical economists such as Michael Reich, argued that "if race prejudice is not accompanied with competitive activities or the subjugation of one group by the other it is soon removed through association."[34] However, as blacks become more competitive with white workers, hostility between the races will increase. Harris never fully explains how this cycle of competition and hostility can be overcome but perhaps we can gain insight into the process from Harris's colleague, E. Franklin Frazier.

If anything Frazier is more critical of the racial romanticism of men like Du Bois than Harris. In his "The Du Bois Program in the Present Crisis," Frazier not only joins Harris in attacking the legitimacy of Du Bois's conversion to Marxism

---

31. Ibid., p. 209.
32. Ibid., p. 211.
33. Young, op. cit., pp. 43–4, Darity, op. cit., p. 204.
34. Darity, op. cit., p. 18.

but goes on to state that Du Bois remained the "genteel" aristocrat who had no real conception of "sympathetic understanding" of the plight of the black proletariat. As for Du Bois' ideal black society, Frazier gratuitously adds that nothing would be more unendurable for him than to live within a Black Ghetto or within a black nation—unless perhaps he were king, and then he probably would attempt to unite the whites and blacks through marriage of royal families."[35] Like Harris, Frazier was concerned that Du Bois' program would split black workers from white workers and create false hopes among blacks for their survival in a capitalistic system. However, the bitterness of the attack is remarkable in that Frazier's early work on the family was much indebted to Du Bois' 1908 report and Du Bois had hired Frazier in the early 1920s to do field work in the deep South.[36]

Frazier was one of five children in a stable and race-conscious family in Baltimore. Although his father was a bank messenger, three of the boys became professional men. Franklin won a scholarship that permitted him to enroll at Howard, from which he graduated cum laude in 1916. He did not take any formal courses in sociology even though Kelly Miller was offering them at Howard as early as 1903. He did read Gidding's *Principles of Sociology* at Howard and became a member of the Intercollegiate Socialist Society. He taught secondary school in Virginia and Baltimore during World War I and privately published a tract he wrote opposing the war entitled "God and War." In 1919, he won a scholarship for graduate study at Clark University in Worchester, Massachusetts, where he came under the influence of Professor Frank H. Hankins and G. Stanley Hall. He appreciated the objectivity of Hankin's statistical approach to sociology but disagreed with his racism. Both Hankins and Hall were a part of the mainstream of scientific racists who supported benevolent social reforms.[37]

After receiving his MA from Clark, Frazier became a research fellow at the New York School of Social Work and was influenced by the psychological work of Bernard Glueck. Frazier's 1921 study of Negro longshoremen in New York City broke new ground in looking at the effects of migration at work and at home. These Southern migrants, Frazier reported, experienced problems in their families and failed to understand the nature of union organization in industry. Frazier was attracted by the socialists of *The Messenger,* supported the first Pan-African Congress, and attended the second Congress in 1921. The following year he spent in Denmark as a fellow of the American Scandinavian Foundation. Influenced by Booker T. Washington's praise of Danish Folk Schools he studied them and their role in the cooperative movement (by 1928 he had given up on coops). Returning to the United States, Frazier became professor of sociology at Morehouse College and later helped set up and then direct the Atlanta School of Social Work. It is during this Atlanta period that Frazier began writing on the disorganization of the Negro family and on the black middle-class. In 1927 he wrote:

> The first fact that makes the Negro family the subject of special sociological study is the incomplete assimilation of western culture by the Negro masses. Generally when two different cultures come into contact, each modifies the

---

35. Young, op. cit., p. 47.

36. Platt, 1991, pp. 18, 133. Frazier and Du Bois established a better relationship in later years with Frazier chairing a controversial dinner honoring Du Bois during the McCarthy era.

37. Blackwell and Janowitz, 1974, pp. 89–90.

other. But in the case of he Negro in America it meant the total destruction of the African social heritage. Therefore, in the case of the family group the Negro has not introduced new patterns of behavior, but has failed to conform to patterns about him. The degree of conformity is determined by educational and economic factors as well as by social isolation.[38]

Among the businessmen of Durham, North Carolina, Frazier found more stable family lives and disciplined individuals than among the poor of Atlanta.

Another work of Frazier's during the Atlanta years demonstrates the influence of psychology on his work. In "The Pathology of Race Prejudice" he compares the mechanisms which operate in prejudiced behavior with those which characterize mental illness. Frazier boldly refers to the operation of projective mechanisms in white women who accuse Negro males of attempted rape. The response to this 1927 article was so emotional (irrational?) among whites that Frazier's life was threatened and he was forced to leave Atlanta almost immediately after the article appeared.[39]

By the time Frazier moved to the University of Chicago for two years of graduate study, his research focus was firmly fixed. Nonetheless, he came under the influence of distinguished teachers and fellow graduate students including Robert E. Park, Ellsworth Faris, Earnest W. Burgess, William F. Ogburn, George H. Mead, Louis Wirth, and Herbert Blumer. Frazier's dissertation, later published in 1932 as *The Negro Family in Chicago* was clearly reflective of the Chicago tradition of empirical study of one aspect of community life to illuminate larger aspects of social reality.[40]

Park, like Du Bois, was a transitional figure who often intermixed biology and sociology. As late as 1931, Park was still attempting to provide a definitive statement on the issue of whether the superior achievement of mulattos was due to their biological or to their cultural inheritance. Frazier disagreed with Park's contention that the two groups differed in temperament. In his writing on the black family, Frazier accounted for the deviation of the great majority of black families from the normative type of family behavior through environmental factors created by the experiences of slavery, emancipation, and urbanization. Older works on the black family had insisted that racial or cultural differences in black families were African survivals. According to the recent anthropological work of Bronislaw Malinowski and Robert Briffault on sexual behavior, primitive peoples had strong sexual impulses that could not be controlled by custom.[41] In short, Frazier denied the possibility of African survivals in order to refute the biological claims that black deviance from the middle-class family norm was due to the less-evolved status of the black race. By charging that slavery and urbanization had left the poor rural peasant with a folk culture unable to cope with city-life, Frazier's view eventually won out over the biological determinists but at the price of accepting conventional white standards of behavior.

For Frazier, Park's race relations cycle of contact, conflict and competition would more quickly lead to acculturation or even assimilation if the Negro be-

---

38. Ibid., p. 92.
39. Edwards, 1968, p. xi.
40. Ibid.
41. Williams, 1989, p. 152.

came an industrial worker receiving an adequate wage that would enable the father to assume his position as chief breadwinner at the head of a stable, conventional family. At this stage, Frazier did not see any role for a unique black culture.
In fact, his condemnation of the life-style behind the blues reveals more than a little of the capitalist ethos he condemned in others: "the Negro has succeeded in
adopting habits of living that have enabled him to survive in a civilization based
upon laissez faire and competition, it bespeaks a degree of success on taking on
the folkways and mores of the white race."[42] At least one writer states that "if
Frazier wanted to see the end of the race in the future, Ralph Bunche often ignored its existence in the present."[43]

Bunche had gone to Howard from Harvard in 1928 where his on-campus home
served as base for a small circle of progressive colleagues known as the "thinkers
and drinkers." In fact, it was this group of scholar-activists that helped attract Frazier to Howard in 1934. Yet while all three of the core members of this circle had
attended elite white graduate schools—Harris/Columbia, Frazier/Chicago,
Bunche/Harvard—Bunche's background diverged sharply from theirs during his
formative years. Ten years younger than Frazier and five years younger than Harris, Bunche was born in Detroit in 1903 rather than in the South like Harris and
Frazier. Bunche's father Fred worked as a barber and the family lived in a mostly
white neighborhood where Ralph's early friends were white. In 1914, after brief
stays in Toledo, Ohio, and Knoxville, Tennessee, the family moved to Albuquerque, New Mexico, hoping the climate would help his mother's rheumatic
fever. Unfortunately illness claimed both of Bunche's parents within two years—
leading his grandmother (the unquestioned head of the family) to move Ralph and
his sister, Grace, to Los Angeles. In Los Angeles, the Bunche's were denied housing
in a predominantly white neighborhood. However, Ralph did attend a predominantly white high school and won a scholarship to UCLA. He graduated magna
cum laude and was valedictorian of his class. Bunche's academic success made him
a local hero among Los Angeles blacks and won him a fellowship at Harvard.[44]

On the eve of his departure for the East Coast and his first contact with black
leaders, Bunche outlined his goals in a letter to W.E.B. Du Bois:

> But I have long felt the need of coming in closer contact with the leaders of our
> race, so that I may better learn their methods of approach, their psychology
> and benefit in my own development by their influence. That is why I am anx-
> ious to come east and anticipate enjoying the opportunity extremely. Now
> specifically, I would like to inquire if there is any way that I can be of service to
> my group this coming summer, either in the east or in the south? Admittedly my
> resources are limited, but I am willing to tackle any problems or proposition
> which will give sufficient return for bare living expenses. I feel that there must
> be some opportunity for me either connected with the NAACP or as a teacher. I
> have a liberal education, extensive experience in journalism, forensics and dra-
> matics, as well as athletics, and am young and healthy. I can furnish the best of
> recommendations, both from the faculty of the University and from the Race
> leaders of the Pacific Coast.[45]

---

42. Young, op. cit., p. 53.
43. Ibid.
44. Haskins, 1992, pp. 67–9; Interview with Mrs. Ralph Bunche, October 18, 1985.
45. Rivlin (ed.), 1990, p. 218.

Within a few years, Bunche would be a critic of Du Bois and race leaders in general, although he was never as close to Du Bois as Harris and Frazier.

More perhaps than Harris and Frazier, Bunche was the logical successor to Du Bois's intellectual legacy. Although separated by thirty years, Bunche had completed the first doctorate by a black in political science at Harvard and the nation as a whole.[46] Bunche's scope of interest ranging from African American politics to the politics of colonial African administration paralleled Du Bois' expertise. Bunche cited philosophers at UCLA and Harvard as his most significant influences.[47] Remarkably his lecture notes from the early years at Howard reveal some of the racial sentimentality he so strongly attacks in Du Bois:

> Fundamentally, the Negro is a being most sensitively sentimental; a being endowed with the most natural of artistic talents...(which historically leads to two very obvious truths)—one is that any distinction so far won by a member of our Race, here, has been invariably in some one of the arts...—the other is that any influence so far exerted by the American Negro upon American civilization has been primarily in the realm of art (he cites Douglass's oratory, Dunbar, Tanner)...the Negro Race of all races, whether it be generally known or not, is endowed with that greatest of racial blessings,—a *soul* (which might be poetically traced back to Africa)...—no race has ever,—no race *shall* ever, rise to the heights of artistic achievement until it has suffered and mourned and received deliverance...(Given that every race has its outstanding trait of genius)—Then it appears from past indications that the American Negro is destined to attain his greatest heights of successful achievement in the realm of art—just as he has in the past (Cites folklore, dances, spirituals, composers)—The final measure of the greatness of any people of whatever creed or race, religious or political affiliation, is the amount and standard of the artistic production of that people (Cited Coleridge—Taylor in England; Dumas in France; Pushkin in Russia, and Robeson, Gilpin & Roland Hughes in U.S.)[48]

It seems clear from these notes that Bunche did not fully reject Du Bois racial views until the onset of the Depression and under the influence of first Harris and then Frazier.

By 1936, Bunche has a decidedly different perspective on race as expressed in his only book length publication, *A World View of Race*. Race, he says, first appears in the English Language in the 16th century and has become an effective instrument of national politics. However, existing racial diversions are arbitrary, subjective, and devoid of scientific meaning. Thus, according to Bunche, all existing human groups are of definitely mixed origin.[49]

Although much conflict is labeled as racial its real causes are social, political, and economic. Racial attitudes are primarily social inheritances based on stereotypes. Like Frazier, Bunche sees racial prejudice and conflict existing as long as easily identified groups are forced into economic competition. Once society guarantees economic security to all peoples, the chief source of group conflict will be

---

46. Aptheker reports that Du Bois initially hoped to study political science at Harvard. Private conversation, Fall, 1988.

47. Ralph Bunche Papers, UCLA, Box 126, "Letters to Dean Rieber," June 10, 1947.

48. Ibid., Box 134, folder "Governments of Europe," lecture notes on "The American Negro and His Achievements."

49. Bunche, 1936, pp. 3–14.

removed. Bunche implies that race war might be avoided by transforming it into class war:

> If the oppressed racial groups, as a result of desperation and increasing under-standing, should be attracted by the principles of equality and humanitarianism advocated by the Soviet Union (and it is both logical and likely that they will) then racial conflict will become intensified. In such case, however, racial conflict will be more directly identified with class conflict, and the oppressed racial groups may win the support of oppressed, though previously prejudiced, work-ing-class groups within the dominant population.[50]

Drawing on his dissertation Bunche cites Africa as imperialism's greatest and most characteristic expression. He condemns the "extreme egoism" of British and French culture as expressed in their colonial policies yet he sees West Africans as culturally in a transition stage between primitivism and civilization.[51] He ends the section on Africa by comparing Lord Lugard's views on "equality in things spiri-tual," but agreed divergence in the physical and material to Booker T. Washing-ton's famous "separate as the fingers, yet one as the hand in all things essential to mutual progress" analogy and the familiar legal fiction of "separate but equal rights."[52] In the last chapter of his work, Bunche asks "is the plight of the Negro the plight of a race?" He contends that the policies of Washington, Garvey, Kelly Miller, and others represent a plea for conciliation with the white moneyed-class and at least a tacit acceptance of group segregation. "Dr. Du Bois," says Bunche, "has differed from these gentlemen chiefly in the militancy of his tone in his insis-tent demand for fair and constitutional treatment of the Negro as a *race*." How-ever, Du Bois' attack was based on Washington's retreat from civil and political equality and not on Washington's economic philosophy or his misleading racial-ism. According to Bunche such "racial" interpretations by Negro leaders and or-ganizations "reveal a clear understanding of the true group and class status of the Negro in American society" leading him "up the dark, blind ally of black chau-vinism."[53] On the positive side, "the depression, ably abetted by the policies of the New Deal, has made the American population white and black, increasingly class-conscious.[54]

The same year that *A World View* appeared Bunche published two articles sharply critical of the status quo. The first of these articles was perhaps the best critique of early New Deal social planning and its impact on blacks. In it Bunche contends that the New Deal represented "merely an effort to refurbish the old in-dividualistic—capitalistic system and to entrust it again with the economic des-tinies and welfare of the American people."[55] "Relatively few Negro workers were even theoretically affected by the labor provisions of the National Recovery Administration," stated Bunche, and the Agricultural Adjustment Act deprived Negro tenants of their benefit from the crop reduction program.[56] In short, the

---

50. Ibid., p. 36.
51. Ibid., pp. 41–57.
52. Ibid., p. 60.
53. Ibid., pp. 83–4.
54. Ibid., p. 90.
55. Bunche, 1936a, p. 60.
56. Ibid., p. 358.

New Deal was a program to benefit the middle-class which barely existed in the black community.

The second article in this unusually productive year asks the question of whether separate schools for blacks raise any separate educational problem in terms of course content. In an article that reveals many of the issues that would rise after the *Brown* decision Bunche writes:

> The fact is that under our present system it is impossible to achieve educational equality for all members of any group in the society. Public schools for example, are supported by taxation. The revenue derived from taxation will depend largely upon the relative prosperity of the propertied interests in the particular locality. Since wealth is unequally distributed in the country the present glaring inequalities in the distribution of funds for the support of education will persist even for "White education." The basic question for all schools is to one of copying the "white man's education," which will afford both white and black students a sound basis for understanding the society in which they live and for attacking the problems confronting them. White as well as Negro schools are woefully deficient in this respect.[57]

For Bunche, the culture of capitalism controlled Negro education as well as White education, and while Negro schools could be much more progressive than at present, they would never be permitted to remodel the social order of the position of the Negro group in that order.[58]

By the mid-thirties, Bunche, Harris, and Frazier held identical views. While Bunche may have ranged across a wider range of issues, they all gave primacy to class over race thus breaking with the racial paradigm of the preceding generation of black intellectuals. The racial chauvinism and narrow legal and political orientation of the older race men was decidedly rejected. In its stead they offered not a program of minority advancement but rather a program of majority advancement through the vehicle of white and black labor solidarity.

Howard and the Assimilationist Paradigm

The Howard School of Thought represented one of several transitional theories that broke away from the dominant biological/genetic paradigm. New approaches to race problems included the Chicago School of Sociology, Donald Young's comparative analysis of minority groups, Howard Odum's regional sociology, Melville Herskovits's cultural anthropology, and John Dollard's "caste and class" approach. When the Carnegie Foundation decided to fund a major study on race relations in the late thirties, they decided no black or white American social scientists could approach the subject objectively. After first considering several former British colonial administrators, they chose the Swedish economist Gunnar Myrdal.[59]

Myrdal was a liberal social Democrat active in Swedish politics. He saw in the Carnegie Foundation president, Francis Keppel, an educated white American who would take action on the civil rights issue if he just knew the facts. Myrdal fo-

---

57. Bunche, 1936b, p. 355.
58. Ibid., p. 358.
59. Jackson, 1990, pp. 93–95.

cuses his study on the alleged contradiction within American society between a strong commitment to democratic values on the one hand and the presence of racial oppression on the other. Although Myrdal had strong economic views he emphasizes the moral contradiction between belief and practice for white America as the root of race relations problems. He states:

> at bottom of our problem is the moral dilemma of the American—the conflict between his moral valuations on various levels of consciousness and generality. The American Dilemma... is the ever raging conflict between, on the one hand, the valuations preserved on the general plane which we shall call the "American Creed," where American thinks, talks and acts under the influence of high national and Christian precepts, and on the other hand, the valuations on specific planes of individual and group living, where personal and local interest, economic, social and sexual jealousies; considerations of community prestige and conformity; group prejudice against particular persons or types of people and all sorts of miscellaneous wants, impulses and habits dominate his outlook.[60]

By casting the basic conflict in moral rather than economic terms, Myrdal's work set the research agenda in race relations for the next two decades. If the root of the problem was white attitudes then the answer must lie in psychological examination of the "nature of prejudice."

The displacement of an economic framework with a moral/psychological paradigm was not opposed by the Howard radicals because they were by-in-large a part of the Myrdal study. Bunche was hired as a principle researcher because Myrdal felt that he should have at least one "negro social scientist." Myrdal described Bunche as "extraordinarily intelligent, open-minded and cooperative" and added "it would be a great advantage to have at least one Negro on the staff, who would serve as intimate contact with the Negro world."[61] Also on the core staff was the well-known black Communist Doxy Wikerson. Bunche's Howard colleague, Sterling Brown, was commissioned to do one of the thirty-one independent research monographs for the study. Frazier was asked to review the entire manuscript. His work on the black family had influenced Myrdal's approach to black culture and the family. Frazier attempted to get Myrdal to abandon his use of the class and caste concept to no avail.[62] Charles S. Johnson and a young Kenneth Clark also worked on the project.

The black social scientists working on the project as well as Du Bois defended the final product and generally hailed it as the most complete study ever done on American race relations. These black scholars hoped the study would generate increased attention and funding for their research projects. And, indeed, the Myrdal work popularized the study of race among white scholars to an unprecedented extent. However, these studies were applications of the paradigm rather than challenges to it. Black scholars did not do as well. No black university had a Ph.D. program and even such well-known scholars as Frazier, Du Bois, and Charles Johnson were unable to institutionalize the study of race.[63]

---

60. Myrdal, 1964, p. lxxi.
61. Jackson, op. cit., pp. 108–111.
62. Platt, op. cit., p. 107, 165–66.
63. Jackson, op. cit., p. 104.

The new paradigm had a number of important consequences. First, it moved the intellectual community away from biological and genetic explanations for racial difference. By posing a moral dilemma revolving around the gap between mainstream belief and practice, Myrdal shifted the debate to the area of social psychology.[64] This moral emphasis could be used to combat any emergent Nazism but it also moved away from social science neutrality. He believed that a social scientist should explicitly state his or her value premises. However, to be an effective social engineer, Myrdal argued, one must select as one's "instrumental norm" valuations held by a substantial proportion of the population.[65]

Second, the shift to a focus on the social psychology of race relation submerges the emphasis on class put forward by the Howard school. While Bunche acknowledged the "American Creed," he found that most thinking is "largely reflex" and finds convenient streamlined expression through the "pat response" and "conventionalized stereotype." Myrdal had once held similar views but his interviews with Americans convinced him that moral ideas were a real social force. The upper classes, in particular, were less racist because they were not in direct economic competition with blacks. According to Myrdal, the problem for the social engineer was "first to lift the masses to security and education and then to work to make them liberal."[66] In short, he agreed with Du Bois that white and black unity under the banner of inter-racial unionism was premature.

Third, while Du Bois agreed with Myrdal in the primacy of race over class, he fundamentally disagreed with the Swedish economist on the utility of black culture. Myrdal had accepted the social pathology model of black culture suggested by Frazier. He saw black history as a "waste field" and after witnessing the emotionalism of a black church service suggested it be studied as abnormal psychology.[67] The emphasis of Herskovits, Du Bois, and Woodson on the Africanness of American Negroes Myrdal felt was dangerous because it fed the tirades of extreme racists like Senator Bilbo.[68] Thus, Myrdal and his Howard colleagues encouraged blacks to adopt white middle-class behavior. Because they believed black status to be unique in that blacks accepted mainstream values even though their environment sometimes effected their behavior, they did not develop a general theory of race or ethnicity. Instead, they promoted what in essence is a theory of assimilation.

Du Bois, on the other hand, disagreed with the cultural pathology model although he chose not to publicly attack *An American Dilemma*. In his *Black Reconstruction*, Du Bois had enlisted the support of moral imperatives (over economic interests) as a prime motive behind the abolition movement. The class structure Du Bois used was more complex than Marx or the Howard school was willing to admit. Although race was formed as a social category from economic conditions, it takes a central, partly subconscious, role due to the cultural milieu.[69] To counter the problem of discrimination in the ranks of organized labor,

---

64. Myrdal influenced by John Dewey's Freedom and Culture (1939); see Jackson, op. cit., p. 105.

65. Ibid., p. 114.

66. Ibid., pp. 129–130.

67. Ibid., pp. 107, 112.

68. Ibid., p. 120.

69. Antonio Gramsci's work accords culture a more central role in Marxism.

Du Bois suggested support for a United Negro Trades modeled after the United Hebrew Trades which would eventually allow blacks a chance to enter the labor movement with their own organizational power base. Moreover, Du Bois believed his economic cooperatives could work because they were based on black culture, e.g the cooperative spirit of African tribes and Church groups.[70] Thus Du Bois sought to use the given racial divisions to construct an economic alternative that might eventually serve a more general audience.

Fourth, by locating the fundamental problem in the attitudes of whites, the development by racial subordinates of power bases among themselves was obscured. This action serves to move political science [71] to the margins in terms of analysis and replace it with social psychology. Modernization emerges as a model along with a theory of assimilation. Traditional values of social solidarity, ascriptive criteria and religious orientations are to be replaced with secular, achievement-oriented, individualistic values of modern society. Of course, politics has a role in this process of transforming the rural peasants into an urban worker. However, the emphasis is on leadership and political parties not on values, culture, movements, or class. Thus, political science tends to focus on how well political elites and sub-elites function in guiding this transformation (assimilation).[72]

Why did the young Howard radicals moderate their views and accept Myrdal's analysis? The onset of World War II had a profound effect on Bunche and his colleagues. If fascism could rise up with such deadly consequences in Europe, could it not also engulf the United States? Bunche, Hastie, and a number of black scholars move to government service in defense of the "American Creed." Their work on the Myrdal study convinced Bunche and others that the New Deal had indeed brought a measure of progress to black America. Myrdal's influence as a social Democrat and social engineer led to a more evolutionary reform of American society. Finally, both Marx and Myrdal saw assimilation as the ultimate end. Neither Bunche, Frazier, nor Harris saw in black culture a viable challenge to the status quo. Hence it was Du Bois and not the Howard radicals that the scholars of the black power generation looked to for inspiration.

Conclusion

The social psychology approach or assimilationist paradigm remained dominant in the field of race relations until the mid-1960s. Bunche moved from Howard to the State Department to the United Nations where he won a Nobel Peace Prize for his mediation of the Palestinian conflict in 1950. Shortly after winning the Nobel Peace Prize he was elected president of the American Political Science Association. Although he ceased to produce scholarly work after joining the UN, his views remained closer to the assimilationist paradigm than Harris and Fazier. Indeed, in the eyes of many his fame became so great that he rose above

---

70. Demarco, p. 155.

71. Certainly the development of pluralist theory falls within the assimilationist framework that emerges during this period. See Robert Dahl's, *Who Governs?* and Dianne Pinderhughes' *Race and Ethnicity in Chicago Politics*.

72. See James Q. Wilson's *Negro Politics* or Harold Gosnell's *Negro Politicians*.

race. Today, one might guess, that the work of William Wilson, a sociologist at Harvard, would find favor with Bunche.

Abram Harris left Howard for the University of Chicago in 1945. He was the first black scholar to receive a teaching appointment at an elite white university. At Chicago his emphasis shifted almost entirely to the history of economic thought, specifically to the critical examination of proposals and schemes advanced by economic theorists for social reform. When he did write on racial matters he argued that the conferring of equal legal rights on blacks would be meaningless unless preexisting racial differences originating in inadequate socialization of the young in black homes were addressed. Thus Harris's views bear a remarkable resemblance to these of another black economist trained at Chicago— Thomas Sowell.[73] The market-oriented views of Sowell in economics have their counterpart in the individualism of rational or social choice theory in political science.

The only member of the Howard school to remain at Howard, with brief stints abroad, was E. Franklin Frazier. After his death in 1962, he was widely hailed by conservatives and praised by liberals for his social pathology model of the black family. This link to neoconservative thought is a misreading of Frazier according to a recent biography. Frazier's goal in his work on the black family was to demonstrate that their problems were socially constructed rather than culturally inherited. In his latter years, he would move closer to Du Bois' position and was grappling to formulate a set of values that would develop a notion of cultural self-determination in the context of American society.

The Howard School of Thought represents a clear break with the biological paradigm of the past. Bunche, Frazier, and Harris denied that there were any significant biological differences between the races. Using their training as social scientists they attempted to demonstrate that it was the socio-economic factors of black urban existence that explained differences between the races. They promoted a class analysis of race relations that favored the unity of black and white workers in opposition to capitalism and saw black culture as dysfunctional. However, their views constituted only a transitional paradigm. They were rejected by mainstream black activists and later absorbed by the social psychological approach of Myrdal. World War II served to further weaken their class approach and strengthen the importance attached to race. It is ironic that the only racial paradigm that black scholars would participate in developing, a theory of assimilation, would call for their disappearance as a racial group. Yet these scholars were undoubtedly reflecting the views of a significant segment of the black community in the thirties.[74]

References

Aptheker, Herbert, ed. (1985). *Against Racism*. Amherst: University of Massachusetts Press.
Banks, William M. and Joseph Jewell (1992). "The Intellectual Society Revisited." Berkeley: unpublished paper.

---

73. Darity and Ellison, pp. 614–17.
74. Banks and Jewell, 1992.

Barker, Lucius J. (ed.) (1992). "Ethnic Politics and Civil Liberties." *National Political Review*, Vol. 3, New Brunswick, NJ: Transaction.

Blackwell, James E. and Morris Janowitz, eds. (1974). *Black Sociologists*. Chicago: University of Chicago Press.

Bunche, Ralph (1939). "The Programs of Organizations Devoted to the Improvement of the Status of the American Negro." *Journal of Negro Education* 8:3, July.

————(1936). "Education in Black and White." *Journal of Negro Education* 5:3, July.

————(1936). "A Critique of New Deal Social Planning as It Affects Negroes." *Journal of Negro Education* 5:1, Jan.

————(1936). *A World View of Race*. Washington: Lyon Press.

————(1935). "A Critical Analysis of the Tactics and Programs of Minority Groups." *Journal of Negro Education* 4:3, July.

————(1934). "French Administration in Togoland and Dahomey," Ph.D. Dissertation, Harvard University.

————Papers, UCLA, Collection #2051.

Dahl, Robert A. (1961). *Who Governs?* New Haven: Yale University Press.

Darity, William, Jr., ed. (1989). *Race, Radicalism, and Reform*. New Brunswick, NJ: Transaction.

Darity, William, Jr. and Julian Ellison (1990). "Abram Harris, Jr. the economics of race and social reform." *History of Political Economy* 22:4.

Dawson, Michael C. and Ernest J. Wilson, III (1989). "Paradigms and Paradoxes: Political Science and African American Politics" a paper prepared for the Midwest Political Science Association Annual Meeting, Chicago, Ill., April 13–15.

DeMarco, Joseph P. (1983). *The Social Thought of W.E.B. Du Bois*. Lanham, Maryland: University Press of America.

Du Bois, W.E.B. (1968). *Dusk of Dawn*. New York: Schocken.

Edwards, G. Franklin, ed. (1968). *E. Franklin Frazier On Race Relations*. Chicago: University of Chicago Press.

Fredricksen, George M. (1981). *White Supremacy*. New York: Oxford University Press.

Gates, Henry Louis, Jr. (1968). *The Signifying Monkey* New York: Oxford University Press.

Genovese, Eugene D. (1976). *Roll Jordan Roll*. New York: Vintage.

George, Hermon, Jr. (1984). *American Race Relations Theory*. Lanham, Maryland: University Press of America.

Gosnell, Harold F. (1967). *Negro Politicians*. Chicago: University of Chicago Press.

Gramsci, Antonio (1971). Selections from the Prison Notebooks, edited and translated by Quentin Hoare and Geoffrey Nowell Smith. New York: International Publications.

Haskins, Jim (1992). *One More River to Cross*. New York: Scholastic.

Jackson, Walter A. (1990). *Gunnar Myrdal and America's Conscience*. Chapel Hill: University of North Carolina Press.

Kirby, John B. (1974). "Ralph J. Bunche and Black Radical Thought in the 1930s" *Phylon* 25:2, Summer.

Kuhn, Thomas S. (1970). *The Structure of Scientific Revolutions*. Chicago: University of Chicago Press.

Logan, Rayford, W. (1968). *Howard University*. New York: New York University Press.

Lynch, Hollis R. (1970). *Edward Wilmont Blyden*. London: Oxford University Press.

Martin, Robert E., ed., and E. Franklin Frazier (1964). *The Negro and Social Research*. Washington: Howard University Press.

Mensh, Elaine and Harry Mensh (1991). *The IQ Mythology*. Carbondale, Ill.: Southern University Press.

Morris, Milton D. (1975). *The Politics of Black America*. New York: Harper and Row.

Moses, Wilson Jeremiah (1988). *The Golden Age of Black Nationalism*. Handen, Conn.: Archer.

Mudimbe, V. Y. (1988). *The Invention of Africa*. Bloomington, Indiana: Indiana University Press.

Myrdal, Gunnar (1964). *An America Dilemma*. New York: McGraw-Hill.

Pinderhughes, Dianne M. (1987). *Race and Ethnicity in Chicago Politics*. Urbana: University of Illinois Press.

Platt, Anthony M. E., and Franklin Frazier (1991). *Reconsidered*. New Brunswick, New Jersey: Rutgers University Press.

Raboteau, Albert J. (1978). *Slave Religion*. New York: Oxford University Press.

Rivlin, Benjamin, ed. (1990). *Ralph Bunche*. New York: Holmes and Meier.

Ross, B. Joyce J.E. (1972). *Spingarn and the Rise of the NAACP*. New York: Atheneum.

Stuckey, Sterling, ed. (1972). *The Ideological Origins of Black Nationalism*. Boston: Beacon.

Toll, William (1979). *The Resurgence of Race*. Philadelphia: Temple University Press.

Turner, Ralph H., ed. (1967). *Robert E. Park*. Chicago: University of Chicago Press.

Van den Berghe, Pierre L. (1967). *Race and Racism*. New York: Wiley.

Ware, Gilbert (1984). *William Hastie*. New York: Oxford University Press.

Wilkens, Roy (1984). *Standing Fast*. New York: Oxford University Press.

Williams, Verson Jr. (1989). *From A Castle To A Minority*. Westport, Conn: Greenwood.

Wilson, James Q. (1960). *Negro Politics*. Glencoe: The Free Press.

Wolters, Raymond (1970). *Negroes and the Great Depression*. Westport, Conn: Greenwood.

Young, James O. (1973). *Black Writers of the Thirties*. Baton Rouge: Louisiana State University Press.

Section VII

Education and Development

18

Race, Intelligence, and Income

Edward M. Miller

The Bell Curve is making waves, and it should. Yet most of its controversial findings were no surprise to the specialists in intelligence (for instance see Gottfredson, 1986a, Gottfredson & Sharf, 1988, Hartigan & Wigdor, 1989, Jensen, 1981), even if they were to the media. Most of the book is new research using the National Longitudinal Survey of Youth (abbreviated NLSY), a large scale study starting in 1979 of 12,486 youths. These have been followed from high school, through college, and into early adulthood. Fortunately, intelligence data in the form of the Armed Forces Qualification Test was obtained for almost 94% of these youths.

Although from the commentary in the media one might think *The Bell Curve* was a book about racial differences, most of it actually discusses only non-Hispanic Whites.

The book proceeds by first examining how variables such as income, poverty, crime, and illegitimacy are affected by intelligence and socioeconomic status among white, non-Hispanics. The major finding is that intelligence is much more important than socioeconomic class for many of these variables. For instance, Whites in the bottom 5% of intellectual ability are 15 times more likely to be in poverty than those in the top 5%. Intelligence was more important than the socioeconomic class of their families (a combination of parents' education, occupation, and income). With both intelligence and socioeconomic class in the equation, intelligence was more important.

A major surprise was how often socioeconomic class seemed to serve as a surrogate for intelligence. It had been known from previous studies that those born into poverty did worse as adults than those born into good families. Most of these studies lacked a measure of intelligence, preventing most economists and sociologists from realizing how often class of birth acted as a surrogate for intelligence.

Similar findings were found for schooling. Intelligence was much more important in determining who dropped out of high school, or who completed college, than being born into a high status family.

Racial Differences in Intelligence

The really explosive part of the book is the discussion of race. This book openly discusses the intellectual differences between the races. After pointing out

293

that East Asians (Chinese, Japanese) appear to be slightly more intelligent than Whites, it moves on to the Black-White differences. The Blacks test about one standard deviation below the Whites, which for the non-statistically trained implies that the average White is superior to 84% of the Blacks, although about 16% of the Blacks do better than the average White. Since most readers of this textbook are in universities and are, hence, well above average in intelligence, an African-American reader can presume himself to be in this superior 16% and hence to be smarter than the average White. He can also feel proud of his willingness to look at facts that are unpopular to recognize.

Some very striking graphs (Figure 1) show the data from the National Longitudinal Survey of Youth. One graph shows the distribution of intelligence in the White and Black parts of the US population with the vertical axes being equal. Another makes the vertical axes proportionate to the number of individuals in each group. What is striking is how the number of Blacks on the graph with IQs over 120 is scarcely visible, while there are actually more Black Americans with IQs below 80 than there are Whites.

This tendency for the racial disparities to become more pronounced at a distribution's extremes is well known to the specialists, but has seldom been discussed in the media presentations to the public. It is a mathematical result of the distribution of abilities in both groups being described by bell (normal) curves whose means differ. This property of normal curves is extremely important in understanding why so few Blacks will be in the professions or in graduate schools without aggressive affirmative action, and why Blacks are over represented in classes for the retarded. The category of what the book calls the very dull (those with IQs below 75) accounts for 25% of the Blacks but only 5% of the Whites. Many of the country's social problems in both races are concentrated in this group.

Are the tests biased against Blacks? In spite of the impression left in media discussions, the experts have concluded that they are not. One reason is that the racial differences on the most culturally based parts of tests (general knowledge, for instance) are actually smaller than on the more abstract problem solving parts. The tests predict school and job performance equally well for both races, although the media appears to believe otherwise. The Herrnstein & Murray discussion draws heavily on Jensen (1980).

Intelligence and Other Social Problems

Is part of the difference in intelligence related to socioeconomic status? Yes. *The Bell Curve* concludes that 37% of the difference between the races is statistically related to socioeconomic differences. Of course, this does not mean that these socio-economic differences are causing the intelligence disparities. Instead, those of low intelligence end up with low socioeconomic status. The genes for low intelligence, along with environmental disadvantages, are then passed on to their children. A major reason many Blacks are poor is that their low intelligence makes it hard for them to finish high school or college or to obtain and hold high paying jobs.

Is there discrimination against Blacks? It is well known that Blacks earn less than Whites and get less schooling. However, most studies showing this fail to

Figure 1. Black and White IQ Distributions in the NLSY

Frequency distributions for populations of equal size

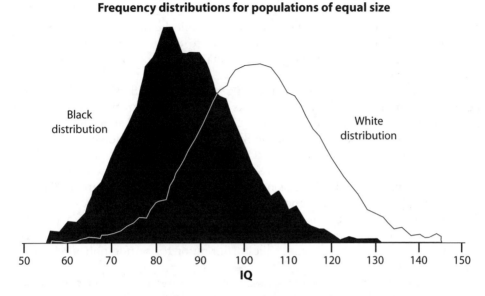

**Frequency distributions proportional to the ethnic composition
of the U.S. population**

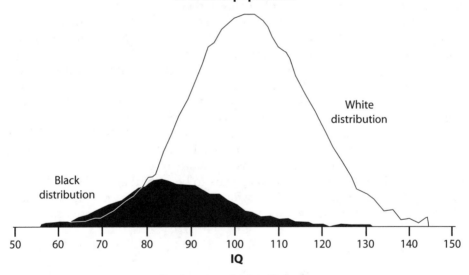

control for IQ differences. The data in *The Bell Curve* show the importance of controlling for intelligence. A White of the study's average age (29 years) would earn $27,372. A Black of that age would earn only $20,994. However, a White of average age and average IQ (100) would earn $25,546, while a Black of the same age and intelligence would earn $25,001. However, more working Blacks than Whites are females. Thus, gender should be controlled for. Once this is done the average Black is found to earn 101% of what a White would earn. The vast bulk of the Black/White wage difference appears to be due to the intelligence difference, not to discrimination. There appears to be very little scientific basis for blaming discrimination for most of the lower wages Blacks receive.

What about poverty? For those 29 years old, the equations show that only 7% of the Whites in the study versus 26% Blacks would be in poverty. For those of average age and intelligence, the figures shrink to 6% for Whites and 11% for Blacks. The Black poverty problem seems primarily, but not completely, related to lower intelligence.

We hear a lot about Black difficulties in getting into and finishing college. Supposedly discrimination is preventing Blacks from getting through college as easily as Whites do. The Bell Curve shows that 27% of Whites of average age (29) have finished college, while only 11% of the Blacks have done so. However, for a person of the same age and the average IQ for college graduate (114), 50% of the Whites have finished college, but 68% of the Blacks have. Of two people with same IQ in high school, the Black is more likely to finish college than the White. If there is any discrimination, it appears to be against Whites, not Blacks. Incidentally, an implication of this is that the typical Black college graduate will be of lower intelligence, and know less, than the typical white graduate. This observation may be of use to those responsible for hiring or for setting policy related to hiring.

The Bell Curve (p. 493) provides data on pass rates for teacher competency exams (which Blacks consistently fail at greater rates than Whites) that suggest that the Black college graduates do indeed know less than White ones. For other fields, data from their sample (p. 488) shows that there are indeed Black-White differences in intelligence and that these range from 1.1 standard deviations (managerial jobs, clerical, craft, and low-skill labor) up to 1.5 standard deviations (technical occupations) in all of the categories listed.

What about entering the high IQ occupations (such as lawyers, doctors, scientists, college professors, etc.)? There is constant publicity about Black under-representation in such jobs. Blacks are indeed under-represented. Only 3% of them at age 29 had made it into these professions, while 5% of the Whites had. However, for those of the average IQ for these professions (117), 10% of the Whites had made it versus 26% of the Blacks. For two individuals with the same ability, the Black appeared 2½ times as likely as the White to make it into these professions. The Black under-representation appears to be more than explained by their lower IQs. Affirmative action is the obvious explanation for the large advantage of Blacks over Whites with the same IQ in getting into these occupations.

Affirmative Action

The later chapter on higher education affirmative action makes clear the advantage given to Blacks. The data assembled shows that at the elite campus, the average Black is in the bottom 10th to 15th percentile in abilities (a result of a 180 point difference in the SAT test scores).

The difference appears to be even greater in graduate schools. For all law schools, the average Black first year student would be better than only 7% of the White first year students. For ten highly selective law schools, the average Black would be at the ability level of the bottom 1% of the Whites. The problem is that there are very few Blacks with extremely high ability. In 1993, there were 1,100 Whites with scores on the Law School Aptitude Test of better than 170, but only 3 Blacks. The only way to get large numbers of Blacks into the elite law schools was to greatly lower admission standards.

The situation is similar for other graduate schools and for medical schools. The average entering Black in medical school is at the level of the bottom 8 to 10% of the Whites on the Medical College Admission Test (p. 457). "In none of the three subtests did more than 19 Blacks score in the 12 to 15 range (on a scale that goes from 1 to 15), compared to 1,146; 1,469; and 853 Whites (for the biological sciences, physical sciences, and verbal reasoning tests respectively)." While this very strong Black preference clearly benefits the few high ability Blacks who receive well paying medical jobs, it is clearly not in the interest of Whites and probably harms most Blacks. Blacks are disproportionately treated by Black doctors (Jaynes & Williams, 1989), and the lower intellectual ability of the Blacks entering medical school by affirmative action probably results in poorer medical care for the typical Black.

The book does not devote a lot of space to the policy implications. Contrary to the impression left by the press, most of the policy discussion is not directed at race related policy. The authors express concern about the increasing division of the country into a cognitive elite and others. A striking chart (p. 516) shows that about 1970 the growth of median family income for Americans slowed, while the percentage of families with incomes over $100,000 continued to grow. Economic growth is benefiting less those whose intellectual abilities limit them to unskilled occupations. While the book doesn't go into great detail on reasons for this, it has become easier to mechanize the most mechanical tasks (which creates a demand for those smart enough to maintain the machines, while reducing the number of operators and laborers the economy requires). Also, as the world economy becomes increasingly integrated, many unskilled jobs can be easily moved to third world countries where wages for low skilled labor are low.

It is argued that there is an increasing division of America (and presumably other countries) into the mass of ordinary citizens and a cognitive elite, which is typically now university educated and often descended from those who are university educated. The policy makers may not realize how limited in cognitive ability (and knowledge) the masses are. Policy makers are virtually always from the cognitive elite, even if they claim to be representing the working classes. A casual inspection of tax forms or government regulations shows they are hard to understand even for those in the cognitive elite and almost impossible to understand for most others.

One chapter (Chapter 16) discusses the prevalence of low cognitive ability in Americans suffering from different problems, showing how frequently they are of disproportionately low cognitive ability. This fact needs to be taken into account in designing programs.

As the authors put it (p. 387), "Do we wish to persuade poor single teenagers not to have babies? The knowledge that 95% of poor teenage women who have babies are also below average in intelligence should prompt skepticism about strategies that rely on abstract and far-sighted calculations of self-interest. Do we favor job training programs for chronically unemployed men? Any program is going to fail unless it is designed for a target population half of which have IQs below 80."

The concluding chapter discusses in a philosophical manner the problem of building a society where those of average and below average ability can find a useful role. Even for those whose cognitive limitations prevent them from achieving high socioeconomic status, supporting and rearing a family, and being law abiding and productive citizens in the local community appear possible routes to self esteem.

The Dysgenic Trend

The Bell Curve contains a chapter on the dysgenic trend by which those of low IQ are having more offspring than those of high IQ. After summarizing the literature as (p. 341), "The professional consensus is that the United States has experienced dysgenic pressures throughout either most of the century (the optimists) or all of the century (the pessimists)," the discussion turns to data for the '90s. Current Population Survey data is used to show that the average number of children born to US women ages 35–44 in 1992 was 71% greater for high school dropouts than for college graduates. The new research reported using the NLSY shows that the average IQ of the mothers in the sample was less than 96. However, because many of the higher IQ women had not yet completed their childbearing, it is estimated that the overall IQ of American mothers was a little less than 98. This implies that a slow generation-to-generation decline in US IQ is to be expected.

A point not made in *The Bell Curve* is that the tendency for those with a high IQ to have fewer children appears to be more pronounced among women than among men. This is primarily because childbearing interferes more with schooling and careers among women than among men. Also, the higher status of high IQ men probably helps them get younger more fertile wives if they remarry, and helps them get more extramarital mating opportunities. Since children inherit genes from both parents, the dysgenic effect is a little weaker when both parents are considered. There is an additional factor that is often neglected. The high IQ have their children later than those with a low IQ (partially because most women defer childbearing until their education is completed, and high IQ women seek higher levels of education). The data from the NLSY shows that women in the top 5% for IQ have their first child at an average age of 27.2 years, while those in the bottom 5% have their first child at an average age of 19.8 years (p. 352). The difference is less for the average over all births, but it appears that those in the bottom 5% will complete 5 generations for every four generations completed by those in the top 5%.

The discussion of differences in birthrates by ethnicity shows that the ethnic differences are much reduced when women of the same levels of education are compared (p. 353) with fertility declining in all three ethnic groups with education. A surprising finding is that after "assigning IQ equivalents based on the relationship of educational attainment and cognitive ability in the NLSY, it appears that after equating for IQ, Black women at a given IQ level may have lower fertility rates than either White or Latino women" (p. 353). A footnote suggests that the fertility depressing effect of high IQ is due to the educational and career effects that accompany it and suggests the lower Black fertility may be because at any IQ level Blacks are more likely to be in school.

A fascinating table (p. 354) shows the percentage of births to mothers of different ethnic groups among those in the NLSY (whose members have yet to finish childbearing). Among White births 19% were to mothers with IQs below 90, and 22% to those with IQs above 110. However, for Black births 69% were to mothers with IQs below 90 and only 2% to mothers with IQs above 110. This suggests that the racial differences will increase over time. Incidentally, for Latinos the figures were 64% and 2%.

The NLSY also includes test results for the offspring of the original sample. This makes it possible to compare the IQ gap between the racial groups in parents with the gap in children. Between White and Black mothers the gap was 13.2 IQ points. However, among these parents' children, the IQ gap was 17.5 points, with a major cause plausibly being that the low IQ mothers among the Blacks had relatively more children. It appears likely that the racial IQ difference is increasing rather than decreasing in America.

Eugenics

A few very controversial topics that the book might have discussed are not discussed. An obvious policy proposal is eugenics. If a child's intelligence and life chances are heavily influenced by intelligence, and intelligence is partially dependent on the genes, it would seem desirable to have a high percentage of children born with genes for high intelligence. How this might be accomplished is another question.

If the benefits to children of good genes were publicized, some people might consider a potential spouse's genes before marriage. While in American culture, the problem of choosing a spouse appears to be most often conceptualized as choosing a companion for life (with the choice presumably based on the spouse's entertainment value, or on the ability to provide financial and emotional support), in some other places (and to some extent in America) it is conceptualized as "choosing a mother or father for my children." With the latter conceptualization, those aware of the importance of genetic heritage may give it weight in selecting mates. In general, if males and females are looking for high IQ mates (which they appear to do even if they aren't aware of the inheritance of intelligence), the major effect is to increase the probability that high IQ males and females mate with others of similar IQ, and those of low IQ mate with each other. Because most genes that affect intelligence appear to act additively, such an increase in associative mating for IQ should not raise the average IQ of the population. However, it should increase the variance of IQ, leaving the population with more high IQ individuals and more low IQ ones. This may be desirable. Most of the inventions, discoveries, and cultural creations come from the cognitive elite. Likewise, they occupy most of the leadership positions (even when they act in the name of the working class or union members). Raising the ability of the cognitive elite could easily bring benefits that exceed the offsetting decline in the ability of the working classes and the underclass.

However, there is one mechanism by which increased emphasis on intelligence in selecting mates might raise the intelligence of a society. A young woman might trade off acceptance of an older mate and the greater risk of a longer period of widowhood for better genes for her children. Such behavior should actually raise the IQ of the populations. Decisions of this type might result from publicizing the data in *The Bell Curve*. However, intelligence is a trait that is highly valued in a mate in most cultures (see the surveys discussed in Buss, 1994) so an awareness of its importance and partially genetic transmission may not greatly change behavior.

Other eugenic measures are more controversial. A simple measure would be to use only sperm from highly intelligent males in artificial insemination programs. Currently they appear to be typically screened for most genetic diseases (as well as for AIDS), but typically not for intelligence (Seligson, 1995). Supposedly, there is a current bias towards intelligence in donors because many of the donors are medical or other students, but the typical procedure does not guarantee this.

Yet the cost of giving intelligence tests would be relatively low. If some donors were to be rejected because of low intelligence, it might be desirable to enlarge the pool of potential donors, but that could be done by increasing the fees paid, or possibly by a public campaign to persuade high quality donors to provide sperm as a public service. The genetic quality of the sperm used could be raised by relaxing other less desirable constraints such as restrictions on the number of children that can be fathered from a single donor or by relaxing efforts to choose donors with particular hair, eye, or skin color. Certainly, if parents are willing to pay many tens of thousands to get their children into and through Ivy League colleges, potential parents should be willing to pay a few dollars more for quality sperm. If well-heeled parents seek the best designer jeans for their offspring, why shouldn't they seek the best genes?

In spite of the apparently very high benefit-cost of ratio from selecting sperm on the basis of the donor's intelligence, an Italian medical group has decided "There should be no selection of sperm based on the social, economic or professional standing of the donor" (Montalbano, 1995), all cheaply ascertained surrogates for intelligence, and other genetic traits that contribute to obtaining these types of status.

A lot of proposed public policies appear to have eugenic implications, which are typically not even discussed. Should conjugal visits be permitted in prisons? In *The Bell Curve* study (p. 376), 62% of the men ever interviewed in jail or prison came from the bottom 20% in intelligence. The offspring resulting from conjugal visits to these men are likely to be of below normal intelligence (as well as having inherited whatever other genes contribute to a criminal career).

The textbook reasons for imprisonment are deterrence and keeping the criminal off the streets so he can't commit another crime. An undiscussed benefit is preventing the criminal from reproducing for several years. Feminists occasionally propose castration as a punishment (usually for rape). This measure would appear to have positive eugenic effects on intelligence and on any other genes contributing to rape.

Should Lesbians or single women become mothers by artificial insemination? If the sperm used is of high quality, it is very likely that the offspring will be of high intelligence and unlikely that they will become public burdens. Should postmenopausal women have babies using advanced technology and their husbands sperm, as a 62 year old women recently did in Italy (Montalbano, 1995)? Given the high cost of such technologies, it is very likely that their husbands had genes for high intelligence. Yet this measure was to be banned by the new Italian doctor's code, as was artificial insemination after a partner's death.

How should population growth be slowed? Typical proposals involve each family having fewer children but with all being subject to equal limits. The possibility of disproportionately discouraging reproduction by the less intelligent is seldom discussed by those concerned with over population.

The Bell Curve does contain some data (p. 379) that points to an eugenic effect for any program that successfully reduces illegitimacy. Of the illegitimate children in the NLSY sample a third were born to women in the bottom 10% of the IQ sample, and 85% were born to women in the bottom half of the cognitive distribution. Of the children born to poor, single, teenage girls, 64% were born to women in the bottom 20% of the cognitive ability distribution and 95% to women in the bottom half.

Anything that successfully reduced the number of children born to single, poor, unmarried women would serve to increase the nation's IQ level and to reduce the incidence of the social problems that are most common among the children of such mothers. While the data in *The Bell Curve* implies it would be desirable to reduce births of such children, it does not specifically propose measures to do so. The closest it comes is to suggest that the welfare system enables poor, low IQ women to have children who would not otherwise do so.

Perhaps the most practical eugenic measure that is even close to politically feasible would be to offer welfare to unwed mothers only if they agree to having a Norplant contraceptive device (which would prevent pregnancy for several years) inserted or to use of the new three month contraceptive injections. This would somewhat reduce the birth rate among those with a low IQ and appears more humane than simply refusing assistance to unmarried teenagers, as has been proposed by the Republicans in the US Congress. Incidentally, sex education classes do not appear to reduce illegitimacy rates.

Implications for Anthropology

The Bell Curve is basically a book about America, drawing on data to show how differences in intelligence affect its citizens. There is only a brief discussion of the IQs of various races when tested outside of the United States. However, its conclusions should readily extend to other industrialized countries where most citizens are offered the opportunity for schooling and the brighter ones can be educated at taxpayer expense through the university level. Indeed, in some countries the economic obstacles to education are even smaller than in the US, and one would expect access to the universities and professions to depend even more on intellectual ability (and the genes that determine it) than in the US.

However, in many third world countries the sorting by cognitive ability is less effective. *The Bell Curve* suggests that low intelligence is the most likely reason to "Why Johnny can't read" in the US (where virtually all children have been given the opportunity to learn how). However, in many countries the most likely reason is still that he did not go to school. Genetic heritage will be less important in such countries and the environmental factor of access to schooling more important.

The material showing that a large part of racial differences in income and in various social variables is explained by the lower IQ of Blacks may also be relevant to other countries that have a Black minority.

Intelligence, the genetics of intelligence, and racial differences in intelligence are not well covered in anthropology textbooks. In many circles they are not considered suitable topics for discussion. Textbooks either ignore them or present what in America is called the "politically correct" view, without mentioning that any other views are widely held by respectable scholars or even providing references to the scientific literature. *The Bell Curve* does provide a short discussion of these topics along with references to the primary scientific literature. The discussion is far superior to what can be found in any anthropology textbook. However, as discussed below, the literature review is already dated.

Genes and Racial Differences

The Bell Curve presents the evidence that a large proportion of the variability in intelligence in America is genetic (pp. 105–108). Is part of the racial difference genetic? The book summarizes well the evidence (pp. 295–311) that was available to the authors when it was being written. The authors conclude (p. 311), "It seems highly likely to us that both genes and the environment have something to do with racial differences. What might the mix be? We are resolutely agnostic on that issue; as far as we can determine, the evidence does not yet justify an estimate." This mild statement was upsetting to many in the US media, although an earlier survey sent to 1020 experts (Snyderman and Rothman, 1988) showed that there were three times as many who thought it was both genetic and environmental as thought it was solely environmental.

There has been considerable press discussion of racial differences in intelligence following the publication of *The Bell Curve* (for a review of this discussion see Murphy, 1995). What the press was not aware of is that *The Bell Curve* is not the latest scientific work on racial differences. Since it went to press, several new papers have been published which greatly strengthen the case for racial IQ differences being at least partially genetic. A recent development is new adoption data. The best way, theoretically, to discover if Black/White differences are due to something they were born with (presumably genetic) is to rear them in the same families (or at least families randomly chosen) and see how they turn out.

Scarr & Weinberg (1976) had earlier reported the results of a study of Black children at age seven adopted into middle class White families, which they interpreted as not supporting genetic differences. In particular, their finding that Black children raised in White families had childhood IQs of 106 was widely interpreted (correctly) as evidence that childhood intelligence could be affected by the environment (for instance, Tucker, 1994, p. 230). However, since a purely environmental theory would suggest that racial origin (between those with two Black biological parents and those with one Black and one White biological parent) would make no difference for children raised in the same families, and there was a difference, the study also provided evidence for a genetic difference between the races.

Recently, the results of a follow-up of the children when they were about seventeen appeared. The published report (Weinberg, Scarr, Waldman, 1992) primarily discussed the IQ change between the first and second testing (even though the use of different tests complicated comparison) rather than the absolute values of the IQs (although these were given in the paper). The authors interpreted their results in terms of demonstrating the power of the environment.

Two recently published comments point out how the new results provide evidence for genetic differences between the races. One is by Levin (1994). With good reason, he points out how their results are just as would be expected if most racial differences in IQ were genetic.

Lynn (1994) points out that when Black and White children are reared in matched social environments (educated White families) they have an IQ difference of 17 points. This slightly exceeds the 15 points observed when each are in their own environments. This is very close to a controlled experiment, and suggests that altering environments after infancy does nothing to reduce the racial IQ differences. The IQ of the mixed race children is 98, halfway between that of the study's Whites and Blacks. As he points out, this is as predicted by genetic theory, but is hard to explain environmentally, since both mixed race and Black adopted children are socially classified as Black. He gives other powerful arguments I find convincing.

In their reply (Waldman, Weinberg & Scarr, 1994), the authors of the study appear to disagree, claiming "results from the Minnesota Transracial Adoption Study provide little or no conclusive evidence for genetic influences underlying racial differences in intelligence and achievement." They give their reasons, of which the strongest is that the children were not perfectly matched on early childhood experience, since the Whites were adopted at an earlier age (probably because they had been easier to place) and also pointing out that an inherited characteristic, skin color, might have led to different treatment of the children even in liberal Minnesota.

However, there is support for the genetic explanation in their article. Notice they are denying "conclusive evidence" from their study. They do not deny it is strong evidence. They readily concede there are IQ differences between White and Black adoptees (and make no argument about biased tests). They later say "We think it is inherently implausible that these differences are either entirely genetically based or entirely environmental based" (p. 31). The reader, not being familiar with the role Sandra Scarr has played in the controversy about racial differences in IQ may not realize the significance of this sentence. She has been a leading opponent of the idea of genetic differences. She is now saying that it is highly implausible that the differences are entirely environmental. This is news.

It contrasts strongly with the impression most of the media has that no respectable scientist believes there are genetic differences and that all the experts believe the differences are entirely due to environmental causes. The leading opponent among professional behavior geneticists now believe "We think it is inherently implausible that these differences are . . . entirely environmental based."

There have been some interesting findings reported regarding head size and intelligence recently. Rushton & Osborne (1995) have reported on a study of Black and White twins showing smaller head size in Black twins than in White twins in a sample where the Blacks have lower IQs. His analysis shows a high heritability for head size (and presumably brain size) in Whites, although for an unknown reason the heritability is lower (but still appreciable) in Blacks.

Jensen (1994) shows that the tests that measure intelligence best are those most sensitive to head size differences, and that the tests most sensitive to head size show the largest Black/White differences.

Jensen and Johnson (1994) of the University of California at Berkeley studied head size and intelligence in Black and White children, males and females, using the very large database from the National Collaborative Perinatal Study. Its importance is not merely in showing that brain size and intelligence are covariants (this has been shown in several recent studies using MRI measurements of brain size) or that there are racial differences in head and brain size (this has been shown by autopsy data). Comparing siblings, Jensen showed that the large-headed tended to be the more intelligent in Black males, Black females, White males, and White females. This result indicates that there is something biological (almost certainly genetic) that affects both brain size and intelligence. (Miller, 1994a, argued that this biological factor affecting both intelligence and brain size could be the thickness of layers of myelin). By showing that much of the racial difference in IQ disappears when children of the same head size are compared, Jensen and Johnson provide strong evidence that whatever is causing the racial head size differences is also causing at least part of the racial differences in intelligence. In turn, it is known that the racial differences in intelligence are closely related to the racial differences in school performance, which are known to be related to the differences in poverty (see *The Bell Curve*). This is a very exciting lead for those concerned with the causes of poor school performance and poverty in Blacks.

The Jensen and Johnson's finding that one gene or set of genes seems to affect both head size and intelligence could help explain an intriguing finding reported in *The Bell Curve*. This is that 45% of low-birth weight babies had mothers in the bottom 20% of intelligence (p. 381). One possible explanation is that low intelligence mothers adopted behavior patterns that led to low birth weight babies. However, there is another possibility that *The Bell Curve* does not discuss. It is now known that brain size and IQ are correlated from MRI studies (Andreason, et al. 1993; Wickett, Vernon, & Lee, 1994; Willerman, Schultz, Rutledge, and Bigler, 1991), and that head size at birth correlates with childhood intelligence (Broman, Nichols, Shaughnessy, Kennedy, 1987). The latter effect is probably because small headed babies are small brained. The brain at birth uses a large percentage of the body's metabolic energy. This would imply that a larger brain would have to be supported by larger lungs, heart, and digestive system. It is plausible that the genes for high adult IQ produce at least part of their effect by affecting brain size at birth (or something correlated with brain size). Since half of a baby's genes come from the mother, the existence of genes that affect both intelligence and birth weight would produce a concentration of low-birth-weight babies among the offspring of low IQ mothers, as *The Bell Curve* reports. It would be interesting to do a sibling analysis similar to that done by Jensen and Johnson of the birth weights and later intelligence to see if the higher birth weight siblings typically were smarter.

The Evolutionary Origins of Racial Differences in Intelligence

Not surprisingly, in a book that does not take a position on the extent to which racial differences are genetic, there is no discussion of how such differences could have arisen. That there could be differences in behaviorally relevant gene frequencies should be no surprise. Recently, a massive compilation of data on the world wide distribution of gene frequencies has become available (Cavalli-Sforza, Menozzi, & Piazza, 1994). As a review pointed out (Miller, 1994c) there is no polymorphic gene known in humans whose frequency does not vary among populations. This observation makes it very likely that as specific genes are identified that affect intelligence, that the frequency of the alleles that contribute to high intelligence will be found to differ between populations.

Recently, the first case of explaining a major racial difference in behavior by a single gene has been reported (Tu & Israel, 1995). Orientals consume significantly less alcohol and show less alcoholism than Caucasians. Most anthropologists, sociologists, etc. would casually refer to this as a "cultural" difference. This study shows that most of the differences in alcohol consumption within Orientals in North America is determined by a single locus, which determines how well they digest alcohol. Those with the genetic defect are protected against alcoholism because alcohol produces a flushing reaction and makes them mildly sick. The cultural effect of exposure to the US culture is controlled for and plays only a minor role.

Caucasians lack this gene. Orientals lacking this gene do not differ significantly from Caucasians. Thus, the Oriental-Caucasian differences seems to have been explained.

Recently, a specific dopamine receptor gene has been shown to be related to reduced visual ability (Berman & Noble, 1995). The spatial test used required aligning two lines. This appears to be the first report of a gene affecting a specific mental ability that differs in frequencies between racial groups, with non-Caucasians higher (.43 vs. .19) in the form that has the lower spatial ability. In this study, most of the non-Caucasians were other than Blacks.

Recently, the APOE*4 allele has been shown to be a significant risk factor for Alzheimer's disease, which adversely affects intelligence. In one study the risk increased from 20% with no copy of the APOE*4 allele to 47% and 91% with one and two copies of the APOE*4 allele respectively (Corder et al. 1993). "Although only 14% of Asians and 25% of Whites carry the APOE*4 allele, almost 50% of Africans, Polynesians, Melanesians, and Australian Aborigines do." (Kamboh, 1995, p. 203). This provides a documented case of racial differences in the frequency of a gene relevant to intelligence, although admittedly the effect occurs through susceptibility to a disease.

Recently progress has been made toward identifying other genes that affect intelligence (Plomin et al, 1994, 1995), with there being evidence for several intelligence related genetic markers. Most likely the alleles of these genes will be found to differ in frequency in racial groups.

This study (Skuder et al., 1995) provided evidence that a mitochondrial DNA gene affects intelligence. The probability from combining two samples that this result would have occurred by chance was less than .01.

The paper reported that in several populations the frequencies "of the two alleles (called MspI-morph 1 and Msp-morph) were similar to the frequencies of 86% and 14% in the present study." All of the populations mentioned were Eurasian ones. Knowing one of the groups mentioned had African data, I tracked it down. In one study I found, "Africans, on the other hand, lack MspI-morph4, which is instead common in Caucasians and Oriental." (Scozzari et al, 1988, p. 543) It is perhaps fortunate that the first *intelligence lowering* allele (version of a gene) identified should be virtually absent in Blacks, while present in Whites.

At first glance, the finding of an intelligence lowering allele in a population argued to have been selected for intelligence (Whites) is surprising, and not predicted by many theories. However, with intelligence known to be affected by many different genes, favorable mutations known to move slowly even with positive selection (Rouhani, 1989), and intelligence under unidirectional selection, a prediction is that the highest intelligence will be found in the most centrally located populations. However, there may be some intelligence raising mutations that have not reached such populations (Miller 1996).

However, most theories for the evolution of racial differences in intelligence depend on the strength of selection for intelligence varying with climate. Rushton (1995) has proposed a theory to explain racial differences in a large number of traits. He argues that Negroids are more r selected than Caucasoids, who in turn are more r selected than Mongoloids. In turn, he argues a less predictable environment selects for r traits and that such an environment existed in sub-Saharan Africa during the period in which racial differences evolved. In biology, r selected organisms have more offspring and invest less in them than K selected ones. He argues intelligence is a K trait. Miller (1993, 1995) has presented arguments against this view to which Rushton and Ankney (1993) have replied.

Miller (1994b) has provided an alternative theory to explain most of the facts explained by Rushton's differential K theory. Miller points out that in the tropics during hunter-gatherer times, females were able to support themselves and their offspring year round. The males who left the most descendants would have been those that adopted a "love them and leave them" strategy with relatively weak pair bonds and more effort invested in obtaining mating opportunities. Obtaining sexual access would often require fighting other males.

In contrast, in colder climates, the problem is to get through the winter, which is normally done by some combination of food storage and hunting. Large game hunting could not be efficiently done by females carrying babies, or by pregnant females. Thus females were dependent on male provisioning. The males who left the most descendants were those who formed strong pair bonds and provisioned their mate's loyally. Provisioning selected for a somewhat different set of traits than a high mating effort environment did.

Intelligence and the Differing Importance of Paternal Investment

Recently, Miller (1995) has extended his differential paternal investment theory to explain differences in intelligence in different parts of the world. Sociobiologists (Symons, 1979; Hrdy, 1981) have argued that resources provided by men are important to female reproductive success and that women select mates partially on the basis of the male's ability and willingness to provide such resources. This induces men to try to persuade women that they have such resources and will provide them to the woman and her children.

Buss (1994) emphasizes how often in human mating deception is used. For instance, men try to convince women that they have, or will have, resources and will devote them to the well-being of the woman and her children (and not squander their resources on other women and their children), while women try to convince men of their sexual loyalty (while possibly seeking better genes from other men).

Buss states (p. 155) "Because the deceived can suffer tremendous losses, there must have been great selection pressures for the evolution of a form of psychological vigilance to detect cues to deception and to prevent its occurrence. The modern generation is merely one more cycle in the endless spiral of an evolutionary arms race between deception perpetuated by one sex and detection accomplished by the other. As the deceptive tactics get more subtle, the ability to penetrate deception become more refined." With northern women more dependent on male provisioning than tropical women, selection would have been stronger in the cold areas for the intelligence needed to recognize deception.

Men can also be deceived. They can waste many resources if they raise another man's child. Women try to deceive men as to their loyalty. The more dependent a man's reproductive success is on accurately directing his provisioning to his own biological offspring and to those females who have or will bear their children, the stronger the selection for male intelligence. In the northern climates, where provisioning directly impacts their children's survival, selection for intelligence will be greatest.

Differences in the importance of paternal investment may even explain the pattern of racial abilities. Detecting deception in a mate calls for reasoning, which would show up in high intelligence. Merely impressing potential sex partners with conversation and song would call for high verbal skills, memory, and verbal fluency. This does resemble the observed pattern of racial differences (Jensen & Reynolds, 1982; Jensen, 1985).

The only alternative to hunting for surviving the winter is food storage, which can be shown to be more common in cold climates. Successfully storing food calls for the ability to defer gratification, the ability to imagine winter conditions when times are warm, and simple quantitative skills to manage the accumulation and consumption of stores. Thus, the need for storage should select for intelligence (Miller 1991). Storage also leads to a settled lifestyle which leads to the use of more artifacts

Lynn (1991b) has tried to explain the racial differences in intelligence, which he had earlier described (Lynn 1991a), by the greater need for hunting in cold climates and hunting's greater intellectual demands.

Further research will be needed to pin down the exact role of the different selective forces that could have produced racial differences in intelligence. There is now strong evidence that such differences exist, and there is no shortage of mechanisms that could explain their existence.

Conclusions

The Bell Curve shows that intelligence is an important determinant of many socioeconomic variables. Many effects that sociologists have attributed to social class appear to be really due to intelligence. Races differ in intelligence. Many racial disparities shrink or disappear when intelligence is controlled for. In particular, discrimination is not needed to explain low Black income or occupational status.

Since *The Bell Curve* was written additional evidence has appeared that the racial difference in intelligence is primarily genetic. These come from adoption studies and from studies of the relationship between head size and IQ. Plausible hypothesises exist for how such a difference emerged. One possibility is that selection for intelligence was strongest where paternal provisioning was most important.

The Bell Curve is an important book that should be read by those interested in the role of intelligence in modern societies or in the causes of racial inequality.

References

Andreason, N. C., Flaum, M., Swayze, V., O. Leary, D. S., Alliger, R., Cohen, G., Ehrhardt, J., & Yuh, W. T. C. (1993). Intelligence and brain structure in normal individuals. *American Journal of Psychiatry, 150*, 130–134.

Berman, S. M. & Noble, E. P. (1995). Reduced visuospatial performance in children with the D2 dopamine receptor A1 allele. *Behavior Genetics, 25*, 45–58.

Berman, S. M. & Noble, E. P. (1995). Reduced visuospatial performance in children with the D2 dopamine receptor A1 allele. *Behavior Genetics, 25*, 45–58.

Broman, S., Nichols, P. L., Shaughnessy, P., & Kennedy, W. (1987). *Retardation in young children*, Hillsdale: Lawrence Erlbaum,

Buss, D. M. (1994). *The evolution of desire*. New York: Basic Books.

Cavalli–Sforza, L. L., Menozzi, P., & Piazza, A. (1994). *The history and geography of human genes*. Princeton: Princeton University Press.

Corder, E. H., Saunders, A. M., Strittmatter, W. J., Schmechel, D. E., Gaskell, P. C., Small, G. W., Roses, A. D., Haines, J. L., & Pericak-Vance, M. A. (1993). Gene does of apolipoprotein E type 4 allele and the risk of Alzheimer's disease in late onset families. *Science, 261*, 921–923.

Gottfredson, L. S. (1986a). *The g factor in employment: A special issue of the journal of vocational behavior, 29 (3)*.

Gottfredson, L. S. & Sharf, J. C. (1988). *Fairness in employment testing: A special issue of the journal of vocational behavior, 33 (3)*.

Hartigan, J. A. & Wigdor, A. K. (1989). *Fairness in employment testing*. Washington: National Academy Press.

Herrnstein, R. J. & Murray, C. (1994). *The bell curve: Intelligence and class structure in american life*. New York: The Free Press.

Hrdy, S. B. (1981). *The women that never evolved*. Cambridge: Harvard University Press.

Jaynes, G. D. & Williams, R. M, Jr. (1989). *A common destiny: Blacks and american society*. Washington: National Academy Press.

Jensen, A. R. (1980). *Bias in mental testing*. New York: The Free Press.

Jensen, A. R. (1981). *Straight talk about mental tests*. New York: The Free Press.

Jensen, A. R. (1985). The nature of the black-white differences on various psychometric tests: Spearman's hypothesis. *Behavioral and Brain Sciences, 8*, 193–219.

Jensen, A. R. (1994). Psychometric g related to differences in head size. *Personality and Individual Differences, 17*, 597–606.

Jensen, A. R. & Johnson, F. W. (1994). Race and sex differences in head size and IQ. *Intelligence, 18*, 309–333.

Jensen, A. R. & Reynolds, C. R. (1982). Race, social class, and ability patterns on the WISC-R. *Personality and Individual Differences, 3*, 423–438.

Jensen, A. R., & Sinha, S. N. (1993). Physical correlates of intelligence. In Vernon, P. A. (Ed.). *The biological basis of intelligence*. Norwood: Ablex, 139–142.

Kamboh, M. I. (1995). Apolipoprotein E polymorphism and susceptibility to Alzheimer's disease. *Human Biology, 67*, 195–217.

Levin, M. (1994). Comment on the Minnesota transracial adoption study. *Intelligence, 19*, 13–20.

Lynn, R. (1991a). Race differences in intelligence: A global perspective. *Mankind Quarterly, 31*, 254–296.

Lynn, R. (1991b). The evolution of racial differences in intelligence. *Mankind Quarterly, 32*, 99–121.

Lynn, R. (1994). Some reinterpretation of the Minnesota transracial adoption study. *Intelligence, 19*, 21–28.

Miller, E. M. (1993). Could *r* selection account for the African personality and life cycle. *Personality and Individual Differences, 15*, 665–676.

Miller, E. M. (1994a). Intelligence and brain myelination: A hypothesis. *Personality and Individual Differences, 17*, 803–833.

Miller, E. M. (1994b). The relevance of group membership for personnel selection: A demonstration using Bayes Theorem. *Journal of Social, Political, and Economic Studies, 19*, 323–359.

Miller, E. M. (1994c). Tracing the genetic history of modern man. *Mankind Quarterly*, Vol. 35, No. 1-2, 71–108.

Miller, E. M. (1995). Environmental variability selects for large families only in special circumstances: Another objection to differential *k* theory. *Personality and Individual Differences, 19*, 903–918.

Miller, E. M, (1996). Geographical centrality as an explanation for racial differences in intelligence. Working paper.

Montalbano, W. D. (1995). Code of ethics given to fertility doctors. *Times-Picayune*, April 17, 2.

Murphy, D. (1995). Rethinking the American dream: Reactions of the media to *The Bell Curve*. *Journal of Social, Political, and Economic Studies, 20*, 93–128.

Plomin R., McClearn, G., Smith, D., Vignetti, S., Chorney, M., Venditti, C., Kasarda, S., Thompson, L., Detterman, D., Daniels, J., Owen, M., & McGuffin P. (1994). DNA markers associated with high versus low IQ: The IQ quantitative trait loci (QTL) Project. *Behavior Genetics, 24*, 107–118.

Plomin, R., McClearn, G., Smith, D., Skuder, P., Vignetti, S., Chorney, M., Chorney, K., Kasarda, S., Thompson, L., Detterman, D., Petrill, S., Daniels J., Owen, M., & McGuffin P. (1995). Allelic associations between 100 DNA markers and high versus low IQ. *Intelligence, 21*, 31–48.

Rouhani, S. (1989). Molecular genetics and the pattern of human evolution: Plausible and implausible models. In *The human revolution*, Mellars, P. & Stringer, C., Eds., 47–61.

Rushton, J. P. (1995). *Race, evolution and behavior: A life history perspective*. New Brunswick: Transaction Publishers.

Rushton, J. P. & Ankney, C. D. (1993). The evolutionary selection of human races: A response to Miller. *Personality and Individual Differences, 15*, 677–680.

Rushton, J. P. & Osborne, R. T. (1995). Genetic and environmental contributions to cranial capacity in black and white adolescents. *Intelligence 20*, 1–13.

Scarr, S., & Weinberg. (1976). IQ performance of black children adopted by white families. *American Psychologist, 31*, 726–739.

Scozzari et al., 1988. Genetic studies on the Sengal population. I. mitochondrial DNA polymorphisms. *American Journal of Human Genetics, 43*, 534–544.

Seligman, D. (1992). *A question of intelligence*. New York: Birch Lane Press.

Seligson, S. (1995). Seeds of doubt. *The Atantic Monthly, 275* (3), 28–39.

Skuder, P., Plomin R., McClearn, G., Smith, D., Vignetti, S., Chorney, M., Chorney, K., Kasarda, S., Thompson, L., Detterman, D., Petrill, S., Daniels J., Owen, M., & McGuffin P. (1995). A polymorphism in mitochondrial DNA associated with IQ? *Intelligence, 21*, 1–12.

Symons, D. (1979). *The evolution of human sexuality*. New York: Oxford University Press.

Snyderman, M. and Rothman, S. (1988). *The IQ controversy, the media and public policy*. New Brunswick, Transaction Books.

Tu, G. & Israel, Y. (1995). Alcohol consumption by Orientals in North America is predicted largely by a single gene. *Behavior Genetics, 25,* 59–65.

Tucker, W. H. (1994). *The science and politics of racial research.* Urbana: University of Illinois Press.

Waldman, I. D., Weinberg, R. A., & Scarr, S. (1994). Racial group differences in IQ in the Minnesota transracial adoption study: A reply to Levin and Lynn. *Intelligence, 16,* 29–44.

Weinberg, R. A., Scarr, S., & Waldman, I. D. (1992). The Minnesota transracial adoption study: A follow-up of IQ test performance at adolescence. *Intelligence, 16,* 117–135.

Wickett, J. C., Vernon, P. A. & Lee, D. H. (1994). *In vivo* brain size, head perimeter, and intelligence in a sample of healthy adult females. *Personality and Individual Differences, 16,* 831–838.

Willerman, L., Schultz, R., Rutledge, J. N. & Bigler, E. D. (1991). In vivo brain size and intelligence. *Intelligence, 15,* 223–228.

19

No More Than Skin Deep: Ethnic and Racial Similarity in Developmental Processes

David C. Rowe
Alexander T. Vazsonyi
Daniel J. Flannery

In an integrated school in an American city, two boys with similar academic problems might be taking a standardized test. Both boys fidget at their seats and strike up conversations with classmates rather than pay attention to the teacher's recitation of test directions. Both boys read a year and one half behind grade level. They may have different non-academic gifts—one being good at sports, the other at drawing. If both these boys were ethnically White, we would look naturally to influences in their home environments to understand their academic slowness and hyperactivity. We would expect similar influences to be responsible for both boys' conditions—we might expect to find two lower class families lacking in financial resources and two single mothers who, in their stressful lives, were unable to encourage their children's school work. If genetic influences play a role in hyperactivity (Goodman & Stevensen, 1989), we might expect that their biological fathers both had childhood histories of overactivity and inattentiveness.

But suppose one boy were ethnically Black and the other ethnically White. Or one boy were ethnically Hispanic and the other White. With this knowledge, in social science, one response has been to generate *different developmental explanations* for the boys' behavior (Helms, 1992; Ogbu, 1991; Spencer, 1990). The ethnic minority family may socialize different values. For instance, one group may emphasize the importance of school achievement, whereas the other emphasizes peer popularity. Or the minority boy may have been teased and taunted by his majority classmates—to the detriment of his self-esteem and academic performance.

An earlier version of this essay appeared in *Psychological Review,* 1994, 101, 3, July, 396–413, and is adapted/reprinted with the permission of the copyright holder/author.

The authors thank Joseph L. Rodgers, Mark Roosa, George Knight, Stephan A. Cernkovich, Nancy Darling, Larry Steinberg, Janine Goldman-Pach, and Travis Hirschi for providing us with the covariance matrices reanalyzed for the present article.

The aim of this paper is to explore these two contrasting explanations of behavioral variation in minority and majority ethnic and racial groups: (1) common developmental processes, versus (2) minority unique developmental processes.

The article's focus is on English-speaking ethnic and racial minorities living in America, mainly Blacks and Hispanics compared with Whites, although one study detailed later also includes Asians. We acknowledge that ethnic and racial minorities are themselves heterogeneous in genetics and social histories. Through inter-marriage, genetic isolation among racial and ethnic groups has been relaxed; for instance, about 25% of the autosomal genes in American Blacks originate from inter-mixing with the White population (Chakraborty et al., 1992). Great heterogeneity also exists within the "White" majority culture. Although people of English background predominate, American Caucasians may trace family histories to France, Germany, the Netherlands, Scotland, or to other places. Once in America, these diverse racial and ethnic groups adopted English as their first language. Their unique cultural backgrounds absorbed changes from, and exerted influence upon, a broader American culture.

Nevertheless, we believe that racial/ethnic classifications carry important information about peoples' genetic and cultural backgrounds—and as such, that they can be useful in scientific studies. First, these classifications carry information about evolutionary phylogenies (Stringer & Andrews, 1988). For instance, American Blacks originated on the African continent, and so they are racially Negro, a group distinguishable from other races on the bases of heritable, physical characteristics. American Whites mainly originated in Western Europe and would be racially Caucasian. Asians came from China, Japan, and southeast Asia and from a "Mongoloid" racial grouping distinctive from both Caucasians and Negroes. Hispanics, while racially Caucasian, mainly originated in Spain and Portugal, and first resided in Mexico, the Caribbean, or South America before moving to the U.S. Although the exact number of existing racial groupings depends on the particular classification system used, it is indisputable that generations of geographic separation have given rise to racial subdivisions, traceable by different biological lineages. Second, these classification carry information about cultural backgrounds as well. For example, "Anglo" culture is distinctive from that which arose in the Hispanic Americas, and African culture is distinctive from European and Hispanic ones. Thus, race or ethnicity qualifies as a nominal variable *correlated* with individuals' genetic and cultural histories. For instance, the dichotomous Black/White variable would correlate with extent of African genetic heritage strongly, but imperfectly. In social science, many approximately valid measures are used to capture sources of behavioral variation, and racial and ethnic classifications are no exception. Most studies use peoples' *self-classifications* of race or ethnicity as the basis for groupings; we would therefore accept individuals' self-classifications as a basis for their racial/ethnic group membership. The subtle issue of the conceptual relation between developmental process and *average* group levels has been discussed previously in the developmental literature (McCall, Appelbaum, & Hogarty, 1973). Nonetheless, confusion often remains between these two concepts, which are at times genuinely difficult to distinguish. We define a group average level as a group's statistical mean on either independent variables (e.g., "influences") or dependent variables (e.g., outcomes). In contrast, we refer to developmental processes as the biological or psychosocial mechanisms relating the independent variables (influences) to the dependent ones (outcomes). It is sometimes thought that, if ethnic group A has a higher mean level on an outcome than ethnic group B, then some different developmental process is necessarily implied; but of course, this is not so. Identical developmental processes may occur in both groups, but they may also differ in *average* levels on developmental antecedents ("influences"), so that they consequently differ in the outcome as well.

For example, blood pressure readings have been reported as higher in Black than White men. Blood pressure is, to some degree, sensitive to dietary salt intake. Suppose the causal influence of salt on blood pressure is represented as a regression coefficient of .17. Assuming that the physiological processes linking salt to blood pressure were the same in Blacks and Whites, then this coefficient would be .17 in both populations. Nonetheless, if Black men culturally had diets higher in salt than white men, then this common developmental process could produce a part of the *average racial difference* in blood pressure. Suppose dietary salt levels were measured in a combined population of an equal number of Black and White men. We may discover that Black men had a mean dietary intake of .6 standard deviation units above the combined group mean (X = 0 for a standardized variate); white men, −.6 units below it. Then the mean blood pressures of Black and White men should differ by about .2 standard deviation units (that is, .6*.17 − (−.6)*.17). In this hypothetical blood pressure example, a common developmental process partly explains both *individual differences* and the *average* differences between racial groups.[1]

Alternatively, developmental processes could differ from one racial/ethnic group to another. In the blood pressure example, suppose, for instance, that Black men were affected by dietary salt but White men were unaffected, at least for typical exposures. In this case, the regression of blood pressure on salt intake would be .17 in Black men but .00 in White men. White men and Black men could have identical levels of dietary salt intake, but because salt intake raises blood pressure in Black men due to their greater salt sensitivity, just the latter would develop higher *average* blood pressure levels.

Neither example was intended to be a true analysis of salt metabolism and its relation to blood pressure; rather, they were presented here as illustrations of a subtle distinction between two contrasting alternatives—(1) group *average* differences due to common processes but different antecedent conditions, versus (2) group *average* differences due to dissimilar biological or psychosocial processes.

In the next section, some theoretical arguments for the different developmental processes among ethnic/racial groups are considered. They are followed by a separate section making arguments for common developmental processes in all ethnic/racial groups.

Argument for Ethnic/Racial Group Differences

Americans belonging to different ethnic/racial groups may possess separate cultural histories that lead to different mechanisms of socialization within different

---

1. Salt intake is not actually the explanation for racial differences in blood pressure. These differences persist after controlling statistically for dietary salt; our example was hypothetical.

groups (Harrison et al., 1990; Steinberg, Dornbusch, & Brown, 1992). One hypothesis is that because ethnic group A has been socialized differently from ethnic group B, a difference in developmental outcome may occur as well.

Helms (1992) advances such a cultural explanation for the lower IQ test performance of Blacks than Whites. She argues that the culture of American Blacks, despite its geographic and temporal separation from African roots, maintains significant elements of African culture through its traditions. According to Helms, at least eight cultural elements are more widespread among American Black culture than among American White culture (p. 1096); they include (1) spirituality, the "greater validity of the power of immaterial forces in everyday life over linear, factual thinking"; (2) movement, "personal conduct is organized through movement"; and (3) social time, "time is measured by socially meaningful events and customs." Helms further connects these cultural values with difficulty on standardized tests because they either interfere with the acquisition of test-relevant material or with test-taking motivation. Thus, a preference for "social time" may interfere with the rigors of a timed IQ test, in which "time is a valuable commodity." Helms summarized Heath's (1989) argument that a gulf in thought and emotion separate Blacks from other ethnic groups:

> Black Americans are socialized in Black communities to develop spontaneous, creative, interactive, and expansive thinking skills. Consequently, upon reaching testable age, it is difficult for them to reconcile the contrasting socially oriented worldview of their communities with the ascetic Eurocentric view that presumably underlies test construction. (p. 1097)

A second hypothesis about group differences is the direct psychological effects of discrimination. On one hand, minority groups may socialize children differently because they possess positive cultural traditions, independent of the majority culture's; on the other, they may develop values that are destructive in the long run, but that represent a means of adapting to social discrimination.

This latter explanation features strongly in Ogbu's (1991) explanation of "involuntary" minorities poor school achievement. He defines as "involuntary" those minorities brought into another society through slavery, conquest, or colonization. Because their incorporation into another society was imposed, the involuntary minority, according to Ogbu, develops a psychological identity in opposition to that of the mainstream culture. Members of an involuntary minority perceive institutionalized discrimination against them, and therefore, they loose faith in their ability to compete successfully in institutions like schools. Although these minority parents may verbally value schooling as a means of social advancement, their lack of personal academic effort and success may undermine their exhortations. In these groups, young people may channel their energies away from conventional routes to success and into "survival" strategies of petty crime and other oppositional behavior. In their generally poor schools, they also see evidence of discrimination—that they are given less just because they are minorities. In overview, minority-unique experience with social discrimination may lead to their (relative) failure in schooling and later in conventional economic competition.

Unlike some explanations for group differences, though, Ogbu accepts the existence of individual differences, noting that "I do not claim all . . . involuntary minorities are academically unsuccessful" (p. 29). In this context, he mentions several strategies for making good academic progress while not offending peers' values contrary to achievement, such as using sports success as a "cover" for genuine academic achievement.

Ogbu's views, and others like his advocating deep cultural differences, have been widely influential in social science. In a recent issue of *Child Development* devoted to minority children, a variety of "cultural difference" explanations were advanced (for instance, Coll, 1990; Harrison et al., 1990; McLoyd, 1990; Slaughter-Defoe, Nakagawa, Takanishi, & Johnson, 1990). A sampling of these explanations includes (1) value on mother-infant enmeshment vs. autonomy, (2) a culturally rooted value on power assertion among American Blacks deriving from traditional African values, (3) minority groups' emphasis on cooperative rather than on competitive views of life, and (4) traditional Asian values such as respect for authority and group cooperation. As shown in these different examples, many social scientists now argue for different developmental processes as a source of group *average* differences.

In summary, although the emphasis has been on differences between American Whites and Blacks, the general idea that ethnic groups may have different cultural values, given their pre-existing traditions, and their conflicts with a majority culture, forms a basis for expecting group differences in causal developmental process. In opposition to ethnic and racial difference are those arguments favoring similarity in the developmental process, as discussed next.

Argument for Ethnic/Racial Group Similarities

In social science, there is a great awareness of human universals (Brown, 1991; Buss, 1989; Russell, 1991). Two examples of cultural diversity, color names and facial expressiveness, on more recent empirical examination, show universals. Around the world, people parse the color spectrum into similar components and name them, and they can read and express the same emotions using nearly identical configurations of facial expression. The list of cultural universals extends into all behavioral domains—specific mate preferences, love of kin, preferential altruism directed towards kin, play, deceit, enduring mateships, and many more. Social scientists involved in studying psychological traits among cultures also adopt a "universalistic" perspective: that characteristics of different cultures result from organism-culture interactions and so are constrained and not purely arbitrary (Berry et al., 1992).

Although genetic arguments are sometimes marshaled as an explanation of ethnic *average* differences (Jensen, 1969; Rushton, 1988), a strong justification for universal developmental processes is also provided. About 25% of genetic loci are *polymorphic* (i.e., their genes exist in multiple forms such as the genes A, O, and B in the ABO blood group). Genetic explanations for group differences focus on those polymorphic loci at which genotype frequencies may differ among ethnic groups. In most polymorphic genetic loci, however, genetic variation is more prominent *within* than between ethnic and racial classifications (Lewontin, 1982). And by current estimates, about 75% of genetic loci contain no genetic variability at all across humans—genetically, we are much more alike than different.[2] At

---

2. The genetic difference between humans and Chimpanzee amounts to changes in about 1% of total DNA. Thus it is possible for a relatively small number of genetic changes to pro-

these nonvariable loci, the genes in Asians, Blacks, and Whites would be exactly identical—this shared genetic heritage makes all people belong to one human species, with many common characteristics. This great degree of genetic similarity leads to the expectation that people of different ethnic groups will be alike in many complex, behavioral adaptations, because the genes that form them tend to be shared by all ethnic groups. Of course, this conclusion only applies to traits with a partly genetic basis, but as argued by Berry et al., many traits may result from "organism-environment" interactions.

A common American culture also encourages the expectation of similar developmental processes. Although Americans of different ethnic backgrounds have some unique heritage, they also may share in common many aspects of American culture—second generation American Hispanics are probably more familiar with MTV, MacDonalds, classroom schooling, presidential inaugurations, and the NCAA basketball playoff tournament than they are with Mexican games or Peruvian oral traditions. Indeed, these aspects of American culture are pervasive, reaching most Hispanics, Asians, Blacks, and the majority Whites as well. So, an argument against the ethnic "difference" view may combine these two observations (1) that biological processes in most humans would be necessarily alike, and (2) that in America, they may interact with many common cultural features. Consequently, developmental processes leading to outcomes for different American ethnic groups would be highly similar.

Clearly, the arguments on the "difference" versus "similarity" sides are both strong ones, deserving our serious consideration. As social scientists, we want to produce empirical data bearing on which of these contrasting alternatives best describes the development of behavioral traits.

Empirical Methods of Evaluating Developmental Process

If we had some marvelous technology that would make the developmental process visible, we could just aim this machine at children from different ethnic groups and make a direct comparison of the developmental process leading to particular traits. Lacking such a wonderful device, we must resort to indirect strategies that examine the strength of different developmental processes using statistical associations (e.g., correlations and covariances).

One way of testing for process difference is to compare the covariances or unstandardized path coefficients between variables that are "influences" and those that are developmental "outcomes" across ethnic groups. In general, if these statistics differ significantly from one ethnic group to another, and if the magnitude of this difference is appreciable, we may conclude (in the absence of statistical artifacts) that developmental process also differs between groups. In contrast, if the statistics were the same for different ethnic groups, we may accept that develop-

---

duce striking morphological and psychological differences between species. Nonetheless, all humans would be substantially more closely related genetically to one another than to Chimpanzees or other primate "out-groups."

mental process was the same (given a large sample, so statistical power would be available to detect group differences).

Comparing Covariance Matrices

In this article, our general analytic strategy will be to compare covariance matrices computed on different racial/ethnic groups. It is more efficient to test the statistical similarity of total covariance matrices, rather than to investigate specific causal models. For any matrix, many different models would be possible—offering specific ones would be open to the criticism that alternative models were not considered, and we cannot be sure which model is the correct one. Comparing the statistical similarity of matrices is a "model-free" statistical test. If the matrices were statistically identical, however, the correct analytic procedure is to pool them before investigating specific causal models, and of course, the *same* causal model must apply to each racial/ethnic group. In later analyses, each matrix is about 10 x 10. They contain both widely accepted "influence" variables and major developmental outcomes. The "influence" variables may include family functioning and peer relationship variables; the developmental outcomes may include academic achievement, conduct problems or delinquency, and depression. The research question is: Are the statistical associations found in these covariance matrices the *same* or *different* in different ethnic groups?

In answering this question, several weak statistical procedures must be avoided. Merely counting the number of statistically significant correlations (i.e., greater than zero) would be a poor procedure. If one group gave a correlation of .20 ($p < .05$), another one of .17 ($p > .05$), they might be seen as different: but both associations may be statistically significant in large samples that provide greater statistical power. The correct statistical approach is one of testing the statistical significance of the *difference* between two correlation coefficients. Given the number of correlations in a 10 x 10 matrix, however, many pairwise comparisons can easily lead to Type I statistical errors (i.e., inferring non-existent relationships). Instead of piecemeal procedures, we adopt a strategy of testing for significant differences between entire covariance matrices using linear structural equation modeling (LISREL). Although many social science applications use correlation matrices, we follow a more stringent test of comparing *covariance* matrices. In the latter comparison method, the equivalence of variances is tested simultaneously with that of covariances. In addition, in group comparisons statistical estimates of standard errors and model-fit lie on firmer mathematical grounds when covariance matrices are used (Cudeck, 1989).

The analytic approach and general argument may be illustrated with a hypothetical example. Table 1 presents covariance matrices (2 x 2) for majority and minority individuals separately. The variable X_1 is a developmental influence (e.g., parental involvement); the variable Y is a developmental outcome (e.g., children's educational aspirations). The matrices suggest different developmental processes: the X_1 – Y association is stronger for the minority group (where the *r* calculated from the covariance matrix equals .62) than for the majority group (where *r* = .30). The X_1 and Y variables also possess greater variance in the minority group (5 versus 9.40 and 5 versus 9.18, respectively).

What could be happening? Figure 1 shows the structural model that generated the majority and minority matrices. In the minority group, a variable that is not di-

Table 1. Hypothetical Matrices for Majority and Minority Groups

Group	X1	Y
Majority		
X_1	5.00	
Y	1.50	5.00
Minority		
X_1	9.40	
Y	5.71	9.18

Note: $a = .3$, $b = .9$, and $c = .35$. In majority group, variance of $X_1 = 5$, residual on $Y = 4.55$. In minority group, residual on $X_1 = 2.11$, variance of $X_2 = 9.0$, and residual on $Y = 5.50$. Matrices were computed from a BASIC language program, major.bas.

rectly observed (X_2) exerts an influence on both X_1 and Y variation. This variable would be some factor unique to minority group members; it might be variation in exposure to racial taunts and insults; it might be variation in individuals' reactions to discriminatory social practices (e.g., red-lined housing, job discrimination). Note that this variable must vary *within* the minority group; correlational analysis, of course, cannot detect an influence that is exactly constant for all group members. Whatever its exact source, it influences variation in, to use the earlier choices, both parental involvement and children's own educational aspirations. According to Wright's rules for reading a structural diagram, the correlation of X_1 and Y has the following mathematical expectation in the majority group,

(1) $r = a$,

(2) and in the minority group, $r = a + bc$,

where a, b, and c are the path coefficients, as shown in Figure 1. The existence of X_2 also induces greater variance in X_1 and Y, because it is causally linked to them. Notice, though, that these diagrams say nothing about the groups' *average* levels on X_1 or Y. The analysis of developmental process may be done independently of variables' *average* levels. The two perspectives may be conjoined if ethnic/racial differences in *average* levels were found on antecedent variables (X_1, X_2) and developmental outcomes (Y), but the focus in this article is on developmental process *per se*.

Figure 1. Path Models for Minority and Majority Groups

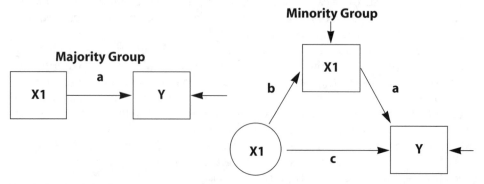

Standardized Path Coefficients, $a = .3$, $b = .9$, and $c = .35$; Y = developmental outcome; X_1 = developmental influence; X_2 = minority-unique developmental influence.

Table 2. LISREL Model Fit to Majority and Minority Matrices

Fitted Matrix	X1	Y	Statistics
X_1	7.20		Chi square 16.9, P < .001
Y	3.61	7.09	Degrees of Freedom 3
			GFI Majority Group .88
			GFI Minority Group .95
			X^2/N .085

Note: Fitted using LISREL 7, with total N = 200, 100 "individuals" in majority group; 100 in minority group. GFI = goodness of fit index. Model line for first group, mo nx=2 nk=2 lx=id td=ze; model line for second group, mo ph=in.

Table 2 gives results from a LISREL comparison of the covariance matrices in Table 1, with a hypothetical sample size of 100 majority persons and 100 minority persons. LISREL generates a covariance matrix that is the average of the two covariance matrices (when sample sizes are equal). Table 2 gives this "fitted matrix," which is the average of the two covariance matrices in Table 1. The more the matrices deviate from this "fitted matrix," the worse is the statistical fit.

In structural equation models, several indices of goodness-of-fit are available. The chi square test takes a value of zero if the fitted and observed matrices were exactly equal and a value greater than zero if they were unequal. If the chi square is statistically significant (on the basis of the degrees of freedom for the comparison), then the hypothesis that the two matrices were equal would be rejected statistically against one that they were unequal. However, the sensitivity of the chi square test depends directly on sample sizes, and in large samples (*Ns* > 200) it is almost impossible not to obtain a nonsignificant value of the chi square (Green, 1992; Tanaka, 1987). For this reason, alternative indices of fit have been developed (Green, 1992; Loehlin, 1992a). The LISREL program (Joreskog & Sorbom, 1988) provides a goodness-of-fit index (GFI) constrained to fall between 0 and 1 that assesses the match of the expected and observed covariance matrices. GFI values greater than .90 are usually considered to provide a good fit to the observed covariance matrix (Green, 1992).[3] Another way to eliminate the effect of sample size is to calculate the x^2 divided by the sample size. Although this index lacks a general interpretation, it is useful when matrices of the same dimensionality are being compared. Because of its generality, we emphasize the GFI index as the best measure of goodness-of-fit.

In the hypothetical example, the chi square showed the groups differed statistically (x^2 = 16.9, p < .001). The chi square per observation equalled .085. And at least in one group, the GFI index was unsatisfactory (GFI = .88 in the majority group, .95 in the minority; discrepancies between larger-dimensioned matrices would produce lower GFIs). The statistical differences between the minority and majority group, of course, were expected in this example because it was constructed to produce group differences.

---

3. The accuracy of the GFI is not entirely independent of sample size, but according to Marsh, Balla, & McDonald (1988), it "performed better than any other stand-alone index (p. 396)" in a study of the influence of sample size on fit indices. In many comparisons, we have samples sufficiently large as to avoid biases introduced by using small samples.

In later statistical analyses, one additional comparison is employed. The sensitive chi square fit index as derived from different ethnic/racial groups is put against chi squares derived from *random* halves of a single ethnic group. If different developmental processes exist between ethnic/racial groups, then greater statistical "strain" would result from the comparison of different ethnic groups than from arbitrary halves of a single ethnic/racial group.

Data Sources

In this section, we describe the principal data sources used in our analyses. We report results for six data sources. One data source, the National Longitudinal Survey of Youth, was used twice: once when treating the surveyed persons as individuals and a second time when matching individuals as sibling pairs from the sampled households. The results from sibling pairs will be discussed separately in a later section.

Data Sources Analyzed for This Study

Space limitations prohibit a detailed discussion of the reliability and validity of variables used in the following studies. However, most variables had been carefully chosen as representing accurately different developmental constructs. For example, the Home Observation for Measurement of the Environment (HOME) is one of the most widely used measures of family environment (Caldwell & Bradley, 1984). The Peabody Picture Vocabulary Test is a high quality, nationally-standardized instrument (Dunn & Dunn, 1981). An extensive literature exists in criminology showing the reliability and validity of self-report delinquency variables (Hindelang, Hirschi, & Weiss, 1981). The Youth Self-Report is a widely used self-assessment of behavior and social competence that possesses national norms on different ages and ethnic groups (Achenbach, 1991). Although no set of variables is perfect, for the most part the ones selected in the following studies satisfy current guidelines for behavioral assessment.

Tucson Substance Use Study. Table 3 gives the characteristics of each source and lists the variables with which covariance matrices were computed. The first source, the Tucson Substance Use Study, was collected by this article's authors in Tucson, Arizona. Children in grades 6–7 were recruited through a Tucson area school district. All students attending school on a particular day were sampled. A "passive" consent procedure was used at most schools, so that students were only omitted from the sample if their parents had requested so in writing. Students completed the survey questionnaires during homeroom sessions under the supervision of study staff. Of the original available number of 1,437 students, 67 students (4.7%) did not participate due to parental concerns, and 134 students were absent during data collection (9.3%). The approximate participation rate was about 86%. An additional 66 surveys (4.6%) were not usable due to incomplete or missing data, defined as completion rates below 50% of all items.

The final sample had 1,022 Caucasian and Hispanic students (for an overall, 81.4% completion rate). It was about equally divided between males and females

Table 3. Data Sources for Covariance Matrices

Matrix Size and Variables	Sample	Source
Tuscon Substance Use Study		
Matrix 11 x 11	Tucson, AZ 1993	Flannery et al.
Peer Pressure	Hispanic, N=278	
Friends Drug Use	White, N=744	
Parental Involvement	Mean Age 12.7 years	
Parental Monitoring	Males & Females	
Self-efficacy		
Academic Adjustment		
Lifetime Drug Use		
YSR Aggression		
YSR Depression		
YSR Impulsivity		
Grades		
National Longitudinal Study of Youth (Individuals)		
Matrix 10 x 10	Nationwide	Baker & Mott, 1989
Mother's Education	Black, N=59	
Age of Child	Hispanic, N=335	
HOME Cognition	White, N=836	
HOME Emotion	Males and Females	
School Self-esteem	6–9 Years	
Selfworth		
Math Achievement		
Reading Recogniton		
Reading Comprehension		
Problem Behavior (Total)		
National Longitudinal Study of Youth (Siblings)		
Matrix 6 x 6	Nationwide	Baker & Mott, 1989
Achievement	Black, N pair=156	
Problem Behavior	Hispanic, N pair=128	
HOME	White, N pair=319	
Variables repeated for each sibling	Males & Females	
	6–18 years	
Wisconsin/California Study		
Matrix 10 x 10	Wisconsin/California	Steinberg, Dorn-
Academic Engagement 1987	Black=635	busch & Brown,
Academic Engagement 1988	White=3943	1992
Behavioral Control	Asian=906	
Psychological Autonomy—granting	Hispanic=827	
Involvement—Warmth	Males & Females	
Parents School Involvement	Grades 9–12	
Parents School Encouragement '87		
Parents School Encouragement '88		
GPA 1987		
GPA 1988		

Table 3 *continued*. Data Sources for Covariance Matrices

Matrix Size and Variables	Sample	Source
Bowling Green Study		
Matrix 8 x 8	Toledo, Ohio	Cernkovich & Gior-
Parental Communication	Black, N=469	dano, 1992
School Involvement	White, N=409	
Attachment to Teachers	Males & Females	
School Commitment	12–19 Years	
School Involvement		
Risk of Arrest		
Perceived Opportunity		
Delinquency		
Richmond Youth Project		
Matrix 10 x 10	Richmond, VA	Hirschi, 1969
Participation with Father	Black N=1427	
Supervision by Father	White N=1872	
Overall GPA	Males & Females:	
Mother's Education	Junior & Senior High School	
Participation with Mother		
Supervison By Mother		
Peer Orientation		
IQ		
Standard Self-Report		
Delinquency		
Official Offenses to 1967		
Prevention Study		
Matrix 9 x 9	Southwestern city	Roosa, Tein, Grop-
CRPBI Acceptance	Hispanic N=70	penbacher,
CRPBI Rejection	White1, N=70	Michaels, &
CRPBI Inconsistent Discipline	White2, N=70	Dumka (1993)
CRPBI Control	Mothers and 8- to 14-year-old	
CRPBI Hostile Control	children	
Open family communication		
Problems in family communication		
Mean value on Kovacs Conduct		
Disorder Index		
CBCL Conduct Disorder Subscale		

Note: YSR = Youth Self-Report; HOME = Home Observation for Measurement of the Environment (Caldwell & Bradley, 1984); GPA = grade point average; CRPBI = Children's Reports of Parental Behavior Inventory; CBCL = Child Behavior Check List. Children's achievement in the National Longitudinal Survey was assessed with the Peabody Individual Achievement Test reading, mathematics and comprehension tests.

and between 6th and 7th graders. Their mean age was about 13 years at the time of data collection. About 28% of the sample were living with a single parent. Variables classified as developmental outcomes were drug use, aggression, depression, grades, impulsivity, school adjustment, and self-efficacy. Variables classified as antecedents were peer pressure, friends' drug use, parental involvement, and parental monitoring (see descriptions in Flannery et al., 1994).

National Longitudinal Survey of Youth (Individuals). In 1979, the original National Longitudinal Survey of the Work Experience of Youth (NLSY) used standard stratified probability sampling methods to locate households representative of the American population. Blacks, poor Whites, and Hispanics were over-sampled to gain more detailed information on them. The original sample consisted of 14 to 21-year olds. In 1986 and 1988, children born to women in the NLSY study were brought into the study (in 1986, ages 1–14; Baker & Mott, 1989). In this report, we focus on these NLSY children, who because of the original sample composition, were disproportionately minority and poor. In the NLSY children, the Black mothers had a slightly higher average educational level than the White or Hispanic parents. The mothers were about the same age (in their late 20s).

The NLSY is a rich data set, with many possible structures for analysis. In the individual data set, we decided to focus on middle childhood (ages 6–9), an age range not represented in our other data sources. The ten variables used are listed in Table 3 (for detailed description, see Baker & Mott, 1989). One noteworthy measure is an abbreviated version of the Home Observation for Measurement of the Environment (HOME) that was used to index the quality of the HOME environment (Caldwell & Bradley, 1984). This version included both interviewer observations and maternal self-reports. Children's achievement was assessed with the Peabody Individual Achievement Test (PIATs) reading, mathematics, and comprehension tests. Other measures included appear in Table 3.

National Longitudinal Survey of Youth (Siblings). As many mothers in the original NLSY sample had more than a single child, it was possible to construct biologically-related sibling pairs. Details on the construction of sibling pairs are given in Rodgers, Rowe, and Li (in press). Except for 14 opposite-sex twin pairs, the rarer twin, cousin, and half-sibling pairs, also identified from the NLSY children, were not used in this article. In this analysis, the matrix was restricted to variables for which missing data were few in number. To maximize sample size, the full biological siblings and opposite-sex twins were permitted to be 6–18 years old at the time of the 1988 survey. The age adjusted 1988 HOME total score was used as an index of the quality of family environment. Unlike the individual matrix, which included age and was based on a limited age range, we choose to use developmental outcomes already adjusted for age and sex differences (Center for Human Resource Research, 1991). Problem behaviors were assessed by the age-and-sex adjusted 1988 survey problem-behavior total score— academic achievement, by the *mean* of the 1988 survey PIAT reading, math, and comprehension measures, all normed variables. It is important that the HOME measure was not identical for siblings, because some items were child-specific. Thus, a sibling matrix contained six variables: sibling A's achievement, problem behavior, and HOME variables; and the same variables repeated for sibling B.

Covariance Matrices Provided to This Study

California/Wisconsin Study. Students attending nine high schools in California and Wisconsin each completed two self-report questionnaires (Steinberg, Mounts, Lamborn, & Dornbusch, 1991). These schools were selected to provide a diverse sample in terms of family structure, socioeconomic status, and type of community (rural, suburban, and urban). Of the approximately 10,000 students, 9% of the students were black, 14% were Asian, 12% were Hispanic, and 60% were White (the remainder belonged to other ethnic groups). Questionnaires were completed for about 80% of the target sample.

Bowling Green Study. The Bowling Green study provides data on both Blacks and Whites. To avoid biases associated with school based studies, the Bowling Green Study probabilistically sampled geographic areas in Toledo, Ohio, to locate youths between 12 and 19 years of age. Geographic stratification was based on the 1980 area census. Within strata, households were selected to identify eligible respondents, who were interviewed in their homes. A total of 942 face-to-face interviews were successfully completed. About half the sample was female, half male; about the same relative division applied to race with 45% of the sample White, 50% Black.

Richmond Youth Project. This study of delinquency recruited from a population of 17,500 students entering eleven public junior and senior high schools in the Richmond, Virginia, area (Hirschi, 1969). A stratified sampling procedure yielded 4,077 students, about 45% of whom were Black. The sampling procedure yielded a group diverse in levels of family income and education.

Prevention Study. This study was part of an evaluation program that recruited children in fourth, fifth, and sixth grades into a prevention program for the children of alcoholics (Roosa et al., in press; Knight, Tein, Shell, & Roosa, 1992). Families were recruited in a southwestern city using a variety of procedures (e.g., newsletters distributed to students and taken home, telephone recruitment, and door-to-door canvassing). One hundred thirty-four one-parent families and 169 two-parent families were interviewed. Family incomes ranged from less than $5,000 per year (12%) to more than $40,000 per year (14%) with the modal income range being from $5,001 to $10,000 (17%). Most families could be described as lower to lower middle class. The ethnic distribution was 60% White, 20% Hispanic, 13% Black, and 6% other. Because of their relatively larger sample sizes, we requested covariance matrices from this research group only for Whites (N = 170) and Hispanics (N = 70). Based on a diagnostic interview, 36% of the mothers were either problem drinkers or alcoholic; 57% of fathers had similar diagnoses.

As shown in Table 3, extensive data were obtained on family functioning (obtained from the mothers). In addition to these parenting-style variables, two developmental outcome variables focused on childhood conduct problems. The Prevention study sent us three covariance matrices. One was computed for the 70 Hispanics; the others were based on two groups of 70 random White families, with the stipulation that no White family appeared in both random subgroups.

Results for Covariance Matrices (Individuals)

For all covariance matrices, the general result was one of striking and consistent similarity between ethnic and racial groups. Although space does not permit a detailed description of covariance matrices, it is worthwhile to give a few details of the matrices obtained from several sources.[4] In Whites, greatest correlation in the Tucson Substance Use matrix was between academic adjustment and substance use ($r = -.51$). Substance use also correlated highly with aggression,

---

4. Except for Roosa's prevention study, the covariance matrices used here may be obtained by writing the first author.

Table 4. Tuscon Substance Use Study

Measure	Hispanic (278) vs. Whites (743)	Hispanic (278) vs. Whites (278)	Hispanic1 (139) vs. Hispanic2 (139)	White1 (372) vs. White2 (372)	Misspecified
Chi Square	144.5	129.8	87.0	122.0	2236.9
GFI (First)	.94	.96	.95	.97	.67
GFI (Second)	.99	.96	.95	.97	.67
x^2/N .14	.23	.31	.16	4.0	

Note: Degrees of freedom, 66. All chi square statistically significant ($p < .05$).

friends' drug use, and parental monitoring (absolute rs, .34 to .51). School grades were associated with greater academic adjustment and less susceptibility to peer pressure (rs, .38 and –.28, respectively). Self-efficacy found few correlates among the ten remaining variables (maximum $r = -.33$ with depression). Overall, the matrix presents a rich set of association for testing models of etiologic influences on substance use.

Table 4 presents the goodness-of-fit tests comparing these 11 x 11 covariance matrices. Whites and Hispanics were compared twice: once with the entire samples (column 1), another time with equal sample sizes (column 2). According to the goodness-of-fit test (GFI), the White and Hispanic matrices were equivalent (GFIs > .90). When data sets contain unequal Ns, the LISREL program makes the common, estimated matrix closer to the White's matrix that was based on the larger sample size (N = 744). When a random White sample equally large as the Hispanic sample was drawn (N = 278), then the two matrices received equal weight in the fitting process, giving closer GFIs (.96).

Despite the close, quantitative similarity of these covariance matrices, the chi square tests yielded statistical rejections of their equality ($p < .05$). As noted earlier, in structural equation modeling, it is understood that this chi square is exquisitely sensitive to slight differences between model-expected and observed covariances (Tanaka, 1987). For this reason, we adopted other yardsticks for comparing the adequacy of model fits: the GFI fit index, the chi square per observation, and the statistical fit of halves of one ethnic/racial group. By randomly assigning individuals of one ethnic group to one of two equivalent subgroups, *within*-ethnicity, racial group covariance matrices were computed. If ethnic/racial groups differ, then the GFI, chi square, and chi square per observation statistics for different ethnic/racial groups should greatly exceed those on random halves of a single group.

As shown in Table 4, a comparison of random, within ethnicity subgroups also yielded significant chi squares (Hispanic1 vs. Hispanic2, 87.0; White1 vs. White2, 122.0, $p < .05$). These statistical rejections may reflect imperfections in social science data—the eleven variables fail to satisfy strict multivariate normality (e.g., drug use is negatively skewed) and they lack exact interval scaling. Given these distributional and measurement inadequacies, any two covariance matrices may be statistically non-equivalent, as compared with two covariance matrices drawn from a true multivariate normal population. Nonetheless, on the basis of these measurement imperfections, it would be improper to postulate different causal models for the random halves of one ethnicity. Here, a better guide to matrix similarity was clearly the high GFI values, not statistically significant chi squares (.96

Table 5. National Longitudinal Study of Youth

	Hispanic (335) vs. Black (335)	Hispanic (335) vs. White (335)	Black (335) vs. White (335)	White1 (418) vs. White2 (418)
Chi Square	140.7	209.7	171.0	193.3
GFI (First)	.96	.94	.96	.96
GFI (Second)	.96	.94	.95	.96
x^2/N	.21	.31	.26	.29

Note: Degrees of freedom = 55. All chi squares statistically significant ($p < .05$).

for Hispanics vs. Whites in column 2, .95 for Hispanic1 vs. Hispanic2, .97 for White1 vs. White2). As shown by the GFI values, random halves of Whites or Hispanics were as statistically similar as White vs. Hispanics. Similarly, the per observation chi square from Hispanic1 vs. Hispanic2 (x^2/N = .31) was actually *greater* than those from the two cross-ethnicity comparisons. In the comparisons just described, no evidence existed for differential causal processes operating within the Hispanic vs. White groups.

Under any circumstances, could the statistical similarity of any two Tucson Study matrices be rejected? Given the many statistically significant variances and covariances within them, the answer would seem to be in the affirmative. To demonstrate this statistically, an analysis was conducted comparing the Hispanic1 versus Hispanic2 groups, except that now the Hispanic2 matrix was purposely computed incorrectly, with variables entered into it in the reverse order. These two Hispanic matrices must satisfy an assumption of grossly "different causal processes"; hence, they should be statistically unequal. As shown in Table 4, the chi square test in this comparison was 2,236, with GFIs equal to .67. There was no question that these two matrices fit one another poorly, so covariances and variances as found in the Tucson Study, if organized differently, can be shown to be unequal.

In the *National Longitudinal Study of Youth* matrices, the three academic achievement level variables correlated highly (> .68). As these were raw score variables, they also correlated with age (about .65). The HOME cognition variable had statistically significant relationships with achievement and problem behavior (mean *r*s .19, −.20, respectively).

As shown in Table 5, the results from the NLSY were substantively similar to those from the Tucson Substance Use Study, but this time in a nationally representative study with three ethnic groups and an over-representation of economically disadvantaged families. As the ethnic groups were unequal in size, we drew random samples of N = 335 from the White and Hispanic groups and used an equal number of Blacks. The tabled results show comparisons for these equal sized groups: the goodness-of-fit index ranged from .94 to .96, all very high values. Furthermore, the cross-ethnic comparisons of White vs. Blacks, Blacks vs. Hispanics, and Hispanics vs. Whites were no more different than two random halves of the Whites (GFI = .96). Other analyses, not shown here, used all individuals when comparing ethnic groups; no evidence was found for developmental differences in them either, but of course the goodness-of-fit was always better in the numerically larger groups. These findings again confirm the great similarity of covariance structure within and between different ethnicities.

Table 6. Wisconsin/California Study

Measure	Black (635) vs. White (3943)	Black (635) vs. Asian (906)	Black (635) vs. Hispanic (827)	Asian (906) vs. White (3943)	Hispanic (827) vs. White (3943)	Asian (906) vs. Hispanic (635)
χ^2	302.8	221.1	171.6	176.7	378.8	209.1
GFI (1st)	.93	.96	.97	.97	.93	.97
GFI (2nd)	1.0	.98	.99	1.0	1.0	.98
χ^2/N	.07	.14	.12	.04	.08	.14

Note. Degrees of freedom, 55. All chi squares statistically significant ($p < .05$).

In Table 6, Wisconsin/California data comparisons of four ethnic groups—Blacks, Whites, Hispanics, Asians—are presented. It is evident that all pairwise comparisons produced excellent fits. The goodness-of-fit indices equalled or exceeded .93 (mean GFI for all twelve matrices = .97). Although .93 is a very good fit, it tends to understate the degree of similarity—because the matrices producing this value involved comparisons of very dissimilar group sizes: nearly 4,000 Whites versus a smaller number of either Hispanics or Blacks. Notice, too, that even over an apparent cultural distance of Blacks and Asians, the fit to a common covariance matrix remained an excellent one. The GFIs were .97 and .99 for Blacks and Asians, respectively, and the "stress" of chi square per observation was only .12. Unfortunately, we lack comparisons for random halves of these ethnic groups; but given the previous results and the close similarity of these matrices, little reason exists to believe that they could show any greater degree of identity of covariance pattern than found in the cross-ethnic comparisons here.

Table 7 presents the remaining data sets. The fits of Bowling Green's and Richmond Youth Project's Black and White matrices, both computed from studies of self-reported delinquency, were excellent. The Prevention Study had one of the smallest samples, and it was unique in that it was a clinical sample (about 60% of families had alcohol abuse problems). The Hispanic's matrix fit the White1 random half ($x^2 = 69.0$) about as well as the two random White halves fit one another ($x^2 = 66.0$). The goodness-of-fits were lower than what we have seen in other samples, but this difference may reflect greater sampling variation due to smaller samples and the presence of parental psychopathology, which may have

Table 7. Bowling Green, Richmond Youth, and Prevention Studies

Measure	Bowling Green Study — Black (409) vs. White (469)	Richmond Youth Project — Black (1427) vs. White (1872)	Prevention Study — Hispanic (70) vs. White1 (70)	Prevention Study — Hispanic (70) vs. White2 (70)	Prevention Study — White1 (70) vs. White2 (70)
χ^2	.50[a]	557.8	87.8	69.0	66.0
GFI (1st)	1.0	.96	.91	.93	.91
GFI (2nd)	.90	.97	.85	.87	.92
χ^2/N	.00	.17	.63	.50	47

Note. Bowling Green Study, df = 36; Richmond, df = 55; Prevention, df = 45.
[a] Chi square non-significant

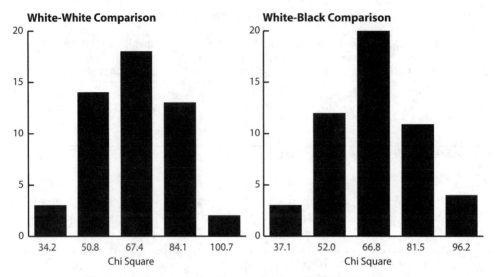

Figure 2. Monte Carlo Comparisons of Within Group vs. Between Group Covariance Matrices

influenced developmental process (N = 70 per group). In summary, the analyses of "provided" data in Tables 6 and 7 reinforced what we discovered in the analyses of the Tucson and nationally-based NLSY samples: a tremendous similarity of covariance structure within and between ethnic groups.

Monte Carlo Comparisons

In the previous within-ethnic group comparisons, one random half of an ethnic/racial group was compared to another. Of course, many random subdivisions of any population are possible. To explore variability in the *distributions* of chi square values, we ran a "bootstrapping" study for the NLSY Blacks (N = 549) and NLSY Whites (N = 836). One hundred random samples were drawn with replacement first from the Whites (each sample N = 125). These samples were used to form 50 comparisons. For each random W:W comparision, LISREL estimated a chi square under the assumption of equality of covariance matrices. Fifty random samples (N = 125) were also drawn from the Black group, and another set of fifty random samples (N = 125) from the White group. They were placed into 50 pairs of W:B covariance matrices, and for each pair, chi square values were estimated by LISREL.

Figure 2 presents the histograms of chi square values for the comparisons of Whites vs. Whites and Whites vs. Blacks. The distributions were nearly identical, approximately normal in shape, and showed equal mean values (W:W, M = 67.4; W:B, M = 66.8, s = 16.6 and 14.7, respectively). Although either mean chi square would be a statistical rejection of matrix equality, this rejection occurred when Whites' random samples were compared with one another as well as when Blacks' samples were compared with Whites'. In summary, repeated comparisons made on 200 random samples confirmed that covariance matrices across racial groups were no more dissimilar than covariance matrices *within* a racial group.

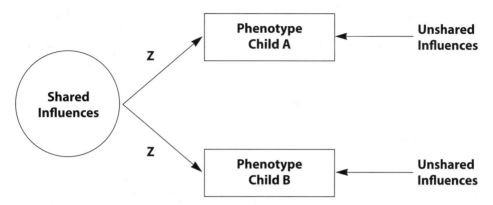

Figure 3. Path Model For Shared Influences On Siblings

Results for Covariance Matrices (Siblings)

The NLSY data provide a unique opportunity to compare familial covariance patterns across ethnic/racial groups. These data play a somewhat different role from the "individual" matrices in the determination of similarity of developmental process. In the "individual" matrices, a large number of measured variables were provided that may assess familial process, for instance, parental monitoring and intellectual stimulation. These measured variables, however, captured only that variation in family developmental process directly associated with those particular variables. In behavior genetic studies, correlations computed on pairs of biological or social relatives are used to capture variation associated with different theoretical processes.

As shown in Figure 3, the correlation of sibling A and B on a trait phenotype can be apportioned between two variance components: (1) shared variation that makes family members alike in a trait phenotype (but different from persons in another family) and (2) unshared variation that operates uniquely on each individual. The latter component would make family members dissimilar in a trait phenotype. The sibling correlation represents the influence of all shared variables tied to the family unit that are a source of behavioral resemblance among siblings. If this correlation were .30, then 30% of variation in the trait phenotype is attributable to "shared" variation and 70% to unshared.

Notice that in this apportionment, the correlation coefficient was not squared to yield "variance explained." Using the rules of path analysis, it can be seen that the variance in sibling A's trait phenotype (or B's) is just the path coefficient, z squared. Yet the correlation of the sibling A's with sibling B's trait phenotypes also has the mathematical expectation of z^2; hence, the trait phenotype's "variance explained" by shared developmental process is also the sibling correlation. In other words, the issue is not how well one can predict one siblings' trait score from the other's; but instead, how well all familial variation relates to trait variation. The remainder of phenotypic variation is attributable to unshared influences.

The advantage, then, of sibling correlations is that they detect the *maximum* influence of a particular type. In research inspired by a family study, shared familial variation may be assigned further to specific genes shared by siblings, or to

Table 8. National Longitudinal Study of Youth Siblings

Measure	Hispanic (128) vs. Black (156)	Hispanic (128) vs. White (319)	Black (156) vs. White (319)	White1 (160) vs. White2 (160)	Black1 (78) vs. Black2 (78)
χ^2	18.46[a]	26.90[a]	41.27	12.61[a]	7.28[a]
GFI (1st)	.96	.96	.95	.99	.99
GFI (2nd)	.98	.99	.99	.99	.99
χ^2/N	.07	.06	.09	.04	.05

Note. 21 degrees of freedom. Sample size is the average number of sibling pairs per matrix.
[a] Statistically nonsignificant (p > .05).

shared environmental processes, such as books available, parental surveillance of children and so on. Before these steps, however, familial covariance matrices can be used to ask, "Is shared family variation the same in different ethnic groups?" With additional groups of relatives, the behavioral variation within ethnic groups may be further apportioned among genetic variation, shared environmental variation and nonshared environmental variation (see Osborne, 1980).

To estimate familial effects, 6x6 covariance matrices were computed for NLSY Blacks, Hispanics, and Whites using the variables listed in Table 3. All data were double entered.[5] The matrices yielded sibling correlations for HOME environment, problem behavior, and academic achievement, respectively. Besides these sibling correlations, the matrices included the ordinary intercorrelations (on individuals) among the HOME, problem behavior, and achievement, and also sibling "cross-correlations," that is, the correlation of variable 1 in sibling A with variable 2 in sibling B (e.g., sibling A's achievement with sibling B's problem behavior). For the ethnic groups, pairwise comparisons of covariance matrices were conducted (B vs. W, B vs. H, and H vs. W). Pairwise comparisons were also constructed from random halves of the White and Black sibling groups.

Table 8 presents the LISREL fits of an estimated covariance matrix. These fits were all excellent, with goodness-of-fit values equal to or exceeding .95. The Whites fit the Blacks and Hispanics well (GFIs = .95–.99). The Hispanics also fit the Blacks well (GFIs .96–.99). The random subdivisions of both Whites and Blacks fit extremely closely (GFIs = .99). In terms of chi square per observation, the random fits were slighly better than the between group fits (random fits, .04–.05; between ethnic group fits, .06–.09). Although still excellent, the worse statistical fit was obtained in the comparison of the Whites and Blacks. It yielded the largest chi square per observation (x^2/N = .09), but nonetheless had GFIs (.96 to .99) that were satisfactory.

To present one familial correlation matrix, another analysis was done fitting Hispanic, White, and Black covariance matrices using a "3 group" LISREL solution. A maximum-likelihood estimate of the common correlation matrix was obtained from the standardized solution. In this analysis, the overall chi square was

---

5. In double entry data, the number of observations is twice the number of sibing pairs; it equals the number of individuals. The first N/2 cases in a variable consist of sibling A; the second N/2 cases consists of sibling B. Entered in this way, a sibling correlation closely approximates an analysis of variance intra-class correlation. Double-entried correlations are used routinely in behavior genetic studies.

Table 9. Pooled Sibling Correlation Matrix

Measure	HOME1	HOME2	ACH1	ACH2	PROB1	PROB2
HOME Quality1	1.0					
HOME Quality2	.76	1.0				
Achievement1	.29	.27	1.0			
Achievement2	.27	.29	.41	1.0		
Prob. Behav1	−.24	−.19	−.17	−.09	1.0	
Prob. Behav2	−.19	−.24	.09	−.17	.49	1.0
SD	14.7	14.7	11.8	11.8	14.4	14.4

Note. Double-entry sibling correlation matrix. Sibling correlations shown in bold. HOME scores scaled as HOME = 1/10 x HOME.

60.7 (df = 42), and the respective goodness-of-fit values were .96 for Hispanics, .95 for Blacks, and .98 for Whites. Table 9 presents this correlation matrix. Substantial sibling correlations were found for all three variables (achievement, .41; problem behavior, .49; and HOME, .76). The HOME was associated with better achievement and with fewer problem behaviors (r equalled .29 and −.24, respectively). The two developmental outcomes were only weakly related to one another (within individuals, −.17, within siblings, −.09). Thus, although both achievement and problem behavior were strongly familial, their familial causes may be distinct. Because the GFIs were all very good in all ethnic groups, this *pooled* correlation matrix would be the appropriate one for fitting more specific developmental models.

Discussion

Our main result was that developmental processes in different ethnic/racial groups were statistically indistinguishable. "Developmental process" refers to the association among variables in these groups and to the variables' total variances. This conclusion held for the examination of six data sources, containing a total of 3236 Blacks, 1643 Hispanics, and 8272 Whites, and in one data source, 906 Asians. The pattern of covariances and variances were essentially equal when one ethnic or racial group was compared with another, and this structural similarity *between* ethnic or racial groups was no less than that *within random halves* of a single ethnic or racial group. In the National Longitudinal Study of Youth data source, Blacks, Whites, and Hispanics were sampled to be nationally representative but to over-represent economically poor families; thus, these findings apply more broadly than just to middle class populations. Similarly, the measures used were varied, with some matrices based entirely on adolescents' self-reports and others based on parental reports and/or direct observations of the family. Few studies, however, employed direct observational assessments of behavioral outcomes. Outcomes included academic achievement, conduct disorders, delinquency, depression, IQ, and academic adjustment.

As discussed earlier, a test of a 10 x 10 covariance matrix not only rules out differences in measured variables, but also differences in *unmeasured* (minority unique) ones that causally relate to either antecedent variables or developmental outcomes. Nonetheless, our findings have failed to confirm this widespread belief: If these (unmeasured) influences existed, then covariance matrices on measured variables *that resulted from them* would be unequal across ethnic and racial groups. That is, a statistical model specified for one group would be misspecified for another. In a related approach, unmeasured familial influences would be expected to change *within* sibling pair correlations from one ethnic/racial group to another. Again, in sibling data for large samples of different ethnic/racial groups, we found that Hispanics, Whites, and Blacks were alike in familial influences on achievement and problem behavior. Process similarity, of course, does not mean that ethnic/racial group *average levels* would be the same for either antecedent variables or developmental outcomes.

The Cultural Bias Argument and IQ

In overview, our position has been that the causal processes leading to individual differences in developmental outcomes may be similar across American ethnic/racial groups. Comparable issues arose in an earlier controversy that centered on the "equivalence" of intelligence test scores for American Blacks and Whites. The critics of IQ tests argued that they were "culturally biased" against Blacks (and other minorities). In its strong form, the cultural bias argument assumed a different causation of IQ within Black and White populations. In a weaker form, this argument was no more than pointing out that Blacks and Whites may experience intellectual environments that were differentially stimulating.

In its strong form, the cultural bias argument is another "difference" argument, of the type weakened by the data reviewed in this article. The argument postulated that, in Blacks, IQ test scores would have the ordinary causes present in Whites, as well as causes unique to Black populations (e.g, a distinct Black dialect that interfered with the acquisition of standard English). In all these hypotheses, some culturally unique influence would act to suppress obtained IQ test scores. With these mutually canceling influences, an IQ score of 90 in a Black child might underestimate his/her true intellectual ability—an ability which would have shown itself in the absence of the culturally unique influences.

Social scientists began to doubt this cultural bias explanation as evidence accumulated showing that IQ scores had the same network of correlates in Blacks and Whites (Jensen, 1980). If an IQ score of 90 actually under-estimated a Black child's intellectual ability (at least over the short term), then this child would be able to show a greater ability to learn academic material than a White child with the same tested IQ. By comparing the regression lines of IQ score on later academic achievement (e.g., first year college grades), computed separately for Blacks and Whites, researchers discovered little support for this expectation—children with IQs of 90 got approximately the same grades (or other nonacademic outcomes), regardless of their racial groupings. In a special issue of the American Psychologist on IQ testing, Cole (1981) observed:

> From a large number of educational and employment studies, the most common conclusion has been that many tests predict various educational and employment performances about as well for minority groups (blacks and women being by far the most frequently studied minority groups) as for majority groups. (p. 1070)

In the same journal volume, Reschly (1981) seconded this conclusion:

> "Conventional tests are nearly always found to be largely unbiased on the basis of technical criteria—for example, internal psychometric properties, factor structure, item content, atmosphere effects, and predictive validity. (p. 1098)

Or, as Berry et al. (1992) concluded,

> It appears that earlier views that sought to put the blame for unequal test scores primarily on the tests have lost much of their momentum...a serious concern about cultural bias has become and will remain an inherent aspect of assessment, just as there is continuing concern for validity and the establishment of norms....It is now generally recognized that within a society intergroup differences in test scores often are a reflection of a real state of affairs. (p. 313)

When IQ tests do show a slight bias, it lies in opposite direction to that predicted by cultural bias theory—a single regression line slightly overpredicting Blacks' academic performance. In summary, the emerging consensus among testing experts is that cultural bias in the IQ tests themselves is no more than a minor source of group IQ difference (Barrett & Depinet, 1991; Synderman & Rothman, 1987).

With regard to our analytic strategy, investigating the predictive validity of an IQ test would be equivalent to comparing two x two covariance matrices (e.g., variable 1 = IQ test score, variable 2 = chemistry grades) computed for the majority and minority groups separately. We know, from this research literature on "bias" in IQ testing, that these matrices must be statistically similar—as their equality would be a prerequisite to that of regression lines.

Our analysis has been more demanding, however. We have included both independent variables and developmental outcomes in larger matrices than the 2x2 IQ matrix, permitting greater possibility for violations of equivalence. In addition, the defenders of IQ tests merely argued that "IQ" was the same construct in majority and minority groups—that it could do equally well the task of predicting academic or job performance, regardless of individuals' ethnic identities. We make here a stronger claim about causal process for the variables examined in this article—that all the influences giving rise to individual differences in developmental outcomes are essentially equivalent in majority and minority groups. Although only one of our matrices directly included an IQ outcome, several others had proxy measures for it, such as grades or standardized achievement tests. And in all these comparisons, including the earlier sibling analysis of latent family influences, causal process appeared to be similar across ethnic and racial lines. Thus, our claim would be that IQ, as with its related variables, is not only the same construct in different ethnic or racial groups but that it would also possess identical developmental determinants in different racial or ethnic groups.

In this article, we have not tested for equivalence in means. In the IQ situation, minority populations tend to have lower mean IQ scores and lower academic performance scores than the majority population. Although the source of *average*, level differences between ethnic and racial groups has not been emphasized thus far in the article, it is clearly essential to integrate mean levels with our understanding of the etiology of individual differences in any complete theory of behavioral development.

Two views of ethnic/racial mean differences may be defended: (1) that they arise from different causal processes than individual differences, and (2) that they arise from different antecedent levels in a common causal process. In the next two sections, both alternatives are discussed, and we give several reasons for favoring the latter.

Different Causal Processes

It is conceivable that the causal processes leading to *average* levels would be different from those creating *within* group variation in behavior. This possibility is real in the mathematical sense in that *averages* and *correlations* are statistically independent. However, for this alternative to hold requires also that Factor X (minority unique) contributes to *average* level but does *not* contribute to variation among individuals.

For example, consider that Down's syndrome children are mentally retarded because they inherit a chromosomal abnormality—three copies of chromosome 22. There are clearly large mean differences between normal children (IQ range 70–130) and Down's syndrome ones (IQ range 25–70). Consider, however, that other familial influences may be similar for the two groups. If mothers' IQs (range: 70–130) were plotted on the "X" axis, and children's IQs on the "Y", the parent-child regression on IQ could be .50 for both groups of children. In this example, the Down's children's mean IQ level would be affected by a different developmental process from that influencing their variation around that mean. That is, the latter variation might have similar familial causes in both Down's and normal children.

But this argument—influences on means separate from those on individual differences—is a strong one because it requires nearly *equal exposure to and influence of* the unique causal mechanism in all exposed persons. Although this may make sense for a chromosomal abnormality with devastating developmental consequences, it is more difficult to imagine that *psychosocial* processes affect all persons within a given group equally. For example, Ogbu (1987) acknowledged that not all Black Americans would experience racial discrimination in the same way:

> Of course, not everyone feels this way. Some black Americans do not identify with the oppositional identity and cultural frame of reference; some do so only marginally. (p. 165)

If Factor X (minority unique) contributed to both group *averages* and to *within* group variation, then its influence should have been apparent in our earlier analyses (at least for the developmental outcomes which were chosen). The greater the number of measured variables in our matrices, the less likely some "ghost" process exists as a unique developmental mechanism in any one minority group. Indeed, the example just given—of a chromosomal abnormality—is a poor one for arguing that ethnic and racial differences exist: Down's syndrome would affect all racial/ethnic groups in the same way.

Different Levels on Common Antecedents

The other explanation of group *averages* is that they result from different average levels on antecedents in the pan-ethnicity, common developmental pathways. Large average level differences in common antecedents may work through causal pathways to become smaller but still socially and statistically significant differences in the developmental outcomes. From this viewpoint, a focus on "averages" *or* on within-group "individual variation" would be misleading; they are simply different summaries of the total variation. Turkheimer (1991) noted that, insofar as IQ variation is concerned, any developmental process that has been postulated to influence group averages should also influence within-group variation, and vice versa:

> Although the two-realms [group and individual] hypothesis is now the received view of nature and nurture... it is implausible to suggest that the forces shaping the IQs of groups are different from those shaping the IQs of individuals; environmental and genetic factors can affect only individuals, one at a time.... *There are two realms of variance, between and within groups; there is only one realm of development.* (pp. 393–394, italics added)

The "one realm" model, with its universalistic assumptions, possesses great theoretical parsimony. It permits generalization of findings from one ethnic/racial group to another, and it eliminates hypotheses that refer to minority unique variables. One must wonder, therefore, why so little theorizing in social science has followed this route. In the next section, we consider this issue and its possible remedies.

Genetic Differences and the IQ Issue

In the main, opposition to a "one developmental" process theory arose from the IQ controversy, namely, from the observation of lower *average* IQs in American Blacks than Whites. This average IQ difference, with its socially meaningful implications for securing higher education and more prestigious jobs, demanded some explanation from social scientists. One explanatory route—common process, different levels on the developmental antecedents,—was acceptable so long as those antecedents were environmental (e.g., social class, home environmental quality) but not if they were genetic. The problem for social scientists has been that 50%–70% of the within ethnic/racial group variation owes to a genetic etiology (Plomin, DeFries, & McClearn, 1990; Bouchard et al., 1990). The common developmental pathway model merely asserts that the cause of group average differences lies in common antecedents, environmental and/or genetic.[6] But with scientific evidence of genetic influences on individual differences in IQ increasingly secure, the common process model automatically raised for social scientists the issue of racial/ethnic differences in genetic alleles related to IQ variation. According to Shepard (cited in Cole, 1981),

> One reason that bias in mental testing is so volatile an issue is that it involves the specter of biological determinism, i.e., whether there is a large difference in

---

6. The antecedent variables in this article are usually presumed to represent "environmental" influences because they are labeled as environmental variables (e.g., social class, parental monitoring). However, genetic variation has been found in measures labeled environmental when they are treated as phenotypes in behavior genetic analyses (Plomin & Bergeman, 1991). Thus, there is a further reason to hypothesize genetic influences on *average* ethnic/racial differences.

intelligence (IQ) between black and white Americans which can be attributed largely to inherited differences. (p. 1067)

One way for social scientists to avoid the implication of genetic variation in ethnic/racial *average* differences was to postulate different causal processes for IQ in minority versus majority groups in the U.S. Like a walk down a garden path, the way at first looks good, with hereditarian hypotheses about ethnic/racial differences safely silenced.

But a pretty garden path can lead into brambles of brush and scrub oak; it may carry considerable theoretical cost. The assumption of "difference" meant that developmental findings from one group could not be generalized to another. It provokes a search for "difference" through the few statistically significant correlations among the greater number computed on minority and majority groups. Furthermore, these significant correlations are often given complex, psychosocial explanations—but with what prospect for independent replication? It also may reinforce group stereotypes—leading to a neglect of the considerable overlap between ethnic/racial groups in behavioral traits. It allows one developmental outcome—tested IQ scores—to drive thinking about many other outcomes, many of which correlate only weakly with IQ variation. In our view, all these liabilities have been accumulating at considerable cost to social science research.

It is not the aim of the article to settle the nature/nurture controversy for average racial IQ differences; the data do not permit a resolution that would be convincing to most social scientists (Loehlin, Lindzey, & Spuhler, 1975; Mackenzie, 1984). But we do want to encourage social scientists to think more in terms of common developmental pathways and less in terms of "difference."

Research Designs

One mechanism for thinking about common developmental processes is to consider offspring from inter-racial (ethnic) marriages. In these marriages, which are increasingly common in America, children would be genetically admixed. In addition, through contact with biological relatives on both sides, they may be culturally admixed as well. These children form a linking *bridge* between different social groups, which are not so culturally or genetically distant as widespread social stereotypes maintain. Indeed, they offer the opportunity for a unique and powerful research design for investigating the commonality of genetic and family environmental influence.

Consider, for example, the kinships pictured in Figure 4. This research design can demonstrate commonality of (familial) developmental processes. All families would be sampled through a racially or ethnically inter-married couple, who have an inter-racial (ethnic) child (cf. Family 2). Two additional families would be ascertained through the inter-racial couple via each parents' brother or sister. Thus, Family 1 would be a minority family with at least one child. The other would be a majority (White) family with at least one child (cf. Family 3).

In these families, there are covariance matrices for parent-child, child—uncle/aunt, child—spouse of uncle/aunt, and cousins. If (familial) developmental processes were identical for all children, regardless of racial group, than covariance matrices computed from the starting point of a majority child in Family 3,

Figure 4. Family Pedigree From Inter-Racial Child Proband

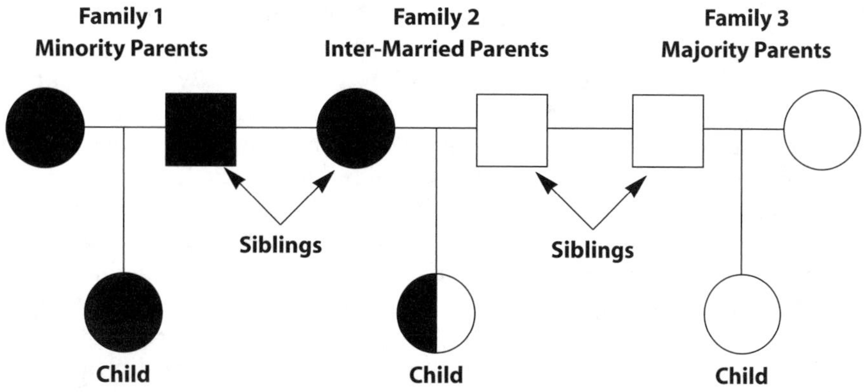

an inter-racial child in Family 2, and a minority child in Family 1, should be identical. Genetic influences would be indicated by a child's correlation to an uncle or aunt greater than to an uncle or aunt's *spouse*. Family environmental influences would be indicated by equal correlations to uncle/aunt versus their spouses (e.g., the child's resemblance to them is on the basis of similar social class levels in the adult siblings' families). Specific models, allowing for spousal resemblance and for direct measures of family environment, could be constructed for the covariance matrices available in Figure 4's research design (Neale & Cardon, 1992).

In this research design, it is also possible to investigate the origin of racial/ethnic mean differences. If *average* levels as well as individual differences were genetically influenced, then the interracial child should have an average (trait) score midway between that of his/her cousins on both sides. If no genetic influence exists, then all cousins would have equal means. However, if sampling of particular families were unrepresentative, it may result in offsprings' average differences, which would then simply reflect these sampling biases. Therefore, a better test of the "mean difference" hypothesis would be to compare the intercepts of the regression of child on mid-parent scores. The intercept has the mathematical expectation: a = child mean – b (midparent mean), where a is the intercept, b is the pooled (if developmental processes are common) regression coefficient, the mid-parent mean is the average of the mother's and father's trait scores, and child mean is the offsprings' average trait score. For a genetically-influenced trait that has a higher majority than minority mean, the intercepts should order Minority Family 1 < Inter-married Family 2 < Majority Family 3.[7]

---

7. As this research design is used for purposes of illustration here, we do not detail its possible strengths and weaknesses. To mention a few issues, if a variable correlates strongly with the decision to marry inter-racially (ethnically), then its variance might be restricted in these families. Comparisons of inter-racial (ethnic) parents and others from their respective populations could reveal the degree of selection bias, and various statistical approaches may be adopted to deal with it. For other variables, self-selection may not be a problem. For the test of genetic mean levels, it would be necessary that the minority parent have little majority biological parentage in his/her own parents or grandparents. Finally, this design would require solving practical problems of recruitment of the proband families and the families of the parents' siblings. A design involving three families presents difficult practical problems, because cooperation is needed from siblings of the proband family.

Of course, other research designs have been proposed to investigate whether racial/ethnic average differences in traits possess a partly genetic basis, including transracial adoption studies (Weinberg, Scarr, & Waldman, 1992) and non-familial genetic admixture studies (MacKenzie, 1984). In these research designs, the focus is on racial differences—rather than on a *commonality* of developmental process—nonetheless, they are methods, each with strengths and limitations, for evaluating empirically hypotheses about a genetic basis to ethnic/racial mean differences. Avoidance of this issue should not allow social science to take an enticing "garden path" of assuming development differs among racial/ethnic groups. Over the long run in our opinion, it will be better to settle this issue with well-designed empirical studies. Perhaps research in this volatile area might move forward if researchers would heed Loehlin's (1992b) advice for behavioral genetic studies of racial differences in IQ: (1) Say clearly what your results mean and what they do *not* mean, (2) Put matters in a quantitative perspective, and (3) Be tactful.

Applications

In work on ethnic/racial groups, the results of this article can suggest a few "DON'TS." The "DON'TS" all relate to statistical pitfalls in the comparison of groups:

(1) when a covariance is significantly greater than zero in one group but not in another group, DON'T automatically interpret this finding as a group difference
(2) when separate multiple regression equations are computed for the majority and minority groups, DON'T attribute a group difference to different unstandardized regression weights, or to different orders of extracted variables

Although both procedures are common, they are flawed because they fail to show that a *difference* between majority and minority groups is statistically significant. The statistically correct procedures are either to (1) test for the significance of the difference of two unstandardized regression coefficients, or (2) test race x variable interactions, in addition to main effects, in multiple regression equations using unstandardized variables.

Although the latter represent proper statistical tools, we believe that they, as well, may be too liberal. With neither prior hypotheses nor independent replications, we believe that researchers should accept the null hypothesis of no group differences until such time as scientifically acceptable evidence for differences is forthcoming. Furthermore, this argument extends beyond racial and ethnic group differences that have been our primary example. In studies of males and females, or of families with dual and single earners, or of children with and without day care experiences, many of the same problems would exist. As in the case of racial and ethnic group differences, these other group comparisons are often done without prior hypotheses about different processes; without replications across different samples; and without concern for whether correlation coefficients are actually statistically different from one another (nor do many studies compare the variance-covariance matrices, which is the more stringent and proper test). The techniques illustrated in this paper offer a methodological approach that should be extended generally for the study of group differences with respect to developmental processes.

In conclusion, in the realm of IQ/achievement and social adjustment, we found that the developmental process was not specific to any racial or ethnic group. Our finding, of course, does not exclude group-unique developmental processes in other developmental outcomes not covered by our data matrices. Nonetheless, we expect that the results shown for the groups studied in this article, which were ethnically diverse (Hispanic, White, Black, and Asian), and which were also diverse in social class origin, geographic location, variables sampled, and identity of target respondents, will generalize widely: *that the developmental process is indeed invariant across U.S. racial and ethnic groups.* Substantively, these findings imply that researchers should seek the determinants of *average level* differences between ethnic and racial groups in average levels of antecedent variables that act through common developmental pathways. Researchers should also be encouraged: results they obtain for one ethnic group, in one U.S. geographic location, will probably generalize to other groups and locations. Powerful generalization is the hallmark of a successful scientific enterprise; it bodes well for the future success of social science that developmental processes are alike in many subgroups of *Homo sapiens.*

References

Achenbach, T. M. (1991). *Manual for the youth self-report: A profile.* Burlington: University of Vermont, Department of Psychiatry.

Baker, P. C., & Mott, F. L. (1989). *NLSY child handbook 1989: A guide and resource document for the National Longitudinal Survey of Youth 1986 child data.* Columbus, Ohio: Ohio State University, Center for Human Resource Research.

Barrett, G. V., & Depinet, R. L. (1991). A reconsideration of testing for competence rather than for intelligence. *American Pschologist, 46,* 1012–1024.

Berry, J. W., Poortinga, Y. H., Segall, M. H., & Dasen, P. R. (1992). *Cross-cultural psychology: research and applications.* New York: Cambridge University Press.

Bouchard, T. J., Jr., Lykken, D. T., McGue, M., Segal, N. L., & Tellegen, A. (1990). Sources of human psychological differences: The Minnesota study of twins reared apart. *Science, 250,* 223–228.

Brown, D. E. (1991). *Human universals.* Philadelphia, PA: Temple University Press.

Buss, D. M. (1989). Sex differences in human mate preferences: Evolutionary hypotheses tested in 37 cultures. *Behavioral and Brain Sciences, 12,* 1–49.

Caldwell, B. M., & Bradley, R. H. (1984). *Home observation for the measurement of the environment.* Little Rock, Arkansas: University of Arkansas.

Center for Human Resource Research. (1991). *Home observation for measurement of the environment.* Columbus, Ohio: Ohio State University.

Cernkovich, S. A., & Giordano, P. C. (1992). School bonding, race, and delinquency. *Criminology, 30,* 261–291.

Chakraborty, R., Kamboh, M., Nwankwo, M., & Ferrell, R. (1992). Caucasian genes in American Blacks: New data. *American Journal of Human Genetics, 50,* 145–155.

Cole, N. S. (1981). Bias in testing. *American Psychologist, 36,* 1067–1077.

Coll, C. T. G. (1990). Developmental outcome of minority infants: A process-oriented look into our beginnings. *Child Development, 61,* 270–289.

Cudeck, R. (1989). Analysis of correlation matrices using covariance structure models. *Psychological Bulletin, 105*, 317–327.

Dunn, L. M., & Dunn, F. C. (1981). *PPVT—Revised manual.* Circle Pines, Minnesota: American Guidance Service.

Flannery, D. J., Vazsonyi, A. T., Torquati, J., & Fridrich, A. H. (1994). Ethnic and gender differences in risk for early adolescent substance use. *Journal of Youth and Adolescence, 23*, 1–19.

Goodman, R., & Stevenson, J. (1989) A twin study of hyperactivity—II. The aetiological role of genes, family relationships and perinatal adversity. *Journal of Child Psychology and Psychiatry, 30*, 691–709.

Green, J. A. (1992). Testing whether correlation matrices are different from each other. *Developmental Psychology, 28*, 215–224.

Harrison, A. O., Wilson, M. N., Pine, C. J., Chan, S. Q., & Buriel, R. (1990). Family ecologies of ethnic minority children. *Child Development, 61*, 347–362.

Heath, S. B. (1989). Oral and literate traditions among Black Americans living in poverty. *American Psychologist 44*, 367–373.

Helms, J. E. (1992). Why is there no study of cultural equivalence in standardized cognitive ability testing. *American Psychologist, 47*, 1083–1101.

Hindelang, M. J., Hirschi, T., & Weiss, J. G. (1988). *Measuring delinquency.* Beverley Hills, CA: Sage.

Hirschi, T. (1969). *Causes of delinquency.* University of California Press.

Jensen, A. R. (1969). How much can we boost IQ and scholastic achievement? *Harvard Educational Review, 39*, 1–123.

Jensen, A. R. (1980). *Bias in mental testing.* New York: Free Press.

Joreskog, K. G., & Sorbom, D. (1988). *LISREL 7: A guide to program and applications.* SPSS Inc.

Knight, G. P., Tein, J. Y., Shell, & Roosa, M. R. (1992). The cross-ethnic equivalence of parenting and family interaction measures among Hispanic and Anglo-American families. *Child Development, 63*, 1392–1403.

Lewontin, R. (1982). *Human diversity.* New York: Scientific American Books.

Loehlin, J. C. (1992a). *Latent variable models: An introduction to factor, path, and structural analysis* (2nd ed). Hillsdale, NJ: Lawrence Erlbaum Associates.

Loehlin, J. C. (1992b). Should we do research on race differences in intelligence? *Intelligence, 16*, 1–4.

Loehlin, J. C., Lindzey, G., & Spuhler, J. N. (1975). *Race differences in intelligence.* San Francisco, CA: W. H. Freeman.

Mackenzie, B. (1984). Explaining race differences in IQ: the logic, the methodology, and the evidence. *American Psychologist, 39*, 1214–1233.

Marsh, H. W., Balla, J. R., & McDonald, R. P. (1988). Goodness-of-fit indexes in confirmatory factor analysis: The effect of sample size. *Psychological Bulletin, 103*, 391–410.

McCall, R. B., Appelbaum, M. I., & Hogarty, P. S. (1973). Developmental changes in mental performance. *Monographs of the Society for Research in Child Development, 38*(Serial 150), 1–84.

McLoyd, V. C. (1990). The impact of economic hardship on Black families and children: Psychological distress, parenting, and socioemotional development. *Child Development, 61*, 311– 346.

Neale, M. C., & Cardon, L. R. (1992). *Methodology for genetic studies of twins and families.* Dordrecht: Kluwer Academic Publishers.

Ogbu, J. (1987). Cultural influences on plasticity in human development. In J. Gallagher & C. Ramey (Eds.), *The malleability of children.* New York: Brookes Publishing Co.

Ogbu, J. U. (1991). Immigrant and involuntary minorities in comparative perspective (pp. 3–33). In M. A. Gibson & J. U. Ogbu (Eds.), *Minority status and schooling: A comparative study of immigrant and involuntary minorities.* New York: Garland Publishing.

Osborne, R. T. (1980). *Twins: Black and white*. Athens, Georgia: Foundation for Human Understanding.

Plomin, R., & Bergeman, C. S. (1991). The nature of nurture: Genetic influences on "environmental" measures. *Behavioral and Brain Sciences, 14*, 373–427.

Plomin, R., DeFries, J. C., & McClearn, G. E. (1990). *Behavior genetics: A primer*. 2nd ed. San Francisco, CA: W. H. Freeman.

Reschly, D. J. (1981). Psychological testing in educational classification and placement. *American Psychologist, 36*, 1094–1102.

Rodgers, J. L., Rowe, D. C., & Li, Chengchang (in press) Beyond nature vs. nurture: DF analysis of nonshared influences on problem behaviors. *Developmental Psychology*.

Roosa, M. W., Tein, J., Groppenbacher, N., Michaels, M., & Dumka, L. (in press). Mothers' parenting behavior and child mental health in families with a problem drinking parent. *Journal of Marriage and the Family, 55*.

Rushton, J. P. (1988). Race differences in behavior: A review and evolutionary analysis. *Personality and Individual Differences, 9*, 1009–1024.

Russell, J. (1991). Culture and the categorization of emotions. *Psychological Bulletin, 110*, 426–450.

Slaughter-Defoe, D. T., Nakagawa, K., Takanishi, R., & Johnson, D. J. (1990). Toward cultural/ecological perspectives on schooling and achievement in African- and Asian-American children. *Child Development, 61*, 363–383.

Snyderman, M., & Rothman, S. (1987). Survey of expert opinion on intelligence and aptitude testing. *American Psychologist, 42*, 137–144.

Spencer, M. B. (1990). Development of minority children: An introduction. *Child Development, 61*, 267–269.

Steinberg, L., Mounts, N. S., Lamborn, S. D., & Dornbusch, S. M. (1991). "Authoritative parenting and adolescent adjustment across varied ecological niches." *Journal of Research on Adolescence, 1*, 19–36.

Steinberg, L., Dornbusch, S. M., & Brown, B. B. (1992). "Ethnic differences in adolescent achievement." *American Psychologist, 47*, 723–729.

Stringer, C. B., & Andrews, P. (1988). Genetic and fossil evidence for the origin of modern humans. *Science, 239*, 1263–1268.

Tanaka, J. S. (1987). "How big is big enough?": Sample size and goodness of fit in structural equation models with latent variables. *Child Development, 58*, 134–146.

Turkheimer, E. (1991). Individual and group differences in adoption studies of IQ. *Psychological Bulletin, 110*, 392–405.

Weinberg, R. A., Scarr, S., & Waldman, I. D. (1992). The Minnesota transracial adoption study: a follow-up of IQ test performance at adolescence. *Intelligence, 16*, 117–135.

20

Interpersonal Relationships and African-American Women's Educational Achievement

Sue Hammons-Bryner

Through ethnographic interviewing and participant observation, a year-long investigation examined social forces that inspired success in higher education among women of different class backgrounds attending college and majoring in social work. This paper explores the link between achievement and intimate relationships, emphasizing older brothers, for rural African-American females who enter college as first-generation students.

Importance and Uniqueness of the Focus

This inquiry challenged conventional perceptions about peripheral groups. The analyses suggested new ways of thinking about persons who work with—or care for—those who differ from the "norm." The in-depth study suggested that the concepts of "achievement" and "motivation" may be much more complex than previous studies have assumed and that parenting in one-parent families could have additional unexplored elements.

Existing literature claimed to establish motivational factors using white, urban, middle-class males; researchers chose to neglect or disparage the experiences of lower-status groups, in part because they found them puzzling or confounding. The dominant view associated academic achievement with the Protestant work ethic and success orientation, as measured by grades and test scores. Repeatedly, researchers in the most often cited studies (McClelland 1961, 1975; McClelland & Atkinson, 1948; McClelland et al., 1953; McClelland and Winter, 1969) reported the characteristics of women or members of minority groups as anomalies; studies of family configurations assumed that a few categories sufficed. Their findings, such as family characteristics that distinguish high-, middle-, and low-

An earlier version of this essay appeared in *SAGE*; 1995, 9, 1, Spring, 10–17 and is adapted/reprinted with the permission of the copyright holder/author.

achieving males, have been universalized. These generalizations have puzzled scholars because of their subsequent inability to explain variations in other groups. (For a complete listing of this era of achievement research, see Dweck & Elliot, 1983 or Hammons-Bryner, 1991.)

"No Crystal Stair": Redefining Achievement

As I studied women who persisted in education despite odds that overwhelmed the majority with these circumstances (Hammons-Bryner, 1991, 1992), I remembered a poem by Langston Hughes (1969), in which a mother urges her son to continue in the face of obstacles:

> So, boy, don't you turn back.
> Don't you set down on the steps
> 'Cause you finds it kinder hard.
> Don't you fall now—
> For I'se still goin', honey,
> I'se still climbin',
> And life for me ain't been no
> crystal stair (p. 20).

Like the woman in Hughes's poem, these participants did not have a "crystal stair" to success.

Psychological factors, such as achievement, were constrained for these women by color, age, power, and gender; the social and cultural contexts in which they lived interacted with the effects of relationships on motivation (Hammons-Bryner, 1993). Findings from this investigation often clashed with the established literature, which discusses motivation as competitiveness or as the desire to excel (McClelland, 1961, 1975). According to the standard view, a highly motivated person performs best in competitive situations, generally experiences little anxiety or fear of failure, and prefers an occupation that provides rewards for *individual* achievement, such as sales, engineering, architecture, or law, rather than a job such as social work, where seniority may count more than performance in the salary calculation.

For the women in this study, the common idea of the need for achievement (competition against a standard of excellence) might have been less important than striving toward goals that relate to responsibility, such as financial and family obligations. This inquiry evaluated factors, including relationships, that motivate achievement for poor, rural women who are in college. Society views college as a vehicle that less-valued groups can use to escape their immediate environments. Research is warranted to analyze the validity of this view as applied to rural women, the working class, or people of color.

The assumption of some mainstream sociologists that problems lie with the contestants, rather than the standards, is too simple (Macleod, 1987).

Research Methodology

Eight of the women involved in the study were African-Americans, aged 19 to 42, who came from low-income rural backgrounds in the southeastern United

States. For this investigation, I defined achievement as the motivation to enroll and persist in higher education. An intimate relationship became one reported by an informant as close or influential. The influence of older brothers was a focus that evolved from a discussion of relationships that affected college enrollment and attendance. In the first set of interviews, several women discussed brothers who had acted in various ways to inspire them to concrete behaviors, such as homework, which eventually conveyed them to a level of learning that resulted in college enrollment. This brothers' confidence guided them to self-concepts that enabled them to dare to become the first in their families to enroll in college; this encouragement was particularly important because they lacked positive signals from teachers or friends.

To identify the participants, I surveyed all the social work majors at "Rural College." They answered a questionnaire that I had prepared to assess a variety of characteristics. When I interviewed the ones selected, I was interested in role models as one aspect of the influence of social structure on motivational levels and expected to find information by asking both prepared questions and any follow-up questions that occurred to me. As I interviewed the 8 women who were African-Americans, several began to discuss influential older brothers.

The interviews averaged one hour and were taped and transcribed in full. They were conducted in the building where the students took classes in their major and where 3 of the 8 women worked as student assistants. For the most part, the women surprised me by their eagerness to talk. I think that their need to speak, especially about the pain that lack of intimacy brought, probably encouraged this rapport as much as the bond that we formed. Because I did not know at the outset what the particularities of each woman's relevant experience would be, I limited the number of questions that were preset. Rather, responses greatly influenced the order of topics, the time spent on each subject, and the introduction of subsequent concerns.

In these first interviews, the areas about which I sought information were motivation for enrollment, factors affecting persistence, post-enrollment changes in motivation and autonomy, and modifications in achievement anticipated after graduation. Additional issues that emerged in early interviews and that I incorporated in later ones included the influence of grandmothers, older brothers, and children (Hammons-Bryner, 1995).

The second phase of the project consisted of another round of interviews conducted four months after the first. I had assumed by this stage that older brothers were significant and that the answers to my questions in the second interviews would help explain their influence in homes that are usually classified as single parent. The format for these interviews was more focused than the first, because I was intent on developing observed patterns as well as seeking information that might contradict the initial findings.

At the end of the formal interviews, observation began because I believed that this method would yield a more holistic picture than my original questionnaire or the interviews alone could do. While observing, I watched the informants react to events and discovered factors that led to changes in analysis.

The stories that I heard about older brothers were similar to some earlier literature that described achievement patterns among Asian-American immigrants. In these households, parents speak little English and cannot help with homework but demonstrate respect for education by turning off the television, giving the children treats as a reward for good grades, and holding the oldest sibling responsible for the younger ones' education (Caplan, Whitmore, & Choy, 1989). Many of my respondents went to college from absent-father homes with a mother who could not read or write; yet, a combination of circumstances gave the student a picture of herself as a person who could succeed in higher education. None of these women had a teacher or parent who was inspiring, as often occurs for middle-class students.

Other family members, including grandmothers and older brothers, nurtured a sense of self that led these women to use grammar, select interests, and comport themselves unlike others in the same circumstances. These characteristics, linked with societal factors, led to enrollment in college. By discussing achievement in classifications that restricted family types to choices such as nuclear, extended, and single-parent, the literature separates into categories that distort. In some homes, a brother at least ten years older than his sister influences her to succeed despite all odds against her. This pattern seems to appear more often in rural and urban homes than in the suburbs. Age, birth order, and family income probably bear upon achievement and sibling influence as well. More research should explore these ideas and provide additional details, which are necessarily limited by studying one set of individuals in one place at one time.

The pattern of older children helping younger ones is common in many families of a certain size. However, it is astonishing to find that younger siblings could experience greater upward mobility than older ones without extensive changes in the income of the family of origin as well as a decrease in the opportunity structure caused by a recession during the time of the study. In addition, the idea of male older siblings encouraging younger sisters contradicts tales of fear-of-success socialization. The differences between Euro- and African-American attitudes toward female academic achievement may help to explain this finding. Traditionally, African-American families have stressed education for daughters as much as (or more than) for sons.

During the initial interviews, the women appeared to receive little or no encouragement from any support network because, on the questionnaire, I had asked about "inspiring teachers" or parental role models. Later, I found that having an older brother gave women in homes without a father the sense of security, added income, and a feeling of nurturing that many researchers assume to be some key advantages for nuclear families. This pattern distorts the findings of most comparative studies. Taken together, these women's stories reveal a picture of African-American males in a positive family role, which is different from the "endangered species" discussion (Austin & Dodge, 1992; Brown et al., 1992; Greenberg & Schneider, 1992; Zimmermann & Maton, 1992).

In claiming that these males aided achievement motivation, I assert that stories of females struggling to rear children alone, of educational gender bias in homes, and of absent-father homes are but a fraction of the familial interaction patterns in America. I am aware that there are homes where the family dynamics are different from those that my participants discussed. However, women in similar circumstances may be touched significantly by *some* pattern.

At root—the thesis of this article—is a story of women who grow up in rural poverty, are poorly educated in classrooms where they suffer from denigrating remarks about their success potential, yet who form dreams, do more than wish, become change agents, make goals come true, and live them out. Women's success struggles are different from men's, in a similar manner and for reasons of expectations, as other female experiences differ from males'. According to Chodorow's (1978) views in *The reproduction of mothering*, feminine personality in any society comes to define itself in relation and connection to other people more than masculine personality does. Nested in this study inside relationships of care, responsibility, and sometimes violence, the participants' lives were interwoven with others. Family complexity strains female students' educational focus more dramatically than it does males'. This different success motivation may not always be negative; however, it may be formed in nurture and for nurture. That aspect is also part of the unfolding story.

Patterns of Achievement and Relationships

Respondents reported that college enrollment changed their existing relationships, that a form of distancing prevented new associations from intimacy, that the lack of intimacy, past and present, affected achievement, and that older brothers had helped to impell them toward college.

Achievement and Intimacy in Rural Women

For these women, and perhaps for others with similar characteristics, many traditional motivators were missing, muffled, or obstructing. For example, women are often depicted as viewing college attendance as a marriage market (Fine and Zane, 1989; Holland and Eisenhart, 1990), for the pursuit of the so-called "MRS degree." This attitude did not surface in my interviews nor in observation with the informants and their families. Abeline, Alice, Cora, and Karora, who were all women in their twenties, did not date at all and did not want to date. As part of their search for success, they may even have avoided intimate relationships. Even Beverly, who was older, had not had a serious relationship in years and "wasn't looking."

Among her sample, Higginbotham (1980) found that a larger proportion of women from working-class backgrounds was single. She explained this statistic in terms of class differences in socialization and mobility strategies. She theorized that the parents of women from working-class backgrounds stressed educational achievement more than other personal goals. These women never viewed marriage as a means of mobility and focused primarily upon education, postponing interest in, and decisions about, marriage. In contrast, women from middle-class backgrounds were expected to marry and were encouraged to integrate family and educational goals throughout their schooling. Thus a perspective that considers reference group theory as it may apply at the intersections of class, race, and gender is needed to analyze individuals whose conditions vary from dominant culture models.

None of the women sought or found romance from their college experience or dated other students. They rarely formed campus same-sex friendships either. Many reported growing away from the friend and family relationships that they had before enrollment. When I asked about support systems, some women hesitantly mentioned a relative. None responded by naming a friend. When I asked, "How about friends?" the immediate response was some form of "I don't really have any friends." Some of them added, "I don't have time." Even the three women who seemed to be friends (Mona Faye, Monnie, and Sandy) gave this response. Long-term friendships in their communities seemed to have changed when one person entered college while the other remained in the old patterns.

As an achievement strategy, my participants who persisted in college seemed to have divorced themselves to some extent from classmates. Especially the students in their twenties also avoided (by not dating, for example) intimate relationships with the opposite sex, as observed in studies by Faunce (1980) and Holland and Eisenhart (1990). Their approach may support Fordham's (1988) concept expounded in her article, "Racelessness as a factor in black students' school success" in that some students may be employing role distancing.

In the close relationships that participants did keep, change was evident, especially with parents or spouses who had local roots and extended kin networks. These rural residents frequently perceived formal schooling as the way that one prepares to leave the community (Deyoung, Huffman, & Turner, 1989). Unsurprisingly, these parents or spouses viewed school success for the participants with uneasiness. The school's accomplishment of creating norms for independence and achievement might cost the students the support of their peers or familial groups.

In *Educated in Romance: Women, Achievement, and College Culture*, Holland and Eisenhart (1990) state that two-thirds of the women in their study enrolled in college with sound educational histories and high professional aspirations but left with intensely reduced ambitions. The authors attribute much of this change to the power of peer groups. Perhaps this influence explains why many of the women in my inquiry discouraged relationships to facilitate success. (See also McKenna, 1990.) Several women experienced changes in relationships with significant others during their time in college. They were genuinely and ardently dedicated to clarifying (and even recreating) their own sense of personal identity.

One woman's comments seemed to indicate vacillation. Monnie's remarks about her marriage often contradicted what she had said previously. On one occasion, she reported that she told her husband that they were moving if she obtained a job elsewhere; on two others, she told me that she would not think of moving because of her husband. Once, I suspected from her appearance that she was the victim of physical abuse; on another day she described her husband as "sweet." This relationship may have been in a state of flux.

The only participant who mated during college, Sandy, married someone from her hometown. Sandy had no relationship at the beginning of the study and made statements similar to the ones that Cora, Karora, Alice, Beverly, and Abeline made. During the study, she formed a serious relationship, which she described as "leading to marriage." She was constantly comparing her boyfriend favorably with the father of her children. Her twelve-year-old son, though, did not like the new friend, which worried Sandy. She reported that her boyfriend seemed to support her in her drive for success and in other ways. However, Sandy, who graduated from junior college with a B average and dreams of a career as an elementary teacher or a school social worker, took a job at a fast-food restaurant after marriage and, at this point, has not pursued senior college.

Because they are so interwoven, the importance of any one factor, such as race, gender, or class, is hard to assess. In her research, Mickelson (1989) suggests that being female is much more important for determining achievement for African-Americans than for whites and that middle-class black women receive the best returns on higher education of *any* black group. (This idea is challenged by Higginbotham, 1980). One of the differences between the African-American college and the white college that Holland and Eisenhart (1990) studied is a contrast in the attitude toward academic effort. More often, black students perceived courses as hurdles in a race for credentials; white students spoke more often of the desire to perform "well" that McClelland (1961) discussed.

Rejection

Lack of a desired intimate relationship could also affect motivations for achievement. One difficult situation to accept or overcome is parental rejection, an event that can leave the child emotionally bare and afraid to be dependent. One woman, Mona Faye, was still struggling to deal with the effects of being the sole child given up for adoption by her mother.
She expressed the pain this way:

> MF: If I had had somebody to come into my life when I was eight years old, that would have helped me. That would have let me be a child a little while longer. 'Cause I had to be an adult almost by the time I was eight years old.
>
> If I could have been a child just a little while longer, I'd have been better. On another day, she explained further:
>
> MF: You see, my mother she gave me up for adoption, and she didn't give up any of the others, and even today if I try to sit down and talk with her about it and ask her why, she won't say, she just won't say (pauses), and I can't understand, from being a mother myself, how anyone could give up a child.
>
> SHB: Would you say that you are bitter?
>
> MF: I can't never forgive it.

Her adoptive mother, a cousin of her biological mother, lived next door to Mona Faye and provided much of the care for her two children. Her biological mother and siblings lived in the same town. Working as a house cleaner, the adoptive mother, with her husband, reared her three children with Mona Faye. The adoptive mother had a sixth-grade education, and her adoptive father, a third-grade one. Mona Faye stated that neither of them could read or write and that she did all the reading and writing for the family. Somewhere in her childhood, the man of the house deserted them. Often working seasonal farm jobs, the family never received any form of public assistance.

Anger could cover hurt feelings; in my study, perhaps it stemmed from a sense of loss. The participants longed for the women who nurtured them as children; even more, they missed the women whose love and support they never received. The necessity of "going it alone" hurt. One might compare some of these women to immigrants, who left close relatives in the old country and never saw them again.

Lack of a positive intimate relationship impelled some women into college in another way. Women revealed traumatic relationships with fathers, stepfathers, or husbands that had effects on self-esteem and financial well-being. These experiences sparked and strengthened their determination to get a college degree and professional status. To them, education was the main avenue for escaping dependence on men, a situation that they viewed as unpleasant.

The Influence of Older Brothers

Several women were reared by the combination of their mothers and brothers at least ten years older than they were. Taken together, their stories revealed a special relationship; these individuals reported coming straight home from school and customarily mentioned playing in the neighborhood (for example, ball games with brothers). They used the term "father figure" to describe their brothers, not referring to any contact with, memory of, or sometimes knowledge of, biological fathers. The women reported that their older brothers helped supervise their homework in grade school and encouraged them to further their education, a particularly direct example of the interweaving of close family relationships and achievement.

Alice reported that her brother, 10 years older than she, had, along with the mother, taken care of her all Alice's life. He worked at a nonunionized carpet factory that employed all the adults in the extended family.

Another participant, Karora, was Alice's only friend. Living with her mother, grandmother, two brothers, and two sisters, Karora, also 22-years-old, similarly illustrates those who grew up in a single-parent extended household. Because Karora's mother, her brother, and her grandmother graduated from high school and always had factory employment, the combined family income enabled them to avoid welfare. Karora had evidently felt some discomfort because she had no contact with her biological father, but thinking of her brother as fulfilling the roles that a live-in father would have played provided her with some comfort. Her brother contributed to the household expenses, listened to the younger children, and discussed their problems with his mother and grandmother. His interest in their welfare was solidly felt by the younger siblings.

Abeline typified the poor and working-class women in the study who sought to improve their socioeconomic status. The family relationships that she formed encouraged her, by negative example, to attend college. She did not mention her father in interviews; as she grew up, her household contained her mother, her grandmother, and three siblings. Her mother had an eighth-grade education, had been on relief for 4 years, and had been employed as a cook and a factory worker.

Abeline remained childless at 27 and had attended vocational-technical school before entering college. After graduating from high school, she began to work at the factory that employed her mother, older brother, and grand-mother, as well as her younger siblings. In part she enrolled in college to avoid the low-paid factory work that was traditional in her family. Her brother encouraged her to attend classes and to allot homework a high priority; he told her that she was too smart not to make something of herself. Six of the eight women lived in family situations with such meager income that welfare supplements often became necessary. One, Alice, seemed to avoid intimacy as part of an achievement strategy. Like three other participants, this 22-year-old student's mother cleaned houses. Single-parent families, lack of education, and early motherhood presented a combination of obstacles for other participants. Monnie's family characteristics, for example, rarely program women for success (no "crystal stair"). Because her father, a cotton mill worker, died during Monnie's babyhood, and because her mother had only a second-grade education (and could not read), the family of eight lived on Social Security checks for 18 years. Monnie explained that watching the struggles of her family, particularly those of her mother, had taught her how to persist in college and in life. Monnie became particularly close to one of her four older brothers,

> It was sixteen years between my oldest brother and me...
> He died sometimes since I was in college. He was my daddy, my brother, my best friend.

Schools still frequently view students as though they all lived in dorms with no financial or family responsibilities to interfere with the demands of college. School administrators prefer not to consider students' families and communities. The consequences of this artificial, but enforced, position remain many for low-income women. Ignoring a woman's family status or increasing her barriers to academic success because of it—a revealing intersection of race, class, and gender alienation—seriously discourages high achievement. Women become forced to make a choice between relationships and achievement (Hammons-Bryner, 1995). Exactly as Weis (1985a, 1985b) reports, instructors translate responsibilities at home as a lack of motivation at school. Women students feel the emotional toll of competing demands.

Especially for low-income women, being female means caring for relatives and neighbors. For many college students, the concept of one acceptable standard for academic behavior—"first things first"—may not be a problem. For women who enrolled past the traditional age, as members of the working class or a minority group, the standard and its implications posed nearly insurmountable obstacles. Sometimes worrying about a brother interfered with school success; for example, Monnie had a brother addicted to drugs.

During the Persian Gulf War, many male and female students at Rural College waited for the call to go overseas or had relatives who were in a similar state of limbo. Mona Faye had trouble studying because she was worried about her brother.

> MF: I'm trying. It's getting better. I guess the tireder I get, the harder it is. My brother...is going to Kuwait. I cried all the way to school this morning. He came to see me last night, and he cried. I've never seen him look like that. Only one time. And I didn't say anything. 'Cause I knew if I said something, both of us would really be crying. He went home, but he kept coming back over there, and I know he had to go either tomorrow or Saturday. And so I got a "bother." I don't know how I'll make it, but I'll make it somehow.

Although these informants came from families that had not set a precedent of college attendance, family relationships directly influenced their desire for higher education. Abilene stated, "My family told me I should go to college because there is nothing out there in the world worth anything without a college degree." Cora's family believed, "You will not be able to get a decent job without an education." As inspirations, all the women who had older brothers reported encouragement toward education from them from kindergarten through college.

Although the poorer parents or brothers could not function as college role models or advise from experience, they offered support in whatever way they could. They supplied abstract verbal support for the usefulness of education, furnished students without cars transportation to and from the college campus each term, supplied babysitters, and insisted that the students complete assignments.

Implications for Research and Policy

Among the African-American women in this study, social forces leading to the desire to matriculate in a community college and to the ability to persevere differed from those reported in typical respondents. The established catalysts for success from studies of high-achieving, white, metropolitan, middle-class males appeared either absent, muted, or inhibiting in these women's lives. Even studies of females did not always report the same motivators because researchers using females normally conducted their studies at large state universities using traditional-aged informants with college preparatory backgrounds and no dependents. Whereas "mainstream" studies found mate selection to be among women's reasons for attending college, this qualitative examination revealed the desire for independence from a mate as a more important motivator for enrollment. Habitually, studies of the effects of parenting categorize families of origin as "nuclear" or "single parent." Several women in this study had brothers ten or more years older who served as father figures and influenced the women's motivation to achieve despite odds. Many of the homes reported statistically as "single-parent homes" may not *feel* that way to the younger children. Both Karora and Alice referred to their oldest brothers as father figures. Grandfathers or older brothers can fulfill many of the functions of biological fathers. Some of the concerns of those analysts who write about single parenthood—only one income in the house, no male role model—may not truly exist. Women in the "single-parent" homes in my study often had four adult earners. Younger family members felt nurtured by mature siblings who dispensed advice, exhorted them to success, and encouraged concrete behaviors, such as homework, which would facilitate long-term achievement. Other concerns, like the chance to observe a stable marriage firsthand, may be important only to middle-class researchers. If women perceive that they had virtually two parents, their perception confounds reports that compare their aspirations and achievements with those of persons who grew up in homes with fathers. The conceptual features acquired could produce new counseling perspectives and other programs that would simplify these individuals' struggles to mainstream in the American Dream.

This ethnographic data conflicted with the customary conceptions of poor, rural African-American women as unmotivated or uninterested in pursuing higher education. Brothers who encourage younger sisters to achieve more than others in a circle of relatives, friends, and neighbors must be considered in discussions of role models, motivation, dysfunction, gender relations, black males, upward mobility, birth order, and fear of success.

Program developers and administrators seeking to encourage motivation among students have adopted perspectives on these topics that do not apply to the substantial portion of the population who do not conform to the mainstream.

Further study of subordinate groups would be useful for policy makers, college recruiters, educators, and researchers because of the need for new data about groups generally neglected in the social sciences literature. Even more important, new research often challenges the conventional perceptions about motivation of peripheral groups, especially groups increasingly "at risk" in the American educational system. There is more diversity among groups, such as poor single-parent families, than we thought in the past.

This study suggests policy for institutions serving nontraditional students. The findings could produce new teaching strategies, counseling perspectives, and academic programs that would simplify these students' struggle for achievement.

We need more research on what motivates members of nontraditional groups to attend college because conventional perceptions may not apply. If ignored in research, females, members of minority groups, older students, or those with uneducated parents cannot be included when effective and efficient social and educational policies are shaped. These students do not always choose to follow a different, less highly valued road to achievement; rather, the traditional route to success presents them with additional problems.

Even when members of subordinate groups accept the theoretical idea that equal opportunity exists for all people, they receive a distinct message that those who are "different" should not seek higher-level jobs if all their superiors at work have different group characteristics such as gender or skin color. Women, then, may be forced to choose between academic or occupational success and conformity to traditional views of femininity (Faunce, 1980; Horner, 1972); African-Americans may find their achievement-related behavior labeled "white" (Fordham, 1988; Fordham & Ogbu, 1986). Both women and members of minorities may experience the "impostor" syndrome, a feeling that success is the result of a false positive image (Turner et al., 1983).

Complex characteristics of multifaceted pluralistic societies, such as the United States, render analyses on or for a single group highly unreliable. In those studies with participants from marginal groups, few combine racial and ethnic groups, social class, and gender to include all the nontraditional phenotypical elements; an investigation that focuses on race, for example, usually overlooks gender (Clark, 1974; Faunce, 1980; Horner, 1972; Kerckhoff & Campbell, 1977; Portes & Wilson, 1976).

Supplementary studies are warranted at the college level both because of the declining numbers of subordinate group members who register for college and because of the low retention rate of those who do enroll. Too often studies address precollegiate factors; for instance, they concentrate on why persons of color do not take upper-level courses in high school. Although these studies are necessary, they should not stand in isolation. As a remedy, societal dynamics should be explored in search of other variables that moderate success. Special attention should be paid to variations within groups.

Because two-year institutions contain higher than usual proportions of members of subordinate groups, they should be an integral part of research on college achievement. Since the beginnings of the American civil rights movement, these institutions have been perceived as the great equalizer for students not formerly considered college material. The success of the community college in America is linked directly to demands for further education among previously excluded groups; students may enter through remedial programs on a "second chance" basis (Astin, 1977). In addition, community colleges attract persons interested in social mobility, a factor that should be considered in the research.

Although the participants had "no crystal stair" to achievement and no mothers who exemplified academic success, they did not "set down on the steps" when life got "kinder hard." They are "still goin' and still climbin'," perhaps in spite of their educational backgrounds rather than because of them. Brothers and other relationships could be part of the difference why they have succeeded in circumstances where others often fail. Nurturing can be as intertwined with achievement in first-generation students as the need for independence from kin.

References

Astin, A.W. (1977). *Four critical years: Effects of college on beliefs, attitudes, and knowledge*. San Francisco: Jossey-Bass.

Austin, R.L., & Dodge, H.H. (1992). Despair, distrust and dissatisfaction among blacks and women, 1973–1987. *Sociological Quarterly, 33*, 570–98, Winter.

Brown, D.R., et al. (1992). Patterns of social affiliation as predictors of depressive symptoms among urban blacks. *Journal of Health & Social Behavior, 33*, 242–53, Summer.

Caplan, N., Whitmore, J.K., & Choy, M.H. (1989). *The boat people and achievement in America: A study of family life, hard work, and cultural values*. Ann Arbor: University of Michigan.

Chodorow, N. (1978). *The reproduction of mothering*. Berkeley: University of California.

Clark, R. (1974). *Family life and school achievement: Why poor black children succeed or fail*. Chicago: University of Chicago.

Deyoung, A.J., with Huffman, K., & Turner, M.E. (1989). Dropout issues and problems in rural America, with a case study of one central Appalachian school district. In L. Weis, E. Farrar & H.G. Petrie (Eds.), *Dropouts from school: Issues, dilemmas, and solutions* (55–77). New York: State University of New York.

Dweck, C.S., & Elliot, E.S. (1983). Achievement motivation. In P.M. Mussen (Ed.), *Handbook of child psychology* (4th ed., vol. 4, 643–691). New York: Wiley.

Faunce, P.S. (1980). *Women and ambition: A bibliography*. Metuchen, NJ: Scarecrow.

Fine, M., & Zane, N. (1989). Bein' wrapped too tight: When low income women drop out of high school. In L. Weis, E. Farrar, & H.G. Petrie (Eds.), *Dropouts from school: Issues, dilemmas, and solutions* (23–53). New York: State University of New York.

Fordham, S. (1988). Racelessness as a factor in black students' school success: Pragmatic strategy or pyrrhic victory? *Harvard Educational Review, 58*, 54–84.

Fordham, S., & Ogbu, J.U. (1986). Black students' school success: Coping with the "burden of 'acting white'." *The Urban Review, 18*(3), 176–206.

Greenberg, M., & Schneider, D. (1992). Blue Thursday? Homicide and suicide among urban 15–24-year-old black male Americans. *Public Health Reports, 107*, 264–268, My/Je.

Hammons-Bryner, S. (1991). "No Crystal Stair": An ethnographic study of the social construction of achievement in rural females. Doctoral dissertation, Florida State University, Tallahassee.

Hammons-Bryner, S. (1992). Educational connections: Aspirations of rural college women. Presented at the Ethnography in Education Research Forum. Philadelphia.

Hammons-Bryner, S. (1993). African-American women's educational achievement and intimate relationships: An ethnographic study of connections and dilemmas. *Proteus: A Journal of Ideas*, Fall.

Hammons-Bryner, S. (1995). "No crystal stair": Rural women's collegiate enrollment and persistence. *Qualitative Studies in Education, 8*(2), 121–136.

Higginbotham, E. (1980). Issues in contemporary sociological work on black women. *Humanity and society, 4*, 226–242.

Holland, D.C., & Eisenhart, M.A. (1990). *Educated in romance: Women, achievement, and college culture.* Chicago: University of Chicago.

Horner, M.S. (1972). Toward an understanding of achievement-related conflicts in women. *Journal of Social Issues, 28*, 157–175.

Hughes, L. (1969). Mother to son. In L.B. Hopkins (Ed.), *Don't you turn back: Poems by Langston Hughes* (p. 20). New York: Knopf.

Kerckhoff, A.C., & Campbell, R.T. (1977). Black-white differences in the educational attainment process. *Sociology of Education, 50*, 15–27.

Macleod, J. (1987). *Ain't no makin' it: Leveled aspirations in a low-income neighborhood.* Westview: Boulder.

McClelland, D.C. (1961). *The achieving society.* Princeton, NJ: Van Nostrand. [Reissued 1967, by NY: Free Press].

McClelland, D.C. (1975). *Power: The inner experience.* New York: Irving ton.

McClelland, D.C., & Atkinson, J.W. (1948). The projective expression of needs: 1. The effects of different intensities of the hunger drive on perception. *Journal of Psychology, 25*, 205–222.

McClelland, D.C., Atkinson, J.W., Clark, R.W., & Lowell, E.L. (1953). *The achievement motive.* New York: Appleton-Century-Crofts.

McClelland, D.C., & Winter, D.G. (1969). *Motivating economic achievement.* New York: Free.

McKenna, A. (1990). The "talk" of returning women graduate students: An ethnographic study of reality construction. Doctoral Dissertation, Florida State University, Tallahassee, 1990.

Mickelson, R.A. (1989). Why does Jane read and write so well? The anomaly of women's achievement. *Sociology of Education, 62*, 47–63.

Portes, A. & Wilson, K.L. (1976). Black-white differences in educational attainment. *American Sociological Review, 41*, 414–431.

Turner, H.M., et al. (1983). *Factors influencing persistence/achievement in the sciences and health professions by black high school and college women.* Atlanta: Center for Research on Women in Science (1–108).

Weis, L. (1985a). *Between two worlds: Black students in an urban community college.* Boston: Routledge & Kegan Paul.

Weis, L. (1985b). Without dependence on welfare for life: Black women in the community college. *The Urban Review, 17*, 233–255.

Zimmermann, M.A., & Maton, K.I. (1992). Life-style and substance use among male African-American urban adolescents: A cluster analytic approach. *American Journal of Community Psychology, 20*, 121–38, Fall.

21

Legal and Executive Journey: African Americans' Search for Social and Educational Equality

Beverley J. Anderson

Social inequality in the United States has never been, nor is it now, a creation of God, a manifestation of white superiority, or evidence of black inferiority as some would have us believe. Rather, it is a social construction of white privilege previously maintained by the force of law, currently supported by custom and vested interest, and designed to provide social, educational, and economic advantages to white beneficiaries.

For more than one hundred and thirty years a variety of laws and executive orders have been used to aid in the deconstruction of this social arrangement in an attempt to fashion a society based on equal access and opportunity. However, in spite of legal and executive relief at various times, the problem remains intractable.

This work discusses how structured social inequality has functioned to keep people of African descent in a race based caste system. It further explores the link between denial of educational opportunity and low caste status. Also, it examines various legal and executive decisions designed to redress these problems. It concludes that social inequality exists because it provides benefits for many and its demise will be accelerated only when it is widely regarded as dysfunctional for the larger society.

If one accepts Horace Mann's position that "Education, beyond all other devices of human origin, is the great equalizer of the condition of men—the balance wheel of the social machinery" (1851, p. 1) one could only conclude that the denial of quality education to children of African descent is the denial of the great equalizer.

Imagine that it is January 1, of the year 2000 and all students of African descent in the United States are well educated with ongoing access to equal education in all sectors of educational institutions. How would such a phenomena change the status of people of African descent in relation to the population of European ancestry? The period between 1865 and 1996 has generated a number of

This article was informed to some extent by a previous essay which appeared in *Journal of Negro Education*; 1994, 63, 3, Summer, 443–450 and is adapted/reprinted with the permission of the copyright holder/author.

laws and executive orders designed ostensibly to enhance opportunities for people
of African descent. With the eminent arrival of the "fin de siecle," attempts to
evaluate the status of education and the attendant employment status of Americans of African descent in the United States produced enormous contradictions.
Careful analysis of available evidence indicates tremendous gains, significant
losses, as well as obvious areas of stagnation. The impact of the educational institution on African Americans is of special concern because of its enormous influence on their economic and social well-being as well as on the larger society. The
importance of education has always been acknowledged by those in power and
therefore helps to explain the pattern of carefully guarding and allocating this
valuable resource to the poor in general, and racial and ethnic minority groups in
specific. Whenever it is deemed to be in the best interest of the power structure,
education has been available to, or withheld from, these groups to meet specific
national needs at various historical periods. Not all countries view education in
this manner. Some provide as many educational opportunities as possible to all
citizens. Such traditions are usually evident in countries that are generally racially
and ethnically homogenous. A few examples are Greenland, Japan, and Norway.
This is less likely to be the case in countries that are racially and ethnically diverse
and has never been the case in the United States. Since the arrival of Africans to
this country, decisions regarding their education, or lack thereof, have always
been and continue to be political, with emphasis on how little education, if any, to
make available to them. History bears witness to a tradition in the United States
of forbidden education; begrudging, segregated miseducation; and bloody legal
struggles for access to quality education.

A cursory review of the literature indicates that the current status regarding access to quality education by Americans of African descent presents a picture that
in a word is best described as confusing (Anderson, 1994). Some historically Black
institutions of higher education are experiencing a resurgence and growth largely
because many Black students find the quality of education to be excellent and the
atmosphere on predominantly White campuses often hostile. On the other hand,
other Black institutions are barely continuing to exist because of poor financial resources and a lack of ability to attract students. Clearly, *de jure* segregation in education has been eliminated. The courts have spoken, the laws are clear, there no
longer exist any legal basis for segregated institutions in education or any other
social institutions. *The Brown v. Board of Education of Topeka, Kansas* (1954)
decision sounded the final death knell for de jure segregation and removed the hu-
miliating "separate but equal" decision of *Plessy v. Ferguson* (1896).

Today, we can attest to the positive impact of *Brown* by the presence and meritorious functioning of persons of African heritage as students, faculty, staff, and
administrators in predominantly White colleges and universities across the nation. In fact there are some who have emerged as superstars in their disciplines.
They are recipients of scholarships of merit and occupy lofty positions in a number of these prestigious predominantly White institutions. However, while some
Americans of African heritage flourish intellectually and socially on predominantly White campuses, others find themselves scarcely tolerated or met with
open hostility on other campuses. Skolnick & Currie (1982) discuss this in detail.
In recent years however, as the number of Blacks have increased on these campuses, so have the opportunities for controversies surrounding their presence.
Dartmouth College is one such example. On its campus Blacks in the capacity of

both students and faculty have experienced equal opportunity of ill treatment. This has become such an established pattern of behavior, that the institution has become as well known for its prestigious "Ivy" position as for its ability to mistreat people of African heritage on its campus (see "The Cole Example," 1990; "Dartmouth Professor," 1990). Minorities at fellow "Ivy" institution, Harvard University, have not fared much better. Ongoing unpleasant racial issues among various factions in its student body, and thinly veiled racial utterances by some White faculty about the presence of Blacks on the campus, have only recently been eclipsed by its intractable stand on the issue of the lack of diversity in its law school. What has sometimes been referred to as the "Derrick Bell affair" brought national attention to this problem ("Legal Beat," 1992; "Complaint," 1992). Magner and Smolensky (1989) note:

> Ugly and embarrassing incidents between white and black students continue to plague colleges and universities across the country. Hundreds of institutions of all sizes have been affected—some by brawls, others by racist flyers or graffiti, still others by fraternity or ghetto themes. Many administrators and scholars who have studied the incidents have concluded that they are not simply isolated and extremist acts, but that they reflect a disturbing pattern. (p.1)

The suggestion here is that while de jure segregation is a thing of the past, attitudes, patterns of behavior, and vested interest keep de facto segregation fixed firmly in place.

Structured Social Inequality

Of the eight social institutions generally recognized to make up the network through which the nation organizes itself to meet the needs of its citizens, the two that bear the greatest responsibility for one's social position are the family and education. The family determines the ascribed standing in the social and economic hierarchy at birth and this generally carries over into adulthood. Education, on the other hand, is the gateway to achieved social and economic standing. Furthermore since theoretically the nation defines itself as a form of meritocracy, the place of education becomes almost supreme. Additionally, for a number of critically important, prestigious, and financially lucrative occupations such as medicine, law, engineering, and academics, access to quality education is mandated. Therefore, from a national standpoint, this social institution fulfills the nation's agenda as the gatekeeper for access to desirable goods and services and entrance into the upper echelons of the society for those not born into them.

Both manifest and latent functions of the educational institution are often commonly recognized as being: (a) to socialize children into the cultural values of the society, (b) to introduce children to the principles of democracy, (c) to prepare students for the world of work, and (d) to facilitate upward mobility. Access to quality education is then a route to enjoyment of the fruits of the nation. The pervasive role of education in the quality of life of citizens and the quality of citizenry was recognized by the advocates of *Brown* when they made this important point:

> Education is perhaps the most important function of state and local governments. Compulsory school attendance laws and the great expenditure for edu-

cation both demonstrate our recognition of the importance of education to our democratic society. It is required in the performance of our most basic public responsibilities, even service in the armed forces. It is the very foundation of good citizenship. Today it is a principal instrument in awakening the child to cultural values, in preparing him for later professional training, and in helping him to adjust normally to his environment. In these days it is doubtful that any child may reasonably be expected to succeed in life if he is denied the opportunity of an education. (*Brown,* p. 493)

One is therefore immediately confronted with the following question: "If education is so critical to individual success and the national agenda, how could the nation's interest be served by its denial or rationing to a significant segment of citizens?" Many scholars have engaged in substantial discussions that largely emanate from this question. This debate can best be made within the context of structured social inequality. Many sociologists have presented theories and arguments in support of, as well as denial of, the need for social and economic hierarchical structuring of citizens in societies in general, and the United States specifically. Some scholars do not believe that it is even possible to organize social life without inequality. According to Anderson (1994):

Some sociologists have formulated theories that attested the importance, inevitability, inherence, and universality of social stratification.... One may be informed by the conflict perspective, which proposes that social inequality is not inevitable but inherent in capitalism.... Conversely, one may subscribe to the functionalist perspective—the theoretical position more congruent to the national philosophy, of the United States—which suggests a necessity for structured social inequality.... This point of view suggests that inequality is necessary to motivate those at the bottom to strive to improve their lot. Inequality serves to make available the necessary cheap labor for menial jobs. Furthermore, some work requires long and difficult training, and to motivate the most talented to undergo such preparation, they have to be able to look forward to being differentially rewarded. (p. 444)

Race, like caste, as a basis for social inequality makes convenient the distribution of desirable goods and services in the society. One group can readily be deemed more or less worthy simply on the basis of membership in a caste or racial grouping. In the United States, this has permitted those of European ancestry to classify themselves as fully human and therefore worthy of the prestigious tasks of control, management, decision making, and appeal to the gods. They further classified the Africans, who were brought as slaves, as less than humans and therefore unable to fully participate in activities reserved exclusively for those designated as completely humans.

Later, after emancipation, and under "Jim Crow," the politically powerful constructed and enforced laws that mandated segregated existence and exclusion from meritorious and prestigious activities solely on the basis of race. It must be emphasized that during the historical periods of slavery and "Jim Crow" character, ability, hard work, or talent were never qualities sought in, or attributable to, the African population. They were simply ascribed roles at the bottom of the social and economic ladder and excluded from access to quality education on the basis of their phenotype. Furthermore, at the same time they were characterized as ineducable. Notwithstanding, when they attempted to seek education, in many instances it was deemed to be illegal. In other instances tremendous efforts, both legal and extralegal were engaged to thwart their efforts. The following is offered as an example of the concerted efforts that members of the legitimate bureaucracies have used to frustrate attempts to educate Black students:

- Oath of all white Teachers and Principals.
- All white high schools will write up as many suspensions on Negroes as they occur, small or large.
- All white high schools will bring about the suspensions of 25 Negroes who are supposed to graduate (15 boys and 10 girls).
- All white high schools will send Negroes home for any little thing they do so that we may have on record their lack of interest in school.
- Nigger is not a bad word to call Negroes, so use the name at will.
- Be aware that all maids and yard boys will do as we tell them because in their eye-sight white is still the best thing they have ever seen.
- All white school board members are with us (except one).
- K.K.K. are doing a thing too, so together we will have Niggers in a turmoil.
- Junior high is the area where we get Niggers prepared for 12th and 14th grades.
- This paper is not to get in the hands of any negro mothers (don't worry about the fathers, they don't show up for nothing) or Negro children.
- The good we are doing for the reading of this nature should be read and burned up before it gets in the hands of your maids or yard boys.
- Reappointment of the School Board (one man one vote to a single member district vote went like white supremacy is supposed to go?).
- Anyway, we feel that Negroes are getting more education now than they will ever use.
- Our goal is to average 240 Negroes suspended per month to aid drop out inferior education. (Skolnick & Elliot, 1988, p. 147)

Practices such as these by the powerful, directed toward a specific population, effectively removed Africans from competition with European phenotypes for prestigious occupations and economically lucrative occupations. Furthermore, since they arrived in this nation under aegis of slavery, family background effectively precluded them from prestigious ascribed status. Access to prestigious achieved status could only effectively come through the gateway of education which was effectively blocked by White gatekeepers.

Economic exploitation theory supports the point of view that prejudice helps to maintain economic privileges from which Whites benefit at the expense of Blacks. Stratification on a racial basis provides better access to education, occupation, and incomes for Whites, and so creates a vested interest in its continued existence. Furthermore, if Blacks are defined by the power structure as being inferior, it makes it easier to keep them in low-status, low-paying jobs. A caste system that allocates to Blacks a permanent low caste position is socially and economically less costly to maintain. Likewise, Whites will better be able to access the higher-status, better-paying jobs if they are defined as permanently superior (Ogbu (1990) discusses this issue extensively).

These social and political decisions constructed Blacks in the United States as inferior and relegated them to a type of generalized semi-permanent subordinate status in all spheres of their lives. "Jim Crow" laws governed public accommodations and segregated Blacks in areas of transportation, movie theatres, restaurants, hotels, and other areas of public life. As *Plessy v. Ferguson* (1896) confirmed, those in power were able to dictate the laws of separation that relegated Blacks to lives of public degradation and shame. Furthermore the chronically unfair structure while making a case for "separate but equal" in fact structured and maintained a system based on "separate and unequal." For example, it is curious that while Black women in the work place were permitted to engage in such intimate task performance activities as "wet nurses," in public they could not drink at water fountains reserved for Whites, or eat at "Whites only" restaurants.

Early Attempts to Ameliorate Inequality

For more than 130 years now, as early as 1865, intermittent attempts to provide opportunities to persons of African heritage have been introduced. Each attempt, however, was swiftly stifled, with the result that successive generations of people of African descent have viewed a window of opportunity which was quickly nailed shut, permitting only a few to enter but leaving large numbers behind. The Freedman's Bureau and jobs for freed slaves were established in 1865 immediately after emancipation. However just 10 years later, by 1875, these initiatives were significantly reduced due to resistance of White southerners and the removal of federal troops who had the responsibility to protect the newly-freed population (see Carter & Wilson, 1996).

The approach to, and conclusion of, World War II also afforded opportunities that permitted some Black citizens to access jobs and education in spite of general White resistance. In 1940 Black advocates led by A. Phillip Randolph petitioned then President Franklin Roosevelt, under promise of demonstration, for access to lucrative jobs in the defense industry of the North. From this, Executive Order 8802 was born. It prohibited discrimination on the basis of race or national origin in industries with government contracts. Another important window of opportunity came during the immediate post-War period. The Servicemen's Readjustment Act of 1944, commonly known as the "G.I. Bill of Rights," provided veterans free college education or job training in addition to access to loans for the purchase of homes. The college funding permitted access to educational institutions for a large percentage of Black citizens for the first time. This access had several benefits. First, many Black veterans availed themselves of the educational opportunity. Second, since many veterans, White as well as Black, were ill-prepared for college, these institutions had to provide remediation across the board—they gave extra points on entrance examinations or waived them altogether. Third, Black colleges experienced a resurgence because of the large number of applicants with government vouchers. Fourth, many White institutions, particularly Northern ones, experienced integration, since they accepted government vouchers from all comers.

Brown and the Paradox of Achieving Equality

In time, Blacks would use the same legal instruments, the courts, and political support, in the form of executive dictates, that had previously been used to restrict them to gain levels of freedom and equality previously denied. Although the law would provide some legal relief from deprivations and provide opportunities for some blacks as well as hope for a great many others, racial privileges for whites, though threatened, would not disappear any time soon. They had the accumulated strength of custom, power, privilege, and inertia of the status quo—formidable opponents with which to contend.

Legal advocates such as Thurgood Marshall and social advocates such as Martin Luther King persuaded the nation to redefine itself by discarding the tools of race and caste in its social construction. Now, more than forty years after the *Brown* decision, there have been some contradictory circumstances which suggest stagnation in some areas, leading some to believe little has changed. Nevertheless, significant gains have been made toward the achievement of equality of opportunities and treatment, especially in the area of education.

Although the heart of *Brown* relates to the end of "separate but equal" in public education, a brief review of the current status of this sector reveals that there is still much to be done. *De facto* segregation in the urban public schools remains difficult if not impossible to resolve. More than forty years after *Brown,* with the "fin de siecle" imminent, several states are either currently engaged in negotiations to correct such situations, or are defendants in lawsuits brought against them to gain legal redress ("Justice for Hartford's schools," 1996).

The existence of continued segregation at the elementary and secondary schools are to a large extent the mirror of segregation in the United States. These schools mirror the politics of race that exist in the larger society. The end of *de jure* segregation became merely the beginning of *de facto* segregation. The wholesale abandonment of the cities by White families for the suburbs is inextricably tied to school integration. Analysis of residential patterns in many cities indicate that prior to the 1970s many White families lived in ethnic enclave communities. Prior to court ordered busing, many White children attended city public schools in what were euphemistically called "neighborhood schools." This residential pattern permitted Whites to live in segregated communities within city boundaries and send their children to all-White neighborhood schools. However, during the 1970s many Black families sought and got court ordered relief to end this pattern of segregation. Whites, however, never intended to permit the courts or any other institution to thwart their policy of segregated schools. Pervasive belief in White superiority and Black inferiority created White resistance to integration. Examples of resultant White resistance, which in some extreme cases such as Boston, Massachusetts, are well known. Rather than permit their children to share classrooms with Blacks, they fled the cities for White suburbs. When Whites fled the cities they took their tax monies and their wealth with them, leaving the cities with eroded tax bases and diminished school systems. Curiously, middle-class Black families who also fled declining city schools often found themselves in segregated Black sections of White suburban communities or all Black suburbs, leading to the new concept of "slurbs." Another variation on this theme is Bloomfield, Connecticut. This community, a suburb of Hartford, has a majority White population with a greater than 90% Black student body.

The *Sheff v. O'Neill* case bears reviewing at this time. In 1989, Milo Sheff was a fourth-grade student in Hartford public schools when a lawsuit was filed in his name, asking the court to rule that the school, 95% Black and Latino, was unconstitutionally racially segregated and that the state be resonsible for redressing the problem. Some six years later, in April, 1995, the court ruled against the petitioners. Many Whites in adjoining suburban communities, along with Governor John Rowland, celebrated that decision. In July 1996, the state supreme court reversed the earlier decision and, though it was too late for him to benefit from the decision, Milo Sheff, now a high school senior, was vindicated. Some suburban officials responded to the decision by predicting "war" if children from their communities were asked to go outside to school. Another trend that occurs more frequently in the South is to have integrated schools with segregated classes. The schools frequently place White students in college preparatory classes and Black students in remedial or basic classes. In one school district, a White student who scored below Black classmates recounted that she was advised she would be placed in the higher sections since she would not be comfortable in classes with Blacks. One Black student who achieved high scores but was placed in the basic section was told that it must have been an accident that he scored so highly on his placement test.

Underlying all the strategies to avoid integrated residential neighborhoods, and especially integrated schools, is the fundamental belief in White superiority. This belief system tends to surface strongest at those times when it appears that the gains of Blacks are becoming significant enough to threaten White privilege. The cyclical appearance of the ideology of intelligence test scores as an indicator of worthiness for desirable goods and services is a case in point. The 1994 arrival of *The Bell Curve* by Herrnstein and Murray was truly notice of a dramatic and definitive change in the political ideology of the notion of equity for all citizens.

In spite of these problems, gains have been made. The increasing Black middle class has been able to make slow but consistent progress in suburban communities, as well as take advantage of private schools. Additionally, some suburban communities have entered into voluntary agreements with Black inner city students to assist in achieving the goals of equality. Two examples from the Boston area are the Metropolitan Council for Educational Opportunity Incorporated (METCO) which busses one way—Black students from Boston to suburban towns—and "A Better Chance," which makes scholarships to private schools available to talented city students. Tushnet (1994) points out that there can be little doubt that much of this progress is directly attributable to *Brown* .

The Post- *Brown* Journey

The post-*Brown* journey has been a long and arduous one. Although it directly addressed the "separate but equal" doctrine at the public elementary school level, it also became an instrument of change in many other areas. These areas include but are not limited to bilingual education, special education, and education for the gifted and talented, access to admission to institutions of higher education, expanded rights for women, and employment opportunities. In spite of these efforts, however, subsequent legislation and litigation have failed to resolve conclusively the issues surrounding the policies, programs, and practices in admissions to institutions of higher learning, as well as discriminatory employment practices. In both cases of education and employment, litigation results appear to have achieved only abiding ambiguity. As a result, we frequently hear the complaint that reliance upon a "case-by-case adjudication of concerns by courts and administrative agencies has proved inadequate." (Blinick, 1975). Even though the 5th and 13th Amendments, along with the Civil Rights Acts of 1866, have long undergirded what we have come to know as affirmative action, the 14th Amendment provided the principal rationale for modern affirmative action programs.

The slow pace of change and many reversals have prompted some observers to suggest that those who have sought to circumvent *Brown* have willfully hampered progress, and some potential beneficiaries have lost faith in the ability of the system to enforce the law. Others argue that those responsible for monitoring and enforcing the law simply lack the resources to confront its most obvious violators.

Brown and Affirmative Action

What has been the impact of *Brown* on employment practices and admissions to institutions of learning? Perhaps the most accurate answer is that the results have been mixed. The major supportive instruments have been the Civil Rights Act of 1866 augmented by the 14th Amendment, titles VI and VII of the Civil Rights Act of 1964, which requires the elimination of artificial, arbitrary, and unnecessary barriers to employment that operate invidiously to discriminate on the basis of racial or other impermissible classifications. Title VII was amended on March 24, 1972, to cover educational institutions, whether they receive federal funds or not.

Executive Order 11246, which became effective 1968, prohibiting federal contractors from discriminating against employees on the basis of race, religion, color, or national origin was amended by Executive Order 11375, to include discrimination on the basis of sex. This also influenced non-discrimination and affirmative action policies in higher education. The implementation framework for Executive Order 11375 was stipulated in Revised Order Number 4, which states that institutions with federal contracts of more than $50,000 and 50 or more employees must develop written affirmative action programs assuring equal opportunity to women and minorities. Specifically, institutions must:

1. develop a data base for all job classifications;
2. maintain a policy statement forbidding discrimination;
3. appoint an individual to be in charge of the program;
4. examine recruiting, hiring and promotion policies, salaries, and all other conditions of employment for conformity with the order;
5. identify areas of under-compliance and develop specific plans for bringing these areas into compliance; and
6. develop numerical employment goals and timetables.

The Higher Education Act provides victims of discrimination with two additional avenues of appeal: (a) it prohibits discrimination on the basis of sex, race, and national origin in any educational program or activity receiving federal aid, and (b) extends the 1963 Equal Pay Act to cover executive, administrative, and professional employees.

Often one hears numerical goals confused with quotas, but the courts have clearly distinguished them. Quotas are illegal because they exclude individuals. Goals, on the other hand, are "targets for inclusion of people previously discriminated against." Persons who intentionally or otherwise fail to grasp the difference have resorted to accusations of "reverse discrimination."

Higher Education and *Brown*

It is instructive to recall that to a large extent the journey toward racial equality in this century began in higher education, and that racial discrimination has long been violative of the Fourteenth Amendment (Stefkovich & Leas, 1994). *Brown I* brought an extension of the principles invalidating the separate-but-equal doctrine; *Geier v. Dunn* (1972) demonstrated the relationship between discriminatory practices in higher educational institutions and secondary education. The district judge held that:

> [I]n cases involving higher education, the interests of the state in setting its own education policy are to be given especially great weight by a federal court framing relief from segregation and an open door policy, coupled with good faith recruiting efforts (as well, perhaps, as provision for remedial education for the educationally underprivileged), is sufficient a basic requirement; but when the basic approach of an open door policy fails to be effective, the interest of the state in completely settling its own educational policy must give way to the interest of the public and the dictates of the Constitution, and the Court may exact more. (p. 573)

He went on to say, "There is an affirmative duty imposed upon the State by the Fourteenth Amendment to dismantle the dual system of higher education" (p. 573). Meanwhile, during the 1960s and 1970s, preferential admissions became controversial in higher education: "The importance of the issue derives from the fact that the admissions policies of an educational institution largely determine its mission and character," (O'Neil, 1971, p.699). In the background, the courts ominously warned that racial classification was "constitutionally suspect" (*Bolling v. Sharpe*, (1954); subject to the "most rigid scrutiny"; and "in most circumstances irrelevant" (*Korematsu v. United States*, 1944); to "any constitutionally acceptable legislative purpose," (*Hirabayshi v. United States*, 1943).

In the case *DeFunis v. Odegaard*, the University of Washington Law School had denied admission to Marco DeFunis, Jr., a White college graduate, but did admit thirty-six minority applicants who had scored lower than DeFunis in the Law School Admission Test, and who also had lower undergraduate averages. The Supreme Court, however, declared the case moot because DeFunis was already attending the law school under a lower court order pending his appeal and his graduation was imminent. Whether it is lawful for a public institution of higher education to favor the admission of minority group members was a question left unanswered.

Within four years, the Court again faced the constitutionality of an "affirmative action admissions program" (Gregory, 1994) in *Bakke v. Regents of the University of California* (1978). In this case, an unsuccessful white male applicant alleged that the affirmative action admissions program at the university's medical school at Davis violated the equal protection clause of the Fourteenth Amendment. The program required that a specified percentage of the student body be allocated to selected classifications of persons. In its opinion the Court said:

> It is evident that the Davis special admission program involves the use of an explicit racial classification never before countenanced by this court. It tells applicants who are not Negro, Asian, or "Chicano" that they are totally excluded from a specific percentage of the seats in an entering class. The fatal flaw in petitioner's preferential program is its disregard of individual rights as guaranteed by the Fourteenth Amendment. (pp. 319–320)

Why the continued distress over Affirmative Action? Perhaps the programs themselves were never thoroughly thought out, and the motivation behind them was often other than noble. Also, because of these reasons a national discussion was never engaged to articulate its *raison d'etre*. Skrentny (1996) suggests that these policies never had strong support or a mandate from the electorate. According to Hacker (1996) discussing Skrentny's work:

> The first coherent affirmative action measure was Nixon's "Philadelphia Plan" of 1969, which required federal contractors to show they were hiring blacks. The plan arose from mixed motives. The Republicans needed to make some response to the rioting of the 1960s, and jobs were clearly an issue. But Nixon, who won the 1968 election by less than one percentage point, was also looking for a long-term strategy to undercut the Democrats. Affirmative action was useful to him,...since it "placed on the table something to help African-Americans at the expense of unions, producing discontent and factional rivalry in two of the liberal establishment's major supporters," Nixon gambled that white workers would direct their anger at those taking "their" jobs, and overlook those who had put the plan in place. The strategy paid off in 1972 and he won reelection by a large majority, including white blue-collar voters who would later be dubbed "Reagan Democrats." A quarter of a century later, Republicans are still betting that affirmative action will stir racial resentments in their favor. (p. 21)

If the above discussion has merit, then in fact the major objective of some affirmative action tools was designed to buttress politicians' careers. It is further instructive to note, in the above example, if the first outcome is resentment of Blacks by Whites, then these goals have been accomplished. The callous disregard for the social and economic distress of Blacks that these self-serving policies indicate should bring shame to politicians. Further, the acrimonious political struggles that involve nomination of justices to the highest courts demonstrate the determination to control the national agenda through political ideology long after various presidents are out of office. These examples, as well as current contradictory rulings by the courts on cases involving affirmative action, lend credence to the charges of "case by case adjudication." Equality and fairness in the work place both in and outside of the field of education has lost out to ideological rulings on affirmative action. In four widely studied decisions, the Supreme Court failed to support programs designed to redress past discriminatory practices in the workplace. The following four well-debated cases are examples:

In *City of Richmond v. J.A. Croson Company* (1989), the Court invalidated, in a 6–3 decision, a program requiring the city to set aside 30 percent of its public works funds for minority-owned construction companies. Justice Sandra Day O'Connor, writing for the majority, stated that the program could be justified only if it served the "compelling state interest" of redressing "identified discrimination." Otherwise such "set-aside programs" constitute a form of reverse discrimination against nonminority contractors and violate their constitutional right to equal protection under the law. Further, "an amorphous claim that there has been past discrimination in a particular industry cannot justify the use of an unyielding ratio quota."

The ruling in *Richmond* has already routed several affirmative action programs similar to *Richmond*'s, and in a prescient dissent, Justice Thurgood Marshall argued that the Court was making "a full-scale retreat from [its] longstanding solicitude to race-conscious remedial efforts directed toward deliverance of the century-old promise of equality of economic opportunity."

In a later 5–4 decision, *Wards Cove Packing Company v. Antonio* (1989), the Court placed the burden of proof on plaintiff minority workers charging racial discrimination in employment, redefining the boundaries it established in *Griggs v. Duke Power*: a plaintiff could offer "statistical proof" that employment policies had a discriminatory effect, regardless of the existence of any proof of intent by the defendant. The ruling in *Griggs* represented the Court's interpretation of Title VII of the Civil Rights Act of 1964 that prohibited discrimination in employment. The *Wards Cove* case brought the *Griggs* perspective into question.

In *Griggs*, black employees had brought action against Duke Power Company, challenging its employment and/or promotion criteria: a high school diploma and satisfactory performance on a standardized general intelligence test. In the majority opinion, Chief Justice Warren Burger stated that it was the intent of Congress under Title VII of the Civil Rights Act that a relationship exist between the criteria for employment and the job to be performed, so that an employer "measure the person for the job and not the person in the abstract." For the majority in *Wards Cove*, Justice Byron White wrote that an employer of seasonal workers at Salmon Canneries in Alaska might justify policies that had a discriminatory impact by providing a reasonable business explanation. The burden of proving discrimination remained with the workers, and a statistical implication of discrimination was, by itself, inadequate to shift that burden to the defendant. The Court simply ruled that the employees must associate specific employment practices with their discrimination-impact assertion. In a dissenting opinion, Justice Harry Blackmun, joined by Justices William Brennan and Thurgood Marshall, charged that the majority decision represented a step backward in the struggle against racial discrimination. "One wonders whether the majority still believes that race discrimination...is a... problem in our society, or even remembers that it ever was."

In another 1989 case, *Martin v. Wilks*, White firefighters in Birmingham, Alabama, challenged an eight-year-old court-approved settlement structured to assure more hirings and promotions for blacks. The firefighters declared that the plan deprived them of due-course promotions and thereby violated the 1964 Civil Rights Act prohibiting discrimination in employment based on race and sex. The Court ruled, 5–4, that they could seek redress under civil rights legislation. For the majority, Chief Justice William Rehnquist wrote, "A voluntary consent decree between one group of employees and their employer cannot possibly settle, voluntarily or otherwise, the conflicting claims of another group of employees who did not join in the agreement." The decision cast doubt on the use of consent decrees to arrive at affirmative action settlements.

The fourth 1989 case, *Patterson v. McLean Credit Union* (1989), focused on employment and had implications for higher education. The Court, which reaffirmed its 1976 landmark civil rights ruling in *Runyon v. McCrary* (1976) implemented a post-Civil War rights law. In another 5–4 split, the Court narrowed the application of the older law so as to exclude claims of racial harassment in the workplace. Justice Anthony Kennedy in the majority opinion stressed that the statute "expressly prohibits discrimination only in the making and enforcement of contracts." He went on, "[T]he right to make contracts does not extend, as a matter of either logic or semantics, to conduct by the employer after the contract relation has been established, including breach of the terms of the contract or imposition of discriminatory working conditions." In his dissent, Justice Brennan observed that the decision failed to recognize the wide use of the 1866 law envisioned by Congress (*Patterson*). Civil rights proponents called *Patterson* a blow against fairness and justice in the workplace. The ruling still raises questions over whether workers are protected from racial harassment, even in what is perceived to be the civilized and contemplative precincts of higher education.

Conclusions

Discussions in this paper indicate that, regardless of the significant inconsistencies in the post-*Brown* journey to educational and occupational equality, on balance many Blacks were making progress. We also see that the courts as well as the executive branch of government provided windows of opportunities for a limited number of Blacks. As we approach the next century, however, a curious picture begins to emerge. The future of Blacks seem less secure. The very instruments that initially were used to suppress Blacks—the judicial decisions and executive orders— and which were later used, beginning with *Brown*, to forge new opportunities, have returned full circle to shut off opportunities.

Why? Earlier, we discussed the reasons used in 1969 by then-President Nixon to impose, according to Lemann (1995), the Government's harshest, most explicit quota plan ever on building contractors in Philadelphia. Diaries and notes of Ehrlichman and Haldeman indicate that Nixon thought of the Philadelphia plan as a wonderful way to pit two key Democratic constituencies, Blacks and labor, against each other, and endorsed it partly for political reasons. The case has been and continues to be made that Blacks, as a powerless minority, have little or no control of the powerful institutions of this land. They must therefore always depend on white goodwill for favorable dispositions. This being the case, Whites who provide these generally do because it is or seems to be in their best interest—as long as this remains the case Blacks can count on the goodwill and support of Whites. In support of this point of view, Lemann presents some speculation that bears repeating:

> The Establishment's reasoning, never openly stated, would have gone something like this: Sure, affirmative action generates white victims of reverse dis-

crimination, but there aren't very many of them and they don't suffer too greatly. They go to Colgate instead of Cornell. Big deal. The most clearly outstanding whites—people the meritocracy set up to spot and train for leadership—don't suffer at all. In return, we are able to take some of the edge off of what has been the most explosive issue in our history, the one that set off our bloodiest war and our worst civil disturbances. We create an integrated authority system. We give blacks a stake. It promotes the peace. In addition, case by case, it creates a feeling of doing something to correct our worst historic wrong. (p. 36)

Although Lemann's speculations may in part be generally accurate, there were always those who, for a number of reasons, opposed the whole idea of affirmative action and the judicial decisions. Furthermore, there had never been legislation that mandated these activities, so that when new power groups emerged with oppositional ideology, those programs became vulnerable. Former Presidents Reagan and Bush campaigned against affirmative action but did not choose to abolish it. In 1985 a concerted attempt by some in the White House almost succeeded in that mission. Attempts failed because of duplicitous behaviors of members of the group. Executive order 11246 was saved because attempts to kill it were leaked to the press. In the words of Lemann "The internal argument was, 'We're expending a lot of political capital on this issue. It's getting in the way of other things that are more important. The less problems for Reagan the better. Let's don't carry this further now. We can always revisit it later.'" This pattern continued over a period of years as similar attempts to banish various aspects of affirmative action continued and were withdrawn because of press leaks.

Appointments to federal courts originate within the executive branch. Clearly, those appointments reflect a common ideology. It is therefore understandable that the courts would swing to reflect the changing ideology of its appointers. Recent court decisions began to undermine affirmative action. By 1994 conservative politicians had launched an all out attack on affirmative action. Furthermore, as many supporters discovered, it had become a broad based issue in White communities. The tolerance for it was gone. And Blacks control nothing in the United States.

The 1996 decision in the *Texas v. Hopwood* case represented this swing in judicial ideology and sent shock waves across academia to those in support of affirmative action. This ruling made the administrators in institutions with such programs more vulnerable. The lack of clear directions from the courts, the case by case adjudication, the seemingly contradictory rulings, all conspire to end programs designed to foster equality. Curiously, these programs were initially designed to redress problems of Americans of African descent who were grievously wronged due to the history of slavery, Jim Crow laws, and the attendant beliefs in racial superiority by Whites. Currently affirmative action programs have been expanded so that they serve a variety of individuals. To a large extent, however, those discontented with the programs have construed Blacks as the beneficiaries and Whites as the victims. In 1970 two-thirds of affirmative action candidates were Black; today less than half are. White women make up a large percentage of participants, as do Asians, handicapped persons and others, including newly arrived immigrants.

It is important to note that preferential treatment has always been a part of the admissions process to prestigious institutions of higher learning and for employment opportunities as well. Children of alumni euphemistically called "legacies" have always been given preferential admission status. For example, Princeton

University accepts only approximately 15% of its applicant pool but 40% of legacies, which gives Princeton approximately 10% of each class as legacies. Furthermore, there is every reason to believe that these "legacies" have admission scores less than some who were denied admission. These legacies therefore bear the same burden for displacement as candidates of affirmative action. However, recently the courts have seen fit to protect preferential treatment of legacies while rejecting affirmative action. With reference to charges of less than qualified affirmative action candidates, available evidence reveals that the graduation rates of those students remain competitive. Also the students who were admitted in the cases that have been brought before the courts, are perhaps the best advertisement for these programs. While they had scores somewhat lower than those they were claimed to have displaced, they have not only graduated from their universities but have passed their various boards and bar examinations. It is important to note that the courts have now ruled irrelevant the very reasons that initially were lauded as important to the mission of affirmative action. A few curious conclusions that can be drawn from the court's recent rush to abolish affirmative action are: preferential treatment through affirmative action is wrong because it favors less qualified Blacks over more qualified Whites; preferential treatment through legacies is right because it favors less qualified Whites above less qualified Blacks and or Whites; and preferential treatment to Blacks to achieve diversity in a diverse society is of no consequence to the larger society.

The quest for full equality continues. It is likely to follow a different path, but the journey remains the same: equal access for all citizens. Those who have benefited from these programs, people like Colin Powell, have shown that there are indeed national treasures who would not have been able to shine without these programs. More Blacks who have benefited will have to carry the torch and lead the way until these programs are no longer needed.

References

Anderson, B.J. (1990). Sport, play and gender-based success in Jaimaica. *Arena Review,* 14(1), 59–67.

———. (1994). Permissive social and educational inequality 40 years after *Brown. Journal of Negro Education,* 63(3), 443–450.

Bakke v. Regents of the University of California, 98 S. Ct. 2733 (1978).

Blinick, (April, 1975). Avoiding Affirmative Action Pitfalls. *Practical Lawyer,* 21(3), 45–46.

Bolling v. Sharpe, 347 U.S. 499 (1954).

Brown v Board of Education, 347 U.S. 483 (1954).

Carter, D.J. & Wilson, R. (1996). Special focus affirmative action and higher education. Minorities in Higher Education. Fourteenth Annual Report. American Council on Education.

Christian Science Monitor, (1993, Nov. 2), p. 10.

City of Richmond v. Croson Company, 109 S. Ct. 706 (1989).

Civil Rights Act of 1964, 42 U.S.C. § 2000 c, d (1993).

The Cole example. (1990, Sep. 17). *National Review,* p. 18.

Complaint on Harvard Law School hiring. (1992, Mar. 4). *New York Times.*

Dahrendorfm R. (1959). *Class and class conflict in industrial society.* Stanford, CA: Stanford University Press.

Dartmouth professor quits after feud. (1990, Sept. 10). *Jet*, p. 36.

Davis, K. & Moore, W. (1945). Some principles of stratification. *ASA*, 10, 242–249.

DeFunis v. Odegaard, 416 U.S. 312 (1974).

Gans, H. (1971, March–April). The uses of poverty: The poor pay all. *Social Policy*, 20–24.

Geier v. Dunn, 337 F. Supp. 578 (1972).

Giroux, H. (1983). Theories of reproduction and resistance in the new sociology of educa-
ton. *Harvard Educational Review*, 52(3), 257–293.

Gregory, D.L. (1994). The continuing vitality of affirmative principles in professional and
graduate school student admission and faculty hiring. *Journal of Negro Education*,
73(3), 421–429.

Griggs v. Duke Power Co., 401 U.S. 424, 431 (1971).

Hacker, A. (1996, July 11). Goodbye to affirmative action? *The New York Review*.

Hartford bill on integration. (1993, June 5), *New York Times*, p. 23.

Hirabayshi v United States, 320 U.S. 81 (1943).

Justice for Hartford's schools. (1996, July 16), *The Boston Globe*, A14.

Korematsu v. United States, 323 U.S. 216 (1944).

Landtman, Gunnar. 1968. *The Origin of Inequality of the Social Class*. New York: Greenwood.

Legal beat: Harvard law. (1992, July 2). *Wall Street Journal*, p. 11.

Lemann, N. (1995, June 11). *New York Times Magazine*, p. 36.

Lenski, G. (1966). *Power and privilege: A theory of social stratification*. New York:
McGraw-Hill.

Magner, D. & Smolensky, E. (1989, Apr. 26). Blacks and Whites on the campuses: Behind
ugly racist incidents, student isolation and insensitivity. *The Chronicle of Higher Education*, p. 1.

Mann, H. (1851). *Slavery: Letters and speeches*. Boston: B.B. Mussey and Co.

Martin v. Wilks, 109 S. Ct. 2188 (1989).

National Review, (1990, Sept. 17). 42(18).

New York Times, (1993, June 5), L23.

———, (1992, March 4), B6.

Ogbu, J.U. (1990). Minority education in comparative perspective. *Journal of Negro Education*, 59(1), 45–57.

O'Neil, R. (1971). Preferential admissions: Equalizing the access of minority groups to
higher education. *Yale Law Journal*, 80, 699.

Parsons, T. & Bales, R.F. (1955). *Family, socialization, and interaction process*. Glencoe:
The Free Press.

Patterson v. McLean Credit Union, 109 S. Ct. 2363 (1989).

Runyan v. McCrary, 427 U.S. 160 (1976).

Sheff v. O'Neill, 15255 (1996).

Skolnick, J. & Currie, E. (1988). *Crisis in American institutions*. Boston: Little Brown.

Skrentny, J. (1996). *The ironies of affirmative action: Politics culture and justice in America*.
Chicago: University of Chicago Press.

Stefkovich, J. & Leas, T. (1994). A legal history of desegregation in higher education. *Journal of Negro Education*, 63(3), 406–420.

Texas v. Hopwood, No. 95-1773 (1996).

Tushnet, M. (1994). *Making civil rights law: Thurgood Marshall and the Supreme Court,
1936–1961*. New York: Oxford University Press.

Wards Cove Packing Co. v. Antonio, 109 S. Ct. 215 (1989).

Wright, Erik O. (1980a). Class and Occupation. *Theory and Society*, 9, 177–214.

———. 1980b. Varieties of Marxist Conceptions of Class Structure. *Politics and Society*, 9,
323–370.

———, D. Hachen, C. Costello, and J. Sprague. (1982). The American Class Structure.
American Sociological Review, 47, 709–726.

Section VIII

Crime and Punishment

22

Courts, Sentences, and Prisons

Cassia C. Spohn

Introduction

"The whole judicial system of courts, sentences and prisons in the South is overripe for fundamental reforms,"[1] concluded Gunnar Myrdal in *An American Dilemma*. Relying primarily on anecdotal accounts of differential treatment of African Americans and whites in Southern court systems, Myrdal documented widespread discrimination in assignment of counsel, bail setting, jury selection, court processing, and sentencing. Myrdal noted that although the danger of discrimination was greatest in lower state courts, where judges with limited education were more susceptible to the pressures of public opinion, it was found to some extent in all state courts in the South. He stated, "In a court system of this structure, operating within a deeply prejudiced region, discrimination is to be expected."[2]

Although Myrdal clearly was dismayed by the racial inequities he observed, he was optimistic that Southern courts would become more impartial. Myrdal saw numerous signs of change. He noted that the U.S. Supreme Court and lower federal courts were increasingly willing to censor state courts for violating the rights of criminal defendants and that it was becoming easier for African Americans to obtain the services of competent attorneys. He also predicted that socioeconomic changes in the South, coupled with the growing activism of civil rights groups and the increasingly important "Negro vote,"[3] would lead to reform. As he stated, "It is the author's observation that, *in principle, the average white Southerner is no longer prepared to defend racial inequality of justice.*"[4]

Some observers might contend that Myrdal's predictions were overly optimistic and that the reforms he envisioned have not produced the results he anticipated.

An earlier version of this essay appeared in *Daedalus;* 1995, 124, 1, Winter, 119–141 and is adapted/reprinted with the permission of the copyright holder/author.

1. Gunnar Myrdal, et al., *An American Dilemma: The Negro Problem and Modern Democracy* (New York: Harper and Brothers, 1944), 555.
2. *Ibid.*, p. 550.
3. *Ibid.*, p. 556.
4. *Ibid.*, p. 556.

It is certainly true that the past 50 years have witnessed significant changes. The U.S. Supreme Court has handed down decisions designed to protect the rights of criminal defendants and to prohibit racial discrimination in selection of the jury pool, use of peremptory challenges, and imposition of the death penalty. States likewise have enacted legislation and adopted policies designed to decrease the likelihood of overt class and race discrimination in the processing of criminal defendants.

Despite these reforms, inequalities persist. African Americans continue to suffer direct and indirect discrimination in decisions regarding bail, charging, jury selection, and sentencing. As Mark Mauer recently concluded, "the extended reach of the criminal justice system has been far from uniform in its effects upon different segments of the population...as has been true historically, but even more so now, the criminal justice system disproportionately engages minorities and the poor."[5]

In the sections that follow, we evaluate Mydral's findings concerning the inequities inherent in the Southern criminal justice system. We also discuss reforms designed to eliminate these inequities and review recent research on the effect of race on court processing decisions. We conclude that while the reforms Myrdal envisioned may have eliminated "the more blatant forms of deviation from fair trial in the lower courts,"[6] they have not produced equality of justice.

Decisions Regarding Counsel and Bail

Myrdal found that Southern blacks suffered both class and race discrimination in decisions regarding appointment of counsel and bail. Although he cited no statistics or empirical evidence in support of his claims (a problem found throughout the chapter), he concluded that African Americans charged with crimes frequently were unable to obtain competent counsel or pretrial release. Myrdal admitted that poor whites faced similar problems, but argued that African Americans were at a greater disadvantage because of their race. He noted that white lawyers were reluctant to take cases with African American defendants, and that bail "was most often refused or made prohibitively high to accused Negroes, particularly when the alleged crime is against whites."[7]

Right to Counsel

Myrdal clearly regarded lack of access to competent counsel as a serious problem. In fact, he concluded that success in reforming the Southern court system hinged on the establishment of "legal aid agencies...to assist poor whites and Negroes to enforce their rights under existing laws in civil and criminal cases."[8]

5. Mark Mauer, *Young Black Men and the Criminal Justice System: A Growing National Problem*. Washington, D.C.: The Sentencing Project, 1990.
6. Myrdal, *An American Dilemma*, p. 555.
7. *Ibid.*, p. 548.
8. *Ibid.*, p. 556.

Myrdal argued that use of court-appointed attorneys, whom he suggested were often young and inexperienced, was not sufficient. He recommended that Southern jurisdictions establish independent agencies staffed by professional lawyers who would not only defend those charged with crimes but who would also monitor the treatment of racial minorities in courts and prisons.

In discussing the right to counsel, Myrdal stated, incorrectly, that in criminal cases courts will "appoint a lawyer for anybody who cannot afford to provide himself with proper legal aid."[9] In fact, until the early 1960s, several Southern states, in compliance with the Supreme Court's decision in *Powell v. Alabama*,[10] guaranteed the right to counsel only to defendants in capital cases. The Court's decision in a 1938 case, *Johnson v. Zerbst*,[11] required the appointment of counsel for all indigent defendants in federal criminal cases, but the requirement was not extended to the states until *Gideon v. Wainwright*[12] was decided in 1963.[13] In subsequent decisions the Court ruled that "no person may be imprisoned, for any offense, whether classified as petty, misdemeanor, or felony, unless he was represented by counsel,"[14] and that the right to counsel is not limited to trial, but applies to all "critical stages" in the criminal justice process.[15]

At the time the *Gideon* decision was handed down, 13 states, including five states in the South, had no statewide requirement for appointment of counsel except in capital cases.[16] Other states relied on members of local bar associations to defend indigents, often on a pro bono basis. Following *Gideon*, it became obvious that other procedures would be required if all felony defendants were to be provided attorneys.

States moved swiftly to implement the constitutional requirements articulated in *Gideon* and the cases that followed, either by establishing public defender systems or by appropriating money for court-appointed attorneys. The number of public defender systems grew rapidly. In 1951 there were only seven public defender organizations in the United States; in 1964 there were 136 and by 1973 the total had risen to 573.[17] A 1981 survey of indigent defense services found that 66% of U.S. counties used assigned counsel or contract attorneys and that 34% used public defender systems; the survey also revealed that over half of the case assignments were made within 48 hours of arrest.[18]

---

9. *Ibid.*, p. 548.

10. *Powell* v. *Alabama*, 287 U.S. 45 (1932).

11. *Johnson* v. *Zerbst*, 304 U.S. 458 (1938).

12. *Gideon* v. *Wainwright*, 372 U.S. 335 (1963).

13. *Gideon* v. *Wainwright* required the states to provide counsel for indigent defendants charged with felonies. In 1972 the Supreme Court ruled that "no person may be imprisoned for any offense, whether classified as petty, misdemeanor, or felony, unless he was represented by counsel [*Argersinger* v. *Hamlin*, 407 U.S. 25 (1972)].

14. *Argersinger* v. *Hamlin*, 407 U.S. 25 (1972).

15. A defendant is entitled to counsel at every stage "where substantial rights of the accused may be affected" that require the "guiding hand of counsel" (*Mempa v. Rhay*, 389 U.S. 128, 1967). These critical stages include arraignment, preliminary hearing, entry of a plea, trial, sentencing, and the first appeal.

16. Anthony Lewis, *Gideon's Trumpet*. New York: Vintage Books, 1964.

17. Lisa J. McIntyre, *The Public Defender: The Practice of Law in the Shadows of Repute*. Chicago: University of Chicago Press, 1987.

18. Bureau of Justice Statistics, *Criminal Defense Systems: A National Survey*. Washington, D.C.: U.S. Government Printing Office, 1984.

In sum, while Myrdal's recommendations regarding the establishment of independent legal aid agencies have not been implemented, significant changes have occurred. As a result of Supreme Court decisions expanding the right to counsel and the development of policies implementing these decisions, African American defendants are no longer denied legal representation at trial or at any of the other "critical stages" in the criminal justice process.[19] Although questions have been raised about the quality of legal representation provided to indigent defendants,[20] it is no longer true that "Negroes are without a voice"[21] in Southern courts.

Bail Decision Making

Myrdal's examination of the bond and bail system was extremely brief. He noted that the system "works automatically against the poor classes."[22] He added that African American defendants, particularly those accused of crimes against whites, were more likely than white defendants to be detained prior to trial, either because the judge refused bail or because the judge set bail at an unaffordable level. Myrdal did not discuss the consequences of pretrial detention and made no specific recommendations for reforming the bail system.

The issue of bail reform did not reach the national political agenda until nearly 20 years after the publication of *An American Dilemma*. Concerns about the rights of poor defendants led to the first bail reform movement, which emerged in the early 1960s and emphasized reducing pretrial detention. Those who lobbied for reform argued that the purpose of bail was to insure the defendant's appearance in court and that the amount of bail therefore should not exceed the amount necessary to guarantee that the defendant would show up for all court proceedings. Proponents of this view asserted that whether a defendant was released or detained prior to trial should not depend upon his or her race or economic status. They also cited research demonstrating that the type and amount of bail imposed upon the defendant and the time spent by the defendant in pretrial detention affected the likelihood of a guilty plea, the likelihood of conviction at trial, and the severity of the sentence.[23]

---

19. In a series of cases, the U.S. Supreme Court decided that the right to counsel is not limited to the trial, but applies to all critical stages in the process. A defendant is entitled to counsel at every stage "where substantial rights of the accused may be affected" that require the "guiding hand of counsel" (*Mempa v. Rhay*, 389 U.S. 128, 1967). These critical stages include arraignment, preliminary hearing, entry of a plea, trial, sentencing, and the first appeal.

20. Studies comparing the quality of legal services provided by private attorneys and public defenders are inconclusive. A study in Cook County, Illinois found that clients represented by public defenders were more likely than those represented by private attorneys or assigned counsel to plead guilty (Dallin H. Oaks and Warren Lehman, *A Criminal Justice System and the Indigent*. Chicago: University of Chicago Press, 1968). Other studies found no differences (see Jean Taylor, Thomas Stanley, Barbara Deflorio and Lyne Seekamp, "An Analysis of Defense Counsel in the Processing of Felony Defendants in Denver, Colorado, *Denver Law Journal* 50 (1973): 9–44; Paul Wice, *Criminal Lawyers: An Endangered Species*. Beverly Hills: Sage Publications, 1978.

21. Myrdal, *An American Dilemma*, p. 547.

22. *Ibid.*, p. 548.

23. Celesta A. Albonetti, "An Integration of Theories to Explain Judicial Discretion," *Social Problems* 38 (1991): 247–266; Ronald A. Farrell and Victoria L. Swigert, "Prior Offense Record as a Self-Fulfilling Prophecy," *Law and Society Review* 12 (1978): 437–453; C.

Arguments such as these prompted state and federal reforms designed to reduce pretrial detention. Encouraged by the results of the Manhattan Bail Project, which found that the majority of indigent defendants released on their own recognizance did appear for trial,[24] local jurisdictions moved quickly to reduce reliance on money bail and to institute programs modeled after the Manhattan Bail Project. Many states revised their bail laws and in 1966 Congress passed the Bail Reform Act, which proclaimed release on recognizance the presumptive bail decision in federal criminal cases.

Then, as Samuel Walker has noted, "the political winds shifted."[25] The rising crime rate of the 1970s generated a concern for crime control and led to a reassessment of bail policies. Critics challenged the traditional position that the only function of bail was to assure the defendant's appearance at trial. They argued that guaranteeing public safety was also a valid function of bail and that pretrial detention should be used to protect the community from "dangerous" offenders.

These arguments fueled the second bail reform movement, which emerged in the 1970s and emphasized preventive detention. Conservative legislators and policymakers lobbied for reforms allowing judges to consider "public safety" when making decisions concerning the type and amount of bail.[26] By 1984, thirty-four states had enacted legislation giving judges the right to deny bail to defendants deemed dangerous.[27] Also in 1984, Congress passed a law authorizing preventive detention of dangerous defendants in federal criminal cases.[28]

The Effect of Race on Bail Decision Making. Proponents of bail reform argued that bail decisions should rest either upon assessments of the likelihood that the defendant would appear in court or upon predictions of the defendant's dangerousness. The problem, of course, is that there is no way to guarantee that race will not influence these assessments and predictions. As Caranae Mann has asserted, even the seemingly objective criteria used in making release on recognizance decisions and in determining dangerousness "may still be discriminatory on the basis of economic status or skin color."[29]

Studies examining the effect of race on bail decisions have yielded contradictory findings. Some researchers have concluded that bail decisions are determined

Foote, "Compelling Appearance in Court: Administration of Bail in Philadelphia," *University of Pennsylvania Law Review* 102 (1954): 1031–1079; Joan Petersilia, *Racial Disparities in the Criminal Justice System* (Santa Monica: Rand Corporation, 1978); G. R. Wheeler and C.L. Wheeler, "Reflections on Legal Representation of the Economically Disadvantaged: Beyond Assembly Line Justice," *Crime and Delinquency* 26 (1980): 319–332.

24. Wayne Thomas, *Bail Reform in America* (Berkeley: University of California Press, 1976), pp. 37–38.

25. Samuel Walker, *Taming the System: The Control of Discretion in Criminal Justice, 1950–1990* (New York: Oxford University Press, 1993), p. 54.

26. J. Austin, B. Krisberg and P. Litsky, "The Effectiveness of Supervised Pretrial Release," *Crime and Delinquency* 31 (1985): 519–537; John S. Goldkamp, "Danger and Detention: A Second Generation of Bail Reform," *The Journal of Criminal Law and Criminology* 76 (1985): 1–74; Samuel Walker, *Taming the System.*

27. Goldkamp, "Danger and Detention."

28. This law was upheld by the U.S. Supreme Court in *United States* v. *Salerno,* 481 U.S. 739 (1987).

29. Coramae Richey Mann, *Unequal Justice: A Question of Color* (Bloomington and Indianapolis: Indiana University Press, 1993), p. 168.

primarily by legal variables such as prior record and offense seriousness and that race has no effect once controls for these legal variables are taken into consideration.[30] Other researchers contend that it is the defendant's economic status, rather than the defendant's race, that determines the likelihood of pretrial release.[31] If this is the case, one could argue that bail decision making reflects *indirect* racial discrimination, since African American defendants are more likely than white defendants to be poor.

There are several studies that conclude either that defendant race directly affects bail outcomes[32] or that defendant race interacts with other variables that are themselves related to bail severity.[33] One study, for example, found that African Americans and Native Americans were less likely than whites to be released on their own recognizance.[34] Another study of bail decision making in ten federal district courts found that race did not have a direct effect on bail outcomes, but did interact with a number of other variables to produce harsher bail outcomes for some types of African American defendants.[35] More specifically, the authors found that having a prior felony conviction had a greater negative effect on bail severity for African American defendants than for white defendants, while having more education or a higher income had a greater positive effect for whites than for African Americans.

Although the findings are somewhat contradictory, it thus appears that the reforms instituted since the 1960s have not produced racial equality in bail decision-making. There is evidence that judges in some jurisdictions continue to take race into account in deciding on the type and amount of bail. There is also evidence that race interacts with other factors to produce higher pretrial detention rates for African American defendants than for white defendants. Given the serious negative consequences of pretrial detention, these findings are an obvious cause for concern.

---

30. Celesta A. Albonetti, "Bail and Judicial Discretion in the District of Columbia," *Sociology and Social Research* 74 (1989): 40–47; C. E. Frazier, E.W. Bock, and J.C. Henretta, "Pretrial Release and Bail Decisions: The Effects of Legal, Community, and Personal Variables," *Criminology* 18 (1980): 162–181; John S. Goldkamp and Michael Gottfredson, "Bail Decision Making and Pretrial Detention: Surfacing Judicial Policy," *Law and Human Behavior* 3 (1979): 227–249; Ilene H. Nagel, The Legal/Extra-Legal Controversy: Judicial Decisions in Pretrial Release," *Law & Society Review* 17 (1983): 481–515; and R. Stryker, Ilene Nagel and John Hagan, "Methodology Issues in Court Research: Pretrial Release Decisions for Federal Defendants," *Sociological Methods and Research* 11 (1983): 469–500.

31. S.H. Clarke and G.G. Koch, "The Influence of Income and Other Factors on Whether Criminal Defendants Go To Prison," *Law & Society Review* 11 (1976): 57–92; Ronald A. Farrell and Victoria L. Swigert, "Prior Offense Record as a Self-Fulfilling Prophecy," *Law & Society Review* 12 (1978): 437–453; and J.D. Unnever, "Direct and Organizational Discrimination in the Sentencing of Drug Offenders," *Social Problems* 30 (1982): 212–225.

32. E. Britt Patterson and Michael J. Lynch, "Biases in Formalized Bail Procedures." In Michael J. Lynch and E. Britt Patterson (eds.) *Race and Criminal Justice* (New York: Harrow and Heston, 1991).

33. Margaret Farnworth and Patrick Horan, "Separate Justice: An Analysis of Race Differences in Court Processes," *Social Science Research* 9 (1980): 381–399.

34. Tim Bynum, "Release on Recognizance: Substantive or Superficial Reform?" *Criminology* 20 (1982): 67–82.

35. Celesta A. Albonetti, Robert M. Hauser, John Hagan, and Ilene H. Nagel, "Criminal Justice Decision Making as a Stratification Process: The Role of Race and Stratification Resources in Pretrial Release," *Journal of Quantitative Criminology* 5 (1989): 57–82.

Jury Selection

Myrdal's examination of the Southern court system revealed that the typical jury was an all-white jury.[36] Myrdal noted that some courts, in response to a 1935 Supreme Court decision[37] stating that African Americans could not be systematically excluded from the jury pool, had taken steps "to have Negroes on the jury list and call them in occasionally for service."[38] He added, however, that many Southern courts, and particularly those in rural areas, had either ignored the constitutional requirement or had developed techniques "to fulfill legal requirements without using Negro jurors."[39]

Since 1943 the Supreme Court has made it increasingly difficult for court systems to exclude African Americans from the jury pool. The Court has consistently struck down the "techniques" used by Southern jurisdictions to circumvent the requirement of racial neutrality in the selection of the venire. The Court, for example, ruled that it was unconstitutional for a Georgia county to put the names of white potential jurors on white cards, the names of African American potential jurors on yellow cards, and then "randomly" draw cards to determine who would be summoned.[40] Similarly, the Court struck down the "random" selection of jurors from tax books where the names of white taxpayers were in one section, the names of African American taxpayers in another.[41] As the Court stated in *Avery* v. *Georgia*, "... the State may not draw up its jury lists pursuant to neutral procedures but then resort to discrimination at other stages in the selection process."[42]

Myrdal's analysis of the jury selection process did not address the use of peremptory challenges to exclude African Americans from the jury. This oversight is understandable. Historically, attorneys "enjoyed carte blanche freedom in exercising peremptory challenges."[43] The assumption was that these challenges were being used to achieve a fair and impartial jury. In reality, of course, peremptory challenges often were used to strike African American jurors from cases with African American defendants. Critics charged that this practice "both reduces minority participation on criminal juries and frustrates the interest of minority defendants in a jury of peers."[44]

The Supreme Court initially was reluctant to restrict the prosecutor's right to use peremptory challenges to excuse jurors on the basis of race. In the 1965 case of *Swain* v. *Alabama*, the Court ruled that the prosecutor's use of peremptory challenges to strike all six African Americans in the jury pool did not violate the equal protection clause of the Constitution. The Court reasoned:

---

36. Myrdal, *An American Dilemma*, p. 549.

37. *Norris* v. *Alabama*, 294 U.S. 587 (1935).

38. Myrdal, *An American Dilemma*, p. 549.

39. *Ibid.*, p. 549.

40. *Avery* v. *Georgia*, 345 U.S. 559 (1953).

41. *Whitus* v. *Georgia*, 385 U.S. 545 (1967).

42. *Avery* v. *Georgia*, 345 U.S. 559 (1953) at 562.

43. David W. Neubauer, *America's Court & the Criminal Justice System*, 3rd ed. (Pacific Grove: Brooks/Cole Publishing, 1988), p. 307.

44. Brian J. Serr and Mark Maney, "Racism, Peremptory Challenges, and the Democratic Jury: The Jurisprudence of a Delicate Balance," *The Journal of Criminal Law & Criminology* 79 (1988): 1–65, p. 9.

The presumption in any particular case must be that the prosecutor is using the State's challenges to obtain a fair and impartial jury... The presumption is not overcome and the prosecutor therefore subjected to examination by allegations that in the case at hand all Negroes were removed from the jury or that they were removed because they were Negroes.[45]

The Court went on to observe that the Constitution did place some limits on the use of the peremptory challenge. The Justices stated that a defendant could establish a prima facie case of purposeful racial discrimination by showing that the elimination of African Americans from a particular jury was part of a pattern of discrimination in that jurisdiction.

The problem, of course, was that the defendants in *Swain*, and in the cases that followed, could not meet this stringent test. As Wishman observed, "A defense lawyer almost never has the statistics to prove a pattern of discrimination, and the state under the *Swain* decision is not required to keep them."[46] The ruling, therefore, provided no protection to the individual African American defendant deprived of a jury of his peers by the prosecutor's use of racially discriminatory strikes.

Despite harsh criticism from legal scholars and civil libertarians,[47] who argued that *Swain* imposed a "crushing burden... on defendants alleging racially discriminatory jury selection,"[48] the decision stood for twenty-one years. It was not until 1986 that the Court, in *Batson* v. *Kentucky*,[49] rejected *Swain*'s systematic exclusion requirement and ruled "that a defendant may establish a prima facie case of purposeful discrimination in selection of the petit jury solely on evidence concerning the prosecutor's exercise of peremptory challenges at the defendant's trial."[50] The Justices added that once the defendant makes a prima facie case of racial discrimination, the burden shifts to the state to provide a racially neutral explanation for excluding African American jurors.

Although *Batson* seemed to offer hope that the goal of a representative jury was attainable, an examination of cases decided since 1986 suggests otherwise. State and federal appellate courts have ruled, for example, that leaving one or two African Americans on the jury precludes any inference of purposeful racial discrimination on the part of the prosecutor[51] and that striking only one or two jurors of the defendant's race does not constitute a "pattern" of strikes.[52] Trial and appellate courts have also been willing to accept virtually any explanation offered by the prosecutor to rebut the defendant's inference of purposeful discrimina-

45. *Swain* v. *Alabama*, 380 U.S. at 222.

46. Seymour Wishman, *Anatomy of a Jury: The System on Trial* (New York: Times Books, 1986).

47. See Comment, "*Swain* v. *Alabama*, A Constitutional Blueprint for the Perpetuation of the All-White Jury," *Virginia Law Review* 52 (1966): 1157; Note, "Rethinking Limitations on the Peremptory Challenge," *Columbia Law Review* 85 (1983): 1357.

48. Serr and Maney, "Racism, Peremptory Challenges, and the Democratic Jury," p. 13.

49. *Batson* v. *Kentucky*, 476 U.S. 79, 93–94 (1986).

50. *Ibid.*, at 96.

51. *United States* v. *Montgomery*, 819 F.2d at 851. The Eleventh Circuit, however, rejected this line of reasoning in *Fleming* v. *Kemp* [794 F.2d 1478 (11th Cir. 1986)] and *United States* v. *David* [803 F.2d 1567 (11th Cir. 1986)].

52. *United States* v. *Vaccaro*, 816 F.2d 443, 457 (9th Cir. 1987); *Fields* v. *People*, 732 P.2d 1145, 1158 n. 20 (Colo. 1987).

tion.[53] Thus, "The cost of forfeiting truly peremptory challenges has yielded little corresponding benefit, as a myriad of 'acceptable' explanations and excuses cloud any hope of detecting racially based motivations."[54]

Although it is no longer true that "the vast majority of the rural courts in the Deep South have made no pretense of putting Negroes on jury lists, much less calling or using them in trials,"[55] the jury selection process remains racially biased. Prosecutors continue to use the peremptory challenge to exclude African American jurors from cases with African American defendants[56] and appellate courts continue to rule that their "racially neutral" explanations adequately meet the standards articulated in *Batson*. Supreme Court decisions notwithstanding, the peremptory challenge remains an obstacle to impartiality.

Court Processing and Sentencing

Myrdal's examination of the Southern court system uncovered widespread racial discrimination in case processing and sentencing. Myrdal observed that cases involving African American defendants were handled informally and with a lack of dignity, and that convictions often were obtained upon presentation of "scanty evidence." He noted that grand juries routinely refused to indict whites for crimes against African Americans, and added that "It is notorious that practically never have white lynching mobs been brought to court in the South, even when the killers are known to all in the community and are mentioned by name in the local press."[57]

A common theme in Myrdal's analysis of court processing and sentencing is the differential treatment of interracial and intraracial crimes. Noting that "It is part of the Southern tradition to assume that Negroes are disorderly and lack elementary morals,"[58] Myrdal concluded that African American defendants who victimized other African Americans were treated with great leniency. He observed that white Southerners viewed the more lenient treatment of black-on-black crime "as evidence of the friendliness of Southern courts toward Negroes," but that "the Southern Negro community is not at all happy about this double standard of justice."[59]

According to Myrdal, interracial crimes evoked very different responses from Southern courts, depending on the race of the offender. Whites who committed crimes, even very serious crimes, against African Americans were rarely convicted; those who were convicted received only the mildest punishment. African

---

53. Serr and Maney, "Racism, Peremptory Challenges, and the Democratic Jury," pp. 43–47.

54. *Ibid.*, p. 63.

55. Myrdal, *An American Dilemma*, pp. 547–548.

56. A study of peremptory challenges issued from 1976 to 1981 in Calcasieu Parish, Louisiana, for example, found that prosecutors excused African American jurors at a disproportionately high rate. See Billy M. Turner, Rickie D. Lovell, John C. Young and William F. Denny, "Race and Peremptory Challenges During Voir Dire: Do Prosecution and Defense Agree?" *Journal of Criminal Justice* 14 (1986): 61–69.

57. Myrdal, *An American Dilemma*, pp. 552–553.

58. *Ibid.*, p. 551.

59. *Ibid.*, p. 551.

Americans charged with (or even suspected of) offenses against whites, on the other hand, were treated very harshly. Myrdal noted that African Americans charged with serious crimes against whites often faced a white lynching mob. He stated that in situations like this, "the court makes no pretense at justice; the Negro must be condemned, and usually condemned to death, before the crowd gets him."[60]

Race and Pretrial Decision Making

Since 1943 there has been a virtual explosion of research investigating the relationship between the defendant's race and court processing decisions. Although most of this research has focused on the effect of race on sentencing, there are a number of studies that examine decisions made prior to trial for evidence of racial discrimination. As noted earlier, several studies have analyzed the relationship between defendant race and bail decision-making. The results of these studies are contradictory, but some do conclude that race affects the type and amount of bail imposed by the judge.

There also is evidence that prosecutors' charging decisions are affected by race. An analysis of the prosecutor's decision to reject or dismiss charges against defendants in Los Angeles County, for example, revealed a pattern of discrimination in favor of female defendants and against African American and Hispanic defendants.[61] A study by Joan Petersilia,[62] on the other hand, found that white suspects were *more* likely than African American or Hispanic suspects to be formally charged. Her analysis of the reasons given for charge rejection led her to conclude that the higher dismissal rates for non-white suspects reflected the fact that "blacks and Hispanics in California are more likely than whites to be arrested under circumstances that provide insufficient evidence to support criminal charges."[63]

Two studies concluded that both the race of the defendant *and* the race of the victim are significant factors. Gary LaFree[64] found that African Americans arrested for raping white women were more likely to be charged with felonies than were either African Americans arrested for raping African American women or whites arrested for raping white women. Another study found that defendants arrested for murdering whites in Florida were more likely to be indicted for first-degree murder than those arrested for murdering blacks.[65]

---

60. *Ibid.*, p. 553.

61. Cassia Spohn, John Gruhl, and Susan Welch, "The Impact of the Ethnicity and Gender of Defendants on the Decision To Reject or Dismiss Felony Charges," *Criminology* 25 (1987): 175–191.

62. Joan Petersilia, *Racial Disparities in the Criminal Justice System* (Santa Monica: Rand, 1983).

63. *Ibid.*, p. 26.

64. Gary D. LaFree, "The Effect of Sexual Stratification by Race on Official Reactions to Rape," *American Sociological Review* 45 (1980): 842–854.

65. Michael L. Radelet, "Racial Characteristics and the Imposition of the Death Penalty," *American Sociological Review* 46 (1981): 918–927.

The Effect of Race on Sentencing

Fifty years after publication of *An American Dilemma*, the issue of racial discrimination in sentencing continues to evoke controversy and spark debate. Citing statistics showing that African American males account for one-half of all state and federal prisoners,[66] critics charge that African American criminal defendants are more likely to be incarcerated, and are incarcerated for longer periods of time, than are white defendants. They argue that judges' sentencing decisions are racially biased. Other researchers suggest that the harsher sentences imposed on African American defendants reflect not racial discrimination on the part of judges, but the fact that African American defendants commit more serious crimes and have more serious prior criminal records than white defendants. They argue that racial disparities in sentencing will disappear once these legal factors are taken into consideration.

There is now a substantial body of research examining the relationship between defendant race and sentence severity.[67] Early studies consistently documented overt bias against African Americans,[68] but more recent studies have produced contradictory findings. These more methodologically rigorous studies have not always supported the proposition that "blacks or other nonwhites will receive more severe punishment than whites for all crimes, under all conditions, and at similar levels of disproportion over time."[69] Although a number of studies have found that African Americans are sentenced more harshly than whites,[70] others have found either that there are no significant racial differences[71] or that African Americans are sentenced more leniently than whites.[72]

---

66. Patrick A. Langan, *Race and Prisoners Admitted to State and Federal Institutions, 1926–1986* (U.S. Department of Justice, Washington, D.C.: U.S. Government Printing Office, 1991).

67. For a review of these studies and for a discussion of the four waves of research on sentencing disparities, see Marjorie S. Zatz, "The Changing Forms of Racial/Ethnic Biases in Sentencing," *Journal of Research in Crime and Delinquency* 24 (1987): 69–92.

68. See, for example, Hugo A. Bedau, "Death Sentences in New Jersey," *Rutgers Law Review* 19 (1964): 1–2; E. H. Johnson, "Selective Factors in Capital Punishment," *Social Forces* 58 (1957): 165–169; E. M. Lemert and J. Rosberg, "The Administration of Justice to Minority Groups in L.A. County," *University of California Publications in Culture and Society* (1948): 1–27; and Thorsten Sellin, "Race Prejudice in the Administration of Justice," *American Journal of Sociology* 41 (1935): 212–217.

69. Hawkins, "Beyond Anomalies: Rethinkin the Conflict Perspective on Race and Criminal Justice," *Social forces* 65 (1987): 719–745.

70. Joan Petersilia, *Racial Disparities in the Criminal Justice System*. Santa Monica: Rand (1983); Cassia Spohn, John Gruhl and Susan Welch, "The Effect of Race on Sentencing: A Re-Examination of an Unsettled Question," *Law & Society Review* 16 (1981–82): 71–88; and Marjorie S. Zatz, "Race, Ethnicity, and Determinate Sentencing: A New Dimension to an Old Controversy." *Criminology* 22 (1984): 147–171.

71. Stephen Klein, Joan Petersilia and Susan Turner, "Race and Imprisonment Decisions in California," *Science* 247 (1990): 812–816.

72. Ilene Nagel Bernstein, William R. Kelly, and Patricia A. Doyle, "Societal Reaction to Deviants: The Case of Criminal Defendants," *American Sociological Review* 42 (1977): 743–795; James L. Gibson, "Race as a Determinant of Criminal Sentences: A Methodological Critique and a Case Study," *Law & Society Review* 12 (1978): 455–478; and Martin A. Levin, "Urban Politics and Policy Outcomes: The Criminal Courts." In George F. Cole (ed.), *Criminal Justice: Law and Politics* (Belmont: Wadsworth).

The failure of research to produce uniform findings of racial discrimination in sentencing has led to conflicting conclusions. Some researchers[73] assert that racial discrimination in sentencing has declined over time and contend that the predictive power of race, once relevant legal factors are taken into account, is quite low. Others[74] claim that discrimination has not declined or disappeared but simply has become more subtle and difficult to detect. These researchers argue that race affects sentence severity *indirectly* through its effect on variables such as bail status,[75] type of attorney,[76] or type of disposition,[77] or that race *interacts* with other variables and affects sentence severity only in some types of cases,[78] in some types of settings,[79] or for some types of defendants.[80]

---

73. John Hagan, "Extra-Legal Attributes and Criminal Sentencing: An Assessment of a Sociological Viewpoint," *Law & Society Review* 8 (1974): 357–383; Gary C. Kleck, "Racial Discrimination in Sentencing: A Critical Evaluation of the Evidence with Additional Evidence on the Death Penalty," *American Sociological Review* 43 (1981): 783–805; and Charles R. Pruitt and James Q. Wilson, "A Longitudinal Study of the Effect of Race on Sentencing," *Law & Society Review* 7 (1983): 613–635.

74. Steven Klepper, Daniel Nagin and Luke-Jon Tierney, "Discrimination in the Criminal Justice System: A Critical Appraisal of the Literature." In Alfred Blumstein, Jacqueline Cohen, Susan E. Martin and Michael H. Tonry (eds.), *Research on Sentencing: A Search for Reform*, Vol. 2 (Washington, DC: National Academy Press, 1983: pp 55–128); Marjorie S. Zatz, "The Changing Forms of Racial/Ethnic Biases in Sentencing," *Journal of Research in Crime and Delinquency* 24 (1987): 69–92.

75. Gary D. LaFree, "Official Reactions to Hispanic Defendants in the Southwest," *Journal of Research in Crime and Delinquency* 22 (1985): 213–23; Alan J. Lizotte, "Extra-legal factors in Chicago's Criminal Courts: Testing the Conflict Model of Criminal Justice," *Social Problems* 25 (1978): 564–580.

76. Spohn, Gruhl and Welch, "The Effect of Race on Sentencing."

77. Gary D. LaFree, "Adversarial and Nonadversarial Justice: A Comparison of Guilty Pleas and Trials," *Criminology* 23 (1985): 289–312; Cassia Spohn, "An Analysis of the 'Jury Trial Penalty' and Its Effect on Black and White Offenders," *The Justice Professional* 7 (1992): 93–112; and Thomas M. Uhlman and J. Darlene Walker, "'He Takes Some of My Time, I Take Some of His': An Analysis of Sentencing Patterns in Jury Cases," *Law & Society Review* 14 (1980): 323–341.

78. Arnold Barnett, "Some Distribution Patterns for the Georgia Death Sentence," *U.C. Davis Law Review* 18 (1985): 1327–1374; Cassia Spohn and Jerry Cederblom, "Race and Disparities in Sentencing: A Test of the Liberation Hypothesis," *Justice Quarterly* 8 (1991): 305–327.

79. Darnell F. Hawkins, "Beyond Anomalies: Rethinking the Conflict Perspective on Race and Criminal Punishment," *Social Forces* 65 (1987): 719–745; Kleck, "Racial Discrimination in Sentencing"; and Martha A. Myers and Susette Talarico, "The Social Contexts of Racial Discrimination in Sentencing," *Social Problems* 33 (1986): 236–251.

80. Theodore G. Chiricos and William D. Bales, "Unemployment and Punishment: An Empirical Assessment," *Criminology* 29 (1991): 701–724; Gary D. LaFree, *Rape and Criminal Justice: The Social Construction of Sexual Assault* (Belmont: Wadsworth, 1989); Ruth Peterson and John Hagan, "Changing Conceptions of Race: Toward an Account of Anomalous Findings in Sentencing Research," *American Sociological Review* 49 (1984): 56–70; Cassia Spohn, "Crime and the Social Control of Blacks: The Effect of Offender/Victim Race on Sentences for Violent Felonies." In George Bridges and Martha Myers (eds.), *Inequality, Crime and Social Control* (Westview Press, 1994); and Anthony Walsh, "The Sexual Stratification Hypothesis and Sexual Assault in Light of the Changing Conceptions of Race," *Criminology* 25 (1987): 153–173.

Differential Treatment of Interracial and Intraracial Crime

As noted above, Myrdal emphasized differences in the treatment of interracial and intraracial crime in Southern courts. He observed that African Americans who victimized whites received the harshest punishment, while African Americans who offended against other African Americans were often "acquitted or given a ridiculously mild sentence...."[81] Myrdal also noted that "it is quite common for a white criminal to be set free if his crime was against a Negro."[82]

Race and Sentences Imposed for Sexual Assault. Recent empirical research confirms these conclusions. There have been a number of studies comparing the processing of interracial and intraracial sexual assaults. LaFree,[83] for example, examined the impact of offender/victim race on the disposition of sexual assault cases in Indianapolis. He found that African American men who sexually assaulted white women were sentenced more severely than were other defendants, while African American men who assaulted African American women were sentenced more leniently than were other defendants. Anthony Walsh[84] reached a similar conclusion. When he examined the sentences imposed on African American and on white defendants convicted of sexual assault in a metropolitan Ohio county, he found that neither the defendant's race nor the victim's race affected sentence severity. Further analysis, however, revealed that black-on-white sexual assaults received more severe sentences than black-on-black assaults.

Spohn's[85] study of sentences imposed on defendants convicted of violent felonies in Detroit also highlighted the importance of testing for race-of-victim and type-of-crime effects. When the author examined the sentences imposed on all felony defendants, she found that offender/victim race did not affect sentence severity in the predicted manner. When she analyzed the effect of offender/victim race on sentence severity *separately* for the various types of crimes, on the other hand, she found that offender/victim race did influence judges' sentencing decisions in sexual assault and murder cases. African Americans who sexually assaulted whites faced a greater risk of incarceration than either African Americans who sexually assaulted African Americans or whites who sexually assaulted whites; similarly, African Americans who murdered whites received longer sentences than did offenders in the other two categories. For these two crimes, then, the author found discrimination based on the race of the offender *and* the race of the victim.

Race and the Death Penalty. Myrdal devoted surprisingly little attention to the issue of racial discrimination in the application of the death penalty. Citing statistics on the numbers of African Americans and whites sentenced to death, he simply noted that "The South makes the widest application of the death penalty, and Negro criminals come in for much more than their share of the executions."[86]

---

81. Myrdal, *An American Dilemma*, p. 551.
82. *Ibid.*, p. 553.
83. LaFree, *Rape and Criminal Justice*, Chap. 6.
84. Anthony Walsh, "The Sexual Stratification Hypothesis in Light of Changing Conceptions of Race," *Criminology* 25 (1987): 153–173.
85. Spohn, "Crime and the Social Control of Blacks," pp. 249–268.
86. Myrdal, *An American Dilemma*, p. 554.

Statistics collected since the early 1940s suggest that little has changed, in the South or elsewhere. African Americans continue to be executed at a disproportionately high rate. Over 50% of the prisoners executed between 1930 and 1977 were African Americans; indeed, nearly 90% of those executed for rape from 1930 to 1977[87] were African Americans, and most were African Americans convicted of raping white women.[88] Between 1977 and 1992, 157 persons were executed by 16 states; of these, 94 (60%) were white and 63 (40%) were black.[89]

African Americans also are overrepresented among those sentenced to death. Data collected by the NAACP Legal Defense and Educational Fund (NAACP-LDF) indicate that nearly 40% of the current death row inmates in the United States are African Americans; the data also reveal that there is a disproportionate number of minorities awaiting death in most of the 35 states with capital punishment statutes.[90] In 1992, for example, the percentage of African Americans on death row was 64% (84/132) in Illinois, 60% (82/137) in Pennsylvania, 59% (30/51) in Mississippi, 54% (20/37) in Louisiana, and 53% (59/111) in Ohio.[91]

Although these statistics indicate racial disparity in the application of the death penalty, they do not prove that states impose the death sentence in a racially discriminatory manner. Recent studies of the imposition of the death penalty, however, suggest that the disparities do reflect discrimination. There is a substantial body of research demonstrating that African Americans who murder whites are much more likely to be sentenced to death than African Americans who murder other African Americans, or whites who murder African Americans or whites.[92] The most widely

87. In 1977 the Supreme Court ruled that imposition of the death penalty for the rape of an adult woman was a violation of the Eighth and Fourteenth Amendments [*Coker* v. *Georgia*, 433 U.S. 584 (1977)].

88. Marvin E. Wolfgang and Marc Riedel, "Race, Judicial Discretion, and the Death Penalty," *The Annals* 407 (1973): 119–133.

89. Lawrence A. Greenfeld, *Capital Punishment 1991*. Washington, D.C.: U.S. Department of Justice, Bureau of Justice Statistics, 1992, p. 2.

90. National Association for the Advancement of Colored People–Legal Defense Fund (NAACP–LDF), *Death Row U.S.A.* (New York: NAACP–LDF, Inc., 1992).

91. *Capital Punishment 1991*, p. 8.

92. Steven D. Arkin, "Discriminations and Arbitrariness in Capital Punishment: An Analysis of Post-*Furman* Murder Cases in Dade County, Florida, 1973–1976," *Stanford Law Review* 33 (1980): 75–101; David C. Baldus, Charles Pulaski, and George Woodworth, "Comparative Review of Death Sentences: An Empirical Study of the Georgia Experience," *Journal of Criminal Law and Criminology* 74 (1983): 661–753; David C. Baldus, George Woodworth, and Charles Pulaski, "Monitoring and Evaluating Contemporary Death Sentencing Systems: Lessons From Georgia." *U.C. Davis Law Review* 18 (1985): 1375–1407; William J. Bowers and Glenn L. Pierce, "Arbitrariness and Discrimination under Post-*Furman* Capital Statutes," *Crime and Delinquency* 74 (1980): 1067–1100; Samuel R. Gross and Robert Mauro, *Death & Discrimination: Racial Disparities in Capital Sentencing* (Boston: Northeastern University Press, 1989); Thomas J. Keil and Gennaro F. Vito, "Race, Homicide Severity, and Application of the Death Penalty: A Consideration of the Barnett Scale," *Criminology* 27 (1989): 511–531; Peter B. Lewis, "Life on Death Row: A Post-*Furman* Profile of Florida's Condemned. In P.W. Lewis and K.D. Peoples (eds.), *The Supreme Court and the Criminal Process—Cases and Comments* (Philadelphia: Saunders, 1978); Raymond Paternoster, "Prosecutorial Discretion in Requesting the Death Penalty: A Case of Victim-Based Racial Discrimination," *Law & Society Review* 18 (1984): 437–478; Michael L. Radelet, "Racial Characteristics and the Imposition of the Death Penalty," *American Sociological Review* 46 (1981): 918–927; and Paige H. Ralph, Jonathan R. Sorensen, and James W. Mar-

cited of these studies[93] found that defendants convicted of killing whites were over four times as likely to receive a death sentence as defendants convicted of killing blacks. David Baldus and his colleagues also found that African Americans who killed whites had the greatest likelihood of receiving the death penalty.

Some commentators have questioned the national significance of findings of victim-based racial discrimination in the capital sentencing process, noting that almost all of the studies address capital sentencing in Southern states. Recent research by Gross and Mauro,[94] however, demonstrates that discrimination based on the race of the victim is not confined to the South. Gross and Mauro found capital sentencing disparities by the race of the victim in each of the eight states— Florida, Georgia, Illinois, Oklahoma, North Carolina, Mississippi, Virginia, and Arkansas—included in their study. They concluded that their data showed "a clear pattern" of victim-based discrimination "unexplainable on grounds other than race...."[95]

Evidence such as that cited above has been used to mount constitutional challenges to the imposition of the death penalty. African American defendants convicted of raping or murdering whites have claimed that the death penalty is applied in a racially discriminatory manner in violation of both the equal protection clause of the Fourteenth Amendment and the cruel and unusual punishment clause of the Eighth Amendment. These claims have been consistently rejected by federal appellate courts. In a series of decisions, the Courts of Appeals ruled, first, that the empirical studies used to document systematic racial discrimination did not take every variable related to capital sentencing into account and, second, that the evidence presented did not demonstrate that the appellant's *own* sentence was the product of discrimination.[96]

The Supreme Court addressed the issue of victim-based racial discrimination in the application of the death penalty in the case of *McCleskey* v. *Kemp*.[97] Warren McCleskey, an African American, was convicted and sentenced to death in Georgia for killing a white police officer during the course of an armed robbery. McCleskey claimed that the Georgia capital sentencing process was administered in a racially discriminatory manner. In support of his claim, he offered the results of the study conducted by Baldus and his colleagues.[98] As noted above, this study found that African Americans who were convicted of murdering whites had the greatest likelihood of receiving the death penalty.

The Supreme Court rejected McCleskey's Fourteenth and Eighth Amendment claims. Although the majority accepted the validity of the Baldus study, they nonetheless refused to accept McCleskey's argument that the disparities documented by Baldus signaled the presence of unconstitutional racial discrimination.

---

quart, "A Comparison of Death-Sentenced and Incarcerated Murderers in Pre-*Furman* Texas," *Justice Quarterly* 9 (1992): 185–209.

93. Baldus, Woodworth and Pulaski, "Monitoring and Evaluating Contemporary Death Penalty Systems."

94. Gross and Mauro, *Death and Discrimination*.

95. *Ibid.*, p. 110.

96. See, e.g., *Maxwell* v. *Bishop*, F.2d 138 (8th Cir. 1968); *Spinkellink* v. *Wainwright*, 578 F.2d 582 (5th Cir. 1978); *Shaw* v. *Martin*, 733 F.2d 304 (4th Cir. 1984); and *Prejean* v. *Blackburn*, 743 F.2d 1091 (5th Cir. 1984).

97. *McCleskey* v. *Kemp*, 481 U.S. 279, 107 S.Ct. 1756 (1987).

98. Baldus, et al., "Monitoring and Evaluating Contemporary Death Penalty Systems."

The Court argued that the disparities were "unexplained" and stated that "At most, the Baldus study indicates a discrepancy that appears to correlate with race."[99] They Court also ruled that the Baldus study was "clearly insufficient to support an inference that any of the decisionmakers in McCleskey's case acted with discriminatory purpose."[100]

Legal scholars and civil libertarians have questioned the Supreme Court's reasoning in *McCleskey*. Citing the inconsistency inherent in assuming the validity of the Baldus study but then refusing to acknowledge the existence of racial discrimination, Gross and Mauro conclude, "The central message of the *McCleskey* case is all too plain; de facto racial discrimination in capital sentencing is legal in the United States."[101]

Racial Discrimination in Sentencing: Summary and Analysis

Research conducted since the publication of *An American Dilemma* suggests that racial discrimination in sentencing persists, in the South and elsewhere. It is no longer true that whites accused of crimes against African Americans are routinely "set free" or that African Americans suspected of raping or murdering whites are routinely threatened by white lynching mobs bent on vengeance. Although these types of overt racism have been eliminated, discrimination in sentencing has not. African Americans convicted of crimes against whites, and particularly those convicted of sexual assault or murder, continue to be punished more harshly than other offenders. They are more likely than other offenders, particularly African Americans who victimize other African Americans, to be sentenced to prison or to be sentenced to death.

Explanations for Disparate Treatment. Researchers have advanced two interrelated explanations for the harsher treatment of crimes involving African American offenders and white victims, the more lenient treatment of crimes involving African American offenders and African American victims. The first explanation builds on conflict theory's premise that the law is applied to maintain the power of the dominant group and to control the behavior of individuals who threaten that power.[102] It suggests that crimes involving black offenders and white victims are punished most harshly because they pose the greatest threat to "the system of racially stratified state authority."[103]

Researchers have advanced a similar explanation for the harsher treatment of African Americans who sexually assault whites. Using the concept of sexual stratification, LaFree[104] argues that one measure of the dominant group's power is its ability to control sexual access to women in the dominant group, who are regarded as the scarce and valuable sexual property of men of their own race. The sexual assault of a white woman by an African American man, then, threatens the

---

99. 107 S.Ct. at 1777.
100. 107 S.Ct. at 1769.
101. Gross and Mauro, *Death & Discrimination*, p. 212.
102. Quinney, *The Social Reality of Crime; Austin Turk, Criminality and Legal Order* (New York: Rand McNally, 1969).
103. Hawkins, "Beyond Anomalies," p. 726.
104. LaFree, *Rape and Criminal Justice*.

power of the dominant group by violating the group's sexual property rights. This, according to Walsh,[105] "accounts for the strength of the taboo attached to inter-racial sexual assault." It also explains why sexual assaults of African American women, who are seen as less valuable sexual "commodities," are perceived as less serious crimes.

The second explanation for the harsher penalties imposed on those who victimize whites emphasizes the race of the victim rather than the racial composition of the victim/offender dyad. This explanation suggests that crimes involving African American victims are not taken seriously and/or that crimes involving white victims are taken very seriously; it suggests that the lives of African American victims are devalued relative to the lives of white victims. Thus, crimes against whites will be punished more severely than crimes against African Americans regardless of the race of the offender.

Most researchers have failed to explain adequately *why* those who victimize whites are treated more harshly than those who victimize African Americans. Gross and Mauro[106] suggest that the explanation, at least in capital cases, may hinge on the degree to which jurors are able to identify with the victim. The authors argue that jurors take the life-or-death decision in a capital case very seriously. To condemn a murderer to death thus requires something more than sympathy for the victim. Jurors will not sentence the defendant to death unless they are particularly horrified by the crime, and they will not be particularly horrified by the crime unless they can identify or empathize with the victim. According to the authors,

> In a society that remains segregated socially if not legally, and in which the great majority of jurors are white, jurors are not likely to identify with black victims or to see them as family or friends. Thus jurors are more likely to be horrified by the killing of a white than of a black, and more likely to act against the killer of a white than the killer of a black.[107]

The same line of reasoning obviously could be applied to judicial sentencing decisions. One might argue that judges, the majority of whom are white, will identify more readily with white victims and thus will be more horrified by crimes against whites. As a consequence, they will be more willing to impose harsh penalties on those who victimize whites.

Conclusion

The court system described by Myrdal in *An American Dilemma* no longer exists, in the South or elsewhere. Reforms mandated by the U.S. Supreme Court or adopted voluntarily by the states have eliminated much of the overt racism against African American criminal defendants documented by Myrdal. Implementation of these reforms, however, has not produced equality of justice. African Americans who find themselves in the arms of the law continue to suffer discrimination in court processing and sentencing.

---

105. Walsh, "The Sexual Stratification Hypothesis," p. 155.
106. Gross and Mauro, *Death & Discrimination*.
107. *Ibid.*, p. 113.

Myrdal described a court system characterized by flagrant racism against African American criminal defendants. Most of these blatant injustices have been eliminated. In the 1990s, whites who commit crimes against African Americans are not beyond the reach of the criminal justice system, African Americans suspected of crimes against whites do not receive "justice" at the hands of white lynching mobs, and African Americans who offend against other African Americans are not immune from punishment. As a result of reforms instituted during the past 50 years, African American criminal defendants are no longer routinely denied bail and then tried by all-white juries without attorneys to assist them in their defense.

Despite these significant changes, discrimination persists. Social scientists and legal scholars have shown that defendant race continues to affect decisions regarding bail, charging, jury selection, and sentencing. Some researchers conclude that race has a direct and obvious effect on these decisions; they contend that African Americans are more likely than whites to be detained, charged, sentenced to prison, or sentenced to death.

Other researchers conclude that discrimination in court processing and sentencing has become more subtle and difficult to detect. They assert that discrimination against African Americans is not universal but is confined to certain types of cases, certain types of settings, and certain types of defendants. These researchers argue, for example, that African American defendants who murder or rape whites will be punished more harshly than other defendants. They also suggest that being unemployed, having a prior criminal record, or being detained prior to trial have more negative effects on court outcomes for African Americans than for whites.

In sum, while the reforms envisioned by Myrdal may have eliminated the more obvious examples of racial discrimination in the criminal justice system, they have not produced an equitable, or color blind, system of justice. Fifty years after the publication of *An American Dilemma*, African Americans continue to suffer discrimination at the hands of criminal justice officials in the United States.

23

Crime and the Racial Fears of White Americans

Wesley G. Skogan

"Fear of black crime covers the streets like a sheet of ice."
—Sen. Bill Bradley[1]

It is widely assumed that expressions by many whites of concern about crime are rooted to a significant degree in their fear of black people. One popular news magazine states that many whites seem to be unduly troubled by black people, especially by young black men; white people are often afraid of danger that may exist solely in their imagination.[2] Of course, fear is not necessarily a bad thing; it can be a rational response to the conditions of one's life, and guide purposeful action. As other articles in this volume document, fear reflects people's individual vulnerability to crime and its harmful consequences, risks in their neighborhood, and their personal victimization experiences and those reported by their family and friends. However, it may also be that white Americans translate their unease about race relations into beliefs about crime, and *vice-versa*, a linkage of potentially great divisiveness. This article reviews research on the nexus between them. It examines linkages between fear and white attitudes toward blacks and the anxiety created by close residential proximity between the two groups.

Focusing on the fears of whites should not obscure the fact that black Americans are even more fearful. Research documents that they are fearful mostly for the same reasons that whites are fearful, and their higher level of fear reflects the fact that those common causes afflict their communities more severely. This article focuses on white fear because it is one of the most compelling political constructs of our time. It is evoked as an explanation for white backlash against progressive social and economic policies, the declining prospects of the Democratic Party, and as a source of divisiveness that threatens the fabric of urban life. Concern about common crime—street mugging, sexual assault, and the like—is not the only outcropping of the racial fears of whites. Another is resistance to school busing.[3] In both instances, white fear partly is deliberately constructed by those

An earlier version of this essay appeared in *Annals of the American Academy of Political and Social Science;* 1995, 539, May, 59–71 and is adapted/reprinted with the permission of the copyright holder/author.

1. *Congressional Record*, March 26, 1992, p. S4242.
2. *U.S. News & World Report*, May 11, 1992, p. 36.
3. D. Garth Taylor (1986). *Public Opinion and Collective Action: The Boston School De-*

who are in a position to profit from its divisiveness. Most prominently, they are politicians, among whom "playing the race card" is a time-tested political ploy. In 1988, Presidential candidate George Bush horrified audiences with his story of a man convicted of murder who raped a Maryland woman while he was on furlough from a Massachusetts prison. The President personally made no reference to Willie Horton's race, but someone was quick to come up with his picture. In that campaign Willie Horton was a "wedge issue."

There is only a limited amount of useful research on the nexus of race and fear, for several reasons. For one, so many aspects of American life are racially encoded that it is difficult to tease out statistically the separate consequences of factors such as crime, school quality, neighborhood satisfaction, property values, neighborhood racial change, and the like. In a segregated society, many things covary strongly with race. For another, what Senator Bradley termed a "cloak of silence and denial" surrounds the general race-crime nexus in many circles.[4] Prominent among them has been the federal agencies which pay for expensive research ventures involving large sample surveys; they have been, in my experience, unwilling to fund investigations which touch too closely on controversial racial attitudes. Crime is also an issue area where the "facts of the case" as measured by arrests, reports by crime victims, and self-reports of offending all point to higher rates of criminality among black Americans, confounding "prejudiced" attitudes with doses of realism that make it difficult to interpret the pulse of white opinion.

Some research closely skirts the two issues. For example, there is a great deal of it on the social and economic determinants of how much cities spend on policing. These studies, which are summarized in a book by Pamela Irving Jackson,[5] find that police strength is politically determined by a complicated set of socially patterned interests, and that the local level of crime plays only a limited role in the process. More straightforward seems to be the role played by indicators of economic inequality by race, inner-city riots, and the relative size of the minority population. More is spent on policing in cities where white interests appear to be threatened.

This report reviews direct studies of the problem. A few are ethnographic reports by researchers who immersed themselves in the lives of residents of urban neighborhoods and emerged to tell their story. The other studies are based on interviews with large samples of survey respondents who were quizzed about crime, fear, and the character of their neighborhoods. Some of these surveys also questioned white respondents concerning their racial attitudes, and those studies present the most complete—and complex—view of the topic.

The Stinchcombe Model of Race and Fear

Perhaps the best known statement of the problem was advanced in 1980 by Arthur Stinchcombe and his associates.[6] Their explanation of fear of crime, which

segregation Conflict. Chicago: University of Chicago Press, pp. 44–61.

4. *Congressional Record*, op. cit.

5. Pamela Irving Jackson (1989). *Minority Group Threat, Crime, and Policing*. New York: Praeger, pp. 1–46.

6. Arthur Stinchcombe, Rebecca Adams, Carol A. Heimer, Kim Lane Scheppele, Tom W.

Figure 1. Stinchcombe Model of Fear

is illustrated in Figure 1, hinges on the racial composition of people's neighborhoods. They examined the problem using data from the General Social Survey (GSS), a yearly national survey. The GSS measures fear by asking if there is a place within a mile of their home where respondents are afraid to walk alone at night. Stinchcombe *et al* began by equating the distribution of black people with the distribution of crime. They cited what they dubbed "well known statistics" to argue that "the most fear-producing crimes are all 'ghetto crimes'" and that "crimes that make people afraid are more concentrated among black people."[7] For example, they showed that blacks were arrested for murder, robbery and rape at a rate that is disproportionate to their numbers in the population, and that blacks were more frequently victimized by violent crime. As part of the argument, they used the GSS to document that victimization of whites was disproportionately high when they lived closer to black people. Whites living in integrated neighborhoods were a little more than twice as likely as those living in segregated neighborhoods to be robbed, and about 1.4 times as likely to be burglarized. They therefore felt justified in using reports by survey respondents of how close they live *to* concentrations of black people as a "measure of objective risk" of victimization *by* black people.[8] The latter construct is depicted in italics in Figure 1, for risk of victimization was not actually measured in the data that they used to test their explanation of fear.

It is important to note that this part of Stinchcombe's model is intended to explain fear of crime among *all* Americans, not just whites. In the data, blacks were more fearful than whites, a finding that is consistent from study to study. However, Stinchcombe did not directly examine the question of whether blacks living in black neighborhoods were more fearful than those living in integrated surroundings, because the number of blacks doing so is painfully small in a national survey. Because of the numbers involved, when he examined the data for "everyone" he was in practice examining the views of whites. He found that the proportion of people who were fearful was substantially higher in integrated areas even when controlling for other factors. These included living in big cities (more fear), sex (women are more fearful), age (fear is higher among old people), household

Smith and D. Garth Taylor (1980). *Crime and Punishment—Changing Attitudes in America.* San Francisco: Jossey-Bass Publishers, pp. 39–73.

7. Ibid., pp. 43 and 47.
8. Ibid., p. 44.

composition (living alone magnifies fear), and individual victimization (fear pro-voking). Gun ownership was at first glance reassuring, for people who owned them were less fearful. However, self-reports of gun ownership were *lower* than usual among whites (and blacks) living in big cities, and among whites living near blacks. When these and the other factors enumerated above were controlled for, the effect of gun ownership disappeared.

The other part of Stinchcombe's model, what he dubbed the "irrational" part, applies only to whites. As illustrated in Figure 1, he also examined the statistical relationship between fear and a three-question measure of white views of black people. It combined responses to questions about laws against interracial mar-riage, objecting to someone in the family bringing a black person home to dinner, and whether or not anyone in the family had actually brought a black person home for dinner. As it was weighted heavily toward intimate social activity, it is not clear that this was the best possible indicator for a study of attitudes related to street crime. However, those falling at the prejudiced end of the scale were more fearful even controlling for the racial composition of their neighborhood.

It is important to note that the link between prejudice and fear was *not* due to higher levels of prejudice among whites in close contact with blacks; in fact, quite the opposite was the case. Figure 2 presents the results of my own reanalysis of data from more recent years of the GSS (1988, 1989 and 1990). It uses a different indicator of racial prejudice, an index combining responses to two measures of whites' views of black participation in society's most public institutions. The first measure assesses their views of the acceptability of white and black children going to school together under the circumstance of varying racial composition of the school. The most prejudiced whites (only 4 percent of the total) objected to white children going to school with even a few blacks, while the most liberal (40 per-cent) did not object to their going to school mostly with blacks. The second com-ponent of the prejudice measure is based on responses to a question about "white people's right to a racially segregated neighborhood." At the most liberal end, 50 percent of respondents strongly disagreed that whites had such a right, while the polar group (8 percent of all whites) agreed strongly that they did. In combina-tion, 28 percent of whites took the most liberal stance on both questions, while 2 percent of whites took the most prejudiced (the questions are presented in an ap-pendix to this article).

As before, fear was measured by the presence of a location nearby where re-spondents were afraid to go alone after dark. Whites' proximity to blacks was measured by a question asking if blacks lived nearby, and a follow-up question determining "how far away" measured in city blocks, using the response cate-gories presented in Figure 2.

As Figure 2 illustrates, on a national basis racial prejudice was in fact some-what *lower* among whites who reported living in close proximity to blacks. As the left side of the Figure indicates, average prejudice scores *dropped* with increasing proximity. This was true of both the school attendance and residential segregation sub-components of the measure. The causes for this might run both ways. Cer-tainly, many whites are financially and socially able to distance themselves from blacks to an extent appropriate to their racial attitudes; many of the more preju-diced just move away. At the same time, people living together *may* (the evidence is mixed) learn to get along, especially if they share cultural values or are not

Figure 2. Racial Prejudice and Fear Among Whites

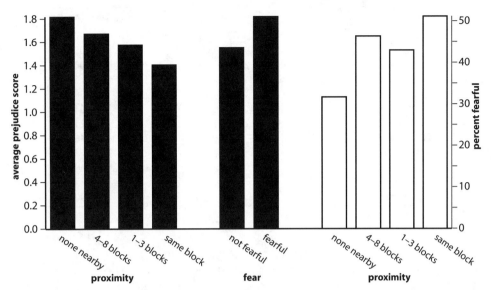

Source: National Opinion Research Center, General Social Survey, 1988–90.

competitors for the same jobs or houses.[9] In either event, the decline in both measures of prejudice with increasing proximity is impressive, in light of the fact that interracial proximity is not at all an abstract, far-away issue for whites who indicated that black people lived within 8 blocks of their home.

On the other hand, Figure 2 indicates that whites who were fearful were also somewhat more prejudiced, so there may be a causal link between the two. Again, the relationship between the two could run in either direction. Stinchcombe argued that fear leads to prejudice, as whites rationally assessed official and media images of the extent of black crime and then generalized the results into beliefs about the appropriate place of blacks in society. The argument that "fear of crime is a code word for racism" takes the opposite view, that whites project their general attitudes toward black people onto resonant social issues such as crime. These data are not very suitable for deciding between the two views, but it is an important research question.

Figure 2 also documents that whites' proximity to blacks was related to fear. Those who reported that no black people lived nearby were the least fearful, while those living closest to blacks were the most fearful. The gap between the two polar groups was 20 percentage points. Stinchcombe's rationality-of-fear argument was that it is simply riskier for whites to live near blacks, so proximity leads to fear.

---

9. Cf. Carolyn Adams, David Bartelt, David Elesh, Ira Goldstein, Nancy Kleniewski, and William Yancey (1991). *Philadelphia: Neighborhoods, Division, and Conflict in a Postindustrial City*. Philadelphia: Temple University Press, pp. 22–25; Elijah Anderson (1990). *Streetwise: Race, Class, and Change in an Urban Community*. Chicago: University of Chicago Press, pp. 28–30; Sally Engle Merry (1980). "Racial Integration in an Urban Neighborhood: The Social Organization of Strangers," *Human Organization*, 39(1): 59–69 (Spring, 1980); Lee Sigelman and Susan Welch (1993). "The Contact Hypothesis Revisited," *Social Forces*, 71(3): 781–795 (March).

Table 1. Logistic Regression Analysis of Fear Among Whites

	Coefficient	Significance
Proximity	.2039	.0002
Prejudice	.1409	.0012
Live in south	.5134	.0002
Female	1.8375	.0000
City size (log)	.2298	.0000
Crime victim	.4991	.0416
Elderly	.2508	.2159
Have children	−.1150	.4656
Age & sex	.0042	.4870
Live alone	.0760	.6029
Education	.0278	.6523
Constant	3.4207	.0000

Note: Overall 72.6% correctly classed. Number of cases 1396.

The tenacity of the link between racial prejudice, proximity to blacks, and fear of crime is illustrated in Table 1. It presents the results of a logistic regression analysis examining the impact of those factors on fear while simultaneously controlling for a host of other well-established correlates of fear. The list of control factors is longer than Stinchcombe's tabular analysis allowed. It includes age, gender, education, whether respondents lived alone, if they had children living at home, a control for region of the country, city size, and whether each respondent has been the victim of a burglary or robbery. It also includes a control for being old *and* female in combination. However, when all of these factors are controlled for, both the residential proximity of blacks and prejudice (measured by whites' views of the appropriate role of black people in society) remained independently linked to fear.

The Liska Model of Race and Fear

A second prominent statistical model of the determinants of fear of crime was advanced by Allen Liska and his associates.[10] It takes into account objective risk of victimization, measured directly by city-wide victim surveys, and the city size factor that was so prominent in the results of the GSS. It does not include a direct measure of the racial attitudes of whites, but takes into account several important features of their environment: the relative size of the black population in the city where they live, the extent of racial segregation in housing patterns there, and the likelihood that crimes against them will be interracial in character. Liska finds that residential segregation calms white fear, while interracial crime exacerbates it.

The factors comprising the Liska model are illustrated in Figure 3. Unlike Stinchcombe's, it is cast at the *city* rather than at the individual level. The data on crime and fear were drawn from official sources and large (10,000 respondent)

---

10. Allen E. Liska, Joseph J. Lawrence and Andrew Sanchirico (1982). "Fear of Crime as a Social Fact," *Social Forces*, 60(3): 760–770 (March).

Figure 3. Liska Model of Race and Fear

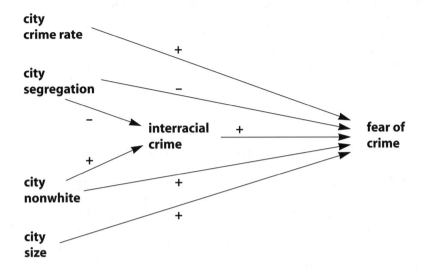

surveys conducted by the Census Bureau in 26 large cities. The cities varied considerably in levels of fear. In the surveys, respondents were asked how safe they feel out alone in their neighborhood at night. Only 27 percent of those interviewed in San Diego felt either unsafe or very unsafe; the comparable figure for residents of Newark, NJ, was 58 percent.

Liska's causal explanations for this large variation are illustrated in Figure 3. Unlike Stinchcombe, he measured crime rates directly, using official FBI statistics. He found that the robbery rate was a strong predictor of fear among whites, and that it was much more potent than city size. However, the interesting parts of the model lie in the middle of the diagram. Whites were more fearful in cities with larger black populations, independent of the crime rate. A measure of residential segregation was included that indicated how separately blacks and whites lived their lives in each city, and there was also a direct effect of this on white fear. Where blacks and whites lived separately, whites were less fearful.

In addition, the extent of *interracial* crime in each city had an added effect on white fear; in fact, it's effect was the strongest of all the elements in the model. Interracial victimization was measured in the city surveys by asking victims to describe their attackers. For statistical purposes Liska used the percentage of robberies against whites in each city that were perpetrated by nonwhites. He notes that "[r]obbery...is the epitome of dangerous street crime in which the offender is a stranger whose racial identity is generally known to the victim."[11] As depicted in Figure 3, interracial robbery was more common in cities with more nonwhites, and in cities that were less segregated. In turn, the extent of interracial crime was the strongest determinant of white fear, followed by the robbery rate.

In Liska's model, it is both risk of victimization and *who* is doing the victimizing that matters to white city residents. He interprets his data as suggesting that "...cultural dissimilarity between whites and nonwhites makes interracial crime

---

11. Ibid., p. 764.

appear particularly uncertain, violent, and dangerous to whites."[12] Residential segregation was directly related to lower levels of white fear, perhaps by reducing the day-to-day visibility of blacks and the frequency with which whites come into contact with them. Segregation was also linked to lower levels of fear indirectly, by dampening the rate of interracial crime. Statistically, the effects of segregation and the racial composition of the cities was most strongly felt *via* the extent of interracial crime.[13]

Other Research on Race and Fear

Beyond these studies, most research examining fear of crime and racial fears of white Americans puts the problem in simpler terms and does not include measures of whites' racial attitudes. Instead, these studies focus solely on the link between racial proximity and fear. For example, Gertrude Moeller conducted interviews with 764 residents of Illinois during the early 1980s.[14] Based on questions in the survey, she classified respondents as living in neighborhoods that were virtually all black, of mixed composition, or virtually all white. Like other studies, hers found that blacks and whites lived in proximity primarily in big cities. She measured fear of crime using the same "is there a place where you would be afraid to walk alone..." question used by the General Social Survey. The survey found that blacks were generally more fearful than whites, and fear went up sharply with city size. When she statistically controlled for such known correlates of fear as age, gender, education, income and size of place, she found that whites living in black or integrated neighborhoods were distinctively more fearful. Differences in fear associated with this condition were less than differences in fear due to gender or city size, but otherwise whites living in proximity to blacks were more fearful than anyone else, including the elderly.

Jeanette Covington and Ralph Taylor found roughly the same pattern in a survey of residents of Baltimore.[15] Their "subcultural diversity" approach to the issue postulated that "...fear of crime...results from living in proximity to others whose cultural background is different from one's own. The manners and behaviors of persons belonging to these different groups is difficult to interpret and thus fear-inspiring."[16] Their research controlled for an impressive list of factors that have been shown to be related to fear, including both personal factors (age, gender, education) and neighborhood-level factors (crime rate, various social disorders, and racial composition). They measured fear by combining responses to

---

12. Ibid., p. 767.

13. In otherwise unrelated research on the statistical correlates of police strength, Liska also finds that the relative size of the black population is more strongly linked to city expenditures on policing in less segregated cities than it is in highly segregated cities. See Allen E. Liska, Joseph J. Lawrence and Michael Benson, "Perspectives on the Legal Order: The Capacity for Social Control (1981)." *American Journal of Sociology,* 87: 413–426.

14. Moeller, Gertrude L., "Fear of Criminal Victimization: The Effect of Neighborhood Racial Composition (1989). *Sociological Inquiry,* 59(2): 208–221 (May).

15. Jeanette Covington and Ralph B. Taylor (1991). "Fear of Crime in Urban Residential Neighborhoods," *The Sociological Quarterly*, 32(2): 231–249.

16. Ibid., p. 232.

questions asking how fearful respondents would feel being out alone in their neighborhood during the day and at night. Controlling for many other factors, they found that residents of mostly black neighborhoods were more fearful. Further, fear was higher than expected among people whose racial identity did not fit their context. They found that the more "different" people were from their neighbors in terms of the racial composition of their neighborhood, the more fearful they were. This effect was apparent for both blacks living in white areas and whites living in black areas, leading them to characterize it as the effect of "cultural diversity" rather than simply "white fear." This was an important conclusion, and runs contrary to Stinchcombe's argument that proximity to whites makes all Americans feel safer. Black residents of white neighborhoods, sometimes facing threats or harassment and more often the targets of humiliation and contempt, would recognize the concept.

What about the *benefits* of living together? Sally Engle Merry studied the consequences of residential racial integration in a small multi-racial housing project in San Francisco.[17] She evaluated the proposition that integration leads to increased social contact between racial and ethnic groups, which in turn leads to increasing tolerance of one another among residents. I noted above that the evidence for this hypothesis is quite mixed, and Merry's contribution is a pessimistic one. She found instead that living together exacerbated tensions between the black, white, Hispanic and Chinese residents of the project. Frictions among residents were all interpreted racially, and prejudice and hostility grew rather than diminished over time. Residents hung on because the housing was good and the price was right, but members of each ethnic group kept to themselves or found social ties outside the project. They did not trust others enough to sustain anti-crime efforts; in fact, they victimized each other with relative impunity because they remained strangers. No one could criticize or exercise control over children of another background. Chinese residents in particular lived in fear of black youths, who remained strangers even while living in their midst.

Conclusions

These studies suggest several conclusions. First, racial differences in fear usually are smaller than differences associated with gender or age, but often they are next on the list. Blacks are much more fearful of crime and these studies document that there are good reasons for this. Blacks are more likely to be victimized, and to live in neighborhoods where serious crime is more frequent. Some of this race-related difference is due to the concentration of black survey respondents in bigger cities, where everyone is more fearful. Another fraction of the racial difference in fear documented in surveys is due to neighborhood-level differences in social disorder, physical decay, and economic collapse. In a segregated society, race "goes along with" many other area-level factors that contribute to fear, and the more segregated that conditions are in any particular research environment, the more closely they covary and the more difficult it is to untangle their effects.

---

17. Engle, "Racial Integration," pp. 59–69.

Second, among whites, residential proximity to black people is related to fear of crime. The link between the two is both direct and further exacerbated by the tie between residential integration and the extent of interracial crime. These links persist even in studies controlling for alternative explanations for fear. It is important to note in this regard that the bulk of whites reporting that black people live nearby themselves live in larger cities. Cities are places where levels of victimization, social disorganization, and aspects of physical decay that are linked to fear of crime are more common.[18] In cities, whites also live closer to all of the other factors that cluster with race in our segregated society, and which themselves have an impact on fear. The statistical controls described above doubtless do not account for all of the effects of these city and neighborhood factors. Race brings with it so many tightly coupled social and economic factors that these studies probably overestimate how much white fear is due to racial proximity and how much it is due to proximity to other factors that scare all Americans but cannot be statistically untangled from race.

Third, the link between residential proximity and fear persists despite the fact that whites living close to blacks register *lower* levels of prejudice than those who are more distant. Whites living in close proximity to blacks voice fewer objections to sharing their schools and neighborhoods with them. This may because they have learned to get along, but it is more likely because through choices about where they live many whites have sorted themselves into residential patterns that reflect their attitudes. Research generally suggests that close contact between blacks and whites breeds favorable attitudes only under unlikely circumstances: when they are of roughly equal status, yet not in competition with one another for jobs, housing, or power. The statistical analysis described above indicated that this measure of prejudice was indeed related to fear of crime, but its effect was independent of the proximity of whites to black people.

In this regard, it is important that white society is becoming more tolerant and egalitarian with regard to selected racial attitudes. A 1942 national poll found that 72 percent of Americans thought black people should eat in separate restaurants, a response that is virtually unheard of today. The percentage of whites tolerant of abstract or personal issues like interracial marriage or bringing people of color home for dinner has climbed to near universality. Very few whites object to mingling with blacks at the workplace. In addition, whites' opinions about blacks have become more variegated; their views on one dimension do not necessarily correspond with their views on another, and they have become linked to larger political and ideological views on such issues as individual responsibility, the role of the government, and compensatory public policies generally. This leads Paul Sniderman and Thomas Piazza to conclude that "racism" *per se* is a minor force in contemporary American politics, especially when defined in Gordon Allport's classic terms as outright hostility and rejection based solely on categorical criteria. Instead, racial cleavages are driven by bundles of social and economic issues which involve or have implications for race but are not—among whites—dominated by it.[19]

---

18. Wesley G. Skogan (1990). *Disorder and Decline: Crime and the Spiral of Decay in American Cities*. New York: The Free Press, pp. 21–50.

19. Paul M. Sniderman and Thomas Piazza (1993). *The Scar of Race*. Cambridge: Harvard University Press, pp. 19–34. See also Mary R. Jackman (1994). *The Velvet Glove: Pa-*

However, whites continue to be particularly resistant to proposals that involve school bussing or close residential proximity to black people, or more generally to policies that promise to interfere with their ability to act on their preferences via markets, and through them to maintain their dominant position.[20] These issues were raised by the school and neighborhood integration components of the racial attitudes measure employed above, and they—not who is coming to dinner—lie near the problematic core of black-white relations at the end of the 20*th* Century. And the image of black lawlessness remains pervasive. In one 1991 national survey, the statement that "blacks are aggressive or violent" was the most frequently endorsed negative stereotype on a list of five, approved by 52 percent of whites.[21] As Andrew Hacker put it, "The dread whites feel of black crime goes beyond actual risks or probabilities. The visage of Willie Horton stirred fears in parts of the country where black faces are seldom seen. . . . The feeling is not simply that crime is out of control. Far more troubling is the realization that white citizens can be held in thrall by a race meant to be subservient."[22] The persistent links between fear, proximity, and white desire to retain their dominance of their most intimate institutions are not likely to wain anytime soon.

Appendix: Measuring Racial Prejudice

The GSS administered fear of crime, racial proximity, and racial prejudice measures to half of a national sample for the years 1988, 1989 and 1990. 1396 respondents answered these and the list of demographic questions discussed in the text. The racial prejudice measure was created by combining responses to questions about school and neighborhood integration. The correlation between the two subcomponent measures was .42.

Attitude toward school integration

Score		Frequency
0	does not object to children going to school with mostly blacks	40%
1	objects to children going to school with mostly blacks, but does not object to children going to school with half blacks	38%
2	objects to children going to school with half blacks, but does not object to children going to school with a few blacks	18%
3	objects to children going to school with even a few blacks	4%

ternalism and Conflict in Gender, Class and Race Relations. Los Angeles: University of California Press, pp. 33–43.

20. Benjamin I. Page and Robert Y. Shapiro (1992). *The Rational Public.* Chicago: University of Chicago Press, pp. 67–80.

21. Sniderman and Piazza, *The Scar of Race*, p. 45. Interestingly, this view was also endorsed by 59 percent of black respondents; Sniderman and Piazza think this is because both views are "rooted in part in a common reality," and are also consistent with views of black violence represented by the mass media.

22. Andrew Hacker (1992). *Two Nations.* New York: Charles Scribners, p. 188.

Attitude toward neighborhood integration

Score		Frequency
0	disagree strongly that whites have a right to live in a segregated neighborhood	50%
1	disagree slightly that whites have a right to live in a segregated neighborhood	26%
2	agree slightly that whites have a right to live in a segregated neighborhood	15%
3	agree strongly that whites have a right to live in a segregated neighborhood	8%

Section IX

Outstanding Sociological and Economic Issues

24

The Ideological Attack on Transracial Adoption in the United States and Britain

Peter Hayes

In the late 1960s and early 1970s, the transracial adoption (TRA) of minority children by white parents became increasingly common in the USA (Day 1979; Fricke 1965). The times were propitious; racial stereotypes were being challenged, racial integration was widely seen as a desirable political goal, and the legalisation of abortion in 1969 was followed by a slight drop in the number of white babies available for adoption, while the number of available black babies rose.[1]

Opposition to TRA by child care professionals dwindled rapidly; it was increasingly confined to the Southern States. In 1970, for example, a baby placed with a white couple in Georgia when she was three days old was forcibly removed nine months later when welfare officials discovered that she was partly black. ('Two Atlanta' 1971). In the eyes of liberals this kind of case appeared to be part of the USA's past, not its future. It was a reactionary vestige of the policy of segregation, a policy whose scope and legitimacy had been greatly diminished by efforts to promote integration.

Much of the credit for the liberalisation of social attitudes in the USA belongs to civil rights campaigners. However, not all civil rights activists were in favour of racial integration. Malcolm X and Stokely Carmichael advocated a policy of separatism. They condemned integration as a movement of middle class blacks to subsume their distinct identity within dominant white culture. This aspiration, they argued, was not only objectionable in itself; it also weakened the collective position of the majority of blacks who remained unassimilated.[2]

An earlier version of this essay appeared in *International Journal of Law and the Family*; 1995, 9, 1, April, 1–22 and is adapted/reprinted with the permission of the copyright holder/author.

1. According to Day between 1969 and 1970 the number of white babies available for adoption declined by 7%. Available black babies rose by 16% (1979, 10). Day explains this rise as being the result, in part, of adoption agencies being more willing to accept black babies.

2. X 1971; Carmichael 1969. This position owed something to the extension of Marxist class analysis to explain other forms of social division, including cultural and ethnic divisions. Particularly important was Marx's contention that the ruling class claimed moral authority for rules that were designed to enforce its dominance, and that beneath its moral code lay the objective of maintaining its power through the repression and exploitation of other classes.

The split between integrationists and separatists entered the area of adoption policy in 1972, when TRA was one of the three main topics at the annual meeting of the National Association of Black Social Workers (NABSW) in Tennessee. Attendees at the conference heard how researchers into sickle cell anaemia had selfish financial motivations and how the English language was having a pernicious effect on black health, unity and well-being. It was, however, Audrey Russell's attack on TRA that galvanised the meeting.

When Russell addressed liberal audiences or white audiences, she adopted a comparatively moderate position, contending that whites, with the best of intentions, hurt rather than helped individual black children who were transracially adopted because they were unable to give them a sense of black identity: 'You can take care of a black child, give him shelter and feed him, but you cannot give him a black identity because you don't have it yourself to give' (Russell 1972; also see Brooton 1971). The NABSW, however, received a much more radical message. TRA was a deliberately hostile attack on blacks by whites. It was a policy designed to perpetuate the unequal power relationship between these ethnic groups by weakening the black community. Thus Russell condemned TRA as a 'diabolical trick,' and a 'lethal incursion on the black family'. She went on to attack the adoption of mixed-race children: 'By immutable law, a drop of black blood has made one black for generations... and now to satisfy the whims of arrogant white America, they have suddenly become something different and are adopting the whiteness in them' (Fraser 1972a).

Russell's attack was enthusiastically taken up by the NABSW, which announced its 'vehement opposition' to TRA, and the launch of a campaign to challenge social welfare organizations that promoted it, particularly 'the white bastion of professional child welfare work standards and practices—the Child Welfare League of America' (Fraser 1972b).

A year after the NABSW announced its anti-TRA campaign, the CWLA changed its *Standards for Adoption Service* to accommodate their demands. The new guidelines returned to the old position that same race adoption was preferable to TRA (CWLA 1973, 92–3). Other organisations followed suit (Fraser 1973; McRoy and Zurcher 1983, 142; Bartholet 1991). In 1978 the Indian Child Welfare Act was passed in the USA. Inspired by the same ideas that had been put forward by the NABSW with respect to black children this Act virtually prohibited the adoption of Indian children by whites.[3] In the 1980s several states passed legislation that prohibited or regulated TRA of any minority child (Bartholet 1991, 1189–90).

In Britain TRA did not come under sustained attack until the early 1980s, when the arguments developed in the USA became increasingly influential. The British Agencies for Adoption and Fostering established a Black Perspectives Advisory Committee, and in 1983 the Association of Black Social Workers and Allied Professionals (ABSWAP) was founded. This organisation deliberately modelled itself on the NABSW, went to it for advice, and then began to campaign amongst social workers (Rhodes 1992, 19, 53). Legislation and guidelines followed; in the 1989 Children Act race is one factor to be taken into 'due consideration' in local authority care of children, while in 1990 the Social Services Inspectorate issued guidelines that made the same point in more detail. 'Due

---

3. The act is aptly criticised by Rosettenstein 1993.

consideration' has been wilfully misinterpreted to mean 'paramount consideration,' with some authorities prohibiting TRA altogether, while others strictly vet
white applicants.(Weise 1988, 25–6; Ahmad 1990, 91). This problem has been
recognised in the 1993 White Paper on adoption in Britain, which promises new
guidelines that will make explicit that while ethnicity and culture should be 'considered' in placing children they should not be made central to the choice of
prospective parents. (*Adoption* 1993, 4.30–4.34).

The formal policies in place in these countries are, to use Bartholet's phrase, no
more than the 'tip of the iceberg' (1991, 1189). Opposition to TRA has become a
virtually unchallenged orthodoxy amongst child care professionals and is constantly reflected in adoption practice, by such methods as actively recruiting
prospective black parents and discouraging white ones, refusing to consider
prospective white parents altogether, or turning to white parents only as a last resort. The general result of these policies has been that minority children in need of
adoptive homes are more likely to remain in institutional care or temporary foster
homes for longer periods of time. Older and handicapped minority children are
more likely remain in foster care or institutions throughout their childhood. The
precise effects of the policies, however, are difficult to calculate, and of necessity
involve a degree of speculation. TRA was expanded rapidly in the late 1960s and
early 1970s in the USA but at what rate might this expansion have continued?
There are conflicting claims about the abilities of adoption agencies to make same-
race placements for minorities, so how far has the positive campaign to recruit minority parents offset the attempt to discourage or prohibit TRA? In order to recruit minorities, parenting requirements have been relaxed; how might minority
children have fared if uniform standards for whites and minorities were maintained? What might have happened if the campaign to recruit minorities was accompanied by a parallel campaign to promote TRA? I can answer these questions
only with the general observation that the more parents that are available to adopt
minority children the better it is for the children, so that if TRA had been encouraged in Britain and the USA it would have would have continued to help minority
children to find the best possible permanent home in the shortest amount of time.

The Argument Against TRA

The key propositions of the argument against TRA are that minority children
have a *right and need* to develop a *positive ethnic identity* and awareness of their
cultural heritage within their own *community*. Without this identity they will face
inevitable problems as they get older and will be unable to develop *survival skills*
or *coping mechanisms* to deal with the *reality of racism*.

Where TRA is not prohibited, it is subject to special regulations that are based
on the same propositions. A white family for a minority child is seen as a second
best option to a minority family,[4] but if such a family cannot be found, even with

---

4. In fact Jones and Else have logically enough suggested that would-be white parents who
are anxious to instil a strong sense of ethnic identity and cultural awareness in minority children are preferable to would-be minority parents who repudiate these objectives (1979,
378–9).

very lax selection criteria, then a much more rigorous list of criterion is drawn up that must be fulfilled by prospective white parents. The parents must be willing to teach their minority child to have a strong ethnic identity; take active steps to equip him with knowledge of his cultural heritage; live in a mixed or minority community, and acknowledge the reality of racism. Sometimes it is stipulated that prospective white parents should also be required to attend 'group encounter sessions' or 'therapy' to make them admit to their own (undoubted) racism.

Given the influence that these arguments have had, it might be expected that they would be supported by social scientific research on minority children placed for adoption in white homes. But they are not; almost all of the evidence presented in these investigations suggests that TRA is as successful as in racial adoption. The only apparently reliable study I have located that suggests otherwise is Bagley's analysis of the adoption of American Indian children in Canada (1991). Against this, however, must be placed a long list of studies that using a variety of assessment measures and techniques have all concluded that the adoption of a minority child by white parents is no more problematic than in racial adoption, and that transracially adopted children are as happy, successful, and socially integrated as other adopted children. This research includes early studies by Raynor (1970) and Fanshel (1972), which predate the anti-TRA campaign. They also include Simon and Alstein's long-term study of over 90 transracial adoptees from the time of their adoption into adulthood (1977, 1981, 1987); Gill and Jackson's study of TRA in Britain (1983); McRoy and Zurcher's comparison of transracial and in racial adoptees (1983); Grow and Shapiro's study of 125 children (1974, 1975) and studies by Simon and Alstein (1991), Saetersdal and Dalen (1991), Rorbech (1991) and Hoksbergen (1991) on minority children from the third world adopted by Westerners.

The fact that the overall proportion of successful transracial adoptions is the same as the proportion of successful in racial adoptions is indicative of a further finding uncovered by researchers: white parents who fulfil the list of special requirements for TRA are no more likely to be successful than ones who do not.

The success of the argument that TRA should be banned or subject to special regulation, cannot, therefore, be explained by research. But if the evidence refutes the position, why has it not been abandoned? To begin to answer this question it is necessary to analyse the intellectual dishonesty that underlies the maintenance of the argument against TRA in the face of such a convincing refutation: its tenets have been developed in such a way as to make them impervious to criticism, to be unfalsifiable, in that attempts to test the propositions are deliberately avoided.[5]

Unfortunately, this aspect of the opposition to TRA helps to account for its success in gaining widespread acceptance rather than its failure. In the face of evidence that refutes them, opponents of TRA have defended their position in a forceful, persuasive, seemingly scientific and apparently convincing manner. This has been done in three ways: (1) By distorting and fitting empirical evidence to support the claim that TRA is harmful, rather than using evidence to test this claim; (2) By adopting absolutist positions that admit to no exceptions and justifying these

---

5. Grow and Shapiro mention that no amount of research that shows TRA to have worked will ever convince its opponents (1977, 91); Simon and Alstein say that it would be naive to expect that the results of social scientific research will be heeded by opponents of TRA (1987, 142).

claims through logical deductions without reference to empirical evidence; (3) By discounting current evidence for predictions concerning the future. These predictions are highly speculative; however, they are presented as inexorable.[6]

The interpretation of research findings by opponents of transracial adoption, and the claims they make in court cases illustrate their use of these arguments

Interpretation of Research Findings

Those who contend that TRA should be banned or regulated—and this sometimes includes researchers whose findings support TRA—have responded to the research evidence in several ways. A common response is to recommend that TRA should be banned or regulated regardless of the research findings. For example, in her British Government sponsored review of adoption law, Thoburn says that Ladner and Small have identified a list of the qualities that white parents need if they are to bring up minority children successfully (a list which requires these parents to live among minorities and so on). Thoburn then rightly points out that 'there is no research which links these characteristics with successful outcome'. But despite her acknowledgement of this fact, Thoburn goes on to recommend that parents who wish to adopt minority children from abroad should be investigated by someone trained in 'ethnically sensitive social work' to ensure that they fulfil the criteria demanded by Ladner and Small (Thoburn 1990, 58, 71; Ladner 1977, 231–2; Small 1984, 140). Similarly, Gill and Jackson conclude their study of transracially adopted children by writing: 'It is not necessary to imply that the many children who have been adopted transracially are suffering major difficulties in order for us to support the call for same race placements.' As these researchers actually found that the children they studied suffered *no difficulties at all* as a result of being transracially adopted their conclusion ignores their own findings (1983, 139, 131–2).

A second response is to distort research findings. For example, in the study cited above, Bagley draws a comparison between his findings on Canadian Indian adoptees with research on black adoptees by stating that 'the adoption of black children by white parents has been problematic compared with within race adoption' (1991, 74). This statement is followed by a parenthetical reference to Feigelman and Silverman's *Chosen Children*. In fact these two authors reach the opposite conclusion: 'black transracial adoptees showed no more evidence of maladjustment than similar white in racial adoptees'.[7]

Another method of distorting research, used by opponents of the TRA of American Indians, is to identify genuine problems that are unrelated to TRA, and then to cite these problems as if they are caused by TRA. Thus, the ill treatment suffered by Indian children in *institutional* care is cited as a reason not to remove children from their tribe for fostering or adoption (Bagley 1991). Similarly, high rates of al-

---

6. Sartori discusses how some belief systems base their assumptions on logic rather than experience (1969); Arendt criticises absolutist logic (1973); Popper criticises predictions that are presented as inevitable (1966).

7. Feigelman and Silverman 1983, 237. These authors also argue that while TRA is not harmful to minority children in need of adoption, delayed placement (which is caused by extended efforts to recruit parents of a matching ethnic group) *is* harmful (Silverman and Feigalman 1981). A distortion similar to Bagley's is found in Fletchman-Smith's summary of Grow and Shapiro's *Black Children White Parents* (Fletchman-Smith 1984, 126).

coholism, drug abuse, suicide and crime among Indians in the USA *in general* are said to have been directly contributed to by TRA in particular—as they are in the Indian Child Welfare Act (1977; 1978)—although there is no evidence that the incidence of these problems is unusually high among adopted children.

A further response is to use one particular research finding as a point of departure into the argument against TRA. Transracially adopted children have often been found to have a weaker sense of their ethnic identity than inracially adopted children. This claim is based on interviews in which transracially adopted children are more likely to describe themselves as first and foremost a human being rather than a member of a specific ethnic group; or say that their racial background is not important to them; or that they do not want to follow their ethnic culture; or that they feel no special affinity with other people of the same skin colour.[8]

The obvious conclusion to be drawn from this evidence is that there is more than one viable form of identity, and if transracial adoptees without a strong sense of *ethnic* identity are otherwise well-adjusted then, their comparative lack of ethnic identity does not cause them any problems. But this is not the desired conclusion, so instead this weak sense of ethnic identity is treated as a problem *in itself*. For example, Chimezie criticises Grow and Shapiro's study of transracial adoptees for not seeing ethnic identity as 'the most important basis for any statement on rate of success' (1977, 85). Similarly Dominelli interprets the research of Gill and Jackson (who she rather unjustly accuses of promoting 'white supremacist values'), as showing that transracial adoptees 'have been successfully indoctrinated into thinking they are white...they have had either to repress or reject their black identity and become *colour-blind*'.[9]

The colour blind philosophy held by some white parents and transracially adopted children is one that contends that people ought to be treated as individuals irrespective of their colour, that they should not be prejudged or stereotyped on the basis of their colour, and neither should they be obliged to conform to certain patterns of behaviour, beliefs, or cultural mores because of their colour. This philosophy, deriving from humanism, is the subject of particular criticism by opponents of TRA.

Some opponents of TRA think of heritage and culture as an aspect of a person that is akin to biology, so that just as genes determine skin colour, etc., so culture is a natural and essential rather than an artificial and conventional part of someone's makeup. This comes out in attacks on the colour blind philosophy for 'equating the concept "we are equal" with the concept "we are the same"' (British Agencies 1991, 6). A colour-blind philosophy does not, however, deny that there are cultural differences between people; rather, it claims that different cultures, including those that parallel racial distinctions, are conventional and that no one is naturally predestined to conform to any particular culture, nor should they be forced to do so.

---

8. Bartholet develops the argument that 'more sophisticated comparative research indicates that transracial adoptees have essentially as strong a sense of black identity and racial pride as other minority children' (1991,1217).

9. Dominelli 1988, 99. Gill and Jackson had found that 'The children...saw themselves as 'white' in all but skin colour and had little knowledge or experience of their counterparts in the black community. There was no general evidence, however, that the absence of racial pride or identity was, at this stage, associated with low self esteem or behavioral disorder' (1983,130).

Others attack the colour-blind philosophy by a facile distortion of its proposition that people *ought not* to be discriminated against on the grounds of colour. Opponents of TRA reformulate this proposition by suggesting that parents who espouse a colour blind philosophy believe that people *are not* discriminated against on the grounds of colour, and tell this to their transracially adopted children. This palpable misrepresentation of humanism is followed by a rhetorical question: how will such an ill-informed child be able to cope on encountering racism? (Ladner 1977, 111) In fact, the answer to this question is that a humanist philosophy provides both the grounds for self-esteem in the face of racism and a belief system that repudiates it. Children who hold such beliefs are able to cope with racism as well as those with a strong sense of their distinct ethnic identity.

In making their claims to the contrary, opponents of transracial adoption treat a strong sense of ethnic identity not as an optional part of the human psyche, but as one that is essential. This unwarranted assumption allows opponents of TRA to contend that a strong sense of ethnic identity is vital to mental health (Lansberry 1992). In other words they assume that their particular political perspective of the kind of identity a person ought to have has an absolute validity and admit to no viable alternative.

At this point, the already tenuous connection between research findings and the argument against TRA is abandoned altogether for a process of logical extrapolation. Thus if a strong sense of ethnic identity is *needed* for good mental health, then anyone without this identity *must* suffer from problems as a consequence. Given this deduction, it follows that research which finds that transracial adoptees have neither problems nor a strong sense of ethnic identity is logically impossible. To resolve this paradox opponents of TRA claim either (1) that the success of TRA is illusory, or (2) that there has not been time for problems to develop.

Thus on the one hand, opponents of TRA frequently make the distinction between what is described as the *appearance* of flourishing and well adjusted children and the alleged underlying reality of a painful lack of identity (Kim 1978). Similarly, the problem of identity allows the successful outcome of TRA to be reformulated as 'conventional measures of success' or 'success' placed in inverted commas.

On the other hand, it is often suggested that the lack of strong ethnic identity will cause 'inevitable problems' to arise in the future (Ladner 1977, 248). In other words, evidence that TRA is successful is discounted by the simple expedient of placing the problems that it is alleged to cause at the end of an ever receding rainbow; problems predicted for children are replaced by problems predicted for adolescents, which are replaced by problems predicted for young adults, which are replaced by problems that occur well into adult life (Ladner 1977; Jones and Else 1979; British Agencies 1991).

Claims Made in Court

A second front in the campaign against transracial adoption lies in the courts. Here too one can see the process of (1) distorting or discounting evidence in favour of TRA, (2) making absolutist claims about the 'needs' of minority children, and (3) making dire predictions about the future of minority children that are left in the care of white parents that are based on the logical consequences of these claims, regardless of their current well-being. The effectiveness of these techniques, can be illustrated by two British court cases in which social workers successfully sought to remove a minority child from white foster parents.

In the first case, social workers holding the position that TRA should be regulated, defended their decision to remove a coloured child from the care of white foster parents with the wrong attitudes and place him with other white parents who held the right attitudes. The foster parents, who had wished to adopt the child, applied to have the social workers' decision overturned. Their application was denied, in part, because:

> D is a child of mixed parentage, who has cultural needs associated with this. This issue will become more important as he grows older. [The applicants'] attitude has been one of "colour-blindness". They do not accept that colour is significant and do not see D as a different race/colour. However much they may choose to ignore this issue, it may not be long before D's colour becomes important to him. Whilst [the female applicant] has said that members of the extended family are mixed race, [the applicants'] general attitude does not bode well for them coping with issues of cultural and racial identity as D grows older.

By contrast, the adoptive parents selected by the social workers have already adopted two children who are half black/Afro-Caribbean. These children are aware of their background and origins and this has been openly addressed. They appear to be happy and well adjusted ('R v. Lancashire' 1992).

In the second case social workers were against the TRA altogether. They removed a child from a white foster mother who wished to adopt him even though she and her prospective husband expressed willingness to support his 'cultural background and needs' and 'take part in any necessary therapy'. The judge supported the social workers' decision. The child, he concluded in light of the evidence provided by social workers, 'is still too young for any problems with his cultural background and identity to arise but the time is not far off when they will begin to do so'. The foster mother appealed. Her appeal was rejected. The appeal court judges said that despite the general agreement that the foster mother 'has cared admirably for D and that he has thrived in her care', the first judge had been entitled to find that the trauma of removing the child was outweighed by evidence that a mixed-race child was better off in a black family ('Re P' 1990).

In neither case, therefore, is it claimed that the child has already suffered from the colour-blind philosophy or the whiteness of his foster parents, rather, it is confidently predicted that he will do so *in the future*. The advantage of making this claim in a court case is that it *cannot be empirically evaluated,* at least not directly. Furthermore, evidence that the child thrived in the care of his foster parents is made to seem irrelevant.

It would be possible to counter this groundless argument, by referring to researchers (e.g., Simon and Alstein) who refute it. However, what may actually happen is that the argument is judged, first, by assessing its logical coherence, and second, by evaluating the professional expertise of the social workers who put it forward.

It is in these respects that the argument against transracial adoption can appear convincing. It is presented in absolute terms of the 'need' a child has for a sense of ethnic and cultural identity. Once this premise is accepted, there is no room for equivocation; the conclusion that a lack of such an identity will cause problems follows inevitably. The argument therefore, seems logical. Furthermore, the claim that a strong sense of ethnic identity is a 'need' can help to obscure the partial political perspective of the social workers, by presenting it as a neutral psychological expertise.

The idea that you can raise a coloured child to be colour-blind, the view of the applicants in the first case, is a perfectly viable alternative to providing him with a strong sense of ethnic identity. By claiming that this ignores a psychological need in the child, however, the foster parents' philosophy, is redefined as a shortcoming, a failure to openly address an issue that will, inevitably, arise in the future.

In the second case, the foster mother accepted the psychological expertise of social workers by offering to enter 'therapy'. But once the need for therapy is conceded, it is hard to disagree with the conclusion that the child's 'cultural and identity needs would be better met' by black parents (Re P 1990).

The spurious expertise with which opponents of TRA lay claim, therefore, is partly the result of the way that they present one particular form of identity—a strong sense of ethnic identity—as a universal psychological need.[10] However, the political objectives that are tied to this notion of identity are often obscured not only by presenting it in psychological terms, but also by the *omission* of the more radical elements of the argument against TRA.

Radical Opposition to TRA

So far I have presented opposition to TRA as a single ideology. But to analyse and criticise it further, it is necessary to recognise that opponents of TRA do not hold identical beliefs, but are ranged along a continuum between those whose position forms part of a radical critique of Western society, and those whose views are more moderate. This distinction between radicals and moderates has some correlation between the two types of argument against TRA identified earlier in the paper. Radicals tend to be completely opposed to TRA; moderates tend to favour special regulations for the vetting of white parents.

Moderate opponents of TRA place it within a framework of three liberal assumptions: (1) Many whites are well-meaning, (2) The welfare of the child is paramount, (3) Opposition to TRA is based on reason, social work expertise, or professional experience. This moderate position is the one presented in court, either because it is genuinely believed, or because it is expedient when faced with a liberal judge to present a liberal perspective.

The radical position, which is frequently advanced in professional literature, makes the opposite assumptions: (1) All or almost all whites are racist, (2) The minority community has a paramount claim in determining the future of a minority child, (3) Opposition to TRA can be advanced only through power.

The moderate position that opposition to TRA is based on reason has been shown to be false, at least within liberal terms. However, it was the holders of radical views who initiated and organised the campaign against TRA, and although the moderate position has now acquired its own momentum, radicals continue to

---

10. For a discussion of how the claim that minority children have various 'needs', allows opponents of TRA to present a political perspective in psychological terms see Hayes 1993.

be an active and influential source of opposition to it. It is necessary, therefore, to examine these views critically and to ask why they have been persuasive.

Racism

Radical opponents of TRA stress that white racism is omnipresent, there is 'prevailing racism', 'endemic racism'; racism is the 'scourge pervading every aspect of social interaction' (Kim 1978, 485; Hill and Peltzer 1982, 558; Dominelli 1988, 6). This view is quite distinct from the position that there is racism *in* society. It is saying that racism can be found to be 'permeating all aspects of it', that it is 'a normal feature of interaction between blacks and whites' (Dominelli 1988, 8). Once this position is conceded then the argument against TRA appears to be much stronger. A member of a minority group, it can be claimed, must learn 'survival skills' or 'coping mechanisms' to deal with this ubiquitous racism (Chestang 1972; Chimezie 1977). These techniques can only be learned from minority family members and peers. Furthermore, if all or almost all whites are racist a transracial adoptee will be rejected by those whose culture he has assimilated.

Three arguments are used to justify the position that racism is ubiquitous. The first is similar to the contention that a colour-blind philosophy is flawed because different cultures are naturally (rather than conventionally) linked to people of different colours. These critics of TRA interpret racism in quasi-Lamarkian terms as an acquired characteristic that has become an inherited instinct. It is claimed that blacks and whites

> belong to different racial and cultural groups, and in the past these groups were related to each other as colonial masters and slaves or exploited labourers. On both sides there are culturally inherited attitudes that make us instinctively feel that one group is superior to the other, however much we repudiate these feelings.

Racism, therefore, is one of the 'unconscious attitudes which survive in all of us' (Association of British Adoption 1981, 160, 161). By identifying racism as an unconscious force impervious to conscious human resolve, proponents of this argument are able to identify it as ubiquitous and to discount empirical evidence to the contrary as merely the manifestations of conscious anti-racism that leaves unconscious racism intact.

In response, it might be said that most whites in the last few hundred years were themselves 'exploited labourers' rather than 'masters'. But my prime objection to such claims concerns not their interpretation of history, but the assumption that people today are bound by history and cannot escape from the past. Fanon makes the point eloquently:

> Am I going to ask the contemporary white man to answer for the slave-ships of the seventeenth century?
> Am I going by every possible means to cause Guilt to be born in minds?
> Moral anguish in the face of the massiveness of the Past? I am a Negro, and tons of chains, storms of blows, rivers of expectoration flow down my shoulders.
> But I do not have the right to allow myself to bog down. I do not have the right to allow the slightest fragment to remain in my existence. I do not have the right to allow myself to be mired in what the past has determined.

I am not the slave of the Slavery that dehumanized my ancestors (1967, 230).

The second argument that racism is ubiquitous has as its starting point statistics that show minorities to be disadvantaged in various dimensions: life expectancy, income, chance of going to prison, educational attainments, unemployment, and so on. The general picture presented by these statistics for some minority groups such as American Indians is undeniably bleak. What is open to question, however, are the implications of these statistics. For some opponents of TRA they show that every aspect of Western society is racist, and every member of Western society who is a member of the comparatively well off white-majority is racist (and sometimes that no member of a minority group is racist). As Weise puts it:

> When a person belonging to the race-superior group (or when organizations and institutions representing its values and norms) consciously or subconsciously, overtly or covertly, propagate or collude with a system which maintains the oppression of non-members, be that by design or default, then that person is racist; the organizations and institutions become ethnocentric and racist in orientation.... Black people, non-members of the race-superior group and lacking one of the essential sets of ingredients—economic and political power—*cannot* be 'racist' (1988, 8).

It might be countered that many aspects of Western society are not racist, for example, laws that prohibit racial discrimination. It could also be said that to attribute systemic disadvantage only to racism does not allow for the influence of cultural variables (except insofar as racism is an aspect of culture). But even if it is conceded that the disadvantages suffered by some minorities are wholly attributable to racism, a key objection remains. Transracially adopted children do not suffer *disproportionately* from this form of racism, if anything, the reverse may be the case.[11] As Chimezie, a strong opponent of TRA says: 'Practically no published argument against transracial adoption contends that transracial adoption adversely affects the child's physical health or academic performance' (1977, 82). In effect this means that transracial adoptees can 'survive' and 'cope' with racism as well as anyone else. Furthermore, there is no reason to assume that transracial adoptees will be uniformly rejected by 'racist' whites as the meaning of the term 'racism' denoted by the argument is a narrow one that refers to a position of privilege in society and not to racist beliefs and acts of prejudice. Part of the persuasive force of this argument, however, relies upon its unjustifiable slippage between (i) the definition of white racism as the automatic result of white privilege, which allows the deduction that *all* whites are racist regardless of their personal attitudes towards and interaction with members of minority groups, and (ii) the commonly understood meaning of the term racism to mean prejudiced beliefs and actions, something that it is much harder to claim is universal among whites.

The third argument that racism is ubiquitous focuses on racial divisions and their implications. This argument begins with the observation that whites and minorities segregate themselves from each other. Given this it is possible to predict that transracial adoptees may be rejected wherever they go; they may be 'defined

---

11. A study by Womack and Fulton (1981) finds that transracially adopted black children have a comparatively high IQ compared to blacks in general. The authors attribute this finding to environmental factors. This and other research is summarised by Bartholet 1991, 1222–3, fn, 159.

as an alien in the white community and a traitor in the black community' (Chestang 1972, 103–4).

It is true that there is some societal segregation between whites and minorities, particularly whites and blacks in US cities. Yet we also know from the research into the lives of transracial adoptees that Chestang's fear has proved to be unfounded, if anything transracial adoptees find themselves in the socially advantageous position of being able to interact with both whites and minorities relatively easily (Bartholet 1991).

To explain why the societal segregation has not, in fact, placed transracial adoptees in an untenable position, it is necessary to challenge the assumption on which the argument is based: that such segregation is indicative of tightly bound, monolithic, homogeneous communities. This assumption does not characterise modern Western society for three reasons: (1) Segregation is by no means absolute, there is also considerable evidence of integration in the West including areas of racially mixed housing and racial intermarriage. Where there is segregation, there is still social contact between races at work and in public places. (2) Racial divisions are only one of a number of *intersecting* social divisions in society. Others, including class, religion, social and cultural interests and political affiliations, bring people of different races together. (3) Societal segregation has not generally gone so far as to impose a racially defined 'community' in which everyone shares or is forced to conform to the same racial attitudes and beliefs. In short, the experiences of transracial adoptees cannot be predicted by making blanket assumptions about their reception by different racial communities as there is sufficient pluralism and scope for individualism in Western society to confound any such predictions.

In making their claims to the contrary, radical opponents of TRA claim their political *objective* of dividing society into completely separate racial communities as 'reality'. TRA, a policy which runs counter to these separatist objectives, can then be described as 'ignoring reality'.

The Community

All the claims about transracially adopted children that I have examined so far, claims concerning their precarious mental health, their identity problems, their rejection by society, are ostensibly concerned with the welfare of the child. However, the argument that it is the minority community that should decide the fate of a minority child in need of adoption is very different. This argument does not rely upon the 'right' and 'need' of a minority child to a sense of ethnic identity. Rather the child has a duty to the 'community' which has the right to determine its fate.

The claim that the community has the right to determine the fate of minority children regardless of their interests is brought into unusually sharp focus by Fanshel. In one of the earliest systematic studies of the effect of TRA on minority children, Fanshel summarises his findings on American Indians adopted by whites as follows:

> When one contrasts the relative security of their lives with the horrendous growing up experiences endured by their mothers...one has to take the posi-

tion that adoption has saved many of these children from lives of utter ruination. In this sense, the research offers supporting evidence for the continuation
and expansion of these adoptions (1972, 339).

Nonetheless, Fanshel concluded that American Indian children did not have the
right to be saved from lives of utter ruination if this was perceived as being un-
helpful or harmful to the collective aspirations or feelings of 'the Indian people':

> Whether the adoption by white parents of the children who are in the most ex-
> treme jeopardy...can be tolerated by Indian organizations is a moot question.
> It is my belief that only the Indian people have the right to determine whether
> their children can be placed in white homes. Reading a report such as this one,
> Indian leaders may decide that some children may have been saved by adoption
> even though the symbolic significance of such placements is painful for a proud
> people to bear. On the other hand even with the benign outcomes reported
> here, it may be that Indian leaders would rather see their children share the fate
> of their fellow Indians than lose them in the white world. It is for the Indian
> people to decide (1972, 341–2).

The same ordering of priorities is found among opponents of TRA influenced
by separatist arguments, although they assume (a) that the interests of the child
and of the community are the same, (b) that 'the community' is opposed to TRA,
and (c) that TRA is harmful to the community. For example, the President of the
NABSW said in Senate Hearings on adoption in 1985: 'We view the placement of
Black children in white homes as a hostile act against our community. It is a blatant form of race and cultural genocide'.[12]

The concept of the paramouncy of the community cannot be criticised in quite
the same way as claims that TRA damages the child. It is not enough to show that
it is factually wrong, the moral issue of the relative claims of the group as opposed to the individual must also be addressed.

Having said this both (a) the concept of the community and (b) the claim that
the community is opposed to TRA are highly suspect. Ambiguity over what is
mean by the community comes out in Fanshel's statement, cited above, where 'Indian organizations' 'the Indian people' and 'Indian leaders' are used interchangeably as if there can be expected to be a natural unanimity between them. In Fanshel's case we see a naive and ill-considered (and unfortunately fairly typical)
notion that a *gemeinschaft* can be expected to emerge that expresses the general
will of a minority group on transracial adoption. Organisations actively opposed
to TRA, such as the NABSW and ABSWAP have made use of simplistic assumptions of this sort to legitimise themselves by laying claim to speak for the community, where in fact they are imposing their views on the community.

I have argued that pluralism, and scope for individualism in Western society
means that racially defined communities are not at all unanimous in their attitudes and beliefs, and that this diversity of opinion includes attitudes towards

---

12. Cited in Simon and Alstein 1987, 143 fn 1. Some members of the NABSW now adopt
a more moderate position. Ladner discusses early descriptions of TRA as 'genocide' (1977,
87–90). The claim that TRA constitutes 'cultural and ethnic genocide' is still made by opponents of TRA purporting to speak for minority communities (Rosario 1994).

Leading Issues in African-American Studies

TRA. There has been little systematic evidence collected on this subject, although opponents of TRA within social work sometimes admit that their views are often contradicted by members of minority groups with whom they have professional contact. Rhodes's observations on the views of black people recruited in a same-race placement campaign for foster parents are particularly interesting in this respect. Rhodes found that although some supported the goals of the campaign, many rejected the ideology of same race placement, and 'nearly all were opposed to a rigid same race placement policy' with comments such as:

> It doesn't matter what colour the child is, whether it is black, white, pink or blue. A child is a child. It's love that counts.

> You have to look at each child individually, regardless of colour.

> [Transracial fostering is] better than being put in a home. Much better.

> Underneath [the skin] we are the same. I don't see why people should look at other people's skin.

> Why not [allow whites to foster black children]? Sometimes they lead better lives.

> I don't believe in segregation.

> It doesn't matter what culture you are. It is being able to give a child a home that is important. As long as you can love and care for that child, that is what is important. It doesn't really matter what culture that child is.

> What's having 'Black identity'? We all eat, drink, sleep. Black people must realise that they aren't any different. I don't know what they mean by 'Black identity'.[13]

Rhodes's observations would suggest that if one were to generalise about 'the black community' in Britain, then the majority might well be in favour of TRA rather than against it. A study of the 'black community perspective' in the USA, reaches the same conclusion in its interpretation of 150 interviews of blacks selected by random sampling: 'the majority of blacks do not oppose the idea of transracial adoptions and a large majority could be described as favorable to this alternative under certain conditions' (Howard 1977, 188).

The question of the views of 'the community' and its significance, however, cannot be settled by a majority vote. On the one hand, radical opponents of TRA can always interpret an unfavourable reaction to their views as coming from those who require 'consciousness raising'. This explanation of minorities who repudiate the ideology of same-race placement performs a similar function to the 'therapy' that is sometimes recommended for whites. It defines alternative opinions as inherently deficient. On the other hand, the argument in favour of TRA put forward here does not depend on it being supported by the majority of any particular ethnic group. This is (a) because the interests of the child are seen as paramount, and therefore (b) the viability of TRA does not depend upon the majority and minority opinions within ethnically defined communities but only on there being sufficient diversity of views and attitudes among members of society

---

13. Rhodes 1992, 'Reactions to the campaign within the black community', 146–149. Rhodes adds that blacks who 'were proud of their cultural heritage...did not necessarily think that it was a particularly important consideration when placing a child in a family' (149).

for someone who is transracially adopted to be able to integrate into the community in which they grow up, and in which they choose to live.

Power

The third argument that tends to characterise the more radical opponents of TRA is that the campaign against it must be conducted through power rather than through reason. The assumption that policies are formulated as the expression of the power of ethnic groups is often seen as axiomatic by critics of TRA. Thus Gill and Jackson say 'We take it as self-evident that the one-way traffic of black and mixed race children from the black to the white community indicates the relative power and position of the different ethnic groups in British society' (1983, 5). If this assumption is combined with the notion of ubiquitous white racism, then it follows that 'the black community must be involved at all levels and its professionals, collectively, must strive to wrest power from the white social service structures as power is the major platform upon which racism is exercised' (*Caribbean Times*, 8 April 1983, cited in Rhodes 1992, 51).

This analysis, however, is untenable. The very fact that TRA programs have collapsed so quickly shows that adoption policies for minority children cannot be explained in terms of an ethnic power-struggle. If this were so the campaign against TRA should have failed as whites continue to form the majority of child care professionals and key decision makers. This is not to say that opponents of TRA, of whatever race, have not used power whenever possible, they have. But the assumption that those in favour of TRA have used power politics to get their way is misplaced. In fact, the success of the campaign against TRA is partly the result of the asymmetry between opponents of TRA, who have used any means necessary in pursuit of their objectives, and its supporters who have tried to counter them with reason.[14]

In her analysis of the debate between supporters and opponents of transracial adoption and fostering, Rhodes interprets these asymmetric positions in terms of ethnic stereotypes. Blacks and whites, she contends, adopt different 'cultural styles' of argument. Blacks are excitable, emotive, confrontational, use *ad hominem* arguments, and are completely one-sided; whites are cool, quiet, restrained, dispassionate, impersonal and consider both sides of an argument. The implications of this analysis might seem to be insulting for anyone who is black and considers himself rational. Rhodes, however, claims that the only difference between these supposed black and white styles of argument is their style, they are otherwise indistinguishable, neither rely upon reason, both are manipulative. The 'white' style, however, is the more subtle as 'listeners may be seduced into agreement' while falsely assuming that 'they have been persuaded by a careful consideration of the arguments and evidence'.[15]

Rhodes's claim that blacks and whites argue in different ways can quickly be discounted. Many blacks make dispassionate arguments and consider both sides

---

14. The classic comparison between proceeding through reason and proceeding through power is found in Plato's *Gorgias*.

15. Rhodes 1992, 58. She quotes T. Kochman (1981) *Black and White Styles of Conflict*, Chicago, in support of these claims.

of a question, many whites use bombastic and emotive rhetoric and are close-minded. But what of the claim that reason and objectivity play no part in choosing sides in a political debate like the debate over transracial adoption?

Rhodes defends this position by arguing that to be open minded is impossible, as everything new that a human being perceives is interpreted according to prior assumptions.[16] But to assume that everyone is subjective in this way need not lead one to the conclusion that rational argument is impossible. Popper, who like Rhodes says that we interpret all that we perceive, says that we are nonetheless able to test our ideas, change our minds when confronted with new evidence, and to be self-critical (1966). Subjectivity does not, therefore, mean that we must be dogmatic, fit evidence to support our ideas, discount rational views that oppose our own without considering them, and refuse to countenance that our ideas might be wrong.

This takes us back to the discussion of research into TRA and its interpretation. We have seen how opponents of TRA have distorted, discounted and denied the evidence in its favour, and this is one manifestation of their use of power over reason to pursue their objectives. By contrast, researchers into TRA who cautiously conclude in favour of it, nonetheless often go to great lengths to consider the case against it and to test their assumptions. They frequently stress that their findings are provisional, and are often self-critical to the extent of conceding that inracial adoption is preferable to TRA without examining this claim (e.g. Grow and Shapiro 1977).

In the face of single minded and vehement opposition to TRA was this open-mindedness and dispassion really likely to persuade, or even more unlikely, to 'seduce' liberal white child care professionals? We know that the answer is no, and that opponents of TRA have successfully obscured, discounted, denied the gap between their claims that TRA has harmed minority children and the fact it has helped them.

The Success of the Attack on TRA

It might be thought that the more radical elements of the arguments against TRA would have hindered rather than helped the campaign against it, especially as I have earlier suggested that opponents of TRA have prudently omitted radical elements of their case in legal arguments. Among child care professionals, however, and particularly among those trained in social work, the radical arguments may help to explain the success of the campaign against TRA. This is because proponents of these arguments can exploit the susceptibilities of those whose general political orientation is liberal or moderate rather than radical but who also combine a tendency to self-criticism, with feelings of white guilt.[17]

Those who are painfully conscious of the great racial injustices of the past may tend to be susceptible to the idea that nothing has changed, and that every problem among minority groups is caused by racism. They may also be unusually sen-

---

16. Rhodes 1992, 58. She quotes V. Harris, (1987) 'Changing Minds', *Social Services Insight,* 17 July, 18–19.

17. Richards (1987) briefly analyses feelings of white guilt among opponents of TRA.

sitive to the charge that they are complicit in this process, that they are the racist upholders of white power. To repudiate white power and white racism they may wish to demonstrate their affinity with minority groups and this may lead them to side, more or less uncritically, with anyone who claims to speak from the perspective of the minority community.

The extent to which these feelings may have influenced decisions by white professionals to limit or abandon TRA is difficult to gauge as they remain unstated beneath the ostensible claim that opposition to TRA is in the best interests of the child. This justification for opposing TRA, however, may be best understood as part of an implicit bargain that has developed between radical opponents of TRA and more moderate child care professionals. Considered schematically, this bargain can be analysed as the final step in a three stage process: (1) Radical opponents of TRA, for all their talk of challenging the 'power' of liberal white professionals, instead relied upon their ability not to unseat white decision makers, but to make them feel guilty. (2) The radicals succeeded; White professionals *were* made to feel guilty. But this placed whites in a dilemma: by supporting TRA they believed that they were seen as enemies by the minority 'community', yet if they opposed TRA they were also guilty: guilty of denying prospective homes to minority children in need of adoption. (3) To resolve this dilemma a compromise was reached. The conscience of white liberals was to be salved by explaining opposition to TRA in *language* that put the best interests of the child first and foremost, while the *substance* of these policies conformed to a separatist agenda that placed the aspiration for distinct, homogeneous communities above the interests of individual children.

The result has been that minority children have been torn from loving foster parents or left languishing in institutional homes in the name of 'the best interests of the child'. This stance is justified by arguments common to radicals and moderates: claims that a minority child has a psychological need to a strong sense of ethnic identity and predictions of inevitable future problems if this is not the case. As has been shown, these ideological claims have been designed in such a way as to make them irrefutable, and have been advanced despite of all the evidence that TRA is a success.

Once these ideological pretensions are stripped away, it becomes possible to understand why it is that as research shows ever more conclusively that TRA works very well, so its critics have become ever more adamantly opposed to it. It is not the failure of TRA that has lead to the attacks upon it but its success. The very fact that TRA is successful is an embarrassment to moderates who claim to support the best interest of the child. It is a threat to the radicals as it undermines their vision of separate and distinct racial communities.

References

"Adoption Guide Urges New Goals" (1969), *New York Times*, 19 Jan., 76.

Adoption: The Future (1993), London: HMSO, CM 2288.

Ahmad, B. (1990), *Black Perspectives in Social Work*, Birmingham: Venture Press.

Allen, A. (1992), "Responses to 'Where do Black Children Belong,'" *Reconstruction*, 1 (4), 46–8.

Arendt, H. (1973), *The Origins of Totalitarianism,* New York: Harcourt Brace Jovanovich.

Association of British Adoption and Fostering Agencies (1981), "Working with West Indian Applicants in Fostering and Adoption: A Discussion Paper," in J. Cheetham *et al.* (ed), *Social and Community Work in a Multi-Racial Society,* London: Harper and Row.

Bagley, C. (1991), "Adoption of Native Children in Canada: A Policy Analysis and a Research Report," in H. Alstein and R. J. Simon (ed), *Intercountry Adoption: A Multinational Perspective* (55–79), New York: Praeger.

Bartholet, E. (1991), "Where Do Black Children Belong," *University of Pennsylvania Law Review,* 139 (5) 1163–1256.

British Agencies for Adoption and Fostering (1991), "The Importance of culture, race, religion and language—placement needs of children and the Children's Act 1989" (Draft).

Brooton, G. (1971), "The Multiracial Family," *New York Times,* 26 Sept., Section 6, 78, 80.

Carmichael, S. (1969), "Stokely Carmichael Explains Black Power to a Black Audience in Detroit," in R. L. Scott and W. Brockriede (ed), *The Rhetoric of Black Power,* New York: Harper and Row, 84–95.

Chestang, L. (1972), "The Dilemma of Biracial Adoption," *Social Work,* 17 (3), 100–105.

Child Welfare League of America (1959), *Standards for Adoption Service,* New York: CWLA.

Child Welfare League of America (1973), *Standards for Adoption Service: Revised,* New York: CWLA, Third Printing.

Chimezie, A. (1977), "Bold but Irrelevant: Grow and Shapiro on Transracial Adoption," *Child Welfare,* 56 (2), 75–86.

Day, D. (1979), *The Adoption of Black Children: Countering Institutional Discrimination,* Lexington MA: Lexington Books.

Dominelli, L. (1988), *Anti-Racist Social Work,* London: Macmillan.

Fanon, F. (1967), *Black Skin White Masks,* tr. C. L. Markmann, New York: Grove Press.

Fanshel, D. (1972), *Far from the Reservation: The Transracial Adoption of American Indian Children,* Metuchen, NJ: Scarecrow Press.

Feigelman, W. and Silverman, A. R. (1983), *Chosen Children: New Patterns for Adoptive Relationships,* New York: Praeger.

Fletchman-Smith, B. (1984), "Effects of Race on Adoption and Fostering," *International Journal of Social Psychiatry,* 30 (1 and 2), 121–8.

Fraser, G. C. (1972a), "Disease Programs Scored by Blacks," *New York Times,* April 9, 29.

Fraser, C. G. (1972b), "Blacks Condemn Mixed Adoptions," *New York Times,* April 10, 27.

Fraser, C. G. (1973), "Educator Scores Fellow Blacks for Failure to take Leadership," *New York Times,* July 26, 33.

Fricke, H. (1965), "Interracial Adoption: The Little Revolution." *Social Work,* 10 (3), 92–97.

Gill, O. and Jackson, B. (1983), *Adoption and Race: Black, Asian and Mixed Race Children in White Families,* Batsford Academic and Educational Ltd.

Grow, L.J. and Shapiro, D. (1974), *Black Children-White Parents: A Study of Transracial Adoption,* New York: CWLA.

Grow, L.J. and Shapiro, D. (1975), "Adoption of Black Children by White Parents," *Child Welfare,* 54 (1) 57–59.

Grow, L.J. and Shapiro, D. (1977), "Not So Bold and Not So Irrelevant: A Reply to Chimezie," *Child Welfare,* 56 (2), 86–91.

Hayes, P. (1993), "Transracial Adoption: Politics and Ideology." *Child Welfare,* 72 (3), 301–310.

Hill, M. and Peltzer, J. (1982), 'A Report of Thirteen Groups for White Parents of Black Children' *Family Relations,* 31 (4), 557–65.

Hoksbergen, R. K. (1991), "Intercountry Adoption Coming of Age in the Netherlands: Basic Issues, Trends and Developments," in H. Alstein and R. J. Simon (ed), *Intercountry Adoption: A Multinational Perspective* (141–158), New York: Praeger.

Howard, A. *et al.* (1977), "Transracial Adoption: The Black Community Perspective," *Social Work,* 22 (3), 184–189.

Indian Child Welfare Act (1977), 95th Congress, 1st Session; Senate Report No. 95-597; Calendar No. 550; S963-20; November 3.

Indian Child Welfare Act (1978), *United States Statutes at Large,* Vol. 92 Part 3; Public Law 95-608; 95th Congress, 3069–3078.

Jones, C. E. and Else, J. F. (1979), "Racial and Cultural Issues in Adoption," *Child Welfare,* 58 (6), 373–382.

Kim, D. S. (1978), "Issues in Transracial and Transcultural Adoption," *Social Casework,* 59 (8), 477–486.

Ladner, J. A. (1977), *Mixed Families: Adopting Across Racial Boundaries,* New York: Anchor Press/Doubleday.

McRoy, R. G. and Zurcher, L. A. (1983), *Transracial and In-Racial Adoptees: The Adolescent Year,* Springfield IL: Charles C. Thomas.

Popper, K. R. (1966), *The Open Society and Its Enemies,* 2 vols, Princeton: Princeton University Press.

"R v. Lancashire County Council Ex Parte M" (1992), *Family Law Reports,* 1, 109–114.

Raynor, L. (1970), *Adoption of Non-White Children: The Experience of a British Adoption Project,* London: George Allen and Unwin.

"Re P (A Minor) (Adoption)" (1990), *Family Law Reports,* 1, 96–102.

Rhodes, P.J. (1992), *"Racial Matching" in Fostering,* Aldershot, Avebury.

Richards, B. (1987), "Family Race and Identity." *Adoption and Fostering,* 11 (3), 10–13.

Rorbech, M. (1991), "The Conditions of 18 to 25-Year-Old Foreign-Born Adoptees in Denmark," in H. Alstein and R. J. Simon (ed), *Intercountry Adoption: A Multinational Perspective* (127–139), New York: Praeger.

Rosario, D. (1994, April), Speech delivered at a meeting on "Transracial Adoption: A Focus on Racial, Cultural and Permanency Issues," Association of the Bar of New York Meeting Hall.

Rosettenstein, D. S. (1993), "Custody Disputes Involving Tribal Indian in the United States," in J. Eekelaar and P. Sarcevic (ed), *Parenthood in Modern Society: Social and Legal Issues for the Twenty First Century,* Martin Nijhoff.

Russell, A. (1972), "White Adoptions," Paper presented at the Annual Meeting of the National Association of Black Social Workers, Tennessee, 1972.

Saetersdal, B. and Dalen, M. (1991), "Norway: Intercountry Adoptions in a Homogeneous Country," in H. Alstein and R. J. Simon (ed), *Intercountry Adoption: A Multinational Perspective* (83–106), New York: Praeger.

Sartori, G. (1969), "Politics Ideology and Belief Systems," *American Political Science Review,* 398–411.

Silverman, A. R. and Feigelman, W. (1981), "The Adjustment of Black Children Adopted by White Families," *Social Casework,* 62 (9), 529–536.

Simon, R.J. and Alstein, H. (1977), *Transracial Adoption,* New York: Wiley.

Simon, R. J. and Alstein, H. (1981), *Transracial Adoption: a Follow-Up,* Lexington MA: Lexington Books.

Simon R. J. and Alstein, H. (1987), *Transracial Adoptees and their Families: A Study of Identity and Commitment,* New York: Praeger.

Simon, R. J. and Alstein, H. "Intercountry Adoption: Experiences of Families in the United States," in H. Alstein and R. J. Simon (ed), *Intercountry Adoption: A Multinational Perspective* (23–53), New York: Praeger.

Small, J. W. (1984), "The Crisis in Adoption," *International Journal of Social Psychiatry,* 30 (1 and 2), 129–142.

Thoburn, J. (1990), *Inter-Departmental Review of Adoption Law, Background Paper Number 2: Review of Research Relating to Adoption,* Department of Health (UK).

"Two Atlanta Whites Yield Black Child," (1971), *New York Times,* 8 Jan., 36.

Weise, J. (1988), *Transracial Adoption: A Black Perspective,* Norwich, University of East Anglia Social Work Monographs No. 60.

William M. Womack and Wayne Fulton (1981), "Transracial Adoption and the Black Preschool Child," *Journal of the American Academy of Child Psychiatry,* 20, 4, Autumn, 712–724.

X, M. (1971), "God's Judgment of White America," in M. X, *The End of White World Supremacy: Four Speeches* (121–148), New York: Merlin House.

25

Adolescent Development and Adolescent Pregnancy Among Late Age African-American Female Adolescents

Joyce West Stevens

Introduction

Adolescent pregnancy is a major social problem in inner city communities. The social consequences of prematurely constituted families is costly in both human and monetary terms. Adolescent parents often become welfare dependent throughout the life span of their offspring. Adolescent parentage has been associated with problems of emotional neglect as well as severe forms of physical abuse. Additionally, the educational achievement of both adolescent males and females is often terminated prematurely because of early parenthood (Hayes, 1987). On this account, some scholars have suggested that adolescent parenthood sets up failed social trajectories (Chilman, 1979; Franklin, 1988; Furstenberg, 1988; McAnarney & Hendel, 1989). Clearly, the consequence of the psychosocial dysfunction of adolescent parenthood has special significance to the field of social work.

Yet, one can argue that there is a growing need in the profession to permit analysis of normative problematic behavior that is free of assessments which stress pathology and a disease model. Moreover, clinical social workers purport to treat but lack a nonpathological conceptual model or definition of the indices of psychological-social health or well being (Saari, 1991). Clinical social workers treat from a pathological medical model of disease. Adolescent development is undergoing theoretical reappraisal (Palombo, 1985, 1990; Offer, 1988; Gilligan, 1990; Surrey, 1990). Contemporary views of adolescent development hold that

An earlier version of this essay appeared in *Child Adolescent Social Work Journal;* 1994, 11, 6, December, 433–453 and is adapted/reprinted with the permission of the copyright holder/author.

adolescent mental health no longer need be seen as being solely grounded in theoretical formulations of what should occur during the adolescent period. There is a decided shift away from the notion of adolescence as a recapitulation of earlier conflicts concomitant with a homogenous youth culture of rebelliousness and turmoil (Esman, 1990). Thus, we are confounded, on two accounts, in an examination of adolescent development and adolescent childbearing: First, on the meanings we attach to adolescence and second, on the meanings we attribute to sexuality.

Research findings herein reported support three theoretical perspectives: (1) pregnancy can serve as a primary way of confirming existence and providing a sense of identity rather than being the result of sexual acting out behavior; (2) parenthood is perceived as a viable route to an adult social identity when opportunities for alternate routes of negotiating an adulthood status are blocked; and (3) the adolescent does not have to disconnect or individuate from familial relationships for the development of self. Following a discussion of general theoretical frameworks in which adolescent pregnancy is examined, this paper describes research which utilized quantitative and qualitative procedures to compare and contrast a random sample of pregnant and nonpregnant late age adolescent African-American females' perceptions about negotiating status and adulthood. A description of the sample and protocol instruments is set forth including a culturally sensitive protocol which elicited in-depth narrative accounts about respondents' commonsense ways of understanding and knowing themselves, others, and the world around them. Results of the study are presented, and the paper concludes with a discussion of findings and implications for clinical adolescent pregnancy intervention/ prevention program models.

Review of Theoretical Issues

Paradigms of Adolescent Pregnancy

Horowitz, Klerman, Kuo, and Jekel (1991) have identified three explanatory models utilized in the examination of adolescent pregnancy: (1) the psychological, (2) the behavioral, and (3) the alternate life style. Chiefly, explanatory models of psychological dysfunction and behavioral deviancy frame most theories about adolescent childbearing. Such theoretical explanations tend to view the female adolescent's behavior as disordered, diseased or as intergenerational transmission of psychological dysfunction. For instance, the psychological model, primarily influenced by classical psychoanalytic theory, emphasized personality dynamics and interpreted adolescent childbearing as one of sexual acting out behavior or failure of individuation, i.e., pre-oedipal narcissistic fixations (GAP, 1986; Horowitz, 1991; LaBarre, 1972; Sanders, 1991; Schaffer & Pine, 1972; Young, 1954). Stewart (1981) argues that an examination of pregnancy at adolescence requires that deviancy not be attributed to normative characteristics associated with the status of female and adolescent. She contends that theorists have claimed that role confusion, narcissism, passivity, and dependency are normative developmental features for the female adolescent. Yet, these features are often descriptive of the psychological dysfunction of pregnant adolescents. On the other hand, the behavioral model focused on illegitimacy, culture, and poverty as correlates of deviant social actions (Clark, 1965; Rainwater, 1970; Reiss, 1970). Indeed, the psychological model gives scant attention to the social context of the female adolescents situated behavior. Although the behavioral model examines social structural factors it does so at the expense of personalism. In addition, the behavioral paradigm does not address satisfactorily the interrelationship of race, class, and gender and their impact on the problem.

The third and less commonly held explanation is that adolescent pregnancy represents an alternate life course and is a pathway to adulthood, especially when opportunities for social mobility are blocked (Ladner, 1971). The alternate life course paradigm stresses deficits in environmental opportunities and as such gives notable attention to the social context of the adolescent experience. A growing body of creditable empirical research supports this alternate life style model. Research findings suggest that the outlook of some adolescent females is that pregnancy and parenthood is a way of attaining adulthood status (Ladner, 1971; Schwab, 1984; Williams, 1991). Such findings inform about ascribed and achieved social roles. In some respects they advance a sociological view of an ascribed role of motherhood—that is the notion that female fertility has value and worth. Fertility may be perceived by some adolescents as having primary and singular importance in their development. The social role of motherhood signifies adult responsibilities, validates identity and, consequently, may serve as a vehicle for maturation. Conversely, the alternate life style model implies that when pathways for social mobility opportunities are open achieved social roles serve as vehicles for maturation and social identities.

In short, the alternate life style model attempts to place the private troubles of adolescent single parenthood within a social context. Albeit, an examination of mental process is not a component of the paradigm, there is nothing inherent in the model that precludes its incorporation. The explication of the problem of adolescent pregnancy both within the context of psychological and sociological domains is useful. Clearly, then, this explanatory model lends itself to a multidimensional theoretical focus when psychological variables are incorporated alongside social-cultural factors. Psychological and sociological paradigms of adolescent pregnancy provide models for the analysis of selfhood or identity. It is within identity that one finds embedded both personal and social factors. As Erikson (1969; 1968; 1964) has cogently expressed, the core issue of adolescent development is the fashioning of an identity within the social order. Even so, the examination of sexuality relative to identity among adolescent childbearers has been restricted to acting out behaviors, again highlighting pathology rather than normal development.

Sexuality

Brooks-Gunn and Furstenberg (1989) have noted that adolescents are seldom studied in any detail relative to the personal meanings of sexuality and to the strategies that are used to incorporate these meanings into their everyday lives. Current research on adolescent sexuality is mostly focused on females and is therefore gender specific. Female fertility regulation is viewed as a female issue not a male one. Scholars contend that gender specificity is a focus in research on adolescent sexuality because there is a remarkable gender difference in the meanings attached to sex. Females are more likely to stress the importance of relationship variables when deciding to engage in sexual coitus, whereas males are more likely to stress physical pleasure at the expense of relational factors. Moreover, it is noted that the long term social cost of pregnancy for early adolescent sexual activity is far greater for females than males; whereas near rewards for early coitus are far less (Strouse and Fabes, 1987).

Yet, marital status may be the most single determinant in the designation of adolescent pregnancy as deviant. Surely, to be single and childbearing raises the explicit issue of illegitimacy. Adelson (1966) observes that despite changes in sexual mores, marriage before parenthood continues to be the normative expected social adjustment. Historically, female adolescent premarital sex activity has been viewed psychodynamically as sexual acting out behavior. Traditional psychoanalytically based theories which posit adolescent pregnancy as a form of sexual acting out behavior is postulated on an instinctual model of development which sets forth sexuality as discharge. The current meaning that sexual behavior has on psychological development has, however, been clarified by Litchtenstein (1977) who contends that sexual activity is a way of affirming identity.

Class, Race, and Gender

To be sure, the adolescent period, inherently, has a unique and profound dynamic given the impetus of physiological changes and the anticipation of future adult roles. The need, during this period, to reorganize and strengthen a new meaning system can be prompted by inner experiences of change and anticipated changes. As noted by Kett (1977) the social reality of the transitional passage of adolescence from an asexual world to a sexual one is a remarkable transformative one. And while the adolescent period is not always beset by angst, rebellion, and intergenerational conflict, it usually is a period which is problematic (Offer, 1988). The transitional passage of adolescence and how it comes to be structured will be greatly influenced by the social categories of class, race and gender.

Socioeconomic class is a variable of considerable import in structuring the adolescent experience. The lower class female, regardless of race, may be more dependent on environmental vicissitudes for adulthood preparation, resulting thereby, in less familial or institutional control over the trajectory toward adulthood. Middle class youth, for instance, are more likely than low income youth or poor youth to use college as a socialization preparatory experience for obtaining adulthood status (Coleman, 1974). Schwab (1984) has explained that there is great similarity between impoverished black and white female pregnant adolescents. Both subpopulations, she contends, deem pregnancy and motherhood as a rite of passage to adulthood. Moreover, she argues that motherhood for the pregnant teen signifies adult responsibilities. The mothering role is viewed as a source of empowerment as it influences social relationships and promises a voice for self definition and self valuation. At the same time, however, interlocking race and class variables create a potent dynamic which impacts on the social trajectories of black female adolescents. Wilson (1987) claims that the unemployability of the black male may be a primary contributing factor to the problem of black adolescent pregnancy and illegitimacy. The economic insolvency of poor black males make for a meager marriageability pool. Few impoverished black males have the wherewithal to assume future spousal and parental responsibilities.

The trajectory to adulthood raises a number of issues and problems for the adolescent which are negotiated within the experiences of everyday living. The most significant question is, "What is required of the adolescent to participate in society as an empowered adult engaging in reciprocal personal and social exchanges"? Every adolescent wants answers, guidance, and direction relative to this question. Further, how this question comes to be understood and answered is dependent on the meanings we attached to adolescence. New theoretical developments supported by empirical evidence suggest that there is a separate line of psychological development for the female adolescent. Emerging theories stress the psychological aspects of development but do so within a theoretical framework of intersubjectivity. Benjamin (1988), a feminist theorist, maintains that self development is centered in reflexive dialectical interactions. She contends that self assertion, recognition by another and the discovery of self in that recognition become conceptual nexus points in theorizing about self development. Others argue that mutually interdependent relationships of care, nurturance, and connection provide the context for the development of self (Belenky, 1986; Gilligan, 1982; Gilligan, Lyons, & Hanner 1990; Gilligan, Ward, & Taylor 1988; Rothman, 1989; Ruddick, 1989; Surrey, 1991). Surrey and her associates (1991) have summarized and conceptualized these theoretical innovations into a psychodynamic theory identified as self-in-relation.

The notion that the adolescent must separate and disconnect from familial relationships to mature may no longer be tenable. Self-in-relation theory postulates that the self is constructed within a matrix of significant relationships of care, nurturance, connection and relation to others. Arguably, this theorization of adolescent self development is remarkably different from what we have come to understand as the second separation-individuation crisis of adolescence (Blos, 1967). Surrey contends that the adolescent wishes to sustain connection with primary relationships while changing the form and content of those relationships in an evolving development of self. There is no need, in her view, to sacrifice relationships or disconnect for self development. Still, one of the main omissions of the theory is that it ignores the impact of social variables such as race, and ethnicity on adolescent psychological development. A theory which takes into account the self embedded in social praxis will allow for the values and norms discovered in social interactions. For instance, it has been postulated that Black females may experience a convergence of feminist and Africentric values insofar as an Africentric ethos represents values of care, mutuality, and connection (Collins, 1990). As a consequence, of this focalization of values female fertility may then come to define personal and social worth.

Social Norms

Although social role and social norms are concepts inherent in the social status of adolescence, few studies have attempted to explicate these concepts when examining adolescent pregnancy. One can conceptualize that social roles have meanings embedded in dialectical social interactions. Meanings can formulate social norms from which a social identity is formed. Norms then can represent situated or social actions which cause others to validate identity (Cancian, 1975). In some communities the most visible validation of adulthood identity for females is parenting actions and parenting responsibilities.

Accordingly, the social structuring of motherhood could provide, for the female adolescent, a social identity. Parenthood, with its corresponding duties, responsibilities and obligations, is a socialization experience for adult social functioning. Certainly, one function of adulthood is the capacity and ability to care for another. The female adolescent who views limited opportunities for social mobility may, indeed, view parenthood as the most available means for achieving an adult social identity. On this account, a modified alternate life style paradigm was utilized as a theoretical framework for this current research.

The objective of this current research is to examine whether some African-American inner city females perceive the use of pregnancy and motherhood, within their environments, as a way to negotiate an adulthood status and affirm a social identity. Research findings are consistent with the theoretical constructs of social norms, self-in-relation theory, and the notion that sexuality is a way to confirm identity. This research specifically argues that, for some inner city Black females, it is not so much the desire for pregnancy as much as the desire for motherhood which represents a social identity.

Methodology

Design

The present study effort was designed to contrast and compare pregnant and nonpregnant Black female adolescents' self understandings about what it means to be a grown up woman. It was expected that:

1. Black female adolescents from both groups would view pregnancy and motherhood as a means through which to attain adulthood status; and
2. that there would be a significant difference between the pregnant and nonpregnant adolescents in that nonpregnant girls are more likely to establish linkages beyond the immediacy of family and peers.

In short it was expected that nonpregnant girls selected to postpone pregnancy to realize social mobility goals whereas pregnant girls would view parenthood as a rite of passage to adulthood.

For purposes of this study adulthood status was defined as an achieved status that confers the right to secure goods and services for the care of self and others as well as the right to influence others so that they recognize the legitimacy of the claim to such a right. The achievement of the status is considered problematic by those conferring the status as well as by those on whom the status is conferred. (Hence, the need for its negotiation). Negotiation is defined as the act of changing the perception of self in the social interaction with another and having that self image recognized as changed. This negotiation is carried out within a situation that has been self evaluated as problematic (Horowitz, 1981).

Subjects

The sample consisted of 20 pregnant and 16 nonpregnant African-American female adolescents between 17 and 19 years of age. Late age adolescents were selected because it was thought that they would have made significant decisions regarding their trajectories to adulthood. The research was conducted at a large metropolitan hospital which serves inner city communities. These communities are representative of urban problems such as poverty, school drop out, unemployment, and teen births (1990 census data analyzed by *The Chicago Reporter*, July, 1992.) The sample was selected from the Family Planning and Prenatal clinic registration. An active listing of some 100 clinic registrants was maintained until the total random sampling of 40 was achieved.

The initial design called for equal numbers of subjects but some of the non-pregnant girls selected proved difficult to reach. Some of them were away at college or working full time. Both study populations had a medical history of no living children. The pregnant sample did not include any females in the first trimester to ensure that subjects had made a decision to have and keep the baby. Respondents with an experience of a prior elective abortion were not eliminated from the study since this was viewed as an exercise of choice and a form of birth control. Finally, two atypical cases emerged, one in each sample. The pregnant population included a 19-year-old married teen living with her employed 21-year-old spouse. Within the nonpregnant population there was an 18-year-old virgin teen who was an active user of birth control pills but had not selected a young man with whom she wanted to be sexually active.

Measures and Procedure

The research utilized two instruments. The first was a 24-item structured interview schedule which yielded basic demographic data. The second instrument was a 27-item semi-structured interview schedule identified as the Pregnancy Adulthood Negotiation of Status Interview (PANSI). The PANSI was constructed to elicit information from respondents about psychosocial developmental domains and their ways of understanding their personal experiences. The schedule was rendered culturally sensitive by utilizing an Africentric perspective for focus and direction of narrative content. Collins' (1990) epistemological categories provided the definitional framework for an Africentric ethos. Collins has categorized the ways in which African-Americans come to know and understand their experience of the world as: (1) concrete experience as a criterion of meaning; (2) the use of dialogue in assessing knowledge claims; (3) the ethic of caring; and (4) the ethic of personal accountability. These conceptual categories were translated into culturally sensitive language and meanings that related to research subjects' daily existence.

Subjects were contacted by phone and letters to schedule interview appointments. They were interviewed at the hospital over a 7-month period and were seen on or independent of clinic visit days. Funds were offered to purchase a meal when subjects were interviewed on their scheduled clinic days; transportation funds were given for the research interviews. The informed consent was taken when the instrument was administered.

Data Analysis

Both qualitative and quantitative procedures for data analysis were employed. The raw data were reviewed and sorted to select variables that could be reduced to quantifiable form. Quantifiable data was coded and entered for computer analysis using the Statistical Package for the Social Sciences (SPSS-X). The Chi-Square, Mann-Whitney U Test, and T test were used to analyze the coded data. A significance level of $<.05$ was selected for all analyses.

The ETHNOGRAPH, a qualitative data analysis computer program, was selected as a descriptive-interpretative program to aid in the analysis of the text-based data (Whalen, 1992) from the PANSI QUESTIONNAIRE. The PANSI questionnaire text was adjusted and transcribed for coding. Conceptual categories and themes were developed and organized based on a review of subject responses to questions. A total of 40 questions were selected as being the most salient for the development of thematic material. Themes were related to theoretical concepts and/or hypotheses that had developed in the course of the project. Once the thematic codes were conceptualized, the computerized text was saturated with these thematic codes. The text-based data was coded based on content (i.e., chunks of meaning) and not on the occurrence of words, since the former better captured the meaning of responses.

Seven thematic categories emerged from review of the data and were conceptualized as constitutive of norm modeling actions. These were defined as those actions or behaviors which a person has deemed appropriate or inappropriate for the development of a social identity. Each theme was operationally defined. The seven themes were: 1) Adulthood Preparation; 2) Role Model Formulation; 3) Decision Making; 4) Care Protective Sensibility; 5) Sex/Gender Role Commitment; 6) Opportunity Mobility; and 7) Mate Selection. Results related to the thematic categories of Care Protective Sensibility; Opportunity mobility; and Mate Selection are discussed in this paper. These categories were selected for this paper as they provide a nexus to the alternate life style paradigm of adolescent pregnancy. Data regarding other themes will be reported in future publications. The coded themes were transferred into quantifiable form by the Qualitative Data Analysis computer program. A Chi-Square test was used to determine how the two sample populations differed in relation to the thematic categories. Examples from the text representing subjects' thematic concerns are presented to document findings.

Results

Biographical Data

Demographically the two groups were more similar than different. Subsamples tended to be equally poor; their mean age was 18 years; and they resided mainly in female-headed households. On the whole, the population tended to be high school graduates, attending high school, or attending college (Table 1). As regards age, class, and family constellation variables, the research population was representative of the geographical communities from which the sample population was drawn. Well over 50% of the population in these communities were below the poverty line (U.S. Census data 1990; The Chicago Reporter, 1992).

The mean age for both groups for sexual initiation was 16 years of age. One hundred per cent of the total sample population reported a history of contracep-

Table 1. Demographic Characteristics of Pregnant and Non-Pregnant Teen Samples

Characteristics	Pregnant (N=20)		Non-Pregnant (N=16)		
	N	%	N	%	χ^2 P value
Receipt of public welfare funds	18	90.0	11	68.8	.109
Presence of father in home	1	5.0	4	25.0	.084
Education—H.S. diploma	9	75.0	8	88.9	.435
College attend	1	33.3	7	87.5	.023
Employment history part-time	1	45.0	12	75.0	.069
Registered voter	6	46.2	8	88.9	.040
Church attendance	13	65.0	15	93.8	.039
Spontaneous abortion	5	25.0	0	.0	.031
	Mean	SD	Mean	SD	T-Test p val.
Age	18.1500	.933	18.000	.966	.470

tive use. However, the two groups did differ significantly in that the pregnant females were more likely to have had a spontaneous abortion, whereas the non-pregnant females never had a spontaneous abortion. Pregnant females were significantly more likely to have had a prior pregnancy that was aborted involuntarily. Findings suggest that nonpregnant females were more likely to have a church affiliation, to be attending college, to be registered voters, to have an active-sustained work history, and to be contraceptive users.

Thematic Categories

The two groups differed significantly in the thematic categories of Care Protective Sensibility, Opportunity Mobility, and Mate Selection (Tables 2 & 3). Differences were found among the two groups because of the thematic psychological-attitudinal responses reflected in question items. Statistical test were not run on each item, but percentages were used to exemplify where the subgroups were in contrast in an overall theme. Thematic responses provided anecdotal information to lend support to theory.

Care Protective Sensibility referred to a sense of care and protection in relation to self and others, that is, to the perception of the importance of affective and behavioral expressions of care, loyalty, and nurturance in relation to others as an evolving self defining personal view. Pregnant girls were more likely to view care and protection in relation to a parental role. Still, the pregnant girls were more involved with partnered mates for nurturance and care than were the nonpregnant

Table 2. Thematic Categories

Observed Theme Occurrences	Pregnant (N=20)		Non-Pregnant (N=16)		
	N	%	N	%	χ^2 P value
Care Protective Sensibility	125	48.3	134	51.7	.05
Opportunity Mobility	94	40.3	139	59.7	.01
Mate Selection	84	63.6	48	36.4	.10

Table 3. Thematic Responses

Themes	Example Answers* (Phraseologies)
Care Protective Sensibility	Nice and considerate
	Thoughtful
	Tries to help
	Understanding
	Patient, kind
	Helps others
	Loving, caring
	Good listener
Opportunity Mobility	Getting a job
	Going to college
	Having goals
	Carrying out goals
	Having a career
	Getting an education
	Being responsible
Mate Selection	Trouble keeping jobs
	Admirable
	Gets girls pregnant
	Immature
	Deals drugs
	Gang banger
	Caring, responsible

* Source: Across protocol

girls. Yet, nonpregnant girls tended to identify more nurturing relationships among female peers and older relative male role models than did the pregnant girls (Tables 4 & 5). These findings were consistent with the theoretical explanation of self-in-relation model which posits that the self is developed through connection with others rather than individuation from primary relationships.

Opportunity Mobility Theme referred to self-expectancies for social mobility goals, that is career, education, etc. It also referred to the self-actualization of social mobility goals reflected in an active engagement in pursuing pathways to en-

Table 4. Care Protective Sensibility Theme: Peer-Friendship Relationships

Sample Group	Number (N = 36)	% Responses
Pregnant Teen	4 (N = 40)	15.0
Non-Pregnant Teen	12 (N = 16)	75.0

Source: A4. Now think about your friends who are your age and are really important to you. Who are they?
A5. Now describe what you and your friends talk about and do together.

Example answers: We're each other's support.
We're the best of friends.
When I need someone, she's right there.
We cry together.

**Table 5. Care Protective Sensibility Theme:
Positive Male Role Model Characteristics**

Sample Group	Number (N = 36)	% Responses
Pregnant Teen	3 (N = 20)	15.0
Non-Pregnant Teen	8 (N = 16)	50.0

Source: Now think about a man you feel is the best kind of man he can be. Who is this man?
          B9. What do you think it takes to be this ideal man or role model?

Example answers: Always there for me
                  Kind and understanding
                  Good provider
                  Hard worker

hance upward mobility, for example, in jobs, schooling. The Opportunity Mobility Theme was more often associated with the nonpregnant girls and less often associated with the pregnant girls. The pregnant girls were less likely to articulate social mobility goals for the future, whereas the nonpregnant girls were more likely to comment about social mobility goals and to be engaged in self-actualizing activities to realize such mobility goals. Some pregnant females tended to view the pregnancy as a problematic situation that could interfere with the realization of social mobility goals. They articulated the possibilities of missed opportunities.

At the same time, however, pregnant females could distinguish between their feelings about the situation of pregnancy and their feelings of self-worth. In other words self-esteem could be positive, although the situation was perceived as problematic. This observation is supported by previous research findings which show that early childbearing does not have to be emotionally incapacitating and may not diminish self-esteem. Moreover, it is supported by a report that African-American females tend to sustain positive self-esteem, and confidence about self did not diminish at the onset of adolescence (Sadker & Sadker, 1994). African-American females are more dependent on the symbolic definitions of those in their proximal environments to give definitional meaning to their behavior. They are less dependent on those persons external to their environment who are likely to attribute negative definitions to their behavior (Rains, 1971).

The Mate Selection Theme referred to valuative judgments about the behavior of male peers. These judgments were made about males with whom the subjects were involved in a committed supportive relationship, i.e., boyfriend or expectant father. Judgments were also made about noncommitted partner relationships (i.e., who experienced disillusionment and breakup of a previously emotionally committed relationship) and/or the observations of the behavior of male peers within the neighborhood. The study population was contrasted in their dating and mating selection patterns. Pregnant girls were such that they tended to be in a sustained relationship with the expectant fathers of their unborn children. Pregnant girls were especially concerned about the relationship between marriage and economic opportunities of Black males (Franklin, 1988; Wilson, 1987). Nonpregnant girls tended to be involved in general dating rather than being attached to one single boy. Both subsample groups tended to be concerned about the involvement of neighborhood boys in the street culture of gangs and drugs.

Discussion

In summary, nonpregnant females manifested a sense of care and responsibility to others in varied relationships and articulated more frequent self expectancies for social mobility. Nonpregnant females were less restricted in their dating and mating behaviors, experiencing multiple dating partners. All together, these findings suggest that these behavioral, situational, and psychological-attitudinal variables herein reported serve as indices of social mobility aspirations for the nonpregnant population. Differences between the two subpopulations argue for the hypothesis that nonpregnant adolescents are more likely to establish linkages beyond their immediate family and peers as reflected in their engagement in church, community, employment, and educational environments.

Finally, study findings supported the expectation that pregnancy and parenthood are viewed as a way to manage developmental concerns for personal and social maturation. The self-reports of well over 50% of the research sample indicated that they perceived that adolescent parentage as providing a maturational experience and a benchmarker for adulthood status. Both groups believed that their age group had achieved the maturity to assume the adulthood responsibility of parenthood. Thus, pregnant females appeared to believe that having a baby was a way of testing themselves for adulthood and that if one were a parent others would treat them as parents.

Overall these findings were undergirded by the theoretical framework set forth in the modified alternate life course explanatory model. Indeed, this model served as a framework for integrating several theoretical approaches. An alternative explanation for study findings is that the pregnant status of the pregnant sample may have biased subject responses. Once pregnant, girls may modify their views substantially. A longitudinal study of younger teens studied before and after pregnancy would address this issue.

Demographic findings tended to support the view that late age poor African-American female adolescents are likely to remain in high school as well as attend college. This finding is not consistent with previous research in which pregnant teens were likely to be high school drop outs (Chilman, 1980; Phipps-Yona, 1980). Findings of the nonpregnant respondents' reports of their abortion history suggest that girls in this sample were inconsistent contraceptors and could have become pregnant at an earlier age than the present age reported in this study. Yet, at the same time, the findings also imply that the decision to engage in sexual activity can represent personal responsibility for sexual desires and sexual activity. This particular finding is also consistent with previous research findings which suggest that adolescents do assume responsibility for their sexual behavior and the consequences thereof (Patten, 1981). The theoretical explanation to account for these findings is one espoused by psychoanalytic theory which proposes that sexual activity can be viewed as a primary way of confirming existence and a sense of identity (Lichtenstein, 1977; Saari, 1986).

Present findings suggest that the socialization process for *Adulthood* was based on perceived prescriptions for becoming a grown up. Over half of the sample population believed parental responsibilities were a determinant in developing adult social competence. These data support previous research findings that lower class adolescent females view pregnancy as a rite of passage to adulthood status and as an enhancer in attaining social and personal maturation (Gabriel & McAnarney, 1983; Ladner, 1971; Schames, 1990; Schwab, 1984; Williams, 1992). Mainly, the *Care Protective Sensibility Theme* findings indicated that the pregnant females were more limited than nonpregnant females in their reliance on selected mates rather than on peers in meeting affiliate needs outside the familial environment. On the surface this appears to be a reasonable response, but pregnant respondents seem to be less engaged with female peers because they were distrustful of them and felt competitive in regard to their selected mates. In contrast, the nonpregnant females perceived nurturing and affective characteristics in the identified male role models in their familial environments and in their relationship with female peers. Theories of self development in relation to connection to others suggest that the nonpregnant females had a greater expectation for mutual empathic interaction to occur in all their relationships. Thus, nonpregnant females may exhibit a greater level of complexity and articulation in their connection to others and in the development of their social norms and social identities. They experienced relationships which were more extensive and expansive.

Conclusion

The implications of these study findings are that they sound a caveat for the need to reconceptualize the theoretical knowledge base of adolescent development to a model of attachment and connection. In adolescent prevention programs the mother-daughter dyad and peer group may be targeted for intervention in so far as female adolescents desire connection, not separation from primary relationships. Early intervention-prevention programs are likely to be particularly helpful in primary-middle school settings before sexuality decisions are made. Mentor-apprenticeship programs to enhance and promote the development of mobility opportunities and to secure employment is suggested. The development of clinical social work programs with institutions in inner city communities (i.e. churches) to mount reach out youth based programs to extend social networks beyond family and peers is recommended. Finally, further research is needed to explore how some lower class Black female adolescents are able to postpone pregnancy and motherhood and seek to negotiate more complex social identities within their environments. Such information would help elucidate the preventive factors that may be important in designing clinical programs.

References

Adelson, Joseph & Donovan, Elizabeth. (1966). *The Adolescence Experience*. New York: John Wiley and Sons.

Belenky, Mary Field; McVicker Clinchy, Blythe; Goldberger, Nancy Rule; & Tarule, Jill Mattrick. (1986). *Women's Ways of Knowing*. New York: Basic Books.

Benjamin, Jessica. (1988). *Bonds of Love*. New York: Pantheon Books.

Blos, P. (1967). The Second Indivduation Process of Adolescence. *Psychoanalytic Study of the Child*. 22, 161–186.

Brooks-Gunn, Jeanne and Furstenberg, Frank, Jr. (1989). Adolsecent Sexual Behavior. *American Psychologist*. 64(2), 249–257.

Cancian, Frances M. (1975). *What Are Norms*. New York: Cambridge University Press.
    Chicago Reporter (The). (1992). Twenty Years Later: A City Still Divided. 21, 7, July.

Chilman, Catherine S. (1980). Teenage Pregnancy: A Research Review. *National Association of Social Workers*. 492–498.

Clark, Kenneth B. (1965). *Dark Ghetto*. New York: Harper and Row Publishers.

Coleman, James (1974). Youth: Transition to Adulthood. Chicago: Univeristy of Chicago Press.

Erikson, Erik. (1969a). *Identity and the Life Cycle*. New York: International Universities Press.

Erikson, Erik. (1968b). *Identity, Youth and Crisis*. New York: W.W. Norton and Company.

Erikson, Erik. (1964c). *Insight and Responsibility*. New York: Morton Publishers.

Esman, Aaron H. (1990). Adolescence and Culture. New York: Columbia University Press.

Feagin, Joe R. and Sikes, Melvin P. (1994). *Living with Racism*. Boston: Beacon Press.

Franklin, Donna L. (1988). Race, Class, and Adolescent Pregnancy: An Ecological Analysis. *American Journal of Orthopsychiatry*. 58(3) 339–354.

Furstenberg, F.F., Brooks-Gunn, J., & Morgan, S.P. (1987). *Adolescent Mothers in Later Life*. New York: Cambridge University Press.

Furstenberg, F.F., Brooks-Gunn, J., & Morgan, S.P. (1985). Sex Education and Sex Experience Among Adolsecents. *American Journal of Public Health*. 75(11), 1331–1332.

Gabriel, Ayola and McAnarney, Elizabeth R. (1983). Parenthood in Two Subcultures: White Middle Class Couples and Black Low Income Adolescents in Rochester, New York. *Adolescence*. XIII(71), 595–608.

GAP (Group for the Advancement of Psychiatry). (1986). *Crisis of Adolescence Teenage Pregnancy: Impact on Adolescent Development*. New York: Brunner Mazel Publisher.

Gilligan, Carol. (1982a). *In A Different Voice*. Cambridge: Harvard University Press.

Gilligan, C., Ward, Janie Victoria, & Taylor, Jill Mclean. (1988b). *Mapping the moral domain*. Cambridge: Harvard University Press.

Gilligan, C.; Lyons, Nona P.; & Hanmer, Trudy J. (1990c). *Making Connections: The Relational World of Adolescent Girls at the Emma Willard School*. Troy, New York: Emma Willard School.

Hacker, Andrew. (1992). *Two Nations*. New York: Charles Scribner's Sons.

Hayes, Cherly D. (Ed.). (1987). *Risking the Future, Adolescent Sexuality, Pregnancy, and Childbearing, vol 1*. Washington, DC: National Academy Press, Washington.

Horowitz, Ruth. (1984). Passion, Submission and Motherhood: The Negotiation of Identity by Unmarried Inner City Chicanos. *The Sociological Quarterly*. 22(Spring), 241–252.

Horowitz, Sarah M., Klerman, Lorraine V., Kuo, Sung H., & Jekel, James F. (1991). Intergenerational Transmission of School Age Parenthood. *Family Planning Perspectives*. 23(4), 168–172.

Kett, Joseph. (1977). Rites of Passage. New York: Basic Books.

LaBarre, Maurine. (1972). Emotional Crisis of School-Age Girls During Pregnancy and Early Motherhood. *Journal of American Academy of Child Psychiatry*. 11, 536–557.

Ladner, Joyce. (1971). *Tomorrow's Tomorrow: The Black Woman*. Garden City, New York: Doubleday and Company, Inc.

Lichtenstein, Heinz. (1977). The Dilemma of Human Identity. New York: Jason Aronson.

McAnarney, Elizabeth R. & Hendel, William R. (1989). Adolescent Pregnancy and Its Consequences. *JAMA*. 262(1), 74–82.

Miles, Matthew B. & Huberman, A. Michael. (1991). *Qualitative Data Analysis*. Newbury Park: Sage Publications.

Offer, Daniel. (1988). *The Teenage World: Adolescents' Self-Image in Ten Countries*. New York: Plenum Medical Book Company.

Palombo, J. (1985). An Outline of Adolescent Development. Paper presented at the Tenth Annual Self-Psychology Conference, Chicago, Illinois.

Palombo, J. (1990). The Cohesive Self, The Nuclear Self, and Development in Late Adolescence. Chicago: Univerity of Chicago.

Patten, Marie. (1981). Self Concept and Self-Esteem: Factors in Adolescent Pregnancy. *Adolescence*. XVI(64), 765–778.

Phipps-Yonas, Susan. (1990). Teenage Pregnancy and Motherhood: A Review of the Literature. *American Journal of Orthopsychiatry*. 50(3), 430–431.

Powers, Sally I., Hauser, Stuart T. & Kilner, Linda A. (1989). Adolescent Mental Health. *American Psychologist*. 44(2), 200–208.

Rains, Prudence Mars. (1971). Becoming An Unwed Mother. Chicago: Aldine Publsihing Company.

Rainwater, Lee. (1970). *Behind Ghetto Walls*. Chicago: Aldine Publishing Company.

Reiss, Ira L. (1970). Premarital Sex as Deviant Behavior: An Application of Current Approaches to Deviance. *American Sociological Review*. 35, 78–88.

Reid, William & Smith, Audrey D. (1981). *Research in Social Work*. New York: Columbia Univeristy Press.

Rothman, Barbara Katz. (1989). *Recreating Motherhood*. New York: W.W. Norton and Company.

Ruddick, Sara. (1989). *Maternal Thinking*. New York: Ballantine Books.

Saari, Carolyn. (1986). *Clinical Social Work Treatment: How Does It Work?* New York: The Guilford Press.

Saari, Carolyn. (1991). *The Creation of Meaning in Social Work*. New York: The Guilford Press.

Sadker, Myra & Sadker, David. (1994). *Failing At Fairness*. New York: Scribners.

Sanders, Joelle. (1991). *Before Their Time*. New York: Harcourt Brace, Jovanovich, Publishers.

Schaffer, Carole & Pine, Fred. (1972). Pregnancy, Aortion, and the Development Tasks of Adolescence. *Journal of American Academy of Child Psychiatry*. 11, 511–536.

Schamess, Gerald. (1990). Toward and Understanding of the Etiology and Treatment of Psychological Dysfunction Among Single Teenage Mothers: Part I: A Review of the Literature. *Smith Studies*. 60(3), 153–168.

Schamess, Gerald. (1990). Toward and Understanding of the Etiology and Treatment of Psychological Dysfunction Among Single Teenage Mothers: Part II: A Review of the Literature. *Smith Studies*. 60(3), 244–261.

Schwab, Brenda Ruth. (1984). Someone To Always Be There: Teenage Childbearing As an Adaptive Strategy in Rural New England. (Doctoral Dissertation, Brandeis University, 1984). *Dissertation Abstracts International,* 45-01, 231a.

Steward, Mary White. (1981). Adolescent Pregnancy: Status Convergence for the Well Socialized Adolescent Female. *Youth and Society*. 12(4), 443–464.

Strouse, Jeremiah S. And Fabes, Richard A. (1987). A Conceptualization of Transition to Nonvirginity in Adolescent Females. *Journal of Adolescent Research*. 2(44), 331–348.

Surrey, Janet. (1991). The "Self-In-Relation": A Theory of Women's Development, in Jordan, Judith V. et al. (Eds). *Women's Growth in Connection*. New York: The Guilford Press.

Whalen, Margaret H. (1992). *Qualitative Data Analysis*. Unpublished Manuscript. Smith College School for Social Work.

Williams, Connie. (1991). *Black Teenage Mothers*. New York: Lexington Books.

Wilson, Julius W. (1987). *The Truly Disadvantaged*. Chicago, Illinois: University of Chicago Press.

Young, Leontine R. (1954). *The Unwed Mother*. New York: McGraw-Hill.

26

Family Life and Teenage Pregnancy in the Inner City: Experiences of African-American Youth

Sandra K. Danziger

Introduction

Of the many public policy dilemmas in the area of teen pregnancy, the causal roles and relative importance of structural conditions versus family processes and dynamics hold center stage. How do the effects of such factors as poverty status, employment opportunities in local communities, the availability of welfare, etc., compare to those of intra-familial mechanisms such as values transmission, parent-child communication patterns, role modeling of employment and marital relations, etc.? This paper examines the relationships among early sexual experience, teen motherhood, and the perceived quality of family life and early schooling experiences among inner-city African-American young women.

Previous research on adolescent childbearing, particularly within "truly disadvantaged" ghetto communities (Wilson, 1987, 1991), emphasizes two different types of antecedent variables. I characterize these as reflecting a family process model versus a structural opportunities model (see also Moore and Miller, 1990). Some research has identified the combined effects of both structural and process conditions of the family environment. For example, Hogan and Kitagawa (1985) found that structural factors such as family composition, parental income and education level, and neighborhood characteristics, as well as the dynamics of parental supervision time and the young women's educational aspirations, affected black teen fertility rates.

Studies that offer a more descriptive portrait of who becomes a young mother suggest that families where this occurs are stressed, overburdened, and provide

An earlier version of this essay appeared in *Children and Youth Services Review;* 1995, 17, 1–2, 183–202 and is adapted/reprinted with the permission of the copyright holder/author.

fewer constraints and supports in the children's lives. Constance Williams (1991), for example, identifies a common socialization pattern. Most of her sample of African-American young mothers in Boston grew up seeing early single parenthood as a way of life, with their teenage social lives characterized by "only casual supervision" (p. 81). Williams also found that many of the women were unhappy with their schooling experiences prior to the point at which they became pregnant, a finding that might be construed as consistent with the structural opportunities model.

If the school environment is alienating and/or frustrating, a young girl may seek alternative outlets for identity development. For example, John Ogbu (1988), Claude Steele (1992), and Reginald Clark (1983) emphasize the ways in which schools, families, and peer culture within impoverished minority communities discourage children from investing their identities, hopes, and aspirations in the educational arena. This may begin with the chasm between the home and school environment and thus have structural origins.

Elijah Anderson (1991) compares those in inner city Philadelphia who do and do not "succumb to the streets" and become teenage mothers and also points to the importance of both familial processes and educational opportunities. He documents the differences between these two groups of young women in their sense of future school and work opportunities and in the level of protectiveness and discipline provided by their families.

In this paper, I assess the relative plausibility of the two explanations by comparing the perceived social hardships within families and the early attachment to schooling among youth who differ by age of sexual initiation and parental status. My analysis is based on retrospective and subjective descriptions of early family and school environments. Based on the prior studies, I hypothesize that, in these data, family process conditions primarily affect the onset of sexual risk-taking behavior, whereas a more positive early attachment to school (structural opportunity) reduces the chances of becoming a teen mother (regardless of when a young girl first became sexually experienced). The combination of a difficult family life and a negative introduction to school contributes both to early sexual activity and young, single motherhood.

Data and Methods

The data are based on an in-depth qualitative study of a purposive sample of young women in Detroit (described in Danziger and Farber, 1990). Life history interviews, averaging more than 2 hours, were conducted between 1987–1989 with 80 African-American women ranging in age from 15 to 20. We recruited a sample of teen mothers and a comparable group of non-parent peers who lived in impoverished inner city communities. We drew respondents from clients of youth-serving social programs and snowball referrals and paid them $25 for the interview.[1]

Using open-ended questions, we elicited from each participant an account of her "life story" (Denzin, 1989). We conducted two interviews, each lasting 45

---

1. Only one or two who were approached about the study refused to be involved.

minutes–1½ hours, with nearly all of the young women.[2] We held most interviews in the sites of the referring agencies, in offices, corners of libraries, or on a few occasions, in a local fast-food restaurant or in the home. Interviews were audio-taped and transcribed verbatim.[3]

The interviews were framed to probe the young women's perceptions of opportunities and their impacts on sexual behavior, pregnancy resolution, school and work (see also Moore and Miller, 1990). We also discussed their perceptions of family life and history, school and community environments, values, ideals and sense of self to achieve a fuller understanding of their social and emotional context.

Analysis and Coding

Perceptions of family life. In response to a general question, "What was your life like at home?", the young women gave a wide range of assessments. Rather than coding these descriptions so as to label each person's family life "positive" or "negative," we coded family life along the several dimensions which emerged as common points of reference for the women themselves. In talking about family, they most consistently referred to three aspects: (1) feelings about family members and the extent to which family closeness was present or absent; (2) the extent to which supervision and routine patterns of rules and household activities were in place; and (3) instances of stress or trauma within the family, such as abuse or violence, serious health problems, family disruption such as desertion, divorce, death of a parent, or a child welfare placement in a foster family or group home.

In coding on the first dimension, feelings toward family members and sense of overall closeness or absence, we identified assessments of all family members mentioned (including those who may not be in the household, such as a father or grandmother). In addition, we judged which family member was reported to be the most central and significant for the young woman; then, overall closeness was rated by assigning positive versus negative feelings toward those most important to her. In some cases, conflicts were reported between the girl and family members, such as siblings. However, most young women talked primarily about their mothers or those who were their longest primary caretakers and gave this relationship a rather consistent overall evaluation over the course of the interview.

Where there was inconsistency, or where their feelings changed over different periods in their lives, we looked for the overall balance of feelings. If a respondent was rather evenly split, we coded her as having the absence of positive or close feelings. In addition, where the young women reported very little either positive or negative about family members, we coded the data as indicating the absence of closeness (same as having reported negative feelings). Because most of the women

---

2. In a few instances, we were unable to locate a young woman for the second interview.

3. The interviews were conducted by the author or by author-trained doctoral students in social work, most of whom were white; one interviewer was African-American. All were women.

spoke easily of these feelings and were fairly animated in characterizing their primary relationships, cases where little emotional content was revealed were suggestive of family problems.

A second component was the issue of supervision and routinization. Stories of family life varied greatly in the range of regularity of household activities, discipline, and the level of organization present in the children's roles and behaviors. The young women talked about the monitoring parents did to keep them "in line" and how involved the parents were in the children's school work, friendships, social activities, and general moral and personal habit development. In addition, they sometimes talked about the extent to which family chores and household activities were rule-governed versus ill-defined and unstructured.

The young women were not always pleased with the extent of supervision and routinization in their family life. As might be expected from teenagers, they preferred a middle-level of order in their lives, finding the lack of routines and supervision a sign of neglectful parenting, and an "excess" of order a sign of a repressive environment. Because it is difficult to tell what range of reported harshness of regimen is excessive versus age-appropriate (and because of possible great discrepancies in judgments had the parents been the narrators instead of the youth), we coded the presence versus absence of order in the home. Where present, it received mixed appraisals. Many who described high levels of restrictions saw them as necessary and a sign of parental concern, while others considered this regimentation as problematic. On the other hand, those who reported a lack of such routines and supervisory behavior were universal in attributing its absence to a lack of concern and/or capability on the part of their parents. None of the women considered the absence of routine to be particularly positive.

With respect to the third component of family life, many of the young women referred to stressful incidents or conditions in their families. They mentioned a wide range of family stresses and strains, but for this paper, we code the presence or absence of very serious traumas. Because of the high frequency of these problems, and because they often come in at least pairs in troubled families, we felt that families where these reports were not made should be compared to those with one or more traumas. Families where the youth reported no extraordinary negative events represented a special type of family, one that managed to survive the inner city environment of the late 1980s without being internally ravaged by drugs, violence, disruption of a particularly conflictual nature, and/or one or more chronic health or mental health stressors.

Perceptions of early schooling. Most reports about "life at school" dealt with current or recent experiences. However, many young women compared what it was like for them in school with how they felt about middle school and/or their elementary school years. The two most common points of reference in these earlier experiences were (1) how they felt as a student, whether they liked school, did well or not, liked other classmates, teachers, etc.; and (2) whether their parents made investments in them as students, i.e., showed concern about their grades, participated in meetings with the teachers, exerted pressure or help to perform well, acted as positive or negative academic role models, etc.

In both types of experiences, the young women generally recalled the extent to which their first encounters with going to school felt inviting, captivating, etc., versus alien, unappealing, or discouraging. What they emphasized was a perception of the school environment as a hospitable, engaging atmosphere in their earliest memories. Similarly, the recall of parental involvement in schooling centered around issues of reinforcing or encouraging student behavior versus not responding to or even undermining the educational orientation. Here, their focus was on the consistency across the two environments.

Due to the paucity of information on their early years, we code these two components as either positive or negative, with absence of information treated as missing data. In contrast to information about perceived quality of family life, we do not consider omissions of description here as having negative connotations for the youth. Similarly, where there is extensive description of a mother's lack of help during the most recent pregnancy, for example, but no data on how she helped or hindered the daughter's prior classroom experiences, we make no assumptions about early familial support for schooling. Our purpose here is to assess whether references to the quality of early experiences in schooling, given that they are described, differentiate either the age at which girls became sexually experienced or whether or not they became school-age mothers.

Thus, for both components of early schooling, we coded whether they mentioned themselves in the student role in a relatively positive or negative connotation, and whether they mentioned helpful or hindering parental behaviors in relation to schooling.

Age of sexual experience. In describing their relationships with boyfriends and/or pregnancy and contraceptive experiences, the young women often talked about their first physical sexual encounter. To be consistent with fertility studies based on survey data, we coded the first time they are likely to have had intercourse. Often, the interviewer probed for this information; at times, however, the earliest sexual experience was alluded to in the context of abuse or assault. Where the girl's sexual introduction occurred in the context of an incestuous or rape situation, but the degree of sexual assault was not clear, the interviewers did not always probe for the precise sexual behavior that occurred. If, for example, a stepfather's behavior eventually led to a major family confrontation and significant repercussions such as medical treatment or changes in the household, we coded it as her first sexual encounter. If she indicated that this person "bothered" and "frightened" her, but it seemed to be of a non-physical nature and less serious in both frequency and impact for her and for others, we did not code it as her first sexual initiation.

In addition, interviewers did not always probe for the exact age at which the first sexual experience took place. For this analysis, we coded for early versus later sexual debut, and used age 15 as the cut-off point. If the young girl described her first experience as occurring at or before age 15 or definitely before high school entry, we coded her as having early age of first sex. Whereas if she placed the first encounter at age 15 or later, as having occurred while she was in 10th grade or above, we coded her as "late" sexual debut. Many of those who began sex early had abusive first encounters, whereas many more of those who began later had their first experiences in the context of a boyfriend/girlfriend relationship of a more positive and/or consensual nature (see also Gershenson et al., 1989).

Parenting status. With respect to teenage motherhood, we coded all those who gave birth before age 18 as mothers, the others as non-parents. Three women who finished high school or reached the age of 18 as peers went on to have babies at age 19. In each case, they described themselves as actively avoiding becoming a

Table 1. Age of Sexual Debut and Parenting Status

	Did not become mothers	Teen mothers in school	Teen mothers who left school
Sex before age 15	10	9	15
n=34 (100%)[a]	(.29)	(.27)	(.44)
Sex at age 15 or later	28	9	7
n=44 (100%)[a]	(.64)	(.21)	(.16)
Total Sample	38	18	22
n=78 (100%)[b]	(.49)	(.23)	(.28)

NOTES: a. The percentage of the total sample that began having sex before age 15 is 44%, and 56% at age 15 or later. Totals may not sum to 100% because of rounding.
b. One non-parent peer and one teen mother in school were not explicit about the age of first sexual encounter; they are omitted from this table.

mother at earlier points, either through contraceptive use, avoiding having sex, or ending a pregnancy through abortion. We have other interviews with young women who are still in school and, while they may as yet not be mothers, their peer status may not "last" through age 20. Within this set of interviews, the more realistic comparison may well be the school-age cut off point rather than the conventional demographic marker of age 20. A more realistic transition time for these inner city youth was finishing high school and what one does with one's life before or after age 18, rather than what happens during the ages of 19 and 20.

Finally, we found that within our interview group, the school-aged mothers comprised two very different groups—those who stayed in school and those who dropped out. Those who continued with their schooling while raising a child were, on the whole, more fortunate than those who left school and had not returned at the time of the interview. This is similar to the Furstenberg et al. study (1987). While some of the out-of-school mothers expressed aspirations to return to their studies, many seemed unlikely to organize their lives and their support systems accordingly. In contrast, those who returned or stayed in school after motherhood did so with a great deal of familial help, high motivation to study or compete in school activities, and access to a supportive school environment. All of these resources bode well for the future of these women and their children. For our purposes, they seem to differ in early familial and schooling experiences from the mothers who dropped out. In fact, they may look more like the non-parent peers than like the other mothers in terms of the combination of early advantages/disadvantages.

Relationships in the data. Table 1 presents the relationship between early sexual experiences and parental status. We report the distributions of adolescents who fall into these various categorical or theoretical groups. The trends can only be suggestive as the sample is not random. Statistical tests of significance of these associations would be inappropriate. Nonetheless, the patterns and variations in life experiences and perceptions identified here generate fruitful questions for further study. In this group of 78, 34 of the young women had their first sexual experience before age 15; 44 delayed sexual activity until later in high school or even post-high school ages. The first row shows that among those who became sexually active before age 15, over 70 percent became teen mothers (24 out of 34), whereas young mothers comprise just 37% (16 out of 44) of those who de-

Table 2. Family Life and Age of Sexual Debut

	Sex before age 15	Sex at age 15 or later
Close family relationships (n=49)	13	36
(100%)	(.27)	(.73)
Conflictual family relationships (n=29)	20	9
(100%)	(.69)	(.31)
Presence of house-hold rules, routines (n=53)[a]	17	36
(100%)	(.32)	(.68)
Absence of rules (n=16)[a]	11	5
(100%)	(.69)	(.31)
Absence of major family trauma (n=30)	7	23
(100%)	(.23)	(.77)
Serious family traumas (n=48)	26	22
(100%)	(.54)	(.46)
Total sample (n=78)[b]	34	44
(100%)	(.44)	(.56)

a. Of those who could be categorized by age of sexual debut, 9 did not refer to this dimension of family life; they are excluded from these rows.
b. This table omits the two women who were not clear about age of sexual debut.

layed until after age 15 (row 2). Early sexual activity is highly correlated with becoming a teen mother *and* leaving school—44% of the girls in row 1 were in this group, compared to only 16% of those in row 2.

Of those who avoided early sex, just under two-thirds (28 out of 44) remained non-parents. Thus, age of first sexual experience appears to differentiate not only teen motherhood but also dropping out among those who become teen mothers. However, age of first sex does not predict the teen mothers who stay in school. This group appears equally likely to have had early and later sexual experiences; they are 27% of those with early debut (row 1) and 21% of the late debut group (row 2).

Family life, schooling, and sexual activity. We turn to the perceptions of early life, and first examine how family relationships and schooling opportunities differ by age of sexual involvement. Table 2 presents the association between family life quality and sexual debut. In first set of rows that examine emotional ties, it is important to note the overall high level of positive reports in the sample as a whole. Forty-nine of the 78 inner city youth, 63%, reported close positive relationships with at least one family member, most often their mothers. The first 2 rows suggest that most of those with close ties delayed sex, 73%, whereas most who reported family conflict or lack of ties began sex before age 15, 69%. Rows 3 and 4 relate age of sex and frequency of parental monitoring of child behavior, consistency and the presence of rule-governed structure to family life. For 9 of the women, this aspect of family life was not discussed in the interview. Of the 69 who discussed it, 53 noted its presence. Again, most who experienced familial routines had delayed sex, 68%, whereas most whose families were described as chaotic or disorderly engaged in early sex, 69%.

The last set of rows presents the absence or presence of family trauma. Only 30 of 78 women reported the absence of multiple problems, 40%. Those protected from these stresses (row 5) tended to postpone their sexual debut, 77%, whereas

Table 3 Schooling Experiences and Age of Sexual Debut

	Sex before age 15	Sex at age 15 or later
Positive sense of self as student (n=56)[a]	22	34
(100%)	(.39)	(.61)
Negative sense of self as student (n=15)[a]	10	5
(100%)	(.67)	(.33)
Family encouragement of school (n=34)[b]	8	26
(100%)	(.24)	(.76)
Lack of familial encouragement or		
discouragement (n=22)[b]	15	7
(100%)	(.68)	(.32)
Both positive sense of self and family		
encouragement in school (n=28)	7	21
(100%)	(.25)	(.75)
Neither personal nor familial orientation to		
schooling (n=11)	8	3
(100%)	(.73)	(.27)
Total sample (n=78)[c]	34	44
(100%)	(.44)	(.56)

Notes: a. Seven of the young women did not describe this dimension and are omitted from these rows.
b. Many of the women, 22, did not describe this dimension and are omitted from these rows.
c. This table omits the two women who were not clear about age of sexual debut.

the majority of those exposed to these problems (row 6) were more likely to have initiated sex before age 15.

Table 3 examines the relationships between perceived schooling opportunities and sexual debut. Recall that where interviews did not cover "life at school" before high school or prior to sexual activity, the observations were excluded. Most of the women who did refer to their elementary and/or middle school years talked about a sense of self as a student. Many in the sample did not discuss the second dimension, family encouragement, but those who did mentioned specific activities of family members focused upon their early schooling. Of those who did elaborate on these aspects of their childhood, most were positive. Of the 71 who talked about themselves as beginning students, 56 or 79% cited positive memories. Of the 56 who talked about the family's involvement, 34 or 61% recalled encouraging or supportive behaviors.

In each dimension of earliest schooling opportunities, the differences by sexual debut group are marked. Rows 1 and 2 compare those who described positive versus negative connotations of being in school. Only 39% of those with positive experiences but 67% of those with negative early experiences had sex prior to age 15. In rows 3 and 4, on their reports of familial involvement with schooling, the disparities between the groups are equally great. About 3/4 of the women who described early attentiveness toward school in their homes had delayed sex. Just under a third of those who described an early discrepancy between educational emphasis at home and at school had delayed sex to age 15 or over.

Finally, rows 5 and 6 show the association between age of sex and the *combined* factors of enjoyment of early schooling and receiving familial rewards or discouragement related to school. While the overall numbers in the group with this information are small, the differences are again very sharp. About 3/4 of those who perceived both a positive sense of being a student and family encouragement of school delayed first sex, while an equally high proportion (almost 3/4) who had negative experiences in both dimensions became sexually active at a young age.

With respect to early involvement in sex, then, both the quality of family life and schooling opportunities (and how school is reinforced at home) were experienced in profoundly different ways by those who began sex early versus late. While the Table 2 results on family life and age of sexual debut were somewhat expected, based on other study findings, the connections between early sense of schooling and early sex were stronger than expected. The young women's perceptions indicate that the late sexual debut group more frequently had a context of home-school interrelations which provided the protection and support to pursue their goals. Examples from the interviews illustrate how these family and school factors could help to defer sexual risk-taking.[4]

Home-school linkages and avoidance of early sex. Many of the girls who experienced late and/or little sexual activity described one of two family conditions: either a strong emphasis on doing well in school and/or a well-developed set of rules and regulations surrounding dating and socializing opportunities. One young woman, who was not a teen mother, stood out in her family's emphasis on school—"Brenda" was among the youngest of 13 children, all of whom had completed high school and many of whom had gone to college. When interviewed at 19, she had graduated from high school, and was attending a local business college. While she had been admitted to a state university in the South, she could not afford to go. She described every sibling as well as her mother and grandmother, with whom she had lived, as encouraging her to study hard as an alternative to "messing with boys."

From early on, her mother had said "to get your education" because "the streets were not going to change." Her brothers had said that if she "got a boyfriend, she would fall behind in her school work." Her mother not only pushed schooling, but had a policy of getting every daughter on birth control by the 10th grade. Brenda was never allowed to go out until her homework was done. The clarity with which Brenda perceived this connection was unique, but comparable to the views of many of the peers and only some of the teen mothers.

These relationships between early sex and early family-school supports also point to what happens when the young women's early memories are negative in both of these dimensions. The majority of young women with both problems in family life and in schooling experiences began sex early and many of them became teen mothers who left school. The depths of the chasm between a traumatic home life and a school life from an early age may indeed have contributed to a "nothing to lose" sense of self for these girls. One example of this great disjuncture and the sense of despair it wrought is evident in the story of "Valerie."

Early despair at home and at school. At 21, the mother of two boys, Valerie spoke of wanting to return to high school to graduate and eventually go on to college. Her goal was to become a therapist with handicapped children and to provide a better life for her children. Starting from early childhood, Valerie's life was peppered with trauma and chaos. She was raped at age 10; a sexual abuse incident at age 14 resulted in her first pregnancy and abortion. From as early as she can remember, she was constantly moving in and out of homes with her drug

---

4. Fictitious names will be used in the examples that follow, so as to protect anonymity.

abusing, violent, welfare-dependent and otherwise troubled parents and an alcoholic and "mean" grandmother; these problems led to stays in a runaway shelter and an adolescent group home.

Her elementary school years were described as "hard" and "embarrassing." While she seemed to have tried to be a student, e.g., she talked about staying up late in her bed to try to teach herself to read, her grandmother never helped her and instead called her "you stupid dummy." She attended three different elementary schools in five years and claimed that after going to a special parochial middle school while in the group home, she finally learned to read and write at the age of 12. She had to drop out when she was pregnant at age 15. She first returned to a high school that had day care, but eventually left this and several other schools having eked her way through 11th grade.

Valerie's pregnancies and births only further confounded a very serious and long term contextual assault on her ability to be a self-directed and successful person. Neither home life nor early school were perceived as positive enabling experiences that would have helped her develop a sense of effectiveness and/or personal options. While the long term and complex set of problems vary among those girls whose early sexual careers resulted in becoming a teen mother and dropping out, those who described their early childhood dwelled mainly on these painful and stigmatizing experiences at home and at school.

At one point in her interview, Valerie discussed her reasons for not remaining in a relationship with her baby's father, who used drugs and lacked ambition. She described the effect of associating with people who do not have goals and in so doing, she expressed the need for support identified by almost all of the young women who shared their life stories with us.

> You cannot be successful with people around you that don't want nothing. You can't have a dream, if you have a person around you who is not a dreamer. If you don't believe, if he don't believe in himself, you can't believe. Because he will make it hard for you to understand what it is that you want to believe in.

Family life, schooling, and early motherhood. Tables 4 and 5 illustrate differences in perceptions of early family life and schooling opportunities according to whether young women avoided motherhood in high school, had a baby and stayed in/returned to school, or had a baby and had not returned to complete their studies. The most interesting group here is the teen mothers in school, because they combine a mix of those who begin sexual activity both early and late (as shown in Table 1). On the other hand, the avoiders of parenthood and the teen mother dropouts should look very much like early sexual debut versus late sexual debut groups in their accounts of early family and school life. With respect to family experiences, shown in Table 4, the school-age mothers who maintained or resumed school attendance were not as strongly differentiated across positive and negative family life categories as were the two other groups. They were a third of those who reported family conflict versus less than a fifth with closeness (rows 1–2); however, they were a smaller percentage of those who reported absence than of those who reported presence of familial order and routines in the home (rows 3–4). There were similar proportions of those who reported traumatic families and non-traumatic ones (rows 5–6).

In Table 5, teen mothers who stayed in school appear to have gotten personal benefit from school despite their lack of familial help in this arena. In rows 1–2,

Table 4. Family Life and School Age Motherhood

	Did not become mothers	Teen mothers in school	Teen mothers who left school
Close family relationships (n=50)	31	9	10
(100%)	(.62)	(.18)	(.20)
Conflictual family relations (n=30)	8	10	12
(100%)	(.27)	(.33)	(.40)
Presence of household rules, routines (n=54)[a]	31	14	9
(100%)	(.57)	(.26)	(.17)
Absence of rules (n=16)[a]	4	2	10
(100%)	(.25)	(.13)	(.63)
Absence of major family trauma (n=30)	21	6	3
(100%)	(.70)	(.20)	(.10)
Serious family traumas (n=50)	18	13	19
(100%)	(.36)	(.26)	(.38)
Total sample (n=80)	39	19	22
(100%)	(.49)	(.24)	(.28)

Notes: a. Ten of the women did not refer to this dimension of family life; they are excluded from these rows.

they are a larger proportion of those with a happy sense of self than they are of those with negative early student experiences. In contrast, in rows 3–4, teen mothers in school were a smaller proportion of those who recalled familial encouragement, and they more frequently described being discouraged in school at an early age. When the two schooling factors are combined, in rows 5–6, again

Table 5. Schooling Experiences and School Age Motherhood

	Did not become mothers	Teen mothers in school	Teen mothers who left school
Positive sense of self as student (n=58)[a]	32	16	10
(100%)	(.55)	(.28)	(.17)
Negative sense of self as student (n=15)[a]	3	2	10
(100%)	(.20)	(.13)	(.67)
Family encouragement of school (n=34)[b]	25	4	5
(100%)	(.73)	(.12)	(.15)
Lack of familial encouragement or discouragement (n=24)[b]	5	9	10
(100%)	(.21)	(.37)	(.42)
Both positive sense of self and family encouragement in school (n=28)	21	3	4
(100%)	(.75)	(.11)	(.14)
Neither personal nor familial orientation to schooling (n=11)	2	2	7
(100%)	(.18)	(.18)	(.64)
Total sample (n=80)	39	19	22
(100%)	(.49)	(.24)	(.28)

Notes: a. Seven of the young women did not describe this dimension and are omitted from these rows.
b. Many of the women, 22, did not describe this dimension and are omitted from these rows.

the teen mothers who remain in school are a small proportion of those who have all positive or all negative schooling experiences.

Two factors from these tables seem to be the most significant for those who remained in school after bearing a child as a young teen. In Table 4, 14 of the 19 young mothers who returned to school had structured household routines to live by and in Table 5, 16 of these 19 women reported an early positive student identity as a student. Thus, both family process and early schooling opportunity were perceived as very positive and important factors in the lives of young mothers in school. How these factors might have promoted the perseverance to keep up with schooling, even when they do not prevent early sex and pregnancy, may be illustrated in two case examples.

Holding on to school through family support. Two of the teen mothers who had stayed in school described with particular clarity their determination to continue their education. In one case, the love of school, coupled with the emotional support of her mother, made staying in school possible. In the second, the precarious structure of a home life created a familial obligation to finish school as the responsible thing for her to do.

"Nola" was 15 and pregnant at the first interview. By the second interview, she had given birth and continued school without missing 8th or 9th grade. She was attending a special school for pregnant and parenting teens, which had a day care program for her son. She described the great effort and level of organization required to get up extra early, get herself and the baby ready, and board the school bus with her books, stroller, and diaper bag, and travel across town to be there on time. She described herself as a really good student who was happy in school and had a very close, supportive relationship with her mother. She also enjoyed a lot of support from the teen mother social service program she attended. Nola's mother had dropped out of high school when she became pregnant with Nola. Her mother had openly discussed obtaining "protection" prior to her first becoming sexually active. Nevertheless, Nola's pregnancy came unexpectedly as a result of having sex without using birth control with her first boyfriend at age 14. Nola said that at the time, becoming pregnant "wasn't really on my mind," that she felt she would not get pregnant.

She saw herself saddled with substantial responsibilities for a person starting out her high school years. While she wished she had waited to have the baby after she finished school, she felt she had the help to stick to a routine and pursue all goals. Her mother was with her "100%," but also expected her to obey rules and behave in school. In her words, her mother has always stressed that, "You can't do anything you want to do when you want to do it."

"Rolanda" managed to stay committed to her schooling goal through the strength and consistency of a grandmother's care. Since her elementary years, Rolanda and her five younger siblings had been in her grandmother's custody, where she watched her mother's drug addiction, divorce, and an inability to relate to her children. Rolanda felt her mother was more like a "sister" to her, or a "long distance aunt." While her grandmother told her about sex and contraception when she first began menstruating at age nine, she did not want Rolanda to use birth control prior to marriage. When she became pregnant in 11th grade with her boyfriend of two years, her grandmother wanted her to get an abortion, but she discovered the pregnancy too late and claimed she had not thought about the possibility.

At Rolanda's side during the birth, her grandmother seems to have inspired her to finish school. She returned to classes three weeks after the birth and had college aspirations. Her motivation to finish high school, "I have to, I just have to," and to not have a second child, stemmed in part from a desire to become responsible for her grandmother. "She didn't have to take us into her home. She could have left us. Ain't no telling where we would be living, in a foster home...She took what she had and shared it with us."

Discussion

Despite the fact that these young women grew up in very disadvantaged neighborhoods and low-income families, many were successful in avoiding early sex and pregnancy and in graduating from high school. Two factors occurring early in their lives were perceived among those who were successful in these arenas—a strong self-perception of enjoying school at early ages and strong family encouragement and supervision. The general structure of family life as well as its emotional quality and how it is consistent with or discouraging of schooling were all perceived by these youth as important components in their lives.

The dynamics of family life and experiences of opportunity (via schooling experiences) influence teen pregnancy in African-American inner-city communities in complex and sometimes unpredictable ways. Most of these families were described as providing rich and supportive emotional ties, in spite of the very common frequency of serious stresses and often turbulent, threatening conditions. Many of the teen women reported experiencing these crises as children, but had enough support and a variety of types of support from their families to enable them to avoid early motherhood. For others, the presence of routinization within the home buffered the more deleterious effects of some of these crises, one of which could be the teen's early sex and/or pregnancy itself. When the home life was more ordered and regular practices were in place, the young mothers were better able to continue their schooling, especially if they had developed and maintained a positive identity as a student from early schooling experiences. In these interviews, teen mothers who remained in school were unlikely to have experienced a disorderly and chaotic rhythm to family life; they identified this routinization as an important feature of supportive families, which they noted as helping them keep up with their studies.

In addition to general processes within the home environment, the young women cited the importance of early connections forged between home and school. While many felt enthusiastic about their introduction to schooling, those who felt discouraged were at greater risk of early sex and pregnancy. Where the home and school provided mutually-reinforcing and positive support, they facilitated the youth's investing herself in the student role. In these interviews, this early blending protected some girls from early sex and thereby early motherhood. Where the early years of schooling were negatively experienced as a clash of worlds, this usually resulted in the child's becoming an out-of-school young mother. In this latter group, their future outlook was bleak, despite the love and hope they held for their children. Rather than structural or family process models of pathways to teen pregnancy, the interweaving and interactions of these conditions differentiate the young women who escape early mothering and school disruption.

Policies and programs that are targeted to helping families support children in their school experiences, from early years through high school completion, would be consistent with the perceptions of need expressed by these young women. Examples would be programs such as James Comer's that target the early school/family linkage (1984, 1993) and comprehensive teen parent programs that target parenting skills, school completion, and support services to the broad circle of the baby's caregivers (Hayes, 1987).

Policies that are oriented toward long-term family support might also be encouraged by these young women. Those who felt supported and consistently pushed in their schooling from an early age and those who missed such help attached utmost significance to this factor. While this paper does not address the reasons for its presence or absence in the lives of inner city women, family support, in terms of nurturing, consistent, and routinized ways of caring, is a dominant influence in their life stories. Programs such as Headstart and Early Start that promote parenting skills and early educational enrichment in the home target the development of the type and quality of parent-child interaction that these young women noted (see also National Commission on Children, 1991).

Lastly, the relationship between early age of sexual exposure and early motherhood that results in high school drop out underscores the significance of helping inner-city youth with pregnancy prevention (see a survey of successful programs in Dryfoos, 1990.) While not consistently utilizing effective birth control, the mothers in this study were almost universal in wishing they had waited to have children after finishing school. Many had desires to further their education but experienced difficulties in maintaining their course of study. Had they better exposure to reproductive health care, they might have been able to delay motherhood even if early sexual debut had already occurred. Expanded access to comprehensive family planning, then, might reduce the linkage between early sexual debut and school drop out in disadvantaged communities.

References

Anderson, E. (1991). Neighborhood effects on teen poverty. In C. Jencks and P. E. Peterson (Eds.), *The Urban Underclass*. Washington, DC: The Brookings Institution, pp. 375–398.

Clark, R. M. (1983). *Family life and school achievement: Why poor Black children succeed or fail*. Chicago: The University of Chicago Press.

Comer, J. P. (1984). Home-school relationships as they affect the academic success of children. *Education and Urban Society*, 16, 323–337.

Comer, J. P. (1993). *School power*. New York: Free Press.

Danziger, S. K., & Farber, N. B. (1990). Keeping inner-city youth in school: Critical experiences of young black women. *Social Work Research and Abstracts*, 26, 32–39.

Denzin, N. (1989). *Interpretive biography*. Beverly Hills, CA: Sage Publications, Inc.

Dryfoos, J. G. (1990). *Adolescents at risk: Prevalence and prevention*. New York: Oxford University Press.

Furstenburg, F., Brooks-Gunn, J., & Morgan, S. P. (1987). *Adolescent mothers in later life*. New York: Cambridge University Press.

Gershenson, H. P., Musick, J. S., Ruch-Ross, H., Magee, V. (1989). The prevalence of coercive sexual experience among teenage mothers. *Journal of Interpersonal Violence*, 4, 204–219.

Hayes, C. (1987). *Risking the future: Adolescent sexuality, pregnancy and childbearing.* Washington, DC: National Academy Press.

Hogan, D., & Kitagawa, E. (1985). The impact of social status,structure and neighborhood on the fertility of black adolescents. *American Journal of Sociology*, 90, 825–855.

Moore, K., & Miller, B. (1990). Adolescent sexual behavior, pregnancy and parenting: Research through the 1980's. *Journal of Marriage and the Family*, 52, 1025–1044.

National Commission on Children. (1991). *Beyond rhetoric: A new American agenda for children and families.* Washington, DC: National Commission on Children.

Ogbu, J. U. (1988). Black education: A cultural-ecological perspective. In H. P. McAdoo, (Ed.) *Black Families*, Second Edition. Sage Publications, pp. 169–184.

Steele, C. M. (1992). Race and the schooling of Black Americans. *The Atlantic Monthly*, April, 68–78.

Williams, C. W. (1991). *Black teenage mothers: Pregnancy and childbearing from their perspective.* Lexington Books.

Wilson, W. J. (1987). *The truly disadvantaged: The inner city, the underclass, and public policy.* Chicago and London: The University of Chicago Press.

Wilson, W. J. (1991). Studying inner-city social dislocations. *American Sociological Review*, 56, 1–14.

27

Influences on Parental Involvement of African-American Adolescent Fathers

David B. Miller

Research on adolescent parental involvement has focused primarily on the adolescent mother, while the adolescent father has received cursory attention at best (Sawin & Parke, 1976; Connolly, 1978; Hendricks, 1981). Parental involvement of adolescent fathers has not received a systematic examination by social researchers (Battle, 1990). This is especially true of African-American adolescent fathers who have been neglected to the extent that they currently are identified as "invisible men" in family studies (Hill, 1988).

The importance of examining the parental involvement of African-American adolescent fathers is particularly critical considering limited empirical investigation in this area. The majority of information on adolescent fathers, especially African-American, often depicts a shadowy and irresponsible individual (Parke, Power, & Fisher, 1980) who is concerned more with proving his masculinity or establishing a reputation within the community than actively being involved in parenting. The adverse portrayal of the adolescent father is a result of society's negative opinion of the unwed father (Barret & Robinson, 1982 & 1985; Robinson, 1988). This negative perception also exists among service providers to adolescent parents (Freeman, 1988; Robinson & Garret, 1985).

As evidenced by limited empirical literature and contrary to popular belief, most adolescent fathers are willing to undertake active parenting roles with their children (Battle, 1990). Such literature also indicates that the father's participation in the child's development decreases the likelihood of subsequent behavioral problems (Barret & Robinson, 1985).

The purpose of this study is to explore the factors that affect the parental involvement of African-American adolescent fathers, such as: (1) social support, (2) father-role readiness, (3) stress, and (4) involvement in the decision making process. The study addresses the following research questions:

An earlier version of this essay appeared in *Child and Adolescent Social Work Journal*; 1994, 11, 5, October, 363–378 and is adapted/reprinted with the permission of the copyright holder/author.

1. a. What community resources are available to the African-American adolescent father in terms of social support?
   b. Does a relationship exists between social support and parental involvement?
2. a. What effect does age, education, and employment have on the African-American adolescent father's perception of his readiness for fatherhood?
   b. Does a relationship exists between the degree of perceived father-role readiness and parental involvement?
3. a. What are the primary sources of stress experienced by African-American adolescent fathers?
   b. Does a relationship exists between the level of stress and parental involvement?
4. Does the African-American adolescent father's participation in the decision-making process regarding the pregnancy and subsequent child rearing increase his likelihood of being involved with the child and mother?

Literature Review

Social Support

According to Hendricks (1980), the social support system of African-American adolescent fathers comprises three sources: (1) family, (2) peers, and (3) community resources. These sources of social support promote competence in parental involvement (Coates, 1987). Financial, material, emotional, and/or educational support can be obtained through formal or informal sources (Thomas, Milburn, Brown, & Gary, 1988). In a study of African-American adolescent fathers in the inner-city, Sullivan (1985) found that the most involved fathers receive some type of support from their environments.

Father-Role Readiness

Hendricks (1981) indicates that African-American adolescent fathers frequently report an uneasiness with the pregnancy, initially, but as it progresses and they become included in the preparation of the newborn, their apprehensions decrease. Their readiness is shown in part by supportive behaviors, such as caregiving extended to the mother and child (Westney, Cole, & Munford, 1986). Although the literature indicates that adolescent fathers are not ready for fatherhood, some of them maintain a strong desire to remain involved with the mother and child and to develop parental competencies.

Self-image also has been associated with the level of father-role readiness displayed by the African-American adolescent (Christmon, 1990). In his study, Christmon indicates that African-American adolescent fathers with positive self-images are more likely to assume some type of responsibility for their children.

Stress

African-American adolescent fathers reported that they experienced problems in the areas of immediate family support, understanding the mothers of their children, and obtaining employment to meet their children's financial obligations (Hendricks, 1988). The stress experienced by the father may directly or indirectly affect his involvement with the child. As he struggles with the issues of adolescence, the adolescent father must also struggle with the issues associated with becoming a father. The literature also suggests that the nature of stress and how it impacts the father's attitudes and behaviors are other areas that require further examination.

Involvement in Decision-Making

The adolescent father's participation in the decision-making process has been virtually non-existent in literature on adolescent parents (Anderson, 1989; Marsiglio, 1987). According to a study by Redmond (1985) the majority of adolescent fathers want to be involved in any decisions related to the pregnancy. Based upon these findings, Redmond suggests that eliminating the father from the decision-making process may cause him to experience a sense of isolation, confusion, and having little control over the status of the child (McAdoo, 1988; Robinson & Garret, 1985). This situation could possibly contribute to problems between the adolescent father and mother, and also serve as the father's avenue of escape from responsibility.

Evidence suggests that the adolescent father's involvement in the decision-making process diminishes stress (Elster & Lamb, 1982) as well as strengthens his commitment following the child's birth (Redmond, 1985; Vaz, Smolen, & Miller, 1983). These findings appear to support Robinson's (1988) subsequent research in which fathers involved in the decision-making process reported less isolation and feelings of loss than those not involved.

Parental Involvement

According to Lamb (1987), the father's parental involvement comprises three components: 1) interaction with the child; 2) accessibility to the child, i.e., the nearness of the father to the child, even if no direct interaction occurs; and 3) responsibility for the child's well-being.

Methodology

Since literature and theoretical perspectives on parental involvement of African-American fathers are limited, the employment of an exploratory research design was most appropriate for this study. As Babbie (1983) indicates, if an area is relatively new or has not been researched, the exploratory approach is an appropriate vehicle for empirical study. This approach allows for the use of qualitative and quantitative techniques for data collection.

Through the use of qualitative methods, data concerning these fathers reflect the depth and breath of their parental involvement. The data obtained through the use of this strategy could then generate hypotheses that could be examined later through the use of more rigorous strategies (Allen-Meares & Lane, 1990; Hakim, 1987). The quantitative methods were utilized to enhance the understanding of the relationship among variables.

Sample & Population

A purposive sampling method was employed to recruit adolescent fathers. Existing literature suggests that the non-random sampling method, while not the preferred choice, is acceptable until a data base can be developed that will completely assess this population (Brown, 1983). Previous studies on adolescent fathers have revealed a wide range of sample sizes, from as few as nine to as many as 100 (Hanson, Morrison, & Ginsburg, 1989; Smith, 1988). An intended sample size of 25 was selected for this study. Although the sample size was relatively small, it was an appropriate number for an exploratory study (Hakim, 1987). It allowed the researcher to expend the necessary time exploring in greater depth the parental involvement of these fathers.

The metropolitan area in which this study was conducted has a network of agencies that offer services to adolescent parents. These agencies were contacted to recruit adolescent fathers from their programs for participation in this study. Additional fathers were recruited by placing an announcement in the newsletter of a project that provides services to families living in socio-economically disadvantaged communities. Fliers announcing the study also were distributed in African-American communities to reach those fathers who were served by the project but were not connected with the identified agencies.

Respondents were between 14 and 20 years of age. The author contends that young men between 18 and 20 who become fathers experience similar normative developmental and transitional issues as the younger fathers. This age range also provided the opportunity to investigate the consistency and extent of involvement in parenting because of greater variations in the length of time these young men have been fathers.

Data Collection

Data were collected from respondents using a questionnaire adapted from existing measures and information collected from the literature. This instrument, which was pre-tested with eight adolescent fathers, was refined and restructured to assure clarity and accuracy.

The author conducted a structured, personal, in-depth interview with each participant to gather data for this study. To assure reliability, validity, and confidentiality, the interviews took place at the social agency or the participant's residence. After receiving written permission, the interviews were audio taped. Contrary to Hendricks et al. (1981), none of the participants objected to this method of questioning. These audio-tapes provided a complete review of the interviews for reference during data analysis.

Measures

Dependent Variables

The dependent variables for this study comprised three components of the father's parental involvement: parenting attitudes, parenting behaviors, and relationships with the child and mother.

Parenting Attitudes. This variable was defined as the father's attitudes and beliefs about his parenting role, and includes assessing his perception of how to instruct the child in certain behaviors.

Parenting attitudes were measured using two instruments adapted from the Steeltown Fathers study (Coontz, Martin, & Sites, 1989). A 13-item instrument — the Child Care-Should Scale — pertained to attitudes about the father's role. A 6-item instrument measured the respondent's level of enjoyment of certain parenting behaviors, such as buying clothes for the child. In addition, open-ended questions were developed to explore in greater detail the respondent's parental involvement.

Parenting Behaviors. This variable was defined as the father's behavior in certain areas in relation to the child. Significant areas include, but are not limited to, care giving, playing, financial obligations, and interaction with the mother on issues related to the child's well-being. Parenting behaviors were measured through the use of a 13-item instrument.

Relationship with Child and Mother. This variable was defined as the father's actual interaction with the child and mother that produces either a positive or negative outcome; e.g., the latter would be the father not being able to visit the child following a disagreement with the mother. Also included in this variable are the duration of the relationship prior to the pregnancy, and the father's perception of his relationship with the mother and the maternal grandparents. This dimension was measured through several open-ended questions; e.g., respondents were asked "How do you get along with the mother of your child?"

Independent Variables

Since there have been few studies of the parental involvement of adolescent fathers, a limited number of measures were available to address this study's variables. In previous studies on African-American adolescent fathers, the particular variable(s) under study often necessitated the development of newly constructed measurement instruments (Brown, 1983; Christmon, 1990; Smith, 1988).

Social Support. This variable was defined as the assistance that a black adolescent father receives to facilitate his parental involvement. In this study, support was either emotional or practical (Koeske & Koeske, 1990). Emotional support was characterized as offering advice, counseling, or just listening to the father's concerns. Practical support was characterized as offering financial resources and actual assistance in child care activities.

Social support was measured using a modified version of the instrument developed by Koeske & Koeske (1990). The instrument consisted of 11 items divided into the categories of emotional and practical support. Responses to the items were based on a 5 point Likert scale: (1) none at all, (2) a little, (3) a fair amount, (4) quite a bit or (5) a great deal. In addition, eight open-ended questions were developed to obtain additional data about these fathers' social support networks. For example, respondents were asked, "Who specifically in your family helps you take care of your child? In what way(s) does that person help you?"

Father-Role Readiness. This variable was defined as the father's beliefs and activities as indicated in his understanding of the responsibilities of fatherhood. These beliefs and activities are characterized by the father's ability to provide care and nurturing to the child. Four dimensions constitute this variable: (1) self-confidence, including self image and motivation; (2) behaviors; (3) attitudes; and (4) preparedness for fatherhood. In addition, the father's age, education, and employment status are factors that influence father-role readiness as identified by Westney et al. (1986), and included for measurement in this study.

The dimensions of father-role readiness were measured using an 11-item instrument designed by the author. Answers were based on a 5 point Likert scale, ranging from: (1) strongly agree to (5) strongly disagree. Eleven open-ended questions were designed to provide additional insight into this variable. For example, respondents were asked, "As a father, what do you feel are the most important responsibilities that you have toward the mother?"

Stress. This variable was defined as the concerns and issues that influence the adolescent father's involvement with the child. These concerns and issues may be financial, emotional, relational or informational. Relational variables represent the extent of the father's relationship with the mother, maternal grandparents, and peers.

Stress was measured through the use of an 11-item instrument developed from a combination of items in previous studies of adolescent fathers. The following dimensions of stress were measured: 1) becoming a parent; 2) relationships; 3) financial matters; 4) health of child and mother; 5) vocation; and 6) future of self and child. Responses were based on the same 5 point Likert scale used for social support.

Seven open-ended questions were designed to obtain additional insight into the impact of stress on the parental involvement of adolescent fathers in this sample. For example, respondents were asked, "How do you/did you get along with the mother?"

Decision-Making. This variable was defined as active participation in decision-making during pregnancy and post-pregnancy, e.g., whether the adolescent mother should carry the pregnancy to term; involvement with the mother in prenatal care and educational activities; selecting a name for the child, and continued input into issues involving the child's growth and development.

Decision-making was measured through the use of a 10-item instrument designed by the author. Answers were either yes (1) or no (0). Six questions were designed to obtain additional information regarding the adolescent father's involvement in decision-making regarding the pregnancy. Follow-up questions concerning the areas in which these fathers make decisions allowed the respondents to detail their involvement.

Data Analysis

Pearson's product-moment correlation was used to measure possible linear relationships among the variables in this study. Although those variables are ordinal, as Kerlinger (1986) points out, the use of the product-moment correlation is

Table 1. Significant Correlation Coefficients (n = 29)

Independent Variables	Dimensions of Parental Involvement		
	Parenting Behavior	Parenting Attitude	Enjoyment of Parenting Activities
Emotional Support	r=.3616 p=.027	****	****
Practical Support	****	****	****
Father-Role Readiness	****	r=.3481 p=.032	r=.4337 p=.009
Decision-Making	r=.5493 p=.001	****	****
Stress	****	r=.3866 p=.019	r=.3894 p=.018

**** Indicates that there was no significant correlation.

appropriate with ordinal variables using the assumption of equality of interval. The author exercised care in the construction of the measures and in the interpretation of the findings in consideration that the usage of the product-moment correlation with ordinal measures does violate some assumptions for statistical analysis. Content analysis was used to determine themes and patterns specific to this sample based upon the adolescent fathers' responses to the open-ended questions. These responses were aggregated by themes and patterns into units for analysis (Allen-Meares, 1990; Babbie, 1983). The interpretation of these units then led to the development of categories that illustrated variation within the variables.

Findings

Sample Characteristics

Twenty-nine African-American fathers agreed to participate in this study. The average age of the participants was 17.9 years, with ages ranging from 15 to 20 years. The average age these respondents became fathers was 16.9 years; approximately two-thirds of the respondents had become fathers by the age of 17. Seven of the respondents were employed full time and one was employed part time. All but one, an emergency medical technician, held low-skill positions such as fast food worker or dietary aide. Of the unemployed respondents, 75.9% reported that they were able to provide financial support to the child and mother. These fathers indicated that their incomes were obtained from casual labor, e.g., painting houses, washing cars, or illegal activities such as selling drugs, and armed robbery. Twenty respondents reported that their parent(s) also had adolescent pregnancies, and 22 indicated that their siblings had adolescent pregnancies. Nearly one-half reported that they had been involved with the mothers of their children for over a year prior to the pregnancies; a slight majority are still involved.

Table 1 highlights the significant correlations among the variables.

Social Support

Thirty six percent of the respondents reported that their mothers play important roles in assisting them with child rearing activities, as well as teaching them about fatherhood; 32% indicated that they receive little or no assistance in learning how to be parents. Emotional support was significantly correlated with parenting behaviors (see Table 1). Emotional support is associated with improved parenting behavior in that the father perceives that he can obtain the necessary guidance within the environment in order to perform his responsibilities. Through this type of support, the young father is able to gain an understanding of what is expected of him as a father. There was no significant correlation between practical support and parental involvement.

Father-Role Readiness

Twenty-one respondents reported moderate to high father role-readiness. As their levels of education increased, the uneasiness experienced with their roles as fathers decreased. Respondents' perceptions of father role-readiness were significantly correlated with positive parental attitudes and enjoyment of parenting activities (see Table 1). These findings suggest that if the father perceives himself ready to assume the responsibility of fatherhood, his attitudes will reflect his beliefs about his role in child rearing. When fathers perceived themselves as being prepared to act as fathers, they were more likely to express positive parenting attitudes and enjoyment of parenting activities as one father stated, "It (becoming a father) made me look at things a whole lot more seriously. The more I be out on the streets and not doing something for myself, the more my downfall later in life when its time to really help my daughter out. It made me look into the future."

Stresses of African-American Adolescent Fathers

Twenty-one respondents reported moderate to high levels of stress associated with being fathers. Stress appeared to have a negative impact on parenting attitudes. As the father's stress increased his attitudes toward parenting roles began to reflect a perception that child rearing was primarily the mother's responsibility. Also, as stress increased these fathers experienced less satisfaction in parenting activities. Although it is conjecture at this stage, the source of stress that seems to produce the most change in attitude originates from the father's relationship with the maternal grandparents. This source of stress is evident in the words of one father who stated, "There were real assholes, because they played like they liked me but after their daughter became pregnant with my child, they disowned her and stopped communicating with me."

As assessed from the interviews, during the pregnancies these fathers were concerned with one of three areas: 1) health of the child, 2) health of the mother, or 3) health of the child and mother. The majority of the respondents, 36%, were concerned with the child's health. Conditions within their social environments were considered to be other sources of stress. Violence directed at some of these fathers caused them to resort to selling drugs, armed robbery, and other at risk behaviors in order to provide financial support for their child(ren).

Involvement in Decision-Making

Twenty respondents reported moderate to high involvement in decision-making responsibilities, and nine reported no involvement. When fathers were involved in the decision-making process, there was a significant relationship with the parental involvement dimension of parenting behavior (see Table 1). As the findings suggest, fathers who participated in the decision-making process regarding those pregnancy reported more involvement in parenting behaviors. This finding is the result of the father's perception that his decisions are valued, and therefore, he is a more active and involved parent. It also appears that when the father's decisions are taken into consideration, provides an intangible reward for his involvement. These fathers appeared to be most involved with the children in the areas of discipline, safety, and clothing. Clothing is an important issue because the wrong color could possibly place the child in jeopardy, unintentionally signaling gang affiliation. Contrary to popular belief, 52% of the fathers indicated that they had discussed with the pregnant mother the possibility of keeping the child and other relevant issues, such as living arrangements and maintaining their relationship.

Discussion

This study explored the relationship among factors that, according to a the literature, influence parental involvement of adolescent fathers, specifically African-American. Although the sample size was limited, the results of this study suggest that many adolescent fathers are attempting to assume responsible roles. This finding does not negate the fact that this study also revealed that some of these fathers personify the stereotype of adolescent father. As Parke et al. (1980) suggest, some adolescent fathers are shadowy and irresponsible, concerned only with establishing reputations and proving their virility. Fathers in this study exhibited more parental involvement than is perceived by the general public. Data reveals that many of these fathers are involved in the lives of the child and mother. The findings also suggest that parental involvement is influenced by factors present in the father's immediate environment. Therefore, it is essential that social workers and program developers understand the factors explored in this study in order to facilitate the parental involvement of adolescent fathers.

Limitations

The manner in which participants were selected was a limitation, in that they were self-selected and, thus, may not represent all black adolescent fathers. The financial stipend associated with the study may have yielded these fathers solely because of the monetary reward. The inability to verify their activities and attitudes, through observation or by confirmation from the mother, presented an additional limitation to this study. The issue of social desirability also should be considered a limitation because it is likely that these fathers want to be perceived as responsible and involved parents.

Implications/Suggestions

Given that adolescent fathers of all racial and ethnic groups have received limited empirical attention from social researchers it is important that both qualitative and quantitative measures be employed to investigate these fathers. The qualitative measures will provide a rich and broad base of understanding to these fathers that can not be uncovered from quantitative measures. As one of the fathers said, "Finally, someone wants to hear our story, from us, by us and for us. We are not all hanging out trying to make babies, then leave the baby and the mother, and brag about it but there are many of us who do care, and try to do the right thing for our child. It is these young fathers that need to be heard about more than those that do not do anything for their child except fade away."

Policy considerations for programming for adolescent parents should include parenting skills training for adolescent fathers. From an intervention perspective, early involvement may increase the likelihood of a long-term, consistent parental commitment. As discovered in this study, most parenting programs provide adolescent fathers with education and employment training and adolescent mothers with training in parenting skills. Although education and employment are important in assuming the father role, these factors do not fully prepare these fathers for parenting. Thus, it is imperative that they also receive training in parenting skills.

Support systems (i.e., the family) must be strengthened to assist these fathers' in being responsible parents. As advocates, social workers can seek assistance from appropriate welfare organizations on behalf of support systems, while simultaneously instructing the fathers how to use available services.

The development of instructional programs that address sexuality and fatherhood is essential for social workers associated with the educational system. These programs should be geared toward all adolescent males. Those at risk of becoming adolescent fathers could be identified by assessing the family history of the adolescent pregnancy. Pregnancy prevention and the responsibilities of fatherhood should be the focus of these programs. Policy formulation and implementation also should address how the educational system encourages adolescent parents to remain in school and continue their education.

Agencies that offer services to adolescents could implement a group for adolescent fathers, co-led by a facilitator and an adolescent father functioning as a peer counselor. This group could be incorporated within the context of existing services and provide a forum for these father to discuss issues that affect them. The time also could be used to instruct them on the basics of child care, such as feeding, diapering the child, and the roles of play and discipline. This type of group could be gender specific to help these fathers become more concerned with fatherhood and less concerned with impressing members of the opposite sex.

Future Research

Future research into the adolescent father's role in parenting is essential. As the literature illustrates, the African-American adolescent father's role as parent has not been adequately investigated by researchers. As the findings of this study suggest, these fathers exhibit characteristics of parental involvement that have not been typically associated with them. For example, future research might investigate the father's sense of responsibility to the mother and child, his availability to the child, and the process through which he makes decisions regarding his child's health and future. Further investigation into these and other characteristics will undoubtedly provide a more accurate representation of a young man's activities as a father.

Future studies of adolescent fathers would benefit by employing longitudinal designs in order to follow the fathers for a specific period. Such designs would give researchers the opportunity to track changes in parental involvement. It would also provide an opportunity to examine the variables which affect the consistency and level of his parental involvement and those factors which contribute to his not being involved with the child and mother. In future studies, parent-child interaction should be illustrated and categorized through the use of established measures of observation. In addition, the adolescent mother also should be interviewed to ascertain her perceptions of the father's parental involvement.

References

Allen-Meares, P., & Lane, B. A. (1990). Social work practice: Integrating qualitative and quantitative data collection techniques. *Social Work, 35(5)*, 452–458.

Anderson, E. (1989). Sex codes and family life among poor inner-city youths. *The Annals of the American Academy, 501*, 59–78.

Babbie, E. (1983). *The practice of social research* (3rd ed.). Belmont, CA: Wadsworth Publishing.

Barret, R. L., & Robinson, B. E. (1982). A descriptive study of teenage expectant fathers. *Family Relations, 31*, 349–352.

Barret, R. L., & Robinson, B. E. (1985). The adolescent fathers. In S. M. H. Hanson & F. W. Bozett (Eds.), *The Dimensions of Fatherhood* (pp. 353–368). USA: Sage Publications.

Battle, S. F. (1990). African-American male responsibility in teenage pregnancy: The role of education. In D. J. Jones & S. F. Battle (Eds.), *Teenage pregnancy: Developing strategies for change in the twenty-first century* (pp. 71–81). USA: Transaction Publishers.

Bohrnstedt, G. W. & Knoke, D. (1988). *Social for Social Data Analysis* (2nd ed.). Itasca, Ill: F.E. Peacock Publishers.

Brown, S. V. (1983). The commitment and concerns of black adolescent parents. *Social Work Research and Abstracts, 19(4)*, 27–34.

Christmon, K. (1990). Parental responsibility of African-American unwed adolescent fathers. *Adolescence, 25(99)*, 645–653.

Coates, D. L. (1987). Gender differences in the structure and support characteristics of black adolescents' social networks. *Sex Roles, 17(11/12)*, 667–687.

Connolly, L. (1978). Boy fathers. *Human Behavior, 7(1)*, 40–43.

Coontz, P. D., Martin, J. A., & Sites, E. W. (1989). *Steeltown Fathers: Rearing Children in an Era of Industrial Decline.* Pittsburgh: University of Pittsburgh, School of Social Work. A Final Report submitted to the Staunton Farm Foundation.

Elster, A. B., & Lamb, M. E. (1982). Adolescent fathers: A group potentially at risk for parenting failure. *Infant Mental Health Journal, 3(3)*, 148–155.

Freeman, E. M. (1988). Teenage fathers and the problem of teenage pregnancy. *Social Work in Education, 11(1)*, 36–52.

Hakim, C. (1987). *Research Design: Strategies and Choices in the Design of Social Research.* London: Allen & Unwin.

Hanson, S. L., Morrison, D. R., & Ginsburg, A. L. (1989) The antecedents of teenage fatherhood. *Demography, 26(4)*, 579–596.

Hendricks, L. E. (1980). Unwed adolescent fathers: Problems they face and their sources of social support. *Adolescence, 15*(60), 861–869.

Hendricks, L. E. (1981). Black unwed adolescent fathers. In L. E. Gary (Ed.), *Black Men* (pp. 131–138). USA: Sage Publications.

Hendricks, L. E. (1988). Outreach with teenage fathers: A preliminary report on three ethnic groups *Adolescence, 23*(91), 711–720.

Hill, R. B. (March 1988). Adolescent male responsibility in African-American Families. *National Urban League Conference on Manhood and Fatherhood: Adolescent Male Responsibility in Black Families*, Atlanta, GA.

Kerlinger, F. N. (1986). *Foundations of Behavioral Research* (3rd ed.). USA: Holt, Rinehart and Winston.

Koeske, G. F., & Koeske, R. D. (1990). The buffering effect of social support on parental stress. *American Journal of Orthopsychiatry, 60*, 440–451.

Lamb, M. E. (1987). Introduction: The emergent American father. In M. E. Lamb (Ed.), *The Father's Role: Cross-Cultural Perspectives* (pp. 3–25). Hillsdale, NJ: Lawrence Erlbaum Associates.

McAdoo, H. P. (1988). Foreword. In B. E. Robinson (Ed.)., *Teenage Fathers*, (pp. ix–xi). Lexington, MA: D. C. Heath and Company.

Marsiglio, W. (1987). Adolescent fathers in the United States: Their initial living arrangements, marital experience and educational outcomes. *Family Planning Perspectives, 19*(6), 240–251.

Parke, R. D., Power, T. G., & Fisher, T. (1980). The adolescent father's impact on the mother and child. *Journal of Social Issues, 36(1)*, 88–106.

Redmond, M. (1985). Attitudes of adolescent males toward adolescent pregnancy and fatherhood. *Family Relations, 34*, 337–342.

Robinson, B. E. (1988). Teenage pregnancy from the father's perspective. *American Journal of Orthopsychiatry, 58(1)*, 46–51.

Robinson, B. E., & Garret, R. L. (1985, December). Teenage fathers: Many care about their babies whether they walk away or are pushed away from fatherhood. *Psychology Today*, pp. 66–70.

Sawin, D. B., & Parke, R. D. (1976). Adolescent fathers: Some implications from recent research on paternal roles. *Educational Horizons, 55*(1), 38–42.

Smith, L. A. (1988). Black adolescent fathers: Issues for service provision. *Social Work, 33*(3), 269–271.

Sullivan, M. L. (1985, April). *Teen Fathers in the Inner City: An Exploratory Ethnographic Study*. A Report to the Ford Foundation Urban Poverty Program, Prudence Brown Program Officer.

Thomas, V. G., Milburn, N. G., Brown, D. R., & Gary, L. E. (1988). Social support and depressive symptoms among blacks. *The Journal of Black Psychology, 14*(2), 35–45.

Vaz, R., Smolen, P., & Miller, C. (1983). Adolescent pregnancy: Involvement of the male partner. *Journal of Adolescent Health Care, 4*(4), 246–250.

Westney, O. E., Cole, O. J., & Munford, T. L. (1986). Adolescent unwed prospective fathers: Readiness for fatherhood and behaviors toward the mother and the expected infant. *Adolescence, 21*(84), 901–911.

28

Comparable Mates: What Shortage of Good Black Men?

Stanley O. Gaines, Jr.
Jacqueline C. Jones-Mitchell

> Besides that fear and the fear of fear, there was another authentic loathing she felt for the man. With him she was in strange waters. She had not seen a Black like him in ten years. Not since Morgan Street. After that in the college she attended the black men were either creeps or so rare and desirable they had every girl in a 150-mile radius at their feet. She was barely noticeable in (and never selected from) that stampede.
> —Toni Morrison, *Tar Baby* (p. 126)

A central theme pervading scholarly and popular discourse on African American male-female relationships is that of the presumed shortage of "good Black men." This theme has surfaced repeatedly in the works of certain prominent African American female novelists, as in the above quotation from Toni Morrison's *Tar Baby* (1981) attests (see Bell, 1992). The preoccupation with the "shortage of good Black men" also has been evident in the writings of certain African American male social scientists, dating back to E. Franklin Frazier (1939; see Martin & Martin, 1989). Add the highly publicized and reckless sexual exploits of once-respected public figures such as Marion Berry, Wilt Chamberlain, and Magic Johnson, and one well might conclude (as did Reynolds, 1994) that African American men increasingly are a menace to society in general and to the institution of the Black family in particular.

Such negative pronouncement regarding the availability of African American men are as inaccurate as they are racist. Lost amidst the seemingly endless attacks on African American males' suitability for dating and marriage is the simple fact that many Black male-female relationships are stable and mutually satisfying (Bowman, 1992). Successful African American male-female relationships belie the still-pervasive stereotype of the "black [male]-beast-rapist" (Painter, 1992) implicit in much of the discourse on Black male eligibility. In this chapter, then, we shall present evidence that in spite of scholarly and/or lay arguments to the contrary, it really is possible for African American women (not to mention other potential mates of African American men) to find "lots of good Black men out here."

Faulty Premises Regarding Black Males' "Marriageability"

Of course, by acknowledging that at least some potential mates of Black men may be women who are not Black, we raise the sensitive question as to whether a substantial exodus of African American men (especially those whose socioeconomic status is sufficiently high as to make them particularly "marketable" in a strictly materialistic sense) has resulted in a depleted pool of possible mates for African American women (see Spickard, 1992). The fact that Black men are more likely to marry White women than Black women are to marry White men has been interpreted by some critics as support for such a claim (i.e., approximately two-thirds of all Black-White marriages involve Black men paired with White women; Spigner, 1994; Staples, 1994a; Wilkinson, 1993). However, more than 90% of all Black men *and* Black women who marry will have Black spouses (Staples, 1994b). Moreover, even though the ratio of unmarried Black men to unmarried Black women has inched upward since 1970 (Aldridge, 1991; National Research Council, 1989), the number of Black male-White female marriages since that time has *decreased* while the number of Black female-White male marriages has *increased* (Spigner, 1994; Staples, 1994b). These statistical trends do not lend credence to the belief that interethnic or interracial romance *per se* poses a widespread threat to the sanctity of Black male-Black female marital relationships.

Apart from the impact of interethnic marriage on the pool of unmarried African American men presumably available to African American women, we might ask whether the harsh socioeconomic conditions facing Black men currently are sufficient to prevent them from marrying at all (Darity & Myers, 1995; Hatchett, 1991; Staples, 1994a; Wilson, 1987). Actually, the proportion of never-married African American men between the ages of 35 and 44 (i.e., 14%) not only is virtually identical to that of African American women in the same cohort (i.e., 13%; National Research Council, 1989) but also is highly similar to that of Americans as a whole (i.e., approximately 10%; Skolnick, 1993). Furthermore, although a number of authors have voiced concern about the plight of college-educated Black women who face a chronic shortage of college-educated Black men (e.g., Aldridge, 1991; Lindzey, 1994; National Research Council, 1989; Staples, 1994a), the fact remains that the economic disadvantage of African American women relative to African American men (i.e., 74% of the average annual income earned by African American men) is nearly identical to that of African American men relative to European American men (i.e., 73% of the average annual income earned by European American men; French, 1985). As the National Research Council (1980) acknowledged in describing the post-1960s decline in the number of two-parent Black families, "Faltering male earnings alone cannot be the whole story" (p. 534).

Prevailing Stereotypes: Domineering Black Women and Ineffectual Black Men

Why have popular and academic discussions of African American male-female relationships focused so narrowly on the supposed deficits of Black men? Part of the answer lies in the still-prevalent societal stereotypes of Black men as weak and ineffectual when compared to Black women (Bowman, 1992; Gaines, 1994; Marable, 1994; Sudarkasa, 1993). Even though the intent of many past and present critiques of the socioeconomic strains placed by the existing social order upon African American men and women alike was to call the public's attention to the precarious situation faced by many African American families (e.g., Frazier, 1939; Moynihan, 1965; see Dodson, 1988), the actual result generally has been the reification of pernicious stereotypes concerning African American male-female relationships (Bowman, 1992; Gaines, 1994; Marable, 1994; Sudarkasa, 1993). That is, any conflict among African American married couples could be blamed (albeit incorrectly) on African American women's tendency to usurp power from African American men and/or African American men's abdication of the traditional male role as head of household (e.g., Frazier, 1939; Moynihan, 1965).

Opinions such as those expressed by Toni Morrison in *Tar Baby* (1981), described at the beginning of this chapter, may carry a hollow ring of truth precisely because they constitute vivid, anecdotal "evidence" that the majority of African American men really are no good after all (see also Wallace, 1979). Even worse, some observers (e.g., Ali, 1990) have advocated that Black men put Black women "in their place" through violent means if necessary (hooks, 1992). Granted that some Black men do behave in a manner consistent with negative stereotypes (e.g., Clark, Beckett, Wells, & Dungee-Anderson, 1994; Pinkney, 1993; Staples, 1994a; Uzzell & Peebles-Wilkins, 1994), the preponderance of books and articles on Black male (in)eligibility scattered throughout the humanities and the social sciences does little to inform either academicians or laypersons as to the ways in which many African American men actively reject those stereotypes in words as well as deeds (see Gaines, 1994; hooks, 1992).

The common wisdom among critics of the "marriageability" of Black men seems to be that because prejudice and discrimination have placed severe constraints upon African American men's economic and social mobility, African American men inevitably take out their rage on African American women—whether actively (e.g., abusing Black women physically and/or verbally) or passively (e.g., refusing to marry or date Black women; deserting Black women with whom they have had offspring). However, empirical evidence linking African American men's socioeconomic circumstances with actual socioemotional behavior in Black male-female relationships is nearly nonexistent (Gaines, 1994; Hecht, Collier, & Ribeau, 1993). Unfortunately, the aforementioned "common wisdom" is perpetuated by Black as well as Whites, men as well as women, scholars as well as laypersons. In fact, it often seems as if "experts" on Black men's supposedly flawed interpersonal characteristics spend more time defending each other from rigorous cross-examination than they do evaluating the entire premise of Black male dysfunctionality in a critical manner (e.g., Loury, 1994).

Contrasting Portrayals of Black Male-Female Relationships in Contemporary African American Women Novelists' Literature

At the beginning of this chapter, we cited Toni Morrison's *Tar Baby* as an example of the oft-encountered view that "good" Black men are impossible to find. Indeed, much of the popular fiction written by contemporary African American women writers can be characterized as the search for a good Black man. Among others, Terry McMillan (author of *Disappearing Acts* and the best-selling *Waiting to Exhale*) expands and perpetuates the myth that there exists a shortage of available, desirable African American men. By no means, however, is this view upheld monolithically in all works by African American women novelists. For example, Gloria Naylor (who, perhaps, has not received the same media attention as Morrison or McMillan) quietly refutes the myth in her novel, *Mama Day* (1988).

The way in which the term "good" typically is interpreted in relation to African American men severely restricts the number of men who would qualify. Though they occasionally claim to want sensitive, honest men, two of the four female characters in Terry McMillan's *Waiting to Exhale* (1992) define "good" as possessing the following attributes in large quantities: Money, property, physical attractiveness, and sexual prowess. The failure of most African American men to meet this set of criteria is a theme apparent throughout the novel. Through her characters, McMillan provides a litany of complaints about those men who are available:

> They're not all with white girls, they're not all homosexuals, they're not all married...What about the rest? They're ugly. Stupid. In Prison. Unemployed. Crackheads. Short. Liars. Unreliable. Irresponsible. Too possessive. Dogs. Shallow. Boring. Stuck in the sixties. Arrogant. Childish. Wimps. Too ***damn old and set in their ways. (p. 332)

Not once do the women praise African American men or acknowledge the obstacles that they face. By employing the standards of the dominant (i.e., European American) culture to African American men, McMillan's ultimately unsuccessful heroines are doomed to attract shallow, inconsequential men. Certainly, the popularity of Terry McMillan's *Disappearing Acts* (1989) and *Waiting to Exhale* (1992) sustain, to a large degree, the myth of the rare "good" Black man. Most of the men in these novels are uneducated (e.g., Franklin in *Disappearing Acts*), adulterers (e.g., Bernadine's husband in *Waiting to Exhale*), materialistic, and violent. It is the unusual man who is kind, considerate, caring, secure, and available.

Savannah Jackson, perhaps the central figure in *Waiting to Exhale*, desperately wants a husband. Her ideal man would, according to her description, focus all of his attention exclusively on her. "What would be nice is to know you're with one [man] who's looking out for your best interests, one who makes you feel special, safe, and secure. And one who excites you...I want a man to go out of his way for me" (p. 12). Examined more closely, Savanna's wish reveals a desire for a middle-class lifestyle. She doesn't seek a partner, a friend, or a lover, but a husband in the traditional sense. Coupled with her exceedingly materialistic descriptions of her current life and hopes for the future, one can only wonder why a good man would be attracted to *her*. Later, Savannah is still alone and has "lowered" her sights: "A lot of times all I want is somebody I can talk to, act silly and bull**** with. Somebody I can trust. He doesn't have to be a candidate for a husband" (p. 198).

Ironically, it is the two characters who *yearn* for, yet do not *seek*, companionship and understanding who have mates by the novel's end. By chance, these two women meet men with whom they have a spiritual and cultural connection. Nevertheless, the presentation of two loving, nurturing relationships between Black men and Black women is overshadowed by the novel's relentless message concerning the scarcity of "good" Black men.

In contrast, Gloria Naylor's *Mama Day* (1988) opens with Cocoa, a thirtysomething African American woman who resists her family's encouragement to find a mate. Cocoa (who believes that the way a man chews his food reveals much about his personality) is grounded culturally, emotionally, and spiritually in her Black Southern upbringing. The singles scene (a major element in McMillan's novels) doesn't fit Cocoa: "I'd never graduated to the bar scene because I didn't drink and refused to pay three-fifty for a club soda until the evening bore returns" (p. 17). Naylor's characters, equipped with a strong sense of self and a healthy dose of common sense, build a life together in which mutual respect and family play important roles.

The fact that she has a good marriage by the first third of the novel is due to the fact that both Cocoa and her mate, George, are both securely anchored by the moral values stressed during their childhoods. Both take the time to notice small details about each other. Mannerisms that reveal personal history are assessed and filed away before a single word is exchanged. Cocoa and George are drawn together, not because of physical attraction, but by fate. They become acquainted by exploring the boroughs of New York City on fall weekends.

Mama Day can be interpreted as a testament to the often overlooked "good" African American man. The male protagonist, George, is not flashy, not especially well-off, yet is not shallow. A quiet, thoughtful man who was raised in a rather strict orphanage, George realizes why he is ignored by women in college:

> ...those too bright, too jaded colored girls...They made no bones about their plans to hook into a man who...was going somewhere....All the guys who were going somewhere had been able to take girls to the fraternity dances on Friday and Saturday nights where they could show off their brand-name clothes. They only needed a pair of jeans to go to the park with me, or to sit in my room and study....They would have thought I was crazy if I had told them that seeing them flow around me like dark jewels on campus was one of the most beautiful sights on earth. (p. 32)

In sum, Terry McMillan and Gloria Naylor offer strikingly different portraits of African American men in their respective novels. McMillan provides numerous variants on the general theme of "so few good Black men," whereas Gloria Naylor dares to probe the possibility that "good Black men" are not nearly as hard to find as societal stereotypes would lead one to believe.

Reconceptualizing the Functionality
of Black Male-Female Relationships

As noted above, one of the ingredients to a successful Black male-female relationship presented in Gloria Naylor's *Mama Day* (1988) was a shared set of values promoted in African American culture. But which of those values can be identified as facilitating social-psychological well-being among African American couples? The relationship between Cocoa and George in *Mama Day* may offer important literary insights into those values that only recently have gained prominence in social scientists' accounts of functionality in Black male-female relationships.

According to Asante (1981), one such cultural value is *collectivism*, or an orientation toward the welfare of one's community (however broadly defined that community may be; see Nobles, 1980; White & Parham, 1990). Specifically, Asante contended that African American men and women who strongly embrace collectivism as a cultural value orientation will tend to express that orientation within the context of personal relationships. Drawing upon Asante's (1981) theory of Afrocentricity as well as Foa and Foa's (1974) resource exchange theory, Gaines (1994) developed a conceptual model explicitly positing collectivism as a positive and significant predictor of *interpersonal resource exchange* (i.e., mutual giving or affection and/or respect) among African American couples.

Another possible social-psychological influence on adaptive relationship processes among African American couples is *ethnic identity* (Cross, 1980; Gudykunst, 1991; Hecht, Collier, & Ribeau, 1993; Helms, 1993a, c; Jackson, McCullough, & Gurin, 1998; Milliones, 1980; White & Parham, 1990), or the degree to which individuals identify with the socially defined ethnic groups of which they are members. Given that the correlation between ethnic identity and self-esteem is strongly positive among African American men (Phinney, 1991; see also Brown, 1986; Whaley, 1993), we might speculate that ethnic identity (like collectivism) will promote affectionate and respectful behaviors by Black men toward Black women (and vice versa). Regrettably, though, neither collectivism nor ethnic identity has been tested empirically as a predictor of individual differences in socioemotional behavior among African American men or African American women.

By the same token, at least some empirical research has been initiated concerning Black self-consciousness and individuals' general stance toward exchanging tangible resources (e.g., goods, services) and intangible resources (e.g., affection, respect) with other Black persons. Perhaps we will witness a gradual shift in the intellectual *Zeitgeist* (Kuhn, 1962) toward the study of individual differences in African American men's propensity toward behaving affectionately and respectfully in relationships with African American women (e.g., Chapman, 1988; Helms, 1993b; Khatib, 1980; Staples, 1988; White & Parham, 1990). For now, though, we encourage African American scholars and others concerned with the issue of Black male "marriageability" or "eligibility" to reconsider their assumptions about the nature of Black male-female relationship processes.

Concluding Thoughts

The fact that the proportion of African Americans in two-parent homes (i.e., approximately 50%) has remained constant throughout the twentieth century (e.g., Du Bois, 1908/1969; Glick, 1988), combined with the predominance of egalitarian gender-role arrangements (Billingsley, 1968; McAdoo, 1988; Staples, 1988; White & Parham, 1990), both argue against the assumption that the institution of the African American family is on the brink of collapse. Similarly, the oft-repeated view that most African American men are "unmarriageable" does not fit the continued tendency for virtually all African American men *and* women to marry at some point in their lives. Although the attempt to connect Black male unemployment with relatively low incidence, stability, and satisfaction is laudable (Dodson, 1988), Black family advocates' emphasis on societal-level structural factors *to the exclusion of relational-level interpersonal factors* (Staples, 1988) likely will leave unaddressed important issues concerning the functionality of African American male-female interaction patterns. Furthermore, such inattention to mutually satisfying African American male-female relationships only serves to fuel an unproductive debate over the "marriageability" of Black men.

We acknowledge that the frustrations voiced by many never-married African American women deserve to be heard. One of the most telling dramatizations of this frustration occurred during the scene in Spike Lee's *Jungle Fever* in which a diverse group of African American women assembles to assuage a friend whose husband has just had an affair with a White woman (Gates, 1991; but see also hooks, 1992). Ironically, it is the protagonist herself who answers the voices of frustration with an affirmation regarding the availability of marriageable African American men: "He's out there." This sense of hope in the face of despair has enabled many African American women to maintain their resolve in a society in which the beauty of Black women is devalued relative to that of White women (Guerrero, 1993).

In conclusion, we are *not* questioning the reality of socioeconomic disadvantage, racism, prejudice, or discrimination in the lives of African Americans. The "problem of the color line," as Du Bois (1903/1969) accurately put it, in many ways is as intractable near the end of the twentieth century as it was at the beginning (Cose, 1993; Sigelman & Welch, 1991; Tatum, 1987; Zweigenhaft & Domhoff, 1991). Rather, our goal in this chapter has been to review the literature on Black male marriageability with a critical eye. Only by approaching the public and private discourse on Black male-female relationships from a perspective that allows for compatibility (hooks, 1992) can we as social commentators—whether in literature or in the social sciences—hope to facilitate personal growth among African American men, personal growth among African American women, and relational growth among African American couples.

References

Aldridge, D. P. (1991). *Focusing: Black male-female relationships*. Chicago: Third World Press.

Ali, S. (1990). *The Blackman's guide to understanding the Blackwoman*. Philadelphia: Civilized Publications.

Asante, M. K. (1981). Black male and female relationship: An Afrocentric context. In L. E. Gary (Ed.), *Black men*. Beverly Hills, CA: Sage, pp. 75–82.

Bell, B. W. (1992). The contemporary Afro-American novel, 1: Neorealism. In F. W. Hayes III (Ed.), *A turbulent voyage: Readings in African American studies*. San Diego: Collegiate Press, pp. 330–362.

Billingsley, A. (1968). *Black families in White America*. New York: Touchstone.

Bowman, P. J. (1992). Coping with provider role strain: Adaptive cultural resources among Black husband-fathers. In A. K. H. Burlew, W. C. Banks, H. P. McAdoo, and D. A. Azibo (Eds.), *African American psychology: Theory, research, and practice*. Newbury Park, CA: Sage, pp. 135–159.

Brown, R. (1986). *Social psychology*, 2nd ed. New York: Free Press.

Chapman, A. B. (1988). Male-female relations: How the past affects the present. In H. P. McAdoo (Ed.), *Black families*, 2nd ed. Newbury Park, CA: Sage, pp. 190–200.

Clark, M. L., Beckett, J., Wells, M., & Dungee-Anderson, D. (1994). Courtship violence among African American college students. *Journal of Black Psychology*, 20, 264–281.

Cose, E. (1993). *The rage of a privileged class*. New York: Harper Collins.

Cross, W. E., Jr. (1980). Models of psychological nigrescence: A literature review. In R. L. Jones (Ed.), *Black psychology*, 2nd ed. New York: Harper & Row, pp. 81–98.

Darity, W., Jr. & Myers, S. L., Jr. (1995). Family structure and the marginalization of Black men: Policy implications. In M. B. Tucker and C. Mitchell-Kernan (Eds.), *The decline in marriage among African Americans: Causes, consequences, and policy implications*. New York: Russell Sage Foundation, pp. 263–308.

Dodson, J. (1988). Conceptualizations of Black families. In H. P. McAdoo (Ed.), *Black families*, 2nd ed. Newbury Park, CA: Sage, pp. 77–90.

Du Bois, W. E. B. (1903/1969). *The souls of Black folk*. New York: Signet.

Du Bois, W. E. B. (1908/1969). *The Negro American family*. Westport, CT: Negro Universities Press.

Foa, U. G. & Foa, E. B. (1974). *Societal structures of the mind*. Springfield, IL: Thomas.

Frazier, E. F. (1939). *The Negro family in the United States*. Chicago: University of Chicago Press.

French, M. (1985). *Beyond power: On women, men, and morals*. New York: Ballantine.

Gaines, S. O., Jr. (1994). Generic, stereotypic, and collectivistic models of interpersonal resource exchange among African American couples. *Journal of Black Psychology*, 20, 294–304.

Gates, H. L., Jr. (1991). *Jungle Fever*; or, guess who's not coming to dinner? In S. Lee (Ed.), *Five for five: The films of Spike Lee*. New York: Stewart, Tabort & Chang. pp. 163–169.

Glick, P. (1988). Demographic pictures of Black families. In H.P. McAdoo (Ed.), *Black families*, 2nd ed. Newbury Park, CA: Sage, pp. 111–132.

Gudykunst, W. B. (1991). *Bridging differences: Effective intergroup communication*. Newbury Park, CA: Sage.

Guerrero, E. (1993). *Framing Blackness: The African American image in film*. Philadelphia: Temple University Press.

Hatchett, S. J. (1991). Women and men. In J. S. Jackson (Ed.), *Life in Black America*. Newbury Park, CA: Sage, pp. 84–104.

Hecht, M. L., Collier, M. J., & Ribeau, S. A. (1993). *African American communication: Ethnic identity and cultural interpretation*. Newbury Park, CA: Sage.

Helms, J. E. (1993a). An overview of Black racial identity theory. In J. E. Helms (Ed.), *Black and White racial identity: Theory, research, and practice*. Westport, CT: Praeger, pp. 9–32.

Helms, J. E. (1993b). Applying the interaction model to social dyads. In J. E. Helms (Ed.), *Black and White racial identity: Theory, research, and practice* (pp. 177–185). Westport, CT: Praeger.

Helms, J. E. (1993c). The measurement of Black racial identity attitudes. In J. E. Helms (Ed.), *Black and White racial identity: Theory, research, and practice*. Westport, CT: Praeger, pp. 33–47.

Hooks, B. (1992). *Black looks: Race and representation*. Boston: South End Press.

Jackson, J. S., McCullough, W. R., & Gurin, G. (1988). Family socialization, environment, and identity development in Black Americans. In H. P. McAdoo (Ed.), *Black families*, 2nd ed. (p. 242–256). Newbury Park, CA: Sage.

Khatib, S. M. (1980). Black studies and the study of Black people: Reflections on the distinctive characteristics of Black psychology. In R. L. Jones (Ed.), *Black psychology*, 2nd ed. New York: Harper & Row, pp. 48–55.

Kuhn, T. S. (1962). *The structure of scientific revolutions*. Chicago: University of Chicago Press.

Lindzey, L. L. (1994). *Gender roles: A sociological perspective*, 2nd ed. Englewood Cliffs, NJ: Prentice-Hall.

Loury, G. C. (1992). The Black family: A critical challenge. In F. W. Hayes III (Ed.), *A turbulent voyage: Readings in African American studies*. San Diego: Collegiate Press, pp. 422–431.

Marable, M. (1994). The Black male: Searching beyond stereotypes. In R. Staples (Ed.), *The Black family: Essays and studies*. Belmont, CA: Wadsworth, pp. 91–96.

Martin, E. P. & Martin, J. M. (1989). Black families. In J. M. Henslin (Ed.), *Marriage and family in a changing society*, 4th ed. New York: Free Press, pp. 46–55.

McAdoo, H.P. Transgenerational patterns of upward mobility in African-American families. In H.P. McAdoo (Ed.), *Black families*, 2nd ed. Newbury Park, CA: Sage, pp. 148–168.

McMillan, T. (1989). *Disappearing acts*. New York: Viking.

McMillan, T. (1992). *Waiting to exhale*. New York: Viking.

Milliones, J. (1980). Construction of a Black consciousness measure: Psychotherapeutic implications. *Psychotherapy: Theory, Research, and Practice*, *17*, 175–182.

Morrison, T. (1981). *Tar baby*. New York: Knopf.

Moynihan, D. P. (1965). *The Negro family: The case for national action*. Washington, DC: Office of Policy Planning and Research, U. S. Department of Labor.

National Research Council (1989). *A common destiny: Blacks and American society*. Washington, DC: National Academy Press.

Naylor, G. (1988). *Mama Day*. New York: Ticknor & Fields.

Nobles, W. W. (1980). Extended self: Rethinking the so-called Negro self-concept. In R. L. Jones (Ed.), *Black psychology*, 2nd ed. New York: Harper & Row, pp. 99–105.

Painter, N. I. (1992). Hill, Thomas, and the use of racial stereotype. In T. Morrison (Ed.), *Race-ing justice, en- gendering power: Essays on Anita Hill, Clarence Thomas, and the construction of social reality*. New York: Pantheon, pp. 200–214.

Phinney, J. (1991). Ethnic identity and self-esteem: A review and integration. *Hispanic Journal of Behavioral Sciences*, *13*, 193–208.

Pinkney, A. (1993). *Black Americans*, 4th ed. Englewood Cliffs, NJ: Prentice-Hall.

Reynolds, A. L., III. (1994). *Do Black women hate Black men?* Mamaroneck, NY: Hastings House.

Sigelman, L. & Welch, S. (1991). *Black Americans' views of racial inequality: The dream deferred*. New York: Cambridge University Press.

Skolnick, A. (1993). Changes of heart: Family dynamics in historical perspective. In P. A. Cowan, D. Field, D. A. Hansen, A. Skolnick, and G. E. Swanson (Eds.), *Family, self, and society: Toward a new agenda for family research*. Hillsdale, NJ: Erlbaum, pp. 45–68.

Spickard, P. R. (1992). The illogic of American racial categories. In M. P. P. Root (Ed.), *Racially mixed people in America*. Newbury Park, CA: Sage, pp. 12–23.

Spigner, C. (1994). Black/White interracial marriages: A brief overview of U. S. Census data, 1980–1987. In R. Staples (Ed.), *The Black family: Essays and studies*. Belmont, CA: Wadsworth, pp. 149–152.

Staples, R. (1988). An overview of race and marital status. In H. P. McAdoo (Ed.), *Black families*, 2nd ed. Newbury Park, CA: Sage, pp. 187–189.

Staples, R. (1994a). Changes in Black family structure: The conflict between family ideology and structural conditions. In R. Staples (Ed.), *The Black family: Essays and studies*. Belmont, CA: Wadsworth, pp. 11–19.

Staples, R. (1994b). Interracial relationships: A convergence of desire and opportunity. In R. Staples (Ed.), *The Black family: Essays and studies*. Belmont, CA: Wadsworth, pp. 142–149.

Sudarkasa, N. (1993). Female-headed African American households: Some neglected dimensions. In H. P. McAdoo (Ed.), *Family ethnicity: Strength in diversity*. Newbury Park, CA: Sage, pp. 81–89.

Tatum, B. D. (1987). *Assimilation blues: Black families in a White community*. New York: Greenwood Press.

Uzzell, O. & Peebles-Wilkins, W. (1994). Black spouse abuse: A focus on relational factors and intervention strategies. In R. Staples (Ed.), *The Black family: Essays and studies*. Belmont, CA: Wadsworth, pp. 104–111.

Wallace, M. (1979). *Black macho and the myth of the superwoman*. New York: Dial.

Whaley, A. L. (1993). Self-esteem, cultural identity, and psychosocial adjustment in African American children. *Journal of Black Psychology, 19*, 406–422.

White, J. L. & Parham, T. A. (1990). *The psychology of Blacks: An African American perspective*, 2nd ed. Englewood Cliffs, NJ: Prentice-Hall.

Wilkinson, D. (1993). Family ethnicity in America. In M. P. P. Root (Ed.), *Racially mixed people in America*. Newbury Park, CA: Sage, pp. 15–59.

Wilson, W. J. (1987). *The truly disadvantaged: The inner city, the underclass, and public policy*. Chicago: University of Chicago Press.

Zweigenhaft, R. L. & Domhoff, G. W. (1991). *Blacks in the White establishment? A study of race and class in America*. New Haven, CT: Yale University Press.

29

The Continuing Significance of Race in Minority Male Joblessness

Ronald D'Amico
Nan L. Maxwell

Race and ethnicity provide or deny access to many of life's chances. Residence, socioeconomic status, income, and employment opportunities are all decided, to some extent, by the race and ethnicity of the individual. Residential space also is correlated with many of the same factors, although the causation is often less clear. One key dimension to the ethnicity, race, and space intersection is joblessness. In fact, spatial elements of minority[1] employment difficulties recently have gained attention, primarily because employment rates diverged between minorities and whites between 1970 and 1980. In 1970, minority and white employment-to-population ratios for males 16 and older were nearly equivalent, with the minority rate being 98.6% of the white rate. By 1980,[2] black employment fell dramatically to 87% of white levels while relative Hispanic employment fell only slightly to 96%.

One explanation for increased minority joblessness is that spatial mismatches between minorities and employment opportunities were exacerbated when shifts in product markets increased the demand for skilled workers, requirements that many minorities were unable to meet (e.g., Kasarda 1983). When low-skill jobs and high-wage workers migrated out of the central city, increased spatial inaccessibility to jobs created employment difficulties (Kasarda 1985) and social isolation (Wilson 1987) for urban minorities. These trends left inner-city minorities concentrated in areas with high rates of joblessness, welfare dependency, crime, and single-parent families, and left them excluded from job network systems, con-

An earlier version of this essay appeared in *Social Forces;* 1995, 73, 3, March, 969–991 and is adapted/reprinted with the permission of the copyright holder/author.

1. We define *minorities* as Hispanics and blacks. Our discussion may not reflect all minority subpopulations because the relatively large black population overshadows trends for other subgroups. We use the terms *black* and *Hispanic* because these terms most often reflect reported data.

2. Since the largest relative employment changes occurred during the 1970s, our analysis centers around this decade. Numbers here were computed from data in the *Statistical Abstract of the United States* (U.S. Bureau of the Census 1983a, 1991). Trends reversed only slightly during the 1980s. The relative employment ratio rose to 89.2 for blacks and 96.0 for Hispanics.

fined to poor quality schooling, and socialized into behavior patterns not conducive to good work habits.

In this context, we examine the nexus of race, ethnicity, and space in determining minority joblessness. We use the 1980 census to estimate the prevalence of minority joblessness across local labor markets or their subareas and to assess both the amount and the concomitants of spatial variation in minority access to jobs. By using the local labor market or its subarea (i.e., county group) as the ecological unit of analysis and by examining the extent of minority disadvantage across each area, we analyze the extent to which minority access to jobs is created by geography and/or by race and ethnicity. We find that, after controlling for local conditions, a large, pervasive employment disadvantage for blacks still exists, a disadvantage that is much smaller for Hispanics. Thus, while we show that spatial mismatches between minorities and employment opportunities may exacerbate minority joblessness, we also show a pervasiveness of the black disadvantage and a striking contrast with Hispanics that suggests that race and ethnicity play a key role in determining access to jobs.

Framework

In 1968 John Kain posited that residential segregation, by isolating minorities from areas of employment growth, increased job search and commuting costs for minorities and fostered discrimination by employers who were concerned about alienating white customers. Since that time, a great deal of research has focused on the spatial dimension to Kain's analysis, in part, because social tolerance of minorities increased (e.g., Tuch 1987) and the significance of race in determining socioeconomic outcomes declined (Wilson 1978).

Consistent with Kain's residential segregation hypothesis, research shows that minorities, especially blacks, are segregated within metropolitan areas (e.g., Massey & Denton 1989, 1988), often with high concentrations of poverty (Massey 1990). Upward socioeconomic mobility of minorities does not always produce movement into the suburbs (Alba & Logan 1991) and, once residential mobility occurs for blacks, does not bring the same amenities as for whites (Massey, Condran & Denton 1987). In terms of employment, a mismatch of skills exists between minorities and their jobs (Lichter 1988), with both black (Ihlanfeldt & Sjoquist 1990) and Hispanic (Ihlanfeldt 1993) *youth* suffering from a lack of proximity to jobs. Skilled minorities must commute farther to obtain employment in *large Northeast cities* (Ihlanfeldt 1992), probably because expanding job opportunities are not located in areas that have a high proportion of blacks (Schneider & Phelan 1990).

This line of research provides strong *prima facie* support for Kain's thesis of a spatial dimension to minority employment difficulties. This support, combined with the arduous task of proving that race or ethnicity provides the basis for employment, makes it easy to downplay the racial component to Kain's analysis. However, a closer examination of the research shows that, while spatial dimensions might contribute to minority joblessness for youth and residents of large northeastern and midwestern industrial cities, the universality of residential segregation in contributing to minority employment disadvantages has not been established and cannot be assumed (see Jencks & Mayer 1990). For example, because youth often have low wages and a schooling alternative, commuting may increase their employment costs above the employment benefit. Hence, the relationship between job proximity and employment may be stronger for youth than adults. As a result, empirical studies based solely on youth may overstate support for spatial mismatch models because restricted analysis focuses on the least mobile subpopulation within a local labor market. Research conducted on samples in large metropolitan areas in the Northeast and Midwest also may be misleading since both urban poverty (Massey & Eggers 1990) and residential segregation (Massey & Denton 1987) are strongest in these areas. Furthermore, the decline in manufacturing production during the 1970s caused dramatic employment declines in these areas. Thus, empirical analysis using data from large Northeast and Midwest urban areas may overstate the influence of spatial mismatch on minority joblessness by restricting analysis to areas of strongest segregation and weakest job growth.

In comparison, few studies have focused on the race-ethnic dimension to Kain's analysis, yet evidence suggests that this component also contributes to increased minority joblessness. Face-to-face interviews with employers show that blacks (e.g., Bendick, Jackson & Reinoso 1993; Kirschenman & Neckerman 1991) and Hispanics (e.g., Cross 1990) receive fewer job offers (and fewer interviews) than whites with equivalent employment credentials. If this evidence is correct, then race or ethnicity creates an employment barrier for minority males because it is used as a proxy for skill (e.g., DeFreitas 1986; Welch 1990) or dysfunctional characteristics created by social isolation (e.g., Wilson 1991), a potential that may have been exacerbated when employers responded to industrial changes in the 1970s. Furthermore, increased affirmative action enforcement, immigration, or concentration may have increased the visibility of minority populations during the 1970s, and as a result, discrimination may have intensified (Fossett & Kiecolt 1989; Moore & Pinderhughes 1993). In other words, there is a renewed possibility that race or ethnicity *causes* employment difficulties (Shulman 1987). "The problem (of joblessness) isn't space. It's race." (Ellwood 1986:181).

Adding a race-ethnicity dimension (back) into Kain's analysis is complicated by the cultural differences that exist between blacks and Hispanics and within the Hispanic population. Because much of the literature on inner-city concentration of minorities has focused on blacks, modifications to the traditional analysis are necessary when Hispanics are involved (Moor & Pinderhughes 1993). Specifically, the role of cultural differences among Latinos, immigration, and positive concentration effects for ethic enclaves, which may play a crucial role in employment opportunities for Hispanics, have been downplayed in most analysis of inner-city joblessness. Therefore, minority employment difficulties cannot be fully understood without a model that differentiates between cultural determinants of black and Hispanic labor market outcomes. In fact, research has shown that, in contrast to their black counterparts, many Latino immigrants benefit from isolation from mainstream society because their ethnic concentration can encourage both a comfortable cultural ambiance and access to useful economic and social networks (e.g., Portes & Truelove 1987; Sanders & Nee 1987; Tienda & Lii 1987).

Our framework suggests that economic restructuring, spatial concentration of minorities, and race and ethnicity all contribute to minority employment opportunities. We examine each of these dimensions of black and Hispanic employment by estimating the magnitude and variation in joblessness among males within local labor markets or their subareas, holding basic skill levels constant. We posit that if space is of primary importance to employment opportunities, only modest differentials in joblessness will exist once we look within smaller, more localized areas. That is, if minority joblessness arises because of concentration in areas where jobs are scarce, then employment differentials will be much more modest within circumscribed areas, where all groups presumably face similar access to jobs. The modest differences that remain should follow patterns associated with economic restructuring. They will be largest in the urban core and Northeast and Midwest cities and much smaller elsewhere.

Alternatively, if race or ethnicity is of primary importance in hiring, minorities will experience a sizable employment disadvantage throughout the country and this disadvantage will persist even within localized areas. While the size of the disadvantage may vary somewhat across cities or regions (the use of proxies in hiring may vary across labor markets) and between blacks and Hispanics (differing roles of race and ethnicity), a minority disadvantage in employment will be pronounced throughout the country.

Data and Methods

To examine minority joblessness within localized areas, we analyzed the 5 in 100 sample (the A sample) of the 1980 census for black, Hispanic, and non-Hispanic white males.[3] From these data we define local labor markets or their subareas and analyze joblessness within each area for noninstitutionalized males aged 18 to 55 who were not enrolled in school. Using basic demographic and population information, including survey week labor force status and yearly work experience, we first compute and compare measures of minority joblessness within each area. These areas then become the unit of analysis to determine spatial determinants of minority access to jobs.

The lowest level of geographic aggregation on the 1980 census tape, called county groups, consists of over 1,100 distinct areas that reflect a mutually exclusive and exhaustive mapping of the land area in the U.S. These geographic units can be a city, a county, a part of a county, or a collection of these.[4] We use these county groups as a crude approximation of local labor markets. While a more appropriate unit of economic activity may be the metropolitan statistical area (MSA), the county group represents a smaller, more localized area. Minority employment variation *between* these smaller areas reflects spatial variation in both residence and economies. In contrast, minority employment variation between the

---

3. We examine joblessness only for males to avoid the potentially confounding effect of sex discrimination.

4. Appendix A discusses construction of these county groups, which vary greatly in size. To ensure that size heterogeneity did not confound results of our analysis, we explicitly control for (log) population size in our multivariate estimations. Furthermore, in distributional analysis, we contrast the largest county groups, where within county-group variation in residence may produce greater differences in relative minority access to jobs, with all county groups to uncover potential differences in minority joblessness associated with county group size.

larger MSAs reflects mainly spatial variation in economic activity. While areas smaller than county groups would better capture residential differences between minority and whites, this level of disaggregation is not available in the census.

To estimate minority joblessness, we first develop three individually based gauges of minority access to jobs *within* each county group: survey week unemployment (restricted to those in the labor force), survey week employment, and hours worked in the calendar year preceding the survey.[5] By examining all three outcomes we analyze access to jobs (unemployment), discouraged worker potential (employment), and instability in labor force movement (hours worked). Because some of the differential in these outcomes results from individual skill differences, we control for demographic attributes of individuals. The limited number of variables available in the census restricts these independent predictors to variables indicating the respondent's age and education, in addition to race and ethnicity.[6]

The concentration of blacks and Hispanics in circumscribed areas of the country means that some county groups have too few minority sample members to compute reliable estimates of the size of their disadvantage. Accordingly, the analysis of county-group differences in access to jobs is restricted to the 416 county groups with at least 100 black male respondents meeting our age and enrollment restrictions (for the analysis of black joblessness) and to the 200 county groups with 100 or more Hispanic male respondents meeting sample restrictions (for the analysis of Hispanic joblessness). All county groups have at least 100 white respondents meeting the sample restrictions. Within these 416 county groups reside 93.1% of the nation's black population. Within these 200 county groups reside 87.4% of the nation's Hispanic population.

The first stage of our analysis estimates the following ordinary least squares (OLS)[7] regression equations for *individuals* within each county group:

$$E_i^j = \alpha + \alpha_1 B_i + \alpha_2 H_i + \Sigma \alpha A_i + \Sigma \alpha S_i$$

where:

E_i^j = unemployment, employment, or hours or work for each individual *i* within a county group *j*

---

5. Survey week unemployment is coded 1 = unemployed, 0 = employed, with "out of the labor force" omitted from analysis. Survey week employment is coded 1= employed, 0 = unemployed or out of the labor force. Total hours worked is obtained by multiplying total weeks worked last year by usual hours worked per week with 0 assigned for those who did not work at all. Total hours is capped at 2,400 because individual variation in hours worked above a fulltime, full-year work week are not of immediate interest.

6. The census microdata file actually contains a limited number of additional characteristics of respondents, but these are of limited utility as control variables for our purposes. Their use would select on the dependent variables (e.g., commute time to work), have limited theoretical relevance (e.g., veteran status), or, arguably, "overcontrol" our estimations by masking the very effects of race and ethnicity that we are examining (e.g., country of origin, language spoken at home). The exclusion from our model of variables in this latter category would, if anything, cause us to overstate the effects of being Hispanic and, as we shall see, these effects are generally modest.

7. The prohibitive expense involved in estimating 816 equations with logit analysis dictates using OLS even though two of the three dependent variables are dichotomous. Preliminary analysis on a handful of county groups verified that logit coefficients, when converted to expected probabilities near the white mean, yielded comparable results and that qualitative interpretations were unchanged by the OLS analysis.

B_i = a binary variable with 1 indicating a black respondent
H_i = a binary variable with 1 indicating a Hispanic respondent[8]
A_i = a vector of age variables (age, age2, and age3)
S_i = a vector of binary schooling variables (high school drop out, attended college).[9]

Since the dependent variables measure individual-level joblessness within each county group, the coefficients on the black and Hispanic dummies (α_1 and α_2) represent the net effect of minority status on work. Negative coefficients in the employment and hours worked equations and positive coefficients in the unemployment equation represent minority disadvantage in each county group. Comparisons of the coefficients quantify differences in access to jobs, net of age, and education differences across county groups. To interpret the employment and unemployment binary measures in percentage terms, the race coefficients (α_1 and α_2) were multiplied by 100.

The second stage of our analysis examines determinants of the minority disadvantaged, α_1 and α_2, *across* county groups. This analysis necessitates linking county groups with data to describe their characteristics. Because data sources generally are available for all counties and for all cities of 25,000 population or more, we used county-level data to describe the characteristics of those county groups comprising a whole county or counties, city-level data for those comprising cities, and county-level data from which characteristics for cities in the county had been netted out for county groups with nonurban portions of counties.[10]

Using the county group as the unit of analysis, we estimate space, race, and ethnic determinants of minority joblessness with controls for economic activity and labor force composition using the six measures of relative minority joblessness: one each with the black coefficient from the unemployment, employment, and hours-worked models as the outcome, and one each with the Hispanic coefficient from the same three models. In this estimation, minority joblessness, which is quantified from the individual-level estimation, is modelled as a function of aggregate-level characteristics of the county group.

This two-stage estimation, with the second stage dependent variable constructed from the first-stage estimation, has the advantage of being an efficient generalized least squares estimation in what could be a more elaborate model (Saxonhouse 1976). Our method is simpler and more feasible than the relatively new hierarchical linear models (Bryk & Raudenbush 1992). While the latter have the advantage of simultaneous estimation of the two-equation system, their sensitivity to violation of model assumptions is still being questioned. Therefore, we adopted the more conventional approach where model strengths and weaknesses are known. We estimated the following equations using weighted least squares:[11]

---

8. The left-out racial category is non-Hispanic white. The small number of black Hispanics were coded as Hispanic. The geographic concentration of Hispanic subpopulations negated the possibility of entering separate dummies for the subcategories of Hispanic origin within each county group.

9. The omitted category is high school graduate.

10. Some county groups were recombined to provide groups that allowed their characterization. See Appendix A for full description

11. Appendix C provides the empirical definition, mean, and standard deviation for each variable. County-group observations were weighted by the inverse of the estimated standard

$$\Sigma \beta_1 Ecologyj + \Sigma \beta_2 Mincompj\ \Sigma \beta Popj + \Sigma \beta Realwagej + \Sigma \beta Empj$$

where:

α_j^1 = the coefficients on the black binary variables for each county group's *j* measure of joblessness (estimated from equation 1)

α_j^2 = the coefficients on the Hispanic binary variables for each county group's *j* measure of joblessness (estimated from equation 1)

Ecology$_j$ = a vector of variables measuring locational attributes of the county group

Min comp$_j$ = a vector of variables measuring minority composition in the county group

Pop$_j$ = a vector of variables measuring attributes of the population in county group

Rel wage$_j$ = a measure of relative minority wages in the county group

Emp$_j$ = a vector of control variables measuring the economic activity in the county group.

Appendix C provides the variables' definitions, means, and standard deviations.

The ecological variables in our model (*ecology*) measure whether the county group is the central city of a MSA, whether it is located in the Northeast or Midwest region, and whether it has a large proportion of residents who work outside its boundaries. We include these variables because central city and Northeast and Midwest residence may exacerbate spatial mismatches between residents and jobs (e.g., urban poverty and hypersegregation), and location outside the central business district (i.e., high proportion of residents who work outside the area) generally is in suburbs where spatial mismatches may be equally problematic for white and minority residents.

The minority concentration variables capture concentration effects, which have been shown to produce social isolation for blacks and ethnic enclaves for Hispanics. Minority concentration is quantified as the relative size of the minority population. Specifically, for equations with black coefficients as the outcomes, we include a variable for the percent of the population in the county group that is black. For equations with Hispanic coefficients as the outcomes, we include one variable for the percent of the population in the county group that is of Spanish origin and three variables that measure the percent of the Hispanic population in the county group that is Puerto Rican, Cuban, and other Hispanic. The comparison category is Mexicans.

Additional controls for the characteristics of the population in the county group include the percent of the Hispanic population claiming limited English-speaking ability (for the Hispanic equation only), population size, and female labor-force participation. Because English is often required for employment, a county group with a large proportion of individuals who do not speak English may facilitate Hispanic employment opportunities by providing an economic enclave (McManus 1990) or a social network with non-English speakers.[12] The log

---

error of the dependent variable from the microlevel analysis to correct for hetroskedasticity. The variance inflation factors (VIFs) indicated that multicollinearity did not confound our estimations.

12. Because we examine the impact of an enclave on employment and not earnings, our analysis is less concerned with the distinction between workers and bosses that Sanders and

of the size of the population controls for the size of the market and the degree of spatial mismatch that could exist within the county group. Our final population measure is the female labor-force participation rate of the county group, which captures the potential effects of competition for jobs between women and minority males.

We also control for the relative wages of minorities in the county. Because the law of demand predicts that lower relative wages of minorities will increase relative employment, lower minority wages should decrease minority joblessness as lower-paid minorities are substituted for capital and white workers. Alternatively, lower minority wages may indicate a high level of discrimination. If this is the case, a positive empirical relationship between wage and job disadvantages should exist.[13] Unfortunately, measuring relative minority wages within a county group is not straightforward. As an approximation, we again use an individual-level analysis of the 1980 census and estimate a log hourly wage equation *within* each county group. In this estimation, the dependent variables in equation 1 are replaced with a log hourly wage variable.[14] The coefficients on the black and Hispanic dummies represent measures of the county group disparity in *wages*, net of age and education,[15] and quantify relative minority wages in each county group. (See Appendix C for a statistical portrait of these variables).

Our final set of variables controls for the economic conditions in the county group (*employment*). Research suggests that declining manufacturing employment (e.g., Nord 1989) and secular downturns in the economy (e.g., Juhn 1992) increase joblessness, especially among low skilled, minority workers. As such, we include county-group measures of the white male unemployment rate and the extent of income growth (1979 to 1985) as controls for the economic health of the local labor market.[16] We also include the percent of the labor force that is employed in manufacturing to capture the employment base of the county group.

Nee (1990) raise. That is, we are merely assuming, in line with McManus (1990), that *employment* opportunities for ethnic minorities with limited English are greater within an enclave.

13. The a priori empirical ambiguity of this variable produces ambiguity in its modeling. If we argue that simultaneity exists in minority wage and job disadvantages, two-stage least square regression should be used to estimate equation 2. However, because the focus of this study is on minority access to jobs and because economic theory clearly predicts a negative relationship between access to jobs and wages, we model minority access to jobs causally and estimate equation 2 using OLS.

14. The respondent's hourly wage was estimated by dividing wage and salary income of the previous year or by the product of weeks worked the previous year and usual hours worked per week. Those who did not work the previous year, as well as those whose estimated hourly wage was less than $1 or greater than $80, were omitted.

15. There are, however, limitations to using the wage equation coefficients in this way. These wage equations are scarcely well specified and the disparity in wages between groups may reflect unmeasured productivity differences between groups. In fact, the same omitted unmeasured productivity variables could give rise to differences in joblessness and wages. While these problems suggest that the magnitude of the relationship between the minority coefficients from the wage and joblessness equations should not be interpreted too earnestly, we believe it provides at least a directional measure of relationship.

16. Because part of the income growth variable postdates our dependent variable, we use it to capture the long-term economic growth and our unemployment rate variable to capture short-term economic activity, a concept that is better measured with the white male rate than the minority rate.

Table 1. Distribution of Black and Hispanic Jobless Coefficients: Percent Distribution[a]

Dependent Variable	Black Coefficient		Hispanic Coefficient	
	Black Counties	Black-Hispanic Counties	Hispanic Counties	Black-Hispanic Counties
Unemployment				
Less than 0	3.6	2.7	28.0	29.1
0 to 2.5	16.3	17.3	49.0	50.0
2.5 to 5.0	34.6	32.7	15.0	15.5
5.0 to 7.5	24.5	28.2	6.0	2.7
7.5 to 10.0	13.2	14.5	1.5	1.8
10.0 or above	7.7	4.5	0.5	0.9
Mean coef. value	5.06	4.91	1.33	1.22
Standard deviation	(3.27)	(2.94)	(2.37)	(2.23)
Employment				
Less than −15.0	15.1	15.5	1.0	1.8
−15.0 to −10.0	37.3	36.4	3.5	4.5
−10.0 to −5.0	37.3	34.5	14.5	13.6
−5.0 to 0	9.9	12.7	48.0	43.6
0 or above	0.5	0.9	33.0	36.4
Mean coef. value	−10.57	−10.50	−1.80	−1.97
Standard deviation	(4.52)	(4.80)	(4.31)	(4.55)
Hours worked last year				
Less than −400	19.7	11.8	1.5	2.7
−400 to −300	34.9	30.9	3.0	2.7
−300 to −200	32.5	37.3	8.0	9.1
−200 to −100	12.0	19.1	36.0	30.9
−100 to 0	1.0	0.9	43.0	47.3
0 or above	0	0	8.5	7.3
Mean coef. value	−314.13	−290.49	−109.68	−115.41
Standard deviation	(96.85)	(101.71)	(101.11)	(108.57)
N	416	110	200	110

a. Mean coefficient values represent the average value of the estimated coefficients on the race, α_j^1 (black coefficient), and ethnic, α_j^2 (Hispanic coefficient), variable from text equation 1. The remaining numbers reflect the percentage distribution of the coefficients. Coefficients in the (survey week) unemployment and employment equations were multiplied by 100 to reflect a percentage change. "Black counties" contain at least 100 black men aged 18 to 55, "Hispanic counties" contain at least 100 Hispanic men aged 18 to 55, and "Black-Hispanic counties" contain at least 100 black and 100 Hispanic men aged 18 to 55. *T* tests for differences in mean coefficient values revealed than only the hours worked mean coefficient for blacks was different ($p \leq .05$) between single race and black-Hispanic counties.

Results

Our initial analysis of county-group differences in minority joblessness is shown in Table 1, which displays the distribution of the black and Hispanic coefficients (α_1 and α_2) from the estimation of the microequations (equation 1). In this analysis, a positive coefficient in the unemployment equation and a negative coefficient in the employment and hours worked equations represent a minority disadvantage in access to jobs. Several findings stand out. First, blacks suffer sizable disadvantages relative to whites on all three outcomes (column 2). Blacks experience a significant disadvantage ($p \leq .05$) in 93.3% of the county groups on the employment outcome, in 73.1% of the county groups on the unemployment outcome and in 99% of the county groups on the hours worked outcome.[17] Furthermore, the average black coefficient (multiplied by 100) on the employment outcome is −10.57, suggesting that, net of age and education, blacks are over 10 percentage points less likely than whites to be employed in the average county group. Similarly, as compared to whites, blacks face about 5 percentage points more unemployment and work about 300 fewer hours per year.

Second, the small dispersion in this disadvantage suggests that the size of the black disadvantage varies only modestly across county groups. In fact, since sampling error alone would produce some differences, the limited variation across county groups is rather startling. For example, in 75% of the county groups the estimated black disadvantage in employment falls within 5 percentage points of the mean value (i.e., between −5.0 and −15.0). Furthermore, blacks rarely achieve parity with whites in any county group. The black coefficient is never zero or positive for the hours-worked outcome. It is zero or positive in only two (i.e., 0.5%) of the county groups in the employment model, and it is zero or negative in only 3.6% of the county groups for the unemployment outcome. In short, the picture is one of a pervasive black disadvantage in access to jobs.

Table 1 also shows that Hispanics fare much better than blacks on each outcome (column 4). The Hispanic coefficients, in fact, are relatively small on average. Moreover, in about 80% of the county groups, the coefficients suggest that Hispanic joblessness is not significantly different ($p \leq .05$) from whites.[18] As Table 1 shows, in 77% of the counry groups the coefficient on the unemployment outcome is less than 2.5 and in 81% of the county groups the coefficient on the employment outcome is greater than −5.0. A final observation from Table 1 reveals that the pervasive black disadvantage in access to jobs and the small Hispanic disadvantage do not result from differences in their spatial distribution around the country. When analysis is limited to county groups that contain a sufficient sample size of both black and Hispanic men (columns 3 and 5), the same conclusions hold.

We next analyze whether the modest county-group differences in the minority disadvantage vary systematically with spatial characteristics of county groups. As a preliminary examination, Table 2 displays the mean values of the black and Hispanic coefficients by characteristics of the county group. Along all dimensions (columns 2–4), and consistent with spatial mismatch models, blacks fare most poorly in the north central region, an area that encompasses county groups of greatest industrial decline, and they do better in the suburban portions of SMSAs, consistent with equal access outside of the central business district. However, the most striking finding presented in this table is that the black disadvantage remains sizable in all regions and in all county-group types and sizes. Analysis therefore provides mixed support for attributing black joblessness solely to spatial mismatches. Although we find small regional and urban differences in black disadvantages that

---

17. These results are not shown here but are available from the authors.

18. The coefficients showed a significant ($p \leq .05$) Hispanic disadvantage in only 22% of the employment estimations, 18% of the unemployment estimations and 60% of the hours estimations. In 5.5% of the employment estimations and 0.5% of the unemployment estimations Hispanics had a significant advantage in joblessness.

Table 2. Mean of Jobless Coefficients by Region, SMSA Status, and Size of County Group: Blacks and Hispanics[a]

	Black Coefficients			Hispanic Coefficients		
	Unem-ployment	Employ-ment	Hours Worked	Unem-ployment	Employ-ment	Hours Worked
Overall mean	5.06	−10.57	−314.13	1.33	−1.80	−109.68
Region[b]						
Northeast	5.42	−10.17	−260.60	1.42	−3.96	−156.08
North Central	7.88	−13.74	−351.91	2.01	−2.66	−110.81
South	4.27	−9.84	−321.45	0.49	−.061	−112.25
West	5.65	−11.35	−276.57	1.72	−1.54	−89.02
SMSA status[c]						
Central city of SMSA	6.28	−11.72	−299.15	1.72	−2.33	−106.65
Balance of SMSA	4.13	−8.64	−276.41	1.24	−1.40	−98.98
Both central city and						
balance of SMSA	5.31	−11.10	−327.11	1.28	−2.13	−137.29
SMSA and non-SMSA	3.94	−10.06	−325.73	0.27	−0.78	−103.78
Non-SMSA	5.01	−11.03	−350.05	1.50	−1.68	−99.73
Population[d] (in thousands)						
100 to 199	5.16	−10.89	−333.43	1.52	−2.04	−118.18
200 to 299	4.91	−10.43	−311.07	1.34	−1.50	−102.98
300 to 499	4.89	−10.01	−285.63	1.17	−1.31	−113.35
500 and above	5.01	−10.00	−267.42	1.14	−1.90	−98.29
N	416	416	416	200	200	200

a. Numbers reflect the mean coefficient values of the minority disadvantage across county groups (i.e., α_j^1 and α_j^2 from text equation 1). *T* tests on mean differences between each category were performed. Results are delineated in footnotes below.

b. Significant ($p \leq .05$) differences exist between all region *except* the Northeast and West for blacks, between the South and the other regions for Hispanics (on unemployment only), and between the Northeast and West for Hispanics (on employment and hours worked only).

c. For blacks, significant ($p \leq .05$) differences exist by SMSA status but do not follow a predictable pattern. Most relevant, significant differences exist between central city county groups and county groups with SMSA balance and SMSA and non-SMSA only for employment and unemployment; between central city and county groups containing both central city and balance of SMSA only for unemployment and hours; and between central city and non-SMSA county groups for only hours. For Hispanics, the *only* significant difference by SMSA status is between central city and the SMSA and non-SMSA combinations for unemployment.

d. The *only* significant ($p \leq .05$) difference by population size is between county groups with 100–199 and 300–499 population and between county groups with 200–299 and 500+ population for black hours worked.

are consistent with a mismatch model, we also find the black disadvantage to be pervasive, suggesting the importance of race in determining access to jobs.

The pronounced regional location of Hispanic subgroups makes interpreting regional variation in Hispanic joblessness somewhat problematic, an issue that will be addressed later. For example, the greater Hispanic joblessness in the Northeast, shown in Table 2, may exist because Puerto Ricans, a group with poor labor market success, predominate in this region. In any case, only modest regional differences exist in Hispanic labor market disadvantages.

We next examine more systematically the extent to which the variation in minority joblessness is determined by racial and spatial factors by estimating equation 2. To facilitate interpretation, we multiplied the employment and hours worked dependent variables by −1 so that a larger positive value on each dependent variable indicates a greater minority disadvantage and a negative coefficient represents less of a minority disadvantage. Results of this analysis, presented in Table 3, once again provide modest support for spatial mismatches and strong support for race and ethnic-based hiring.

For blacks (columns 2–4), joblessness is not significantly larger in central cities (*central city*) than elsewhere. However, residence does determine minority disadvantage as measured by the proportion of residents that work outside of the county group and by region of the country. Results show that, for both blacks and Hispanics, areas with a high proportion of individuals who commute to work have less minority joblessness. This suggests that minorities who work in areas without a job base, typically more affluent suburbs, face similar job access as their white counterpart, presumably because migration into these areas is highly selective (see Jencks & Mayer 1987 for a discussion). Spatial determinants of minority joblessness are also supported by the significant increase in black joblessness for residents in the Northeast and Midwest, areas of intense residential segregation, inner city poverty, and industrial decline. Furthermore, localized indicators of economic health are significantly related to black joblessness, with both a strong economy (*income growth*) and decreased "aggregate" unemployment reducing relative joblessness for blacks.

In addition to the support for spatial mismatch determinants of joblessness for blacks, our analysis shows strong evidence of race-based hiring, as seen by the significant race and minority concentration variables. Specifically, the negative, significant relationship between wage and job disadvantages in two of the three equations for blacks suggests that these factors are positively related across county groups.[19] That is, where blacks lag behind whites in wages received, they also lag in employment and hours worked. Although the limitations on the variable measuring the black wage disadvantage dictate caution in interpreting these results, we nonetheless conclude that these two important facets of black disadvantage in the labor market move in tandem. One explanation for this phenomena is that employers make both hiring and salary decisions based, in part, on race (Shulman 1987). This argument is strengthened by the positive relationship between the proportion of the population that is black and black joblessness on all three outcomes. This finding, in combination with the work by Burr, Galle, and Fossett (1991), suggests that the increased presence of blacks is perceived as a "threat" by whites and, as a result, economic inequality in opportunity is increased.

Results from the estimation of similar models of Hispanic joblessness are subject to a somewhat different interpretation because the mean Hispanic disadvantage across county groups is close to zero for each outcome (Table 1). Perhaps because of this distinction or perhaps because race and ethnicity play different roles in determining labor market outcomes, results of the Hispanic estimations differ from black estimations. For example, a queuing model may be less applicable for Hispanics since the economic vitality of the county group is, at best, weakly related to the size of Hispanic joblessness. More generally, few of these regressors significantly and consistently relate to relative Hispanic access to jobs. The Hispanic disadvantage in employment and hours worked is significantly greater in areas where Puerto Ricans predominate, but is no different in county groups where Cubans and other Hispanics predominate. Also, the percent of the population that is of Spanish

---

19. The negative sign on the minority relative wage coefficient indicates a positive relationship between wage and joblessness because values on the employment and hours worked variables were multiplied by −1.

Table 3. WLS Analysis of County Group Differences in Joblessness: Blacks and Hispanics

	Blacks			Hispanics		
	Unemployment	Employment	Hours	Unemployment	Employment	Hours
Locational attributes						
Central city	0.576	−0.865	−9.994	0.235	0.402	−5.135
	(.356)	(.492)	(10.348)	(.411)	(.680)	(16.383)
Northeast or Midwest	1.678**	2.101**	32.936**	−0.130	−0.380	3.964
	(.402)	(.545)	(11.379)	(.654)	(1.072)	(25.814)
Jobs	−0.023**	−0.040**	−1.006**	−0.015	−0.035*	−0.840*
	(.008)	(.011)	(.231)	(.010)	(.016)	(.395)
Minority composition						
Black	0.031**	0.034*	0.967**	—	—	—
	(.010)	(.014)	(.296)			
Puerto Rican	—	—	—	0.015	0.098**	2.201**
				(.013)	(.020)	(.485)
Cuban	—	—	—	−0.005	−0.019	−0.760
				(.014)	(.025)	(.609)
Other Hispanic	—	—	—	0.016	0.025	0.080
				(.012)	(.019)	(.461)
Spanish	—	—	—	0.012	0.030	0.537
				(.012)	(.021)	(.507)
Population						
Language	—	—	—	0.017	−0.105*	−0.483
				(.030)	(.049)	(1.187)
Log population	−0.221	−0.318	−19.474**	−0.432*	−0.912**	−26.394**
	(.176)	(.241)	(5.066)	(.193)	(.318)	(7.656)
Female labor force participation	−0.018	−0.106**	−4.124**	0.004	0.010	1.875
	(.027)	(.038)	(.805)	(.033)	(.057)	(1.410)
Relative wages of minorities						
Black wage disadvantage	−0.847	−9.308**	−146.125**	—	—	—
	(2.167)	(3.035)	(63.984)			
Hispanic wage disadvantage	—	—	—	0.841	−8.063	66.945
				(2.730)	(4.541)	(109.871)
Economic activity						
Aggregate unemployment	0.359**	0.486**	0.637	0.126	0.062	−2.926
	(.088)	(.118)	(2.432)	(.018)	(.134)	(3.211)
Income growth	−0.070**	−0.163**	−4.264**	−0.016	−0.054	−0.991
	(.025)	(.034)	(.728)	(.018)	(.030)	(.730)
Manufacturing	0.003	−0.002	−0.629	0.017	0.038	−0.161
	(.015)	(.021)	(.438)	(.026)	(.043)	(1.051)
Intercept	11.580**	29.744**	1041.848**	3.550	10.111*	260.595**
	(2.998)	(4.182)	(88.296)	(2.352)	(4.049)	(99.292)
Adjusted R^2	0.278	.330	.327	.017	.214	.164
N	416	416	416	200	200	200

a. Values on the employment and hours worked dependent variables have been multiplied by −1 so that higher values on all three outcomes represent greater minority disadvantage. This means that larger values on the "minority relative wage" independent variables represent greater minority joblessness. Numbers represent coefficients estimated from text equation 2. Standard errors are in parentheses. County-group observations were weighted by the inverse of the standard error of the dependent variable in text equation 1 to correct for heteroskedasticity.

*p ≤ .05 **p ≤ .01

origin has no effect on relative Hispanic joblessness. The significant, positive influence of limited English (*language*) confirms the evidence of concentration effects shown in Moore and Pinderhughes (1993). Finally, the Hispanic measure of relative wages is never significantly related to Hispanic joblessness and the sign of this variable is inconsistent across outcomes, suggesting that no clear relationship exists between relative wages and access to jobs for Hispanics.

Discussions and Conclusions

This study empirically examines the race, ethnic, and space dimensions to minority joblessness. The dramatic increase in minority joblessness during the 1970s, a phenomena from which minorities never fully recovered, necessitates this exploration if parity in economic outcomes across all subpopulations is a goal. Our analysis strongly suggests that, while spatial mismatches between minorities and jobs contribute to minority joblessness, race plays a key role in determining access to jobs. Therefore, policy makers cannot close employment gaps between minorities and whites by simply relying on policies that eliminate spatial mismatches between minorities and employment opportunities.

Our most striking finding is that a pervasive black disadvantage in access to jobs exists, a phenomenon that is not shared with Hispanics. Across all county groups examined, and net of the respondent's age and education, black males work over 300 fewer annual hours than whites. Furthermore, their unemployment rate is 5 percentage points higher and their employment-to-population ratio is 10 percentage points lower. For blacks, racial disparities in joblessness apparently do not vary greatly across regions of the country or between central cities and suburbs or rural areas. In only a handful of county groups is the black disadvantage near zero on any outcome. In contrast, the labor force behavior of Hispanic males is more often zero, or a difference in favor of Hispanics as large as the average disparity between whites and blacks, once basic demographics have been taken into account.

This pervasive black disadvantage in access to jobs may override the more localized spatial mismatch that increases black male joblessness. Although our multivariate results suggest that the black disadvantage is somewhat larger in areas of industrial decline, the more limited black access to jobs is a national phenomenon that demands a unified, national solution. This is not to say that the insights of the spatial mismatch model are not valid or that they hold no utility. Indeed, a responsibility for the increased impoverishment experienced by ghetto blacks in America's northeastern and midwestern cities must be laid at the door step of the massive industrial shifts that these same cities have experienced over recent decades. Results presented in this article, however, strongly suggest that lagging black access to jobs is a general and widespread social problem, one that cannot be eliminated by simply locating blacks and jobs in closer proximity.

The difference between black and Hispanic levels and determinants of employment disadvantages also places in question the assumptions underlying both homogeneous labor market and declining significance of race arguments. Our study shows that, while blacks face a pervasive disadvantage in access to jobs, the Hispanic employment difficulties may be alleviated by increased concentration. The heterogeneity in labor market operations between blacks and Hispanics explains, for example, why economic vitality in the community decreases black joblessness but has little impact on Hispanics, whose employment may be more sheltered in enclaves. This heterogeneity in labor market operations also means that our nation can never reach its full employment potential without recognition that race and ethnicity are still key dimensions to labor market operation.

While our study provides strong support for these statements, its reliance on 1980 census data dictates that it be replicated and validated. Census data are both confining and liberating. The variables available for this type of analysis are crude but they lend themselves to a *national* examination of the race, ethnicity, and space interactions. Only census data have the observations necessary to obtain *individually based* estimates of county levels of discrimination (our first-stage estimations), but the cost of this estimation is parsimony in variable selection. Future research should, at a minimum, include better controls for human capital and wage discrimination and verify our results with different definitions of local labor markets. Updating our analysis to include the 1980s is also necessary. Our examination of the 1970s is important because this decade produced the dramatic divergence between white and minority employment, an event from which we have not recovered. This decade also saw deindustrialization in the Midwest and Northeast come of age and urban concentration of minorities increase. During the 1980s firms continued to migrate out of the central city, deindustrialization continued to polarize jobs into high and low wages/skills, and minority concentration in inner cities intensified. While our analysis has established the continuing and significant role that race and ethnicity plays in employment outcomes, updating the analysis and validating its measures would solidify its linkage with wage and employment determination.

Appendices

Appendix A: Construction of County Groups

The U.S. Census Bureau formed county groups with the proviso that no county group should contain fewer than 100,000 residences and often fit them to state planning districts. Quite a few county groups were designed to make the 100,000 threshold while others contained as many as 4.1 million people. While the mean county group contained about 200,000 persons, the median value was substantially smaller. About 235 of the 1,100 original county groups necessitated measuring characteristics of cities smaller than 25,000. In many cases, only a small portion of the county group was made up of cities this small, but in many other cases, the county group was made up largely of them. Since available data sources do not permit characterizing cities below the 25,000 size threshold, some measurement imprecision resulted. About 200 of the affected county groups—those where more serious mismeasurement would result—were combined to form a smaller number of county groups whose characteristics could be measured accurately. In the remaining 35 cases, mismeasurement was presumed to be sufficiently slight that no recombination seemed necessary. In these cases, the area whose characteristics were measured constitutes no less than 85% and no more than 115% of the county group's actual population. In the majority of these 35 cases, the precision of measurement is actually within the 95% and 105% range.

In our analysis, the 416 county groups retained for black joblessness analysis and the 200 county groups retained for the Hispanic joblessness analysis constitute a small part of the country's total county groups (41% and 20%) but a large part of the minority population (93.1% and 87.4%). Appendix B shows the spatial distribution of these country groups. As expected, county groups retained in the study are located disproportionately in the South (for the black sample) or the West (for the Hispanic sample) and are more likely than average to be central cities and areas with large populations.

Appendix B. Distribution of County Groups in Total, Black, and Hispanic Samples by Region, SMSA Status, and Size: Percent Distribution

| | | Percent Distribution | |
| | | Black | Hispanic |
County group characteristics	Total	Sample	Sample
Region			
Northeast	16.4	13.7	17.5
North Central	29.4	14.7	9.5
South	39.2	64.0	29.5
West	15.0	7.7	43.5
SMSA status			
Central city of SMSA	11.3	22.6	27.5
Balance of SMSA	21.5	21.9	27.5
Both central city and balance of SMSA	20.5	24.8	21.0
SMSA and non-SMSA	15.5	10.8	9.0
Non-SMSA	31.3	20.0	15.0
Population (in thousands)			
100 to 199	73.5	56.7	41.0
200 to 299	12.4	16.1	16.0
300 to 499	7.5	12.3	16.5
500 and above	6.7	14.9	26.5
N	1,011	416	200

Appendix C. Definition, Means, and Standard Deviations of Key Variables in County-Level Estimation (Text Equation 2) [a]

Construct		Data Source	Mean	Std. Dev.
Dependent variables:				
Minority joblessness				
α_u^b	The black coefficient from the OLS estimation of within-county group individual unemployment	1980 Census	5.06	3.27
α_e^b	The black coefficient from the OLS estimation of within-county group individual employment	1980 Census	−10.57	4.52
α_h^b	The black coefficient from the OLS estimation of within-county group individual hours worked	1980 Census	−314.13	96.85
α_u^h	The Hispanic coefficient from the OLS estimation of within-county group individual unemployment	1980 Census	1.33	2.37
α_e^h	The Hispanic coefficient from the OLS estimation of within-county group individual employment	1980 Census	−1.80	4.31
α_h^h	The Hispanic coefficient from the OLS estimation of within-county group individual hours worked	1980 Census	−109.68	101.11
Independent variables				
Locational Attributes *Locational attributes of the county group*				
Central city	1 = central city; 0 = other	1980 Census	0.21	0.41
Northeast or Midwest	1 = in state located in the Northeast or Midwest; (New England, Middle Atlantic, East North Central, West North Central states)	1980 Census	0.24	0.43
Jobs	Percent of workers who work outside of the county group	City County Data Book	23.60	17.44
Minority composition *Minority composition of the county group*				
Black	Percent black in county group	City County Data Book	17.48	14.39
Puerto Rican	Percent of Hispanic population that is Puerto Rican	City County Data Book	12.93	18.39
Cuban	Percent of Hispanic population that is Cuban	City County Data Book	4.38	7.82
Other Hispanic	Percent of Hispanic population that is other Hispanic	City County Data Book	29.99	16.37
Spanish	Percent of population that is of Hispanic origin	City County Data Book	7.47	12.55

Appendix C continues on next page

a. All data from the *County and City Data Book* (U.S. Bureau of the Census 1983b) were drawn from the 1980 census. The dependent variables and wage disadvantage variables were computed from individual-level estimation of 1980 census data.

Appendix C *continued*

Construct		Data Source	Mean	Std. Dev.
Population	*Attributes of the population*			
Language	Percent of the Hispanic population over age 5 that speaks English poorly	City County Data Book	12.59	7.98
Log population	Log population in county group	1980 Census	5.38	0.68
Female labor	Female labor force participation (*100)	City County Data Book	49.63	5.98
Relative wages of minorities	*Relative minority wages*			
Black wage disadvantage	The black coefficient from the OLS estimation of within-county group individual wage	1980 Census	−0.15	0.08
Hispanic wage disadvantage	The Hispanic coefficient from the OLS estimation of within-county group individual wage	1980 Census	−0.12	0.08
Economic base	*Economic base in the county group*			
Aggregate unemployment	White male mean unemployment rate for the county group	City County Data Book	4.72	2.31
Income growth	1985 (1985 dollars) to 1979 per capita income ratio (*100)	City County Data Book	99.89	7.98
Manufacturing	Percent of the labor force employed in manufacturing	City County Data Book	21.52	10.09

Appendix D. Mean of Minority Wage Coefficients, by Region, SMSA Status, and Size of County Group: Blacks and Hispanics[a]

County group characteristics	Black Coefficients	Hispanic Coefficients
Overall mean	−.154	−.120
Region		
Northeast	−.110	−.157
North Central	−.063	−.041
South	−.187	−.146
West	−.131	−.104
SMSA status		
Central city of SMSA	−.113	−.111
Balance of SMSA	−.141	−.115
Both central city and balance of SMSA	−.157	−.124
SMSA and non-SMSA	−.191	−.155
Non-SMSA	−.192	−.118
Population (in thousands)		
100 to 199	−.169	−.122
200 to 299	−.141	−.119
300 to 499	−.134	−.095
500 and above	−.130	−.131
N	416	200

a. Numbers represent mean values of the coefficients on black and Hispanic binary variables computed from individual-level log wage estimation of the 1980 Census.

References

Alba, Richard D., and John R. Logan. 1991. "Variations on Two Themes: Racial and Ethnic Patterns in the Attainment of Suburban Residence." *Demography* 28:431–53.

Bendick, Marc Jr., Charles W. Jackson, and Victor A. Reinoso. 1993. *Measuring Employment Discrimination Through Controlled Experiments*. Washington, D.C.: Fair Employment Council.

Bryk, Anthony S., and Stephen W. Raudenbush. 1992. *Hierarchical Linear Models: Applications and Data Analysis Methods*. Sage.

Burr, Jeffrey A., Omer R. Galle, and Mark A. Fossett. 1991. "Racial Occupational Inequality in Southern Metropolitan Areas, 1940–1980: Revisiting the Visibility-Discrimination Hypothesis." *Social Forces* 69:831–50.

Cross, Harry, with Genevieve Kenny, Jane Mell, and Wendy Zimmermann. 1990. *Employer Hiring Practices: Differential Treatment of Hispanic and Anglo Job Seekers*. The Urban Institute Press.

DeFreitas, Gregory. 1986. "A Time-Series Analysis of Hispanic Unemployment." *Journal of Human Resources* 21:24–43.

Ellwood, Daniel T. 1986. "The Spatial Mismatch Hypothesis: Are There Teenage Jobs Missing in the Ghetto?" pp. 147–85 in *The Black Youth Employment Crisis*, edited by Richard B. Freeman and Harry H. Holzer. University of Chicago Press.

Fossett, Mark A., and K. Jill Kiecolt. 1989. "The Relative Size of the Minority Populations and White Racial Attitudes." *Social Science Quarterly* 70:820–35.

Ihlanfeldt, Keith R. 1993. "Intra-Urban Job Accessibility and Hispanic Youth Employment Rates." Georgia State University, Policy Research Center, memo.

———. 1992. "Intraurban Wage Gradients: Evidence by Race, Gender, Occupational Class, and Sector." *Journal of Urban Economics* 32:70–91.

Ihlanfeldt, Keith R., and David L. Sjoquist. 1990. "Job Accessibility and Racial Differences in youth Employment Rates." *American Economic Review* 80:267–76

Jencks, Christopher, and Susan Mayer. 1990. "Residential Segregation, Job Proximity and Black Job Opportunity." pp. 187–222 in *Inner City Poverty in the United States* edited by Laurance E. Lynn Jr. and Michael G.H. McGeary. National Academy Press.

Juhn, Chinhui. 1992. "Decline of Male Labor Market Participation: The Role of Declining Market Opportunities." *Quarterly Journal of Economics* 102:79–121

Kain, John. 1968. "Housing Segregation, Negro Employment, and Metropolitan Decentralization." *Quarterly Journal of Economics* 82:32–59.

Kasarda, John D. 1985. "Urban Change and Minority Opportunities." pp. 33–67 in *The New Urban Reality*, edited by Paul E. Peterson. The Brookings Institute.

———. 1983. "Entry-Level Jobs, Mobility, and Urban Minority Unemployment." *Urban Affairs Quarterly* 19:21–40.

Kirschenman, Loleen, and Kathryn M. Neckerman. 1991. " 'We'd Love to Hire Them, But...': The Meaning of Race for Employers." pp. 203–34 in *The Urban Underclass*, edited by Christopher Jencks and Paul E. Peterson. The Brookings Institution.

Lichter, Daniel T. 1988. "Racial Differences in Underemployment in American Cities." *American Journal of Sociology* 93:771–92.

McManus, Walter S. 1990. "Labor Market Effects of Language Enclaves: Hispanic Men in the United States." *Journal of Human Resources* 25:228–52.

Massey, Douglas S. 1990. "American Apartheid: Segregation and the Making of the Underclass." *American Journal of Sociology* 96:329–57.

Massey, Douglas S., Gretchen A. Condran, and Nancy A. Denton. 1987. "The Effect of Residential Segregation of Black Social and Economic Well-being." *Social Forces* 66:29–56.

Massey, Douglas S., and Nancy A. Denton. 1987. "Trends in the Residential Segregation of Blacks, Hispanics, and Asians: 1970–1980." *American Sociological Review* 52:802–25.

————. 1988. "Suburbanization and Segregation in U.S. Metropolitan Areas." *American Journal of Sociology* 94:592–626.

————. 1989. "Hypersegregation in U.S. Metropolitan Areas: Black and Hispanic Segregation Along Five Dimensions." *Demography* 26:373–91.

Massey, Douglas S., and Mitchell L. Eggers. 1990. "The Ecology of Inequality: Minorities and the Concentration of Poverty, 1970–1980." *American Journal of Sociology* 95:1153–88.

Moore, Joan, and Raquel Pinderhuges. 1993. *In the Barrios: Latinos and the Underclass Debate*. Russell Sage.

Nord, Stephen. 1989. "The Relationship among Labor Force Participation, Service-Sector Employment, and Underemployment." *Journal of Regional Science* 29:407–21.

Portes, Alejandro, and Cynthia Truelove. 1987. "Making Sense of Diversity." pp. 359–85 in *Annual Review of Sociology*. Vol. 13, edited by W. Richard Scott and James F. Short, Jr.

Sanders, Jimy M., and Victor Nee. 1987. "Limits of ethnic Solidarity in the Enclave Economy." *American Journal of Sociology* 52:745–73.

Saxonhouse, Gary R. 1976. "Estimated Parameters as Dependent Variables." *American Economic Review* 66:178–83.

Schneider, Mark, and Thomas Phelan. 1990. "Blacks and Jobs: Never the Twain Shall Meet?" *Urban Affairs Quarterly* 26:299–312.

Shulman, Steven. 1987. "Discrimination, Human Capital, and Black-White Unemployment." *Journal of Human Resources* 22:361–76.

Tienda, Marta, and Ding-Tzann Lii. 1987. "Minority Concentration and Earnings Inequality: Blacks, Hispanics, and Asians Compared." *American Journal of Sociology* 93:141–65.

Tuch, Steven A. 1987. "Urbanism, Region, and Tolerance Revisited: The Case of Racial Prejudice." *American Sociological Review* 52:504–10.

U.S. Bureau of the Census. 1983a. *Statistical Abstract of the United States*. Government Printing Office.

————. 1983b. *County and City Data Book*. Government Printing Office.

————. 1991. *Statistical Abstract of the United States*. Government Printing Office.

Welch, Finis. 1990. "Employment of Black Men." *Journal of Labor Economics* 8 (1, pt. 2):S26–S74.

Wilson, William Julius. 1991. "Public Policy Research and 'Truly Disadvantaged'." pp. 460–82 in *The Urban Underclass*, edited by Christopher Jencks and Paul E. Peterson. the Brookings Institution.

————. 1987. *The Truly disadvantaged: The Inner City, the Underclass, and Public Policy*. University of Chicago Press.

————. 1978. *The Declining Significance of Race*. The University of Chicago Press.

30

The Impact of Local Labor Markets on Black and White Family Structure

Michael C. Seeborg
Kristin Jaeger

I. Introduction

In recent years the U.S. has experienced rapid increases in the incidence of female-headed households. The adverse effects that these increases have on overall poverty rates and income levels are well documented (Bane, 1986; Danziger, Jakubson, Schwartz & Smolensky, 1982), as are the adverse effects on certain subsegments of the population, especially women and children. While the increase in the incidence of female-headed families has been great for white families, going from 9.1 percent of all white families in 1970 to 12.9 percent in 1988, it has been even more pronounced for black families, going from 28.3 percent in 1970 to 42.8 percent in 1988 (U.S. Bureau of the Census, 1990).

Not all geographic areas, however, mirror the national averages. For example, in comparing metropolitan areas (SMSAs) with populations in excess of 250,000 we find that in 1980, the percentage of black families headed by women ranged from 22.8 percent in Tacoma, Washington to 49.6 percent in Milwaukee, Wisconsin; and for white families the range was from 8.1 percent headed by women in Beaumont, Texas to 18.9 percent in Jersey City, New Jersey (U.S. Bureau of the Census, 1983). Cross-sectional variation in family structure of this magnitude makes it possible to use SMSA level data to analyze a number of the economic determinants of family structure.

Evidence that there may be a relationship between economic characteristics of metropolitan areas and family structure is suggested in Table 1, which shows summary statistics for black populations in our sample of 99 SMSAs from the continental United States. To derive the three groups shown in the table, the 99

An earlier version of this essay appeared in *Journal of Socio-Economics;* 1993, 22, 2, Summer, 115–130 and is adapted/reprinted with the permission of the copyright holder/author.

Table 1: Summary Statistics Across SMSAs by Percent of Black Female-Headed Families

Variable	Low %BFHEAD (<35.81%)	Middle %BFHEAD	High %BFHEAD (>40.1%)	Total Sample
Mean Black Poverty Rate	22.3	25.2	26.4	24.6
Median Black Family Income	$13,765	$13,166	$12,794	$13,242
Black Marriagable Male Index	62.0	56.3	51.5	56.6
Black Female Emp. to Population %	56.4	59.6	62.1	59.4
Mean Public Assistance	$2,244	$2,291	$2,605	$2,380
% Employed Blacks in Durable Goods	12.3	14.4	18.5	15.0
% Employed Blacks in Government Jobs	29.1	27.3	26.1	27.5
Number of SMSAs	33	33	33	99

SMSAs were ranked from high to low by the percentage of black families which were female-headed and then divided into three equal groups of 33. In the first group are the SMSAs with the largest percentage of female-headed black families (above 40.1 percent). The table shows that these SMSAs had, on average, higher black poverty rates, lower median black family incomes, a higher percentage of black women with employment, a lower percentage of black men with employment, and higher average public assistance outlays for black families who receive public assistance.

This study employs 1980 Census data for a sample of SMSAs with populations in excess of 250,000 to determine how economic characteristics such as employment opportunities for men, employment opportunities for women and the average level of welfare support determine the incidence of female-headed families in metropolitan areas. The study also attempts to determine if black family structure responds differently than white family structure to changes in these variables. The data base is described in detail in the Appendix.

II. Determinants of Family Structure

Modeling the economic determinants of family structure has been a long-time concern of sociologists and more recently of economists. We believe that much can be learned from both perspectives. In fact, hypotheses of the determinants of female-headed households to be developed and tested in this article are derived from both the theoretical and largely deductive work of neoclassical economist Gary Becker (1981) and from the more inductive approach of liberal sociologist William J. Wilson (1986, 1987). Becker's neoclassical theory of the family suggests a number of hypotheses concerning the economic determinants of family structure which are equally applicable to black and white families while Wilson's theory of the urban underclass suggests hypotheses concerning differences in the sensitivity of black and white family structures to changes in economic variables. That is, the "neoclassical" theory explains why family structure in general responds to economic change and the "underclass" theory explains why black family structures may be more responsive than white family structure to these changes.

From Becker's choice theoretic perspective, the decision to form or retain a traditional married couple family unit is based, in part, on perceived gains which can be received from a division of labor within the household. In a survey article on family change among black Americans, Ellwood and Crane (1990) explain some of the implications of Becker's work on the family.

> ...Becker's theory has been extended and interpreted in numerous ways. If one of the chief gains from marriage involves exploiting comparative advantages, and if one assumes sexually stereotypical roles of men and women, men will tend to specialize disproportionately in market work and women disproportionately in "home production." Any worsening of the economic position of men would seem to make marriage less attractive (or at least they will be able to gain a smaller share of the gains from marriage), since they have less comparative advantage in market work. Conversely, the comparative advantages of marriage might be weakened by factors leading to increased earnings of women (like reduced discrimination in the labor market, increased opportunity, or heightened desire to work) since the comparative advantages are lessened and the gains from specialization reduced. Similarly, an increase in the availability of other income that can be used to support a family in the absence of a male, like government welfare payments, would be expected to reduce the marriage desires of women. (p.71).

Therefore, three major implications of the Becker model for our purpose are that the percentage of female-headed households 1) will be greater in cities where welfare support is high; 2) will be greater where employment opportunities for men are poor; and 3) will be greater where employment opportunities for women are good.

Becker (1981) explains some of the possible effects of welfare on family structure as follows:

> Payments to mothers with dependent children are reduced when the earnings of parents increase, and are raised when additional children are born or when fathers do not support their children. It is a program, then, that raises the fertility of eligible women, including single women, and also encourages divorce and discourages marriage (the financial well-being of recipients is increased by children and decreased by marriage). In effect, welfare is the poor woman's alimony, which substitutes for husband's earnings. The expansion of welfare, along with the general decline in the gain from marriage, explains the sizable growth in the ratio of illegitimate to legitimate birth rates despite the introduction of the pill and other effective contraceptives. (pp. 251–252).

Although most would agree that public assistance will have some influence on family structure, there is still disagreement as to the magnitude of its effects. At one extreme, Charles Murray (1984) argues that high levels of welfare support for female-headed households (e.g., AFDC support) destroys work incentives and discourages the formation of married couple families. Sociologist William J. Wilson, on the other hand, attempts to demonstrate that current levels of welfare support have little to do with family structure and posits that joblessness is the major determinant of the incidence of female-headed families (1987).

In his research on the economic and social effects of the economic decline of many predominantly black central city neighborhoods, Wilson (1987) follows a different line of reasoning to reach the same conclusion as Becker regarding the direct relationship between male joblessness and the incidence of female-headed families. He links the "marriageability" of young adult males directly to their employment. Recent increases in black male joblessness in depressed urban neighborhoods have sharply reduced the supply of "marriageable" males and, according to Wilson, caused rapid increases in the incidence of black female-headed families.

Wilson's conclusion, restated in the context of Becker's theory of the family, is simply that increasing black male joblessness—which manifests itself in the form of rising unemployment, withdrawal from the labor force and increasing rates of incarceration—reduces the economic advantages of marriage and results in a higher incidence of female-headed families.

One strength of Wilson's theory and that of other sociologists working on the emergence of black "underclasses" in central city areas, such as Kasarda (1985) and Sampson (1987), is the attention given to urban transformations which have contributed to the high rates of joblessness for poorly educated black males. One of the most profound changes in urban labor markets has been the rapid decline in manufacturing jobs in central city areas and a resultant loss of many blue-collar jobs. For example, Wilson (1987) points out that between "1953 and 1984 New York City lost about 600,000 jobs in manufacturing but gained nearly 700,000 jobs in white-collar service industries" (p. 102). Analysis of the effects of the deindustrialization of central cities on the economic situation of residents have also received some attention by economists such as Kain (1968), and Ihlanfeldt and Sjoquist (1990), who argue that movement of manufacturing out of the central cities, combined with the lack of mobility of less-educated, largely minority populations in the central city has resulted in a serious "spatial mismatch" between that population and job opportunities.

Demographic trends have also worsened the economic and social structure of many central city neighborhoods. Most notable have been the exodus of white and middle class black families. Those who remain are often poor, less-educated minorities who lack both economic opportunities and role models.

The natural result of these changes has been the development of an urban, largely black, underclass which exhibits high rates of joblessness and associated social pathologies such as youth gang activity, high crime rates, drug and alcohol abuse, and high dropout rates. An important implication of the underclass theory regarding the issue of family structure is that participation of jobless males in underclass behavior may well decrease their "marriageability" even more than would unemployment alone.

This line of reasoning has important implications for our research on the economic determinants of the incidence of female-headed families. If, as Wilson and his associates would argue, a strong interaction exists between economic opportunity and underclass activity for the black urban population, black family structure may be more strongly influenced by economic variables than white family structure.

III. The Model

To determine the influence of employment opportunities for men and women and the level of welfare support on black and white family structure, two equations are estimated:

Table 2: Variable Definitions and Summary Statistics

Variable	Mean	Std. Dev.	Definition
%BFHEAD	37.6	5	Percent of all black families which are female-headed
%WFHEAD	11.3	2	Percent of all white families which are female-headed
B-MMPI	56.6	9	Employed black males aged 20 through 34 as percent of the black female population aged 20 through 34
W-MMPI	81.4	5	Employed white males aged 20 through 34 as percent of the white female population aged 20 through 34
B-%FEMEMP	59.4	7	Employed black females aged 20 through 34 as percent of the black female civilian population aged 20 through 34
W-%FEMEMP	63.5	5	Employed white females aged 20 through 34 as percent of the white female civilian population aged 20 through 34
B-POV	24.6	5	Poverty rate for black families in the SMSA
W-POV	5.8	2	Poverty rate for white families in the SMSA
B-FAMINC	$13,597	$2,314	Real median black family income
W-FAMINC	$22,274	$2,410	Real median white family income
B-DUR	15	9	Percent of all employed black workers in durable goods producing industries
W-DUR	13.6	7	Percent of all employed white workers in durable goods producing industries
B-GOV	27.5	7	Percent of all employed black workers in government jobs (local, state and federal)
W-GOV	16.6	6	Percent of all employed white workers in government jobs (local, state and federal)
EMPCHANGE	44.3	33	Percent change in total employment in the SMSA between 1970 and 1980
AID	$2,379	$383	Real mean public assistance to families who are on public assistance

$$\%BFHEAD = \alpha_0 + \alpha_1(B\text{-}MMPI) + \alpha_2(B\text{-}\%FEMEMP) + \alpha_3(B\text{-}DUR\%)$$
$$+ \alpha_4(B\text{-}GOV\%)\ 1) + \alpha_5(EMPCHANGE) + \alpha_6(AID)$$

$$\%WFHEAD = \beta_0 + \beta_1(W\text{-}MMPI) + \beta_2(W\text{-}\%FEMEMP) + \beta_3(W\text{-}DUR\%)$$
$$+ \beta_4(W\text{-}GOV\%)\ 2) + \beta_5(EMPCHANGE) + \beta_6(AID).$$

Variable definitions and summary statistics are in Table 2. Of principle concern is how our measures of male employment opportunities (B-MMPI and W-MMPI), female employment opportunities (B-%FEMEMP and W-%FEMEMP) and public assistance levels (AID) effect the incidence of female-headed families in SMSAs (%BFHEAD and %WFHEAD). The rationale for inclusion of each of these variables in the model is presented below.

Employment Opportunities for Men

According to Becker's theory of the family, reduced employment opportunities for men decreases the returns from specialization (i.e., division of labor) within the family. Consequently, deterioration in the employment prospects for men should result in an increase in the proportion of female-headed families.

Wilson (1987) provides additional explanations for why the relationship between male employment and family structure may be especially strong for blacks. He links marriageability of black males to joblessness by defining the male marriageable pool index (MMPI) as the ratio of employed men to women of the same age and race. This measure is "intended to reveal the marriage market conditions facing women, on the assumption that to be marriageable a man needs to be employed." (p. 95) In our model we define an MMPI for 20 through 34 year old blacks (B-MMPI) and another for whites in the same age group (W-MMPI). The marriageable pool indexes, thus computed, are presented in Table A-1 in the Appendix for each of the cities in our sample. There is significant variability in the index across the 99 metropolitan areas in our sample and the index for whites is much greater, on average, than for blacks (81.4 percent vs. 56.6 percent).

On the basis of both Becker's and Wilson's theories, we hypothesize that the MMPI will be inversely related to the incidence of female-headed households. That is, the coefficients α_1 and β_1 are expected to be negative. Also, an implication of Wilson's work on the underclass, is that α_1 should be more negative than β_1. This is because marriageability of jobless black males should be decreased further by participation in urban underclasses. Jobless white males, on the other hand, will be more geographically diffused and consequently less likely to be exposed to the further debilitating effects of contact with "underclass" environments.

Employment Opportunities for Women

From his economic analysis of trends in family structure, Becker concludes that one of the most important determinants of the increased incidence of female-headed families (%FHEAD) has been secular improvement in the employment opportunities of women (see, Becker 1981, pp. 245–47). Wilson would agree, but argues that improvements in employment opportunities for women may have been more important in explaining trends in white family structure than black family structure where the rate of joblessness of black men appears to be the most important determinant. (see, Wilson 1987, pp. 83–84).

Our proxy for the employment opportunities of women is the percentage of the 20 through 34 year old female population which is employed in the SMSA, shown as %FEMEMP in equations 1 and 2. We hypothesize that %FEMEMP will be directly related to %FHEAD (i.e., $\alpha_2 > 0$ and $\beta_2 > 0$).

Public Assistance

To determine the extent that the average level of welfare support effects family structure across SMSAs, we include the average level of welfare support (AID) in the model. Following Becker, we expect a direct relationship between AID and the %FHEAD for both black and white populations. We also expect the effect to be stronger for blacks than for whites since a larger percentage of the black population is impoverished and eligible for welfare support. In terms of equations 1 and 2, α_6 should be more negative than β_6.

Control Variables

The remaining three variables in our model—DUR% GOV% and EM-PCHANGE—are included to control for factors on the demand side of local labor markets which could effect family structure. The first two are measures of the industrial structure of the local economy.[1] The third is a measure of the growth of total employment in an SMSA over time. It is included to capture the effects of the long term economic health of a community on family structure after taking into account job opportunities for men and women at a point in time as well as the overall structure of employment across industries. Our proxy for the economic health of the community is the percentage change in total SMSA employment between 1970 and 1980 (EMPCHANGE).

IV. Results

Table 3 presents the results of the regression analysis of %FHEAD as specified in equations 1 and 2. In general, they support the hypotheses suggested by Becker's theory of the family. Also, an examination of the absolute values of the coefficients reveals that black family structure is far more responsive to differences across metropolitan areas in economic characteristics. For example, black families respond more than white families to economic opportunities facing men and women (MMPI and %FEMEMP), to the level of welfare support (AID), to differences in industrial structure (DUR% and GOV%), and to long term economic growth of metropolitan areas (EMPCHANGE).

In support of both Becker and Wilson is the finding of an inverse relationship between the marriageable male pool index (MMPI) and %FHEAD. This finding is consistent with inferences drawn from Becker's argument that marriage is less likely when the employment and earnings of men decrease because of fewer opportunities for specialization, and also consistent with Wilson's argument that marriage is less likely when employment of men decrease because joblessness of males decreases their attractiveness as marriage partners.

Further support for Wilson is the finding that $\alpha_1 > \beta_1$, which indicates that black family structure is more responsive to changes in their MMPI than is white

---

1. Previous research on Mid-West SMSAs found that the higher the level of durable goods manufacturing in the SMSA, the more favorable the relative income position of black families compared to white families (Seeborg, 1990). One reason to expect DUR% to be inversely related to %FHEAD is that entry level jobs in manufacturing often offer higher wages than entry level jobs in other industries. This would increase the marriageability of males who hold these jobs and decrease the incidence of female-headed families (i.e., $\alpha_3 < 0$ and $\beta_3 < 0$).

It is more difficult to hypothesize the effect that high levels of government employment (GOV%) will have on family structure. First, government employment tends to be female dominated. Perhaps by increasing employment opportunities for women, a high level of government employment will increase %FHEAD. But this is not likely to be reflected much in the coefficient to GOV% since we have already included a direct measure of employment of women (%FEMEMP) in the model. Second, government employment tends to be more stable and consequently males employed by the government may be considered more marriageable. If, as we expect, the second explanation dominates there would be a negative relationship between the level of government employment and %FHEAD (i.e. $\alpha_4 < 0$ and $\beta_4 < 0$).

Table 3: Regression of Percent Female-Headed by Race
(t Statistics in Parentheses)

Variable	White %FHEAD	Variable	Black %FHEAD
W-MMPI	−0.122 (−3.56)**	B-MMPI	−0.345 (−5.59)**
W-%FEMEMP	0.072 (2.63)**	B-%FEMEMP	0.223 (2.75)**
W-DUR%	−0.04 (−1.78)*	B-DUR%	−0.074 (−1.33)
W-GOV%	−0.064 (−2.11)**	B-GOV%	−0.258 (−3.79)**
EMPCHANGE	−0.0107 (−2.41)**	EMPCHANGE	−0.0503 (−3.22)**
AID	0.00127 (3.20)**	AID	0.00286 (2.32)**
CONSTANT	15.72	CONSTANT	47.62
Sample	99		99
R-squared	0.32		0.46

** indicates significance at the 5 percent level.
 * indicates significance at the 10 percent level.

family structure. This is consistent with Wilson's theory that, in many black communities, joblessness of young black males leads to the formation of "underclasses". Where underclasses develop, higher incidences of criminal activity, drug abuse, and teen pregnancy are observed along with higher high school drop out rates. These developments reinforce the adverse effects of joblessness on family structure. Since joblessness of white males is typically more diffused, underclass social pathologies are less likely to develop.

These results are stronger than those derived from a time series study by Hess (1990) which included MMPI, and several other control variables in an analysis of the percentage of female-headed families for several age-race cohorts between 1968 and 1984. His estimates were very sensitive to model specification and not always consistent across cohorts. We suspect that multicollinearity could account for at least some of the econometric difficulties encountered in this study. Other cross-sectional studies (e.g., Sampson, 1987) have found strong effects of MMPI on family structure, but generally are subject to the criticism that they did not control, in a parallel way, for the employment opportunities available to women. Our analysis gives equal treatment to female employment by including %FEMEMP in equations 1 and 2 along with MMPI.

Hypothesis 2 also finds support in our results. There is a direct relationship between the proxy for employment opportunities for women (%FEMEMP) and the incidence of female-headed families. This supports Becker's hypothesis that better employment opportunities for women reduce the gains from marriage; single women may have an economic incentive to delay marriage and married women may be in a better economic position to end bad marriages. It is interesting to

Table 4: Means and Coefficients by Race

Variable	White Mean	Black Mean	White Coef.	Black Coef.
MMPI	81.4	56.6	−0.122	−0.345
%FEMEMP	63.5	59.4	0.072	0.223
AID	N/A	N/A	0.00127	0.00286

note that black family structure is about 3 times as sensitive as white family structure to changes in female employment.

The third hypothesis also receives support. Our measure of welfare support (AID) is directly related to %FHEAD for both black and white families. Also, as expected, black family structure is more responsive than that of white families to changes in AID.

Regarding the control variables, we found that cities with higher levels of employment in durable goods producing industries (%DUR) and higher levels of employment in government (%GOV) tended to have lower %FHEAD. Also, employment growth in the metropolitan area (EMPCHANGE) is inversely related to %FHEAD.

V. Implications and Concluding Thoughts

An important implication of the above results is that changes in employment of men and women may have profound effects on family structure. Consider Table 4, which presents coefficients and mean values for the key variables in our analysis.

An examination of the marriageable male pool index (MMPI) shows that blacks have a much lower mean MMPI and a much more negative coefficient than whites. Consider the effects of a public policy which increases the demand for black male labor. If the policy were successful in raising the black MMPI to the same level as the white MMPI (from 56.6% to 81.4%), black %FHEAD would decline by about 8.6 percentage points. This is computed by multiplying the difference in black and white mean MMPI times the coefficient to MMPI in the black regression equation.[2]

But this is not the entire story. It is possible that the same policy would effect the magnitude of the black MMPI coefficient. We argued earlier that increases in black male joblessness could have an indirect effect on %FHEAD by adding to the underclass. Social pathologies associated with the underclass further decreases the marriageability of those who have fallen into it. Because residential segregation in-

---

2. The procedure used in this paragraph and those which follow amounts to a partial decomposition analysis of two regression equations. The work is patterned after the that of Blinder (1973) and Oaxaca (1973). Their purpose was to separate wage differentials into a component which is due to differences in endowments (i.e., differences in means) and a component which is due to differences in discrimination (i.e., differences in coefficients). Our purpose is limited to explaining the effects of black/white differences in the means and coefficients of three variables (MMPI, %FEMEMP and AID) on black/white differences in %FHEAD.

creases the likelihood that jobless black males will find themselves in underclass activity, black family structure is more responsive to changes in joblessness as measured by MMPI. If this is the case, public policy to reduce joblessness among black males will also reduce the underclass and, in terms of our model, make the coefficient to black-MMPI closer in value to the coefficient to white-MMPI.

To simulate the effect that this has on family structure, assume that the difference between the black and white coefficients is reduced by 50 percent via an increase in the black coefficient from −.345 to −.233. The reduction in black %FHEAD from the change in the black coefficient is then computed as the change in coefficient times the white mean MMPI (i.e., .112 times 81.4). The result is a 9.1 percentage point reduction in black %FHEAD.

In sum, the estimated effect of eliminating differences in mean MMPIs between whites and blacks is the combination of the direct effect (8.6 percentage points) and the indirect effect that the reductions in black male joblessness has via changes in coefficients (9.1 percentage points). The total effect is a 17.7 percentage point reduction in black %FHEAD. Therefore, under the assumptions of our simulation, policies to equalize black and white male MMPIs would reduce the 26.3 percentage point differential in %FHEAD between black and white populations to 8.6 percentage points.

Although equalization of employment rates of white and black males would have a large impact on narrowing the gap between white and black %FHEAD, policies which decrease the employment differentials between white and black females have quite different effects. Consider again the means and coefficients presented in Table 4. The average black female employment to population ratio expressed in percentage terms (%FEMEMP) is 4.1 percentage points less than white %FEMEMP. If black %FEMEMP were raised to the white level, and the coefficients did not change, the percentage of black families headed by women would increase by .91 percentage points (.223 times 4.1). If public policy also had the effect of reducing the difference in black and white coefficients by 50 percent, the percentage of families headed by black women would decrease by about 4.8 percentage points. The total effect of this simulation is a 3.9 percentage point decrease in the incidence of female-headed households.

Therefore, equalization of black and white female employment rates would have a much smaller effect on the total black/white differences in family structure. We have identified three reasons: first, the difference in employment rates is not large; second, the responsiveness of black family structure to a unit change in %FEMEMP is less than the responsiveness of black family structure to a unit change in MMPI; and third, the effect of increasing the mean level of black %FEMEMP on family structure is offset by the effect of reductions in the magnitude of the coefficient to black %FEMEMP.

Our results also indicate that policy to change the level of welfare support (AID) in a SMSA can effect family structure. For example, if the average level of AID in an SMSA were increased by $500 (from $2380 to $2880), the incidence of black female-headed households would increase by 1.1 percentage points and the incidence of white female-headed households would increase by 0.36 percentage points. This moderate, but significant effect is consistent with other empirical work (Danziger, et. al., 1982; Ellwood & Bain, 1985). In a review of the literature, Ellwood and Crane (1990) point out that it appears that changes in welfare support have the most impact on young single mothers as they decide whether to live with their parents or to live independently as a female-headed family unit. Levels of support appear to have much less impact on divorce and separation rates of older women.

Overall, the results are quite consistent with the theory of the family posited by Gary Becker (1981). Family structure changes in predictable ways to changes in economic opportunities facing men and women. Increases in the employment opportunities for men (i.e., increases in B-MMPI) leads to *reductions* in the incidence of female-headed families for whites and blacks, while increases in the employment opportunities for women (i.e., increases in %FEMEMP) leads to *increases* in the incidence of female-headed families for both groups. Also, nonwork income in the form of welfare assistance for female-headed families has its predicted effect even though this effect is not very strong.

The most remarkable set of findings, however, are in support of Wilson's theory of the underclass. Black family structure is much more responsive to the joblessness of black males (B-MMPI) than white family structure is to joblessness of white males (W-MMPI). Our simulations show that high rates of black male joblessness is a major factor in accounting for racial differences in the incidence of female-headed families. If true, the most effective way of reducing the incidence of female-headed black families is to pursue policies to expand job opportunities for black men.

Appendix A

The Data Base and Adjustments of Nominal Values

The data base used in this study is Standard Metropolitan Area (SMSA) level data primarily from the 1980 census (U.S. Bureau of the Census, 1983, Chapters C and D). Included in our sample are 99 SMSAs in the continental United States which met all of the following criteria:

1. A total population of at least 250,000;
2. A black population of at least 3,000;
3. No more than 20 percent of the black population enrolled in colleges and universities.

The last criterion is designed to eliminate from the sample those SMSAs which have a large black transient student population whose labor market participation patterns and family structure are unrepresentative of the black population. Only Madison, Wisconsin, which has 22 percent of its black population enrolled in college, was eliminated from the sample because of the college enrollment criterion.

There are four SMSAs which met the above criteria which were excluded from the sample because comparable boundaries were not available for 1970 and 1980. Therefore, it was not possible to compute the employment change variable (EMPCHANGE) used in this study. These SMSAs are Lakeland, Daytona Beach, Long Beach and New Brunswick. For all other SMSAs, we were able to match counties in the SMSA in 1980 with the same counties in 1970 (U.S. Bureau of the Census, 1973). Therefore, the employment change data are based on the same geographic areas.

Table A-1: Summary Statistics

SMSA	%BFHEAD	%WFHEAD	BMMPI	WMMPI
AKRON	39.4	11.2	47.0	80.8
ALBANY	42.7	13.0	60.6	78.4
ANAHEIM	21.3	12.3	97.8	88.6
ANN ARBOR	35.8	11.3	51.1	75.8
ATLANTA	39.0	10.7	59.4	85.1
AUGUSTA	34.3	11.2	55.1	73.7
AUSTIN	32.5	10.5	65.7	83.3
BALTIMORE	42.2	11.5	52.5	82.9
BATON ROUGE	33.5	9.1	61.8	86.7
BEAUMONT	28.8	8.1	63.3	91.9
BIRMINGHAM	34.7	9.9	56.8	84.7
BOSTON	44.9	14.8	56.4	78.4
BRIDGEPORT	44.4	13.2	56.0	84.1
BUFFALO	47.2	12.6	40.8	76.9
CHARLESTON	32.9	9.8	59.4	71.2
CHARLOTTE	37.7	10.7	57.0	76.3
CHATTANOOGA	39.1	10.9	52.8	81.1
CHICAGO	41.7	11.3	48.0	85.8
CINCINNATI	40.4	11.5	51.4	83.1
CLEVELAND	37.9	11.4	50.6	84.7
COLUMBIA	32.6	10.9	57.4	79.8
COLUMBUS, OHIO	38.7	12.1	59.6	81.3
DALLAS	34.7	10.2	66.2	89.3
DAYTON	38.6	10.6	45.6	77.3
DENVER	32.7	11.3	77.1	87.0
DETROIT	40.8	11.8	43.3	79.5
FLINT	41.4	12.4	46.5	73.5
FORT LAUDERDALE	34.8	9.7	66.4	88.5
FORT WAYNE	40.2	10.0	50.2	83.0
FRESNO	38.7	11.9	49.9	81.4
GARY-HAMMOND	37.0	10.3	51.6	85.3
GRAND RAPIDS	45.4	10.4	50.5	84.6
GREENSBORO	36.5	10.3	59.7	84.6
GREENVILLE	35.8	10.0	65.3	94.0
HARRISBURG	41.1	10.1	52.1	83.5
HARTFORD	41.6	11.5	58.8	85.0
HOUSTON	29.5	9.2	73.1	96.5
HUNTSVILLE	31.8	10.4	54.5	80.1
INDIANAPOLIS	37.4	11.0	55.8	82.8
JACKSON	34.3	10.0	58.4	81.0
JACKSONVILLE	40.1	12.0	53.3	77.7
JERSEY CITY	46.3	18.9	47.1	80.8
KANSAS CITY	38.1	10.2	57.3	83.9
KNOXVILLE	39.0	11.6	55.6	81.3
LANSING	36.5	11.9	58.9	75.1
LAS VEGAS	35.1	12.2	64.1	83.0
LEXINGTON	41.4	11.8	51.9	79.6
LITTLE ROCK	37.5	11.1	58.2	78.3
LOS ANGELES	38.6	14.4	57.7	85.7
LOUISVILLE	41.9	12.5	53.8	82.0
MACON	36.9	10.6	53.6	78.8

Table A-1: Summary Statistics *continued*

SMSA	%BFHEAD	%WFHEAD	BMMPI	WMMPI
MEMPHIS	38.4	11.0	54.2	81.8
MIAMI	36.0	13.0	62.7	77.5
MILWAUKEE	49.6	10.9	50.6	86.1
MINNEAPOLIS	42.3	11.2	75.7	84.7
MOBILE	37.9	10.0	57.5	85.8
MONTGOMERY	37.1	10.0	53.1	78.1
NASHVILLE	37.7	10.8	59.3	82.5
NASSAU	31.4	9.8	55.1	80.9
NEW HAVEN	45.6	12.2	52.1	79.3
NEW ORLEANS	39.0	11.8	58.7	87.1
NEW YORK	43.7	14.9	47.3	77.5
NEWARK	41.6	11.4	50.8	83.4
NEWPORT NEWS	33.6	9.2	58.8	73.6
NORFOLK	36.8	11.7	54.7	69.4
OKLAHOMA CITY	34.0	10.6	63.7	84.7
OMAHA	43.5	11.5	51.7	76.6
ORLANDO	38.6	11.0	57.3	83.3
PATERSON	47.5	13.0	47.8	82.1
PENSACOLA	40.8	11.6	48.2	69.1
PHILADELPHIA	42.2	12.1	46.3	80.5
PHOENIX	29.4	10.8	73.4	84.0
PITTSBURGH	40.4	11.6	47.3	79.3
PORTLAND	35.1	12.1	74.4	83.4
RALEIGH	34.2	10.4	61.1	80.0
RICHMOND	35.7	10.8	58.8	83.7
RIVERSIDE	27.6	11.0	58.2	78.7
ROCHESTER	44.4	11.3	55.6	82.2
SACRAMENTO	35.4	13.4	51.6	73.4
SAN ANTONIO	30.7	13.6	44.8	72.5
SAN DIEGO	32.5	12.8	54.9	75.6
SAN FRANCISCO	38.7	12.8	55.9	83.8
SAN JOSE	27.2	12.6	84.4	88.2
SEATTLE	35.9	11.3	72.9	85.0
SHREVEPORT	35.1	10.0	59.2	79.9
SPRINGFIELD	44.4	13.9	50.1	77.9
ST. LOUIS	40.8	10.6	46.7	81.4
SYRACUSE	45.0	12.1	54.9	75.0
TACOMA	22.8	11.2	48.6	70.1
TAMPA	41.4	10.3	55.1	81.7
TOLEDO	40.1	11.2	44.8	77.2
TRENTON	44.1	12.2	46.4	80.9
TULSA	36.7	9.4	65.1	87.4
VALLEJO	27.0	10.5	49.7	74.0
WASHINGTON DC	35.6	10.8	60.0	80.8
WEST PALM BEACH	32.8	8.8	69.6	90.4
WICHITA	37.0	10.1	59.6	91.8
WILMINGTON	39.4	10.7	54.7	81.8
YOUNGSTOWN	35.0	11.0	42.6	79.0
Mean	37.6	11.3	56.6	81.4
Standard Deviation	5.2	1.5	9.0	5.1

To account for differences in the cost of living across SMSAs, nominal values of levels of welfare support (AID) were deflated by the Inter-City Cost of Living Index developed by the American Chamber of Commerce Researchers Association (ACCRA) for the second and third quarter of 1979 (1979, June; 1979, September). Since the index was only computed for 56 out of the 99 cities in our sample, it was necessary to estimate it for the remaining 43. This was achieved by estimating the following OLS regression for the 56 cities for which the ACCRA index existed:

$$INDEX = 99.04 + 0.0000029POP + 0.0696POPCHG - 4.98SOUTH$$
$$(6.32)(2.08)(-3.39)$$

Adjusted R^2 = .56 (t statistics are in parentheses).

This equation was then used to estimate the cost of living index for the 43 cities for which no index existed.

An advantage of the metropolitan area (SMSA) level data used in this study compared to neighborhood specific data used in other studies is that there is less likely to be serious biases caused by selective migration, a problem discussed in a survey article on black family structure by Ellwood and Crane (1990). If highly motivated blacks with high levels of educational attainment tend to migrate to middle and upper class suburban neighborhoods they would still be in our sample along with more economically disadvantaged populations which remain in segregated low-income central city neighborhoods. Our results, therefore, are more representative of the entire metropolitan population. The SMSAs included in our sample, along with summary statistics for each, are listed in Table A-1.

References

American Chamber of Commerce Research Association (ACCRA) (1979, June). *Intercity Cost of Living Indicators, Second Quarter 1979*. Indianapolis, Indiana: ACCRA.

American Chamber of Commerce Research Association (ACCRA) (1979, September). *Intercity Cost of Living Indicators, Third Quarter 1979*. Indianapolis, Indiana: ACCRA.

Bane, M. J. (1986). Household Composition and Poverty: Which Comes First? In *Fighting Poverty. What Works and What Doesn't,* edited by S. Danziger, and D. Weinberg. Cambridge: Harvard University Press.

Becker, G. S. (1981). *A Treatise on the Family,* Cambridge: Harvard University Press.

Blinder, A. S. (1973). Wage Discrimination: Reduced Form and Structural Estimates. *The Journal of Human Resources* 8: 436–55.

Danziger, S., G. Jakubson, S. Schwartz, and E. Smolensky (1982). Work and Welfare as Determinant of Female Poverty and Household Headship. *The Quarterly Journal of Economics* 98: 519–534.

Ellwood, D.T., and M. J. Bane (1985). The Impact of AFDC on Family Structure and Living Arrangements. In *Research in Labor Economics* Vol. 7, edited by R.G. Ehrenberg. Greenwich, Connecticut: JAI Press.

Ellwood, D. T., and J. Crane (1990). Family Change Among Black Americans: What Do We Know. *Journal of Economic Perspectives* 4: 65–84.

Hess, S. C. (1990). The Effect of Employment and Welfare on Family Structure: Explaining the Time Trend of Female-Headed Families. *The American Economist* 34: 76–82.

Ihlanfeldt, K. R. and D.L. Sjoquist (1990). Job Accessibility and Racial Differences in Youth Employment Rates. *American Economic Review* 80: 267–276.

Kain, J. F. (1968). Housing Segregation, Negro Employment and Metropolitan Decentralization. *Quarterly Journal of Economics* 82: 175–197.

Kasarda, J. D. (1985). Urban Change and Minority Opportunities. In *The New Urban Reality*, Edited by P.E. Peterson, Washington, D.C.: Brooking Institution.

Murray, C. (1984). *Losing Ground: American Social Policy: 1950–1980.* New York: Basic Books.

Oaxaca, R. (1973). Male-Female Wage Differentials in Urban Labor Markets. *The International Economic Review* 14: 693–709.

Sampson, R.J. (1987). Urban Black Violence: The Effect of Male Joblessness and Family Disruption. *American Journal of Sociology* 93: 348–382.

Seeborg, M.C. (1990). The Effect of Industrial Structure on Black-White Family Income Differentials. *Eastern Economic Journal* 16: 41–48.

U.S. Bureau of the Census (1973). *1970 Census of the Population: Characteristics of the Population* Vol. 1.

U.S. Bureau of the Census (1983). *1980 Census of the Population: General Social and Economic Characteristics* Vol. 1, Chapter C.

U.S. Bureau of the Census (1983). *1980 Census of the Population: Detailed Population Characteristics* Vol. 1, Chapter D.

US. Bureau of the Census (1990). *Statistical Abstract of the United States: 1990,* 110th ed.

Wilson, W. J. (1987). *The Truly Disadvantaged.* Chicago: Chicago University Press.

Wilson, W. J. and K. M. Neckerman (1986). Poverty and Family Structure: The Widening Gap between Evidence and Public Policy Issues, in *Fighting Poverty. What Works and What Doesn't,* edited by S. Danziger and D. Weinberg. Cambridge: Harvard University Press, 1986, pp. 232–259.

Section X

Theology and Liberation

31

The Effects of Religious Messages on Racial Identity and System Blame Among African Americans

Laura A. Reese
Ronald Brown

The relationship between race and political participation has been a critical issue in political research for several decades. Studies have examined connections between race and voting behavior (see for example Babchuk and Thompson, 1962; Verba and Nie, 1972), race and other forms of participation (Verba and Nie, 1972; Shingles, 1981; Ellison and Gay, 1989), race and self-esteem, efficacy and trust (Shingles, 1981), and race, group identity and political participation (Verba, Ashmed and Bhatt, 1971; Verba and Nie, 1972). More recent work has combined a number of these approaches to develop and test models of political behavior and participation (Miller et al., 1981; Allen, Dawson, and Brown, 1989). While large and complex, this literature has posited conclusions about political participation without significant attention to the demographic, psychological, and organizational interrelationships which ultimately lead to differing forms and levels of political participation.

This research examines the relationships between racial consciousness or identity, system blame, and religiosity for African Americans, with a particular focus on the effects of church-based education and activism on racial group consciousness. While other researchers have focused on the political impacts of religion (Morris, 1984; Brown and Jackson, 1988; Allen, Dawson, and Brown, 1989), few have separated the effects of religiosity and the messages and activities promoted by religious organizations. This is an important deficit since religion has and continues to significantly influence American civic culture. Further, while past research has focused on participation among African Americans and the impact of racial identity, even complex analyses such as that presented by Allen, Dawson,

This research was supported by Eastern Michigan University. The authors would like to thank Professor Joseph Ohren for helpful comments and editorial assistance, and Professors David Fasenfest and John Strate for statistical advice.

An earlier version of this essay appeared in *Journal of Politics;* 1995, 57, 1, February, 24–43 and is adapted/reprinted with the permission of the copyright holder/author.

and Brown (1989) have failed to fully specify the connections between various aspects of racial consciousness. The focus on system blame as the dependent variable here allows a more careful consideration of these connections and introduces religious messages into the equation.

Literature Review

While research has addressed race, racial consciousness, church activity and participation, each project has tended to examine only some of the issues. Racial differences appear to be critical in understanding political behavior. Indeed, a recent summary of the literature finds that being African-American impacts protest behavior, attitudes about civil rights, identification with the Democratic party, voting in presidential and congressional elections, and cynicism about government (Peterson and Somit, 1992). Further, African Americans appear to have a unique racial consciousness and belief system (Miller et al., 1981; Robinson, 1987), and blacks and whites have differing "world views," with African Americans still overwhelmingly liberal and Democratic (Brady and Sniderman, 1985; Verba and Orren, 1985; Dawson, 1986).

Research on black political participation has identified racial identity or consciousness as an important explanatory factor. Miller and his colleagues (1981) provide one of the most complete analyses of the operation of racial consciousness. Building on the work of Verba and Nie (1972) and Miller, Gurin, and Gurin (1978), they posit an interactive model of the effects of racial identity. Four components of a system of group consciousness are identified: group identification, a sense of having shared interests with other members of a group; polar affect, a preference for one's own group over other groups; polar power, a dissatisfaction with the relative power position of one's group; and system blame, a belief that the responsibility for the group's status lies in the economic or governmental rather than the personal realm. In the model, group consciousness occurs through the following process; individuals realize that they are members of a particular group, prefer that group over others, notice that their group is disadvantaged, and look to government for redress. The ultimate outcome is increased political participation. African Americans, through greater group consciousness, are prone to higher levels of participation, even controlling for socio-economic status (SES).

Other authors have found similar relationships using different measures and combinations of variables. For example, Shingles (1981) examines the impact of efficacy and trust on black political participation with explicit attention to both allegiant and non-conventional activities. He concludes that racial consciousness accounts completely for internal efficacy differences between poor blacks and whites. Disadvantaged blacks are more efficacious than expected due to race consciousness, with system blame operating as a critical element. While important in linking trust and efficacy, Shingles' work is not as refined in its use of racial consciousness in that it does not include the intermediate stages present in Miller and associate's work.

Peterson and Somit (1992) also address the impact of racial consciousness and conclude that racial consciousness explains alienation from the political system but not political participation. Rather, political empowerment appears to have the most significant impact on political participation. The measures of group consciousness employed, however, more closely resemble Miller's definition of power imbalance, making the connection to alienation more reasonable.

Further refinements were added by the work of Allen, Dawson, and Brown (1989) in constructing a schema of an African-American racial belief system. They suggest that religiosity is a central determinant of racial consciousness or a racial belief system, with those who are more religious showing greater feelings of closeness to other blacks. Religiosity did not appear to be connected to feelings of black autonomy, however. These researchers did not examine the various elements of race consciousness defined by Miller et al.; instead, they employed only measures of closeness to other group members. Further, the components of the black autonomy index appear to be more reflective of polar effect than group identity (Miller et al., 1981, pg. 429).

Finally, little work has been done to date to differentiate various aspects of religiosity. Most research has considered such factors as how often one attends a place of worship or how important religion is perceived to be in an individual's life (Allen, Dawson, and Brown, 1989). Little attention has been given to the messages received, however. As Allen, Dawson, and Brown note, there is a "complexity of black religiosity." Indeed, Hunt and Hunt (1977) suggest that non-sectarian black churches may have the strongest impact on race consciousness and subsequent political participation. Similarly, Allen and colleagues (1989) suggest that this relationship should be stronger in black churches where liberation theology is stressed. Recent work by Brown and Wolford (1994) shows that exposure to political information at a place of worship is a strong correlate of electoral and protest-demand political activism.

In summary, the literature reflects several gaps in understanding the connections between race, racial consciousness, religion and political participation. Some treatments have carefully examined racial consciousness but have ignored ties to religion. Others have included religion but have not focused on the interdependencies of the elements of group consciousness. And, in attempting to move too quickly to the ultimate outcome, political participation, the critical element of system blame often gets lost. As noted by Gurin, Gurin, and Beattie (1969) and Gurin and Epps (1975), an individual's ability to "transfer responsibility" or blame for their life situation to the larger system is critical in enhancing self-esteem, efficacy, and self-confidence in trying to impact the system (Yancy, Rigsby, and McCarthy, 1972; Hulbary, 1975).

The effects of racial identity have been explored using several dependent variables: political participation, political preferences, support for a particular president, and intergroup conflict (Miller et al., 1981; Bobo, 1983; Dawson, 1986; Allen, Dawson, and Brown, 1989). However, system blame tends to precede such outcome variables since it plays a pivotal role in the decision to participate. Laying blame for life's problems or status on external forces and looking to government for redress is critical in determining feelings of personal efficacy, and ultimately, participation (Hulbary, 1975; Shingles, 1981; Miller, et al., 1981).

Given the necessary role system blame plays in political participation and finding that religiosity is a critical part of a racial belief system defining the position of the group vis-à-vis larger society, it becomes particularly important to more carefully examine the connections between religion and system blame. Does religiosity and/or the messages heard at a place of worship play a role in the development of feelings of system blame? How does religion compare to demographic variables in creating perceptions of system blame? The following section presents specific hypotheses regarding these relationships.

Hypotheses

The preceding analysis identified a number of variables important to understanding the political behavior of African Americans. This research focuses on the following factors: demographic characteristics, religion, racial consciousness, and system blame. These factors were selected because of their central role in the literature and because they have yet to be fully developed in a single model. Specific hypotheses to be tested are as follows:

H1: Religiosity is affected by demographic factors such as gender, age and income. Specifically it is expected that women will be more religious than men (Brown, Tate and Theoharris, 1990), that older blacks will be more religious than younger, and that African Americans with higher incomes will evidence lower levels of religiosity (Allen, Dawson, and Brown, 1989).

H2: Increased attendance at a place of worship will lead to greater incorporation of particular messages. Previous research has suggested that black churches socialize individuals to believe that they have a personal and collective obligation to improve the status of group members (McAdam, 1982; Morris, 1984; Branch, 1988). This socialization occurs through various distinct messages transmitted by the individual religious body. Those attending worship more frequently are more likely to report hearing two separate messages; information about upcoming elections or issues, i.e. civic awareness messages, and/or a more objectively political behavior message as candidates and political activities are brought into the place of worship. This differentiation of religious message is critical in that church attendance or religiosity alone has not uniformly been found to affect racial consciousness (Allen, Dawson, and Brown, 1989).

H3: African Americans hearing more political behavior and civic awareness messages at their place of worship will have higher levels of identity as belonging to a unique racial group (Cone, 1986; Dawson, 1986; Allen, Dawson, and Brown, 1989).

H4: Those with a stronger sense of group belonging or identity will feel closer to other members of minority groups than those with a lower sense of group identity (Allen, Dawson, and Brown, 1989).

H5: African Americans who feel close to other minority group members will also perceive a distance between their racial group and other racial groups (Miller, et al., 1981).

H6: Respondents perceiving a distance or separation between their group and other groups are also more likely to perceive a power imbalance between the groups (Miller, et al., 1981).

H7: A stronger perception of power imbalance between groups will lead to higher levels of system blame as individuals externalize the sources of the imbalance (Gurin, Miller, and Gurin, 1980; Miller, et al., 1981).

Figure 1. Hypothesized Model

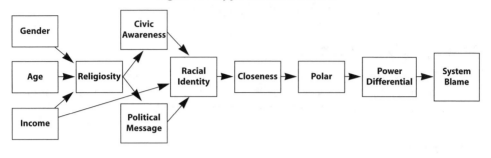

H8: Demographic factors such as gender, age, and income will also have direct affects on racial consciousness and system blame.

Since some of these relationships have proved conflicting or insignificant in past research, no *a priori* assumptions are made regarding direction of affects for hypothesis 8. Further research has been urged to more carefully examine the correlations between age, gender, and group consciousness for African Americans (Allen, Dawson, and Brown, 1989). It is expected here that the previously hypothesized relationships will hold even while controlling for demographic factors (Miller, et al., 1981). Figure 1 presents the model which would result if the proceeding hypotheses were to be supported. The possible affects of the demographic variables have been left out, however, to simplify the presentation. The hypotheses are now explained and tested and a model of system blame is developed.

Methodology and Variables

The hypotheses are tested using data from the 1984 National Black Election Study conducted by the Inter-University Consortium for Political and Social Research at the University of Michigan. The 1984 study comprised two waves of telephone surveys, prior to and after the 1984 presidential election. A total of 1150 respondents were included in the pre-election and 872 in the post-election waves. The response rate was 57% for the pre-election survey and 61.9% for the post-election group. While many of the same questions were asked in both waves, this was not the case for all variables. Post-election data were employed for this analysis since many of the variables of interest were only included in that wave.[1]

The variables are operationalized based on previous literature, with appropriate variation to accommodate specific survey questions. In most cases these variables are indexes of several survey questions combined through factor analysis

---

1. Post-election questions were used uniformly because the pre-election survey did not contain questions regarding closeness to other groups, political behavior messages, polar power, and power differential. Because most of the key variables of interest were contained only in the post-election wave all responses were taken from that survey to control for change in attitudes over time. Although this reduces sample size somewhat, the post-election sample is still sufficiently large for robust analysis.

(Appendix A presents the factor loadings and composite variables for the indexes).[2] The variables are operationalized as follows.

Demographic Variables

Three demographic variables were chosen for analysis. Age and gender were considered in order to refine their role in explaining political behavior among African Americans. Income was employed to represent SES.[3]

Religiosity

In past research, a single religiosity variable has been employed including such measures as numbers of religious books read, religious programs attended, requests for prayer, and how religious the respondent perceived him or herself to be (Allen, Dawson, and Brown, 1989). However, according to Wuthnow (1988), western Judeo-Christianity is a public religion which requires interaction among a collection of believers. Thus, this research includes how often the individual attends a place of worship, how important religion is to the individual, and how much guidance is provided by religion.

Religious Messages

Based on factor analysis two separate messages appear to be presented at places of worship for black Americans. The first is a *civic awareness* measure comprised of whether there is political discussion at the place of worship, whether the religious organization encouraged voting, and whether the respondent felt that the religious body should be involved in politics.

The second variable represents the extent to which *political activity* occurs at the place of worship. This includes whether the respondent attends political meetings at the place of worship, whether the religious organization took a collection to support a candidate, and whether other work for a candidate took place at the place of worship. Including these factors helps determine whether religiosity or attendance alone affects racial consciousness or political participation. In other words, attending worship may only be important in that it increases the likelihood of hearing certain messages or increasing exposure to specific activities.

Racial Identity

Based on the work of Miller et al. (1981), a separate variable was specified to measure group identification or identity, defined as being "a psychological feeling

---

2. For the factor analysis, the standard SPSS default modes were employed including varimax rotation, listwise deletion of missing data, and principle components analysis. A .50 or higher loading was the criteria employed for inclusion in a factor and no variable loaded on more than one factor. Factor scores were converted to f or standardized scores due to differences in measurement frame and added to create an index score.

3. Education was rejected as a demographic variable because of correlations between the demographic variables and because, when included individually, education had identical impacts to income. Similar findings are discussed in previous work (Peterson and Somit, 1992).

of belonging to a particular social stratum....and a sense of shared interest with those having the same stratum characteristics but not with those of other strata" (pg. 496). To create a racial group identity index two variables were combined; agreement that what happens to other blacks affects the individual, and agreement that the civil rights movement has directly affected the respondent.[4]

Closeness to Other Groups

As indicated, an important component of a racial belief or consciousness system is the feeling that one is close to other members of the group or similar groups (Miller et al., 1981; Allen, Dawson, and Brown, 1989). To measure this variable an index was created of responses to the following questions: how close do you feel to West Indians, blacks in Africa, and Hispanics?[5]

Polarity

The polarity variable is similar to that employed by Miller et al. (1981). It is designed to measure "a preference for members of one's own group and a *dislike* for those outside the group" (pg. 496). The questions included—blacks should only vote for black candidates, and blacks should not have anything to do with whites—are both clear measures of a desire for separation or distance between groups.[6]

---

4. These variables appear to more directly measure feelings of belonging to a particular group separate from perceptions of closeness to other groups than other measures previously employed. Miller et al. (1981) operationalized this identification through questions asking respondents how close they felt to 16 different groups. This is problematic in practice as a feeling of closeness to groups may be different or separate from a feeling of belonging to a particular group. In other research, Verba and Nie (1972) for example, open-ended questions were employed to determine the extent to which a respondent used race as an organizing principle in thinking about politics. In creating measures of a black belief system, Allen, Dawson, Brown (1989) employed two "closeness measures"—to black masses and black elites—and a separate measure of black autonomy. The principle of examining closeness and identity as distinct phenomena is well taken but the black autonomy index, as the title implies, does not really reflect racial identity. The component variables of support for study of black languages, voting for black candidates, shopping in black-owned stores, and the use of African names for children do represent an autonomy or distancing perspective which may be different than identifying oneself as part of a group. The two questions employed here directly measure feelings of belonging to a particular racial group and being connected to its struggles for civil rights. This corresponds to definitions of racial identity previously used in the literature.

5. A similar question relating to feelings of closeness to American blacks did not factor with this index. Thus, this index is measuring closeness to other groups which might have certain positional commonalities to the group with which the respondent identified. That these variables do not factor together is not surprising in light of research suggesting tension between African Americans and other minority groups such as Latinos (see for example essays in Browning, Marshall and Tabb, 1990). However, feelings of closeness to other blacks is significantly and positively correlated with the closeness index. The relationships between the other variables in the model were examined with closeness to blacks substituted for the closeness index. And, while more demographic variables predicted closeness to blacks, this variable performed no better in explaining system blame than did the closeness index.

6. This index was examined for possible "skewness" of responses which could affect later results. While respondents were unlikely to indicate that blacks should have nothing to do with

Power Differential

Miller and associate's work suggests that polar power differential, an "expressed satisfaction or dissatisfaction with the group's current status, power, or material resources in relation to that of the outgroup," is an outgrowth of perceptions of polarity ultimately leading to system blame (1981, pg. 496). Factor analysis for this research identified a power differential variable comprised of a question measuring whether blacks have too little influence in American life and politics and whether blacks should shop only in black-owned stores.[7]

System Blame

The final variable, system blame, is designed to measure the feeling that the disadvantaged position that some groups find themselves in is due to problems with society or the "system" rather than the individual. The specific question employed to indicate system blame was, "In the United States, if black people don't do well in life, is it because they don't work hard to get ahead or because they are kept back because of their race?"

Findings

Correlation analysis is employed to test the hypotheses and path analysis employed to identify an alternate model. The latter analysis is based on the assumption that error correlations for endogenous variables are zero, thus allowing the use of ordinary least squares regression to estimate path coefficients (beta weights). It is also assumed that random disturbances are not correlated with each other nor with exogenous variables.

Based on the analysis of bivariate correlations it was determined that the hypothesized model could be reduced and simplified. The following discussion examines the "best fitting" model, as presented in Figure 2, and is organized by endogenous variable. All relationships depicted were statistically significant at the .05 level in bivariate analysis.[8]

---

with whites (6% agreed/strongly agreed), the responses regarding voting only for black candidates were more balanced (18% agreed, 82% disagreed). Clearly the trend is away from strong polarity. However, this variable will be excluded from the final model.

7. To measure this concept Miller et al. (1981) employed two questions about the power of subordinate and dominant groups. Respondents were asked to indicate whether groups had "too much" or "too little" power. The question regarding shopping in black-owned stores was included in the index here since factor analysis indicated that it was measuring the same external concept as the question regarding black influence in American life. While questions about shopping in black-owned stores might be perceived as measuring polarity, i.e., a desire to shop only within the group, under present urban conditions it is more likely that it represents a desire toward action which might balance an existing power differential. The push in many urban areas to "shop at home" reflects less a desire for distance or polarity and more an attempt to strengthen and support the economic resources of the group which perceives itself to be disadvantaged in power status.

8. The residuals from the regressions were saved and correlated. Path residuals were significantly correlated only in the case of the paths going to the two religious messages (Pear-

Figure 2. Full Model

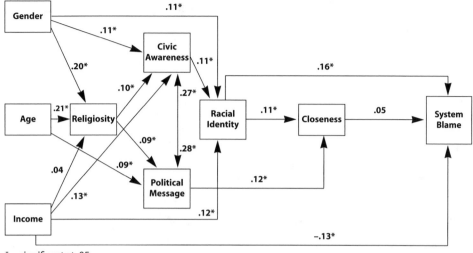

* = significant at .05

Religiosity

The religiosity variable operates essentially as hypothesized (see Figure 2). The demographic variables have direct impacts both on religiosity and the messages heard at the place of worship. Among African Americans, those most likely to attend religious services and see religion as important in their lives are older females with higher incomes. While the gender and age relationship is predictable, the positive correlation between income and religiosity contradicts previous research (Allen, Dawson, and Brown, 1989). However, while income was significantly correlated to religiosity in bivariate analysis, this was not the case in multiple regression (see Table 1). Thus, it appears that income is not related to religion when controlling for age and gender. Ultimately, the strongest predictor of religiosity is age, followed closely by gender, and the three variables together predict 30% of the variation in religiosity.

Religious Message

Gender is also directly related to civic awareness, with women hearing more messages promoting civic awareness at their place of worship. While this is due in part to more frequent attendance at services, it may also be that women are more likely to attend auxiliary functions, with independent effects. Church attendance and income are also predictors of civic awareness messages, with those attending a place of worship more frequently hearing more civic awareness messages as predicted. Thirty-five percent of the variation in civic awareness is explained.[9]

---

son correlation = .28). While this may tend to bias standard error estimates, Bohrnstedt and Carter (1971) suggest that unless the correlation is extreme the bias is not prohibitively serious.

9. The paths for both civic awareness and political messages were examined including both these variables. Thus the r^2 values for each path are probably inflated due to multi-

Table 1. Path Analysis Results

Variables	b	B	Significance
System Blame			
racial identity	.10	.12*	.00
power differential	.08	.10*	.01
r² = .17			
Power Differential			
racial identity	.18	.18*	.00
political message	.03	.04	.40
civic awareness	.11	.11*	.01
age	.01	.12*	.00
income	.04	.12*	.01
r² = .30			
Racial Identity			
gender	.22	.11*	.01
income	.06	.12*	.00
civic awareness	.10	.11*	.01
r² = .27			
Civic Awareness			
gender	.23	.11*	.01
religiosity	.12	.10*	.00
income	.04	.13*	.00
political message	.27	.27*	.00
r² = .35			
Political Message			
religiosity	.11	.09*	.01
age	.01	.09*	.02
civic awareness	.29	.28*	.00
r² = .32			
Religiosity			
gender	.42	.20*	.00
age	.01	.21*	.00
income	.01	.04	.30
r² = .30			

Note: b = regression coefficient; B = standardized regression coefficient (beta);
* = statistically significant at the .05 level.

Age is a direct predictor of political behavior messages received at the place of worship, with older African Americans more likely to hear behavioral messages. However, religiosity is also a predictor of such messages. Together these variables predict 32% of the variation in political behavior messages.

In summary, women and older African Americans are more likely to attend a place of worship, and are thus more likely to hear messages that promote civic awareness and be exposed to politics. These findings lend support to hypotheses 1 and 2.

---

collinearity. When the path to civic awareness messages was run without political messages, the resulting r² was .25; the r² value for the path to political message absent civic awareness was .19. It should also be noted that hearing political messages is the best predictor of civic awareness and vice versa, again reflecting their common roots.

Racial Identity

Civic awareness and political behavior messages, while driven by the same factors, appear to have slightly different affects on racial consciousness. Civic awareness messages tend to increase levels of racial identity as predicted. Civic awareness messages, because they are often more community-focused, may tend to promote greater identity with one's own group. However, being exposed to political activities at the place of worship does not promote feelings of belonging to a specific group.

Gender and income are both directly related to racial identity. Males tend to have higher levels of racial identity than females, and those with higher incomes are also more likely to have higher levels of racial identity. This confirms earlier findings on the affects of both gender (Gurin, Hatchett, and Jackson, 1989; Bledsoe, et al., 1994) and socioeconomic status (Jaynes and Williams, 1989). Both characteristics are significantly correlated even in multiple regression, with income the better predictor.

This also supports the finding that higher incomes lead to greater political and civic awareness and ultimately to increased racial identity (Allen, Dawson, and Brown, 1989). The researchers note that "...African Americans of different strata have different psychological orientations toward racial identity" (Allen, Dawson, and Brown, 1989, pg. 435). Thus, while higher social status may reduce feelings of polarity (Kilson, 1983), education and income increase awareness of black media and racial group accomplishments, hence promoting positive attitudes about the group and hence identity (Allen, Dawson, and Brown, 1989). All variables together explain 27% of the variation in racial identity.

Closeness to Other Groups/Polarity

Hypotheses 4 through 6 are not supported by the analysis. The closeness and polarity variables did not operate as expected and were excluded from Figure 2. While racial identity is significantly correlated to feelings of closeness to other groups, closeness is not related to either polarity or power differential.[10] Nor are polarity and power differential significantly related to each other. Thus, the sequence posited by Miller et al. (1981) and expected here, with racial identity producing feelings of closeness to other similar groups, then to a desire to be separate from groups which are not similar, and finally to a perception of power imbalances between these groups, was not supported by this analysis. This may reflect compositional differences in indexes used here and the fact that Miller et al. proposed a multiplicative model.

Power Differential

Hypothesis 7 is supported by the data. Respondents perceiving a greater power differential between their group and other groups are significantly more likely to blame systemic discrimination for failure to achieve life goals. Perception of power imbalance is significantly predicted by strong racial identity, the reception of civic awareness messages at a place of worship, higher income levels, and older

---

10. The single variable "closeness to blacks" was positively correlated to power. However, it was not related to polarity as suggested by Miller et al. (1981).

age in multiple regression. Thirty percent of the variation in perceptions of power imbalance can be explained by these variables with racial identity serving as the best predictor.

While it was expected that racial consciousness would affect perceptions of power differential, older African Americans with higher incomes are also more likely to perceive power differences. Further, exposure to civic awareness messages at religious events is also likely to increase feelings that power is different between groups. While political behavior messages at a place of worship significantly increase perceptions of power imbalance in bivariate correlation, the relationship was not significant in multiple regression.

System Blame

Racial identity directly influences system blame and indirectly increases blame through perceptions of group power imbalance. Thus, those with higher levels of racial consciousness and perceptions of power differential are more likely to blame the system for individual problems. Seventeen percent of the variation in system blame can be accounted for by racial identity and feelings of power imbalance, with racial identity the strongest predictor of system blame.

It appears that racial identity produces higher levels of system blame without being filtered through polarity. This partly reflects the influence of income on racial identity. Since higher status significantly increases identity but significantly decreases feelings of polarity, it is reasonable that perceptions about distance between groups are less critical to system blame than a recognition of power imbalance. Thus, it is the acknowledgement of power imbalance that leads those with stronger racial identity to place blame on the system rather than the individual. Further, recent research suggests that racial identity leads to increased feelings of racial victimization due to systemic discrimination (Bledsoe, et al., 1994).

Gender Differences

Since there appears to be gender differences in racial identity, attendance at a place of worship, and the concomitant messages received, the model was applied to males and females in separate path analyses. Figures 3 and 4 present modified models for each group. Gender-specific analysis is particularly important in this case since 61% of the sample is female.

The best-fitting model for black males (see Figure 3 and Table 2 for regression results) closely resembles the overall model, and accounts for 15% of the variation in system blame. Feelings of system blame are directly affected only by racial identity. Males who are more frequent churchgoers are more likely to hear both political and civic awareness messages and have higher levels of racial identity, and finally higher system blame. The path between politics and racial identity is not significant in multiple regression, however. The most significant variation from the full model is that perceptions of power differential between groups has no impact on system blame. Thus, African-American males develop feelings of system blame only through racial identification.

Figure 4 presents a somewhat different picture for black women. Racial identity does not appear to have the independent affects operating for men or for the sample as a whole (see Table 3 for regression results). Rather, higher feelings of

Figure 3. Males

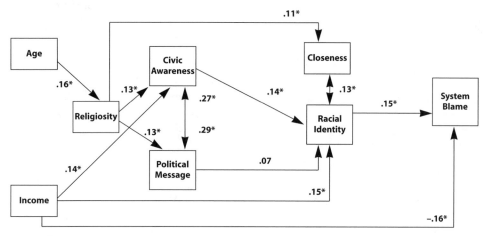

* = significant at .05

identity lead to greater perception of power differential and then to system blame. For women, age also directly affects system blame. Older women are more likely to blame the system for being disadvantaged in life, although this relationship was not significant in multiple regression. Overall the model predicts 16% of the variation in system blame for African-American women.

The impacts of religiosity and religious messages are different for women as well. While attendance at a place of worship leads to greater exposure to political and civic awareness messages, neither lead to racial identity for black women. Further, in multiple regression the paths between religiosity and political behavior and civic awareness messages are not significant. Thus, demographic factors such as income, in the case of awareness messages, and age, in the case of political exposure, are more important in predicting messages received. Thus, since questions specifically focused on receiving such messages at a place of worship, it is clear

Figure 4. Females

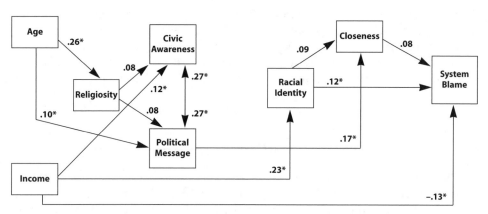

* = significant at .05

Table 2. Path Analysis Results—Males

Variables	b	B	Significance
System Blame			
racial identity	.16	.15*	.01
$r^2 = .15$			
Power Differential			
racial identity	.18	.18*	.00
political message	.03	.04	.40
civic awareness	.11	.11*	.01
age	.01	.12*	.00
income	.04	.12*	.01
$r^2 = .30$			
Racial Identity			
political message	.07	.07	.30
civic awareness	.13	.14*	.03
income	.04	.15*	.03
$r^2 = .25$			
Political Message			
religiosity	.13	.13*	.03
civic awareness	.27	.29*	.00
$r^2 = .33$			
Civic Awareness			
religiosity	.14	.13*	.04
income	.04	.14*	.03
political message	.28	.28*	.00
$r^2 = .36$			
Religiosity			
age	.01	.16*	.00
$r^2 = .16$			

Note: b = regression coefficient; B = standardized regression coefficient (beta);
        * = statistically significant at the .05 level.

that women are more likely to attend special events where such messages are presented, quite apart from the worship experience.

For women it appears that exposure to civic awareness messages at a place of worship increases perceptions of power differentials and, in turn, system blame. In short, the activist tenor of civic awareness messages appears extremely important for women, particularly in the formation of feelings of power imbalance among groups in society. Political behavior messages do not appear to be sufficient in politicizing black women. Rather, exposure to general civic awareness messages is necessary to establish a realization of imbalance which in turn heightens feelings of system blame.

Summary

With few exceptions, most hypotheses were supported in the analysis. Religiosity is affected by demographic factors, particularly gender and age, with female and older African Americans more religious. Two different messages appear to be presented at places of worship; one promoting civic awareness, the other political

Table 3. Path Analysis Results—Females

Variables	b	B	Significance
System Blame			
power differential	.11	.14*	.00
age	.003	.06*	.17
$r^2 = .16$			
Power Differential			
racial identity	.19	.19*	.00
civic awareness	.12	.12*	.00
age	.01	.12*	.00
income	.03	.12*	.00
$r^2 = .30$			
Racial Identity			
income	.07	.23*	.00
$r^2 = .23$			
Political Message			
age	.01	.10*	.04
religiosity	.10	.08*	.11
civic awareness	.28	.27*	.00
$r^2 = .32$			
Civic Awareness			
income	.04	.12*	.02
religiosity	.10	.08	.12
political message	.26	.27*	.00
$r^2 = .32$			
Religiosity			
age	.01	.26*	.00
$r^2 = .26$			

Note: b = regression coefficient; B = standardized regression coefficient (beta);
         * = statistically significant at the .05 level.

activity. Those that attend a place of worship more frequently are more likely to hear both messages. Greater exposure to civic awareness messages tends to produce higher levels of racial identity and greater sensitivity to power imbalances between racial groups. Finally, racial identity and perceptions of power differential affect system blame. Perceptions of group polarity or closeness to similar groups do not appear to be necessary factors in this process. While this finding conflicts with previous work—perhaps due to differences in the index or the data set employed—it obviously suggests the need for more careful analysis of the impact of religion and religious attendance on political participation.

Other interesting connections are also suggested. While income is not an important predictor of religiosity, it does have direct affects on both racial identity and perceptions of power differentials. Higher income African Americans are likely to have greater racial identity, producing perceptions of power imbalance and ultimately system blame.

The analysis also suggests different dynamics for men and women. Males are more likely to have higher levels of racial identity, leading to system blame. For women, no such direct relationship exists. For African-American women, perceptions of power imbalance are essential to feelings of system blame. These perceptions are heightened through three routes: higher income leading to stronger racial identity leading to power differential, directly from higher income to power differential, and higher income to increased civic awareness messages at a place of worship to power differential. Thus, while African-American males with greater racial identity are more likely to blame discrimination for life's problems, females must also feel that their group is disadvantaged relative to others.

Especially pertinent to this analysis is the significant role civic awareness messages at a place of worship play in developing a sense of power differential for African-American women. The broader world view and civic consciousness reflected in such messages are important to the development of perceptions about group placement in the power hierarchy and perceptions as to cause. And, because higher income directly increases both racial identity and perceptions of power differential, the role of civic awareness messages may be particularly critical for low income black women. Analysis of the model separately for male and female respondents supports the conclusion that different processes are at work and suggests the utility of further gender specific analyses. This reinforces the call by Allen and associates (1989) for research which more carefully addresses the effects of gender on political attitudes.

Finally, the analysis highlights the importance of considering religious messages separate from religiosity. Clearly, separate phenomena are at work. The fact that religiosity is related to racial identity and system blame only through the messages is telling. Future research should explore this connection more fully. While examination of different denominations might prove useful, such analysis should include variation within denominations as well. This research suggests that the messages presented in individual religious settings may be critical, and a more careful operationalization of religiosity is clearly in order.

References

Allen, R.L., M.C. Dawson, and R.E. Brown. 1989. "A Schema-based Approach to Modeling an African-American Racial Belief System." *American Political Science Review* 83:421–441.

Babchuk, N. and R.V. Thompson. 1962. "The Voluntary Association of Negroes." *American Sociological Review* 27:647–655.

Bledsoe, T., S. Welch, L. Sigleman, and M. Combs. 1994. "Suburbanization, Residential Integration, and Racial Solidarity Among African Americans." Presented at the annual meeting Midwest Political Science Association, Chicago.

Bobo, L. 1983. "Whites' Opposition to Busing: Symbolic Racism or Realistic Group Conflict?" *Journal of Personality and Social Psychology* 45:1196–1210.

Bohrnsted, G.W. and T.M. Carter. 1971. "Robustness In Regression Analysis." In *Sociological Methodology*, ed. H.L. Costner. San Francisco: Jossey-Bass.

Brady, H.E. and P.M. Sniderman. 1985. "Attitude Attribution: A Group Basis for Political Reasoning." *American Political Science Review* 79:1061–1078.

Branch, T. 1988. *Parting the Waters: America in the King Years 1954–63.* New York: Simon and Schuster.

Brown, R.E. and J.S. Jackson. 1988. "Church-based Political Participation." Eastern Michigan University. Typescript.

Brown, R.E., K. Tate, and J. Theoharris. 1990. "The Black Church, Religious Faith, and the Political Activism of Black Women." Presented at the Afro-American Religion and Politics Conference, Boston.

Brown, R.E., and M. Wolford. 1994. "Religious Resources and African-American Political Action." *National Political Science Review* 4:30–48.

Browning, R.P., D.R. Marshall, and D.H. Tabb. 1990. *Racial Politics in American Cities.* New York: Longman.

Cone, J.H. 1986. *Speaking the Truth: Ecumenism, Liberation, and Black Theology.* Grand Rapids: William B. Erdmans.

Dawson, M. 1986. *Class and the Formation of Afro-American Political Attitudes: 1972–1983.* Ph.D. diss. Harvard University.

Ellison, G.G. and D.A. Gay. 1989. "Black Political Participation Revisited: A Test of Compensatory, Ethnic Community, and Public Arena Models." *Social Science Quarterly* 70:101–119.

Gurin, P. and E. Epps. 1975. *Black Consciousness, Identity and Achievement.* New York: John Wiley.

Gurin, P., G. Gurin, and L.M. Beattie. 1969. "International-External Control in the Motivational Dynamics of Negroes." *Journal of Social Issues* 25:29–53.

Gurin, P., S. Hatchett, and J. Jackson. 1989. *Hope and Independence: Black's Response to Electoral and Party Politics.* New York: Russell Sage.

Gurin, P., A.H. Miller, and G. Gurin. 1980. "Stratum Identification and Consciousness." *Social Psychology Quarterly* 43:30–47.

Hulbary, W.E. 1975. "Race, Deprivation, and Adolescent Self-Images." *Social Science Quarterly* 56:105–114.

Hunt, L.L. and J.G. Hunt. 1977. "Black Religion as Both Opiate and Inspiration of Civil Rights Militance: Putting Marx's Data to the Test." *Social Forces* 56:1–14.

Jaynes, G.D. and R.M. Williams, Jr. 1989. *A Common Destiny: Blacks and American Society.* Washington, DC: National Academy Press.

Kilson, M. 1983. "The Black Bourgeois Revisited." *Dissent* 30:85–96.

McAdam, D. 1982. *Political Process and the Development of the Black Insurgency 1930–1970.* Chicago: University of Chicago Press.

Miller, A.H., P. Gurin, and G. Gurin. 1978. "Electoral Implications of Group Identification and Consciousness: The Reintroduction of a Concept." Presented at the annual meeting of the American Political Science Association, New York.

Miller, A.H., P. Gurin, G. Gurin, and O. Malanchuk. 1981. "Group Consciousness and Political Participation." *American Journal of Political Science* 25:494–511.

Morris, A.D. 1984. *The Origins of the Civil Rights Movement: Black Communities Organizing for Change.* New York: Free Press.

Peterson, S.A. and A. Somit. 1992. "The Political Behavior of American Blacks: A Research Note on Three Contending Theories." *Social Sciences Research Working Paper Series* 9:2–19.

Robinson, D. 1987. *The Effect of Group Identity Among Black Women on Group Consciousness.* Ph.D. diss. University of Michigan.

Shingles, R. 1981. "Black Consciousness and Political Participation: The Missing Link." *American Political Science Review* 75:76–91.

Tate, K., R.E. Brown, and S.J. Jackson. 1989. *The 1984 National Black Election Study Sourcebook.* Ann Arbor: Institute for Social Research.

Verba, S., B. Ashmed, and A. Bhatt. 1971. *Caste, Race and Politics.* Beverly Hills: Sage.

Verba, S., N.H. Nie. 1972. *Participation in America: Political Democracy and Social Equality.* New York: Harper & Row.

Verba, S. and G.R. Orren. 1985. *Equality in America: The View From the Top.* Cambridge: Harvard University Press.

Wuthnow, W. 1988. *The Restructuring of American Religion.* Princeton: Princeton University Press.

Yancy, W.L., L. Rigsby, and J.D. McCarthy. 1972. "Social Position and Self-Evaluation: The Relative Importance of Race." *American Journal of Sociology* 78:338–359.

32

Martin and Malcolm as Cultural Icons

Ralph W. Hood Jr.
Ronald J. Morris
Susan E. Hickman
P.J. Watson

A major theme in the studies of African-American religion is the extent to which religious participation is associated with particular forms of secular activities, especially militancy. For instance, Nelsen and Nelsen (1975) argued that church activity is directly related to militancy while sect activity is inversely related to militancy. Lincoln and Mamiya (1990) found empirical support for this claim insofar as among African-American churchgoers, those attending more church-like denominations such as Baptist and Methodist approved of civil rights activities while those attending the more sect-like Church of God in Christ were less likely to approve of civil rights activities. Similarly, Chaves and Higgins (1992) demonstrated that African-American churchgoers are not more likely to engage in secular activities in general, but only in certain types of secular activities such as civil rights.

These studies must be understood in the context of an established historical literature documenting the powerful role of African-American churches in the organization of community life and the support of secular social services for the Black community (Frazier, 1964/1974; Lincoln, 1974; McAdam, 1982; Morris, 1984; Wilcox & Gomez, 1990). In addition, the complex roles various African-American churches played and continue to play in the civil rights movement are a focus of continual debate.

While many have claimed that African-American religion serves to counter significant social militancy by essentially providing illusory escapist theologies (Marx, 1967), several investigators question what appears to be at best a generalization with little firm empirical support (Alexander, 1991; Jacobson, 1992).

Paper presented at the annual meeting of the Southeastern Psychological Association, New Orleans, Louisiana, March, 1994. An earlier version of this paper was presented at the Society for the Scientific Study of Religion, Raleigh, North Carolina, October, 1993. We wish to thank Ms. Bonnie Kelley for her extraordinary assistance in obtaining some of the participants for this study.

An earlier version of this essay appeared in *Review of Religious Research*; 1995, 36, 4, June, 382–388 and is adapted/reprinted with the permission of the copyright holder/author.

While the relationship between militancy and church participation remains an intriguing empirical question, little of this research has focused upon the role of the African-American minister in fostering secular activities, including civil rights activities. Even more impoverished is empirical literature on the image of African-American ministers and their differential perception among ethnic groups.

In particular, we are intrigued by what initially is more a guess than a hypothesis. It appears to us that in recent years, especially among alienated lower class African-American males, there has been a shift away from the acceptance of Martin Luther King, Jr., to a focus upon Malcolm X. This shift occurred much earlier among radical African Americans, but has been accentuated more recently to influence alienated African-American males whose explicit political knowledge may be minimal. Furthermore, among whites, knowledge of Malcolm X has been influenced by the recent media shifts in presentations and discussions of Malcolm X. We see cultural phenomena such as Spike Lee's film, "Malcolm X" and the inevitable commercialization of Malcolm X's image less as facilitating this turn than capitalizing upon it. Furthermore, we suspect that the turn to Malcolm X is motivated by what can be seen as some whites' cynical concern with civil rights and ethnic equality in which Martin Luther King, Jr., serves as a conservative cultural icon to placate otherwise militant tendencies among alienated African-Americans.

Briefly stated, we suspect many whites prefer that African-American males identify with Martin Luther King, Jr., rather than Malcolm X precisely because the former is likely to be perceived as more socially acceptable insofar as his message of nonviolence can be construed to mean nonaction. We suspect that alienated African-American males have seen through this cynical icon use of Martin Luther King, Jr., and have identified more with Malcolm X, the African-American leader largely ignored (when not vociferously condemned) by the white press. We hasten to emphasize that what might be cynical use of these cultural icons as well as their differential perception by different ethnic groups in no way argues for the reality or actual effectiveness of strategies and tactics adopted by these two African-American ministers.

Cone (1991) has provided a compelling comparative analysis of Martin and Malcolm in which their divergences and compatabilities are explored. In terms of social representations, facts yield to the image and to the myth makers (Keller, 1984; Marcuse, 1964). The switch from Martin's "I have a dream" image to Malcolm's "by any means necessary" image may be perceived as threatening to whites precisely to the extent that it is perceived as empowering African-Americans to militancy. Martin's nonviolence may be rejected by alienated African-American males insofar as it is perceived to foster a dream that mitigates militancy and serves the cynical interests of at least some whites in their desire to minimize the empowerment of African-Americans. Despite a national holiday, numerous boulevards, and schools across the nation named after Martin Luther King, Jr., few parallels exist for Malcolm X. We have admittedly painted a broad and speculative picture in need of numerous conceptual and empirical refinements. It is presented as the backdrop from which two specific hypotheses emerged.

The two specific hypotheses tested were: (1) both white and African-American males would rate MX as having significantly higher potentiality than MLK, Jr., and (2) these groups would differ in their evaluative ratings of these two leaders, with white males evaluating MX lower than MLK, Jr., We assume these differences to be driven more by affective and emotional responses than explicitly cognitive and ideological awareness. Thus, we tested our hypotheses by means of semantic differential ratings. The semantic differential is a widely accepted means by which to assess affective or connotative meanings and are not dependent upon cognitive or objective meanings (Osgood, Suci, & Tannenbaum, 1957).

Method

Our interest was in the semantic differential ratings of both Malcolm X and Martin Luther King, Jr., thus we first independently established the usefulness and reliability of our rating scales. For this purpose an independent sample of 104 volunteer undergraduate psychology students completed a semantic differential rating of "significant public and historical figures." Using standard instructions (Osgood et al., 1957; 82–84), participants rated a variety of historical (e.g., Jack Kennedy, Martin Luther King, Jr., Richard Nixon, and Malcolm X) and contemporary political figures (e.g., Bill Clinton, George Bush, Albert Gore, Dan Quayle). In addition, current nonpolitical figures were rated (e.g., Bill Cosby, Richard Pryor, and Robin Williams). The semantic differential is widely recognized to measure the subjective dimensions or meanings of responses to public figures (Osgood, Suci & Tannenbaum, 1957). Our use of the phrase *cultural icon* is meant to suggest this subjective reaction to public figures which is grounded less in explicit ideological terms that in the affectively shaded meanings such figures have for individuals. The semantic differential is designed to measure precisely such affectively shaded, connotative meanings.

Seven each of evaluative, activity, and potency words were utilized along with the same number of masking items. Scales were randomly presented and counterbalanced. Two figures, Bill Clinton and George Bush, were utilized to perform principal components factor analyses with oblique rotation. We simply wanted to confirm the value of using semantic differential technique to assess public figures. In particular, we wished to obtain at least two scales: one evaluative and the other dealing with potency, or power. A screen test was utilized to determine the number of factors.

For both ratings, two factors emerged. Factor 1 was clearly an evaluative factor consisting of nine items (e.g., kind/cruel, successful/unsuccessful). Factor 2 also consisted of nine items that were primarily a mixture of activity and potency items (e.g., weak/strong, active/passive). Since identical factors emerged for ratings of both Clinton and Bush, the relevance of both evaluative ratings (Factor 1) and potentiality ratings (Factor 2) of significant political figures seemed reasonable. Further refinement to maximize reliability produced two eight item scales: the evaluative scale with a reliability of .86 and the potentiality scale with a reliability of .82. These scales are presented in Table 1.

To obtain a sample of African-American lower class males and a comparison sample of lower class white males, various assistants were employed to obtain the relevant samples. The requirements of both samples were that all participants (a) be male; (b) have no education beyond high school; (c) be on some form of public assistance, including but not restricted to public housing, and (d) be either marginally employed or unemployed. This procedure was followed to permit the assumption of

Table 1. Evaluative and Potentiality Ratings Scale

Evaluative	Potentiality
1. kind/cruel	1. active/passive
2. positive/negative	2. ornate/plain
3. violent/gentle*	3. heavy/light
4. successful/unsuccessful	4. soft/hard*
5. timely/untimely	5. slow/fast*
6. foolish/wise*	6. feminine/masculine*
7. near/far	7. weak/strong*
8. harmonious/dissonant	8. calm/excitable*

* Indicate reversed scored item; a seven pt. format is used. Higher scores indicate greater evaluation or potentiality.

alienation from the social system and the practical rather than academic awareness of issues involved in social change. Eventually, matched samples of 53 African-American males and lower class white males were obtained. Average age was 18 in both samples.

Same-race interviewers presented all participants with the rating forms utilized in the first portion of this study as outlined above. This procedure successfully served to mask the central concern of this study which was to directly compare evaluative and potentiality ratings of Martin Luther King, Jr., and Malcolm X by lower class African-American and white males.

These data were collected over a period of several months. Further, all data were collected prior to the 1992 presidential election and prior to the release of the film "Malcolm X" in this region of the country. Participants generally completed their ratings individually, although some participants required assistance from the interviewer in order to complete the forms. Interviewers noted that most participants felt this study was about "the election." Few focused upon discussion of ratings for either Martin Luther King, Jr., or Malcolm X.

Results

Our hypothesis required a comparison between evaluative and potentiality ratings of Martin Luther King, Jr., and Malcolm X for both African-American and white lower class, alienated males. Relevant means and standard deviations are presented in Table 2.

The overall correlations between evaluative and potentiality ratings for each sample are only of marginal relevance to our hypotheses.[1] After obtaining a significant triple order interaction in a preliminary 2x2x2 analysis of variance [$F(1/104) = 16.64$; $p < .001$], separate 2x2 analyses of variance with one between

---

1. Among African-American males, the correlation between evaluative ratings for the MLK, Jr., and MX was .48 while the correlation for potentiality ratings was .31. The parallel correlations among white males were .20 and .36 respectively. Using the total sample (coding white male 1 and African-American male 0), the correlation between evaluative ratings for MLK was −.20 while it was −.81 for MX. The parallel correlations for potentiality ratings were −.15 for MLK, Jr., and .10 for MX.

Table 2. Evaluative and Potentiality Ratings of MLK, Jr., and MX by African American and White Males

	Evaluative Rating		Potentiality Rating	
	MLK, Jr.	MX	MLK, Jr.	MX
African-American Males				
Mean	36.19	44.66	33.02	46.17
SD	9.95	6.96	9.35	5.79
White Males				
Mean	32.13	24.87	30.49	47.28
SD	9.81	7.76	8.06	5.26

groups factor (race) and one repeated measures factor (person rated) were run to directly test our two specific hypotheses.

The first hypothesis, that both white and African-American males would rate MX higher on potentiality than MLK, Jr., was supported by the significant main effect for person rated [F (1/104) = 318.21; $p < .001$) and the lack of a main effect for race [F (1/104) = 0.38]. As predicted, both whites and African-American males saw Malcolm X as having greater potentiality than MLK, Jr. In addition, the interaction term was significant [$F(1/104) = 4.71$; $p < .05$]. While not specifically hypothesized, this interaction is consistent with our hypothesis in that whites tend to see the potentiality difference between MX and MLK, Jr., as even greater than African-American males see the same difference. Thus, in terms of the potentiality analysis of variance, both whites and African-American males rate MX as having much more potentiality than MLK, Jr., with whites seeing the difference between MLK, Jr., and MX as being even greater than do African-American males.

The second hypothesis was that African-American males would evaluate MX higher than MLK, Jr., while whites would evaluate MLK, Jr., higher than MX. This explicitly demands a significant interaction term which was obtained [$F(1/104) = 63.47$; $p < .001$]. The hypothesis is further supported by the finding that the main effect for person rated was not significant [$F(1/104) = .37$] but the main effect for race was [$F(1/104) = 75.06$; $p < .001$]. The latter main effect simply indicates that African-American males evaluate the two black leaders higher overall than do whites, a not surprising finding even though not one of our hypotheses.

Inspection of standard deviations in Table 2 for MX and MLK, Jr., across all ratings shows a strong tendency to have greater variability in assessments of MLK, Jr., than MX for both white and African-American males. Thus, whatever one's view, there is greater consistency in how MX is perceived than in how MLK, Jr., is viewed.

Discussion

These data clearly support the two specific hypotheses. First, both white and African-American males affectively rate MX higher on potentiality than MLK, Jr. This is as predicted. A bit surprising, but clearly consistent with our first hypothesis, is that whites and African-American males overall do not differ in their potentiality ratings. Both see MX as higher than MLK, Jr. However, whites' differential evaluation of MLK, Jr., and MX is greater than that of African-American males. This supports our hunch that white males have a sense of a greater difference in potentiality between MX and MLK, Jr., and indeed, this sense of difference exceeds in magnitude a similar difference perceived by African-American males.

The second hypothesis specifically requires an interaction to support the prediction that white males would evaluate MLK, Jr., higher than MX while the reverse would hold for African-American males. The data clearly supported this prediction. While African-American males evaluated both MX and MLK, Jr., higher than whites, the powerful interaction revealed that whites evaluated MLK, Jr., higher than MX while African-American males evaluated MX higher than MLK, Jr.

It is admittedly a large leap from demonstrating whites' evaluative preference for MLK, Jr., in light of their documented lower potentiality rating of this black leader relative to MX to the claim that this motivates them to prefer African-Americans to identify with MLK, Jr., over MX. This speculation was not tested by these data. Indeed, it may be that whites cannot evaluate MX as effectively as they can MLK, Jr., due to limited historical information regarding MX among lower class white males. Yet even if this were proven true, the powerful iconic effect of MX on primarily affective grounds is that he is high on potentiality, and this message apparently has gotten through to both African-American and white lower class males. This claim is consistent with the smaller variations in ratings of MX across all scales for both whites and African-Americans. Why the high potentiality rating of MX relative to MLK, Jr., for both groups leads to differential evaluations among these groups deserves further research.[2]

It is apparent that these data are quite robust. We have obtained correlations and effects in relatively small samples that are unlikely to be obtained in work with undergraduate psychology students. Whether these results are due to saliency of the issues studies, or to the nature of our samples, can only be determined by more refined empirical research.

References

Alexander, B. C. (1991) "Correcting Misinterpretations of Turner's Theory: An African American Pentecostal Illustration." *Journal for the Scientific Study of Religion* 30: 26–44.

Chaves, M. & L.M. Higgins (1992) "Comparing the Community Involvement of Black and White Congregations." *Journal for the Scientific Study of Religion* 31: 425–440.

Cone, J.H. (1991) *Martin & Malcolm & America*. Maryknoll, New York: Orbis Books.

Frazier, E. Franklin (1974) *The Negro Church In America*. New York: Schocken Books (Originally published 1964).

Jacobson, C.K. (1992) "Religiosity in a Black Community: An Examination of Secularization and Political Variables." *Review of Religious Research* 33: 215–228.

Keller, D. (1984) *Herbert Marcuse and the Crisis of Marxism*. Berkeley: University of California Press.

Lincoln, C.E. (1974) *The Black Church Since Frazier*. New York: Schocken Books.

---

2. Tests for homogeneity of related variance were all significant. For African American males the t value for potentiality was 3.16 ($p < .01$) and for evaluation it was 4.29 ($p < .001$). For white males the respective t values were 1.89 ($p < .05$) and 3.91 ($p < .001$).

Lincoln, C.E. & L.H. Mamiya (1990) *The Black Church in the African American Experience*. Durham: Duke University Press.

McAdam, D. (1982) *Political Process and the Development of Black Insurgency*. Chicago: University of Chicago Press.

Marcuse, H. (1964) *One-Dimensional Man*. Boston: Beacon Press.

Marx, G.T. (1967) "Religion: Opiate or Inspiration of Civil Rights Militancy Among Negroes." *American Sociological Review* 32: 64–72.

Morris, A. (1984) *The Origins of the Civil Rights Movement: Black Communities Organization for Change*. New York: Free Press.

Nelsen, H. & A.K. Nelsen (1975) *Black Church in the Sixties*. Lexington: University Press of Kentucky.

Osgood, C.E., G.J. Suci, & P.H. Tannenbaum (1957) *The Measurement of Meaning*. Urbana: University of Illinois Press.

Wilcox, C. & Gomez, L. (1990) "Religion, Group Identification, and Politics Among African American Blacks." *Sociological Analysis*, 51: 271–285.

Section XI

Political Identification and Political Strategies

33

Black and White Perceptions of Party Differences

James M. Glaser

Educationally, African Americans lag behind white Americans, reflecting a long history of segregation, discrimination, and institutional neglect. The deficit in education that blacks suffer from has numerous potential consequences in the political arena. For a variety of very direct reasons (and some not so direct), there is a strong relationship between education and most every aspect of political sophistication—political interest, knowledge, understanding, and participation.

Against this background, the political thinking and behavior of African Americans is distinctive. For despite the comparative disadvantage in education (and other resources that contribute to political sophistication), blacks do show signs of being a rather politically sophisticated group of people. They tend to participate in politics in numbers greater than one might expect given their socio-economic disadvantage (Verba and Nie, 1972, Wolfinger and Rosenstone, 1980). And, as I argue elsewhere with Michael Hagen (1992), while blacks lag behind whites on many measures of political sophistication, in certain circumstances, they do appear to be as knowledgeable, politically interested, and efficacious as whites. The reason, we argue more generally, is that blacks expend their relatively scarce political resources more efficiently and selectively than whites.[1] With less, they do more. The reason for this is that blacks are more sensitive to political context than whites, and spend their political energies where the payoffs are greatest. They thus appear more politically sophisticated than one might expect given the fact that they are, on the whole, younger, less educated, and less affluent than whites.

What is to follow is another example of the surprising political sophistication of blacks. One of the marks of a sophisticated voter is an understanding of what makes Democrats and Republicans different.[2] To the political sophisticate, poli-

---

An earlier version of this essay appeared in *Political Behavior*: 1995, 17, 2, June, 155–177 and is adapted/reprinted with the permission of the copyright holder/author.

1. A very large literature has developed on the meaning of the term *sophistication* as applied to politics and on the measurement of the concept (see Luskin, 1987 for an excellent summary of much of this literature). I do not wish to take part in that debate here and use the term simply to connote an involvement in and an understanding of politics.

2. By this statement, I mean politicians and party officials. While followers of the two parties may not diverge much in the positions they take on issues, party leaders often take starkly different issue positions and hold different ideological principles not all that well un-

tics is not just a bewildering muddle. It is a struggle between two distinct camps and the sophisticated citizen can distinguish between them. Various studies show that those with greater affluence, education, exposure to information, and cognitive ability are significantly better able to recognize partisan differences as well as the character of these differences (Campbell et al., 1960; Hamill et al., 1985; Luskin, 1985). And it is not just that political sophisticates see differences between the parties. As Sniderman, Glaser, and Griffin (1991) argue, those who best understand American politics tend to overstate these differences:

> This tendency to accentuate dissimilarities between candidates and parties seems to us the mark of the well-informed voter; indeed, it may not exaggerate to say that the mark of the person who understands American politics is precisely that he accentuates—that is, that he exaggerates—the differences between the parties and the candidates who represent them. (Sniderman, Glaser, and Griffin 1991, p. 175)

The point, of course, is that while accentuation may not necessarily be more accurate, it is of greater utility. It helps people figure political things out.

In this article, I compare blacks and whites in their perceptions of the two parties and argue that blacks, more than whites, have an accentuated view of the partisan landscape. Many appear to grasp an important aspect of American partisan politics despite a comparative disadvantage in education and all the benefits it affords the individual. Not only is this another example of the efficiency of black political thinking, but it is a possible explanation for some of the other such findings. If such efficiency stems from a greater sensitivity to political context, the claim here is that blacks may have a better read of that context, a more accessible map with which to approach politics, an aid or guide that many whites do not have. This map helps blacks compensate for their relative disadvantage in other political resources as both its racial and political elements can be of great utility in making political decisions. This article is an exercise in political cartography, an attempt to show how black and white maps, or at least some aspects of these maps, are different.

Data

The data for this exercise come from the National Election Studies,[3] conducted biennially since 1952. In several surveys, respondents are presented with an issue and two policy alternatives and asked to place themselves on a seven-point scale with regard to the issue. Those respondents who have an opinion on the issue then are asked to place various groups and politicians on the scale. Most of my analysis is based on attributions of issue positions to the Democratic Party and the Republican Party. Data from the 1980, 1982, 1984, 1986, 1988, and 1990

---

derstood by their constituents (McClosky, Hoffman, and O'Hara, 1960; Jackson, Brown, and Bositis, 1982; Verba and Orren, 1985).

3. The N.E.S. data used here were made available by the Inter-University Consortium of Political and Social Research. They were collected originally by the Center for Political Studies of the Institute for Social Research, the University of Michigan, under a grant from the National Science Foundation. Neither the original collectors of the data nor the Consortium bear any responsibility for the analysis or interpretations presented here.

surveys (the Reagan-Bush years) are pooled to bolster the number of respondents, which is particularly important in analyzing blacks, and to make statistically safe generalizations. I also examine estimates of the issue positions of other groups, such as whites and blacks, men and women, young and middle-aged people, and working class and middle-class people. These questions were included only in the 1972 and 1976 surveys, which are pooled here for analysis. Again only those who could answer the original self-placement question pass through the filter to the attribution questions. Black respondents are less likely to meet this criterion—a matter I take up below—but this fact is without consequence for the analysis to follow.

Differences between the Parties

I start by comparing blacks and whites in their general perceptions of partisan differences. Separate from the battery of attribution questions just described, respondents are asked if there are any "important differences in what the Republicans and Democrats stand for." As shown in Table 1, blacks are more likely than whites to believe that this is the case.[4] Sixty-one percent of whites and 66 percent of blacks answered that there were important partisan differences. While this difference may not seem very remarkable, the 95-percent confidence intervals do not overlap given the large number of respondents in each racial category.

More important, this difference exists despite the fact, noted above, that blacks lag behind whites in educational attainment.[5] And, as shown in Table 1, education has a profound impact on perceiving an important difference between the parties. Seventy-five percent of all college graduates see an important difference, while only 51 percent of those who did not graduate high school perceive such a difference. This makes the black-white gap all the more interesting. It is driven by the larger numbers of less educated blacks who perceive a difference in the parties. There is a 13-percentage-point difference between less-educated blacks and less-educated whites on this question.

This is but the first of a battery of questions. It is worth looking at the follow-up questions as well, for they ask the respondent to identify specifically some of the differences he perceives. Up to three responses to these open-ended questions are recorded by the N.E.S. Here, the racial difference is evened out a bit. Blacks are slightly more likely than whites not to name any specific differences and are slightly more likely to name just one difference. While 37 percent of blacks can name three important differences between the parties, 51 percent of whites can do so. Thus while blacks are more likely to perceive a difference between the parties, their list of differences is not as long as whites. This is certainly more consistent with expectations, given the comparative disadvantage blacks have in political re-

---

4. Non-white, non-black racial minorities are not included in this analysis or in any of the analyses to follow.

5. Whites are substantially more likely to have gotten a high school diploma or have attended more than 12 years of school (80 percent to 65 percent) and are almost twice as likely to have a college degree or to have attended more than 17 years of school (24 percent to 13 percent). These percentages are derived from the NES dataset analyzed throughout this article.

Table 1. Blacks Are More Likely to See a Difference Between the Parties

		All	Less Educ. (< high school)	Med Educ. (high sch. diploma+)	High Educ. (college degree+)

Do you think there are any important differences in what the Republicans and Democrats stand for? (cells represent percent of respondents who perceived a difference)

All		62%	51%	59%	75%
		(4656)	(925)	(2569)	(1127)
Whites		61	49	59	75
		(4098)	(756)	(2268)	(1045)
Blacks		66	62	65	79
		(558)	(169)	(301)	(82)

What are these differences? (up to three responses were coded; cells represent percent of respondents listing a certain number of differences)

All	0	4%	7%	4%	1%
	1	13	22	13	9
	2	34	36	36	29
	3	49	35	48	61
		(2866)	(475)	(1523)	(847)
Whites	0	3%	7%	4%	1%
	1	13	22	13	9
	2	33	36	34	28
	3	51	36	49	62
		(2497)	(371)	(1326)	(782)
Blacks	0	5%	7%	6%	2%
	1	17	25	14	11
	2	42	38	43	45
	3	37	30	38	43
		(369)	(104)	(197)	(65)

Source: N.E.S. 1980–1990 (pooled)

sources. Still, what is most intriguing here is that the broad general idea that the parties represent different alternatives has clearly penetrated black public opinion *even though* blacks have fewer specifics supporting this idea.

This tendency of blacks to see a general difference between the parties also translates into a propensity to see larger differences between the parties when it comes to specific issues. Four sets of questions are analyzed here, three on specific issues, the fourth on a measure of general ideology. One set of questions, dealing with whether the government should help minorities (point 1 on the scale) or whether individuals should help themselves (point 7 on the scale), has an obvious racial connection. The other two sets of issue questions—one asking whether the government should guarantee jobs and a decent standard of living or let people get ahead on their own, the other asking whether the government should cut spending or should increase and enhance services—round out the set.[6]

---

6. Only four domestic issues were used consistently by the N.E.S. in this battery of questions. The fourth, dealing with equal rights for women is analyzed later in this paper in a different context. See the Appendix for question wording.

Figure 1. Blacks Perceive Larger Partisan Differences on Issues

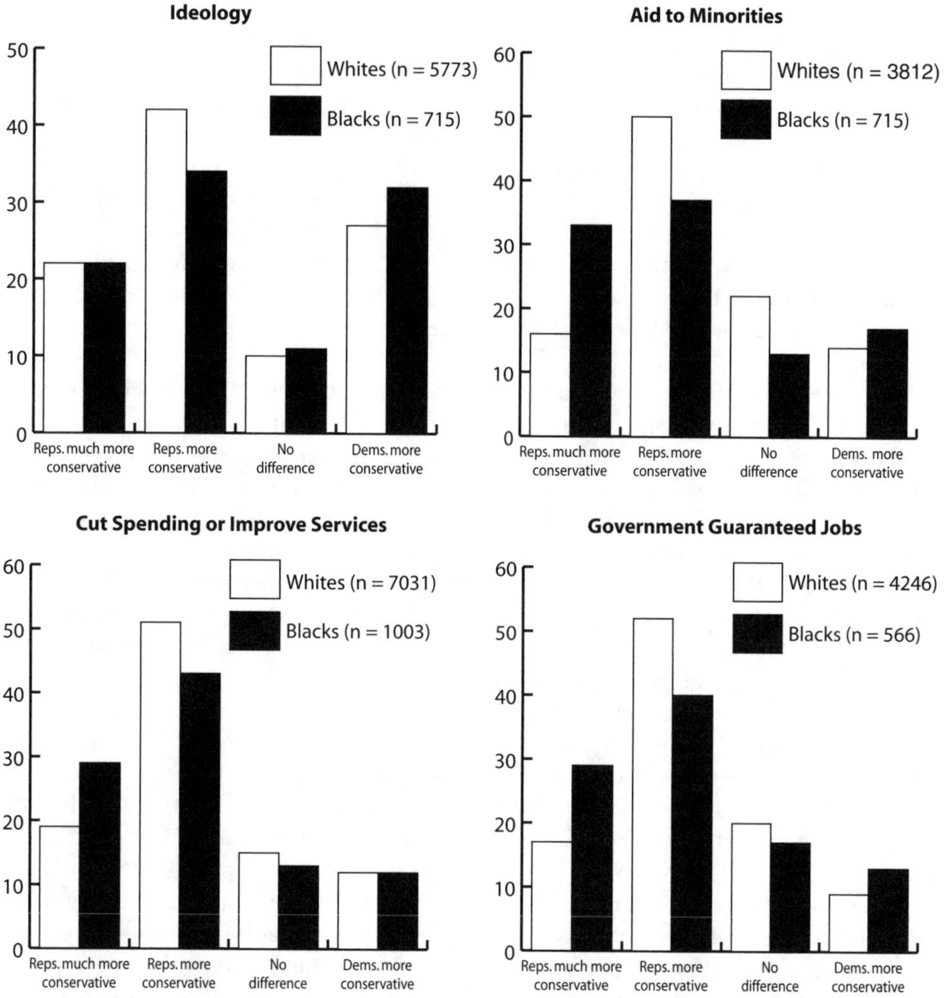

Note: Vertical scale measures the percent seeing various relationships between the Democratic Party and the Republican Party on an issue. All data come from the National Elections Studies, 1980–1990 (pooled).

On each of the issues in Figure 1, respondents are classified into one of four categories: those who saw the Democrats as more conservative (placing the Democrats at a more conservative point on the issue scale than the Republicans), those who saw no difference between the parties on the issue (placing both parties at the same point on the scale), those who saw the Republicans as the more conservative party but did not see a large difference between the parties on the issue (placing the Republicans at a more conservative point on the scale, but placing the Democrats less than four points away), and those who viewed the Republicans as considerably more conservative on the issue (seeing a four- to six-point difference between the parties). People who did not express their own opinion on the issue are not included in this analysis as they were not asked to place the parties on the scale. Respondents who did not place both of the parties on the scale also are filtered out. Thus the denominator for each of the bars in Figure 1 is the number of respondents who are able to place both parties on the scale on the issue.

On the three issues (excluding general ideology) the pattern is essentially the same. Blacks are considerably more likely than whites to perceive a large difference (in the correct direction) between the two parties. On the aid to minorities question, for example, twice as many blacks as whites perceive a large difference between the parties (32 versus 16 percent), while whites are more likely to perceive a modest difference between the parties or to see no difference at all. There is hardly any racial difference in the percentage of people who perceive the Democrats to be less sympathetic to minorities. On the other two (non-racial) questions, this is the pattern as well: blacks are much more likely to perceive a large difference between the parties and whites are more likely to perceive a smaller difference.

Only on the question of general ideology is this pattern broken. Here blacks are equally likely to perceive a large difference and eight percentage points less likely to perceive a modest difference while they are more likely to see no difference or a difference the other way, the Democrats being more conservative. It is likely that this divergence from the pattern is simply the result of some general confusion about the terms associated with ideology (Converse, 1964; Conover and Feldman, 1981). And while the other questions provide some guidance in their preamble and are more specific in their alternatives, this question requires an understanding of abstractions. It is here that the advantage whites have in education and other political resources reveals itself.

What accounts for this tendency of blacks to see more dramatic partisan differences than whites? Several alternatives come to mind. One possible explanation for these results is that blacks are more likely to be filtered out of the analysis from the start (thus generating misleading racial differences). It is true that blacks are more likely not to have their own opinion on all four items. But the differences on the three issues are minimal (three to six percentage points), and only on the question of ideology is there a significant racial difference. While 30 percent of whites cannot place themselves on the seven-point ideological self-placement scale, this is the case for 47 percent of blacks. Others purged from the analysis are those who can place themselves on the issue or ideological self-placement scales but cannot place one or both of the parties on the scale. On all four items, blacks are not more likely than whites to be eliminated from the analysis on this count. In the end, blacks are only slightly more likely to be filtered out of the analysis on three of the four items. Only on the fourth question, ideology, is there a significant racial difference in the percentage of people able to place both parties on the scales, and on this item, there is no difference in perceptions of the parties to explain in the first place. Including those eliminated from the analysis in the denominators of the percentages in Figure 1 does not change the racial differences I have reported. The general finding is not an artifact of how the battery of questions was prepared, and the racial differences on the three issues are genuine.

A General Propensity to Perceive Stark Differences?

Another possible explanation for the proclivity of blacks to see wider partisan differences than whites is that they are more inclined to see everything as more polarized. Perhaps these findings simply are the consequence of a more general tendency of blacks to see starker differences everywhere. If this is the case, it most certainly would show up when black and white respondents evaluate the positions of other groups—young people and middle-aged people, men and women, even blacks and whites—on other issues. I test this proposition with data from the 1972 and 1976 National Election Studies, where these groups were included as part of the battery of questions. In the 1980s, the N.E.S. dropped these questions from the instrument. Though the sample for this exercise is different and the analysis is covering a different time period, the results are enlightening and allow for an evaluation of the hypothesis (see Figure 2). The issues chosen for this test are equal rights for women, the adoption of a more progressive income tax (albeit in less technical terms), withdrawal from Vietnam (only asked in 1972), and once again, the question of government aid for minorities. I chose these issues because the battery of questions included attributions for groups that may be thought to take opposite sides of the issue.

In this analysis, blacks, in fact, are not consistently more likely to view these groups in polar terms. On the question of government aid to minorities, for example, respondents are asked to place the positions of most whites and most blacks on the seven-point scale. On the basis of these evaluations, whites are actually more likely than blacks to perceive a stark racial difference on the issue, 38 percent of whites versus 29 percent of blacks seeing a large gap. In fact, whites also are more likely to perceive a moderate racial gap while blacks are much more likely to perceive most blacks and most whites as holding the same position on the issue. On two other issues, there is little difference in how blacks and whites evaluate the issue positions of what might be considered opposing groups. On the question of withdrawal from Vietnam, whites are slightly more likely to perceive most young people and most middle-aged people as being far apart in their opinions. On the question of a more progressive income tax, blacks are only slightly more likely to perceive "most workingmen" and most middle-class people as being sharply opposed. Only in the attributions of men and women on the question of equal rights for women do significantly more blacks than whites perceive stark group differences, and this racial difference is about eight percentage points.

The question here is not whether blacks or whites are more accurate in their perceptions of different groups on different issues.[7] It is whether blacks tend to see the world through a more polarized lens than whites do. The results above lead one to reject this hypothesis with confidence. Blacks may be more likely than whites to perceive stark partisan differences but it cannot be because they tend to perceive everything that way.

---

7. See O'Gorman (1979) and Brady and Sniderman (1985) for analyses of the perceptual accuracy of group attributions such as these.

Figure 2. Blacks Are Not More Likely to View the World in Polar Terms

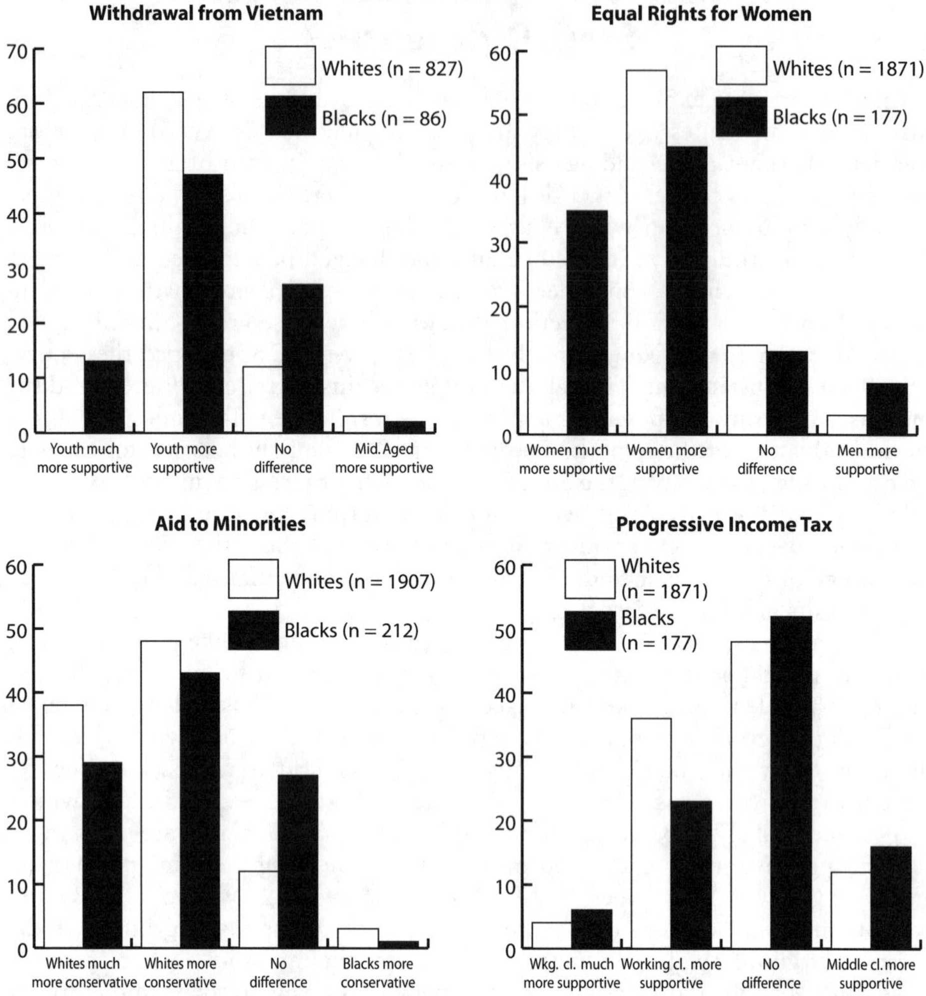

Note: Vertical scale measures the percent seeing various relationships between different groups on an issue. All data come from the National Elections Studies, 1972, 1976 (pooled).

Race, Education, and the Perception of Partisan Differences

So how is that blacks have a more distinct view of the partisan system, a mark of political sophistication, when they hold fewer of the resources that lead to greater sophistication? For one thing, while blacks have fewer of the resources that aid one in understanding and participating in politics, these resources appear to matter less for blacks than for whites. Education, for instance, makes a big difference in perceiving partisan differences on the various issues under investigation here. Well-educated people tend to have a more distinct picture of the political system and to understand the basic philosophies of the parties. This enables them to better reason downward on issues and they are better able to point to where

Table 2. Education Matters More for Whites in Perceiving a Gap

	Aid to Minorities		Government Guaranteed Jobs		Ideology		Cut Spending or Improve Services	
	Whites	Blacks	Whites	Blacks	Whites	Blacks	Whites	Blacks
Low Educ.	1.76	2.88	1.72	2.85	1.97	2.12	1.22	2.21
	(378)	(97)	(462)	(117)	(533)	(97)	(849)	(217)
Med Educ.	1.89	2.96	1.84	2.54	2.36	2.39	1.65	2.22
	(1901)	(254)	(2188)	(297)	(2345)	(281)	(3310)	(494)
High Educ.	2.43	2.78	2.43	2.52	2.83	2.99	2.53	2.89
	(981)	(58)	(1175)	(67)	(355)	(96)	(1831)	(146)
All	2.04	2.91	2.01	2.61	2.46	2.46	1.86	2.33
	(3260)	(409)	(3825)	(481)	(4233)	(474)	(5990)	(857)

Note: Cells represent mean partisan gap perceived on the issue. Those who perceive the Democrats as more conservative on the issue are not included in this average.

the parties stand.[8] This is true for blacks and for whites. But in a most interesting twist, and one that sheds some light on the basic phenomenon being discussed here, education has much more of an effect on whites than on blacks in perceiving more dramatic partisan differences.

In Table 2, I break down the original racial differences in partisan perception by education to illustrate the point. Here I present the average perceived gap for the entire black and white sample before breaking down the sample by education. It should be noted that only those people who perceive the Republicans as more conservative or who perceive no difference between the parties are included in this analysis. This is because it is not clear how people who perceive the Democrats to be the more conservative party on an issue should be categorized. Should someone who perceives the Democrats to be much more conservative than the Republicans (six points more conservative, for instance) be coded as a '6' or a '–6'? Are they most like people who see the Republicans as much more conservative or most different from them? Both perceive large partisan differences, though in opposite directions. Moreover, given that 80–90 percent of those who are able to attribute positions to both parties (on the three issues) see the Republicans as the more conservative party or see no difference between the parties, and given that blacks are only slightly more likely to perceive the Democrats as more conservative, removing those who perceive the Democrats as more conservative from the analysis does not distort the substantive findings here.

On the question of whether or not the government should aid minorities or whether they should help themselves, the average partisan difference perceived by whites is 2.04; for blacks it is 2.91. Controlling this relationship by education enhances this original difference, particularly in the less-educated categories. Among those blacks who did not attain a high school diploma, the average perceived gap

---

8. One assumption running here is that seeing starker differences between the parties is somehow correct. It would be foolish not to acknowledge that the astute political observer might take into account the nuances and exceptions that muddy the differences between the parties. Still, as noted above, on issues like those discussed in this paper, Democratic and Republican elites really do stand quite far apart.

between the parties is 2.88, about what it is for the black sample as a whole. The average perceived difference for less-educated whites is 1.76. Compare this racial difference of 1.12 with the racial difference among the well educated. Well-educated whites perceive an average gap of 2.43. The mean gap for well-educated blacks is 2.78, only a slightly larger gap than perceived by whites. This pattern repeats itself on the guaranteed jobs and government spending batteries of questions (though not on the ideology battery).

There are two conclusions to be derived from this exercise. First, education makes a big difference for whites, but not for blacks. Blacks at all levels of education perceive a large difference between the parties on specific issues. In some cases, those blacks with less education perceive the largest partisan differences. Second, it is less educated blacks who are driving the original relationship. The major reason for the original difference in partisan perceptions is that less educated blacks (those who have not attended college) have acquired the idea that the parties represent quite different choices. Something associated with more sophisticated citizenship, seeing party positions with greater clarity, has percolated through the entire black community.

Testing Other Explanations for Racial Differences

Other variables also should be considered in evaluating the original racial differences observed here. To test some alternatives, I have conducted two ordinary least squares regression analyses on the three issues discussed above. In the first equation, I regress perceived partisan difference on race.[9] In the second, I regress perceived partisan difference on race and several other important independent variables. The variables included in the multivariate equation are two dummy education variables (one measuring the impact of a high school degree or more than 12 years of school, the other the impact of a college degree or at least 17 years of school), region of residence, strength of partisanship, and the intensity of one's own opinion on the issue. I also include interaction terms of race with all these variables in an attempt to capture any additional effect they may have among blacks. The results, displayed in Table 3, show again that there is something quite distinctive about black political thinking.

It is no surprise in the bivariate case that race has a strong and significant effect on perceiving a difference between the parties. This effect is strongest on the minorities question, but it is quite powerful in the other two cases as well. The multivariate findings also parallel the findings in Table 2. The coefficients associated with education are strong and statistically significant. In particular, the acquisition of at least some college experience leads one to be much more likely to maximize perceived party differences on the issues. As discussed above, college education is associated (for direct and indirect reasons) with a more sophisticated understanding of American politics and this finding simply confirms this. The in-

---

9. As in Table 2, and for the same reasons, I eliminate those who perceive the Democrats as more conservative than the Republicans from the analysis.

**Table 3. Accounting for Some of the Racial Difference in
Perceiving Partisan Differences**
(Unstandardized O.L.S. Regression Coefficients)

	b	SE(b)	b	SE(b)
Aid to Minorities				
Race	.87	(.08)*	.44	(.31)
High School			.18	(.09)**
College			.72	(.10)*
South			.09	(.06)
Issue Strength			.16	(.03)*
Partisan Strength			.21	(.03)*
Race x High School			− .04	(.21)
Race x College			− .78	(.28)*
Race x South			− .88	(.17)*
Race x Issue Strength			.19	(.07)*
Race x Partisan Strength			.28	(.09)*
Constant	2.04	(.03)*	1.12	(.11)*
R^2	.03		.10	
n	3686		3630	
Government Guaranteed Jobs				
Race	.61	(.08)*	.20	(.29)
High School			.20	(.08)*
College			.78	(.09)*
South			.00	(.06)
Issue Strength			.22	(.02)*
Partisan Strength			.25	(.03)*
Race x High School			− .36	(.19)
Race x College			− .86	(.26)*
Race x South			− .74	(.16)*
Race x Issue Strength			.13	(.07)
Race x Partisan Strength			.35	(.09)*
Constant	2.01	(.03)*	.87	(.10)*
R^2	.01		.10	
n	4339		4297	
Cut Spending or Improve Services				
Race	.46	(.06)*	.35	(.23)
High School			.26	(.07)*
College			.80	(.07)*
South			−.05	(.05)
Issue Strength			.17	(.02)*
Partisan Strength			.28	(.02)*
Race x High School			− .21	(.15)
Race x College			− .50	(.19)*
Race x South			− .62	(.12)*
Race x Issue Strength			.04	(.05)
Race x Partisan Strength			.23	(.07)*
Constant	2.17	(.02)*	1.07	(.08)*
R^2	.01		.09	
n	6939		6657	

*p < .01 **p < .05

teraction coefficients capturing the additional effect of education for blacks are also consistent with the findings of the previous table for they are negative and achieve statistical significance. Education, particularly post-secondary education, makes much less of a difference for blacks than whites, even when the relationship is evaluated in the context of several important controls.

Region of residence is introduced into the equation for obvious reasons. The key here is to control for a different reality. As southern Democrats (politicians and partisans) are considerably more conservative than their northern brethren, placing the parties on an issue scale is likely to be a somewhat trickier business in the South. This is not to say that the parties cannot be differentiated. Southern Republican politicians and activists also are more conservative than northern Republicans and certainly southern Democrats (Glaser, 1996; Moreland, Steed and Baker, 1988), making the parties distinguishable but moving the political spectrum a couple of notches to the right. Nonetheless, given that in recent memory, southern Democrats epitomized conservatism and southern Republicans hardly existed, there is likely to be less certainty in attributing positions to the parties in the South. This makes it important to take account of region in evaluating the original racial difference.

Surprisingly, the coefficient associated with southern residence does not achieve statistical significance in any of the three equations and, in fact, there seems to be no pattern to its effect. The expected pattern does appear, though, with the interactions' terms. The effect of being from the South for blacks is significantly negative, southern blacks being much less likely to see differentiation between the parties than northern blacks, all else the same. Why this is the case for blacks but not whites is unclear. But coupled with the fact that southern blacks comprise half of all blacks while southern whites only comprise one quarter of all whites, the original racial relationship is suppressed. In other words, blacks overall perceive more difference between the parties than whites despite the fact that a much larger percentage of blacks than whites are from the South, where partisan murkiness lessens the likelihood of southern blacks drawing starker party differences.

This makes the other two controls (and their sibling interaction effects) even more important. How strongly one feels about an issue is likely to have some bearing on how one perceives the parties on that issue. Actually, one can envision two very different possibilities here. Those who feel strongly about an issue may perceive that neither party satisfies them completely, leading them to place both the Democrats and the Republicans closer to the middle. Or these individuals may bring the party that is more inclined to support their position closer to them and "push" the other party away, thus creating a larger perceived partisan gap. To test these alternatives, I have folded the seven-point self-placement variables over to create four-point control variables whereby those who hold strong positions on either side of the issue are grouped together at "3" while those who are middle of the road on the issue are coded at "0." An interaction term also is added to the regression equation to test whether strength of position has an additional impact on blacks that it does not have on whites.

My analysis clearly supports the latter hypothesis that stronger opinions lead to perceptions of starker partisan differences. On all three issues, the stronger one's opinion on an issue, the larger the partisan difference one is likely to perceive on that issue. This effect is even stronger for blacks than it is for whites, particularly on the question of aiding minorities, where the interaction term yields a large and statistically significant coefficient. To illustrate, whites taking a very strong stand on this issue (putting themselves at 1 or 7 on the scale) see a partisan difference that is a bit less than one-half of a point larger than whites taking a middle-of-the-road position on it, all else the same.[10] For blacks, taking a strong stand as opposed to a moderate stand has more than twice the impact that it has for whites (increasing the perceived partisan difference by about one point). On the guaranteed jobs question and the government spending question, the strength of one's issue position again has an important impact on the size of the perceived partisan gap though it does not appear to have a much larger impact for blacks than it does for whites. In both instances, the coefficients associated with the interaction terms are small (though positive) and statistically insignificant. Holding a stronger opinion on an issue clearly leads one to perceive more differentiation between the parties on that issue. When that issue has a racial connection, moreover, blacks are likely to perceive even starker differences.

Certainly the fact that blacks are more strongly partisan than whites also might have some bearing on the racial difference in partisan perceptions. Forty-three percent of blacks identify strongly with a party (most, obviously, with the Democrats), while 27 percent of whites identify themselves as a strong partisan. One might argue that being very supportive of a party might lead one to exaggerate the differences between one's favored party and the opposition, to draw a more severe picture of these differences. This is in fact the case.[11] People who are more attached to a party do see larger differences between the parties, as the coefficient associated with partisan strength is positive and achieves statistical significance in each of the three multivariate equations.[12] For blacks, on all three issues, this effect is even more accentuated and considerably so. The coefficients for all three interactions are large and easily achieve significance. On the question of government guaranteed jobs, for example, white strong partisans perceive a partisan difference that is .75 larger than the gap perceived by white independents. For blacks, the effect is more than twice that, the difference in perceived differences at 1.80. While blacks are more partisan than whites, this is only part of the reason they perceive larger Democratic–Republican differences. Being a strong partisan carries more information for blacks than for whites.

One other possible explanation for blacks seeing larger partisan differences than whites is that they have some sort of racial consciousness. The idea here would be that an individual's very conscious identification with blacks as a group

---

10. The maximum possible perceived difference is six points.

11. Alternatively, one might argue that perceiving more vivid partisan differences leads to a stronger attachment to one of the parties or at least that the line of causality may run both ways. This is probably true though some rudimentary empirical evidence suggests that partisan identification is the more likely independent variable. In these situations, Rosenberg (1968) advises looking at the "fixity or alterability of the variables" (p. 11). Logically, the more stable attitude or property is more likely to generate change in the less stable attitude or property than vice versa. Using panel data from the National Election Studies, I correlate partisanship in 1990 with partisanship in 1992 and party perceptions on the government spending issue in 1990 with such perceptions in 1992. Partisanship was clearly the more stable attitude, correlating at .78, while party perceptions correlated at .17.

12. In the regression equations in Table 3, the party identification strength variable, as above, is created by folding the party identification variable so that pure independents are the base category, independent leaners, Democrat and Republican, are coded "1," weak partisans "2," and strong partisans "3."

would lead to greater awareness of party differences in answering the question, "Who's best for us?" Greater awareness of party differences would, in turn, lead to a stronger expression of these differences on the survey items.

Testing for this as an explanation of black–white differences is tricky as the variable for black consciousness is so highly correlated with race–not that all blacks identify with blacks but hardly any whites do. I therefore just look at blacks and regress party placements on black consciousness, education (again measured with two dummy variables), strength of party identification, strength of one's stand on the issue, and region (Table 4). The measure for black consciousness is created by putting together a variable measuring identification with blacks as a group with a variable tapping comparative affect toward blacks and whites (a thermometer score for blacks minus a thermometer score for whites).[13] While not a perfect measure of the concept, it does capture its most important elements.[14]

Black consciousness does lead people to accentuate party differences in all three cases. Those blacks more strongly racially identified do perceive the parties to be further apart, though only on the aid to minorities issue does the coefficient associated with racial consciousness achieve significance at the .01 level. On that issue, not surprisingly, there is a very clear connection between being racially conscious and holding a picture of starker party positions. Scoring a '1' instead of a '0' on the racial consciousness scale leads one to stretch the perceptual distance between the parties over one point, quite dramatic when the maximum perceived distance is six points.

Given that only blacks are being analyzed in this equation, the education coefficients fail to reach statistical significance and are very small substantively. This brings back the question: Why do less-educated blacks view this aspect of the political world much like better-educated blacks? I introduce interaction terms to the equation in Table 4, interactions combining the two education dummies with the other independent variables, to begin to get at this puzzle. The coefficients for each of the original variables thus now represent the effect of that variable only for the least educated segment of the black sample. The coefficients for the two interactions represent the additional effect each variable has for that portion of the black sample with a high school degree (or more than 12 years of school) and that portion with a college degree (or more than 17 years of school). Different factors emerge as most important for different educational groups.

---

13. The feeling thermometer asks respondents to place a group or a political personality on a 100-point scale measuring affect running from 0 degrees (very cold) to 100 degrees (very hot). A rating of 50 degrees indicates neutrality. The identification question reads: "Here is a list of groups [which includes blacks]. Please read over the list and tell me the letter of those groups you feel particularly close to—people who are most like you in their ideas and interests and feelings about things."

14. There are other aspects of the concept that are not captured in my measure. Miller et al. (1981) identify four components of group consciousness, two of which are included in this measure. In addition to group identification and polar affect, the concept, they argue, involves polar power, "the expressed satisfaction or dissatisfaction with the group's current status, power, or material resources in relation to that of the outgroup," and individual versus system blame, "the belief that the responsibility for a group's low status in society is attributable either to individual failings or to inequalities in the social system" (pp. 496–497). Unfortunately, while the National Election Studies data set constructed here does include survey questions tapping these latter dimensions, they are asked infrequently and are not asked in the same years as the questions measuring the first two dimensions.

**Table 4. Strength of Partisanship, not "Black Consciousness,"
Appears to Make the Difference for Less Educated Blacks**
(Unstandardized O.L.S. Regression Coefficients; Blacks Only)

	b	SE(b)	b	SE(b)
Aid to Minorities				
High School	− .03	(.28)	−1.93	(1.01)
College	− .25	(.38)	−1.18	(1.42)
South	− .60	(.23)*	− .68	(.23)*
Issue Strength	.32	(.09)*	.26	(.21)
Partisan Strength	.28	(.13)*	- .11	(.32)
Black Consciousness	1.14	(.46)*	.49	(.93)
H.S. x Issue Strength			.16	(.24)
Col x Issue Strength			− .29	(.36)
H.S. x Partisan Strength			.55	(.35)
Col x Partisan Strength			.35	(.46)
H.S. x Black Consciousness			.68	(1.06)
Col x Black Consciousness			.88	(1.74)
Constant	1.31	(.48)*	2.72	(.94)*
R^2	.14		.16	
n	266		266	
Government Guaranteed Jobs				
High School	.12	(.26)	− .04	(.90)
College	.29	(.35)	− .61	(1.19)
South	− .51	(.21)*	− .53	(.21)*
Issue Strength	.39	(.09)*	.15	(.22)
Partisan Strength	.45	(.11)*	.77	(.27)*
Black Consciousness	.86	(.41)**	.19	(.80)
H.S. x Issue Strength			.30	(.24)
Col x Issue Strength			.22	(.34)
H.S. x Partisan Strength			− .34	(.30)
Col x Partisan Strength			− .63	(.37)
H.S. x Black Consciousness			.59	(.94)
Col x Black Consciousness			3.09	(1.51)**
Constant	.37	(.44)	.58	(.82)
R^2	.15		.17	
n	319		319	
Cut Spending or Improve Services				
High School	− .23	(.28)	− .62	(1.02)
College	− .12	(.36)	−1.22	(1.40)
South	− .41	(.21)	− .43	(.22)**
Issue Strength	.03	(.09)	− .14	(.23)
Partisan Strength	.44	(.12)*	.60	(.28)**
Black Consciousness	.74	(.44)	.11	(.88)
H.S. x Issue Strength			.19	(.25)
Col x Issue Strength			.37	(.34)
H.S. x Partisan Strength			− .10	(.32)
Col x Partisan Strength			− .59	(.41)
H.S. x Black Consciousness			.46	(1.03)
Col x Black Consciousness			3.07	(1.62)
Constant	1.55	(.45)*	1.89	(.93)*
R^2	.08		.10	
n	299		299	

*$p < .01$ **$p < .05$

Black consciousness is a more important influence on the partisan perceptions of the better-educated group. In all three equations (even on the aid to minorities issues), black consciousness has only a small effect on the partisan perceptions of the least educated. The additional effect black consciousness has for the most educated blacks is considerable. While this interaction term achieves statistical significance only on the guaranteed jobs issue, the errors associated with all the interaction terms in the equation are so large as to substantially raise the standard of statistical significance. There is little doubt, though, that racial consciousness is a very powerful influence on the perceptions of educated blacks.

The strength of one's partisan identification, on the other hand, appears to be more important to less-educated blacks. On both the guaranteed jobs issue and the government spending issue (though not on the aid to minorities issue), strength of partisanship has a sizable and significant effect on perceiving broader partisan differences for the least educated. The effect of partisanship diminishes for those with more education. While still an important influence for these blacks, its effect is more muted as reflected in the negative interaction coefficients. This pattern does not hold in the aid to minorities equation, but the other two equations suggest that for those blacks with least education, it is partisan strength more than some sort of connection to the racial group that leads to a more polar view of the parties.

In sum, blacks have a more vivid picture of the differences between the parties than whites, and this is despite the fact that they are more likely to come from the South (where the partisan picture is in flux and more difficult to read) and that they are less advantaged by education. The multivariate analyses here offer insight into why blacks see larger partisan differences. A major reason is that blacks are more partisan than whites are (more of them classifying themselves as strong partisans), and being a strong partisan has a powerful effect on the sharpness of attributions. But being more partisan has an effect on blacks over and above the effect it has on whites; and this is particularly true for blacks with lower levels of education. Some sense of connection to the racial group also leads to the likelihood of seeing broader partisan differences as individuals likely draw conclusions about which party is best for blacks as a group. Group consciousness, however, is most important in shaping the party perceptions of the best-educated African Americans and not so much the least educated. And it is the least educated whose perceptions are most surprising and in need of explanation.

Conclusions

Here and elsewhere, I probe the idea that African Americans invest political resources more efficiently than whites, that they do more with less. Indeed, herein is an example of this efficiency, of how black public opinion is more sophisticated than one might predict given the usual models devised by social scientists. In this case, a very important idea about American politics is understood by a great many African Americans. This is true even—indeed especially—for those blacks with less education who might not be expected to have a very sophisticated understanding of American politics. That this idea has so permeated the entire black community, even in rudimentary form, is remarkable.

How blacks, particularly those with less education, have acquired this idea is open to speculation, though this analysis offers some clues. It may be that, among blacks, the Democratic Party has become identified as the party fully aligned with black interests (Tate, 1993).[15] If this is the case, particularly those individuals with a sense of connection to other blacks could be expected to be more likely to stretch the perceptual distance between the favored Democratic Party and the hostile Republican Party. But this connection between racial consciousness and a sharp definition of the parties involves several links in a chain of thinking. First, it necessitates having a sense of racial consciousness, a tie to other blacks and an understanding of the black condition. Second, it requires knowing which party is more favorable and hospitable to blacks, which less. Third, it entails using that information to place the parties on a spectrum of views. That racial consciousness appears to be most important to well-educated blacks indicates that this chain is vulnerable, that it is easily short-circuited, especially on non-racial issues.

An alternative (and not mutually exclusive) explanation of how blacks, particularly less-educated blacks, have acquired this important understanding of American politics is that political communication from black elites to black followers is less filtered and/or more persuasive. Put another way, opinion leadership is simply more common in black communities. As a white southern Democratic congressman said to me in response to a question about campaigning for black votes, "I've found in the black community that they truly have opinion leaders. There was a time that it was more prevalent in the white community too. But that's not the case anymore and it sure makes a difference in how you reach for black votes" (Glaser, 1996). His point is rather specific to campaign strategy, but it has broader implications. If he is correct, an opinion leadership explanation may be quite viable. Opinion leadership would have a direct effect, the transmission of the basic idea that Democrats and Republicans represent quite different alternatives (as well as what these alternatives are). It likely would have an indirect effect, leading blacks to be more partisan than whites, which, in turn, has a clear effect on partisan perceptions. And those getting one message (the parties are different) would also likely get the other (support the Democrats), which would account for strength of partisanship having even more of an effect on blacks (and less-educated blacks, at that) than on whites.

Informal social communication between blacks who have received these same messages further reinforces their strength. The segregated nature of society and the general inclination for people to befriend, marry, socialize, live near, and work with others like themselves ensures that some basic ideas about the political world (and the world in general) receive little challenge. Both the leadership and organizational structure of the community and the social workings of the community thus contribute to phenomena like that studied here.

However they do acquire this picture of American politics, my argument is that in some ways the political world has greater clarity to blacks than to whites, that blacks have a more accessible map of the terrain of American politics, one with some clearly demarcated landmarks (and even, perhaps, an "X" labelled "You are here"). This article represents an investigation into what this map, or at least one aspect of this map, might look like, if not how it might be used. This map also

---

15. There are compelling arguments that many whites, particularly in the South, also have come to believe this statement (see Huckfeldt and Kohfeld, 1989 and Carmines and Stimson, 1989).

may help to explain some of the other findings of black political sophistication. It is a political resource that helps guide many blacks through political decisions they might not otherwise be prepared to make.

References

Brady, Henry E. and Paul M. Sniderman (1985). "Attitude Attribution: A Group Basis for Political Reasoning." *American Political Science Review* 79:1061–78.

Campbell, Angus, Philip E. Converse, Warren E. Miller, and Donald E. Stokes (1960). *The American Voter*. Chicago: The University of Chicago Press.

Carmines, Edward G. and James A. Stimson (1989). *Issue Evolution: Race and the Transformation of American Politics*. Princeton: Princeton University Press.

Conover, Pamela Johnston and Stanley Feldman (1981). "The Origins and Meaning of Liberal/Conservative Self-Identifications." *American Journal of Political Science* 25:617–45.

Converse, Philip E. (1964). "The Nature of Belief Systems in Mass Publics." In David E. Apter (ed.), pp. 202–261. *Ideology and Discontent*. New York: Free Press.

Glaser, James M. (1996). *Race, Campaign Politics, and the Realignment in the South*. New Haven: Yale University Press.

Glaser, James M., and Michael G. Hagen (1992). "Race and the Investment of Political Resources." Paper presented at the Workshop on Race, Ethnicity, Representation, and Governing, Harvard University.

Hamill, Ruth, Milton Lodge, and Frederick Blake (1985). "The Breadth, Depth, and Utility of Class, Partisan, and Ideological Schemata." *American Journal of Political Science* 29:850–870.

Huckfeldt, Robert and Carol Weitzel Kohfeld (1989). *Race and the Decline of Class in American Politics*. Urbana: University of Illinois Press.

Jackson III, John, Barbara Leavitt Brown, and David Bositis (1982). "Herbert McClosky and Friends Revisited: 1980 Democratic and Republican Party Elites Compared to the Mass Public." *American Politics Quarterly* 10:158–180.

Luskin, Robert C. (1985). "Explaining Political Sophistication." Paper presented at the annual meeting of the Midwest Political Science Association, Chicago, Illinois.

Luskin, Robert C. (1987). "Measuring Political Sophistication." *American Journal of Political Science* 31:856–899.

McClosky, Herbert, Paul J. Hoffman, and Rosemary O'Hara (1960). "Issue Conflict and Consensus Among Party Leaders and Followers." *American Political Science Review* 54:406–427.

Miller, Arthur H., Patricia Gurin, Gerald Gurin, and Oksana Malanchuk (1981). "Group Consciousness and Political Participation." *American Journal of Political Science* 25:494–511.

Moreland, Laurence W., Robert P. Steed, and Tod A. Baker (1988). "Ideology, Issues, and Realignment among Southern Party Activists." In Robert H. Swansbrough and David M. Brodsky (eds.), pp. 268–281. *The South's New Politics: Realignment and Dealignment*. Columbia: University of South Carolina Press.

O'Gorman, Hubert J. (1979). "White and Black Perceptions of Racial Values." *Public Opinion Quarterly* 43:48–59.

Rosenberg, Morris (1968). *The Logic of Survey Analysis*. New York: Basic Books, Inc.

Sniderman, Paul M., James M. Glaser, and Robert Griffin (1991). "Information and electoral choice." In Paul M. Sniderman, Richard A. Brody, and Philip E. Tetlock (eds), pp. 164–178. *Reasoning and Choice: Explorations in Political Psychology*. Cambridge: Cambridge University Press.

Tate, Katherine (1993). *From Protest to Politics: The New Black Voters in American Elections.* Cambridge: Russell Sage Foundation and Harvard University Press.

Verba, Sidney and Norman H. Nie (1972). *Participation in America.* New York: Harper and Row.

Verba, Sidney and Gary R. Orren (1985). *Equality in America: A View from the Top.* Cambridge: Harvard University Press.

Wolfinger, Raymond E. and Steven J. Rosenstone (1980). *Who Votes?* New Haven: Yale University Press.

Appendix
Question Wordings

Aid to Minorities: Some people feel that the government in Washington should make every effort to improve the social and economic position of blacks and other minority groups. Others feel that the government should not make any special effort to help minorities because they should help themselves. Where would you place yourself [the Democratic Party/the Republican Party] on this [7-point] scale, or haven't you thought much about this?

Government Guaranteed Jobs: Some people feel the government in Washington should see to it that every person has a job and good standard of living. Others think the government should just let each person get ahead on his own. Where would you place yourself [the Democratic Party/the Republican Party] on this [7-point] scale, or haven't you thought much about this?

Ideology: We hear a lot of talk these days about liberals and conservatives. Here is a seven-point scale on which the political views that people might hold are arranged from extremely liberal to extremely conservative. Where would you place yourself [the Democratic Party/the Republican Party] on this scale, or haven't you thought much about this?

Cut Spending or Improve Services: Some people think the government should provide fewer services, even in areas such as health and education, in order to reduce spending. Other people feel it is important for the government to provide many more services even if it means an increase in spending. Where would you place yourself [the Democratic Party/the Republican Party] on this scale, or haven't you thought much about this?

Withdrawal from Vietnam: With regard to Vietnam, some people think we should do everything necessary to win a complete military victory, no matter what results. Some people think we should withdraw completely from Vietnam right now, no matter what results. And, of course, other people have opinions somewhere between these two extreme positions. Where would you place yourself [most young people/most middle-aged people] on this scale, or haven't you thought much about this?

Equal Rights for Women: Recently, there has been a lot of talk about women's rights. Some people feel that women should have an equal role with men in running business, industry, and government. Others feel that women's place is in the home. Where would you place yourself [most women/most men] on this scale, or haven't you thought much about this?

Progressive Income Tax: As you know, in our tax system people who earn a lot of money already have to pay higher rates of income tax than those who earn less. Some people think that those with high incomes should pay even more of their income into taxes than they do now. Others think that the rates shouldn't be different at all—that everyone should pay the same portion of their income, no matter how much they make. Where would you place yourself [most workingmen/most middle class people] on this scale or haven't you thought much about this?

34

Racial Differences in the Support for Democratic Principles: The Strategy of Political Emancipation

Darren W. Davis

Exposure to and experience with democratic principals are not encountered in pure form or in isolation, but in substantive contexts which influence the way individuals react to them. Indeed, in areas in which individuals perceive a greater personal threat from their political enemies individuals have been willing to deny them democratic and constitutional rights (Stouffer, 1955; Sullivan, Piereson, and Marcus, 1982; Gibson, 1986; Pefley and Sigelman, 1990; Davis, 1995) and as a consequence, individuals may become more accepting of constraints on their own personal freedom (Gibson, 1992; 1995). Behaving somewhat rationally (or perhaps justifiably), individuals can be viewed as going through a decision calculus in which the costs associated with tolerating behavior they perceive as threatening are weighed against the democratic rules being challenged, and in the end, a trade-off is made in favor of the behavior that protects them from such threats. Support for democratic and constitutional principles are invariably sacrificed in specific situations as it takes an extraordinary measure of forbearance and a strong will to suffer repugnant opinions and threatening behavior (McClosky, 1964).

With respect to racial differences in support for democratic principles, the concept of rationality has not been used to describe African Americans' orientations to democratic norms.[1] Rather, the social situation of blacks and the rigidity of black culture have gained widespread acceptance as explanations predisposing blacks to authoritarian values and beliefs (Bachrach, 1967; Dahl, 1956; Lipset,

---

1. The evidence on blacks' commitment to the principles of democracy has been largely tangential in the sense that black intolerance is usually assessed by the simple inclusion of a race dummy variable into a political tolerance equation (recent exceptions to this include Gibson (1995) and Davis (1995). With no attempt to explain the inclusion of race, this certainly admits to a lack of knowledge concerning the underlying motivations of black intolerance (see Davis (1997) for a similar argument). This also assumes that the impact of the predictors of tolerance is equivalent among blacks and whites. For instance, an additional year of education is considered to have the same influence on tolerance for blacks and whites. Although not explicitly addressed in this paper, the analysis does indeed reveals that this is certainly not the case.

1960). It has been frequently argued that lower levels of education and the deficiency of certain psychological attributes (i.e., self-esteem and dogmatism) essential to learning the general norms of democracy interfere with blacks being able to apply democratic principles to specific situations (McClosky and Brill, 1983; Zellman, 1975; Sullivan, Pierson, and Marcus, 1982). Further insulating blacks from the learning and acceptance of democratic values are feelings of political cynicism, political inefficacy, and distrustfulness of political leaders and democratic institutions (Gibson and Caldeira, 1992; Abramson, 1983). Consequently, if one's culture and social situation interfere, either socially or psychologically, with the acquisition of democratic values and beliefs, it seems only by chance that one would be able to apply such principles selectively. Thus, black political intolerance becomes nearly involuntary and unpredictable.

This paper challenges this view of black intolerance. Given that blacks show a more fragile commitment to democratic principles and, in turn, claim little freedom for themselves (Gibson, 1992), it is important to examine closely the extent to which black intolerance is a manifestation of the rigidity of black culture and social learning. Or is black intolerance a focused and calculated decision? The basic hypothesis of this paper is that black political intolerance can be viewed as an emancipatory strategy used to defend and protect blacks from racial hatred and violence. Considering the persistence of groups in American society that have sought the eradication of black people, it seems reasonable (actually rational) for blacks, in order to secure basic civil and human rights and seek protection from racial hatred, to consciously and selectively deny procedural rights to such groups that threaten their existence directly (Bay, 1981). On the basis of this framework, black support and tolerance of the Ku Klux Klan's ability to speak publicly, to hold rallies and demonstrations, and to publish racist material can be viewed as passivity, submissiveness, and political acquiescence.

From the perspective of democratic theorists, democracy is secure when blacks and other groups are unconditionally committed to democratic principles and "tolerate" such behavior. However, that American democracy is somehow jeopardized when a sizeable portion of its population is not firmly committed to the application of democratic principles is generally not accepted (Herson and Hofstetter, 1975; McClosky, 1964; Prothro and Grigg, 1960; Stouffer, 1955).[2]

In adopting a defensive posture, black intolerance may be used to assert the distinctiveness of the African-American experience and to exert greater control over the determination of acceptable values and norms established by the dominant culture. Recent research by Gibson (1995) suggests that this form of response to victimization is a plausible hypothesis for black intolerance.

---

2. This should not be too surprising since, according to the elitist theory of democracy, democracy is preserved among political elites who generally accept the norms of civil liberties and are prepared to apply them to specific circumstances (Bachrach, 1967). Conversely, those who are most confused about democratic ideas are also more likely to be politically apathetic.

Table 1. Targets of Intolerance

Communists	4.8%	33.5%
Ku Klux Klan	79.4	24.1
Atheists	7.3	11.6
Nazis	1.0	12.2
Militarists	2.0	13.1
Homosexuals	5.5	5.5

Members of the [*least-liked group*] should be banned from running for public office.

Agree	77.5	64.2
Uncertain	4.4	6.8
Disagree	18.1	28.8

Members of the [*least-liked group*] should allowed to teach in public schools.

Agree	12.0	19.6
Uncertain	7.9	11.0
Disagree	80.1	69.4

The [*least-liked group*] should be outlawed.

Agree	68.9	51.0
Uncertain	8.3	14.5
Disagree	22.8	34.5

Members of the [*least-liked group*] should be allowed to make a speech in this city.

Agree	35.2	53.2
Uncertain	12.4	10.5
Disagree	52.4	36.3

The [*least-liked group*] should be allowed to hold rallies in our city.

Agree	18.5	36.0
Uncertain	7.6	11.8
Disagree	73.9	52.2

Note: The agree and disagree percentages are a combination of those who gave agree (disagree) strongly with those that simply agreed (or disagreed). Source: 1987 GSS.

Racial Differences In Political Tolerance

The literature has documented the intolerance levels among blacks (Hofstetter, 1975; Sullivan et al., 1985), though a few studies have detected a little tolerance or no racial differences (Bobo and Licari, 1989; Seltzer and Smith, 1985). Others observed that once other factors are held constant racial differences in political tolerance disappear (Green and Waxman, 1987; Sullivan, Piereson, and Marcus 1982). Thus, racial differences in political tolerance are primarily viewed as a function of racial differences in education and the perceived level of threat posed by various groups (Davis, 1995). More recently, Gibson (1992; 1995) shows that black intolerance is partly driven by one's social and political context and that it has real-life consequences. Since blacks are generally less committed to certain democratic principles, they, in turn, do not claim much freedom for themselves and censor their own behavior. This is the extent of our knowledge concerning black intolerance.

Clearly, there are many lingering questions. For instance, to the extent that whites and blacks target different groups to deny civil liberties, are there racial differences in the intensity of intolerant attitudes? Put more broadly, is the concept of intolerance comparable between blacks and whites? And, what accounts for the divergent views of political tolerance?

To help answer some of the basic questions concerning the nature of racial differences in tolerant attitudes, the distribution of blacks' and whites' least-liked groups and the support for civil liberties of that group are displayed in Table 1. Obviously, there is no mass consensus on the least-liked group in American society. While the selection of least-liked groups among whites is more dispersed, blacks basically agree on the group they like the least. A higher percentage of whites select Communists as their least-liked group. This is followed by members of the Ku Klux Klan, Militarists, Nazis, and Atheists. A very small percentage of white respondents mention homosexuals as the group they dislike the most. In sum, white intolerance is basically pluralistic (Sullivan, Piereson, and Marcus, 1982; Gibson, 1988).[3]

The explanation for blacks is quite different. Considerably less polarized than whites, blacks are clearly threatened by the Ku Klux Klan. More than three-fourths of the black respondents mention the Klan as their most disliked group in American society. In a time in which racial tensions are expected to have diminished, blacks continue to acknowledge the racial hatred and threat posed by the Klan.[4] As McClosky and Brill (1983) noted, "a cross burning by the Ku Klux Klan might more easily be tolerated in a field outside of a southern town than in Harlem (p. 24)." A very small percentage of blacks dislike Atheists, Homosexuals, and Communists, respectively.

When asked questions pertaining to the extension of civil liberties to their least-liked group, both whites and blacks give intolerant responses. On all the items, the majority of respondents are willing to deny civil liberties to their least-liked group. So, in one sense, black intolerance is not all that unusual since intolerance still appears pervasive in American society. But, blacks are much less tolerant of their least-liked group than whites, and blacks are also more certain of their intolerant responses. For instance, while 77.5 percent of the black respondents agree that their least-liked group should be banned from running for public office, only 64.2 percent of whites hold this opinion. Additionally, blacks are less likely to give uncertain responses on most of the tolerance items. This trend holds

---

3. In its original form, the questions were asked in such fashion to solicit four groups respondents dislike the most. Whites' second least-liked groups are Nazis (27.4%), Ku Klux Klan (23.6%), Communists (14.8%), and Atheists (11.9%). Blacks' second least-liked groups are Nazis (27.1%), Communists (19%), Atheists (14%), and Ku Klux Klan (11.5%).

4. From a psychological standpoint, some individuals may be predisposed to perceive threats whether they exist or not, or even past events. Few would question whether blacks are responding to the historical legacy of the Klan or whether they are reacting to the current intimidation of the Klan. Nevertheless, the behavior of state legislatures in strengthening old laws and writing new laws aimed at Klan activity, and subsequent constitutional tests of such statutes are taken as an indication of the current level of violence and terrorism. From 1983 to 1990, many states have enacted and strengthened existing laws in response to the growing racial and religious terrorism. Most of these statutes prohibit acts of harassment, intimidation and defacement of property (i.e. cross burning or religious symbol burning) (CA, CT, FL, GA, ID, MD, MA, NJ, NY, NC, PA, OR, RI, TN, VT, VA, WA), forbid mask-wearing or the carrying of weapons in certain circumstances (CT, FL, GA, IL, ID, LA, MI, MN, MT, NJ, NC, PA, RI, SC, TN, VT, VA, WV), and prohibit private paramilitary organizations (AL, AZ, CA, CT, FL, ID, IL, IA, KY, LA, ME, MD, MA, MI, MS, NE, NV, ND, WA, WV, WY). Constitutional tests to these laws and subsequent invalidations have occurred in California and Florida.

for all of the civil liberties items. As a group, black intolerance of the Klan is very durable. The interesting question, then, is to the extent that blacks are presented with the behavior of other disliked groups in American society, are blacks willing to extend such groups civil liberties? Theories of political emancipation and social learning make different predictions.

Political Emancipation vs. Social Learning

Christian Bay in *Strategies of Political Emancipation* (1981) argues that the commitment to civil liberties is secondary to security and survival needs. According to Bay "the right to stay alive and healthy or the right of everyone to protection against avoidable dangers to life and limb is the most basic of all human rights (Bay, 1981, p. 102)." For social contract theorists (e.g., Hobbes, Rousseau), this protection from continual threats to security and the preservation of life is the primary objective of the state. Therefore, all forms of political emancipation admit to the limitation of governmental institutions in making one secure and tacit acceptance of racial bigotry.[5] When individuals return to this "state of war" they must become their own police, their own adjudicator, and their own executioner.[6] Political emancipation, then, is the reduction of specific dangers threatening the destruction of human beings or the destruction of what is most dear to them, such as their health and dignity (Bay, 1981).

Given that most individuals can identify a group in American society they dislike and to some degree feel threatened by it, to what extent is the political intolerance expressed by some whites considered political emancipation? This distinction is critical to understanding the underlying motivations of black intolerance. The primary difference in racial perceptions of threat is the internalized anxiety and fear generated by different groups in American society. Simply put, white intolerance does not come from the same degree of internalized fear and anxiety as black intolerance. The argument follows that no group in American history has endeavored to terrorize and demean whites for simply being white. In fact, an analysis of Table 1 indicates that the groups whites dislike the most do not seek to harm whites or even terrorize them. Moreover, the threat that whites perceive from Communists, the Ku Klux Klan, Militarists, and Nazis manifests itself indirectly by challenging certain beliefs whites consider valuable. For instance, the threat posed by Communists comes from their potential threat to certain democratic values but not from a direct destruction of whites in America. This is also obvious in whites' dislike of the Ku Klux Klan. While whites and blacks basically

---

5. According to Kuklinski et al., (1997), emotionally charged prejudice and racial bigotry remain a significant problem in American society. While their results indicate that nearly one in every twelve whites express anger over the suggestion that a black family may move next door, six out of every ten whites are angry over affirmative action. Consequently, the possibility that blacks face racism in their everyday lives is quite high.

6. That the limitation of certain types of behavior destructive to the ends of civil society is justifiable is reflected in the writings of J.S. Mill. According to Mill, "the sole end for which mankind are warranted, individually or collectively, in interfering with the liberty of action of any their number, is self protection (*On Liberty*, p.15)." The only justifiable limitation of individual rights is to prevent harm to others.

agree that the Klan is "threatening to the American way of life," "likely to engage in illegal activity," and "[made up of] extremists," only 35 percent of whites consider them as "personally threatening" as opposed to 77 percent for blacks.[7] Thus, white intolerance is tied to the survival of the democratic system and constitutional order.

By contrast, black perceptions of danger and insecurity stem from and are directed toward groups that seek to harm them directly. Following the concept of political emancipation, black intolerance is tied to personal survival. Still, according to Table 1 a few blacks reflect the concerns of the dominant culture and are most threatened by Atheists, Homosexuals, and Communists. Whites are probably no different from blacks in that they would deny civil liberties to groups they perceived as "out to get them."[8]

From the perspective of social learning, black political intolerance due to the rigidity of black culture—the emphasis on authoritarian values—and its interference with the learning of democratic principles is less controllable. Accordingly, blacks learn the norms of intolerance much as they learn other social norms. What is more important is that the factors that shape the socialization to cultural norms pretty much determine the acquisition of democratic values: limited access to information and exposure to democratic norms, low levels of education, feelings of political cynicism, and low levels of self-esteem and open-mindedness. Added to this is that the perceived benefits of upholding democratic values are not always intuitively obvious among blacks. Simply, "not all persons in the society are in an equally good position to learn why their presumed beliefs in freedom obliges them to permit offensive or frightening conduct—especially if they, or their associates, happen to be the victims (McClosky and Brill, 1983, p. 214)."

Since black intolerance is merely the reflection of the rigidity of black culture, low levels of education, environmental differences, and psychological deficiencies, blacks do not go through any form of decision calculus to express their intolerance. Furthermore, the social and psychological constraints on black political behavior render them incapable of making a decision when it comes to political tolerance and reduce the available choices for blacks. Theories of social learning predict that blacks do not discriminate in their denial of civil liberties.

This paper attempts to make explicit racial differences in the underlying motivations of intolerance. Although social learning and political emancipation appear to be reasonable hypotheses, they clearly make different predictions for intolerance.

A Model of Political Tolerance

Political tolerance is frequently referred to as the willingness of citizens to support the extension of rights of citizenship to all members of society, that is, to

---

7. These data come from the 1987 GSS.

8. This strategy of political emancipation is certainly applicable to some subgroups of whites in American society (e.g. Jews, gays and lesbians, and women). Since the empowerment of such groups invoke negative reactions among some segments of society and are singled out to demean and intimidate, it is possible in some instances for a subgroup of repressed whites to behave in an emancipatory fashion.

allow political freedoms guaranteed in a democracy. A politically tolerant individual, then, is one who does not restrict ideas that challenge the basic principles and norms of democracy (Crick, 1973). In this vein, political tolerance is closely associated with the idea of procedural fairness. Political tolerance implies the degree to which individuals are committed to the "rules of the game" and also committed to apply these rules to all equally.

However, Sullivan, Piereson, and Marcus (1982) suggest that political tolerance is not that simple. One cannot be tolerant of something one already supports. Political tolerance implies a willingness to permit the expression of ideas or interests one opposes. Therefore, persons are considered tolerant to the extent they are prepared to extend such constitutional guarantees like the right to speak, the right to publish, the right to run for office to those with whom they disagree. It takes no tolerance to put up with people with whom one agrees. Conversely, an intolerant person might feel that blacks should not be allowed to run for public office, that Communists should not be allowed to teach in public schools, and that members of the Ku Klux Klan should not be allowed to hold rallies.[9]

Political tolerance is not the same as acceptance. Tolerance only requires that individuals respect the right of people to express different views; political tolerance in no way implies that individuals accept those views. Moreover, tolerance is not the same as a lack of prejudice although prejudice may be a cause of intolerance. A tolerant person might be prejudiced toward a certain group, yet respect the civil liberties of that group.

Nonetheless, to reflect this concern over what political tolerance is exactly and the best measurement strategy, political tolerance is examined in several ways. I examine racial differences in political tolerance using a content-controlled measure of political tolerance proposed by Sullivan, Piereson, and Marcus (1979; 1982) and a group specific measure similar to that proposed by Stouffer (1955). The content-controlled measurement scheme allows respondents to select functionally equivalent groups as not to contaminate the tolerance scale with one's personal beliefs. The group-specific measurement scheme, on the other hand, relaxes this assumption and makes it possible to examine political tolerance toward groups that may or may not be disliked.

More importantly, this measurement scheme permits a rigorous and conservative test of the expectations of political emancipation and social learning theories. Political emancipation predicts that blacks focus their intolerance on the Ku Klux Klan only. This expectation should not be confused with the black tolerance of racists. That is, everyday racists or bigots do not invoke the same degree of fear and anxiety among blacks as the Klan. Since it is not unusual for a person to consider blacks inferior and yet not seek to terrorize and destroy them, there should be no racial differences in the tolerance of racists, or at the very least, whites may be less tolerant of racists. When blacks go through the decision calculus to express intolerance they are expected to identify the Klan's historical torment as well as current anxiety, fear, and threats to their security. In this regard, in all situ-

---

9. This view of political tolerance is not universally accepted. McCutcheon (1985), representing the traditional Stouffer approach, argues that the willingness to curtail civil liberties to any group, whether one loves it, despises it, or is indifferent to it, is an intolerant attitude. The refusal to permit civil liberties to any group, liked or disliked, constitutes intolerance. Sniderman et al. (1991) also argue that dislike is not a necessary condition of intolerance.

ations except those pertaining to the Klan, blacks should be just as committed to the "rules of the game" as whites.

The test of social learning is also a conservative test. Social learning predicts that since black intolerance is the product of black culture and its interference in the acquisition of democratic norms black intolerance should be indiscriminant. Blacks are not familiar with the "rules of the game" because their social context interferes with the acquisition of democratic values. That is, every group has an equal chance of being targeted by blacks. Social learning theory is credited if black intolerance is not focused, or several groups are targeted.

Explanations of Political Tolerance

Previous research has directed attention to both psychological and social context explanations of political tolerance. Political intolerance is generally most prevalent among the less educated, members of the lower social class, religious fundamentalists, and individuals from rural communities. Psychologically, political intolerance is associated with low self-esteem, direct personal threat, and dogmatism. These explanations are used to construct a model of political tolerance. An exposition of these factors is important to understanding the social learning explanations of racial differences in political tolerance.

The degree to which people feel insecure, untrusting, and powerless has been found to be related to political tolerance. Sniderman (1975) demonstrates that low self-esteem not only makes a person an instrument of fear but also seriously retards political learning, which characterizes those weakly committed to democratic principles. Persons high in self-esteem, compared to those low in self-esteem, are more likely to be exposed to more information. It is the superior capacity for social learning of persons with high self-esteem that strengthens their chances of learning the norms of political culture and the ideas of democratic restraint. Bagley (1979) points out that people with poor self-esteem are likely to be prejudiced. Such persons may also use intolerance to enhance their self-esteem, defend their egos, and alleviate their anxieties. Lack of self-esteem is likely to lead to various kinds of attempts to re-establish the primacy of the self in relation to others. One way of doing this is by devaluing others who are identifiable in terms of their ethnic characteristics (Bagley, 1979).

Dogmatism is another psychological factor that increases political tolerance. According to Rokeach (1960), a less dogmatic or an open-minded person is more receptive to new information and ideas and evaluates them on a logical basis. The acceptance or rejection of new ideas is made on the basis of its merit. Conversely, the close-minded or dogmatic person adopts a closed system of beliefs. This overall system of beliefs is not very susceptible to change because it satisfies psychological needs of the individual.

Equally important, the perceived threat of one's least-liked group has been strongly and consistently related to political tolerance. Individuals who view a group as a serious threat are very likely to be intolerant toward that group. Following Sullivan, Piereson, and Marcus, (1982) logic, the notion of tolerance seems to be based on a threat of some kind. Political tolerance is directly related to perceptions of threat posed by dissident groups. Intolerance arises from perceptions that dissident groups threaten important values or constitute a danger to the constitutional order. Yet, it is conceivable that many people who perceive dissident groups as threatening are nevertheless prepared to tolerate them and to defend their procedural claims.

The influence of education on levels of support for civil liberties has been a central concern of students of political tolerance. Since Stouffer's strong positive relationship between education and political tolerance, subsequent analyses have found education to be a key determinant of political tolerance (one obvious exception is Sullivan, Piereson, and Marcus 1982). According to Stouffer, "to be tolerant, one has to learn further not only that people with different ideas are not necessarily bad people but also that it is vital to America to preserve this free market place, even if some of the ideas traded are repugnant or even dangerous to the country (p.127)." Nunn, Crockett, and Williams (1978) stressed that increasing years of education were part of a learning process that enhanced cognitive skills, cultural knowledge, and cognitive flexibility. Similarly, McClosky (1964), Prothro and Grigg (1960), Lawrence (1976), and Bobo and Licari (1989) maintain that democratic values are complex ideas requiring considerable education and social learning. Education, furthermore, exposes people to greater social diversity, and it leads to greater learning of democratic norms.

Stouffer found that religion and religiosity made a substantial difference in political tolerance. There was a 29 percent difference in political tolerance between people who regularly attend church and people who did not attend church. Subsequent research in political tolerance, however, suggests that it is not religiosity per se, but religious denomination (Nunn, Crockett, and Williams 1978). Protestants and religious fundamentalists closely link God and political authority and are also likely to see political nonconformity as the work of the Devil.

Last, urban experience is included in the model because it promotes tolerance by enabling individuals to "rub shoulders" with people unlike themselves and exposes individuals to different cultures. It is through the urban experience and the exposure to diversity that individuals learn to "live and let live" (Stouffer, 1955, p. 222).

Data and Measures

The data used in this analysis come from the National Opinion Research Center's 1987 General Social Survey. This is a national representative multi-stage probability sample of English-speaking adults. The main GSS sample included a total of 1,466 respondents, with 191 blacks, 1,222 whites, and 53 non-black non-whites (excluded from this analysis), with an overall response rate of 75.4 percent. The 1987 GSS also includes a large black oversample (N = 353). The black oversample had a response rate of 79.9 percent and brings the total sample size of blacks to 544.[10]

It is important to recognize that most psychological concepts cannot be observed directly, and that no measurement, particularly single question items, is ever error free. Since random measurement error emanates from any number of sources and reduces the reliability of variables, where there are multiple indica-

---

10. Respondents are required to give a valid response to a large majority of item in order to be included in the analysis. "Don't know" and "uncertain" responses were dropped.

tors of a concept factor, scores are created from multiple items to reduce random measurement error. Yet, some single item indicators are inescapable.

Political tolerance is measured the way Sullivan, Piereson, and Marcus (1982) proposed. First, each respondent was given a list of potentially unpopular groups that ranged from socialists and Black Panthers on the left to Ku Klux Klan and John Birch society members on the right. Some groups, however, were more difficult to categorize as being ideologically extreme, such as atheists, liars, and people who drink. Respondents were then asked to identify the group they like the least and presented with the following questions:

1. Members of the ___ should be banned from running for public office.
2. Member of the ___ should be allowed to teach in public schools.
3. The ___ should be outlawed.
4. Members of the ___ should be allowed to make a speech in this city.
5. The ___ should be allowed to hold rallies in our city.

The statements were read as they appear above with the blanks filled with the group selected by each respondent. According to Sullivan, Piereson, and Marcus (1982) the intention was to avoid contaminating the tolerance–intolerance scale with the respondent's political beliefs concerning different groups.

An index using factor scores was created from the previous five items. The five items resulted in a single factor solution on which all items load approximately .7 or higher and which accounts for 57 percent of the variance in the underlying correlations. This single dimensionality of the items does a reasonably good job in tapping the hypothesized abstract dimension. The reliability coefficient of the least-liked group items and the political tolerance scale is quite high (alpha=.77).

An alternative to the least-liked approach is to use the same stimuli for all subjects. Here, I utilize responses to Communists, Homosexuals, Militarists, Atheists, and Racists. All respondents were asked three standard questions about these groups (i.e. allow them to teach, to speak publicly, and to publish). Factor scores were also used to construct a scale for each group.[11]

A self-esteem index was created using four of Sniderman's (1975) measures of self-esteem. Using principle components extraction the five self-esteem items resulted in a single factor solution with an eigenvalue of 1.75 and an explained variance of 60 percent (alpha = .53). Each item loaded approximately .60 or better.[12]

---

11. Unfortunately, all of the questions pertaining to one's least-liked group were not asked in the group-specific items. Nonetheless, each scale appears to be very reliable. The eigenvalues and reliabilities are as follows.

Index	Eigenvalue	Alpha
Racists	2.45	.72
Militarists	2.67	.75
Homosexuals	2.02	.63
Communists	2.23	.66
Atheists	2.75	.77

12. The Sniderman (1975) items used to construct a self-esteem scale include:
"I never try to do more than I can for fear of failure."
"I think that in some ways I am really an unworthy person."
"When I look back on it, I guess I really haven't gotten as much out of life as I has once hoped."
"I often feel I have done something wrong or evil."

A dogmatism scale was constructed using four of the Rokeach (1960) items: having like-minded friends, ideas worth the paper they are printed on, compromise is dangerous, and group existence. The questions resulted in a single factor solution with an eigenvalue of 2.43 and an explained variance of 55.8 (alpha = .58).[13]

The last variable constructed using factor scores is the perceived threat of one's least-liked group. The items used in the construction of a threat scale are three semantic differential items of one's most disliked group. Respondents were asked whether their least-liked group was threatening to the American way of life, likely to engage in illegal activity, extremist, un-American, and personally threatening. The result is a single factor solution with an eigenvalue of 2.02 and an explained variance of 40 percent (alpha = .53). [14]

Race, age, education, religious fundamentalism, and social status are single item indicators. Urbanism is the population size of the city in which the respondent resides.

Analysis and Results

Table 2 shows the preliminary estimates of the significance of race on the predictors of political tolerance. The coefficients for democratic norms suggest that there are no racial differences in the support abstract democratic principles. Controlling for other factors (not reported), there is essentially no distinction between blacks and whites in their support for abstract democratic principles. Clearly, racial differences are more significant when there is an attempt to apply them to specific situations or when such principles are presented in substantive contexts. Mostly everyone tends to respect freedom of speech, trial by jury, and due process in the abstract.

Though there are racial differences in self-esteem in the bivariate case, such differences can be explained away by the incorporation of other relevant factors. Racial differences in self-esteem can be masked by racial differences in other fac-

---

13. The Rokeach (1960) items used to construct a dogmatism scale include:
   "There are two kinds of people in this world: those who are for the truth and those who are against it."
   "Most ideas that get printed nowadays aren't worth the paper they are printed on."
   "To compromise with our political opponents is dangerous because it usually leads to the betrayal of our own side."
   "A group which tolerates too many differences of opinion among its own members cannot exist for long."
14. A factor score was obtained from the ratings of one's least-liked group using the following items:
   "Not threatening to the American way of life versus threatening to the American way of life."
   "And how would you rate [least-liked group] in terms of being "non-extremist versus extremist?"
   "And in terms of 'not likely to engage in illegal activity' versus 'likely to engage in illegal activity'?"
   "And in terms of 'American versus un-American'?"
   "Finally, how would you rate [least-liked group] in terms of not personally threatening to me versus personally threatening to me"?"

Table 2. Ordinary Least Squares (OLS) Estimates of Race on Various Dependent Variables (Predictors of Political Tolerance)

Dependent Variable	(race) b	SE	t
Democratic Norms	−.06	.07	−1.36
Self-Esteem	−.09	.07	−3.36**
Perceived Threat	−.46**	.07	7.63**
Dogmatism	.32**	.06	−9.04**

Note: Each dependent variable is a predictor of political tolerance in tables 3 and 4. The b coefficients were estimated separately using the following the equation: y = race + education + gender + social class + income + region + urbanicity. The results for the full equations may be obtained from the author. The t coefficients represent simple significance of t test assuming a two-tailed test.
 * significant at .05
** significant at .01

tors. But, controlling for other influences significant racial differences exist in perceptions of threat and the level of dogmatism.

Results from the Ordinary Least Squares (OLS) estimates of the model of political tolerance are reported in Table 3. That black political tolerance is a focused decision used to protect blacks from racial hatred is supported nicely. Blacks un-

Table 3. OLS Estimates of Political Tolerance Model Using Least-Liked Group and Group Specific Measures

Independent Variables	Least Liked Group	Left Wing Groups		Right Wing Groups		
		Communists	Homosexuals	Militarists	Racists	Atheists
Race (1 = Black)	−.225**	−.087	−.069	.011	.121	.022
	(.060)	(.051)	(.051)	(.053)	(.151)	(.047)
Education	.073**	−.078**	−.075**	−.082**	−.035**	−.078**
	(.009)	(.008)	(.007)	(.008)	(.007)	(.007)
Social Class	.017	.064*	.048	.065	.068	.085*
	(.041)	(.035)	(.035)	(.036)	(.035)	(.033)
Religious Fundamentalism	−.027**	.034**	.062**	.045**	.040**	.059**
	(.011)	(.009)	(.009)	(.009)	(.009)	(.008)
Population Size (x 1000)	.494**	−.079	−.055	−.395*	−.484**	−.663**
	(.192)	(.165)	(.166)	(.173)	(.166)	(.153)
Dogmatism	.237**	−.212**	−.191**	−.161**	−.136**	−.162**
	(.029)	(.025)	(.025)	(.026)	(.025)	(.023)
Self-Esteem	−.056*	−.025	−.018	−.013	−.015	−.021
	(.028)	(.024)	(.024)	(.024)	(.024)	(.022)
Perceived Threat	−.202**					
	(.027)					
Intercept	−1.01**	.657**	.517**	.699**	.213	.547**
	(.144)	(.124)	(.122)	(.129)	(.122)	(.113)
Pairwise N	1170	1116	1190	1118	1181	1182
R^2	.23	.22	.21	.19	.10	.23

Note: Values in parentheses are standard errors.
*significant at .05; **significant at .01.

Table 4. Percentage of Black Intolerant Responses to Tolerance Items for Unpopular Groups

Tolerance Items	Least Liked Group	Left Wing Groups		Right Wing Groups		Atheists
		Communists	Homosexuals	Militarists	Racists	
Allow to Teach	75.7%	46.4%	42.7%	61.5%	43.2%	53.8%
Allow to Publish	87	39	43.7	48.7	42.8	38.6
Allow to Speak	60	36.7	33.3	48	42.9	35.6

Note: The numbers indicate the percentage of black respondents giving intolerant responses to political tolerance items. Source: 1987 GSS.

doubtedly play favorites and direct intolerance to their most disliked group in American society, the Ku Klux Klan. Apparently, blacks look at the historical violence and current attempt by the Klan to demean and terrorize blacks and respond by placing constraints on the Klan's freedom. Thus, limiting the Klan's civil liberties can be added to the list of available strategies to make blacks more secure from racial hatred.

More decisively, blacks are able to differentiate between the threat posed by "everyday racists" and the Klan. In this respect, there are no racial differences in the extent to which racists and bigots are prohibited from speaking publicly, publishing racist material, and teaching in public schools. Blacks are not particularly intolerant of bigots. Logically, bigots invoke different reactions than the Klan. Because everyday racists want to make life unpleasant and not destroy it, they do not appear too ominous. Perhaps, this comes from the frequency with which blacks come into contact with racial bigots and individuals who think they are inferior and the development of coping mechanisms by blacks to insulate themselves from insults and general disrespect (Davis, 1997). [15]

Further evidence of political emancipation is the lack of racial differences in the tolerance of Communists, Homosexuals, Militarists, and Atheists. Everything else being equal, blacks and whites are not different in the extent to which they would extend civil liberties to other disliked groups in American society.

Another test of the hypothesis that blacks are able to distinguish between the threat and terror posed by different groups in American society would be to compare black responses to tolerance items of their least-liked group to their responses for other unpopular groups. Support for a theory of intolerance as a strategy for political emancipation suggests that blacks overwhelmingly give intolerant responses to their least-liked group (the Ku Klux Klan).

Table 4 reports the black percentage of intolerant response to tolerance items for unpopular groups. As expected, black intolerance for unpopular groups is not as restrictive for their least-liked group. More importantly, when presented with the allow certain type of behavior for racists, blacks appear to be just as willing to tolerate such behavior as much as they tolerate the same actions by Communists, Homosexuals, Militarists, and Atheists. Somewhat surprisingly, blacks do not place any particular restrictions on Atheists.

---

15. This model of political tolerance using the least-liked group approach was also generated without individuals' perception of threat of their least-liked group. Although the overall performance of the model was reduced slightly, racial differences in political intolerance remained significant (b = .30, p. < .01).

Table 5. OLS Estimates of Political Tolerance Model Using Least-Liked Group Measures

Independent Variables	Unstandardized Regression Coefficients	
	Blacks	Whites
Education	.034**	.092**
	(.014)	(.012)
Social Class	–.018	.019
	(.047)	(.054)
Religious Fundamentalism	–.003	–.035**
	(.019)	(.013)
Population Size (x 1000)	.254	.969**
	(.221)	(.037)
Dogmatism	.156**	.252**
	(.047)	(.038)
Self-Esteem	–.064	–.189**
	(.046)	(.035)
Perceived Threat	–.229**	–.189**
	(.046)	(.032)
Intercept	–.580**	–1.02**
	(.227)	(.183)
Pairwise N	408	762
R^2	.10	.25

Note: Values in parentheses are standard errors.
* significant at .05; ** significant at .01.

Clearly, black intolerance is very selective. What is less obvious, however, are racial differences in the strength of factors that interfere with the acquisition of democratic values. Does education have the same impact on blacks and whites? To the extent that blacks and whites find groups threatening, do self-esteem, dogmatism, urbanism, and social class status further insulate blacks from racial hatred? Using the least-liked approach, another set of equations separated by race were run to help answer these questions. The separation by race permits an analysis of the racial differences in the predictors of intolerance. Because of the different sampling variances among the predictors' tolerance, the unstandardized regression coefficients reported in Table 5 allows for comparisons across samples.

It should first be noted that the model explains a considerable amount of the variance in tolerance among whites. As expected, the tolerance of whites is fairly well explained by their social and psychological attributes, while the intolerance of blacks is not.

A comparison of the intercepts in the black and white equations indicates that whites start off almost twice as low on the intolerance scale as blacks, everything else being equal. Because the size of the coefficients of the other predictors of tolerance are much larger for whites, this relationship reverses very quickly. Except for the level of perceived threat, the explanatory variables pack a "bigger bang" for whites than blacks. That is, at the same levels of education, open-mindedness, and self-esteem, whites are clearly more tolerant. However, the potential for such

**Figure 1. Conditional Predictions of Political Tolerance
Using Threat and Education—Black Equation**

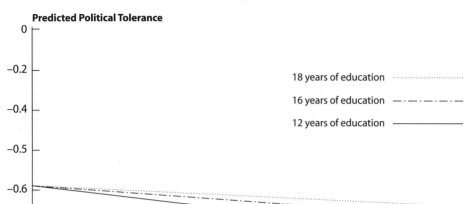

y = −.58 + threat (−.229) + education (.034). All other variables in the equation are held at their means.

factors increasing the tolerance levels among blacks is not inconsequential. Blacks with higher levels of education are more supportive of the application of democratic principles than blacks with lower levels of education. This is consistent with the effects of self-esteem and open-mindedness. Thus, such factors can be said to some degree reduce the interference of black culture with the acquisition of democratic values and beliefs.

But, these factors are up against a very powerful effect of the perceived threat of the Klan. Considering the relative impact of education, dogmatism, and self-esteem, the threat posed by the Klan can not be overpowered easily. When the threat posed by the Klan is at its highest level among blacks, no single factor nor a combination of factors can compel blacks to tolerance. Conversely, the levels of self-esteem, dogmatism, urbanism, and education among whites certainly outweighs the saliency of threat in their support of civil liberties. The only factor pushing whites toward more intolerant beliefs is religious fundamentalism.

Conditional Predictions of Political Tolerance

Based on the OLS estimates in Table 5 it is possible to extend the analysis further by examining how education and perceptions of threat may conditionally influence one's commitment to political tolerance. Figures 1 and 2 show racial differences in the predictions for political tolerance based on perceptions of threat by different levels of education. The conditional predictions allow us to question whether racial differences in the influence of education has an effect on the relationship between perceptions of threat and political tolerance. It would appear that individuals with higher levels of education would perceive a lesser threat and

Figure 2. Conditional Predictions of Political Tolerance Using Threat and Education—White Equation

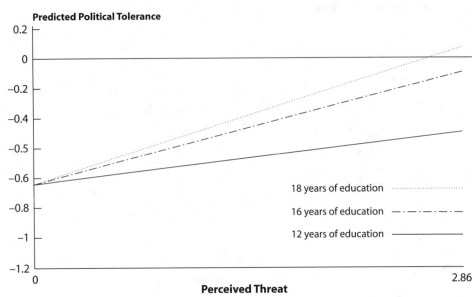

y = −1.02 + threat (−.189) + education (.092). All other variables in the equation are held at their means.

that this lesser threat might also influence support for democratic principles. The basic question is—does education have the same impact for whites and blacks in the sense that education reduces perceptions of threat or do perceptions of threat transcend levels of education?

The noticeable decline in all of the lines in Figure 1 suggests that as the perceived level of threat increases among blacks, the support for democratic principles decreases. This is basically a reproduction of the effect of perceived threat in Tables 4 and 5. An important and new finding is that the influence of education on threat continues to lead to political intolerance. In other words, perception of threat among blacks with some graduate school experience translates into political intolerance, but not as much for blacks with only a college education or a high school diploma. Education does have an effect for blacks but only in the sense that blacks become less politically intolerant as education increases but the differences are not very large (and the line never shifts to positive slope).

Figure 2 indicates that the effect of education for whites may reverse the relationship between threat and political tolerance. First, taken by itself, perceptions of threat among whites translates into intolerance (see table 5). However, because the slope for education is much larger for whites, combining this effect with what would be predicted based on the perception of threat increases their support for democratic principles. In a sense, whites' level of education saves their support for democratic norms from perceptions of threat. As the level of education increases, whites' perception of threat translates into greater political tolerance.

Clearly, the conditional relationship between education and perceived threat makes different predictions about political tolerance. Education makes blacks slightly less intolerant while the influence of education on whites reverses the en-

Table 6. Percent Supporting Their Least-Liked Group To Demonstrate Under Different Situations

	Percentages		
	Blacks	Whites	t
Suppose that the [*least-liked group*] wanted to hold a demonstration here in your neighborhood to advocate its political views. Would you:			
Do nothing to try to stop the demonstration from taking place.	41.8	62.2	7.47**
Get the government to stop the demonstration.	56.1	41.5	5.28**
Get people to go to the demonstration and stop it in any way possible, even if it meant breaking the law.	22.2	12.1	4.67**
Suppose the members of your local legislature—the city council or county government—voted to allow the demonstration to take place. Would you:			
Get the legislature decision reversed by some other government body or court.	49.2	40.4	3.17**
Do nothing at the moment but vote against the members of the local legislature at the next election.	65.6	65.0	.22

Note: These questions were asked concerning the least-liked group selected by each respondent.
**significant at .01.

tire relationship. It is also worth noting that whites and blacks start at different levels of political tolerance.

From Intolerant Attitudes to Behavior

The foregoing analysis has sought to explain black political intolerance as a conscious decision used by blacks to make them more secure and to protect them from racial hatred. Obviously, other means to constrain the behavior of the Klan are also available. Perhaps in some situations, merely limiting the freedom of the Klan may not be enough. To what extent will blacks go to limit the freedom of the Klan? Are blacks likely to resort to illegal acts and anti-systemic means to control the behavior of the Klan?

Included in the data are several items assessing individual behavior under different conditions. Respondents were presented with different scenarios involving their least-liked group after which they were asked several questions about their own behavior. Table 6 reports the questions and responses to the different scenarios.

Several conclusions are warranted. Compared to whites, a lower percentage of blacks would do nothing to try to stop the Ku Klux Klan from demonstrating in their neighborhood. In an effort to keep the Klan from demonstrating in their neighborhood, blacks are more likely to seek help from government, and more willing to organize people to stop the demonstration, even if it meant doing things that are illegal. Although whites would follow the similar strategy involving their least-liked group, a higher percentage of whites would do nothing while a lower percentage would try to stop the demonstration and organize people to stop it.

Another set of behavioral questions were prefaced with the condition that the local legislature, the city council or county government voted to allow the demonstrations to take place. Here, the racial differences are much smaller. While a larger percentage of blacks would seek to get the decision reversed by some other governmental body, blacks and whites are pretty much identical in that they would vote against the members of the city council in the next election. From the previous responses among whites, it appeared that they were not at all concerned about their least-liked group demonstrating in their neighborhood. But, clearly, their disapproval would be expressed at the polls.

Moreover, while expressing intolerant beliefs, blacks would confine themselves to the use of systemic means to limit the freedom of the Klan. To some, this may appear hopelessly tautological since the reason such behavior is perceived as necessary in the first place is due to the limitation of government making them secure.

Conclusion and Discussion

The hypothesis tested in this research is very simple: to what extent is black intolerance selective (rational) or involuntary due to cultural norms? I have argued that black political intolerance need not be viewed so pessimistically. The analysis indicates that, contrary to conventional wisdom, black intolerance is not a function of being socialized into a rigid culture stressing authoritarian values, low levels of education, nor is black intolerance a function of the absence of certain psychological attributes. Rather, blacks, in order to defend and protect themselves from anxiety and fear that comes from racial hatred, consciously and selectively deny procedural rights to such groups that threaten their existence directly, such as the Ku Klux Klan. Clearly, blacks identify the historical and current effort of the Klan to demean and terrorize them, and thus, blacks attempt to restrain its behavior.

Reacting more decisively, blacks are not particularly intolerant of everyday racists and bigots. Logically, blacks can distinguish between everyday racists and bigots who want to make life unpleasant and the Klan who wants to destroy it. If everyday racists were to become more terroristic and violent, blacks can be expected to respond by attempting to limit their freedom, as well. From this perspective, blacks are certainly committed to the rules of the game. Equally important, blacks would use systemic means to control such behavior.

Considering the various factors that interfere with the acquisition of democratic values, blacks with higher levels of education are certainly less intolerant of the Klan than blacks with lower levels of education. Although this applies to levels of self-esteem and dogmatism as well, they just do not achieve enough importance to outweigh the threat blacks perceive from the Klan. For whites, this process is very different. Because whites do not view their least-like group as particularly threatening, their levels of education, self-esteem, dogmatism, and urbanism are such that they can withstand such a threat. However, if there were groups in American society who were "out to get them" and destroy whites for simply being white, tolerance among whites might prove to be less resilient.

References

Abramson, Paul R. 1983. *Political Attitudes In America*. San Francisco: Freeman.
Bachrach, Peter. 1967. *The Theory of Democratic Elitism: A Critique*. Boston: Little Brown.

Bagley, Christopher. 1979. "Self-Esteem as a Pivotal Concept in Race and Ethnic Relations," in *Research in Race and Ethnic Relations*. eds. Cora Bagley Marret and Cheryl Leggon.

Bay, Christian. 1958. *The Structure of Freedom*. Stanford: Stanford University Press.

Bay, Christian. 1981. *Strategies Of Political Emancipation*. Notre Dame: University of Notre Dame.

Bobo, Lawrence, and Frederick C. Licari. 1989. "Education and Political Tolerance," *Public Opinion Quarterly*. 53: 283-308.

Crick, Bernard. 1973. *Political Theory and Practice*. New York: Basic Books.

Dahl, Robert. 1956. *A Preface to Democratic Theory*. Chicago: University of Chicago Press.

Davis, Darren W. 1997. "The Direction of Race of Interviewer Effects: Donning the Black Mask," *American Journal of Political Science* forthcoming.

Davis, Darren W. 1995. "Exploring Black Political Intolerance," *Political Behavior* 17: 1-22.

Gibson, James. 1995. "The Political Freedom of African Americans: A Contextual Analysis of Racial Attitudes, Political Tolerance, and Individual Liberty," *Political Geography* 14: 571-599.

Gibson, James. 1992. "The Political Consequences of Intolerance: Cultural Conformity and Political Freedom," *American Political Science Review* 36: 560-577.

Gibson, James L., and Gregory Caldeira. 1992. "Blacks and the United States Supreme Court: Models of Diffuse Support," *Journal of Politics* 54: 1120-1145.

Gibson, James. 1988. "Political Intolerance and Political Repression During the McCarthy Red Scare," *Journal of Politics*, 51: 13-35.

Gibson, James. 1986. "Pluralistic Intolerance in America: A Reconsideration," *American Politics Quarterly*, 14: 267-293.

Gibson, James. 1986. "Homosexuals and the Ku Klux Klan: A Contextual Analysis of Political Tolerance," *Western Political Quarterly*, 40: 427-448.

Green, Donald P. and Lisa M. Waxman. 1987. "Direct Threat and Political Tolerance: An Experimental Analysis of the Tolerance of Blacks Toward Racists," *Public Opinion Quarterly* 51: 149-165.

Herson, L. J. R. and C. R. Hofstetter. 1975 "Tolerance, Consensus, and the Democratic Creed: A Contextual Exploration," *Journal of Politics*, 37: 1007-1032.

Kuklinski, James H., Paul M. Sniderman, Kathleen Knight, Thomas Piazza, Philip E. Tetlock, Gordon Lawrence, and Barbara Millers. 1997. "Racial Prejudice and Attitudes Toward Affirmative Action," *American Journal of Political Science* 41: 402-419.

Lawrence, David G. 1976. "Procedural Norms and Tolerance: A Reassessment," *American Political Science Review*, 70: 80-100.

Lipset, Seymour Martin. 1960. *Political Man*. New York: Doubleday.

Lipsitz, Lewis. 1972. "Freedom and the Poor," *Western Political Quarterly*, 25: 151-62.

McClosky, Herbert. 1964. "Consensus and Ideology in American Politics," *American Political Science Review*, 58: 361-82.

McClosky, Hebert, and Alida Brill. 1983. *Dimensions of Tolerance: What Americans Believe About Civil Liberties*. New York: Russell Sage Foundation.

McCutheon, A. L. 1985. "A Latent Class Analysis of Tolerance for Nonconformity in the American Public," *Public Opinion Quarterly*, 49: 474-488.

Mill, John Stuart. [1859] 1989. *Three Essays: On Liberty, Representative Government, The Subjection of Women*. New York: Oxford University Press.

Nunn, Clyde Z., Harry Crockett, Jr., and J. Allen Williams, Jr. 1978. *Tolerance for Conconformity*. San Francisco: Jossey–Bass.

Peffley, Mark, and Lee Sigelman. 1990. "Intolerance of Communists during the McCarthy era: A General Model," *Western Political Quarterly* March 43: 93-111.

Prothro, James W. and Charles M. Grigg. 1960. "Fundamental Principles of Democracy: Bases of Agreement and Disagreement," *Journal of Politics*, 22: 276-94.

Rokeach, Milton. 1960. *The Open and Closed Mind*. New York: Basic Books.

Seltzer, Richard and Robert Smith. 1985. "Race and Civil Liberties," *Social Science Quarterly* 66: 155-62.

Simmons, Roberta, Leslie Brown, Diane Bush, and Dale Blyth. 1978. "Self-Esteem and Achievement of Black and Whites Adolescents," *Social Problems*, 76: 86-96.

Sniderman, Paul M., Philip Tetlock, James Glaser, Donald Philip Green, and Michael Haut. 1991. "Principled Tolerance and the American Mass Public," *British Journal of Political Science* 19: 25-45.

Sniderman, Paul M. 1975. *Personality and Democratic Politics*. Berkeley: University of California Press.

Stouffer, Samuel. 1955. *Communism, Conformity, and Civil Liberties*. New York: Doubleday.

Sullivan, John L., James E. Piereson, and George E. Marcus. 1979. "An Alternative Conceptualization of Political Tolerance: Illusory Increases, 1950's–1970's," *American Political Science Review*, 73: 233-49.

Sullivan, John L., James E. Piereson, and George E. Marcus. 1982. *Political Tolerance and American Democracy*. Chicago: The University of Chicago Press.

Sullivan, John L., Michal Shamir, Patrick Walsh, and Nigel S. Roberts. 1985. *Political Tolerance in Context: Support for Unpopular Minorities in Israel, New Zealand, and the United States*. Boulder: Westview Press, Inc.

Verba, Sidney and Norman H. Nie. 1972. *Participation in America*. Chicago: The University of Chicago Press.

Zalkind, S. S., E. A. Gaugler, and R. M. Schwartz. 1975. "Civil Liberties Attitudes and Personality Measures: Some Exploratory Research," *Journal of Social Issues*, 31: 77-91.

Zellman, Gail. 1975. "Anti-Democratic Beliefs: A Survey and Some Explanations," *Journal of Social Issues* 31: 31-53.

35

From Black Power to Black Perspectives: The Reconstruction of a Black Political Identity

Kalbir Shukra

Introduction

Strategies of contesting racism deployed by African-Caribbean and Asian political organisers today are dominated by the politics of ethnicity, that is an emphasis on cultural difference and identity in a search for a share of resources, influence and representation within the existing social framework. The growing recognition that the resulting divisions and disunity are undesirable has given rise to the 1990s alternative to ethnicity: the creation of black perspectives.

A high proportion of 1990s black[1] organisers, public sector professionals, academics and politicians seem to have been party to the development and normalisation of black perspectivist thought and social regulation. Whether in developing local authority policies, procedures and practices; promoting new agendas within organisations; developing black caucuses; demanding black representation or producing reports which specify the effects of a particular concern on black communities, contemporary black political contestation of racism tends to take the form of black perspectivism. The key characteristics of black perspectivist strategies can be summarised as:

1. Promoting ethnic pride, identity and self-esteem.
2. Allowing for self-definition.
3. Recognising a common 'black' experience by coordinating ethnic identities.
4. Supporting black autonomous organisation.
5. Contesting racial discrimination at a local, often institutional level.

An earlier version of this essay appeared in *Youth and Policy* 49 (Summer 1995): 5–19 and is adapted/reprinted with the permission of the copyright holder/author.
1. I use the term 'black' in this paper to refer to people of African-Caribbean or South Asian origin or descent.

6. Seeking the inclusion of marginalised groups in the mainstream.

Both ethnic pluralism and black perspectivism represent a shift of black politics, community and youth work into mainstream managerialism. In order to critically evaluate the impact of this development on community work and young black people in the 1990s, it is necessary to go beyond an examination of the minutiae of policy and take a broad sociological view of the nature of black perspectivism. This means examining its descent through revolutionary marxist, pluralist and town hall versions of black power to highlight the changing objects of black political contestation as indicative of a shift from aspirations of social change to operating a bureaucratised form of black power.

It also involves tracing the emergence of black perspectivist thought and identifying the continuities as well as the discontinuities between black radicalism, ethnicity and perspectivism. In this way, what I seek to reveal is that far from being contradictory political strategies, ethnicity and black perspectivism share fundamental ideological connections. In community and youth work circles, the notion of 'theory' is all too often derided as being too distant from people's real experiences. However, in adopting a theoretical approach which situates the role of black organisers in its wider context and refuses to confine itself to a narrow experiential or policy perspective, I have attempted to reveal that the implications of these developments for black youth today have been enormous. Young blacks were active in the militant campaigns of the 1960s and 1970s as well as the street rebellions of the 1980s. Their direct action was crucial in forcing the State to re-think its strategy and allowing some black activists to press for black representation and resources. During the 1980s professionalisation process when a new layer of black public sector professionals was created, many youth activists were also incorporated. By the 1990s, however, the institutionalisation of black organisers and their politics has resulted in two forms of experience: on one hand there are the majority of black youth and on the other there are professionals and politicians who purport to represent their interests.

A key consequence of this has been a redirection of black youth anger away from street confrontation and towards bureaucratic settlements. It is this broader shift rather than individual policies which have made black politics ineffectual and alienated black youth from it. This raises questions about today's black political outlook which community and youth workers who wish to change the position of black people need to address.

Black Radicalism

My analysis begins with black radicalism, which was a version of black power that made its presence felt in Britain from 1967-79 and has since become a source of inspiration and contention in black politics. Black radicalism emerged from the visits to Britain of Malcolm X in 1965 and Stokely Carmichael in 1967 (Hiro, 1991) when black militants in Britain encouraged existing race related organisations to adopt a black militant position. Splits and coups in the United Coloured People's Alliance (UCPA); Institute of Race Relations (IRR); Campaign Against Racial Discrimination (CARD) and other organisations were evidence of the radicalisation that was occurring in black communities and the support that black power was gaining amongst activists. However, 'black power' was a diffuse political identity which accommodated a wide range of ideas including promotion of black pride and identity; black history; black cultural heritage; black separatism; black control; a return to Africa; black revolution; black capitalism; and black community. That black power coexisted with so many diverging approaches weakened the newly black power-led organisations. Black Power activist Obi Egbuna described the problem faced by the UCPA thus:

> Within that single organisation, there were members who believed that the answer to the Black man's problem lay in the overthrow of the capitalist system, and there were others who felt it lay in the Black man going to the House of Lords; there were some who saw themselves as part of the international Black revolution, and there was a faction who believed that the Black man in this country should concern himself only with what goes on in this country... in short, it became all too clear that what we had was not one movement, but movements within a movement. (Egbuna, 1971:19-20)

The contradictions and tensions in the notion of black power produced constant conflicts, splits and new formations. (Ibid:21) Nevertheless, the different approaches that were evident in both Britain and the USA were held together by a common inner dynamic. That was the idea that black people needed to redefine themselves by asserting their own history and culture to project an image which they would develop without white people. This alternative identity and counter-discourse became known as a 'positive image' and was intended to counter the dominant 'negative' images of black people. (Carmichael and Hamilton, 1969:51) Whilst neither small revolutionary black power organisations nor black capitalism were successful in 1970s Britain, black power politics in the form of black radicalism gained a significant level of support, especially among young people.

At first sight, black radicalism appeared to be a revolutionary movement in Britain. Black radical intellectuals sought to develop a 'black marxist' political position and activists deployed language associated with enthusiasm for change. In practice, however, black radicals adopted an approach which coincided with the Carmichael and Hamilton school of pluralist black power thought. Carmichael and Hamilton had promoted black 'pride and identity' in the context of seeking effective leverage for black people in the USA to obtain more resources from the existing social structure. In 1970s and 1980s Britain, black intellectuals such as Ron Ramdin, A. Sivanandan, Darcus Howe and American academic Cedric Robinson[2] struggled to balance race and class factors in their writing to develop a black marxist political position. They adopted the US 'black power' slogan which referred to African-Americans and applied it to refer to Asian as well as African-Caribbean communities in Britain. They also used it to promote concepts such as 'black struggle'; 'black solidarity'; 'black resistance' and 'black consciousness'—all of which were linked to the notion of politicising black communities to achieve 'black liberation'. (Ramdin, 1987; Sivanandan, 1982; Howe, 1988; Robinson, 1983) In processing the race-class dynamic they drew on a com-

---

2. These individuals are connected in that they have at some point been based at or worked from the Institute of Race Relations, which Sivanandan currently leads.

bination of marxist analyses and black nationalism. (Callinicos, 1992:4-6) In 1973 Sivanandan described the problem as:

> the confused historical position in which black people find themselves placed in white capitalist society. Whereas the working class sees itself exploited as a class and comes face to face with its exploiter, capital, the capitalist exploitation of blacks is veiled by racial oppression. As a result they are caught up in a two-fold consciousness: as a class and as a race, each of which often contradicts the other without affording a synthesis. (*Race Today*, June 1973)

Whereas class-based social theories sought to provide an analysis of the position of working class people in economic terms and black nationalist theories sought to provide an analysis of the position of black people in terms of race, Sivanandan sought a combination of the two so that the issues of race and class could be addressed simultaneously. Sivanandan saw the solution as 'an organic fusion of forces'. He argued that the prerequisites for this were that black people should:

> through the consciousness of their colour, through the consciousness, that is, of that in which they perceive their oppression, arrive at a consciousness of class; and the white working class must in recovering its class instinct, its sense of oppression, both from technological alienation and a white oriented culture, arrive at a consciousness of racial oppression. (Sivanandan, 1982:96)

For Sivanandan, in order for one to reach a comprehension of the other, each social group needed to look inwards at itself. In this way each group could develop an awareness of the factors which militated against itself before and in order to develop an awareness of the other. The implication was that neither group could understand the other without understanding itself first. This analysis translated into black people needing to seek a black consciousness whilst white workers developed a parallel class consciousness prior to any fusion occurring.

The 'black consciousness' which the black radicals promoted in their writings, referred to a growing awareness of Asian and African-Caribbean people as a group of black people with specific collective interests defined by their collective experience of racism and consequent resistance to it. This concept is worth exploring further as it forms the basis of continuities between black radicalism, ethnicity and black perspectivism.

Although in processing the race-class equation the four writers sought a black marxist position their emphasis on black consciousness coincided with pluralist concepts in two key respects. Firstly, the search for a black consciousness called for the acquisition of a black identity through the recognition of a distinct culture[3] through black solidarity, pride and history—a concept rooted in pluralist black power, as promoted by Carmichael and Hamilton. This reconciled the black radicals to the pluralist objective of inclusion into the mainstream through using self-identification as a social group to lever a share of rights, policies and resources for the black community from the existing society. Secondly the radicals' objective of black consciousness was rooted in the pluralist conception of society as made up of competing interest groups which gain influence and resources through negotiation, dialogue, strength and solidarity. (Jacobs, 1988:33) Thus, al-

---

3. In this context 'culture' implied religion, language, style, aesthetics and customs as vehicles for the creation of a black (often African) identity.

though the black radicals may have started out with a view to promoting black marxism, the analyses that they developed were rooted in pluralist black power.

This gap between the intention and the end result of the analyses had the effect of creating a gap between what black radicals claimed to do and the strategies which they adopted. This was evident in the campaign organised around the trial of the 'Mangrove 9.'[4] (Howe, 1988:41; Carter, 1986:107) The campaign had two main elements to it: the legalistic and the mobilisational. The legalistic element involved the defence of the nine through the judicial system, an unsuccessful jury challenge, the demand for a black jury of peers and the tabling of motions for the rights of the defendants. (Howe, 1988:47). Meanwhile the mobilisational element served to put the cases under public scrutiny through lobbying of courts, organising rallies and distributing publicity material. The inconsistency between activist claims and this strategy lay in the focus of the mobilisational activity. Activity was focused predominantly within black communities although, as well as encouraging black community self-organisation, leading campaign activists had hoped that it would pose a challenge to racism amongst the white working class. This is apparent from Darcus Howe's evaluation that 'Racism as a basis for the division of the working class took a beating'. (Ibid:48) However, the campaign neither sought nor won the active support of any section of the white working class. At most, white workers remained quiet and white jurors seemed sympathetic. (Ibid:48) A challenge to the white working class was necessarily limited by the focus on autonomous black self-organisation and mobilisation, which was primarily within the ranks of black communities.

A revolutionary linguistic style was also used by the black radical Race Today Collective in its monthly journal *Race Today* to argue in its 'Editorial' for a 'mass organisation, of unemployed youth, students and parents' to fight police harassment. (*Race Today*, Jul/Aug 1976) Like the Asian Youth Movements, the alliance between the Black Parents Movement and the Black Students Movement (BPM/BSM) was portrayed as an example of the way forward. John La Rose, leading figure in the BPM asserted in the columns of *Race Today* that 'There was no turning back from independent revolutionary black politics' (*Race Today*, Mar. 1976) What he described could more accurately be termed a form of 'community politics'. There was little evidence of 'revolutionary black politics' amongst these groups in the sense that they sought fundamental social and economic change. The approach which they adopted in practice was a pluralist one of seeking to obtain the maximum out of the existing system. This took the form of, for example, taking on defence casework and helping defendants through the legal system; publicising each case within the local black community; lobbying the Home Secretary and Police Commissioner. (*Race Today*, Oct. 1976)

The black radicals did not match their revolutionary claims with their practice, which was based on the particularist pursuit of black consciousness, 'particularist' because the search for a black consciousness was rooted in the idea of there being a corporate black history and identity which is accessible only to individuals by

---

4. The Mangrove 9 were arrested on 8/9/70 during clashes with the police at a demonstration against police raids on the Mangrove restaurant. They were charged with riot, conspiracy, affray and assault. The ten week trial which followed formed the basis of a national campaign among black communities and marked a turning point in the development of black community campaigning.

virtue of their experience of being black. Within this analysis, racism was specifically a black experience alone. Hence, Ron Ramdin, argued that the development of black solidarity reflected the 'failure of white radicals to recognise the special problems of the black working class'. (Ramdin, 1987:499-500) Cedric Robinson was more explicit in *Black Marxism* in which he argued that 'the black radical tradition' rather than a broader working class is the agency of social change. A white marxist commentator, Alexander Callinicos, took issue with the black radicals in their belief that 'white workers materially benefit from racism'. (Callinicos, 1992:22) Callinicos posited that the 'fundamental reason why Marxists argue that racism is not in the interests of white workers is that, by dividing the working class, it weakens white as well as black workers'. (Ibid:25) In contrast to this, Ramdin and the other black radicals suggested that racism remained a 'special problem' for black people and that marxism was incapable of addressing the issue of racism since its very epistemology is 'Eurocentric'. (Robinson, 1983)

The effect of identifying racism as problematic only insofar as it is experienced by a single section of society, was to lose the totality of the experience. The specificity emphasised in the work of the black radicals reflected the black radical tendency to localise the experience of racism to the effects that it had on a particular social group rather than generalising it to indicate the overall experience and effects. The logic of viewing racism as a black experience alone was that contesting it involved raising black consciousness and organising black resistance. It then followed that if the negative experience of racism was turned into a positive experience of being black, an identity could be acquired as a vehicle for the pursuit of equality. Hence, several years later, Sivanandan argued:

> We don't need a cultural identity for its own sake, but to make use of the positive aspects of our culture to forge correct alliances and fight the correct battles. (Sivanandan, 1983:11)

A consequence of this was the promotion of a black-only form of community organisation or what Ramdin referred to as 'black autonomous organisations'. (Ramdin, 1987:508) Although the labels 'Black Self-help' and 'autonomous organisation' imply self-reliance, the key feature of these organisations was a shift in focus away from seeking white working class support and putting pressure on officialdom for support instead. Thus, the Brent Defence Committee called on the Home Secretary to intervene in the harassment of black people by the Metropolitan police. (*Race Today*, Jul/Aug 1976) Similarly, the campaign 'Bookshop Joint Action' called on letters of protest to be written to the Home Secretary with a view to seeking state protection against racist attacks. (*Race Today*, Jan 1978)

In this process, the black radicals' attempt to fuse race and class had the effect of focusing on black communities to oppose racism but left the role of other social groups as a side issue. Whereas the early post-war black organisations arose from an isolated and defensive position of exclusion, the influence of pluralist black power on black radicalism resulted in an emphasis on separateness, differentness and fragmentation despite efforts to seek a balance between race and class factors in community campaigns. Black radicalism, in turn, endorsed different, separate and exclusive experience, and therefore, black-only organisation as a conscious strategy for emancipation. This occurred in the context of the wider development of New Separatism which is examined next.

Black radicalism was one element in New Separatism. In the black radical tradition, a hermetically sealed Black Experience was treated as impenetrable by any non-black people. Marxism was considered 'Eurocentric' because it 'was formulated in a European context'. (Sivanandan, 1982; Ramdin, 1987; Robinson, 1983) It was immutably so because 'to understand fully the burden of blackness they (white marxists) require the imagination and feeling systematically denied them by their culture'. (Sivanandan, 1982) From this viewpoint, even if white marxists tried to make sense of the black experience, they could not because the experience would be alien to them. Consequently, separatism remained the logical form of expression and organisation for developing a black political movement. As Kobena Mercer noted, the importance attached to developing a group identity based upon cultural and subjective experience was not lost on other social movements, such as feminists and the gay liberation movement:

> the radicalisation of sexual politics from 1970 onwards derived significant momentum from imaginary equivalences with black struggle as 'black pride' and 'brotherhood' acted as metonymic leverage for the affirmation of 'gay pride' and the assertion of sisterhood is strength. (Mercer, 1990:61)

In addition to a similarity of language and labels these social movements were based on particularist ideologies. Each group localised its experiences as women, black people or homosexuals. In doing so the group formed a membrane around its corporate experience, thereby dividing itself from other groups. As part of the emergence of this wider development, Black radicalism formed the race dimension of New Separatism in the 1970s. This progressed into the identity politics and black perspectivism of the 1980s and 1990s. Although identity politics and black perspectivism were different in form, they both emerged from the ideology of ethnicity and were consistent with mainstream power structures. It is therefore necessary to examine how ethnicity derived from New Separatism before moving on to examine identity politics and black perspectivism.

Ethnicity

The concept 'ethnic group' emerged from urban anthropology to emphasise the self-identification of groups based on cultural difference. (Lyon, 1972; 1972-3; 1973) Amongst Barthian ethnic relations researchers in Britain such as Michael Banton, Sandra Wallman and V.S. Khan, it is the perception and attribution of meaning to difference which forms the basis of 'ethnicity'. (Rex and Mason, 1986:175; Miles, 1982:60-4) Therefore, for these writers, ethnic relations research begins with a group's perception of a sense of difference ('us') against the rest ('them') with phenotype as one element in the 'repertoire of ethnic boundary markers'. (Wallman, 1986:229)

Just as the 1970s debate amongst academics about the relationship between race and class broadened to include ethnic group (Miles, 1982:44; Sivanandan, 1983:4; Jenkins, 1986:180-181) so ethnicity became another factor in New Separatism. Ethnicity broke down the race section of New Separatism into competing histories and identities within black communities: Indians, Bangladeshis, Africans, Caribbeans and other ethnic groups made separate demands for resources and status based upon their cultural differences. The value placed upon subjective experience created an unbridgeable gap between all of these groups and deemed the experience exclusive. At most they forged alliances but generally they became competitors in the bargaining for power.

Black radicals were critical of ethnicity and presented black radicalism as oppositional to the development of ethnicity. The connection which they missed was the pluralist black power influence on black radicalism which emphasised a need to recognise a cultural identity based on a different past. This analysis suggests that ethnicity was a logical extension of this promotion of difference, separateness and particularist experience. Where they differed was in the use of cultural distinctiveness to create ethnic identities to lever resources and status out of local government. As municipal socialism and the race dimension of New Separatism converged, it gave rise to the identity politics of the 1980s.

Identity Politics

So far this paper has characterised the main features of 1960s/70s black power politics and shown how it developed into a section of New Separatism and laid the foundation for the emergence of a new ethnicity. The reforged ethnicity converged with the rise of Labour left politics in local government to produce identity politics and perspectivism. The changing response of black activists to the establishment's race relations initiatives can be used as a marker for the development of these black political strategies. The dominant response changed from activist hostility to critical discussions and then integration into the mainstream.

The non-cooperation and hostility towards establishment initiatives shown by some black activists in the immediate aftermath of the 1981 revolts was rooted in the black radical outlook which was carried over from the previous decade. (Goulbourne, 1990:111) The primary response of militant black activists and local groups was a refusal to cooperate with Lord Scarman's inquiry into the Brixton events, arguing that it was a containment exercise. (Tompson, 1988:101; CARF, 1981) The use of the tool of non-cooperation with state representatives was not unusual amongst black radicals at the time, for example, on 22 May 1980 Black community leaders in Bristol refused to meet their MP (CARF, 1980); on 15 Aug. 1981 the Caribbean community in Sheffield suspended all contact with police after 17 youths were arrested. This was repeated on 3 March 1982 and on 13 September 1982 when the Asian community in Sheffield adopted the tactic. Furthermore, on 29 June 1980 more than a hundred delegates from at least 40 black organisations met at the Afro-Asian Caribbean Convention to set up a National Council of Black Organisations. A proposal at the conference calling for Caribbean and Asian people not to cooperate with the police received much press publicity. (*Times* 6/30/80; *Guardian* 7/1/80; *West Indian World* 7/4/80; *New Statesman* 7/25/80)

The pluralist politics of the black radicals which was dressed in revolutionary marxist rhetoric, however, left the activists short of what Brian Jacobs calls a 'political programme which would take them beyond a critique of the state, government and police'. (Jacobs, 1986:149) Sivanandan encouraged the growth of anti-racist black organisations and argued that in order to be effective they would need to adopt a more coherent political strategy which could defend the interests of black people. (*Race and Class*, 1981) He did not, however, indicate how this could be brought about. Similarly, *Race Today* editor Darcus Howe described the events as revolts against the police and predicted more to come. (*Times*, 11/26/81). Jacobs notes that such analyses in practice led some radicals to expect a spontaneous up-turn in political activity, only to become demoralised when it did not materialise. (Jacobs, 1986:148) The inadequacy of these black radical strategies left activists open to alternative ideas. Initially this meant that when the establishment looked to build bridges with black community activists in the aftermath of the 1981 re-volts, many radical black activists were prepared to shift from hostility towards state initiatives to critical cooperation. The work of the Labour left in local gov-ernment to woo hitherto excluded groups to participate in local politics was a key factor in facilitating this shift. (Shukra, 1990:169; Wainwright, 1987)

When the pioneering Labour controlled, local authorities began to face the task of establishing a race relations network, those activists who commanded some grass roots support were generally hostile towards establishment initiatives. The hostility was rooted in the legacy of the campaigning and mobilisational approach of 1970s black power-led community politics. This was reflected, shortly after the 1981 riots, in Sivanandan's endorsement of organisations which had not "compromised with government policy or fallen prey to government hand-outs...or looked to the Labour Party for redress". (*Race And Class* Aut. 1981/Winter 1982) The chief al-liance made by black radicals had been with Trotskyist groupings such as the Inter-national Marxist Group, Workers Revolutionary Party and Socialist Workers Party which also operated outside of the mainstream. As some of the Trotskyist groups de-veloped closer relationships with the Labour Party, some of the black people who were active in them joined the Labour Party along with their white counterparts. Thus, Black Section members who were wary of the Labour Party nevertheless joined it because there were moves to democratise the Party and explained their move as a political recognition of the need to join a mainstream party in order to make a politi-cal impact.... (Wainwright, 1987; Shukra, 1990) These individuals were part of the rise of the left in local government and were, thereby, also part of bridging the gap between black activists who maintained their stand against joining the Labour Party and state institutions, for it was through the rise of left wing local authorities, that many black activists began to develop a critical dialogue with radical wings of Labour authorities. Black radicals and theoreticians such as A. Sivanandan; Farrukh Dhondy; Cecil Gutzmore and CLR James, agreed to appear on the platform of the 1983 GLC conference 'Challenging Racism in London' and spoke critically of the initiative. The Feature Address, for example, was delivered by Sivanandan, under the guise of a 'heretic and a disbeliever' who, nevertheless, argued:

> Don't let's be purists and stand outside, for we can't fight the system bare-handed. We don't have the tools, brothers and sisters; we've got to get the tools from the system itself and hope that in the process five out of ten of us don't be-come corrupt. (Sivanandan, 1983)

Although these radicals had argued immediately after the 1981 disorders for the creation of an independent black political force, they now seemed to recognise that they did not have a strategy which could achieve this and their reasoning shifted towards the view that some kind of involvement was practical and neces-sary, despite the risks. In this way they approved local authority patronage amongst radical audiences who may otherwise have remained uncertain. From non-cooperation, black militants moved towards a sceptical cooperation which proved to be a bridge towards a working relationship between activists and the local state.

Groups enticed by local authority offers of recognition went on to negotiate a share of limited resources, status and political influence. In order to gain recognition, representatives needed to convince the authority that they were members of a group which shared experiences that constituted a distinct culture within British society. The reasoning went on that the group was disadvantaged by its exclusion from the mainstream in terms of recognition, resources, status and political influence. Thus by arguing a case of difference, distinctiveness and separateness, group activists would seek recognition, participation and inclusion in the distribution of power and resources. This approach concurred with the efforts of some of the Labour left-led authorities to link up with some of these groups. (Shukra, 1990:169)

Competing Identities

One of the consequences of this process was the institutionalisation of rivalry between groups seeking access to resources. These identities began with broad categories of race, class, sexuality and gender and multiplied into subcategories and combinations of sub-categories. This trend was described by contributors to a conference entitled 'Changing Identities' in 1989 in a variety of ways: 'a plurality of particularisms', (Mercer, 1990:65) 'identity politics', 'cultural politics of difference', (Rutherford, 1990:20) 'a hierarchy of oppression' (Parmar, 1990:107). Whatever the label commentators applied to the process, they generally agreed that one effect of this was to legitimise a series of competing identities between different social groups:

> ...one group's loss was another group's gain. In this zero sum game the only tangible consequence of diversity was dividedness. (Rutherford, 1990:47)

As limited resources became dwindling resources in local government, the dividedness which developed sometimes manifested itself in local conflict. In some areas this generated conflict over consultation and representation between the established groups such as Community Relations Councils (CRC) and the new organisations. Enthusiastic young workers recruited in new grant-aided organisations found it necessary to set up new consultative structures which they considered to be more representative of the local black community. (Black People's Forum, 1983; Eade, 1989:105-112) The effect of these developments was disunity, depoliticisation and a tendency towards fragmentation. This fragmentation sometimes took an ethnic form.

Fragmentation and Depoliticisation

The development of politics based upon competing identities institutionalised and reinforced fragmentation amongst black groups into more specific ethnicities.

One of the symptoms of this was a widespread debate amongst black activists during this time related to the definition of 'black'. 'Black' also became divided into 'Asian' and 'Afro-Caribbean'; then 'Asian' was broken down into 'Indian', 'Pakistani' and 'Bengali'; then 'Afro-Caribbean' into 'African' and 'Caribbean'; and sometimes into other groupings under the headings of 'ethnic', 'cultural' or 'national' minorities.

This signified a shift in thinking amongst black organisers. Their primary concern was less one of creating unity amongst Asian, African and Caribbean communities in the search for a black consciousness to be used to bring about wider social change. As increasing emphasis was put on culture and ethnicity, the particularist approach of seeking a black alternative view fragmented into a search for smaller, minority perspectives. Each perspective was based upon differential experience and the rejection of the idea of a universal human history in favour of the notion of different histories and identities (Furedi, 1992:230). In this context, many small changes were regarded as more viable than one big one.

The Localisation of Change

In accepting that there are many experiences, approaches, histories and meanings, the idea of a single truth was rejected. With a plurality of perspectives, communities and histories, the question of change also became localised. As Furedi argued, 'Local histories and small narratives call into question the making of history on a societal level'. (Ibid:239)

In this context of rising perspectivism, the main concern of black people shifted towards a search for small movements in policy, working methods, representation and resourcing to ensure that diverse lifestyles, religions, perspectives and heritage, as represented amongst 'ethnic minority' communities, were taken into account. Thus, multi-culturalism in education (Jacobs, 1988:122) and equal opportunities in employment and service provision were promoted. (Ball and Solomos, 1990) Some organisers sought provision for single ethnic or religious minorities, as represented by the demands for non-white minority schools; Halal meat in schools; and separate youth, community and leisure provision for ethnic groups. It was at this time that one commentator, Tariq Modood, argued in favour of 'Ethnic self-definition' and against the 'black' of identity politics. (Modood, 1988) He argued that the 'black' identity could not adequately serve Asian communities because it was rooted in Pan-Africanist/black power influence and signified 'the acceptance by Asians of an Afro political leadership'. (Ibid) In arguing this, however, Modood did not account for what were seen by some Asian activists as positive effects of black power on Asian community organisations in the 1970s. First, 'black power' had contributed to a new militant mood of Asian militancy in which Asian Youth Movements thrived and Asian workers—often women as in the cases of Grunwick and Imperial Typewriters—engaged in industrial disputes. Second, some of the first black power initiatives had been led by Asian activists such as Sivanandan in transforming the Institute of Race Relations, and Jagmohan Joshi in creating and leading the Black People's Alliance. Third, black power had contributed to efforts to break down prejudices between Asians and African-Caribbeans as exemplified by the Organisation of Women of African and Asian

Descent (OWAAD) which brought together African-Caribbean and Asian women to develop a black feminist strategy. (Parmar, 1990) The strength of Modood's case lay in the fact that these events occurred in the late 1960s through to 1980 whereas Modood argued against the 'black' identity in the late 1980s in the midst of the controversy over *The Satanic Verses*. At this time, political strategies were less about solidarity and militancy and more about representation in the mainstream based on ethnic identities. In the context of changed political objectives, Modood's case was coherent. His approach supported deregulation of 'black' and promoted ethnic self-identification.

Black Perspectivism

Whilst Modood gave support to the developing ethnic perspectives, those black people who were uncomfortable with the emphasis on ethnic and cultural difference turned to black radicalism. In doing so, they became black perspectivists. Black perspectivists represented the revival of the black power/black radical approach of pursuing a joint Asian-African-Caribbean approach. However, rather than channel it into campaigns, protests and mobilisation, the black perspectivists introduced the black identity into policy development, the professions and mainstream politics. They acknowledged ethnic identities but promoted the use of 'black' to avoid ethnic disunity.

Black perspectives were claimed and deployed by the all-black review panel investigating the 'Handsworth Rebellions of September 1985'; (Bhavnani et al., 1986) Labour Party Black Sections in *The Black Agenda* (1988); the Parliamentary Black Caucus; the participants of the 1990 National Black Workers and Trainers Conference in their response to Ministerial proposals for a core curriculum for Community and Youth Work (National Black Workers and Trainers Standing Conference, 1990); the National Black Caucus at its annual conferences and by other black professionals and academics in their work. The chief and clearest attempt to define the term can be found in the report of the 1990 National Conference of Black Workers and Trainers. Although it took four pages to explain the term, it was summarised as:

> the collective capacity for Black people to define, develop, defend and advance their own political, economic, social education (sic) and cultural interests. (Ibid:10)

By this definition it seems that the 1980s/90s 'black perspective' is related to 1960s 'black power' and 1970s 'black autonomous organisation'. It brought together the key elements of its antecedents: the search for pride and identity to develop a high self-esteem; self-definition; recognition for black experience; and self-organisation. It also shared with its progenitors their tendency to localise experience. Within the broad term 'black', black perspectivists continued to recognise ethnic difference in a way that the 1970s use of 'black' did not. 'Black' shifted from being a single political identity stemming from resistance to racism to a mechanism through which the separate ethnic groups could be called together, coordinated and linked. In Sivanandan's words, black lost its 'political culture' and became a 'cultural colour'. (Interview with Sivanandan)

What distinguished the black perspectivist tendency was the way it combined the continued localisation of experience with the localisation of change to the point of seeking political solutions through bureaucratic measures. The localisation of change saw a further shift in attitudes amongst black activists as the emphasis moved away from the declarations for wider social change towards a reconstruction of black political activity through institutionalisation and bureaucratisation. During the 1980s, this was further confined to modifications within specific organisations as the focus of change became policies and individual practices. Black perspectivists sought to apply a new way of seeing to issues or cases in hand to ensure that black experiences were accounted for.

In addressing the question of the changing nature of anti-racism, Gilroy described how the local authority became the 'primary site of anti-racist struggle' and the search for anti-racist change became 'atomised' (Gilroy, 1987:144-6) and Tompson (1988) demonstrated how the bureaucratisation of 'anti-racism' occurred through the integration of black people into local government machinery. The concern of this paper is how black people came to redefine their objectives such that small changes rather than social transformation became their concern. The inclusion of black individuals in local power structures was partly made possible by their desire to play a part in the mainstream.[5] Manifested through identity politics, this desire for inclusion converged with the objectives of the local state of increasing the participation of fringe groups in the political process. This integration in turn affected black political activity. It changed the outlook of black leaders. As Tompson argued:

> It was not so much that radicals were bought off (though some undoubtedly were) but rather that their whole outlook became shaped by the new race-relations machinery. Activists grew dependent upon council grants, resources and facilities to maintain their momentum. Oak-panelled committee rooms, dingy community centres—these became a way of life. (Ibid:100)

The decline in numbers mobilised to the few demonstrations that were organised from 1985 suggests that protest and opposition was no longer the primary concern of black activists. (Ibid:107-8) Instead of mass protest marches in response to racist murders and injustice as seen in 1981,[6] the sense of 'realism' preoccupying the left affected black activists too. Effective black responses became equated with policy changes, committee reports, establishing new organisations, recruiting more black staff, increasing black representation at every level of the establishment and adopting 'a black perspective'.

Whereas a sense of major injustice up to 1981 might have resulted in a large mobilisation, thereafter the predominant activities were calls for official inquiries, more resources and increased representation in officialdom. The 1985 events at Broadwater Farm alone gave rise to two inquiries by Lord Gifford, an investigation by Amnesty International, a report compiled by black American judges Margaret Burnham and Lennox Hinds and, finally, an investigation by the Metropolitan Police. Similarly the 1985 Handsworth disorders resulted in a government

---

5. The desire for inclusion did not suddenly materialise in the 1980s but was the main impulse behind pluralist black power.

6. 1981 saw the Black People's March for Justice in south London, an outcry against the murder of the Khan family in East London and a national mobilisation against the killing of Satnam Singh Gill in Coventry.

inquiry conducted by the police; a City Council inquiry conducted by a retired local MP, Julius Silverman; and a West Midlands County Council inquiry from 'a black perspective' by a black team. A year later, the murder of 13-year-old Ahmed Ullah in his school playground gave rise to a Manchester Council sponsored inquiry. Some of these inquiries were boycotted by militant organisations and others were supported. They were all attempts to manage the crises and reestablish cooperation between black leaders, their constituents and the establishment.

In Manchester, for example, an inquiry was suggested to the council by the moderate Greater Manchester Bangladeshi Association in a bid to restore calm and regain influence as militant groups set up the Ahmed Ullah Memorial Committee. (Burnage Report, 1989:x and 81) In Handsworth, a black-inquiry was set up because militants continued to threaten boycotts of the police and Silverman inquiries and the Council sought to gain the confidence of Black people through such an inquiry (*Birmingham Post*, 10/12/85; Bhavnani, et al.:6). The all-black panel was able to adopt a different approach and appeal to black militants and critics in a way that the others could not. Firstly, members of the panel held black militant credentials. They included well-known black people such as Stuart Hall, Herman Ousley, Keith Vaz, Paul Gilroy, Juliet Coke, and Reena Bhavnani. Secondly, the panel gained the support of local black organisers at the launch of the inquiry by listening to the criticisms and suggestions of those present, and stating that they 'would only proceed if there was extensive community backing and support for the initiative'. (Ibid:7) Consequently most groups present 'pledged their cooperation.' (Ibid:7)

The inquiry's findings concurred with the conciliatory approach of Scarman, Gifford and Silverman urging increased black participation in the mainstream. It called for more resources and investment from mainstream state expenditure, increased black representation and structures of police accountability. (Ibid:76-89) Such black militant-led inquiries symbolised the bureaucratisation of black activists and was a long way from notions of the black revolution.

Conclusion

The institutionalisation of black political activity into the Labour Party and mainstream institutions has had the effect of creating a growing gap between black people who achieved office, became black professionals or were absorbed into the mainstream in some other way and the majority of black youth who experience rising repression. Hence, Labour Party Black Section, Race Today, National Black Caucus, Anti-Racist Alliance and other organisations, have been unable to go beyond attracting young black people to occasional benefit concerts. They have been unable to attract and maintain a significant young black membership. Whilst the gap in the experiences of young black people and the growing stratum of black professionals has allowed for the development of alternative leaderships for angry black youth, this leadership opportunity has been appropriated by religious/ethnic leaders rather than young black people themselves. Alienated and isolated, young blacks have turned to streetlife, escapism, cultural solutions and away from both organised activity and mainstream party politics. The widespread mobilisation of young Asians for the campaign against *The Satanic Verses* was in stark contrast to the Asian Youth activities of the 1970s and illustrated the new direction of black politics. In the 1970s the anger against racism of young Asians in cities like Bradford culminated in campaigns such as the Bradford 12 and the formation of the Asian Youth Movements. As the militant Asian youth of the 1970s gradually became involved in local politics, the Labour Party and the race relations industry, they stopped being leaders of local conflicts with the authorities. In the late 1980s, the main conflicts became depoliticised. Ethnic and religious expressions of local tension overwhelmed political issues. Campaigns around halal meat and separate education led by mosque leaders, for example, gained more prominence than the matter of racial violence.

The late 1980s generation of young Asians in Bradford became followers rather than leaders of ethnic campaigns. They seemed isolated, alienated and angry to the point that many gave up on politics altogether and adopted a more individualistic outlook. When Muslim religious leaders in Britain bolstered their own declining influence by mobilising against Rushdie, they were able to win the support of young Asians for demonstrations. Nevertheless, tensions between the elders and the youth came to the fore when young Asians vented their frustrations against the police and the organisers lost control of marches. The attraction of the anti-Rushdie campaign for many Asian youth underlined the extent of the vacuum in organised black resistance to racism resulting from the depoliticisation of black activity which occurred in the 1980s. The question now facing practitioners and commentators alike is how can black politics be transformed to make it applicable to the real needs of today's black young people and adults?

References

Ball, W. and Solomos, J. (1990). *Race and Local Politics*. Macmillan.

Black People's Forum (1983). Report on Black People's Conference.

Bhavnani, R., Coke, J., Gilroy, P., Hall, S., Ouseley, H., and Vaz, K. (1986). *A Different Reality*. West Midlands County Council.

Burnage Report (1989). *Murder In The Playground*. Longsight Press.

Birmingham Post (1985). October 12.

Callinicos, A. (1992). 'Race and Class' in *International Socialism*, no. 55.

C.A.R.F., 'Calendar of Racism 1981' in *Searchlight*.

C.A.R.F., 'Calendar of Racism 1980' in *Searchlight*.

Carmichael, S. and Hamilton, C.V. (1969). *Black Power: The Politics of Liberation in America*. Gretna, LA: Pelican.

Carter, T. (1986). *Shattering Illusions: West Indians In British Politics*. Lawrence and Wishart.

Eade, J. (1989). *Politics of Community*. Avebury.

Egbuna, O. (1971). *Destroy This Temple*. Granada.

Furedi, F. (1992). *Mythical Past, Elusive Futures*. Pluto Press.

Gilroy, P. (1987). *There Ain't No Black In The Union Jack*. Hutchinson.

Goulbourne, H. (1990). *Black Politics in Britain*. Avebury 'Guardian' 1/7/80.

Hiro, D. (1991). *Black British, White Britis*. Grafton.

Howe, D. (1988). *From Bobby to Babylon*. Race Today Publications.

Jacobs, B. (1986). *Black Politics and Urban Crisis in Britai*. Cambridge University Press.

Jacobs, B. (1988). *Racism in Britain*.

Jenkins, R. (1986). 'Social Anthropological Models' in *Theories of Race and Ethnic Relations*, eds. Rex and Mason. CUP.

Labour Party Black Sections (1988). *The Black Agenda*. Hansib.

Lyon, M. (1972). 'Race and Ethnicity in Pluralistic Societies' in *New Community*, Vol. 1:256-62

Lyon, M. (1972-3). 'Ethnicity in Britain: the Gujarati tradition' in *New Community* Vol. 2, no. 1.

Lyon, M. (1973). 'Ethnic Minority Problems: an overview of some recent research' in *New Community*, Vol. 2, no. 4.

Mercer, K. (1990). 'Changing Identities' in *Identity*, ed. J. Rutherford.

Miles, R. (1982). *Racism and Migrant Labour*. Routledge and Kegan Paul.

Modood, T. (1988). 'Black racial equality and Asian identity' in *New Community*, Vol. 14 no. 3.

National Black Workers and Trainers Standing Conference (1990). Report of National Black Workers and Trainers Conference On A Core Curriculum For Community And Youth Work And Training From A Black Perspective

New Statesman (1980). July 25.

Parmar P. (1990). 'Black Feminism: the Politics of Articulation' in *Identity*, ed. J. Rutherford. Lawrence and Wishart.

Race and Class (1981). Autumn.

Race and Class (1982). Winter.

Race Today June 1973; March 1976; July-Aug 1976; Sept. 1976; Oct. 1976; Jan 1978,

Ramdin, R. (1987). *The Making of the Black Working Class in Britain*. Gower.

Rex and Mason (1986). *Theories of Race and Ethnic Relations*. CUP.

Robinson, C. (1983). *Black Marxism*. Zed Press.

Rutherford, J. (1990). *Identity*. Lawrence and Wishart.

Shukra, K. (1990). 'Black Sections in the Labour Party', in *Black Politics in Britain*, ed. H. Goulbourne.

Sivanandan, A. (1982). *A Different Hunger*. Pluto Press.

Sivanandan, A. (1983). 'Challenging Racism: strategies for the '80s', in *Race and Class*.

Times of London (1980). June 30.

Times of London (1981). November 26.

Tompson, K. (1988). *Under Siege*. Penguin.

Wallman, S. (1986). 'Ethnicity and the Boundary Process', in *Theories of Race and Ethnic Relations*, eds. Rex and Mason.

Wainwright, H. (1987). *Labour: A Tale of Two Parties*. The Hogarth Press.

West Indian World (1980). July 4.

Section XII

Pan-Africanity Reconsidered

36

Afro-Americans and United States Foreign Policy

Vernon D. Johnson

Since the presidency of Jimmy Carter, Afro-Americans have been more visible in the United States foreign policy arena. Before Carter took office in 1977, Black interests in foreign policy toward Africa were being articulated by Congressman Charles Diggs (D–Mich.) via his chairmanship of the House of Representatives sub-committee on African Affairs. Also, the Congressional Black Caucus, of which Diggs was a leading member had consolidated its power by 1976 to the point where it could convene a Black Leadership Conference on Africa policy to make policy proposals and begin to mobilize Black communities around African issues. It was at that conference that the seeds for the Black lobbying organization, TransAfrica, were planted. TransAfrica would emerge a year later as a powerful new voice representing Afro-American policy aspirations toward Africa and the Caribbean.

President Carter increased Black involvement in foreign policy as a whole by appointing Andrew Young as United States Ambassador to the United Nations; and his elevation of human rights to primacy as a foreign policy goal coincided with traditional Black interests, especially regarding White minority rule in Southern Africa. If the appointment of Andrew Young made Black interests in foreign affairs more visible, his sudden resignation in 1979 following the disclosure of his secret meeting with the Palestinian Liberation Organization (PLO) representative to the United Nations made the importance of conflicts outside of Africa more apparent to the Black community. In 1984 the presidential campaign of the Reverend Jesse Jackson featured the Black interests in promoting social justice and peace in foreign affairs. Finally, the promulgation of the new South African constitution in the fall of 1984, with its continued denial of African political rights, followed by increased unrest and the awarding of the Nobel Peace prize to Bishop Desmond Tutu, set the stage for the "Free South Africa Movement" in the United States. The November sit-in at the South African embassy in Washington by TransAfrica Executive Randall Robinson, District of Columbia Congressional Delegate Walter Fauntroy and U.S. Civil Rights Commissioner Mary Frances Berry set off a chain of similar demonstrations at South African consulates across the country. Afro-Americans were in the forefront of the Free South Africa Move-

An earlier version of this essay appeared in *Humboldt Journal of Social Relations* 14, 1–2 (Fall-Summer 1987): 214–235 and is adapted/reprinted with the permission of the copyright holder/author.

ment. Motivated by the suffering of their African brethren, Afro-Americans were projecting themselves onto the foreign affairs stage in an unprecedented fashion.

Yet, Black Americans have always been involved in America's relationship with Africa either through private association or official channels. Paul Cuffee, a wealthy Black shipbuilder in Massachusetts, began to research the possibility of Black emigration to Africa in 1788, and in 1815 sent thirty-eight free Afro-Americans to Sierre Leone in West Africa. In 1817 free Blacks joined with White abolitionists and slaveholders seeking to deport "undesirable" slaves to form the American Colonization Society (ACS) with the goal of sending some Blacks back to Africa to establish a new nation. That goal was realized in 1847 when Liberia became an independent republic (Pinckey, 1976, p. 52).

Black-missionaries journeyed to Africa in large numbers during the nineteenth century. Their presence, however, caused tension with their White counterparts. Black missionaries tended to favor independence for African colonies, while Whites were content to save souls in the name of the status quo. Consequently, by the twentieth century White American churches were sending very few Afro-American missionaries to work in their ancestral homeland. Black missionaries, however, continued to find an outlet for their energies in Africa under the auspices of the African Methodist Episcopal Church (AME) after 1880. Under the leadership of Bishop Henry McNeal Turner AME missionaries combined Pan-Africanist ideology with the gospel and some were even implicated in a small armed uprising in Nyasaland (Malawi today) in 1915 (Jackson, 1982, pp. 131–33).

The largest Afro-American initiative of any kind toward Africa was Marcus Garvey's Universal Negro Improvement Association (UNIA). Founded in 1914, the UNIA bred new pride among Afro-Americans in their African Heritage. Propelled by the slogan "Africa for Africans," Garvey raised millions of dollars through a variety of business enterprises, the most ambitious of which was the Black Star Line shipping company designed to establish trade among African peoples everywhere and allow Blacks in the Diaspora to emigrate back to Africa. Efforts to transport Afro-Americans to Liberia were never realized, probably due to pressures placed upon the Liberian government by neighboring colonial powers. Still, at its height in the 1920s the UNIA had approximately six million members worldwide, most of whom were Afro-Americans (Jackson, pp. 136–139).

The Italian invasion of Ethiopia in 1935 sparked a great deal of movement in Black communities. Ethiopia held great symbolic significance for Blacks in the Diaspora. Until 1935 it was the only region of Black Africa to escape European colonialism. In an era when Blacks were everywhere subjugated, Ethiopian independence demonstrated that Blacks were capable of ruling themselves. During the Italian occupation, a number of Black organizations in the United States mobilized to send medical and financial assistance for Ethiopians. A boycott of Italian-American businesses was organized, and the Nationalist Negro Movement even attempted to send Black volunteers to fight in Ethiopia, but their recruits were denied passports by the State Department (Du Bois, 1935, p. 88).

Black American interest in Africa was rekindled as a result of the national liberation movements of the post-war era. In 1957 the reverend James H. Robinson initiated Operation Crossroads Africa to work on economic development projects. Operation Crossroads Africa became the prototype for the Peace Corps initiated by President Kennedy in the 1960s. Africare is another Black run development-oriented organization sustained largely by grants from the United States

Agency for International Development and a number of sources in the Black community (Jackson, pp. 146–147). When the news of severe drought across North Africa hit Black America in 1973, a broad coalition of groups came together to form Relief for Africans in Need in the Sahel (RAINS). RAINS and other Black organizations such as People United to Save Humanity (PUSH) and Africare raised over $500,000 for Sahelian drought relief (Challenor, 1981, p. 168).

Significant Black efforts to affect United States policy toward Africa began with the Pan-African Congress (PAC) movement under the leadership of W.E.B. Du Bois. The first congress was held in London in 1900, but it was at the second one in Paris in 1919 that the Black foreign policy lobby began to take effect. The Second PAC was scheduled to coincide with the Versailles Peace Conference following World War I. With Du Bois in the forefront, the Second PAC petitioned the Allies for the placement of the German colonies under international administration in preparation for eventual self-government. That proposal is believed to have had an effect on the establishment of the League of Nations Mandate System (Padmore, 1972, pp. 10–103; Du Bois, 1965, pp. 10–12). Greater Black influence on the peace Conference was subverted by the United States government. The administration of President Woodrow Wilson pressured the French government to prevent the PAC from meeting in Paris, and failing in that effort, denied passports to Black Americans planning to attend. Du Bois sailed to France secretly, and though PAC delegates were denied the opportunity to testify before the Peace Conference, they were able to influence the proceedings because of the coverage given the PAC in the French press (Challenor, p. 151). Wilson also worked successfully to prevent a statement promoting racial equality from being included in the preamble to the League of Nations Covenant (Blumenthal, 1963, p. 18).

The National Association for the Advancement of Colored People (NAACP) provided most of the financing for the Second and Third PACs and retained an interest in United States foreign policy toward the Black world in the 1920s and 30s. The civil rights organization was active around the issue of American hypocrisy in protesting forced labor in Liberia in the 1930s, while ignoring it in European colonies in Africa. The NAACP also lobbied for an end to the American military occupation of Haiti during the same period. In both cases the organization's activity contributed to reasonable resolutions of the issues at hand. After breaking off diplomatic relations with Liberia in 1930, they were resumed in 1935; and U.S. military occupation of Haiti ended in 1935 (Challenor, pp. 149–150, 153–154).

The Council on African Affairs, formed in 1937, was a multiracial grouping dominated by Black intellectuals such as Du Bois, Paul Robeson, Ralph Bunche, and Adam Clayton Powell, Jr. Its goals were providing material assistance to African nationalist organizations, educating the public about Africa, and lobbying the U.S. government for policies supporting African independence. After a brief hiatus during which domestic civil rights struggles were emphasized, Afro-American leaders refocused their attention on Africa with the formation of the American Negro Leadership Council on Africa (ANLCA) in 1962. The ANLCA included Martin Luther King, Jr., Whitney Young, Roy Wilkins and A. Philip Randolph. Its goal was the advancement of national independence efforts in Africa. Among other things, ANLCA called upon the U.S. to proscribe investment and oil shipments to the apartheid regime in South Africa. The ANLCA wielded little influence and disintegrated after an abortive effort at mediating the Nigerian

Civil War in 1968 (Jackson, pp. 142–146). Herschelle Challenor points out, I think correctly, that the ANLCA might have been more influential if Black leaders had chosen to mobilize Black communities around African issues as they had been activated concerning domestic civil rights. By confining the discussion of Africa to "brokerage politics" among political elites, the ANLCA was unable to effectively counter government opposition to what was viewed as a racialist approach toward foreign policy (Challenor, pp. 163–164).

After 1970 brokerage politics among civil rights leaders in the area of foreign affairs became impossible. The Black-Power movement emerged in the late 1960s and by the early 1970s, Black nationalism, in one or another of its formulations, was the dominant ideology in Black communities across the country (Marable, 1984, Chap. 6). Nationalism affected Black-American politics in many ways, two of which are germane to this discussion. First, Black nationalism coincided with unprecedented Black participation in electoral politics. This meant that the numbers of Black elected officials had spiraled by the 1970s and that these newly ascendant representatives would be indebted to nationalism for placing them in power. Secondly, the spread of Black consciousness precipitated a greater awareness of the conditions facing Black people internationally. This Pan-Africanism was manifested in opposition to colonialism, neocolonialism and apartheid in Africa. In 1972 the Pan-Africanist African Liberations Support Committee (ALSC) attracted 20,000 people to its African Liberation Day rally in Washington, D.C. Among the speakers that day were Congressional Black Caucus members Charles Diggs and Walter Fauntroy. In 1973 over 100,000 people participated in African Liberation Day marches in a number of locations across the country (Marable, p. 151).

In 1971 the Congressional Black Caucus (CBC) was formed, including all twelve Black members of the House of Representatives. After consolidating itself as the Afro-American voice on domestic politics, the CBC began to exert itself in the area of African Affairs. One of the Caucus's leading members, Charles Diggs of Michigan, had become the chairman of the House subcommittee on African Affairs in 1969. Under Diggs the subcommittee undertook extensive research on Africa and sponsored several official visits to the continent (Morris, 1972, pp. 460–461). It was in 1975 that Black nationalist mobilization around African politics converged with what were considered the vital strategic interests of the United States. In the summer of 1975, still licking its wounds from the debacle of Vietnam, the U.S., nevertheless, got involved in the civil war in Angola. Fourteen million dollars were sent covertly to the National Front for the Liberation of Angola (FNLA) and the National Union for the Total Independence of Angola (UNITA). These movements were fighting for control of the country against the Marxist and pro-Soviet Popular Movement for the Liberation of Angola (MPLA) (Stockwell, 1978). Africa had traditionally been considered low politics in State Department circles, and Secretary of State Henry Kissinger lacked a firm grasp of African realities. In a meeting with the CBC over the Angolan crisis in August 1975, Kissinger admitted that he did not have an African policy (Challenor, pp. 168–169). Yet, that meeting occurred at a time when the covert aid to FNLA–UNITA forces was already in the pipeline.

Kissinger's duplicity would catch up with him through the autumn of 1975, as a massive Soviet-Cuban military buildup in support of the MPLA occurred, and it was disclosed that South African troops were fighting alongside U.S. backed

UNITA (Stockwell, 1978, p. 202). In December of 1975 the CBC held a jam-packed press conference and delivered the first comprehensive critique of the Angola situation and U.S. policy regarding it. The Caucus proposed the withdrawal of South African troops, an end to all external intervention, a ceasefire, U.S. recognition of the MPLA as the legitimate Angolan government, and aid for postwar reconstruction. Although the press conference received no coverage in the Washington press, it was part of the general climate contributing to the termination of covert U.S. aid to the FNLA–UNITA forces in February 1976.

By 1975, African affairs had become critical enough that Secretary of State Kissinger enlisted Black Caucus input into his search for a coherent policy. Yet the exchange of information was clearly one-sided, since the Secretary did not disclose the fact that his hand had already been played via covert operations established a month earlier. The December press conference held by the Caucus received extensive attention, but no press. Decision makers and opinion leaders in Washington wanted to know what was going on in Angola, but they did not wish to credit the CBC with a valuable contribution to the clarification of the debate, perhaps because the Caucus's attendant policy proposals were unpalatable in mainstream foreign policy circles.

Although Black nationalism and Pan-Africanism among politically active sectors of the Black community, had pushed the CBC to take a more active role in U.S. Africa policy, the Caucus chose to employ the brokerage politics which had thwarted previous Black attempts to influence that policy. The result was the continued frustration of Black aspirations for a voice in America's relationship with their ancestral homeland. In September of 1976 the CBC sponsored a Black Leadership Conference on United States Africa Policy. The goals of the conference were to support African peoples in their struggles for self-determination and Pan-Africanism, and to mobilize the Afro-American community toward those ends (Challenor, p. 170). As I mentioned above, Afro-American communities had already mobilized themselves around African issues, and it was that mass movement that compelled Black elected officials to articulate an interest in those same issues. Still, the September 1976 conference marked a qualitative leap for Black foreign policy influence, because it led to the birth of TransAfrica in 1977—the lobby for Black American interests in U.S. policy toward Africa, the Caribbean and the Black World. TransAfrica had pushed Black concerns to center stage in foreign policy debates by the mid-1980s, but before we survey its successes, let us take a detour to review the traditional perceptions of U.S. national security which have historically limited the extent to which Black concerns were taken seriously. It is these perceptions that continue to pose obstacles to Black inclusion in the U.S. foreign policy-making establishment.

The Traditional Notion of National Security

At the end of the Second World War the United States and the Soviet Union inherited the leadership of the international state system from the old Great Powers of Europe. That system had featured a handful of states arrayed in a multipolar balance of power in order to manage international relations and maintain their own national security (Morgenthau, 1985, pp. 360–363). National security was defined in geopolitical terms. That is, it was believed that national security inhered in the control of territory. Since many states occupied regions that were geographically vulnerable to attack, they frequently sought satellite or client states as buffer zones. Military power became the ancillary of geopolitical security in order to conquer weak states at the periphery, as well as to defend the national homeland (Sprout and Sprout, 1971, pp. 402–404). In the age of global empires, from the fifteenth to the twentieth century, national security came to include the defense of overseas dominions and the protection of the overland and sea routes connecting them to respective mother countries. By the twentieth century most of the non-European world was controlled by European states (except Latin America). International politics was little more than the acquisition and maintenance of colonial empires by Europeans.

The delicate European-centered global balance of power unravelled in the present century, leading to two inter-imperialist world wars and a loss of their will to maintain overseas possessions (Morgenthau, pp. 360–363). The United States and the Soviet Union, though allies during WWII, quickly became adversarial superpowers managing a bi-polar global balance of power after 1945. This superpower conflict was exacerbated by the vast differences between the socioeconomic systems and political cultures of the two countries. The Russian Revolution in 1917 had established the world's first communist state with a leadership promoting Karl Marx's vision of worldwide proletarian revolution. Although the Soviet regime had consolidated itself around the primacy of establishing socialism in one country, it still sought to aid and abet the emergence of new communist states. The old colonial empires were bastions of monopoly capitalism providing raw materials, markets, and cheap labor for industrial enterprises headquartered in Europe. It was the reluctance of capitalist Britain and France to forge an early alliance with communist Russia that led to Stalin's ill-fated association with Hitler. After the war, Western capitalist suspicion about the Soviet Union continued and was fueled by Soviet creation of a sphere of influence in Eastern Europe. The United States was the only vital capitalist power following the war, and thus took the lead in preventing further communist expansion. Since World War II, and especially after the establishment of the North Atlantic Treaty Organization (NATO) in 1949, U.S. national security has been perceived as virtually synonymous with the security of its counterparts in global capitalism (including Japan) in their worldwide confrontation with encroaching Soviet-sponsored communism (Nathan and Oliver, 1976, Chap. 4). Both superpowers retained a geopolitical sense of their national security; the Soviets in their belief that the defense of their homeland required the acquisition of peripheral states as buffer zones and the United States in its presumption that the emergence of communist or socialist regimes anywhere in the world was a threat to the global free market economy (Gray, 1977, Chap. 3; Klare, 1981).

Despite their differences over domestic politics, both the Republican and Democratic parties in the United States felt the need to present a strong united stance in the struggle against communism. This led to the bi-partisan U.S. foreign policy of "containment" that was initiated by President Truman and in one way or another has informed American strategic security thinking across Democratic and Republican administrations until the present (Sanders, 1983).

Although pre-Vietnam foreign policy-making did not receive the consistent public scrutiny given to domestic policies, certain ethnic groups were able to exert considerable influence on U.S. policy toward regions in which they were interested. Martin Weil (1974) has demonstrated that ethnic groups which present an electoral threat to one of the major parties, possess an effective lobbying apparatus, and harmonize their aspirations with the symbols of the American tradition, can dominate United States foreign policy toward the regions of their concern. The Polish electoral threat and lobby compelled President Truman to take a hard line on the Soviet Union in the 1948 election. The same factors were involved in Truman's support for the establishment of a Jewish state in Palestine during the same period. In both cases geopolitical thinking informed U.S. policies. The Polish issue was one of several that helped to crystallize the consensus for the policy of containment, a geopolitical doctrine linking U.S. security directly to the existence of democracy and "free institutions" around the world (Truman, 1947, pp. 178–179; U.S. Congress, 1947, pp. 30–31). While geopolitics originally had little to do with the establishment of the state of Israel, they quickly became involved with the emergence of militant Arab states with Soviet backing committed to the destruction of Israel.

The foreign policy aspirations of Afro-Americans were not part of the post-war consensus. Unlike Poles and Jews, Blacks did not possess a viable electoral threat or an effective foreign policy lobby. Black electoral participation did not become a pivotal force until after the passage of Voting Rights legislation in 1965. As we have seen, though Blacks lobbied the government around foreign policy concerns, their efforts were usually ineffectual. Also, Black interests tended to focus on Africa. The United States did not have an independent foreign policy toward Africa when decolonization began to take place. The State Department Bureau of African Affairs was not established until 1958, and President Eisenhower did not recognize newly independent African states before leaving office in 1961. Africa was considered part of the former European colonial powers' sphere of influence. Therefore, the U.S. foreign policy toward the continent was, in the words of Henry F. Jackson, one of "Eurocentrism" (1982, p. 51). Despite heavy U.S. involvement in the Congo Crisis (1960–65) and its growing interests in the African Middle East during the 1960s, Jackson points out that the U.S. continued to pursue its objective in Africa through "moribund colonial networks" (see p. 52). Only a powerful Afro-American lobby providing consistent pressure as well as policy direction could have changed U.S. African policy during the 1960s, and that did not yet exist.

Vietnam and the End of Consensus

The failure of the United States intervention in Vietnam to ward off the establishment of a communist state sent the foreign policy-making apparatus into disarray shattering the consensus for containment. After the demonstration of resilience by Vietnamese communists during the Tet Offensive in early 1968, many foreign policy elites began to doubt the wisdom of employing American military power in places like Vietnam where America's vital security interests were not endangered. At issue was not whether international communism should be contained, but rather, what should be the primary instruments of that containment in the 1970s and beyond. Liberals were impressed by the dramatic way in which the war demonstrated the decline in American power, and the way the deficit spending of the military buildup set off a chain reaction that threatened to undermine the global economic order. Thus, these liberal elites proposed collective management by advanced capitalist nations of both the international economic and military security systems. But in this new formulation economic policies were primary. International communism was to be defeated by increasing economic cooperation between advanced capitalist states and the promotion of expanded international trade, as much as possible, under conditions favorable to the advanced economies. It was believed that the greater vitality and technological advancement of capitalism would eventually entice even communist countries into increased trade, and ultimately into the economic orbit of capitalism on a global scale (Gardner, et al., 1977). Economic containment became the cornerstone of the strategy adopted by the Trilateral Commission and the administration of President Jimmy Carter. In opposition were those who continued to believe that the essence of containment resided in military superiority and the willingness to use it anywhere in the "free" world (Ravenal, 1975; Tower, 1976).

The Vietnam war also saw the emergence of a growing number of Americans who did not view their own interests in foreign affairs in terms of geopolitics or the security of the nation-state. The anti-war movement was part of the counter-culture of the 1960s which eschewed almost everything about the world its forefathers had created including racism, sexism, environmental damage and the superpower competition which spawned gunboat diplomacy and the threat of nuclear holocaust. As Jerry Sanders puts it:

> ...The organizational style of these movements placed a high premium on participation and authenticity, displaying little patience with bureaucratic hierarchy, and compromise. Among grass roots movements there was a palpable distrust of authority, suspicion of institutions, disdain of expertise, and general hostility toward planning. Formed in rebellion in universities, the ideological foundation of these movements rested on a deep cultural critique of technocratic rationality which was held responsible for the domination and exploitation of non-Western people, women, and the natural environment (1983, p. 111).

Neither the hard line of Cold Warriors nor the soft containment of the Carter years appealed to the counter culture, since both ultimately saw national security resting in the domination of foreign countries.

A re-examination of contemporary international relations reveals that the counter-cultural perspective regarding U.S. foreign policy is more accurate than the views of either wing of the foreign policy establishment. The notion that national security is based on geopolitical maneuvering is anachronistic in today's world. Abdul Aziz Said (1981, p. 6) observes that "the [nation] state is essentially a territorial form of organization in a century where security is no longer a function of geopolitics, but one of technology." He sees that with the advent of nuclear weapons and increasingly sophisticated conventional ones, states can now realize security not by controlling foreign territories, but rather, by possessing the latest military technology. It may be argued that advanced industrial nations must have access to raw materials produced in foreign countries if their industries are to operate smoothly, that their commercial shipping fleets must be able to pass safely across international waters to engage in trade, that their military vessels must be able to patrol global seas to protect the interests of their citizens and allies, and that those vessels need to have access to friendly ports for fueling and repairs. Those who would put forward such a set of assertions would conclude by saying that if the interests just stated are not safeguarded, then the national security of the nation-states having those interests is jeopardized (Klare, 1981; Gann and Duignan, 1981).

It is in this way that many politicians, military leaders, and scholars continue to rationalize a geopolitical understanding of national security in the late twentieth century. The argument continues to be compelling for most policy-makers, but it proceeds as if the contemporary world is the same as the world of the turn of the century in which most of the planet was colonized by a few European states and the rest labored under a quasi-colonialism imposed from the United States. Since 1945 the old colonial empires have disintegrated and over one hundred new nations have appeared on the map. These nations, which we have come to categorize as the Third World, happen to perceive themselves as something more than the terrain upon which Western or Soviet geo-strategic interests are secured. Although these nations are weak, unstable and underdeveloped, they are independent and are now positioned, however tenuously, to pursue their own interests. Primary among those interests are economic development and the creation of legitimate indigenous structures of political authority. The decline in American power alluded to earlier is really part of the diminution of the hegemony of advanced industrial states within the global political economy of capitalism, and the decline of the capitalist mode of production itself as some new states select non-capitalist or socialist models for development (see Krasner, 1985, for a lucid discussion of structural conflict within global capitalism). The ability of former colonial areas to control their resources and territories has meant less favorable terms of trade and less political allegiance toward advanced capitalist states. Decolonization has also meant stiffer economic competition as several new states industrialized successfully. But more expensive resources or labor, and less access to ports and military bases does not mean less national security. It simply means that desired goods, services, facilities, and relationships with emerging states may be more difficult to realize. It means that the quantity of life in advanced states is likely to diminish causing lower real incomes and higher unemployment (at least until broad economic reforms occur). But if by national security we fundamentally mean military security, then countries such as the United States have little to fear from Third World countries as long as they possess high technology defense systems.

Many from the Vietnam generation also recognize that the problems confronting the world today cannot be solved by nation-states pursuing military security Abdul Aziz Said makes this point eloquently.

> The national interest's emphasis on military power and control over territory does not fit the new conditions of the global system. The present challenges of the world cannot be solved by any one nation-state. The care of the planet's life-support systems, the control of nuclear weapons, and the appropriate use and fair distribution of the earth's resources affect all of us and the whole planet. National interest has long ceased to coincide with human and planetary interests (1981, p. 16).

Seeing that nation-states are reluctant to think about security in this new, more humanitarian context, many individuals and groups are pursuing international relations that are at odds with the goals of their own governments, Said continues by citing a number of factors causing citizens to oppose the foreign policies of their governments.

Global Economic Development and Political Communication

Mercantilism and colonialism eventually pulled virtually the whole world into the capitalist system. In the process, traditional social structures were disrupted and sometimes dismantled as societies were forced to orient themselves to the mandates of the market economy. The sense of community derived from a common cultural tradition began to break down. Capitalist class differentiation occurred alongside, and at the expense of, traditional social hierarchies. This socioeconomic assimilation corresponded to an overall acculturation process wherein elements of colonial populations acquired European education and came to adhere to Western political values such as democracy and equality. With the postwar explosion of new nations in constant contact via international organizations, the availability of an international mass media and international travel on an unprecedented scale, peoples of the world became increasingly aware of similarities among disparate societies in their efforts for self determination and social justice.

The breakdown in traditional communities and subsequent appearance of an inchoate sense of international community in turn gave rise to a lack of consensus among citizens within nation-states regarding the direction of foreign policies and a concommitant growth in political solidarity and feelings of community among actors from different nation-states.

Said's analysis is of great moment in understanding the historical development of Afro-American politics in the United States. The presence of millions of Black people in the United States is a manifestation of international capitalist development. Due to slavery, Afro-Americans lost their traditional culture altogether and regrouped into an Afro-American culture, a process involving considerable assimilation to the larger society. Paradoxically part of that assimilation meant for some, acquiring American education and becoming aware of the condition of Black people under colonialism in Africa. A Pan-Africanist spirit has been evident among Afro-Americans since the earliest days of the republic, and has been manifested politically since 1900 with the first Pan-African Congress. Afro-Americans have unusually been at odds with U.S. foreign policy in general and particularly its policy toward Africa. Therefore, Afro-Americans are at the center of the international re-alignment of political forces that Said has identified.

The factor of growing solidarity and community among actors across national boundaries is of particular significance here. The international political and economic systems are stratified along racial lines. With the exception of Japan, the dominant states in both international orders are ruled by Caucasians of European ancestry; and the poor and less powerful states in the world are, by and large, ruled by people of color. Racism played a role in justifying the international division of labor along color lines and it continues to play a role in U.S. foreign policy today (Shepherd, 1970, p. 221). In 1969 the National Security Council under Henry Kissinger recommended that the United States strengthen its ties to White minority regimes in Southern Africa, since it seemed unlikely that black national-ist movements in the region could become "realistic or supportable alternatives to continued colonial rule" (Stockwell, 1978, p. 51). In 1978, with Black national-ism the victor in Angola and Mozambique, and soon to be ascendant in Zim-babwe, another National Security Advisor, Zbigniew Brzezinski circulated a memorandum proposing that the FBI and CIA be mobilized to forestall "durable ties between U.S. black organizations and radical groups in African States (Brzezinski, 1978).

The Brzezinski memo was written in the context of over a decade of active politico-cultural communication between Afro-Americans and Africans among Black nationalists as well as mainstream politicians such as Congressman Charles Diggs. More specifically, Dr. Brzezinski wrote at a time when a newly emergent Black foreign policy lobby, TransAfrica, was in the process of spearheading a suc-cessful drive for Congressional retention of economic sanctions against Rhodesia following its announcement of puppet Black majority rule in March 1978. As I mentioned earlier, TransAfrica was born due to the concerted efforts of Black leaders seeking to generate a more powerful voice in debates over U.S. policy to-ward the African world. The organization's board of directors included promi-nent Afro-Americans from all walks of life including congressmen, local political leaders, members of the clergy and entertainers. Its Executive Director was Ran-dall Robinson, a Harvard Law School graduate and former aide to Congressman Diggs (Challenor, p. 170). The fledgling lobby was able to score such an early vic-tory in part because Robinson knew his way around Capitol Hill so well. What was particularly troubling for Brzezinski and the foreign policy establishment was the explicit alliance between TransAfrica and key actors on the African continent. Robinson relayed information regarding the possibility of a U.S. withdrawal of sanctions to the Organization of African Unity (OAU) during its annual summit. The OAU responded by declaring that such an action would be frowned upon in Africa (Challenor, p. 171).

Following Robinson's leakage of documents detailing the Reagan Administra-tion's plans for "constructive engagement" with South Africa, high-ranking offi-cials were incensed. Assistant Secretary of State for African Affairs, Chester Crocker, refused to appear on a television program with Robinson, and Secretary of State Alexander Haig stonewalled a meeting between himself and Black leaders when notified that Robinson would be invited. These events prompted one ob-server to characterize the actions of government officials toward Robinson as "... sour grapes, [because] Robinson, like growing numbers of Black leaders, is making waves in American foreign policy" (Beaubien, 1982, p. 39).

The actions of TransAfrica and other Black organizations and individuals in-terested in foreign policy will continue to infuriate many in established foreign policy circles. Blacks have always opposed a U.S. foreign policy dominated by the geopolitical game of chess in which Third World countries are won and lost like pawns at the bidding of the super-power gamesmen. Instead, Black Americans will continue to uphold the ability of developing countries to pursue self-determi-nation and, if they so choose, non-alignment and even socialism. In the process they will often feel more allegiance to foreign governments and movements than they feel for the United States government and its view of the national interest. This is because many Afro-Americans see themselves as victims in the historical development of the capitalist world economy, albeit in a manner different from peoples of the Third World. The latter were colonized where they were found, while the former were transported across the Atlantic to be subjugated. Furthermore, Afro-Americans have discovered some twenty years after the passage of civil rights legislation that their collective standard of living has declined in the face of the deindustrialization characterizing advanced capitalism. This is at the same time that developing countries continue to be jerked around by competing superpowers a generation and more after political independence. Of course, the dominant groups both within the United States and internationally are White and as Said (p. 15) points out, "the black lacks cultural and physical affinity with the dominant groups." Thus, Afro-Americans are seeking a sense of political community with Africans in particular and the rest of the Third World to a lesser extent; and many actors in Africa and the developing world are identifying with the plight of Afro-Americans (Nyerere, 1968, p. 70; Cabezas, 1986). This foreign policy dissensus poses serious problems to the United States as it gropes for a coherent international posture in the late 1980s and 90s.

Afro-Americans and Their Future in International Relations

As we approach the twenty-first century, the debate over U.S. policy toward the Third World will continue to revolve around alternative ways of responding to the inevitable push for changes both within those societies, and between them and the advanced capitalist world. Some analysts such as Robert W. Tucker (1977, pp. 197–201) have posited that in the economic realm, the inequality among states that characterizes the international system is a fact of life that powerful states are not necessarily compelled to alter. In Tucker's mind only a handful of Third World states can really ever hope to present a serious economic challenge to the Western world. Included here are states such as Brazil, Nigeria, India, and Indonesia (and one might add China)—states with populations and development potentialities that make them too salient for industrialized states to ignore. He says that advanced states should engage in the "co-optation of these states into the management of the international system," while we are left to assume that the rest of the underdeveloped world will remain just that—underdeveloped! In the area of international political relations many, if not most, elites will continue to aver that the U.S. should make the countering of communist expansion the hallmark of its foreign policy (See Reed, 1985, for an analysis of Reagan administration policy). Afro-American visibility will continue to increase in the foreign policy arena in years to come. The expansion of Black political power into the area of foreign affairs assures that they will now be heard.

Oliver Cox was right when he posited that the most effective strategy for achieving social justice for Black Americans "entails infighting—not separatism (1976, p. 281). Most Afro-Americans have always had the wisdom to prefer being a part of American society to isolation from it, even in periods when few others were pursuing an agenda including Black concerns. Today many others are struggling for the same broad vision of a better, more humane world. Since the United States is the most influential nation-state in the global community, and the leader of the dominant international political and economic blocs, changing the direction of U.S. foreign policy is essential for improving the conditions under which the world's people live. In order to change it, the disparate elements of the post-Vietnam counterculture, who initially caused the dissensions in U.S. foreign policy thinking, must coalesce formally and place their platform before the public. Gabriel Almond put the matter eloquently more than a quarter of a century ago:

> ...The central question of American foreign policy in the 1960s is whether or not the United States still possesses this capacity for growth—not simply economic growth which will enable us to hold our lead over the Soviet Union—but cultural and psychological growth which will enable us to provide moral and political leadership over an expanding free world (1960).

What Almond put forward in 1960 is even truer today, and his question hangs in the balance. Now that Afro-Americans are directing their political energies toward foreign policy, they are likely to play a critical role in determining its answer.

References

Almond, Gabriel. *The American People and Foreign Policy.* New York: Frederick A. Praeger, Publishers, 1960.

Beal, Frances M. and Depass, Ty. "The Black Presence in the Struggle for Peace." *Black Scholar*, Jan.-Feb. 1986, pp. 2–8.

Beaubien, Michael. "Making Waves in Foreign Policy." *Black Enterprise*, April 1982, pp. 38–40, 42.

Blumenthal, Henry. "Woodrow Wilson and the Race Question." *Journal of Negro History,* January 1963, pp. 1–21.

Brzezinski, Zbigniew. *National Security Council Memorandum,* 46, 1978.

Cabezas, Omar. Vice-Minister of the Interior, Republic of Nicaragua. "King: The Third World's Heroic Symbol." *La Voz,* March 1986, pp. 6–7.

Challenor, Herschelle Sullivan. "The Influence of Black Americans on U.S. Foreign Policy Toward Africa." In Abdul Azia Said (ed.), *Ethnicity and U.S. Foreign Policy.* New York: Praeger Publishers, 1981, pp. 143–182.

Cox, Oliver C. *Race Relations: Elements and Social Dynamics.* Detroit: Wayne State University Press, 1976.

Du Bois, W.E.B. "Inter-racial Implications of the Ethiopian Crisis: A Negro View." *Foreign Affairs,* October 1935, p. 88.

————. *The World and Africa.* New York: International Publishers, 1965.

Gann, Lewis H. and Duignan, Peter. *Africa South of the Sahara: The Challenge to Western Security.* Stanford, CA: Hoover Institute Press, 1981.

Gardner, Richard N. and Okita, Saubro, and Udink, B.J. "A Turning Point in North-South Economic Relations." *Trilateral Commission Task Force Reports.* New York: New York University Press, 1977, pp. 57–74.

Jackson, Henry F. *From the Congo to Soweto: U.S. Foreign Policy Toward Africa Since 1960.* New York: William Morrow and Company, Inc., 1982.

Johnson, Vernon D. "Black Voter Education and the 1984 Election." Paper delivered at the Third Annual Conference of the National Council for Black Studies, Pacific Northwest Region. Cheney, WA, February 2–4, 1984.

Karenga, Maulana. "Jesse Jackson and the Rainbow Coalition. The Invitation and Oppositions of History." *Black Scholar*, Sept.–Oct., 1984, pp. 57–67.

Klare, Michael T. *Beyond the Vietnam Syndrome: U.S. Intervention in the 1980s*. Washington, DC: Institute of Policy Studies, 1981.

Kopkind, Andrew and Cockburn, Alexander. "The Left, the Democrats and the Future." *The Nation*, July 21–28, 1984, pp. 33, 42–45.

Krasner, Stephen D. *Structural Conflict: The Third World Against Global Liberalism*. Berkeley, CA: University of California Press, 1985.

MacEoin, Gary (ed.). *Sanctuary: A Resource Guide for Understanding and Participating in the Central American Refugees' Struggle*. Harper & Row, Inc., 1985.

Marable, Manning. *How Capitalism Underdeveloped Black America*. Boston: South End Press, 1983.

———. *Race, Reform and Rebellion: The Second Reconstruction in Black America, 1945-1982*. Jackson, MS: University Press of Mississippi, 1984.

Meredith, Martin. *The Past is Another Country*. London: Andre Deutsch, Ltd., 1979.

Morgenthau, Hans J. *Politics Among Nations*, 6th ed. New York: Alfred A. Knopf, Inc., 1985.

Morris, Milton D. "Black Americans and the Foreign Policy Process: The Case of Africa." *Western Political Quarterly*, September 1972, pp. 451–463.

Nathan, James A. and Oliver, James K. *United States Foreign Policy and World Order*. Boston: Little, Brown & Company, Inc., 1976.

Nyerere, Julius K, *Freedom and Socialism*. Oxford: Oxford University Press, 1968.

Padmore, George. *Pan-Africanism or Communism*. Garden City, NY: Doubleday & Company, Inc., 1972.

Pinckney, Alphonse. *Red, Black and Green: Black Nationalism in the United States*. Cambridge, England: Cambridge University Press, 1976.

"Protests Going Strong," *Africa News*, November 4, 1985, pp. 5, 12.

Ravenal, Earl C. "Consequences of the End Game in Vietnam." *Foreign Affairs*, July 1975, pp. 651–657.

Reed, Gail. "Low Intensity Conflict: A War for All Seasons." *Black Scholar*, Jan.–Feb. 1986, pp. 14–22.

"Rockers Raise Money, Awareness." *Africa News*, July 1985, pp. 1, 2, 14, 15.

Said, Abdul Aziz. "A Redefinition of National Interest, Ethnic Consciousness, and U.S. Foreign Policy." In Said (ed.), *Ethnicity and U.S. Foreign Policy*, revised ed. New York: Praeger Publishers, 1981, pp. 1–19.

Sanders, Jerry W. "Breaking Out of the Containment Syndrome." *World Policy Journal*, Fall 1983, pp. 101–125.

Shepherd, George, Jr. "The Racial Dimension of United States Intervention in Africa and Asia." In Shepherd (ed.), *Racial Influences on American Foreign Policy*, New York: Basic Books, Inc., 1970, pp. 220–228.

Sprout, Harold and Sprout, Margaret. *Toward a Politics of the Planet Earth*. New York: Van Nostrand Reinhold, 1971.

Stockwell, John. *In Search of Enemies*. New York: W.W. Norton, Inc., 1978.

Tower, John G. "Foreign Policy for the Seventies." In Anthony Lake (ed.), *The Vietnam Legacy: The War, American Society and the Future of American Foreign Policy*. New York: New York University Press, 1976, pp. 242–255.

Truman, Harry S. "The Truman Doctorine: Special Message to Congress on Greece and Turkey, March 12, 1947." *Public Papers of President of the United States*, Harry S. Truman, 1947. Washington, DC: U.S. Government Printing Office.

Tucker, Robert W. *The Inequality of Nations*. New York: Basic Books, Inc., 1977.

U. S. Congress. Senate Foreign Relations Committee, *Hearings on S 938 Assistance to Greece and Turkey*, 180th Congress, First Session, March 24, 1947.

Weil, Martin. "Can Blacks Do for Africa What the Jews did for Israel." *Foreign Policy*, Summer 1974, pp. 109–130.

37

The Barrier Inside: Afro-Consciousness, Identification and the Impact on Foreign Policy

Nikongo BaNikongo

Introduction

Consciousness, said the writer Marx, is what moves a group from "a class in and of itself" to "a class for itself." Consciousness may be considered to be a self-knowledge of the group, its heritage, where it stands in relationship to other groups and what changes need to be made to improve its situation. The development of consciousness presupposes knowledge, knowledge of the various elements of group situation and does not proceed in the absence of it, since consciousness by definition, is knowledge. Nor does it advance in a vacuum but rather takes place in an environment of other group interaction. The dynamic of group interaction is unquestionably affected by differing group strength, but likewise, group strength is affected by the nature and dynamic of group interaction. Strength has many dimensions in the context of groups: economic, numeric, political. Yet influence may well transcend all of these and lay instead in conscious assertion. This is not to say that some of these variables are unimportant in the determination of influence, but it is the constitution of a the mass as a group which takes primacy in the determination of influence. Cultural anthropologists understand that ethnic boundaries are defined by the degree of commonality, cohesiveness, peculiarity/idiosyncracy within one group which separates it from others. It is, therefore, those commonalities, understood, recognized, demonstrated and sustained which allow a group to be forceful, exert maximum influence and become an entity for itself. Group members must know, understand and display group identifiers, must know what distinguishes "us" from "them" suggesting then not only group identification but group solidarity and group pride as well. While the group could in fact share some particularities of other cultures in the larger environment, these variants must, in the main, be secondary to its internal culture if even important. For identification suggests the viewing by individual members of themselves as part of the group structure, outside of which it is incomplete since the individual must be nothing more than a part of the group, nothing outside of the group and always subordinate to it. Such a view-point must not be mistaken for Leviathanism as it does not seek to steal from the individual his autonomy, but rather allows for the fullest expression of that individuality within the context of the group. As such, one's highest goal must always be what can be done not merely for oneself, but what one can do to enhance the position of the group vis a vis its relation to other groups and in the pursuit of improving the livelihood and lifestyles of its internal parts even while one is oneself uplifted.

As consciousness presupposes knowledge, so to does identification. Identification within the group suggests knowing group aims, group goals, group hurdles and group strategies. One cannot be an effective and meaningful part of something without knowing what it is about or one is likely to retard or find oneself part of a thing that is not necessarily in one's interest. This was essentially the shortcomings of the French peasantry and working class in whose name the revolution of 1789 was fought, who provided the numbers and bloodshed for the revolution, but whose situation did not significantly alter once the old order was replaced. Knowledge, then, is critical since it provides not only perceptive but cognitive and analytic elements as well. Knowledge not only allows for a concrete and correct definition of the enemy, but provides also for correct strategies to oppose and overcome it.

Knowledge teaches us not only about others, but more importantly about ourselves and disallows alienation within the group even when physical barriers to communication exist. Knowledge of the parts maintain group cohesiveness even when geographic proximity is absent and permits splintered and dispersed elements to retain group allegiance since one is always part of the group and struggles for it. Knowledge makes the individual know what is happening to himself by knowing what is happening to the group, for nothing happens to the group which does not affect the individual most especially when viewed by external groups within the larger sociological environment. But knowledge is insufficient and inadequate if not coupled with acceptance.

Acceptance is natural on the part of the group for its individual units. Therefore, it is for the individual to accept the group as his own. Acceptance marries group members each to the other and in the creation of this matrimonial bond, makes us indispensable to each other. Acceptance is the embracing of the group as one's own, recognition of one's existence as not being separate or distinct from the group and understanding the irrefutability of group supremacy. Acceptance not only denotes that each member shares in the fortunes and misfortunes of the group, but strives in his/her individual acts to advance group objectives and goals. In the final analysis, it is acceptance which determines the degree of consciousness an individual has of himself.

Consciousness produces awareness and allows group energy to be focussed. The important variables, then, in the position of a group (particular a minority group), vis à vis the larger community in which it interacts are knowledge, identification and influence. Does the African born in the United States of America possess that knowledge and identification which would allow for influence, particularly with regard to U.S. foreign policy towards the rest of his/her group? This is the issue at hand.

What are the parameters of concern for the Afro-community in these United States? How much do we know about other and numerically major parts of the group and to what extent we identify with them? These are three basic questions we raise. These issues are raised, however, only in the context of the primary consideration which is the nexus between the demonstrated degree of concern and the relatively low influence the Afro-community has in the formulation and implementation of U.S. foreign policy toward Africa and the Afro-diaspora.

It is generally assumed that the American people, by and large, are ignorant concerning foreign policy issues (Kegley & Wittkopf, 1987:281). A noted student on the subject argued that their interest peak only in times of crisis and peril, otherwise they are indifferent. (Almond, 1960:158). But while the American people, so defined, as a collectivity of White Anglo Saxson Protestants can afford to demonstrate indifference, as the leadership reflects their cultural background, one must wonder if the Afro-community could do likewise.

Of course much has been made on the relevance of public opinion to the making of foreign policy, but in light of Vietnam (protest) and the Gulf War (support), it is difficult to wholly sustain this argument. It is true also that foreign policy seems to influence the public more so than vice versa (Klingberg, 1979; Holmes, 1985).

Nie and Andersen (1974:543) argue that the masses, as opposed to elites, are particularly ignorant and that only a few elites actually understand the workings of foreign policy. On this point, disagreement has been registered as others have argued that the masses have in their political attitudes both structure and ideological sophistication (Wittkopf, 1990:14). Therefore, relying on Holsti's description of a belief system as one which "[organizes] perceptions into a meaningful guide for behavior . . . [and] . . . has the function of the establishment of goals and the ordering of preferences" (1962:245), Wittkopf (op. cit.) argues that this is indeed the case with the American masses.

As to the nature of public sentiment on issues of foreign policy, if even one concedes that their role in its formulation is at best miniscule, there is the suggestion that much conflict does not exist. It is suggested that some "general ideological consensus" exists, the hallmarks of which are anti-communism, containment, alliances, foreign aid and whatever is deemed best in the national interest of the United States (Almond, op. cit.). These views were elsewhere supported as others noted that such policies enjoyed a consensus of political opinion and was the source of what was termed "centrism and majorityship." (Destler, Gelb & Lake, 1984:19). Indeed, appealing to these broad, yet specific tenets is seen as "the guranteed means of gaining congressional and public support" (Chace, 1978:3). Chace goes on to note that even when fluctuations are seen over time across the political spectrum from isolationist tendencies to interventionist tendencies, a consensus still seems to prevail, since what emerges are majority mood shifts as opposed to the fracturing of political opinion.

For us, a major concern has been whether the Afro-community could, as part of this mainstream consensus, find adequate expression of the idiosyncracies of its legitimate concerns; disturbing is the fact that while some statistical studies have demonstrated some variance of outlook between the Afro and mainstream communities on some particular subject matter (Brown & Baker, 1985:1–3), no study has demonstrated that on the overall direction of U.S. foreign policy, the Afro-community finds itself at odds with the political majority. This has been most recently demonstrated in the Gulf War. The question, then, becomes whether the Afro-community in these United States ought to have foreign policy concerns separate and distinct from mainstream society (and we suggest that it does) and if so, can it and is it poised to influence that process?

Weil (1974) suggested that ethnic groups which presented an electoral threat to one of the major parties and possess an effective lobbying apparatus can influence, if not dominate U.S. foreign policy toward the region of their concern; he uses as his example Jewish Americans. While it is true that the electoral threat which they possess is based significantly on their use of wealth to influence both sides of the political equation, their strength lies primarily in their cohesiveness, since they lack strength of numbers. It is their persistence of group identifiers and their maintenance of ethnic boundary lines that allow for the effectivity of their lobbying which they do quite efficiently.

The ability to mobilize the group around internal issues has been noted by other writers. Johnson (1987) believes that in the period from 1976 and thereafter, when an Afro-American was U.S. Ambassador to the United Nations, such an opportunity manifested itself for Afro-Americans. Hence, he argues that the rise of Trans Africa and interest in South Africa could be traced directly to this event. For Johnson, the history of African-American awareness and concern goes as far back as Paul Cuffee's Black emigration to Africa in 1788, the Founding of Liberia in 1847, Du Bois' Pan African Congresses, Garvey's UNIA, the NAACP's argument against U.S. occupation of Haiti in the 1920s and 1930s, and the 1957 Council on African Affairs. One should note, however, that Garvey's well-meaning, if even ill-conceived, Back-to-Africa movement was designed to repatriate African-Americans, not to challenge U.S. policy in Africa, and that the Council on African Affairs was, like the NAACP, a multi-racial association. Moreover, these activities occured in spurts and erratic formation, never assuming a sustained interest that one would associate with ingrained policy. Still, Johnson sees these as a continued process reaching its zenith in the 1970s.

The expansion of this so-called "Black Consciousness" in the 1970s, Johnson contends, precipitated a fuller understanding of the conditions facing African peoples internationally. This cannot be regarded as true when all focus was principally on South Africa proper, with little regard to U.S. policy elsewhere. In a real sense, the issue of South Africa was en vogue in the late 1970s and early 1980s to be championed by Afro-Americans and Caucasian liberals alike. Therefore, Johnson's suggestion that African Liberation Day had real meaning must be shunned as faulty logic as it testified less to rising consciousness than it does to a willingness for festivity. Johnson, I believe, is correct when he notes that prior to 1976, the Afro-community had mobilized themselves around African issues, but I'm not altogether sure if it could be considered as a mass movement. He is likewise correct, I think, when he underscores the point that traditional perceptions of U.S. national security limited the extent to which African-American concerns were seriously taken. Still, it is doubtful if this ought to be seen as damaging to consciousness and the extent to which the Afro-community could identify with causes abroad.

The nature, character and extent of Afro-American and African identification have been explored elsewhere. One writer concluded that there is a complex identification of shared common identifiers based upon external (i.e., political, social and economic) and internal (i.e., color/ancestry) factors (Moikobu, 1981). The writer, however, fails to adequately demonstrate this existence and while color and ancestry do define linkage, it is often not analytically valuable and too often insignificant as a bond of cohesiveness in an atmosphere where race begins to lose its salience, especially to the socially upward mobile. And while Moikobu, like Johnson, points to Du Bois as the patron saint of this Afro-consciousness, it is worth remembering that Du Bois' brand of Pan Africanism was continental, not hemispheric nor universal.

Pan Africanism in the 1900s and thereafter, then, had certain idiosyncracies which suggested an almost exclusive interest in the welfare of Africans in America than Africans wherever they were found. In this regard it was Garvey, more so than Du Bois, who was the genuine Pan Africanist.

Other writers refer to the long history of awareness and involvement. Jacobs (1990) refers to a closeness between slaves up to and until 1865 by virtue of the repatriation activity of the African Colonial Society (1816–1866) and Paul Cuffee's attempt in 1815. Yet she does not make any attempt to demonstrate that it continued after the passage of the 13th and 14th Amendments. Furthermore, most individuals who were repatriated, she notes, were "free blacks" and indeed freedom was often granted on condition that they emigrated to Liberia. Since many left on the basis that they had no chance for a good life in the U.S., one must wonder if a halt in emigration interest suggests a change in that outlook. In any event, to equate emigration with awareness demands a quantum leap of logic.

Much, too, has been written on the cause of the low awareness and thus the low participatory level of Afro-Americans in the making and formulation of U.S. foreign policy. Their ineffectiveness in foreign policy, even on an issue of vital concern to them Diggs (1980) writes, results from the recency of their involvement, absence of political power and the low esteem accorded to Africa and Africans by the people and government of the United States. While I may take some issue with the idea of low esteem in light of the role Africa plays in supplying American industry, I have no doubt that Diggs' points are well taken, yet it is questionable if we have touched on a principal factor, i.e., the knowledge and attitude of the Afro-American population itself.

Like many of the writers referred to, Morris (1972) speaks on the issue of association and obstacles. He gives much credit to the Black revolution for arousing interest in Africa and African affairs. The diaspora concept itself, he argues,—here citing Okun Uga in his essay "Black Brotherhood"—emerged in this movement. Identification, he infers, led to pride in African independence, citing Niel Friedman's *Africa and Afro-America: The Changing Negro Identity*. And, Morris writes, they would have been much more involved were it not for centuries of racial oppression which has denied them the economic means and technical skills needed. Morris himself notes that it has been left up to U.S. officials to point out why Africa is important to America by virtue of the 10% argument. More importantly, he recognizes that Afro-Americans have not, by the evidence, substantially affected U.S. policies there at a time when Africa loomed low on the totem pole and when significant domestic pressure combine to limit resource expenditure there.

Morris continued to assume what he called "a growing interest black Americans have in the future of Africa's struggle" as if it was anything more than superficial and as if the Afro-community was a monolith in its understanding and regard for Africa and its people; this is simply not the case as our research will show.

Morris' point of departure is that the masses are limited in the formulation of foreign policy anyway, as others have demonstrated. But how sustainable is such an argument in the context of Jewish masses influence on U.S. Israeli policy and does not foreign policy reflect the interest of some portion(s) of the polity? While, then, it may be correct to note that a major impediment is the absence of available channels to contribute, Morris himself cites Giardina (Morris, op. cit.) on the lack of a concerned constituency even within the Afro-American community, not just mainstream society, with regard to Africa. As to this "record of neglect and apparent unconcern" for U.S. relations with Africa, Morris suggested two points of explanation:

1. Socio-economic factors that limit attentiveness. These include poverty; low education; racial oppression; and pre-occupation with domestic affairs by the leadership; feeling of political powerlessness.

2. Lack of political access born of institutional racism, i.e., few blacks strategically placed.

By 1970, Morris argues, the only sustained attempt at organizing group activity on behalf of Africa was the American Negro Leadership Conference on Africa formed in 1912 (Morris, op. cit.). Had he been writing much later he might have included Trans Africa and the Institute for Afro-American Scholarship with which I was affiliated. The NAACP, he argues correctly, for the most part, did not.

That the character of American foreign policy is not significantly shaped by its possible impact on Afro-Americans or by any role they play in it, is a given. The question is why. Based on our research findings we contend that Afro-Americans do not, beyond fadish considerations, identify with Africans in Africa and the rest of the diaspora and demonstrate less commitment to what happens to Africa and Africans.

While one may consider the history of their particularity and the extent of their contemporary domestic problems and concerns, the fact remains, that in the making of American foreign policy toward Africa and the African diaspora, they may be divorced as much owing to a lack of any real commitment as much as a result of institutional exclusion. In a real sense, Afro-Americans, whether it is due to their pre-occupation with domestic concerns of which they have more than most, or their long separation from the continent of their ancestral ties, display an alienation and socio-anthropological distance quite detrimental to their group interest.

The point here is not to demonstrate that Afro-Americans are isolationist in their foreign policy views; that has been done before (Hero, 1959; Watts & Free, 1973; Hughes, 1978). Rather, it is to show that they are uninformed, and that this may well be the basis of both their isolationist tendencies as well as their underclassness.

We conclude, therefore, that the lack of political consciousness and lack of identification necessarily translates in a lack of commitment and an inability to harness the direction of U.S. foreign policy in what ought to be major areas of concern. Other conclusions will be later offered.

On Methodology

The survey employed the use of a questionnaire drawn up at the Institute for Afro-American Scholarship in the summer of 1991. The questions were designed to extract general patterns of foreign policy awareness and disposition based on a premise that attitude and influence result primarily from cognition. There were three batches of questions designed to elicit different categories of information. The number of questions totalled one hundred.

The first batch of questions sought to obtain socio-economic and personal data on respondents regarding such things as gender, age, educational achievement and income. These data allowed for cross-tabulation of information and allowed inquiry into modes of attitudinal differentiation among subgroups. Since there was no appreciable analytic statistical deviation among cohorts, we excluded meaningless discussion of these data.

The second batch of data probed for the actual knowledge of respondents to issues of the group abroad. Information such as political, social and military dimensions of African states were stressed as well as information concerning the dimensions of U.S. policy there. Responses here give a picture of the extent of alienation which exists.

The third batch of questions investigated the personal attitudes of respondents toward issues of international and foreign policy concerns. Here the objective was to give respondents an opportunity to offer personal perspectives on subjects ranging from U.S. policy in the African world to identifying what they consider as the most salient issues today.

Almost 200 items were examined in the formulation of the survey. The respondents represented a stratified random sample from the District of Columbia. Stratification took into consideration gender and geographic location. Geographic location was extremely important in that, by and large, each of the four quadrants (NE, NW, SE, SW) represents differing socio-economic structures and ensures a cross-section of the population which otherwise could not be achieved if one wished to stratify for income and education. The survey did exclude anyone who was not ethnically African or was not a citizen of the U.S. by birth; the idea here was to avoid any skewing of the data by including respondents who could possibly have a different cultural background and, likewise, differing political outlooks. The survey which included 520 respondents was conducted in the Washington, D.C. area. There is no pretense here that it does not suffer from geographic flaws. However, there is no existing literature to suggest that the African-American population in Washington, D.C. differs markedly in its political opinion from African-Americans elsewhere. Au contraire, one would expect that they would, on average, be more informed by virtue of being geographically closer to the center of politics, albeit not politically closer. Nor was there any attempt to compare the outlook of other Americans; this was simply not a relevant concern. The degree of similar non-consciousness among others, while it may something about the American population in general, does little to explain the impact of understanding for the African-American community, which alone, suffers from the kind of alienation seen in American society.

A Note of Caution

Quite inadvertently, the survey was conducted during the Gulf Crisis (Operation Desert Shield) and Gulf War (Operation Desert Storm) which had some influence on some of the responses given and some of the important issues identified. However, it is safe to assume that it did not interfere with nor impair the value of information that was being sought since it would tend to increase awareness not reduce it.

The Results

What We Know about Each Other

The study had at its centerpiece the determination of the degree of political consciousness among the study group. Certainly, we asked objective questions to this effect. However, we felt it important to have respondents give a personal assessment of what they considered their own level of political consciousness to be (granted that political culture means different things to different people). Perhaps not surprisingly, less than 20% of individuals viewed themselves as having a low level of political consciousness. Instead, better than 40% felt that theirs was average and less than one-third viewed theirs as very high.

Table 1.1 Self-Evaluation of Political Consciousness

Very High	30.2
Average	43.4
Low	18.9

As a group, we assume that our level of consciousness is relatively good, yet when analyzed by objective measures, the opinion seems not to be well founded. When asked where most Africans outside of Africa reside, an overwhelming 40% believed it to be in the United States. One-fifth had no idea (DK) and almost as many believed it to be in one of the Caribbean islands. Less than 4% knew the correct answer to be Brazil (Table 1.2). Indeed, almost 40% could not say where around the globe Africans were to be found in considerable numbers (Table 1.3).

Table 1.2 Habitat of Most Africans Outside of Africa

USA	41.5
DK	20.8
Caribbean Islands	17.0
Other Places	9.3
Brazil	3.8
England	3.8
Europe	3.8

Table 1.3 Habitat of Africans Outside of Africa

DK	39.6
USA	24.5
Everywhere	13.2
Caribbean Islands	9.4
Europe	7.5
South America	3.8
Canada	1.9

If one conceded that identification and knowledge are indispensable one to the other, then the ability to identify must rest upon how well members of a group know each other. While it is clear that American education fails to stress multilingual capabilities, as do many English-speaking societies, it was nonetheless interesting to enquire about knowledge of African languages. While a significant percentage (43%) was able to identify Swahili as a native African language, half of the respondents had no clue (Table 1.4).

Table 1.4 Indigenous African Languages

DK	50.9
Swahili	43.4
French	1.9
Spanish	1.9
Afrikans	1.9

The strength of groups lie, as well, in the presence of heroes and role model or image builders. Therefore, the study asked respondents to list individuals they consider as major African personalities, living or dead. More than one-third listed Nelson Mandela; this is perhaps best explained by the recency of his release, the high media profile accorded to him and the fact that he made a public visit to the United States. But almost as many respondents could name no one (DK) and while Nkrumah and Tutu gained a respectable 8%, Gandhi, who is not even African was named as often as Nyerere and Kenyatta, as was Botha, which raises serious questions (Table 1.5).

Table 1.5 Recognized Africans Heroes/Personalities

N. Mandela	35.8
DK	34.0
K. Nkrumah	7.5
D. Tutu	7.5
M. Makeba	7.5
W. Mandela	1.9
J. Kenyatta	1.9
J. Nyerere	1.9
W. Sisula	1.9
P.W. Botha	1.9
M. Gandhi	1.9

We earlier hypothesized that the best interest of African states could not be accomplished in the absence of lobbying organizations to champion their causes. This is particularly true in the American political process where lobbying is viewed as part of the constitutional rights of groups and through which benefits and privileges are obtained. Most Afro-Americans, however, knew of no such organization for African interest in the United States. It would be difficult, then, for them to influence policy if they are unaware of avenues to do so. About 15% were aware of Trans Africa which emphasized much of its work on Southern Africa (Table 1.6).

Table 1.6 African Lobby Organizations

DK	73.6
Trans Africa	15.1
NAACP	9.4
AARPP*	1.9

* All African Revolutionary Peoples Party

The United States in Africa

A major section of the law-making process involves policy to foreign states and foreigners. In the 1980s, the Reagan/Bush era, this was particularly true regarding Africa and Africans. In this light we asked the simple question, "Do you know of any bills in Congress affecting Africans outside the U.S.?" Tables 2.1 and 2.2 show that more than 85% of Afro-Americans were unaware of the existence of any. Even among those who claimed to know, 85% could not identify the subject of the proposed legislation (Table 2.2).

Table 2.1 Awareness of Afro-Interest in Congress

No	84.9
Yes	15.1

Table 2.2 Awareness of Afro-Interest Bills in Congress

DK	86.8
South African Sanctions	9.4
Arms Control	1.9
Aids	1.9

Probing further into knowledge of United States African policy, we asked if economic aid was given to African or Afro-Caribbean states. About half said yes and 40% said no. The data, however, showed that no one had any clear idea as to the amount of aid given in cases where it was. As this was an open-ended question, it was interesting to find that some respondents were sure that it was not much or certainly not sufficient. The same kinds of questions were asked of U.S. military aid with roughly the same results. Just about half did not know, with 26% of respondents saying yes. Likewise, over 90% could not say how much, but again some felt it was not much or insufficient. An additional question was attached here seeking to look at kinds of assistance which a consistent 90% plus could not identify (Tables 2.3, 2.4, 2.5).

Table 2.3 Amount of U.S. Economic Aid Africans Get

DK	83.0
Not Much	9.4
Not Enough	3.8
Millions	3.8

Table 2.4 Amount of Military Aid Africans Get

DK	90.6
Not Much	7.5
Millions	1.9

Table 2.5 Kind of Military Aid

DK	92.5
Arms/Equipment	3.8
Financial	3.8

Quite recently, the United States has been involved in major events concerning African peoples. African-American soldiers have been deployed to fight their brothers outside the U.S. These are the sort of escapades that one would think group members would not easily forget. Upon inquiry, however, we did not find this to be the case. Table 2.6 indicates that fewer than 6% of respondents thought of the invasion of Grenada in 1983 as a noteworthy event. Fewer still (2%), understood the impact of the 1989 raid on Panama upon Afro-Panamanians. While just above 15% noted South Africa, it is clear that they could not describe the nature of the involvement as testified to in earlier questions, and even though some did recall the raid on Libya in 1986, more than half could give no response.

Table 2.6 U.S. Involvement in Major Events Concerning African Peoples

DK	52.8
South Africa	15.1
None	7.5
Liberia Destabilization	7.5
Grenada	5.7
Haiti	3.8
Panama	1.9
Ethiopian Food Aid	1.9
Mandela U.S. Visit	1.9
Persian Gulf	1.9

As the Reagan administration came into its own in the early 1980s, its South African policy took shape rapidly. The policy of constructive engagement came to define that relationship. By most accounts, the policy was seen as detrimental to the interest of Africans, yet it dictated what the United States was officially and unofficially prepared to do in their interest extending an olive branch to a repressive regime. Based on what we saw, most African-Americans never heard of the policy by name and of those who claimed to have heard of it, few could be specific on its content.

Table 2.7 Awareness of Constructive Engagement

No	84.9
Yes	15.1

Table 2.8 What Is Constructive Engagement?

DK	88.7
Policy Of Apartheid	5.7
Good Relations With South Africa	5.7

As constructive engagement came to define the South Africa policy, the Caribbean Basin Initiative defined the economic policy toward the Caribbean states. The CBI was extremely political in that it was designed and used to reward friends and punish enemies. Even in its rewards it worked more to the advantage of multi-nationals than to Caribbean economies and it was most noteworthy for what it excluded than what it included. Here we found that less than 6% of respondents ever heard of this policy (Table 2.9) and less than 4% could specify its contents (Table 2.10).

Table 2.9 Awareness of C.B.I.

No	94.3
Yes	15.1

Table 2.10 What Is C.B.I.?

DK	96.2
Caribbean Basin	3.8

Africans in the World Today

How do we as a group, subdivided into nations, stand in comparison to other groups and nations? What is our comparative power measured in real politic terms? In the contemporary world, the power of nations is determined first and foremost by their military prowess even if that strength is dependent upon economic fortitude; economic strength can be harnessed and guaranteed by military prowess. We were concerned then about how well informed the external group is about the strength of its majority. We asked whether there were any militarily powerful African and Afro-Caribbean states and found that almost 30% said yes and roughly the same said no. Again almost four-fifths could not name any state that they considered militarily powerful. Since military power is the power to defend, to declare independence, autonomy of domestic and foreign policy and assist friends and neighbors, a group ought to think of its vital position in this field.

Table 3.1 Militarily Powerful African States

DK	45.3
Yes	28.3
No	26.4

Table 3.2 Which Are the Militarily Powerful States?

DK	77.4
Nigeria	7.5
Liberia	5.7
South Africa	3.8
Chad	1.9
Haiti	1.9
Senegal	1.9

Indeed the shift from a world defined by the Balance of Power to one defined by a Balance of Terror meant that the powerful are those in possession of nuclear capability. It is the nuclear capability of states and its potential for Mutually Assured Destruction which, for super and medium powers, have assured their defense and guranteed the peace. It is the knowledge of its ability to provide equality, too, which led to the destruction of sites in Libya and Iraq. Do African states, politically controlled by Africans possess such capability? Half of our respondents did not know, just above 13% said yes, and only one-third said no (Table 3.3). It is interesting that about 8% of respondents regarded South Africa as possessing nuclear capability and thereby presenting a real threat to the rest of Africa.

Table 3.3 Nuclear Capable African States

DK	52.0
No	34.0
Yes	13.2

Table 3.4 Which Are The Nuclear Capable States?

DK	88.7
South Africa	7.5
Uganda	1.9
Libya	1.9

The South African threat is perhaps among the greatest that Africans face on the continent, and by extension, elsewhere. Particularly grave in years gone by has been the situation of those states immediately on the borders of South Africa otherwise known as the Frontline States (Namibia, Botswana, Zimbabwe, Mozambique, Swaziland, Lesotho). This is a threat to the entire group, yet almost 75% of Afro-Americans could not identify one of these states and an equal amount could not even place them geographically. An analogy would be to find three-quarters of Jewish-Americans not knowing a single state surrounding Israel.

Table 3.5 Frontline States

DK	73.6
Nigeria	7.5
Zimbabwe	5.7
Mozambique	5.7
Namibia	3.8
Angola	1.9
South Africa	1.9

How Do We Feel/Disposition of the Group Abroad

Important Issues

Looking at perceived important issues tells what is significant and what is ever-present in the group interest. It was not very surprising that among those issues identified as most important, domestic concerns loomed high with economic worries being extremely prominent (Table 4.1).

Table 4.1 Most Important Issues

Drugs	17.0
Economy/Unemployment	15.1
DK	13.2
Peace	9.4
Black-on-Black Crime	7.5
Domestic Racism	7.5
Apartheid	7.5
Education	7.5
Health Care	5.7
Religion	3.8
Black Family	3.8
Global Oppression of Africans	1.9

However, when we probed for important international issues, it was significant that South Africa ranked below the military and economic position of the U.S. in the world, merely equalled the continuing might of the U.S. as a super-power and its relations with Europe. The fact that almost 40% named the Gulf situation was clearly reflective of the timing of the survey (Table 4.2).

Table 4.2 Most Important International Issues

Gulf Crisis/War	39.6
DK	32.1
U.S. Global Economic Position	5.7
U.S. Defense Position	5.7
South Africa	3.8
U.S. Position as a Superpower	3.8
U.S. Relations with Europe	3.8
Enforcing the New World Order	1.9
Palestinian Issue	1.9
Other	1.9

As to what respondents felt should be more prominent issues, 13% mentioned apartheid in South Africa. Only 9% and 6% respectively felt that South Africa and Africa in general should be given more media coverage, with fairly similar amounts (15% and 6%) feeling that these issues should take a greater place in presidential debates.

Table 4.3 International Issues That Should Be Prominent

DK	37.7
Other Issues	28.5
World Peace	20.8
Apartheid	13.2

Table 4.4 International Issues Needing More Media Coverage

DK	24.5
Other Issues	22.8
South Africa	9.4
Africa	5.7

Table 4.5 International Issues Needing More Coverage in Presidential Politics

DK	56.5
Other Issues	22.8
South Africa	15.1
Africa	5.7

Interest Abroad

Does U.S. foreign policy affect the lives of Afro-Americans at home? Most Afro-Americans could not say (62%). Of the remaining 38% who believed that it did, less than one-fifth identified U.S.–African policy. And while close to two-thirds said that they have a direct interest in what happens outside of the U.S., only one-fifth noted Africa as that location. Therefore, when we enquired as to membership in African/Afro-Caribbean interest groups in the United States, it was no surprise that almost three-quarters said no. Importantly though, is that close to one-half of respondents claim to have given support to such organizations at some time with about one-third having given financial support.

Table 4.6 Aspects of US Foreign Policy Having An Effect Upon Afro-Americans

DK	62.3
Economic Relations with U.S./Japan	11.3
Policy On Africa	7.5
Arms Control	7.5
Foreign Economic Aid	3.8
Immigrants	3.8
Iraqi Sanctions	3.8

Table 4.7 Interest in Events Outside US

Yes	56.6
No	22.6
DK	20.8

Table 4.8 Location of Interest Outside US

DK	47.2
Other Locations	24.5
Africa	22.6
South Africa	5.7

Table 4.9 Membership in Afro Interest Groups

No	73.6
NR	15.1
Yes	11.3

Table 4.10 Support for Afro Interest Groups

Yes	47.2
No	39.6
NR	13.2

Table 4.11 Kind of Support Given

NR	52.8
Financial	30.2
Lobby/Protest	7.5
Other	9.4

American Support & Policy

Are Afro-Americans happy with the treatment of their group members abroad, and how do they see U.S. policy there? Interestingly, more than 70% of respondents believe that African and African-Caribbean states should get economic aid from the U.S. Just above a quarter of respondents held that view because they feel that it is needed and that others get help. Nine percent suggested it was owed as a result of past exploitation (Tables 5.1, 5.2). In the case of military aid, the viewpoint was significantly more divided. Only 40% said yes even though a mere 20% gave as a reason defense needs and that the United States gives it to others. Of the significant percentage who were undecided or opposed on the subject, most could not say why, with others raising concerns about the potential for promoting war and perhaps it not being in the interest of the U.S.

Table 5.1 Right to Economic Aid

Yes	71.7
DK	24.5
No	3.8

Table 5.2 Reason For Economic Aid

DK	34.0
Need	28.3
Others Get	22.6
Past Exploitation	9.4
Other Reasons	5.7

Table 5.3 Right To Military Aid

Yes	43.4
DK/NR	41.5
No	15.1

Table 5.4 Reasons For Military Aid

NR/DK	62.3
Defense Needs	18.9
Others Get	18.9

Table 5.5 Reasons For Witholding Military Aid

DK	86.6
Promotes War	9.4
Against U.S. Interest	3.8

Similarly, less than 20% of respondents wished to see African/Afro-Caribbean states in possession of nuclear power and of these, more than 30% cited its destructiveness with an additional 8% feeling that these states cannot be trusted with such weaponry.

Table 5.6 Nuclear Weapons For African States

No	41.5
DK/NR	39.6
Yes	18.9

Table 5.7 Reasons For Withholding Nuclear Weapons

NR/DK	60.4
Destructive	32.1
Untrustworthy States	7.5

If most of our other probes involved abstract issues, we included specific issues on which personal opinions could be offered. Our purpose was to determine how much the group relates to U.S. policy against the greater part of the group. Here, responses seemed to suggest more ignorance of the subject matters than anything else. On the question of agreement with the policy of Constructive Engagement, only 25% of respondents could offer an opinion and of those almost one-half said yes. On the view of U.S. action in Libya, more than 50% offered no opinion but of those who did, it was opposed by a margin of three to one. As for the U.S. invasion of Grenada, 45% offered no opinion but a full half of respondents opposed this action. Likewise, almost two-thirds of those who offered opinions on the raid on Panama opposed that action, but again almost 40% of interviewees gave no response. Finally, with regard to past U.S. support for the insurgency movement in Angola, an overwhelming two-thirds seemed not to have had any idea of it, with one-third viewing it negatively.

Table 5.8 Attitude Toward Constructive Engagement

NR/DK	75.5
No	13.2
Yes	11.3

Table 5.9 Attitude Toward U.S. Actions

Action	Approve	Disapprove	NR/DK
Raid on Libya	11.3	34.0	54.7
Grenada Invasion	5.7	49.1	45.3
Raid on Panama	17.0	45.3	37.7
Civil War in Angola	5.7	30.2	64.2

What do the above responses say about the disposition of the Afro-community in the United States toward U.S. policy in the African world? We found that just about 70% had no opinion on it or found it neither good nor bad, about 26% felt it was bad and about 6% felt it was good. In addition, better than 35% could not offer an opinion on what was a driving force behind U.S. policy there with just about 50% saying that it was racially determined. (Tables 5.10, 5.11).

Table 5.10 Opinion On U.S. African Policy

NR	49.0
Bad	26.4
Indifferent	18.9
Good	5.7

Table 5.11 Determining Force In U.S. African Policy

Racially Determined	50.9
DK	35.8
Economically Determined	11.3
Militarily Determined	1.9

Self-Image

In the final analysis, we wanted to know how African-Americans view themselves. Whether their African origins take primacy or is secondary to their American heritage was very important in determining the perspective of the group. Therefore, the survey asked individuals to describe themselves as African, American, or some other specified category. Only thirteen percent wished to identify themselves as African, and twice as many wished to have themselves classified as

American. More significantly, however, most wished to lay claim to the duality of their heritage as a full 47% indicated a preference to think of themselves as African-Americans.

Table 6.1 Ethnic Self-Description

African-American	47.2
American	26.4
African	13.2
NR	13.2

Conclusion

Based on our findings, several conclusions can be drawn. Firstly, most African-Americans lack the conscious knowledge of their external group to make judgements of U.S. foreign policy there. Secondly, their pre-occupation with pressing, unresolved, and growing domestic issues relating to their own place in American society, which has left them politically denied, economically deprived and socially outcast, has left little room for considerations of international issues. Moreover, the fact that they make little and unconcerted demands upon the U.S. foreign policy process, presents little incentive for demonstrated U.S. sensitivity to these concerns. In fact, owing to the limited nature of organizations to function as lobby groups and the overall limited parameters of concerns of those lobby groups, the ability to have meaningful impact is greatly undermined.

No one could doubt that the African-American community has, on numerous occasions, displayed significant concern for its external group. Nevertheless, we would be hard pressed to suggest that such concern has been widespread, broad-based or sustained. Nor could an argument suggesting that the Pan Africanist idea in theory did, at any point, enjoy universal practical acceptance, be easily upheld. What is true is that several efforts on the part of individuals and organizations have made significant impact upon the outlook of the African-American community and direction of U.S. policy toward parts of the Afro-dominant world; certainly this has been true of the Congressional Black Caucus and Trans Africa. But efforts by groups such as the Washington Office on Haiti went largely ignored in Washington and fell by the wayside of U.S. geo-strategic and economic thinking. And how often, one can inquire, do ideas such as the "Sullivan Principles" find their place as cornerstones of official U.S. policy, if even often undermined?

Finally, it ought to be recognized and understood that while the dominant political culture of these United States may well have served to exclude the African-American from considerations of the group abroad, and kept him/her mired in the struggle of domestic survival, it is necessary to look to other causes which assist in the absence of positive policies toward the dominant African world.

In the development of political development of a group, particularly minority groups, there are understandably barriers from outside, but often there are barriers inside which in the case of the African-American community has, as far as its exclusion from consideration in the making of foreign policy is concerned, derived in a large way, most assuredly from its lack of political consciousness and identification with the greater of its parts, numerically.

References

Almond, Gabriel A. (1960). *The American People & Foreign Policy*. New York: Praeger.

Brown, Diane and C.A. Baker (1985) "Attitude Differentiation at the 1980 Presidential Conventions: Aspects of Race & Party Identification." *Urban Research Review*, 10, 1: 1–3, 11.

Chace, James (1978). "Is A Foreign Policy Consensus Possible?" *Foreign Affairs*, 57 (Fall): 1–16.

Destler, I.M., Leslie H. Gelb., and Anthony Lake (1984). *Our Own Worst Enemy: The Unmaking of American Foreign Policy*. New York: Simon & Schuster.

Diggs, Irene (1980). "The Biological & Cultural Impact of Blacks on the United States." *Phylon*, 41, 2 (June): 153–166.

Hero, Alfred O. Jr. (1959). *Americans In World Affairs*. Boston: World Peace Foundation.

Holmes, Jack E. (1985). *The Mood/Interest Theory of American Foreign Policy*. Lexington: Univ. of Kentucky Press.

Holsti, Ole R. (1962). "The Belief System and National Image: A Case Study." *Journal of Conflict Resolution*, 6 (Sept.): 244–52.

Hughes, Barry B. (1978). *The Domestic Content of American Foreign Policy*. San Francisco: Freeman.

Jacobs, Sylvia (1990). "Pan African Consciousness Among Afro-Americans," in Talmadge Anderson (ed.). *Black Studies: Theory, Method, Cultural Perspectives*. Pullman: Washington State Univ.

Johnson, V.D. (1987). "Afro-Americans and U.S. Foreign Policy." *Humboldt Journal of Social Relations*, 14, 1–2: 214–235.

Kegley, Charles W. Jr., and Eugene R. Wittkopf (1987). *American Foreign Policy: Patterns and Process*. New York: St. Martins.

Klingberg, Frank L. (1979). "Cyclical Trends In American Foreign Policy Moods and Their Policy Implications," in C.W. Kegley, Jr., and Patrick J. McGowan (eds.). *Challenges to America*. Berkeley, CA: Sage. 37–55.

Moikobu, Josephine (1981). *Blood and Flesh: Black Americans and African Identification*. Westport, CT: Greenwood Press.

Morris, Milton D. (1972). "Black Americans & The Foreign Policy Process: The Case of Africa." *The Western Political Science Quarterly*. 25. 3: 451–463.

Nie, Norman H., with Kristi Andersen (1974). "Mass Belief Systems Revisited: Political Change and Attitude Structure." *Journal of Politics*, 36 (August): 540–91.

Watts, William, and Lloyd A. Free. (1973). *State of The Nation*. New York: Universe Books.

Weil, Martin. (1974). "Can Blacks Do For Africa What Jews Did For Israel?" *Foreign Policy*, 109–130.

Wittkopf, Eugene R. (1990). *Faces of Internationalism: Public Opinion and American Foreign Policy*. Durham: Duke Univ. Press.

Other References

Blackwell, James E. (1975). *The Black Community: Diversity and Unity*. New York: Dodd, Mead & Co.

Chancellor, Herschelle (1981). "The Influence of Black Americans on U.S. Foreign Policy Toward Africa" in Abdul Said (ed.). *Ethnicity and U.S. Foreign Policy*. New York: Praeger Pubs., 143–182.

Davis, John (1969). "Black Americans and United States Policy Toward Africa." *International Affairs*, 23: 241–43.

Jacobs, Sylvia (1981). *The African Nexus: Black American Perspectives on the European Partitioning of Africa, 1880–1920*. Westport, CT: Greenwood Press.

Lee, Barbara (1987). "The Black Community and the Non-Aligned Movement." *Black Scholar*, 18, 2 (Mar-Apr.): 2–8.

Obatala, J. K. (1975). "Black Consciousness and American Policy In Africa." *Trans-Action*, 12, 2, 94 (Jan-Feb): 61–64 & 74.

Shepperson, George (1960). "Notes on Negro American Influence on the Emergence of African Nationalism." *Journal of African History*, 1: 299–312.

38

Diaspora African Repatriates in Ghana, West Africa: Intersections Between Socio-Cultural and Political Pan-Africanism

Obiagele Lake

The diasporization of African people into all corners of the earth has been answered by a less forceful, but consistent centrifugal response back to the continent of Africa. This paper addresses the dialectical nature of Pan-African identity as expressed by Diaspora Africans from the United States, the Caribbean and South America who have maintained their diaspora identities and at the same time have symbolized their African identities by returning to the motherland. These experiences inform the notion proposed by Kwame Toure (formerly Stokely Carmichael) that continental and Diaspora Africans constitute "one people" (Carmichael 1969).

In the late 1960s Toure, a former civil rights activist, evolved into one of the most influential Pan-Africanists of the twentieth century. He founded the All African People's Revolutionary Party in 1969 and has promulgated the return of Diaspora Africans and the liberation of African territory from European suzerainty. Toure's Pan-African ideas were heavily influenced by Kwame Nkrumah,

> one of the fathers of modern Pan-Africanism, who had been overthrown as Ghana's president in a 1966 coup and was living under the protection of President Sekou Toure in Guinea. Addressing the opening of the Malcolm X Liberation University in Greensboro, North Carolina in October 1969 from Guinea, [Toure] said 'Now we must recognize that [B]lack people, whether we are in Durham, San Francisco, Jamaica, Trinidad, Brazil, Europe or in the mother continent, are all an African people. We are Africans, there can be no question about that[1] (Walters 1993:187).

An earlier version of this essay appeared in *Anthropoligical Quarterly* 68,1 (January 1995): 21–36 and is adapted/reprinted with the permission of the copyright holder/author.
1. Cited in Stokely Carmichael, *Stokely Speaks*. New York: Vintage/Random House 1971, p. 20.

Toure further proposed that by definition the struggle for African people worldwide is Pan-Africanist. He reasoned that sovereignty was based on land, that our land base must be Africa, and that Diaspora Africans must fully participate in the development of Africa's resources (Carmichael 1969).

The purpose of this paper is to show the multifaceted aspects of Pan-Africanism as experienced by contemporary Diaspora African repatriates and how these experiences articulate with Toure's notion of "one people." The data for this discussion comes from empirical research that I conducted in Ghana between 1987 and 1989. Interviews with diaspora informants present primary data that speaks to the process of identity formation. This discussion is significant insofar as it links psycho-cultural identity with political-economic aspects of Pan-Africanism. Although the philosophy of Pan-African has as many interpretations as it has proponents, there are at least two basic tenets that describe this idea and movement. One well-known theory was proposed by Kwame Nkrumah (1963, 1957), the first Prime Minister of independent Ghana, who asserted that Pan-Africanism encompasses the unification of Africa and the development of political and economic self-determination. Under this system the continent would operate like a United States of Africa with one government, one economic system, and one army. Nkrumah was dedicated to this concept, but the newly independent leaders of many other African nations were more concerned about their nationalistic chauvinism than they were in a strong continent of Africa.[2] In spite of the fact that Nkrumah's united Africa has not yet emerged, ideas of Pan-Africanism persist.

Another form of Pan-Africanism, what I call holistic Pan-Africanism, embraces Nkrumah's idea and also promulgates Diaspora Africans as Africans and promotes their "return" to the motherland. These ideas have been advanced throughout the centuries by scholar activists such as Bishop Henry Turner (1834–1915) and Edward Blyden (1832–1912) (Blyden 1967). Marcus Garvey (1887–1940) (Lewis 1988) joined the ranks of nationalist leaders in the first quarter of the twentieth century and asserted that a land base in Africa was necessary in order for Diaspora Africans to obtain self-respect and self-determination. Garvey is central to our discussion of Diaspora African repatriates since he formulated the largest organization of African descended people in the western hemisphere and reinvigorated pride in one's African ancestry.

In 1916 Garvey formed the Universal Negro Improvement Association (U.N.I.A.) which, among other accomplishments, served as the vehicle for promoting repatriation to Africa. Garvey purchased three ships toward these ends, but was unable to fulfill his dreams. Resistance from sectors of the African American elite, intimidation from the United States government, and lack of business acumen combined to thwart his scheme. In 1925 Garvey was convicted for mail fraud[3] and subsequently deported back to Jamaica in 1927. While many scholars look to Garvey's back-to-Africa campaign as a failure, he might also be considered successful because of his pioneering ideas and his commitment to African development. Garvey's U.N.I.A. branches not only spread to many parts of the Caribbean and South America, but were influential in Africa as well (Martin 1983). In spite of Garvey's

---

2. The compromise solution that would assuage those who promulgated Pan-Africanism and those who did not was the formation of the OAU in 1963.

3. This conviction was based on very flimsy evidence, namely, an empty envelope that Garvey allegedly used to send information to prospective stock holders of his Black Star Line.

influence on the concept of a global African identity in many parts of Africa and the Diaspora, and the longevity of other Pan-African experiences, anthropologists have paid scant attention to Pan-African identity formation.

Anthropology and African Identity

Anthropologists have routinely investigated identity issues in terms of "ethnic identity" or "ethnicity"[4] and have been divided into two camps. The first consists of those who believe that ethnic alliances are predicated on "blood ties," such as race and kinship (Geertz 1973:259–260; Shils 1957; Van den Berghe 1978). Other scholars assert that ethnicity is defined in social terms and suggest that ethnic alliances are founded on factors that are perceived to advance a group's political-economic status (Fischer 1986; Keyes 1981; Nagata 1976).

It is my contention that these two approaches are not mutually exclusive, but that biological ties bring with them cultural affinities that act to create allegiances. This approach has been discussed by others (e.g., Trottier, 1981; Trosper 1981; Nagata, 1975) who suggest that common origins serve as charters for people of different cultures to formulate pan-cultural identities that are forged around issues of mutual concern.

We see this mechanism at work in a number of different communities where people form fictive kinship alliances in order to more effectively combat European and European American hegemonic institutions. Pan-cultural relations among Native American groups are a case in point and one which articulates with the neo-colonial dilemma in which Africans exist. Like African Americans, First Nation people are divided in their response to European American suzerainty. Progressive Native Americans emphasize their assimilation to European American society (Hertzberg 1971:31–58), while traditionalists focus on traditional ways and the repossession of their stolen lands. This latter emphasis was most clearly exemplified by the occupation of Alcatraz on November 20, 1969 by Native Americans from various cultural groups and led by the American Indian Movement (AIM). This group utilized the history of stolen land and broken treaties as the basis for their consolidation as one people.

> We join the dance and feel the magic which is passing from hand to hand. All Tribes and unity are the words of the drum and all tribes in the unity are the dancers. The vast differences separating our many tribes is (sic) forgotten as are the man-made boundaries. Indians from Alaska to South America are here to dance as brothers and sisters. The ancient drum of Indian unity is begun.
> We dance on our turtle island and draw strength from one another and from the past. Isolated, we will learn unity and learn to speak out our demands to a deaf government. This temporary isolation is necessary. We must build our strength. Self-determination is our goal. We must forever survive as Indians. (Bluecloud 1972:20–21)

---

4. While these terms are frequently used in the social sciences and other literatures, wherever possible, I try to avoid this usage since the term is used very selectively and some times perjoratively. For example, when "ethnicity" is used in the United States it refers mainly to people of African or Hispanic origin and not people of European descent.

This treatise conveys the dialectical relationship between the primordialist (innate or biological) and circumstantial factors as discussed by Trottier (1981); Trosper (1981); and Nagata (1981) among others. Racial, territorial and cultural factors have been promordialized by a number of groups in order to build common identities around issues of shared concern.

The literature is replete with such formulations among Asian groups who prioritize their self-representation over those imposed upon them by government decree (Nagata 1981, 1976). These disparate formulations among Asians (Obeyesekere 1975; Ichioka 1971; Thomas 1972) as well as many other groups (Lee and DeVos 1984; Glick 1982; Neusner 1989) are instructive insofar as they underscore the confluence between the political-economy and the designation of cultural and national categories. The historical and contemporary political-economic marginalization of Diaspora Africans has been similarly influenced by external sources that encouraged the formation of a global African identity. Even though many Diaspora Africans are committed to life in the metropole, others have been in search of their homeland where they can experience a Pan-African identity. Since the eighteenth century, this movement from North to South has been continuous and has taken on a number of permutations.

Not only have Diaspora/Continental relations been factored out of the literature, but the very basis of an African identity among Diaspora Africans is denied (Van den Berghe 1976:242–255). This misconception emanates from the penchant among many people of European descent to ignore the reality of slavery and our exorcism from Africa. In order to render this misrepresentation complete, anthropologists have also ignored the long socio-cultural and political history of Pan-African relations that have been in place throughout the centuries. Instead, scholars use linguistic, cultural and geographic differences to assert what they infer is antagonistic relations between these societies (Van den Berghe 1976:242–255; Safran 1991:89–90; Legum 1962).

> I suggest that this ideological separation of indigenous and diaspora Africans is a result of and is consistent with the hegemonic forces that inhered during the European extraction of Africans from their motherland. That is, the power to remove millions of people from the continent of Africa was accompanied by the removal of African languages and other cultural constructs from these diasporized peoples...(Lake 1995:21).

Diaspora Africans in the Americas, Europe and other parts of the globe have maintained aspects of their African heritage (Moore 1970:385–403; Thompson 1983; Asante and Asante 1985), and at the same time they have merged their cultures, like European immigrants in the Americas, with those of other groups in their new settings. As Keyes (1981:15) has noted, "the formation of ethnic groups involves the formation of new identities or the investment of new meaning in old identities." What is important to underscore here is that cultural identity is an active, organic entity, one which assumes different expressions depending on the social and/or political moment (Basch, Schiller and Blanc 1994:268).

Historical and Contemporary Pan-African Linkages

The current repatriation of diaspora Africans to Ghana, West Africa, follows a movement of African descended people from the western hemisphere to the motherland since the eighteenth century. A full discussion of these movements can be found in a number of sources (Uya 1971; Dunbar 1968; Jenkins 1975; Redkey 1969) thus only a brief overview is necessary here.

Beginning in the eighteenth and nineteenth century Diaspora Africans were either forced to migrate to Africa or repatriated with the hope of escaping the evils of slavery and racism. After the emancipation of slavery in Brazil in 1888 many people repatriated to Nigeria (Turner, J.M. 1975; Turner, L. 1942). Africans from England and African Americans who had fought on the side of the British during the American Revolution were first transported to Nova Scotia and then to Sierra Leone (Walker, W. 1976:229–231; Fyfe 1962:136, 147, 291; Kup 1975). The bulk of nineteenth century repatriates were transported to Liberia (Shick 1980) by the European American controlled American Colonization Society (Staudenraus 1961; Liebenow 1973).[5] Even though these early African American pioneers were criticized for their dominance over indigenous Africans, there were many Diaspora Africans such as William Sheppard (Williams 1982:135–153) and Edward Blyden (1967) who made important contributions to the Congo, Liberia and other African societies. Sheppard and Blyden were joined by a number of other scholar-activists and missionaries who struggled for the self-determination of continental Africans and the repatriation of Diaspora Africans to the motherland (Jacobs 1982; Esedebe 1994; Essien-Udom 1964). Although it was these leaders who initiated and experienced the concept of Pan-Africanism[6] it was not until the twentieth century that the term Pan-Africanism was born.

The term Pan-African was initiated by Trinidadian Henry Sylvester Williams, a lawyer who organized the first Pan-African Conference in England in 1900. Several other conferences followed from 1919 until 1945 that laid the groundwork for independence movements in Africa. From 1919 to 1927 William Du Bois organized these fora which were predominantly attended by Diaspora Africans; however, in 1945 Kwame Nkrumah organized the first Pan-African meeting where continental Africans were in the majority. African leaders such as Jomo Kenyatta and Peter Abrahams were two of many dignitaries who went on to become the first leaders in the struggle for African independence. Diaspora and continental Africans also collaborated in Tanzania in 1974 at the first Pan-African Conference held in Africa. The most recent meeting was held in 1993 in Uganda. In addition to these conferences there were many other arenas where Diaspora Africans demonstrated their eagerness to express their commonality with continental sisters and brothers.

Diaspora Africans volunteered to fight for Ethiopian independence during the 1930 Italian invasion; participate in transnational meetings such as the African-

---

5. Other nineteenth century repatriates included missionaries who were sent to the Congo, South Africa and many other countries in Africa. Some of the better expositions of this missionary history include works by Sylvia Jacobs (1982) and Walter Williams (1982).

6. Edward Blyden was a leading nineteenth century Pan-Africanist who used the term Pan-Negro to describe the interconnections between Diaspora and continental Africans.

African American Summits in 1991 and 1993 (Walker, S. 1993:12–15); the Pan-African Conference on Reparations in Abuja, Nigeria, in 1993; and the fund raising work of the South African Support Project (Walters 1993:87) are only a smattering of events that are indicative of positive transnational relations. In addition to these more political linkages, Diaspora African cultural expressions point to continuing links with Africa (Whitten and Szwed 1970; Moore 1970:385–403; Thompson, R. 1983; Holloway 1990). Cultural and political issues bring various communities of African descent together in a number of academic circles. St. Clair Drake (1982:341–405) speaks to the importance of these transnational linkages when he writes that

> [w]hat makes [these activities] Pan-African is the conceptualization on the part of the participants in these local struggles of their being part of a larger world-wide activity involving [b]lack people everywhere, with the various segments having obligations and responsibilities to each other (Ibid:343).

These opportunities to experience our collective struggle and develop a collective consciousness do not suggest that Diaspora and continental Africans are the same people, nor, as Gellner argues (1987) does it suggest that African people are suffering from a collective amnesia in terms of intercultural conflict on the continent and the complicit role of Africans in the continental and transatlantic slave trade. Instead, these fora are predicated on our common struggle for liberation and the affirmation of our Africanness. These meetings also place Africa "in the foreground of [our] assertions of cultural identity and community" (Scott 1991:273).

Following the work of Basch, Schiller, and Blanc (1994), which seeks to broaden the identity discourse to include transnational African communities (among other populations), I argue that many Diaspora Africans do not consider themselves as minorities, but as part of a wider African society. Such a vision is crucial for African people and one that must precede political-economic forms of Pan-Africanism. While Europeans dismembered African communities and cultures, this process also serves as a link that transgresses geographic and temporal boundaries.

Attention to the interface between the political and the cultural is significant since the colonization of Africa encompassed both of these aspects. African people were divested of their land and other raw materials while Europeans created a cultural ideology that deemed African people as lazy, unintelligent, and otherwise inferior. Because of the long history and the pervasiveness of these ideas, people of African descent

> were forced to deny a decisive part of their social being: to detest their faces, their colour, the peculiarities of their culture.... All this was done so that they would idealize the colour, history and culture of Europeans (Campbell 1990:39).

While many Africans have internalized these notions of inferiority, other continental and Diaspora Africans see themselves

> against a reclaimed background, in a perspective that [gives] pride and self-respect ample scope, and makes history yield for him (sic) the same values that the treasured past of any people afford (Schomburg 1925:237).

While some contemporary scholars are content with imagining *imagined* communities (e.g., Anderson 1987; Hall, S. 1993; Rushdie 1991), the cultural legacy of African descended people acts as an actual stimulus that compels them to their *real* homelands. This is a significant exodus since it occurs in spite of poor economic conditions in Africa and in spite of cultural differences that inhere between continental and Diaspora Africans.

Ronald Cohen (1978:379–403) and other scholars have discussed other societies whose cultural and ideological solidarity have taken precedence over material advantages. In light of these findings, it is worth emphasizing that the distribution of material resources is not separate from other affinities, but sets the stage for cultural and psychological conditions. For Africans everywhere, racism has meant being far removed from the means of production; this economic impoverishment has been matched by a virulent assault on the cultural and psychological economies. Even though these relationships have persisted throughout history, past and contemporary scholars are eager to erase race from the identity discourse.

While more than a few European American and African American scholars are eager to dismiss race as a real entity, many Diaspora Africans assume race to be one of the important factors that contributes to their sense of peoplehood and one which forges their commonality with continental Africans. For repatriates in Ghana, the commonality of race serves as the underpinning of face-to-face and political alliances. Like transmigrants to other areas, Diaspora Africans in Africa

> have reinscribed their newly unbounded hyperspace into reconceptualised categories of deterritorialized nation-states and of race (Basch, Schiller, and Blanc 1994:268).

While Basch et al. (Ibid:291) describe paying attention to race as replicating the ideology of "white" superiority, they also acknowledge that race thinking provides

> sites of resistance [which] challenge colonially derived constructions in which "white" and "British" were the primary standards of national culture (Ibid:283).

Indeed, attempts by scholars to erase race is in tandem with efforts by political figures to eradicate set-aside programs that have the potential of creating equal opportunity, especially in the case of African Americans in the United States. At the more cultural level, it is ironic that just at a time when more and more Diaspora Africans are embracing Africanness, non-African people are defining race as a non-issue. The recognition of a Pan-African identity is central to the creation of a communal African environment. While this African community may be diverse in its cultural constructions, it may also be seen as a manifestation of "one people." Sorenson (1992:201) suggests that the utility of such a construction is to

> counterbalance the profound sense of loss that accompanies it. To describe as myths these forms of remembering, of constructing new shared identities, and of formulating particular visions of the future is not necessarily to dismiss them as illegitimate aspirations, false versions of history, or invalid types of identity, but rather to emphasize their *social* (emphasis in original) character.... Myths are not relics of some antique past but mechanisms for organizing experience and reworking the present.

Diaspora Repatriates in Ghana

In the 1950s and 1960s there was a resurgence of Diaspora African repatriation to various parts of the continent. Those areas most frequently chosen were Ghana, Nigeria, Kenya, Togo, and Zimbabwe.[7] I chose Ghana as my host community since Nkrumah was one of the first Africans who had encouraged Diaspora Africans to participate in the African experience. Other literatures on migration to Africa also highlight Ghana as a mecca for repatriates (Jenkins 1975; Dunbar 1968:39–109).

The major factors underlying African American migration include systemic discrimination and violence (Pinkney 1984). In the Caribbean the continuation of neo-colonialism (Edmonson 1979; 1968) encouraged Jamaicans, Triniadians and others to migrate. The fact that Kwame Nkrumah was one of the first continental Africans to advocate holistic Pan-Africanism was a major pull factor for Diaspora Africans who migrated in the 1950s and 1960s.

For the most part, it has been skilled Diaspora Africans who have settled in Ghana. Those heads of state who have encouraged Diaspora Africans to return have emphasized the need for skilled repatriates who could accelerate the process of African development (Weisbord 1973:126–127, 132ff). During his visit to Harlem in 1958 Kwame Nkrumah was very explicit in his call for

> bonds of blood and kinship [and encouraged] doctors and lawyers and engineers to come and help us build our country (Kihss 1958:4).

Many of the repatriates during Nkrumah's incumbency were doctors, lawyers, owners of insurance companies, electricians, and other professionals. A number of people taught at the University of Ghana while others, e.g., George Padmore and Arthur Lewis, were advisors to Nkrumah's government. Although Du Bois railed against Garvey's repatriation agenda in the first quarter of the twentieth century, he migrated to Ghana in 1961. Nkrumah's presidency also encouraged many lesser known Diaspora Africans to emigrate to Ghana. Along with a range of technical and professional skills these repatriates came to Ghana with a great deal of hope of an egalitarian society free of systemic discrimination based on race. While race may not have been an inhibiting factor in Ghana, Nkrumah's incumbency (1957–1966) was fraught with coups, droughts, and the continuation of dependence on western governments (Ungar 1978:383; Howell and Rajasooria 1972; Bretton 1966). The current regime under Jerry Rawlings is also marked by austerity programs orchestrated by the IMF (Sarris 1991; Sawyer 1990). Beginning with Nkrumah's departure many Diaspora Africans came back to the United States. Others migrated to Tanzania or other parts of Africa. Still there are several families in Ghana who have been there since the Nkrumah days and who are continually joined by new repatriates.

Prior research in this area has focused on the testimony of a few contemporary returnees (Jenkins 1975; Dunbar 1968) and larger nineteenth century movements.

---

7. The literature (Jenkins 1975; Thompson, E. B. 1969), as well as anecdotal evidence indicates that in addition to Ghana, Diaspora Africans are found in the largest numbers in Nigeria, Tanzania, Togo, and Zimbabwe. Since Zimbabwe's independence in 1980, increasing numbers of Diaspora Africans have been migrating there (Washington 1989). There has been no in-depth research that reports the numbers of Diaspora Africans in these countries.

Figure 1. Diaspora African Population in Ghana, 1989

	AA	AC	ASA	Total	Total Percentage
Men	30	5	2	37	30.8
Women	42	35	6	83	69.2
Total	72	40	8	120	100.0

My research offers an empirical in-depth view of repatriates' lives and how these every-day experiences articulate with broader Pan-African themes.

In 1989 there were approximately 120 Diaspora Africans[8] in Ghana. Most of these repatriates were African Americans and African Caribbeans (see Fig. 1) who had settled in urban areas in Accra and Kumasi (shown in Fig. 2). The larger number of African Americans is mainly due to the presence of a group of African Americans who refer to themselves as The Nation (and who are called Black Hebrews by others) (Gerber 1977; Weisbord and Kazarian 1985:61–91).

The Nation, who have their headquarters in Dimona, Israel, have lived in an area in Accra called Medina since 1965. Members of this group profess to be "The Chosen People" whose original home is Israel. According to Hebrew Israelites, Israel is a part of northeast Africa and the ancestral home of African people. While the Hebrew Israelites live as a community in Medina, most repatriates live in nuclear or extended families.

I interviewed eighty-four of these individuals (seventy percent of whom were women) (Lake 1997). Some of these repatriates remember the Nkrumah days; however, the majority migrated between 1960 and the present. Most of these Diaspora Africans had at least an undergraduate degree and were professionals in the fields of education, medicine, law, or religion. Even though most repatriates would have been considered middle-class by Diaspora or African standards, the vagaries of day-to-day life were nevertheless challenging.

In addition to cultural adjustments, repatriates must learn to accommodate for the infrastructural inadequacies. Ghanaians and returnees are obliged to deal with medical services that are inferior or grossly undersupplied. In addition, many general consumer items are either hard to get or are overpriced. Services, such as transportation, are very poor and add to the frustration of daily life. While most informants had their own cars, there were occasions when they were dependent on public transportation which is usually in the form of *tro tros* or minibuses that are in a state of disrepair. Even though fares are quite inexpensive, there are a limited number of these vehicles which are usually grossly overcrowded. Moreover, their dilapidated state contributes to an uncomfortable ride that often does not reach its destination before breaking down or running out of gas.

The condition of these vehicles is compounded by poor roads. While some of the interregional roads, e.g, from Accra to Kumasi, are in very good condition other roads are badly eroded and are full of pot holes. This inefficiency in transportation infrastructure has consequences on other aspects of life that affect the efficiency of the country.

---

8. Since my research in Ghana, anecdotal evidence, the appearance of new repatriates in the film *Sankofa*, and articles in popular magazines indicate that the Diaspora population in Ghana in steadily increasing.

Figure 2. Regional Map of Ghana

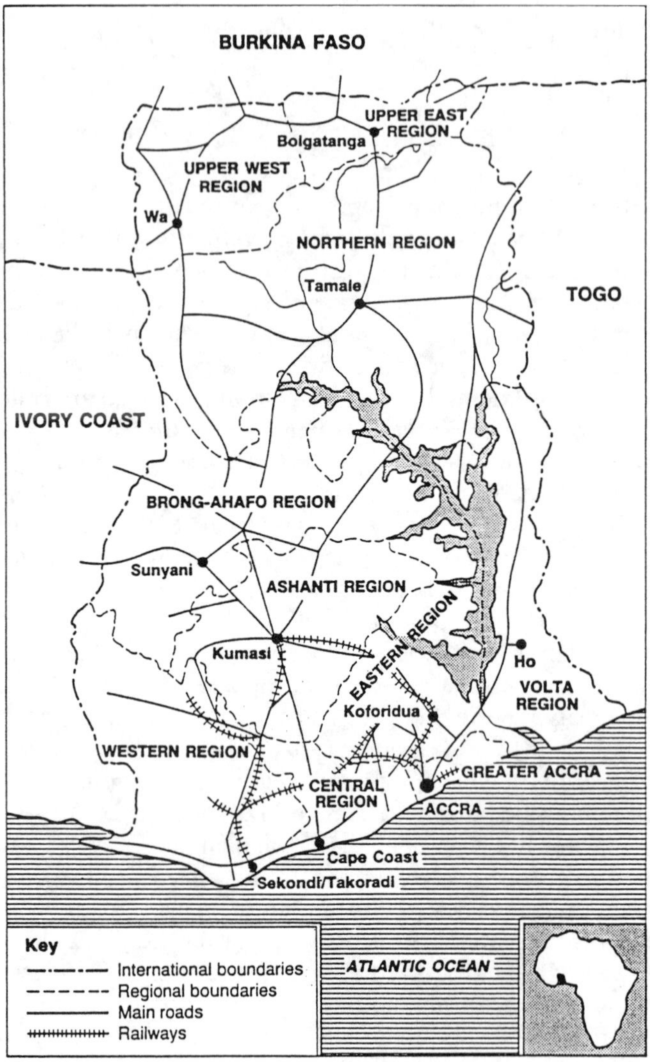

Other facilities such as water, communications, and electricity are also wanting. Even though the apparatus for these services are in place, they are old and in need of repair. Many households have running water and electricity, but it is common for both to be inoperable. Water is also problematic since it must be treated before consumption. There are some foreigners who claim that the water is completely potable, yet they have no explanation for their frequent non-malarial illnesses. I point out these exigencies in order to indicate the setting, although constantly changing, in which indigenous and Diaspora Africans in Ghana find themselves. In a general sense, these conditions are true for all of Africa (Ungar 1978); however, my research and findings pertain only to Ghana. Further research may point to similarities or differences in other African countries regarding relationships between indigenous and Diaspora Africans.

Although each interview included information regarding many different aspects of these peoples' lives, for the purposes of this article I have extracted portions that speak directly to Pan-African issues. One of the ways that I attempted to ascertain peoples' sense of connection to Africa was by asking them "What made you come to Africa?", and asking what their experiences have been in Ghana, and how they perceived the concept of Pan-Africanism.

The kind and quality of repatriates' experiences were influenced by such factors as sex,[9] education, class, and general knowledge about Africa. Even though each repatriate's experience is different, they can be divided up into three heuristic categories which reflect their orientation to the idea of Pan-Africanism and their views relative to the concept of "one people." "Africanists" refers to repatriates who considered themselves Africans and who felt that Africa was as much theirs as it was continental Africans. "Citizens of the world" are those individuals who either did not identify with Africa or who were more concerned about agape love among all human beings than they were in stronger relations between Diaspora and continental Africans. These two groups are situated at either end of a spectrum where "Diasporafricans" constituted the majority. People in this category embraced both their national identities (i.e., their places of birth) and their African ancestry. These individuals were also very concerned about the development of holistic Pan-Africanism. Even though there is overlap within and between these categories, I use them in order to provide a structural basis for analyzing people's responses and experiences. To the extent possible I use interview excerpts in order to allow informants to tell their own stories.

The experiences of repatriates were as varied as the reasons for migration. Some informants migrated because they were influenced by their parents who were part of the Garvey movement. Some had made earlier trips to Africa through Crossroads Africa, organized by James Robinson in 1958, and were stimulated to return. Other Diaspora Africans came to "find their roots." A number of repatriates were responding to the newly won independence of African nations and wanted to participate in this process.

Pan-African Perspectives

Informants reported a number of experiences and observations that were not related to their Pan-African orientation, but yet inform the Pan-African discourse. While most Pan-African discussions focus on political or economic issues, informants' stories addressed more interactive, face-to-face encounters with Ghanaians. Many of these informants stated that they had a long-standing interest in Africa but could not explain where this interest came from.

While in secondary school, a Jamaican woman told me that she "always wrote stories about African children." Another told of how her mother took pride in being of African descent which compelled my informant to romanticize about becoming an African princess. Another woman from St. Nevis, West Indies, "always wanted to have a day care center in Africa"—a dream she was fulfilling.

---

9. Obiagele Lake (1997) focuses on the particular experiences of women in Ghana.

In a more general sense there were a number of cultural practices in Ghana that reminded repatriates of their homes in the Diaspora. The annual *Homowo* celebration reminded many informants from the Caribbean and South America of their Carnival or *Candoble* celebrations. A few informants were convinced that they were from Ghana because they found family names among Ghanaians.

It has been proposed more than once in the literature that names are part of a historical and socio-cultural framework (Isaacs 1967:46–52; Frazer 1911: 318–386; Stuckey 1987:194–198; Herskovits 1958:17, 190–194ff). Stuckey notes that "(i)n West Africa the names of many of the people constitute their 'essence', producing deep and permanent psychological effects." That Diaspora Africans also find names to be meaningful and historically commemorative is indicated by the following informants:

> I do remember that my father has…a middle name [that is African.] And he dropped that name when he got grown because he said it was ridiculous. He didn't like it and he dropped it, not knowing that name comes from northern Ghana, a name from the Bolgatanga area.

Another informant, Bajan,[10] who is a Catholic priest, came to Africa to acquire the experience of rootedness. The use of Ghanaian names in his family contributed to feeling of family resemblances.

> I can remember my mother had a very good friend whose name was Efe. And now since I've been here I've found that Efe is a Ghanaian name. That is no [proof], but, I remember this lady called Efe. Now I know this girl next door called Efe. Efe means a girl born on Friday.

Other informants also remembered names in common. One informant told me that his grandmother used to speak Twi. He is one of the few people who felt he had direct connection with Ghana because his grandparents kept family histories.

Emotional similarities also played a role in forging connections between repatriates and Ghanaians. One informant not only insisted that her people were from Ghana, based on similarities in temperament, but believed that she had located the exact ancestral area.

> I don't know the tribe, but the village is Bolgatanga [see Fig. 2 above]. And those are some fightin' people….They fight all the time, mad! And my father's people are some fightin' people. They argue…it's experience that has caused this temperament. I've discovered it's not. It's hereditary, you know. So I believe definitely that Daddy's people come from the north, from Bolgatanga.

Other informants found linkages in styles of communication. Even though Europeans robbed Diaspora Africans of their indigenous languages, similar language behaviors are evident. Baber (1987:33) suggests that Africans worldwide have a "proclivity toward expressive performance" which was evident among Ghanaians and repatriates. In heated debates, it is common to observe Ghanaians dramatically calling attention to themselves and drawing an audience in the process. These dramatic public disputes are not unusual in sectors of the Caribbean or African American communities. Abrahams and Szwed (1983:77) speak to the ubiquitousness of African Americans speech behavior.

---

10. All informants' names used in this paper are pseudonyms.

We see a tremendous significance attached to speech in all its forms: the use of talk to proclaim presence of self, to assert oneself vocally in the most anxious and most unguarded situations. We are shown the value of arguing in the daily prosecution of life, as one technique of dramatizing oneself.

Many scholars have addressed the persistence of African verbal and non-verbal communication styles and words in the Diaspora. Avoidance of eye contact is one similarity (LaFrance and Mayo 1978). Often while they are speaking Diaspora Africans do not look at the person they are conversing with. There is similar eye contact behavior among Ghanaians.

Black culture as manifested in communication cannot be taken out of its historical context, because present behavior cannot be isolated from past patterns.... Even though Africans came from diverse backgrounds, the specific vocabularies and particular cultural traits that could have separated them from each other were overcome by the similarity of the basic structure of their languages and cultures (Baber 1987:77).

There were other factors such as physical resemblances and celebrations of newborn children (outdoorings) that made Diaspora Africans feel more at home. Even in the face of these similarities, there were a number of adjustments that repatriates were obliged to make.

Nobari, a piano teacher from Jamaica, shared portions of her cross-cultural experience in terms of her relationship with her Ghanaian husband, Thomas.

Nobari: I am African basically, but I still think Caribbean. I still think so. I tend to think I mustn't lose my identity. I feel that for marriage and for life. I feel that one should not try to submerge themselves into somebody else's culture or somebody else's life for that matter. So...we meet each other halfway on some things. On other things we are poles apart.

African food, for example—-I choose the ones I like and I leave the ones I don't like. So sometimes I feel he suffers. He doesn't get half as much African food as he would like. So he says, 'Oh don't worry, I don't care so much for fufu and that sort of thing.' But if his sister cooks fufu, he will *enjoy* it! (Laughter, Nobari and Lake).

So, deep down in my heart I think maybe one day I ought to just die and let this man have a proper wife (Laughter, Nobari). I think I've tried to introduce him to the Caribbean...like I say, we eat bananas boiled. At first he would resist that. He'd say, 'Oh, no, we don't eat such things here.' Until 1983 when we had famine in Ghana, near-famine—then he was ready to eat anything.

Nobari clearly falls into the Diasporafrican category and exemplifies the balance that many repatriates pursue in their lives in the mother country. One of the ways that she and other Diaspora Africans maintained connections with their diaspora homelands was to form the Ghanaian Caribbean Association. This group consists mainly of African Caribbeans, but there are also Ghanaian members. The group started as a social organization, but has extended into a support group that aids families in legal matters, in times of death, and other stressful circumstances. The women in the Ghanaian Caribbean Association find community among themselves and with Ghanaians; however, some informants were adamant about making stronger links with Ghanaians and Ghanaian life styles.

Egala, an informant from Trinidad, considers herself Ghanaian and suggests that

> You have to be in touch with the customs if you want to get along. Doing it any other way, you won't achieve anything...trying to change things willy-nilly. When I came here I didn't want to associate with West Indians to the detriment of maintaining close relationships with Ghanaians. I felt if you did, you would not be able to integrate into Ghanaian society really. You would be trying to live like West Indians in Ghana.
>
> In earlier days West Indian women only moved together and it became more difficult to be accepted. Sometimes it depends on the household they had. They may have accepted West Indian ways. This can lead to problems and the husband may decide he wants to go somewhere else to get his Ghanaian food. My husband certainly wasn't going to tolerate my making a West Indian household. My mother-in-law taught me to prepare a lot of dishes.

Ironically, African American women thought that life for Caribbean women was easier because some of the foods were the same as those found in many Caribbean countries. Caribbean women, however, were very clear that while some foods may have been similar the methods of preparation were very different. In general, repatriates were unfamiliar with other dimensions of the physical and social landscape, but soon became accustomed to them. This level of incorporation is important since it speaks to the process of every-day interactions between Diaspora and continental Africans. As Moerman (1988:2) points out

> it is only in interaction that things social are manipulated....The main reason for an interest in "micronotions" is that they tell us about the actual encountered life experiences and circumstances of the people we study.

Even though their experiences and perceptions of Ghana and Pan-Africanism varied in detail, Diaspora Africans constructed their identities along a broad spectrum of Pan-African ideas. Informants whom I call "Africanists" are those who tended to have had relationships with continental Africans before coming to Ghana and were also more cognizant of African political issues than some other informants. The following informant is unusual in that she had been to several African countries before deciding to settle in Ghana. She was also unusual in that she was a political activist. While many informants were involved in the civil rights movement in the United States or the Caribbean, most were not forming political alliances in Ghana or even making political statements. Adjety's views on global Pan-Africanism are redolent of prominent nationalists in the United States when she suggests that

> our plight in the United States is so intertwined with Africa. I think after eighteen or nineteen years of activism in the States, it is time for me to share what I think is the central component of our development in the world, as well as developing my own consciousness about solving our problems in the world, because they're pretty much the same. I see it as a responsibility. I am in a unique position in terms of knowing the way of the West. It's only being in Africa, but being with Africans in Europe. I learned a lot about Africans in Europe.

Adjetey's dissatisfaction with the stagnating Pan-Africanism in the United States also prompted her to migrate to the motherland. Her views on the international nature of Pan-Africanism are reminiscent of those of Malcolm X when speaking to continental Africans.

[O]ur people here in America consider ourselves inseparably linked with [Africans], that our origin is the same and our destiny is the same, and that we've been kept apart now for too long (Brietman 1970:145).

Even though many Africanists identified as African and were proponents of the Pan-African idea, they were also well aware of the difficulties in making this concept a reality. Jeunef, an African American woman who taught primary school, recounted her experiences and feelings about the complexity of identity formation. In the United States, she was a member of Toure's All African People's Revolutionary Party where she had the opportunity to meet continental Africans.

> Jeunef: It was a blessing to get an in-depth view of material reality. You're not going to live in trees, yet you're not going to be in a situation like the United States. But in the long run, it's going to be a better life—which I agree it is.
> Lake: Better in what sense?
> Jeunef: Better in that the quality of living is better here. I have a better sense of who I am. Even despite the little prejudices here where many Black people say I don't have an identity because I'm a Black American. But I do have an identity because I am a combination of everything. Yes, I'm a descendant of slaves and I am from Africa. So I have the advantage. I can take a little of Yoruba's (culture), I can take a bit from the Gas,[11] and just shape it into what I am. So I don't even get offended *anymore* because I don't have a specific group. I even think it's best because I don't get into that tribalistic mentality.

Jeunef was joined by other "Africanists" who considered themselves Africans; however, this self-identification was sometimes at variance with that of the host community. Diaspora repatriates are not unusual in this regard since "self definitions and other definitions do not necessarily adjust at the same rate" (Horowitz 1975:131).

Nguyen is an African American woman who came to Ghana in 1957 with her Ghanaian husband. As is true for most Diaspora Africans, she places an great deal of importance on race as the unifying factor among people of African descent. She also explicates the difference between nationality, race, and culture in her comments regarding Muslims who originally came to the continent of Africa through slave trading and colonialism.

> Nguyen: Pan-Africanism to me means a united Africa. Well, it's supposed to be the whole of Africa including North Africa, but I don't think those Arabs think of themselves as Black or Africans. They're only Africans when it's their interest politically. They really don't identify with Black Africa. So I think the idea that Nkrumah had was beautiful, but I don't think the Arabs adopted it as such. So I think that we have to somehow limit that Pan-Africanism to sub-Saharan Africa. We should be able to communicate with the Northerners, but I don't think it's going to be integrated, united like the United States of America was envisioned. I don't think it's possible because the two cultures are too different, you know. And it's such a different race of people.
> Lake: Do you think that Diaspora Africans have a role to play in the development of Pan-Africanism in Africa?
> Nguyen: Yes, certainly. And we have the heroes who started long before even Nkrumah had the idea of Pan-Africanism. That West Indian . . . Marcus Garvey,

---

11. Ga is the name of a Ghanaian ethnic group found predominantly in the Accra Region.

he had the idea. You know, I admire him. And there are others. Frantz Fanon, he's a Black. So indeed, we should bring in all our people. If they're in the Caribbean or wherever they're from. As long as they are Black they have a role to play in uniting Africa—I mean sub-Saharan Africa.

Many Ghanaians I spoke with also felt that it was time for Diaspora Africans to "come home." Even though some Ghanaians may feel a kinship with Diaspora Africans, they do not speak for the entire population. Historically, there have been tensions between these populations based on cultural differences. While Diaspora Africans view their problems as racial ones,

> the racial edges of the Ghanaian were not as sharp as those of the Americans....Ghanaian psycho-social framework did not utilize generalized race identity as a basis for relationships, but rather utilized culturally specific references. The questions was: "Are you Ga, or Ewe, or Ashanti, or Fanti?" (Walters 1993:104–105).

In addition to the cultural chauvinism of continental Africans, there is often a certain amount of envy and suspicion at play (Walters 1993:89–126). My own experience, anecdotal evidence, and much of the literature also speak to the fact that communication is sometimes difficult since many continental Africans are unfamiliar with the slave trade or are only vaguely aware of the systemic discrimination faced by Diaspora Africans (Walters 1993:89–126; Lacy 1970; Angelou 1987:20).

This is a curious phenomenon since African enslavement was as much a reality on the continent as it was in the Diaspora. Moreover, European racist ideology that deemed Africans to be physically, intellectually, and culturally inferior was first put forth in terms of continental Africans. European neo-colonist control of African economic systems continue to racialize the North and South. The fact that African people are in the majority in African nations masks the internalization of European norms and values that are also pervasive.

Crossroads and Roadblocks

The few informants who I call citizens-of-the world thought that Diaspora and continental Africans should "get along," but were more concerned about global agape love than they were in forging an African family. One woman from Jamaica, who identifies as African, but also called herself a "citizen-of-the-world," emphasized class over race relations.

> I'm much more concerned with individuals making their way through the community. I haven't had many adjustments to make here in Ghana because I've not had to mesh. I've not had to mix well out of my class. I'm very conscious of class.

> Out of the eighty-four people I interviewed, only four identified themselves as citizens-of-the-world—all were upper middle class. Even Droller, who became a Ghanaian citizen, emphasized the cosmopolitan quality of his life and the opportunities to mix with people from all over the world over his ties with

Ghanaians. Droller was one of the first African Americans to migrate during the 1950s; however, he emphasizes a more diffuse identity over his Africanness.

> I think of myself as being fundamentally American even though technically I may be a Ghanaian in a legal sense. But generally speaking, I can go into the U.S.A. almost anywhere because I was born there. I can't do that here. I can't get in certain parts of the country. I don't even know what they're talking about. Or when they do certain things, it's just so different from what I would do. So I know I couldn't live in that particular area. Accra is a cosmopolitan area. There are lots of people from all over the world. It's almost a miniature New York. In New York you can meet a Romanian, a Spanish person from Spain, a Russian, a Chinaman. Well, Accra is like that too. I play golf with a Scotsman, an Englishman, and two Africans, one from Ghana, one from Sierra Leone. So you see, you can be with anybody and that's the way I like it.

Although Droller is heavily involved with the Du Bois Center in Ghana, most of his comments were based on his class status. Another Jamaican informant in this category thought that Pan-Africanism was important, but that looking for "understanding [among] a broad network of countries" took precedence over African consolidation.

While these views are ideally important, they fail to address the disparaging image that Europeans have had for Africans throughout history and how this image has served as a justification for the material plunder of Africans around the world. The coming together of African people is a process of centering that establishes continuity and self-esteem. The fact that all people look to their own beginnings and their own cultures as anchoring points has been addressed in the literature more than incidentally.

> Ethnicity is intimately related to the individual need for collective continuity. The individual senses to some degree a threat to his own survival if his group or lineage is threatened with extinction. Ethnicity...includes a sense of personal survival in the historical continuity of the group (DeVos 1975:19).

Diaspora/African/Woman

Both men and women found integration into Ghanaian society an ongoing process. Although they shared many problems in common, women encountered problems *as* women. Many women found the extended African family to be a curse as well as a blessing. When Diaspora Africans marry continental Africans, they marry more than a husband, they marry a family. This has been much written about by Diaspora women in other parts of Africa (see e.g., Golden 1987; Kayode 1979:81, 106–110; Angelou 1987). Almost all of the Diaspora women in Ghana related stories about visiting relatives or in-laws who were living with them. (Most of the Diaspora men were married to women of the same nationality.) The nature and quality of these domestic arrangements depended heavily on the nature of the marriage.

One woman from Brazil, who I call Centero, is married to a Ghanaian and has two children. She considered herself Brazilian, but also embraces her African roots. She recalled the warm welcome she received from her in-laws in the Volta Region.

> I was very well accepted in the family, I must say. We had a very nice reception when we went to his hometown with not only the family, but practically the whole tribe came to see us, first of all because my husband was away for six and a half years. And, of course, he had brought the wife from abroad.
> The reception was really, really nice, I was much impressed. I was very happy to be welcomed in such a fashion. Everything went alright for a while.

Most of the relatives who come to live with these families are children. In Centero's case, it was her nieces and nephews who came. In Ghanaian families girls are expected to help with the daily chores of child care, cooking and cleaning. According to Centero, her in-laws felt that they did not have to assume these duties since she was an *oburuni* (foreigner). This proved to be onerous for her since not only was she obliged to come home from her full-time job and take care of her children, but her house guests as well. In addition to these daily chores, Centero and her husband were expected to pay school fees and other expenses for these children. She was persistent in her struggle against these intrusions and with the help of her husband, the visits ended and financial support was diminished. Even though these were trying times for Centero she offered that in other instances her husband's family was also very supportive.

Other informants were also impressed with how much more supportive their in-laws were compared to their families back home. A woman from Jamaica commented on the fact that elderly people are "kept within the family." Other women commented on the help received from in-laws when repatriates gave birth to children.

Witness the following excerpt:

> Ocran: First of all, when I came to Ghana, I didn't have a mother-in-law to deal with because the father never remarried. And my husband had only one sister. So he's not from a large family.
> His sister is an educated person. She's a graduate of the Winneba Specialist Training College. And she works quite independently. In fact, she was the supporter of her father until the brother returned from Europe [where Ocran met her husband]. And I didn't have any family *palaver* [disagreement], not that I know about anyhow. In fact when I started having babies my sister-in-law was right there.
> And my mother came over when I had the second child and she said, "I have never seen a sister-in-law like this." Ordinarily, in Ghanaian society, the sister-in-law is the bane of your life. I mean she really makes your life miserable.

Clearly Diaspora African women have a range of experiences that preclude generalizations about the extended family; however, the majority of women's lives were also affected by their husband's extra-marital affairs and other wives. Ocran's husband was disappointed because his wife bore "only girls" and decided to take another wife in his village. Another informant's husband decided to have an affair with his cousin in the same household. This woman from Trinidad told a story to boggle the minds of the most staunch cultural relativists.

In addition to his cousin, Pouver's husband had children by other women who, all together, bore him nine children in addition to Pouver's own five. Her husband belongs to Ewe, a patrilineal group, so it was natural for the children to be reared in his household.

> So I've raised all of his children. I've raised every one of them! I'm not afraid of [the other women] coming back, but I just do think about it and it makes me nauseated at times where it seemed like I've swallowed something and don't want it. And then suddenly it comes. It's like a dog lapping up what he doesn't want.... [My husband] is by nature a polygamous person.

Diaspora women experience these trying events even after their husbands' die since in-laws come to claim husband's and wife's property. In some cases, in-laws have been successful and sent repatriates packing. Some Ghanaian men have anticipated these problems by spelling out inheritors in their wills. It is important to emphasize here that Diaspora women are not alone in their problems with other women and property rights.

There is a growing literature that speaks to similar problems among continental Africans (Cohen and Odhiambo 1992; Potash 1986). Repatriates are quick to point out these similarities, but hasten to add that African women are in a position to return to their families, usually within the same country whereas Diaspora women have no one to turn to and are forced to traverse the Atlantic once again. Even though their analysis of continental African women may be true in one sense, it is important to point out that although African women have their own families of orientation to turn to, they are often involved in litigation of burial and property rights when their husbands die.

In spite of these marital issues, many Diaspora women have lived in Ghana for twenty or more years. It remains a matter of further research to assess whether conditions have significantly changed in their favor. As for Diaspora Africans on the whole, there are problems of another kind.

"We" and "They"

Although there are many Ghanaians who accept Diaspora Africans, there are many problems of cultural integration. This aspect is important since it demystifies the concept of global Pan-Africanism and addresses cultural and nationalist differences between the two populations. These differences are clearly expressed by Ghanaians who use the term *oburuni* to refer to Diaspora Africans.

Oburuni, a Ga word, is a term that means "White person" or foreigner. Although originally used to refer to people of European descent it is now used to refer to African descended people as well. Although some Ghanaians use the term openly and suggest that it is not used derisively, Diaspora Africans consider it a pejorative term. As Droller points out, the emphasis in Ghanaian culture is culture, not color.

> There has been quite a movement from America and the Caribbean. Just as your people [informant's reference to African Americans] on that side have gotten distorted ideas of life in an African community, Africans have gotten a distorted idea of Black Americans. So when you come into this town, he [a Ghanaian] sees you as some kind of White man. He doesn't see you as a skin color, but rather as a culture color. And it takes him a while.

Ghanaians also use the term *oburuni* to refer to non-Ghanaian Africans or Ghanaians who are lighter-skinned. Sometimes the term is even used positively to refer to newborns who have light skin and curly hair as "cute little *oburuni* baby." But then even this usage speaks to a preference for European features over African ones. Equivalents of the word *oburuni* are also used in other African countries and are not specific to Diaspora African populations (Legum 1962:110). Nevertheless, this widespread usage does nothing to lessen the sting felt by Diaspora Africans. As voiced by an African American woman,

> I find that people still see me as an Afro-American. For instance, there was a woman I met here in the early seventies. She was from Costa Rica and I asked her, "Do you know that people still refer to me as being White?" I said, "look at my skin." And she said, "Oh, don't worry about that, I've been here for thirty-five years and I'm still considered "White." And she was browner than me. She was an old lady married to a Ghanaian. I said, "But maybe it's because I don't speak the language." She said, "I speak fluent Ga, it doesn't matter. They know you have a western culture so when they say 'White,' they mean that your culture is different. They're referring more to culture than color." Because, you know, I didn't like being called White. Here you think you're coming home and you're called White.

Even though unwelcoming labels are troublesome, they are not overwhelming enough to warrant another voyage across the Atlantic. Another informant who was painfully aware of Ghanaian's lack of receptivity to change also noted that this did not begin and end with Diaspora Africans.

> People come here thinking that Ghanaians should be glad they are here because after all they have something to teach them, you see. And that's not what they're [Ghanaians] looking for because there are other Ghanaians who have gone out and gotten so many degrees and they come back and they have been rejected. So what would make an outsider think that they will be accepted?

The level of acceptance experienced by individual repatriates depended on several factors, including personality, class, the level at which they were involved in social institutions, and how well informed they were about African culture and events before they came to Ghana. Even given these factors, it has been shown that in other diaspora communities in homelands there is a reluctance to accept returnees. American, European, Russian, or North African Jews in Israel is a case in point (Isaacs 1967; Deshen 1974:281–310).

Most repatriates felt that they were accepted socially, but not culturally. Despite these differences Diaspora Africans preferred this to the racism encountered in America and the Caribbean (Walters 1993:107). It could also be said that even though Ghanaians are very "tribalistic" there are Diaspora behaviors that preclude their cultural assimilation. One of the most important was language. Repatriates themselves stated that they did not feel part of the culture "because they didn't know the language." As already mentioned, although many informants have been in Ghana for over twenty years, only four or five of the people I spoke with had bothered to learn a Ghanaian language. Even though there are over forty-seven (Hall, E. 1983) Ghanaian languages, learning any of the major languages, such as Ga, Twi, or Ewe would be sufficient since most Ghanaians speak several languages. The reasons given for not learning a local language were weak.

People say you have to learn it, but I think it's limited so I don't bother. And I don't pick up languages easily. I pick up a few words here and there. The children pick up languages quite easily so they can speak Ga quite well.

Another informant from Jamaica stated that not knowing any other languages made her feel left out on many occasions. Although she offered that her husband was very understanding and spoke only English to her, she also averred that in the long run this may not have been the best thing because if

> he had insisted in speaking *the vernacular* [emphasis mine], maybe I would have learned it. So the adjustment was really about language. I didn't understand.

The reluctance of most Diaspora Africans to learn a Ghanaian language might stem, in part, from the fact that the vast majority of Ghanaians are fluent in English. Nevertheless, it is common to hear them using their native tongue. A member of the Hebrew Israelites offered another reason.

> [In America] they always taught us that we're not speaking anything other than English. And we were made to feel that way. Anybody getting on a bus [in the U.S.] speaking their native tongue, people would just tell you silently to "shut up" if you weren't speaking English. Even though you were taught another language in high school, we were not encouraged in society to use it. You were always taught that English was a superior language. And you can see that in the way it's been spread around the world as sort of a universal language.

Not only would knowledge of a Ghanaian language be useful in communicating in more situations, but this would also send a message to Ghanaians that repatriates are making a serious effort to be included at a deeper level into their cultures since language not only gives us the tools to speak, but determines what we are capable of thinking. Similarly Nielsen (1987:16) reminds us that

> We have our local attachments and they simultaneously fetter us and define us in ways that are inescapable. They are in part given in our very language and thought structures with their distinctive and culturally differentiated categories and ways of seeing the world.

Given that language is more than a means of communication, Diaspora Africans could forge stronger bonds with continental Africans by adopting an important symbol of affinity. Even with the problems of assimilating into Ghanaian culture, the vast majority of informants were steadfast in their matriculation into Ghanaian society and were hopeful about the prospects of Pan-Africanism.

Conclusion

This research does not exhaust the debate on the question of "one people," but underscores the complexity of cultural and political Pan-Africanism. While the majority of informants have maintained their national identities, they have also embraced the African aspects of these identities. For the majority of informants, "one people" may not signify that we are all the same, but it does underscore the ancestral, territorial, and cultural foundations for African solidarity. Even though the existence of African culture in the Diaspora has been gainsaid, it is also clear that much of African culture remains an integral part of Diaspora societies. This assertion is based on my own life experiences, testimonies from informants and an abundance of evidence in the literature (Moore 1970; Thompson, R.F. 1983; Holloway 1990). I should hasten to add that the necessity of *proving* one's culture is also part and parcel of a people who have been forcefully separated from their roots. Nevertheless, because culture is also very particular and is tied into day-to-day political relationships, Diaspora Africans, in many instances, find it difficult to melt into certain areas. Moreover, culture in Ghana (as in other African nations), has to do with *being* Ewe or Ashanti (among others) which constitutes a hindrance to full incorporation of Diaspora peoples into these societies.

Other internal factors that bode poorly for the development of holistic Pan-Africanism include internecine warfare (i.e., Liberia and Somalia) and nationalistic tendencies that preclude the creation of Africa as a major world power. As indicated by many informants internal conflicts are an indication of how Diaspora Africans, as long-distance relatives, will be received. At the national level, governmental leaders remain more concerned about their individual wealth than they are in the wealth of their country or their nation. These factors are directly related to the capability of foreign governments to maintain control over African economies.

African countries will remain Third World as long as their day-to-day survival depends on the largess of Europeans or European Americans. Development continues to be defined as an increase in African exports and a decrease in Africa's capacity to produce food and other raw materials for local consumption. These factors cannot be separated from the attitude by and toward Diaspora Africans since the degree to which they are accepted or encouraged to migrate depends on how this is viewed by foreign concerns.

In the face of these issues, it is important to emphasize that culture and identity are ever-changing dimensions that are influenced by material and psychological, internal and external factors. Many scholars (e.g, Walters 1993:333; Shepperson 1962:346–358) make sharp distinctions between the "back-to-Africa" brand of Pan-Africanism and political-economic versions. Walters (1993:333) suggests that Diaspora Africans can be most effective in building Pan-Africanism outside of Africa. Although the contributions made by Diaspora Africans organizations to Africa have been useful, I do not think that they are mutually exclusive to Diaspora African migration where they can participate in their own development while lending a hand in Africa. An African American informant speaks clearly to the benefits that would be received on either side.

> Andoh: We [African Americans] still don't have the confidence that it takes to put us where we could be. No matter how much we talk about it and how much Black history they teach, there are certain things that have to come through experiences, through really getting something done—really seeing Blacks [Andoh is referring to indigenous Africans here] doing things and really being proud. Black Americans are still not proud of themselves. They can talk about it as much as they like, but deep down in their subconscious, it isn't there. And it will never be there until they come down and assist here in Africa—to make Africa what it could be—and until Africa really opens its doors and realizes that they have a lot to learn from what the Black Americans have done in America. Because they basically built the U. S., but nobody has really realized that.

There were other Diaspora Africans who felt that there needed to be a reciprocal exchange between Diaspora and continental Africans. Most informants thought that they had a number of useful skills to share with their estranged kin and were eager to absorb aspects of Ghanaian culture. Their views suggest that these dimensions are permutations of a singular theme and that Pan-Africanism exists along a continuum where cultural and political dimensions overlap. Ideally, the development of Africa and Diaspora Africans will be part of the same process.

To a certain degree Pan-African development is taking place since most repatriates are professionals who have been working in Ghana—in some cases, for more than twenty years. While there may be problems of cultural integration, there are many Ghanaians (usually better educated intellectuals) who are eager for Diaspora Africans to "come home." Even though there are African beliefs and practices that deter this process, there are others that are in keeping with those in the Diaspora. Ironically, the intrusion of European culture in Africa and among Africans in the Diaspora has served as common link among African and Diaspora societies.

Due to the ubiquitous presence of Christian churches in Ghana,[12] Diaspora Africans are right at home and attend the same Christian churches as other Africans. Style of dress is another arena where people meet since European styles are in the majority. One of the most important commonalities is the English language, another vestige of colonialism that serves as a common denominator. These factors are counterpoised against those practices and beliefs that are foreign to Diaspora repatriates.

The fact of common African and European practices serves as foundation for friendships and marital relations which bridge the gap created centuries ago by colonial invasion. Further, repatriate's statements regarding the development of their African identities is indicative of what Michael Fischer (1986:230) refers to as "a family of resemblances." Some informants explicitly stated that they were African in features and heritage and to some degree in experience. These resemblances engendered a sense of pride and self esteem which is evident from the following excerpts.

> Droller: ... Meeting Africans, genuine Black Africans, when you talked with them, you felt more respect for yourself. You saw that, left alone, you could do these things that other people could do.
> Momree: ... (Becoming a member of the Nation [Black Hebrews] gave me an awareness of what my purpose should be. Before then, I was, you know, kind of mixed up, to the point where I didn't have anything to steer me in the right direction... in regard to (Black) people. It gave me an awareness of who I was and just about Black people in general... We're the Chosen People of God.
> Conway: ... I've always thought of myself as just being a Black female—a woman. But I'd say over the years I see where I really am African to a great extent. Since being here, I've seen all of my family, all of your family, and all my friends and everyone I've ever known—the whole range of shades and features. And they're all African... (Being in Africa has) made me feel more open in terms of knowing who I am.
> Abuaka: ... I was three years with the (Black) nationalist group in Newark. What struck me more was the consciousness that I am an African person. To

---

12. Over 40% of Ghanaians are Christians.

me, I see that Black people have a common history and a common experience, and I think it's very valuable to recognize it. I like roots in general. If you're Jewish, you should know what that is. If Irish, you should know something about it — celebrate it. If I were a Jew, I'd be an orthodox Jew. I'd want to know the deep, deep stuff.

The "deep, deep stuff" for most repatriates was feeling "spiritually and psychologically free," "being free of racism," and "feeling at home." These experiences not only provide opportunities for face-to-face encounters between Diaspora and continental Africans in Ghana, but for relatives of informants as well. Informants who travel back to their places of birth for visits and relatives who visit Ghana unwittingly serve as ambassadors of Pan-Africanism and create stronger ties between these societies. Moreover, children of Diaspora/African unions embody the values and experiences of Africa and the Diaspora and increase the possibilities of greater understanding.

Informants' testimonies are at variance to scholarly rhetoric (Fanon 1968:216; Legum 1962:108–110) that characterizes Diaspora/African relations as antithetical. The presence of Diaspora Africans in Ghana and the broad spectrum of Pan-African ideas that they offer calls into question the separation of political and cultural Pan-Africanism since existential participation and the development of ideology must precede political-economic action. This study of Diaspora Africans in Ghana is just the beginning of an area of research that focuses on what Geertz (1973:308–309) calls the "comparative sociology (or social psychology...)" of identity formation. Repatriates offer a unique perspective of holistic Pan-Africanism since they witness, first hand, not only the political aspects of African life, but the psychological and social dimensions of what it means to be African and of the Diaspora.

References

Abrahams, Roger and John Szwed (1983). *After Africa*. New Haven: Yale University Press.

Anderson, Benedict (1987). *Imagined Communities: Reflections on the Origin and Spread of Nationalisms*. London: Verso.

Angelou, Maya (1987). *All God's Children Need Traveling Shoes*. New York: Vintage Books.

Asante, Molefi and Kariamu Asante (1985). *African Culture. The Rhythms of Unity*. Westport, CT: Greenwood Press.

Baber, Ross Ceola (1987). "The Artistry and Artifice of Black Communication." In *Expressively Black: The Cultural Basis for Ethnic Identity*. Ed. Geneva Gay and Willie Baber. New York: Praeger.

Basch, Linda, Nina Glick Schiller and Christina Szanton Blanc (1994). *Nations Unbound. Transnational Projects, Postcolonial Predicaments, and Deterritorialized Nation-States*. Switzerland: Gordon and Breach.

Bluecloud, Peter (1972). *Alcatraz Is Not an Island*. Berkeley: Wingbow Press.

Blyden, Edward (1967). *Christianity, Islam and the Negro Race*. Edinburgh: University of Edinburgh Press. (Originally published in London in 1887).

Brietman, George (1970). *By Any Means Necessary. Speeches, Interviews and a Letter by Malcolm X*. New York: Pathfinder Press.

Bretton, Henry L. (1966). *The Rise and Fall of Kwame Nkrumah. A Study of Personal Rule in Africa*. New York: Frederich A. Praeger.

Campbell, Horace (1990). *Rasta and Resistance. From Marcus Garvey to Walter Rodney.* Trenton, NJ: Africa World Press, Inc.

Carmichael, Stokely (1969). "Pan-Africanism, Land and Power." *Black Scholar.* November, 1(1):36–43.

Cohen, Ronald (1978). "Ethnicity: Problem and Focus in Anthropology." *Annual Review of Anthropology.* 7:379–403.

Cohen, David and E. S. Atieno Odhiambo (1992). *Burying SM.* Portsmouth, NH: Heinemann.

Deshen, Shlomo (1974). "Political Ethnicity and Cultural Ethnicity." In *Urban Ethnicity.* Ed. Abner Cohen, pp. 281–310. England: Tavistock Publications.

DeVos, George (1975). "Ethnic Pluralism: Conflict and Accommodation." In *Ethnic Identity: Cultural Continuities and Change.* Ed., Lola Romanucci-Ross. Palo-Alto: Mayfield Publishing.

Drake, St. Clair (1982). "Diaspora Studies and Pan-Africanism." In *Global Dimensions of the African Diaspora.* Ed. Joseph Harris. Washington, DC: Howard University Press.

Dunbar, Ernest (1968). *Black Expatriates.* New York: Dutton.

Edmondson, Locksley (1979). "Black Roots and Identity: Comparative and International Perspectives." *International Journal.* Summer, 34(3):408–429.

——— (1968). "The Internationalization of Black Power: Historical and Contemporary Perspectives. *Mawazo.* 1(4):16–30.

Esedebe, P. Olisanwuche (1982). *Pan-Africanism. The Idea and the Movement.* Washington, DC: Howard University Press.

Essien-Udom, E.U. (1964). *Black Nationalism: The Idea and the Movement.* New York: Dell Publication Company.

Fanon, Frantz (1968). *The Wretched of the Earth.* New York: Grove Press, Inc.

Ferkiss, Victor C. (1966). *Africa's Search for Identity.* New York: George Braziller.

Fischer, Michael M. (1986). "Ethnicity and the Post-Modern Arts of Memory." In *Writing Culture.* Eds. James Clifford and George Marcus, pp. 194–233. Berkeley, CA: University of California Press.

Frazer, J.G. (1911). "Taboo and the Perils of the Soul." In *The Golden Bough: A Study in Magic and Religion,* pp. 318–386. London: MacMillan and Company.

Fyfe, Christopher. (1962). *History of Sierra Leone.* London, England: Collier Books.

Geertz, Clifford. (1973). "The Integrative Revolution: Primordial Sentiments and Civil Policies in the New States." In *The Interpretation of Culture.* New York: Basic Books, Inc.

Gellner, Ernest (1987). *Culture, Identity, and Politics.* Cambridge: Cambridge University Press.

Gerber, Israel (1977). *The Heritage Seekers. Black Jews in Search of Identity.* Middle Village, NY: Jonathan David Publishers.

Glick, Edward Bernard (1982). *The Triangular Connection: America, Israel, and American Jews.* Boston: George Aleen and Unwin.

Golden, Marita (1987). *Migrations of the Heart.* New York: Ballantine Books.

Hall, Edward (1983). *Ghanaian Languages.* Accra, Ghana: Asempa Publishers.

Hall, Stuart (1993). "Culture, Community, Nation." *Cultural Studies.* October, 7(3):349–363.

Herskovitz, Melville (1958). *The Myth of the Negro Past.* Boston: Beacon Press.

Hertzberg, Hazel W. (1971). *The Search for an American Indian Identity: Modern Pan-Indian Movements.* Syracuse: Syracuse University Press.

Holloway, Joseph E. (1990). *Africanisms in American Culture.* Bloomington: Indiana University Press.

Horowitz, Donald (1975). "Ethnic Identity." In *Ethnicity. Theory and Experience.* Eds. Nathan Glazer and Donald Moynihan, pp. 111–140. Cambridge: Harvard University Press.

Howell, Thomas A. and Jeffrey P. Rajasooria (1972). *Ghana and Nkrumah.* New York: Fact on File, Inc.

Ichioka, Yuji (1971). "A Buried Past: Early Issei Socialists and the Japanese Community." *Amerasia Journal.* 1(2):1–25.

Isaacs, Harold (1967). *American Jews in Israel*. New York: The John Day Company.

Jacobs, Sylvia (1982). *Black Americans and the Missionary Movement in Africa*. Westport, CT: Greenwood Press.

Jenkins, David (1975). *Black Zion. The Return of Afro-Americans and West Indians to Africa*. London: Wildwood House, Ltd.

Kayode, Bernette (1979). "African/Afro-American Marriages." *Essence*. July, 81: 106–110.

Keyes, Charles (1981). *Ethnic Change*. Seattle, WA: University of Washington Press.

Kihss, Peter (1958). "Harlem Hails Ghanaian Leader as Returning Hero." *The New York Times*. July 28, pp. 1, 4.

Kup, A.P. (1975). *Sierra Leone. A Concise History*. London: David and Charles.

Lacy, Leslie Alexander (1970). *The Rise and Fall of the Proper Negro*. New York: Macmillan.

LaFrance, Marrianne and Clara Mayo (1978). "Gaze Direction in Interracial Dyadic Communication." *Ethnicity*. 5(2):167–173.

Lake, Obiagele (1997). "Diaspora African Repatriation—The Place of Diaspora Women within the Pan-African Nexus." In *Cultural Encounters: Gender at the Intersection of the Local and the Global in Africa*. Eds. Maria Grosz Negate and Omari Kokole. New York: Routledge.

Lake, Obiagele (1995). "Toward a Pan-African identity: Diaspora African Repatriates in Ghana." *Anthropological Quarterly*. 68(1):21–36.

Lee, Changsoo and George DeVos (1984). "Koreans in Japan: Ethnic Conflict and Accommodation." *Man*. March, 19:173.

Legum, Colin (1962). *Pan-Africanism. A Short Political Guide*. London: Pall Mall Press.

Lewis, Rupert (1988). *Garvey, Anti-Colonial Champion*. Trenton, NJ: African World Press, Inc.

Liebenow, J. Gus (1973). *Liberia. The Evolution of Privilege*. Ithaca: Cornell University Press.

Martin, Tony (1983). *The Pan-African Connection: From Slavery to Garvey and Beyond*. Dover, MA: The Majority Press.

Moerman, Michael (1988). *Talking Culture. Ethnography and Conversation Analysis*. Philadelphia: University of Philadelphia Press.

Moore, Richard B. (1970). "African Conscious Harlem." In *Old Memories, New Moods. Americans from Africa*. Ed. Peter Rose. New York: Atherton Press.

Nagata, Judith (1981). "In Defense of Ethnic Boundaries: The Changing Myths and Charters of Malay Identity." In *Ethnic Change*. Ed. Charles Keyes. Seattle: University of Washington Press.

—— (1976). "The Status of Ethnicity and the Ethnicity of Status. Ethnic and Class Identity in Malaysia and Latin America." *International Journal of Comparative Sociology*. September–December, 17(3–4):242–260.

—— (1975). "Perceptions of Social Inequality in Malaysia." In *Pluralism in Malaysia: Myth and Reality*. Ed. J. Nagata, pp. 113–36. Leiden: E. J. Brill.

Neusner, Jacob (1989). *Who, Where, and What is "Israel"?: Zionist Perspectives on Israeli and American Judaism*. Lanham: University Press of America.

New York Times (1958). "Nkrumah Praises Ghana's Ties Here." July 29, p. 10.

Nielsen, Kai (1987). "Undistorted Discourse, Ethnicity, and the Problem of Self Definition." In *Ethnicity and Language*. Ed. Winston A.Van Horne. Madison, WI: The University of Wisconsin System, Institute of Race and Ethnicity.

Nkrumah, Kwame (1963). *Africa Must Unite*. New York: International Press.

—— (1957). *Ghana: The Autobiography of Kwame Nkrumah*. New York: Thomas Nelson and Sons.

Obeyesekere, Gananath (1975). "Sinhalese-Buddhist Identity in Ceylon." In *Ethnic Identity: Cultural Continuities and Change*. Ed. George DeVos and Lola Romanucci-Ross, pp. 231–58. Palo Alto, CA: Mayfield Publishing.

Pinkney, Alphonso (1984). *The Myth of Black Progress*. London: Cambridge University Press.

Potash, Betty, ed. (1986). *Women in African Societies: Choices and Constraints*. Stanford, CA: Stanford University Press.

Ray, Donald Iain (1986). *Ghana: Politics, Economics, and Society*. London, England: F. Pinter Publishers.

Redkey, Edwin S. (1969). *Black Exodus. Black Nationalist and Back to Africa Movements, 1890–1910*. New Haven, CT: Yale University Press.

Rushdie, Salman (1991). *Imaginary Homelands. Essays and Criticism 1981–1991*. London: Granta Books.

Safran, William (1991). "Diasporas in Modern Societies: Myth of Homeland and Return." *Diaspora*. Spring, 1(1):83–99.

Sarris, Alexander (1991). *Ghana Under Structural Adjustment: The Impact on Agriculture and the Rural Poor*. New York: New York University Press.

Sawyer, Akilagpa (1990). *The Political Dimension of Structural Adjustment Programmes in Sub-Saharan Africa*. Accra: Ghana Universities Press.

Schomburg, Arthur (1925). "The Negro Digs up His Past." In *The New Negro*. New York: Atheneum.

Scott, David (1991). "That Event, This Memory: Notes on the Anthropology of African Diasporas in the New World." *Diasporas*. 1(3):261–284.

Shepperson, George (1962). "Pan Africanism or 'Pan-Africanism.'" *Phylon*. 23(4):346–358.

Shick, Tom (1980). *Behold The Promised Land. A History of Afro-American Settler Society in Nineteenth Century Liberia*. Baltimore, MD: Johns Hopkins University Press.

Shils, Edward (1957). "Primordial, Personal, Sacred and Civil Ties." *British Journal of Sociology*. June, 1:130–141.

Shiner, Cindy (1991). "The Changing Face of Africa." *Africa News*. December 23, 1991–January 6, 1992:15.

Smith, William (1970). *Return to Black America*. Englewood Cliffs, NJ: Prentice-Hall.

Sorenson, John (1992). "Essence and Contingency in the Construction of Nationhood: Transformation of Identity in Ethiopia and its Diasporas." *Diaspora*. 2(2):201–228.

Staudenraus, P.J. (1961). *The African Colonization Movement, 1816–1865*. New York: Columbia University Press.

Stuckey, Sterling (1987). *Slave Culture: Nationalist Theory and the Foundation of Black America*. New York: Oxford University Press.

Thomas, Robert K. (1972). "Pan-Indianism." In *The Emergent Native Americans*. Ed. Deward E. Walker, Jr., pp. 739–46. Boston, MA: Little, Brown.

Thompson, Era Bell (1969). "Are Black Americans Welcome in Africa?" *Ebony*. January, 24(3): 44–50.

Thompson, Robert F. (1983). *Flash of the Spirit: African and Afro-American Art and Philosophy*. New York: Random House.

Toure, Kwame. (n.d.) "The Relevance of the People's Revolutionary Party to Africans World-Wide." Mimeograph No. 3. All African People's Revolutionary Party.

Trosper, Ronald (1981). "American Indian Nationalism and Frontier Expansion." In *Ethnic Change*. Ed. Charles Keyes. Seattle: University of Washington Press.

Trottier, Richard (1981). "Charters of Panethnic Identity: Indigenous American Indians and Immigrant Asian-Americans." In *Ethnic Change*. Ed. Charles Keyes. Seattle: University of Washington Press.

Turner, Jerry M. (1975). "Les Brasiliens—The Impact of Former Brazilian Slaves upon Dahomey." Ph.D. Dissertation, Boston University.

Turner, Lorenzo (1942). "Some Contacts of Brazilian Ex-Slaves with Nigeria, West Africa." *Journal of Negro History*, January, 27(1):55–67.

Ungar, Sanford (1978). *Africa. The People and Politics of an Emerging Continent*. New York: Simon and Schuster.

Uya, Okon (1971). *Black Brotherhood. Afro-Americans and Africa*. Lexington, MA: D.C. Heath.

Van den Berghe, Paul L. (1978). "Race and Ethnicity. A Sociobiological Perspective." *Ethnic and Racial Studies*. 1:401–11.

——— (1976). "Ethnic Pluralism in Industrial Societies." *Ethnicity*. 3:242–255.

Walker, Sheila (1993). "A Summit Fueled by a Common Past: A Reunion of African Americans." *African World*. November–December, 1(1): 12–15.

Walker, W. St. G. James (1976). *The Black Loyalists*. New York: Africana Publishing Company.

Walters, Ronald W. (1993). *Pan Africanism in the African Diaspora. An Analysis of Modern Afrocentric Political Movements*. Detroit: Wayne State University Press.

Washington, Elsie B. (1989). "The Front Line—Ten Proud Years of Freedom." *Essence*. October, 20(6):97–110.

Weisbord, Robert (1973). *Ebony Kinship*. Westport, CT: Greenwood Press.

Weisbord, Robert and Richard Kazarian, Jr. (1985). "Black Hebrew Israelites and Other Non-Whites." In *Israel in the Black American Perspective*, pp. 61–92. Westport, CT: Greenwood Press.

Whitten, Norman and John Szwed (1970). *Afro-American Anthropology. Contemporary Perspectives*. New York: Free Press.

Williams, Walter (1982). "William Henry Sheppard, Afro-American Missionary in the Congo, 1890–1910." In *Black Americans and the Missionary Movement in Africa*. Ed. Sylvia Jacobs. Westport, CT: Greenwood Press.

39

Afrocentrism and a New World Order

V. Oguejiofor Okafor

This paper attempts to articulate the Present Moment—that is, the contemporary state of the African-American community in the United States. As some, if not most people, are aware of, a disproportionate number of the present generation of African-American families are headed by Black women. In fact, about sixty percent of the households in the African-American community are headed by women.[1] Those of them with children represent thirty point seven percent of the national total at a time the overall population of African Americans constitutes roughly twelve percent of the U.S. national population.[2] While African Americans constitute over thirty-one percent of the poor in the United States (the figure for Whites is eight-point-eight percent), more than forty-eight percent of African-American female-headed households are classified as poor (the figure for white female-headed households is twenty-six point eight percent).[3]

These figures paint the picture of an unduly harsh burden on the shoulders of African-American women; they also indicate that Black men no longer participate significantly—that is, in sufficient numbers—in the upbringing of children. In the absence of appropriate male support, single mothers are left to bear alone the difficult burden of nurturing their sons and daughters. Worse still, the environment in which most of these sons and daughters are raised, more likely than not, hardly qualifies as a bed of roses of role models. Several scholarly works have been done on this issue, including Haki R. Madhubuti's nerve-wrecking book entitled, *Black Men: Obsolete, Single and Dangerous?* One of the sad realities of the present moment is that the socialization of African young ones is, for the most part, no longer a balanced process—that is, a process that ought to be enriched with the inputs of the male and female leaders of the family.[4]

An earlier version of this essay appeared in *Western Journal of Black Studies* 18, 4 (1994): 185–194 and is adapted/reprinted with the permission of the copyright holder/author.

1. Haki R. Madhubuti, *Black Men: Obsolete, Single, Dangerous?* Chicago: Africa WP, 1990: 72.
2. *U.S. Bureau of the Census, Statistical Abstract of the United States: 1992* (112th edition.). Washington, D.C., 1992: 39.
3. James Jenning, *Understanding the Nature of Poverty in Urban America*. Westport: Praeger, 1994:58, 61.
4. Haki R. Madhubuti, *Black Men: Obsolete, Single, Dangerous?* Chicago: Africa WP, 1990: 72–73.

Although this state of affairs is attributable to a host of factors from within and without, including structural changes in the economy[5] and high levels of incarceration of black males, Madhubuti, in his work, points the most serious accusing finger at the system of white supremacism as a debilitating influence on Black families and Black manhood. Among other things, he states, the system not only seeks to incapacitate Black men economically, it systematically rewards black men and women who assist in the oppression of the Black community. In like manner, the system targets, labels and harasses black men and women who dare to speak out on behalf of the community. Prime examples include Martin Luther King, Jr. and Malcolm X.[6] There are, of course, lesser examples.

Notice also the glaring disproportionality in the number of young African Americans who are in prison, in jail, on probation or parole. Between 1989 and 1995, the proportion of African Americans between the ages of 20 and 29 under the criminal justice system rose from twenty-three to thirty-two point two percent.[7] Although thirteen percent of drug users in America are African American, seventy-four percent of those who received prison sentences for drug possession are black.[8] While the nation's efforts to control drug usage and possession have been hailed—and rightly so—as necessary means of discouraging drug addiction and its multifarious harmful effects on the social well-being of society, critics have, however, pointed to what appears to be a case of unequal justice in the whole affair. For instance, there is a mandatory prison term of five years for possession of five grams of crack cocaine; whereas, in the case of powder cocaine, the threshold for the same punishment is five hundred grams.[9] Because African Americans constitute eighty-eight percent of those charged with possession of crack cocaine,[10] critics point to the differential punishment as tantamount to racial injustice.

Lamentations of the preceding picture run through almost the entire spectrum of contemporary African-American sociopolitical thought. The scholars may differ in their choice of words, but their message remains basically the same. Somewhat differently from Madhubuti's analysis, another scholar, one who is nationally known, Cornel West, frames the African situation this way.

New World African modernity consists of degraded and exploited Africans in American circumstances using European languages and instruments to make sense of tragic predicaments—predicaments disproportionately shaped by white supremacist bombardments on black beauty, intelligence, moral character and creativity.[11]

---

5. William Julius Wilson offers a penetrating discussion of such structural changes in the economy, along with factors he describes as social dislocations in his 1987 work, *The Truly Disadvantaged: The Inner City, the Underclass, and Public Policy*, published by the University of Chicago P.

6. Madhubuti, 73.

7. "A Shocking Look at Blacks and Crime," *U.S. News & World Report*, Oct. 16, 1995: 53.

8. *U.S. News & World Report*, 54.

9. *U.S. News & World Report*, 54.

10. *U.S. News & World Report*, 54.

11. Cornel West, *Keeping Faith: Philosophy and Race in America*. New York: Routledge, 1993: xii.

In the face of these tragic predicaments, the following question becomes logical: is there not an urgent need for the community, like any other self-conscious group, to strengthen itself by conscientiously enhancing its *structural capacity*, including forging a sense of cohesion—a collective consciousness—necessary for an effective and creative response to the challenges of the day? The survival of a group of people, as well as its potential for self-fulfillment, has a great deal to do with that group's capacity to define, develop and defend its interests.

It has been suggested that, generally-speaking, African people do not believe in themselves and do not know who they are. As Molefi Kete Asante puts it, "many people of African descent are dislocated, and alienated from their own history, suffer amnesia, and believe in white supremacy.[12] Na'im Akbar, a noted psychologist, writes about sociopsychological forces that threaten Black life and development. He describes one of these as anti-self disorder, which manifests itself in "overt and covert hostility towards the groups of one's origin and thus one's self."[13] No doubt, this is not a pleasant state of human affairs, but it must be remembered that it is a product of history. During the time of enslavement, for instance, Africans were negatively reinforced for trying to be themselves. Overtime, Africans in this part of the world in particular, developed an ambivalence about their Africanness. Vincent Bakpetu Thompson, a well-known and authoritative scholar of African Diasporic History, had the following to say about this phenomenon.

> The process of conditioning Africans to accept slave status began even as they were leaving the shores of Africa; it was intensified in the form of psychological warfare on the far side of the Atlantic in the Americas, with adverse consequences for the [enslaved] themselves.[14]

He continues by observing as follows:

> It is not difficult to imagine the havoc wrought on the enslaved Africans' psychology in this long period of acculturation to the New World environment. It is, therefore, easy to understand the many and conflicting tendencies exhibited by Africans and their descendants in the diaspora resulting from centuries of sustained conditioning, propaganda, badgering and brutalization.[15]

Even though times have changed measurably, contemporary society is still saddled with vestiges of the past, among which is the fact that, at this time, some of the actions that spew forth from the system tend to generate an impression that the system's psychological orientation and philosophical underpinning remain anti-African. Up until the present time, individuals are punished for their Blackness—not through overt lynching as was the case in the nineteenth and early twentieth centuries,[16] but

---

12. Molefi Kete Asante, *Open Letter to Dr. Henry Louis Gates, Jr.*, July 25, 1992.

13. Na'im Akbar, quoted in Maulana Karenga, *Introduction To Black Studies*. 1982. Los Angeles: University of SP, 1993: 444.

14. Vincent Bakpetu Thompson, *The Making of the African Diaspora In the Americas 1441–1900*. New York: Longman, 1987: 119.

15. Thompson, 153.

16. Readers are referred to Ralph Ginzburg's *100 Years of Lynchings* for insights into the magnitude and odium of racial prejudice and the attendant violence. I imagine that readers would be intrigued by a December 30, 1900 report, in this hair-raising and chilling book, which quoted one Professor Albert Bushnell Hart of Harvard College as suggesting, before a convention of the American Historical Convention, that "if the people of certain States are

through stealthy, *"high-tech lynching."*[17] In a 1992 best seller entitled *Two Nations: Black and White, Separate, Hostile, Unequal,* Andrew Hacker spoke to this fact of contemporary life. He reports:

> Many black men and women are concluding that they can best be described as African-Americans, considering how much their character and culture owe to their continent of origin. A pride in this heritage and history has helped them survive slavery and subsequent discrimination...However, most white Americans interpret the African emphasis in another way. For them, it frequently leads to a more insidious application of racism.[18]

Hacker concludes with a climactic confession of sorts:

> There persists the belief that members of the black race represent an inferior strain of the human species. In this view, Africans—and Americans who trace their origins to that continent—are seen as languishing at a lower evolutionary level than members of other races.[19]

Needless to say, the right to define oneself is a fundamental human right. Thus, a people cannot allow others to tell them who they are or who they should be. Alienation from self ought to be viewed not as a strength but a weakness—a major weakness. How could this be solved? African students (diasporic and continental) need to be educated to understand and appreciate their cultural roots and to identify with, and thus, show respect for not only themselves, but also their communities. "Migrating Back to Africa" in a symbolic, philosophical sense has historically been espoused as a remedy to the anti-self orientation which this paper mentioned earlier.

Historically, the "Back to Africa" concept has been espoused from two broad angles: one is literal; the other is symbolic. This paper examines those contexts as well as other implications of a trend which, in some quarters, has been characterized as "Migrating Back to Africa." The first context—that is, the literal—is what this writer calls the Marcus Garvey Movement. The second, symbolic context is labelled as the Malcolm X Movement.

In the early part of this century, Marcus Garvey had championed a movement for the creation of a United African Nation free from what he described as "the hands of alien exploiters."[20] Such a nation, he believed, would be "strong enough to lend protection to [Africans] scattered all over the world and to compel the respect of the nations and races of the earth."[21] Garvey wanted "talented" diasporic Africans to return to the continent in order to help build a strong African society.

---

determined to burn colored men at the stake, those States would better legalize the practice." Ralph Ginzburg. *100 Years of Lynchings.* Baltimore: Black CP, 1962: 36.

17. The reader's attention is drawn to an illuminating article on forms of "high-tech" lynching: Esmeralda Barnes. "Watched: Scholars Urge Blacks To Counter the Federal Government's Surreptitious Scrutiny of Black Leaders." *Black Issues In Higher Education.* April 22, 1993: 14–17. A major work on this subject is Kennedy O'Reilly, *Racial Matters: The FBI's Secret File On Black America, 1960–1972.* New York: Free Press, 1989.

18. Andrew Hacker, *Two Nations: Black and White, Separate, Hostile, Unequal.* New York: Ballantine, 1992: 23.

19. Hacker, 23.

20. Tony Martin, *Race First: the Ideological and Organizational Struggles of Marcus Garvey and the Universal Negro Improvement Association.* Dover: The Majority P, 1976: 41.

21. Martin, 41.

However, Garvey was not the first notable diasporian to call for the return of the Africans. It will be recalled that long before him, between 1817 and 1857, the American Colonization Society resettled 13,000 African Americans in Liberia[22] although for different motives. In his time, Garvey advocated this cause with such vehemence that the theme of migrating back to Africa almost went down in history as a synonym for his name.[23]

Garvey lived in the United States during one of the ugliest chapters of American history—an ugliness whose odium was surpassed only by the Great Enslavement. It was a time of legally sanctioned racial segregation in America—otherwise known as Jim Crow. The only difference between Jim Crow and the Great Enslavement was that enslavement meant compulsory and unrequited labor. Jim Crow, just like the era of enslavement, retained the institutions and legal instruments of racism—the pillar of the ideology and practice of white supremacism. Also characteristic of Jim Crow were the Anti-African, academic doctrines promulgated and propagated by the masters of objectivity. Those doctrines include Biological Determinism, Social Darwinism, and Kindly Paternalism. Prominent names in academia (some of whom were located in so-called prestigious schools), churned out Anti-African ideas which helped to give the stamp of academic objectivism to the blatant racial oppression of the period. These dogmas were ingrained into the consciousness of private and official America through the help of the masters of objectivity. Thus, Anti-African ideas, over time, became a part of the bedrock of the system's definitional framework.

For Malcolm X, "Back to Africa" had a different meaning from Garvey's—a symbolic meaning. For him, it did not mean the physical return of U.S. Africans to Africa. Malcolm's vision was that Africans in the United States should return to Africa culturally, philosophically and psychologically.[24] A reinvigorated spiritual bond with continental Africa, he argued, would strengthen the position of Africans in America. In essence, Malcolm advocated Afrocentric consciousness for African Americans. He believed that Afrocentric consciousness would strengthen the position of U.S. Africans—in the form of a sense of cohesion that a group would need to navigate effectively through America's pluralist democracy. Afrocentric education would give African Americans the cultural and historical "centeredness" which had been severely impaired by the systemic brain-washing that has, more or less, been the lot of the African. The educational and mass communication order appears, for the most part, to be characterized by a psychological orientation and philosophical underpinning which inevitably yields anti-African consciousness. Carter G. Woodson, in his classic work, *The Miseducation of the Negro*, articulated a sobering viewpoint. Lamenting the consequences of miseducation, he declared that many an African lacks "both a clear understanding of [the] present state and sufficient foresight to prepare for the future."[25] That's a profound thought which calls for sober reflection on our part.

---

22. Olisanwuche P. Esedebe, *Pan-Africanism: the Ideas and Movement, 1776–1963*. Washington, D.C.: Howard UP, 1982: 10.

23. Martin, 136–137.

24. George Breitman, *The Last Year of Malcolm X: the Evolution of a Revolutionary*. New York: Pathfinder, 1967: 63.

25. Carter G. Woodson, *The Miseducation of the Negro*. 1933. New York: AMS P, 1977: 96.

This writer concurs with Malcolm X's perspective on the question of symboli-
cally migrating back to Africa, but it must be pointed out that a spiritual bond has
always existed between Diasporic and Continental Africans. This bond was not
broken by the Great Enslavement. Indeed, it lives on and can only be strengthened.
Ironically, the anguish, the injustices, the institutional and subtle racism which
have been inflicted upon Africans in the Diaspora have had the effect of keeping
Africa alive in the memories of succeeding generations. This view is amply supported by Dona Marimba Richards, a leading African Americanist, in her articulation of the markings and vitalism of African spirituality in the Americas as a
whole. She, like several other scholars who have written on this subject, observes
that besides the skin pigment, African spirituality remains one of the enduring
threads that bind the African Diaspora with the Continentals. In fact, the African
world-view, she writes, is distinguished by unity, harmony, spirituality, and organic
interrelationship.[26] Richards observes that African spirituality accounts for the resilience of the Diasporic African and was the major factor that enabled enslaved
Africans to survive the brutality of their bondage.[27] Richards explains:

> Faced with the realities of slave existence we had to find ways of expressing, en-
> ergizing and revitalizing the spiritual being we had salvaged from the wreckage
> of the holocaust...Out of the chaos and trauma of slavery, the spirit of Africa
> was reborn in the form of the African American ethos.[28]

Ethos refers to the emotional flavor of a cultural group; Richards characterizes
the African-Diasporic ethos as "our unique spirit and spiritual being. It is a result
of our shared cultural history and is derived from Africa."[29] This ethos is reflected
in the African-American music, language, dance, thought patterns, laughter, and
walk.[30] Expounding on this theme, Richards adds:

> They took from us everything they could, but there was something left inside
> that slavery couldn't touch. That something was the fragmented pieces of a
> shattered world-view, so different from that of the Europeans, that in time it re-
> pudiated the materialism that they [had] assumed. The African world-view
> stresses the strength of the human spirit. It places paramount value on human
> vitality as the ground of spiritual immortality.[31]

An expression of this vitality takes the form of a phenomenon which has been described as the African-Diasporic Soul-Force. Leonard Barrett describes it:

> Soul-Force is that power of the Black man that turns sorrow into joy, crying
> into laughter, defeat into victory. It is patience while suffering, determination
> while frustrated and hope while in despair. It derives its impetus from the an-
> cestral heritage of Africa, its refinement from the bondage of slavery, and its
> continuing vitality from the conflict of the present.[32]

---

26. Marimba Dona Richards, *Let the Circle Be Unbroken: the Implications of African
Spirituality in the Diaspora.* New York: Djifa, 1980: 51–53.
27. Richards, 51–53.
28. Richards, 23–24.
29. Richards, 3.
30. Richards, 14.
31. Richards, 14.
32. Leonard Barrett, quoted in Marimba Dona Richards, *Let the Circle Be Unbroken:
the Implications of African Spirituality in the Diaspora.* New York: Djifa, 1980: 34.

But there are concrete forms of African retentions in the Diaspora. These include the African-Brazilian musical tradition known as the Candomble, the Caribbean Calypso, the use of proverbs as pedagogical tools in the Caribbean, and such religious systems as the Haitian Vodun. The continued practice of African historical medicine in the Caribbean represents another manifestation, among others, of African imprints on the diasporic landscape.[33]

Besides Malcolm X, Martin Luther King, Jr. and W.E.B. Du Bois, as well as others, had, in various ways, also wrestled with the issue of how to strengthen the African capacity for full-fledged citizenship. In discussing this subject, these heroic activists pointed to an undeniable reality of America: Africans have made mighty contributions to the economic, technological and sociopolitical development of this country, including two hundred and fifty years of unrequited labor. In addition, they have fought side by side with other Americans in the battles that this country has fought to preserve and advance itself. In *The Souls of Black Folk*, Du Bois called for an America which would respect the pluralistic character of its cultural landscape—an America which would not place overt and covert obstacles to the full-fledged citizenship of Africans in America. As part of what could be described as a philosophy of live and let live, Du Bois stated:

> the [African American] simply wishes to make it possible for a man to be both [an African] and an American without being cursed and spat upon by his fellows, without having the doors of Opportunity closed roughly in his face.[34]

Reflecting similar concerns in *The Miseducation of the Negro*, Woodson pinpointed the significance of educating African children in a manner that would infuse them with correct historical and cultural consciousness. He criticized the educational order for being exclusive of the historical and cultural experiences of a major segment of the American population. He also criticized the Black Church for being mired in Eurocentric theology and for being more imitative than creative.[35] Woodson emphatically stated that the education of Africans in the United States must include African and African-American history, African literature, African religion and the African philosophy of human existence. Even though Woodson had obtained his doctoral education from none other than Harvard University, he came to a realization, later in his life, that centered education was indispensable to the attainment of intellectual maturity—was vital to cultivating the capacity for critical reasoning.[36]

Eighteenth, nineteenth and early twentieth century scholars of the African experience had also called for the scientific study and promotion of the African cultural heritage at a time the African was systematically denigrated as a biologically inferior being through a string of racist dogmas. Such African scholars/writers include Olaudah Equino, Alexander Crummell, James Africanus Beale Horton, David Walker, Edward Wilmot Blyden and J.E. Casely Hayford.

These scholar-activists had boldly challenged racist doctrines about Africa. Horton in particular contended that in human history, civilizations had risen and fallen and that Africa, like other human centers, had had a glorious past as exem-

---

33. Richards, 14–15, 17, 19 & 20.
34. W.E.B. Du Bois, *The Souls of Black Folk*. New York: Penguin Books, 1969: 46.
35. Woodson, 61.
36. Woodson, 150.

plified by the magnificence of ancient Egypt. This line of argument was reinforced by Blyden's "African Personality" concept which stated, among other things, that human races are equal and complementary.[37]

Horton called for the establishment of a West African university which, he believed, would serve to cleanse the minds of Africans of the poison of negative self-consciousness and also help the continent to take advantage of its huge mineral and human resources. It is pertinent to note that Horton called for not just a business-as-usual university, but one which would be African-centered in its epistemological frame of reference.[38]

The idea of a West African university makes sense for a number of reasons: one, such a university would strengthen the process of economic and political cooperation and coordination across the Atlantic by serving as a major intellectual power house and center of research; two, the university would experience greater academic freedom than national universities, which in Africa, tend to operate under the suffocating influence of state authorities; three, given its greater academic freedom, a West African university would be more effective in pursuing African-centered epistemology; and lastly, given the preceding reasons, the university would be in a better position to pull diasporic and continental intellectuals— the combination of which would give the African world an unfettered and much-needed academic prop.

Although the African intellectual ancestors mentioned in the preceding passage did not employ the terminology of Afrocentrism, they had a clear understanding of the necessity for correct historical and cultural training for African children. In the current era, Molefi K. Asante has advanced a theoretical framework for "centeredness" in the education of Africans through his Afrocentric Idea. In three seminal works, *The Afrocentric Idea* (1987), *Afrocentricity* (1988) and *Kemet, Afrocentricity and Knowledge* (1990), Asante articulates the straight-forward idea that Africans should be studied as the subjects of their own history rather than as appendages of someone else's history and culture. Afrocentric research, therefore, "seeks to uncover and use codes, paradigms, symbols, motifs, myths, and circles of discussion that reinforce the centrality of African ideals and values as a valid frame of reference for acquiring and examining data."[39] Other scholars who have contributed profoundly to the promotion of African-centered scholarship include Cheikh Anta Diop, Chancellor Williams, John G. Jackson, Theophile Obenga, Ivan Van Sertima, C. Tsehloane Keto, Maulana Karenga, Dona Marimba Ani, Abu Abbary, Abdias Dos Nascimento, Na'im Akbar, Linda James Myers, Asa Hilliard, and Wade Nobles. There are several others who could not be listed here for lack of space.

To some individuals, all this talk about culture may sound like much ado about nothing. But this writer hastens to suggest that they're mistaken. The centrality of culture to a people's life was brilliantly articulated by Ngugi Wa Thiong'O in his new and riveting work, *Moving the Centers*:

> Culture carries the values, ethical, moral and aesthetic, by which people conceptualize or see themselves and their place in history and the universe. These

---

37. Esedebe, 33–37.
38. Esedebe, 28.
39. Molefi K. Asante, *Kemet, Afrocentricity and Knowledge*. Trenton: Africa WP, 1990: 6.

values are the basis of a society's consciousness and outlook, the whole area of a society's make-up, its identity. A sense of belonging, a sense of identity is part of our psychological survival. Colonialism [and enslavement] through racism tried to turn us into societies without heads. Racism, whose highest institutionalized form is apartheid, is not an accident...Thus psychological survival is necessary. We need values that do not distort our identity, our conception of our rightful place in history, in the universe of the natural and human order.[40]

Wa Thiong'O's thought-provoking paragraph comes at a time of cultural aggression—a time when there exists a greater need than ever before to protect African culture from "decadent" influences—particularly those mass media images and messages which are tailored after the least common denominator. In effect, Wa Thiong'O's position represents a challenge to scholars and writers who have committed their lives to the systematic study of diasporic and continental African cultural experiences.

This writer believes that a human being is both a biological and a cultural organism. Therefore, to exclude the cultural and historical experiences of a group from the curriculum of education is to negate the other half of its humanity. It is another way of saying: "you are not human enough." As a concept which is rooted in history and culture, Afrocentricity belongs to the pluralist perspective, and pluralism constitutes one of the core elements of American democratic ideals. Afrocentricity incorporates Malcolm's vision of a cultural and philosophical return to Africa. Afrocentricity, this writer contends, does not represent the black version of Hegemonic Eurocentrism, which, as empirical experience has shown, can operate as an ideology and practice of exclusion and objectification of the cultural other.[41] Asa G. Hilliard, III, captures this fact rather succinctly when he recalls as follows:

At the turn of the century, theologians in seminaries were debating whether African people had souls, psychologists were debating whether Africans were genetically inferior mentally, anthropologists were labeling Africans 'primitive,' historians were saying that Africans had no history, biologists were even debating the fundamental humanity of Africans.[42]

Such bombardments of the human mind against the African apparently laid the foundation for the mind-set (the persistence of a belief in African inferiority in the current era) which Hacker addressed earlier in this article.

Afrocentric scholars and students conceptualize America as a mosaic of cultures[43] where Africans should co-exist alongside others—not below or above anyone else.[44] The African-American community's consciousness of its collective his-

---

40. Ngugi Wa Thiong'O, *Moving the Centre: the Struggle for Cultural Freedoms*. Portsmouth: Heinemann, 1993: 77.

41. Dona Marimba Ani's latest explosive and highly-documented book, *Yurugu: An African-Centered Critique of European Cultural Thought and Behavior*. Trenton: Africa WP, 1994, represents a rich resource for readers who may want to explore the historical, ideological and even religious roots of Hegemonic Eurocentrism.

42. Asa G. Hilliard, III, "Afrocentrism In a Multicultural Society," *American Visions* (August 1991): 23.

43. Ella Forbes, "The African American View of America," a Presentation at a Debate on Multicultural Education. Mount Pocono, PA.: East Strausbourg University, Sept. 25, 1992.

44. Molefi Kete Asante, "Multi-Culturalism: An Exchange," *The American Scholar* (Spring 1991): 268.

torical and cultural heritage that goes back to Africa with its thousand year history is important for the collective survival and self-fulfillment of the community. It is, by and large, true that the American model of the free market economy hinges on individual initiative, but it is also true, as realists would argue, that a person's life chances as an American do not depend solely on his/her personal efforts. Harold Cruse articulates this point succinctly in *The Crisis of the Black Intellectual*. In it, Cruse points out the significance of "ethnic group democracy" in America. He states that American ethnic group democracy manifests itself through the self-conscious activities of such segments of the population as the White Anglo Saxon Protestants (WASP), White Catholics, White Jews, and Asian-Americans.[45] Apparently, it was the Rev. Jesse Jackson's realization of this thinly-veiled truth of American multicultural life which compelled him to declare in 1989 that "African Americans" should become the official name for Africans in the U.S.[46] In making this declaration, Jackson stated that the term "African America" had cultural integrity. Jackson could not be more correct. Africans are not known to cry wolf when others assert their Irishness or Jewishness. In fact, China towns abound in America. No one complains about this fact; and, in fact, no one should. These groups assert their self-consciousness because it strengthens them; it makes them stronger Americans. Why then, one may ask rhetorically, does the body politic respond with hysteria to the African's quest for self-definition? Why is that which is a sweetener for others, a sour pill for the African?

It can be said with confidence that the Second African Revolution of the 1960s, which is popularly referred to as the 1960's Protest Movement, owed much to ethnic group democracy. Thus, Affirmative Action, as well as other offshoots of that revolution, including the 1964 Civil Rights Act and the 1965 Voting Rights Act,[47] was designed to open doors that had hitherto been closed to the Africans although as a policy instrument, Affirmative Action is intended to promote equality of access but not equality of results.

For Africans in general, migrating back to Africa philosophically implies, among other things, a reconnection with or strengthening of African *humanistic* heritage. The ancient Egyptians were the first in the world to place on record a philosophy of *humanism* under a system which they called *Maat*. *Maat* was the name the African ancestors in ancient Egypt gave to the set of principles which governed the Code of Conduct of a humanistic society. *Maat* means order, harmony, balance, righteousness, and truth.[48] Those principles determined what the Egyptians, and in fact other historical African societies, considered to be correct

45. Harold Cruse, *The Crisis of the Negro Intellectual*. New York: Bazel E. Allen and Ernest J. Wilson, 1984: 317.

46. "'African-American' Favored By Many of America's Blacks." *New York Times*, January 31, 1989: Sec. A(1).

47. It is pertinent to recall that the passing of the Civil Rights and Voting Rights Acts in the '60s was a re-invention of the wheel. During the Great Reconstruction (1865–1877), Congress enacted Civil Rights Acts in 1866 and 1875. (It was the Supreme Court of the United States which outlawed the 1875 Civil Rights Act in 1883). John Hope Franklin & Alfred A. Moss, Jr., *From Slavery to Freedom: A History of Negro Americans*. New York: McGraw-Hill, 1988: 238.

48. Rjnhild Bjerre Finnestad, *The Religion of the Ancient Egyptians: Cognitive Structures and Popular Expressions (Proceedings of Symposia in Uppsala and Bergen 1987 and 1988)*. Stockholm, Sweden: Tryckeri Balder AB, 1989: 23.

human conduct, correct societal norms and values. *Maat* was central to the Egyptian philosophy of life. *Maat* conceives life as an orderly system. Maulana Karenga, an African Americanist who has done impressive work in the area of Egyptology, interprets *Maat* as "the foundation of both nature and righteousness in human society."[49] Karenga observes that *Maat* was the Kemites' "spirit and method of organizing and conducting the relations of human society."[50]

Dona Richards, who was cited earlier, notes that "the [African] culture from which the diasporians had been taken was humanly oriented and organized on the basis of the recognition of the human need for love, warmth, and interrelationship."[51] That is, indeed, true, and, at this point, this writer would like to share with you a question which students raise when *Maat* is discussed in class. They ask, "is it pragmatic to practice *Maat* in a hedonistic and ravenous society where the kind of values enshrined in *Maat* appear to be taking a back-stage?" This writer's response has always been as follows: the real question should be about how the African community, riven by internal disharmony, as well as black-on-black spiritual and physical killings, can put its divided and troubled house in order; as the saying goes, a house divided unto itself cannot stand. Furthermore, *Maat* does not dilute the imperative for *intellectual vigilance*, on the part of the community, and for taking all ethical and morally-defensible measures necessary for the defense and protection of its vital and legitimate interests. It is been well-stated that as a victimized people "fighting for survival and development, Afrikan Americans must see our children as future 'warriors' in [the] struggle for liberation."[52]

Maat embodies the concept of an ideal human being. The ancients viewed the ideal human being as a silent, moderate, and sensible person who lives up to society's norms and values. The ideal person, who is also known as the "silent one," manifests self-control, modesty, kindness, generosity, discretion, truthfulness, and serenity. The contrast to the ideal person is an individual whom the ancients described as the fool or the hothead—a person who is controlled by "his emotions and instincts which lead to a behavior disapproved by society."[53] The hothead is given to gluttony, greed, arrogance, bad temper, and vindictiveness.

In effect, to return to the motherland philosophically would mean ordering one's life in accordance with the teachings of *Maat*. A cultural return to Africa would mean much more than the adornment of African motif—attires, home decorations and what have you even though they serve a useful purpose of nourishing aesthetic sensibilities. It could also mean much more than the acquisition of knowledge of African history. After all, without the ability or will to apply whatever knowledge a person has acquired to his/her daily life, knowledge becomes wasted information. Returning to Africa also means a conscious attempt to lead a life of honesty, self-control, self-respect and respect for fellow human beings, refinement in spoken and written language, hard-work, and excellence. In fact, *Maat* enjoins its adherents to strive for excellence in all endeavors "so that no

---

49. Maulana Karenga, *Selections From the Husia*. Los Angeles: The University of Sankore P, 1989: 29.
50. Karenga (1989), 30.
51. Richards, 13.
52. Madhubuti, 192.
53. Finnestad, 81.

fault can be found in [our] character."[54] *Maat* also calls for a temperament for deferred gratification and a consciousness that "I exist because we exist." Migrating back to Africa would mean respect for elders and a keen sense of family. It means a willingness to serve as one's brother's or sister's keeper.

This writer contends that the ultimate test of Afrocentric consciousness would be the extent to which the mind has been freed of the bondage of "slave" or "colonial" mentality. Killing each other, physically and spiritually, does not reflect Afrocentric consciousness on the part of the killer. Rather, Afrocentricity enjoins its adherents to inspire and uplift each other. What is expected is creative courage, as opposed to destructive courage. While Afrocentric consciousness allows for healthy competition amongst the people, it, however, simultaneously stresses cooperative endeavors. For instance, if Africans do not patronize the businesses in their neighborhoods, who would?

Furthermore, it is not enough for individuals or groups to lament (as should be done from time to time) African community's lack of control over its economic sector—a situation which is, in part, a legacy of slavery, Jim Crow and dashed promises like the unfulfilled promise of forty acres and a mule; it is important that Africans initiate personal business enterprises and try to strengthen them through cooperative ventures, among other measures. It is necessary that the inhabitants of a given neighborhood work together to keep that neighborhood safe and to dissuade juvenile children from defacing the structures that individuals labored hard to put up in such communities. Through collective vigilance over the neighborhoods, the inhabitants can deter those who live by infesting the environment with drugs, and neighborhood vigilantes can also deter those who threaten lives and property.

The history of African institution-building teaches an important lesson: there is a splendid record of building institutions, but, often, a poor job is done of sustaining them. This writer postulates that the causal factors stem from within and without. The internal factors appear to be failure to groom successors, in-fighting, poor planning and poor management. Yes, the community is confronted with a clear and present threat from without—that evil known as racism that ever looms large! African women face the double jeopardy of racism and sexism. It is a world where whiteness per se gives an individual an advantage in the struggle of life. This psychological malady prompted W.E.B. Du Bois to declare in 1900, at the 2nd Pan-African Congress[55] in London, that the major problem which confronts the twentieth century is the problem of the color line. Ninety-four years later, that profound statement remains, by and large, a valid truth. As happens from time to time, the questions and innuendos which preceded the collegial basketball championship of April 4, 1994, brought the problem of the twentieth century to the fore.

Be that as it may, migrating back to Africa philosophically would help rebuild collective African consciousness which had been shattered by the major interventions in African history. Global African consciousness would augur well for the recovery process that is going on now in the African world, for it is this writer's informed conviction that the African world, like a convalescing patient, is still at the stage of recovering from the devastating consequences of the Great Enslave-

---

54. Maulana Karenga, "Towards a Sociology of Maatian Ethics: Literature and Context," *Egypt Revisited*. Ed. Ivan Van Sertima. New Brunswick: Transaction Books, 1993: 373.

55. Olisanwuche P. Esedebe. *Pan-Africanism: the Ideas and Movement, 1776–1963*. Washington, D.C.: Howard UP, 1982: 37.

ment and colonial exploitation and brainwashing. Global African consciousness would facilitate educational, political and socioeconomic linkages between diasporic and continental Africa—linkages which are necessary if the African world is to become a real actor on the world stage. In the last five hundred years, the African world has found itself at the receiving end of history. This hope for a global African consciousness need not be viewed with alarm by non-Africans; for to seek to promote the African interest is not to stand against anyone's interest. The world is large enough to accommodate everyone. Rather, non-Africans should understand that to seek to promote the African interest is to promote the interest of humanity as a whole through one of its branches. This is not a doctrine for how others could be dominated or exploited; this is a quest for universal racial justice, for the improvement of the lot of the long-suffering African.

In the wake of the disintegration of the Eastern Bloc's ideological camp and the consequent demise of the Cold War, scholars of international geopolitics and even politicians have been discussing the contours of an emerging world order. In order to become a force to be reckoned with in the emerging world order, Diasporic and Continental Africans must build more linkages and strengthen existing ones.

Apart from bringing direct pressures to bear on the U.S. foreign policy formulation process, African-American organizations and intellectuals should expand and create Pan-African linkages. Without Pan-African linkages, the African world can not exert a significant influence on the emerging world order let alone define and direct it in its own interest.

International politics is power politics. The greater the leverage at the disposal of the strategically-placed individual, the more likely that he/she can make the system work in the desired direction. Walter Rodney, the late distinguished African-American historian, left behind an eloquent truth about the centrality of power to human life. As he put it,

> Power is the ultimate determinant in human society, being basic to the relations within any group and between groups. It implies the ability to defend one's will by any means available. In relations between peoples, the question of power determines maneuverability in bargaining, the extent to which one people respect the interests of another, and eventually the extent to which a people survive as a physical and cultural entity.[56]

Pan-African linkages would increase the leverage open to the institutions and individuals who shape the place of the African world in the global scheme of things. Examples abound of successes achieved through Pan-African cooperation. African Americans rose to the occasion when Italy invaded Ethiopia in 1935, despite the fact that this was a time when the diasporic Africans themselves were reeling under the weight of virulent white racism[57] in America. Historians John Hope Franklin and Alfred A. Moss, Jr., recall a memorable display of diasporic solidarity with the Ethiopians.

> Almost overnight even the most provincial among Negro Americans became international-minded. Ethiopia was a black nation, and its destruction would

---

56. Walter Rodney, *How Europe Underdeveloped Africa*. Washington, D.C.: Howard UP, 1982: 224.

57. I hope the reader would not interpret this statement to imply that racism is a phenomenon of the past.

symbolize the final victory of whites over blacks. In many communities funds were raised for the defense of the African Kingdom, while in larger cities elaborate organizations were set up.[58]

The general Decolonization effort in Africa stands out as another example. Among others, W.E.B. Du Bois's Pan-African Congresses and literary campaigns not only helped to inspire a generation of African nationalist leaders, but also brought the plight of colonized Africa to the attention of world opinion. Champions of African independence like the late Kwame Nkrumah and Dr. Nnamdi Azikiwe, the Owelle of Onitsha, had been inspired by the works of Du Bois. In turn, the decolonization process in Africa doubled as a psychological boost for oppressed and abused African men and women across the Atlantic, resulting in the just struggle known as the Civil Rights Movement. Franklin and Moss, Jr., recall, with relish, that august moment in the history of the African world.

> The emergence into independence of the [African] nations enormously changed the worldwide significance of the American race problem and provided a considerable stimulus to the movement for racial equality in the United States....It seemed that black men from the Old World had arrived just in time to help redress the racial balance in the New.[59]

Pan-African interaction has thus been a symbiotic process despite vicissitudes in relations between Africans and African Americans. There are examples of this symbiosis from contemporary times. Without the activism of Trans Africa, African American/African Student Unions across American college campuses, and the Black Congressional Caucus, the sanctions and divestments achieved against South Africa, when it was under an apartheid regime,[60] would not have been possible. The same argument can be made about Namibian independence in 1990.

Economic, educational and technological progress in the African world would profit from Pan-African linkages. African-American Studies departments and African-American businesses are the appropriate channels for Pan-African economic, educational and technological linkages. In 1991, a Pennsylvania African-American business mission visited Nigeria and other African countries where it explored investment opportunities. Similarly, the 1990s have witnessed significant economic investments in Ghana, West Africa by a growing number of African Americans.[61] These were steps in the right direction, and there should be more of such business missions to Africa. The Congressional Black Caucus should initiate talks with the Organization of African Unity (OAU), the Economic Community of West African States (ECOWAS) and the South African Development Community (SADC) for special economic investment terms for African Americans, including land acquisition.

---

58. John Hope Franklin, *From Slavery to Freedom: A History of Negro Americans*. New York: McGraw-Hill, 1988: 385.

59. Franklin & Moss, Jr., 438.

60. South Africa has now come under a black majority rule. Nelson Mandela, easily the foremost leader of what was a world-wide movement against apartheid in South Africa, took office on May 13, 1994, as the first president of a free South Africa. He had paid a heavy price for his dogged struggle, including spending twenty-seven years of his youthful life behind bars.

61. "Ghana Black Star of Africa Growing Nation Welcomes African-Americans Eager to Trace Their Roots and Invest in its Future," *Detroit Free Press* June 6, 1996: 1a & 12a–13a.

Communications technology represents a major lever of power. Whoever controls the apparatus for global communications exercises immeasurable influence on the flow and ideological slant of information and thus helps to determine how people view the world and also themselves. To a large degree, the international media decide what and who get priority attention on the agenda of world affairs. Needless to say, communications technology and manpower deserve priority attention from Pan-African strategists.

As this paper discussed at length in the preceding pages, the cultural vitality of the African diaspora will profit from Pan-African linkages. Besides rejuvenating the cultural life of the African diaspora, Pan-African linkages would bear collateral economic fruits. Diasporic cultural groups and think tanks are the appropriate channels for such linkages. Visible action is already being taken in this direction as more and more U.S. Africans have demonstrated practical interest in tourism to Africa.

This writer believes that a new world order and your place in it are not simple matters of definition and theorizing or wishful thinking. A world order is directed by the activities of individuals and institutions. The task of protecting and advancing the just interests of the African community requires not only domestic coalitions and alliances, but also international networks, including, most importantly, the Pan-African connection.

In conclusion, this writer suggests that African governments should grant automatic citizenship to African Americans so as to give them the option of dual citizenship. Nigeria has taken a step in this lofty direction by providing for dual citizenship for Nigerians;[62] it should grant African Americans the unfettered option of taking up the citizenship of Nigeria if they so wish. This should not be viewed as a favor. It is a measure that is overdue. African Americans are entitled to automatic citizenship in African countries of their choice by virtue of the self-evident truth that Africa is their historical homeland.

References

"'African-American' Favored By Many of America's Blacks." (1989). *New York Times*, 31, January: Sec. A(1).

Ani, Marimba. (1994). *Yurugu: An African-Centered Critique of European Cultural Thought and Behavior*. Trenton: Africa WP.

Asante, Molefi. (1988). *Afrocentricity*. Trenton: Africa WP.

Asante, Molefi. (1987). *The Afrocentric Idea*. Philadelphia: Temple UP.

Asante, Molefi. (1990). *Kemet, Afrocentricity and Knowledge*. Trenton, N.J.: Africa WP.

Asante, Molefi Kete. (1991). "Multi-Culturalism: An Exchange." *The American Scholar*, Spring.

Asante, Molefi Kete. (1992). *Open Letter to Dr. Henry Louis Gates, Jr.* July 25.

"A Shocking Look at Blacks and Crime." (1995). *U.S. News & World Report*, 16, Oct.: 53–54.

Barnes, Esmeralda. (1993). "Watched: Scholars Urge Blacks to Counter the Federal Government's Surreptitious Scrutiny of Black Leaders." *Black Issues In Higher Education*, April 22: 14–17.

---

62. "Dual Nationality at Last," *West Africa*, November 2–8, 1992: 1867.

Breitman, George. (1967). *The Last Year of Malcolm X: the Evolution of a Revolutionary.* New York: Pathfinder.

"Dual Nationality At Last." (1992).*West Africa*, November 2–8: 1867.

Du Bois, W.E.B. (1969). *The Souls of Black Folk.* [1903.] New York: Penguin Books.

Esedebe, Olisanwuche P. (1982). *Pan-Africanism: the Ideas and Movement, 1776–1963.* Washington, D.C.: Howard UP.

Finnestad, Bjerre Rjnhild. (1989). *The Religion of the Ancient Egyptians: Cognitive Structures and Popular Expressions (Proceedings of Symposia in Uppsala and Bergen 1987 and 1988).* Stockholm, Sweden: Tryckeri Balder AB.

Forbes, Ella. (1992). "The African American View of America." A Presentation at a Debate on Multicultural Education. Mount Pocono, PA.: East Strausbourg University, Sept. 25.

Franklin, John Hope. & Moss, Jr., Alfred A. (1988). *From Slavery to Freedom: A History of Negro Americans.* New York: McGraw-Hill.

Ginzburg, Ralph. (1962). *100 Years of Lynchings.* Baltimore: Black CP.

"Ghana Black Star of Africa Growing Nation Welcomes African Americans Eager to Trace Their Roots and Invest in its Future." (1996). *Detriot Free Press*, June 6: 1A & 12A–13A.

Hacker, Andrew. (1992). *Two Nations: Black and White, Separate, Hostile, Unequal.* New York: Ballentine.

Hilliard, III, Asa G. (1991). "Afrocentrism in a Multicultural Democracy." *American Visions*, August 23.

Jenning, James. (1994). *Understanding the Nature of Poverty in Urban America.* Westport: Praeger, 1994.

Karenga, Maulana. (1984). *Selections From the Husia.* Los Angeles: The University of SP.

Madhubuti, Haki R. (1990). *Black Men, Obsolete, Single, Dangerous?* Chicago: Third WP.

Martin, Tony. (1976). *Race First: the Ideological and Organizational Struggles of Marcus Garvey and the Universal Negro Improvement Association.* Dover: The MP.

Ohaegbulam, Festus Ugboaja. (1980). *Towards an Understanding of the African Experience from Historical and Contemporary Perspectives.* Lanham: UP of America.

O'Reilly, Kennedy. (1989). *Racial Matters: The FBI's Secret File On Black America, 1962–72.* New York: Free Press.

Richards, Dona Marimba. (1980). *Let the Circle Be Unbroken: the Implications of African Spirituality in the Diaspora.* New York: Djifa Publishers.

Rodney, Walter. (1972). *How Europe Underdeveloped Africa.* Washington, D.C.: Howard University.

Thiong'O Wa, Ngugi. (1993). *Moving the Centre: the Struggle for Cultural Freedoms.* Portsmouth: Heinemann.

Thompson, Vincent Bakpetu. (1987). *The Making of the African Diaspora In the Americas 1441–1900.* New York: Longman.

(1992) *U.S. Bureau of the Census, Statistical Abstract of the United States: 1992* (112th edition.). Washington, D.C.

West, Cornel. (1993). *Keeping Faith: Philosophy and Race in America.* New York: Routledge.

Woodson, Carter G. (1977). *The Miseducation of the Negro.* [1933.] New York: AMS Press.

Section XIII

Intellectual Wars

40

Black Intellectuals in Conflict

Manning Marable

African-American and white liberal academic circles are still buzzing about Adolph Reed's controversial essay in the April 11, 1995, issue of *The Village Voice* on "The Current Crisis of the Black Intellectual." The Northwestern University black political scientist launched a major polemical broadside against some of America's best-known and most publicized black scholars. Although Reed's title echoes the classic critique of an earlier generation of black scholars published in 1967 by Harold Cruse, *The Crisis of the Negro Intellectual*, Reed's fundamental criticism was aimed against only two individuals, who are both professors of African-American Studies at Harvard University: Cornel West, the author of *Race Matters* and other works; and Black Studies chairperson and literary scholar Henry Louis Gates. Other black scholars who Reed criticized were black feminist bell hooks, a professor of literature at the City University of New York; cultural critic Michael Eric Dyson, professor of communications and African-American Studies at the University of North Carolina; and New York University history professor Robin Kelley.

Reed's basic argument was that these scholars presented themselves as "authentically black" spokespersons, who actually lacked viable constituencies or any genuine accountability within the African-American community. In stark departure from the black intellectual tradition, which engaged in a serious and lively conversation on "such questions as the definition, status, and functions of black literature, the foundations of black identity (and) topical critiques of ideological programs and tendencies in social affairs," Reed claims that the new breed "exhibit little sense of debate or controversy among themselves." He charges that this group's absence of controversy betrays a lack of critical content and purpose. Reed equates the new intellectuals with the Tuskegee Institute founder Booker T. Washington, a conservative black Republican and chief architect of black capitalism a century ago. To Reed, Washington was simply a purely freelance race spokesman; his status depended on designation by white elites rather by any black electorate or social movement. Similarly, the politics and statements of these black "public intellectuals exude *pro forma*" moralism, not passion, and are supposedly disconnected from the masses of black folk.

If Reed had left matters there, perhaps there would be the basis for the political engagement or dialogue which theoretically he claims to be seeking. But for good measure, Reed found it necessary to add a series of mean-spirited criticisms against those characterized as "the children of Booker T. Washington." Gates was defined as "the voice" of a "black, self-consciously petit bourgeois centrism." West was nothing less than "freelance race relations consultant and Moral Voice for white elites." Kelley was charged with "spinning narratives that ultimately demean political action by claiming to find it everywhere." And hooks and Dyson were slurred as simply "hustlers, blending bombast, cliches, psychobabble, and lame guilt-tripping in service to the 'pay me' principle."

If one did an informal poll among most black intellectuals today, many might agree with part of Reed's analysis. There is a growing sense that a significant number of black scholars speak primarily to white elites, rather than addressing the specific problems of the African-American community. But the two major factors for this are: (1) the growth of class stratification and social fragmentation within black civil society, in which large institutions like the black church, civic associations and civil rights organizations have lost much of their influence; and (2) the decline of the black freedom movement, and more generally, the deterioration of progressive and liberal political coalitions in which blacks were a significant element. Black intellectuals during the era of racial segregation were forced to maintain contacts with all-black organizations, professionally and socially. With the legal integration of civil society and the assimilation of black students and faculty within formerly all-white academic institutions, the linkages which kept black intellectuals in the orbit of African-American political culture and society were largely ruptured. Few black intellectuals today maintain an authentic, organic relationship with multi-class, black formations which have significant constituencies among working class and poor people.

Political clout among black intellectuals these days is all too often measured by one's ability to leverage policy within powerful white circles, rather than inside social protest formations. For example, probably the most influential social scientist in America today is University of Chicago's sociologist William Julius Wilson. The author of the controversial *The Declining Significance of Race*, Wilson's ties with the Clinton administration and his criticisms of affirmative action carry much greater weight in public policy circles than any of the intellectuals Reed cites. On the right, the work of conservative scholars like economist Thomas Sowell, the apologist for Reaganism, has been devastating to blacks' collective interests. Sowell, Walter Williams, Alan Keyes, Clarence Thomas, Glen Loury and other black conservatives proudly proclaim their distance and lack of accountability to the African-American community. Reed certainly has the right, and even the responsibility to critique any political tendency within the black community. But to single out black scholars who are to the left-of-center in a manner which is abusive and nearly intolerant in tone comes close, given this context, to confusing our friends for our enemies.

The greatest reservoir of antagonism one finds today against any single liberal intellectual within the African-American community is probably targeted against Gates, who has been described publicly and privately as something of a "modern Booker T. Washington," at least in the realm of cultural studies and literary criticism for the past five years. Like the "Wizard of Tuskegee," Gates sees himself as something of an entrepreneur; he has extensive influence within foundation circles and inside the white media. Gates broke into the public sphere with a controversial op-ed essay in *The New York Times* which condemned anti-Semitism within the black community. The essay evoked deep anger and outrage among many blacks, who felt it pandered to elements within the Jewish community which had become alienated from black issues and interests. In the context of national politics, Gates is unambiguously a liberal, but implicitly he embraces a social philosophy of inclusionist integration, appealing to the liberal wing of white corporate and political power. But simultaneously, he has a strong grasp of currents within black popular culture, and has the political imagination to build personal and political bridges with leaders and intellectuals who are ideologically to his left. Gates is a thoughtful and gifted writer, who has no aspirations to play the role of a contemporary race leader of the masses.

Although frequently associated with Gates, West has a very different political history. West developed a distinct constituency among blacks by first working in progressive and black nationalist-oriented religious and political circles fifteen years ago. West became associated with the white moderate left in his capacity as nominal leader of the Democratic Socialists of America, following the death of socialist writer Michael Harrington. West also became closely linked with writer Michael Lerner, and the liberal Jewish publication *Tikkun*. Criticism of West within some black circles began several years later, as he spoke out against the sentiments of nihilism and social alienation found within contemporary urban culture. But when he accepted an academic appointment at Harvard in late 1993 in the African-American Studies program directed by "Skip" Gates, West increased the general perception that he had become part of Gates entourage. After the publication of *Race Matters*, black academicians who had never taken part in a protest action or walked a picket line in their lives, began to attack West's politics. As in the case of Gates, some of this criticism was jealousy, pure and simple. Part of it was the distrust West generated among some blacks by his efforts to reach out to liberal whites and Jews with his message of coalition-building and radical democracy. But part of the trouble was that West's more recent work, especially in *Race Matters*, tended to be framed in a language and style which was more at home with traditional liberalism than with the left. Some radicals such as Stephen Steinberg felt that West was prepared to sacrifice the importance of race on the high altar of class. In a essay for *New Politics* in the summer, 1994, Steinberg accused West of shifting "the focus of analysis and of blame away from the structures of racial oppression," and of engaging in a "tortuous reasoning that subverts the whole logic behind affirmative action."

Reed's analysis captures some of these details, but misses the mark by lumping together scholars with widely divergent interests, styles of communication, and political orientations. For example, bell hooks established her reputation as a feminist critic and social commentator with the publication of her book *Ain't I A Woman* in 1982. A series of books have followed, increasingly moving toward themes which focus on gender and social relations, cultural behavior and issues of representation within black contemporary life. It is true that the real impact of her books and essays is less evident within the traditional academy than among hundreds of thousands of black women, who find her idea and commentary inspirational. Hooks has never treated class with the sharpness of focus in her work that other feminist scholars, such as Angela Davis, have done. But it seems like Reed is hostile and impatient with hooks because she doesn't engage in the kink of research or detailed political analysis that he values; he should recognize that political intervention can and often does take a variety of forms. Challenging sexism and forms of patriarchy within the black community, the central concern of hooks, makes a fundamental political contribution.

Reed's criticisms of Dyson and Kelley seemed especially petty. Dyson has produced a collection of social essays and a book assessing the cultural and social impact of the Malcom X phenomenon of the 1990s; Kelley has written several books, including an invaluable study of black rural protest form the Great Depression, *Hammer and Hoe*. Both younger scholars are thoughtful and have a special awareness of the centrality of popular cultural forms, such as Hip Hop, to the construction of a political consciousness of resistance and group empowerment. They represent a vanguard of the post-civil rights generation of new scholarship on black identity, cultural and history.

Reed fails to capture this diversity among this group of scholars. But the greatest errors within his analysis were essentially historical and conjunctural. First, Reed's characterization of Washington and the politics of the Tuskegee Machine was grossly inaccurate. Washington was certainly a black Republican, an opponent of labor unions and publicly an apologist for Jim Crow segregation, but without question, he had a strong following among a segment of the black community. Washington was actively promoted by white capitalists and conservatives, but he also constructed his own effective constituency by establishing the National Negro Business League. He was deeply interested in Pan-Africanism, encouraged students from Africa to attend Tuskegee, and inspired an entire generation of early African nationalists, including the founder of the African National Congress, John Langalibalele Dube. He was an astute politician who fought secretly against segregation, hiring lobbyists to oppose Jim Crow laws. These aspects of Washington's program explains why black nationalists such as Marcus Garvey praised and respected him. Reed is a serious scholar of black political history. He surely understands the profound significance of the black capitalist and accommodationist tradition within black political history, and its intimate connections with conservative black nationalism. In the final analysis, Du Bois was right: Washington's accommodationist approach toward white power was profoundly flawed, and at times even criminal, in that it gave legitimate to the lynching and disfranchisement of black people. However, that doesn't make him an "Uncle Tom." Washington's primary role was to articulate the interests of the entrepreneurial, conservative wing of the emerging black middle class to the representatives of corporate and political power in the white world.

The new black public intellectuals, a century later, are engaged in a totally different political enterprise. They are not building educational institutions like Tuskegee Institute, or political machines which negotiate for influence within the white establishment. They utilize the power of words to impact the contours of political culture and the public discourse. Unlike Washington, their commitment is to theoretical and cultural engagement, analyzing the meaning of race, gender and class issues in the context of a post-civil rights reality of unrelenting attacks against affirmative action, welfare and multicultural education. To be sure, many of them are sadly disconnected from the social forces and struggles of working class and poor peoples communities. And as a result, their political discourse is frequently obtuse, and they lack any intimate or textured awareness of the efforts for empowerment and social change being waged by most African-Americans today. Reed accurately understands this. But by wielding a polemical sledgehammer against West, hooks, *et al.*, Reed ignores a far greater danger to the possibilities for progressive black politics.

Since the early 1990's, the Far Right has waged an ideological war against the politics of liberal democratic social change. With the declining strength of the organized labor movement, the deterioration of the liberal wing of the Democratic party and the disarray of the Civil Rights Movement, one of the few sectors of growing left-of-center influence in national political culture is the black intelligentsia. The black population overall is significantly to the left of the general society on socioeconomic issues; this permits many progressive, anti-corporate capitalist intellectuals like Angela Davis to exercise significant influence.

White conservatives made a strategic decision to delegitimate the liberal-left black intelligentsia several years ago. After Clinton's election to the presidency, for example, conservatives attacked prominent black anthropologist Johnetta Cole, the president of Spelman College, to deny her possible nomination as Secretary of Education. In 1994, legal scholar Lani Guinier was publicly smeared as the "Quota Queen" by the Far Right, after being nominated as the Assistant Attorney General for Civil Rights. Clinton's retreat from Guinier's nomination signaled a victory for conservatives which led directly to today's assault against affirmative action, minority economic set-asides and an entire range of civil rights initiatives.

In *The New Republic* this March, Cornel West was viciously attacked in a vitriolic polemic by Leon Wieseltier. Accurately described by Michael Lerner as the "errand boy and hatchet man" for Martin Peretz, the publisher of *The New Republic*, Wieseltier denounced West's writings as "almost completely worthless." Reed backhandedly defends Wieseltier's thesis as being "right-for-the-wrong-reasons." This position is not only irresponsible, but directly feeds into the retreat from an antiracist politics among white liberals and so-called radicals who are among *The Village Voice* readers. To join the chorus of the Far Right, to deplore and denounce the works of an entire group of black intellectuals espousing progressive ideas, is alien to the best traditions of black scholarship. Many black activists suspect that the real motivation behind Wieseltier was West's principled decision to participate in the National African American Leadership Summit, called by former NAACP national secretary Benjamin Chavis, last June. West strongly defended the political initiatives taken by Chavis to revitalize the NAACP, and vigorously opposed Chavis's ouster. His well-publicized defense for the need to dialogue directly with Nation of Islam leader Louis Farrakhan, and his endorsement of the Senatorial campaign of Al Sharpton in New York last fall, may have triggered the polemical attack in *The New Republic*.

Growing up in a Midwestern industrial town in the 1960s, I witnessed hundreds of petty quarrels between representatives of our small black community, which were animated by jealously and a desire for influence within the white elite. Among ourselves, we used to complain that middle class Negroes frequently responded to each others' successes like "crabs in a barrel"—pulling each other down. Reed identifies himself with the radical left, but all too often seems to behave in the same manner. In many ways, the sharply confrontation style of Reed is reminiscent of other voices of independent black radicalism, such as William Monroe Trotter. Reed is often unfairly dismissed, like Trotter, as something of a loner, so ideologically "left" that his criticism carries little weight among most black activists. His scathing book on the 1984 presidential campaign of the Rainbow Coalition was so hostile to Jesse Jackson that most blacks concluded erroneously that Reed was a "black conservative" like Sowell, Loury and Thomas. But the supposed virtue of being further to the left than anyone else may mean that one is really outside the real experiences of one's people.

Reed himself apparently has few connections with real social forces, with the present-day struggles of women and men who are attempting to halt the tide of political reaction against black folk by the Republican Right. For if he did, Reed would not so easily be convinced that West, Gates and company should be the primary objects of his political scorn and contempt. At a time when we need to construct a new left-of-center paradigm as an alternative to mass conservatism, we need to engage in a thoughtful, civil dialogue among ourselves—not a public mugging of black intellectuals who share democratic, progressive values.

41

Paradoxes of Black American Leadership

Martin Kilson

I begin with a straightforward proposition that there have been three types of black political leadership in twentieth century America: (1) pragmatic-activist, (2) systemic-radical, and (3) ethno-radical. The first of these refers to what we commonly think of as the mainstream pattern, pioneered by W.E.B. Du Bois from the Niagara Movement and the founding of the National Association for the Advancement of Colored People (NAACP), in the years 1905 to 1910 and onward. Pragmatic activism has produced, in our era, a full-fledged, electoral-based black political class. Members of this class accept both the basic parameters of the democratic capitalist system and the broader cultural matrix within which this system is embedded. But there is one crucial refusal. They insist that America must purge itself of white supremacy and of the social institutions and cultural identities in which it is reflected.

The second category refers to a minority but quite persistent strand of black leadership whose representatives reject the basic parameters of American capitalism. Their ideological inspiration has been largely Marxist, and in the 1930s and 1940s, they came together mostly in the American Communist party (CP). They include James W. Ford (a CP presidential candidate), Benjamin Davis, Paul Robeson, Richard Wright, even Ralph Ellison. Du Bois, too, formally joined the Communist party during his last years, which suggests that there is some movement between the first and second categories. People in both of them, of course, accept the larger American culture, which marks them off from the ethno-radicals.

This last group has exhibited what we might call a three-sided schizophrenia toward the democratic capitalist system. First, its representatives endorse the capitalist mechanisms for producing and distributing wealth. But, second, they are indifferent or hostile to democratic politics. And, third, they do not accept the underlying cultural matrix. This cultural antipathy is manifest in various ways. Depending on personality and organizational style, leaders adopt different postures of rebellion. They indulge in aggressive verbal and symbolic challenges to mainstream culture. They seek some specific black-ethno replacement for standard features of the culture, in diet, consumption, personal adornment, and so on. Or they aim deeper, countering and seeking to replace basic cultural patterns in religion, family, gender, and historical identity.

An earlier version of this essay appeared in *Dissent;* 1995, 42, 3(180), Summer, 368–372 and is adapted/reprinted with the permission of the copyright holder/author.

Terms such as black nationalists, black militants, Garveyites, Black Muslims, and Afrocentrists refer to this third category. "The legacy of Malcolm X" makes the same reference. What gives this ethno-radicalism its radical edge is the rejection of the American cultural mainstream and the demand for a black replacement.

Ethno-Radical Politics

Operationally, black ethno-radicalism has been mainly ritualistic (emotive and cathartic) rather than rationalist (means-and-end focused, accountable, committed to modernity). Exactly why the pattern has taken this shape, I don't quite know, and I prefer to leave this question to the philosophical, culture-probing analysis of writers like Cornel West and Anthony Appiah. I want simply to describe the unanticipated outcomes and the internal contradictions of this leadership pattern.

What is its empirical track record? If we take the official membership of the most prominent ethno-radical organization, the Nation of Islam, as a gauge, then some twenty thousand blacks have been hived off from the American cultural matrix—out of thirty million in the country as a whole. Data from an earlier period, when Elijah Muhammad and Malcolm X rather than Louis Farrakhan were the leading ethno-radicals, suggest a following of about two hundred thousand. It is reasonable to conclude, then, that this leadership style has achieved a rather low penetration of African-American ranks. But its influence, and the sympathy it has won, extend far beyond the membership of its organizations.

How far? Before trying to answer this question, I want to note one curious paradox of black ethno-radicalism: though it is directed toward the "black masses"—the poor and the underclass—its actual followers are mainly upper-working class and lower-middle class in background. Afrocentric elementary and middle schools in Baltimore, Detroit, Chicago, and Philadelphia draw their students from these same classes, and don't reach beyond them. What has happened to the ethno-radical commitment to fashioning a sense of efficacy among poor blacks in the inner city, reeling from social disarray and macho-male youth fratricide? Where have all these masses-trumpeting black nationalists gone?

The Reach of Malcolm X

Malcolm X produced the first systematic challenge to the pragmatic-activist style of black leadership. But this challenge, although quite real, is not a function of the institutional success of Afrocentrism—not of the direct heirs of Malcolm, like Farrakhan's organization, or of the indirect heirs like the groups around, say, Ron Karenga and Molefi Asante. It isn't their institutions but their personal flamboyance and the ritual catharsis that they make possible that accounts for the success they have had. Again, ritualism, not rationalism, has been overwhelmingly prominent in this challenge to the mainstream of black leadership.

Boundaries are sharply drawn in this leadership contest. On one side are the pragmatic activists, who are made up of the heads of the civil rights organizations and their followers among the black intelligentsia (clergy, professionals, and so on), the eight thousand elected black politicians, and the many thousand and more black administrators and the bureaucrats at all levels of the American polity. (The systemic radicals, insofar as they still have a presence in the black political world, are allied with this first group.) On the other side are the ethno-radicals, now popularly called Afrocentrists, who are themselves divided. First, there is a xenophobic type of Afrocentrism, represented by Farrakhan and Khalid Muhamad; and second, there is a more intellectual type, focused on a type of Afro-catechism, represented by people like Asante or Ivan Van Sertima, who do not usually indulge in rhetoric demonizing white Americans or denouncing Jews. They are concerned mainly with fashioning cultural theories and a new, assertive, pro-black historiography.

The appeal of Afrocentrism is a matter of real concern to the mainstream, pragmatic-activist leadership, which is itself at a critical stage of its development within American politics. Its expanding public policy role depends increasingly on its ability to forge biracial legislative and electoral alliances. But the triumph of a militant conservatism focused on policy issues like welfare and affirmative action has weakened this ability, and the high visibility of Afrocentrism compounds the difficulty of maintaining or expanding the necessary ties. The normal, racist-tinged resistance among white Americans is now provided with a rationale: one racist thrust begets another. And without a strong biracial alliance, mainstream black leaders cannot fashion effective legislative programs or private sector initiatives that respond to the deep crises of joblessness and social disorganization among the one-third of African-American households that are submerged in poverty.

Evaluating Afrocentrism

Given this dilemma, it is important to sharpen our understanding of the appeal of ethno-radical xenophobia. How deep is the penetration now? And how can we gauge its political significance? In the short run, at least, there are many thousands of "attentive ears" straining toward Farrakhan and Khalid Muhammad. I use the term "attentive ears" advisedly; "supporters" is too strong when we try to measure the seriousness or tenacity of the Afrocentrist appeal. Many thousands of everyday black folks in urban areas (some suburbs too) turn out to hear the mean and twisted utterances of these men, crowding sports stadiums in Baltimore with twenty thousand people or in New York with twelve thousand. This kind of popular emotional response once given to another variant of ethno-radical leadership, the "sacred" ethno-radicals represented by black clergymen like Father Divine, Elder Michaux, Bishop "Sweet Daddy" Grace and Prophet Jones, among others. Pragmatic activists, whether they are politicians or intellectuals, have seldom sparked a comparable popular response among African-Americans (Martin Luther King is the sole exception). No contemporary representative of this type, however stellar in their fields and professions, could draw twenty thousand everyday black folk out of "the hood" as Farrakhan can—not Toni Morrison, Marian Wright Edelman, Gwendolyn Brooks, Alice Walker, David L. Lewis, John Lewis, Ishmael Reed, Julian Bond, Cornel West, not even Jesse Jackson. No combination of pragmatic activists is capable of competing today with the xenophobic Afrocentrists in gaining the attentive ears of ordinary black Americans.

Why is this so? Mainly because there is a deep need for catharsis in the black community, for the release of emotion. But there is something more too: Afrocentrism contains a massive entertainment component, sheer flamboyance, designed to make black people feel good. And, one must be candid about this, inasmuch as black Americans have been massively traumatized by this country's white supremacist structures and values, there inevitably has been and will be a demand for the catharsis, the flamboyance, and the good feeling. It has been the special burden of the pragmatic-activist leaders that they took on mainly the rationalist, problem-solving tasks of the black community, while also, always, having to show sensitivity to the ritual tasks as well. And except in the Kennedy–Johnson era, they have never had anything like significant help from American power structures for either of these tasks. So the success of the ethno-radicals cannot be a surprise to any honest and serious observer of American realities. It is still a question, however, what this success in catharsis and entertainment means in institutional and pragmatic terms.

A recent poll of black attitudes provides data for an empirical analysis of the relationship between everyday black folk and the Afrocentrists. The poll was conducted for *Time* by the Yankelovich Survey in February 1994, and it shows that along what might be called a political cathartic trajectory, the xenophobic Afrocentrists exert a strong influence among black Americans, but along a oliotical-substantive trajectory, their influence is more limited. For example, when asked whether Farrakhan says things the country should hear, some 70 percent of blacks say yes. When asked whether Farrakhan speaks the truth, 63 percent say yes; whether he is good for the black community, 63 percent say yes; a role model for the black youth, 53 percent say yes.

But when asked to compare an ethno-radical organization like the Nation of Islam with a pragmatic-activist organization like the NAACP, the latter was favored by 74 percent to 31 percent. To the question of who is the most important black leader today, respondents give Jesse Jackson 34 percent to Farrakhan's 9 percent and Colin Powell's 4 percent. There is, then, a discrepant pattern here, with Afrocentrism showing more emotional than substantive political strength. It provides a certain salve for deep wounds, but its candidates in city council elections in Chicago, Detroit, and Washington, D.C., do not win many votes. And of the thousands who listen to Farrakhan or someone like him in a big city sports stadium, barely a hundred will sign on as members of the Nation of Islam as they exit. The 20,000 Farrakhan followers have to be set against the 840,000 African-Americans who now practice standard or orthodox Islam.

But even a merely cathartic politics, xenophobic in character, which scapegoats whites in general and Jews in particular (and Catholics, gays, and feminists too), though it has little substantive or institutional strength, nonetheless poses a major political dilemma for the mainstream African-American leadership. The Afrocentrist appeal is counterproductive in the context of a democratic politics. The point requires emphasis, and then some specification. Groups such as blacks, Hispanics, and women, who struggle for social standing and mobility, depend upon electoral and legislative alliances, while Afrocentrist xenophobia generates negative feelings among the necessary allies. Already resistant to biracial alliances, white Americans now have a new rationale for their resistance—while at the same time Afrocentrism resonates among ordinary blacks. These two facts together make for a kind of double jeopardy for the black pragmatic activists. The escape from this dangerous dynamic is complicated by the special circumstances associated with black–Jewish discord over the past twenty-five years.

Blacks and Jews

The antecedents of this discord go back at least to the Ocean Hill–Brownsville school district election in New York City 1968, but for my purposes here the viciously anti-Semitic speech by Khalid Muhammad at Kean College in New Jersey in November 1993 is a suitable starting point. Understandably, prominent Jewish intellectuals published major articles attacking Muhammad's speech. But, beyond that, they also attacked what they viewed as an overall softness toward anti-Semitism among the mainstream black leadership. This criticism was sharpened as a result of another event in the fall of 1993: the creation of a cross-cutting alliance involving ethno-radicals and pragmatic activists in the black community. From my perspective on the African-American leadership dynamics, criticism of this latter effort was off the mark, unbalanced, and analytically shallow.

For one thing, the charge that the African-American intelligentsia has been soft on black anti-Semitism is just factually wrong. No one close to this intelligentsia can be unaware of its vigilance against extremism. Although the white media have virtually never recognized it, this vigilance has prevented or, at least, helped to prevent the export from the African-American community of demented extremists to crisis-ridden areas of Africa. During the dangerous and protracted period of intense black/white conflict in the Republic of South Africa, for example, not one Afrocentric-inspired American crossed the Atlantic to advocate or practice terrorism in South Africa. Figures like Leon Sullivan, Jesse Jackson, Andrew Young, John Conyers, John Lewis, Leon Higginbotham, William Coleman, Julian Bond, Toni Morrison, Alice Walker, Marian Wright-Edelman, and Cornel West, to name just a few, exerted steady pressure—intellectual, moral, organizational—against terrorist discourse among black Americans.

In this business of reining in ethnocentric extremists, the African-American intelligentsia has a much better record than, say, the Irish-American intelligentsia, though the latter group has never been subjected to the same kind of broad brush criticism. Until 1994, few Irish-Americans were vigilantly or boldly engaged in criticizing and checking the many ties between Irish extremists and their American supporters. The dangerous and intellectually shameful coddling of ethnocentric extremists by mainstream leaders, for which some Jewish leaders have criticized the black community, is far more prominent among white ethnic groups. One could just as easily add to the Irish-Americans, the Greeks, Armenians, Serbs, and Croats, among others. Indeed, until the Hebron massacre of 1994, most Jewish-American leaders and the intellectuals virtually ignored extremists like those of the Kach movement, largely recruited and financed here.

It was also a mistake to pick a fight with mainstream black leaders because of their bid for ties between themselves and the Afrocentrists—ties aimed at a specific task of coping with the runaway drug crisis and criminal crisis in inner-city black communities. No doubt, the intrinsic illegitimacy of Farrakhan-type Afrocentrists in the eyes of Jewish leaders is valid, and black leaders are obligated to address sensitively this Jewish concern. With Ben Chavis's self-destruction as executive secretary of the NAACP, the immediate issue is now moot. But the deeper question of odd-bedfellow alliances within a democratic polity remains relevant for discussion and evaluation. I want to argue that, while such alliances are potentially counterproductive to long-run democratic purposes, every instance of cross-cutting ties isn't necessarily counterproductive; and this most recent example should not jeopardize the quest for black-Jewish concord.

In general, cross-cutting ties involve minimal reciprocity for the sake of some larger interest that none of the groups alone can achieve. Such alliances are, after all, commonplace in a pluralistic and highly competitive democratic polity like ours, and the mainstream black leaders are not innocents in this matter. For example, FDR's New Deal policy advances, which have benefited broad sections of the American working class, poor, and the middle class, were the work of some very odd bedfellows. The New Deal coalition included Ku Klux Klan-supported white politicians from the South. Yet, though infuriated and embittered by these partners, pragmatic-activist black leaders (the NAACP, the National Urban League, the National Negro Congress [a Marxist-oriented organization], and much of the black church leadership) did nothing to fracture the political basis of the New Deal. Why not? Because the reciprocal goals that sealed the alliances were, however minimal the returns for African-Americans, beneficial enough to justify the ties to Klan supporters. It is within this kind of democratic give-and-take that, I suggest, the ties between mainstream black leaders and Afrocentrists should be evaluated today.

Still, the long-run legitimacy of the mainstream leaders depends, as I have said, upon the expansion of their alliances outside the black community. Progressive, liberal, and moderate whites, even what might be called proactively conservative whites (conservatives, that is, who wish to solve, not ignore, the multilayered crisis confronting the African-American poor), must carry a special responsibility in this regard. In today's climate of expanding militant and plutocratic conservatism, Republican party politicians, and the interest groups they represent, cannot be expected to facilitate this alliance expansion. Quite the contrary. Their political discourse is riddled with subliminal anti-black or Negrophobic messages—also with antifeminist, anti-Hispanic, and homophobic messages. And if Michael Lind's *New York Review* article is taken seriously as it should be, then we have to add, subliminal anti-Jewish messages too.

It is, then, important to take some steps, even small steps, toward a reduction of black–Jewish tensions. Some signs of movement down this path were apparent in the 1994 elections. The pattern of black–Jewish voting in regard to the candidacy of Carl McCall for comptroller of New York provides a first indication. McCall ran against a Jewish candidate, Herbert London, who started with major support among Jewish voters. But London cynically sought to exploit black–Jewish discord, a tactic that backfired, especially among Jews. A critical shift of Jewish suburban voters away from London, toward McCall, resulted in the election of the first African-American to an executive office in New York state.

Noteworthy too is that after the 92 percent black voter support for Democratic party candidates in 1994, the second largest Democratic vote came from Jews, at 79 percent. After that was the Hispanic vote, 70 percent Democratic. These patterns suggest that it is indeed possible for blacks and Jews to put the past twenty-five years of contention behind them. The expanding neoracist and neonativist militancy in the Republican party demands that this be done.